FAMILY PROPERTY LAW

———

CASES and MATERIALS ON
WILLS, TRUSTS, and FUTURE INTERESTS

by

LAWRENCE W. WAGGONER
Lewis M. Simes Professor of Law
University of Michigan

RICHARD V. WELLMAN
Robert Cotton Alston Professor of Law
University of Georgia

GREGORY S. ALEXANDER
Professor of Law
Cornell University

MARY LOUISE FELLOWS
Everett Fraser Professor of Law
University of Minnesota

Westbury, New York
THE FOUNDATION PRESS INC.
1991

 TEXT IS PRINTED ON 10% POST CONSUMER RECYCLED PAPER

 PRINTED WITH SOY INK

Preface

We derive the title of this casebook on wills, trusts, and futures interests from family law and property law. More than ever before, the law of the family intersects with the law of property in this area. Disputes involving family property often pit one family member against another. To be sure, transmission of family property usually occurs quietly, privately, and harmoniously. But not always. In this book, we will come across intensely personal disputes—siblings against siblings, children of a prior marriage against their deceased parent's surviving spouse. We can safely imagine the aftermath in strained or even severed family relationships. In reading and discussing these sometimes dryly presented cases, the human dimension ought not be overlooked. Family property law can affect not only the wealth but also the emotional lives of real human beings.

Once a static area, family property law has entered a reform-minded phase as it responds to a variety of social and legal developments. These developments include: changing notions of family and society; the acceptance of a partnership theory for assessing the financial aspects of a marriage; a growing recognition that the traditional rules and doctrines advertised as giving effect to intention can work to undermine it; and the need to reshape the law of donative transfers into a unity, thus departing from the status quo under which one set of rules governs wills and another set governs other property arrangements such as life insurance, pension benefits, and revocable trusts.

The casebook centers on the Uniform Probate Code (UPC). The UPC was revised in 1990. These revisions play a prominent role in the reform movement. We believe that the 1990 UPC is destined to be the model for family property law deep into the next century. At the same time, we are mindful that the pre-1990 UPC or non-UPC law still constitutes the law in many states. The 1990 UPC revisions are so comprehensive that significant periods of study will be necessary before large numbers of states will move to enact them. Thus, in this book, we principally study the 1990 version of the UPC but do not neglect the coverage of the pre-1990 version or non-UPC law.

Following an introductory chapter that explores fundamental issues in family property law, we organize the materials in four divisions. Division One covers probate transfers—intestacy, execution and revocation of wills, ademption, abatement, and lapse. Division Two brings nonprobate transfers into the discussion. It covers taxation, revocable trusts and other will substitutes, protection of the family, will contracts, mistake, formation of trusts, spendthrift, discretionary, and support trusts, termination and modification of trusts, and charitable trusts. Division Three covers powers of appointment and future interests, including classification, construction, and the rule against perpetuities. Division Four covers estate and trust administration.

Code Book. The casebook is meant to be used with a companion code book, Selected Statutes on Trusts and Estates (Selected Statutes). The casebook does not reproduce the UPC or the variety of other uniform acts upon which family property law and the casebook are largely centered. We believe that much is to be gained by studying the statutory text and official comments in the context of a code or act as a whole.

Selected Statutes contains the UPC as revised in 1990, the pre-1990 UPC, and the various other uniform acts used in the course and referred to in the casebook. It also contains selected nonuniform and Commonwealth legislation germane to the course. The UPC and other statutes in Selected Statutes are integrated into the casebook by use of "Statutory References," which appear immediately below title headings throughout the casebook. Each "Statutory Reference" identifies, by statute, the principal section or sections that are assigned for study along with the casebook materials under that title heading.

Editorial Conventions. We adhere to the customary casebook convention of omitting footnotes from cases and other extracted sources without disclosure, but we also omit citations within cases without the customary disclosure by way of ellipses. For the most part, citations to precedent within court opinions are omitted except where the citation identifies quoted passages. We only use ellipses to disclose deletion of substantive material from cases or other extracted sources.

Acknowledgments. We express gratitude to John H. Langbein of Yale University, Sarajane Love of the University of Georgia, and Patricia J. Roberts of Wake Forest University for helpful comments on earlier drafts of portions of this book. We also acknowledge, with thanks, the research and editorial assistance of various law students. They include, at the University of Chicago Law School, Edward J. Finley II (Class of '91) and Maxine Lans (Class of '91); at Cornell Law School, Dena Bauman (Class of '91); at the University of Michigan Law School, Jordana R. Enig (Class of '85) and Margaret L. Thompson (Class of '84); and at the University of Minnesota Law School, Jill Bergquist (Class of '92).

Special thanks are due to Barbara Brown of the University of Michigan Law School and Marti Blake of the University of Minnesota Law School, whose diligent, sustained, and skillful use of computers and word processing produced complicated charts and transformed our text into pages, titles, and type of the right size, shape, and location.

Permissions from Authors and Publishers. We acknowledge our gratitude to the authors and publishers who have given us permission to reproduce extracts from their copyrighted works. Full citation and credit appear at the point of reproduction. The following copyright-holders prefer special forms of acknowledgement: for B. Longstreth, Modern Investment Management and the Prudent Man Rule, Copyright (c) 1986 by Oxford University Press, Inc. Reprinted by permission; B. Sparks, Contracts to Make Wills, reprinted by permission of New York University Press, Copyright 1956 by New York University; for ABA Formal Opinion 210, Model Rules of Professional Conduct, and Model Code of Professional Responsibility, Copyright by the American Bar Association. All rights reserved. Reprinted with permission; for Alexander, The Dead Hand and the Law of Trusts in the Nineteenth Century, Copyright 1985 by the Board of Trustees of the Leland Stanford Junior University; for Dobris, Argument in Favor of Fiduciary Divestment of "South African" Securities, 65 Neb. L. Rev. 209 (1986), Copyright 1986, Nebraska Law Review; for French, Imposing a General Survival Requirement on Beneficiaries of Future Interests: Solving the Problems Caused by the Death of a Beneficiary Before the Time Set for Distribution, Copyright 1985 by the Arizona Board of Regents. Reprinted by permission; for Friedman, The Law of Succession in Social Perspective, reprinted with permission from Halbach's Death, Taxes and Family Property: Essays and American Assembly Report, Copyright 1977 by West Publishing Co.; for Gustis, What Makes a Family? Traditional Limits Are Challenged, Copyright 1989 by The New York Times Company. Reprinted by permission; for Pickering, Life at All Costs: Pious "Balderdash," reprinted with permission. Legal Times, Copyright, 1989; for Halbach, Problems of Discretion in Discretionary Trusts, Copyright 1961 by the Directors of the Columbia Law Review Association, Inc. All Rights Reserved. This article originally appeared at 61 Colum. L. Rev. 1425 (1961). Reprinted by permission; for Owens & Jordan, Estate Planning for Parents of Mentally Disabled Children, reprinted with permission from Trusts & Estates, Sept. 1987 (c) 1991, Communications Channels, Inc., Atlanta, GA, USA; for Report of the ABA Section Committee on Succession, Restrictions on Charitable Testamentary Gifts, Reprinted by permission of the American Bar Association.

LAWRENCE W. WAGGONER
RICHARD V. WELLMAN
GREGORY S. ALEXANDER
MARY LOUISE FELLOWS

April 1991

Summary of Contents

Division One: Probate Transfers

Division Two: Probate and Nonprobate Transfers

Division Three: Powers of Appointment and Future Interests

Division Four: Administration

Table of Contents

Division One: Probate Transfers

Table of Contents

Division Two: Probate and Nonprobate Transfers

Division Three: Powers of Appointment and Future Interests

Division Four: Administration

Table of Abbreviations

Am. L. Prop.   American Law of Property (A. Casner ed. 1952)

Atkinson on Wills   T. Atkinson, Handbook of the Law of Wills (2d ed. 1953)

Bogert on Trusts   G. Bogert & G. Bogert, Law of Trusts and Trustees (2d ed. 1984-88)

Gray on Perpetuities   J. Gray, The Rule Against Perpetuities (4th ed. 1942)

IRC   Internal Revenue Code of 1986

Palmer on Restitution   G. Palmer, Law of Restitution (1978)

Page on Wills   W. Page, Law of Wills (W. Bowe & D. Parker rev. eds. 1959-82)

Restatement 2d of Property   Restatement (Second) of Property (Donative Transfers) (1983, 1986, 1988, 1992)

Restatement of Property   Restatement of Property (1936, 1940, 1944)

Restatement 3d of Trusts   Restatement (Third) of Trusts (Prudent Investor Rule) (1992)

Restatement 2d of Trusts   Restatement (Second) of Trusts (1959)

Restatement of Trusts   Restatement of Trusts (1935)

Scott on Trusts   A. Scott, Law of Trusts (4th ed. 1987 -89)

Simes & Smith on Future   L. Simes & A. Smith, Law of Future
Interests   Interests (2d ed. 1956)

Table of Cases

The principal cases are in italic type. Other cases are in roman type. References are to pages.

Table of Cases

Tables of Statutes

TABLE OF 1990 UNIFORM PROBATE CODE SECTIONS

Tables of Statutes

TABLE OF PRE-1990 UNIFORM PROBATE CODE SECTIONS

TABLE OF UNIFORM LAWS
(Other than Uniform Probate Code)

TABLE OF INTERNAL REVENUE CODE SECTIONS

TABLE OF TREASURY REGULATIONS

FAMILY PROPERTY LAW

―――

CASES and MATERIALS ON
WILLS, TRUSTS, and FUTURE INTERESTS

INTRODUCTION TO FAMILY PROPERTY LAW

Family Property Law is an unconventional title for a classroom book on wills, trusts, and future interests. We chose the title to emphasize the relationship between transmission of wealth and family. This theme is made all the more important by the fact that questions about family have become acutely important to American law and society in the past few decades as the American family profile changes. Experts estimate that about two-thirds of all first marriages are likely to disrupt. See Martin & Bumpass, Recent Trends in Marital Disruption, 26 Demography 37 (1989). The high divorce rates are accompanied by high remarriage rates. About one out of three persons who marry has been married before. See U.S. Dep't of Health & Human Services, Pub. No. 89-1923, Remarriages and Subsequent Divorces—United States 1-2, 5 (1989). For additional specifics, see infra p. 278.

In fact, the very meaning of family is no longer self-evident in the 1990s. See Bumpass, What's Happening to the Family? Interactions Between Demographic and Institutional Change, 27 Demography 483 (1990) (describing major changes in marriage, divorce, childbearing, women's employment, parenting, and adult intergenerational relationships). Agreements by women to give birth to a child and then to relinquish the baby to the sperm donor are just one of many recent legal developments requiring us to reconsider what we mean by motherhood, fatherhood, and kinship. Uncertainty over the meaning of family in turn has made the role that property plays in affecting family relationships more controversial.

With these issues in mind, each chapter is designed to illuminate the countervailing policies that are at stake as we consider family property law's role in the structuring of the family.

PART A. TERMINOLOGY

The principal actors in this course, and their activities and documents, are known by a special terminology. So, we begin with a thumbnail sketch of that terminology.

A person dying without a valid will has died "intestate," and is referred to as the "intestate." A person who dies with a valid will is said to have died "testate" and is called the "testatrix" or "testator." When the will of a testatrix or testator does not dispose of all of her or his property, it is usually said that the person has died "partially intestate," rather than "partially testate." Conventional legal jargon distinguishes between the "testator" (if a man) and the "testatrix" (if a woman), but, with the abolition of unuseful gendered words, we no longer consider this practice appropriate. In our text, then, we refer to all persons who died with a valid will as the "testator." The Uniform Probate Code also adheres to this usage, but the term "testatrix" still shows up in court opinions, and we have not used our editing pen to change the term in those opinions.

Intestate property is distributed according to statute. The American statutes on intestate succession are derived in part from two sources in English law: the common-law canons of descent, which determined inheritance of land, and the English Statute of Distribution, 1670, 22 Car. 2, c. 10, which governed succession to personal property.

The separate treatment of land and personal property in the English law of intestate succession gave rise to a special terminology. Inheritance of land was called "descent." In fact, the word "inheritance" itself was reserved for intestate succession to land. Those who took land on intestacy were called "heirs." Succession to personal property was often called "distribution" because of the fact that title to personal property passed to the personal representative, who made distribution to those entitled after paying debts and other charges against the estate. As a consequence, statutes on intestate succession were (and still are) called "statutes of descent and distribution." Those who took personalty on intestacy were called "distributees" or "next of kin."

The history is somewhat the same in testate succession. In older usage, a disposition of land by will was a "devise," and the one to whom the land was given was a "devisee." A disposition of personal property was a "legacy" or "bequest," and the recipient was a "legatee." Today the words are commonly used almost interchangeably, especially "devisee" and "legatee." The Uniform Probate Code (UPC or Code) section 1-201 (1990) defines the word "devise," when it appears in the Code, as "a testamentary disposition of real or personal property." Many lawyers have interpreted (misinterpreted?) this statutory definition as meaning that, in UPC states, the words "devise" and "devisee" are the proper words to use in wills for bequests of personal property as well as for devises of land. We have gone along with this newer usage and in this book we usually refer to testamentary dispositions of land or personal property as "devises" and the recipients as "devisees."

Although the rules for intestate succession to real and personal property have major points of difference in a few American jurisdictions, and minor ones in some others, the tendency from an early time in our legal history has been to eliminate such differences. Today, in well over two-thirds of the states, there is a single pattern of inheritance without regard to the nature of the property.

One important difference remains in most states, however: In accordance with the traditions of English law, title to and the right of possession of land pass directly to the heirs, whereas title to and the right of possession of personal property pass to the administrator, a fiduciary who is now often called the "personal representative." The same difference appears in the law of wills: Title to and possession of land disposed of by will vests in the devisee, whereas title to and possession of personal property goes to the personal representative, the executor, where the will names an executor. Where there is legislation on the point, however, title to both real and personal property usually passes directly to the heirs or devisees, subject to a right of possession in the personal representative for purposes of properly administering the estate. See, e.g., UPC §§ 3-101, -709 (1990). The old difference in concept manifests itself in some states where personal property is to be used ahead of real property in the payment of estate creditors.

With the modern tendency to eliminate differences between succession of real and personal property, the old terminology is disappearing. Lawyers now often use the words "inheritance," "heirs," and "next of kin" without regard to the character of the estate. Nevertheless, disregard of the older usage is still dangerous as long as there is some reason for differentiating between real and personal property. For example, testators sometimes make devises to their own or somebody else's "heirs" or "next of kin." A devise of real property to "next of kin," or a devise of personal property to "heirs," may be ambiguous if the applicable law contains a different pattern for succession of real and personal property.

PART B. DONATIVE FREEDOM

The right to make a donative transfer is viewed generally as a statutory creature that is not constitutionally protected, see Irving Trust Co. v. Day, 314 U.S. 556 (1942), but, as Professor Friedman suggests in the excerpt below, it has a strong historical tradition in Anglo-American law.

Friedman, The Law of Succession in Social Perspective,

in Death, Taxes and Family Property: Essays and American Assembly
Report 14-18 (E. Halbach ed. 1977)

It is often said that the principle of freedom of testation dominates the law of the United States. Every adult of sound mind may make out a *will*; in the will, the testator can dispose of his property as he wishes. There are, however, quite definite, and important, limitations on the principle. . . .

Freedom of testation, in theory, gives a person the right to exclude or disinherit his "natural" heirs. In almost all of the states, however, this freedom does not extend to a surviving husband or wife. The survivor has a claim on the estate—as much as half—which cannot be defeated by will. It is possible, in some states, for an angry or malicious husband or wife to disinherit the spouse through living trusts or other devices of transfer; but it is never easy, and many states have tried to prevent this from occurring. The problem, in fact, arises quite rarely in practice. Studies show little inclination to disinherit spouses; and easy divorce makes the problem less real by providing a better way to end financial entanglements when the emotional tie has been destroyed.

Children, on the other hand, can be disinherited merely by mentioning them. Cohen, Robson, and Bates, who surveyed public attitudes toward law in Nebraska in the 1950's, in *Parental Authority: The Community and the Law* (1958), found that this right to disinherit children was distinctly unpopular. 57.3 percent of their sample disapproved of the right, even with regard to children who were grown and wealthy (as to minor children, 93.4 percent disapproved). In fact, minor children (and surviving spouses) have a right under the law to money from the estate, to maintain them while the estate is in probate. Widow and minor children also often have rights to keep the family homestead. Moreover, spouses and children usually have special claims on pension rights, social security rights, and other welfare benefits. As to these, there is typically no freedom of testation. This means that the law is not really so far from community sentiment as it appears to be on the surface. For most of the lower middle class, most of the estate will in fact be "bound" to the immediate family, and not subject to freedom of testation in any meaningful sense. Furthermore, the "disinheritance" of children by will is actually quite common, and even normal. The average man who dies survived by a wife and children, will want to leave his estate to his wife rather than to his children. Technically, of course, he is disinheriting them. . . .

The inheritance law of the United States derives many of its main institutions from English law, as is true of the law in general. But the changes in the last few centuries have been massive. In medieval England, land was overwhelmingly the most important form of property, the basis for wealth, and the keystone of the social system; personal property was relatively unimportant. Originally, there was little freedom of testation in land. The statute of wills was enacted in 1540, during the reign of Henry VIII. It recognized the validity of wills of land and required them to be in writing. Another landmark was the Statute of Frauds (1640) which prescribed the formalities familiar to this day. . . .

There have been more substantial changes in the law of succession reflecting major social change, in other areas. As the position of women in the law changed, the law of inheritance changed with it. In the older common law, the married woman was not treated as a self-sufficient entity. When a woman married, she lost her legal personality, which merged with her husband's. The two were, as the phrase went, "one flesh"; but the husband was the dominant partner. He managed the property, and the wife had no independent power to dispose of it at all. Beginning around 1840, the states enacted Married Women's Property acts. These gradually altered this situation; by the late 19th century, the married woman had the same rights to deal with and transfer land, and to dispose of it by will, as the married man.

Hodel v. Irving
481 U.S. 704 (1987)

O'CONNOR, J. The question presented is whether the original version of the "escheat" provision of the Indian Land Consolidation Act of 1983, Pub. L. 97-459, Tit 2, 96 Stat. 2519, effected a "taking" of appellees' decedents' property without just compensation. . . .

Towards the end of the 19th century, Congress enacted a series of land Acts which divided the communal reservations of Indian tribes into individual allotments for Indians and unallotted lands for non-Indian settlement. This legislation seems to have been in part animated by desire to force Indians to abandon their nomadic ways in order to "speed the Indians' assimilation into American society," and in part a result of pressure to free new lands for further white settlement. Two years after the enactment of the General Allotment Act of 1887, ch. 119, 24 Stat. 388, Congress adopted a specific statute authorizing the division of the Great Reservation of the Sioux Nation into separate reservations and the allotment of specific tracts of reservation land to individual Indians, conditioned on the consent of three-fourths of the adult male Sioux. Act of Mar. 2, 1889, ch. 405, 25 Stat. 888. Under the Act, each male Sioux head of household took 320 acres of land and most other individuals 160 acres. 25 Stat. 890. In order to protect the allottees from the improvident disposition of their lands to white settlers, the Sioux allotment statute provided that the allotted lands were to be held in trust by the United States. Id., at 891. Until 1910 the lands of deceased allottees passed to their heirs "according to the laws of the State or Territory" where the land was located, ibid., and after 1910, allottees were permitted to dispose of their interests by will in accordance with regulations promulgated by the Secretary of the Interior. 36 Stat. 856, 25 U.S.C. § 373 [25 U.S.C.S. § 373]. Those regulations generally served to protect Indian ownership of the allotted lands.

The policy of allotment of Indian lands quickly proved disastrous for the Indians. Cash generated by land sales to whites was quickly dissipated and the Indians, rather than farm the land themselves, evolved into petty landlords, leasing their allotted lands to white ranchers and farmers and living off the meager rentals. The failure of the allotment program became even clearer as successive generations came to hold the allotted lands. Thus 40-, 80-, and 160-acre parcels became splintered into multiple undivided interests in land, with some parcels having hundreds and many parcels having dozens of owners. Because the land was held in trust and often could not be alienated or partitioned the fractionation problem grew and grew over time.

A 1928 report commissioned by the Congress found the situation administratively unworkable and economically wasteful. Good, potentially productive land was allowed to lie fallow, amidst great poverty, because of the difficulties of managing property held in this manner. . . . In 1934, . . . the Congress acknowledged the failure of its policy and ended further allotment of Indian lands. Indian Reorganization Act of 1934, ch. 576, 48 Stat. 984, 25 U.S.C. § 461 et seq. [25 U.S.C.S. §§ 461 et seq.]

But the end of future allotment by itself could not prevent the further compounding of the existing problem caused by the passage of time. Ownership continued to fragment as succeeding generations came to hold the property, since, in the order of things, each property owner was apt to have more than one heir. In 1960, both the House and the Senate undertook comprehensive studies of the problem. These studies indicated that one-half of the approximately 12 million acres of allotted trust lands were held in fractionated ownership, with over 3 million acres held by more than six heirs to a parcel. Further hearings were held in 1966, but not until the Indian Land Consolidation Act of 1983 did the Congress take action to ameliorate the problem of fractionated ownership of Indian lands.

Section 207 of the Indian Land Consolidation Act—the escheat provision at issue in the case—provided:

> No undivided fractional interest in any tract of trust or restricted land within a tribe's reservation or otherwise subjected to a tribe's jurisdiction shall descendent [sic] by intestacy or devise but shall escheat to that tribe if such interest represents 2 per centum or less of the total acreage in such tract and has earned to its owner less than $100 in the preceding year before it is due to escheat. 96 Stat. 2519.

Congress made no provision for the payment of compensation to the owners of the interests covered by § 207. The statute was signed into law on January 12, 1983, and became effective immediately.

The three appellees—Mary Irving, Patrick Pumpkin Seed, and Eileen Bissonette—are enrolled members of the Oglala Sioux Tribe. They are, or represent, heirs or devisees of members of the Tribe who died in March, April, and June 1983. Eileen Bissonette's decedent, Mary Poor Bear-Little Hoop Cross, purported to will all her property, including property subject to § 207, to her five minor children in whose name Bissonette claims the property. Chester Irving, Charles Leroy Pumpkin Seed, and Edgar Pumpkin

Seed all died intestate. At the time of their deaths, the four decedents owned 41 fractional interests subject to the provisions of § 207. . . .

This Court has held that the Government has considerable latitude in regulating property rights in ways that may adversely affect the owners. The framework for examining the question of whether a regulation of property amounts to a taking requiring just compensation is firmly established and has been regularly and recently reaffirmed. . . .

There is no question that the relative economic impact of § 207 upon the owners of these property rights can be substantial. Section 207 provides for the escheat of small undivided property interests that are unproductive during the year preceding the owner's death. Even if we accept the Government's assertion that the income generated by such parcels may be properly thought of as de minimis, their value may not be. While the Irving estate lost two interests whose value together was only approximately $100, the Bureau of Indian Affairs placed total values of approximately $2,700 and $1,816 on the escheatable interests in the Cross and Pumpkin Seed estates. These are not trivial sums. There are suggestions in the legislative history regarding the 1984 amendments to § 207 that the failure to "look back" more than one year at the income generated by the property had caused the escheat of potentially valuable timber and mineral interests. Of course, the whole of appellees' decedents' property interests were not taken by § 207. Appellees' decedents retained full beneficial use of the property during their lifetimes as well as the right to convey it inter vivos. There is no question, however, that the right to pass on valuable property to one's heirs is itself a valuable right. Depending on the age of the owner, much or most of the value of the parcel may inhere in this "remainder" interest. . . .

The extent to which any of appellees' decedents had "investment-backed expectations" in passing on the property is dubious. Though it is conceivable that some of these interests were purchased with the expectation that the owners might pass on the remainder to their heirs at death, the property has been held in trust for the Indians for 100 years and is overwhelmingly acquired by gift, descent, or devise. Because of the highly fractionated ownership, the property is generally held for lease rather than improved and used by the owners. None of the appellees here can point to any specific investment-backed expectations beyond the fact that their ancestors agreed to accept allotment only after ceding to the United States large parts of the original Great Sioux Reservation.

Also weighing weakly in favor of the statute is the fact that there is something of an "average reciprocity of advantage," to the extent that owners of escheatable interests maintain a nexus to the Tribe. Consolidation of Indian lands in the Tribe benefits the members of the Tribe. All members do not own escheatable interests, nor do all owners belong to the Tribe. Nevertheless, there is substantial overlap between the two groups. The owners of escheatable interests often benefit from the escheat of others' fractional interests. Moreover, the whole benefit gained is greater than the sum of the burdens imposed since consolidated lands are more productive than fractionated lands.

If we were to stop our analysis at this point, we might well find § 207 constitutional. But the character of the Government regulation here is extraordinary. . . . [T]he regulation here amounts to virtually the abrogation of the right to pass on a certain type of property —the small undivided interest—to one's heirs. In one form or another, the right to pass on property—to one's family in particular—has been part of the Anglo-American legal system since feudal times. The fact that it may be possible for the owners of these interests to effectively control disposition upon death through complex inter vivos transactions such as revocable trusts, is simply not an adequate substitute for the rights taken, given the nature of the property. Even the United States concedes that total abrogation of the right to pass property is unprecedented and likely unconstitutional. Moreover, this statute effectively abolishes both descent and devise of these property interests even when the passing of the property to the heir might result in consolidation of property—as for instance when the heir already owns another undivided interest in the property. Since the escheatable interests are not, as the United States argues, necessarily de minimis, nor, as it also argues, does the availability of inter vivos transfer obviate the need for descent and devise, a *total* abrogation of these rights cannot be upheld.

In holding that complete abolition of both the descent and devise of a particular class of property may be a taking, we reaffirm the continuing vitality of the long line of cases recognizing the States', and where appropriate, the United States', broad authority to adjust the rules governing the descent and devise of property without implicating the guarantees of the Just Compensation Clause. The difference in this case is the fact that both descent and devise are completely abolished; indeed they are abolished even in circumstances when the governmental purpose sought to be advanced, consolidation of ownership of Indian lands, does not conflict with the further descent of the property.

There is little doubt that the extreme fractionation of Indian lands is a serious public problem. It may well be appropriate for the United States to ameliorate fractionation by means of regulating the descent and devise of Indian lands. Surely it is permissible for the United States to prevent the owners of such interests from further subdividing them among future heirs on pain of escheat. It may be appropriate to minimize further compounding of the problem by abolishing the descent of such interests by rules of intestacy, thereby forcing the owners to formally designate an heir to prevent escheat to the Tribe. What is certainly not appropriate is to take the extraordinary step of abolishing both descent and devise of these property interests even when the passing of the property to the heir might result in consolidation of property.

BRENNAN, J., concurring, joined by MARSHALL and BLACKMUN, JJ. SCALIA, J., concurring, joined by REHNQUIST, C.J., and POWELL, J. STEVENS, J., concurring, joined by WHITE, J.

Notes and Questions

1. *Lifetime vs. Deathtime Transfers.* In Part C and throughout this casebook we will discuss the similarities and differences between lifetime and deathtime transfers. For now, it is interesting to conjecture whether Justice O'Connor thinks that the right to create will substitutes, such as a revocable lifetime trust, is nearly the equivalent of the right to make a will. Even if she had not appreciated the similarities between these two types of transfers, is her decision to hold section 207 unconstitutional supportable? See Note, 18 Envtl. L. 597 (1988); Comment, 43 U. Miami L. Rev. 739 (1989).

2. *Approval of Wills.* The Secretary of the Interior is authorized under 25 U.S.C. § 373 to approve Indian wills for allotted land. Tooahnippah v. Hickel, 397 U.S. 598 (1970), held that the Secretary does not have unlimited discretion to revoke or rewrite a will that reflects a rational testamentary scheme. The *Tooahnippah* case concerned a will in which the testator devised his estate to a niece, with whom he had a close and loving relationship, and disinherited his daughter, with whom he had no social relationship. The Regional Solicitor, an officer having authority to make a final decision on behalf of the Secretary, disapproved the will because it failed to treat the testator's daughter fairly and equitably. The Court held this standard was inappropriate. "The Regional Solicitor's action was based on nothing more that we can discern than his concept of equity and in our view that was not the kind of degree of discretion Congress vested in him." 397 U.S. at 610.

A testator may have greater testamentary freedom with regard to allotted land than with regard to other property. The Supreme Court held in Blanset v. Cardin, 256 U.S. 319 (1921), that state law had no application to allotted lands. Thus restrictions upon testamentary freedom imposed under state law, such as the spousal elective share, are inapplicable. Applying both *Blanset* and *Tooahnippah* cases together, an Indian may, in some respects, have greater freedom to devise allotted lands than other property. See Akers v. Morton, 499 F.2d 44 (9th Cir. 1974) (state dower rights do not apply under 25 U.S.C. § 348; the Secretary of the Interior is not authorized to impose a spousal protection requirement as part of the process of will approval under 25 U.S.C. § 373).

PART C. THE PROBATE/NONPROBATE DICHOTOMY

Division One (Chapters 2 through 5) of this book is devoted to family property law as it relates to probate property. Chapter 2 focuses on the distribution of probate property when a decedent dies without a will and Chapters 3 through 5 focus on the distribution of probate property when a decedent dies with probate's exclusive instrument—a valid will. Division Two (Chapters 6 through 13) brings nonprobate transfers into the discussion. Nonprobate instruments are plentiful and include the revocable trust, the life-insurance contract, the pension–account contract, and the joint bank or stock account. Chapters 7 and 11 through 13 discuss the formation and operation of trusts in detail. Chapter 18 is devoted to the subject of fiduciary administration. It describes the powers, duties, and liabilities of fiduciaries, including both probate representatives and trustees. In other words, it establishes the legal contours of the term "fiduciary."

Sometimes trusts are created by will. These trusts are referred to as "testamentary trusts." Trusts can also be created by nonprobate instruments, which are referred to as "lifetime trusts," "inter-vivos trusts," or "non-testamentary trusts." However created, a trust is a fiduciary relationship with respect to property, in which title and beneficial ownership are separate. The trustee holds title to and manages the trust property for the benefit of another person or persons, who are called the beneficiary or beneficiaries. A lifetime trust can be irrevocable or revocable. If it remains revocable until the settlor's death, it operates as a will substitute and serves the function of avoiding probate.

Although Chapters 7, 11 through 13, and 18 will go into more detail about the formation and operation of trusts, it is useful to appreciate at the outset that a trust is conceptually simple and is a powerful estate planning tool. A good deal of the discussion in this book is devoted to trusts because, as we shall see, they are used by estate planners to maximize flexibility and minimize administrative complexity as they accomplish their clients' family property goals.

By addressing probate transfers first, we do not mean to indicate that they are more important than nonprobate transfers. Nor do we mean to suggest that intestate succession and wills are more important forms of transfer than other forms, such as lifetime trusts. On the contrary, our organization is designed to show that intestate succession is a default mechanism that becomes operative when a property owner dies without having executed a will or without having executed any will substitutes, such as acquiring a life-insurance contract and designating a beneficiary to receive the proceeds. A will, in turn, operates as a default mechanism by controlling the distribution of property that is not otherwise controlled by a nonprobate instrument. How and why nonprobate transfers have come to overshadow probate transfers is the subject of the following excerpt.

Langbein, The Nonprobate Revolution and the Future of the Law of Succession
97 Harv. L. Rev. 1108, 1108-09, 1113-25 (1984)

The law of wills and the rules of descent no longer govern succession to most of the property of most decedents. Increasingly, probate bears to the actual practice of succession about the relation that bankruptcy bears to enterprise: it is an indispensable institution, but hardly one that everybody need use. . . .

I. The Will Substitutes

Four main will substitutes constitute the core of the nonprobate system: life insurance, pension accounts, joint accounts, and revocable trusts. When properly created, each is functionally indistinguishable from a will—each reserves to the owner complete lifetime dominion, including the power to name and to change beneficiaries until death. These devices I shall call "pure" will substitutes, in contradistinction to "imperfect" will substitutes (primarily joint tenancies), which more closely resemble completed lifetime transfers. The four pure will substitutes may also be described as mass will substitutes: they are marketed by financial intermediaries using standard form instruments with fill-in-the-blank beneficiary designations. . . .

Although the revocable trust is the fundamental device that the estate-planning bar employs to fit the carriage trade with highly individuated instruments, the revocable trust also keeps company with the mass will substitutes. Standard-form revocable trusts with fill-in-the-blank beneficiary designations are widely offered in the banking industry and were at one time aggressively promoted in the mutual fund industry. The Totten trust, an especially common variant, is simply a deposit account in which the beneficiary designation is thinly camouflaged under language of trust. The depositor names himself trustee for the beneficiary, but retains lifetime dominion and the power to revoke. . . .

Either by declaration of trust or by transfer to a third-party trustee, the appropriate trust terms can replicate the incidents of a will. The owner who retains both the equitable life interest and the power to alter and revoke the beneficiary designation has used the trust form to achieve the effect of testation. Only nomenclature distinguishes the remainder interest created by such a trust from the mere expectancy arising under a will. Under either the trust or the will, the interest of the beneficiaries is both revocable and ambulatory. . . .

The "pure" will substitutes are not the only instruments of the nonprobate revolution; "imperfect" will substitutes—most prominent among them the common-law joint tenancy—also serve to transfer property at death without probate. Joint tenancies in real estate and in securities are quite common; joint tenancies in automobiles and other vehicles are also fairly widespread. Because they ordinarily effect lifetime transfers, joint tenancies are "imperfect" rather than "pure" will substitutes. When the owner of a house, a car, a boat, or a block of IBM common stock arranges to take title jointly, his cotenant acquires an interest that is no longer revocable and ambulatory. Under the governing recording act or stock transfer act, both cotenants must ordinarily join in any subsequent transfer. Yet like the pure will substitutes, joint tenancy arrangements allow the survivor to obtain marketable title without probate: under joint tenancy, a death certificate rather than a probate decree suffices to transfer title. . . .

II. The Hidden Causes Of The Nonprobate Revolution

. . . The will substitutes differ from the ordinary "last will and testament" in three main ways. First, most will substitutes—but not all—are asset-specific: each deals with a single type of property, be it life insurance proceeds, a bank balance, mutual fund shares, or whatever. Second, property that passes through a will substitute avoids probate. A financial intermediary ordinarily takes the place of the probate court in effecting the transfer. Third, the formal requirements of the Wills Act—attestation and so forth—do not govern will substitutes and are not complied with. Of these differences, only probate avoidance is a significant advantage that transferors might consciously seek.

. . . The probate system has earned a lamentable reputation for expense, delay, clumsiness, makework, and worse. In various jurisdictions, especially the dozen-odd that have adopted or imitated the simplified procedures of the Uniform Probate Code of 1969 ("UPC"), the intensity of hostility to probate may have abated a little. There are, however, intrinsic limits to the potential of probate reform. As Richard Wellman, the principal draftsman of the UPC, forthrightly declared: "The assumption that administration of an estate requires a judicial proceeding is as doubtful as it is costly." Because the Anglo-American procedural tradition is preoccupied with adversarial and litigational values, the decision to organize any function as a judicial proceeding is inconsistent with the interests that ordinary people regard as paramount when they think about the transmission of their property at death: dispatch, simplicity, inexpensiveness, privacy. As long as probate reform still calls for probate, it will not go far enough for the tastes of many transferors, who view probate as little more than a tax imposed for the benefit of court functionaries and lawyers.

The puzzle in the story of the nonprobate revolution is not that transferors should have sought to avoid probate, but rather that other persons whose interests probate was meant to serve—above all, creditors—should have allowed the protections of the probate system to slip away from them. Probate performs three essential functions: (1) making property owned at death marketable again (title-clearing); (2) paying off the decedent's debts (creditor protection); and (3) implementing the decedent's donative intent respecting the property that remains once the claims of creditors have been discharged (distribution). . . . Although the will substitutes are not well suited to clearing title and protecting creditors, a series of changes in the nature of wealth and in the business practices of creditors has diminished the importance of these functions. . . .

The probate court is empowered to transfer title to a decedent's real property and thereby to restore it to marketability under the recording system. The cautious procedures of probate administration have seemed especially appropriate for realty, because the values tend to be large and the financing complex. In theory, the probate court should exercise a similar title-clearing function for all personalty, down to the sugar bowl and the pajamas, because only a court decree can perfect a successor's title in any item of personalty. Of course, ordinary practice quite belies the theory. Beyond the realm of vehicles and registered securities, which are covered by recording systems and thus resemble realty in some of the mechanics of transfer, formal evidence of title is not required to render personalty usable and marketable.

The preoccupation of probate procedure with the transfer of title to single-tenancy real estate reflects the wealth patterns of the small-farm, small-enterprise economy of the nineteenth century that shaped our probate tradition. . . . Promissory instruments—stocks, bonds, mutual funds, bank deposits, and pension and insurance rights—are the dominant component of today's private wealth. Together with public promises (that is, government transfer payments) these instruments of financial intermediation eclipse realty and tangible personalty.

The instruments of financial intermediation depend upon an underlying administrative capacity that is without counterpart in the realm of realty and tangible personalty. Financial intermediation is, as the term signifies, intrinsically administrative. . . . Once a bureaucracy appropriate to such tasks is in operation, only a scant adaptation is necessary to extend its functions and procedures to include the transfer of account balances on death.

The probate system nonetheless backstops the practice of financial intermediaries in important ways. The standard form instruments of the nonprobate system all but invariably name the transferor's probate estate as the ultimate contingent beneficiary. If, therefore, the named beneficiaries predecease the transferor or cannot be identified, the financial intermediary remits the fund to probate distribution. Messy heirship determinations are foisted off onto the courts. Likewise, if the proper course of distribution is for some reason doubtful, or if contest threatens, financial intermediaries can force the probate (or other) courts to decide the matter. . . . In this way the nonprobate system rides "piggyback" on the probate system. . . . In the nonprobate system, genuine disputes still reach the courts, but routine administration does not. . . .

The other set of changes that underlie the nonprobate revolution concerns another great mission of probate: discharging the decedent's debts. Many of the details of American probate procedure, as well as much of its larger structure, would not exist but for the need to identify and pay off creditors. These procedures are indispensable, but—and here I am asserting a proposition that has not been adequately understood—only for the most exceptional cases. In general, *creditors do not need or use probate.*

I have undertaken to verify this point within the retail and consumer credit industry. Without mounting a systematic empirical study, I have tried to inquire broadly among credit officers and credit information specialists and their lawyers. Among those I interviewed, I found unanimity both on the central proposition that probate plays an inconsequential role in the collection of decedents' debts, and on the reasons why.

In the vast majority of cases, survivors pay off decedents' debts voluntarily and rapidly. . . .

Creditors know that survivors behave in this way, and they rely upon voluntary notice from survivors as their primary means of learning about a debtor's death. . . . In the remainder of cases, which usually involve unmarried decedents, the creditor commonly discovers the death when the account becomes delinquent and collections personnel begin making inquiries. None of the large retail creditors with whom I spoke made any effort to take advantage of the formal notice-of-death procedures contained in the probate codes for their protection, nor did they have anyone assigned to read newspaper obituaries or inspect official death registers. . . .

Creditor protection is also intertwined with a variant of the principal will substitute, life insurance. So-called credit life insurance typically discharges an insured's account balance at death. . . .

Toward the upper end of the scale of consumer debt, where we encounter automobile finance, we find a different mode of creditor protection, the security interest. . . . This leverage over survivors ordinarily leads to out-of-court settlement of such debts. . . .

When this formidable battery of out-of-court payment and collection practices fails to clear a debt, the creditor protection system of probate may also be unavailing. Although the safeguards of notice, court filings, hearings, adjudication, and so forth are meant to protect creditors, they are often self-defeating, because they make probate proceedings too expensive to be cost effective for collecting routine debts. Account balances are often so small that collection costs would exceed the likely recovery even if nonlawyers handled most of the filings and subsequent steps.

Nonetheless, creditors do use probate. The large creditors with whom I spoke were prepared to go to probate to attempt to collect debts of several thousand dollars when preliminary investigation by credit information agencies or in-house personnel revealed the likelihood of substantial assets in a probate estate. None seemed concerned to trace nonprobate assets. . . .

In the late twentieth century, creditor protection and probate have largely parted company. Had this development been otherwise, the rise of the will substitutes could not have occurred. If creditors had continued to rely significantly upon probate for the payment of decedents' debts, creditors' interests would have constituted an impossible obstacle to the nonprobate revolution. For—make no mistake about it—the will substitutes do impair the mechanism by which probate protects creditors. Even though the substantive law governing most of the major will substitutes usually recognizes the priority of creditors' claims over the claims of gratuitous transferees (life insurance is sometimes an exception), the decentralized procedures of the nonprobate system materially disadvantage creditors.

Notes and Questions

1. *Probate Administration.* Chapter 18 is devoted to a consideration of many probate administration issues. The purpose of this Note is to give you a general sense of the personal representative's responsibilities and the procedures. Any discussion of probate administration quickly becomes complicated because of the nonuniform state of the laws and the diverse

practices in local probate offices. Nevertheless, a general description of the probate administration process and the responsibilities of the personal representative of the decedent's estate is possible. If a decedent dies without a will or if the decedent's will fails to name an executor, courts, in accordance with statutory direction, will name an administrator. If the will names an executor and that person is willing and able to serve, she or he will act as personal representative of the estate. An executor or administrator have the same responsibilities. They are fiduciaries and are entrusted with the decedent's property. They are accorded powers that they must exercise on behalf of those persons who have a claim to the decedent's estate—beneficiaries and creditors.

In preparation for beginning the probate administration process, the personal representative should consult with the family and assist, as requested, with funeral arrangements. She or he should also ascertain surviving kin and obtain their addresses, notify the decedent's banks, employer, insurers, and annuity obligors of the death, identify and protect the decedent's moveable assets, and review records for business contracts, property transactions, debts, and credits. The personal representative should locate the will and obtain copies of the death certificate.

The personal representative then should file a petition for probate of the will and obtain a court appointment as the personal representative. The will should be probated in the county in which the decedent was domiciled at the time of death. If real property is located in another jurisdiction, she or he will also have to seek ancillary administration in that jurisdiction. She or he should arrange for probate bond, if necessary, and give required notices to creditors of the decedent.

The personal representative's next responsibility is to collect, protect, inventory, and appraise all probate assets. She or he should deposit all estate cash and checks payable to the decedent in a personal representative's estate account. She or he should collect insurance proceeds, if any, that are payable to the estate. She or he should collect any sums owed to the decedent. She or he should take possession of, store, or otherwise secure, tangible personal assets. She or he should prepare an inventory of estate assets for court filing, if necessary, and arrange for appraisal of estate assets as may be required by the court or dictated by federal and state tax rules. She or he should set up a record system to identify probate and nonprobate assets passing at death to surviving joint tenants and death beneficiaries. This information will be required for reporting on state inheritance and federal estate tax returns. Finally, she or he should investigate business arrangements that may require attention and make appropriate protective and managerial arrangements.

The personal representative must also consider all claims presented to her or him or the court against the estate. She or he should gather the necessary information needed to reject or allow each of the claims. She or he should discharge undisputed and minor obligations as soon as possible. In making these decisions, she or he should consider the amount of all known claims against the estate and the estate's liquidity. She or he should obtain information necessary to file necessary tax returns, including federal and state transfer taxes, the decedent's final income tax return, and the estate's income tax return. She or he should pay all taxes when due.

In addition to discharging claims, the personal representative should consider the other cash demands on the estate. These would include payments for family allowance, which are statutorily provided, see infra Chapter 8, administrative expenses, and legacies. The personal representative must make decisions about how needed cash may be best raised and what assets, if any, need to be liquidated. She or he must also make investment decisions taking into consideration market conditions and the estate beneficiaries. She or he has the responsibility for investing the probate assets prudently and for managing them conservatively pending distribution.

Finally, the personal representative must determine the distributive rights of estate beneficiaries. She or he must prepare an accounting of receipts and disbursements. This accounting must indicate whether those receipts and disbursements are related to income or principal. She or he must also prepare a distribution plan for the court and obtain the beneficiaries' approval of the plan. The personal representative should consider whether to make partial distribution in cash or in kind. That decision will be influenced by tax consequences for the estate and for the beneficiaries. Final distribution will occur upon order of the court or upon receipt of a release from the beneficiaries.

2. *Creditors' Claims.* Professor Langbein writes that creditors do not rely much on probate administration to secure discharge of debts owed them. His analysis, however, focuses exclusively on voluntary creditors. Do you think that persons who have tort claims against the decedent would rely on the protections afforded by probate administration? Do you think property passing by will substitutes, such as life-insurance proceeds and joint bank accounts, should be beyond the reach of tort claimants? This question is discussed infra in Chapter 7. We will see that the rights of creditors to reach nonprobate property is frequently determined by statute and depends on the type of will substitute involved.

The United States Supreme Court held in Tulsa Professional Collection Services, Inc. v. Pope, 485 U.S. 478 (1988), that the due process clause requires that creditors of the decedent who are known to, or reasonably ascertainable by, the estate fiduciary be given actual notice of court proceedings serving to bar creditors' claims. The Court held that notice by publication is insufficient. For further discussion of this case and its impact on probate procedure, see infra Chapter 18.

3. *The Will/Will Substitute Distinction.* Professor Langbein writes that "[t]he owner who retains both the equitable life interest and the power to alter and revoke the beneficiary designation has used the trust form to achieve the effect of testation. Only nomenclature distinguishes the remainder interest created by such a trust from the mere expectancy arising under a will." Langbein, supra, at 1113. That passage was probably particularly confusing when you read it, because it seems to say that what the law calls a will and what the law calls a revocable lifetime trust has the same substantive consequences. If that is so, why distinguish the two

instruments at all? The answer is that family property law is in a transitional stage, moving toward the elimination of the will/will substitute distinction.

The twentieth-century nonprobate revolution has significantly affected family property law. Many important issues ignore the distinction. For example, statutory protections of spouses provide that nonprobate as well as probate property is reachable by spouses who decedents have disinherited. See infra Chapter 8. Similarly, the federal and state income and transfer tax laws treat property passing by wills and will substitutes alike. See infra Chapter 6. On the other hand, full integration of the law of wills and will substitutes is not yet complete. Many legal consequences still turn on whether an instrument is labelled a will or a will substitute. For example, a marital dissolution accompanied by a property settlement operates to void any devise to one spouse in the other spouse's will. The legislatures generally have failed to reform these statutes to void will-substitute transfers made to former spouses. But see UPC § 2-804 (1990). Throughout the study of family property law, the will/will substitute distinction requires the following inquiries: Does this rule apply only to wills? Ought the rule, or a variant of it, apply to will substitutes? A still further question is: Does, or ought, the rule apply to *all* donative transfers, including lifetime transfers that are not will substitutes, such as irrevocable lifetime trusts?

PART D. ESTATE PLANNING CLIENTS: THE SMITH /WILLIAMS FAMILY

What follows is a description of a hypothetical family with hypothetical property and problems. This client profile is used to explore further the probate/nonprobate dichotomy discussed in Part C. It also is used as the basis for many of the issues raised in Part E, which deals with another major theme that pervades the study of family property law: the professional responsibility of the estate planning attorney.

Name	*Relations*	*Age*	*Health*
Barbara Smith	Wife	44	Good
James Williams	Husband	43	Good
Nelson Jordan	Biological son of Barbara; Stepson of James	13	Hearing impairment
Ella Williams	Biological daughter of Barbara and James	8	Good

Marital Status and Occupations of Spouses. This is a second marriage for both Barbara and James. They were both divorced when they married each other ten years ago. James had no children from his prior marriage. Barbara had one child, Nelson, from her prior marriage. The court awarded custody of Nelson to Barbara. She receives $500 per month child support from his father. These payments will continue until Nelson attains the age of 18. Although in the past, these support payments were irregular, Nelson's father has made every payment for the last year on a timely basis.

Barbara teaches science and James teaches mathematics at public high schools in Baltimore, Maryland.

Parents. Barbara's mother, Taunya Smith, is 76 years old and lives in Michigan. Her father died five years ago of cancer. James' mother, Susan Williams, is 78 and lives in North Carolina. His father died of a heart attack at age 67. Both mothers live modestly but comfortably, thanks to pension and social security benefits. Neither mother requires financial assistance from her children at this time. Both continue to be healthy enough to maintain their own homes and care for themselves. Barbara does not expect to inherit any significant amount of property from her mother. Susan Williams told James that she has written a will that names him as taker of her North Carolina home. She explained her plan to her other children by reminding them that James had spent several summers repairing and remodeling the home for her and had always expressed a great fondness for it.

Collateral Relatives. Barbara has four siblings and six nieces and nephews. James has a brother and sister, four nephews, and three grandnephews. One of Barbara's sisters is financially successful and has no children. She is likely to leave some of her property to her nieces and nephews, including Nelson and Ella, after she provides financial security to her domestic partner, Mary Mitchell. She is also likely to assist her nieces and nephews through college and graduate or professional school should they decide to attend.

Barbara has one maternal uncle surviving and James has one maternal aunt surviving. Both the uncle and aunt have surviving children and grandchildren and Barbara and James do not expect to inherit from either.

ASSETS

Type	Estimated Value
Tangible personal property, including furnishings, clothing, and jewelry	$ 15,000
Cars:	
(1) BMW: Title in James. It is subject to a $9,000 debt.	$ 15,000
(2) Mercury Topaz: Title in Barbara. It is subject to $4,000 debt.	$ 7,000

Intangible personal property:
(1) Bank accounts:

Joint checking account: James and Barbara	$ 2,000
Savings account: James	$ 4,000
Savings account: Barbara	$ 6,000

(2) Certificate of Deposit: Barbara and James as joint owners with right of survivorship — $ 10,000

(3) Series EE U.S. Savings Bonds: Barbara owner and payable-on-death to Nelson — $ 1,000

(4) Brokerage stock account: Barbara and James as joint owners with right of survivorship — $ 5,000

Family residence:
Deed states: "Barbara Smith and James Williams as joint tenants with right of survivorship." It is subject to mortgage of $85,000. — $140,000

Employee benefits:
(1) Group term life insurance on Barbara; double the face value in case of accidental death — $150,000
(2) Group term life insurance on James; double the face value in case of accidental death — $150,000
(3) Disability insurance on Barbara (annual salary at time of injury) — ---
(4) Disability insurance on James (annual salary at time of injury) — ---
(5) Qualified pension plan for Barbara; allows election of joint and survivor annuity at age 62. James is eligible to receive Barbara's contributed amount (presently $34,000) if Barbara dies before retiring. — ---
(6) Qualified pension plan for James; same as Barbara's except contributed amount is valued presently at $30,000. — ---

(7) Entire family covered under
   school district's Blue Cross/Blue
   Shield medical plan, which in-
   cludes dental coverage.   ---

LIABILITIES

Real estate mortgage on residence $ 85,000

Car loans
   (1) BMW $ 9,000
   (2) Mercury Topaz $ 4,000

Credit card balances $ 1,500

Pledge to United Negro College Fund (to
be paid over the next three years) $ 2,000

Prior Estate Plans. Barbara has a will leaving all of her estate to her son, Nelson. She wrote this will before she married James. James has never written a will.

———

1. *Probate/Nonprobate.* What assets owned by the couple would be subject to probate administration? Does Barbara's will leave James at serious economic risk if she were to die with it in force? What further investigation regarding these assets do you need to make before you can answer these questions accurately?

Suppose Barbara died in an accident caused by the faulty manufacture of a consumer product she was using. Would any damages paid posthumously by the manufacturer as a result of a settlement or court decision become part of her probate estate?

2. *Creating Nonprobate Instruments.* Do you think that Barbara and James should consider executing revocable lifetime trusts? What assets that they now own would be suitable for a lifetime trust?

3. *Probate as a "Backstop."* Proceeds of life insurance commonly go to the insured's probate estate if the designated primary and secondary beneficiaries predecease the insured. If Barbara designated James, Nelson, and Ella as the beneficiaries of her life insurance policy and they all predecease Barbara, what alternative beneficiaries other than Barbara's probate estate might she consider designating?

PART E. THE PROFESSION AND PROFESSIONAL RESPONSIBILITY

Our main purpose in this Part is to introduce you to the subject of professional responsibility. Before that, here is some information on the profession itself. Lawyers who practice in this area are part of the estate-planning segment of the bar. By a recent estimate, somewhere between 50,000 and 60,000 of the nation's approximately 720,000 attorneys are significantly engaged in estate planning. About six percent of them earn in excess of $300,000 a year; the median annual income is somewhere between $90,000 and $99,000. In the period 1984 to 1989, the median age has shifted from below 40 to the low 40's. See L. Gissel, Reflections of a Fellow on Lawyers, the Law and the Rule of Law after Thirty Odd Years of Exposure 22-23 (1990 Joseph Trachtman Lecture, American College of Trust and Estate Counsel). What accounts for the rise in median age of estate planning attorneys? Why is this likely to change?

With the Smith/Williams family in mind, this Part now begins a discussion of professional responsibility that will continue throughout the book, as different legal doctrines are addressed. Wherever relevant, this Part includes excerpts from the Model Rules of Professional Conduct, which were approved by the ABA House of Delegates in 1983. It also includes relevant excerpts from the ABA's Model Code of Professional Responsibility, which the Model Rules were designed to replace, but which remain effective in some jurisdictions.

1. Conflicts of Interest Among Clients

ABA Model Rules of Professional Conduct

RULE 1.7: CONFLICT OF INTEREST: GENERAL RULE

(a) A lawyer shall not represent a client if the representation of that client will be directly adverse to another client, unless:

(1) the lawyer reasonably believes the representation will not adversely affect the relationship with the other client; and

(2) each client consents after consultation.

(b) A lawyer shall not represent a client if the representation of that client may be materially limited by the lawyer's responsibilities to another client or to a third person, or by the lawyer's own interests, unless:

(1) the lawyer reasonably believes the representation will not be adversely affected; and

(2) the client consents after consultation. When representation of multiple clients in a single matter is undertaken, the consultation shall include explanation of the implications of the common representation and the advantages and risks involved.

Comment. . . . *Other Conflict Situations.* Conflicts of interest in contexts other than litigation sometimes may be difficult to assess. Relevant factors in determining whether there is potential for adverse effect include the duration and intimacy of the lawyer's relationship with the client or clients involved, the functions being performed by the lawyer, the likelihood that actual conflict will arise and the likely prejudice to the client from the conflict if it does arise. The question is often one of proximity and degree. . . .

Conflict questions may also arise in estate planning and estate administration. A lawyer may be called upon to prepare wills for several family members, such as husband and wife, and, depending upon the circumstances, a conflict of interest may arise. In estate administration the identity of the client may be unclear under the law of a particular jurisdiction. Under one view, the client is the fiduciary; under another view the client is the estate or trust, including its beneficiaries. The lawyer should make clear the relationship to the parties involved.

RULE 2.2: INTERMEDIARY

(a) A lawyer may act as intermediary between clients if:

(1) the lawyer consults with each client concerning the implications of the common representation, including the advantages and risks involved, and the effect on the attorney-client privileges, and obtains each client's consent to the common representation;

(2) the lawyer reasonably believes that the matter can be resolved on terms compatible with the clients' best interests, that each client will be able to make adequately informed decisions in the matter and that there is little risk of material prejudice to the interests of any of the clients if the contemplated resolution is unsuccessful; and

(3) the lawyer reasonably believes that the common representation can be undertaken impartially and without improper effect on other responsibilities the lawyer has to any of the clients.

(b) While acting as intermediary, the lawyer shall consult with each client concerning the decisions to be made and the considerations relevant in making them, so that each client can make adequately informed decisions.

(c) A lawyer shall withdraw as intermediary if any of the clients so requests, or if any of the conditions stated in paragraph (a) is no longer satisfied. Upon withdrawal, the lawyer shall not continue to represent any of the clients in the matter that was the subject of the intermediation.

Comment. A lawyer acts as intermediary under this Rule when the lawyer represents two or more parties with potentially conflicting interests. A key factor in defining the relationship is whether the parties share responsibility for the lawyer's fee, but the common representation may be inferred from other circumstances. Because confusion can arise as to the lawyer's role where each party is not separately represented, it is important that the lawyer make clear the relationship. . . .

A lawyer acts as intermediary in seeking to establish or adjust a relationship between clients on an amicable and mutually advantageous basis; for example, in . . . arranging a property distribution in settlement of an estate . . . . The lawyer seeks to resolve potentially conflicting interests by developing the parties' mutual interests. The alternative can be that each party may have to obtain separate representation, with the possibility in some situations of incurring additional cost, complication or even litigation. Given these and other relevant factors, all the clients may prefer that the lawyer act as intermediary.

In considering whether to act as intermediary between clients, a lawyer should be mindful that if the intermediation fails the result can be additional cost, embarrassment and recrimination. In some situations the risk of failure is so great that intermediation is plainly impossible. For example, a lawyer cannot undertake common representation of clients between whom contentious litigation is imminent or who contemplate contentious negotiations. More generally, if the relationship between the parties has already assumed definite antagonism, the possibility that the clients' interests can be adjusted by intermediation ordinarily is not very good.

The appropriateness of intermediation can depend on its form. Forms of intermediation range from informal arbitration, where each client's case is presented by the respective client and the lawyer decides the outcome, to mediation, to common representation where the clients' interests are substantially though not entirely compatible. One form may be appropriate in circumstances where another would not. Other relevant factors are whether the lawyer subsequently will represent both parties on a continuing basis and whether the situation involves creating a relationship between the parties or terminating one.

Confidentiality and Privilege. A particularly important factor in determining the appropriateness of intermediation is the effect on client-lawyer confidentiality and the attorney-client privilege. In a common representation, the lawyer is still required both to keep each client adequately informed and to maintain confidentiality of information relating to the representation. See Rules 1.4 and 1.6. Complying with both requirements while acting as intermediary requires a delicate balance. If the balance cannot be maintained, the common representation is improper. With regard to the attorney-client privilege, the prevailing rule is that as between commonly represented clients the privilege does not attach. Hence, it must be assumed that if litigation eventuates between the clients, the privilege will not protect any such communications, and the clients should be so advised.

Since the lawyer is required to be impartial between commonly represented clients, intermediation is improper when that impartiality cannot be maintained. For example, a lawyer who has represented one of the clients for a long period and in a variety of matters might have difficulty being impartial between that client and one to whom the lawyer has only recently been introduced.

Consultation. In acting as intermediary between clients, the lawyer is required to consult with the clients on the implications of doing so, and proceed only upon consent based on such a consultation. The consultation should make clear that the lawyer's role is not that of partisanship normally expected in other circumstances.

Paragraph (b) is an application of the principle expressed in Rule 1.4. Where the lawyer is intermediary, the clients ordinarily must assume greater responsibility for decisions than when each client is independently represented.

ABA Model Code of Professional Responsibility

Canon 5

A Lawyer Should Exercise Independent Professional Judgment on Behalf of a Client

Ethical Considerations

EC 5-14 Maintaining the independence of professional judgment required of a lawyer precludes his acceptance or continuation of employment that will adversely affect his judgment on behalf of or dilute his loyalty to a client. This problem arises whenever a lawyer is asked to represent two or more clients who may have differing interests, whether such interests be conflicting, inconsistent, diverse, or otherwise discordant.

EC 5-15 If a lawyer is requested to undertake or to continue representation of multiple clients having potentially differing interests, he must weigh carefully the possibility that his judgment may be impaired or his loyalty divided if he accepts or continues the employment. He should resolve all doubts against the propriety of the representation. . . . [T]here are many instances in which a lawyer may properly serve multiple clients having potentially differing interests in matters not involving litigation. If the interests vary only slightly, it is generally likely that the lawyer will not be subjected to an adverse influence and that he can retain his independent judgment on behalf of each client; and if the interests become differing, withdrawal is less likely to have a disruptive effect upon the causes of his clients.

EC 5-16 In those instances in which a lawyer is justified in representing two or more clients having differing interests, it is nevertheless essential that each client be given the opportunity to evaluate his need for representation free of any potential conflict and to obtain other counsel if he so desires. Thus before a lawyer may represent multiple clients, he should explain fully to each client the implications of the common representation and should accept or continue employment only if the clients consent. If there are present other circumstances that might cause any of the multiple clients to question the undivided loyalty of the lawyer, he should also advise all of the clients of those circumstances.

DISCIPLINARY RULES

DR 5-105 *Refusing to Accept or Continue Employment if the Interests of Another Client May Impair the Independent Professional Judgment of the Lawyer.*

(A) A lawyer shall decline proffered employment if the exercise of his independent professional judgment in behalf of a client will be or is likely to be adversely affected by the acceptance of the proffered employment, or if it would be likely to involve him in representing differing interests, except to the extent permitted under DR 5-105(C). . . .

(C) In the situations covered by DR 5-105(A) and (B), a lawyer may represent multiple clients if it is obvious that he can adequately represent the interest of each and if each consents to the representation after full disclosure of the possible effect of such representation on the exercise of his independent professional judgment on behalf of each.

Notes and Questions

1. *Representing the Smith/Williams Couple and Disclosure.* Barbara Smith and James Williams call your office and ask for an appointment to review estate planning matters. Are you allowed to advise both on estate planning issues? Does it matter if you were the attorney that handled Barbara's marital dissolution and that you had advised her when she executed her first will? Are there potential conflicts between them? All you know so far from the phone conversation is that they say they are married and want estate planning advice. Consider this letter published in an Ann Landers column:

> Dear Ann: After 30 years of marriage, my husband and I decided to make out our wills. I assumed that we would go the usual route, name one another as beneficiaries and leave everything to our children if we should die together.
>
> I was wrong. In the lawyer's office, my husband announced that if he died first, he wanted to leave everything to our children, because I would probably remarry and he didn't want another man to live it up on his money. We nearly split up over this. I gave him six beautiful children and am a devoted wife. I also have contributed financially to our marriage, holding part-time jobs all through the years. It was devastating to learn that he doesn't love or trust me enough to leave me financially secure.
>
> After much discussion, he agreed to leave me everything if I promised to divide the money among our children if I should remarry. Reluctantly, I said I would, but I am very bitter.
>
> My friends think he was totally wrong. He insists, however, that most husbands would want the same deal. What do you think?
> —Still Bitter in Madison

Chi. Trib., May 9, 1990, Tempo, at 3. How would you evaluate the resolution reached by the Madison couple? How would you evaluate the lawyer's conduct? In this regard, consider Whitney v. Seattle-First Nat'l Bank, 90 Wash. 2d 105, 579 P.2d 937 (1978), in which a wife brought an action to rescind an agreement executed when she and her husband made their wills. Under the terms of the wills and the agreement, if the husband predeceased the wife, all her property, including her community share, was to be placed into an irrevocable trust, along with that of her husband. When her husband died, the wife realized that she had waived her right to control her half of the community property. The Supreme Court of Washington affirmed the lower court and upheld the agreement because it "was fair and reasonable, and because petitioner has not shown fraud or overreaching." The court went on to say that "there is no absolute requirement that the wife have acted upon the competent, independent advice of counsel, or that she be specifically informed of her right to seek the same." Id. at 111, 579 P.2d at 940. See also infra Chapter 8, discussing standards for determining the validity of premarital and marital agreements, and infra Chapter 9, discussing the formation and enforcement of will contracts.

How should you inform Barbara and James about the potential conflicts between them? At your initial meeting with the couple, you start discussing potential conflicts between the spouses. Barbara and James immediately interrupt you and in unison say, "Look, we love each other. We don't have a lot of extra money to spend on lawyers. All this talk about conflicts is taking time and costing us money. Let's get on to what we came to talk about." What do you do and say now to them?

2. *Representing the Smith/Williams Couple: Waiver of Confidentiality.* Suppose that you successfully worked your way through the conflicts-of-interest maze with the Smith/Williams, and you assisted both in executing their estate plans. A year later, Barbara calls and asks for an appointment to reconsider her estate plan. Should you agree to talk with her without James being present? Should you agree to talk with her only if she agrees to tell James that she has made an appointment with you to discuss changing her estate plan? Cf. Barth v. Reagan, 139 Ill. 2d 399, 564 N.E.2d 1196 (1990).

2. Conflicts of Interest Between Attorney and Clients

ABA Model Rules of Professional Conduct

RULE 1.8: CONFLICT OF INTEREST: PROHIBITED TRANSACTIONS

(a) A lawyer shall not enter into a business transaction with a client or knowingly acquire an ownership, possessory, security or other pecuniary interest adverse to a client unless:

(1) the transaction and terms on which the lawyer acquires the interest are fair and reasonable to the client and are fully disclosed and transmitted in writing to the client in a manner which can be reasonably understood by the client;

(2) the client is given a reasonable opportunity to seek the advice of independent counsel in the transaction; and

(3) the client consents in writing thereto.

(b) A lawyer shall not use information relating to representation of a client to the disadvantage of the client unless the client consents after consultation.

(c) A lawyer shall not prepare an instrument giving the lawyer or a person related to the lawyer as parent, child, sibling, or spouse any substantial gift from a client, including a testamentary gift, except where the client is related to the donee.

Comment. *Transactions Between Client and Lawyer.* . . . A lawyer may accept a gift from a client, if the transaction meets general standards of fairness. For example, a simple gift such as a present given at a holiday or as a token of appreciation is permitted. If effectuation of a substantial gift requires preparing a legal instrument such as a will or conveyance, however, the client should have the detached advice that another lawyer can provide. Paragraph (c) recognizes an exception where the client is a relative of the donee or the gift is not substantial.

ABA Model Code of Professional Responsibility

ETHICAL CONSIDERATIONS ACCOMPANYING CANON 5

EC 5-5 A lawyer should not suggest to his client that a gift be made to himself or for his benefit. If a lawyer accepts a gift from his client, he is peculiarly susceptible to the charge that he unduly influenced or over-reached the client. If a client voluntarily offers to make a gift to his lawyer, the lawyer may accept the gift, but before doing so, he should urge that his client secure disinterested advice from an independent, competent person who is cognizant of all the circumstances. Other than in exceptional circumstances, a lawyer should insist that an instrument in which his client desires to name him beneficially be prepared by another lawyer selected by the client.

EC 5-6 A lawyer should not consciously influence a client to name him as executor, trustee, or lawyer in an instrument. In those cases where a client wishes to name his lawyer as such, care should be taken by the lawyer to avoid even the appearance of impropriety.

DISCIPLINARY RULES

DR 2-103 *Recommendation of Professional Employment.* (A) A lawyer shall not, except as authorized in DR 2-101(B), recommend employment as a private practitioner, of himself, his partner, or associate to a layperson who has not sought his advice regarding employment of a lawyer.

Notes and Questions

1. *Client Naming Attorney as a Beneficiary in a Will or Will Substitute.* The Model Rules and Model Code are reasonably clear that the client should obtain independent counsel if the client wants to provide a substantial gift to her or his attorney. See Matter of Randall, 640 F.2d 898 (8th Cir. 1981); Committee on Professional Ethics v. Randall, 285 N.W.2d 161 (Iowa 1979) (In a series of actions, John D. Randall, Sr., a former president of the American Bar Association, was disbarred from the practice of law in Iowa, the federal district courts for the Southern and Northern Districts of Iowa, and the United States Court of Appeals for the Eighth Circuit, partly on the ground of a violation of Ethical Canon 5-5 of the Iowa version of the Code, which is identical to Ethical Consideration 5-5 quoted above. Mr. Randall had drafted a will for a business partner naming himself as sole devisee of the business partner's $4.5 million estate.). See also Will of Cromwell, N.Y.L.J., Feb. 7, 1989, at 25 (Sur. Ct.) (will upheld, but attorney liable for costs of the action because of breach of rules of professional responsibility). The Model Rules make an exception, however, when the client is related to the attorney. Do you think it would be a good idea for you to provide estate planning advice to your spouse or domestic partner if she or he is intending to make you a beneficiary? See State v. Collentine, 39 Wis. 2d 325, 159 N.W.2d 50 (1968) (holding that the attorney can be the drafter of the will and a beneficiary only when the attorney is a natural object of the testator's bounty and when, under the will, the attorney would receive no more than what she or he would receive had the will not been executed). Do you think the problem is solved if, instead of you, one of your law partners provides the estate planning advice to your spouse or domestic partner?

2. *Attorney Named as Personal Representative of the Estate or as Trustee.* What is the advantage to attorneys of being named as personal representative of the estate or trustee in their clients' estate plans? Should an attorney be able to be compensated for serving both as a fiduciary and as an attorney for the fiduciary? What should an attorney infer from the fact that the Model Rules do not specifically address the practice of attorneys drafting dispository instruments naming themselves as fiduciaries? The following excerpt suggests that uncertainty about the ethics of the matter reigns in this area of estate planning practice:

> A survey of prominent estate administration attorneys throughout the United States conducted by the American College of Probate Counsel [now the American College of Trust and Estate Counsel] revealed that knowledgeable attorneys disagree about the propriety of attorneys serving as fiduciaries. The survey asked whether it is appropriate for an attorney to serve as coexecutor or cotrustee with a corporate representative. Of the forty-five attorneys who expressed an opinion, seven had no hesitancy about serving, nine would refuse to serve in any case, and twenty-nine generally had negative feelings about serving except in extraordinary situations. Of the fifty-one attorneys surveyed, twenty-two had in fact served as a coexecutor or a cotrustee. . . .

The attorney-personal representative is a rare but important phenomenon. Measuring changes over time is beyond the power of our data, but there are indications that the prevalence of attorney fiduciaries may increase. A respected California probate practitioner has written an article vigorously advocating more frequent service by attorneys as personal representatives, claiming that no one is better qualified to serve as personal representative than a competent attorney. Moreover, several law firms have formally established "trust departments" within their firms which allow attorneys to both represent a trust and serve as its trustee, another form of dual representation comparable to that of attorney-representative.[1] Accordingly, both because it is likely to increase and because of differing opinions as to its propriety, this aspect of the attorney's participation in estate administration warrants further attention.

Stein & Fierstein, The Role of the Attorney in Estate Administration, 68 Minn. L. Rev. 1107, 1164-65, 1172 (1984). See also A.B.A. Section of Real Prop., Prob. & Tr. L., Developments Regarding the Professional Responsibility of the Estate Planning Lawyer: The Effect of the Model Rules of Professional Conduct, 22 Real Prop. Prob. & Tr. J. 1 (1987); Coolidge, New Avenue for Lawyers Boasts Old Tradition, 128 Tr. & Est. 20 (Dec. 1989); deFuria, A Matter of Ethics Ignored: The Attorney-Draftsman as Testamentary Fiduciary, 36 Kan. L. Rev. 275 (1988); Johnston, An Ethical Analysis of Common Estate Planning Practices—Is Good Business Bad Ethics?, 45 Ohio St. L.J. 57, 86-101 (1984). It is also interesting to note that most ethics committees and the few courts that have considered the issue view the practice as permissible, although some decisions contain a strong note of caution. See deFuria, supra, at 285-92 for a detailed discussion of the authorities.

3. *Testamentary Appointment of Attorney.* A provision in a will directing that the drafting attorney be hired to represent the personal representative is usually held not binding on the personal representative. Clients have a right to hire their own attorneys, and in these cases, the client is the personal representative. See, e.g., Highfield v. Bozio, 188 Cal. 727, 207 P. 242 (1922); In re Caldwell, 188 N.Y. 115, 80 N.E. 663 (1907); Estate of Sieben v. Phillips, 24 Wis. 2d 166, 128 N.W.2d 443 (1964).

Suppose an attorney, in an effort to defeat the non-binding effect of such an appointment, devises the following provision for wills she or he drafts:

I hereby nominate X to be my personal representative subject to the condition that X agrees to employ [the drafting attorney] as the attorney for my estate; if X refuses, then Y is to be my personal representative, subject to the same condition; if both X and Y refuse, then the court is to appoint a personal representative who will agree to retain [the drafting attorney].

---

1. There is a long standing custom in Massachusetts of using a "Boston Trustee." These trustees are of three kinds, one of which is a law firm with a trust department. There are not many such firms, but most have existed since the mid-nineteenth century and are well established. . . . For a history of the Boston Trustee, see Curtis, Manners and Customs of the Boston Trustee, 97 Tr. & Est. 902 (1958).

Should the courts enforce this provision? Compare Estate of Deardoff, 10 Ohio St. 3d 108, 461 N.E.2d 1292 (1984) (provision held not enforceable) with Estate of Devroy, 109 Wis. 2d 154, 325 N.W.2d 345 (1982) (provision held enforceable). Binding or not, of course, Professor Johnston points out the practical effect of the testamentary appointment.

> [I]t is still likely that the specified attorney will be retained, since the [personal representative] and members of the testator's family generally want to carry out the desires of the decedent. This, too, can be deceptive when the testator had no preference in the matter, and simply acceded to the provision inserted by the drafting attorney in the belief that it was routine boilerplate.

Johnston, supra, at 106. See also Powers, Testamentary Designations of Attorneys and Other Employees, 20 Golden Gate U. L. Rev. 261 (1990).

3. Zealous Representation of Clients

ABA Model Rules of Professional Conduct

Rule 1.14: Client Under a Disability
(a) When a client's ability to make adequately considered decisions in connection with the representation is impaired, whether because of minority, mental disability or for some other reason, the lawyer shall, as far as reasonably possible, maintain a normal client-lawyer relationship with the client.

(b) A lawyer may seek the appointment of a guardian or take other protective action with respect to a client, only when the lawyer reasonably believes that the client cannot adequately act in the client's own interest.

Rule 1.16: Declining or Terminating Representation . . .
(b) . . . a lawyer may withdraw from representing a client if withdrawal can be accomplished without material adverse effect on the interests of the client, or if: . . . .

(3) the client insists upon pursuing an objective that the lawyer considers repugnant or imprudent; . . .

(d) Upon termination of representation, a lawyer shall take steps to the extent reasonably practicable to protect a client's interests, such as giving reasonable notice to the client, allowing time for employment of other counsel, surrendering papers and property to which the client is entitled and refunding any advance payment of fee that has not been earned. The lawyer may retain papers relating to the client to the extent permitted by other law.

Rule 2.1: Advisor
In representing a client, a lawyer shall exercise independent professional judgment and render candid advice. In rendering advice, a lawyer may refer not only to law but to other considerations such as moral, economic, social and political factors, that may be relevant to the client's situation.

Comment. . . . *Scope of Advice.* . . . Advice couched in narrowly legal terms may be of little value to a client, especially where practical considerations, such as cost or effects on other people, are predominant. Purely technical legal advice, therefore, can sometimes be inadequate. It is proper for a lawyer to refer to relevant moral and ethical considerations in giving advice. Although a lawyer is not a moral advisor as such, moral and ethical considerations impinge upon most legal questions and may decisively influence how the law will be applied.

RULE 4.4: RESPECT FOR RIGHTS OF THIRD PERSONS

In representing a client, a lawyer shall not use means that have no substantial purpose other than to embarrass, delay, or burden a third person . . . .

Comment. Responsibility to a client requires a lawyer to subordinate the interests of others to those of the client, but that responsibility does not imply that a lawyer may disregard the rights of third persons. It is impractical to catalogue all such rights . . . .

ABA Model Code of Professional Responsibility

CANON 7

A Lawyer Should Represent a Client Zealously Within the Bounds of the Law

ETHICAL CONSIDERATIONS

EC 7-8 A lawyer should exert his best efforts to insure that decisions of his client are made only after the client has been informed of relevant considerations. A lawyer ought to initiate this decision-making process if the client does not do so. Advice of a lawyer to his client need not be confined to purely legal considerations. A lawyer should advise his client of the possible effect of each legal alternative. A lawyer should bring to bear upon this decision-making process the fullness of his experience as well as his objective viewpoint. In assisting his client to reach a proper decision, it is often desirable for a lawyer to point out those factors which may lead to a decision that is morally just as well as legally permissible. He may emphasize the possibility of harsh consequences that might result from assertion of legally permissible positions. In the final analysis, however, the lawyer should always remember that the decision whether to forego legally available objectives or methods because of non-legal factors is ultimately for the client and not for himself. In the event that the client in a non-adjudicatory matter insists upon a course of conduct that is contrary to the judgment and advice of the lawyer but not prohibited by Disciplinary Rules, the lawyer may withdraw from the employment.

EC 7-11 The responsibilities of a lawyer may vary according to the intelligence, experience, mental condition or age of a client, the obligation of a public officer, or the nature of a particular proceeding. Examples include the representation of an illiterate or an incompetent . . . .

EC 7-12 Any mental or physical condition of a client that renders him incapable of making a considered judgment on his own behalf casts additional responsibilities upon his lawyer. Where an incompetent is acting through a guardian or other legal representative, a lawyer must look to such representative for those decisions which are normally the prerogative of the client to make. If a client under disability has no legal representative, his lawyer may be compelled in court proceedings to make decisions on behalf of the client. If the client is capable of understanding the matter in question or of contributing to the advancement of his interests, regardless of whether he is legally disqualified from performing certain acts, the lawyer should obtain from him all possible aid. If the disability of a client and the lack of a legal representative compel the lawyer to make decisions for his client, the lawyer should consider all circumstances then prevailing and act with care to safeguard and advance the interests of his client. But obviously a lawyer cannot perform any act or make any decision which the law requires his client to perform or make, either acting for himself if competent, or by a duly constituted representative if legally incompetent.

DISCIPLINARY RULES

DR 2-110 *Withdrawal from Employment.* (A) In general. . . .

(2) In any event, a lawyer shall not withdraw from employment until he has taken reasonable steps to avoid foreseeable prejudice to the rights of his client, including giving due notice to his client, allowing time for employment of other counsel, delivering to the client all papers and property to which the client is entitled, and complying with applicable laws and rules. . . .

(C) Permissive withdrawal. . . . [A] lawyer may not request permission to withdraw in matters pending before a tribunal, and may not withdraw in other matters, unless such request or such withdrawal is because:

(1) His client: . . .

(e) Insists, in a matter not pending before a tribunal, that the lawyer engage in conduct that is contrary to the judgment and advice of the lawyer but not prohibited under the Disciplinary Rules.

Notes and Questions

1. *Donative Capacity of Client in Doubt.* A client who has AIDS asks that you visit him in his hospital room to complete his estate plan. He has been discussing his estate plan with you for the past year and was uncertain whether to devise a part of the family farm to his sister or to his domestic partner. The doctors tell you that there is evidence that he has suffered the onset of AIDS dementia. You detect slurred speech, slower movement, and memory loss during your meeting with him. You believe he is telling you

to draft the necessary documents to give a portion of the farm to his domestic partner and bring them to the hospital for him to execute. No lifetime or deathtime gratuitous transfer is valid unless the transferor possesses the necessary mental capacity. See infra Chapter 3. Should you oversee the execution of the documents that your client is requesting? When in doubt about the mental capacity of your client, should you favor drafting the requested documents or not? What precautions might you take to avoid potential litigation about whether the documents are valid? See Mock & Tobin, Estate Planning for Clients With AIDS, 7 St. Louis U. Pub. L. Rev. 177 (1988).

2. *Morally Repugnant Estate Plans.* Your client comes to your office and describes his dispository plan, which disinherits his brother, who is his sole heir. He also asks you to include in the will the following statement: "To my brother I give $1 to purchase a rope strong enough and long enough to kill yourself because you are no good to anyone and you are no good to yourself." Should you include this statement in the revocable lifetime trust you are planning to draft for your client? Should you try to talk your client out of including the statement in the trust? If your client insists on having the statement included, should you withdraw and tell him to find another estate planning attorney?

PART F. SOCIAL AND POLITICAL ASPECTS OF FAMILY PROPERTY LAW

Family property law touches nearly every aspect of a person's life, whether that person is a property owner or is in some way connected to a property owner. The disposition of property at the death of its owner is a central issue for various disciplines, including anthropology, economics, history, political theory, and sociology. The rules of inheritance are a means of exploring the human condition and connectedness with others. They force us to confront our moral obligation to future generations. They create and reflect family and community configurations. They are one of the primary means by which dominant groups maintain their dominance. They are also one of the primary means by which the community defines deviancy and thereby controls the private and public activities of its members.

What follows are excerpts from a variety of sources to help you think about: (1) the role family property law has played in our society and will continue to play in the future and (2) how society, in turn, has influenced and will continue to influence family property law.

1. Sociology

Tappan, The Sociology of Inheritance
in Inheritance of Property and the Power of Testamentary
Disposition 54, 55-73 (E. Cahn ed. 1948)

Put in simplest terms, the specialized law of property devolution serves—as does law generally—both to reflect social needs and to resolve them. It does so peculiarly through the family system as the vortex where most of these problems are centered. Too, like the rest of the law, it leaves many segments of family and social need unfulfilled; it is slow to alter in response to changing requirements, sometimes sacrificing social equity to order. . . .

[I]t is impossible to view the changing family in reference to institutions of property devolution only, without regard to broader economic influences with which inheritance is interrelated. Neither the family nor inheritance functions in a simple and pure reciprocal relation. Viewing the contemporary family system in its more striking manifestations, however, and looking at the forms of property devolution as an essential and characterizing part of the industrial order, we may observe important elements of the relationship between the law and society.

Our contemporary society may be described as a diversely industrialized, corporate-capitalized, highly urbanized, widely differentiated and individualized, socially and spatially mobile, secondary group[2] society. In all these basic qualities, as in many other details, we differ radically from pre-industrial feudalism. Contemporary social organization has lost a greater part of its ancient rooting in kinship ties and the medieval foundations of personal fealty and reciprocity. In their place have developed the specialized and highly transitory relationships to impersonal secondary groups in which most of our economic, religious, social and political interests are mediated. . . . Out of this development have grown impersonality and intense individuation, reflected both in the family system and in our property relationships. . . .

Property has been associated decreasingly with size of landholdings and it has become correspondingly less important to the economy to preserve the integrity of holdings. Money, not land, is power. . . .

Without the necessity to keep landed estates intact, the law of intestate succession has facilitated changes in property division by the shift from a system of primogeniture to one of relatively equitable distribution among surviving heirs. . . .

The principle of equitable distribution of estates to descendants has played some considerable part in an inclination of our families to keep their size small enough to insure a fair patrimony to each. It is symptomatic perhaps that those who are sufficiently well-to-do to leave an

---

2. A secondary group is characteristically impersonal, specialized in function, and consciously organized. A labor union would be an example of such a group.

estate of inheritance are also those who produce the smallest families. Other more important factors related to the property regime and to the industrial organization are involved, however, in the small size of the modern American family. . . .

Modern inheritance and the family organization have abandoned the principle customarily implied under primogeniture that imposed upon the heir a duty to care for the family, so that, although the modern scheme of descent . . . provides with relative generosity (compared to the old system of dower) for the surviving spouse and for immediate descendants, neither custom nor law insures security for the parent. The child in the family has ceased to be a self-liquidating investment since, after an economic dependence upon his parents for a long score of years, he is then emancipated largely from the control of and responsibility to his ascendants, depriving them of both emotional and economic support during their years of reduced productivity. With the increasing proportion of the aged in our society, this becomes a problem of large and growing magnitude. Modern recognition of the serious plight of the aged in our society has led to measures of social security to insure a minimum support of the dependent aged through public funds where the children cannot themselves provide it. . . .

Modern inheritance rules together with the fluidity of contemporary estates serve both economic requirements for capital investment and social interests in a more widely and equitably distributed wealth. They serve our familial interests in the protection of the small conjugal family. All this has represented large-scale and quite rapid evolution of an economy, a family organization, and an inheritance system. It is little wonder that the transitions have been marked by lags and inconsistencies, by failures to provide uniformly well for the diversity of social needs. . . . In a dynamic legal and social system continuous change is an essential trait in the law. Imperfect adjustments of law to society are only natural. An effective system of law is one which is modified by the people as intelligently as possible to meet apparent and important social needs. As Ehrlich has said, "The centre of gravity of legal development . . . is in society itself." The law is both an important part of society and an agency for deliberate and planful social change to meet the evolving necessities of our social institutions.

Notes and Questions

1. *Definition of Family: Adult Partnering.* What kinds of households are being created today to which the inheritance laws might respond in the future?

"A family is a group of people who opt to live together and who should be nurturing each other in one way or another," said John Odom, who has lived in Manhattan with his partner, Barbara Boynton, for 11 years without marrying.

"We went our separate ways during the day but would come home to eat dinner together and then either go to the gym or sometimes the movies together," James L. McFarland, a 24-year old member of the Madison, Wis., Common Council, said of his three-year relationship with Rick Villasenor. . . .

"I feel I have a lot of sisters here," said 92-year-old Edna Freimuth, who shares a home with 13 other elderly people in Ridgewood, N.J. "They are all so kind; they help me. Everybody shares."

"During his sickness, we took care of him and whenever he had to go to the doctor, I would be there to make sure they took care of him," Jimmie Hendrix, 50, said of Henry Pittman, who shared his Harlem apartment with Mr. Hendrix for 25 years and became like a father to him. . . .

"The problem is that it becomes very difficult to determine what is and what is not a family," said William R. Mattox Jr., director of policy analysis at the Family Research Council, a conservative organization in Washington. . . .

[T]he increasing number of laws that [expand the traditional definition of family] raise "all kinds of really ridiculous situations if you attempt to unravel the traditional meaning of marriage and family by so broadening its definition that it becomes meaningless," Mr. Mattox said. . . .

"Society has good reason to extend legal advantages" to heterosexuals who marry, [Mr Sullivan, a former associate editor of the New Republic and currently a doctoral candidate in government,] wrote. "They make a deeper commitment to one another and to society; in exchange, society extends certain benefits to them. We rig the law in its favor not because we disparage all forms of relationship other than the nuclear family, but because we recognize that not to promote marriage would be to ask too much of human virtue." . . .

The Federal Census Bureau reports that in 1988, 27 percent of the nation's 91.1 million households fit the traditional definition of a family: two parents living with children. That was down from 40 percent in 1970. [The 73 percent "nontraditional" households included those with only one person, or only one parent, as well as those with unmarried couples, gay or straight.]

Gutis, What Makes a Family? Traditional Limits are Challenged, N.Y. Times, Aug. 31, 1989, at C1, col. 6 (N.Y. ed.).

What factors influence the traditional view of the family? Friedrich Engels believed he knew the answer to that question. He asserted that society demands female monogamy to guarantee paternity for the inheritance of private property. He believed the rise of private property, class divisions, women's oppression, and the state were coincidental developments and all necessary for the ruling classes successfully to exploit and dominate. See F. Engels, The Origin of the Family, Private Property, and the State 119-43 (Marxist Lib. ed., vol. 22, 1942).

2. *Definition of Family: Parent-child Relationships.* Chapter 2 contains an extensive discussion of the various types of parent-child relationships that arise and how the law treats them. Adoption and biological connection are the primary guideposts used by the law to recognize parent-child relationships. Can you think of situations in which those guideposts may prove inadequate? See Moorman & Hernandez, Married-Couple Families with Step, Adopted, and Biological Children, 26 Demography 267 (1989). With the increasing incidence of divorce and remarriage in the United States today, stepchildren raise new and important questions for inheritance law.

Social scientists in the 1980s published a growing body of research on stepfamily relationships. The findings demonstrate a societal bias against stepfamilies. Perceptions of stepfamily members are less positive than those of traditional, first-married families. People may interpret a stepparent's behavior as negative simply because it fits the image of the "wicked" stepmother or the "abusive" stepfather. . . .

Stepfamilies do face extra challenges not present in traditional, first-married families. Remarriage situations introduce complexities into households and the quality of relationships between stepfamily members varies according to several factors. These factors include the age of the child, the presence of siblings, the degree of contact between the child and the noncustodial parent, and the amount of interaction between the stepparent and stepchild. . . .

Legal circumstances of stepfamilies also may relate to the quality of stepparent-stepchild relations. The legal system generally treats stepparents and stepchildren differently from first-married family members. Laws regulating the rights and obligations of biological family members typically are not extended to stepparents and stepchildren. . . .

One commentator argues that these legal rules may affect relations between stepfamily members. The lack of clear legal obligations between stepparents and stepchildren may lessen their degree of commitment. Legal ambiguities also perpetuate the uncertain status of stepfamilies in society and may exacerbate adjustment difficulties for family members.

Note, The Spousal Share in Intestate Succession: Stepparents are Getting Shortchanged, 74 Minn. L. Rev. 631, 642-48 (1990). See also Fine, A Social Science Perspective on Stepfamily Law: Suggestions for Legal Reform, 38 Fam. Rel. 53, 55 (1989).

3. *Evolutionary Functionalism.* The Tappan excerpt and Notes 1 and 2 are premised on a view of the society in the United States as developing and progressing. They are also premised on the view that the legal system responds to those evolving social needs. This dominant vision of the law contributes to an ideology that law is a facilitator of social good.

That dominant vision currently is being scrutinized. Critics of evolutionary functionalism argue, for example, that: (1) law is nothing but a product of interest-group pressures; (2) law maintains the power of a dominant clan or group; or (3) the legal rules could be radically different and still maintain the community's social and economic structures. See Gordon, Critical Legal Histories, 36 Stan. L. Rev. 57 (1984).

As we study family property law rules, these critiques remind us to explore claims that purport to describe "society's needs" without considering the complexity and differences in the society. If we fail to consider these issues, we will not appreciate the full implications of the legal rules and how they affect different people's social experiences differently at different times.

2. Political Theory

J. Bentham, The Theory of Legislation 177-86
(C.K. Ogden ed. 1931)

Title by Succession. After the decease of an individual, how ought his goods to be disposed of?

In framing a law of succession, the legislator ought to have three objects in view:—1st, Provision for the subsistence of the rising generation; 2nd, Prevention of disappointment; 3rd, The equalization of fortunes.

Man is not a solitary being. With a very small number of exceptions, every man has about him a circle of companions, more or less extensive, who are united to him by the ties of kindred or of marriage, by friendship or by services, and who share with him, *in fact*, the enjoyment of those goods which *in law* belong to him exclusively. His fortune is commonly the sole fund of subsistence on which many others depend. To prevent the calamities of which they would be the victims, if death in taking away their friend took from them at the same time the supplies which they draw from his fortune, it is necessary to know who habitually enjoy these supplies, and in what proportions. Now, since these are facts which it would be impossible to establish by direct proofs, without becoming involved in embarrassing procedures and infinite contests, it is necessary to resort to general presumptions, as the only basis upon which a decision can be established. The share which each survivor was accustomed to enjoy in the property of the deceased may be presumed from the degree of affection which ought to have subsisted between them; and this degree of affection may be presumed from nearness of relationship. . . .

The model of a law will serve instead of a great number of discussions.

Article I. *No distinction between the sexes; what is said of one extends to the other. The portion of the one shall be always equal to that of the other.*

Reason.—Good of equality. If there were any difference, it ought to be in favour of the feebler—in favour of women—who have more wants and fewer means of acquisition, or of employing profitably what they possess. But the stronger have had all the preferences. Why? Because the stronger have made the laws.

Article II. *After the husband's death, the widow shall retain half the common property; unless some different arrangement was made by the marriage contract.*

Article III. *The other half shall be distributed among the children in equal proportions.*

Reasons.—1st. Equality of affection on the part of the father. 2nd. Equality of co-occupation on the part of the children. 3rd. Equality of wants. 4th. Equality of all imaginable reasons on one side and the other. Differences of age, of temperament, of talent, and of strength, may produce some differences in point of wants; but it is not possible for the law to appreciate them. The father must provide for them by the exercise of his right to make a will. . . .

Why to descendants before all others? 1st. *Superiority of affection.* Every other arrangement would be contrary to the inclination of the father. We love those better who depend upon us than those upon whom we depend. It is sweeter to govern than to obey. 2nd. *Superiority of need.* It is certain that our children cannot exist without us, or some one who fills our place. It is probable that our parents may exist without us, as they did exist before us. . . .

Testaments. 1st. The law, not knowing individuals, cannot accommodate itself to the diversity of their wants. All that can be exacted from it is to offer the best possible chance of satisfying those wants. It is for each proprietor, who can and who ought to know the particular circumstances in which those who depend upon him will be placed at his death, to correct the imperfections of the law in all those cases which it cannot foresee. The power of making a will is an instrument intrusted to the hands of individuals, to prevent private calamities.

2nd. The same power may be considered as an instrument of authority, intrusted to individuals for the encouragement of virtue in their families and the repression of vice. It is true that this means may be employed for the contrary purpose; but, fortunately, such cases are an exception. The interest of each member of a family is, that the conduct of every other member should be conformable to virtue, that is, to general utility. The passions may occasion accidental deviations; but the law must be arranged in conformity to the ordinary course of things. Virtue is the dominant regulator of society; even vicious parents are as jealous as others of the honour and the reputation of their children. A man little scrupulous in his own conduct would be shocked to have his secret practices disclosed to his family; at home he is still the apostle of probity; he disregards it in his own behaviour, but he wishes it in those about him. In this point of view, every proprietor is entitled to the confidence of the law. Clothed with the power of making a will, which is a branch of penal and remunerative legislation, he may be considered as a magistrate appointed to preserve good order in that little state called a family. This magistrate may be guilty of partiality and injustice; and as he is restrained in the exercise of his power neither by publicity nor by responsibility, he would seem to be very likely to abuse it. But that danger is more than counterbalanced by the ties of interest and affection, which put his inclination in accord with his duty. His natural attachment to his children and his relatives is as secure a pledge for his good conduct as any that can be obtained for that of the political magistrate; to such a degree that, all things considered, the authority of this non-commissioned magistrate, besides being absolutely necessary to children of tender age, will oftener be found salutary than hurtful, even to adults.

3rd. The power of making a will is advantageous under another aspect, as a means of governing—not for the good of those who obey, as in the preceding article, but for the good of him who commands. In this way the power of the present generation is extended over a portion of the future, and to a certain extent the wealth of each proprietor is doubled. By means of an order not payable till after his death, he procures for himself an infinity of advantages beyond what his actual means would furnish. By continuing the submission of children beyond the term of minority, the indemnity for paternal care is increased, and an additional assurance against ingratitude is secured to the father; and though it would be agreeable to think that such precautions are superfluous, yet when we recollect the infirmities of old age, we must be satisfied that it is necessary not to deprive it of this counterpoise of factitious attractions. In the rapid descent of life, every support on which man can lean should be left untouched, and it is well that interest serve as a monitor to duty.

Ingratitude on the part of children and contempt for old age are not common vices in civilized society; but we must recollect that everywhere, more or less, the power of making a will exists. Are these vices most frequent where this power is most limited? We might decide the question by observing what passes in poor families, where there is but little to give in legacies; but even that method of judging would be deceptive, for the influence of this power, established in society by the laws, tends to form general manners, and general manners thus formed determine the sentiments of individuals. This power given to fathers renders the paternal authority more respectable, and those fathers whose indigence does not permit them to exercise it, unconsciously profit by the general habit of submission to which it has given rise.

But in making the father a magistrate we must take care not to make him a tyrant. . . . The institution called in France a *legitime*, by which each child is protected against a total disinheritance, is a convenient medium between domestic anarchy and paternal tyranny. Even this provision the father should have the power of taking away, for causes specified in the law and judicially proved.

There is still another question. In default of natural heirs, shall the proprietor have the right of leaving his property to whomsoever he chooses, either to distant relations or strangers? . . .

It may be said that, in default of kin, the services of strangers are necessary to a man, and his attachment to them almost the same as to relations. He should have the means of cultivating the hopes and rewarding the care of a faithful servant, and of softening the regrets of a friend who has watched at his side, not to speak of the woman who, but for the omission of a ceremony, would be called his widow, and the orphans whom all the world but the legislator regard as his children.

Again, if to enrich the public treasury you deprive a man of the power of leaving his property to his friends, do you not force him to spend it all upon himself? If he has no control over his capital from the moment of his death, he will be tempted to convert his property into a life annuity. It is to encourage him to be a spendthrift, and almost to make a law against economy.

These reasons are, doubtless, more weighty than any consideration of gain to the public treasury. We ought to leave the proprietor who has no near relations the right of disposing of at least half his property by will, while the other half is reserved for the public; and to be contented with less would, perhaps, in this case, be a means of getting more. Besides, it is a matter of very great importance not to attack the principle which allows every one to dispose of his property after death; and not to create a class of proprietors who will regard themselves as inferior to others, on account of the legal incapacity attached to one-half of their fortune.

Notes and Questions

1. *Kinship as a Proxy for Need.* What proxies could a state use other than "nearness of relationship" to determine who depended on a decedent's financial resources? For example, why should a state not give the property to those who resided in the decedent's home? Would this rule be less simple to administer than determining takers according to blood relationships? See Wendel's Will, 143 Misc. 480, 257 N.Y.S. 87 (1932) (over 1600 claimants contended that they were heirs of the decedent and contested her will).

2. *Private vs. Public.* Bentham conceives of the family "as a little state" in which private and autonomous relationships can flourish. When Bentham accords by law testamentary freedom to the proprietor, however, does he interfere with the private workings of the "family state?" Does he change the family dynamics when he proposes that each child be protected against total disinheritance? Does Bentham suppress the role of the government in will making by using the rhetoric of individual and family autonomy? Cf. Dalton, An Essay in the Deconstruction of Contract Doctrine, 94 Yale L.J. 997, 1010-39 (1985) (describing how the opposing ideas of public and private have dominated the discourse about contract doctrine).

3. *Family Domination.* Both the benefits of control that parents can enjoy over family members by having testamentary freedom and the risks that parents might act as tyrants have intrigued many writers from many different perspectives. For example, Anthony Trollope wrote in his classic work Doctor Thorne that "[People] will spend years in degrading subserviency to obtain a niche in a will; and the niche, when at last obtained and enjoyed, is but a sorry payment for all that has been endured." A. Trollope, Doctor Thorne 246 (1980 ed.). Compare Buchanan, Rent Seeking, Noncompensated Transfers, and Laws of Succession, 26 J. Law & Econ. 71, 83 (1983): "rent seeking [*i.e.*, profit seeking] emerges as wasteful activity in any uncompensated transfer of value, and notably with respect to gifts and bequests among persons."

4. *Mothers Questioning the Fairness of Equal Treatment.* Although Bentham did not consider the possibility of a female-dominated family, historical evidence suggests that during some periods and in some areas of the United States women have been more willing than men to control family members by wielding their testamentary power.

[During the period 1831 to 1860,] of the 131 men who died in Petersburg[, Virginia] leaving more than one child, 71 percent directed that all their children receive equal portions. Of the 43 women who left more than one child, only 16 (37.2 percent) called for an equal division. When there were both male and female children, the temptation to favoritism was greater, and here again the women more often filled their wills with discriminatory provisions. Among the men who left children of both sexes, 61.6 percent (53/86) still divided their property equally; those who favored one child over another usually favored sons. Among the women who left children of both sexes, only 26.7 percent (8/30) made equal divisions. The women, not surprisingly, ordinarily favored their daughters.

S. Lebsock, The Free Women of Petersburg: Status and Culture in a Southern Town, 1784-1860, 135 (1984). As Professor Lebsock notes, "[t]here may have been an element of the power play in this; a propertied woman could keep her heirs on their good behavior for years, as long as she kept them guessing as to the terms of her last will." Id. at 136. She also suggests that women were more likely to reward "special qualities of loyalty and affection . . . [and to] funnel[ ] property into the hands of the heirs who needed it most . . . . [H]ere again the women's penchant for economic security was revealed." Id.

5. *The Role of Testamentary Freedom in the Economy.* Do you agree with Bentham that unless the law accords proprietors testamentary freedom, they will fail to save and will not remain industrious throughout their lives? See infra Section 5, pp. 57-63, which includes excerpts from articles showing how some economists have approached this inquiry.

6. *Intergenerational Justice.* Recent political theorists have focused on the question of what obligation one generation has to another generation. Professor Ackerman explores this issue through a dialogue format:

> Begin with a simple model. Assume that Manic and Depressive are the only members of the first generation and that they have two children, neither of whom genetically dominates the other. Both Manic Junior and Depressive Junior are in the final stages of a perfect liberal education. As they approach full citizenship, their parents approach death. The model's critical assumption is that the two generations share only a single moment during which both coexist as full citizens, each charged with the full burden of dialogue. During this moment, the first generation asserts its right to determine each child's initial wealth.
>
> *Minimal Trusteeship.* To simplify further, assume that Manic and Depressive have, mirabili dictu, ended where they began—each with a single grain of manna under his control. On their deathbeds, each announces his intention to pass on half a grain to his namesake; the two seniors, however, propose to spend the other half on a giant fireworks display commemorating their achievements. Upon hearing this announcement, the two juniors rise in protest. The death scene, then, is dialogue:
> SENIORS: Let there be light!
> JUNIORS: Not if we have anything to say about it.
> SENIORS: Why are you being so selfish? Isn't half a grain enough?
> JUNIORS: This is a question of justice, not selfishness. After all, when you started out in life, each of you received a whole grain as your initial endowment.[3]

---

3. Earlier in Ackerman's parable, the citizens (the first generation) of a liberal state agreed that each would receive manna according to an "equal-manna principle." See B. Ackerman, supra, ch. 2.—Eds.

SENIORS: True.

JUNIORS: And why should we start off with less?

SENIORS: Well, you weren't there when we began.

JUNIORS: Why should that matter? Do you think that citizens who are born early are intrinsically superior to those who are born late?

SENIORS: We can't say that. It would violate Neutrality.

JUNIORS: Well, then, how *can* you justify the fact that your starting point was better than ours promises to be?

SENIORS: (*Silence.*)

JUNIORS: While you are searching for a Neutral reason, let us give you one to support our claim. We think that all citizens are at least as good as one another regardless of their date of birth. If we're as least as good as you are, we should start out in life with at least as much manna as you did.

So far as ideal theory is concerned, the bad trustee stands no better than any other kind of thief. . . .

[W]hat is the difference between taking your neighbor's initial endowment and taking the endowment of a citizen who you know will be your neighbor? While it is true that the aggrieved victim will not challenge the action immediately, we have stipulated, in this model, that there *will* come a time when Senior will be called to account for his conduct by Junior. And at that time, Senior will find nothing Neutral to say in defense of depriving Junior of his right to an equal starting place. . . .

B. Ackerman, Social Justice in the Liberal State 202-04 (1980). Ackerman's trusteeship theory requires only that the first generation assure that the worst off in the next generation are not worse off than the worst off in its own generation. Why should a just society ignore the fact that the first generation had the opportunity to make the next generation better off? Professor Rawls, in developing his "just savings" principle, seems to suggest that this obligation does arise:

No generation has stronger claims than any other. In attempting to estimate the fair rate of saving the persons in the original position ask what is reasonable for members of adjacent generations to expect of one another at each level of advance. They try to piece together a just savings schedule by balancing how much at each stage they would be willing to save for their immediate descendants against what they would feel entitled to claim of their immediate predecessors. Thus imagining themselves to be fathers, say, they are to ascertain how much they should set aside for their sons by noting what they would believe themselves entitled to claim of their fathers. . . .

It is a natural fact that generations are spread out in time and actual exchanges between them take place only in one direction. We can do something for posterity but it can do nothing for us. This situation is unalterable, and so the question of justice does not arise. What is just or unjust is how institutions deal with natural limitations and the way they are set up to take advantage of historical possibilities. Obviously if all generations are to gain (except perhaps the first), they must choose a just savings principle . . . .

See J. Rawls, A Theory of Justice 289-91 (1971). Ackerman rejects Rawls' theory as follows:

He tells us that the contractors must conceive of themselves as family heads who are concerned with the welfare of their entire bloodline; why a person can't be a bachelor (or at least know of the possibility) is left entirely obscure. Yet even this first manipulation will not suffice. After all, *why* must a responsible family head want more for his children than he gets for himself? Why is it not enough to bring the child to a level of welfare equal to that the parent himself enjoys? It is always possible to short-circuit these questions simply by stipulating that *all* contractors have the psychology of the quintessential Jewish mother, but this stipulation will hardly convince parents of other temperaments. . . . This is a contractarianism at its worst, where hard questions are dismissed by painting the "state of nature" to suit one's prephilosophical fancies.

B. Ackerman, supra, at 225. Do you agree with Ackerman's implicit assumption that a "bachelor" would not care about subsequent generations? Does the family head concept used by both Ackerman and Rawls tell us something about how they view the community and an individual's responsibility to the community? Do you agree that a person's responsibility to and expectations of family members, as a matter of justice, should be different than for nonfamily members?

3. Anthropology

Grobsmith, The Lakhota Giveaway: A System of Social Reciprocity
24 Plains Anthropologist 123, 124-29 (1979)

[The following excerpt from this article describes "Giveaways" as they are practiced among Lakhota of the Rosebud Sioux Reservation] In Lakhota, . . . giveaway . . . refers to the general distribution of goods. . . .

[F]easts held in remembrance of the dead . . . [are a] type of Giveaway [that] is by far the most common. Traditionally, upon someone's death, the family would go to the home of the deceased and give away all his or her belongings. Gifts were given randomly to non-kinsmen. While this is no longer done, it is still traditional to distribute some gifts randomly at Giveaways, although more often the majority of gifts are destined for specific individuals. . . .

More prestige is definitely awarded those staging the more elaborate Giveaways. . . . It should be noted that no prestige is afforded those who simply have accumulated wealth; the honor of being labeled generous accompanies the distribution rather than the accumulation of wealth. A brief description of the Giveaway may serve to illustrate the monetary burden, the increased social interaction, and the extension of kin-like bonds resulting from such a feast.

Preparation. The initial stage of the Giveaway is the year-long planning and preparation which such ceremonial distribution entails. Generally, commemoration Giveaways are held on the anniversary of a death, so that a sponsor has one year following the burial to complete arrangements. It is usually a woman who serves as sponsor, although her nuclear or extended family will assist her in nearly all capacities. . . .

Lakhota draw a distinction between hand-made and store bought gifts. It is acceptable for a woman to save store-bought gifts she has received for distribution at her own future ceremony. However, hand-made quilts and shawls are considered generous, prestigious gifts and are always kept by the individual for whom they were intended.

Distribution. The day of the Giveaway, the family gathers all the goods to be distributed and takes them to the outdoor arena ("shade") or hall where the ceremony will take place. . . . Anywhere from one hundred to several thousand people from all over the reservation may attend. Among these are some who do not expect to receive gifts but are welcome to share in the food. Often, newspapers announce that there will be a free public feast and more prestige is awarded the family which feeds the entire community. . . .

[After the Sioux National Anthem and prayer,] [n]ext follows the meal which may be served in a "chow line" or may be brought around to seated individuals. Guests bring their own eating containers and utensils and are expected to take home as much food as they can carry. Little talking or eye contact is made during this distribution. No thanks are expected or due. . . .

After the meal, the announcer [who has been carefully selected] . . . will say a few words about the reason for the Giveaway, either honoring an individual who is present or in remembrance of the dead. . . . During this speech the guests sit in absolute silence, while the sponsoring family may gather and begin to grieve openly, sharing the painful memory of the person's life and the suffering they have experienced since the death. . . . Following this, the women spread the gifts to be distributed: quilts are unfolded as guests silently admire the fine workmanship, patterns, and quantity of goods displayed. Shawls and blankets are removed from suitcases and are spread out, along with fabric, towels and bedding. The sponsor usually stands with the announcer and provides him in writing or orally with a list of individuals to receive specific gifts. . . . Quilts are always distributed first; they are considered the most prestigious gift. It is not uncommon for forty or fifty quilts and quilt-tops to be given away. Shawls and bedding are distributed next, and finally household items and hardware and small gifts may be distributed randomly. Goods are not openly admired, but are left in their folded or packaged state until the distribution is completed. . . .

Discussion. . . . The overall cost of sponsoring a Giveaway is exorbitant; it is not uncommon for a family to spend two to five thousand dollars. While items of great expense such as ponies or horses are rarely given now, sponsoring such a ceremony is an enormous financial burden. In the late 1800's, individuals who gave away most of their possessions, e.g. horses, tipis, buffalo robes and clothing were immediately reincorporated into the community by being given the bare necessities to begin to exist once again. Having no possessions was a temporary inconvenience compared to the great amount of prestige awarded for having been so generous. The exchange cycle created networks of mutual reliance which reinforced the Lakhota value in an egalitarian society, highly integrated by interdependence and mutual obligation. . . .

Today, gift-giving fulfills similar functions: 1) it sets up a chain of reciprocal exchange which requires the development of kin-like relationships with non-kinsmen and 2) gift-giving provides moral lessons which illustrate and reinforce Lakhota values. The first function is evident from the fact that while relatives are generally expected to assist in Giveaway preparations, they are seldom the recipients of gifts. This supports a interpretation of the Giveaway as a means of *establishing* kin-like bonds with non-relatives and as a way of extending and perpetuating the web of obligations with individuals outside the family. Today, as in the past, gifts are given to those outside one's bilateral extended family and usually to members of a different community since it was and is essential to cement bonds beyond one's local group.

The second function is apparent in the manner in which generosity and sharing are revered. Informants say that the generous are always repaid in kind and that reciprocal favors constituted a very basic form of economic and social security. . . . Strong sanctions exist pertaining to how freely one gives: while the generous take comfort in the fact that they will be cared for if necessary, stinginess is criticized and avaricious people ostracized. . . .

Summary. The meaning and function of the Giveaway can be summarized in light of the above data. On the surface, gift-giving provides individuals with material items needed in daily life. However, since everyone either produces or purchases the same items, the importance of gift-giving is not the product but the relationship established by the transaction. Considering the financial burden placed on the sponsoring family, one can only conclude that one gains something more valuable than one has lost. One gives up possessions but gains friends, security, prestige; and one can rely on those alliances created, for recipients are bound into an unspoken agreement to reciprocate. Thus the cycle of gift-obligation-repayment—and, more importantly, its social consequence, mutual aid—is perpetuated.

Notes and Questions

1. *Attitudes Toward Property and Property Transmission.* In what ways do the Lakhota view and use property and gift making? Do the Lakhota understand property to mean private ownership that gives the individual the absolute right to use and to dispose of property? Do you? How do the Lakhota view their rights and duties to family and nonfamily members?

This description of Lakhota giveaways highlights, through cultural comparisons, the fact that family property law rules reflect the interests of the dominant groups in the United States. It also highlights how the family property law rules are constrained and limited by the conceptual framework from which they emanate. The principle of testamentary freedom emphasizes individual rights and creates barriers to imagining a set of customs and rules that is not built on the right of individual ownership of property, the power to transfer that property, and the right to claim property from another if certain conditions of transfer have been met. Cf. Kennedy, Toward an Historical Understanding of Legal Consciousness: The Case of Classical Legal Thought in America, 1850-1940, 3 L. & Soc. 3 (1980).

2. *Quilts*. Quiltmaking was not part of the Native American traditions. It was introduced by the government and church agencies "[a]s part of an overall effort to educate the Sioux in the ways of White people . . . ." Albers & Medicine, The Role of Sioux Women in the Production of Ceremonial Objects: The Case of the Star Quilt, in The Hidden Half Studies of Plains Indian Women 123, 126 (P. Albers & B. Medicine eds. 1983). See also L. Hyde, The Gift: Imagination and the Erotic Life of Property (1979), which was inspired in part by the anthropological literature describing gift making and which explores the thesis that art, by which a quilt is but one example, is a gift.

4. Social History

Speth, More than Her "Thirds": Wives and Widows in Colonial Virginia

in L. Speth & A. Hirsch, Women, Family, and Community in Colonial
America: Two Perspectives 5, 5-35 (1983)

Despite the relative scarcity of historical sources, one area of Virginia does contain records that reveal significant details and provide insights to the lives of eighteenth-century women. Amelia, Prince Edward, and Mecklenburg counties, areas of the eighteenth-century piedmont, have a complete run of court records. The historian can use probate and tax records to indicate patterns of behavior, to identify male attitudes about women, and even to suggest the measure and quality of female participation within the family and the larger agricultural community. In the absence of such traditional sources as letters and diaries, the 394 wills of the three counties are often the only existing personal statements made by male colonists about women, and by a few women about themselves. By analyzing the probate records in this area of Southside Virginia, one can isolate and identify the broad economic and demographic factors that influenced a woman's role and status. . . .

The legal code of the colony and the few literary sources that have survived can help define the status of the Southern woman. But the probate records of the three Southside counties reveal that, although the legal and religious institutions of colonial Virginia relegated women to the home, many Southside women, at least in widowhood, achieved a considerable measure of personal power and responsibility. These legal records, particularly the wills written in the years prior to the Revolution, offer valuable insights into women's access to property, and . . . suggest how members of the colonial family regarded each other.

Wills serve yet another function; they document the transfer of authority from one individual to another. . . .

A study of probate and other manuscript court records can thus be very useful to women's historians in their attempts to answer some of the thornier questions of women's history. At the very least, they give us the opportunity to more deeply explore the fabric of the female experience in the Old Dominion. . . .

Although Virginia intestacy laws clearly favored males, they alone do not accurately represent women's access to property. A man could dispose of his economic assets as he saw fit by his last will and testament; the only legal limitation was that a husband was required to provide his wife with her minimum dower. An examination of the 394 wills probated in the three county courts of the Southside reveals that the testators diverged significantly from the inheritance patterns suggested by the laws regulating property distribution of intestate. As the male testators disposed of the land, cattle, and slaves they had taken a lifetime to accumulate, their primary concern was that when possible, all members of the family, male and female, receive a share of the estate. The testators ignored primogeniture, tried to give all of the sons land, and proved generous in their treatment of the women in their families.

From 1735 to 1775 approximately one-fifth of the Southside fathers bequeathed land to their daughters. . . . Such bequests were at the expense of the eldest sons and reflected the testators' desires that their daughters have an equitable share of their estates, probably to use as dowries or marriage portions.

The men who gave their daughters land were usually among the elite in the Southside; it was only the wealthy who possessed enough economic resources to bequeath sufficient land to all members of the family. As Amelia County became more settled during the course of the eighteenth century, however, the daughters of the wealthy began to receive fewer bequests of land. . . .

It may be that the testators, facing a more populated county, began to perceive that the family resources could not sustain all of the sons and daughters, and still provide for the economic support of the widow. In this competition for family resources, it was daughters who received less land, although many continued to receive substantial legacies of slaves and personal property.

Wives and mothers, on the other hand, had significantly more access to both real and personal property. From 1735 to 1775, slightly more than 77 percent (N=185) of the testators in Amelia and Prince Edward assigned their wives more than traditional legal thirds. . . .

Although the legacies varied, generally the wife tended to receive the dwelling house, land, and the balance of the husband's personal property, usually farm implements, furniture, household goods, and livestock. . . . The legacy a man left his wife constituted the necessary equipment to run an agricultural operation in the eighteenth-century South, and he fully expected his spouse to use her legacy to support herself and their children. . . .

The critical decision to leave a wife a substantial legacy, more than her dower, hinged on the age of the testator and the presence of minor children in the household. Although the Southside birth and death records have been lost . . . , the wills themselves provide important information about the demographic contours of the family which significantly influenced a widow's access to economic resources. . . .

Whenever a man was elderly, he tended to give all of his property to his adult children and grandchildren and charge his eldest son with seeing that his mother had "gentle maintenance." Approximately sixteen of the testators in Amelia and Prince Edward were elderly when they wrote their will, and of these, nine individuals gave their wives less than dower.

At the other extreme of the life-cycle, men recently married and whose children were all very young tended to give their wives far more than their dower. Approximately fifty-six testators died within a few years of marrying, and either had not yet had children, or the children were very young. . . .

Many men in their middle years had young children living within the household as well as adult children who had already left home. Slightly more than 80 percent of these fathers bequeathed substantial legacies to their wives, often with the stipulation that they were to support themselves and their young children. In 1755 Daney Stanly wrote: "My Will is my loving Wife Edith Stanly shall have the use and profits of my whole Estate both real and personal until my Son John shall come to the age of twenty-one years. She giving my children Sufficient Maintenance." . . .

Generous property bequests to Southside daughters were tied more to class lines than were bequests to wives, and the testators' wives always received a far larger amount of the estate than did their daughters.

The age structure of the Southside family, however, did not always operate totally to the wife's economic advantage. The concern for minor children led many testators to restrict their wives' legacies. The Southside husbands did not usually give their wives land outright, . . .; instead they usually bequeathed it to their spouses for their lifetimes or on the condition that the women remain unmarried. . . .

Authority: Guardians and Executrixes. Most of the testators' widows received not only far more property than the legal code ordered but also significant amounts of authority and responsibility. The Southside widow was only rarely deprived of custody of her children, despite the fact that the legal code and books on childrearing at the time downplayed the idea of a mother having any impact on, or being competent to rear her children. . . .

This decision to name the wife as guardian was not made because the father had no other male to turn to. Even during the earliest years of settlement, many men had male relatives living in the area or adult sons they could name as guardians of younger children. . . .

The handful of men who deprived their wives of custody were men of wealth and were among the political and social elite in the Southside. . . . These wealthy planters usually gave their children handsome legacies, often bequeathing them large plantations in different areas of Virginia. In such circumstances they tended to rely on other wealthy planters, often business acquaintances, to oversee the children's legacies and to serve as guardians. . . .

Widows in the Southside also received grants of authority from their spouses that enabled them to enter the legal and economic sectors of society, primarily as their spouses' executrixes. One of the most vital decisions a person made when writing a will was who to name as executor. Legally the executor was responsible for paying the decedent's debts, carrying out personal requests, and dispensing the legacies. Slightly more than half of the Amelia testators appointed their wives to this important position; 78 percent of the Prince Edwards husbands did so; and 57 percent of the Mecklenburg men named their wives.

As Amelia County became more settled, however, the men began to rely less on their spouses. In the first decade of settlement, 65 percent (N=13) of the testators had appointed their wives, but by 1775 this percentage had declined to 43. In the years immediately before the Revolution, the men began to ask their eldest sons to administer their estates. This change may have been due to the maturation of the testators' sons. Traditionally settlement is undertaken by young men, either bachelors or men who had just begun their families. As the original settlers and their families matured, a large group of male children probably reached legal age and were thus able to serve as executors. . . .

Although the wills are useful . . . they are an incomplete source. Ultimately, the probate records just analyzed indicate male perceptions, male concerns, and male attitudes, and they tell us relatively little about how women acted or what they believed. These documents provide a snapshot of the Southside family, frozen at the moment a husband or father wrote his will. Perhaps more importantly for our purposes, is the exploration of women's responses to the social, economic, and legal changes that their spouses' deaths wrought.

The Widow as Feme Sole—Her New Status and Role. . . . The very fact of . . . [a husband's] death altered . . . [his widow's] life more than that of any other member of the nuclear family. Her legal status, her economic position, and her social standing within the community changed dramatically. Since her husband's death dissolved the marriage bond, legally the widow was now a *feme sole*. She could enter into contracts, sue her debtors, control her personal property, manage her land, execute a will, or sign a deed. Economically, her husband's death meant that the material resources of the family unit had been reduced, and she now faced the prospect of a lower standard of living. Socially, much of the status she had derived from her husband's position within the community ended with his death. . . .

For the most part, [historians had] . . . assumed that widows remarried rapidly, and if necessary, frequently. . . .

If widowhood was indeed a temporary and easily rectified condition in the eighteenth century, neither society, the family, nor the widow had to worry about the economic problems associated with that state. Furthermore, given the restrictions imposed by coverture, if widows did not remain single for long, it would follow that most Southside women rarely had significant access to property or played a role within the colonial economy. However, this was not the case, as an examination of marriage bonds and ministers' returns reveals. . . .

The collected and published marriage bonds and ministers' returns for . . . [the three] counties show that relatively few of the testators' widows in the Southside remarried. Less than 9 percent of these widows are known to have contracted a second marriage. . . .

Many Southside widows of either testators or intestate did not economically need to contract a second marriage. With the work provided by either her slaves or her minor children, the widow did not need the labor of a new spouse to help her exploit either her dower rights or her sizable legacy. In addition, since many of the testator's widows lost some of their wealth upon remarriage, it was not to their economic advantage to contract a second marriage unless their prospective spouses' wealth offset the loss. . . .

[C]ourt records indicate that few widows survived their spouses for several decades. The average duration of widowhood was approximately ten years, the median, six years. Women in their middle years with some economic resources may have felt they had enough to support themselves and any minor children . . . .

The primary economic activity of the testator's widow usually involved running her late husband's farm or plantation in addition to performing her traditional domestic duties. . . .

Apparently, the widow assumed most of these responsibilities herself and did not rely on an adult son or male friend of her late husband. . . .

Edmund S. Morgan, in his social history of seventeenth-century Virginia, found that when a widow served as an executrix she frequently delayed paying the other heirs their legacies and enjoyed the wealth of her late husband's estate for a considerable period of time. It is impossible to determine whether this was a common or widespread practice for the Southside widows during the eighteenth century. However, a few wills, left by the widows themselves, reveal that some women did occasionally delay paying the other heirs, usually the couple's children.

In 1759 John Wallace, Sr., . . . appointed his wife Mary as his sole executrix and ordered that as his children came of age they were to receive their share of his estate. When Mary Wallace died twenty-five years later, she had given some of her married sons and daughters their portions but had delayed paying three married daughters their legacies. Jane, Sally, and Molly had attained their legal majority some time previously, but contrary to their father's wishes, they had not received their inheritances. Such delays could reflect a desire to maintain parental authority or an effort to prevent family wealth from going outside the family to sons-in-law. In Mary Wallace's case, however, the delay probably reflected her desire to maintain control of a portion of the family wealth. In her will she made no effort to create separate estates for two of her married daughters and assigned one daughter's portion directly to her son-in-law and named him as the executor of her estate. Whatever her specific motivation, Mary Wallace kept control of a portion of her late husband's estate for several years longer than he had originally stipulated and only relinquished that control at the time of her own death in 1780. . . .

The thirty-two wills left by Southside widows . . . hint at gender differences. For example, in the 394 wills probated in the Southside courts the only bequest to charity was made by a woman. Francis Stokes of Amelia County ordered that her executors were to ensure that the "Poor of Raleigh Parish" received £25 from her estate. Furthermore, women frequently made bequests to female friends and sisters, hinting at the importance of other women in their lives. In 1766 Judith Frank wrote: "I Give and bequeath all my Estate both Real and personal and Cash unto my Friend Mary Finney and to her heirs forever." Judith Frank also requested that her friend serve as the executrix of her estate. Both Dorothy Crowder and Mary Gray left their estates to their sisters and appointed them as executrixes. Oftentimes, such bequests and appointments were made at the expense of male relatives. Widows also turned to other women when they were worried about their young children. Judith Booker directed by her last will that her young daughter, Judith, "live with and under the care and Tuition of Mrs. [Edith] Cobbs."

Taken together, the wills written by both men and women, as well as local church and court records, suggest the outlines of economic and legal realities—greater access to economic resources, some autonomy in the private sphere regarding decision-making and childrearing, and hint at slightly different value systems for female testators.

Notes and Questions

1. *Same Facts/Different Story.* The Speth study looks at the instances in which women controlled property, such as when they were named executors of their husbands' estates, and concludes that they experienced authority and property ownership. Another historian looking at English property law between 1660 and 1833 suggests that a different interpretation is possible.

> A principal feature of these deeper patriarchal structures was that women functioned to transmit wealth from one generation of men to the next generation of men. . . . In the property regimes of patriarchy, descent and inheritance are reckoned in the male line; women function as procreators and as transmitters of inheritance from male to male.

S. Staves, Married Women's Separate Property in England, 1660-1833, at 4 (1990). Which one of these stories seems more correct? Is either correct?

The thesis that women functioned only as the vessels by which property was transmitted from one generation of males to another is the basis for one explanation of the New England witchcraft trials in the seventeenth and eighteenth centuries.

> A substantial majority of New England's accused females were women without brothers, women with daughters but no sons, or women in marriages with no

children at all . . . . Of the 267 accused females, enough is known about 158 to identify them as either having or not having brothers or sons to inherit: . . . ninety-six (61 percent) did not. More striking, *once accused*, women without brothers or sons were even more likely than women with brothers or sons to be tried, convicted, and executed: women from families without male heirs made up 64 percent of the females prosecuted, 76 percent of those who were found guilty, and 89 percent of those who were executed. . . .

What seems especially significant here is that most accused witches whose husbands were still alive were, like their counterparts who were widows and spinsters, over forty years of age—and therefore unlikely if not unable to produce male heirs. Indeed, the fact that witchcraft accusations were rarely taken seriously by the community until the accused stopped bearing children takes on a special meaning when it is juxtaposed with the anomalous position of inheriting women or potentially inheriting women in New England's social structure. . . .

The amount of property in question was not the crucial factor in the way these women were viewed or treated by their neighbors, however. Women of widely varying economic circumstances were vulnerable to accusation and even to conviction. Neither was there a direct line from accuser to material beneficiary of the accusation: others in the community did sometimes profit personally from the losses sustained by these women . . . , but only rarely did the gain accrue to the accusers themselves. . . .

However varied their backgrounds and economic positions, as women without brothers or women without sons, they stood in the way of the orderly transmission of property from one generation of males to another.

C. Karlsen, The Devil in the Shape of a Woman: Witchcraft in Colonial New England 102-16 (1989).

Woman as vessel for property transfers coincides with social myths surrounding procreation itself.

> With the advent of patriarchal institutions, the male laid eager claim to his posterity. It was still necessary to grant the mother a part in procreation, but it was conceded only that she carried and nourished the living seed, created by the father alone. . . . Under these imaginative hypotheses, woman was restricted to the nourishment of an active, living principle already preformed in perfection.

S. de Beauvoir, The Second Sex 8 (Vintage ed. 1989).

Although today, characterizing a woman as a vessel has a negative connotation, "in primordial terms the vessel is anything but a 'passive' receptacle: it is *transformative*—active, powerful. . . . The transformations necessary for the continuation of life are thus, in terms of this early imagery, exercises of female power." A. Rich, Of Woman Born: Motherhood as Experience and Institution 98 (10th Ann. ed. 1986). Do the different views of vessel help you understand the Lakhota giveaway differently? Are the women acting for and on behalf of others, themselves, or both? Are the women exercising transformative power through their quiltmaking?

2. *Widows and Widows' Property Rights.* The Speth study illustrates how wills serve as windows into the lives and family relationships of ordinary people. Her historical examination of systems of inheritance and probate records simultaneously reveals how women have realized control over

property and, therefore, their lives, and how the constraints on women to obtain and exercise property rights was one of the means by which women were restricted to the domestic sphere. This point is made more generally by Goody:

> The linking of patterns of inheritance with patterns of domestic organization is a matter not simply of numbers and formations but of attitudes and emotions. The manner of splitting property is a manner of splitting people; it creates (or in some cases reflects) a particular constellation of ties and cleavages between husband and wife, parents and children, sibling and sibling, as well as between wider kin. . . .
> The mode of tenure and system of inheritance are linked not only to household structure but also to a constellation of demographic variables, factors which affect growth of population and preferences for male or female children. The ways in which these links occur are many and complex.

Family and Inheritance: Rural Society in Western Europe, 1200-1800, at 3 (J. Goody, J. Thirsk, & E.P. Thompson eds. 1976).

3. *Distinctive Women's Value System or Culture Reflected in Wills—the Post-revolutionary Period.* Professor Lebsock in her study of the free women of Petersburg, Virginia, after the revolutionary war relies on women's wills as evidence that women, unlike their male counterparts, "made economic decisions according to their own standards of propriety and justice." S. Lebsock, supra, at 116.

Lebsock provides evidence that women had different values than their male counterparts by identifying the high incidence of will making by propertied women during the antebellum period. Lebsock writes that "During the period 1831 to 1860, nearly two-thirds of the propertied men who died in Petersburg (324/495 = 65.5 percent) died intestate. Among the women, the intestacy rate was substantially lower. Of those women who died with property and with the legal capacity to write a will [unmarried], fewer than half (106/222 = 47.8 percent) died intestate. . . . [I]n every age category and in every category of wealth, women were more likely to leave wills than were men." Id. at 133. She explains the relatively high incidence of wills written by women by suggesting that women and men had different attitudes toward death, wealth, family, and slavery.

> It may have been that women, who looked at death with every pregnancy and who were more likely to be deeply religious, had less trouble making preparations for their dying.
> To make a will was also to come to terms with one's financial standing. For men who had not done well . . . this was painful. . . . For women, on the other hand, wealth was a less important measure of one's worth as a human being; relative poverty was less likely to prove an obstacle to writing a will. . . . [W]omen handed out their rather puny legacies with a good deal of relish. "I have nothing of consequence sufficient to make it necessary to write a will," Ann Birchett began, but she wrote one anyway, making very particular bequests to her nearest kin. To her son George, she gave her wedding ring and a fruit knife; to her daughter Jane, she gave one share of bank stock, a miniature portrait, and her white counterpane; and to her sister, she gave a cloak, a shawl, and some caps; and so it went.

The care with which Ann Birchett selected particular items for particular persons suggests a third and probably the most important reason why women were more likely than were men to write wills. That is, women were more likely to be dissatisfied with what would be done with their property if they died intestate and left their estates to be distributed according to law. The central principle of Virginia probate law was equality [among children]. . . . This was perhaps laudable democracy, but most of the women had other ideas. While most of the men who left wills went along with the law, dividing their property equally among their children, women tended to play favorites.

Id. at 134-35. See supra Note 4, at p. 41.

Lebsock provides two other reasons why making a will was important for women in Petersburg. First, women were more interested than men in assuring that their daughters' legacies were protected from the control of their husbands and their husbands' creditors. See id. at 136. Second, they wanted, more often than did men, to provide for their slaves.

[M]ore women than men used their wills to set slaves free. . . . (A much larger number of emancipations were performed by deed, and here, too, white women appear to have outdone the men in liberating slaves.) . . . [M]ore women than men . . . inserted clauses either to prevent their slaves from being moved or sold or to restrict the terms of sale. . . .

[W]omen more often than men . . . gave their slaves legacies, single cash payments in some cases, maintenance for life in others. . . .

[W]hite women were in fact a subversive influence on chattel slavery, not so much because they opposed slavery as a system . . . , but because they operated out of an essentially personal frame of reference. The women who wrote special provisions for their slaves into their wills worked from the same mentality that caused women as a group to divide property unevenly among their heirs: Women indulged particular attachments—they were alert to the special case, to the personal exception.

Id. at 137-38. Cf. Stein & Fierstein, The Demography of Probate Administration, 15 U. Balt. L. Rev. 54, Table 4.6, 83-84 (1985) (in a study of a random sample of residents who died during 1972 in five different states, the researchers found that females were more likely to die with a will than were males). But see Crane, The Socioeconomics of a Female Majority in Eighteenth-Century Bermuda, 15 Signs 231, 243-48 (1990) (shows that Caucasian women, who held more property than their counterparts on the mainland, relied on and exploited male and female slaves to engage in commercial activity and were not inclined to free them).

4. *Survivorship.* The Speth and Lebsock studies highlight the instances in which women exercised some control over some property. That control, however, was contingent on wives surviving their husbands. Historians studying England indicate that during the sixteenth to the nineteenth centuries, the risks of childbirth decreased the chances that a wife would survive.

In the seventeenth and eighteenth centuries . . . marriages were broken . . . by the premature death of one spouse or another, since all pre-modern societies had a fairly high death rate among young adults. In the sixteenth century, the chance of dying in one's twenties or thirties was as great as it is today in one's sixties. . . . [I]n early nineteenth-century England, . . . there was a two per cent chance of one spouse or the other dying each year, which means that not far off thirty per cent of all marriages were broken up by death in the first fifteen years. . . .

[R]emarriage was very common, about a quarter of all marriages being a remarriage for the bride or the groom. . . . This means that in the seventeenth century the remarriage rate, made possible by death, was not far off that in our own day, made possible by divorce. In both periods, consecutive legal polygamy has been extremely common. Many of the remarriages were by the fathers of young children whose wives had died in childbirth, and who, therefore, urgently needed a nurse, housekeeper, cook, washerwoman and sexual partner. On the other hand many women who lost their husbands, especially poor women, could not find a new partner, so that in Lichfield in 1695 no fewer than thirty-one per cent of all women over thirty were widows. . . .

For women, childbirth was a very dangerous experience, for midwives were ignorant and ill-trained, and often horribly botched the job, while the lack of hygienic precautions meant that puerperal fever was a frequent sequel. . . . Because of this high mortality from childbirth, at all periods from the sixteenth to the nineteenth century, in three out of four cases of all first marriages among the squirarchy that were broken by death within ten years, the cause was the death of the wife. . . .

L. Stone, The Family, Sex and Marriage In England 1500-1800, at 55-56, 79-80 (1977).

5. *Women and Philanthropy.* The Speth study suggests that review of wills may be telling about women's greater proclivity to make charitable gifts. Professor Lebsock supports this hypothesis by showing that in the antebellum South, Caucasian women were active in religion and organized charity. Lebsock suggests that this interest merely reflects the "fact that women were allowed to do church and charity work while they were not allowed to enter formal politics, the professions, big business, or the military." S. Lebsock, supra, at 142. See also id. at ch. 7. One fundraiser recently wrote that she detected that women had a predisposition to give their time to charities rather than their money, *i.e.,* women remain "active in religion and organized charity."

> Many women compensate for not giving money by donating time, the commodity in shortest supply for career women and mothers of young children, but the one resource they feel is theirs to give. Overall, 45 percent of American women compared to 38 percent of men did volunteer work in 1989. I'm not sure how those respondents defined "volunteer work," but after 20 years of activism, I can testify that women are the quintessential givers when it comes to effort, energy, comfort and service.

Pogrebin, Contributing to the Cause, N.Y. Times, Apr. 22, 1990, § 6 (Magazine) at 22, 23.

6. *Philanthropy's Societal Role.* Philanthropy's proper role in our democratic and pluralistic American society raises difficult issues. Andrew Carnegie, the famous entrepreneur and philanthropist, argued "that to leave

great fortunes to children did not prove true affection for them or interest in their genuine good . . . ; it was not the welfare of the children, but the pride of the parents, which inspired enormous legacies." Carnegie, The Best Fields for Philanthropy, 149 N. Am. Rev. 683, 684-85 (1889). He believed that people owning "enormous fortunes" should "from time to time during their own lives . . . so administer them as to promote the permanent good of the communities from which they have been gathered." Id. at 685. He further hoped "that public sentiment would soon say of one who died possessed of millions of available wealth which he might have administered: 'The man who dies thus rich dies disgraced.'" Id. The remaining part of the article was devoted to identifying some of the best uses to which the wealthy could contribute, including educational institutions, free libraries, hospitals and medical research, public parks, concert halls, swimming pools, and religious buildings.[4] Why do you think Carnegie failed to consider the alternative of requiring that the wealth be given to governmental bodies to decide, through the political process, how it should be used for the community? Even if society concludes that property owners should be able to decide how their wealth should be used, should philanthropic giving relieve the property owner of having to pay income taxes or estate and gift taxes on the amount of property given to charity? Should the charitable organizations enjoy tax-exempt status?

The Internal Revenue Service denied tax-exempt status to Bob Jones University because of its racially discriminatory admissions policy. Bob Jones argued that the Service's action violated its First Amendment freedom of religion rights. That argument was rejected by the Supreme Court in Bob Jones University v. United States, 461 U.S. 574 (1983). The Court upheld the Service's action by relying on the overriding public policy of providing desegregated education. See Devins, Bob Jones University v. United States: A Political Analysis, 1 J.L. & Pol. 403 (1984); Galvin & Devins, A Tax Policy Analysis of Bob Jones University v. United States, 36 Vand. L. Rev. 1353 (1983). See also Cover, The Supreme Court 1982 Term Foreword: *Nomos* and Narrative, 97 Harv. L. Rev. 4 (1983). See also infra p. 783.

5. Economics

Modigliani, The Role of Intergenerational Transfers and Life Cycle Saving in the Accumulation of Wealth
2 J. of Econ. Persp. 15, 15, 17, 38-39 (1988)

The purpose of this paper is to review what economists know at present about the following question: How large a portion of the existing wealth is the result of a bequest motive, that is, of accumulation for the specific

---

4. Carnegie referred only to churches and places where "the whole neighborhood gathers on Sunday." Id. at 696. His exclusive attention to Christian religions exemplifies how a dominant group retains domination by wielding its power to make gifts.

purpose of leaving bequests? I will also endeavor to clarify why an answer to this question is of interest. . . .

[A]cknowledging that aggregate wealth could arise from both transitory hump wealth [a build up of a reserve against unforeseen contingencies or anticipated decline in income to support anticipated future consumption] and from the transfer of wealth through bequests from one generation to the next conveys nothing about the importance of each of these processes in accounting for existing wealth. In particular, is the bequest motive the main source of existing wealth, as supposed by the traditional view, or is it swamped by hump saving?

This question has attracted attention at least since the early 1960s when a number of investigations . . . were undertaken. The interest was spurred, in part, by scientific curiosity. But the question also has relevance for the design of economic policies because the two sources of wealth may be expected to respond to very different stimuli. . . . [H]ump wealth should respond to variables or institutions like length of retirement, family size, liquidity constraints, uncertainty of income (at least from labor), private and public pension arrangements, and health insurance. Most of these variables would likely have little effect on bequests, though, admittedly, economists know rather little as to what, other than estate and gift taxation, would have a significant impact on bequests.

Thus, knowledge of the relative contributions is important to assess the effectiveness of measures designed to affect saving and wealth as well as the effects on wealth of measures intended to achieve other goals, such as estate taxation designed to reduce economic inequalities. . . .

Clearly, part of the private wealth held at any time reflects hump . . . wealth and part reflects wealth transmitted through inheritances and major gifts. The interesting question is: how large is each component? The available evidence . . . consistently indicates that the share of wealth received by transfer does not exceed one-fourth. . . .

[T]he role of bequest motivated transfers . . . seem[s] to play an important role only in the very highest income and wealth brackets. Some portion of bequests, especially in lower income brackets, is not due to a pure bequest motive but rather to a precautionary motive reflecting uncertainty about the length of life, although it is not possible at present to pinpoint the size of this component.

Kessler & Masson, Bequest and Wealth Accumulation: Are Some Pieces of the Puzzle Missing?
3 J. of Econ. Persp. 141, 142-45 (1989)

Any measurement of the contribution of transfers to wealth accumulation rests on a specific theory of saving behavior. . . . [W]e list eight issues that appear especially relevant to choosing a perspective on savings behavior.

1. Who makes consumption-saving decisions? Is it the (independent) individual, the household or the dynastic family? The life cycle hypothesis claims that the relevant saving unit is the household, abstracting from the intra- or inter-generational relations among its members, and giving limited consideration to the links between parents and children in different households. The individual approach will, to the contrary, take into account some intra-household transfers that may affect individual accumulation. In a dynastic approach . . . the relevant saving decision unit is the dynastic family whose foundation lies precisely in transfers.

2. Is it reasonable to assume separability between material bequests and expenditures made on behalf of children? What about assuming separability between saving choices and labor supply or human capital decisions? The life cycle hypothesis assumes this separability: in this model, the bequest motive is considered in isolation and the process of asset accumulation can be considered relatively apart from labor supply or family-related decisions. Other models assume a large substitutability between material transfers from parents to children and expenditures by parents on behalf of children . . . .

This question is illustrated in the decision by . . . [some economists] to count the cost of a college education as an intergenerational transfer, because such payments appear to be a main component of the expenditures parents make on their "adult" children (above the age of 18). To evaluate their position, one has first to look at parents' motivations: college tuition may be assimilated to transfers if parents substitute such educational expenses with material gifts bestowed to other children, or if some parents prefer to invest in the college education of their children while others choose to make bequests. But a complete assimilation supposes also, on the recipient side, that college education has the same impact on later accumulation as a cash transfer. In practice, it is not sure that both conditions are satisfied; moreover, in keeping with this perspective, almost any expenditure on behalf of children or family could be counted as an intergenerational transfer, leading to an inflated measurement of the ratio of inherited wealth (in human and nonhuman form) to existing nonhuman wealth. . . .

3. How can economists identify the inherited and life cycle components of wealth, since the two types of accumulation interact? Receiving inherited wealth does change life cycle savings, with the effect depending on the size and timing of the bequest. An inheritance received at a young age is likely to boost accumulation, especially given strong market imperfections and uncertainties. How can such interactions be quantified and be divided between the two factors to reach a true measure of the impact of bequests? . . .

5. Should people be considered primarily life cyclers or inheritors and bequeathers? Given the skewed distribution of wealth and the even more skewed distribution of inheritances, it is insufficient to consider only the importance of transfers in aggregate accumulation. The statement that bequests lead to half of total wealth could correspond to two very different situations: in one, the (age-adjusted) share of inheritance in total wealth is 50 percent for everybody; in the second, the top quintile of wealth holders owns three-quarters of total assets (as in the United States) and has inherited two-thirds of its wealth, whereas the bottom 80 percent of the wealth distribution receives and bequeaths nothing. The role of inheritance on wealth inequality and the relevance of the life cycle hypothesis are not at all the same in the two situations.

6. Why do people bequeath? The debate offers a distinction between true, planned bequests and accidental unplanned bequests. Unintended bequests may be due to uncertain length of life in a world of imperfect annuity markets or to imperfect rental markets for housing and other durable assets . . . . Either way, they blur the black-white distinction between life cycle and bequest accumulation. [One economist] . . . has shown that the precautionary motive alone (unintended bequests providing no direct utility) can lead to sizeable transfers that are not caused by a genuine bequest motive. However, [other economists] . . . point out that households do derive some utility even from an unintended bequest, so that the two motives interact. For example, dwellings are held at old age both for the services they yield or as insurance of consumption against longevity, and as a source of bequests to the children if not used up. Although it might be said that life cycle motives are more important for more households in this context, the absence of separability makes it virtually impossible to distinguish life cycle from bequest savings.

The motivation of inheritance . . . is also important to understand for policy purposes. For instance, if bequests are of a "compensatory" type, driven by strong altruism, the consumer will react to higher estate taxation by "increasing his bequest so as to cushion the impact on his heirs" . . . . The inheritance elasticity of wealth may then be very small or even negative. . . .

7. Are life cycle savings and bequests the only two motives for accumulation? This dichotomy may seem reasonable, since all excess life cycle accumulation winds up as bequeathed wealth. But economists may be understating other motives for holding wealth, such as power, entrepreneurship, social prestige, and so on, motives which may not be confined to the super-rich. Those determinants of saving are more or less ignored in most saving models, but they may play an important role in the debate concerning the status of accumulated interest on inheritance. Consider how the effect of bequests on total wealth will differ in two models of social savings behavior.

Consider first the case of the capitalists . . . whose income is derived almost entirely from property, initially inherited. Their lifecycle accumulation is assumed to be negligible in relative terms, and nearly all their wealth is destined to be bequeathed. But these [capitalists] . . . will also save simply because they derive utility directly from owning assets. Indeed, to keep their social position and their economic power, they have to maintain their relative wealth share, which means that their wealth must increase as quickly as general economic growth. If the available rate of return equals the rate of growth, then all the income from inheritance must be saved to preserve the relative size of the bequest. . . . [It would be wrong to treat this saving as motivated by the lifecycle model because it was] never intended to be spent.

Consider next a traditional stationary society where . . . someone inheriting a given *bien de famille* may use the income from it, but has to hold the asset intact until he dies, when it passes to the next generation. There are no other transfers. Since the rate of saving out of bequest income is nil, this society is closer to [the lifecyle's approach of measuring] . . . inherited wealth.

Notes and Questions

1. *Recent Empirical Research Regarding Bequest Motive.* Professor Hurd concludes that

> [a]n inoperable bequest motive cannot be detected empirically because it does not lead to behavior any different from the complete absence of a bequest motive. . . .
>
> An implication of the tests of the bequest motive is that bequests appear to be largely accidental, the result of uncertainty about the date of death.

Hurd, Research on the Elderly: Economic Status, Retirement, and Consumption and Saving, 28 J. of Econ. Lib. 565, 628 (1990).

2. *Current Wealth Predictions of the Older Segment of the Population.* Whatever the motivations for wealth accumulation, estimates indicate that the older segment of the population is wealthier than ever. Increases in the value of housing and decades of strong economic performance have resulted in the older segment of the population becoming increasingly wealthy as compared to the national average. In 1960, the segment of households headed by 45- to 69-year olds was 33% more wealthy than the national average. In 1990, that segment was 75% wealthier. It is estimated that $6.8 trillion of wealth will be transferred at death between 1987 and 2011. See N.Y. Times, July 22, 1990, § E, at 4 (Midwest ed.).

3. *Production and Reproduction.* If intergenerational transfers play a role in wealth accumulation, then should we view family as an integral part of the United State's economic order and economic productivity even though family enterprises are no longer the norm in the economy and families are no longer the major production unit? Professor Langbein believes that the twentieth century has brought about a shift in the motivation of wealth accumulation for the middle class and believes the lifecyle model is controlling. See Langbein, The Twentieth-Century Revolution in Family Wealth Transmission, 86 Mich. L. Rev. 722 (1988). He further suggests that "the patterns of wealth transmission for the broad middle classes have also touched the holders of great wealth. The new pattern has become a social norm, a norm so powerful that it has begun to chip away at the ethos of older notions of inheritance." Id. at 737. He detects the beginnings of a "hostility towards conventional succession." Id. This conclusion is particularly important in view of the increased wealth in the hands of the older segment of the population. See supra note 2. How would Andrew Carnegie greet this predicted transformation? If Langbein is right, what is the role families will play in the economic order? Will the economic order

look any different if "power, entrepreneurship, [and] social prestige" become more important as intergenerational transfers become less important?

4. *Women's Role and the Emerging Transformation of Inheritance.* Langbein and Carnegie suggest that a "defense against death" other than through inheritance by children, is philanthropic giving. If Langbein is right that there is an emerging transformation of inheritance, might it have an effect on the role women will play in the culture? Will that role necessarily be a better one for women? Professor MacKinnon's tentative explanation of the connection of the concept of private property to inheritance by a man's children may provide some insight into this question. She hypothesizes that "[i]f . . . private property ownership reflects positively on personality in a given culture, and if death culturally means the end of personality, one might want to pass on property to someone with whom one identifies. Inheritance becomes a defense against death by perpetuation of self through the mediation of property ownership, to which end monogamous marriage is (at least for men) a means." C. MacKinnon, Toward a Feminist Theory of the State 29-30 (1989). See also M. Foucault, The History of Sexuality 36-37 (Vintage ed. 1990) ("All this garrulous attention which has us in a stew over sexuality, is it not motivated by one basic concern: to ensure population, to reproduce labor capacity, to perpetuate the form of social relations: in short to constitute a sexuality that is economically useful and politically conservative?").

5. *How are Large Fortunes Generated and Distributed?* The Modigliani and Kessler and Masson articles ask the question why people want to accumulate wealth as a basis for determining economic and social policy. Another related question is how wealth is generated and distributed. Professor Thurow suggests that the answer to that question lies in "a phenomenon called the 'random walk'." L. Thurow, Generating Inequality: Mechanisms of Distribution in the U.S. Economy 142 (1975). He goes on to explain the phenomenon in more detail.

> Large instantaneous fortunes are created when the financial markets capitalize new above-average rate of return investments to yield average rate of return financial investments. It is this process of capitalizing disequilibrium returns that generates rapid fortunes. Patient savings and reinvestment has little or nothing to do with them. To become very rich one must generate or select a situation in which an above-average rate of return is about to be capitalized. . . .
>
> The random walk is a process that will generate a highly skewed distribution of wealth regardless of the normal distribution of personal abilities and regardless of whether the economy does or does not start from an initial state of equality. Once great wealth has been created, the holder diversifies his portfolio and after that is subject to diversification and to earning the market rate of return. Because most holders of wealth eventually diversify their portfolios, great fortunes remain even after the underlying disequilibrium in the real capital markets disappears. . . .
>
> The net result is a process that generates a highly skewed distribution of wealth from a normal distribution of abilities. Fortunes are created instantaneously or in very short periods of time. Personal savings behavior has little

or nothing to do with the process. Once created, large fortunes maintain themselves through being able to diversify and through inheritance.

Id. at 149, 151-52. Does Thurow's thesis make you more or less inclined to favor high death taxes? In thinking about this question, one should of course distinguish between inheritance of large fortunes—excessive inheritance—and more modest inheritance. For a proposal for eliminating excessive inheritance through the federal transfer-tax system, see Ascher, Curtailing Inherited Wealth, 89 Mich. L. Rev. 69 (1990).

PART G. THE UNIFORM PROBATE CODE

With the preceding background in mind, we are now prepared to begin studying American family property law as it exists and as it is likely to take shape in the future. In pursuing that objective, this book centers on the Uniform Probate Code (UPC). The UPC was originally promulgated by the Uniform Law Commissioners (ULC) in 1969. It has had a profound effect on American law. The UPC is the first effort, ever, at comprehensive codification of the law of estates and probate. Its major divisions cover the substantive and procedural law of intestacy, wills, donative transfers, guardianship, conservatorship, and estate and trust administration.

The UPC is not a static Code. Unlike nearly all other uniform acts, the UPC is constantly monitored by a supervisory body called the Joint Editorial Board for the Uniform Probate Code (JEB-UPC). The JEB-UPC is composed of nine members—three from the ULC, three from the American Bar Association, and three from the American College of Trust and Estate Counsel. Six of the nine members (including the chair) are practitioners of national reputation; three are academic lawyers. There are, in addition, an Executive Director, a Director of Research and Chief Reporter, and three liaisons, one to probate judges and two to law teachers.

Throughout the twenty-plus years since the UPC's origination, the JEB-UPC has, with the approval of the ULC, revised a section here, a section there, to eliminate unintended consequences and, in some cases, to reflect changed policy choices. But the supervisory process took a dynamic turn in the mid-1980's. The heightened activity culminated, in 1989, in a thoroughly revised Article VI, dealing with multiple-party accounts and related areas, and, in 1990, in a dramatically revised Article II, the core substantive article of the UPC. The 1990 Article II makes significant changes in the law of intestacy, wills, elective-share law, and constructional law. In addition, the ULC is moving toward promulgating the new Article II in 1991 as a freestanding Uniform Act on Intestacy, Wills, and Donative Transfers, in order to facilitate its adoption in states that do not employ the UPC's procedural system.

The 1990 UPC Article II reflects four fundamental policy objectives: (1) to respond to the changes in the American family, especially the multiple-marriage society; (2) to extend the partnership theory of marital property, now recognized in divorce law, into the laws protecting surviving spouses from disinheritance; (3) to move toward unification of the law of probate and nonprobate transfers; and (4) to diminish the formalistic barriers to the implementation of transferors' intentions. Consistent with these objectives, major changes have been introduced into virtually every chapter of the law.

We believe that 1990 UPC Article II is destined to be the model for American family property law deep into the next century. At the same time, we must bear in mind that the pre-1990 version of UPC Article II or non-UPC law still constitutes the law in many states. The 1990 UPC revisions are so comprehensive that it will take significant periods of study before large numbers of states will move to enact them. Thus, in this course, we principally study the 1990 version of the UPC but do not neglect the coverage of the pre-1990 version or non-UPC law.

Statutory References. This book is meant to be used with Selected Statutes on Trusts and Estates, a code book that reproduces both the 1990 and pre-1990 versions of the UPC, various other uniform laws that are germane to family property law, and a small selection of nonuniform and Commonwealth legislation.

The casebook and the code book are integrated by the freestanding captions in the casebook denominated Statutory References. These Statutory References direct you to the major statutory material reproduced in the code book that you should examine in conjunction with the topic you are about to study.

DIVISION ONE
PROBATE TRANSFERS

Chapter 2

INTESTATE SUCCESSION AND RELATED MATTERS

PART A. INTRODUCTION TO INTESTATE SUCCESSION

Statutory References: *1990 UPC §§ 1-107, 2-104, -108*
                              Pre-1990 UPC §§ 2-104, -108

Who Is Likely to Die Intestate? Conventional wisdom is that most people die intestate. Conventional wisdom also is that the older and wealthier you are, the more likely you are to have a will.[1] An empirical study corroborated the points that age and wealth are good predictors of will-making, but cast some doubt on the notion that most people die intestate. See Fellows, Simon & Rau, Public Attitudes About Property Distribution at Death and Intestate Succession Laws in the United States, 1978 Am. B. Found. Res. J. 319, 336-39. The results of a telephone survey conducted in five states in 1977 reveal the following demographic characteristics of the respondents who said they had a will and those who said they did not have one:

	Have Will	*No Will*
Family income:[2]		
Under $50,000	34.6%	65.4%
$50,000 and above	65.4%	34.6%
Estate size:[3]		
$0-$99,999	27.7%	72.3%
$100,000-$199,999	50.2%	49.8%
$200,000-$1 million	69.0%	31.0%
Age:		
17-30	12.3%	87.7%
31-45	34.6%	65.4%
46-54	60.7%	39.3%
55-64	63.4%	36.6%
65 and over	84.6%	15.4%

---

1. There will always be exceptions. A striking one is Howard Hughes, who died intestate in 1976. In his case, however, he apparently once had a will, but it could not be found after his death and the proponent and principal beneficiary of the will, the Howard Hughes Medical Institute, was unable to probate it as a lost will. The story is told infra p. 263.

2. The family income and estate size figures presented above have been adjusted for inflation. Between 1977, when the survey was conducted, and 1990, when this book was prepared, the consumer price index has nearly doubled. To reflect this increase due to inflation, we doubled the original figures.

3. See supra note 2.

Family status:

No children	10.9%	89.1%
Some minor children	32.2%	67.8%
All adult children	72.6%	27.4%

Although, overall, nearly 55 percent of the respondents interviewed said they had no will, the above table shows that those without a will were young and unlikely to die in the near future. About 73 percent of the population dies between ages 60 and 90. If this survey is accurate for the country as a whole, and if 60.7 percent of the 46-54 population, 63.4 percent of the 55-64 population, and 84.6 percent of the 65-and-over population have wills, the conventional wisdom that most people die intestate may be unfounded. Perhaps it is more accurate to suggest that most people who die prematurely die intestate.[4]

Besides age and income, what additional factors might explain why some people do not make wills? See Astrachan, Why People Don't Make Wills, 118 Tr. & Est. 45 (Apr. 1979).

Of course, even for those people who die intestate, intestacy is often not the prevailing form of family property transfer. Many decedents will die having provided for the disposition of at least some of their property through a will substitute, such as a joint tenancy with right of survivorship or a life-insurance contract. Data gathered in a study of probate administration conducted in the 1970s show that, although life-insurance proceeds represent a relatively small percentage of property transferred by decedents at death, most of them have life insurance. The data from this study also show that joint tenancy property is commonly found in decedents' estates. See Stein & Fierstein, The Demography of Probate Administration, 15 U. Balt. L. Rev. 54, 102-04 (1985).

Historical Roots of Intestacy Rules. The intestacy rules of modern America have roots deep in medieval England. Under the medieval English canons of descent (which developed from customary rules), only persons related by blood to the decedent could be heirs. Blood relatives were divided into three groups: (1) descendants (or issue), (2) ancestors (those in the ascending line), and (3) collaterals. A collateral relative is a blood relative who shares a common ancestor with the decedent, but is neither an ancestor nor a descendant. Examples of collateral relatives are: brothers and sisters, who have parents in common with the decedent, and first cousins, who have grandparents in common with the decedent.

The intestate's land was inherited by his descendants so long as any descendant was living at his death. This was true also under the English Statute of Distribution, 1670, and is true under all American statutes on succession, except that the English statute made provision for a surviving

---

4. The results of a public attitude survey conducted in England and Wales in 1988 and 1989 provide further support for the view that intestacy is more likely to control the disposition of young people's property. See U.K. Law Comm'n, Family Law: Distribution on Intestacy (No. 187), app. C, at 25-26, 32-33 (1989).

wife and American statutes typically make provision for a surviving spouse, either wife or husband.

The English canons, which in fact were not uniformly applied throughout England, provided that a male descendant should be preferred over a female descendant and that, among male descendants, the eldest should take the entire estate (primogeniture). In a society such as England's, which was dominated by a landed and male aristocracy, one purpose of primogeniture was to preserve the unity of the patrimony, the large family estates, in the male line.[5] Primogeniture was not abolished until 1926 by the Administration of Estates Act, 1925, 15 Geo. 5, c. 23, § 45. Neither of these rules was followed in the English Statute of Distribution, which basically codified well established customary rules for dividing personal property equally among the decedent's children. See J. Baker, An Introduction to English Legal History 321-22 (2d ed. 1979).

If the intestate died without leaving any living descendant, his land passed to collateral heirs; ancestors were completely excluded from inheriting land. The exclusion of ancestors was not followed in the English Statute of Distribution, nor has it been followed in any American jurisdiction, though our statutes vary considerably on the order of inheritance by ancestors. Under many statutes, for example, parents inherit ahead of collaterals, such as brothers and sisters, while under others they inherit equally with brothers and sisters.

In America, rejection of the preference for males over females and of primogeniture among male descendants began during the colonial period. There was considerable reform of intestacy law during the Revolutionary era. These reforms, including the elimination of primogeniture in virtually all of the states in favor of a rule that treated the children equally, reflected the influence of the political tradition of republicanism that animated the Revolution. The preambles to the Revolutionary and post-Revolutionary acts governing inheritance expressed the republican abhorrence of aristocracy, family dynasties, and large estates.[6] This ideology co-existed uneasily with the commitment to individual rights of ownership. The conflict between individual freedom of disposition and the prevention of dynastic wealth is one of the recurrent stories throughout American succession law, and we will see several examples of it throughout the book.

---

5. The purposes and effects of the rule of primogeniture are subjects much debated among legal historians. English lawyers themselves did not agree on its purposes. Sir Matthew Hale, for example, defended primogeniture by making the improbable claim that it ensured socially useful occupations for younger sons, who otherwise would have "neglected the Opportunities of greater Advantage of enriching themselves and the Kingdom." M. Hale, The History of the Common Law of England 142 (C. Gray ed. 1971) (first published in 1713). The great English legal historian, Sir Frederic Maitland, claimed that primogeniture obliterated class distinctions. 2 F. Pollock & F. Maitland, A History of English Law 274 (1898).

6. See, e.g., 2 Laws of the State of Delaware, ch. 53 (S. & J. Adams pub. 1797); 1 Public Acts of the General Assembly of North Carolina, ch. 22 (J. Iredell ed., F. Martin rev. 1804). For further discussions of the relationship between early American inheritance law and republican political ideology, see Alexander, Time and Property in the American Republican Legal Culture, 66 N.Y.U. L. Rev. 273 (1991); Katz, Republicanism and the Law of Inheritance in the American Revolutionary Era, 76 Mich. L. Rev. 1 (1977).

Policy Bases of Intestate Succession. What objectives do and should guide policymakers in developing a system for succession of property upon the death of a person who lacked a valid will or will substitute? The rationale that today is commonly ascribed to intestacy laws is expressed in the following passage from the court's opinion in King v. Riffee, 309 S.E.2d 85, 87-88 (W. Va. 1983):

> Our laws concerning intestate succession are designed to effect the orderly distribution of property for decedents who lack either the foresight or the diligence to make wills. The purpose of these statutes . . . is to provide a distribution of real and personal property that approximates what decedents would have done if they had made a will. Spouses and children enjoy a favored position under the laws of intestate succession because, on statistical average, they are the natural objects of most peoples' [sic] bounty.

In Fellows, Simon & Rau, supra, at 324, the authors suggest that effectuating probable intentions of decedents is not the only objective of intestacy statutes:

> The alternative . . . rationale for adopting a particular distributive pattern in an intestacy statute is that it serves society's interests. There are four identifiable community aims: (1) to protect the financially dependent family; (2) to avoid complicating property titles and excessive subdivision of property; (3) to promote and encourage the nuclear family; and (4) to encourage the accumulation of property by individuals. If society's well-being requires a distributive pattern different from the determined wishes of intestate decedents, the decedents' wishes should be subordinated.

To this list, we would add another objective: to produce a pattern of distribution that the recipients believe is fair and thus does not produce disharmony within the surviving family members or disdain for the legal system.

Requirement of Survivorship of the Decedent. Only persons who survive the decedent are entitled to succeed to the decedent's property by testate or intestate succession. Unless altered by statute, survivorship by only an instant is sufficient. On occasion, decedents and their devisees or heirs die in circumstances—such as an automobile or airplane accident—in which it is impossible to determine the order of deaths. To meet this problem, almost all states have passed a statute identical to or closely patterned after the Uniform Simultaneous Death Act (1953) (USDA), section 1 of which provides:

> *No Sufficient Evidence of Survivorship.* Where the title to property or the devolution thereof depends upon priority of death and there is no sufficient evidence that the persons have died otherwise than simultaneously, the property of each person shall be disposed of as if he had survived. . . .

Why does it make sense to presume that the testator or intestate survived? Dissatisfied with the USDA, the pre-1990 UPC provided that "any individual who fails to survive the decedent by 120 hours is deemed to have predeceased the decedent," and the 1990 UPC provides that "any individual who is not established by clear and convincing evidence to have survived the decedent by 120 hours is deemed to have predeceased the decedent." UPC § 2-104. See also UPC § 2-702 (1990) (adopts 120-hour requirement of survival for all donative dispositions, including life insurance, and for joint tenancies and joint accounts with a survivorship feature); pre-1990 UPC § 2-601 (adopts 120-hour requirement for devises). Do you see the reason for the dissatisfaction with the USDA?

In 1991, the Uniform Law Commissioners revised the USDA to adopt the UPC's 120-hour requirement of survivorship.

The Uniform Determination of Death Act (1980) defines death as follows:

> *Section 1. [Determination of Death.]* An individual who has sustained either (1) irreversible cessation of circulatory and respiratory functions, or (2) irreversible cessation of all functions of the entire brain, including the brain stem, is dead. A determination of death must be made in accordance with accepted medical standards.

The Uniform Determination of Death Act has been enacted in 32 states and was incorporated into section 1-107 of the UPC and the revised USDA in 1991.

Relatives in Gestation at the Decedent's Death. For purposes of intestacy and for purposes of devises of any present interest in property, persons who are born after the decedent's death generally are not eligible to receive the decedent's property.[7] The common law treats children in gestation at the decedent's death as if they were alive at the decedent's death if they subsequently are born alive. This principle is codified in some states and in both the pre-1990 and 1990 versions of UPC section 2-108.

In administering this principle, there is precedent suggesting a rebuttable presumption that the date of conception was nine months prior to the date of birth. See, e.g., Equitable Trust Co. v. McComb, 19 Del. Ch. 387, 396, 168 A. 203, 207 (1933); In re Wells, 129 Misc. 447, 456, 221 N.Y.S. 714, 724 (Sur. Ct. 1927). To be entitled to share in the decedent's estate, a child in gestation at the decedent's death must be born alive and probably must be born viable. See, e.g., Ebbs v. Smith, 59 Ohio Misc. 133, 394 N.E.2d 1034 (1979); 70 Mich. L. Rev. 729, 735 (1972). Under section 2-108 of the UPC, the child must survive birth by at least 120 hours.

---

7. Some exceptions to this rule can arise with regard to devises made to a class of persons. See infra Chapter 16.

PART B.   GENERAL PATTERNS OF INTESTATE SUCCESSION

1. Spouse

Statutory References: *1990 UPC § 2-102*
Pre-1990 UPC § 2-102

One of the major concerns about intestacy law is whether the surviving spouse is granted an adequate share. To be sure, the surviving spouse generally inherits the entire estate if the decedent leaves no surviving descendants or parents. But, if the decedent does leave descendants, the surviving spouse may have to share part of the estate with them. This is so even when some or all of them are minors, in which case any portion the minors inherit must be placed in a normally cumbersome and expensive guardianship form of ownership. See infra p. 86. It is also so even when some or all of them are able-bodied adults with adequate means of support, in which case the surviving spouse may be elderly and in far greater need. Also, if the decedent leaves no descendants but does leave a parent or parents, the spouse may have to share the estate with the parent or parents, even though the parents may be financially self-sufficient ("WOOPS," in newspeak, standing for well-off older people).

Pre-1990 Uniform Probate Code. As originally promulgated in 1969, section 2-102 of the UPC granted the decedent's surviving spouse the entire intestate estate if the decedent left neither surviving issue nor surviving parents. If either issue or a parent survived the decedent, the surviving spouse received only the first $50,000[8] plus one-half of the remaining balance of the estate. If one or more of the decedent's issue were not the surviving spouse's issue, however, the pre-1990 UPC did not give the spouse priority on the first $50,000. Instead, it limited the spouse's share to one-half of the intestate estate.

The use of the lump-sum-plus-a-fraction-of-the-remaining-balance device enabled the pre-1990 UPC to pay (or appear to pay) a proper obeisance to tradition while assuring the spouse the entire estate in the modest estates of $50,000 and under, and assuring the spouse the bulk of the estate if it did not have an appreciably greater value than $50,000. In a $100,000 estate, for example, the spouse's share was $75,000, with $25,000 going to the decedent's descendants or parents. In a $150,000 estate, the spouse took $100,000, with $50,000 going to the descendants or parents.

The pre-1990 UPC introduced another twist in the distribution pattern not typically found in intestacy statutes. It addressed the question of step relationships. If the decedent was survived by a child (or descendants of a

---

8. Some states adopting a lump-sum-plus-a-fraction-of-the-remaining-balance approach have used a different figure, ranging from a low of $20,000 in Florida and Missouri to a high of $100,000 in Alabama.

deceased child) who was not the surviving spouse's child, the lump-sum-plus-a-fraction device was abandoned in favor of a fifty/fifty split between the decedent's spouse and descendants.

Non-Uniform Probate Code Law. Contrasted with the intestacy patterns generally in effect when the pre-1990 UPC was promulgated, and which are still in effect today under non-UPC law, the surviving spouse's share granted by pre-1990 section 2-102 was quite generous. Under non-UPC law, if the decedent is survived by children (or descendants of deceased children), the spouse's share will likely be one-third, with the remaining two-thirds going to the decedent's descendants.[9] If the decedent is not survived by children (or descendants of deceased children), but is survived by one or both parents, the spouse's share will likely be one-half, with the other half going to the decedent's parent or parents.[10]

Public Attitudes. Except perhaps for the wealthy, whose behavior should have very little relevance to the proper design of an intestacy law, studies have identified a strong social preference to give the entire estate to the surviving spouse, even when the decedent has surviving children or parents. Some of these studies were based on an examination of the probated wills of similarly situated decedents who died during a particular time frame in a particular locality.[11] Other studies were based on interviews with living

---

9. Other variations exist. Some non-UPC statutes provide for a 50/50 split between the surviving spouse and the descendants. Others provide the spouse a one-half share if there is one descendant but a one-third share if there is more than one descendant, the remaining half or two-thirds going to the descendants. Still others provide a variety of unique patterns of division between the spouse and descendants. Normally, no distinction is drawn between decedent's descendants who are also descendants of the spouse and those descendants who are not also the spouse's descendants. For a compilation of the various statutory patterns as of 1978, see Fellows, Simon & Rau, Public Attitudes About Property Distribution at Death and Intestate Succession in the United States, 1978 Am. B. Found. Res. J. 319, 357 n.128.

10. Other variations exist. In a few states, the spouse must share the estate with the decedent's siblings if both parents have predeceased. Others have unique systems for allocating the estate between the spouse and parents. Some non-UPC law gives the entire estate to the surviving spouse and nothing to the decedent's parents. See id. at 348-50.

11. See, e.g., M. Sussman, J. Cates & D. Smith, The Family and Inheritance 86-87, 89-90, 143-45 (1970) (for those testators survived by spouse and lineal kin, 85.8 percent of the decedent testators (N=226) and 85.3 percent of the testators (N=367) in the survivor population provided that the spouse receive the entire estate; in 33 of 37 cases where the testator was not survived by lineal descendants or ascendants but was survived by a spouse, the spouse received the entire estate); Browder, Recent Patterns of Testate Succession in the United States and England, 67 Mich. L. Rev. 1303, 1307-09 (1969) (26 of the 54 testators left their entire estates to their spouse and not to their issue; of those 18 testators who distributed the estate to both spouse and issue, six designed their wills to give the spouse only that amount equal to the maximum marital deduction available for federal estate tax purposes at that time; in 9 of the 13 instances in which the testator was survived by a spouse and no children, the testator gave the spouse the entire estate); Dunham, The Method, Process and Frequency of Wealth Transmissions at Death, 30 U. Chi. L. Rev. 241, 252-53 (1963) (in the 22 testate estates where the deceased was survived by spouse and children, 100 percent left all of the property to the spouse; in all but one of the six cases in which the testator was survived by a spouse but no children, the testator gave the spouse all of the property).

persons.[12]

These empirical studies confirm that the pre-1990 UPC was aligned more closely with public attitudes than the non-UPC laws. Although the pre-1990 UPC retained the traditional approach of splitting the estate between the spouse and the descendant or parent, it used the lump-sum-plus-a-fraction device that, as noted above, made an actual split less likely, and made the spouse's share greater than fifty percent when a split did occur.

1990 Uniform Probate Code. The UPC's approach in 1969 significantly increased the share of the intestate estate that passed to the surviving spouse. For medium to larger intestate estates, however, it still failed to reflect society's preference to have the surviving spouse receive the entire estate. In those estates, the pre-1990 UPC still called for a split between the spouse and children (or descendants of deceased children) and between the spouse and parents if there were no children (or descendants of deceased children).[13]

Rethinking of this approach led to significant revisions of the spouse's share in section 2-102 of the 1990 Code. It continues the pattern of giving the surviving spouse the entire estate when the decedent is not survived by descendants or parents. It goes further, however, and provides that the surviving spouse also receives the entire estate when the decedent is

---

12. Fellows, Simon & Rau, supra note 9, at 351-54, 358-64, 366-68 (found the majority favored granting the entire estate to the spouse regardless of the level of wealth involved); Contemporary Studies Project, A Comparison of Iowans' Dispositive Preferences with Selected Provisions of the Iowa and [Pre-1990] Uniform Probate Codes, 63 Iowa L. Rev. 1041, 1089 (1978) (found the percentage who favored granting the entire estate to the spouse decreased as the level of wealth increased); U.K. Law Comm'n, supra note 4, at app. C, at 36-37, 40-45 (1989) (well over 70 percent of the respondents favored the spouse receiving the entire estate regardless of whether the decedent was also survived by minor children, adult children, or siblings).

13. A report of the United States National Commission on the Observance of International Women's Year criticized this aspect of the pre-1990 version of the UPC.

Although the provisions of the [pre-1990] Uniform Probate Code [were] an improvement over the existing law in many States, it is apparent that the [pre-1990] Code was drafted from a strictly male point of view.

The Committee does not agree with the intestacy provisions for a surviving spouse (a) when there are children of the marriage; (b) when there are no children but there are surviving parents; and (c) the provisions for a "forced share."

When the decedent's only surviving children are those of the marriage to the surviving spouse, the committee believes the surviving spouse should receive the entire estate. If the children are minors or unable to earn a living, the surviving spouse will be responsible for their support. When they are able-bodied and grown, they are no longer dependent, and the surviving spouse is likely to be at least approaching old age.

The provision on disposition of an estate when there are surviving parents but no children is arbitrary and may result in great inequity. In this case the [pre-1990] Uniform Probate Act [gave] the surviving spouse the first $50,000 plus one-half of the balance, with the remainder going to the parent or parents. If the parent or parents of a decedent husband have been dependent completely on the couple for a number of years and the marriage is of long duration, should the wife receive everything? If the decedent husband is young and the marriage has been of short duration and the parents have been partially supporting the couple, should the parents receive at least some of the estate?

U.S. Nat'l Comm'n on the Observance of Int'l Women's Year, ". . . To Form a More Perfect Union . . ." Justice for American Women 227-28 (1976).

survived by descendants if they are also the descendants of the surviving spouse and if the surviving spouse has no descendants who are not the decedent's descendants.

The move to have the spouse inherit the entire estate is aligned with trends in intestacy laws throughout the U.S. and Europe.[14] In her recent book, Mary Ann Glendon has identified this trend, which she calls the "shrinking circle of heirs" phenomenon. See M. Glendon, The Transformation of Family Law 238 (1989). By this she means that, over time, throughout the U.S. and Europe, "the position of the surviving spouse has steadily improved everywhere at the expense of the decedent's blood relatives." Id. She goes on to point out that this trend "strikingly illustrate[s]" the movement of modern marriage into the foreground of family relationships." Id. at 239. It recognizes "the gradual attenuation of legal bonds among family members outside the conjugal unit of husband, wife, and children," id. at 238, and "[t]he tendency to view a marriage that lasts until death as a union of the economic interests of the spouses . . . ." Id. at 240.

As Professor Glendon noted, granting the surviving spouse the entire intestate estate comes "at the expense of the decedent's blood relatives." Notice the *categories* that lose out to the surviving spouse under section 2-102. Under section 2-102(1)(i), the losers are the decedent's collateral relatives and/or ancestors more remote than parents; under subsection (1)(ii), the losers are the decedent's children (or descendants of deceased children).[15]

As between these two categories, decedents presumably view their children as having higher claims to at least some portion of their property than the claims of their collateral relatives and/or ancestors more remote than parents. Section 2-102(1) appears, however, not to recognize any distinction between these two categories of claimants—after all, it grants a surviving spouse the entire estate to the exclusion of both. In fact, section 2-102(1) can be understood to distinguish between the two categories.

Section 2-102 is predicated on the notion that the decedent's children are not losing. Rather, surviving spouses are viewed as occupying two roles—one as the decedent's primary beneficiary and one as a conduit through which to benefit their children. If the decedent died prematurely, at a time when the couple's children were still minors, the surviving spouse is seen as being in a better position to use the decedent's property for the benefit of their children, as well as for herself or himself.[16] For a decedent who lives out her or his life expectancy, the surviving spouse is likely to be older and have greater economic needs than their children. By then the children are probably middle-aged working adults whose needs may be less

---

14. A recent report of the U.K. Law Commission recommended granting the surviving spouse the entire intestate estate in all circumstances. U.K. Law Comm'n, supra note 4, at 8-12.

15. The distribution pattern when the decedent is survived by a surviving spouse and a parent or parents is discussed infra pp. 78 & 90.

16. See infra p. 86, for a discussion of the disadvantages of guardianships when minor children inherit property in their own right.

than the surviving spouse's. That does not mean, however, that the conduit theory does not operate for adult children. The statute assumes that the adult children will inherit any unconsumed portion of the decedent's property at the surviving spouse's death.

The conduit theory does not apply to a decedent's collateral relatives and/or ancestors more remote than parents. Section 2-102 is predicated on the notion that their "loss" is permanent. When a decedent leaves a surviving spouse and collateral relatives and/or ancestors more remote than parents, a surviving spouse is the sole beneficiary of the estate. The statute assumes that the surviving spouse, while alive or at death, is unlikely to share any significant portion of the decedent's property with those other relatives.

When there are other than joint children in the family, the conduit theory becomes problematic. If the state gives the entire estate to the surviving spouse of a decedent who leaves surviving children (or descendants of deceased children) who are not the surviving spouse's, the risks of permanent "loss" to those children appear greater because the surviving spouse is related to them only by marriage. Similarly, if the state gives the entire estate to the surviving spouse who has children (or descendants of deceased children) who are not the decedent's, the risk exists that the surviving spouse will share at least some of the decedent's property with the decedent's stepchildren at the expense of the decedent's children.[17] Thus, the dilemma facing the states in the stepparent situations becomes one of striking a reasonable balance between the objective of granting the surviving spouse an adequate share and the objective of providing for the economic needs of a decedent's minor children and reducing the risks that the decedent's adult children are not permanently disinherited.

Section 2-102 resolves that dilemma by invoking the lump-sum-plus-a-fraction device for these situations. The intent is not to restrict the spouse's share to no more than necessary to provide her or him with the bare necessities of life, but to grant a share that is commensurate with the size of the estate and the circumstances of the family make-up. In the typical intestate estate of small to modest size, this approach still allows the surviving spouse to take the entire estate. A factor that makes this even more likely is that, under the UPC scheme, the lump-sum portion of the formula is in addition to the probate exemptions and allowances, which run in favor of the surviving spouse and amount to a *minimum* of $43,000. See UPC §§ 2-402 to -404 (1990).[18]

In the larger intestate estates, infrequent though they may be, the UPC approach is predicated on the notion that the decedent would feel that some provision for her or his children would not deprive the surviving

---

17. The possibility that the same moral conflict will arise after the decedent's death, should the surviving spouse remarry and have children by her or his new spouse, exists but must be disregarded. As currently constituted, intestacy law requires the decision as to how much to award the surviving spouse to be made on the basis of the facts existing at the decedent's death.

18. See infra Chapter 8 for further discussion of these provisions.

spouse of an adequate share. Economic security for the surviving spouse is likely to be further enhanced in most estates because the decedent is apt to have executed will substitutes providing for the spouse, such as joint tenancies, joint checking, savings, or money-market accounts, life-insurance contracts, and pension plan arrangements. For large estates, the lump-sum-plus-a-fraction device assures that the *decedent's* children receive some inheritance.

Section 2-102 recognizes that the surviving spouse's conflicting loyalties are more intense when the decedent has children by a prior marriage than when only the surviving spouse has children by a prior marriage. In the former case, the surviving spouse is granted the first $100,000 ($143,000 including the minimum probate exemptions and allowances) plus fifty percent of any remaining balance. In the latter case, the surviving spouse is granted the first $150,000 ($193,000 including the minimum probate exemptions and allowances) plus fifty percent of any remaining balance.

The approach taken is admittedly a crude solution to the survivor's loyalty conflicts. Can you think of a more responsive solution? Would a statutory trust do the trick? Under this approach, the surviving spouse would be granted the *use* of all the property for life, but at death the unconsumed portion of that property would be returned to the decedent's own children.[19]

The final circumstance in which section 2-102 gives the surviving spouse less than the entire estate if it is large is when a decedent dies survived by a surviving spouse and parent, but no descendants. Here, section 2-102(2) grants the surviving spouse the first $200,000 ($243,000 including the minimum probate exemptions and allowances) plus three-fourths of the remaining balance. Since very few intestate estates exceed $243,000, and fewer still exceed this value by any substantial margin, the surviving spouse *in practice* will almost always receive the entire intestate estate when a parent survives the decedent. Why do you think section 2-102 does not provide that the surviving spouse receive the entire intestate estate when the decedent is childless, but leaves a surviving parent?

EXTERNAL REFERENCE. Fisher & Curnutte, Reforming the Law of Intestate Succession and Elective Shares: New Solutions to Age-Old Problems, 93 W. Va. L. Rev. 61 (1990); Waggoner, Spousal Rights in our Multiple-Marriage Society: The Revised Uniform Probate Code, 26 Real Prop. Prob. & Tr. J. 683 (1992).

---

19. The U.K. Law Commission recommended abandonment of this type of statutory trust, which is presently provided for under English law. See Administration of Estates Act 1925, §§ 46, 47(1)(i). They viewed it as cumbersome and complicated. See U.K. Law Comm'n, supra note 4, at 10.

2. Descendants

Statutory References: *1990 UPC §§ 2-103, -106, 5-202, -423*
Pre-1990 UPC §§ 2-103, -106

a. Descendants' Share

In the absence of a surviving spouse, the law of all states—UPC and non-UPC law, alike—gives the entire estate to the decedent's descendants, *i.e.*, to the decedent's children and descendants of deceased children. The descendants universally inherit to the exclusion of the decedent's ancestors, such as parents and grandparents, and to the exclusion of collateral relatives, such as brothers and sisters.

When a decedent dies leaving a surviving spouse as well as descendants, the descendants' share is determined in accordance with the applicable distribution patterns outlined above. Under some non-UPC statutes and under UPC-law in the small to modest estates, the spouse may receive the entire estate to the exclusion of the decedent's descendants. Under other non-UPC statutes and under UPC law in the larger estates, the spouse and descendants share the estate.

b. Representation Among Descendants

Any share that goes to the decedent's descendants is divided among them by representation.[20] The term "descendants" (or "issue") denotes a multiple-generation class, which includes not only children, but also grandchildren, great-grandchildren, and so on all the way down the descending line.

To explore the idea of representation, we give you G, a 78-year old widow who has just died, leaving some married surviving children in their late forties or early fifties, a somewhat greater number of surviving grandchildren in their twenties or early thirties, a few of whom are married with young children.[21]

---

20. The idea of taking by representation is traceable to the canons of descent, which provided that lineal descendants should represent their deceased ancestors in inheritance. The idea of taking by representation was also carried over into the Statute of Distribution. In one form or another, representation appears in all the American statutes.

21. With average life expectancy now projected to be about 75 years (78 for women, 72 for men) (U.S. Bureau of the Census, Statistical Abstract of the United States: 1990, Table 105, at 73 (111th ed. 1991)), three-generation families are quite common and four-generation families such as G's are not at all unusual. Many people now live long enough to have grown grandchildren and young great-grandchildren.

We made all persons with children married in the hypothetical to avoid issues regarding the law's treatment of children whose parents are not married to each other. We will address those and other status questions in Part E. For now, the purpose of the hypothetical is to help you understand the concept of representation and the different representational systems found

G's four-generation family is depicted in Chart 1, except that it does not show the descendants' spouses, G's ancestors, or G's collateral relatives. The parenthetical figures show each survivor's age. For Chart 1 and the other charts that follow, the brackets indicate those family members who have died. The bold type indicates those persons who will share in G's estate.

CHART 1

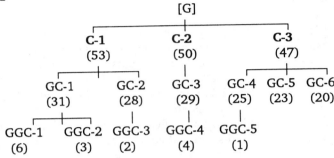

One of the principal features of representation is that the property is divided among the living persons who are nearest to the decedent in each descending line. A descendant who has a living ancestor who is also a descendant of the decedent is not an eligible taker. Consequently, the only descendants who share in G's estate are C-1, C-2, and C-3, each taking a one-third share. G's grandchildren and great-grandchildren take nothing.[22]

Because descendants more remote than children who have living ancestors are not eligible intestacy takers, the possibility of representation comes into play only if at least one child predeceases G. Chart 2 depicts G's family with C-1 having predeceased G.[23]

CHART 2

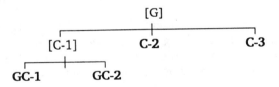

C-2 and C-3 continue to receive their one-third shares. Having predeceased G, C-1 is not eligible to take. C-1 is represented by GC-1 and GC-2. They divide C-1's one-third share equally, *i.e.*, each receives a one-sixth share.

In Chart 2 above, two facts converge to make for a simple and straight-forward application of the representation principle: (1) only one of G's

---

in the intestacy statutes around the country.

22. The spouses of married descendants do not share in the decedent's estate.

23. To avoid unnecessary clutter, Chart 2 and the charts that follow show only the first living person or persons in each descending line. Other descendants might or might not exist, but even if they do, they are not relevant for determining the distributional shares passing to the descendants under an intestacy statute.

children predeceased G and (2) neither child of C-1 predeceased G leaving
surviving descendants. When more than one child or one or more
grandchildren predecease G leaving surviving descendants, representation
becomes more complicated, and the outcome depends on which system of
representation the jurisdiction follows.

We start exploring the different systems of representation with the
situation where more than one child predeceases G and the predeceased
children leave surviving descendants. Chart 3 depicts the unlikely situation
where all three of G's children predecease her.

CHART 3

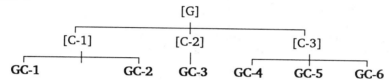

Depending on the representation system used, G's estate is divided in one
of two ways among G's grandchildren. The different distributional outcomes
resulting from applying different representational systems is described
below:

(1) One set of representational rules initially divides the estate equally
among the children's families, *i.e.*, into three shares. The one-third share for
C-1's family is then divided into two sub-shares, giving GC-1 and GC-2 one-
sixth of G's estate each. The one-third share for C-2's family passes to C-2's
lone representative, GC-3. The one-third share for C-3's family is divided into
three sub-shares, giving GC-4, GC-5, and GC-6 one-ninth of G's estate each.

(2) The other set of representational rules initially divides the estate
equally among each of the grandchildren, *i.e.*, into six equal shares.

Per-Stirpes System. The per-stirpes system produces the first outcome
described. This system is faithful to the idea of representation: Each
grandchild or more remote descendant takes not only as a representative
of her or his deceased ancestor, but has the right to share with her or his
siblings or siblings' descendants the same portion of the intestate's estate
as that descendant's parent would have taken if that parent had survived
the decedent. The per-stirpes system was used by the common law under
the canons of descent for land,[24] and about twelve states in this country
prescribe it for intestate succession of both land and personal property.[25]

The per-stirpes system can be described by the following three operational steps:

---

24. See 2 W. Blackstone, Commentaries *218.
25. See, e.g., Fla. Stat. § 732.104; Ga. Code § 53-4-2; Ill. Rev. Stat. ch. 110 1/2, § 2-1;
Va. Code § 64.1-3; W. Va. Code § 42-1-3. The list of states using per stirpes includes a few
that have otherwise adopted the pre-1990 UPC's general pattern of intestacy. See, e.g., Tenn.
Code Ann. § 31-2-106; Utah Code Ann. § 75-2-106.

Step One: Divide the estate into primary shares at the generation nearest to the decedent (*i.e.*, at the children generation). This primary-share generation is often described by the courts as the generation at which the "stocks" or "roots" are determined. The number of primary shares is equal to the number of children alive at the decedent's death plus the number of children who predeceased the decedent leaving descendants who survived the decedent. If there are any deceased children who have no living descendants, those children are disregarded in determining the number of primary shares. The number of primary shares is determined at the children generation even though no children survive the decedent, which is the situation depicted in Chart 3. (Step one applied to Chart 3 results in three primary shares.)

Step Two: Allocate the primary shares. One share goes to each living member of the children generation, if any. (There were no living children in Chart 3.) One share also goes to the descendants of each deceased child with living descendants, if any. (There were three predeceased children with living descendants in Chart 3.)

Step Three: Divide and subdivide each primary share allocated to the living descendants of a deceased member of the children generation. Each of the primary shares is divided and subdivided among the deceased child's descendants in the same manner as if the deceased child and other younger-generation descendants who have died were the decedent. (This is why C-1's primary share was divided between GC-1 and GC-2, and so on, in Chart 3.)

The per-stirpes system stands alone in the way it divides G's estate in Chart 3. All the other systems, discussed below, opt for the second outcome in that chart—giving a one-sixth share to each grandchild.

Per-Capita-with-Representation System. With the exception of the first step, this system is identical to the per-stirpes system. *Step One* in this system is to divide the estate into primary shares at the generation nearest to the decedent *that contains at least one living member.* Thus, if *all* of the decedent's children are deceased, as in Chart 3, but at least one grandchild is alive, the primary shares are determined at the grandchildren generation rather than at the children generation. In a strict sense, then, the grandchildren take in their own right, *per capita,* and not as representatives of the decedent's deceased children.

If, however, one of the grandchildren in Chart 3 had also predeceased G, leaving living descendants, the descendants of that deceased grandchild would take in a representative capacity. Hence, the system is called "per capita *with representation,*" a term that really means per capita at the nearest generation with a living member, with descendants of deceased members of that generation taking by representation.

Since the second and third steps in this system and in the per-stirpes system are the same, this system is sometimes called "modified per stirpes." Indeed, it is sometimes employed under the statutory term "per stirpes."[26]

---

26. See, e.g., Ark. Stat. § 61-135; Ohio Rev. Code §§ 2105.06, .12, .13, as interpreted in Kraemer v. Hook, 168 Ohio St. 221, 152 N.E.2d 430 (1958).

Pre-1990 Uniform Probate Code System. As promulgated in 1969, UPC section 2-106 adopted a variation of the per-capita-with-representation system. Nineteen states have enacted the pre-1990 UPC's representation system.[27] Although the statutory language could have been drafted more clearly, section 2-106 was meant to codify *Step One* of the per-capita-with-representation system and to fix the primary-share generation at the nearest generation to the decedent containing at least one living member.[28]

The pre-1990 UPC departed from the per-capita-with-representation system at *Step Three.* Under the pre-1990 version of section 2-106, each share allocated to the descendants of a deceased member of the primary-share generation was divided and subdivided "in the same manner." The same manner meant as if the deceased member of the primary-share generation were the decedent with respect to her or his primary share and, therefore, required that the primary share be subdivided at the nearest generation to the deceased descendant containing at least one living member. Perhaps a useful way of describing the pre-1990 UPC's system is that it is per capita with per capita representation.

In contrast, the per-capita-with-representation system is in reality *per capita with per stirpes representation. Step Three* of that system divides and subdivides each of the primary shares as under *Step Three* of the per-stirpes system. The primary shares are divided and subdivided at the nearest generation to the deceased descendant regardless of whether that generation contains any living member. Chart 4 illustrates this point. It depicts the situation in which G is predeceased by C-1, GC-1, and GC-2:

CHART 4

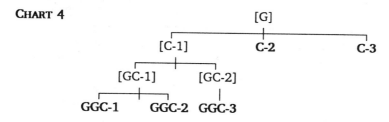

The per-capita-with-representation system also is sometimes invoked by a statute like the one found in Massachusetts:

If all [the] descendants are in the same degree of kindred to the intestate, they shall share equally; otherwise, they shall take according to the right of representation.

Mass. Gen. Laws Ann. ch. 190, § 3, interpreted by Balch v. Stone, 149 Mass. 39, 20 N.E. 322 (1889). But see Maud v. Catherwood, 67 Cal.App.2d 636, 155 P.2d 111 (1945), interpreting a similar (but now repealed) statute as invoking the per-stirpes system only when the takers are in unequal degree. Other states that have similar statutes include Nevada and South Dakota. See Nev. Rev. Code § 134.040; S.D. Code § 29-1-5.

27. In New Hampshire, the enactment of the pre-1990 UPC omitted § 2-106. The system prescribed by pre-1990 § 2-106 was, however, judicially adopted in Estate of Martineau, 126 N.H. 250, 490 A.2d 779 (1985).

28. The statutory phrase "surviving heirs in the nearest degree of kinship" would have made this point more clearly had it said "surviving heirs in the nearest degree of kinship that contains one or more surviving heirs."

Under the pre-1990 UPC, C-1's one-third primary share is divided equally among GGC-1, GGC-2, and GGC-3, giving each a one-ninth share. Under the per-capita-with-representation system, C-1's primary share would be subdivided at the deceased grandchildren generation, giving GGC-1 and GGC-2 a one-twelfth share each and giving GGC-3 a one-sixth share.

1990 Uniform Probate Code—Per Capita At Each Generation. UPC section 2-106 (1990) adopts a still different system of representation—the per-capita-at-each-generation system. The pre-1990 version of section 2-106 neither assured equality among the children's families nor equality among members of the same generation whose parents had predeceased the decedent. The 1990 version of section 2-106 assures equality among members of the same generation whose parents predeceased them. To see how it accomplishes this result, consider Chart 5 below, which depicts the situation in which C-2 and C-3 predecease G.

CHART 5

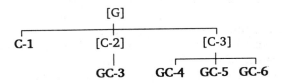

Both the pre-1990 and 1990 versions of section 2-106 of the UPC give a one-third share to C-1. However, under the pre-1990 version, the four grandchildren did not receive equal shares. GC-3 represented C-2 and got a full one-third share. The other three represented C-3 and each took a one-ninth share. Under the 1990 version, however, equality among the four grandchildren is achieved. The 1990 version achieves equality by the device of treating the four grandchildren as representing both C-2 and C-3. Another way to think about the operation of this representational system is that it treats C-2 and C-3 as if they were one person who had four children. This device gives each grandchild an equal one-sixth share.

The per-capita-at-each-generation system can be described by the following three operational steps:

Step One: Divide the estate into primary shares at the nearest generation to the decedent that contains at least one living member. The number of primary shares is the number of living persons in that generation plus the number of deceased persons in that generation who have living descendants.

Step Two: Allocate one primary share to each living member of the primary-share generation.

Step Three: Combine the remaining primary shares, if any, into a single share and assume that the descendants already allocated a share and their descendants had predeceased the decedent. Then distribute that single share among the decedent's descendants in accordance with Step One.

This system, which consistently results in "horizontal equality," (*i.e.,* equality among members of the same generation) as distinguished from the "vertical equality" (*i.e.,* equality among children's families) consistently accomplished by the per-stirpes system, is now in force in North Carolina and Maine.

As recounted in the Official Comment to UPC section 2-106 (1990), the results of recent client surveys have found that the public finds the per-capita-at-each-generation system considerably more to its liking than the other systems. See Young, Meaning of "Issue" and "Descendants," 13 Prob. Notes 225 (Am. C. of Tr. & Est. Couns. 1988) (client survey in which 71% of the respondents chose the per-capita-at-each-generation system; 19% chose per-stirpes; 9% chose the pre-1990 UPC system); Contemporary Studies Project, A Comparison of Iowans' Dispositive Preferences with Selected Provisions of the Iowa and Uniform Probate Codes, 63 Iowa L. Rev. 1041, 1108-16, 1135-37 (1978) (survey of public at large in which 87% of the respondents chose the per-capita-at-each-generation system; 12% chose per stirpes).

Use of the Various Systems of Representation in Planning. In the planning and drafting of wills and trusts, multiple-generation class gifts are frequently used. For example: "to A for life, remainder to A's descendants who survive A." It is obviously desirable in this type of case to select, and explicitly designate in the will or trust instrument, a system for determining the share to which each of A's surviving descendants is to be entitled. What system is to be used in the absence of an express designation? See infra Chapter 16; UPC § 2-708 (1990).

Without doubt, the most frequently designated system in these types of gifts is per stirpes: "to A for life, remainder to A's descendants who survive A, per stirpes." Although the per-stirpes system has a commonly understood meaning (as described above), some courts have held that the phrase "per stirpes" invokes the system described above under the label "per capita with representation." See, e.g., Kraemer v. Hook, 168 Ohio St. 221, 152 N.E.2d 430 (1958); Estate of Dakin, N.Y.L.J., May 10, 1988, at 12, col. 2 (Sur. Ct.). Therefore, the use of the term "per stirpes" without further clarification risks litigation over the term's meaning. See 1990 UPC section 2-709 for a statutory rule of construction defining "per stirpes." In the absence of such a statutory rule of construction, it is good practice to insert a clause in the will or trust that defines the term. In this regard, it is especially important to clarify whether the initial division into primary shares is to be made at the children generation of A, even when no member of that generation is living, or whether the initial division into primary shares is to be made at the nearest generation to A that contains at least one living member.

Litigation has arisen in a number of cases over the use of phrases such as "to my brothers and sisters, per stirpes," or "to my nieces and nephews, per stirpes." See, e.g., Teller v. Kaufman, 293 F. Supp. 1397 (E.D. Mo. 1968); Hartford Nat'l Bank & Trust Co. v. Thrall, 184 Conn. 497, 440 A.2d 200 (1981); Bennett v. Lloyd, 245 Ga. 706, 267 S.E.2d 3 (1980); Will of Griffin, 411 S.2d 766 (Miss. 1982); Wachovia Bank & Trust Co. v.

Livengood, 306 N.C. 550, 294 S.E.2d 319 (1982); Richland Trust Co. v. Becvar, 44 Ohio St. 2d 219, 339 N.E.2d 830 (1975); Restatement 2d of Property § 25.1 comment i, illustration 14 (stating that "children" means issue); cf. Estate of Walters, 519 N.E.2d 1270 (Ind. Ct. App. 1988) ("to my wife, Jessie E. Walters, per stirpes"). Surely language whose meaning is so doubtful that it has caused so much recent litigation is to be avoided in drafting legal documents.

Uncertainty about the level at which the primary shares are to be determined is not the only ambiguity contained in phrases such as "to my nieces and nephews, per stirpes." If one of the nieces dies leaving a descendant, should that descendant be able to share in the gift? How would you edit this language to provide that descendants of nieces and nephews share in the gift?

It would appear from the client surveys and other empirical studies alluded to above that, if asked, most clients would prefer the horizontal equality accomplished by the per-capita-at-each-generation system. At the same time, surveys also indicate that the great majority of lawyers believe that most clients prefer the system that we have called per stirpes. See Young, supra (85% of lawyers surveyed indicated that most clients prefer this system). Why do you suppose this discrepancy exists? How would you pose the representation question to a client?

c. Guardianships for Minors and Legally Incapacitated Persons

If an intestate decedent leaves heirs who are minors or are otherwise legally incapacitated, a guardian, who is referred to as a "conservator" in some states, must be appointed to receive and manage the intestate assets passing to the minor or incapacitated heirs. A surviving parent is the natural guardian of her or his minor child, but only of the child's person. A court appointment is necessary to give the parent responsibility over the child's property. If there is no parent, a court will have to appoint someone to take responsibility for the heir's custody and care, a "guardian of the person." A guardian may be responsible for the minor's or incapacitated heir's person or property or both, but often the appointment is unclear about the extent of the guardian's responsibility. It is generally assumed that a guardian is appointed for both the person and the property of a ward unless the terms of the appointment provide otherwise.

One of the major estate planning concerns of parents with minor children is to designate a particular person, usually a close friend or relative, to act as guardian of the child's person. The need arises if both parents die, together or separately, before the child reaches the age of majority. The need also arises when a minor child is reared by a single parent and that parent dies. In most states, a guardian may be designated by a will. Under the UPC, the appointment is made by probate of the parent's will and acceptance by the designated person. Court confirmation is unnecessary. See UPC § 5-202 (1990).

If the parents die intestate, obviously they have no say over who will be appointed guardian of their minor child or children. There must be a court proceeding, and the court will appoint a guardian from a list of available relatives.

Gay or lesbian parents with minor children cannot rely on courts to appoint their surviving domestic partner as guardian of the child's person if the surviving partner is neither the biological nor adoptive parent of the child. The legally recognized parent needs to execute a will naming the surviving partner as guardian so that she or he can retain custody of the child. Executing a will is not a fool-proof solution, however, because courts have been known to disregard the guardianship clauses of a gay or lesbian parent's will. See Ms., Oct. 1989, at 69.

Procedures for appointment of the guardian, both of the person and the property, are often slow and expensive. Even after appointment, further judicial proceedings are usually needed, increasing the delay and cost of guardianship. This is especially so for guardianship of the ward's property. If there are multiple children, separate guardianships must be taken out for each child, even though the same person will usually be appointed guardian for each child. The guardian does not have title to the ward's property. Rather, the guardian is merely custodian of the property with limited powers. These powers are defined by statute, and typically statutes define powers inadequately, both in the sense of uncertainty of meaning and failure to grant certain important powers, particularly concerning investment of protected property. These deficiencies make it necessary in most instances for the guardian to obtain court authorization for actions in dealing with the ward's property, generating expenses that diminish the ward's assets. Required accounting and bonds may further deplete the wealth available to the ward.

Modern guardianship or conservatorship statutes that ameliorate some of these problems have been enacted in several states. The UPC, for example, grants the appointed person, called a "conservator," the type of title to the protected property that a trustee would have and grants powers, duties, and liabilities comparable to those of a trustee. Relaxing the extensive and mandatory judicial supervision that characterizes traditional property guardianships, the UPC specifically grants substantial management powers to the conservator, exercisable without court order. These powers include the power to lease, sell, mortgage, or exchange assets; to borrow money; to pay creditor claims; to invest (subject to the same requirements applicable to trustees); and to distribute income and principal for the child's support, education, care, or benefit. See UPC § 5-423 (1990). The UPC's guardianship and related provisions are also promulgated as a free-standing uniform law called the Uniform Guardianship and Protective Proceedings Act (1987).

Where no such modern guardianship legislation exists, several devices are available to avoid the problems associated with property guardianship. These include a so-called contingent trust for minors, lifetime transfers to minors under the Uniform Gifts to Minors Act (1966) or lifetime or testamentary transfers to minors under the newer Uniform Transfers to

Minors Act (1986), and the so-called durable power of attorney ("durable" because the agency relationship continues despite legal disability of the principal). Legislation in some states provides statutory durable-power-of-attorney forms which, by standardizing these powers, may make them more acceptable to financial intermediaries and others who deal with the attorney-in-fact. See, e.g., Cal. Civ. Code § 2400, et seq. More recently, the Uniform Custodial Trusts Act (1987) provides for the creation of statutory custodial trusts to protect adult beneficiaries and their dependents against problems in the event of the beneficiaries' future incapacity. See infra p. 439.

3. Ancestors and Collaterals

Statutory References: *1990 UPC §§ 2-102 to -103, -105 to -107*
                               Pre-1990 UPC §§ 2-102 to -103, -105 to -107

Apart from the decedent's own descendants, her or his blood relatives are either ancestors or collaterals. A collateral relative is descended from an ancestor of the decedent.[29] The category of collateral relative is narrower than that, however, because a descendant of an ancestor may be a descendant or an ancestor of the decedent.[30] So, a collateral relative is a descendant of an ancestor, excluding, however, the decedent's own descendants and ancestors. Examples of collateral relatives are: brothers, sisters, nephews, and nieces (descended from the decedent's parents); aunts, uncles, and cousins (descended from the decedent's maternal or paternal grandparents), and so on. See the Chart of Relationships Through a Common Ancestor and the Table of Consanguinity, opposite.

---

29. A collateral relative *of the whole blood* is descended from a pair of the decedent's ancestors. A collateral relative *of the half blood* is descended from one of the decedent's ancestors, but not from a pair of them. The status of collateral relatives of the half blood is discussed infra p. 91.

30. The decedent's daughter is not only a descendant of the decedent, but also of the decedent's parents. Each of the decedent's parents is not only an ancestor of the decedent, but also a descendant of one set of the decedent's grandparents.

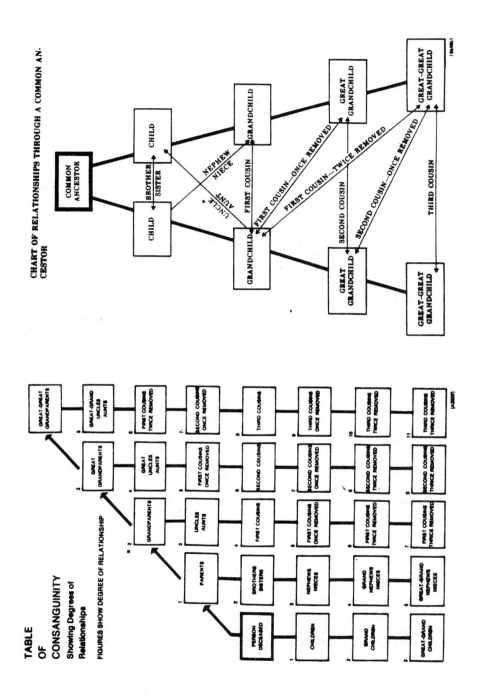

a. Parents and Their Descendants

Parents. The decedent's parents and their descendants inherit to the exclusion of more remote ancestors and their descendants.[31] The decedent's parents and their descendants inherit, however, only if the decedent leaves no surviving descendants of her or his own. Under UPC sections 2-102 and -103 (1990), parents of decedents with large estates inherit if the decedent leaves a surviving spouse but no descendants. The parents take one-fourth of that part of the probate estate, if any, that is in excess of $200,000.

Non-UPC law often gives the parents a much greater share. Often the parent will be granted half and the spouse half when the decedent leaves a surviving spouse, but no descendants. The pre-1990 UPC gives the parents half of that part of the estate, if any, that is in excess of $50,000.

If the decedent leaves neither a surviving spouse nor surviving descendants, the decedent's parents inherit to the exclusion of the decedent's surviving siblings or their descendants under most intestacy statutes. This is the rule under both the pre-1990 and the 1990 versions of UPC section 2-103. In a few states, under various formulas, the decedent's parents, brothers, and sisters share in the estate.[32]

Ancestral Property. At common law, land returned to the branch of the family from which the decedent inherited it. See 2 W. Blackstone, Commentaries *220. Some type of ancestral-property rule—usually restricted to land, but not always—still persists in a few states. When the rule is followed, it sometimes applies only to the estates of unmarried minors.[33]

Neither the pre-1990 UPC nor the 1990 UPC contain an ancestral-property rule. While this type of rule seems appealing, most legislatures have decided that its benefits are outweighed by its administrative costs, such as tracing and accounting for accretions.

Descendants of Parents. If neither of the decedent's parents survives, the descendants of the decedent's parents inherit by representation. The system of representation employed in the jurisdiction most likely will be the same system employed in the jurisdiction for representation among the decedent's own descendants. UPC section 2-106 (1990) applies the per-capita-at-each-generation system.

---

31. Under the English canons of descent, as condensed by Blackstone, an intestate's land "shall linearly descend to the issue of the person who last died seized, *in infinitum*; but shall never linearly ascend." 2 W. Blackstone, Commentaries *208. The preclusion of ancestors from inheriting land has never been adequately explained. Ancestors were not excluded in the English Statute of Distribution, nor has the idea been followed in any American jurisdiction.

32. In Illinois, for example, parents, brothers, and sisters take equal shares; if only one parent survives, that parent takes a double share; if a brother or sister is deceased, the surviving descendants of that brother or sister take the deceased sibling's share, per stirpes. Ill. Rev. Stat. ch. 110 1/2, § 2-1(d). Other variations are catalogued in Fellows, Simon & Rau, supra note 9, at 342-43.

33. For a discussion of ancestral-property statutes, see id. at 343-44.

Relatives of the Half Blood. Today, the principle is generally—though not universally—recognized that relatives of the half blood are treated the same as relatives of the whole blood. This principle is codified in some states and in UPC section 2-107 (1990). A relative of the half blood is a collateral relative who shares one common ancestor. If, for example, the decedent's mother or father has children from a prior marriage, those children will be the decedent's half brothers or half sisters. Descendants of a decedent's half brothers or half sisters are also related to the decedent by the half blood.

Relatives by Affinity. Blood or adopted relatives of the decedent's spouse, such as the spouse's parents, siblings, or descendants of siblings, and spouses of the decedent's blood or adopted relatives, such as daughters- and sons-in-law, are relatives by affinity. Almost all jurisdictions exclude them from inheriting under their intestacy statutes.

b. More Remote Ancestors and Collaterals

Parentelic System. To summarize the preceding description of intestacy statutes, excepting the discussion of the share passing to the surviving spouse, we have identified the first two steps of the "parentelic system." That system was utilized by the canons of descent and to a lesser degree by the Statute of Distribution. A parentela consists of an ancestor and that ancestor's surviving descendants. The parentelic system of inheritance is based on a preference for persons who are in the nearest parentela to the decedent. Thus, the parentelic system provides that the first parentela (the decedent's own surviving descendants) inherit first; if that parentela contains no surviving members, the second parentela (the decedent's parents and their descendants) inherit next; and so on.[34] Thus the grandson of the intestate's sister, being a descendant of the intestate's parents, takes in preference to an uncle, who descended from the intestate's grandparents. This is so even though under the civil-law method of determining degrees of kinship the uncle is a closer relative to the intestate than the grandnephew. See infra p. 92.

This procedure—going, step by step, up the ladder of ancestral seniority—can theoretically continue forever, but no state does that. Under UPC (1990), the parentelic system is carried out through the third parentela (grandparents and their descendants).

The Table of Consanguinity, supra p. 89, makes the parentelic system appear simpler than it is. Not depicted by the Table is the fact that each step up the ladder brings about a geometric increase in the number of ancestors at the head of each parentela. A decedent has two parents, four grandparents, eight great-grandparents, sixteen great-great-grandparents, and so on.

---

34. As noted above, the canons of descent did not permit ancestors to inherit. So, under the canons of descent, the second parentela was only comprised of the descendants of the decedent's parents, and did not include the parents themselves, and so on.

Under UPC section 2-103(4) (1990), the estate is first divided into paternal and maternal halves (if there is at least one grandparent or descendant of a grandparent in each half).[35] If both of the grandparents on one side predeceased the decedent, that half is a separate parentela for purposes of representation among the descendants of the grandparents who head up that half.

Nearest Kindred—Determining Degrees of Kinship. Many American statutes (but not the UPC) provide that, if no member of any of the specifically designated parentela survives the intestate, the estate passes to the intestate's "nearest kindred" or "next of kin." The phrases "in equal degree" and "without representation" are frequently tacked on.

Such provisions make it necessary to determine degrees of kinship between the intestate and those claiming a share of the estate. Under the "nearest kindred" part of the statute, the relatives in the *lowest* degree of kinship, being the intestate's nearest living relatives, share the estate equally. This type of distribution is *nonrepresentational.* In other words, it might be described as "per capita without representation." Each relative must take, if at all, in her or his own right and not as a representative of a deceased ancestor. Each heir takes an equal share, because all the relatives who are entitled to participate in the estate will be in the same degree.

In its primary sense, each degree reflects a difference of one generation. Thus, a parent of the intestate is related to the intestate in the first degree, a grandparent is in the second degree, and so on. The determination of the degree relationship is somewhat more complicated when it comes to collateral relatives, as discussed below.

The Civil-Law Method. As to collateral relatives, the method for computing degrees of kinship used in American law goes back to the interpretation by the English judges of the Statute of Distribution of 1670. It provided for distribution of personal property to "next of kindred in equal degree" in the event the intestate left no descendants.

The English judges adopted the civil-law method of computing degrees, which consists of counting generations under the following formula: count the number of generations (1) up from the intestate to the intestate's ancestor who is also an ancestor of the collateral relative and (2) down from that common ancestor to the collateral relative. The total of these two figures constitutes the degree of kinship for each collateral relative.[36] See

---

35. If the surviving grandparents or descendants of a grandparent are all on one side, that side takes the whole.

36. At one time, another method, the canon-law/common-law method, had some following. This method differs from the civil-law method in that, instead of using the total of the two figures (the number of generations from the intestate to the common ancestor plus the number of generations from the common ancestor to the claimant), only the larger of the two figures is used.

The canon law employed this method for determining which marriages between relatives were prohibited and the common law employed this method for limiting the number of successive donees in frankmarriage. See Atkinson on Wills § 7, at 45.

Although this method was never used for inheritance purposes in England, Blackstone erroneously reported that it was. 2 W. Blackstone, Commentaries *204. Blackstone's error led

4 R. Burn, Ecclesiastical Law 538-543 (9th ed. 1842). This means, for example, that a sister or brother is related to the decedent in the second degree, a niece or nephew is related in the third degree, and an aunt or uncle is also related in the third degree. See the chart, supra p. 89. Many American statutes explicitly provide that degrees shall be computed according to the method of the civil law. And when the statute is silent on the point, most courts have used this method.

The Modified Civil-Law System. Under a fairly widespread statutory modification of the civil-law method, when there are two or more collateral relatives in equal degree who claim through different common ancestors, those claiming through the ancestor nearest to the decedent take to the exclusion of the others. Is this system any different from the parentelic scheme?

Problems

In the chart below, the decedent, D, died intestate without leaving a spouse or descendants.

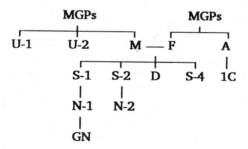

In the following alternative circumstances, how is D's property divided under UPC sections 2-103, -106 (1990)? Under a statute that provides for an intestate's property to be distributed to her or his "nearest kindred" and uses the civil-law method? Compare these results with those under a statute referring to "nearest kindred" that uses the modified civil-law method?

1. All of D's relatives depicted in the above chart survived him.

---

to adoption of that method for inheritance purposes in a few American states. But it has now disappeared. The last remaining jurisdiction in which it was used for inheritance purposes, Georgia, repealed it in 1972.

2. All of D's relatives depicted in the above chart survived him, except for M, F, MGPs, PGPs, and the following relatives, all of whom predeceased him:

    (a) S-1.

    (b) S-1, S-2, and S-3.

    (c) S-1, S-2, S-3, and N-1.

    (d) S-1, S-2, S-3, N-1, N-2, and GN-1.

c. Limitations on Inheritance

Both the English canons of descent and the Statute of Distribution provided for inheritance by any blood relative no matter how remote the relationship. Through the first half of the twentieth century, this was also true under nearly all of the American intestacy laws. By giving remote heirs inheritance rights, however, the rule of universal inheritance makes probate administration more complex. It increases the number of problems regarding proof of heirship and it requires these relatives to be identified and located so that they might have the opportunity to contest wills offered for probate. The increased administrative costs are hard to justify when the potential takers of the probate estate are distant relatives with whom the decedent had no personal or social ties—so-called "laughing heirs." See 1 R. Ely, Property and Contract in Their Relations to the Distribution of Wealth 422 (1914); Cavers, Change in the American Family and the "Laughing Heir," 20 Iowa L. Rev. 203 (1935). Indeed, the Sussman, Cates and Smith study revealed that such heirs "saw themselves as [unworthy takers]. They had rendered the deceased no service of any kind; they could not justify their windfall to themselves. Unlike Irish Sweepstakes winners, they did not even risk a shilling for their good fortune." M. Sussman, J. Cates & D. Smith, The Family and Inheritance 144-45 (1970).

An important change was made in English law in 1925 when intestacy succession was limited so as to exclude remote relatives. If there is no relative in any of the categories named in the statute, the estate passes to the state, which is empowered by section 46 of the Administration of Estates Act, 1925,[37] to "provide, in accordance with the existing practice, for dependents, whether kindred or not, of the intestate, and other persons for whom the intestate might reasonably have been expected to make provision."

A "Model Probate Code" was published in 1946 as the product of a research project carried on at the University of Michigan Law School in cooperation with a committee of the American Bar Association. That Model Code limited inheritance by collateral relatives to grandparents and those descended from grandparents. Legislation of several American states followed that recommendation and limited inheritance before the exhaus-

---

37. 15 & 16 Geo. 5, c. 23, § 46, as amended, 15 & 16 Geo. 6 & 1 Eliz. 2, c. 64, § 1 (1952).

tion of blood lines. Likewise, both the pre-1990 and 1990 versions of the UPC abandon the universal inheritance rule. See UPC §§ 2-103, -105.

PART C. REARRANGING INTESTATE SUCCESSION

The intestacy statutes make it appear that decedents' estates must be distributed in accordance with the statutory rules unless the decedent executes a will. The statutes also make it appear that heirs have no power to vary an intestacy statute's operation. The following materials show that the situation is not as inflexible as it appears.

1. Agreement Among the Heirs

Statutory References: *1990 UPC §§ 1-403, 3-912*

If an intestate's heirs are not satisfied with the distribution under the intestacy statute, they normally can divide up the decedent's assets in a different way. UPC section 3-912 (1990) contains a provision authorizing private agreements among successors.

Problem of Unascertained Successors or Successors Who Lack Capacity. Utilization of this procedure is, of course, quite tricky. It only works if all the successors are competent adults. UPC section 1-403 (1990) provides (in the absence of a conflict of interest) for a conservator to represent the person whose estate she or he controls, for a trustee to represent the beneficiaries of a trust, for a parent to represent her or his minor child under certain conditions, and for the appointment of a guardian ad litem to represent the interests of unborn and unascertained parties. It only applies, however, to "formal proceedings [and] judicially supervised settlements." (A proposal from the State Laws Committee of the American College of Trust and Estate Counsel is currently before the Joint Editorial Board for the Uniform Probate Code to revise and extend the coverage of section 1-403 to nonjudicial settlements and agreements.)

Potential Adverse Tax Consequences. This procedure can also have adverse tax consequences to the parties. To the extent the agreed-upon distribution differs from that which the intestacy laws would have directed, federal gift taxes may be incurred. In this sense, an agreement under section 3-912 is the substantive equivalent of the heirs having received their inherited portions under the intestacy laws and then having made gifts of part or all of those assets to one or more of the other parties to the agreement. In this respect, a voluntary agreement under section 3-912 should be distinguished from an agreement settling a bona fide controversy.

It is noteworthy that the Internal Revenue Service instructs its revenue agents to be alert to possible gift tax consequences where heirs agree to have property distributed in some way other than that provided by the state statute. See Internal Revenue Service, Estate Tax Examiner's Handbook (1988), which provides:

> ¶ *(24)932. The Estate Tax Return as a Source for Unreported Gifts.* . . . (11) . . . . Have the heirs agreed to share the decedent's property or to have the property pass in some way other than provided by will or by laws of descent and distribution, i.e., a non-adversary proceeding? Agreed changes can constitute gifts among the heirs.

Qualified Disclaimer as an Alternative Course of Action. If the heirs want to rearrange the intestacy pattern of distribution, a better course of action might be to utilize qualified disclaimers to accomplish the desired rearrangement. If executed properly, this approach avoids federal gift tax liability.

INTERNAL REFERENCES. For a discussion of settlement of will contests and for a discussion of the duty to probate, see infra pp. 237, 275.

2. Disclaimers

Statutory References: *1990 UPC § 2-801*
                              Pre-1990 UPC § 2-801

Disclaimers at Common Law. A disclaimer, sometimes called a renunciation, is the refusal to accept gratuitously transferred property. For lifetime transfers, the right to disclaim frequently is expressed in terms of the donee's nonacceptance of a gift. The acceptance requirement for a completed gift and the right to disclaim an inheritance or a devise are conceptually the same—both reflect a policy that ownership cannot be forced upon a transferee. The common law, which originated the disclaimer doctrine, broadly protected a transferee's right to just say no. The courts adopted a relation-back doctrine, under which a disclaimer was considered to relate back to the date of the transfer and operate as a nonacceptance. Under relation-back, all claims of creditors and governmental taxing authorities seeking to attribute ownership rights to the disclaimant were ineffective. The only exception to the courts' general willingness to protect people's right to just say no was that heirs could not prevent title from passing to them by intestate succession.[38]

State Disclaimer Legislation. The breadth of the relation-back doctrine led to the growing popularity of disclaimers. Disclaimers have now become a

---

38. See, e.g., Watson v. Watson, 13 Conn. 83 (1839); Coomes v. Finegan, 233 Iowa 448, 7 N.W.2d 729 (1943). The theory was that intestate succession cannot be refused because it arises by operation of law. See Lauritzen, Only God Can Make an Heir, 48 Nw. U.L. Rev. 568 (1953).

matter of statutory law in most jurisdictions.[39] Although the legislation increases the formalities for accomplishing a disclaimer, it should not be interpreted as reflecting dissatisfaction with the common law. On the contrary, these statutes are designed to make disclaimers more useful to beneficiaries through regularization. Perhaps the clearest proof of legislative approval of the right to disclaim is the statutory extension to property passing by intestacy and to new types of nontestamentary transfers.

Notwithstanding the significant efforts made to obtain uniform legislation through the promulgation of the Uniform Acts by the National Conference of Commissioners on Uniform State Laws, including UPC section 2-801 (1990), and by a Special Committee of the American Bar Association,[40] disclaimer legislation varies greatly.

Federal Disclaimer Legislation. Disclaimers are used for many tax motivated purposes, which would be defeated if a disclaimer were not treated as a refusal to accept, but rather as a taxable transfer on the part of the disclaimant. State statutes are not uniform on a number of subsidiary questions, such as the time allowed after the decedent's death or after the date of the transfer to file the disclaimer. The Tax Reform Act of 1976 introduced provisions on disclaimers into the Internal Revenue Code "to achieve uniform treatment" and to "provide a uniform standard . . . for determining the time within which a disclaimer must be made." H.R. Rep. No. 94-1380, 94th Cong., 2d Sess. 65 (1976).

Under IRC sections 2518, 2046, and 2614(c), no federal transfer tax consequences are incurred by a disclaimant if the disclaimer meets the IRC's definition of a "qualified disclaimer." Generally speaking, a qualified disclaimer must be in writing and filed within nine months of the later of the time of the transfer or the disclaimant's 21st birthday; the disclaimant must not have accepted the interest or any of its benefits; and the property must pass to either the transferor's spouse or a person other than the disclaimant.

The enactment of these federal provisions has diminished the significance of the state law requirements. With federal tax savings a major motivating factor when a beneficiary considers a disclaimer, qualification under the

---

39. The National Conference of Commissioners on Uniform State Laws approved a Uniform Disclaimer of Property Interests Act in 1973, which covered the disclaimer of property interests created by either lifetime or testamentary transfers. Because state codifiers frequently are unwilling to include statutes relating to nontestamentary transfers in the probate codes, the Commissioners promulgated two companion acts: the Uniform Disclaimer of Transfers by Will, Intestacy or Appointment Act, dealing exclusively with disclaimers of deathtime transfers, and the Uniform Disclaimer of Transfers Under Nontestamentary Instruments Act, dealing exclusively with disclaimers of lifetime transfers. In 1978, the Uniform Disclaimer Acts were amended in response to the federal transfer tax changes made in 1976 regarding disclaimers.

The Uniform Act relating to disclaimers of deathtime transfers was included in the pre-1990 UPC. When the UPC was revised in 1990, the broader Uniform Disclaimer of Property Interests Act, with some modification, was integrated into the Code, replacing the narrower one included in the pre-1990 version of the UPC.

40. For a discussion of the American Bar Association's work in this area, see Special Committee on Disclaimer Legislation, Disclaimer of Testamentary and Nontestamentary Dispositions—Suggestions for Model Acts, 4 Real Prop. Prob. & Trust J. 658 (1969).

federal statute naturally becomes of primary importance. See, e.g., Linck v. Barokas & Martin, 667 P.2d 171 (Alaska 1983) (recognized claim for negligence for failure of attorneys and accountant to advise a surviving spouse to disclaim a devise for purposes of avoiding transfer taxes).

State disclaimer statutes are now playing secondary roles as spoilers and facilitators. A state's disclaimer law may affect the manner of obtaining qualification of a disclaimer for tax purposes if it contains more restrictive rules than the federal statute. In a few situations, a more restrictive requirement can prevent a disclaimer from being "qualified" for federal tax purposes.[41] State laws also indirectly affect federal taxation because they control the devolution of disclaimed property. By selecting devolution patterns that most frequently coincide with the disclaimant's dispositive intent, the state can remove a potential disincentive to disclaim and encourage its citizens to take advantage of tax-saving opportunities.

Partial Disclaimers. The statutes recognize partial disclaimers. They, however, provide very few guidelines for distinguishing between a partial disclaimer and an acceptance of some of the benefits from the property, which would bar making a valid disclaimer. There are very few reported cases deciding the question about whether an attempt to make a partial disclaimer is valid. If a testator makes a gift of two different properties to the same devisee, the courts have permitted the disclaimer of one of the gifts once they assured themselves that the testator did not consider the separate gifts to be interrelated. See, e.g., Brown v. Routzahn, 63 F.2d 914 (6th Cir. 1933). Not only do the courts need to be concerned about frustrating the testator's estate plan, however, but they must also consider the tax policies at stake of allowing a beneficiary to enjoy many rights and interests with respect to the property without suffering adverse tax consequences. See Estate of Koerner, 133 Cal. App. 3d 209, 183 Cal. Rptr. 769 (1982).

Creditors' Rights. The prevailing view in the United States is that a beneficiary can disclaim an interest to prevent creditors from reaching the property. Creditors' rights may be defeated even if the disclaimer would otherwise qualify as a fraudulent conveyance. See, e.g., Tompkins State Bank v. Niles, 127 Ill.2d 209, 537 N.E.2d 274 (1989). But see, e.g., Estate of Clark, 488 Pa. 1, 410 A.2d 796 (1980); Fla. Stat. §§ 689.21(6), 732.801(6)(a); N.J. Stat. Ann. § 3A:25-46(3).

A disclaimer apparently will not defeat creditors' rights under the Federal Bankruptcy Code. See In re Cornell, 95 Bankr. 219 (1989) (inheritance from debtor's mother, who died about four months after confirmation of the plan, was property of the estate, and, therefore, the trustee could avoid the

---

41. IRC § 2518(c)(3) provides that if the beneficiary transfers the property or interest to the person or persons who would have taken the property had the disclaimer been effective under local law, the disclaimer will qualify for federal tax purposes. Although this rule eliminates reliance on local law in the majority of disclaimer cases, it remains inadequate for interests that are not transferable. That can happen if the interest is subject to a spendthrift provision. See infra Chapter 12. The problem can also arise if local law does not permit a personal representative of a beneficiary who is dead or incompetent to make a disclaimer or a gratuitous transfer.

post-petition disclaimer); In re Watson, 65 Bankr. 9 (1986) (proceeds of life-insurance policy that the debtor became entitled to acquire as beneficiary within 180 days of petition filing constituted property of the estate, and, therefore, the trustee could avoid a post-petition disclaimer). But see In re Atchison, 925 F.2d 209 (7th Cir. 1991) (a disclaimer that was filed within one year before the bankruptcy filing was held not to be a transfer in accordance with state law, and, therefore, held not to be a "transfer" that the bankruptcy trustee could avoid); see also Hoecker v. United Bank, 476 F.2d 838 (10th Cir. 1973) (same result in case decided under the 1898 Bankruptcy Act).

Another issue related to creditors' rights and disclaimers, which arises with frequency in recent years, concerns the effect of a disclaimer on a person's eligibility for public assistance and the right of the agency to reimbursement. Some courts take the view that a disclaimer causes a loss of eligibility for public assistance, while others hold that it has no effect on eligibility. Compare, e.g., Estate of Srivani, 116 Misc. 2d 204, 455 N.Y.S.2d 505 (Sup. Ct. 1982) with, e.g., Neilsen v. Cass County Social Services Bd., 395 N.W.2d 157 (N.D. 1986). Some courts hold that a fiduciary cannot disclaim an interest to defeat the agency's right to reimbursement, while others hold that a disclaimer by a fiduciary for a ward on public assistance is permissible. Compare, e.g., Dep't of Income Maintenance v. Watts, 211 Conn. 323, 558 A.2d 998 (1989) with, e.g., Estate of Schiffman, 105 Misc. 2d 1025, 430 N.Y.S.2d 229 (Sur. Ct. 1980).

Jointly Owned Interests. The majority of state statutes allow a joint tenant to disclaim the survivorship interest obtained through joint ownership of property. The statutes typically do not distinguish between joint tenancies, tenancies by the entirety, joint bank accounts, or jointly owned U.S. Savings Bonds, even though the rights of the parties vary depending on the type of joint ownership in question.[42]

The federal transfer tax effect of disclaimers of jointly owned property has only recently been clarified. Although Treas. Reg. § 25.2518-2(c)(4)(i) currently provides that a disclaimer of the right of survivorship must be made no later than nine months after the transfer creating the joint tenancy and that a joint tenant cannot disclaim any portion of the property attributable to consideration provided by that tenant, these positions have been rejected by several Courts of Appeals. Estate of Dancy v. Commissioner, 872 F.2d 84 (4th Cir. 1989); Kennedy v. Commissioner, 804 F.2d 1332 (7th Cir. 1986); McDonald v. Commissioner, 853 F.2d 1494 (8th Cir. 1988). Following this string of defeats, the Internal Revenue Service issued Action on Decision 1990-06 (Feb. 7, 1990), providing:

> Where a joint tenant has the right to sever the joint tenancy or cause the property to be partitioned under state law, the Service will no longer litigate that the transfer relative to which the timeliness of the disclaimer of a

---

42. Federal, and not state law, controls questions of ownership regarding U.S. Savings Bonds. See United States v. Chandler, 410 U.S. 257 (1973); Free v. Bland, 369 U.S. 663 (1962). Federal regulations make no provision for disclaimers.

survivorship interest is measured refers to the transfer creating the joint tenancy. The Service will also no longer contend that a joint tenant cannot make a qualified disclaimer of any portion of the joint interest attributable to consideration furnished by that joint tenant. Treas. Reg. section 25.2518-2(c)(4)(i) will be revised accordingly.

Disposition of Disclaimed Property. If the testamentary or nontestamentary instrument provides for an alternative disposition in the event of a disclaimer, that alternative disposition controls. See, e.g, Estate of Devlin, 46 Misc. 2d 399, 259 N.Y.S.2d 531 (Sur. Ct. 1964). In the absence of an alternative disposition, a disclaimed interest passes as provided by the disclaimer statute or by the common law. In general, the states apply the fiction that the disclaimant predeceased the decedent or, for property passing by nontestamentary instrument, that the disclaimant predeceased the instrument's effective date.

Representation Revisited. Can a disclaimer by used to manipulate shares under the various systems of representation? Suppose that G devised the residuary of her estate to her descendants and directed the distribution to be based on a per-capita-at-each-generation system. G was survived by her son, A, and by three grandchildren, X, Y, and Z. X and Y are A's children. Z is the child of a predeceased son, B. Consequently, under the distribution called for by G's will, half of her residuary estate would go to A and half to Z.

But what if A disclaims all his interest in his mother's will? By engaging in this maneuver, can or should A be permitted to manipulate the distributive pattern of G's residuary estate and obtain for X and Y a two-thirds share?

In analyzing whether the law prevents such a manipulation, notice the difference between a disclaimer statute that provides that the decedent's "estate" devolves as if the disclaimant predeceased the decedent and one that provides that the "disclaimed interest" devolves as if the disclaimant predeceased the decedent. If the statute provides that the "estate" devolves as if the disclaimant predeceased the decedent, the initial division of G's residuary estate would probably be recalculated so as to give X and Y a two-thirds share. But if the statute provides that the "disclaimed interest" devolves as if the disclaimant predeceased the decedent, only the one-half share that A disclaimed is affected. Consequently under pre-1990 UPC section 2-801(c), the portion of G's estate that devolves as if A predeceased G is the interest that A disclaimed—one half of G's residuary estate.

But there is a further problem. Does that disclaimed one-half share go to X and Y, as it should, or does it go to X, Y, *and Z*? If the statute merely provides that the disclaimed one-half devolves as if the disclaimant, A, predeceased the decedent, then that disclaimed one-half would appear to go to X, Y, *and Z*. If so, A's disclaimer would end up depriving his own children, X and Y, of part of his one-half share. Note how UPC section 2-801(d)(1) (1990) cures this further problem and assures that X and Y take A's disclaimed one-half share.

INTERNAL REFERENCE. For the effect of disclaimers by present-interest beneficiaries on remainder interests, see infra Chapter 15.

EXTERNAL REFERENCES. Hirsch, The Problem of the Insolvent Heir, 74 Cornell L. Rev. 587 (1989); Martin, Perspectives on Federal Disclaimer Legislation, 46 U. Chi. L. Rev. 316 (1979); Roche & Carlson, The Dynamic Disclaimer, 14 New England L. Rev. 399 (1979); Note, Disclaimer of Joint Tenancy Interest—When Does the Nine-Month Time Limit in I.R.C. Section 2518 Begin to Run?, 21 Ind. L. Rev. 669 (1988).

3. Formality versus Discretion in Intestate Succession

If the decedent's heirs can voluntarily rearrange intestacy patterns of distribution, should the courts have a power to vary the shares on the petition of one or more parties in interest? Under American law, as under the English canons of descent and the Statute of Distribution, intestate shares are determined mechanically. A surviving spouse's share, for example, is determined solely by reference to the decedent's other surviving relatives (or, under the UPC, by reference also to the surviving spouse's relatives). Traditional legislation does not authorize a court to inquire into the harmony or disharmony in the marital relationship. It does not allow for inquiry into the surviving spouse's contribution to the decedent's wealth.[43] It does not allow for any inquiry into the surviving spouse's needs, such as might be determined by the extent of the survivor's own assets and earning power.[44] All these issues are deemed irrelevant. In this sense, the current American law of intestate succession can be characterized, at least based on statutory language, as having a high degree of formality.

Although the pre-1990 UPC was pathbreaking in important ways, it did not break with tradition on this point. The basic statutory scheme of the former UPC still looked to the decedent's surviving relatives to determine the share of any particular relative. When the UPC was revised in 1990, it still determined the shares passing to a relative by applying mechanical factors relating to the existence of a surviving spouse and descendants and their biological (or adoptive) ties to the decedent or the surviving spouse. No judicial discretion was introduced into the statutory scheme.

---

43. See infra Chapter 8, Part A, discussing the relevance of the length of the marriage for determining the spouse's share. See also Ark. Stat. Ann. § 28-9-214(2) (permitting a spouse of a childless decedent to receive the entire estate only if the decedent and spouse were married for three years or more).

44. Such information is relevant, however, under family allowance statutes that are in effect in most states. We will study these statutes in Chapter 8, but at this point we need to bear in mind that they permit a judge to make a discretionary support allowance out of certain assets of the estate for the needs of the surviving spouse and children during the period of estate administration. In practice, these discretionary allowances often consume a substantial portion or all of a small estate.

This tradition of formality in intestacy law can usefully be compared with two examples of highly discretionary legal regimes. The first is the present American law of property division upon divorce. All or almost all states now confer upon courts the discretionary power to make an "equitable" division of assets belonging to the wife or husband or both and discretion in providing for the support of one party and the children. The second is the existing English system for distribution of property at death. The Inheritance (Provision for Family and Dependents) Act of 1975 allows the surviving spouse to apply for an award of provision that is "reasonable in all the circumstances." The statute instructs the court to take into account a number of factors that resemble the guidelines set for discretionary distribution upon divorce.

In view of the existence of these two discretionary systems, should American intestacy law provide more discretion to courts in distributing property at death? Are there good reasons for having a discretionary system of property division upon divorce and child support but a (largely) non-discretionary intestacy system? The question of formality versus discretion will come up again in several other areas of succession law. At this point, it will be useful for you to begin thinking about the reasons for and against discretion and formality and about whether the cogency of these reasons varies from one context to another.

EXTERNAL REFERENCE. Glendon, Fixed Rules and Discretion in Contemporary Family Law and Succession Law, 60 Tul. L. Rev. 1165 (1986).

PART D. WHO IS A "SURVIVING SPOUSE"?

The Transformation of the American Family. One of the more interesting stories of the latter half of the 1970s and into the present is the transformation of the American family. Although the traditional "Leave It to Beaver" family, consisting of a wage-earning husband, a housekeeping and child-rearing wife, and two or three joint children, has not disappeared, it is no longer the predominant pattern. Divorce rates are high, and many married couples have children from prior marriages on one or both sides. Families are increasingly headed by a single parent. Many couples with children have two adults working outside the home. More couples are choosing to postpone or forgo having children (called "DINKS" in newspeak—the acronym standing for double income, no kids). Unmarried heterosexual and homosexual couples, including some with children, are also increasingly prevalent in American society.

The challenge facing courts and legislators is to design family property laws that reflect the major changes occurring in American households. This Part and the next one present material to help you understand how family property law is responding currently to different family arrangements and to ponder what alternative approaches might be considered.

1. Formal Marriage

The rights accruing to a surviving spouse in probate law are based on status. These rights include the right to a share of the estate if the decedent dies intestate. See supra p. 73. States also provide a surviving spouse other statutory rights, such as a family allowance, protection against intentional disinheritance (traditionally referred to as an "elective share"), and protection against unintentional disinheritance by a premarital will that the decedent failed to revise after the marriage. In most states, these and other similar rights accrue only to a person who was lawfully married to the decedent when the decedent died. See infra Chapter 8.

2. Divorce, Separation, Misconduct

Statutory References: *1990 UPC § 2-802*
                              Pre-1990 UPC § 2-802

Not surprisingly, if the decedent's marriage was dissolved, by divorce or annulment, the decedent's former spouse loses the status of surviving spouse. Likewise, if the decedent's marriage was void because it was bigamous, incestuous, or preceded by an invalid divorce decree, the decedent's would-be spouse does not have the status of surviving spouse. But what if the decedent's divorce or annulment was itself invalid? Or, what if the decedent and her or his spouse were separated? Or, what if a divorce suit was pending but not final at the time of the decedent's death?

UPC section 2-802 (1990) addresses some but not all of these status questions.[45] Note that section 2-802 is not framed as a definition of "spouse." Instead, it gives a list of situations in which a person is *not* a surviving spouse. The most obvious of these is the case where the couple were validly divorced or their marriage was validly annulled. The others are where the person obtained or consented to a final decree or judgment of divorce or annulment, even though the decree turned out to be invalid; where the person, following an invalid decree obtained by the decedent, participated in a marriage ceremony with a third individual; and where the individual was a party to a valid proceeding purporting to terminate all marital property rights.

A few states, by statute, go farther and bar the surviving spouse from taking for desertion or adultery.[46] A few courts, without statutory authority

---

45. Section 2-802 appeared in the pre-1990 UPC, and was carried forward in the 1990 revisions without substantive change.

46. Ky. Rev. Stat. § 392.090 (spouse barred if spouse "leaves the other and lives in adultery," unless the spouses "afterward become reconciled and live together as husband and wife"); N.H. Rev. Stat. Ann. § 560:19 (spouse barred "if at the time of the death of either husband or wife, the decedent was justifiably living apart from the surviving husband or wife because such survivor was or had been guilty of conduct which constitutes cause for divorce"); N.Y. Est. Powers & Trusts Law § 5-1.2 (spouse barred if spouse "abandoned the deceased spouse, and such abandonment continued until the time of death" or if the spouse "who,

to vary the rights provided to surviving spouses, have denied claims against decedents' estates by persons who were lawfully married to the decedents when they died. See, e.g., Estate of Abila, 32 Cal. 2d 559, 197 P.2d 10 (1948) (wife barred because interlocutory decree of divorce, granted to decedent before his death, terminated decedent's obligation of support, though it did not dissolve the marriage).

3. Putative Spouses

A few courts have adopted a putative-spouse doctrine. See, e.g., Walker v. Walker, 330 Mich. 332, 47 N.W.2d 633 (1951); Annot., 81 A.L.R.3d 6 (1977). Under the Uniform Marriage and Divorce Act section 209 (1973), enacted in eight states as of 1991, a putative spouse acquires the "rights conferred upon a legal spouse."[47] A putative spouse is defined in the Act as "any person who has cohabited with another to whom he is not legally married in the good faith belief that he was married to that person." Courts have used the putative-spouse doctrine to recognize a claim for an intestacy share by an unmarried cohabitor. See, e.g., Estate of Leslie, 37 Cal. 3d 186, 689 P.2d 133, 207 Cal. Rptr. 561 (1984).

Neither the pre-1990 nor 1990 UPC explicitly confers rights upon or denies rights to putative spouses. If the decedent participated in a marriage ceremony with a third individual while she or he was lawfully married to another individual, the individual to whom the decedent was lawfully married remains the decedent's spouse. This is true even if the decedent

---

having the duty to support the other spouse, failed or refused to provide for such spouse though he or she had the means or ability to do so, unless such marital duty was resumed and continued until the death of the spouse having the need of support"); 20 Pa. Cons. Stat. § 2106 (spouse barred "who, for one year or upwards previous to the death of the other spouse, has wilfully neglected or refused to perform the duty to support the other spouse, or who for one year or upwards has wilfully and maliciously deserted the other spouse"); Va. Code § 64.1-23 (spouse barred if spouse "wilfully desert[s] or abandon[s] his or her consort and such desertion or abandonment continues until the death of the consort"). See also Haw. Rev. Stat. § 533-9.

47. Section 209 goes on to declare:

If there is a legal spouse or other putative spouses, rights acquired by a putative spouse do not supersede the rights of the legal spouse or those acquired by other putative spouses, but the court shall apportion property, maintenance, and support rights among the claimants as appropriate in the circumstances and in the interests of justice.

The Official Comment accompanying § 209 further explains:

It is possible for a person to have more than one putative spouse at the same time, since good faith is the test. In addition, a putative spouse and a legal spouse may be able to claim from a single estate or from other funds legally available to a spouse. A common situation of the latter type might involve a bigamous marriage in which the second spouse was never married or had been divorced. In such cases, the court is instructed to apportion property and the other financial incidents of marriage between the legal and the putative spouse, or among putative spouses. A fair and efficient apportionment standard is likely to be the length of time each spouse cohabited with the common partner.

had obtained or consented to an invalid decree or judgment of divorce or annulment. The UPC does not explicitly grant that third individual any rights to the decedent's estate. This is not to say, however, that the courts in a UPC state are not free to adopt a putative-spouse doctrine or that a putative-spouse doctrine cannot be recognized in a state that enacts both the UPC and the Uniform Marriage and Divorce Act.

4. Common-Law Marriage

Most states have abolished common-law marriage by statute. See, e.g., Mich. Comp. Laws § 551.2. Only thirteen states (Alabama, Colorado, Georgia, Idaho, Iowa, Kansas, Montana, Ohio, Oklahoma, Pennsylvania, Rhode Island, South Carolina, and Texas) and the District of Columbia still recognize the concept. H. Clark, Law of Domestic Relations § 2.4 (2d ed. 1987). The requirements necessary to establish a common-law marriage vary somewhat from state to state, but can be summarized as follows:

> The jurisdictions which recognize common law marriages all require that the parties presently agree to enter into the relationship of husband and wife. Most jurisdictions also require cohabitation, or actually and openly living together as husband and wife. . . . Some jurisdictions further require that the parties hold themselves out to the world as husband and wife, and acquire a reputation as a married couple. However, other jurisdictions hold that cohabitation and reputation are not requirements of a valid common law marriage, but solely matters of evidence.
>
> Under all of these definitions, evidence that the parties have stated "We're not married, we're just living together" will destroy the claim of a common law marriage.

Lovas, When Is a Family Not a Family? Inheritance and the Taxation of Inheritance Within the Non-traditional Family, 24 Idaho L. Rev. 353, 361 (1987).

Negative judicial and legislative reaction to the concept of common-law marriage grew during the late nineteenth century. One criticism of the concept was that the informality of common-law marriages makes them highly vulnerable to fraud and perjury. More prominent was the argument that common-law marriage undermined the sanctity of marriage. See, e.g., Sorenson v. Sorenson, 68 Neb. 500, 504, 100 N.W. 930, 932 (1904). See generally M. Grossberg, Governing the Hearth: Law and the Family in Nineteenth-Century America (1985).

In codifying a statutory version of common-law marriage, New Hampshire introduced a three-year bright-line rule:

> *N.H. Rev. Stat. Ann. § 457:39. Cohabitation, etc.* Persons cohabiting and acknowledging each other as husband and wife, and generally reputed to be such, for the period of 3 years, and until the decease of one of them, shall thereafter be deemed to have been legally married.

In some states where common-law marriage has been abolished, courts have applied a de facto common-law marriage doctrine to couples who lived together in a common-law marriage state. In Kellard v. Kellard, 13 Fam. L. Rep. (BNA) 1490 (N.Y. Sup. Ct. 1987), a New York woman and man, unmarried but cohabiting with one another, took an automobile trip to Disney World in 1978. During the trip, they stayed overnight in a motel in South Carolina where they registered as wife and husband, and engaged in sexual intercourse. They also stayed for two nights in a motel in Georgia. Some years later, in defense to a divorce suit filed in New York by the woman, the man claimed that no divorce was necessary because he was not married to the plaintiff. A New York court rejected his defense, holding that the couple's behavior enroute to Disney World satisfied the common-law marriage requirements of South Carolina and Georgia. This, along with the lengthy history of the couple's relationship, led the court to recognize them as married. See also Taylor, Increased Mobility Adds to Common Law Claims, Nat'l L.J., Aug. 14, 1989, at 24.

5. Unmarried Cohabitors

Demographics. Approximately six percent of the nation's 91 million households are headed by unmarried couples. That six percent includes a variety of living arrangements, including both domestic partnerships, meaning partners who are sexually intimate and financially interdependent, and friends who share a home. Of the domestic partnerships, about forty percent are gay or lesbian. See Time, Nov. 20, 1989, at 101.

Demographers have taken a special interest in the cohabitation phenomenon and have arrived at a variety of findings:

> About 40 percent of cohabiting unions in the U.S. breakup without the couple getting married, and this tends to occur rather quickly. By about one and one-half years, half the cohabiting couples have either married or broken up. . . . Only about 1 out of 10 remain cohabiting after 5 years without either marrying or breaking up. Nonetheless, this does not mean that at any point in time there are a few cohabitations of longer duration. Longer cohabitations tend to "accumulate" in the population, so there are more in the cross-section than we might expect from a cohort perspective. . . . [Twenty] percent of cohabiting couples have lived together for 5 or more years. The duration of cohabiting unions is longer among previously-married persons. . . .
>
> [C]ohabiting unions are much less stable than those that began as marriages. . . . [M]arriages that are preceded by living together have 50 percent higher disruption rates than marriages without premarital cohabitation. Several factors may be at work. On the one hand, it may just be that persons who are willing to cohabit are less traditional in their family values, and hence, at the same level of marital unhappiness, more likely to accept divorce as a solution. For example, among unions of 10 or fewer years duration, cohabitors are much less likely to agree that "Marriage is a lifetime relationship and should never be ended except under extreme circumstances."

Bumpass, Sweet & Cherlin, The Role of Cohabitation in Declining Rates of Marriage, Working Paper No. 5, at 6-13 (Nat'l Survey of Families and Households, 1989). This latter point was later amplified as follows:

> If many couples are using cohabitation to test their relationship, and if 40% split up without marrying, then we expect those who do marry to have more stable marriages than would have been the case in the absence of cohabitation. Despite all the attention given the results on the higher divorce rate of marriages preceded by cohabitation, this finding is not contrary evidence on this point. Cohabitation is selective and includes a lower proportion of couples who hold traditional family attitudes and a higher proportion of those who are uncertain about their relationship.

Bumpass, What's Happening to the Family? Interactions Between Demographic and Institutional Change, 27 Demography 483, 487 (1990).

Legal Rights. The respective rights of domestic partners upon dissolution of the partnership during life or at death are governed almost exclusively by court-made law. Why is that, in an age of legislation?

Heterosexual Couples. The unmarried-cohabitors cases that come to public attention nearly always involve a defendant who is a wealthy celebrity, entertainer, or professional athlete. But the less celebrated come to court also. As a Houston divorce attorney recently remarked: "You don't need millions of dollars for people to fight. Give two people a house worth $200,000 and they'll consider an action." Taylor, supra, at 24.

These suits are sometimes grounded on a common-law marriage claim, but, when that claim is unavailable, they can still go forward as a "palimony suit."[48] Not surprisingly, most of the cases arise in the context of a dissolution during life. Claims arising at death are less common because, if the partners remain devoted to each other, the surviving partner is probably provided for in the decedent partner's will or other parts of the estate plan. Therefore, it is unusual for cases to arise in which a surviving partner is making a claim to a share of a decedent's estate. The most famous of the "palimony" cases is Marvin v. Marvin, below.

Plaintiffs have no problem in stating a cause of action when they allege that they made a monetary contribution toward the purchase of specific property on the understanding that they would be the owner or part owner. The fact that the property is not titled in the name of the plaintiff is not a defense. A cause of action for the imposition of a purchase-money resulting trust or a constructive trust on the specific property is well established.[49] See, e.g., Estate of Eriksen, 337 N.W.2d 671 (Minn. 1983) (surviving cohabitor entitled to constructive trust in her favor of a one-half interest in home purchased with joint funds but titled in decedent's name alone).

---

48. The term "palimony" is misleading because the plaintiff is usually seeking a division of the couple's property, not an award of periodic payments similar to alimony.

49. For a discussion of these remedies, see infra Chapter 11.

The *Marvin* case confronted the problem of whether there can ever be a remedy and, if so, under what circumstances, when the plaintiff's contribution came in the form of services.

Marvin v. Marvin
18 Cal. 3d 660, 134 Cal. Rptr. 815, 557 P.2d 106 (1976)

[The plaintiff, Michelle Triola, brought a breach of contract action against the defendant, Lee Marvin. Because the trial court granted judgment on the pleadings for the defendant, the question on appeal was whether the plaintiff's complaint stated a cause of action or could be amended to state of cause of action.]

TOBRINER, J. . . . Plaintiff avers that in October of 1964 she and defendant "entered into an oral agreement" that while "the parties lived together they would combine their efforts and earnings and would share equally any and all property accumulated as a result of their efforts whether individual or combined." Furthermore, they agreed to "hold themselves out to the general public as husband and wife" and that "plaintiff would further render her services as a companion, homemaker, housekeeper and cook to . . . defendant."

Shortly thereafter plaintiff agreed to "give up her lucrative career as an entertainer [and] singer" in order to "devote her full time to defendant . . . as a companion, homemaker, housekeeper and cook;" in return defendant agreed to "provide for all of plaintiff's financial support and needs for the rest of her life."

Plaintiff alleges that she lived with defendant from October of 1964 through May of 1970 and fulfilled her obligations under the agreement. During this period the parties as a result of their efforts and earnings acquired in defendant's name substantial real and personal property, including motion picture rights worth over $1 million. In May of 1970, however, defendant compelled plaintiff to leave his household. He continued to support plaintiff until November of 1971, but thereafter refused to provide further support.

On the basis of these allegations plaintiff asserts two causes of action. The first, for declaratory relief, asks the court to determine her contract and property rights; the second seeks to impose a constructive trust upon one half of the property acquired during the course of the relationship. . . .

2. *Plaintiff's complaint states a cause of action for breach of an express contract.* In Trutalli v. Meraviglia (1932) 215 Cal. 698, 12 P.2d 430 we established the principle that nonmarital partners may lawfully contract concerning the ownership of property acquired during the relationship. We reaffirmed this principle in Vallera v. Vallera (1943) 21 Cal.2d 681, 685, 134 P.2d 761, 763 . . . .

[W]e can abstract from [our prior] decisions a clear and simple rule. The fact that a man and woman live together without marriage, and engage in a sexual relationship, does not in itself invalidate agreements between them relating to their earnings, property, or expenses. Neither is such an agreement invalid merely because the parties may have contemplated the creation or continuation of a nonmarital relationship when they entered into it. Agreements between nonmarital partners fail only to the extent that they rest upon a consideration of meretricious sexual services. . . .

The principle that a contract between nonmarital partners will be enforced unless expressly and inseparably based upon an illicit consideration of sexual services not only represents the distillation of the decisional law, but also offers a . . . precise and workable standard . . . .

In summary, we base our opinion on the principle that adults who voluntarily live together and engage in sexual relations are nonetheless as competent as any other persons to contract respecting their earnings and property rights. Of course, they cannot lawfully contract to pay for the performance of sexual services, for such a contract is, in essence, an agreement for prostitution and unlawful for that reason. But they may agree to pool their earnings and to hold all property acquired during the relationship in accord with the law governing community property. . . . So long as the agreement does not rest upon illicit meretricious consideration, the parties may order their economic affairs as they choose, and no policy precludes the courts from enforcing such agreements.

3. *Plaintiff's complaint can be amended to state a cause of action founded upon theories of implied contract or equitable relief.* . . . Both plaintiff and defendant stand in broad agreement that the law should be fashioned to carry out the reasonable expectations of the parties. . . .[50]

[A]lthough parties to a nonmarital relationship obviously cannot have based any expectations upon the belief that they were married, other expectations and equitable considerations remain. The parties may well expect that property will be divided in accord with the parties' own tacit understanding and that in the absence of such understanding the courts will fairly apportion property accumulated through mutual effort. We need not treat nonmarital partners as putatively married persons in order to apply principles of implied contract, or extend equitable remedies; we need to treat them only as we do any other unmarried persons. . . .

---

50. We note that a deliberate decision to avoid the strictures of the community property system is not the only reason that couples live together without marriage. Some couples may wish to avoid the permanent commitment that marriage implies, yet be willing to share equally any property acquired during the relationship; others may fear the loss of pension, welfare, or tax benefits resulting from marriage. Others may engage in the relationship as a possible prelude to marriage. In lower socio-economic groups the difficulty and expense of dissolving a former marriage often leads couples to choose a nonmarital relationship; many unmarried couples may also incorrectly believe that the doctrine of common law marriage prevails in California, and thus that they are in fact married. Consequently we conclude that the mere fact that a couple have not participated in a valid marriage ceremony cannot serve as a basis for a court's inference that the couple intend to keep their earnings and property separate and independent; the parties' intention can only be ascertained by a more searching inquiry into the nature of their relationship. [According to Professor Glendon, the reference in this footnote to a searching inquiry raised "the prospect of litigation in which the private lives of the parties can be explored in detail [and] has led already to the settlement out of court of a number of suits by alleged same-sex lovers or clandestine playmates of well-known people." M. Glendon, The Transformation of Family Law 279 (1989). Eds.]

Although we recognize the well-established public policy to foster and promote the institution of marriage, perpetuation of judicial rules which result in an inequitable distribution of property accumulated during a nonmarital relationship is neither a just nor an effective way of carrying out that policy. . . .

We conclude that the judicial barriers that may stand in the way of a policy based upon the fulfillment of the reasonable expectations of the parties to a nonmarital relationship should be removed. As we have explained, the courts now hold that express agreements will be enforced unless they rest on an unlawful meretricious consideration. We add that in the absence of an express agreement, the courts may look to a variety of other remedies in order to protect the parties' lawful expectations.[51]

The courts may inquire into the conduct of the parties to determine whether that conduct demonstrates an implied contract or implied agreement of partnership or joint venture, or some other tacit understanding between the parties. The courts may, when appropriate, employ principles of constructive trust or resulting trust. Finally, a nonmarital partner may recover in quantum meruit for the reasonable value of household services rendered less the reasonable value of support received if he can show that he rendered services with the expectation of monetary reward.

Since we have determined that plaintiff's complaint states a cause of action for breach of an express contract, and, as we have explained, can be amended to state a cause of action independent of allegations of express contract,[52] we must conclude that the trial court erred . . . .

WRIGHT, C.J., and McCOMB, MOSK, SULLIVAN and RICHARDSON, J., concur.
CLARK, J. (concurring and dissenting).

Notes and Questions

1. *Subsequent History.* On remand, the plaintiff failed to prove the existence of an express or implied contract, but the trial court awarded her $104,000 for rehabilitation on the ground of an unspecified equitable theory. On appeal, the judgment granting this award was reversed for want of a "recognized underlying obligation in law or in equity." Marvin v. Marvin, 122 Cal. App. 3d 871, 176 Cal. Rptr. 555 (1981). See also Taylor v. Polackwich, 145 Cal. App. 3d 1014, 194 Cal. Rptr. 8 (1983) ("rehabilitative award" reversed on appeal).

---

51. We do not seek to resurrect the doctrine of common law marriage, which was abolished in California by statute in 1895. Thus we do not hold that plaintiff and defendant were "married," nor do we extend to plaintiff the rights which the Family Law Act grants valid or putative spouses; we hold that she has the same rights to enforce contracts and to assert her equitable interest in property acquired through her effort as does any other unmarried person.

52. We do not pass upon the question whether, in the absence of an express or implied contractual obligation, a party to a nonmarital relationship is entitled to support payments from the other party after the relationship terminates.

2. *Whose Expectations Are They, Anyway?* Justice Tobriner wrote that courts should provide remedies "in order to protect the parties' lawful expectations." Do you think that Michelle and Lee shared the same expectations in entering into[53] and continuing their relationship? On the expectations of unmarried cohabitors in general, Bumpass, Sweet & Cherlin, *supra*, at 14, found:

> In 39 percent of the cases for which we have couple data, one party believes they will marry and the other does not! This difference of perception is surely a factor in the higher instability of these unions. Another 11 percent agree that they will not get married, making just about half of all cohabiting couples where there is disagreement about marriage or no plans to marry. Twenty-nine percent agree that they have definite plans to marry, and in another 20 percent of the cases one partner has definite plans to marry, while the other thinks they will marry but does not have definite plans to do so.

See also Rindfuss & VandenHeuvel, Cohabitation: Precursor to Marriage or an Alternative to Being Single, 16 Population & Dev. Rev. 703, 721 (1990) (empirical study finding that "cohabitors are substantially more similar [in their attitudes toward matters such as marriage and childbearing plans] to the singles than to the married.").

3. *Quasi-Marriage?* Common-law marriage was abolished in part because of the perceived proof problems associated with the lack of a formal ceremony. Is the *Marvin* doctrine subject to the same criticism? Should legislatures create two legal forms of marriage, Marriage I and Marriage II, in response to the lack of formality in *Marvin*-type arrangements? See Pilpel, Marriage I, Marriage II, Harper's, May 1974, at 5.

The state of cohabitation law in western Europe as well as America has been perceptively summarized as follows:

> [T]hough [a good deal of variety exists,] a few generalizations [can be made] about the legal treatment of informal [heterosexual] family behavior in the countries surveyed here [England, France, Sweden, United States, West Germany]. Just as we have seen a universal trend, with varying degrees of strength, to diminish the legal consequences of marriage, we have observed an increasing body of legal effects being attributed to marriage-like cohabitation. Nevertheless, a distinction between legal marriage and cohabitation is maintained everywhere, with marriage even in Sweden being nominally accorded a central position in family law. Where children are concerned, however, the opposite principle governs. Even where some legal distinctions remain, the idea is firmly in place that a child ought not to suffer legal disadvantages because of the marital status of its parents. Thus, it may be that the legally relevant distinction in the future will be between childless unions and those where children are being or have been raised. The law's intervention in the former may be confined to sorting out property problems, while the latter may enjoy a certain privileged status on account of the public interest in the nurture and socialization of future citizens.

---

53. It may be noted that, during the first two years of their relationship, Lee was married to another woman.

M. Glendon, The Transformation of Family Law 289-90 (1989). Notice the focus of the above report on the difference between childless unions and those where children are being or have been raised. Why should the existence or nonexistence of children have a bearing on a domestic partner's right to a recovery? Is this factor being used somewhat as a proxy for distinguishing between marriage-like and non-marriage-like cohabiting unions? Is this factor a reliable proxy? How frequently are children present in such unions? Demographers have reported the following information on this question:

> The common image of cohabiting couples as college students, or at least young couples, does not usually include a family with children. Yet, 4 of every 10 such couples have children present. This proportion is one-third among the never-married and almost half among the previously married. One-sixth of never-married cohabiting couples have a child that was born since they began living together. . . . [T]his represents a significant component of unmarried births (about a quarter) that are not born into single-parent households.
>
> Further, the children in cohabiting households are not all young children. . . . [A] quarter of the households with children have children age 10 or older; mostly living with previously-married parents. In thinking about the meaning of cohabitation and the dynamics of cohabiting households, it is critical to keep in mind that issues of parenting and step-parenting are very much a part of the picture.

Bumpass, Sweet & Cherlin, supra, p. 107, at 10.

As yet, no American legislature has established an institution of quasi-marriage. If one did, should the quasi-marriage status lead to the same rights and obligations accorded married couples, such as the right of inheritance? Or, the right to take advantage of the imputed marital-sharing principles of the divorce laws? See infra Chapter 8.

In the absence of legislative establishment of a quasi-marriage status, should courts assign to unmarried cohabitors, on the basis of their cohabitation alone, or on the basis of cohabitation for a significant period plus some evidence of emotional and financial commitment, the same economic consequences as marriage? Some courts have held that a cohabitation relationship can have the same force and effect as a legal marriage.[54] For example, in Goode v. Goode, 396 S.E.2d 430 (W. Va. 1990), Martha and Carl Goode separated after having lived together for 28 years. Although the couple had never formally married, they had constantly held themselves out to the public as wife and husband. They had four children. Martha, age 47, filed a divorce action against Carl, age 61, seeking an equitable division of the property they had acquired during their 28-year

---

54. For examples of cases providing for equitable division of property acquired while the couple cohabitated before marrying or acquired while the couple cohabitated after having divorced each other, see Eaton v. Johnson, 10 Fam. L. Rep. (BNA) 1094 (Kan. Ct. App. 1983); Pickens v. Pickens, 490 S.2d 872 (Miss. 1986); Marriage of Lindsey, 101 Wash. 2d 299, 678 P.2d 328 (1984).

period of cohabitation. Although West Virginia is not a common-law marriage state, the court held that Martha could recover, saying:

> [W]e hold that a court may order a division of property acquired by a man and woman who are unmarried cohabitants, but who have considered themselves and held themselves out to be husband and wife. Such order may be based upon principles of contract, either express or implied, or upon a constructive trust. Factors to be considered in ordering such a division of property may include: the purpose, duration, and stability of the relationship and the expectations of the parties. Provided, however, that if either the man or woman is validly married to another person during the period of cohabitation, the property rights of the spouse and support rights of the children of such man or woman shall not in any way be adversely affected by such division of property.[55] The expectations of the parties under these circumstances would be equitable treatment by the other party in exchange for engaging in such a cohabiting relationship.

A case going perhaps even farther toward allowing unmarried plaintiffs to utilize the divorce laws is Warden v. Warden, 36 Wash. App. 693, 676 P.2d 1037 (1984). Denise Boursier and Charles Warden began living together in 1963, holding themselves out as wife and husband. They had two children. In 1972, Charles moved to California and formally married another woman. After learning of this, Denise brought suit under the divorce laws for child support and an equitable division of property, which the trial court awarded. Charles appealed that part of the judgment decreeing a division of the property. Although Washington is not a common-law marriage state, the Washington Court of Appeals affirmed, saying:

> We believe the time has come for the provision of [the Washington statute providing for equitable division of property upon dissolution of a marriage] to govern the disposition of the property acquired by a man and a woman who have lived together and established a relationship which is tantamount to a marital family except for a legal marriage.
>
> The trial judge here properly treated Denise and Charles as a marital family and correctly considered the length and purpose of their relationship, the two children, the contributions of the parties, and the future prospects of each. He correctly assumed that both Denise and Charles contributed to the acquisition of the property and divided it in a manner which was "just and equitable after considering all relevant factors."

Id. at 698, 676 P.2d at 1039-40.

---

55. Under the facts of this case, the parties lived together for an extended period of time, considered themselves as husband and wife, and, in fact, pooled their resources to include taking property under three joint deeds. Therefore, in this case, the equities are more easily determined than in a relationship between two parties which was for a shorter duration, or where the parties did not consider themselves to be husband and wife, or where the parties did not pool their resources. Cases in other jurisdictions have noted that "[e]ach case should be assessed on its own merits with consideration given to the purpose, duration and stability of the relationship and the expectations of the parties." Hay v. Hay, 100 Nev. 196, 199, 678 P.2d 672, 674 (1984). [Footnote by the court. Eds.]

Other post-*Marvin* cases have asserted claims based on nonfamily doctrines, such as express contract, contract implied in fact, contract implied in law, quantum meruit, and constructive trust. See, e.g., Watts v. Watts, 137 Wis. 2d 506, 405 N.W.2d 303 (1987) (set forth infra p. 654). Decisions in many of these cases are ambiguous as to whether the court based recovery on a contract implied in fact or on unjust enrichment grounds. Later chapters will study these theories further in the context of other family property law issues. The following materials, however, present some of the contract issues that have arisen.

4. *The Illegal Consideration Problem.* A few post-*Marvin* decisions have held that contracts between unmarried cohabitors are unenforceable on public policy grounds. See, e.g., Rehak v. Mathis, 239 Ga. 541, 238 S.E.2d 81 (1977) ("It is well settled that neither a court of law nor a court of equity will lend its aid to either party to a contract founded upon an illegal or *immoral* consideration. Code Ann. § 20-501. . . . The parties being unmarried and the appellant having admitted the fact of cohabitation in both verified pleadings, this would constitute immoral consideration under Code Ann. § 20-501 . . . ."); Hewitt v. Hewitt, 77 Ill. 2d 49, 394 N.E.2d 1204 (1979) ("Illinois' public policy regarding agreements such as the one alleged here was implemented long ago . . . , where this court said: 'An agreement in consideration of future illicit cohabitation between the plaintiffs is void.' . . . The issue, realistically, is whether it is appropriate for this court to grant a legal status to a private arrangement substituting for the institution of marriage sanctioned by the State. The question whether change is needed in the law . . . [is best left to] the legislative branch . . .").

5. *Express Contract Required?* Some jurisdictions have taken the position that only an express contract concerning property division upon dissolution of a cohabitation relationship is enforceable. They do not recognize an implied contract. See, e.g., Levar v. Elkins, 604 P.2d 602 (Alaska 1980); Estate of Alexander, 445 S.2d 836 (Miss. 1984); Dominguez v. Cruz, 95 N.M. 1, 617 P.2d 1322 (Ct. App. 1980); Morone v. Morone, 50 N.Y.2d 481, 413 N.E.2d 1154, 429 N.Y.S.2d 592 (1980). The *Alexander* court held that if a remedy is to be given to a surviving cohabitant in the absence of an express contract, "the Legislature should provide the remedy." See also Carnes v. Sheldon, 109 Mich. App. 204, 311 N.W.2d 747 (1981) (although prior Michigan cases have held that express contracts are enforceable to the extent they are based on independent consideration, and have enforced contracts implied in fact for wages or for the value of commercial services, the court in the instant case was "unwilling to extend equitable principles to the extent plaintiff would have us do, since recovery based on principles of contracts implied in law essentially would resurrect the old common-law marriage doctrine which was specifically abolished by the Legislature. . . . [J]udicial restraint requires that the Legislature, rather than the judiciary, is the appropriate forum for addressing the question raised by plaintiff. We believe a contrary ruling would contravene the public policy of this state 'disfavoring the grant of mutually enforceable property rights to knowingly unmarried cohabitants.'").

Should only express written contracts be enforceable? Premarital agreements are enforceable only if in writing. See Unif. Premarital Agreement Act § 2 (1983) ("A premarital agreement must be in writing and signed by both parties. It is enforceable without consideration.").

Legislation in Minnesota provides that an express written contract "between a man and a woman who are living together . . . out of wedlock" is valid, even if "sexual relations between the parties are contemplated," but also provides that, in absence of an express written contract, any claim to another's earnings or property must be dismissed as contrary to public policy if it is "based on the fact that the individuals lived together in contemplation of sexual relations and out of wedlock within or without this state."[56] Minn. Stat. §§ 513.075, .076.

6. *Dissolution by Death.* Although most of the cases have involved property disputes between living cohabitors who have separated, some cases have involved contractual or equitable claims by the survivor to a share of the other's estate upon the latter's death. Complaints founded upon breach of oral promises supported by social, domestic, nursing, and business services have been held to state a cause of action. See, e.g., Poe v. Estate of Levy, 411 S.2d 253 (Fla. Ct. App. 1982) (reversing trial court's dismissal of count seeking enforcement of an express support contract and count seeking imposition of a constructive trust in certain property due to a confidential relationship between surviving cohabitor and decedent, but affirming trial court's dismissal of count seeking one-half ownership interest in decedent's property grounded on argument that their relationship had the same force and effect as a legal marriage); Donovan v. Scuderi, 51 Md. App. 217, 443 A.2d 121 (Ct. Spec. App. 1982) (plaintiff entitled to recover damages for breach of express oral promise to pay to plaintiff 1,000 shares of stock of the bank of which the decedent was chairman of the board, in return for which plaintiff made various expenditures and provided loans and services, including "catering services, personal shopping services (clothing, furniture and furnishings)"; decedent, a married man, and plaintiff, an unmarried woman, did not have a full-time cohabitation relationship, but frequently used an apartment plaintiff had obtained at decedent's request)); Tyranski v. Piggins, 44 Mich. App. 570, 205 N.W.2d 595 (1973) (surviving cohabitor entitled to specific performance of decedent's oral promise to convey house to her; plaintiff, a married woman who was separated from her husband, performed various domestic, social, and nursing services for decedent).

Complaints have also been held to state a cause of action when they sought the imposition of a constructive trust on specific property based on a confidential relationship between the cohabitors. See, e.g., Poe v. Estate of Levy, supra. Complaints seeking damages in the amount of the value of such services on the theory of quantum meruit (as much as the plaintiff

---

56. This statute does not prevent a cause of action for a constructive trust or a purchase-money resulting trust where the plaintiff contributed monetary consideration toward the purchase of specific property titled in the decedent's name alone. See Estate of Erickson, 337 N.W.2d 671 (Minn. 1983).

deserved) have also been upheld. See, e.g., Green v. Richmond, 369 Mass. 47, 337 N.E.2d 691 (1975) (surviving cohabitor entitled to quantum meruit recovery of damages for value of social, domestic, and business services performed in reliance on decedent's oral promise to leave a will devising his entire estate to her; set forth infra p. 534); Humiston v. Bushnell, 118 N.H. 759, 394 A.2d 844 (1978) (lack of proof of alleged oral promise to devise a certain parcel of realty prevented surviving cohabitor from recovering damages for breach; surviving cohabitor was entitled to recover in quantum meruit for value of "intimate, confidential, and dedicated personal and business service" she performed for the decedent with the expectation of being ultimately compensated therefor); Estate of Steffes, 95 Wis. 2d 490, 290 N.W.2d 697 (1980) (surviving cohabitor entitled to recover damages for value of housekeeping, farming, and nursing services rendered at decedent's request and with the expectation of being compensated therefor).

Also, complaints seeking the imposition of an implied partnership with respect to a business arrangement have been upheld. See, e.g., Estate of Thornton, 81 Wash. 2d 72, 499 P.2d 864 (1972) (surviving cohabitor entitled to recover on basis of an implied partnership in cattle-raising business). But the dismissal of a complaint seeking a half interest in the decedent's property based on the theory that the parties' relationship had the same force and effect as a legal marriage was affirmed. See, e.g., Poe v. Estate of Levy, supra.

Lesbian and Gay Couples. Formal marriage, common-law marriage, and the putative-spouse doctrine are unavailable to couples of the same sex.[57] In 1989, Denmark became the first industrial nation to allow lesbian and gay couples to register and thereby obtain all but a few of the rights accorded married couples. See N.Y. Times, Oct. 2, 1989, at 15, col. 4 (nat'l ed.).

Although fewer in number, reported cases involving property disputes between lesbian and gay couples occur. As with heterosexual couples, no problem has been encountered in stating a cause of action for the imposition of a purchase-money resulting trust or a constructive trust on specific property when the plaintiff alleges or proves that she or he

----

57. For cases upholding the state's power to limit marital status to heterosexual couples, see Jones v. Hallahan, 501 S.W.2d 588 (Ky. 1973); Baker v. Nelson, 291 Minn. 310, 191 N.W.2d 185 (1971), appeal dismissed, 409 U.S. 810 (1972); Singer v. Hara, 11 Wash. App. 247, 522 P.2d 1187 (1974). Reinforcing these decisions is the Supreme Court's decision in Bowers v. Hardwick, 478 U.S. 186 (1986), which upheld the constitutionality of state laws making homosexual sodomy criminal. But cf. Loving v. Virginia, 388 U.S. 1, 12 (1967) ("the freedom to marry . . . resides with the individual."). See Stoddard & Ettlebrick, Legalizing Lesbian and Gay Marriages: A Conversation for Many Voices (1989) (presenting opposing views by members of the lesbian and gay legal community on the desirability of legalizing same-sex marriage); Law, Homosexuality and the Social Meaning of Gender, 1988 Wis. L. Rev. 18; Note, The Necessity for State Recognition of Same-Sex Marriage: Constitutional Requirements and Evolving Notions of Family, 3 Berkeley Women's L.J. 134 (1988); Note, The Legality of Homosexual Marriage, 82 Yale L.J. 573 (1973).

contributed monetary consideration toward the purchase of that property. See, e.g., Bramlett v. Selman, 268 Ark. 457, 597 S.W.2d 80 (1980). Indeed, this type of cause of action has been recognized even in states such as Georgia that have held that cohabitors' agreements based on services are unenforceable because the consideration is immoral. See Weekes v. Gay, 243 Ga. 784, 256 S.E.2d 901 (1979).

Current law generally refuses to accord lesbian and gay domestic partners any rights or obligations beyond those available under contract and related equitable doctrines. Changing public attitudes may lead to legal changes. Recent surveys found that 65 percent of those surveyed think that a lesbian or gay partner should be allowed to inherit the other partner's property. See Time, Nov. 20, 1989, at 101. And, a number of American cities have extended the same employee benefits such as health insurance to the domestic partners (of the same or different sex) of city employees that are extended to spouses of city employees. Berkeley, Santa Cruz, and West Hollywood, California, Ann Arbor and East Lansing, Michigan, Minneapolis, Minnesota, Ithaca, New York, and Seattle, Washington, are among the cities in the vanguard of this movement. See Treuthart, Adopting a More Realistic Definition of "Family," 26 Gonz. L. Rev. 91, 101-05 (1990/91).

A recent decision by the New York Court of Appeals, Braschi v. Stahl Associates Co., 74 N.Y.2d 201, 543 N.E.2d 49, 544 N.Y.S.2d 784 (1989), distinguished between adoption as a method of establishing family status for gay and lesbian couples for intestacy purposes and the meaning of "family" for purposes of statutory protection against eviction from rent-controlled premises upon the death of the tenant of record. The court held that the term "family," as used in the New York City Rent and Eviction regulation, "should not be rigidly restricted to those people who have formalized their relationship by obtaining, for instance, a marriage certificate or an adoption order." It reasoned that "[i]n the context of eviction, a more realistic . . . view of a family includes two adult lifetime partners whose relationship is long-term and characterized by an emotional and financial commitment and interdependence." Compare the court's approach in *Braschi* to the same court's approach in Robert Paul P., infra p. 147, rejecting the petition of a gay man to adopt his partner.

Jones v. Daly and Whorton v. Dillingham, which follow, are illustrative of the judge-made law regarding the ability of a lesbian or gay domestic partner to obtain a contractual remedy based on contributions in the form of services. Although neither court explicitly distinguished heterosexual from homosexual partnerships when developing its analysis, consider whether the sexual orientation of the parties played a role in either court's reasoning.

Jones v. Daly
122 Cal. App. 3d 500, 176 Cal. Rptr. 130 (1981)

[The plaintiff, Randal Jones, brought an action against the estate of James Daly. Because the trial court sustained the defendant's demurrer without leave to amend, the question on appeal was whether the plaintiff's complaint stated a cause of action.]

LILLIE, J. . . . Plaintiff, Randal Jones, first met James Daly in December 1975. Between that time and March 1976, they "met on frequent occasions, dated, engaged in sexual activities and, in general, acted towards one another as two people do who have discovered a love, one for the other." In March 1976 plaintiff and Daly orally agreed that plaintiff would move into Daly's condominium with Daly, quit his job, go travelling with Daly and "cohabit with him [Daly] as if [they] were, in fact, married." They also entered into an oral agreement (referred to hereinafter, in the language of the complaint, as "cohabitors agreement") whereby each agreed: during the time "they lived and cohabited together," they would combine their efforts and earnings and would share equally any and all property accumulated as a result of their efforts, whether individual or combined, except that Daly would give plaintiff a monthly allowance for his personal use, and they "would hold themselves out to the public at large as cohabiting mates, and [plaintiff] would render his services as a lover, companion, homemaker, traveling companion, housekeeper and cook to Daly"; and "in order that [plaintiff] would be able to devote a substantial portion of his time to Daly's benefit as his lover, companion, homemaker, traveling companion, housekeeper and cook," plaintiff would abandon "a material portion" of his potential career as a model, and in return Daly would furnish financial support to plaintiff for the rest of his life. Pursuant to and in reliance on the "cohabitors agreement," plaintiff and Daly "cohabited and lived together continuously" from March 1976 until Daly's death, and plaintiff allowed himself to be known to the general public "as the lover and cohabitation mate of Daly." Plaintiff performed all of the terms and conditions required to be performed by him under the "cohabitors agreement." During the time that plaintiff and Daly "lived and cohabited together" they acquired, as a result of their efforts and earnings, substantial real and personal property (hereinafter, in the language of the complaint, "cohabitors' equitable property"). Plaintiff does not know the exact nature and extent of such property, but he believes it has a value in excess of $2 million and will amend the complaint to reflect the true value when it is ascertained. Under the "cohabitors agreement," all of the "cohabitors' equitable property" was to be shared and divided equally between plaintiff and Daly. All of such property is in the possession of defendant executors and under their control. Plaintiff has demanded that defendants recognize his interest in the "cohabitors' equitable property," but defendants refuse to do so. . . .

In determining whether the "cohabitors agreement" rests upon illicit meretricious consideration, we are guided by the following principles: "[A] contract between nonmarital partners, even if expressly made in contemplation of a common living arrangement, is invalid only if sexual acts form an inseparable part of the consideration for the agreement. In sum, a court will not enforce a contract for the pooling of property and earnings if it is explicitly and inseparably based upon service as a paramour." (Marvin v. Marvin, supra, 18 Cal. 3d 660, 672.) The complaint herein alleges: Following their initial meeting, plaintiff and Daly "dated, engaged in sexual activities and, in general, acted towards one another as two people do who have discovered a love, one for the other"; plaintiff orally agreed "to cohabit with [Daly] as if [they] were, in fact, married"; at the same time they entered into the "cohabitors agreement" whereby they agreed that during the time "they lived and cohabited together" they would hold themselves out to the public at large as "cohabiting mates" and plaintiff would render his services to Daly as "a *lover*, companion, homemaker, traveling companion, housekeeper and cook" (emphasis added); in order that plaintiff would be able to devote his time to Daly's benefit "as his lover, companion, homemaker, traveling companion, housekeeper and cook," he would abandon his career; plaintiff and Daly "cohabited and lived together" and pursuant to and in reliance on the "cohabitors agreement," plaintiff allowed himself to be known to the general public as the "lover and cohabitation mate" of Daly. These allegations clearly show that plaintiff's rendition of sexual services to Daly was an inseparable part of the consideration for the "cohabitors agreement," and indeed was the predominant consideration. . . .

Marvin states that "even if sexual services are part of the contractual consideration, any *severable* portion of the contract supported by independent consideration will still be enforced." That principle is inapplicable in the present case. There is no severable portion of the "cohabitors agreement" supported by independent consideration. . . . Neither the property sharing nor the support provision of the agreement rests upon plaintiff's acting as Daly's traveling companion, housekeeper or cook as distinguished from acting as his lover. The latter service forms an inseparable part of the consideration for the agreement and renders it unenforceable in its entirety. . . .

The judgment is affirmed.

SPENCER, J. and HANSON, J. concurred.

Questions

Why did the *Marvin* court find it easy to sever the sexual component of the parties' relationship and the *Jones* court find it impossible to do? Do you think that *Jones* would have been decided the same way if the case had involved a heterosexual couple rather than a gay couple?

We know in *Marvin* that Lee Marvin did not want to "give a dime" to Michelle Triola. An antagonistic attitude such as Lee's toward Michelle will typically prevail when the relationship terminates during the defendant's life. Should the court in cases such as *Jones,* where the relationship ended because of the death of one of the partners, assume a similarly antagonistic attitude by the decedent toward the plaintiff? Why did the court not tell us whether James Daly died intestate, or, if he died with a will, when that will was written? How might consideration of these factors have affected the analysis of the case, particularly with respect to *Marvin's* directive "to protect the parties' lawful expectations"?

Whorton v. Dillingham
202 Cal. App. 3d 447, 248 Cal. Rptr. 405 (1988)

[The plaintiff, Dennis G. Whorton, brought a breach of contract action against the defendant, Benjamin F. Dillingham, III. Because the trial court sustained the defendant's demurrer without leave to amend, the question on appeal was whether the plaintiff's complaint stated a cause of action.]

WORK, J. . . . The alleged facts include the following. At the time the parties began dating and entered into a homosexual relationship, Whorton was studying to obtain his Associate in Arts degree, intending to enroll in a four year college and obtain a Bachelor of Arts degree. When the parties began living together in 1977, they orally agreed that Whorton's exclusive, full-time occupation was to be Dillingham's chauffeur, bodyguard, social and business secretary, partner and counselor in real estate investments, and to appear on his behalf when requested. Whorton was to render labor, skills, and personal services for the benefit of Dillingham's business and investment endeavors. Additionally, Whorton was to be Dillingham's constant companion, confidant, traveling and social companion, and lover, to terminate his schooling upon obtaining his Associate in Arts degree, and to make no investment without first consulting Dillingham.

In consideration of Whorton's promises, Dillingham was to give him a one-half equity interest in all real estate acquired in their joint names, and in all property thereafter acquired by Dillingham. Dillingham agreed to financially support Whorton for life, and to open bank accounts, maintain a positive balance in those accounts, grant Whorton invasionary powers to savings accounts held in Dillingham's name, and permit Whorton to charge on Dillingham's personal accounts. Dillingham was also to engage in a homosexual relationship with Whorton. Importantly, for the purpose of our analysis, the parties specifically agreed that any portion of the agreement found to be legally unenforceable was severable and the balance of the provisions would remain in full force and effect.

Whorton allegedly complied with all terms of the oral agreement until 1984 when Dillingham barred him from his premises. Dillingham now refuses to perform his part of the contract by giving Whorton the promised consideration for the business services rendered.

Adults who voluntarily live together and engage in sexual relations are competent to contract respecting their earnings and property rights. Such contracts will be enforced "unless expressly and inseparably based upon an illicit consideration of sexual services. . . ." (Marvin v. Marvin). . . .

The holding in *Marvin* suggests the court determined that the contract before it did not *expressly* include sexual services as part of the consideration, and thus, it did not need to reach the issue of whether there were severable portions of the contract supported by independent consideration. The only reference to sexual services in *Marvin*'s alleged facts was that the parties agreed to hold themselves out to the public as husband and wife, which apparently the court did not interpret as expressly indicating sexual services were part of the consideration. . . .

Unlike the facts of *Marvin*, here the parties' sexual relationship was an express, rather than implied, part of the consideration for their contract. The contract cannot be enforced to the extent it is dependent on sexual services for consideration, and the complaint does not state a cause of action to the extent it asks for damages from the termination of the sexual relationship.

The issue here is whether the sexual component of the consideration is severable from the remaining portions of the contract.[58] . . .

Thus, the crux of our analysis is whether Whorton's complaint negates as a matter of law, a trier of fact finding he made contributions, apart from sexual services, which provided independent consideration for Dillingham's alleged promises pertaining to financial support and property rights. The services which plaintiff alleges he agreed to and did provide included being a chauffeur, bodyguard, secretary, and partner and counselor in real estate investments. If provided, these services are of monetary value, and the type for which one would expect to be compensated unless there is evidence of a contrary intent. Thus, they are properly characterized as consideration independent of the sexual aspect of the relationship. By way of comparison, such services as being a constant companion and confidant are not the type which are usually monetarily compensated nor considered to have a "value" for purposes of contract consideration, and, absent peculiar circumstances, would likely be considered so intertwined with the sexual relationship as to be inseparable. . . .

We hold that Whorton—based on allegations he provided Dillingham with services of a chauffeur, bodyguard, secretary, and business partner—has stated a cause of action arising from a contract supported by consideration independent of sexual services. Further, by itemizing the mutual promises to engage in sexual activity, Whorton has not precluded the trier of fact from finding those promises are the consideration for each other and independent of the bargained for consideration for Whorton's employment.

We believe our holding does not conflict with that in *Jones v. Daly* . . . .

Jones is factually different in that the complaining party did not allege contracting to provide services apart from those normally incident to the state of cohabitation itself. Further, Jones's complaint stated the agreement was premised on that they "would hold themselves out to the public at large as cohabiting mates. . . ." In contrast, Whorton's complaint separately itemizes services contracted for as companion, chauffeur, bodyguard, secretary, partner and business counselor. These, except for companion, are significantly different than those household duties normally attendant to non-business cohabitation and are those for which monetary compensation ordinarily would be anticipated. Accepting Whorton's allegations as true, we cannot say as a matter of law any illegal portion of the contract is not severable so as to leave the balance valid and enforceable, especially where

---

58. Dillingham does not assert *Marvin* is inapplicable to same-sex partners, and we see no legal basis to make a distinction.

it is alleged the parties contemplated such a result when entering into their agreement. . . .

The judgment is reversed.

WIENER, J. and BENKE, J., concur.

———

EXTERNAL REFERENCES. Writings on the topic of the legal rights of unmarried cohabitors are legion. Here are references to a few of them. M. Freeman, Cohabitation: An Alternative to Marriage? (1983); M. Glendon, The Transformation of Family Law ch. 6 (1989); D. Rhode, Justice and Gender 134-41 (1989); Breech, Cohabitation in the Common Law Countries a Decade After *Marvin*: Settled in or Moving Ahead?, 22 U. C. Davis L. Rev. 717 (1989); Casad, Unmarried Couples and Unjust Enrichment: From Status to Contract and Back Again?, 77 Mich. L. Rev. 47 (1978); Folberg & Buren, Domestic Partnership: A Proposal for Dividing the Property of Unmarried Families, 12 Willamette L. Rev. 453 (1976); Krause, Legal Position: Unmarried Couples, 34 Am. J. Comp. L. 533 (Supp. 1986); Lovas, When Is a Family Not a Family? Inheritance and the Taxation of Inheritance Within the Non-traditional Family, 24 Idaho L. Rev. 353 (1987); Prager, Sharing Principles and the Future of Marital Property Law, 25 UCLA L. Rev. 1 (1977); Schwarzschild, Same-Sex Marriage and Constitutional Privacy: Moral Threat and Legal Anomaly, 4 Berkeley Women's L.J. 94 (1988-89); Treuthart, Adopting a More Realistic Definition of "Family," 26 Gonzaga L. Rev. 91 (1990/91); Note, The Necessity for State Recognition of Same-Sex Marriage: Constitutional Requirements and Evolving Notions of Family, 3 Berkeley Women's L.J. 134 (1987-1988); Developments Note, Sexual Orientation and the Law, 102 Harv. L. Rev. 1508 (1989); Note, Marital Status Classifications: Protecting Homosexual and Heterosexual Cohabitors, 14 Hastings Const. L.Q. 111 (1986); Annots., 3 A.L.R.4th 13 (1981); 94 A.L.R.3d 552 (1979); 93 A.L.R.3d 420 (1979); 81 A.L.R.3d 110 (1977); 81 A.L.R.3d 6 (1977).

PART E. WHO IS A "DESCENDANT"?

Finding a satisfactory meaning of the term "descendant" is surprisingly vexing. The question of who qualifies as a descendant is treated as a status question in the sense that the inheritance rights of the decedent's descendants are linked to the identification of a legally recognized parent-child relationship: A decedent's grandchild *is* a grandchild because a legally recognized parent-child relationship exists between the decedent and a parent of the grandchild.

This Part examines the circumstances under which the law does or should recognize a parent-child relationship. The question not only arises for purposes of intestate succession, but also for purposes of construing language in wills, trust instruments, life-insurance policies, and similar documents making gifts to classes such as "children," "descendants," or "issue."

1. Intestate Succession

Statutory References: *1990 UPC §§ 1-201(5), 2-107, -113, -114*
Pre-1990 UPC §§ 2-107, -109, -114

a. Adopted Children/Stepchildren/Foster Children

Intestate Succession By, From, and Through Adopted Children. Formal adoption as a social institution has undergone substantial change within the past half century. Unknown to the English common law, which exhibited a strong preoccupation with blood ties,[59] adoption is now a widely practiced method for creating familial relationships. By one count, 51,157 American children and 10,019 children from other countries were adopted in the United States in 1986, the latest year for which figures were available. N.Y. Times, March 3, 1991, at B1. Legal reaction to this social phenomenon, however, has been far from uniform. In all states, either by statute or decision, adopted children inherit from their adoptive parents. There is less agreement, however, on inheritance by adopted children from their biological parents and from ancestors and collateral relatives of their biological and adoptive parents. What policy concerns are influencing the legislatures when they decide these issues? If a statute is silent on such issues, how should courts construe it? The case of Estates of Donnelly, which follows, raises these questions. For a discussion of these matters, see Rein, Relatives by Blood, Adoption, and Association: Who Should Get What and Why, 37 Vand. L. Rev. 711 (1984).

UPC section 2-114(b) (1990) and most non-UPC statutes treat an adopted person as a child of her or his adoptive parents for all inheritance purposes. In other words, they abrogate the common law's "stranger-to-the-adoption" rule and allow not only a child to inherit from but also through the adoptive parent and allow adoptive family members to inherit from and through the adopted child. A more difficult problem is, to what extent should or does an adopted child retain inheritance rights from her or his biological family.

---

59. A second reason is that alternative methods of child placement, such as apprenticeship, lessened the need for formal adoption.

The English aversion to adoption was initially transplanted to the American colonies, but diminished availability of alternatives produced a more favorable climate for legal recognition of adoption in the mid-nineteenth century. Following enactment of the first adoption acts between 1849 and 1850, the remaining states quickly authorized adoption, either by statute or judicial ruling. See M. Grossberg, Governing the Hearth, supra p. 105, at 268-80.

Estates of Donnelly
81 Wash. 2d 430, 502 P.2d 1163 (1973)

NEILL, J. May an adopted child inherit from her natural grandparents? Both the trial court and the Court of Appeals . . . answered "yes." We granted review . . . and disagree. In speaking of heirs and inheritance, we refer to the devolution of property by law in intestacy and not by testamentary or other voluntary disposition.

John J. and Lily Donnelly, husband and wife, had two children, a daughter, Kathleen M., now Kathleen M. Kelly, and a son, John J., Jr. The son had one child, Jean Louise Donnelly, born October 28, 1945. Jean Louise's father, John J. Donnelly, Jr., died on July 9, 1946, less than a year after her birth. Her mother, Faith Louise Donnelly, married Richard Roger Hansen on April 22, 1948. By a decree entered August 11, 1948, Jean Louise was adopted by her step-father with the written consent of her natural mother. She lived with her mother and adoptive father as their child and kept the name Hansen until her marriage to Donald J. Iverson. . . .

Lily Donnelly, the grandmother, died October 7, 1964, leaving a will in which she named but left nothing to her two children. All of her property she left to her husband . . . .

John J. Donnelly, Sr., the grandfather, died September 15, 1970, leaving a will dated October 16, 1932, in which he left his entire estate to his wife, Lily, who had predeceased him. He, too, named but left nothing to his two children, and made no provision for disposition of his property in event his wife predeceased him. His daughter, Kathleen M. Kelly, as administratrix with wills annexed of the estates of her parents, brought this petition to determine heirship and for a declaration that Jean Louise Iverson, the granddaughter, take nothing and that she, Kathleen M. Kelly, the daughter, be adjudged the sole heir of her mother and father, Lily and John J. Donnelly, Sr., to the exclusion of Jean Louise Iverson, her niece and their granddaughter.

The trial court decided that each was an heir. It concluded that Jean Louise Iverson, daughter of John J. Donnelly, Jr., and granddaughter of his father, John J. Donnelly, Sr., should inherit one-half of the latter's estate and that Kathleen M. Kelly, daughter of John J. Donnelly, Sr., should inherit the other half of the estate.

Kathleen M. Kelly, the daughter of decedent, appealed to the Court of Appeals which affirmed, and now to this court. With the issue recognized to be close and of general importance, we granted review . . . .

As the trial court in its memorandum opinion and the Court of Appeals noted, the issue is whether RCW 11.04.085, which says that an adopted child shall not be deemed an heir of his natural parents, cuts off the inheritance from the natural grandparents as well. The Court of Appeals put the question precisely . . . :

> In Washington, may a natural granddaughter inherit from her intestate grandparents, notwithstanding her adoption by her stepfather after the death of her natural father, the son of the decedent grandparents?

The sole beneficiary under his will having predeceased him, John J. Donnelly, Sr., died intestate. His estate would thus pass by the statutes governing intestacy according to RCW 11.04-.015, which says:

> The net estate of a person dying intestate . . . shall be distributed as follows: . . . .
>
> (2) . . . the entire net estate if there is no surviving spouse, shall descend and be distributed . . .
>
> (a) To the *issue* of the intestate; if they are all in the same degree of kinship to the intestate, they shall take equally, or if of unequal degree, then those of more remote degree shall take by representation.

(Italics ours.)

Issue "includes all the lawful lineal descendants of the ancestor." RCW 11.02.005(4). A descendant is one "who is descended from another; a person who proceeds from the body of another, such as a child, grandchild." Black's Law Dictionary 530 (Rev. 4th ed. 1968). Thus, both the daughter and granddaughter are descendants and issue of John J. Donnelly, Sr. The daughter under the descent and distribution statutes would take as the most immediate descendant, and the granddaughter being of more remote degree would take by representation as the sole issue of her deceased father who stood in the same degree of kinship to John J. Donnelly, Sr., as did Kathleen M. Kelly. RCW 11.04.015.

RCW 11.02.005(3) states:

> [E]ach share of a deceased person in the nearest degree shall be divided among those of his issue who survive the intestate and have no ancestor then living who is in the line of relationship between them and the intestate, those more remote in degree taking together the share which their ancestor would have taken had he survived the intestate.

Thus, a statutory right to inherit one-half of the grandfather's estate is vested in Jean Louise Iverson, the granddaughter, unless that right is divested by operation of RCW 11.04.085, which declares that an adopted child is not to be considered an heir of his natural parents:

> A lawfully adopted child shall not be considered an "heir" of his natural parents for purposes of this title.

When the question of the right of an adopted child to inherit from his natural parents came before us, the intent of the legislature was clear from the literal language of the statute. We held that RCW 11.04.085 prevents an adopted child from taking a share of the natural parent's estate by intestate succession. However, reference to the literal language of RCW 11.04.085 does not answer the instant question, *i.e.*, whether, by declaring that an adopted child shall not take from his natural parent, the legislature also intended to remove the adopted child's capacity to represent the natural parent and thereby take from the natural grandparent.

The purpose of statutory interpretation is to ascertain and give effect to the intent of the legislature. To decide whether RCW 11.04.085 also severs the right of the adopted child to inherit from a remote ancestor, we must first determine why the legislature terminated the rights of inheritance with respect to the natural parent. In so doing, we should be guided by the established principle of statutory interpretation which requires that:

> In placing a judicial construction upon a legislative enactment, the entire sequence of all statutes relating to the same subject matter should be considered.

Connick v. Chehalis, 53 Wash.2d 288, 290, 333 P.2d 647, 649 (1958).

The legislature has addressed itself to the inheritance rights of adopted children in both the probate and domestic relations titles of RCW . . . . For example, RCW 26.32.140 also directly affects the inheritance rights of an adopted child:

> By a decree of adoption the natural parents shall be divested of all legal rights and obligations in respect to the child, and *the child* shall be free from all legal obligations of obedience and maintenance in respect to them, and *shall be* to all intents and purposes, and for all legal incidents, *the child, legal heir, and lawful issue of his or her adopter or adopters, entitled to all rights and privileges, including the right of inheritance* and the right to take under testamentary disposition, and subject to all the obligations of a child of the adopter or adopters begotten in lawful wedlock.

(Italics ours.)

Since RCW 11.04.085 and RCW 26.32.140 each delimit the inheritance rights of an adopted child, the two statutes must be read in pari materia . . . .

It is clear that: (1) the adopted child cannot take from his natural parent because he is no longer an "heir" (RCW 11.04.085); and, (2) the adopted child enjoys complete inheritance rights from the adoptive parent, as if he were the natural child of the adoptive parent (RCW 26.32.140). Both statutes are in harmony with the fundamental spirit of our adoption laws—*i.e.*, that for all purposes the adopted child shall be treated as a "child of the adopter . . . begotten in lawful wedlock."

Legislative intent is to be ascertained from the statutory text as a whole, interpreted in terms of the general object and purpose of the legislation.

The question at bench should, therefore, be decided in the context of the broad legislative objective of giving the adopted child a "fresh start" by treating him as the natural child of the adoptive parent, and severing all ties with the past. We believe it clearly follows that the legislature intended to remove an adopted child from his natural bloodline for purposes of intestate succession.

The trial court and Court of Appeals, however, held that although an adopted child may not take *from* a natural parent dying intestate, the same child may take *through* the natural parent, by representation, if the natural parent dies before the natural grandparent. Little supportive reasoning is offered for this inconsistent result. In reaching its conclusion, the Court of Appeals reasoned that consanguineal ties are so fundamental that an explicit expression of legislative intent is required to deprive an adopted child of the bounty which would normally be his by reason of the "intuitive impulses" generated by the blood relationship. The Court of Appeals reasoned that had the legislature desired to remove an adopted child from its natural bloodline, it could have used the word "kin" in place of the word "parents" in RCW 11.04.085. Thus, since RCW 11.04.085 does not specify that an adopted child may not take from an intestate natural grandparent, this capacity is not lost.

However, where the literal interpretation of a particular word is repugnant to the intent of the legislature plainly manifested by the legislation taken as a whole, such interpretation ought not to prevail. . . .

Obviously, the legislature did *not* consider consanguinity to be of controlling importance where the blood relationship must be presumted [sic] to be strongest—the natural parent. Moreover, RCW 26.32.140 provides that an adopter and his kin shall inherit from an adopted child to the exclusion of the child's natural parents or kin. Thus, if respondent here had predeceased her natural grandfather, he would not have been permitted to inherit from his natural grandchild, any "intuitive impulses" of kinship notwithstanding. And, if consanguinity had *in fact* moved the grandparent to provide for respondent here, he could easily have done so by will.

The legislative policy of providing a "clean slate" to the adopted child permeates our scheme of adoption. The natural grandparents are not entitled to notice of any hearing on the matter of adoption. RCW 26.32.080. RCW 26.32.150 provides that, unless otherwise requested by the adopted, all records of the adoption proceeding shall be sealed and not open to inspection. Pursuant to RCW 26.32.120, a decree for adoption shall provide: (1) for the issuance of a certificate of birth for the adopted child, containing such information as the court may deem proper; and (2) that the records of the registrar shall be secret. RCW 70.58.210 declares that the new birth certificate shall bear the new name of the child and the names of the adoptive parents of the child, but shall make no reference to the adoption of the child. Thus, the natural grandparents have no assurance that they will know the new name or residence of the adopted child. Indeed, in the usual "out of family" adoption situation the administrator of a deceased natural grandparent's estate will be unable to locate—much less to identify—the post-adoption grandchild.

The consistent theme of the relevant legislation is that the new family of the adopted child is to be treated as his natural family. The only conclusion consistent with the spirit of our overlapping adoption and inheritance statutes is that RCW 11.04.085 was intended to transfer all rights of inheritance out of the natural family upon adoption and place them entirely within the adopted family.

Respondent suggests it is most probable that the legislature never considered the problem of inheritance by adopted persons from their remote natural kin when it passed RCW 11.04.085. Thus, respondent contends that the word "parents" should be strictly construed. We disagree.

> On numerous occasions this court has indicated that a statute should be construed as a whole in order to ascertain legislative purpose, and thus avoid unlikely, strained or absurd consequences which could result from a literal reading. That the spirit or the purpose of legislation should prevail over the express but inept language is an ancient adage of the law.

Alderwood Water Dist. v. Pope & Talbot, 62 Wash.2d 319, 321, 382 P.2d 639, 641 (1963).

As we stated in State ex rel. Spokane United Rys. v. Department of Pub. Serv., 191 Wash. 595, 598, 71 P.2d 661, 663 (1937):

> The rule that the expression of one thing will, under certain circumstances, exclude others, should be applied as a means of discovering the legislative intent, and its application should not be permitted to defeat the plainly indicated purpose of the legislature. [Citations omitted.]
>
> In determining the legislative intent, the purpose for which a law was enacted is a matter of prime importance in arriving at a correct interpretation of its parts, and "A thing which is within the object, spirit and the meaning of the statute is as much within the statute as if it were within the letter.'" 2 Lewis' Sutherland Statutory Construction (2d ed.), §§ 369 and 379.

The broad legislative purpose underlying our statutes relating to adopted children is consistent only with the inference that RCW 11.04.085 was intended to remove respondent, an adopted child, from her natural bloodline for inheritance purposes. If the adopted child cannot take from her natural father, she should not represent him and take from his father.

The chain of inheritance was broken by respondent's adoption. Reversed.

HAMILTON, C.J., and STAFFORD, WRIGHT and UTTER, JJ., concur.

[The dissenting opinion of HALE, J., in which FINLEY, HUNTER, and ROSELLINI, JJ., concur, is omitted.]

Notes and Questions

1. *Uniform Probate Code.* Both the pre-1990 and 1990 versions of the UPC adopt the general principle of the Washington statute in *Donnelly* and place adopted persons exclusively in their adopting families for inheritance purposes. 1990 UPC § 2-114; pre-1990 UPC § 2-109. Both versions, however, anticipated cases like *Donnelly* by providing an exception for stepparent adoptions. Thus, Jean not only would have inherited half of her biological grandfather's estate had *Donnelly* been governed by the UPC, but would not have been forced to litigate to gain her inheritance. Can you think of any other circumstances in which you would argue that adopted persons should continue to be treated for inheritance purposes as members of their biological families? Should the exception of section 2-114(b) be extended to adoptions by any relative of a decedent's spouse? Or, is the

exception too inclusive as it is? A more restrictive Florida statute, for example, states:

> *Fla. Stat. Ann. § 732.108(1)(b).* Adoption of a child by a natural parent's spouse who married the natural parent after the death of the other natural parent has no effect on the relationship between the child and the family of the deceased natural parent.

Is any exception for stepparent adoptions justified? Suppose that Faith and Richard, in *Donnelly,* had had children of their own. Would Jean's half siblings be jealous of Jean's inheritance from her biological grandfather, John, precipitating disharmony within the family? Would such jealousy only arise or at least be more intense if John had died while Jean and her half-siblings were still living in Faith and Richard's household?

If a biological relative adopts a person, a question arises about whether the adopted person can inherit both as a biological relative and as an adoptive relative. For example, a daughter's widowed father might marry her maternal aunt, who then adopts her. Under UPC section 2-114(b) (1990), the daughter is a child of her predeceased mother as well as a child of her adoptive mother/biological aunt for inheritance purposes. If her grandmother dies intestate, can the adopted child inherit a share by representation through her biological mother? If the adoptive mother/biological aunt predeceases the child's grandmother, can the child inherit a share by representation of her biological mother as well as by representation of her adoptive mother? See UPC § 2-113 (1990).

2. *Statutory Interpretation in Donnelly.* Does *Donnelly* mean that Jean is not an heir of her mother or her mother's parents? In the case of a stepparent adoption, the practice in some states is for both the stepparent and the custodial biological parent to be listed as adopting parents on the adoption papers.

What legislative policy did the Court of Appeals of Washington rely on to find that the statutory language that "[a] lawfully adopted child shall not be considered an 'heir' of his natural parents for purposes of this title" did not preclude an adopted child from inheriting from her biological grandfather? What legislative policy did the Supreme Court of Washington rely on to find that the same statutory language precluded an adopted child from inheriting from her grandfather? Is one approach to interpreting the statute more "correct" than the other? What facts in this case are treated as irrelevant by both these approaches? Neither the lower courts nor the supreme court considered the argument that a child's status as an heir of a parent and that parent's family should be determined at the parent's death and that a subsequent adoption does not affect that determination. Would such an interpretation be consistent with the "clean slate" legislative policy of adoption that concerned the supreme court? If you had been hired to represent Jean, would you have made or emphasized different arguments than her attorneys apparently did? If you had been Jean's attorney, what further facts would you have tried to prove at the trial level?

3. *Individuated Donative Intent?* Do you think the court furthered John's donative intent in *Donnelly*? Why or why not? What motivated Kathleen to

oppose Jean's inheritance, not only initially but by appealing the decision of the Court of Appeals? Greed? Or a belief that Jean was undeserving? Is individuated intent a relevant factor in interpreting and applying an intestacy statute? To be sure, intestacy statutes establish default rules, but the default rules apply unless the decedent has expressed a contrary intent in a validly executed will, the heirs voluntarily agree to a rearrangement, or an heir disclaims.

Do you think that Faith and Richard Hansen or Lily and John Donnelly thought about the inheritance consequences of the adoption? Did the attorney handling the adoption have a duty to inform the family of these consequences? If so, would that duty extend to Lily and John?

4. *Stepparent Adoptions.* We know very little about residential stepparent adoptions. The facts of *Donnelly* are quite unusual in that Faith was a young widow rather than a divorcee when she married Richard. Are stepparents more likely to adopt their stepchildren in post-death than in post-divorce marriages? Recall Professor MacKinnon's claim that monogamous marriage is a means by which a man can identify with a child for purposes of extending his personality beyond death. See Note 4, supra p. 62. Is this why Richard adopted Jean? Here is what one writer has discovered about the information available (or not available) about residential stepparent relationships and adoptions in post-divorce cases:

> In cases in which the biologic parents have been divorced (in contrast to cases in which one of the biologic parents has died), the course of the stepparent-child relationship is especially difficult to predict because of the very existence of the nonresidential parent and the variations in the frequency and quality of the visits between the child and the nonresidential parent. Indeed, the range of family compositions in the lives of children one or both of whose parents remarry is vast. . . .
>
> State law has had only one mechanism—adoption—to permit a stepparent married to the custodial parent to formalize a role with a child. . . .
>
> Adoptions by stepparents today typically occur, as they always have, with the explicit consent or acquiescence of the parent who is about to be replaced. Laws that once permitted adoption to occur only when there was such consent (or acquiescence or deliberate "abandonment") have now, however, commonly been expanded to permit courts to approve adoptions by stepparents in a wider range of cases, including some in which the noncustodial biologic parent strenuously objects to the adoption. . . .
>
> Almost no information is available about actual patterns of stepparent adoption in this country or about the impact of adoption on the relationships between stepparents and children. For those interested in people's own conception of family and how they use laws to validate those conceptions, distressingly little is known about what stepparents and custodial parents consider when deciding whether to seek adoption[60] or about what biologic

---

60. In a later footnote, footnote 63, the author cited an interview-based study of 55 stepparent adoption cases in a prosperous Pennsylvania county. The study revealed that "the most frequently stated single reason given by the mother and adopting stepfather for wanting the adoption was to permit a name change. The largest grouping of children being adopted were between five and seven, which the authors read as consistent with the desires of many adopters to 'have the child's name changed prior to school enrollment.' Providing access to

parents consider when deciding whether to consent. What we are able to calculate is that only a small percentage of stepparents actually adopt their stepchildren, despite the fact that the high proportion of children of divorce who never see or receive support from their noncustodial parent suggests that the number of stepparents eligible to adopt, even over the absent biologic parent's objection, must be very large. We know nothing about what distinguishes the families in which adoption occurs from the families in which it does not. We do not even know whether stepparent adoptions are increasing in frequency. Because of the more generous standards for stepparent adoption and a supportive atmosphere today for stepparent involvement in children's lives, we could guess that more are occurring. On the other hand, as child support enforcement against absent fathers has become more effective in some states, more custodial parents may wish to hold onto this source of income.

Just as we know little of the incidence of or motivations for stepparent adoption in the United States, so likewise we know almost nothing about the effects of such adoption on children. No researcher has ever compared children who were adopted in order to learn whether adoption affects children's sense of well-being or even clarifies roles within families.

Chambers, Stepparents, Biologic Parents and the Law's Perception of "Family" after Divorce, in Divorce Reform at the Crossroads 102, 104-05, 108, 118-19 (S. Sugarman & H. Kay eds. 1990) (footnotes omitted).

———

Stepchildren and Foster Children. Unless adopted, stepchildren usually are not entitled to inherit from their stepparents or the stepparents' ancestors and collateral relatives. Foster children are not entitled to inherit from members of their foster families. See UPC § 1-201(5) (1990).

In California, a recent breakthrough has occurred. Under the California Probate Code section 6408(e), a stepchild or foster child (and her or his descendants) is entitled to inherit from and through her or his stepparent or foster parent if "the relationship of parent and child" began "during the person's minority and continued throughout the parties' joint lifetimes" and if "it is established by clear and convincing evidence that the foster parent or stepparent would have adopted the person but for a legal barrier." See Estate of Lind, 209 Cal. App. 3d 1424, 257 Cal. Rptr. 853 (1989) (interpreting the statutory phrase "but for a legal barrier"). See also Mahoney, Stepfamilies in the Law of Intestate Succession and Wills, 22 U.C. Davis L. Rev. 917 (1989) (proposing that inheritance be permitted among stepfamily members when certain conditions are met).

———

benefits and insurance was another, occasionally stated reason." Wolf & Mast, Counselling Issues in Adoptions by Stepparents, 32 Social Work 69 (1987). Eds.

Problems

A and B were married and had two children, X and Y. A and B got divorced and B was awarded custody of X and Y. B married C. A married D. B and C had a child, Z. A and D had a child, V.

1. C died intestate, survived by A, B, D, V, X, Y, and Z. Under UPC sections 2-102, -103, and -114 (1990), who are C's heirs and what shares do they take?

2. X died intestate, survived by V, Y, and Z. A, B, C, and D predeceased X. Under UPC sections 2-103 and -107 (1990), who are X's heirs?

3. How, if at all, would your answer in Problem 1 differ if C had adopted X and Y?

———

"Equitable Adoption" of Foster Children. Foster children who have not been formally or legally adopted by their foster parents may nevertheless obtain inheritance rights under a doctrine called "equitable adoption." Courts also refer to this doctrine as "virtual adoption," "de facto adoption," or "adoption by estoppel." Courts in over half the states have recognized such a doctrine, but courts in at least eight states have rejected it. The strongest factual situation presented for applying the doctrine is when the foster parents had expressly contracted to adopt the child, but failed to complete the adoption procedures. Even if the child cannot prove an express contract, however, courts have implied a contract under certain circumstances.

A recent departure from the traditional requirement of either an express or implied contract to adopt was made by the Supreme Court of Appeals in West Virginia. In Wheeler Dollar Savings & Trust Company v. Singer, 250 S.E.2d 369, 373-74 (W. Va. 1978), the court said:

> While the existence of an express contract of adoption is very convincing evidence, an implied contract of adoption is an unnecessary fiction created by courts as a protection from fraudulent claims. We find that if a claimant can, by clear, cogent and convincing evidence, prove sufficient facts to convince the trier of fact that his status is identical to that of a formally adopted child, except only for the absence of a formal order of adoption, a finding of an equitable adoption is proper without proof of an adoption contract.

Circumstances that would satisfy this test were described by the court as follows:

> The equitably adopted child in any private property dispute such as the case under consideration involving the laws of *inheritance* or *private trusts* must prove by clear, cogent and convincing evidence that he has stood from an age of tender years in a position *exactly* equivalent to a formally adopted child. Circumstances which tend to show the existence of an equitable adoption include: the benefits of love and affection accruing to the adopting party; the performances of services by the child; the surrender of ties by the natural parent; the society, companionship and filial obedience of the child; an invalid or ineffectual adoption proceeding; reliance by the adopted person upon the

existence of his adoptive status; the representation to all the world that the child is a natural or adopted child; and the rearing of the child from an age of tender years by the adopting parents. . . . Of course, evidence can be presented which tends to negate an equitable adoption such as failure of the child to perform the duties of an adopted child, or misconduct of the child or abandonment of the adoptive parents; however, mere mischievous behavior usually associated with being a child is not sufficient to disprove an equitable adoption.

b. Children of Parents Not Married to Each Other

The Evolving Legal Status of Nonmarital Children. Historically, the common law labelled nonmarital children as "filius nullius"—the child of no one. These children formally lacked the right to inherit from or through either parent. The law in practice was more complicated, however. Church courts and, later, common-law courts, enforced a father's duty to support his children born out of wedlock, indicating some willingness to recognize the parent-child relationship between nonmarital children and their natural parents. See Helmholz, Support Orders, Church Courts, and the Rule of Filius Nullius: A Reassessment of the Common Law, 63 Va. L. Rev. 431 (1977).

Inheritance Rights of Nonmarital Children. Insofar as the UPC is concerned, the law has come full circle. The general principle of the 1990 Uniform Probate Code is that an individual inherits from and through her or his biological parents regardless of their marital status. UPC § 2-114(a) (1990).

As for non-UPC law, the statutes uniformly entitle nonmarital children to inherit from their mothers, but differences exist concerning the children's right to inherit from their fathers. Ostensibly, because of the then-greater difficulty of proving paternity than maternity, pre-1977 statutes in many states allowed nonmarital children to inherit from their fathers only if the father had married the child's biological mother and acknowledged or recognized the child. In 1977, the United States Supreme Court in Trimble v. Gordon, 430 U.S. 762 (1977), held this type of statute to be an unconstitutional denial of equal protection. The Illinois statute provided:

An illegitimate[61] child is heir of his mother and of any maternal ancestor, and of any person from whom his mother might have inherited, if living; and the lawful issue of an illegitimate person shall represent such person and take, by

---

61. Regarding this vocabulary, consider the following observation:

[T]he court wishes to express criticism of the use of the word "illegitimate" as applied to children. Not only is this term, when used in connection with children, repugnant to this court but its use in any local law, ordinance or resolution or in any public or judicial proceeding or in any process, notice, order, decree, judgment, record, public document or paper, is a violation of law (*see* General Construction Law, sec. 59). Despite this fact Judges, legal writers and others continuously use that term when writing about children born out of wedlock.

Estate of Leventritt, 92 Misc. 2d 598, 599, 400 N.Y.S.2d 298, 299 (Sur. Ct. 1977). Eds.

descent, any estate which the parent would have taken, if living. A child who was illegitimate whose parents inter-marry and who is acknowledged by the father as the father's child is legitimate.

The state argued that the statute served its interest of promoting family relationships, assuring accurate and efficient disposition of property at death, and mirroring the presumed intentions of its citizens. The Supreme Court held that none of the state's interests justified the statutory discrimination against nonmarital children. It held that the state cannot influence the conduct of parents by burdening their child. It refused to address "the question whether presumed intent alone can ever justify discrimination against nonmarital children," because it did not believe that the state enacted the statute for that purpose. The Supreme Court acknowledged that problems of proving paternity might justify a more demanding standard for nonmarital children to claim under their fathers' estates than that required for them to claim under their mothers' estates or than that required for marital children generally. It held, however, that this concern did not warrant "the total statutory disinheritance of illegitimate children whose fathers die intestate."[62]

The Supreme Court revisited the questions of proof and expeditious handling of estates in Lalli v. Lalli, 439 U.S. 259 (1978), in which it considered New York's legislative approach for assuring an accurate and efficient probate process. The statute provided:

> An illegitimate child is the legitimate child of his father so that he and his issue inherit from his father if a court of competent jurisdiction has, during the lifetime of the father, made an order of filiation declaring paternity in a proceeding instituted during the pregnancy of the mother or within two years from the birth of the child.

The decedent's son, Robert Lalli, contended that requiring an order of filiation during the father's lifetime discriminated against him on the basis of his nonmarital-child status in violation of the Equal Protection Clause of the Fourteenth Amendment. The evidence showed that the father had acknowledged his paternity in a notarized document and that he had acknowledged openly and frequently that Robert Lalli was his son. Additionally, the evidence showed that the decedent had provided support to his son, vitiating the need to bring the paternity action that the statute contemplated. The Court concluded that the paternity adjudication requirement was tied to the state interest in an orderly process for wealth succession and found that the statute did not violate the Equal Protection Clause.

Following Lalli, the New York legislature amended the statute so that it now provides in part:

---

62. In Reed v. Campbell, 476 U.S. 852 (1986), the Court gave its decision in *Trimble* retroactive effect where at the time of the child's claim the statute barring inheritance had been declared unconstitutional and the father's estate was still open.

N.Y. Est. Powers & Trusts Law § 4-1.2. Inheritance by or from born out of wedlock persons . . . .

(2) A child born out of wedlock is the legitimate child of his father so that he and his issue inherit from his father and his paternal kindred if:

(A) a court of competent jurisdiction has, during the lifetime of the father, made an order of filiation declaring paternity or;

(B) the father of the child has signed an instrument acknowledging paternity, provided that

(i) such instrument is acknowledged or executed or proved in the form required to entitle a deed to be recorded in the presence of one or more witnesses and acknowledged by such witness or witnesses, in either case, before a notary public or other officer authorized to take proof of deeds and

(ii) such instrument is filed within sixty days from the making thereof with the putative father registry established by the state department of social services . . . or;

(C) paternity has been established by clear and convincing evidence and the father of the child has openly and notoriously acknowledged the child as his own; or

(D) a blood genetic marker test had been administered to the father which together with other evidence establishes paternity by clear and convincing evidence.

(3) The existence of an agreement obligating the father to support the child born out of wedlock does not qualify such child or his issue to inherit from the father in the absence of an order of filiation made or acknowledgment of paternity as prescribed by subparagraph (2). . . .

Who Inherits From Nonmarital Children? The current New York statute not only applies to inheritance rights of nonmarital children but also to inheritance rights from them. The latter context gave rise to a case interpreting the meaning of the phrase "open and notorious acknowledgment" for purposes of subsection (2)(C). The court in Estate of Campbell, N.Y.L.J., March 7, 1984, at 11, col. 2, stated that the father must "publish to the world that the child is [his]." Such publication, the court said, "can take the form of a paper trail of documents, oral declarations, or acts from which an acknowledgment can be logically inferred." A paper trail of documents might include income tax returns on which the father had claimed the child as a dependent, cancelled checks, purchases receipts, birthday cards, letters, or other written material.

In the *Campbell* case itself, the child (an eight-year-old girl) was the decedent; the purported father was claiming as an heir of the child, who was killed in an apartment fire and whose major estate asset was a possible cause of action against the owner of the building. The court discounted the purported father's payment of the child's funeral and cemetery plot as constituting an open and notorious acknowledgment because these actions occurred *after* the prospect of economic recovery had arisen.

Although UPC section 2-114(a) (1990) facilitates inheritance by a nonmarital child merely on proof of parentage, section 2-114(c) precludes a biological mother or father, or the kindred of either, from inheriting from her or his marital or nonmarital child unless the parent "has openly treated the child as his [or hers], and has not refused to support the child." See

Estate of Ford, 552 S.2d 1065 (Miss. 1989) (interpreting a statute similar to section 2-114(c)[63] and holding that a biological father's family was not entitled to inherit from a nonmarital child because the claimants failed to establish by preponderance of the evidence that the father openly recognized the decedent as his child and that the father did not refuse or neglect to support her.)

The Supreme Court of Iowa in Estate of Evjen, 448 N.W.2d 23 (Iowa 1989), was asked to consider the meaning of open and notorious acknowledgment in circumstances where the father died before the child was born. The Iowa statute provided that nonmarital children inherit from their fathers:

> if the evidence proving paternity is available during the father's lifetime, or if the child has been recognized by the father as his child; but the recognition must have been general and notorious, or in writing.

The decedent's estate did not contest paternity. It argued that the statute required that the father also recognize the child as his own. Even though the doctor did not perform a pregnancy test and confirm the pregnancy until after the decedent's death and even though the decedent was killed in an automobile accident a week after the child's mother told the decedent that she believed she was pregnant, the court held that the father had openly and notoriously recognized the child. During the week that the decedent knew of the probable pregnancy he told at least five people that the baby was his. The court held that this evidence was sufficient to find a recognition for the purpose of the inheritance statute. See also Prince v. Black, 256 Ga. 79, 344 S.E.2d 411 (1986) (held that under the doctrine of virtual or equitable legitimation a nonmarital child could inherit from his biological father; the father had tried to get his name on his son's birth certificate, paid all the hospital bills, and ultimately obtained custody of his son when he was six years old).

Proving Parentage. Inheritance under section 2-114(a) of the 1990 UPC depends upon proof of a parent and child relationship. This relationship may be established under the Uniform Parentage Act (1973) in the eighteen states that as of 1990 have enacted it. The Uniform Parentage Act authorizes actions to be brought by the child or any interested person to establish the identity of the child's biological mother or father. In proving paternity, blood tests can be required and the results along with all other relevant evidence are admissible. Unif. Parentage Act §§ 11, 12. The problem of proof is eased by provisions in the Parentage Act that list specified circumstances that give rise to a presumption of paternity; those specified circumstances include the alleged father having received the child into his home and having openly held the child out as his child. Id. § 4.

---

63. The Mississippi statute placed conditions only on a biological father's right to inherit from a nonmarital child. Pre-1990 UPC § 2-109 had a similar rule. The 1990 UPC neither distinguishes between biological mothers and fathers nor between marital and nonmarital children.

In Alexander v. Alexander, 42 Ohio Misc. 2d 30, 537 N.E.2d 1310 (1988), the court ordered disinterment of the decedent's body so that a DNA (deoxyribonucleic acid) test could be conducted to determine if he was the father of a child claiming heirship. In ordering the test, the court said:

> [T]he bottom line to denying an illegitimate child equal inheritance rights is that there is a substantial problem of proof of paternity, especially after the alleged father is dead. Today, however, we are entering into a new area. Science has developed a means to irrefutably prove the identity of an illegitimate child's father. No longer are we dependent upon fallible testimony, nor are we concerned that the decedent cannot be present to defend himself. The accuracy and infallibility of the DNA test are nothing short of remarkable. We live in a modern and scientific society, and the law must keep pace with these developments.

See also Annot., Admissibility of DNA Identification Evidence, 84 A.L.R.4th 313, 355-57 (1991) (reviewing basic genetic principles, different techniques of DNA testing, and decisional law on the admissibility of such tests in establishing parentage).

Presumption of Legitimacy and Paternity. A presumption is recognized at common law that a child born during marriage is legitimate, thus placing paternity of a child born to a married woman in the woman's husband. Although the presumption is rebuttable, it takes persuasive evidence to rebut it. See, e.g., Commonwealth v. Beausoleil, 397 Mass. 206, 490 N.E.2d 788 (1986)(results of HLA blood test admissible in paternity proceedings); Hanley v. Flanigan, 104 Misc. 2d 698, 428 N.Y.S.2d 865 (Sur. Ct. 1980); L.F.R. v. R.A.R., 269 Ind. 97, 378 N.E.2d 855 (1978); Ewell v. Ewell, 163 N.C. 233, 79 S.E. 509 (1913); Adoption of Young, 469 Pa. 141, 364 A.2d 1307 (1976); Unif. Parentage Act § 4 (1973); A.L.I., Model Code of Evidence, Rule 703 (1942); cf. 1 S. Schatkin, Disputed Paternity Proceedings § 1.02 (4th rev. ed. 1985); Annot., Parental Rights of Man Who Is Not Biological or Adoptive Father of Child but Was Husband or Cohabitant of Mother When Child was Conceived or Born, 84 A.L.R.4th 655 (1991).

A related presumption is that "a man who marries a woman while she is pregnant is presumed in law to be the father of the child . . . ." Romweber v. Martin, 30 Ohio St. 2d 25, 282 N.E.2d 36 (1972). But see Thompson, 49ers' Lott Agrees to Pay Temporary Child Support, S.F. Chron., June 16, 1990, at A5, col. 5. (Santa Clara County officials sued for paternity claims against Lott on the mother's behalf. The California Supreme Court refused to overturn a lower court's ruling that the rebuttable presumption that a mother's husband is the father applies only if the husband and wife were cohabiting at the time of conception. The mother married her husband four months before the child was born.).

Children Conceived by Means Other Than Sexual Intercourse. Medical technology allows for conception by means other than sexual intercourse. The medical profession uses three different artificial insemination procedures. Homologous insemination is the process by which the wife is artificially impregnated with the semen of her husband. This procedure is referred to as A.I.H., which stands for "artificial insemination husband." Children conceived by this method are, of course, the biological children of the husband and wife and raise no special legal issues.

Heterologous insemination, called "artificial insemination donor" or A.I.D., occurs when a woman is artificially impregnated with the semen of a third-party donor. "Combined (or confused) artificial insemination" or C.A.I. is the name of the process when the semen of the husband and of a third-party donor are mixed. C.A.I. is no longer a reputable procedure because it creates confusion about the child's genetic history.

Section 5 of the Uniform Parentage Act (1973) declares the husband of a wife who, with the husband's written consent, signed by him and his wife, was impregnated by either of these methods, not the third-party donor of the semen, to be "treated in law as if he were the natural father of a child thereby conceived." As of 1988, twenty-five states have enacted legislation identical or similar to the Uniform Parentage Act. See Restatement 2d of Property, Statutory Note to § 25.3. See McIntyre v. Crouch, 98 Or. App. 462, 780 P.2d 239 (1989), cert. denied, 495 U.S. 905 (1990) (upheld right of sperm donor to enjoy responsibilities of fatherhood based on the Constitution's guarantee of due process if he could prove birth mother had promised that he would be allowed to assist in the child's rearing).

In the absence of legislation, the husband of a married woman who has been inseminated artificially should be advised to adopt the child to clarify paternity. Care should be taken, however, to make sure that the state's adoption statute will not, upon adoption by the husband, operate to terminate the relationship between the child and mother.

Artificial-insemination technology has made it easier for lesbian couples to have children. Having been promulgated in 1973, before the advent of this practice, the Uniform Parentage Act understandably fails to address the question of the relationship between the child and the biological mother's partner. In the absence of legislation, the couples have attempted to use the adoption laws to create a legally recognized parent-child relationship between the child and the mother's partner. A few courts have allowed adoption in these cases. See, e.g., In re EBG, No. 87-5-137-5 (Wash. Sup. Ct. Mar. 15, 1989). The inadequacy of the law in this area is demonstrated most poignantly in recent reports of child custody disputes when the lesbian couples separate. See Alison D. v. Virginia M., 155 A.D.2d 11, 552 N.Y.S.2d 321 (1990) (denied visitation rights to biological mother's estranged domestic partner); Margolick, Lesbian Child-Custody Cases Test Frontiers of Family Law, N.Y. Times, July 4, 1990, at A1. See also Polikoff, This Child Does Have Two Mothers: Redefining Parenthood to Meet the Needs of Children in Lesbian-Mother and Other Nontraditional Families, 78 Geo. L.J. 459 (1990). Recent drafts of a revision to the Uniform Adoption Act suggest some progress is being made. They provide that any individual can adopt any other individual, except that one spouse cannot adopt the other spouse, and the adoption must be intended to create a parent-child relationship.

Artificial-insemination technology creates an array of other questions that currently remain unresolved or controversial in the law. For example: Should a woman be able to demand that she be impregnated with her husband's or partner's sperm after he has died? Should that child be treated as the husband's or partner's child? Does it make a difference if the husband or partner consented to posthumous use of his sperm? Should a man be able to pay a woman to become impregnated with his sperm and to carry the fetus to term? Should a woman who agrees to be artificially inseminated and then to relinquish maternal rights to the child be able to revoke her promise after the birth of the child? Should a woman who carries to term another woman's fertilized egg be able to claim rights as the child's mother? This abbreviated list of issues shows that the technology of artificial insemination creates many ethical issues and raises important class and gender questions for our society. The challenge of the next decade will be for the law to transform its concepts regarding reproductive freedom so that these kinds of issues are seen as something other than a clash of individual rights. See Allen, Surrogacy, Slavery, and the Ownership of Life, 13 Harv. J.L. & Pub. Pol. 139 (1989); Colloquy: In re Baby M, 76 Geo. L.J. 1717 (1988).

EXTERNAL REFERENCE. Annot., Rights and Obligations Resulting from Human Artificial Insemination, 83 A.L.R.4th 295 (1991).

2. Rules of Construction for Class Gifts

Statutory References: *1990 UPC §§ 2-701, -705, 8-101(b)(5)*
Pre-1990 UPC §§ 2-603, -611

a. Adopted Children/Stepchildren/Foster Children

Adopted Children. Wills, trusts, and other donative instruments commonly include gifts to classes of persons, such as "to A's children" or "to A's descendants." Whether adopted children are included within these class gifts depends in the first instance upon the intention of the donor. The drafter should expressly address this matter in the instrument. If the instrument fails to indicate the donor's intent one way or the other, the law must provide an answer. Intestacy statutes are not controlling in these circumstances, but they are often used as guides to what the donor likely intended and to public policy.

The courts or statutes usually treat an adopted child as a member of the class if the donor of the class gift adopted that child. See UPC § 2-705(a) (1990); Restatement 2d of Property § 25.4. The more difficult and controversial situation is when someone other than the donor adopted the child. Suppose, for example, that Alice makes a gift to her nieces and nephews and Alice's brother adopts a daughter. According to the so-called "stranger-to-the-adoption" doctrine developed by the courts, Alice is presumed not to have intended to have her adopted niece share in the class gift. The rationale for this rule of construction is similar to that encountered as the basis for non-recognition of the intestacy rights of adopted persons from the adopting parent's family, which is that the adopting parent should not be permitted to determine the beneficiaries of a gift made by a person who did not participate in the adoption. If circumstances indicate, however, that the donor would likely have intended to include the adopted person (such as evidence that the donor knew that the adoptive parent was incapable of having children), then the presumption is rebutted.

Both the UPC section 2-705(c) (1990) and the Restatement 2d of Property section 25.4 abrogate the "stranger-to-the-adoption" doctrine where, in the case of the UPC, the adopted person lived while a minor, either before or after the adoption, as a regular member of the household of the adopting parent, and, in the case of the Restatement, the adopting person has been or will be raised by the adopting parent.

The *Mills* case, below, tells the story of one state's struggle to dislodge the stranger-to-the-adoption doctrine and raises the question as to whether laws that change or expand the rights of adopted children should apply to documents in existence on the effective date of the statute or only to documents executed subsequently.

Ohio Citizens Bank v. Mills
45 Ohio St. 3d 153, 543 N.E.2d 1206 (1989)

The facts, and procedural background, of this case are as follows. On September 21, 1944, Charles H. Breyman created an inter vivos trust which provided for the ultimate distribution of the trust assets to his "living grandchildren and to the living children of each deceased grandchild" upon the death of his daughter, Marie Breyman Mills. He also permitted his daughter to postpone the time of distribution beyond her death until after the death of her son, Robert E. Mills, Breyman's grandson. Prior to her death in 1973, Marie Breyman Mills did exercise the power of extension and postponed the distribution of the trust assets until 1985, the date of Robert E. Mills' death. Charles Breyman died in 1945. In 1957, Robert E. Mills married Esther K. Mills. Five years thereafter, Robert E. Mills adopted his wife's children from her previous two marriages, Roxanne Mills Pugh and Judith Lynne Muth. Later, [after Esther's death,[64]] Robert E. Mills remarried, and from that marriage emanated one natural child, Robert David Mills, appellant herein.

Following the death of Robert E. Mills in 1985, the trustee commenced a trust construction action to determine the beneficiaries of the Breyman trust. Named as defendants in that action were appellant, Robert David Mills, the natural child of Robert E. Mills, appellees, Roxanne Mills Pugh

---

64. Reported by the appellate court. Eds.

and Judith Lynne Muth, the adopted children of Robert E. Mills, and Elva Marie Bonser, an alleged illegitimate child of Robert E. Mills.

The matter was submitted to the trial court upon the stipulated facts and the parties' cross-motions for summary judgment. In two separate entries, the trial court entered judgment against Elva Marie Bonser and appellees Pugh and Muth, respectively. In the latter entry, the trial court relied upon the law in effect at the time Breyman created his trust and the "stranger to the adoption" doctrine to determine that Breyman did not intend to include adopted children in the designated class of trust beneficiaries. The court found as a matter of law that appellees are not beneficiaries of the Breyman trust.

Upon appeal by Pugh and Muth, the appellate court applied the adoption statute in effect at the time of review to determine that Breyman did intend to include adopted persons and reversed the decision of the trial court.

This cause is now before this court pursuant to the allowance of a motion to certify the record. . . .

HOLMES, J. The issue presented for our consideration is whether R.C. 3107.15(A)(2), which in effect abrogated the common-law "stranger to the adoption" doctrine, may be applied in construing wills or trust documents created prior to the effective date of such statute. We answer such query in the negative, and accordingly reverse the court of appeals.

In determining whether or not an adopted child is included within a class designation in a will or trust instrument, and where a reading of the "four corners" of such instrument does not give a reviewing court the appropriate clues, various additional considerations must be weighed.

First, it is axiomatic that the intent of the testator, grantor, or settlor will be ascertained and given effect wherever legally possible. The express language of the instrument generally provides the court with the indicators of the grantor's intentions, and the words used in the instrument are presumed to be used in their ordinary sense. In his trust instrument, Charles Breyman provided for the distribution of the trust assets to the "living children of each deceased grandchild." Appellant, Robert David Mills, the natural child of Robert E. Mills, is a living child of a deceased grandchild, and is obviously an intended beneficiary of this trust.

With respect to the adopted children of Robert E. Mills, the difficulty arises, of course, as to whether they are included within this class of "living children," where no such intent is stated. We then must look to the history of this area of the law, both the common law and statutory law, regarding the inheritance rights of adopted children.

Within the common law dealing with inheritance by adopted children, courts generally have treated an adoption by the settlor or grantor differently than adoptions by others. In the former situation, courts have readily concluded that the testator is presumed to have intended to include his child or children by adoption as well as his natural children. In the latter situation, the courts have been less likely to hold that an adopted child is to be included within a class in a testamentary gift or inter vivos trust. See, generally, Annotation, Adopted child as within class in testamentary gift (1962), 86 A.L.R.2d 12; Annotation, Adopted child as within class named in deed or inter vivos trust instrument (1962), 86 A.L.R.2d 115.

Courts have traditionally looked to the specific words or terms utilized to designate the class, such as "heirs," "heirs at law," "child," "children," "issue," and "heirs of the body." The courts have tended to ascribe the common or ordinary meaning to such words, and have held that the terms "child," "children," "grandchildren," "heirs of the body," "issue," or "heirs" appearing in a will, trust or other instrument exclude an adopted child, absent a contrary intention within the instrument itself and the surrounding circumstances. In contrast, the term "heirs at law," when given its ordinary meaning, has been held to include an adopted child.

Various presumptions or rules of construction have been historically utilized by the courts in this area of the law. One of these presumptive rules is that of "stranger to the adoption," with which we deal herein. Such rule basically is to the effect that there is a presumption that a testator or settlor intended to include a child adopted by him within a generally stated class, but where the testator or settlor is a stranger to an adoption of another, such as where the adoption takes place after the testator's death, it will be presumed that he did not intend the adopted child to be included within the designated class, unless a contrary intention clearly appears.

The courts also must look to the circumstances surrounding the execution of the will or trust. The most important factor here would be the time of the adoption in relation to the execution of the will or trust, or to the death of the testator or settlor. If the facts show that the adoption took place within the lifetime of the testator or settlor, and he knew about and approved of such adoption, the adopted child may well be included within the class.

Also, of course, reviewing courts must look to the various statutes regulating the rights of an adopted child, including the current statutes and the legislative history of such statutes. Specifically, when construing an inter vivos trust, as here, a court should determine the intent of the settlor in light of the law existing at the time of the creation of the trust, since an inter vivos trust speaks from the date of its creation—not the date upon which the assets are distributed. In construing the words used by a settlor, it is a well-established presumption that the testator or settlor was acquainted with the relevant then-existing statutes, their judicial interpretation and the effect they might have on the devolution of his estate. In 1944, when Charles Breyman created the inter vivos trust at issue, the "stranger to the adoption" doctrine was recognized, and he set forth no provisions in the trust contrary to the presumption that adopted children were not included in a gift to "living children of each deceased grandchild."

However, appellees argue, and the court of appeals agreed, that the "stranger to the adoption" doctrine is no longer a rule of construction in Ohio, by virtue of R.C. 3107.15(A)(2), which "places adopted children on the same footing as natural children." That statute, effective January 1, 1977, provides:

> (A) A final decree of adoption and an interlocutory order of adoption that has become final, issued by a court of this state, shall have the following

effects as to all matters within the jurisdiction or before a court of this state:

. . .

> (2) To create the relationship of parent and child between petitioner and the adopted person, as if the adopted person were a legitimate blood descendant of the petitioner, for all purposes including inheritance and applicability of statutes, documents, and instruments, whether executed before or after the adoption is decreed, which do not expressly exclude an adopted person from their operation or effect.

The timeliness of the applicability of an adoption statute such as R.C. 3107.15, as it relates to the beneficiary rights of adopted children, is an important consideration for a reviewing court, and goes directly to the question of what law governs, in point of time. While the general rule, as stated above, is that the law existing at the time an inter vivos trust is executed is the law which applies, a subsequent legislative enactment which changes the rights of inheritance of adopted persons may apply, depending on the intent of the General Assembly.

In this regard, a statute will not be applied retrospectively unless a contrary intention clearly appears. Where a statute is to be applied prior to its effective date in such a manner as to entirely abrogate a longstanding common-law rule, the General Assembly must clearly state its intention in order to do so.

The adoption statute construed here, R.C. 3107.15, does not specifically state that it should apply retrospectively to all existing wills, but only that it shall apply to instruments, "whether executed before or after *the adoption is decreed.*" (Emphasis added.) Although the presumption embodied in the "stranger to the adoption" doctrine may no longer be applied subsequent to the effective date of the statute, the application of this doctrine has not been totally abrogated by the statutory change. The doctrine may still be utilized in the interpretation of certain wills and trust instruments executed prior to such effective date, January 1, 1977.

Reasonably interpreted, and given the absence of an express intention to apply its provisions retrospectively, R.C. 3107.15(A)(2) shall be applied prospectively, and subsequent to its effective date, January 1, 1977, to those documents, statutes, and instruments, whether executed before or after an adoption is decreed, which do not expressly exclude the adopted person from the law's or instruments' operation and effect. Provisions of an inter vivos trust shall continue to be governed by the law existing at the time of its creation, absent a contrary expression of intent within the trust instrument itself. . . .

Finally, appellees argue that, in any event, the adoption statute in effect at the time Charles Breyman created his trust also abrogated the "stranger to the adoption" doctrine. We are unpersuaded, since appellees' arguments reflect an erroneous reading of the legislative history of the adoption statute and of our cases construing such legislative changes.

Prior to 1932 the rights of adopted persons were set forth in G.C. 8030. That section provided, in pertinent part, as follows:

. . . and the child shall be invested with every legal right, privilege, obligation and relation in respect to education, maintenance and the rights of inheritance to real estate, or to the distribution of personal estate on the death of such adopting parent or parents as if born to them in lawful wedlock; provided, such child shall not be capable of inheriting property expressly limited to the heirs of the body of the adopting parent or parents. . . .

In construing this statute, this court held that adopted children were enabled to inherit from but not through their adopting parents. The "stranger to the adoption" doctrine was a valid rule of construction.

The adoption statute was expanded with the enactment of G.C. 10512-19, effective January 1, 1932. That section added the following language to the prior statute after the limitation to the heirs of the body:

. . . but shall be capable of inheriting property expressly limited by will or by operation of law to the child or children, heirs or heirs at law, or next of kin, of the adopting parent or parents, or to a class including any of the foregoing . . . .

We interpreted these provisions to overrule prior law and allow adopted children to inherit both from as well as through their parents. When G.C. 10512-19 was renumbered G.C. 10512-23 upon the establishment of Ohio's "Adoption Code", effective January 1, 1944, no substantive changes were made to the relevant provisions above. Thus, the law existing at the time of the execution of the Charles Breyman trust was restricted to the rights of inheritance of adopted children, by will or intestate succession, and did not speak to trust instruments. The law existing at this time also recognized the "stranger to the adoption" doctrine.

With the enactment of G.C. 8004-13, effective August 28, 1951, the rights of adopted persons were further expanded by omitting the inheritance rights stated above at G.C. 10512-19 and in lieu thereof adding the following provision:

. . . For all purposes under the laws of this state, including without limitation all laws and wills governing inheritance of and succession to real or personal property and the taxation of such inheritance and succession, a legally adopted child shall have the same status and rights, and shall bear the same legal relationship to the adopting parents as if born to them in lawful wedlock and not born to the natural parents; provided:

(A) Such adopted child shall not be capable of inheriting or succeeding to property expressly limited to heirs of the body of the adopting parent or parents . . . .

This provision, by its express language, was still not made specifically applicable to trust instruments.

G.C. 8004-13 remained basically unchanged as R.C. 3107.13 until 1972, when two significant changes were made. R.C. 3107.13 was amended effective January 26, 1972 to read, in pertinent part, as follows:

. . . For all purposes under the laws of this state, including without limitation all laws, wills, and trust instruments governing inheritance of and succession to real or personal property and the taxation of an estate, a legally adopted child shall have the same status and rights, and shall bear the same legal relationship to the adopting parents as if born to them in lawful wedlock and not born to the natural parents; provided:

(A) Such adopted child shall not be capable of inheriting or succeeding to property expressly limited to heirs of the body of the adopting parents. . . .

Unless an express intention to the contrary appears in a will or trust instrument, "child," "children," "issue," "grandchild," or "grandchildren," includes a legally adopted child, for the purpose of inheritance to, through, or from the adopting parents of such child, irrespective of when such will was executed or such trust was created.

The provisions of the amended statute for the first time made the right to inherit under the adoption statutes applicable to trust instruments. These revisions also provided that when the term "children" is used in a trust instrument, such term includes a legally adopted child irrespective of when the trust was created.

Thus, it was only after 1972 that the "stranger to the adoption" doctrine began to be eroded. The final expansion of the rights of adopted children came with the enactment of current R.C. 3107.15, effective in 1977. This section removed the limitation prohibiting adopted children from inheriting property limited to "heirs of the body" and, thus, although prospectively, fully accorded adopted children the same rights of inheritance as natural born children. The abrogation of the "stranger to the adoption" doctrine has been a slow, deliberate process, and had not yet begun when Charles Breyman executed his trust in 1944.

Accordingly, based upon the law existing in 1944, we conclude that the presumption embodied in the "stranger to the adoption" doctrine is applicable to the Charles Breyman trust, consistent with the grantor's intent. Such intent was to include only natural children in the distribution of assets of his trust estate. The judgment of the court of appeals is reversed, and the judgment of the trial court is reinstated.

Judgment reversed.

MOYER, C.J., and SWEENEY, DOUGLAS, WRIGHT, HERBERT R. BROWN and EVANS, J., concur.

Notes and Questions

1. *1990 Uniform Probate Code.* Had the 1990 UPC governed in *Mills,* the outcome would have been different. Section 8-101(b)(5) provides that "any rule of construction or presumption provided in the Code applies to instruments executed . . . before the [Code's] effective date unless there is a clear indication of a contrary intent." Consequently, section 2-705, which abrogates the stranger-to-the-adoption rule for all governing instruments, not merely for wills as under pre-1990 UPC section 2-611, applies to documents executed before the Code's effective date. If Roxanne and Judith lived while minors as regular members of the Robert E. Mills' household (a

fair assumption), they would have been included in the class gift and each would have taken a one-third share. Robert David Mills would have received only one-third of the corpus, not all of it.

2. *Policy of Pre-Effective Date Application.* As a matter of legislative policy, should statutory changes in rules of construction be expressly restricted to documents executed after the statute's effective date? What justifications are there for the UPC's approach of expressly extending application of its constructional rules to documents executed before the UPC's effective date?

Will of Hoffman, infra p. 149, demonstrates that a change in a common-law rule of construction often applies to documents executed before the court's decision. Is the case for application to pre-effective date documents stronger for common-law changes in rules of construction than it is for statutory changes in rules of construction?

3. *Remainder Interest to "Heirs."* If the remainder interest created by Charles Breyman's trust had been in favor of Robert E. Mills' "heirs" rather than his "children," the predominant rule of construction is that Robert's heirs should be determined by reference to the intestacy statute in existence at Robert's death, not the statute in existence when Charles executed his trust.[65] See Matter of Dodge Testamentary Trust, 121 Mich. App. 527, 330 N.W.2d 72 (1982) (set forth infra p. 942); UPC § 2-711 (1990); Restatement 2d of Property § 29.4.

4. *The 1972 Ohio Statute.* Had Robert E. Mills died between January 26, 1972 and January 1, 1977, would it have been more likely that the Ohio court would have held Roxanne and Judith were eligible to share in the class gift? If your answer is yes, should the fact he died after January 1, 1977, have produced a different result, simply because the 1977 Ohio statute repealed the 1972 statute?

5. *Fact Variations of Mills.* Suppose, in *Mills,* that Esther had not had children by a prior marriage and that Esther and Robert E. had adopted Roxanne and Judith as infants through an adoption agency. Suppose further that Robert E. had not remarried after Esther's death. Does the *Mills* precedent mean that Roxanne and Judith would be excluded from class membership under Charles' trust? If so, who would take the corpus of the trust?

Take a different variation of the original facts. Suppose that Esther did not die, but rather that Esther and Robert E. were divorced and that custody of Roxanne and Judith was awarded to Esther. Would or should Roxanne and Judith take as class members under Charles' trust?

———

Adoption of Adults. Adoption statutes generally permit adoptions of adults.[66] An adoption of an adult devisee may be useful in preventing an

———

65. But cf. Society Nat'l Bank v. Jacobson, 560 N.E.2d 217 (Ohio 1990), infra p. 870, footnote 10.

66. A most extraordinary use of adult adoptions was posed in a biography of Huntington Hartford, heir to the A. & P. fortune. Wishing to rid himself of his first wife, he is reported to have suggested that his mother adopt her and make her his sister! L. Gubernick, Squandered

anticipated will contest. By removing the testator's disappointed collateral relatives as heirs, the adoption prevents them from having standing to contest the will. See, e.g., Collamore v. Learned, 171 Mass. 99, 50 N.E. 518 (1898).[67] Will this planning technique work under the UPC? See UPC § 2-114 (1990).

Can or should an adoption of an adult be used to qualify a person as a member of a class for purposes of sharing in a class gift? Will this technique work under the UPC? See UPC § 2-705(c) (1990). In the absence of clarifying legislation or language in the governing instrument,[68] some courts have treated the adult as an adopted child for purposes of construing the dispositive instrument. See, e.g., Estate of Fortnoy, 5 Kan. App. 2d 14, 611 P.2d 599 (1980) (remainder to "heirs" of life tenant; at age 90, life tenant adopted wife's nephew, age 65). Other courts, however, have refused to construe the dispositive instrument to include a child who was adopted as an adult. In Cox v. Whitten, 288 Ark. 318, 704 S.W.2d 628 (1986), for example, the court excluded a person adopted as an adult sixteen years after the testator died by holding that the testator's reference "to her brothers' children was not selected with the idea of including a person who was not adopted until long after her death." The excluded person was 48 years old when the testator's brother and his wife adopted him. See Mather, The Magic Circle: Inclusion of Adopted Children in Testamentary Class Gifts, 31 S. Tex. L. Rev. 223, 234-37 (1990).

Adoption of a Legal Spouse or Domestic Partner. In a 4-2 decision, the New York Court of Appeals in Adoption of Robert Paul P., 63 N.Y.2d 233, 236-39, 471 N.E.2d 424, 425-427 (1984), denied the petition of a gay man to adopt his partner:

> Our adoption statute embodies the fundamental social concept that the relationship of parent and child may be established by operation of law. . . . Despite the absence of any blood ties, in the eyes of the law an adopted child becomes "the natural child of the adoptive parent" with all the attendant personal and proprietary incidents to that relationship. . . . Indeed, the adoption laws of New York, as well as those of most of the States, reflect the general acceptance of the ancient principle of *adoption naturam imitatur—i.e.,* adoption imitates nature, which originated in Roman jurisprudence . . . , which, in turn, served as a guide for the development of adoption statutes in this country. . . .
>
> In imitating nature, adoption in New York, as explicitly defined in section 110 of the Domestic Relations Law, is "the legal proceeding whereby a person takes another person into the *relation of child* and thereby acquires the rights and incurs the responsibilities of *parent*." (Emphasis supplied.) It is plainly not a quasi-matrimonial vehicle to provide nonmarried partners with a legal imprimatur for their sexual relationship, be it heterosexual or homosexual. . . .

Fortune (1991).

67. But see Adoption of Sewall, 242 Cal. App. 2d 208, 51 Cal. Rptr. 367 (1966) (allowing disappointed collateral heir to attack adoption decree for fraud and undue influence).

68. It is not unusual to find form books for wills and trusts that define class gift terms as including an adopted child "only if the individual was adopted under the age of 18 at the date of adoption." See, e.g., Mich. Will Manual p. XVI-22 (1990).

Moreover, any such sexual intimacy is utterly repugnant to the relationship between child and parent in our society, and only a patently incongruous application of our adoption laws—wholly inconsistent with the underlying public policy of providing a parent-child relationship for the welfare of the child . . .—would permit the employment of adoption as the legal formalization of an adult relationship between sexual partners under the guise of parent and child. . . .

Here, where the appellants are living together in a homosexual relationship and where no incidents of a parent-child relationship are evidenced or even remotely within the parties' intentions, no fair interpretation of our adoption-laws can permit a granting of the petition. Adoption is not a means of obtaining a legal status for a nonmarital sexual relationship—whether homosexual or heterosexual. Such would be a "cynical distortion of the function of adoption." . . . Nor is it a procedure by which to legitimize an emotional attachment, however sincere, but wholly devoid of the filial relationship that is fundamental to the concept of adoption.

While there are no special restrictions on adult adoptions under the provisions of the Domestic Relations Law, the Legislature could not have intended that the statute be employed "to arrive at an unreasonable or absurd result." . . . Such would be the result if the Domestic Relations Law were interpreted to permit one lover, homosexual or heterosexual, to adopt the other and enjoy the sanction of the law on their feigned union as parent and child.

There are many reasons why one adult might wish to adopt another that would be entirely consistent with the basic nature of adoption, including the following: a childless individual might wish to perpetuate a family name; two individuals might develop a strong *filial* affection for one another; a stepparent might wish to adopt the spouse's adult children; or adoption may have been forgone, for whatever reason, at an earlier date. . . . But where the relationship between the adult parties is utterly incompatible with the creation of a parent-child relationship between them, the adoption process is certainly not the proper vehicle by which to formalize their partnership in the eyes of the law. Indeed, it would be unreasonable and disingenuous for us to attribute a contrary intent to the Legislature.

In Minary v. Citizens Fidelity Bank & Trust Co., 419 S.W.2d 340, 343-44 (Ky. 1967), a wife who was adopted by her husband under the state's adoption statute[69] was refused treatment as a child for purposes of determining the takers of a class gift to heirs found in the will of the husband's mother. The court focused on the question of achieving the testator's likely intent rather than on the absence of a parent-child relationship between the husband and wife:

It is of paramount importance that man be permitted to pass on his property at his death to those who represent the natural objects of his bounty. . . . Our adoption statutes . . . should not be given a construction that does violence to the above rule . . . .

---

69. A challenge to the validity of the adoption was dismissed for lack of jurisdiction. See Minary v. Minary, 395 S.W.2d 588 (Ky. 1965).

Stepchildren and Foster Children. Usually, courts do not construe class gifts to include stepchildren. California, however, applies a constructional rule that includes as members of class gifts some stepchildren and foster children (or their issue when appropriate to the class). See Cal. Prob. Code § 6152. The statute incorporates California's intestacy rule, see Cal. Prob. Code § 6408, which recognizes a parent-child relationship if it begins during the stepchild's or foster child's minority and continues throughout the parent's and child's joint lifetimes and if it is established by clear and convincing evidence that the stepparent or foster parent would have adopted the child but for a legal barrier. See supra p. 131 for further discussion of this provision. Section 6152 also incorporates the provision in section 6408 that provides that the judicial doctrine of equitable adoption still applies. See Cal. Prob. Code § 6408.

b. Children of Parents Not Married to Each Other

Will of Hoffman
53 A.D.2d 55, 385 N.Y.S.2d 49 (1976)

BIRNS, J. . . . Mary Hoffman, the testatrix died in 1951. Her will established a trust for the benefit of her two cousins and provided that when the first of the two should die, his one-half share of the income should be paid for the remainder of the trust term "to his issue."

One cousin is still living; the other died in 1965, survived by a daughter and a son named Stephen. Stephen died in 1972 leaving two children, the infants represented by respondent-appellant herein. Stephen never married the mother of these children nor was an order of filiation entered. The Surrogate, however, determined that the two children were indeed the children of Stephen.

Relying on precedent, the Surrogate ruled that . . . the term "issue" as used in the will meant lawful issue only, and absent an intention to the contrary it could not be assumed that the testatrix intended illegitimate descendants as the object of her bounty.

In this court, as she did below, respondent-appellant asserted that inasmuch as the word "issue" in the provision of the will under consideration was not qualified by the word "lawful," the question of legitimacy was not in decedent's mind when she made her will. In addition, the change in conventional attitudes towards illegitimates, as reflected in statutes and decisions, would warrant a construction of the word "issue" as including illegitimates, in the absence of contrary intent to exclude them.

Petitioner-respondent emphasizes that under settled case law, where the word "issue" appears in a will it will be interpreted to mean only lawful descendants in the absence of clear evidence of a contrary intent of a testator.

We recognize that precedents do hold that in the absence of an express intent to the contrary by a testator, the word "issue" presumes lawful issue and not illegitimate offspring. This presumption has its roots in an earlier society where there was no sense of injustice in the teaching that the sins of the fathers were to be visited upon their children and succeeding generations . . . .

Because of changes in societal attitudes and recent developments in constitutional law, we are of the opinion that, to the extent that precedents require this burden to be placed upon illegitimate claimants under a will, the law is not only outmoded, but discriminatory and should be rejected. We would reverse. . . .

Apparently the precise question before us has never been decided by the Court of Appeals or this court. . . .

Our statutes do provide continuing evidence of legislative concern for illegitimate children . . . .

While nothing in the [Estates, Powers, and Trusts Law] provides that illegitimate children are "issue" for the purposes of taking under a will, rights of illegitimates to share in the estates of their kin are expanding. In fact, present attitudes appear to reject an inferior social or legal status for illegitimates.

[Many] statutes, state and federal, . . . demonstrate significant changes in societal attitudes vis-a-vis illegitimate children, each of which was directed toward the elimination of disadvantages, legal and social, suffered by illegitimates. This parade of legislation was well underway, when in 1950, the testatrix executed the will before us.

The question raised is whether social and statutory changes require a reconsideration of the rule which presumed an intent by testatrix to exclude illegitimate descendants in sharing under her will.

Certainly, it cannot be said, as a matter of fact, that the testatrix was aware of these changes in societal attitudes as evidenced by the legislation referred to, or aware of community attitudes towards premarital sex or sex without marriage. Nor can it be said with any degree of assurance that at the time she executed her will she was provided with an explanation of the word "issue" which appeared on the type-written pages of that document. It is just as likely that the word "issue" in her mind had a meaning no different that "progeny" or "offspring".

The will itself supports the conclusion that the bequest to her cousins was of paramount concern in establishing the trust. It is most unlikely that she gave any more than passing thought to the children who now, 25 years after her death, claim under her will, particularly as to whether or not they would be legitimate.

The presumed intent of the testator with which all the precedents are concerned, although represented as rebuttable, is in fact, in most cases irrebuttable. The passage of time has made it impossible to establish that the testatrix did not intend to exclude illegitimate descendants from sharing under her will. . . .

To continue to rely upon these precedents and then declare that in using the word "issue" in her will, testatrix intended only lawful issue and not illegitimates is to attribute to her a frame of mind not at all supported by the facts. We recognize that the testatrix should possess the broadest freedom of choice in making known the objects of her bounty, and that it is the duty of the court to ascertain the testatrix's intent. Nevertheless, the court should not under the guise of determining the testatrix's intent substitute its own preference as to the legatees who shall take under the will. There should be a demonstrable relation between judicial interpretation of a will and the testatrix's actual frame of mind. . . .

We have been instructed that "[t]hat court best serves the law which recognizes that the rules of law which grew up in a remote generation may, in the fullness of experience be found to serve another generation badly, and which discards the old rule when it finds that another rule of law represents what should be according to the established and settled judgment of society, and no considerable property rights have become vested in reliance upon the old rule. It is thus great writers upon the common law have discovered the source and method of its growth, and in its growth found its health and life. It is not and it should not be stationary. Change of this character should not be left to the Legislature."

The Court of Appeals has stated, just recently: " . . . from the earliest times the doctrine of *stare decisis* did not require a strict adherence to precedent in every instance . . ."

There are cases also where "the rule of adherence to precedent though it ought not be abandoned, ought to be in some degree relaxed." In the case before us, we are of the opinion that rigid adherence to precedent will produce a result not warranted by facts but rather by adherence to an anachronistic rule.

Therefore we reject the rule that where the word "issue," standing alone, appears in a will, it will be interpreted to include within its meaning only lawful descendants. We hold that the word "issue" should be construed to refer to legitimate and illegitimate descendants alike in the absence of an express qualification by the testatrix.

Further justification for our decision today can be found in expanding concepts of the Equal Protection Clause (U.S. Constitution, 14th Amendment). To construe "issue" in a will as excluding illegitimate children otherwise entitled to inherit thereunder, is, as stated before, nothing more than the substitution of judicial preference for a testator's intent. Such preference, under the guise of judicial construction, we believe, is state action. (See Shelley v. Kraemer, 334 U.S. 1.) State action is proscribed if it promotes discrimination based upon an unconstitutional classification. . . .

In holding that illegitimates are covered by the Equal Protection Clause, the Supreme Court of the United States [in Weber v. Aetna Casualty & Surety Co., 406 U.S. 164] struck down as discriminatory a statute which provided that illegitimate children did not have the same right to share in the death benefits under a Louisiana workmen's compensation statute as did legitimate children. . . .

Because of the expanding concept of equal protection we should not adhere rigidly to the rules enunciated in the cases cited as precedents herein. To do so would require us to hold that illegitimates enjoyed a lesser status than legitimate children before the law in cases such as the one before us.

In rejecting archaism, we do no more in this appeal than hold that the word "issue" as used by testatrix in her will should have no meaning other than that ordinarily and customarily imputed to persons in its usage in the absence of any manifestation of an intent to the contrary. . . . Accordingly, the law will not be required to discriminate against children labeled illegitimate through no fault of their own. . . .

All concur.

Notes and Questions

1. *Rules of Construction Regarding Nonmarital Children.* The law is clearly moving away from the traditional constructional rule that children of unmarried parents are presumptively *excluded* from membership under class-gift terminology. The rule of construction that should replace the traditional rule is more controversial. Is it to be the opposite rule, as the *Hoffman* court held, under which nonmarital children are presumptively *included* under class-gift terminology? Is some intermediate rule more appropriate, under which children of unmarried parents are included in some circumstances, but excluded in others? Keep in mind that rules of construction supply *presumptive* meaning to the language in a private instrument, such as a will or trust. Transferors are not bound by a rule of construction and well drafted instruments expressly address whether nonmarital children are intended to be takers of gifts made to classes of beneficiaries. The function of the rule of construction is to reflect the likely intent of transferors who fail to indicate whether they want to include nonmarital children as members of a class.

Children of unmarried parents always presumptively included. The Restatement 2d of Property section 25.2 promulgates a rule of construction stating that nonmarital children are presumptively included in class gift terminology. This approach has also been adopted by a number of recent judicial decisions in addition to *Hoffman*. In Powers v. Wilkinson, 399 Mass. 650, 663, 506 N.E.2d 842, 848 (1987), the Supreme Judicial Court of Massachusetts broke from prior Massachusetts precedent dating back about 150 years by holding that "the word 'issue,' absent clear expressions of a contrary intent, must be construed to include all biological descendants." Id. at 662, 506 N.E.2d at 848. This new Massachusetts rule of construction, however, is not to apply retroactively, but "only to trust instruments executed after the date of [the *Powers*] opinion." In Northwestern Nat'l Bank v. Simons, 308 Minn. 243, 246-47, 242 N.W.2d 78, 80 (1976), the Supreme Court of Minnesota, four justices dissenting, held that a nonmarital child of a granddaughter of the settlor of a trust created in 1921 was a beneficiary of the trust under a provision in favor of the settlor's "issue." The court said: "When there is some doubt, either from family circumstances, the behavior or knowledge of a settlor, or from the trust instrument itself, this court will hold that illegitimate issue are to be included as issue." In Estate of Dulles, 494 Pa. 180, 431 A.2d 208, 17 A.L.R.4th 1279 (1981), the Supreme Court of Pennsylvania held that a codified rule of construction declaring that, in the absence of an explicit declaration to the contrary in the governing instrument, a person born out of wedlock is not included in class-gift language (such as "grandchildren"), is in violation of the equal protection clause of the federal constitution.

Children of unmarried parents presumptively included under an agency concept. A competing approach utilizes an agency concept for documents of transferors who are not the parent of the nonmarital child. Under this concept, Mary Hoffman would be presumptively deemed to have viewed Stephen as her agent: If Stephen had treated his nonmarital children as his own, they would be included in Mary's class gift to her cousin's "issue"; if Stephen had not treated them as his own, they would be excluded from the class. Section 2-705(b) of the 1990 UPC adopts this agency-concept approach and so has the Supreme Court of Wisconsin in In re Trust of Parsons, 56 Wis. 2d 613, 203 N.W.2d 40 (1973). Section 2-705(b) states that, in construing a dispositive provision by a transferor who is not the natural parent, an individual born to the natural parent is not considered the child of that parent unless the individual lived while a minor as a regular member of the household of that natural parent or of that parent's parent, brother, sister, spouse, or surviving spouse.[70] The California Probate Code section 6152 promulgates a similar rule. The Supreme Court of Wisconsin held that the traditional presumption against inclusion of a child of unmarried parents is rebutted if the child was "a part of the family circle."

A distinction is sometimes drawn in legal-academic circles between "rules" and "standards." The distinction focuses on the degree of precision with which a legal proposition is formulated: Rules are more specific than standards. Both UPC section 2-705(b) and *Parsons* seek to establish the same agency-concept proposition, but section 2-705(b) formulates it as a rule and *Parsons* formulates it as a standard. What are the pros and cons of each method of formulation? See Ehrlich & Posner, An Economic Analysis of Legal Rulemaking, 3 J. Leg. Stud. 257 (1974); Kennedy, Form and Substance in Private Law Adjudication, 89 Harv. L. Rev. 1685, 1699-1701 (1976); Rose, Crystals and Mud in Property Law, 40 Stan. L. Rev. 577 (1988).

2. *Adopted-Out Nonmarital Children.* After *Hoffman* was decided, a case arose in New York concerning a nonmarital child who, upon birth, was put up for adoption and shortly thereafter was adopted. The case is Estate of Best, 66 N.Y.2d 151, 485 N.E.2d 1010, 495 N.Y.S.2d 345 (1985). In *Best,* the testator died in 1973, leaving a will that devised the residuary of her estate in trust. The trustee was directed to pay income to the testator's daughter, Ardith, for life. On Ardith's death, the testator directed the trustee to pay the income to Ardith's issue for the life of each. Ardith was the mother of two children, David and Anthony. David was born in 1952, out of wedlock. David was immediately placed with an agency for adoption and

---

70. Note that § 2-705(b) applies to marital as well as nonmarital children.

shortly thereafter adopted by the McCollums. Ardith's second child, Anthony, was born in 1963, in wedlock.

The Surrogate applied the presumption established in *Hoffman*, held that it had not been rebutted, and concluded that David was entitled to share in the income from the testator's trust. See 116 Misc. 2d 365, 455 N.Y.S.2d 487 (1982). The Appellate Division affirmed, saying: "Because we agree with the reasoning set forth in the opinion of Justice Birns in Matter of Hoffman (supra), we hold that the Surrogate properly applied the presumption established therein in the case at bar." 102 A.D.2d 660, 662, 477 N.Y.S.2d 431, 432 (1984).

The Court of Appeals reversed. Although the court accepted as a "rebuttable rule of construction" the proposition that "the unmodified term issue [refers] to children born both in and out of wedlock," the court held that adopted-out children posed a different question. As to adopted-out children, the court said: "Only if a child adopted out of the family is specifically named in a biological ancestor's will, or the gift is expressly made to issue including those adopted out of the family, can the child take." 66 N.Y.2d at 156, 485 N.E.2d at 1013, 495 N.Y.S.2d at 348.

The Restatement 2d of Property promulgates a somewhat different rule of construction. Under section 25.5, an adopted-out child is presumptively excluded from a class gift if the adoption "removes the child from the broader family circle" of the biological parent.

How would the facts in *Best* be analyzed under the Restatement or under UPC sections 2-701 and -705 (1990)? Would *Best* have been decided differently had David's mother immediately placed him with an adoption agency, but David was never adopted? How would this factual situation be treated under the Restatement or under UPC sections 2-701 and -705 (1990)?

If Ardith had died leaving a will disposing of her property to "my children," would David be treated as a member of the class under New York or UPC law and share in his biological mother's estate?

3. *Children Conceived by Means Other Than Sexual Intercourse.* The Restatement 2d of Property adopts the following rule of construction:

> § 25.3 *Gifts to "Children"—Child Conceived by Means Other Than Sexual Intercourse.* When the donor of property describes the beneficiaries thereof as "children" of a designated person, the primary meaning of such class gift term includes a child conceived by means other than sexual intercourse who is recognized by the designated person as a child of him or her. It is assumed in the absence of language or circumstances indicating a contrary intent, that the donor adopts such primary meaning.

———

EXTERNAL REFERENCE. Halbach, Issues About Issue: Some Recurrent Class Gift Problems, 48 Mo. L. Rev. 333, 347-50 (1983).

PART F. ALTERING INTESTATE SUCCESSION BY MEANS OTHER THAN TESTAMENTARY DISPOSITION

In Part C, we learned that the heirs are not bound by the distributive pattern of the intestacy statute. What means are available to the decedent for altering the intestacy statute? The most obvious means is to make a valid will disposing of the decedent's entire estate. This is the topic of Chapter 3, infra. Short of that, the decedent can alter the intestacy scheme by making an advancement and possibly by executing a so-called negative will.

1. *Advancements and Related Doctrines*

Statutory References: *1990 UPC §§ 2-101(a), -109*
                             Pre-1990 UPC §§ 2-101, -110

Advancements. An advancement is a gift made by a decedent during life to a family member. It is a gift, however, that has the effect of reducing the share of the probate estate that the family member receives under the intestacy succession statute upon the decedent's death. The primary purpose of the advancements doctrine is to further the intestacy statute's distribution pattern that assures equal treatment among the decedent's children. By taking into account lifetime parental gifts to children, the advancements doctrine achieves a more equal sharing by the children of their parent's wealth when the parent dies without a will.

Most jurisdictions originally modeled their advancements statutes after the English Statute of Distribution of 1670, which provided only the manner for accounting for these lifetime gifts. The English courts apparently treated all gifts made during the life of the decedent as advancements, except gifts of small sums or gifts made for the purpose of maintenance or in satisfaction of the decedent's support obligation. Proof of whether a gift fell within one of the exceptions to the rule rested on objective evidence of the nature or purpose of the gift. See, e.g., Taylor v. Taylor, 20 L.R.-Eq. 155 (1875); Boyd v. Boyd, 4 L.R.-Eq. 305 (1867).

American statutes also made no attempt to define an advancement or to provide guidelines on the type of transfers to be treated as advancements. Unlike their English counterparts, however, the American courts generally refused to adopt any objective tests to identify advancements.[71] Instead,

---

71. South Carolina is the only state in which the courts have held that the specific intent of the decedent is irrelevant. The objective circumstances surrounding the gift, such as the amount or purpose of the gift, are considered to determine if a court should treat a particular gift as an advancement. See, e.g., Heyward v. Middleton, 65 S.C. 493, 43 S.E. 956 (1903); Rees v. Rees, 11 Rich. Eq. 86 (S.C. 1859); M'Caw v. Blewit, 2 McCord Eq. 90 (S.C. 1827).

they interpreted the advancements statutes as authorizing an inquiry to determine if the decedent's specific intent was to make an advancement rather than an absolute gift. See, e.g., Holland v. Bonner, 142 Ark. 214, 218 S.W. 665 (1920); Bulkeley v. Noble, 19 Mass. (2 Pick.) 337 (1824). Predictably, this judicial inquiry created a significant amount of litigation involving factual disputes that were exacerbated by the inevitable unreliability of the evidence admitted to show the decedent's intent.

Disenchantment with the operation of the advancements doctrine led a number of nineteenth-century legislatures to restrict advancements to gifts accompanied by a writing expressing the decedent's intent to make an advancement. The general rule is that a decedent can avoid the operation of the intestacy statute only by executing a will. Why should a writing that does not meet the will formality requirements be sufficient to vary the intestacy law and have a gift treated as an advancement? On the one hand, the advancements doctrine, as it developed through American cases and legislation, reflects an extraordinarily flexible and unrestrictive view as to how a decedent can control property distributions at death. On the other hand, the relaxation of testamentary formalities may be somewhat illusory. A decedent who understands the need to make a contemporaneous writing to accomplish an advancement is likely to be sophisticated enough to execute a will instead. It is also true, however, that a decedent who does not know of the writing requirement may prepare a writing anyway, such as in a letter to the donee enclosing the check. Arguably, that type of clear and convincing evidence should not be ignored.

All American jurisdictions have statutes providing for advancements. The two most typical types of statutes are those that create a presumption that the decedent does not intend a gift to be treated as an advancement and those that create the same presumption against advancements and go on to provide that it can be rebutted only by a writing.

UPC section 2-109 (1990) requires a writing. The writing can be by the decedent indicating an intent to make an advancement or by the donee acknowledging the gift is an advancement. Like other statutes requiring a written document, section 2-109 does not prescribe any formalities other than that it be in writing.

It expands the class of eligible advancees beyond the decedent's children to include all of the decedent's heirs.[72] The original concern for equality among the decedent's children has been extended to the decedent's descendants presumably because, with the writing requirement, the concern about creating difficult litigation is lessened. An eligible advancee is anyone who is an heir at decedent's death. See UPC § 2-109(a) (1990). For example, suppose G makes a lifetime gift to his daughter's child accom-

---

72. Tennessee appears to be the only state that continues to limit the doctrine to children. Tenn. Code Ann. §§ 31-5-101, -102. The language in the statute is ambiguous. In all reported cases, the advancements concerned a transfer from a parent to a child, but no reported case specifically held that the advancements doctrine did not apply to gifts to the decedent's other heirs. See also Robinson v. Robinson, 23 Tenn. (4 Hum.) 392, 393 (1843) (dictum suggesting advancement can be made to a relative).

panied by a writing that he intends the gift to be an advancement. If G dies intestate, G's daughter predeceases him, and her child survives him, section 2-109(a) treats the gift as an advancement. If G's daughter survives him, however, the gift is not an advancement because the grandchild is not an heir.

Under UPC section 2-109(c) (1990), an advancee's descendants are not chargeable with the advancement if the advancee predeceases the intestate decedent unless the decedent's declaration provides otherwise. The rationale, as given in the Comment, is that "there is no guarantee that the recipient's descendants received the advanced property or its value from the recipient's estate."

The commentary to section 2-109 explains the common-law hotchpot method that should be used for computing the shares passing to each heir.

Releases and Assignments. Presumptive heirs (or devisees) can *release* their expectancy interests to the decedent. Presumptive heirs (or devisees) can also *assign* their expectancy interests to third persons. Contracts to release or assign expectancy interests are only enforceable in equity and only if the heir (or devisee) receives fair consideration. If a releasor or assignor predeceases the decedent, should their descendants be bound by their ancestor's dealings? In Donough v. Garland, 269 Ill. 565, 572, 109 N.E. 1015, 1017 (1915), the court said that the descendants of a releasor but not of an assignor are bound:

> [A] release by an heir presumptive of his expectancy operates as an extinguishment of the right of inheritance, cutting it off at its source. The line of inheritance is ended by the release made by the one having the expectancy at the time, and the release is binding not only upon him but upon those who take as heirs in his place, otherwise a release would often be ineffective. That would always be the case where the one executing the release does not survive the one to whom the release is made although he has himself received the consideration for the expectancy. If, however, the expectancy is assigned to another, the right of inheritance is not extinguished but still exists, and the assignment is enforced as a contract to convey the legal estate or interest when it ceases to be an expectancy and becomes a vested estate. The assignee is regarded as bargaining for a legal interest depending on a future, uncertain and contingent event. The assignee acquires a right to the legal estate if it ever vests in the assignor, but if it does not, he acquires nothing.

———

External References. W. Thornton, A Treatise on the Law Relating to Gifts and Advancements (1893); Elbert, Advancements: I, 51 Mich. L. Rev. 665 (1953); Elbert, Advancements: II, 52 Mich. L. Rev. 231 (1953); Elbert, Advancements: III, 52 Mich. L. Rev. 535 (1954); Fellows, Concealing Legislative Reform in the Common-Law Tradition: The Advancements Doctrine and The Uniform Probate Code, 37 Vand. L. Rev. 671 (1984).

2. Negative Wills

Statutory Reference: *1990 UPC § 2-101(b)*

In Brown's Estate, 362 Mich. 47, 49, 106 N.W.2d 535, 536, 100 A.L.R.2d 322 (1960), the testator's will made a devise to Lepha Conlon that was accompanied by the following language:

> This bequest is all that Lepha Conlon shall receive from my estate: and that she shall NOT receive anything else.

The will partially failed, raising the question whether Lepha Conlon was entitled, as one of the testator's heirs, to receive a share of the property passing by intestacy.

The court, following the majority of states, held that a decedent cannot "eliminate an heir from receiving that portion of an estate governed by the statute of descent and distribution except by disposing of the property by will."[73] Why do you think the courts were attracted to a rule that distinguished between a testamentary provision directing that a devisee receive property and one directing that a devisee not receive property?

New York overruled the common law by altering the statutory definition of a will to include a direction by a testator as to "how his property shall not be disposed of." N.Y. Est. Powers & Trusts Law § 1-2.18. If a testator disinherits an heir in a will, the effect of the statute is to treat the heir as having predeceased the testator for purposes of applying the intestacy statute. See, e.g., Matter of Cairo, 35 A.D.2d 76, 312 N.Y.S.2d 925 (1970), aff'd per curiam, 29 N.Y.2d 527, 272 N.E.2d 574, 324 N.Y.S.2d 81 (1971). UPC section 2-101(b) (1990) promulgates a similar provision.

To make clear that a spouse cannot receive both a devise and also elect to take dower, an elective share, homestead allowance, or the like, wills sometimes include a provision like that found in Waring v. Loring, 399 Mass. 419, 422, 504 N.E.2d 644, 645 (1987):

> The provisions of this will for the benefit of my wife . . . are in lieu of dower and of all her statutory rights in or to any part of my estate.

If the will partially fails, as it did in *Waring*, does this language preclude the spouse from taking under the will *and* taking her share as an heir of the intestate portion of the estate? The court in *Waring* held that she could take both. The court reasoned that intestacy, unlike dower and the elective share, does not require the surviving spouse to make an election and does not disrupt the testator's distributive plan. The court limited its decision to the situation in which partial intestacy resulted from an ineffective provision in the will. Contra, e.g., In re Hills, 264 N.Y. 349, 191 N.E. 12

---

73. Id. at 51, 106 N.W.2d 537. *Brown* overruled LaMere v. Jackson, 288 Mich. 99, 284 N.W. 659 (1939), because it conflicted with the prevailing common-law view regarding negative-will provisions.

(1934). See infra p. 451 for a further discussion of the doctrine of equitable election.

EXTERNAL REFERENCES. Note, The Intestate Claims of Heirs Excluded by Will: Should "Negative Wills" Be Enforced?, 52 U. Chi. L. Rev. 177 (1985); Annot., 100 A.L.R.2d 322 (1965).

EXECUTION OF WILLS

Anglo-American law did not always accord property owners the right to make a will. To be sure, the power to dispose of personal property by will was recognized early. The ecclesiastical courts asserted jurisdiction over succession to personal property on death, and encouraged bequests for religious and charitable purposes, as well as for the decedent's family. During the Anglo-Saxon period, testamentary disposition of land was possible, but recognition ceased within about a century after the Norman Conquest. The gift of land by will "stood condemned," Maitland wrote, "because it is a death-bed gift, wrung from a man in his agony. In the interest of honesty, in the interest of the law state, a boundary must be maintained against ecclesiastical greed and the other-worldliness of dying men." 2 F. Pollock & F. Maitland, History of English Law 328 (2d ed. 1911). The church courts never gained jurisdiction over succession to land and the Crown courts were not concerned with seeing that a man atoned for his wrongs by devoting a portion of his property to pious objects. Women, of course, were ignored by both the Crown and ecclesiastical courts during this period.

Land, during this early period, passed by inheritance to the eldest son. Nevertheless, landowners sought means to make provision at death for their other children, for pious uses, and perhaps for a general freedom of testamentary disposition. This became possible after equity began to enforce uses in the early part of the fifteenth century. A landowner would transfer land (enfeoff) to A, to hold to the use of the feoffor for life and then to such uses as the feoffor might appoint in his will. The Chancellor recognized the will appointing the use (for it was not a disposition of legal title to land) and compelled A to carry out the uses.

One of the purposes of the Statute of Uses, passed in 1536 (27 Hen. 8, c. 10), was to eliminate testamentary disposition of land by way of use. The preamble to the statute condemned "wills and testaments, sometimes made by nude parolx and words, sometimes by signs and tokens, and sometimes by writing, and for the most part made by such persons as be visited with sickness, in their extreme agonies and pains, or at such time as they have scantly had any good memory or remembrance." But the demand for power of testation was strong and four years later, in 1540, the first English Statute of Wills was enacted, permitting testamentary disposition of land with certain limitations that are important only to the student of the English history of feudalism. Notably, three years later, another act was passed providing that a married woman's devise was invalid. See 34 & 35 Hen. 8, c. 5, § 14. Every jurisdiction has passed married women's acts that remove a woman's incapacity to make wills.[1]

Studies show that the considerable testamentary freedom Americans now enjoy is highly valued. See, e.g., Fellows, Simon & Rau, Public Attitudes About Property Distribution at Death and Intestate Succession Laws in the United States, 1978 Am. B. Found. Res. J. 319, 333-36. A legal regime that allows wide latitude in directing the disposition of property reflects substantial societal indifference as to how property devolves. The only function the law serves is to make a reasonably reliable determination about whether a particular decedent chose to exercise her or his right of testamentary freedom by making a will and, if so, what that decedent's directions were.

The considerable testamentary freedom Americans enjoy is usually used wisely and maturely. In the hands of an unwise or even vindictive testator, however, a will can do considerable harm to family relationships, as the following extract from an article written by a psychiatrist cautions:

> Making a Will is one of the most important things a person does during his lifetime. Death dramatically interrupts the process of ownership and our culture has set up procedures for the destruction, orderly transfer or legally approved distribution of the assets of the deceased. Yet the Will is more than a legacy of the testator's worldly goods. It is also a human document—an expression of perceived or misperceived family relationships, or both. The Will represents, in a dramatic microcosm, a family's dynamic structure and the relationships between its members. It can be a concrete expression of love that

---

1. For further discussion of the development of women's property rights in the United States, see N. Basch, In the Eyes of the Law: Women, Marriage, and Property in Nineteenth-Century New York (1982); M. Salmon, Women and the Law of Property in Early America (1986); E. Warbasse, The Changing Legal Rights of Married Women 1800-1861 (1987); Chused, Married Women's Property Law, 1800-1850, 71 Geo. L.J. 1359 (1983). See also S. Staves, Married Women's Separate Property in England, 1660-1833 (1990).

strengthens family tradition, or it can be a weapon that destroys the family. As such, the Will has considerable power.

Schneiderman, The Creation of a Will is a Personal Matter, 130 Tr. & Est. 68 (Feb. 1991).

Probate Procedure. Procedurally, the determination about whether a particular decedent left a valid will is made in a proceeding in which the instrument is "offered" for probate by the "proponent." If the instrument is found to be valid, it is "admitted to probate as the decedent's last will." This procedure developed early in English law for wills of personal property, but not for wills of real property (even after wills of land were authorized by statute in 1540). The ecclesiastical courts assumed jurisdiction over wills of personal property, but not of land. Until a probate court was established in England in the mid-nineteenth century and given jurisdiction over the probate of all wills, there was no direct means of establishing the validity of a will of land. Instead, validity was usually put in issue by an action in ejectment or trespass, brought to try the title to land.

Nearly everywhere in this country, some court is given jurisdiction to probate wills, whether the property involved be real or personal or both. In many states there are separate probate courts, although they may go by other names, such as surrogates' courts in New York, or orphans' courts in Pennsylvania. In other states, the court of general jurisdiction, such as a circuit or county court, exercises probate jurisdiction. Although there are many local differences in the jurisdiction of probate courts, in general they not only pass on the validity of wills, but they also appoint executors and administrators and exercise supervision over these personal representatives in the administration of decedents' estates, regardless of whether the decedent died testate or intestate. The appointment of a personal representative is traditionally described as the grant of "letters testamentary" or "letters of administration."

The Relationship Between Substantive Requirements and the Statutory Formalities. Determining that a particular decedent left a valid will has been thought to require: (1) solid evidence of the existence and content of the decedent's directions; (2) some indication that the directions were not casually arrived at; (3) reason to think that the directions were the product of the decedent's free choice; and (4) reason to think that the decedent had the mental capacity to comprehend what property she or he owned and who the so-called natural objects of her or his bounty were at the time the decisions were made.

Throughout American history, these objectives—frequently called the evidentiary, cautionary, and protective functions—have been partly achieved through the establishment of statutory formalities for the execution of a valid will. In broad form, the statutory formalities have remained unchanged. They are that the will must be: (1) in *writing;* (2) *signed* by the testator; and (3) *attested* by credible witnesses. The details of two of these three basic requirements—signature and attestation—vary considerably from state to state. These variations are largely attributable to the fact that, before the widespread adoption of the pre-1990 UPC, American statutes were—and still are in non-UPC states—largely copied from one or the other (or, in some cases, partly from both) of two English statutes: the Statute of Frauds of 1677 and the Wills Act of 1837.[2]

Statute of Frauds, 1677, § 5.[3] [A]ll devises and bequests of any lands . . . shall be in writing and signed by the party so devising the same or by some other person in his presence and by his express directions and shall be attested and subscribed in the presence of the said devisor by three or four credible witnesses or else they shall be utterly void and of none effect.

Wills Act, 1837, § 9.[4] [N]o will shall be valid unless it shall be in writing and executed in manner hereinafter mentioned; (that is to say,) it shall be signed at the foot or end thereof by the testator, or by some other person in his presence and by his direction; and such signature shall be made or acknowledged by the testator in the presence of two or more witnesses present at the same time, and such witnesses shall attest and subscribe the will in the presence of the testator, but no form of attestation shall be necessary.

Notice the direction taken by the later English statute, the Wills Act of 1837: It increased rather than decreased the statutory formalities. Prior to the promulgation of the Uniform Probate Code in 1969, most American states had opted for a statute modelled on the lower-formality Statute of Frauds provision. The pre-1990 UPC lowered the formalities still further in order to "validate the will whenever possible." General Comment to Art. II, Part 5, pre-1990 UPC. Accordingly, pre-1990 UPC section 2-502 required a will to be in writing, signed by the testator, and signed by two persons who witnessed either the testator's act of signing or the testator's acknowledgment of the signature or of the will.

Section 2-502 of the 1990 UPC essentially continues the pre-1990 set of formalities. It takes a further step, however, in the direction of upholding wills whenever responsibly possible by adding a new section, section 2-503. That section provides that a will not executed in conformity with section 2-502 is valid if the proponent can establish by clear and convincing evidence that the decedent intended the document to constitute her or his will.

---

2. In early law, wills of personal property were not required to be in writing, nor were wills of land when they were made through the device of a use. The Statute of Wills of 1540, 32 Hen. 8 c. 1, seems to have established the requirement of a writing, though it was not necessary that the instrument be written or signed by the testator, nor that it be witnessed. The hesitation in making a flat statement that a writing was necessary arises from the language of the statute giving power to any person who should "have" any lands as tenant in fee simple to "give, dispose, will and devise" the same "by his last will and testament in writing, or otherwise by any act or acts lawfully executed in his life . . . ." The authorities state, however, that a writing was required. See, e.g., 7 W. Holdsworth, History of English Law 367 (1926).

3. Statute of Frauds, 1677, 29 Car. 2, c. 3.

4. Wills Act, 1837, 7 Wm. 4 & 1 Vict. c. 26.

PART A. FORMALITIES OF EXECUTION: THE PROPONENT'S CASE

As indicated above, most non-UPC statutes in this country prescribe formalities for the execution of a will modeled on one or the other of the English statutes set forth above. In the majority of non-UPC states, the legislation is based on the Statute of Frauds of 1677, except that only two witnesses are usually required.[5] Some states have added requirements not found in the English statutes, such as the requirement that wills be "published," by which it is meant that the testator must declare to the witnesses that the document is her or his will.

In addition to attested wills (wills subscribed by the prescribed number of attesting witnesses), a substantial and growing number of states also recognizes the validity of certain types of unattested wills. Here we are principally speaking of holographic wills. The formalities prescribed for a valid holographic will are that the will must be written in the handwriting of the testator and signed, and in some states that it must be dated.

The goal of the statutory formalities—writing, signature, attestation (or, in the case of holographic wills, writing in the testator's hand, signature, and perhaps dating)—is, as stated above, to facilitate reasonably reliable determinations about whether decedents chose to exercise their testamentary freedom and, if so, what their distributive plans were. In addition to the evidentiary, cautionary, and protective functions, the formalities serve a channeling function. The following excerpt from an article by Professor Langbein elaborates on the functions that the formalities seek to serve.

Langbein, Substantial Compliance With the Wills Act
88 Harv. L. Rev. 489, 492-97 (1975)

Several discrete functions can be identified and ascribed to the formalities; however, we shall see that in modern practice they are not regarded as equally important.

1. The Evidentiary Function. The primary purpose of the Wills Act[6] has always been to provide the court with reliable evidence of testamentary intent and of the terms of the will; virtually all the formalities serve as "probative safeguards." The requirement of writing assures that "evidence of testamentary intent [will] be cast in reliable and permanent form." The requirement that the testator sign the will is meant to produce evidence of

---

5. Three witnesses were once required in a few states, principally in New England. Of these, only Vermont still retains a three-witness requirement. Restatement 2d of Property, Statutory Note to § 33.1.

6. The term "Wills Act" is used by the author to refer generically to whatever statutory formalities have been enacted in the state; the term is not meant to refer exclusively to the English Wills Act of 1837. Eds.

genuineness. The requirement that he sign at the end prevents subsequent interpolation.

The attestation requirement, the distinguishing feature of the so-called formal will, assures that the actual signing is witnessed and sworn to by disinterested bystanders. When the statute directs the testator to publish his will to the witnesses, he is made to announce his testamentary intent to the persons who may later "prove" the will. Those who survive the testator are available to testify in probate proceedings. The requirement that they be competent, meaning disinterested, produces witnesses whose testimony is not self-serving.

In holographic wills the requirement of handwriting substitutes for that of attestation. Gulliver and Tilson think holographs "almost exclusively justifiable in terms of the evidentiary function." [Gulliver & Tilson, Classification of Gratuitous Transfers, 51 Yale L. J. 1, 13 (1941).] A more ample handwriting sample results than mere signature, should the genuineness of the document be questioned. . . .

2. *The Channeling Function.* What Fuller calls the "channeling" function of legal formalities in contract law is also an important purpose of the Wills Act formalities. Fuller likens the channeling function to the role of language: "One who wishes to communicate his thoughts to others must force the raw material of meaning into defined and recognizable channels. . . ."

The channeling function has both social and individual aspects. Friedman points to the relationship between the formalities and efficient judicial administration. "Formalities must be capable and fit for the job of handling millions of estates and billions of dollars in assets." Compliance with the Wills Act formalities for executing witnessed wills results in considerable uniformity in the organization, language, and content of most wills. Courts are seldom left to puzzle whether the document was meant to be a will.

Standardization of wills is a matter of unusual importance, because unlike contracts or conveyances, wills inevitably contemplate judicial implementation, although normally in non-adversarial litigation resembling adjudication less than ordinary governmental administration. Citizen compliance with the usual forms has, therefore, the same order of channeling importance for the probate courts that it has, for example, for the Internal Revenue Service. Under the principle of free testation, "[t]he *substance* of wills (what they actually say) cannot be standardized. It may be all the more important that the documents be standardized in form."

The standardization of testation achieved under the Wills Act also benefits the testator. He does not have to devise for himself a mode of communicating his testamentary wishes to the court, and to worry whether it will be effective. Instead, he has every inducement to comply with the Wills Act formalities. The court can process his estate routinely, because his testament is conventionally and unmistakably expressed and evidenced. The lowered costs of routinized judicial administration benefit the estate and its ultimate distributees.

Holographic wills serve the channeling function less well, because the required formalities are less likely to resolve whether the document was meant as a will. Whereas the formalities for witnessed wills call for a virtually unmistakable testamentary act, holographic will requirements are closer to the patterns of ordinary nontestamentary communication. . . .

3. *The Cautionary Function.* A will is said to be revocable and ambulatory, meaning that it becomes operative only on death. Because the testator does not part with the least incident of ownership when he makes a will, and does not experience the "wrench of delivery" required for inter vivos gifts, the danger exists that he may make seeming testamentary dispositions inconsiderately, without adequate forethought and finality of intention. Not every expression that "I want you to have the house when I'm gone" is meant as a will. One purpose of many of the forms is to impress the testator with the seriousness of the testament, and thereby to assure the court "that the statements of the transferor were deliberately intended to effectuate a transfer." They caution the testator, and they show the court that he was cautioned.

The requirements of writing and signature, which have such major evidentiary significance, are also the primary cautionary formalities. Writing is somewhat less casual than plain chatter. As we say in a common figure of speech, "talk is cheap." More important than the requirement of written terms is that of written signature. "The signature tends to show that the instrument was finally adopted by the testator as his will and to militate against the inference that the writing was merely a preliminary draft, an incomplete disposition, or haphazard scribbling."

The formalities associated with attestation also serve cautionary policies. The execution of the will is made into a ceremony impressing the participants with its solemnity and legal significance. Compliance with the Wills Act formalities for a witnessed will is meant to conclude the question of testamentary intent. It is difficult to complete the ceremony and remain ignorant that one is making a will.

A principal objection to holographic wills is that they serve the cautionary function poorly. A particular writing may be casual and offhand or considered and testamentary. . . . The inference of testamentary intent is far stronger when explicit testamentary language is used. Nevertheless, the cautionary value of the attestation ceremony is wanting.

4. *The Protective Function.* Courts have traditionally attributed to the Wills Act the object "of protecting the testator against imposition at the time of execution." The requirement that attestation be made in the presence of the testator is meant "to prevent the substitution of a surreptitious will." Another common protective requirement is the rule that the witnesses should be disinterested, hence not motivated to coerce or deceive the testator.

The Gulliver and Tilson article made a persuasive critique of the protective policy, which has borne some fruit in the attestation requirements of the [pre-1990] Uniform Probate Code. Sections 2-502 and 2-505 of the [pre-1990] Code eliminate the presence and competency (disinterestedness) requirements. The official commentary to [pre-1990] section 2-505, explaining the elimination of the competency requirement, repeats the principal arguments advanced by Gulliver and Tilson against the protective policy: (1) The attestation formalities are pitifully inadequate to protect the testator from determined crooks, and have not in fact succeeded in preventing the many cases of fraud and undue influence which are proved each year. (2) Protective formalities do more harm than good, voiding homemade wills for harmless violations. (3) Protective formalities are not needed. Since fraud or undue influence may always be proved notwithstanding due execution, the ordinary remedies for imposition are quite adequate.

The protective policy is probably best explained as an historical anachronism. In the seventeenth century when the first Wills Act was written, most wealth was in the form of realty, and passed either by intestacy or conveyance. Will making could thus be left to end, and the danger of imposition was greater because "wills were usually executed on the deathbed." Today, "wills are probably executed by most testators in the prime of life and in the presence of attorneys."

Because they lack attestation, holographic wills make no pretense of serving the protective function. "A holographic will is obtainable by compulsion as easily as a ransom note."

1. Attested Wills

Statutory References: *1990 UPC §§ 2-502 to -503, -506, 3-407*
                            Pre-1990 UPC §§ 2-502, -506

The Preferred Method for Executing a Valid Will. As indicated earlier, the statutes differ among the states as to various details of formality. Differences in the statutes suggest that execution in compliance with the law of the place where the testator is living at the time of execution may not be a wholly safe procedure. If the testator owns land in another state, the validity of the will as a disposition of this land will be controlled by the law of the state where the land is located. If the testator moves to another state after making the will, the validity of the will as to personal property depends on the law of the state in which she or he was domiciled at death. These, at least, are the common-law rules of conflict of laws.

To be sure, the common-law rules are frequently changed by a statute such as UPC section 2-506 (1990), which in general recognizes a will executed outside the state in accordance with either the law of the place of execution or of the testator's domicile. Several statutes, however, are narrower than the UPC provision. Some recognize a will executed outside the state only if it was executed in accordance with the law of the place of execution. Others recognize validity only if the will was executed in accordance with the law of the testator's domicile. See Restatement 2d of Property, Statutory Note to § 33.1.

The presence of the common-law rules, and the lack of uniformity within the choice-of-law statutes, suggest the advisability of complying with the maximum formalities called for by the law of any state. The excerpt from the Restatement 2d of Property that follows outlines a preferred method for will execution to assure validity in all states.

Restatement 2d of Property
§ 33.1 comment c

Statutory formalities. . . . [I]f the following steps are taken in the execution of a will, the will should have maximum acceptability in the various States:[7]

1. The testator should examine the will in its entirety and the lawyer should make certain that the testator understands the terms of the will.

2. The testator and three persons who are to be witnesses to the will and who have no interest vested or contingent in the property disposed of by the testator's will or in the testator's estate in the event of an intestacy, along with the lawyer supervising the execution of the will, should be in a room from which everyone else is excluded. No one should enter or leave this room until the execution of the will is completed.

3. The lawyer supervising the execution of the will should ask the testator the following question: "Do you declare in the presence of [witness 1], [witness 2], and [witness 3] that the document before you is your will, that its terms have been explained to you, and that the document expresses your desires as to the disposition of the property referred to therein on your death?" The testator should answer "yes" and the answer should be audible to the three witnesses.

4. The lawyer supervising the execution of the will should then ask the testator the following question: "Do you request [witness 1], [witness 2], and [witness 3] to witness the signing of your will?" Again, the testator should answer "yes," and the answer should be audible to the three witnesses.

5. The three witnesses should then be so placed that each can see the testator sign and then the testator should sign in the place provided for the testator's signature at the end of the will. The testator should also sign on the bottom of each page of the will.

6. One of the witnesses should then read aloud the attestation clause, which should provide in substance that the foregoing instrument was signed on such a date by the testator (giving the testator's name); that the testator requested each of the witnesses to witness his signing of the document; that each of the witnesses did witness the signing of the document; that each witness in the presence of the testator and in the presence of the other witnesses does sign as witness, and that each witness does declare the testator to be of sound mind and memory.

7. Each witness should declare that the attestation clause is a correct statement.

---

7. The one exception is Louisiana, where three witnesses are required, one of whom must be a notary public. The Louisiana Codes need to be consulted. See La. Civ. Code Ann. art. 1574, et seq.; La. Rev. Stat. § 9:2442. Eds.

8. Each witness should then sign in the place provided for the signatures of the witnesses following the attestation clause. As each witness signs, the testator and the other two witnesses should be so placed that each one can see the witness sign. Each witness should give an address opposite his or her signature.

If under the controlling local law the observance of certain formalities will make the will self-proving, and additional formalities to those listed above are required to make it self-proving, such additional formalities should be adopted.

———

Attestation Clauses. The Restatement, above, assumes the use of an attestation clause. Attestation clauses are located immediately below the line for the testator's signature, and typically provide:

> The foregoing instrument, consisting of _____ typewritten pages, including this page, was signed, published and declared by the above named testator to be his last will, in the presence of us; we, in his presence, at his request, and in the presence of each other, have hereunto subscribed our names as witnesses; and we declare that at the time of the execution of this instrument the testator, according to our best knowledge and belief, was of sound mind and disposing memory and under no constraint.
>
> Dated at _____, _____, this ___ day of _____,_____.

_____	_____
Witness	Address
_____	_____
Witness	Address
_____	_____
Witness	Address

Although no state requires the use of an attestation clause as a prerequisite to validity, lawyers routinely use them because they raise a rebuttable presumption that the events recited therein actually occurred. In most states, the presumption is regarded as a presumption of fact. That means the presumption remains operative and is entitled to evidentiary weight notwithstanding the introduction of contrary evidence. See, e.g., Morris v. Estate of West, 602 S.W.2d 122 (Tex. Civ. App. 1980). See also Estate of Johnson, 780 P.2d 692 (Okla. 1989) (will held invalid where testimony of witnesses persuasively contradicted attestation clause). If the witnesses' testimony contradicts the events recited in the attestation clause, but is consistent with one of a number of chains of events that comply with the statutory formalities, what result? See Betts v. Lonas, 172 F.2d 759 (D.C. Cir. 1948) (will upheld on the basis of a presumption of regularity arising from fact that will looked regular on its face).

On occasion, a will, regular on its face but without an attestation clause, has been denied probate when the witnesses could not recall whether the required procedures had been followed. For example, in Young v. Young, 20 Ill. App. 3d 242, 248, 313 N.E.2d 593, 597 (1974), the court said, "where the purported will does not contain an attestation clause, the proponent of the will has the burden of proving its proper execution by other evidence. . . . The [proponent] has furnished no such evidence."

Attorney Liability for Invalid Execution. A lawyer who supervises the execution of a will may be liable to the devisees if the lawyer caused the will to be invalidly executed. See, e.g., Biakanja v. Irving, 49 Cal. 2d 647, 320 P.2d 16 (1958); Licata v. Spector, 26 Conn. Supp. 378, 225 A.2d 28 (1966); Guy v. Liederbach, 501 Pa. 47, 459 A.2d 744 (1983); Auric v. Continental Casualty Co., 111 Wis. 2d 507, 331 N.W.2d 325 (1983); Johnston, Legal Malpractice in Estate Planning—Perilous Times Ahead for the Practitioner, 67 Iowa L. Rev. 629, 650-52 (1982); Annots., 45 A.L.R.3d 1181 (1972); 65 A.L.R.2d 1363 (1959). For further discussion of lawyer malpractice, see infra Chapter 10.

a. The Writing Requirement

All the statutes, including the pre-1990 and 1990 Uniform Probate Code, require a will to be in writing. In interpreting this requirement, "probably the courts would insist upon some fairly permanent record—a will scratched on a cake of ice or moulded in the sand might not be allowed." Atkinson on Wills § 63.

A videotape has not yet been recognized as a writing and cannot operate as the will itself. Nevertheless, videotaping a client's will execution ceremony is recommended as a new and effective estate planning tool.

[T]he objective of Wills is to effectuate the desires of the testator in distributing his property and caring for surviving family or friends. Videotape facilitates the realization of these quests. Recording the testator's recitation inexorably links the decedent with the document. Fraudulent writings crumble in the face of such proof. The trier-of-fact sees and hears the decedent personally explain his intentions. This "meeting of minds" is far more intimate and compelling than dry words on yellowing parchment. The testator's mental capacity is crystallized on videotape, enabling judge or jury to appreciate entirely the decedent's mental faculties. The filmed execution establishes satisfactory compliance with statutory precepts. Will opponents' averments accordingly dissipate, and the estate may proceed unaccosted toward rapid distribution and closure.

Practitioners often fear excessive production costs will exceed the benefits videotape bestows. Certainly in many instances the written Will should suffice. Under suitable circumstances, however, videotape can become an invaluable evidential tool to strengthen the paper document. . . .

Within the last decade, considerable caselaw and procedural rules have appeared allowing videotaped evidence of depositions, civil and criminal trials, defendant's confessions, police line-ups, crime or accident scenes, law enforcement "sting" operations, and "day-in-the-life" accounts.[8] Courts have readily

---

8. Indiana has adopted an evidentiary rule pertaining specifically to wills. See Ind. Ann. Stat. § 29-1-5-3(d) ("Subject to the applicable Indiana rules of trial procedure, a videotape may be admissible as evidence of . . . the proper execution of a will."). Eds.

equated videotape with photographs and apply identical standards for admissibility.

Buckley, Videotaped Wills: More Than a Testator's Curtain Call, 126 Tr. & Est. 48, 49 (Oct. 1987). See also Beyer & Buckley, Video Tape and the Probate Process: The Nexus Grows, 42 Okla. L. Rev. 43 (1989); Buckley, Indiana's New Videotaped Wills Statute: Launching Probate Into the 21st Century, 20 Val. U.L. Rev. 83 (1985); Max, Videotaped Wills: Status of Present Statutory Law and Implications for Expanded Use, 4 Conn. Prob. L.J. 125 (1988).

b. The Signature Requirement

All the statutes, including section 2-502 of the pre-1990 and 1990 Uniform Probate Code, require the testator to sign the will. Both versions of the UPC and many non-UPC statutes qualify the signature requirement by the rule that, if the testator does not sign herself or himself, someone else can sign the testator's name if it is done in the presence and at the direction of the testator. A further requirement, sometimes imposed by non-UPC statutes, is that persons who sign for testators must also sign their own names and sometimes also give their addresses. See Restatement 2d of Property, Statutory Note to § 33.1.

Estate of McKellar, below, considered the validity of a will under a statute modeled on the English Statute of Frauds of 1677, supra p. 164.

Estate of McKellar
380 S.2d 1273 (Miss. 1980)

BROOM, J. Execution and attestation of a purported Last Will and Testament are at issue in this case appealed from the Chancery Court of Lauderdale County. In that court Tiny Bell filed for probate a document said to be Greta Meador McKellar's true Last Will and Testament. The matter was contested and after hearing testimony the lower court found that the document was statutorily deficient and therefore invalid. . . .

The purported Last Will and Testament of Greta Meador McKellar (McKellar herein) is a five-page instrument [completely written out in McKellar's own handwriting and] dated August 23, 1977. McKellar died March 29, 1979. . . . According to the document at issue, several beneficiaries of McKellar's purported Will were persons not her heirs at law. Her heirs at law were stated to be Tiny Bell, named by the lower court as her administratrix, Nell Thrash and Jacqueline Field.

First paragraph of the purported Will is in the following language:

To Whom it May Concern
I, Greta Meador McKellar, being of sound mind and body, declare this to be my last Will and testimony [sic] concerning my real and personal property. . . .

The document consists of five pages (four sheets of paper), the last of which is on the reverse side of page 1. Near the bottom of the last page, being page No. 5, is the following:

> The following have witness [sic] my writing of this five page will—
> Luciana Brewer
> Lucille Jay
> Douglas Watkins.

Nowhere on the instrument except in the opening paragraph does McKellar's purported signature appear.

Testimony adduced to the lower court included the three people whose names appear at the end of the document as witnesses. Douglas Watkins testified that she took the deceased McKellar to the hospital, and that while a patient in the hospital, McKellar called Watkins to her room and said, "Sign this." Watkins did not see McKellar write any part of the document; nor did she see McKellar sign her name, nor hear McKellar acknowledge signing the document. According to Watkins, McKellar did not tell her what the document was.

Another witness to the instrument, Luciane Brewer, stated that McKellar called her to McKellar's hospital room where McKellar handed Brewer one page to sign. She testified that in all McKellar had four or five pieces of paper, and that when she (Brewer) signed it, she saw no other names on the paper. Brewer's further testimony was that McKellar discussed the contents of the instrument with her but did not state that McKellar told her that McKellar had signed the instrument. Brewer did not read the instrument.

Lucille Jay testified that McKellar asked her to come to McKellar's room where McKellar said, "This is my Last Will and Testimony [sic]. . . ." Jay stated that when she signed the instrument as a witness, she didn't examine it but that Mrs. Brewer had already signed it when she, Jay, signed it.

The witness Watkins kept the controversial document until the day after the funeral when she opened the envelope containing the document.

The chancellor in his opinion held that the

> [P]urported will was not signed by the purported testatrix as is required by law and the cases in this jurisdiction. It is the opinion of this Court that the statements made to the witnesses by the purported testatrix did not carry with it any words signifying that the purported testatrix had signed the will.

Upon this record we cannot say that the decree against the purported Will was manifestly wrong or that the chancellor's finding was contrary to the law or the evidence. Careful analysis of the testimony establishes that none of the witnesses who testified stated that they saw or read or heard the entire document. None of the pages of the document except near the bottom of page five was signed by a witness, and McKellar's purported signature was at the top of page one. No testimony is in the record that any of the witnesses saw or observed McKellar either affix her signature on the document or heard her acknowledge that she had previously or at any time signed or affixed her signature to the document.

Under the case law of this state, the execution of a Will is a statutory privilege and not a constitutional or common law right. We have held many times that the intention of a testator is the paramount issue in the construction of Wills but one's intention does not become important nor the object of search by a court until there is first established a Will executed according to statutory requirements. *Wilson v. Polite*, 218 S.2d 843 (Miss. 1969). *Wilson* dealt with a purported Will wherein the testatrix did not sign (subscribe) at the bottom. Accordingly we held it not to be a valid holographic Will. In *Wilson*, there were no attesting witnesses to the purported Will, and it could not be valid as a non-holographic Will so it was a nullity. *Wilson* made the following pronouncement concerning a non-holographic or attested Will (the type now at issue):

> [T]he name of the testator may be written at any place on the instrument, so long as it is declared to be his signature, and the instrument is published and signed in the presence of the witnesses.

Our statute applicable here is Mississippi Code Annotated § 91-5-1 (1972) which states in pertinent part that:

> [S]uch last will and testament, or codicil, be signed by the testator or testatrix, or by some other person in his or her presence and by his or her express direction. Moreover, if not wholly written and subscribed by himself or herself, it shall be attested by two (2) or more credible witnesses in the presence of the testator or testatrix. . . .

Upon this record we cannot say that the Will was properly executed . . . and therefore the lower court must be affirmed. Affirmed.

PATTERSON, C.J., SMITH and ROBERTSON, P.JJ., and SUGG, WALKER, LEE, BOWLING and COOPER, JJ., concur.

Notes and Questions

1. *Strict-Compliance Approach.* Writing in 1975, Professor Langbein observed:

> The law of wills is notorious for its harsh and relentless formalism. The Wills Act[9] prescribes a particular set of formalities for executing one's testament. The most minute defect in formal compliance is held to void the will, no matter how abundant the evidence that the defect was inconsequential. Probate courts do not speak of harmless error in the execution of wills. To be sure, there is considerable diversity and contradiction in the cases interpreting what acts constitute compliance with what formalities. But once

---

9. See supra note 6. Eds.

a formal defect is found, Anglo-American courts have been unanimous in concluding that the attempted will fails.

Langbein, Substantial Compliance With the Wills Act, supra, at 489. What formal defect caused Greta McKellar's will to fail? To what do you attribute the court's picky attitude? Does it appear to have been generated by a suspicion that Greta's will was not a reliable expression of her true wishes?

2. *"Signature" in the Exordium?* When Greta McKellar wrote her name in the exordium, was she signing her will or was she identifying herself as the maker of the will? Can a document be "signed" before it has been written? Must a signature be a freestanding handwritten name affixed for the purpose of finalizing a document, or can it also be a name in a handwritten sentence of identification? Courts going as far back as Lemayne v. Stanley, 3 Lev. 1, 83 Eng. Rep. 545 (1681), have accepted a handwritten name in the exordium as the testator's signature, given other proof of finality. See Restatement 2d of Property § 32.1 comment c; Mechem, The Rule in *Lemayne v. Stanley*, 29 Mich. L. Rev. 685 (1931).

If a handwritten name in the exordium can be counted as a signature, can a handwritten name in a dispositive provision also be counted as a signature? Compare Bloch's Estate, 39 Cal. 2d 570, 248 P.2d 21 (1952) (Traynor, J., dissenting) (the court upheld as a will a handwritten document left by Helen I. Bloch in which her name was found only in a devise of "bonds belonging solely to *Helen I. Bloch*") with Nelson v. Texarkana Historical Soc'y and Museum, 257 Ark. 394, 516 S.W.2d 882 (1974) (Fogleman, J., dissenting) (the court held a handwritten document left by Maye Elizabeth Ramage Davis was not a will because the only place her name was found was in a devise to the "Texarkana Museum in memory of my mother and father, W.R. Ramage and brother Robert Ramage and *Maye Elizabeth Ramage Davis*").

3. *Position of the Testator's Signature.* Unlike the English Statute of Frauds of 1677, supra p. 164, and the Uniform Probate Code, the English Wills Act of 1837, supra p. 164, requires the testator to sign "at the foot or end" of the will.[10] In this country, about eight states require the testator's signature to be at the end of the will. See Restatement 2d of Property, Statutory Note to § 33.1. For examples of cases where the will failed because the testator did not meet the requirement of signing at the end, see Sears v. Sears, 77 Ohio St. 104, 82 N.E. 1067 (1907) (The testator, in using a printed will form, failed to sign her name on the indicated dotted line, but did write her name in the attestation clause below the signature line, as follows: "The foregoing instrument was signed by the said *Arminda S. Nicholson* in our presence, and by *her* published and declared as and for *her* last will and testament, etc." The italicized words were in the testator's

---

10. The rigidity of this requirement, or at least of its interpretation, was relaxed somewhat by an amendment in 1852 that permitted, *inter alia*, a signature "so placed at or after, or following, or under, or beside or opposite to the end of the will, that it shall be apparent on the face of the will that the testator intended to give effect by such his signature to the writing signed as his will. . . ." 15 & 16 Vict., c. 24.

handwriting. The "end of the will was self-evident," the court said, and the testator signed not at the end but below it.); Winter's Will, 277 A.D. 24, 98 N.Y.S.2d 312 (1950), aff'd without opinion, 302 N.Y. 666, 98 N.E.2d 477 (1951) (The decedent and the proper number of attesting witnesses signed their names underneath the dispositive provisions of the instrument but above a clause naming certain persons as executors)[11]; Estate of Proley, 492 Pa. 57, 422 A.2d 136 (1980) (Using a printed will form designed to be folded over, the decedent wrote her name on the back portion on a blank line below the printed words "Will of . . .," which appeared at a right-angle to the text of the will on the other side. Whether the decedent actually believed she was signing her will, the signature was invalid, the court said, because "the question is not what a testator mistakenly thinks he is doing, but what he actually does.").

4. *The Sign-First Requirement.* Most courts assume that the testator must sign the will before the witnesses sign. By substantial authority, however, the exact order of signing is not critical if the testator and the witnesses sign as part of a "single (or continuous) transaction." See, e.g., Waldrep v. Goodwin, 230 Ga. 1, 195 S.E.2d 432 (1973); Hopson v. Ewing, 353 S.W.2d 203 (Ky. 1961). A few courts have rejected the single-transaction idea. See, e.g., Barnes v. Chase, 208 Mass. 490, 94 N.E. 694 (1911) (testator's signing in presence of witnesses a few minutes after witnesses had signed invalidated will); Marshall v. Mason, 176 Mass. 216, 57 N.E. 340 (1900); Estate of Hartung, 52 N.J. Super. 508, 145 A.2d 798 (1958). Cases are collected in Page on Wills § 19.139; Annot., 91 A.L.R.2d 737 (1963).

Suppose a testator signs her will before the witnesses arrive. After the witnesses arrive, she asks them to sign her will as witnesses and tells them that she already signed it, but she folds the paper in such a way that the witnesses never see her signature. If the case were governed by a statute modeled on the English Statute of Frauds of 1677, supra p. 164, the will would probably be valid. See Betts v. Lonas, 172 F.2d 759 (D.C. Cir. 1948). But, would the will be valid if the case were governed by a statute modelled on the English Wills Act of 1837, supra p. 164, which requires that the testator's "signature shall be made or acknowledged by the testator in the presence of" the witnesses? See Hudson v. Parker, 1 Rob. Ecc. 15, 163 Eng. Rep. 948 (1844), where the court said: "What is the plain meaning of acknowledging a signature in the presence of witnesses?—what do the words import but this?—'Here is my name written, I acknowledge that name so written to have been written by me; bear witness;' how is it possible that the witnesses should swear that any signature was ac-

---

11. N.Y. Est. Powers & Trusts Law § 3-2.1(a)(1)(A)) now provides that the material above (but not below) the signature can be given effect. See Estate of Mergenthaler, 123 Misc. 2d 809, 474 N.Y.S.2d 253 (Sur. Ct. 1984) (a four-page will, prepared by an attorney, was improperly stapled and its pages were misnumbered prior to execution; what should have been page 3 came after what should have been page 4; the will having been signed at the bottom of page 3, the court gave effect to pages 1 through 3; page 4, which contained the residuary devise, was not given effect, causing the residue to pass by intestacy, fortuitously, to the same person who was to have been the residuary devisee).

knowledged unless they saw it." Accord Patten v. Patten, 171 Mont. 399, 558 P.2d 659 (1976) (will invalid). But see Norton v. Georgia Railroad Bank & Trust Co., 248 Ga. 847, 285 S.E.2d 910 (1982), where the court held that a testator's acknowledgment of his signature to the witnesses "need not be explicit, but may be inferred from conduct." A witness testified that he was not in the house when the testator signed the will. The witness later entered the living room and sat at a table "right by" the testator and across from the attorney who drafted the will. The attorney asked the witness to witness the instrument, and the witness signed it in the presence of the testator. The testator's conduct was held to be a sufficient acknowledgment of his signature to the witness.

5. *Crossed Wills.* W and H go to a lawyer for simple wills. At their request, the lawyer prepares a will for W devising her entire estate to H if H survives her, if not to their joint children, A and B; and prepares a will for H devising his entire estate to W if she survives him, if not to A and B. When W and H go to the lawyer's office to sign the wills, the lawyer gets the wills mixed up and gives W's will to H to sign and H's will to W to sign. The mistake is not discovered until W dies, survived by H, A, and B. Does W have a valid will? In Pavlinko's Estate, 394 Pa. 564, 148 A.2d 528 (1959), the court held that the will signed by H "could not [be] probated as [W's] will, because it was not signed by [her] . . . [and that the will signed by W] is a meaningless nullity." But see In re Snide, 52 N.Y.2d 193, 437 N.Y.S.2d 63, 418 N.E.2d 656 (1981), described infra p. 581.

6. *The Rule/Standard Distinction.* A legal proposition can be formulated as a "rule" or as a "standard." See supra p. 153. In the law of wills, the traditional approach formulates the prescription for a valid will as a rule or set of rules: The statutes require the validity of a document to be determined by whether it is written, signed, and attested in the prescribed form, not by whether it satisfies the evidentiary, cautionary, or protective functions.

One of the leading figures in the Critical Legal Studies movement has written in favor of casting legal propositions as standards, not rules, because, to one degree or another, rules are inherently over-inclusive and under-inclusive. This, he argues, inevitably leads courts to invent means of circumventing the rules in order to do justice in particular cases:

> The argument for casting formalities as rules rests on two sets of assumptions, each of which is often challenged in discussions of actual legal institutions. The first set of assumptions concerns the impact on real participants in a real legal system of the demand for formal proficiency. If the argument for rules is to work, we must anticipate that private parties will in fact respond to the threat of the sanction of nullity by learning to operate the system. But real as opposed to hypothetical legal actors may be unwilling or unable to do this. . . .
>
> The second set of assumptions underlying the argument for rules concerns the practical possibility of maintaining a highly formal regime. . . . Take, for example, the "rule" that a contract will be rescinded for mutual mistake going to the "substance" . . . of the transaction, but not for mistakes as to a "mere quality or accident," even though the quality or accident in question was the whole reason for the transaction. We have come to see legal directives of this

kind as invitations to sub rosa balancing of the equities. Such covert standards may generate more uncertainty than would a frank avowal that the judge is allocating a loss by reference to an open textured notion of good faith and fair dealing. . . .

It is also often possible to make a plausible claim that the reason for the "corruption" of what was supposed to be a formal regime was that the judges were simply unwilling to bite the bullet, shoot the hostages, break the eggs to make the omelette and leave the passengers on the platform. The more general and more formally realizable the rule, the greater the equitable pull of extreme cases of over- or underinclusion. The result may be a dynamic instability as pernicious as that of standards. There will be exceptions that are only initially innocuous, playing with the facts, the invention of counterrules . . . , the manipulation of manifestations of intent, and so forth. Each successful evasion makes it seem more unjust to apply the rule rigidly in the next case; what was once clear comes to be surrounded by a technical and uncertain penumbra that is more demoralizing to investment in form that an outright standard would be.

Kennedy, Form and Substance in Private Law Adjudication, 89 Harv. L. Rev. 1685, 1699-1701 (1976).

Although Professor Kennedy argues for "standards," much can be said for "rules" in the law of wills. Rules (formalities) provide certainty of result—a safe harbor—for those who comply with them. And, those who comply undoubtedly far outnumber those who botch the job on one point or another.[12] In addition, the law of wills does not fit Professor Kennedy's description of law generally. The first discrepancy is that the formalities for a valid will are not both over-inclusive and under-inclusive. They are merely under-inclusive. Wills executed in strict compliance with the statutory formalities constitute reliable enough expressions of intention. The problem, as McKellar surely demonstrates, is that wills that fail to comply with one or another of the statutory formalities, and hence are invalid, may in given cases constitute just as reliable expressions of intention as those executed in strict compliance with the formalities. The second discrepancy is that, in cases like McKellar, the courts seem quite content to "leave the passengers on the platform," rather than "corrupt" the formal regime to do justice. (What makes the courts behave differently under the law of wills than they do under, say, the law of contracts?)

The solution, then, is not to replace the "rules" (formalities) with a "standard," but to supplement the rules with a standard. This general

---

12. A recent empirical study of probate and court records over a nine-year period (1976-1984) in Davidson County, Tennessee (Nashville) revealed that 7,638 (less than 22 percent) of the 36,832 deaths during the period produced a will offered for probate. Of the wills offered for probate, 66 (less than one percent) were contested. Only one of these contests was wholly grounded on a defective-execution claim; eight of the contests coupled a claim of defective execution with other grounds of contest such as undue influence or lack of testamentary capacity, the latter of which were the primary thrust of these cases and the predominant ground of contest in general. See Schoenblum, Will Contests—An Empirical Study, 22 Real Prop. Prob. & Tr. J. 607 (1987). This study does not, of course, reveal the number of defectively executed documents that represented genuine expressions of the decedent's intentions but were not presented for probate.

approach allows the standard to take the form of a harmless-error standard, that is, wills executed in strict compliance with the rules (formalities) are valid, but those not executed in strict compliance are tested under the standard. In broad form, two means of supplementing the formalities with a harmless-error standard are available. Retain the rules, but either: (1) accept substantial compliance with them when strict compliance is absent; or (2) grant the courts a power to dispense with compliance in cases in which it can be established that the underlying purposes of the statutory formalities have been met. The substantial-compliance approach could be adopted judicially but the dispensing power approach calls for a legislative corrective.

7. *1990 Uniform Probate Code.* Section 2-503 of the 1990 UPC adopts the dispensing power approach. Several foreign jurisdictions have had that approach in place for several years. 1990 section 2-503 is quite similar to statutes in effect in Israel since 1965, the Australian state of South Australia since 1975, and the Canadian province of Manitoba since 1983.[13]

8. *Restatement 2d of Property.* On the judicial front, the prospect for adoption of a substantial-compliance doctrine was considerably enhanced when in 1990 the American Law Institute approved in section 33.1 of the Restatement 2d of Property a comment that encourages courts to adopt that approach:

> g. *Will not in strict compliance with statutory formalities.* Because the purpose of the statutory formalities is to give effect to the testator's intention, law-reform organizations, commentators, and legislatures in a variety of common-law jurisdictions have been moving to the view that innocent defects in compliance with the formalities should be excused under a harmless-error rule. To be sure, many American courts have taken the position that any defect in compliance with the statutory formalities is fatal to the validity of a will, no matter how innocent the decedent's mistake. This strict-compliance approach has led to harsh results in many cases. In some of these cases, the court's own opinion has openly acknowledged that the result defeated the decedent's intention. Courts have also long been troubled by the fact that the opposite result is reached in will substitute cases. Consequently, an effort should be made to adopt a rule that excuses harmless errors in the execution of a will—a rule that unifies the law of wills and will substitutes by extending to will formalities the harmless-error principle that has long been applied to defective compliance with the formal requirements for will-substitute transfers. In the absence of a legislative corrective [such as UPC section 2-503 (1990)], the court should apply a rule of substantial compliance, under which a will is found validly executed if the document was executed in substantial compliance with the statutory formalities and if the proponent establishes by clear and convincing evidence that the decedent intended the document to constitute his or her will. . . .

The Restatement's move quickly bore fruit. In a decision of breakthrough proportion, Alleged Will of Ranney, 124 N.J. 1, 589 A.2d 1339 (1991), the

---

13. The South Australia and Manitoba statutes are set forth in *Selected Statutes on Trusts and Estates.*

Supreme Court of New Jersey took the lead in embracing the substantial-compliance approach. Citing the tentative draft version of the Restatement and section 2-503 of the 1990 UPC, the court upheld a will signed by the attesting witnesses on the self-proving affidavit rather than on the will itself (see infra p. 194):

> Rigid insistence on literal compliance often frustrates [the] purposes [of the formalities]. . . . Compliance with statutory formalities is important not because of the inherent value that those formalities possess, but because of the purposes they serve. . . . It would be ironic to insist on literal compliance with statutory formalities when that insistence would invalidate a will that is the deliberate and voluntary act of the testator. Such a result would frustrate rather than further the purpose of the formalities. . . . Generally, when strict construction would frustrate the purposes of the statute, the spirit of the law should control over its letter. . . . Accordingly, we believe that the Legislature did not intend that a will should be denied probate because the witnesses signed in the wrong place. . . .
>
> The execution of a last will and testament, however, remains a solemn event. A careful practitioner will still observe the formalities surrounding the execution of wills. When formal defects occur, proponents should prove by clear and convincing evidence that the will substantially complies with statutory requirements. See Uniform Probate Code . . . § 2-503; Restatement, . . . § 33.1 comment g. Our adoption of the doctrine of substantial compliance should not be construed as an invitation either to carelessness or chicanery. The purpose of the doctrine is to remove procedural peccadillos as a bar to probate.

Problems

How would you expect the following cases to be resolved under UPC section 2-503 (1990)? Under a substantial-compliance doctrine as set forth in the Restatement?

1. G sent a signed letter to his attorney giving directions for the preparation of his will. G died while the will was being prepared. Could either the letter or the will prepared by the attorney be probated? See, e.g., Baumanis v. Praulin, 25 S. Austl. St. R. 423 (1980); cf. Estate of Smith, 108 N.J. 257, 528 A.2d 918 (1987); Estate of Moore, 443 Pa. 477, 277 A.2d 825 (1971); Price v. Huntsman, 430 S.W.2d 831 (Tex. Civ. App. 1968).

If neither the letter nor the unsigned will could be probated, would G's intended devisees, those named in his letter, have a cause of action for malpractice against G's attorney? In Krawczyk v. Stingle, 208 Conn. 239, 543 A.2d 733 (1988), the court said:

> We conclude that the imposition of liability to third parties for negligent delay in the execution of estate planning documents would not comport with a lawyer's duty of undivided loyalty to the client. . . . Imposition of liability would create an incentive for an attorney to exert pressure on a client to complete and execute estate planning documents summarily.

2. Same as Problem 1, except that the will was typed in accordance with G's instructions and G came to his attorney's office to execute it. As the attorney and her secretary looked on, G was struck by a fatal heart attack just as he was preparing to sign the will. Cf., e.g., Estate of Richardson, 40 S. Austl. St. R. 594 (1986) (unsigned will held valid where decedent committed suicide and left a suicide note in which he said that he had "left a will with this;" the suicide note and the will were found in the decedent's automobile).

c. *The Attestation Requirement*

Statutory References: *1990 UPC §§ 2-502, -505*
Pre-1990 UPC §§ 2-502, -505

Presence Requirement. Non-UPC statutes commonly prescribe that the witnesses must sign the will "in the presence of" the testator. Signing by the witnesses outside of the presence of the testator, followed by an acknowledgment of the signature in the testator's presence, generally is not permitted. See, e.g., Chase v. Kittredge, 93 Mass. (11 Allen) 49 (1865). See also Atkinson on Wills § 72, at 344; Annot., 115 A.L.R. 689 (1938). But see, e.g., Brammer v. Taylor, 338 S.E.2d 207 (W. Va. 1985).

Statutes modeled on the English Wills Act of 1837, supra p. 164, commonly impose additional signing-in-the-presence-of requirements: They require that the *testator* sign (or acknowledge her or his signature) "in the presence of" the *witnesses* and that the *witnesses* sign "in the presence of" *each other*.[14] The "presence" requirement has proved to be troublesome, in part, because of the narrow meaning many courts give to the word.

Line-of-Vision Test. The prevailing view is that the witness must have been within the testator's "line of vision." The line-of-vision test requires at a minimum "that the testator, without changing his position, might have seen the will being attested; it is not necessary that he actually saw it." See Newton v. Palmour, 245 Ga. 603, 605, 266 S.E.2d 208, 209-10 (1980). One court even held that the will failed because the testator, ill in bed, could only see the backs of the witnesses as they signed, not their hands or the paper on which they wrote. Presence, the court said, means "'within view' . . . the thing to be seen, or to be within the power of the party to see, is the very act of subscribing by the witness." Graham v. Graham, 32 N.C. 219 (1849). Suppose the testator is blind. Under the line-of-vision test, what result? See, e.g., Welch v. Kirby, 255 F. 451 (8th Cir. 1918) (will upheld).

A case of some note under the line-of-vision test is Estate of Jefferson, 349 S.2d 1032 (Miss. 1977). In that case, attorney E. W. Montgomery, II,

---

14. The English Wills Act did not literally require the witnesses to sign in the presence of each other; it required the testator to sign or acknowledge her or his signature in the presence of the witnesses present at the same time; the witnesses were then to sign in the presence of the testator.

A case of some note under the line-of-vision test is Estate of Jefferson, 349 S.2d 1032 (Miss. 1977). In that case, attorney E. W. Montgomery, II, prepared a will for Alcot Jefferson, and caused it to be signed by the testator in a manner authorized by the statute. Mr. Montgomery then became an attesting witness thereto, signing the document in the presence of the testator. This ceremony apparently took place in Jefferson's home. After the testator and Montgomery signed the will, Montgomery returned to his office in the Deposit Guaranty National Bank Building in Jackson, Mississippi, and showed the document to Gid Montjoy, IV, his law partner, informing Montjoy that the document was Alcot Jefferson's will and that Alcot Jefferson had requested that Mr. Montjoy witness the same as a subscribing witness. Montjoy then telephoned Alcot Jefferson and inquired as to whether the instrument presented was his will, and Alcot Jefferson verified the fact. Whereupon, Montjoy, in Montgomery's presence, signed the document as a subscribing witness. Montjoy testified that he knew the voice of Alcot Jefferson. The will was held invalid.

Conscious-Presence Test. A respectable number of courts have interpreted the "presence" requirement more liberally. They have adopted the "conscious-presence" test, which recognizes that a person can sense the presence of another without seeing her or him. "If [the witnesses] are so near at hand that they are within the range of any of [the testator's] senses, so that he knows what is going on, the [presence] requirement has been met." See, e.g., Demaris' Estate, 166 Or. 36, 110 P.2d 571 (1941).

Uniform Probate Code. Rather than codify the conscious-presence test, the pre-1990 UPC largely dispensed with the "presence" requirement. UPC section 2-502 (1990) substantially carries forward this approach. The only place the "presence" requirement is retained is where the testator does not sign her or his own name but directs someone else to sign on her or his behalf. The pre-1990 Code required that person to sign the testator's name "in the testator's presence." The 1990 version of section 2-502 requires the person to sign the testator's name "in the testator's *conscious* presence." (Emphasis added).

The UPC does not require the *witnesses* to sign in the presence of the testator or in the presence of each other. It requires the witnesses to "witness" the testator's act of signing the will or "witness" the testator's act of acknowledging either the signature or the will. Presumably, the "witnessing" requirement means that they must observe the act. The requirement would not be satisfied by showing simply that the act took place in their line of sight. Would the will in the *Jefferson* case, supra, have been validly executed under UPC section 2-502 (1990)? See Estate of McGurrin, 113 Idaho 341, 743 P.2d 994 (Ct. App. 1987); cf. Matter of Heaney, 75 Misc. 2d 732, 347 N.Y.S.2d 922 (Sur. Ct. 1973).

The UPC's abrogation of the requirement that the witnesses sign in the testator's presence raises a question about whether there is any time limit on when the witnesses must sign the will after they have witnessed the testator's signature or acknowledgement of the signature or of the will. Estate of Peters, below, which was decided under the pre-1990 version of UPC section 2-502, addresses this question. It also addresses the question of whether courts should abandon the strict-compliance approach in favor of a substantial-compliance approach to the statutory formalities.

Estate of Peters
107 N.J. 263, 526 A.2d 1005 (1987)

[Conrad Peters died on March 28, 1985. His wife, Marie, predeceased him by slightly more than five days. Conrad and Marie had no children by their marriage, but Marie had a son, Joseph Skrok, by a prior marriage. Marie's will devised her entire estate to Conrad if he survived her (which he did), but if not, to Joseph. Conrad's will devised his entire estate to Marie if she survived him (which she did not), but if not, to Joseph.

At Marie's request, her sister-in-law, Sophia M. Gall, an insurance agent and notary public, prepared the wills for Marie and Conrad. About two years before he died, Conrad suffered a stroke that put him into the hospital. The stroke affected him physically but not mentally. Marie, Sophia, and Sophia's husband (Marie's brother), came to Conrad's hospital room with Conrad's will. Sophia read the provisions of the will to Conrad, who then assented to it and signed it. None of the individuals who witnessed Conrad's signing of the will signed the will as witness, the apparent intention being to await the arrival of two of Sophia's employees, Mary Gall and Kristen Spock.

Later in the afternoon, after Mary and Kristen arrived, Sophia reviewed the will briefly with Conrad, who, in the presence of Mary and Kristen, indicated his approval and acknowledged his signature. Sophia then signed the will as a notary, but neither Mary nor Kristen placed her signature on the will. Sophia then folded the will and handed it to Marie. When Conrad died fifteen months later, the two witnesses, Mary and Kristen, had still not signed the will.

Joseph Skrok presented Conrad's will for probate. Its validity was disputed by the State of New Jersey, which would succeed to Conrad's estate if his will was invalid. Conrad left no surviving blood relatives.

At the probate proceeding, Sophia testified as to why the two intended witnesses never signed the will:

> As I say, just because of the emotional aspect of the whole situation, my sister-in-law was there, my husband, her brother was there, myself and the two girls. There were six of us. The other patients had visitors. It got to be kind of—I don't know how to explain it, just the situation, and the girls were in a hurry to get back to the office, because they had to leave the office.
> I honestly think in their minds, when they saw me sign the will, they thought that is why they were there. And we folded up the will, gave it [to] my sister-in-law. It was just that type of situation.

The trial court found the will validly executed, by treating Sophia's signature as notary as the valid signature of a witness and by allowing one of the other witnesses to sign the will. The Appellate Division reversed.]

HANDLER, J. . . . The operative statute governing the validity of the execution of a will is N.J.S.A. 3B:3-2. The statute prescribes the formalities necessary for the proper execution of a will. It requires (1) that the will be in writing and (2) that it be signed by the testator (or by someone in his presence and at his direction). It also requires that a will be signed by at least two persons who witnessed either (a) the signing or (b) the testator's acknowledgement of his signature or of the will. . . .

Wills are solely the creatures of positive law. "The right to make a will . . . is derived from the statute." A. Clapp, 5 New Jersey Practice, Wills and Administration § 41, at 173 (3d ed. 1982). . . . Historically, courts have held that, as statutory creations, wills must adhere to the requirements prescribed by the statute. Failure to comply with the statutory requirements has long resulted in a will being declared invalid, no matter how accurately the document may have reflected the wishes of the testator.

This policy of construing the wills statute's formalities strictly came to be criticized for producing inequitable results and for encouraging, in effect, the circumvention of the wills statutes through such means as conveyances in joint tenancy, revocable trusts, tentative or "Totten" trusts, and cash value life insurance policies. . . . The perception of inequitable results, coupled with the decline of wills, relative to other instruments, as means of devising property after death, led the National Conference of Commissioners of Uniform State Laws and the American Bar Association, in August 1969, to propose adoption of the [pre-1990] Uniform Probate Code. The [pre-1990] Code's approach was not to encourage courts to abandon their strict construction of the formalities prescribed, but rather to reduce the number and refine the scope of those formalities so that, if strict construction were employed, "inequities" in individual cases would occur less frequently and would be justified by the importance of the interests protected by the formal requirements that were retained. . . . Thus, the General Comment to Part Five of the [pre-1990] Code states:

> If the will is to be restored to its role as the major instrument for disposition of wealth at death, its execution must be kept simple. The basic intent of these sections is to validate the will whenever possible. To this end, . . . formalities for a written and attested will are kept to a minimum. . . .

A second approach to reform was proposed in 1975 by Professor John Langbein, in "Substantial Compliance With the Wills Act," 88 Harv. L. Rev. 489. According to Professor Langbein, "[t]he finding of a formal defect should lead not to automatic invalidity, but to a further inquiry: does the noncomplying document express the decedent's testamentary intent, and does its form sufficiently approximate Wills Act formality to enable the court to conclude that it serves the purposes of the Wills Act?" Id. Thus, while addressing the same ills, the [pre-1990] Uniform Probate Code and the substantial compliance doctrine endorse different remedies; the [pre-1990] Uniform Probate Code reduces the number and refines the scope of formalities, whereas the "substantial compliance" approach relaxes the extent to which whatever formalities exist must be honored. One approach

1990] UPC approach is to reduce the number of required formalities. Although both techniques work generally in the same direction, they will produce different results in many cases if the [pre-1990] UPC's "minimal formalities" are to be enforced with the same literalism as before. [Id. at 512.] . . .

The current statute, a variant of the [pre-1990] Uniform Probate Code, constitutes a significant statutory change from its predecessor with respect to how a will must be witnessed. In accordance with the [pre-1990] Uniform Probate Code, the thrust of the change is to reduce the number of formalities entailed in the witnessing of the execution of a will and, in doing so, to ease the difficulty of complying with the formalities that are prescribed for witnesses. . . .

Plaintiff argues that the repeal of N.J.S.A. 3A:3-2 and the elimination of the requirement that the witness sign in the presence of the testator indicate that the Legislature intended that a witness could sign a will as a subscribing witness at any time after the testator has signed or acknowledged the will, even after the testator's death. Plaintiff points to the lack of any other restrictions in the statute relating to when witnesses may sign a will. Plaintiff thus argues that the procedure employed here was within the contemplation of the statute. In the alternative, plaintiff argues that, in the absence of any allegation of fraud, the will should be validated as in substantial compliance with the statute. We treat first the argument that the procedure involved here—allowing the witness to sign the will some eighteen months after the will was witnessed, where the testator had died with the will unsigned by witnesses some fifteen months after the will was witnessed—complies with the statute.

It cannot be overemphasized that the Legislature, in reforming the Wills statute, did not dispense with the requirement that the execution of a will be witnessed. Indeed, it is arguable that as the number of formalities have been reduced, those retained by the Legislature have assumed even greater importance, and demand at least the degree of scrupulous adherence required under the former statute.

It is generally acknowledged that witnesses serve two functions, which can be characterized as "observatory" and "signatory." The current statute clearly requires the fulfillment of both functions; a testamentary writing proffered as a will, in the statute's terms, "shall be *signed* by at least two persons each of whom *witnesses* either the signing or the testator's acknowledgement of the signature or of the will."

The observatory function consists of the actual witnessing—the direct and purposeful observation—of the testator's signature to or acknowledgement of the will. It entails more than physical presence or a casual or general awareness of the will's execution by the testator; the witnessing of a will is a concomitant condition and an integral part of the execution of the will.

The signatory function consists of the signing of the will by the persons who were witnesses. The signatory function may not have the same substantive significance as the observatory function, but it is not simply a ministerial or precatory requirement. While perhaps complementary to the observatory function, it is nonetheless a necessary element of the witness-

The signatory function consists of the signing of the will by the persons who were witnesses. The signatory function may not have the same substantive significance as the observatory function, but it is not simply a ministerial or precatory requirement. While perhaps complementary to the observatory function, it is nonetheless a necessary element of the witnessing requirement. The witness' signature has significance as an evidentiary requirement or probative element, serving both to demonstrate and to confirm the fulfillment of the observatory function by the witnesses. There is nothing, therefore, to suggest that in retaining the requirement that a will's execution be witnessed, the Legislature meant to imply that either witnessing function is dispensable. The statutory policy to reduce the required formalities to a minimum should not, in our view, be construed to sanction relaxation of the formalities the statute retained.

Resolution of the issue of when the witnesses must sign the will in relation to their observations of the execution of the will by the testator follows from the purpose of the requirement that the will be signed. Because, as noted, the signatory function serves an evidentiary purpose, the signatures of the witnesses would lose probative worth and tend to fail of this purpose if the witnesses were permitted to sign at a time remote from their required observations as witnesses. Consequently, because the witnessing requirement of the statute consists of the dual acts of observation and signature, it is sensible to infer that both acts should occur either contemporaneously with or in close succession to one another.

We are thus satisfied that it would be unreasonable to construe the statute as placing no time limit on the requirement of obtaining two witnesses' signatures. By implication, the statute requires that the signatures of witnesses be affixed to a will within a reasonable period of time from the execution of the will.

This reading of N.J.S.A. 3B:3-2 to require subscription within a reasonable time from observation is buttressed by a consideration of other statutory provisions. The Legislature clearly required that a witness actually observe directly and in his or her presence the testator's signing of the will or acknowledgement that the will bears the witness's [testator's?] signature. If, indeed, the will is to be "self-proving," that is, susceptible of being validated solely by the signed acknowledgement of the witnesses, the will must be signed by the witness in the presence of the testator either at the time the testator executed the will, N.J.S.A. 3B:3-4, or subsequent to the execution of the will, N.J.S.A. 3B:3-5. If a will cannot be "self-proving," then at the very least N.J.S.A. 3B:3-2 requires that the witness himself sign the will intending that the signature be that of a witness to the testator's signing or acknowledgement, and that the witness' signature be affixed to the will within a reasonable period of time following the testator's execution or acknowledgement of the will. In other words, since the witnessing of the will still constitutes a part of the formal ceremony entailed in the will's proper execution, it follows that the signing of the will by the witnesses must be within a reasonable period of time of the signing or acknowledgement of the will by the testator.

The requirement of subscription within a reasonable time follows also from the consistent policy of this state that execution formalities are substantive requirements, and, therefore, that execution defects are substantive. Because the purpose of execution formalities is to prevent fraud and undue influence, they have consistently been held by our courts to be substantive requirements. The fact that the Legislature has reduced the number of execution formalities required does not diminish the significance of the formalities it retained; if anything, in our view, their significance is heightened. What this Court stated in In re Hale's Will, supra, 21 N.J. at 297, 121 A.2d 511, is no less true under the reformed statute: the purpose of execution formalities is to "forestall[ ] fraud by the living upon the dead [and to] discourage imposition on the unwary. . . ."

Given our conclusion that the witnesses must sign within a reasonable time from observation, the question is whether the time period involved here—in which the testator died with the will still unsigned by witnesses fifteen months after the will was witnessed—is reasonable. Two factors in this case affect our determination of reasonableness: (1) the fact that the witness signed after the testator's death; and (2) the fact that some eighteen months passed between the observatory and signatory functions of the witness. While there have been no New Jersey cases addressing the issue of whether a witness may sign a will after the testator's death, the problem has been treated in other jurisdictions. In In re Estate of Flicker, 215 Neb. 495, 339 N.W.2d 914, 915 (1983), the Nebraska Supreme Court observed that the purpose of the witnessing requirement is to prevent fraud or mistake, and that permitting witnesses to sign after the testator's death "would erode the efficacy of [this] safeguard. . . ." Thus, "[the witnesses'] signatures are the last acts in the ceremony required by the statute. By its terms, the statute requires a witness to sign." See also Matter of Estate of Mikeska, 140 Mich. App. 116, 362 N.W.2d 906, 910 (1985) ("We agree with the holding in *Flicker*, as well as with the rationale"); Rogers v. Rogers, 71 Or. App. 133, 691 P.2d 114 (1984) (a will, as an ambulatory instrument, takes effect at the time of the testator's death; failure to comply with the formalities of execution by the time the testator has died results in an invalid will).

In this case, the Appellate Division declined to adopt a bright-line rule under N.J.S.A. 3B:3-2 requiring witnesses' signatures before the death of the testator. It expressly left open the question raised by In re Leo's Will, 12 Fla. Supp. 61 (Fla. Dade Co. Cir. Ct. 1958), concerning the validity of a will where a testator has died moments after execution, but before the witnesses have had an opportunity to sign. We endorse this conclusion. There may indeed be cases in which the affixation of witnesses' signatures after the testator's death would be reasonable, particularly if the witnesses were somehow precluded from signing before the testator died. This case, however, does not present such a situation. Even if one accepts the testimony that the emotional trauma of the moment prevented the witnesses from signing the will while the testator was hospitalized, there is simply no adequate explanation of the failure to have obtained their signatures in the extended fifteen-month interval prior to his death. If the

Legislature's retention of the signing requirement is to be at all effectual, signing must occur within a reasonable time of observation to assure that the signature attests to what was actually observed, and not to what is vaguely remembered. While this requirement does not necessarily entail subscription prior to the testator's death, the interval here between the observation and the testator's death was simply too long for subscription after death to have been reasonably within the contemplation of the statute.

Plaintiff argues in the alternative, however, that even if compliance with execution formalities was defective, this Court should validate the will in the absence of any allegation of fraud because it was in "substantial compliance" with the statute. Thus, given the historical trend toward liberalization of the wills statute described above, and the policy favoring validation of wills that "meet the minimal formalities of the statute," the ultimate question raised by this case is how courts should construe wills that fail to satisfy even the "minimal formalities" retained in the statute.

As Professor Langbein has explained, "[t]he substantial compliance doctrine would permit defective compliance with . . . ceremonials to be evaluated purposively. It would permit the proponents to prove that in the circumstances of the case the testator executed the will with finality and that the execution is adequately evidenced notwithstanding the defect." Langbein, "Substantial Compliance with the Wills Act," supra, 88 Harv. L. Rev. at 521. The doctrine has been criticized, however, because it reduces predictability of wills:

> The argument in favor of the implementation of the substantial compliance doctrine is that, while it lacks the predictability of the [pre-1990] U.P.C., it does insist upon a higher degree of formality yet with the understanding that where the failure to comply with any formality is shown, proof may be received to demonstrate that the function of the formality has still been met. . . . The problem is that wills are unlike the world of contract where the demands of business often necessitate informality. . . . Wills are more often made without such demands of time pressure. The testator has every opportunity to comply with formality requirements. . . .
>
> A second problem is the ambiguity of "substantial compliance." . . . Does it mean that some formalities are more important than others and that substantial compliance involves completion of only the important formalities?
>
> [Nelson and Starck, "Formalities and Formalism: A Critical Look at the Execution of Wills," 6 Pepperdine L. Rev. 331, 355 (1979).]

In addition, the doctrine's reliability has been questioned because of its emphasis upon evidence of testamentary intention and the recollection of distant, indistinct events. Irmiston, "Formalities and Wills: A Plea for Caution," American/Australian/New Zealand Law: Parallels and Contrasts, A.B.A., 72, 74 (1980). This has led to rejection of the doctrine in some states, where it has been found to "lead to confusion and uncertainty." Hopkins v. Hopkins, 708 S.W.2d 31, 32 (Tex. Ct. App. 1986). . . .

The . . . New Jersey courts have generally rejected a rule of substantial compliance. In In re Hale's Will, supra, 21 N.J. at 295, 121 A.2d 511, this Court stated that "although on at least one occasion in this state it has been suggested that substantial compliance . . . is all that should be required, our more authoritative appellate tribunals have been averse to the adoption of any such view. . . ." Our courts have thus acknowledged the important policy interest advanced by a rule of strict compliance. In In re Taylor's Estate, 28 N.J. Super. 220, 225, 100 A.2d 346 (App. Div. 1953), where the issue was whether the witnesses actually saw the testator execute a will, the court declined to follow the substantial compliance approach. In In re Johnson's Will, 115 N.J. Eq. 249, 253-54, 171 A. 307 (Prerog. Ct. 1934), the court denied probate to a will on defective publication grounds, despite its recognition that the document was clearly intended to be the testator's will. The court stated:

> It is said that such a construction of the demands of the statute as this is harsh and may work an injustice. The answer is that the statute expresses the legislative requirement for a valid will, and until that body sees fit to change it, the courts are not at liberty to do so.

Id. at 244, 171 A. 307.

It is undeniable that in liberalizing execution formalities in accordance with the [pre-1990] Uniform Probate Code, the Legislature was responding to the perceived inequities resulting from strict construction of the former statute. . . . [P]laintiff now asks this Court to take this process of liberalization a step further by holding that, in the absence of fraud, even defective compliance with the remaining formalities may be sufficient.

To do so on the facts of this case would, in our view, effectively vitiate the statutory requirement that witnesses sign the will.[15] We continue to believe that, as a general proposition, strict, if not literal, adherence to statutory requirements is required in order to validate a will, and that the statutory requirements must be satisfied regardless of the possibility of fraud in any particular case. . . .

The doctrine of strict adherence to statutory requirements follows from the status of wills as creatures of statutory law, and from the statutory purpose to prevent fraud upon the estate of the deceased. . . . To adopt the doctrine of substantial compliance on the facts of this case would unsettle the probate process and undermine the reform enacted by the Legislature.

The prophylactic purpose of preventing fraud would be substantially undermined if "witnesses" to a will that contained no witnessing signatures could testify to their presence at execution, no matter how much time had elapsed between execution and the affixing of their signatures. . . . [S]uch an approach would have the effect of eliminating the signing requirement in its entirety. . . .

Accordingly, for the reasons stated, the judgment below is affirmed.

---

15. We are unwilling to foreclose consideration of the substantial compliance doctrine in a case where there is no question of fraud, and where, unlike this case, there has been a clear attempt to comply with a statutory formality but compliance is deficient. In this case, however, the statutory formalities contemplate at a minimum witnessing by two persons; the treatment of a notary's signature as that of a witness does not compensate for the absence of the signature of a second witness.

Notes, Questions, and Problems

1. *Probative Value of Witnesses' Signatures.* What is the probative value of the witnesses' signatures and why is that value lost if the witnesses do not sign at or within a "reasonable" time after the execution ceremony? By what measure is "reasonableness" to be determined? "Reasonableness" to the New Jersey court seemed to require the witnesses to sign "contemporaneously with or in close succession to" the events the witnesses witnessed. But, as long as the witnesses have a firm recollection of the events they witnessed, why is eighteen months not a "reasonable" time? If the two witnesses in *Peters* had signed Conrad's will at the hospital room ceremony, they would have been permitted to testify at the probate hearing as to their recollection of the events they witnessed. Why should their failure to sign preclude their testimony?

The New Jersey court based its imposition of a reasonable-time standard on the ground that "the witness' signature has significance as an evidentiary requirement or probative element, serving both to demonstrate and to confirm the fulfillment of the observatory function by the witnesses." Note that the court did not link its analysis to signing an attestation clause. In the absence of an attestation clause, such as in the case of Greta McKellar's will, supra p. 172, does the witnesses' act of signing at or within a reasonable time after the execution ceremony demonstrate and confirm that the witnesses witnessed the testator's act of signing the will or the testator's acknowledgment of the signature or of the will? If not, what probative value, if any, does the witnesses' act of signing have that arguably justifies requiring it to occur at or within a reasonable time after the execution ceremony?

2. *1990 Uniform Probate Code's Approach.* UPC section 2-502 (1990) altered the pre-1990 version by introducing a reasonable-time standard for signing by the witnesses, but because of the dispensing power granted by section 2-503, the failure of the witnesses to sign the will within a reasonable time or to sign it at all is not necessarily fatal to the validity of the will. Should the witnessing requirement be abandoned altogether by eliminating it from the statutory formalities? See Lindgren, Abolishing the Attestation Requirement for Wills, 68 N.C. L. Rev. 541 (1990). Professor Lindgren argues: "We should reduce the minimum formalities required for a will to only two—that a will be in writing and that it be signed by the testator. Writing makes an estate plan concrete. Signature indicates a decision, final unless later revoked, and supplies evidence of genuineness." Id. at 542. Although Professor Langbein has not argued for abolition of the attestation requirement, he has studied the case law under the South Australia statute, which is similar to UPC section 2-503 (1990), and concluded: "Of the three main formalities—writing, signature, and attestation—writing turns out to be indispensable. . . . Signature ranks next in importance. If you leave your will unsigned, you raise a grievous doubt about the finality and genuineness of the instrument. . . . By contrast, attestation makes a more modest contribution, primarily of a protective

character, to the Wills Act[16] policies. But the truth is that most people do not need protecting, and there is usually strong evidence that want of attestation did not result in imposition. The South Australian courts have been quick to find such evidence and to excuse attestation defects under the dispensing power." Langbein, Excusing Harmless Errors in the Execution of Wills: A Report on Australia's Tranquil Revolution in Probate Law, 87 Colum. L. Rev. 1, 52 (1987).

3. *Status of Substantial Compliance. Peters* was decided under the pre-1990 UPC and before the American Law Institute took a position in the Restatement 2d of Property favoring a substantial-compliance doctrine, as described supra p. 179. The New Jersey Supreme Court is known as a "liberal" court. Influenced by both the Restatement and the 1990 UPC, the court subsequently made good on its statement in footnote 15 of *Peters* and adopted a rule of substantial compliance. See Alleged Will of Ranney, 124 N.J. 1, 589 A.2d 1339 (1991), supra p. 179.

Section 1-102 of the pre-1990 UPC provides that the "Code shall be liberally construed and applied to promote its underlying purposes and policies. The underlying purposes and policies of this Code are: . . . to discover and make effective the intent of a decedent in the distribution of his property. . . ." This provision was left out of the New Jersey enactment of the UPC. When included in an enactment of the pre-1990 UPC, should it be taken by a court as authorizing a doctrine of substantial compliance? An Idaho decision, rendered before the promulgation of the Restatement, decided against giving section 1-102 this effect. See Estate of McGurrin, 113 Idaho 341, 743 P.2d 994 (Ct. App. 1987).

4. *Meaning of Substantial Compliance.* One of the objections to a substantial-compliance doctrine cited by the court in *Peters* was the uncertain meaning of "substantial" compliance. Professor Langbein has reported that in the Australian state of Queensland, which has had the substantial-compliance doctrine in place through legislation since 1981,[17] the Queensland courts have interpreted "substantial" compliance to mean near-perfect compliance. See Langbein, supra, at 41-45. Professor Langbein suggests that this is the wrong approach: "The right question under the doctrine," he argues, "is whether the testator's conduct served the purposes of Wills Act[18] formality."

To test the difference in approaches, suppose that, after G's death, there were found among her important papers a handwritten but unsigned draft of her will and a signed typewritten copy of the handwritten draft. Could either document be probated? See, e.g., Estate of Smith, 38 S. Austl. St. R. 30 (1985).

Take another case. Suppose that, after signing her will, G handed it to her nephew and asked him to "get it witnessed." The nephew took the will to two neighbors, who signed as "witnesses." The nephew then returned the will to G. Under a substantial-compliance doctrine, what result?

---

16. See supra note 6. Eds.
17. The Queensland statute is set forth in Selected Statutes on Trusts and Estates.
18. See supra note 6. Eds.

Suppose that the nephew took the will to only one neighbor, who signed as "witness." See, e.g., Taylor v. Estate of Taylor, 770 P.2d 163 (Utah Ct. App. 1989) ("A standard of substantial compliance would forgive no more than 'slight or trifling departures from technical requirements'. . . . [O]nly one witness . . . amounts to an absolute failure to comply—strictly or substantially—with even the most liberal construction of [our statute requiring that a will be signed by at least two persons in the testator's presence and in the presence of each other].").

Would G's will be valid in the above cases under a dispensing power statute such as UPC section 2-503 (1990)? See, e.g., Re Graham, 20 S. Austl. St. R. 198 (1978).

––––––

Competency of Attesting Witnesses. The English Statute of Frauds of 1677, supra p. 164, required the witnesses to be "credible." In this country, most non-UPC statutes require the witnesses to be either "credible" or "competent." Today in almost all states the conviction of a crime no longer renders a person an incompetent witness to a will. See Page on Wills § 19.82. Mental incompetency, whether from mental deficiency, extreme intoxication, or the influence of drugs, remains a ground of disqualification as a witness. See id. § 19.83. Insofar as age is concerned, a few states specifically provide by statute a minimum age, such as eighteen, for attesting witnesses. See, e.g., Idaho Code § 15-2-505; Utah Code Ann. § 75-2-505. More commonly, however, no age is specified in the statute, and the cases usually allow minors who are old enough to observe, remember, and relate the facts occurring at the execution ceremony to be valid witnesses. See, e.g., Estate of Dejmal, 95 Wis. 2d 141, 289 N.W.2d 813 (1980); Atkinson on Wills § 65, at 320; Page on Wills § 19.81.

Interested Witnesses—Disqualified at Common Law. The Statute of Frauds of 1677 was construed to disqualify a witness who was a devisee under the will and, therefore, presumably interested in sustaining the will. At that time, a person who had an interest in the outcome of litigation was disqualified from testifying as a witness because of that interest. (A party to a lawsuit could not testify in her or his own behalf.) In construing the Statute of Frauds, the courts carried over this incapacity of the "testimonial" witness to the attesting witness. See Evans, The Competency of Testamentary Witnesses, 25 Mich. L. Rev. 238 (1927). The result was that a will wholly failed where one of the necessary attesting witnesses was also a devisee.

Purging Statutes. After a time, it came to be thought in England that the invalidity of the entire will was unnecessarily harsh on the other devisees. To remedy the situation, a statute—sometimes referred to as a "purging statute"—was passed in 1752 that provided that the disposition to the attesting witness should be void, but the witness should "be admitted as a witness to the execution of such will." 25 Geo. 2, c. 6, § 1. By eliminating the witness's interest, the witness was made "credible" and the will was saved.

In this country, as indicated above, most non-UPC statutes require attesting witnesses to be either "credible" or "competent." See Restatement 2d of Property, Statutory Note to § 33.1. Whichever word is used, the devise of a beneficial interest is usually regarded as disqualifying the witness, unless there is a purging statute similar to the English statute of 1752. Almost all non-UPC states have purging-type legislation. Most American purging statutes go on to provide a partial exception for a devisee who is also an heir of the testator or a devisee under the testator's prior will.[19] Under this partial exception, an heir or devisee who is a necessary witness forfeits only that portion of her or his devise that exceeds the amount she or he would have taken by intestacy or under a prior will if the will in question were invalid. Suppose, for example, that G's will devised $10,000 to X. X served as an attesting witness to G's will. G's prior will, which was not witnessed by X and which was revoked by the subsequent will, devised $8,000 to X. Under the heir/devisee exception, X forfeits $2,000 of the $10,000 devise contained in G's subsequent will. Is a witness who is devised less than the share she or he would have taken if the will were invalid an "interested" witness? See Sparhawk v. Sparhawk, 92 Mass. (10 Allen) 155 (1865), and cases cited in Atkinson on Wills § 65 at 315 n. 48.

Spouse of a Witness. The common-law disqualification of a witness who had an interest in the outcome of litigation extended also to the witness' spouse; and this same notion was applied in England to hold that the spouse of a devisee was not a credible witness to a will. Moreover, the 1752 statute did not save the will, since it invalidated a devise only to the attesting witness. The situation was remedied in the English Wills Act of 1837 by invalidating a devise to the spouse of an attesting witness as well as to the witness. See 7 Wm. 4 & 1 Vict., c. 26, § 15.[20]

In this country, the purging statutes in about eight states expressly extend to a devise to the spouse of an attesting witness. The spouse rule has survived constitutional challenge. See Dorfman v. Allen, 386 Mass. 136, 434 N.E.2d 1012 (1982).

In the absence of an express provision in the purging statute voiding all or a portion of a devise to the spouse of an attesting witness, a number of decisions have held that spouses of devisees are not interested witnesses. See, e.g., Estate of Harrison, 738 P.2d 964 (Okla. Ct. App. 1987).

---

19. One court interpreted a purging statute to have the heir/devisee exception, though the statute expressed no such exception. See Manoukian v. Tomasian, 237 F.2d 211 (D.C. Cir. 1956). (The position is now codified in D.C. Code Ann. § 18-104.) But see, e.g., Rosenbloom v. Kokofsky, 373 Mass. 778, 369 N.E.2d 1142 (1977) (refusing to adopt the exception).

20. The same history appears in some of our states, though with a surprising time lag. Thus Illinois and New Hampshire enacted statutes at a fairly early date modeled on the English legislation of 1752. In 1892, the New Hampshire court held that the spouse of a devisee was not a competent witness to the will, that the statute did not apply to the devise, and that the will was not therefore properly executed. See Kittredge v. Hodgman, 67 N.H. 254, 32 A. 158 (1892). In 1909, the same decision was reached in Illinois. See Fearn v. Postlethwaite, 240 Ill. 626, 88 N.E. 1057 (1909). In 1911, each state amended its statute so as to invalidate not only a devise to an attesting witness, but also a devise to the witness' spouse.

Time When Competency is Required. The competency or incompetency of
the witness is determined when the will is executed. Thus, in Estate of
Parsons, 103 Cal. App. 3d 384, 163 Cal. Rptr. 70 (1980), the court held
that a witness who disclaimed her devise was not rendered disinterested,[21]
saying:

> The quintessential function of a subscribing witness is performed when the
> will is executed. . . . [T]he purpose of the statute is to protect the testator
> from fraud and undue influence at the very moment when he executes his
> will, by ensuring that at least two persons are present "who would not be
> financially motivated to join in a scheme to procure the execution of a
> spurious will by dishonest methods, and who therefore presumably might be
> led by human impulses of fairness to resist the efforts of others in that
> direction." Gulliver and Tilson, Classification of Gratuitous Transfers, 51 Yale
> L.J. 1, 11 (1941).

1990 Uniform Probate Code—Interest of Attesting Witness Disregarded. Pre-
1990 UPC section 2-505 charted a new course on the treatment of
interested witnesses. Under section 2-505, an interested witness is neither
disqualified as an attesting witness nor forfeits any portion of her or his
devise. Close to forty percent of the states now follow this rule. See
Restatement 2d of Property, Statutory Note to § 33.1. The rule is continued
without substantive amendment in UPC (1990). The rationale of the UPC
drafters was that disregarding the interest of the witnesses simplifies the
law, prevents unjust results for home-made wills in which family members
innocently serve as witnesses, and does not appreciably increase the
opportunity for fraud or undue influence. See UPC § 2-505, comment
(1990).

d. Self-Proved Wills

Statutory References: *1990 UPC §§ 2-504, 3-405*
                              Pre-1990 UPC § 2-504

At least thirty-four states authorize wills to be made self proved. See
Restatement 2d of Property, Statutory Note to § 33.1. A self-proved will is
a will for which the testator and the witnesses have executed an affidavit
before a notary public or similar officer detailing the procedures followed
in the execution of the testator's will. The effect of a self-proved will varies
among jurisdictions. In some jurisdictions a self-proved will conclusively
establishes that all formalities have been met. The pre-1990 and 1990 UPC
conclusively presume that all the signature requirements imposed by its

---

21. California has recently changed its rule by adopting a modified version of the UPC.
Under Cal. Prob. Code § 6112, "any person generally competent to be a witness may act as
a witness to a will," but "the fact that the will makes a devise to a witness [who is a necessary
witness] creates a presumption that the witness procured the devise by duress, menace, fraud,
or undue influence."

wills statute have been met and create a rebuttable presumption that all other requirements for a valid will have been met. A self-proved will also serves to eliminate the need for having the witnesses testify upon the filing of the will to prove its authenticity. UPC (1990) carries forward the self-proved will provisions found in the pre-1990 UPC versions of section 2-504(a) and (b) without substantive amendment. See also UPC § 3-406 (1990) detailing the effect of having a self-proved will. UPC (1990) adds a new subsection (c) to section 2-504 to respond to the type of situation that arose in Orrell v. Cochran, below.

Orrell v. Cochran
695 S.W.2d 552 (Tex. 1985)

[George Jefferson Cochran died on July 13, 1982. His daughter, Helen Levell Cochran, sought to probate a will that George had executed in 1971 and that devised the residue of his estate to her. George's wife, Iva Dell Cochran, sought to probate a will dated September 28, 1979, which devised George's entire estate to her.

The facts surrounding the execution of the 1979 will were that George, accompanied by Iva, took the will, a form document entitled "Last Will and Testament," to the Seminary State Bank, where they were customers, to get it notarized. The document had already been filled out, except for the signatures. A notary public at the bank, A. Ruth Balega, testified that she and three other bank employees worked to execute the document. She and the other three bank employees affixed their signatures in the presence of each other and the testator. She signed her name on the line reserved for the testator's signature[22] and the testator signed in the blanks for the names of the witnesses in the self-proving affidavit, which was located below the signatures of the witnesses. Nevertheless, the trial court admitted the 1979 will to probate and, on appeal, the intermediate appellate court affirmed. The testator's daughter, Helen, then took an appeal to the Supreme Court.][23]

PER CURIAM. . . . Because we hold that the court of appeals opinion is in conflict with Boren v. Boren, 402 S.W.2d 728 (Tex. 1966), the court, with three justices dissenting, reverses the judgment of the trial court and court of appeals and, without hearing oral argument, renders judgment that the 1979 instrument be denied probate as Cochran's will. Tex. R. Civ. P. 483.

The purported will is set out in the opinion of the court of appeals [see next page]. The only place the testator signed the instrument is in the

---

22. When testifying, Ruth was asked why she did this. Her reply: "I probably goofed." Orrell v. Cochran, 685 S.W.2d 461, 462 (Tex. Ct. App. 1985).

23. The facts, drawn from the opinion of the Court of Appeals, appear in 685 S.W.2d 461 (Tex. Ct. App. 1985).

Last Will and Testament

KNOW ALL MEN BY THESE PRESENTS: That I, **GEORGE JEFFERSON COCHRAN**

of the City/Town of **FORT WORTH** , County of **TARRANT**

and State of **TEXAS** , being of sound and disposing mind and memory, do make, publish and declare the following to be my LAST WILL AND TESTAMENT, hereby revoking all Wills by me at any time heretofore made.

FIRST: I direct my Executrix, hereinafter named, to pay all of my funeral expenses, administration expenses of my estate, including inheritance and succession taxes, state or federal, which may be occasioned by the passage of or succession to any interest in my estate under the terms of this instrument, and all my just debts, excepting mortgage notes secured by mortgages upon real estate.

SECOND: All the rest, residue and remainder of my estate, both real and personal, of whatsoever kind or character, and wheresoever situated, I give, devise and bequeath to my beloved wife:

IVA DELL COCHRAN to be hers absolutely and forever.

THIRD: If my beloved wife does not survive me, I direct that the rest, residue and remainder of any estate shall be divided into **"2"** equal parts, and I give, devise and bequeath one of such parts to each of the following **2** persons, to be his/hers absolutely and forever:

1—My son;**CHARLES ROBERT COCHRAN** of **3919 Montana St.El Paso,Texas.**

2—My daughter ;**Hellen Lovelle COCHRAN ORELL of; Rt.1. Box 264,ROYAL,ARK.**

The share of any person above named who shall not survive me shall be divided among the other beneficiaries named above, in equal shares.

FOURTH: I hereby appoint my wife, **IVA,DELL COCHRAN** as Executrix of this my LAST WILL AND TESTAMENT, if she be living. If she be not living, I appoint **BILLIE LOUISE JANECKI** as Executor/Executrix. I direct that no Executor or Executrix serving hereunder shall be required to post bond.

IN WITNESS WHEREOF, I have hereunto set my hand and seal at **Ft.worth** , this **28th** day of **September** , 1979.

(sign here) _George J. Cochran_   **l.s.**

Signed, sealed, published and declared to be his LAST WILL AND TESTAMENT by the within named Testator in the presence of us, who is his presence and at his request, and in the presence of each other, have hereunto subscribed our names as witnesses:

(1) _____ of _____ Ft.worth, Tx.   State __ Th.

(2) _Betty J. Orr_ of _Ft worth Tx_   State __ Tx.

(3) _Oscar D. Young_ of _Ft. worth_   State __ Tx.

AFFIDAVIT

STATE OF **TEXAS** ss.: #461-09-7428-A

COUNTY OF **TARRANT**

Personally appeared (1) _George J. Cochran_ , (2) _I. Dee Cochran_ and (3).

who being duly sworn, depose and say that they attested the said Will and they subscribed the same at the request and in the presence of the said Testator and in the presence of each other, and the said Testator signed said Will and TESTAMENT, and deponents further state that at the time of the exicution bl said Will the said Testator appeared to be of lawful age and sound mind and memory and there was no evidence of undue influence. The deponents make this affidavit at the request of the Testator.

(1) _____

(2) _____

(3) _____

Subscribed and sworn to before me this **28th** day of **September** 19 **79**

(Notary Seal) _G. Russ Bailey_
       Notary Public

blanks for the names of the witnesses in the self-proving affidavit. This affidavit is located below the signatures of the witnesses to the purported will, and the affidavit itself is not signed by any witnesses.

In Boren v. Boren, this court held that a will which was not witnessed could not be validated by the fact that the witnesses had signed the self-proving affidavit. The self-proving provisions of a will are not part of the will, but concern the matter of proof only. The will and the self-proving affidavit are two separate instruments. The execution of a valid will is a condition precedent to the usefulness of the self-proving affidavit.

We therefore hold that Cochran did not sign his will and his signature in the self-proving affidavit cannot validate the will. Our opinion is not changed by the fact that the self-proving affidavit was not properly executed in this case. When Cochran signed the self-proving affidavit, he was not signing his will. Accordingly, the court reverses the judgment of the trial court and court of appeals and renders judgment that the 1979 instrument be denied probate as George Cochran's last will and testament.

We remand to the trial court for further proceedings on the 1971 instrument filed for probate by Orrell.

Notes and Questions

1. *State of Authorities.* Most courts have taken a view opposite to that of the Texas court in *Orrell* and have upheld wills signed on the self-proving affidavit. Estate of Charry, 359 S.2d 544 (Fla. Ct. App. 1978) ("The Texas view places form over substance and we decline to follow it."); Estate of Petty, 227 Kan. 697, 608 P.2d 987 (1980); Estate of Cutsinger, 445 P.2d 778 (Okla. 1968); Alleged Will of Ranney, supra p. 179 (utilizing substantial-compliance doctrine). In accord with *Orrell*, however, are Estate of Sample, 175 Mont. 93, 572 P.2d 1232 (1977); Estate of Ricketts, 54 Wash. App. 221, 773 P.2d 93 (1989). See Mann, Self-Proving Affidavits and Formalism in Wills Adjudication, 63 Wash. U. L.Q. 39 (1985).

2. *Bank Liability for Improper Execution.* If a bank employee supervises the will execution in the absence of an attorney, such as happened in *Orrell*, do you think the employer-bank should be liable if the execution procedures are flawed? The question was considered in Brammer v. Taylor, 338 S.E.2d 207 (W. Va. 1985), and the court said:

Drafting a will for another person, advising another person how to draft a will or supervising its execution are activities which constitute the practice of law. . . . On the other hand, merely typing a legal instrument drafted by another person or merely reducing the words of another person to writing does not constitute the preparation of a legal instrument and, thus, does not constitute the practice of law. . . .

In the case now before us, there was an allegation that the decedent reasonably relied upon defendants to supervise the execution of the codicil, based upon prior wills of the decedent and of plaintiff having been signed and attested at defendant bank. If defendants had acted not only as typists and attesting witnesses but had actually engaged in the unauthorized practice of law by supervising the execution of these prior wills, the jury might reasonably infer that defendants had engaged in the unauthorized practice of law by supervising the execution of the codicil in question in this case. If defendants had engaged in the unauthorized practice of law in this case, in violation of W. Va. Code, 30-2-4 [1931] and W. Va. Code, 30-2-5 [1972], they would be *prima facie* negligent in their supervision of the execution of the codicil . . . and if such negligence proximately contributed to the invalidity of the codicil, defendants would be liable to plaintiff for the value of the legacy lost by invalidation of the codicil, unless plaintiff is barred from recovering from defendants by her own comparative negligence, if any.

e. Statutory Wills

The term "statutory will" refers to two distinct concepts, the California Statutory Will and the Uniform Statutory Will Act. Both, however, have a feature in common, which is that they offer a state sponsored pattern or patterns of property distribution that differs from the state directed pattern of property distribution under the intestacy laws.

California Statutory Will. The California statutory will is a state sponsored and distributed will form. Actually, two will forms are made available, one with a trust and the other without a trust. Cal. Prob. Code §§ 6200-48. Other states that have enacted the California Statutory Will are Maine, Michigan, and Wisconsin.

Uniform Statutory Will Act (1984). Rather than offer a state sponsored set of will forms, the Uniform Statutory Will Act follows a different approach, called the incorporation-by-reference approach. The pattern of distribution is set forth in the statute rather than in the will. The will adopts (incorporates by reference) the statutory pattern by executing a will that states that all or a specified portion of the testator's estate is to be disposed of in accordance with the enacting state's Uniform Statutory Will Act. Massachusetts and New Mexico have adopted the Uniform Statutory Will Act.

Both the California Statutory Will and the Uniform Statutory Will Act require that the will be executed in accordance with the state's rule for executing an attested will. The will forms supplied to the public under the California Statutory Will legislation provide explicit directions to the maker for the procedures required for valid execution.

2. Unattested Wills

Statutory References: *1990 UPC §§ 2-502(b), (c), -503*
Pre-1990 UPC § 2-503

Unattested wills fall into two categories: holographic wills and nuncupative wills. By far, most of the litigation arises in connection with holographic wills.

Holographic Wills. A holographic will is one that is written entirely or materially in the handwriting of the testator. Although holographic wills were not authorized in England (unless properly attested), over thirty American jurisdictions now have statutes recognizing their validity. All of the statutes require that the testator sign the will and all of them dispense with witnesses to the execution. A few, however, contain a provision concerning the number of witnesses needed to prove the testator's handwriting. A number of the statutes also require that the will be dated. A few require that the will be signed "at the end."

Nuncupative Wills. Over twenty states, by statute, allow personal property (often with a maximum limit on value), and in a few instances real property, to pass under nuncupative or oral wills. "Soldiers in active military service" and "mariners or sailors at sea" traditionally have been excused from the more rigorous testamentary formalities. See Statute of Frauds, 1677, 20 Car. 2, c. 3, §§ 19-21, 23; Wills Act, 1837, 7 Wm. 4 & 1 Vict., c. 26, § 11. Some states allow persons in their "last illness"—"one so violent that the testator has not the time, opportunity, or means to make a written will in legal form"—to make oral wills, provided certain requirements are met. The testator must: (1) be dying and know it; (2) express orally the intent to make an oral will; and (3) call upon "competent" witnesses (usually at least two) to witness that the spoken words are her or his last will. The witnesses must put into writing their testimony within a prescribed time after the act and, generally, the nuncupative act must take place within the testator's home, unless she or he was "surprised" by the "last illness" while on a journey. See Restatement 2d of Property, Statutory Note to § 33.1; Atkinson on Wills §§ 76-78; Page on Wills §§ 20.13-20.31; Note, A Survey, Analysis, and Evaluation of Holographic Will Statutes, 17 Hofstra L. Rev. 159 (1988).

Estate of Black
30 Cal. 3d 880, 641 P.2d 754, 181 Cal. Rptr. 222 (1982)

RICHARDSON, J. Appellant Gene Ray Bouch appeals from the denial of probate of the holographic will of Frances B. Black, deceased, who died on September 6, 1977, a resident of Long Beach, California. [See page 201 for] a copy of the instrument, which purported to leave the bulk of her estate to appellant and his family. . . . It may be seen from an examination that the instrument was handwritten on three pages of a partially preprinted stationer's form. It is conceded by all parties that all of the handwriting, including the date and her name, is that of the testatrix. Probate was denied because of her incorporation of some of the printed language on the stationer's form. Having found that none of the incorporated material is either material to the substance of the will or essential to its validity as a testamentary disposition, we conclude that the trial court erred in rejecting the holograph and reverse its order.

Testatrix used three copies of a stationer's form, which form obviously was intended to be used for a one-page will. In appropriate blank spaces in the exordium clause at the top of each page, and in her own handwriting, testatrix inserted her signature and the place of her domicile. Other printed language on each page of the form relating to residuary gifts, the appointment of an executor, attesting witnesses and a testimonium clause generally was either stricken or ignored by testatrix. At the bottom of her third and last page, however, following all of the dispositive provisions of the will, she inserted in the appropriate spaces of the preprinted form the name and gender of her executor. And although she dated the holograph entirely in her own hand at the top of the first page of her will, she also utilized pertinent blanks to insert the date of the instrument at the end of the last page and to identify the city and state in which she executed it.

Using virtually all of the remaining space on each of the three pages, testatrix expressed in her own handwriting a detailed testamentary disposition of her estate, including specific devises and legacies to individuals and a charitable institution and a bequest of her residuary estate. As noted, no handwriting of any other person appears on any of the three pages.

Probate was denied to the holograph apparently because testatrix was seen to have "incorporated" the indicated preprinted portions of the form "as part of her will," in violation of the presumed, implied prohibition of Probate Code section 53, which provides:

> A holographic will is one that is entirely written, dated and signed by the hand of the testator himself. It is subject to no other form, and need not be witnessed. No address, date or other matter written, printed or stamped upon the document, which is not incorporated in the provisions which are in the handwriting of the decedent, shall be considered as any part of the will.

Where, as here, there is no conflict in the evidence, "the validity of the holographic instrument must be determined entirely by reference to the applicable statutes and principles of law." (Estate of Baker, 59 Cal. 2d 680, 683, 381 P.2d 913, 31 Cal. Rptr. 33 (1963)) Unanimously in *Baker*, we stressed that "The policy of the law is toward a construction favoring validity, in determining whether a will has been executed in conformity with statutory requirements." (Ibid.) Moreover, we affirmed "the tendency of both the courts and the Legislature . . . toward greater liberality in accepting a writing as an holographic will. . . ." (Ibid.) "*Substantial compliance with the statute, and not absolute precision is all that is required. . . .*" (Id., at p. 685, 381 P.2d 913, 31 Cal.Rptr. 33 italics added.)

. . . In construing section 53 we bear in mind the primary legislative purpose of the holographic will statute which was identified by us in Estate of Dreyfus (1917) 175 Cal. 417, 418-419, 165 P. 941, as the prevention of "fraudulent will-making and disposition of property" by virtue of the recognized difficulty of forging an entire handwritten instrument. After reviewing the legislative history of the statute in Dreyfus we had "no doubt that (the holographic provision) owes its origin to the fact that a successful counterfeit of another's handwriting is exceedingly difficult, and that, therefore, the requirement that it should be in the testator's handwriting would afford protection against a forgery of this character." (Id., at p. 419, 165 P. 941.) . . . An overly technical application of the holographic will statute to handwritten testamentary dispositions, which generally are made

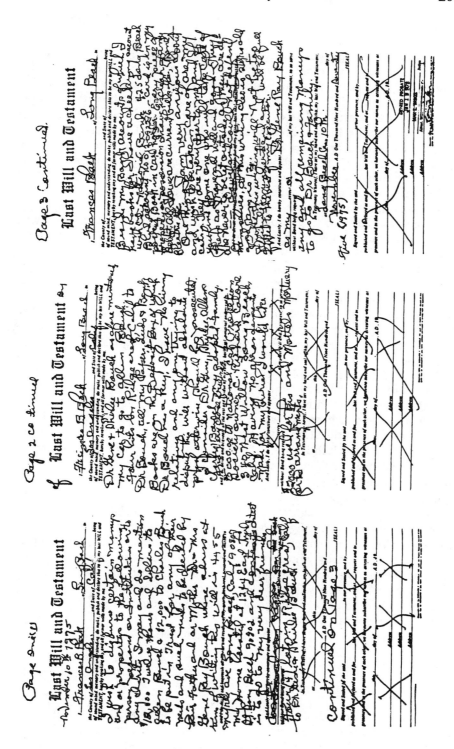

by persons without legal training, would seriously limit the effectiveness of the legislative decision to authorize holographic wills. . . .

Read literally, section 53 requires only that a holographic will be "written, dated and signed" by the hand of testatrix, and that printed matter not incorporated in the handwritten provisions not be considered as any part of the will. . . . Frances Black's will fully satisfies the requirements of the statute. There is no question as to the authorship or authenticity of the handwritten document before us. To reiterate: There is no handwriting on any page of the holograph which is not admittedly that of testatrix. The will is dated both at its beginning and partially at its end in the handwriting of testatrix. She wrote her name on each page and we deem this a sufficient "signature." On each of the first two pages she referred to the instrument as her "will," and on the last page she expressed the hope that "this writing" would be given legal effect. The completeness and integrity of the testamentary disposition written in her own handwriting, in our view, is itself evidence of her intent to authenticate the document as her last will and testament by affixing her signature at the top of each page. We have repeatedly said that "It is settled in California that the signature need not be located at the end (of a holographic will) but may appear in another part of the document, provided the testator wrote his name there with the intention of authenticating or executing the instrument as his will." (Estate of Bloch 39 Cal. 2d 570, 572-573, 248 P.2d 21 (1952)).

No sound purpose or policy is served by invalidating a holograph where every statutorily required element of the will is concededly expressed in the testatrix' own handwriting and where her testamentary intent is clearly revealed in the words as she wrote them. Frances Black's sole mistake was her superfluous utilization of a small portion of the language of the preprinted form. Nullification of her carefully expressed testamentary purpose because of such error is unnecessary to preserve the sanctity of the statute. Moreover, rejection of the instrument as a will would have the unfortunate practical consequence of passing her estate through the laws of intestacy to the daughter of her predeceased husband by a former marriage—in fact, a stranger to her—thereby excluding those whom she described in the holograph as "my very dear friends" and "my adopted family" and the charity which was apparently close to her heart and which she specifically wished to benefit. The resulting frustration and defeat of her testamentary plan would be directly contrary to our Baker reasoning and would serve neither valid public policy nor common sense.

The order appealed from is reversed.

[The dissenting opinion of MOSK, J., is omitted.]

Notes

1. *First Generation Holographic Will Statutes.* Section 53 of the California Probate Code is a first generation holographic will statute. Under this type of statute, most courts have held wills like that in *Black* invalid. See, e.g.,

Wolcotts' Estate, 54 Utah 165, 180 P. 169 (1919). Contra, e.g., Fairweather v. Nord, 388 S.W.2d 122 (Ky. 1965). But see, e.g., Estate of Teubert, 298 S.E.2d 456 (W. Va. 1982) (upholding as a holographic will the handwritten portion of a document containing both handwritten and typed material). Cases are collected in Annot., 37 A.L.R.4th 528 (1985); Annot., 89 A.L.R.2d 1198 (1963).

2. *Second Generation Holographic Will Statutes.* The pre-1990 UPC established the second generation holographic will statute. Pre-1990 section 2-503 retained the signature requirement, deleted the requirement that the will be dated, and replaced the requirement that the will be "entirely" in the handwriting of the testator with the requirement that the "material provisions" be in the testator's handwriting. After *Black* was decided, the California legislature replaced its holographic-will statute with a provision nearly identical to pre-1990 section 2-503. Cal. Prob. Code § 6111(a).

Estate of Johnson, 129 Ariz. 307, 630 P.2d 1039 (Ct. App. 1981), was decided under pre-1990 UPC section 2-503. The decedent, Arnold H. Johnson, died on January 28, 1978, at the age of 79. He was survived by six children. A printed will form was presented for probate. According to the court, the underscored portions shown below were in the decedent's handwriting. In part, the will reads:

THE LAST WILL AND TESTAMENT

I <u>Arnold H. Johnson</u> a resident of <u>Mesa Arizona of Maricopa</u> County, State of Arizona, being of sound and disposing mind and memory, do make, publish and declare this my last WILL AND TESTAMENT, hereby revoking and making null and void any and all other last Wills and Testaments heretofore by me made. . . .

Second—I give devise and bequeath to <u>My six living children as follows</u>

<u>To John M. Johnson 1/8 of my Estate</u>
<u>Helen Marchese</u>	1/8
<u>Sharon Clements</u>	1/8
<u>Mirriam Jennings</u>	1/8
<u>Mary D. Korman</u>	1/8
<u>A. David Johnson</u>	1/8

<u>To W.V. Grant, Souls Harbor Church</u> <u>3200 W. Davis Dallas Texas</u>	1/8

<u>To Barton Lee McLain</u>) <u>and Marie Gansels</u>) <u>Address 901 E. Broadway</u> ~~Phoenix~~) <u>Az</u> <u>Mesa</u>)	1/8

Probate of this document was denied by the trial court, and on appeal the appellate court affirmed, saying in part:

Initially it is to be noted that Arizona has adopted the [pre-1990] Uniform Probate Code, the holographic will provisions being contained in § 2-503 . . .

The statutory requirement that the material provisions be drawn in the testator's own handwriting requires that the handwritten portion clearly express a *testamentary* intent. . . . In our opinion, the only words which establish this requisite testamentary intent on the part of the decedent are found in the *printed* portion of the form. . . .

Admittedly, . . . our decision here might well do violence to the intent of the decedent, Arnold H. Johnson. However, as was stated by our Supreme Court in Estate of Tyrrell, 17 Ariz. 418, 153 P. 767 (1915):

> If the statute requires the testator to sign the instrument and he omits to sign it, although he intended to do so, such omission may not be cured by his intention. The omission is fatal to the validity of the will. The omission of any of the requirements of the statute will not be overlooked on the ground that it is beyond question that the paper was executed by the decedent as his will while he possessed abundant testamentary capacity, and was free from fraud, constraint or undue influence, and there is no question of his testamentary purpose, and no obstacle to carrying it into effect had his will been executed in the manner prescribed by the statute. (Citations omitted) 17 Ariz. at 422, 153 P. at 768. . . .

We thus have stringent requirements for finding that a document, which might appear in a thousand different forms, is a valid and authentic holographic will.

But see Estate of Muder, 159 Ariz. 173, 765 P.2d 997 (1988), reversing 156 Ariz. 326, 751 P.2d 986 (Ct. App. 1988). The court said:

> We hold that a testator who uses a preprinted form, and in *his own handwriting* fills in the blanks by designating his beneficiaries and apportioning his estate among them and signs it, has created a valid holographic will. Such handwritten provisions may draw testamentary context from both the printed and the handwritten language on the form. We see no need to ignore the preprinted words when the testator clearly did not, and the statute does not require us to do so.

3. *Third Generation Holographic Will Statute.* The *Johnson* case and the lower appellate court decision in the *Muder* case prompted the drafters of the 1990 UPC to amend the pre-1990 UPC's holographic will statute. Under UPC § 2-502(b), (c) (1990), only the "material portions of the document" need be in the testator's handwriting and portions of the document that are not in the testator's handwriting, along with other extrinsic evidence, can be used to establish testamentary intent.

4. *Should a Tape Recording Qualify as a Writing?* In Estate of Reed, 672 P.2d 829 (Wyo. 1983), a sealed envelope was found in Robert G. Reed's home after his death on which was handwritten:

Robert Reed To be played in the event of my death only! (signed) Robert G. Reed.

The envelope contained a tape recording, which was filed for probate as a holographic will.

The Supreme Court of Wyoming rejected the proponent's claim that a tape recording can be a valid holographic will:

The Wyoming statutes are clear and unambiguous in their description of a holographic will. A holographic will must be entirely in the handwriting of the decedent. . . .

Handwriting is not an ambiguous word, nor is the word entirely. We are not aware of any definition of "handwriting" that includes voice print, nor do we know of any authority that has held that "handwriting" includes voice prints. It seems to be stating the obvious that a voice print is not handwriting; therefore, the requirement that an holographic will be "entirely in the handwriting of the testator" has not been met in this case.

Appellant urges this court to apply the spirit of the holding in Estate of Black, 30 Cal. 3d 880, 181 Cal. Rptr. 222, 641 P.2d 754 (1982), by reasoning that we have previously shown an inclination to follow California decisions because part of our probate code was derived from California law. . . .

In Estate of Black, supra, the court reemphasized that the policy of the law is toward a construction favoring validity and a tendency of both the courts and legislature toward greater liberality in accepting a writing as an holographic will. We need not agree or disagree with Estate of Black, supra, and its philosophy, as that case is easily distinguishable. . . .

The use of a tape recording or other type of voice print as a testamentary instrument is a decision for the legislature to make. We will not enlarge, stretch, expand or extend the holographic will statute to include a testamentary device not falling within the express provisions of the statute.

PART B. GROUNDS OF CONTEST: THE CONTESTANT'S CASE

Statutory References: *1990 UPC §§ 1-306, 3-407*

1. Lack of Testamentary Intent

Kauffman's Will
365 Pa. 555, 76 A.2d 414 (1950)

This is an appeal from the decision of the Register of Wills of York County refusing to admit to probate a certain undated instrument of writing alleged to be the holographic last will and testament of Annie Kauffman, also known as Annie N. Kauffman . . . , which reads as follows:

> dear bill
> i want you to have farm
> Annie Kauffman.

The decedent died on Sunday, May 22, 1949, unmarried, at the age of eighty-seven years. Her husband, William H. Kauffman, having predeceased her on July 19, 1937. Letters of administration on her estate were granted by the Register of Wills on May 26, 1949, to Noah Kauffman, a son, and Marie E. Zarfoss, a daughter.

On September 23, 1949, William M. Kauffman, a son of the decedent, believing that he was the "dear bill" mentioned in the above quoted instrument, presented his petition to the Register of Wills of York County, asking for the probate of said instrument as the last will and testament of his mother, and that letters of administration c.t.a. on her estate be granted to him. On the same day the Register of Wills refused to admit the alleged will to probate on the grounds that the instrument offered is not testamentary in character. It is from this decision of the Register of Wills that William M. Kauffman has appealed. . . .

The contestants object to the probate of the alleged instrument on the grounds that it purports to be no more than a letter; does not show testamentary intent and that extrinsic evidence to show testamentary intent is inadmissible, but, if such evidence is admissible, the "two witness rule" is applicable thereto. Fraud was also alleged (N.T. 24) but was abandoned at the argument.

That the paper offered for probate was actually written and signed by the decedent is not seriously disputed. The main question for our decision is, Did she write it with testamentary intent? i. e., Did she intend that the paper so written by her should be her will? The ultimate effect of the disputed paper, if found to have been written by the decedent with testamentary intent, is not now before the Court.

A will was defined by Blackstone (2B1. Comm. 499) as "the legal declaration of a man's intentions, which he wills to be performed after his death" and by Kent as "a disposition of real and personal property to take effect after the death of the testator."

The foregoing definition of a will has been universally adopted by the Courts of this state and requires no citations to support it.

While the informal character of a paper is an element in determining whether or not it was intended to be testamentary, this becomes a matter of no moment when it appears thereby that the decedent's purpose was to make a posthumous gift. The mere fact that the instant paper offered for probate was addressed to "dear bill" is of no materiality except in so far as it may aid in identifying the object of her bounty. The mere fact that the paper was in the form of a letter does not affect the result. Neither does the fact that the paper was undated have any particular significance. . . .

In all cases of this kind where a paper is proposed for probate and its testamentary character is denied, it becomes the duty of the Court in the first instance to examine the paper, its form and its language, and therefrom determine as a matter of law whether or not it shows testamentary intent with reasonable certainty. If testamentary intent is satisfactorily revealed from such an examination by the Court, the paper should be probated as a will.

On the other hand, if, from such examination, the paper is shown not to be a testamentary disposition, but is shown to be a document of another type, then it is not to be probated as a will. But, if, from such an examination, the Court should determine that a real doubt or real ambiguity exists, so that the paper offered for probate might or might not be testamentary, depending upon circumstances, then it has been held on numerous occasions by the Appellate Courts that the document presents an ambiguity which will permit the use of extrinsic evidence in aid of resolving the uncertain character of the paper. . . .

The decedent left to survive her as her only heirs at law and next of kin the following named children, to-wit:

(1) Noah N. Kauffman, a son, who, after his marriage, left his parents' home about forty years ago and is now living in the Borough of Glen Rock, in York County, and is one of the contestants.

(2) Marie E. Zarfoss, a daughter, who also married some years ago and lives in the Borough of Dallastown, in said county, and is one of the contestants.

(3) Florence M. Smyser, a daughter, who always lived with her parents and, after her marriage in December, 1946, both she and her husband resided with the decedent until the decedent's death. She is not one of the contestants.

(4) William M. Kauffman, a son who has resided in Spring Garden Township, in said county for the past sixteen years. He is the proponent. . . .

Here . . . we have the case of a disputed paper which is in law either a will in respect to decedent's farm or it is nothing, written by the decedent with her own hand, at age 87 years, while sick in bed and whose approaching death four days later it may be inferred she contemplated when she executed the paper.

The night of May 17 was a restless night for the decedent. Her faithful daughter Florence, who had always lived with her mother and in whom she must have had implicit confidence, had nursed her through the night.

Early in the morning, to her daughter Florence, she said, "Here I was so good and I didn't fix things. You call your husband Roman to go down to Bill (meaning her son William) and tell him to bring a lawyer out here, I want to fix things." Florence told her husband what her mother said and then her husband went into the decedent's room and she told him the same thing. Her message was communicated to her son William, who came to see his mother that morning and she said substantially the same thing to William, who then communicated with Attorney Kohler for his services and, when the decedent was apprised of the fact that the attorney could not come to see her before 6:00 o'clock in the evening, she then said to her daughter Florence, "I want to fix something. Can't I do it myself?" And Florence said to her, "Well, you can write a paper". Florence then procured a pencil and paper for her and, sitting up in bed, unassisted, she wrote the disputed paper, and entrusted it for safe keeping to her daughter Florence, who put it in a bureau drawer in her mother's room, and subsequently that evening she showed the paper to Attorney Kohler and her brother William and then placed it in a box with her mother's other private papers, where it remained until after the decedent's death.

We are of the opinion that . . . whatever ambiguity might appear on the face of the disputed paper, the extrinsic evidence offered, particularly that of the daughter Florence, clearly removed the ambiguity. . . .

PER CURIAM. The decree of the Orphans' Court . . . to admit the written instrument to probate as decedent's last will . . . is affirmed . . . .

Note and Question

A Contrary Approach to Holographic Wills. In Poindexter v. Jones, 200 Va. 372, 106 S.E.2d 144 (1958), Hendley Jones offered the following writing for probate as a holographic will:

> Harrisonburg, Va. August 20, 1953. I give all that I possess to my beloved nephew Hendley Jones.
>
>   Maude R. Snyder

In ordering probate to be denied, the court held that the trial judge had erred in receiving evidence to show that the instrument was intended to be a testamentary disposition:

> As the paper lacks on its face any indicia of *animus testandi,* evidence *aliunde* to prove that it was a will should not have been admitted. . . . Testamentary intent must appear within the four corners of the instrument, and lacking that necessary indicia, it cannot be rightly probated. . . .
>
> Neither the word "give" nor the word "beloved", as used by Maude R. Snyder in this writing, discloses *animus testandi.* Webster's New International Dictionary, 2d Ed., among other definitions of the word "give", lists the following: "to make over or bestow without receiving a return; to confer without compensation; . . . to make over or yield possession of by way of exchange; . . . to hand or hand over; . . . to bestow freely or fully . . . ." It thus appears that the word "give" usually implies an immediate delivery of possession.
>
> The word "beloved" is defined in the same authority as "loved; greatly loved; dear to the heart." It is self-evident that this word carries no testamentary significance but is merely a term of endearment.
>
> In context, when considered alone or together, or along with the entire instrument, the two words "give" and "beloved" have no relation to death nor do they indicate testamentary intent. . . .
>
> The indicia of testamentary intent must be found in the paper itself, and evidence *aliunde* to supply this vital and necessary characteristic is not permitted.[24]

---

24. A later Virginia case took a more enlightened view. In Thomas v. Copenhaver, 365 S.E.2d 760 (Va. 1988), the following handwritten document was offered for probate as the holographic will of Helen L. Thomas:

WILL

3   Rag Doll in Attic -- (Note pinned on her.)
1   Diamond ring to Frances C. Lowe (my boss at N & W Ry.)
2   If my brother does not want the car, I give it to Hazel F. Maultsby.

Is this decision in conflict with Kauffman's Will? With Estate of Johnson, supra p. 203?

Fleming v. Morrison
187 Mass. 120, 72 N.E. 499 (1904)

Appeal from a decree of the Probate Court for the county of Essex made on April 27, 1903, allowing a certain instrument as the last will and testament of Francis M. Butterfield, late of Lynn.

The case was heard by Loring, J., who found that the testator was of sound mind, that no undue influence was exercised, and that the will was executed properly. At the request of the contestants, he reported the case for determination by the full court.

The report contained the following findings of the justice referred to in the opinion:

I find that on or about May 18, 1901, Francis M. Butterfield called upon Sidney S. Goodridge, and requested him to draw up his will, leaving all his property to the Mary Fleming named in the instrument admitted to probate as the will of said Butterfield. Thereupon said Goodridge drew up the said

---

1846 Belleville Rd., S.W.

<u>DIVIDE EVENLY</u>

Grace Pearson   ) 305 Preston Bluefield Virginia Pearson) W. Va.
Barbara J. Brown, Box 774, Spring Lake, N.C.
Mrs. Maryann Durham, Warsaw, Va. 22572
Mr. and Mrs. H.B. Bock, Blacksburg, Va.
Sara Hall -- 1709 Arlington Rd., S.W.
Hazel F. Maultsby

/s/Helen L. Thomas
August 13, 1972

Affirming the admission of the will to probate, the court said:

To be a valid will, the writing must have been executed with testamentary intent. Although no particular form is necessary, testamentary intent must be ascertained from the face of the document, not from extrinsic evidence.

The heirs contend that the document in question "does not evidence the necessary testamentary intent required of a valid will." They assert that "[i]t appears from the face of the document that the decedent was making notes of things she wanted to put in her will at some future time." We do not agree.

The decedent entitled the document a "*Will*." The term "will" is defined as "[t]he legal expression or declaration of a person's mind or wishes as to the disposition of his property, to be performed or take effect after his death." Black's Law Dictionary 1433 (5th ed. 1979). Additionally, the language employed by the decedent, e.g., "[d]iamond ring to Frances C. Lowe," "[i]f my brother does not want the car, I give it to Hazel F. Maultsby," and "*DIVIDE EVENLY*," evinces the decedent's desire to dispose of her property. Finally, the decedent dated the document and signed her name at the bottom, conduct inconsistent with that of a person who was simply making notes of things she wanted to put in her will at some future time.

By looking at the face of the document, it is clear to us, as it was to the trial court, that the writing was executed by the decedent with testamentary intent. Therefore, the trial court did not err in finding that the writing is a valid will.

instrument, said Butterfield signed it, and said Goodridge attested and subscribed said instrument as a witness to the signature of said Butterfield. Before Butterfield and Goodridge parted, Butterfield told Goodridge that this was a "fake" will, made for a purpose.

I find by the evidence in this case that said Butterfield meant by this that he did not intend to complete the instrument by having it attested and subscribed by at least two other witnesses, and that the purpose referred to by him was to induce said Fleming to allow him (said Butterfield) to sleep with her. Afterwards said Butterfield determined to complete the execution of his will, and for that purpose he produced the instrument before the other two attesting witnesses, Bryant and Cheney, told them it was his will, that the signature was his signature, and asked them to attest and subscribe it as witnesses. Goodridge, Bryant, and Cheney were each competent witnesses.

I find that the words appointing Mary Fleming "as administrator" were written on the instrument after it was attested and subscribed by Bryant and Cheney.

The instrument offered as a will was as follows:

Be it remembered that I, Francis M. Butterfield of Lynn, County of Essex *of Massachusetts* in the Commonwealth of Massachusetts, being of sound mind and memory, but knowing the uncertainty of this life, do make this my last will and testament, this 18th day of May, 1901.

After the payment of my just debts and funeral charges, I bequeath and devise as follows:

To Mary Fleming of Lynn State of Massachusetts all of My Possessions at My death of all Real *est* and personal property and all that May Come to Me after My death.

Francis M. Butterfield

I appoint Mary Fleming my Administratrix.

In testimony whereof I hereunto set my hand and in the presence of three witnesses declare this to be my last will this 18th day of May 1901 in the year one thousand and Nine hundred and one.

On this 18th day of May *day of May A.D.* 1901 Lynn State of Massachusetts *Massachusetts*, signed the foregoing instrument in our presence, declaring it to be his last will: and as witnesses thereof we three do now, at his request, in his presence, and in the presence of each other, hereto subscribe our names.

Sidney S. Goodridge,
Eron J. Bryant,
Zella J. Cheney.

LORING, J. All the rulings asked for at the hearing have been waived, and the only contention now insisted upon by the contestants is that, on the finding made at the hearing, the proponent of the will has failed to prove the necessary *animus testandi*. We are of the opinion that this contention must prevail.

The finding that, before Butterfield and Goodridge "parted," Butterfield told Goodridge that the instrument which had been signed by Butterfield as and for his last will and testament, and declared by him to be such in the presence of Goodridge, and attested and subscribed by Goodridge as a witness, "was a 'fake' made for a purpose," is fatal to the proponent's case. This must be taken to mean that what had been done was a sham. This is not cured by the further finding that what Butterfield meant by this was "that he did not intend to complete the instrument by having it attested and subscribed by at least two other witnesses, and that the purpose referred to by him was to induce said Fleming to allow him (Butterfield) to sleep with her."

This is not a finding that Butterfield intended to sign the instrument before Goodridge as and for his last will and testament, leaving the further execution to depend on future events. Much less is it a finding that Butterfield changed his mind after he had signed, and had Goodridge attest and subscribe the instrument. The whole finding, taken together, amounts to a finding that Butterfield had not intended the transaction which had just taken place to be in fact what it imported to be; that is to say, a finding that when Butterfield signed the instrument, and asked Goodridge to attest and subscribe it as his will, he did not, in fact, then intend it to be his last will and testament, but intended to have Mary Fleming think that he had made a will in her favor to induce her to let him sleep with her.

We are of opinion that it is competent to contradict by parol the solemn statements contained in an instrument that it is a will; that it has been signed as such by the person named as the testator, and attested and subscribed by persons signing as witnesses. Lister v. Smith, 3 Sw. & Tr. 282; . . . [w]hen [a will] is signed, or, having been previously signed, when the signature is acknowledged in the presence of three or more witnesses. And where that is done before each witness separately, as it may be done in this commonwealth (Chase v. Kittredge, 11 Allen, 49, 87 Am. Dec. 687), the *animus testandi* must exist when it is signed or acknowledged before, and attested and subscribed by, each of the necessary three witnesses. If this is not done, the statutory requirements have not been complied with.

Assuming that the acknowledgment *animo testandi* of a signature not originally made with that *animus* is enough, the will in the case at bar would have been duly executed had Butterfield subsequently acknowledged the instrument before three in place of two additional witnesses. But he did not do so. The instrument, having been acknowledged and attested and subscribed by two witnesses only, is not a valid will, within Rev. Laws, c. 135, § 1. . . .

Decree to be entered reversing decree of probate court, and disallowing the instrument as the will of Butterfield.

Notes and Questions

1. *Sham Will Precedent.* The *Fleming* court relied on Lister v. Smith, 3 Sw. & Tr. 282, 164 Eng. Rep. 1282 (P. Ct. 1863), for precedent that extrinsic evidence is admissible to show a document, which in all respects looks like a valid will, is not one because the testator lacked the requisite

intent. In *Lister*, the testator executed a codicil to his will, but extrinsic evidence was presented and the jury found that he never intended the codicil to be operative. His purpose in executing the codicil was to force a member of his family to give up a house that she occupied; the codicil revoked a bequest to the woman's daughter. The court held the evidence admissible, saying:

> The momentous consequences of permitting parol evidence . . . to outweigh the sanction of a solemn act are obvious. It has a tendency to place all wills at the mercy of a parol story that the testator did not mean what he said. On the other hand, if the fact is plainly and conclusively made out; that the paper which appears to be the record of a testamentary act, was in reality the offspring of a jest, or the result of a contrivance to effect some collateral object, and never seriously intended as a disposition of property, it is not reasonable that the Court should turn it into an effective instrument. And such no doubt is the law. There must be the *animus testandi*. In Nichols v. Nichols, 2 Phill. 180, the Court refused probate to a will regularly executed, which was proved to have been intended only as a specimen of the brevity of expression of which a will was capable. And in Trevelyan v. Trevelyan, 1 Phill. 149, the Court admitted evidence, and entertained the question whether the document was seriously intended or not. In both cases the Court held that evidence was admissible of the animus testandi. . . . But here I must remark that the Court ought not, I think, to permit the fact to be taken as established, unless the evidence is very cogent and conclusive.

See also Vickery v. Vickery, 126 Fla. 294, 170 S. 745 (1936), where probate was denied to a will, regular on its face, shown to have been executed by the decedent to satisfy a requirement for initiation into a Masonic order. The execution was merely a "ceremonial rite," the court said, and testamentary intent was lacking. Cases are collected in Annot., 21 A.L.R.2d 319 (1952).

2. *When Must the Testator Intend To Make a Will?* When must a testator possess the requisite testamentary intent according to *Fleming*? Why should testators not be able to meet the requirement of testamentary intent by possessing the requisite intent at the time they complete the last procedural formality (e.g., when the last witness signs the will)? Would Francis Butterfield's will have been valid under the dispensing power authority of UPC section 2-503 (1990)?

3. *Conditional Wills.* If a person is about to enter into a life threatening situation, does the will she or he executes in contemplation of this imminent danger remain valid when she or he survives? Would it make a difference if the life threatening activity is described in the will as the reason for executing the will? In Eaton v. Brown, 193 U.S. 411 (1904), the decedent, Caroline Holley, wrote the following document:

> Washington, D. C. Aug. '31"/001
> I am going on a Journey and may not ever return. And if I do not, this is my last request. The Mortgage on the King House, wich [sic] is in the possession of Mr. H. H. Brown to go to the Methodist Church at Bloomingburgh. All the rest of my properday both real and personal to My adopted son L B. Eaton of the life Saving Service, Treasury Department Washington D.C,

All I have is my one hard earnings and I propose to leave it to whome I please.

Caroline Holley

She returned to Washington and resumed her occupation as a clerk before her death on December 17, 1901.

Justice Holmes delivered the opinion of the Court, in effect ordering the will admitted to probate:

> "Courts do not incline to regard a will as conditional where it can be reasonably held that the testator was merely expressing his inducement to make it, however inaccurate his use of language might be, if strictly construed." Damon v. Damon, 8 Allen. 192, 197. . . . . In the case at bar we have an illiterate woman writing her own will. Obviously the first sentence, "I am going on a journey and may not ever return," expresses the fact which was on her mind as the occasion and inducement for writing it. If that had been the only reference to the journey the sentence would have had no further meaning. But with that thought before her, it was natural to an uneducated mind to express the general contingency of death in the concrete form in which just then it was presented to her imagination. She was thinking of the possibility of death or she would not have made a will. But that possibility at that moment took the specific shape of not returning from her journey, and so she wrote "if I do not return," before giving her last commands. We need not consider whether, if the will had nothing to qualify these words, it would be impossible to get away from the condition. But the two gifts are both of a kind that indicates an abiding and unconditioned intent,—one to a church, the other to a person whom she called her adopted son. The unlikelihood of such a condition being attached to such gifts may be considered. And then she goes on to say that all that she has is her own hard earnings and that proposes to leave it to whom she pleases. This last sentence of self-justification evidently is correlated to and imports an unqualified disposition of property; not a disposition having reference to a special state of facts by which alone it is justified and to which it is confined. If her failure to return from the journey had been the condition of her bounty,—an hypothesis which is to the last degree improbable in the absence of explanation,—it is not to be believed that when she came to explain her will she would not have explained it with reference to the extraordinary contingency upon which she made it depend instead of going on to give a reason which, on the face of it, has reference to an unconditioned gift.

Eaton v. Brown exemplifies the general attitude of the courts, which is to resolve doubts in favor of validity, but decisions like Walker v. Hibbard, 185 Ky. 795, 215 S.W. 800 (1919), also occur from time to time. In *Walker,* the decedent, Mame Long, hand wrote a letter that read, in part:

> Dear Aunt Mintie: On Sunday evening I go to St. Elizabeth's Hospital to have a slight operation. I do not anticipate any trouble but one never knows. If anything should happen to me, I want you please to do this for me. See that everything I have in the world goes to George B. Gomersall.

The letter satisfied the formal requirements of a holographic will, which is recognized in Kentucky. Long completely recovered from the operation and died some six months later from a wholly unrelated cause. The court denied the will probate finding that the letter "was only written to provide against the fatality that might follow" from the operation. See Evans, Conditional Wills, 35 Mich. L. Rev. 1049 (1937).

2. Lack of Testamentary Capacity

Statutory References: *1990 UPC § 2-501*
                              Pre-1990 UPC § 2-501

a. Age Requirement

Probate codes commonly establish a minimum age for the execution of a will. UPC section 2-501 (1990) and almost all non-UPC statutes set 18 as the minimum age.[25]

The age requirement is purely a physical requirement and, as illustrated by Estate of Teel, 14 Ariz. App. 371, 483 P.2d 603 (1971), can be over-inclusive and under-inclusive as compared with its purpose of assuring that only a person of mature judgment can execute a will. In *Teel,* the decedent, Marvin Teel, was approximately 54 years of age when he executed his will, but he was mentally retarded and possessed the mental capacity of a 10 to 12 year old. The will was upheld.

b. Mental Requirement

UPC section 2-501 (1990) not only requires a person to be at least 18 years old when executing her or his will, but also requires the person to be "of sound mind." Atkinson on Wills section 51, at 232, defines the "of sound mind" phrase as follows:

> To make a valid will one must be of sound mind though he need not possess superior or even average mentality. One is of sound mind for testamentary purposes only when he can understand and carry in his mind in a general way:
> (1) The nature and extent of his property,
> (2) The persons who are the natural objects of his bounty, and
> (3) The disposition which he is making of his property.
> He must also be capable of:
> (4) Appreciating these elements in relation to each other, and

---

25. The state-by-state compilation contained in Restatement 2d of Property, Statutory Note to § 34.4, lists forty-eight states (including the District of Columbia) that set 18 as the minimum age. The age requirement is occasionally relaxed for married persons, emancipated minors, and persons in the armed forces. In Georgia, the minimum age is 14; in Louisiana, 16; and in Wyoming, 19.

(5) Forming an orderly desire as to the disposition of his property.

As shown above, testamentary capacity is determined according to one's mental ability to make a will; one may have testamentary capacity though he is under guardianship or lacks the ability to make a contract or transact other business.

It is usually thought that the mental capacity needed to execute a will is not as high as that needed to make a lifetime gift. Why not? Despite the conventional view, the Restatement 2d of Property seeks to apply the same definition of mental competency to all donative transfers, whether by will or lifetime gift:

> *§ 34.5 Comment a. Who is mentally incompetent.* A person is mentally incompetent to make a donative transfer if such person is unable to understand fully the significance of such transfer in relation to such person's own situation. Stated another way, to be mentally competent a person must know and understand the extent of his or her property, comprehend to whom he or she is giving his or her property, and know the natural objects of his or her bounty. A slightly different statement of what constitutes mental capacity is that the person must understand the nature and extent of his or her property, know and recall the natural objects of his or her property, and be able to determine and understand how he or she wishes to dispose of his or her property.

See also Meiklejohn, Contractual and Donative Capacity, 39 Case W. Res. L. Rev. 307 (1988-89); Note, The Elderly Client: Mental Capacity and Undue Influence and the Need for Estate and Lifetime Planning, 4 Conn. Prob. L.J. 55 (1988).

The above definitions concern mental *ability*, not actual knowledge. In Williams v. Vollman, 738 S.W.2d 849 (Ky. Ct. App. 1987), an elderly testator was held competent to execute a will at a time when his wife and one of his daughters were deceased, but he was unaware of their deaths because the news was kept from him for fear that it would weaken his resolve to live. The test, the court said, "does not require that the testator have actual knowledge of the objects of his bounty." The test only requires that he have "sufficient mind to know the objects of his bounty."

Fletcher v. DeLoach
360 S.2d 316 (Ala. 1978)

TORBERT, C.J. The appellant, Mary Elizabeth DeLoach Fletcher, is the proponent of Ada B. Padgett's last will and testament, which was executed on April 15, 1970. [T]he testatrix died on October 31, 1975. . . . The appellees, a son and granddaughter of the testatrix, contested the probate of said will . . . , and moved that the contest of the will be transferred to circuit court for a trial by jury. See sections 43-1-70, 43-1-78, Code of Alabama 1975. The probate judge ordered the transfer of the cause to circuit court for trial by jury on April 2, 1976.

The trial . . . judge, after hearing the evidence, ruled that the will had been properly executed and that there was no evidence of undue influence or fraud in the case. Therefore, the only issue submitted to the jury was whether the testatrix possessed testamentary capacity at the time she executed the will of April 15, 1970. The jury found for the appellees (contestants) on the issue of testamentary capacity, and the trial judge ordered that Mrs. Fletcher was not entitled to have the will probated.

Mrs. Fletcher filed a motion for new trial . . . , alleging that the testimony and the evidence failed to support the jury's verdict. The trial judge denied this motion. . . . Mrs. Fletcher appeals from the denial of her motion for a new trial and from the jury verdict on a similar ground—whether the contestants satisfied their burden to prove the testatrix's lack of testamentary capacity. We hold that there was evidence before the jury which would tend to show that the testatrix lacked testamentary capacity at the time she executed the will of April 15, 1970, and we therefore refuse to overturn the verdict of the jury where it has not been shown to be clearly wrong and unjust.

The testatrix must have testamentary capacity in order to execute a valid will; I.e., she must have

> mind and memory sufficient to recall and remember the property she was about to bequeath, and the objects of her bounty, and the disposition which she wished to make—to know and understand the nature and consequences of the business to be performed, and to discern the simple and obvious relation of its elements to each other. . . .

Knox v. Knox, 95 Ala. 495, 503, 11 So. 125, 128 (1892). However, since it is presumed that every person has the capacity to make a will, the contestant has the burden to prove a lack of testamentary capacity. . . . Unless the contestant presents evidence that the testatrix suffered from a permanent type of insanity prior to the execution of the will (which was not shown in this case), the contestant's burden of proof is met when the jury is reasonably satisfied from the evidence that the testatrix did not have testamentary capacity at the time she executed the will.

When mental capacity is at issue, the factual inquiry must necessarily be of the broadest range. . . . Thus, evidence offered as to the mental and physical condition of the testatrix, either before or immediately after execution of the will, is admissible since it tends to indicate her condition when the will was signed. Likewise, testimony regarding the testatrix's "conversations, deportment, acts, and appearance" has been found to be competent on the issue of testamentary capacity. Batson v. Batson, [217 Ala. 450, 456, 117 So. 10, 15 (1928)].

Also relevant to this issue is the character of the testamentary scheme; i.e., the reasonableness of the distributions made by the testatrix in her will. It is permissible for the jury to examine the will to see if its provisions are "just and reasonable, and consonant with the state of the (testatrix's) family relations," since this would reflect on her capacity to recall the natural objects of her bounty. Fountain v. Brown, [38 Ala. 72, 74 (1861)].

This court, in Councill v. Mayhew, 172 Ala. 295, 55 So. 314 (1911), has stated that:

> An *unequal* disposition of property per se raises no presumption . . . of testamentary incapacity, nor is it per se unnatural; but the unequal treatment of those who ostensibly have equal claims upon the testator's bounty, or the preference of one to the exclusion of another, may under the circumstances of a particular case, be deemed *unnatural*. In such a case, an *unnatural* disposition is a fact to be ascertained and considered by the jury [on the issue of testamentary capacity].

The pecuniary condition of the testatrix's heirs, when considered in the light of an unnatural disposition of property, would also reflect on the character of the will and would therefore be admissible.

There was sufficient evidence presented in this case for the jury to find that the testatrix lacked testamentary capacity when she signed her will on April 15, 1970. The testimony indicated that the testatrix became quite depressed after her eldest son died in January of 1970, and there was also evidence presented that she was disoriented when she went to Florida with relatives both before and after April 15, 1970. The evidence indicated a noticeable decline in the testatrix's attention to her appearance and to the cleanliness of her clothing immediately prior to the execution of the will.

The fact that the 1970 will left all of the estate to Mrs. Fletcher, the testatrix's daughter, thus making no provision for her son or granddaughter, could be evidence of an unnatural disposition of her property, and could be considered by the jury on the issue of testamentary capacity. This feature of the 1970 will is significant in that the 1970 instrument revoked the testatrix's prior will of 1959, which provided for the equal disposition of her estate among her three children.

The unnatural disposition manifested by the 1970 will and the pecuniary condition of the testatrix's heirs in 1970 (which did not show a great disparity between Mrs. Fletcher's financial condition and that of the testatrix's son and granddaughter), when considered with the evidence of the mental and physical condition of the testatrix before and after the execution of the will, supports the jury's verdict that the testatrix lacked testamentary capacity. In cases of this nature, the verdict of the jury cannot be overturned unless shown to be clearly wrong and unjust. The refusal of the trial judge to grant the appellant-proponent's motion for new trial strengthens this presumption in favor of the verdict. After a careful consideration of the record in this case, we feel that the jury's verdict is not clearly wrong and unjust, and the judgment entered in favor of the contestants is hereby affirmed.

BLOODWORTH, FAULKNER, ALMON and EMBRY, JJ., concur.

———

The Lucid Interval. The Restatement 2d of Property sets forth the well accepted lucid-interval principle as follows:

§ 34.5 *Comment a. Who is mentally incompetent.* . . . A person who is mentally incompetent part of the time but who has lucid intervals during which he or she comprehends fully the significance of a donative transfer can, in the absence of an adjudication or statute that has contrary effect, make a valid will or a valid inter vivos donative transfer, provided such will or transfer is made during a lucid interval.

Potts v. House
6 Ga. 324 (1849)

LUMPKIN, J.[26] [W]e are not prepared to say that [the trial judge] underrated the degree of testamentary capacity necessary to make a will, in maintaining that *imbecility* of mind did not disqualify, provided it stopped short of *idiocy* or *lunacy*. Before investigating this case, I had supposed that more capacity was required to make a will than I now find warranted by the authorities . . . .

One thing is certain—that *eccentricity*, however great, is not sufficient, of itself, to invalidate a will. Mason Lee, the testator in this case, supposed himself to be continually haunted by witches, devils, and evil spirits, which he fancied, were always worrying him. He believed that *all women are witches.* (In this, perhaps, he was not so *singular!*) He lived in the strangest manner—wore an extraordinary dress, and slept in a hollow log. He imagined that the Wiggins' relatives, whom he desired to disinherit, were in his teeth; and to dislodge them, he had fourteen sound teeth extracted, evincing no suffering from the operation. He had the quarters of his shoes cut off; saying, that if the devil got into his feet, he could drive him out the easier. . . . His wearing apparel, at his death, was appraised at one dollar. He always shaved his head close, as he said that in the contests with the witches, they might not get hold of his hair, and also, to make his wits glib. He had innumerable swords, of all sizes and shapes, to enable him to fight the devil and witches successfully; they were made by a neighboring blacksmith. In the day-time, neglecting his business, he dozed in a hollow gum-log, for a bed, in his miserable hovel; and at night, kept awake fighting with his imaginary unearthly foes. He fancied, at one time, that he had the devil nailed up in a fireplace, at one end of his house, and had a mark made across his room, over which he never would pass, nor suffer it to be swept. . . . But enough of these *whimsicalities.* The will was established; and upon the appeal, the supervisory tribunal, through its organ, Judge *Nott*, declared that "the evidence, (a part of which only I have

---

26. Judge Joseph H. Lumpkin later became the first Chief Justice of the Georgia Supreme Court. One commentator who has studied the role of southern courts in preserving slavery during this period concluded: "The nine men who sat on the three-judge [Georgia] court from its formation to the outbreak of the Civil War formed by far the most politically active, articulate, and doctrinaire southern bench in support of [slavery] . . . This 'triumph' of ardent pro-slavery was in some measure due to the force of personality of one man, Joseph H. Lumpkin. . . ." See Nash, Reason Of Slavery: Understanding the Judicial Role in the Peculiar Institution, 32 Vand. L. Rev. 7, 105 (1979). Eds.

quoted,) seemed very well to have authorized the verdict which the Jury rendered." . . .

Chancellor *Kent* feelingly observes, that, "it is one of the painful consequences of extreme old age, that it ceases to excite interest, and is apt to be left solitary and neglected. The control which the law still gives to a man, over the disposal of his property, is one of the most efficient means which he has, in protracted life, to command the attentions due to his infirmities. The will of such an aged man ought to be regarded with great tenderness, when it appears not to have been procured by fraudulent acts, but contains those very dispositions which the circumstances of his situation, and the course of the natural affections dictated." Van Alst and others, vs. Hunter and others, 5 Johns. Ch. R. 148. . . .

Perhaps there is one principle which I have failed to guard with sufficient accuracy, to wit: the distinction between oddity or caprice, as exhibited in Mason Lee, and derangement.

Because if there be partial insanity only, and the will is the direct offspring of it, it will be invalid, although the general capacity be wholly unimpeached. And this partial insanity may be *quo ad hoc* or *quo ad hanc:* i.e. upon a particular subject, or as to a particular person. In either case, the sound and disposing mind is deficient or wanting in regard to this particular transaction. It is well established, both by medical and legal authorities, that a party may be both sane and insane, at *different* times, upon the *same* subject, and both sane and insane at the *same* time on *different* subjects; and it is in this last sense that the phrase *partial insanity* is generally used. . . .

Insane Delusion/Monomania/Partial Insanity. Mason Lee, the testator whose will was upheld in *Potts*, was a troubled man. He suffered from insane delusions (also called monomania or partial insanity) about women, witches, and the devil, to name a few. An insane delusion is a belief to which the testator adheres against all evidence and reason. "The subject-matter of the insane delusion must have no foundation in fact, and must spring from a diseased condition of mind. It does not mean merely a mistaken conclusion from a given state of facts, nor a mistaken belief of a sane mind as to the existence of facts." Dibble v. Currier, 142 Ga. 855, 83 S.E. 949 (1914).

An insane delusion does not necessarily affect the validity of the will. Mason Lee's will was upheld because it was not "the direct offspring" of the delusions. As the North Dakota court stated in Kingdon v. Sybrant, 158 N.W.2d 863 (N.D. 1968): "[I]t is not sufficient to establish that the testator was the victim of [an insane] delusion, but the evidence must go further and establish that the will itself was the product of that delusion and that the testator devised his property in a way which, except for that delusion, he would not have done."

Notes and Problems

1. G came to believe that people were living in the trees on his farm. His will devised $40,000 so they could be fed, and devised the residue of his estate to his wife, W. Is the $40,000 devise valid?

2. Pearl was elderly and suffered from a variety of medical problems, including diabetic seizures. Her physician recommended that she go into a nursing home where the seizures could be controlled. When her nephew, Henry, whom she had raised from infancy and who had been living in her house and caring for her, suggested that she abide by her physician's wishes, she went into a rage and eventually became convinced that he wanted her to go into the nursing home so he could steal her possessions. She executed a new will in favor of other relatives, with whom she had had little contact, expressly revoking a former will that named Henry sole beneficiary. Is Pearl's new will valid? Compare Johnson v. Dodgen, 244 Ga. 422, 260 S.E.2d 332 (1979), and Spruance v. Northway, 601 S.W.2d 153 (Tex. Civ. App. 1980), with Estate of Bonjean, 90 Ill. App. 3d 582, 413 N.E.2d 205 (1980).

3. In Estate of Koch, 259 N.W.2d 655 (N.D. 1977), Chris Koch and Elizabeth Koch were married in 1940 and divorced in 1974. They had five children. Chris died in 1976. In the 1960s, Chris came to believe that Elizabeth "was bad," that she "never did anything," and "was running around with other men." Chris expressed the view that no one cared for him. More than once, he tried to commit suicide, threatened suicide, and said that he had attempted it. When friends or neighbors visited, however, Chris's personality would change and he would appear and act normal.

A psychiatrist recommended that Chris be admitted to the psychiatric ward of a hospital, but he objected. Chris did allow himself to be admitted to a medical ward of the hospital and stayed there for about a week. A few years later, he suffered a severe heart attack and was hospitalized for over a month. Following this episode, his children noticed further deterioration of his mind, and came to believe that he was sick mentally as well as physically. Chris continued to accuse Elizabeth of being unfaithful to him, and also of being an alcoholic. Chris's medical doctor concluded that Chris needed psychiatric help because of his depression and suicidal tendencies. In 1973, Chris did undergo psychiatric care at various institutions.

In 1973, on the recommendation of one of the psychiatrists, Chris's two eldest daughters signed a petition to have him committed. At the hearing on the petition, the psychiatrist did not appear, but did send a letter describing Chris's depression and beliefs about Elizabeth. Chris's two daughters also testified to the necessity of a commitment, but several neighbors and more remote relatives testified against commitment. The mental health board determined that Chris should not be committed. Shortly after the hearing, Chris wrote letters to two of his children telling them never to come home again, and allegedly executed a will disinheriting Elizabeth and the children.

Later in 1973, a divorce proceeding was commenced. At the divorce hearing, three of the children testified in support of Elizabeth's effort to secure one-half of the property, which she was ultimately awarded. In March 1974, Chris executed a will devising all his property to his brother. Between 1974 and his death in 1976, Chris spent some time with each of his children, but efforts at reconciliation with Elizabeth failed. During this period, Chris was able to function well in society, and his neighbors thought he was mentally competent. Indeed, they had no knowledge of his mental problems and suicidal tendencies. Chris told several people that his children had sided with their mother, Elizabeth, at the commitment and divorce proceedings, and that he thought the commitment proceeding was commenced to get his money.

The court held that Chris's 1974 will was invalid, saying: "[D]ecedent's feelings toward his children were produced by beliefs held by the decedent which were unfounded in fact and . . . these beliefs were the reason the decedent excluded his natural objects of bounty from his will." Did Chris hold beliefs towards his children that were unfounded in fact?

3. Undue Influence/Coercion

A will is invalid to the extent it is procured by undue influence or coercion. Like many other grounds for contesting a will, "undue" influence/coercion is easier to define than apply to the facts of actual cases. Influence is said to be "undue" if it overcomes the free agency of the testator, substituting the perpetrator's volition for that of the testator's. Mere advice, persuasion, or kindness are said not to constitute undue influence. See Atkinson on Wills § 55.

The historical development of undue influence as a ground of contest is traced in Dawson, Economic Duress—An Essay in Perspective, 45 Mich. L. Rev. 253, 262-64 (1947):

> Equity doctrines of undue influence . . . were aimed . . . at protection for the mentally or physically inadequate, whose inadequacy fell short of a total lack of legal capacity. . . . Throughout the formative period doctrines of undue influence were frequently reinforced by other protective doctrines of equity, particularly those evolved for "confidential" and "fiduciary" relationships. Close family relationships frequently provided opportunity for the exercise of "influence"; or if the parties were not related by blood or marriage, a condition of dependence by the weaker party might provide the elements of a "confidential" relationship which supplemented undue influence as ground for overhauling the transaction. . . .
>
> It was not until the nineteenth century that serious efforts were made to explain the undue influence cases in terms of a larger objective. The objective chiefly employed soon acquired a remarkable appeal, since it coincided with main movements in nineteenth century thought. The "wrong" involved in undue influence, it was said, was the interference with another's will, which should ideally be free. The test for the existence of undue influence became the presence or absence of "free agency," whether or not the individual will had been "overpowered." From this it was easy to move to the broader thesis that, whatever the means of pressure used, "the inequity of the act consists in compelling a person to do what he does not want to do." The objective

defined for cases of mental or physical weakness began to seem equally appropriate for situations included in common law duress, such as threats of criminal prosecution and even duress of goods. Inspired by this new conception, the nineteenth century cases seemed to have set off in pursuit of an ideal as attractive as it was unattainable.

Even in the undue influence cases themselves, the ideal of complete freedom for the individual will was incompletely realized. In the first place, it was clear that no legal agencies would entirely eliminate the pressures that operate on the physically, mentally, or emotionally handicapped, or insulate them from all the multiplied stimuli of a complex social environment. The problem, here as elsewhere, is to select the means of pressure that are permissible and to regulate the manner in which they may be exercised. A closer reading of the undue influence cases reveals the operation of some objective tests, side by side with the analysis of individual motives that is chiefly accented in judicial opinions. Transactions must be judged not only in terms of motive but in terms of their effects.

Direct evidence of undue influence/coercion is not likely to be available to a contestant. The contestant's case must usually be based on circumstantial evidence. When cases are such that direct evidence of the truth is unavailable, the law generally responds by establishing presumptions. Will contests based on undue influence are no exception. For a discussion of the case law, see Moller, Undue Influence and the Norm of Reciprocity, 26 Idaho L. Rev. 275 (1990).

Estate of Kamesar
81 Wis.2d 151, 259 N.W.2d 733 (1977)

DAY, J. This is an appeal from a judgment entered July 14, 1975, admitting the will of Samuel Kamesar, deceased, to probate over objections alleging that it was executed as a result of undue influence.

Facts. Samuel Kamesar died on January 16, 1974, at the age of eighty-four years. He was survived by two daughters, Jeanette Feldman and Bernice Lee, a son, Armon Kamesar, and his second wife, Doris Kamesar, to whom he had been married three years.

During the seven years prior to his death, the deceased executed four wills. The first was executed on January 23, 1967 leaving the major portion of his estate to his first wife, Rose. In the event his wife predeceased him, he left $10,000 to a grandson, Richard Feldman, and $5,000 each to his other grandchildren. If his children became beneficiaries, they were treated equally.

The second will was executed March 10, 1969, following the death of his first wife. It gave $10,000 to his grandson, Richard Feldman and $5,000 each to his other grandchildren. It left $6,000 to various charities, divided the residue equally between his children and named them and a corporate fiduciary as co-executors.

The third will executed on March 2, 1971 was drafted because of a reduction in the value of the testator's holdings. It eliminated the corporate fiduciary and the charitable gifts, but the remaining provisions were the same as the 1969 will.

On March 28, 1971, Samuel Kamesar married Doris Kamesar. On June 18, 1971, he executed a fourth will which is the subject of this appeal. This will incorporated the terms of a pre-nuptial agreement. It left $5,000 to Richard Feldman and nothing to the other grandchildren. The will named Bernice Lee as sole executor and left to her the remainder of his estate. The will left nothing to Jeanette Feldman or Armon Kamesar and contained the following statement:

> I make no other provisions herein for my daughter, Jeanette, or my son, Armon, because I have made special provisions for them during my lifetime, making it unnecessary to do so in this will.

The June 1971 will was propounded by Bernice Lee as the last will and testament of the deceased. It was objected to by Armon Kamesar and Jeanette Feldman on the ground it was the result of undue influence by Bernice Lee. In turn, the objectors offered the March 1971 will as the last will of the deceased.

At the time of his death in 1974, Samuel Kamesar suffered from cerebral arteriosclerosis and cancer. One of the physicians who treated him, Dr. Jay S. Goodman, testified the arteriosclerotic condition began years before but he could not state when. Armon Kamesar testified his father became a little forgetful as early as 1967. Several of the deceased's friends and relatives stated he was forgetful, especially of recent events, and confused in June 1971, the time when the will in question was executed.

However, all witnesses except Armon Kamesar, testified he was of sound mind when he remarried in March 1971. His wife Doris, testified he was forgetful when they were married but always knew what he owned and who his children were. Armon testified that while he doubted his father's mental capacity at the time of the March 1971 will, the pre-nuptial agreement and marriage, he never expressed such doubts because he approved of what was done. Dr. Goodman testified that by the last half of 1973, when the decedent entered the hospital, until his death in 1974 the decedent lacked the ability to make a decision.

Samuel Kamesar resided in Milwaukee most of his adult life. For many years he was in the meat packing business, and Armon Kamesar was also active in the management of the business until it terminated in 1960. Jeanette Feldman has lived in California with her husband and children since 1965 and received substantial financial support from her parents, particularly in the early years of her marriage. Armon Kamesar also lives in California with his family. Until 1971, Armon lived in Milwaukee and managed his father's financial affairs. He had a power of attorney from his father that was never revoked. He collected his father's rents, paid the bills, reviewed his taxes and managed his father's investments. He participated in his father's estate planning and knew the contents of the first three wills.

Armon testified he received between $80,000 and $90,000 in gifts from his parents. $50,000 of this amount represented forgiveness of a debt incurred when Armon attempted to return to the meat packing business in 1961. Bernice Lee lived abroad with her children for several years and returned to Milwaukee prior to her mother's death in 1968. When Armon left Milwaukee in 1971, Bernice collected her father's rents, paid his bills and handled his checking account. She managed his investments and communicated with his accountant and his attorney. She also possessed a power of attorney executed by her father in March 1971.

The record does not show any gifts to Bernice Lee or her family until after execution of the June 1971 will. The record shows that Samuel Kamesar gave $3,000 each to Bernice Lee and her two children in the years 1971 thru 1974 inclusive. They were paid by check drawn by Bernice Lee on her father's account. On December 26, 1973, twenty-one days before his death, Samuel Kamesar executed a document setting up a gift program in favor of Bernice Lee and her children of $9,000 in tax free gifts per year.

While the record shows that there was much ill feeling between Bernice and her brother and sister, it seems clear that Samuel Kamesar had equal affection for all of them.

All of the wills were drawn by the deceased's lifetime friend and attorney, Mr. George Laikin. Mr. Laikin testified that on March 18, 1971, when Samuel Kamesar and Doris Kamesar executed the pre-nuptial agreement, Mr. Laikin recommended that Mr. Kamesar amend his will to incorporate the terms of the agreement. Mr. Kamesar told him that "other changes" should be made in the will also and that he would advise him of those changes later. Mr. Laikin testified that Mr. Kamesar did not personally contact him but communicated the changes to be made in the will by telephone through Bernice Lee. Mr. Laikin stated that Mr. Kamesar customarily communicated with him in that manner, first through Armon and later through Bernice.

When the June will was ready to sign, Bernice Lee made an appointment with Mr. Laikin and drove Samuel and Doris Kamesar to his office. Doris Kamesar and Bernice Lee were present when the will was executed. Mr. Laikin and Bernice Lee both testified that Mr. Laikin reviewed the specific terms of the will. Bernice Lee testified Mr. Laikin asked her to go through the terms again with her father and she read it to him. She testified Mr. Laikin told her father that the will would make some people unhappy but her father replied that one has to take a chance in life. Doris Kamesar testified that Mr. Laikin did not review the will but merely gave it to Samuel Kamesar to read and asked him if he understood it. She and Mr. Laikin testified Samuel Kamesar did ask to have the will changed to provide that his wife could remain in the apartment for one year after his death instead of six months.

Mr. Laikin testified that Samuel Kamesar said the will was what they had talked about and said, "let's proceed to sign the will." Mr. Laikin also testified he questioned Samuel Kamesar whether he knew this will left all to Bernice and he said he did. Mr. Laikin believed Samuel Kamesar was competent at the time and not under any undue influence.

Doris testified that some months after the will was signed, when she reminded Samuel Kamesar that he had cut his two children out of the will, he could not remember doing so.

When Bernice Lee offered the June 1971 will for probate, Armon Kamesar and Jeanette Feldman objected, claiming the will was the result of undue influence by Bernice Lee upon her father. The trial court conducted a hearing on the issue and found in favor of Bernice Lee and ordered the June 1971 will admitted to probate.

Issues. There are two avenues by which an objector to a will on the theory of undue influence may challenge its admission.

One is by proving the elements that this court has said show undue influence. Those are: (1) susceptibility to undue influence, (2) opportunity to influence, (3) disposition to influence, and (4) coveted result. The burden is on the objector to prove by clear, satisfactory and convincing evidence that the will was the result of undue influence. However, when three of the four elements have been established by the required quantum of proof, only slight evidence of the fourth is required.

The second method of challenge is to prove the existence of (1) a confidential relationship between the testator and the favored beneficiary and (2) suspicious circumstances surrounding the making of the will.

I. Four Elements Test.

A. *Susceptibility To Undue Influence.* The objectors must establish by clear, satisfactory and convincing evidence that the testator in this case was susceptible to the influence of Bernice Lee. Factors to be considered are age, personality, physical and mental health and ability to handle business affairs. This court has stated that the infirmities of old age, such as forgetfulness do not incapacitate one from making a valid will. The objectors here cite Estate of Larsen, 7 Wis. 2d 263, 272, 96 N.W.2d 489 (1959) for the proposition that evidence of impaired mental powers on the part of a testator is itself a circumstance which gives rise to a reasonable inference that the testator is susceptible to undue influence. However in *Larsen*, a testator described as "senile" also had periods of lucidity and this court also said:

> While we would have had no difficulty in affirming a determination by the trial court that the transfer was made as the result of undue influence, we are not prepared to hold that the finding of the trial court, that Minnie was not susceptible to undue influence at the time she made the transfer, together with the ultimate finding that such transfer was not the result of undue influence, are against the great weight and clear preponderance of the evidence. A finding of fact of a trial court made upon conflicting evidence should not be set aside on review if a judicial mind could, on due consideration of the evidence as a whole, reasonably have reached the conclusion of the court below. Id. at 273, 274, 96 N.W.2d at 494.

The objectors argue that the fact that Samuel Kamesar entrusted the management of his business affairs to Bernice, coupled with his impaired mental powers, made him susceptible to her influence. But the evidence is conflicting. The testator did suffer from arteriosclerosis, and there was testimony that in June of 1971 he was forgetful and confused. But several witnesses testified he was of sound mind three months before when he was married, and his wife testified he never forgot what he owned or who his children were. Mr. Laikin, the attorney, who was present when all the wills were executed and had known the testator for most of his own life, testified that the deceased was of sound mind and not under any undue influence when the will in question was executed. At that conference the testator made one request for a change with regard to his wife's occupancy of the apartment in the event of his death. This request shows his awareness of the will's provisions. The trial court's conclusion that the objectors did not establish susceptibility is not against the great weight and clear preponderance of the evidence.

B. *Opportunity To Influence.* The trial court found and the proponents agree that Bernice Lee had ample opportunity to exert undue influence on the decedent. This conclusion is not against the great weight of the evidence.

C. *Disposition To Influence.* Disposition to unduly influence means more than a desire to obtain a share of the estate. It implies a willingness to do something wrong or unfair.

The evidence in this case shows that Bernice Lee had taken over the decedent's business affairs completely, but as the trial court pointed out, she had merely taken up where her brother had left off when he moved from Milwaukee. Bernice Lee testified that in December 1973, she did consult another attorney other than Mr. Laikin and procured a declaration of intent signed by her father to give her and her children $9,000 in tax free gifts every year. This document was executed twenty-one days before Samuel Kamesar died, at a time when his attending physician testified that he was incapable of making any kind of decision. But this was remote in time from the date of execution of the will in question here. . . .

In the case before us, the . . . evidence . . . is quite clear that Armon Kamesar and Jeanette Feldman received substantial gifts from their parents during the parents' lives and that Bernice Lee had not. Even if she had tried to influence her father to make his will more favorable to her than to her brother and sister who had already benefitted from Samuel Kamesar's generosity, such influence would not necessarily be undue. In the Estate of Brehmer, 41 Wis. 2d at 356, 164 N.W.2d 318, where the decedent's daughter convinced him that his earlier will was unfair to her, this court said that nothing in the record supported a finding that the daughter was disposed to influence her father for the purpose of procuring an improper favor. The trial court's finding in favor of Bernice Lee on this issue is not against the great weight and clear preponderance of the evidence.

D. *Coveted Result.* This element goes to the naturalness or expectedness of the bequest. The fact that the testator has excluded a natural object of his bounty is a "red flag of warning." Estate of Culver, 22 Wis. 2d 665, 673, 126 N.W.2d 536 (1964). But that fact alone does not render the disposition unnatural where a record shows reasons as to why a testator would leave out those who may be the natural beneficiaries of his bounty.

In the case at bar, the will expressly states that Armon Kamesar and Jeanette Feldman are excluded because the testator believed he had adequately provided for them during his lifetime. Mr. Laikin testified that it was [Kamesar] who suggested that this language be used in drafting the will. . . .

While conflicting inferences may be drawn from the evidence presented and even though the June 1971 will manifests a drastic change in attitude from that manifested just three months before when Armon Kamesar had been the close confidant of his father, the trial court's finding in favor of the proponent on this issue is not against the great weight and clear preponderance of the evidence.

We conclude, therefore, that on the basis of the four classic elements the trial court must be sustained.

II. WAS THE TRIAL COURT'S REFUSAL TO RAISE A PRESUMPTION OF UNDUE INFLUENCE CONTRARY TO THE GREAT WEIGHT AND CLEAR PREPONDERANCE OF THE EVIDENCE?

Undue influence may also be proved by the existence of (1) a confidential relationship between the testator and the favored beneficiary, and (2) suspicious circumstances surrounding the making of the will. When the objector proves the existence of both elements by the required quantum of evidence, a presumption of undue influence is raised, which must be rebutted by the proponent. The trial court held that the record did not substantiate a finding of either element.

(1) *Confidential Relationship.* This court has described the confidential relationship that is sufficient to raise a presumption of undue influence as follows:

> The basis for the undue influence presumption lies in the ease in which a confidant can dictate the contents and control or influence the drafting of such a will either as the draftsman or in procuring the drafting. . . . If one is not the actual draftsman or the procurer of the drafting, the relationship must be such that the testator depends upon the advice of the confidant in relation to the subject matter of the will. . . . Estate of Steffke, 48 Wis. 2d at 51, 179 N.W.2d at 849, quoted in Estate of Velk, 53 Wis. 2d 500, 507, 192 N.W.2d 844 (1972).

The objectors argue that Bernice Lee's role in the execution of the June 1971 will made her the procurer of the drafting and execution of the will. To "procure" is "to initiate," "to instigate," or "to cause a thing to be done." Black's Law Dictionary, (1968) page 1373. However, the record shows that it was Mr. Laikin who recommended that Samuel Kamesar change his will to reflect the provisions of the pre-nuptial agreement. Samuel Kamesar himself stated that he intended to make "other changes" as well. Bernice Lee's role in communicating these changes to Mr. Laikin and in arranging for the execution of the will was a role customarily played by one of Samuel Kamesar's children.

The record is clear, however, that Bernice Lee did manage all of her father's business and personal affairs, and this court has held that where a child has also served as a testator's financial advisor that a confidential relationship can be found to exist. Will of Raasch, [230 Wis. 548, 284 N.W. 571 (1939)].

In the case of In re Estate of Malnar, 73 Wis. 2d 192, 243 N.W.2d 435 (1976), this court affirmed a trial court determination that Genevieve Malnar, a relative by marriage of the testatrix, unduly influenced the testatrix to execute a will leaving all of her property to Genevieve Malnar. This court concluded that the objector met its burden of proof under the confidential relationship and suspicious circumstances test. The court held that a confidential relationship existed by virtue of a power of attorney conferred by the testatrix on Genevieve and the role that Genevieve Malnar played in managing the testatrix's affairs. The court pointed out that the testatrix relied heavily on Genevieve Malnar for transportation, maintaining her household, assisting her in taking medication, making translations for her since the testatrix spoke very little English and assisting her in her financial matters. The court concluded that these factors indicated the presence of a confidential relationship.

The close similarity between the services performed for the testatrix in the *Malnar* case and those performed by Bernice Lee for the testator in this case establish the existence of a confidential relationship. Armon Kamesar testified that when he managed his father's affairs he also took an active part in the estate planning. Bernice Lee testified that she took over the role that had previously been played by her brother and it appears to us that the reasonable inference to be drawn from the evidence is that Samuel Kamesar did rely on Bernice Lee in relation to the subject matter of the will. We conclude, therefore, the finding of the trial court, that there was no confidential relationship between Bernice Lee and her father is against the great weight and clear preponderance of the evidence.

(2) *Suspicious Circumstances.* The suspect circumstances requirement is satisfied by proof of facts "such as the activity of the beneficiary in procuring the drafting and execution of the will, or a sudden and unexplained change in the attitude of the testator, or some other persuasive circumstance." Will of Faulks, 246 Wis. at 360, 17 N.W.2d at 440; Estate of Hamm, 67 Wis. 2d at 294, 227 N.W.2d 34. "The basic question to be determined from the evidence is always whether 'the free agency of the testator has been destroyed.'" Estate of Hamm, Id. at 294, 295, 227 N.W.2d at 41.

In *Malnar*, 73 Wis. 2d at 203, 204, 243 N.W.2d 435, the court found that the following evidence supported a conclusion of suspicious circumstances surrounding the making of the will. Genevieve Malnar had called an attorney and asked him to draft the will. The attorney visited the testatrix, who was bed-ridden, in a nursing home. Because she spoke little English, the attorney realized that she did not understand him and Genevieve acted as a translator in communicating to him the terms of the will. When he brought the draft to the testatrix to sign, she was too weak to sit up by herself. Genevieve Malnar propped the testatrix up with pillows, and the testatrix was so weak that she could only sign by using an "x." The attorney who drafted the will was not the testatrix's personal attorney but was Genevieve Malnar's mother's attorney. Nothing in the evidence explained the sudden change in attitude expressed by the testatrix in the will made three years earlier in which she bequeathed her entire estate to her nieces, nephews and charity. The evidence showed the will was made in haste and that the testatrix showed reluctance in making the will, had at first refused to do so and then suddenly, without explanation, changed her mind. None of the nieces and nephews knew about her serious medical condition or her desire to change her will.

In contrast, in the case at bar, although Bernice Lee called the attorney, Mr. Laikin, made the appointment to see him to have the will signed, drove Samuel Kamesar to the lawyer's office and communicated to the attorney the terms of the will which made her the sole beneficiary, these were all routine practices for this particular testator. The evidence showed that at the time of execution, Samuel Kamesar was aware of the terms of his will. The will was also drafted by his long-time personal friend and attorney who testified there was nothing irregular in the drafting or in the execution. The will itself contained the explanation that Samuel Kamesar believed that he had adequately provided for his son and his other daughter during their lifetime, and the fact was that they had received substantial gifts and that Bernice Lee had not received such gifts. The will was not made in haste but over a period of three months. There was no reluctance shown in signing the will and while the testator was forgetful, he was functioning on his own, outside of a nursing home when the will was executed. It was also established that Armon Kamesar had been informed by Doris Kamesar of the new will before his father died and all parties were aware of the testator's failing health. The differences in the proof of suspicious circumstances in the case of Malnar and the one before us support the court's conclusion that no suspicious circumstances were proven. That conclusion is not against the great weight and clear preponderance of the evidence. . . .

Judgment affirmed.

Notes

1. *Effect of Undue Influence on the Validity of the Will.* When undue influence is found to exist, the will as a whole is not necessarily held invalid. The denial of probate is usually limited to that part of the will that was procured by the undue influence. See, e.g., Williams v. Crickman, 81 Ill. 2d 105, 405 N.E.2d 799 (1980); Haman v. Preston, 186 Iowa 1292, 173 N.W. 894 (1919); Estate of Carothers, 300 Pa. 185, 150 A. 585 (1930); Palmer on Restitution § 20.2, at 177-78. Contra, e.g., McCarthy v. Fidelity Nat'l Bank & Trust Co., 325 Mo. 727, 30 S.W.2d 19 (1930) (entire will invalid if any part resulted from undue influence).

2. *Weight of the Evidence.* Although some courts agree with the view expressed in *Kamesar* that evidence of undue influence must be clear and convincing, most courts adhere to the preponderance-of-the-evidence standard normally used in civil cases.

A recurring factual pattern in which wills have been successfully contested on the ground of undue influence, without the aid of a presumption of undue influence, is as follows: The testator, in her or his elderly and failing years, is cared for by someone who is often a nonrelative hired for this purpose. During this time, the testator executes a will leaving all or a substantial portion of her or his estate to the caretaker to the exclusion of her or his relatives. For this type of case where the will was successfully contested, see Sheets v. Estate of Sheets, 345 A.2d 493 (Me. 1975); Estate of Button, 459 Pa. 234, 328 A.2d 480 (1974); Erb v. Lee, 13 Mass. App. Ct. 120, 430 N.E.2d 869 (1982). In each of these cases, there was evidence that the people caring for the decedent sought to isolate the decedent from contact with her or his relatives or old friends. Of course, the contestants cannot always sustain their burden of proof in cases where a substantial portion of the estate is devised to nonrelatives who were hired to take care of an elderly testator. See, e.g., Estate of Corbett, 211 Neb. 335, 318 N.W.2d 720 (1982).

3. *Presumption of Undue Influence.* By most authority, and as held in *Kamesar,* a presumption of undue influence does not arise merely from the fact that a devise is made to one who is in a confidential relationship with the testator. See, e.g., Estate of Fritschi, 60 Cal. 2d 367, 33 Cal. Rptr. 264, 384 P.2d 656 (1963); Estate of Weickum, 317 N.W.2d 142 (S.D. 1982). The situation is different in the case of lifetime gifts, where the presence of a confidential relationship between the donor and donee is commonly said to give rise to a presumption that the gift was obtained by undue influence. See, e.g., Nelson v. Dague, 194 Kan. 195, 398 P.2d 268 (1965); Palmer on Restitution § 19.2.

In the case of testamentary transfers, the fact that a devise to a devisee who is in a confidential relationship with the testator does not, by most authority, give rise to a presumption of undue influence is explained by the fact that "otherwise, too many testamentary dispositions would be placed in jeopardy, since legatees frequently are persons who bear a confidential relation to the testator, and in many instances probably are in a position to exercise undue influence should they choose to do so." Palmer on Restitution § 20.2, at 184. In addition, it must be kept in mind that many devisees do not even know they have been provided for in a will until after the testator is dead. It has been said that "the natural influence of the parent or guardian over the child, or the husband over the wife, or the attorney over the client, may lawfully be exerted to obtain a will or legacy, so long as the testator thoroughly understands what he is doing, and is a free agent." Parfitt v. Lawless, L.R. 2 P. & D. 462 (1872). There is some authority to the contrary. For example in Wood's Estate, 374 Mich. 278, 132 N.W.2d 35, 5 A.L.R.3d 1 (1965), the court held that the mere presence of a confidential relationship between the testator and a devisee was enough to raise a presumption of undue influence. Of more general acceptance is the idea that the presence of a confidential relationship is enough to raise a presumption of undue influence where the testator was unusually susceptible to influence by reason of physical or mental deterioration, and where a substantial portion of the estate was diverted from natural objects of the testator's bounty. Palmer on Restitution § 20.2, at 187-88.

The fact the will was drafted by a devisee usually does not raise a presumption of undue influence, but the drafting of the will by a devisee who was in a confidential relationship with the testator and who was not otherwise a natural object of the testator's bounty has led courts almost uniformly to make the presumption. See, e.g., Franciscan Sisters Health Care Corp. v. Dean, 95 Ill. 2d 452, 448 N.E.2d 872 (1983); Haman v. Preston, 186 Iowa 1292, 173 N.W. 894 (1919); Estate of Reiland, 292 Minn. 460, 194 N.W.2d 289 (1972); Harris v. Sellers, 446 S.2d 1012 (Miss. 1984); Blake's Will, 21 N.J. 50, 120 A.2d 745 (1956); Haynes v. First Nat'l State Bank, 87 N.J. 163, 432 A.2d 890 (1981); Estate of Pedrick, 505 Pa. 530, 482 A.2d 215 (1984); Estate of Thomas, 463 Pa. 284, 344 A.2d 834 (1975); Estate of Smith, 68 Wash. 2d 145, 411 P.2d 879, corrected, 68 Wash. 2d 145, 416 P.2d 124 (1966); Atkinson on Wills §§ 55, 101. The actual preparation of the will by the one in a confidential relationship has not been regarded as essential, so long as she or he participated in procuring its preparation or execution. See, e.g, Knight's Estate, 108 S.2d 629 (Fla. Ct. App. 1959); Estate of Garfield, 192 Neb. 461, 222 N.W.2d 369 (1974); Estate of Malnar, 73 Wis. 2d 192, 243 N.W.2d 435 (1976). Merely referring the testator to an attorney by one who is in a confidential relationship with the testator and who ultimately is named as the principal devisee is probably not sufficient to raise a presumption of undue influence, even when the attorney to whom the testator was referred was the devisee's personal attorney. See, e.g., Rose v. Dunn, 284 Ark. 421, 679 S.W.2d 180 (1984); Calhoun v. Calhoun, 277 S.C. 527, 290 S.E.2d 415 (1982); Wood v. Stute, 627 S.W.2d 539 (Tex. Ct. App. 1982).

Many of the cases cited invoking a presumption of undue influence, such as *Blake's Will, Haynes, Pedrick,* and *Smith,* were cases in which the testator's attorney prepared a will for the client in which the attorney was named as a devisee and sometimes also as the executor or attorney for the executor. Other such cases are collected in Annot., 19 A.L.R.3d 575 (1968). For further discussion of this issue, see supra pp. 26-30.

4. *Devises to Nonmarital Partner.* Do courts consider a nonmarital partner to be a natural object of the testator's bounty, or do they exclusively invoke traditional notions of family? In one early case, Lamborn v. Kirkpatrick, 97 Colo. 421, 50 P.2d 542 (1935), the court clearly came down on the side of the traditional family. Samuel Braden, a childless widower, died at age 60. His will, written for him by Mrs. Rena Lamborn, as she sat at his bedside twelve days before his death, devised over half of his estate to her.

Samuel's will was contested by his sister, Mrs. Elizabeth Kirkpatrick, who alleged the will was the product of undue influence.

The case was tried before a jury, which found for the contestant. An appeal followed, in which the following jury instruction was challenged as being in error:

> The court instructs the jury that if they believe from the evidence that the testator and Rena Lamborn, before and at the time the will was made, were living in unlawful cohabitation, then the burden is upon her to show that such relationship between her and the deceased was not used to influence the deceased in making the alleged will.

The Supreme Court of Colorado upheld the jury instruction, and affirmed the judgment denying probate. Of the jury instruction, the court said:

> We deem it proper to attach to illicit cohabitation . . . [a] moral basis for requiring an affirmative showing against the existence of undue influence from one who is shown to be guilty of illicit cohabitation. . . . The unlawful intimacy of this meretricious relation between a testator and a beneficiary who is not related to him by blood or marriage usually assumes a clandestine form and, after the testator's death, would almost invariably render such undue influence as results therefrom incapable of proof except by the aid of the presumption which the instruction in question undertakes to recognize. In our opinion, the instruction, fully supplemented as it was, is a correct statement of the law in Colorado. Compare Snyder v. Erwin, 229 Pa. 644, 79 A. 124, 140 Am. St. Rep. 737 [(1911)].

See also deFuria, Testamentary Gifts Resulting from Meretricious Relationships: Undue Influence or Natural Beneficence?, 64 Notre Dame L. Rev. 200 (1989) ("[Although only] a few courts [raise] a rebuttable presumption of undue influence . . . whenever the testator willed his estate to a meretricious partner . . . , [m]any more courts emphasized that such a relationship raised a significant suspicion of undue influence, which would be closely scrutinized."); Sherman, Undue Influence and the Homosexual Testator, 42 U. Pitt. L. Rev. 225 (1981) ("[T]here is at least some evidence to suggest that a homosexual testator who bequeaths the bulk of his estate to his lover stands in greater risk of having his testamentary plans overturned than does a heterosexual testator who bequeaths the bulk of his estate to a spouse or lover."); Annot., 76 A.L.R.3d 743 (1977).

4. Fraud/Forgery

The concept of fraud, as applied in the area of wills and succession, is derived from the common-law tort action for deceit. See Atkinson on Wills § 56. The elements necessary to legal relief for deceit are:

> (1) false representation "with scienter" by the defendant to the plaintiff to induce him to make a particular decision or choice; (2) action or nonaction by the plaintiff in justifiable reliance on the representation; and (3) damage. "With scienter" means that the defendant knew that the representation was

false, or had doubts as to its truth or falsity, or did not know its truth or falsity, or acted in reckless disregard of its truth or falsity.

W. Blume, American Civil Procedure 10 (1955).

A testator can be defrauded in a variety of ways. *Fraud in the execution* occurs when the testator is defrauded about the nature or contents of the document she or he is signing. An interesting variation of this type of fraud appears in the following newspaper story.

> The will seemed genuine enough. Typed neatly on a piece of notepaper and bearing an authentic signature, it left everything to the husband of the deceased, directing that "my children shall have no part of my estate."
>
> But the outraged children weren't satisfied and pursued the will a step further. To test its authenticity, they took it to Lucile Lacy, an examiner of questioned documents.
>
> In her well-equipped laboratory, Mrs. Lacy put the document under an ultraviolet light, and beneath the typewriting appeared, in blue traces of the words, "Dutch, please leave money for the washing."
>
> The will, it turned out, had been fraudulently typed over a note bearing the dead woman's signature. The original note had been eradicated, but the traces—invisible to the naked eye—appeared under expert scrutiny.

Wall St. J., Feb. 19, 1971, at 1, col. 1.

Another type of fraud is called *fraud in the inducement.* This type of fraud occurs when the testator is intentionally misled into forming a testamentary intention that she or he would not otherwise have formed. In Estate of Carson, 184 Cal. 437, 194 P. 5, 17 A.L.R. 239 (1920), Alpha O. Carson died, leaving a will devising the residue of her estate to "my husband J. Gamble Carson." In a will contest, it was alleged that, although Gamble had gone through a marriage ceremony with Alpha a year before her death, and she believed that he was her husband, and made her will in that belief, he was not her husband because he was already married to a woman who was still living and from whom he had not been divorced. It was also alleged that Gamble knew he was not free to marry, and yet represented that he was, and that Alpha's belief that she was married to him was induced by these false representations. It was also alleged that solely because of this belief, she made the will in question, leaving the bulk of her estate to him. The court said:

> The gross fraud upon the testatrix is, of course, apparent. According to the evidence, she was seduced by a marital adventurer into a marriage with him which was no marriage in the eyes of the law because of the fact, which he concealed from her, that he had already had at least one, if not more, spouses, legal and illegal, who were still living and undivorced. There can be no question also that if the bequest to Carson were the direct fruit of such fraud, it is void. The only question in the case, assuming the contestants' evidence to be true, as we must, is, Was the bequest in fact the fruit of the fraud? This is a question of fact which it was for the jury to determine; and, unless it can be said that the jury could have reasonably reached but one conclusion concerning it, and that was that the bequest to Carson was not the direct fruit of his fraud, the evidence was sufficient to prevent a nonsuit.

The remedy for the fraud contemplated by the *Carson* decision was the denial of probate of the residuary clause. Fraud or other wrongful conduct can appear in a variety of circumstances surrounding the making or revoking of wills, and in some of these cases merely denying probate of the will or a part thereof will not adequately remedy the fraud. If a wrongdoer resorts to coercion to prevent a testator from executing a will or deceives a testator into believing that a devise to a person was included in the will when in fact it was not, no remedy is available in the probate court. The remedy must be by way of constructive trust.

5. Constructive Trust and Other Remedies

Statutory References: *1990 UPC §§ 2-517, 3-905, -1101 to -1102*

Constructive Trust as a Remedy for Wrongful Conduct. For centuries, Anglo-American courts, both law and equity, have been working out relief in wrongful-conduct situations to prevent unjust enrichment by ordering restitution of the benefit to the one at whose expense it was obtained.

The law courts developed a remedy usually called *quasi-contract.* For example, if the defendant steals the plaintiff's goods and sells them, the plaintiff, suing in quasi-contract, may recover a money judgment for the amount realized on the sale. The action developed out of the common-law action of assumpsit, which was used to recover for breach of express contract. In the theft case, there was, of course, no express contract by which the defendant was to pay over the proceeds to the plaintiff, but the court treated the situation as though there were and allowed the plaintiff to make use of assumpsit. Although the history is somewhat more complicated than this, the process is illustrative of a tendency of lawyers (as well as other people) to make use of the familiar instead of developing a new set of ideas and techniques to meet the demands of the situations facing them. This development occurred in the law courts, and quasi-contract remains today a strictly legal remedy, seeking a money judgment.

While the law judges were working out quasi-contract, Chancery was developing its own remedies to prevent unjust enrichment, the principal one being *constructive trust.* If the defendant steals the plaintiff's money and uses the money to buy land, the plaintiff may sue in equity for a decree ordering the defendant to transfer title to the land to the plaintiff. The equity court treats the defendant as though the defendant were a trustee of the land for the benefit of the plaintiff. There is, of course, no express trust[27] any more than there was an express contract in the first case. The equity judge is giving relief to prevent unjust enrichment, and is making

---

27. Later, we will study the express trust, which is frequently used by transferors in disposing of their wealth. See infra Chapters 7 and 11.

use of a familiar idea for this purpose by "constructing" a trust. Unlike the law court's judgment in quasi-contract, this is not a money judgment but rather a judgment for specific restitution, requiring, that is, the transfer of title to a specific asset. The remedy is wholly in the province of equity.

If a wrongful act prevents a testator from making a will or a particular devise, it was sometimes argued and held in earlier cases that constructive trust relief is not available because the complaining party has only been deprived of an "expectancy," which is not a property interest. The prevailing view, however, is that such relief is available to protect "disappointed hopes and unrealized expectations." See, e.g., Latham v. Father Divine, 299 N.Y. 22, 85 N.E.2d 168, 11 A.L.R.2d 802 (1949); Scott, The Expectant Legatee, 63 Harv. L. Rev. 108 (1949). Again, there is a considerable burden involved in proving that the wrongful act in fact prevented the making of the will or a particular devise. The prevailing view is also that the wrongful act subjects beneficiaries other than the wrongdoer to constructive trust relief.

The case of Pope v. Garrett, 147 Tex. 18, 211 S.W.2d 559 (1948), is typical on this point. Some days before her death, Carrie Simons requested a friend and neighbor, Thomas Green, to prepare a will for her, leaving all of her property to Claytonia Garrett. Simons and Garrett were unrelated. Green prepared the will as requested and read it to Simons. Simons then declared it to be her will and prepared to sign her name to it. Present in the room during this time were Garrett, the Reverend Preacher, Jewell Benson (a friend of Garrett), and several others, including Simons' sister, Lillie Clay Smith, and Simons' niece, Evelyn Jones. As Simons was about to sign the will, Smith and Jones—"by physical force or by creating a disturbance"—prevented her from carrying out her intention. Shortly after this incident, Simons suffered a severe hemorrhage, lapsed into a semi-comatose condition, and remained in that condition until her death a few days later. The court held that Garrett was entitled to the imposition of a constructive trust in her favor.

> Shall the trust in favor of Claytonia Garrett extend to the interests of the heirs who had no part in the wrongful acts? From the viewpoint of those heirs, it seems that they should be permitted to retain and enjoy the interests that vested in them as heirs, no will having been executed, and they not being responsible for the failure of Carrie Simons to execute it. On the other hand, from the viewpoint of Claytonia Garrett, it appears that a court of equity should extend the trust to all of the interests in the property in order that complete relief may be afforded her and that none of the heirs may profit as the result of the wrongful acts . . . .
>
> The texts of Scott, Bogert and Perry seem to support this view, that is that the trust should be impressed even though the wrongful conduct because of which the title was acquired is that of a third person. Scott on Trusts, Vol. 3, pp. 2374-2376, Secs. 489.5, 489.6; Bogert's Trusts and Trustees, Vol. 3, p. 1467, Sec. 473; Perry on Trusts, 3d Ed., Vol. 1, pp. 260, 261, Sec. 211. The same is true of the Restatement. See illustrations 17 and 18, under Sec. 184, p. 754, Restatement of the Law of Restitution.
>
> The policy against unjust enrichment argues in favor of the [position of the text writers and the Restatement]. But for the wrongful acts the innocent defendants would not have inherited interests in the property.

Accord White v. Mulvania, 575 S.W.2d 184 (Mo. 1978); Rogers v. Rogers, 63 N.Y.2d 582, 473 N.E.2d 226 (1984); UPC § 1-106 (1990); Palmer on Restitution § 20.17.

Would Carrie Simon's will have been valid under the dispensing power authority of UPC section 2-503 (1990)?

Tortious Interference With an Inheritance. A person who—by undue influence, duress, fraud, or other tortious conduct—causes a decedent to divert property from one who would otherwise have received it through gift, devise, or intestate succession may be liable for damages in tort for wrongful interference with inheritance or gift. See, e.g., Nemeth v. Banhalmi, 125 Ill. App. 3d 938, 466 N.E.2d 977 (1984); Bohannon v. Wachovia Bank & Trust Co., 210 N.C. 679, 188 S.E. 390 (1936); Restatement 2d of Torts § 774B (1979); W. Prosser, Law of Torts § 130, at 950-51 (4th ed. 1971). It has been held, however, that a tort action for wrongful interference with inheritance will lie only if the claim for wrongful conduct could not have been asserted as part of the proceedings to admit a will to probate or in a will contest. See, e.g., Robinson v. First State Bank, 97 Ill. 2d 174, 454 N.E.2d 288 (1983).

Living Probate. An 1883 Michigan statute unsuccessfully attempted to grant testators an option to "prove" or "validate" their wills while they were still alive.[28] The statute permitted the testator to petition the county probate court, which would then notify the presumptive heirs and others named by the testator of a hearing, at which the testator's testamentary capacity and freedom from fraud or undue influence would be determined. If these were established, the probate court would decree the validity of the will. Appeals from the decree and the testator's right to revoke or alter the will were expressly provided for by the statute. The Michigan Supreme Court, however, held that the statute authorized a proceeding beyond the scope of judicial power and declared it unconstitutional. See Lloyd v. Wayne Circuit Judge, 56 Mich. 236, 23 N.W. 28, 24 Am. L. Reg. (n.s.) 790 (1885). It ought to be noted that, when *Lloyd* was decided, declaratory judgments were quite alien to the law.

Since this early unsuccessful attempt, only three states, Arkansas, North Dakota, and Ohio, have resurrected the idea of living probate,[29] though there has been considerable discussion advocating various forms of the idea in the journals. See, e.g., Alexander, The Conservatorship Model: A Modification, 77 Mich. L. Rev. 86 (1978); Alexander & Pearson, Alternative Models of Ante-Mortem Probate and Procedural Due Process Limitations of Succession, 78 Mich. L. Rev. 89 (1979) (advocating an "administration model," in which a guardian ad litem would conduct an independent investigation and report to the court; the court would hold a hearing and issue a binding judgment, without notice to affected persons); Cavers,

---

28. The Michigan statute is reprinted in Fink, Ante-Mortem Probate Revisited: Can An Idea Have A Life After Death?, 37 Ohio St. L.J. 264, 268 n.8 (1976).

29. Ark. Code Ann. §§ 28-40-201 to -203; N.D. Cent. Code 30.1-08.1; Ohio Rev. Code §§ 2107.081-.085. The North Dakota statute is set forth in Selected Statutes on Trusts & Estates.

Ante Mortem Probate: An Essay in Preventive Law, 1 U. Chi. L. Rev. 440 (1934) (suggesting the appointment of a probate officer to determine the validity of a testator's will based on affidavits of the will drafter and disinterested witnesses as well as interviews of them and the testator); Fink, Ante-Mortem Probate Revisited: Can An Idea Have A Life After Death?, 37 Ohio St. L.J. 264 (1976) (advocating a "contest model" of living probate, in which all affected persons would be notified and given an opportunity to contest the validity of the will in an adversarial proceeding; the court would then issue a declaratory judgment as to testamentary capacity, undue influence, and compliance with formalities of execution; this is the model that has been enacted in Arkansas, North Dakota, and Ohio); Langbein, Living Probate: The Conservatorship Model, 77 Mich. L. Rev. 63 (1978) (advocating a "conservatorship model," in which all affected persons would be represented in an adversarial proceeding by a guardian ad litem); Leopold & Beyer, Ante-Mortem Probate: A Viable Alternative, 43 Ark. L. Rev. 131 (1990) (advocating some form of ante-mortem probate).

In 1932, a proposed uniform law that would have provided for living probate was drafted, but was not submitted to the Commissioners for approval. Handbook of the Nat'l Conf. of Commissioners on Uniform State Laws and Proceedings 463 (1932). No effort is made in the UPC to adopt the idea, and another recent attempt to formulate a uniform law was abandoned in 1981.

In Fellows, The Case Against Living Probate, 78 Mich. L. Rev. 1066, 1080 (1980), the author argued that the living-probate proposals are seriously flawed because:

> First, the proposals will fail to achieve their own stated objectives of improving the evidence available during probate and assuring testators that their dispository schemes will be carried out. Second, all three proposals [i.e., the "contest," "conservatorship," and "administrative" models] make the testator pay a high price for these ephemeral advantages. Finally, and perhaps most important, all three proposals are unfair to presumptive takers, and under the Administrative Model that unfairness may rise to the level of a constitutional due process violation.

Settlement of Will Contests. Will contests are frequently settled rather than tried. See Schoenblum, Will Contests—An Empirical Study, 22 Real Prop. Prob. & Tr. J. 607, 618-24 (1987). UPC §§ 3-1101 and -1102 (1990) contain elaborate provisions concerning the necessity of court approval of such agreements and their binding effect on interested parties.

Property received by an heir of a decedent (or a devisee of a prior will) pursuant to a bona fide settlement of a claim that the decedent's will was invalid is treated, for federal income, gift, and estate tax purposes, as property derived directly from the decedent. See Lyeth v. Hoey, 305 U.S. 188 (1938). For example, suppose that G executed a will devising $100,000 to A, residue to B, and that later G executed a second will, expressly revoking the former one and naming B as the sole devisee. After G's death, A claimed that the second will was invalid because G lacked testamentary capacity, and B agreed to settle A's claim by consenting to A's receiving

$50,000 from G's estate. If the settlement was bona fide, A will be deemed for tax purposes to have received the $50,000 as a devise from G. B will incur no gift tax consequences. If bona fide settlements were not so treated, the tax laws would create a disincentive to settle donative-transfer disputes. A court judgment that A was to receive property as a devisee would clearly not impose adverse tax consequences. To deny those same tax effects to an out-of-court settlement would seriously interfere with the negotiations.

If, however, the claim of an heir or devisee to a share of a decedent's estate is insubstantial and if the so called settlement is not bona fide, then the transaction is treated as a voluntary rearrangement of the decedent's property, which can cause adverse gift tax consequences. See, e.g., Commissioner v. Vease's Estate, 314 F.2d 79 (9th Cir. 1963); Hardenbergh v. Commissioner, 198 F.2d 63 (8th Cir. 1952). See also A. Casner, Estate Planning § 3.7 (5th ed. 1984); Kemp, How to Achieve Optimum Income, Gift, and Estate Tax Benefits in a Will Contest, 38 J. Tax. 285 (1973); Note, The Effect of an Adjudicated Compromise of a Will Contest or Controversy Upon the Right to Dispose of Property by Will, 37 Ind. L.J. 528 (1962).

Rein, An Ounce of Prevention: Grounds for Upsetting Wills and Will Substitutes
20 Gonz. L. Rev. 1, 64-68 (1984/1985)

Two common situations seem to invite a will contest. One is the so-called unnatural will scenario in which the testator either treats his children unequally or disowns his nuclear family in favor of a charity or a friend. The second is the stepparent scenario where the testator favors a spouse of his later years at the expense of his children by a prior marriage. In either case, the disappointed members of the family may become convinced that the decedent would not have made such a disposition had he not been either unbalanced or unduly pressured by the favored beneficiaries. Gifts between unpopular types of unmarried cohabitants (e.g., same sex friends; older woman-younger man) seem particularly vulnerable. Wills made by infirm or mentally impaired testators also invite contest.

It is not enough for a lawyer faced with such a situation to draft a technically perfect instrument. If it reasonably appears that the testator has capacity and he cannot be dissuaded from making the suspicious disposition, the lawyer who drafts a will which strongly suggests the possibility of a contest has a duty to take special precautions to ensure that the desired donative plan will survive the testator's death.

The idea of antemortem probate in various forms as a means of establishing due execution, testamentary capacity and freedom from undue influence during the testator's lifetime has captured the imagination of legal scholars. Several states have living probate statutes on their books. It may be helpful and feasible for a testator to avail himself of such antemortem procedures (also called living probate) in some cases. But even if the many practical and constitutional objections to antemortem probate schemes could be overcome in theory, living probate procedures seem a bit cumbersome and costly for the average testator.

For the most part the drafter and his client will have to rely on non-adjudicative strategies for discouraging contest of the client's last wishes.

No-contest clauses are frequently inserted to discourage will contests.[30] Such clauses (also called *in terrorem* or forfeiture clauses) purport to deprive any legatee or devisee who brings contest from taking his gift under the will. Although this device can be effective, in many cases it is of limited utility in discouraging contests. First, a potential contestant cannot be deterred by such a proviso unless the will leaves him a substantial gift. Second, many courts refuse to enforce such clauses when it appears that the contest was brought in good faith and on probable cause. This salutary exception is made out of concern that the device might otherwise be used by unscrupulous schemers as a weapon to secure the fruits of their misdeeds from challenge by scaring off those worthy contestants who should be encouraged to dispute a truly fishy-smelling will.

Several commentators have suggested the use of will substitute arrangements, particularly the revocable inter vivos trust. The theory is that lifetime transfers are "more resistant" to capacity and undue influence challenges even though the substantive capacity standard is higher for lifetime transactions than for wills. Of course, the effectiveness of this strategy depends on the type of will substitute employed and the atmosphere in which it is arranged. Professor Langbein seems correct in his observation that "the settlor who lives with his trust for a while, conveying property to it and receiving income distributions, has the opportunity to show greater deliberateness than someone who merely signs a will that works no lifetime consequences upon him." As another commentator states, "a contestant might have more difficulty persuading a jury that a revocable inter vivos trust was the product of the ephemeral influence of a beneficiary." But conveyances in joint tenancy with right of survivorship and deeds executed under suspicious circumstances seem no less resistant to contest than wills executed under similar circumstances. Even trust agreements have been successfully challenged, particularly those drafted by an attorney selected by one of the major remainder beneficiaries and executed by an enfeebled, dependent settlor with no business experience. This suggests that lifetime property arrangements made by vulnerable transferors fare no better than wills executed by vulnerable testators. One also suspects the converse—that wills made by strong minded and active testators fare no worse than will substitutes arranged by strong minded and active settlors—also holds true.

Even if the devices and tactics just described are employed, the lawyer will want to take the precautions traditionally relied on by the estate planning bar to protect the donative plan. These center around the preparation and execution of the will itself.

---

30. UPC §§ 2-517, 3-905 (1990) provide that no-contest clauses are unenforceable if probable cause exists for instituting the proceedings. Eds.

All preliminary conferences with the testator should be held out of the presence of the prospective beneficiaries. Because even irregular wills tend to stand where a rational basis for the disposition is shown, it is a good idea to build a record of the reasons for the apparently unnatural will. The testator should be warned of the irregularity of the proposed plan and asked to explain his reasons for desiring such a disposition. The true reason should always be given because a fabricated explanation made to spare the feelings of an excluded heir may arm the potential contestant with a factual basis for claiming that the disposition was the product of an insane delusion. It may sometimes be desirable to include a statement of such reasons, albeit not necessarily in the will itself. Whether in the will or in a separate document, this memorialization should always be done in measured, factual terms, "without the use of extreme or bitter language." This is because hysterical language decreases the testator's credibility and also leaves the estate vulnerable to a suit for testamentary libel.

[L]ay testimony that the testator knew what he was doing often prevails over medical evidence of incapacity. This suggests that a carefully orchestrated execution ceremony is of prime importance. Too many lawyers select as witnesses anyone who happens to be around (usually secretaries) or, worse yet, send the client off with the will to have it witnessed on his own. The will should be attested by more than the minimum number of witnesses required by statute. Some of the persons selected should be acquainted with the testator (e.g., testator's neighbor, banker or clergyman) but all should be completely disinterested. Ample time should be allowed for the witnesses to chat with the testator and to form an opinion regarding the this [sic] testator's capacity on that day. Some lawyers have employed psychiatrists to render an opinion at some stage of the proceedings. This strategy may backfire by suggesting that those who were advising the testator entertained doubts as to his capacity. In special cases it may be desirable to make a videotape or sound recording of the testator's conversation with the witnesses and the execution ceremony itself. This might serve to deter disgruntled relatives from bringing a contest or, if a contest is brought anyway, might permit the triers of fact to form their own impression of the testator's mental state. What case law there is suggests that such evidence is admissible, both in will contests and in proceedings challenging inter vivos transfers, provided "proper foundation has been laid to assure [its] authenticity and its consequent reliability."

PART C. UNATTESTED DOCUMENTS AND EVENTS —INCORPORATION BY REFERENCE, INDEPENDENT SIGNIFICANCE, AND RELATED DOCTRINES

Statutory References: *1990 UPC §§ 2-510, -512 to -513*
Pre-1990 UPC §§ 2-510, -512 to -513

Integration. Wills frequently are composed of multiple pages. No state requires each sheet of paper of a multiple-page will to be separately executed. Writings contained on separate pieces of paper can be effective as parts of a single document. The process of integrating separate papers into one will, however, like the process of integrating separate papers into one contract under the Statute of Frauds, involves some proof of intention that the parts be considered together—proof that would be supplied, for example, by relation of sense or by physical attachment.

Occasionally, a court suggests that either relation of sense or physical attachment is essential to integration, see, e.g., Seiter's Estate, 265 Pa. 202, 108 A. 614 (1919), but the actual decisions tend strongly to support the view that any evidence will suffice so long as the court is satisfied that at the time of execution the separate papers were present and regarded by the testator as parts of the will she or he was making. See, e.g., Cole v. Webb, 220 Ky. 817, 295 S.W. 1035 (1927); Estate of Beale, 15 Wis. 2d 546, 113 N.W.2d 380 (1962).

Incorporation by Reference. In most jurisdictions, unattested papers—papers that were not present when the will was executed—can be regarded as part of the will by incorporation. See Atkinson on Wills § 79; Evans, Nontestamentary Acts and Incorporation by Reference, 16 U. Chi. L. Rev. 635 (1949); Evans, Incorporation By Reference, Integration, and Non-Testamentary Act, 25 Colum. L. Rev. 879 (1925); Annot., 38 A.L.R.2d 477 (1954).

Simon v. Grayson
15 Cal. 2d 531, 102 P.2d 1081 (1940)

WASTE, C.J. The question presented for determination upon this appeal involves the construction and effect to be given a provision in a will purporting to incorporate a letter by reference. Respondent's claim to certain of the estate's funds is based upon the terms of the letter. The appellants, who are residuary legatees under the will, contend that the attempted incorporation by reference was ineffectual. The facts, which were presented to the trial court upon agreed statement, are as follows:

S. M. Seeligsohn died in 1935. His safe deposit box was found to contain, among other things, a will and codicil and a letter addressed to his executors. The will, which was dated March 25, 1932, contained a provision in paragraph four, leaving $6,000 to his executors to be paid by them in certain amounts to certain persons as shall be directed by me in a letter that will be found in my effects and which said letter will be addressed to Martin E. Simon and Arthur W. Green (the executors) and will be dated March 25, 1932.

Paragraph four also provided that any one having an interest in the will "shall not inquire into the application of said moneys" and that the executors "shall not be accountable to any person whomsoever for the payment and/or application of said sum . . . this provision . . . is in no sense a trust."

The letter found in the testator's safe deposit box was dated July 3, 1933, and stated:

> In paragraph VIII of my will I have left you $6,000—to be paid to the persons named in a letter and this letter is also mentioned in said paragraph. I direct that after my death you shall pay said $6,000 as follows: To Mrs. Esther Cohn, 1755 Van Ness Ave. San Francisco, Calif. the sum of $4,000— . . . If any of the said persons cannot be found by you within six months after my death, or if any of the said persons shall predecease me, the sum directed to be paid to such persons . . . shall be paid by you to my heirs as described in paragraph IX of my said Will. . . .

This letter was written, dated and signed entirely in the handwriting of the testator. No letter dated March 25, 1932, was found among his effects.

The codicil to the will was executed November 25, 1933. It made no changes in paragraph IV of the will and contained no reference to the letter, but recited, "Except as expressly modified by this Codicil, my Will of March 25th 1932 shall remain in full force and effect." . . .

It is settled law in this state that a testator may incorporate an extrinsic document into his will, provided the document is in existence at the time and provided, further, that the reference to it in the will clearly identifies it, or renders it capable of identification by extrinsic proof. An attempt to incorporate a future document is ineffectual, because a testator cannot be permitted to create for himself the power to dispose of his property without complying with the formalities required in making a will.

In the case at bar the letter presumably was not in existence when the will was executed, for the letter bore a date subsequent to the date of the will. However, the letter was in existence at the time the codicil to the will was executed. The respondent points out that under the law the execution of a codicil has the effect of republishing the will which it modifies, and argues from this that Seeligsohn's letter was an "existing document" within the incorporation rule. . . . The principle of republication thus applied is unquestionably sound. In revising his scheme of testamentary disposition by codicil a testator presumably reviews and reaffirms those portions of his will which remain unaffected. In substance, the will is re-executed as of that time. Therefore, the testator's execution of the codicil in the present case must be taken as confirming the incorporation of the letter then in existence, provided the letter can be satisfactorily identified as the one referred to in the will. And this is true, notwithstanding the codicil made no reference to the letter and recited that the will should remain in full force "except as expressly modified by this codicil", for the letter, if properly incorporated, would be an integral part of the republished will.

We are also of the opinion that the trial court did not err in concluding that the letter found with the will was the letter referred to in the will. Conceding the contrary force of the discrepancy in dates, the evidence of identity was, nevertheless, sufficient to overcome the effect of that factor. The . . . informal document [need not] be identified with exact precision; it is enough that the descriptive words and extrinsic circumstances combine to produce a reasonable certainty that the document in question is the one referred to by the testator in his will. Here the letter was found in the safe deposit box with the will. It was addressed to the executors, as the will stated it would be. No other letter was found. Moreover, the letter is conceded to have been written by the testator, and its terms conform unmistakably to the letter described in the will. It identifies itself as the letter mentioned in the will and deals with the identical subject matter referred to in that portion of the will. All these circumstances leave no doubt that the letter of July 3, 1933, is the one that the testator intended to incorporate in paragraph four of his will. . . .

The judgment is affirmed.

SHENK, CARTER, CURTIS, and GIBSON, JJ., concur.

Notes and Questions

1. *Incorporation by Reference—Recognition of the Doctrine.* A few states—notably Connecticut, Louisiana, and New York—refuse to recognize the doctrine of incorporation by reference. In Hatheway v. Smith, 79 Conn. 506, 65 A. 1058 (1907), the Connecticut court reasoned that "the only power given by [the statute of wills] is that of disposing of . . . property by means of a writing containing in itself language by which the subject and object of the testamentary gift intended is therein expressed."[31]

---

31. The rejection of incorporation by reference in Connecticut was presaged by a decision some three years earlier, in a case involving William Jennings Bryan. Bryan, a self-styled candidate of the ordinary American, lost three presidential elections as the nominee of the Democrat Party. He opposed the gold standard and delivered the famous "Cross of Gold" speech at the 1896 Democrat Party national convention. A religious fundamentalist, he fought against the teaching of evolution in the public schools and helped prosecute the teacher, John Scopes, in the famous 1925 Scopes Trial in Tennessee.

Bryan's Appeal, 77 Conn. 240, 58 A. 748 (1904), involved the will of Philo S. Bennett. Bennett's will devised $50,000 to Bennett's wife, Grace Imogene Bennett, "in trust, however, for the purposes set forth in a sealed letter which will be found with this will."

In connection with the execution of the will, Bennett, with Bryan's help, prepared a letter to Mrs. Bennett directing her to pay the $50,000 to Bryan. Bennett's letter explained that he believed the welfare of the nation depended upon the triumph of the political principles for which Bryan stood and that he wished to help Bryan financially, "so that he may be more free to devote himself to his chosen field." The letter was enclosed in a sealed envelope addressed to Mrs. Bennett. Both the will and the envelope were placed in the testator's safe deposit box, where they remained until after his death. Mrs. Bennett refused to honor the letter, largely because Bennett's will, which Bryan had helped prepare, left $20,000 to Bennett's mistress.

2. *Incorporation by Reference—Common-Law Elements.* In formulating the necessary elements of an effective incorporation by reference, courts frequently say that the will must refer to the extrinsic writing as one in existence. Thus, in Wagner v. Clauson, 399 Ill. 403, 409, 78 N.E.2d 203, 206, 3 A.L.R.2d 672 (1948), the Illinois court described the essential elements of incorporation as follows:

> (1) the will itself must refer to the paper to be incorporated (a) as being in existence at the time of the execution of the will, (b) in such a way as to reasonably identify such paper in the will, and (c) in such a way as to show the testator's intention to incorporate such instrument in his will and make it a part thereof; (2) such document must in fact be in existence at the time of the execution of the will, and must be shown to be the instrument referred to in the will.

Requirement (1)(a) has led sometimes to the rejection of a writing that was in existence, for the reason that the testator failed to use the correct tense in describing the writing, a situation most likely perhaps to occur in instances of republication by codicil. Thus, in Durham v. Northen, [1895] P. 66, the will created a trust and directed the trustees to set apart properties "which the trustees will find noted by me for the purpose." A paper was found listing such properties, but it was dated later than the will. A codicil republishing the will was executed after the date of this paper. The court held that the paper was not incorporated because the will "does not refer to a document as existing." For an American case with a similar fact pattern and result, see Kellom v. Beverstock, 100 N.H. 329, 126 A.2d 127 (1956).

3. *Statutory Recognition of the Doctrine.* The doctrine of incorporation is codified in about twenty-four states, along the lines of UPC section 2-510 (1990). See Restatement 2d of Property, Statutory Note to § 33.1. If the *Durham* or *Kellom* cases had been governed by UPC section 2-510 (1990), would the result have been different?

4. *Incorporation Into Holographic Wills.* The decisions are divided on the question whether a valid holographic will can effectively incorporate a writing that is not in the testator's handwriting if the statute requires the will to be "entirely" in the testator's hand. Incorporation was upheld in Estate of Plumel, 151 Cal. 77, 90 P. 192 (1907), but rejected in Hewes v. Hewes, 110 Miss. 826, 71 S. 4 (1916). Two leading writers have taken opposing positions on the issue. Compare Atkinson on Wills § 80, at 392 with Mechem, The Integration of Holographic Wills, 12 N.C. L. Rev. 213, 225-29 (1934).

Bryan sued to enforce the letter, but was unsuccessful. The court did not then pass on whether it would recognize the doctrine of incorporation by reference, but placed its decision on the ground that the requirements of a valid incorporation were not satisfied. In its view, the will did not contain "any clear, explicit, unambiguous reference to any specific document as one existing and known to the testator at the time his will was executed."

5. *Incorporation of Otherwise Invalidly Executed Wills.* In Allen v. Maddock, 11 Moore P.C. 427, 14 Eng. Rep. 757 (1858), Anne Foote attempted to execute a will, but it was invalid because it was attested by only one witness. Five years later, on her deathbed, she duly executed a codicil, which recited that it was "a codicil to my last will and testament." No other reference to the will was contained in the codicil, which merely disposed of a small amount of property to Anne's servant, Eliza.

By allowing the invalid will to be incorporated into the codicil, the court held that the will was entitled to probate along with the codicil. The court rejected the contention that

> there is no such distinct reference to this paper in the codicil, as to enable the court to receive parol evidence in order to identify it; that it is not a will; that it is not identified either by date or by any reference to its contents, or by annexation to the codicil, so as to distinguish it from other papers of a like description, if more than one were found; and that to admit this paper to probate on the ground that no other is produced to satisfy the description, would be to incorporate the will in the codicil, merely by parol evidence, and not by the effect of the reference contained in the codicil itself.

It is necessary, the court said, "and it is sufficient, that the description should be such as to enable the court, when the evidence is produced, to say what is the instrument intended."

Republication. Republication of a will by codicil is usually thought of as the equivalent of *re-execution* of the will. This idea did not originate as a device to subvert the incorporation-by-reference requirement that only documents in existence when the will was executed can be incorporated. Instead, it originated as a device to subvert a different rule—the rule that a will could not dispose of land acquired after the will was executed.

From an early time, a will could bequeath after-acquired personal property, but it was not until the Wills Act of 1837, supra p. 164, that English law permitted a will to operate on after-acquired land. The church courts had jurisdiction over wills of personal property and borrowed from Roman law the concept that a will could dispose of after-acquired chattels. But general power of testation over land was first given by the Statute of Wills of 1540, 32 Hen. 8 c. 1, which enabled any person who should "have" any land to dispose of it "by last will and testament . . . ." This language was soon construed as allowing disposition only of land owned by the testator when she or he executed the will. See Brett v. Rigden, 1 Plow. 340, 344, 75 Eng. Rep. 516, 523 (1568); 7 W. Holdsworth, History of English Law 365 (1926); 2 F. Pollock and F. Maitland, A History of English Law 315 (2d ed. 1898).

By section 3 of the Wills Act of 1837, the old rule as to land was changed in England so as to permit a person to dispose by will of "all real estate and all personal estate which he shall be entitled to, either at law or in equity, at the time of his death." In this country, the old rule as to after-acquired land has been everywhere eliminated, in most states by statute. See, e.g., UPC § 2-602 (1990).

Acts Having Independent Significance. All jurisdictions give effect to devises that identify the property or the devisee by reference to acts and facts that have "independent" significance. The independent-significance doctrine has been codified in some states. See UPC § 2-512 (1990).

One of the earliest applications of the independent-significance doctrine occurred in Stubbs v. Sargon, 3 My. & Cr. 507, 40 Eng. Rep. 1022 (Ch. 1838). The testator devised the premises in Little Queen Street to trustees to pay the rents to the testatrix's sister, Mary Innell, during her life, and after her decease, in trust to dispose of and divide the same unto and amongst the testator's partners who were in copartnership with her at the time of her death. The Chancellor upheld the devise, saying:

> In the present case, the disposition is complete. The devisee, indeed, is to be ascertained by a description contained in the will; but such is the case with many unquestionable devises. A devise to a second or third son, perhaps unborn at the time—many contingent devises—all shifting clauses—are instances of devises to devisees who are to be ascertained by future events and contingencies; but such persons may be ascertained, not only by future natural events and contingencies, but by acts of third persons.

The Chancellor's decision affirmed a decision by the Master of the Rolls, 2 Keen 255, 269, 48 Eng. Rep. 626, 632 (1837), who gave this explanation of the doctrine of independent significance:

> [If] the description be such as to distinguish the devisee from every other person, it seems sufficient without entering into the consideration of the question, whether the description was acquired by the devisee after the date of the will, or by the testator's own act in the ordinary course of his affairs, or in the management of his property, and I think that a devise to such person as may be the testator's partners or the disponees of his business may be good.

Examples of the many decisions approving references to circumstances having significance apart from their impact on the testamentary disposition include First Nat'l Bank v. Klein, 285 Ala. 505, 234 S.2d 42 (1970) (devise of part of residuary estate "to the residuary legatees . . . of [my son, Clarence's] estate under his last will and testament,"); Dennis v. Holsapple, 148 Ind. 297, 47 N.E. 631 (1897) ("Whoever shall take good care of me and maintain, nurse, clothe and furnish me with proper medical treatment . . . shall have all of my property."); Gaff v. Cornwallis, 219 Mass. 226, 106 N.E. 860 (1914) (devise of "the contents, if any, of a drawer in said safe . . . ."); Brown v. Clothey, 193 Mass. 271, 79 N.E. 269 (1906) (bequest by a manufacturer of a product "which I may leave on hand at my decease."); Creamer v. Harris, 90 Ohio St. 160, 106 N.E. 967 (1914) ("I give to Sadie Harris . . . one bureau and contents . . . ."); Reinheimer's Estate, 265 Pa. 185, 108 A. 412 (1919) (devise to "the party . . . who may be farming my farm and taking care of me at my death."). In In re Robson, [1891] 2 Ch. 559, a devise of the testator's desk "with the contents thereof" was held to pass title to money found therein and debts due the testator evidenced by notes contained in the desk. A key in the desk unlocked a separate tin box containing securities. The court held that the devisee was not entitled to the contents of the box. Many of the cases noted above involved similar questions of intention.

Reference to Unattested Writing. Pre-1990 UPC section 2-513 introduced a new idea into American probate law. As part of its policy of effectuating a testator's intent by reducing formalities, the pre-1990 UPC permitted testators to dispose of their tangible personal property without having to meet the requirements of the doctrines of incorporation by reference or acts having independent significance. A handwritten document or a signed writing is sufficient so long as the will refers to it. It can be executed before or after the will was written and modified at any time. About twenty-two states have enacted a provision similar or identical to the pre-1990 version of section 2-513. See Restatement 2d of Property, Statutory Note to § 33.1.

The pre-1990 version of section 2-513 has been significantly revised. The 1990 version eliminates some confusion created in pre-1990 UPC section 2-513 about what constitutes tangible personal property. It also repeals the language that allowed an unsigned handwritten document to control the disposition of property. The drafters were concerned that the lack of signature suggests that the testator lacked the requisite testamentary intent. They recognize, however, that UPC section 2-503 (1990) (the dispensing-with-compliance rule) might apply and allow the document to be effective if a proponent proves by clear and convincing evidence that the testator intended an unsigned writing to control the disposition of tangible personal property.

Problem

G's will devised her antique desk to her granddaughter, A. It also contained the following clause:

> I might leave a written statement or list disposing of items of tangible personal property. If I do and if my written statement or list is found and is identified as such by my Personal Representative no later than 30 days after the probate of this will, then my written statement or list is to be given effect to the extent authorized by law and is to take precedence over any contrary devise or devises of the same item or items of property in this will.

After G's death last month, G's will was discovered in the top drawer of her antique desk. In the same drawer was a piece of paper in G's handwriting, dated about a year after the date of execution of her will, that says: "Antique desk to granddaughter, B."

Under either the pre-1990 or 1990 version of UPC section 2-513, who is entitled to G's antique desk, A or B?

Chapter 4

REVOCATION OF WILLS

Part A. Revocation by Instrument
Part B. Revocation by Act to the Document
Part C. Revocation by Changes in Circumstances—Marriage, Divorce, Remarriage
Part D. Revival of a Revoked Will
Part E. Dependent Relative Revocation

A will is said to be "ambulatory," meaning that it does not take effect as a dispositive instrument and, therefore, does not transfer property to the devisees until the testator dies. A will is also revocable throughout the testator's lifetime. The methods and events that revoke wills are statutorily provided in all American jurisdictions and are the subjects of Parts A, B, and C of this Chapter. Parts D and E explore the circumstances under which wills that have been previously revoked are nevertheless given effect at the testator's death. Judicially developed doctrines as well as statutes identify the situations in which previously revoked wills remain effective.

PART A. REVOCATION BY INSTRUMENT

Statutory References: *1990 UPC § 2-507(a)(1), (b)-(d)*
Pre-1990 UPC § 2-507(1)

The Uniform Probate Code and all non-UPC revocation statutes authorize will revocation by valid execution of a subsequent instrument expressly revoking the previous will.[1] See, e.g., UPC § 2-507(a)(1) (1990). Typically, express revocation occurs in wills drafted by lawyers, because standard will forms contain an express clause, such as "this will hereby revokes all wills and codicils heretofore made by me."

The Uniform Probate Code also permits revocation by subsequent instrument that contains only a revocation clause. See, e.g., UPC §§ 1-201(56) (defining a will to include a testamentary instrument that merely revokes another will); 2-507(a)(1) (1990) (referring to a subsequent will

---

1. Most courts hold that a holographic will can revoke a formal, attested will, even in a jurisdiction where the statute provides that a will can be revoked only by an instrument executed with the same formalities as the revoked will. Cases are collected in Annot., 49 A.L.R.3d 1223 (1973).

that revokes a previous will expressly). A testator obtaining legal advice is not likely to execute an instrument that serves only to revoke a previous will, because lawyers typically advise a client to replace one will with another.

The Uniform Probate Code and non-UPC revocation statutes also provide that, in the absence of an express revocation, a prior will is revoked by an "inconsistent" subsequent will. See UPC § 2-507(a)(1) (1990). "Revocation by inconsistency," or "implied revocation" as it is sometimes called, typically occurs when a testator executes a will without the aid of an attorney and fails to include an express revocation provision. When a testator dies with two or more wills and the latest one fails expressly to revoke the earlier ones, litigation can arise about whether the testator intended the subsequent will to replace the prior wills in whole or in part or merely to supplement the prior wills. This was the circumstance in Gilbert v. Gilbert, below.

Gilbert v. Gilbert
652 S.W.2d 663 (Ky. Ct. App. 1983)

PAXTON, J. This is an appeal from a judgment of the Jefferson Circuit Court determining that a holographic instrument, consisting of two writings folded together inside a sealed envelope, was a codicil instead of a second and superseding will. Appellees are a brother of the testator, a niece and three nephews of the testator, and two beneficiaries unrelated to the testator. Appellants are the testator's sisters and remaining brothers.

Frank Gilbert died testate on June 5, 1979. Two writings were offered for probate: an eight-page typewritten instrument, prepared by an attorney, dated April 2, 1976, and the holographic instrument dated December 8, 1978. The "codicil" was written on the back of a business card and on the back of one of Frank's pay stubs. The card and stub were found folded together in a sealed envelope. On the back of the business card, Frank wrote: "12/8/78 Jim and Margaret I have appro $50,000.00 in Safe. See Buzz if anything happens [signed] Frank Gilbert". On the back of the pay stub, Frank wrote: "Jim & Margaret $20,000.00 the Rest divided Equally the other Living Survivors Bro. & Sisters [signed] Frank Gilbert 12/8/78". Written on the envelope is the following: "This day 12/8/1978 I gave to Jim and Margaret this card which I Stated what to do". "Jim and Margaret" are James Gilbert (one of the appellees) and Margaret Gilbert, brother and sister-in-law, respectively, of Frank Gilbert, the testator. The typewritten instrument and the holographic instrument were admitted to probate on September 4, 1979, the holographic instrument being admitted as a codicil.

Appellants subsequently brought a will contest action in Jefferson Circuit Court seeking to have the holographic instrument interpreted as a second and superseding will. After a hearing, the circuit court entered a judgment construing the second instrument as a codicil affecting only the money Frank kept in his employer's safe. This appeal is from that judgment. We affirm.

Appellants argue . . . [that] the separate holographic writings should have been construed as a second and superseding will instead of a codicil. . . . This interpretation would eliminate James Gilbert from sharing in any portion of his brother's estate, except the $20,000.00 bequeathed to him and his wife, Margaret, in the "codicil". Appellees argue, of course, that the "codicil" pertains only to the money in the safe and that James takes both his share under the typewritten will and one-half of the first $20,000.00 of the money in the safe pursuant to the terms of the "codicil". . . .

The second instrument was probated as a codicil, but because it does not refer to the typewritten will, we prefer to characterize it as a second will. A testator can have more than one will effective at the same time, each distributing part of the estate. In such a case the subsequent wills "perform the office of codicils". Muller v. Muller, 108 Ky. 511, 516, 56 S.W. 802, 803 (1900). We believe that to be the situation in this case: the second will serves as a codicil because it does not contain a revocation clause and only distributes part of the residuary estate.

The holographic will does not revoke the typewritten one. We think it is very unlikely that Frank intended to supplant the elaborate distribution of his estate contained in the eight-page typewritten will with a single phrase scratched out on the back of a pay stub. Furthermore, there is no revocation clause in the second will and Kentucky courts have consistently held that one testamentary instrument revokes another only if it is the clear intent of the testator to do so, and even then the revocation is only to the extent necessary. The second will in this case need only re-distribute part of the residue.

We must resolve Frank's intent by looking at the four corners of the two wills, and harmonizing any conflicting provisions to give effect to every provision of each instrument. Here, it is easy to harmonize the two instruments. The only way to give effect to every provision of both instruments is to adopt the trial court's interpretation, to-wit: the two holographic writings comprise a second will that distributes only the money Frank kept in his employer's safe. It was not inconsistent for him to distribute, by a second will, a portion of his estate that would have passed under the residuary clause of the first will.

The judgment of the Jefferson Circuit Court is affirmed. All concur.

Notes, Problems, and Questions

1. *Non-Uniform Probate Code Law*. Most non-UPC statutes fail to elaborate on how one determines whether a subsequent will is sufficiently inconsistent with a prior will to revoke it in whole or in part. Courts and writers have attempted to formulate rules to resolve the inconsistency question caused by multiple wills. The Restatement 2d of Property formulates the following principle:

> § 33.2 *Multiple Wills.* If a donor has multiple wills that are not multiple copies of the same will, each one is fully operative on the donor's death to the extent they are not inconsistent. To the extent they are inconsistent, the later will revokes the earlier wills.

Some courts have been more specific. For example, the California Supreme Court in Estate of Danford, 196 Cal. 339, 238 P. 76 (1925), said that the question depends on whether the later will "was intended to wholly supplant the prior will." And Woerner in his classic treatise, American Law of Administration § 51, at 139 (3d ed. 1923), fills in more detail by suggesting that "if the later or latest will disposes of the whole of a testator's estate, all former wills are thereby revoked."

In trying to determine whether any of these formulations is helpful in resolving the inconsistency question, consider the following situation:

> Five years before her death, G executed a will (Will No. 1), devising her antique desk to A; $20,000 to B; and the residue of her estate to C.
>
> Two years later, A died, and G executed another will (Will No. 2), devising her antique desk to A's husband, X; $10,000 to B; and the residue of her estate to C. Will No. 2 neither contained an express revocation provision nor referred to Will No. 1.
>
> At G's death, her net probate estate consisted of her antique desk (worth $10,000) and other property (worth $90,000).

How should G's estate be divided among X, B, and C? Would your answers change if Will No. 2 had not contained a provision devising the residuary of her estate to C? Should extrinsic evidence be admissible in determining the extent to which Will No. 2 in the above hypothetical is impliedly revoked by Will No. 1?

2. *1990 Uniform Probate Code.* UPC sections 2-507(b)-(d) (1990) substantially revise the pre-1990 UPC to provide guidance to courts in resolving the inconsistency question. These subsections create a presumption, rebuttable only by clear and convincing evidence, that a subsequent will replaces rather than supplements a previous will if the subsequent will makes a complete disposition of the testator's estate. They also create a presumption, rebuttable only by clear and convincing evidence, that a subsequent will supplements rather than replaces a previous will if the subsequent will does not make a complete disposition of the testator's estate. A similar rule is also set forth in comment b, appended to Restatement 2d of Property section 33.2.

PART B. REVOCATION BY ACT TO THE DOCUMENT

Statutory References: *1990 UPC §§ 2-507(a)(2), -515 to -516, 3-912*
Pre-1990 UPC §§ 2-507(2), -901 to -902

The English Statute of Frauds of 1677, § 6, 29 Car. 2, c. 3, permitted revocation of a will by "burning, cancelling, tearing or obliterating the same." The Uniform Probate Code and nearly all non-UPC statutes have a somewhat similar provision.[2]

That the statutes recognize revocation by act to the document exemplifies how the law can be molded by the practices of the people whose affairs it regulates. One reason for recognizing revocation by burning, tearing, etc. is the fact that many people choose this method of revoking their wills.[3]

The law treats a will as revoked because its maker *intended* to revoke it. Just as the law requires a writing to furnish reliable evidence of an intent to make a will, the law also insists upon reliable evidence of a manifestation of intent to revoke. In the main, reliable evidence consists either of another duly executed writing (revocation by instrument) or of some act to the instrument that tends of itself to suggest that the testator meant to revoke the will or some part of it.

Among the prescribed methods of revoking by act, most of the litigation has concerned cancellation. Cancellation occurs when the testator has crossed out or marked through the document or part of it or has written on the document words such as "cancelled" or "null and void."

EXTERNAL REFERENCE. Chaffin, Execution, Revocation and Revalidation of Wills: A Critique of Existing Statutory Formalities, 11 Ga. L. Rev. 297 (1977).

Kronauge v. Stoecklein
33 Ohio App. 2d 229, 293 N.E.2d 320 (1972)

CRAWFORD, J. Plaintiffs, the appellants herein, are the heirs at law of Helen L. White, deceased. Defendants are her executor and the beneficiaries

---

2. Some statutory lists are less comprehensive than the one contained in the English statute. See Comment, American Will Revocation Statutes: The Need for Change and Uniformity, 8 Cumb. L. Rev. 175 (1977). An older study is Rees, American Wills Statutes II, 46 Va. L. Rev. 856, 875-80 (1960). UPC § 2-507(a)(2) (1990) and many non-UPC statutes include "destroying."

3. "The old law enabled a man to revoke his will by cancelling it, and such was the habit of Englishmen." E. Sugden, Speech in the House of Commons upon the Law of Wills Bill 32 (1838). Sir Edward Sugden was criticizing the failure of the Wills Act of 1837 to include "cancelling" as a method of revoking a will by act to the document. He suggested "a few simple rules by which we ought to be governed in the alterations of our law of property," one of which was: "Run not counter to the habits of the people."

under her will, the principal beneficiary being Jennifer L. Jones aka Jennifer L. Manson.

The will of Helen L. White was executed on October 4, 1968. It was drawn upon the stationery of her attorney, Robert J. Stoecklein, who was also one of the witnesses to the will. She never spoke to him thereafter about changing or revoking the will.

On the otherwise blank margin of the will, in the handwriting of the testatrix, but not touching any of the writing in the will, appear these words:

> This will is void. We have never heard or seen Jennifer Jones or did she come to Jess' funeral so I do not leave her anything
>
> April 17, 1971

Plaintiffs brought this action to contest the will. Defendants filed a motion for summary judgment. The facts upon the motion were stipulated.

The court sustained the motion and entered judgment for the defendants, the appellees and proponents of the will. Plaintiffs, the appellants and contestants, have appealed.

The parties agree that the single question before us on appeal is whether the writing on the margin revoked the will.

There is no inherent or common-law right to dispose of one's property by will. Such right depends upon statute. The law is quite specific as to the formalities required to make a valid will, or to revoke it. R.C. § 2107.33 provides the exclusive methods of revoking a will. These must be strictly complied with in order to make the revocation effective.

R.C. § 2107.33 reads:

> A will shall be revoked by the testator by tearing, canceling, obliterating, or destroying such will with the intention of revoking it, or by some person in such testator's presence, or by such testator's express written direction, or by some other written will or codicil, executed as prescribed by sections 2107.01 to 2107.62, inclusive, of the Revised Code, or by some other writing which is signed, attested, and subscribed in the manner provided by such sections. . . .

The intent of the testatrix here is not questioned.

It is conceivable that a writing might be so placed over the text of the instrument as to constitute [a cancellation]. Such is not the case here, where the writing does not touch any part of the wording in the will itself. It must therefore be classified as a writing which is not a canceling; and, of course, the writing does not purport to be "signed, attested and subscribed in the manner provided by such sections." (R.C. §§ 2107.01 to 2107.62.) . . .

Judgment affirmed.

SHERER, P.J. and KERNS, J., concur.

Notes and Questions

1. *Invalid as a Revocation by Cancellation; Valid as a Revocation by Subsequent Instrument.* As the court suggested in the *Kronauge* case, a statement of cancellation, if properly executed, can be given effect as a revocation by subsequent instrument, regardless of whether the statement of cancellation touches any of the words on the will. See, e.g., Kehr Will, 373 Pa. 473, 95 A.2d 647 (1953). Doubtless this is most likely to occur in jurisdictions that recognize holographic wills. See, e.g., Estate of Nielson, 105 Cal. App. 3d 796, 165 Cal. Rptr. 319 (1980); McCarthy v. Bank of California, 64 Or. App. 473, 668 P.2d 481 (1983).

Would the decision in *Kronauge* have been different if the dispensing-power rule of UPC section 2-503 (1990) had applied?

2. *Touching of the Words.* Under the pre-1990 UPC and under non-UPC law, if the words and formalities are insufficient to accomplish a revocation by subsequent instrument, the cases usually hold that, in order to constitute a revocation by cancellation, the testator's marks on the paper must touch the words of the will. See, e.g., Noesen v. Erkenswick, 298 Ill. 231, 131 N.E. 622 (1921); Cox's Estate, 621 P.2d 1057 (Mont. 1980).

Most authority is consistent with the *Kronauge* holding that words of cancellation in the margin or on the back of the will fail to revoke a will by cancellation. See, e.g., Dowling v. Gilliland, 286 Ill. 530, 122 N.E. 70 (1919); Yont v. Eads, 317 Mass. 232, 57 N.E.2d 531 (1944); Thompson v. Royall, 163 Va. 492, 175 S.E. 748 (1934). Contra, e.g., Warner v. Warner's Estate, 37 Vt. 356 (1864). On the other hand, under either the pre-1990 UPC or non-UPC law, no touching of the words is required for revocation by burning or tearing. See, e.g., White v. Casten, 46 N.C. 197 (1853) (burning); Crampton v. Osborn, 356 Mo. 125, 201 S.W.2d 336, 172 A.L.R. 344 (1947) (tearing).

UPC section 2-507(a)(2) (1990) eliminates the distinction between revocation by cancellation and revocation by burning or tearing. Regardless of the type of revocatory act, a touching of the words on the will is not required. Thus, the UPC framers decided to eliminate rather than retain the touching-of-the-words requirement and not to remit cases like *Kronauge* to UPC section 2-503 (1990), which dispenses with formality requirements only if clear and convincing evidence demonstrates that a decedent intended to revoke the will.

Revocatory Act Performed by Another. Like most probate code provisions on revocation, both the pre-1990 and 1990 versions of section 2-507 authorize the performance of a revocatory act not only by the testator, but also by another person. The execution analogue of this procedure is the procedure under which someone other than the testator signs the testator's name on her or his behalf. See supra p. 172. Not surprisingly, the question of whether the other person's act was done in the testator's "presence" arises in this context just as it did in the will execution context. Consider, for example, the case of Estate of Bancker, 232 S.2d 431 (Fla. Dist. Ct.

App. 1970). Adrian G. Bancker died in 1967, survived by his wife, three natural children, and a step-daughter. Shortly before his death, Adrian became dissatisfied with the attorney who drew his 1966 will and who was named alternate executor therein. For the purpose of reviving a former will, Adrian directed his wife, step-daughter, and her husband to destroy the 1966 will. Adrian remained in bed while they went into another room, removed the will from a wall safe, and destroyed it by tearing it into pieces and flushing them down a toilet. The court held the 1966 will was not revoked, saying:

> [The Florida] statute specifically provides the revocation must be made in the presence of the testator. Under this statute, such revocation must take place in the physical and mental presence of the testator. The requirements for a valid revocation of a will must be strictly observed.

Would the outcome of the *Bancker* case have been different if the case had been governed by UPC section 2-507 (1990)?

Wrongful Interference With an Attempt to Revoke. If a testator intends to revoke a will by act to the document and the will is not destroyed by physical act because another person fraudulently intervened to prevent the destruction, the will remains effective. Without the physical act, an intent to revoke is insufficient to revoke a will. The courts, however, will provide a remedy for any wrongful interference with an attempt to revoke and will accomplish a testator's intent through the constructive trust remedy. See supra p. 234.

For example, in Estate of Silva, 169 Cal. 116, 145 P. 1015 (1915), Frank V. Silva died in 1912, survived by his wife and some brothers and sisters. Frank's will devised his entire estate to his wife. Frank's brothers and sisters, his heirs at law, claimed that the will had been revoked. Their petition alleged that Frank had requested his wife to destroy the will; that she, in his presence, burned an envelope, declaring that his will was inside; and that, in fact, some other paper was inside the envelope. The court held that the will was not revoked, saying:

> In order to constitute [a] revocation, there must be an actual burning, tearing, canceling, obliteration, or destruction, with the intention to revoke the document as a will. The mere intent, unperformed, to destroy or burn the will is not sufficient. There must be a joint union of act and intent in order to accomplish the revocation. . . . If relief can be given at all for such a wrong, it must be sought by suit in equity to declare the wrongdoer a trustee for the heirs with respect to the property received by such wrongdoer in virtue of the will.

In response to the court's statement that they had chosen the wrong remedy, the heirs brought a suit in equity for a constructive trust. On appeal in that action, Brazil v. Silva, 181 Cal. 490, 185 P. 174 (1919), the court stated:

> The constructive trust with which it is sought to charge the defendant is based upon her alleged fraud. . . . [T]he alleged fraud . . . consisted in her

preventing by deceit the actual destruction animo revocandi of the will in which she is the sole beneficiary, with the result that it was preserved contrary to the intention and belief of the testator, and the defendant has now acquired the legal title to his property, which otherwise would have gone to the plaintiffs. . . . [T]he general principle upon which relief is asked for in such cases as the present, namely, that where the defendant has by his own wrong obtained the legal title to property, a trust as to such property will be imposed upon him in favor of the party injured . . . is a familiar one, and is based upon the maxim . . . that no one may profit by his own wrong. The instances of its application are as various nearly as the ways in which property can be wrongfully acquired. A most common illustration is the imposition of a trust upon a party holding under a deed fraudulently obtained from the grantor, where admittedly the deed is valid to the extent of conveying the legal title. Nor can there be any doubt that such a case as the present comes within this principle. If the facts alleged in the complaint are true, the defendant has by the grossest fraud acquired the legal title to property which, but for her fraud, would have gone to the plaintiffs. . . . It is a familiar function of equity, and one very characteristic of its peculiar province, to refuse to permit, and affirmatively to prevent, a statute being used as a means whereby to perpetrate a wrong. . . . In this connection, since the cause must go back for trial, it may not be amiss to call attention to the rule that, because of the very nature of these cases, the fraud or other wrong relied on must be proven clearly and satisfactorily. The relief asked for is so extraordinary, and the opportunity for false testimony so great, since the evidence in most cases must be largely parol, that it is only where it is fairly certain that the circumstances calling for the relief actually exist that the extending of it may be justified.

For other decisions holding that a case such as *Silva* is a proper one for imposing a constructive trust upon the devisee, see White v. Mulvania, 575 S.W.2d 184 (Mo. 1978); Morris v. Morris, 642 S.W.2d 448 (Tex. 1982).

Presumption of Intent to Revoke. If will contestants prove that the testator had custody of the will, a will that is found physically mutilated is presumed to be revoked. As demonstrated in Estate of May, below, this presumption is rebuttable.

Estate of May
88 S.D. 313, 220 N.W.2d 388 (1974)

DUNN, J. . . . The decedent lived alone on a farm a few miles from Parker, South Dakota. He executed a document on December 28, 1967 entirely in his own handwriting purporting to dispose of his property upon his death. There was no question raised of undue influence or of testamentary capacity. The decedent told Victor Brandt on at least two occasions that he did have a will, the last time being approximately three days before his death. On February 14, 1973 John R. May died in Turner County, South Dakota.

Pro. 73-12

Dec 28 / 1967

his is my will
my doctor & bills must be
that medcare dos not
pay my socuperton bills
Esther gets 1200, 00
Eva gets 1200. 00
Lamar two adopted girls
miller 600. 00
600.00
my onnerd mothers will
in I passed away, this will
made was not dated
+ hold.
my Ed may died not
other will, on this gets $1.00
of on that I have gets to
1/2 A Conpuence at Parke No 8
n who ever is prudent
unce at that time can be
point the administrator.
would like this house
& and suppins to go into our

John R. may
parker So. Dak

Mrs. Eva Christensen, respondent and a sister of the deceased, searched the decedent's home and bank boxes thoroughly after his death but could find no will. Mrs. Christensen, the sheriff of Turner County and others went through the papers of the deceased in his home; some papers were destroyed and others piled into boxes and stored in a rented barn near the home of a niece, Eva Brandt. Later, Mrs. Brandt found the contested will with the papers moved to the barn and in a box of documents which also contained current receipts, bills, bank statements and current business records of the deceased.

The document purporting to be a Holographic Will is hereby set out in full [see previous page], showing where it was cut out of the book on the right margin, and where it was torn on the left margin.

There is no evidence to show what happened to the document from the date it was executed to the date it was found. It came from decedent's home and the inference would be that it was in decedent's possession at least until the date of his death. All of the witnesses testified that decedent's home was a mess with important documents as well as worthless scraps of paper piled around the house without any system or order. In the light of these facts the trial court ruled that the Holographic Will had been torn and obliterated by the decedent during his lifetime with the intent and for the purpose of revoking the same in accordance with SDCL 29-3-1 which states:

> Except in the cases in this chapter mentioned, no written will, nor any part thereof, can be revoked or altered, otherwise than:
> (1) By a written will or other writing of the testator, declaring such revocation or alteration, and executed with the same formalities with which a will should be executed by such testator; or
> (2) By being burnt, torn, canceled, obliterated, or destroyed, with the intent and for the purpose of revoking the same, by the testator himself, or by some person in his presence and by his direction.

In considering this statute we should also refer to SDCL 29-3-3:

> A revocation by obliteration on the face of the will may be partial or total, and is complete if the material part is so obliterated as to show an intention to revoke; . . . .

As there was no extrinsic evidence that decedent intended to destroy the will, the trial court of necessity in reaching its decision had to rely on the presumption generally set out in 57 Am. Jur., Wills, § 550, which reads as follows:

> It is generally agreed that if a will produced for probate, which is shown to have been in the custody of the testator after its execution, was found among the testator's effects after his death, in such a state of mutilation, obliteration, or cancelation as represents a sufficient act of revocation within the meaning of the applicable statute, it will be presumed, in the absence of evidence to the contrary, that such act was performed by the testator with the intention of revoking the instrument. . . . Whatever presumption arises from

acts of cancelation or mutilation is rebuttable, but the burden of the rebuttal rests upon the proponent.

Proponent of the will rebuts this presumption by evidence that the decedent told Victor Brandt (husband of Eva Brandt, niece of decedent) that he had a will on two different occasions, the last time being some three days before his death. This testimony was corroborated by Mrs. Brandt to the extent that her husband had advised her of decedent's statements at the time that they were made. No other will was ever found. Mrs. Brandt would be an heir of the decedent if the will was not upheld and would take nothing under the will. Accordingly, the testimony of the Brandts on this subject is most credible and convincing and any presumption of intent to revoke the will arising from the tearing while in the possession of the decedent was effectively rebutted. In Fleming v. Fleming, 367 Ill. 97, 10 N.E.2d 641, it is stated:

> Any act of tearing of the paper on which the will is written, however slight, is an act of tearing within the meaning of this statute if done with intent to revoke the will, but it is likewise true that no act of tearing or cutting, unless it be with the intention to revoke the will, accomplishes such purpose. The intent with which the act is done governs. . . .

Thus the trial court's finding No. 6, that the will had been revoked "by tearing and obliterating same with the intent of revoking" is clearly erroneous under the evidence as there was no actual evidence of an intent to revoke, and the presumption of intent arising from the tearing was effectively rebutted.

The next question is whether the contents of the document itself can be determined so as to provide for the disposition of decedent's property.

First it should be noted that the date, the signature, and the fact that it is decedent's will are intact. Reasonable men could not differ that the document provides for the payment of any doctor and hospital bills not covered by medicare. It provides that Esther (sister) gets $1200.00; Eva (sister) gets $1200.00; and Laura's (deceased sister) two adopted girls receive $600.00 each. It provides that Ed May (brother) gets $1.00.[4]

This takes care of the special bequests, after which comes the words "of what I have goes to S D A Conference at Pierre, So.D—who ever is president—frence at that time can be—point the administrator." No one contests that the decedent was referring to the Seventh Day Adventist Conference at Pierre, South Dakota in this sentence, and again reasonable men could not differ that the document calls for the rest of his property, after the

---

4. It also gives the reason for the difference in the bequests. There is evidence in the record that his mother's will was not upheld as it was not dated. The sisters had honored the intent of the will and quit-claimed property to the deceased. The brother did not agree to this and some settlement had to be made with him in order for deceased to obtain title to 80 acres of land he had actually purchased himself. Thus the language "they 'onnerd' mothers will" found in the document.

special bequests, to go to the Seventh Day Adventist Conference and that its president be appointed administrator.

Following the residuary clause, there seems to be some special instructions as to the broom factory and supplies which were on the farm. The document gives no inkling of what the decedent had in mind for this particular property. The words "to go into our" could refer to "our academy" as he once told the Brandts he would like to give this broom factory to one of the South Dakota Adventist academies; or it could just as well refer to "our family." In any event it is such an infinitesimal part of this $55,000 estate that it should not be controlling in this decision, and the property could become a part of the residuary after the definite special bequests are made, or be treated as property not covered by the will.

It is concluded that the opponents of the will have not established that the Holographic Will executed by the testator on December 28, 1967 was ever revoked "By being burnt, torn, canceled, obliterated or destroyed with the intent and for the purpose of revoking the same. . . ." The presumption of intent to revoke arising from the torn document has been rebutted and the will effectively provides for the disposition of decedent's property. Every effort should be made by the courts to uphold a will that has been validly executed. As the only evidence here on earth to indicate decedent's desires as to the disposal of his property upon his death, the Holographic Will should have been upheld.

Judgment reversed. All Justices concur.

Lost or Destroyed Wills. What happens if the decedent is known to have executed a will, but it cannot be found after her or his death? If the will remained in the decedent's possession after execution, there are many decisions that presume the decedent destroyed the will with intent to revoke. See Atkinson on Wills § 101, at 553; Annots., 70 A.L.R.4th 323 (1989); 3 A.L.R.2d 949, 952 (1949). Concerning this presumption, the Supreme Court of Iowa, in Estate of Crozier, 232 N.W.2d 554, 559 (Iowa 1975), remarked:

> There is good reason why the burden of proof on the part of a lost will proponent [where the will was traced to the testator's possession] should not be prohibitive. Wills are carelessly lost and misplaced and a reasonable opportunity should be given to establish such a will. Likewise wills are sometimes suppressed or destroyed for an ulterior purpose. The defeat of that purpose ought not be made too difficult or impossible.

Crozier went on to hold, however, that the presumption is rebuttable only by clear and convincing evidence. But in Estate of Glover, 744 S.W.2d 939 (Tex. 1988), the Texas court held that the presumption is rebuttable by a preponderance of the evidence.

Wills Executed in Duplicate. To execute a will in duplicate means that the formality procedures for executing a will were performed on two copies of a will. The effect of duplicate execution is that the testator has two identical wills. If a will is executed in duplicate, an act of revocation performed with revocatory intent on one of the duplicates also revokes the other duplicate. This rule is sometimes codified, as in Cal. Prob. Code section 6121.

The presumption of revocation becomes a source of special difficulty for wills that are executed in duplicate. If the testator retains one executed copy and the other executed copy is retained by her or his lawyer or delivered to another person (for example, the personal representative), and the copy retained by the testator cannot be found after death, courts have held that there is a presumption of destruction with intent to revoke. See, e.g., Robinson's Will, 257 A.D. 405, 13 N.Y.S.2d 324 (1939); Atkinson on Wills § 101, at 553; Annot., 17 A.L.R.2d 805, 814 (1951). Yet, the fact that an executed copy of the will was safely in the custody of the lawyer or another might cause the testator to be careless in preserving her or his own executed copy. In these circumstances especially, the presumption rests on uncertain ground and its application could lead to a denial of probate in a case where the testator had no revocatory intent. The ambiguity of the situation has been recognized by the courts who nonetheless applied the presumption. See, e.g., Robinson's Will, supra.

On occasion, the fact of duplicate wills was sufficient to conclude the will remains unrevoked. In Stiles v. Brown, 380 S.2d 792 (Ala. 1980), for example, revocation of the will of Claude Stiles was avoided where Stiles' lawyer, James T. Tatum, Jr., twice gave Stiles the legal advice that "if he, Mr. Stiles, desired to revoke [the will], he would have to destroy both the duplicate original in his own possession and the one Mr. Tatum had in his possession." Although Stiles' copy could not be found after his death, the fact that Stiles had made no effort to destroy the duplicate retained by Tatum was considered strong evidence in rebutting the presumption of revocation. See also Estate of Shaw, 572 P.2d 229 (Okla. 1977).

Equally uncertain is the situation in which both executed copies were retained by the testator, but only one can be found after her or his death. Courts have held that the presumption of revocation also applies to this situation as well. See, e.g., Phinizee v. Alexander, 49 S.2d 250 (Miss. 1950); Mittelstaedt's Will, 280 A.D. 163, 112 N.Y.S.2d 166, appeal dismissed, 109 N.E.2d 86 (N.Y. 1952); Shield's Will, 117 Misc. 96, 190 N.Y.S. 562 (Sur. Ct. 1921); Annot., 17 A.L.R.2d 805, 817 (1951).

Leading writers on wills preach against duplicate execution. See, e.g., J. Price, Contemporary Estate Planning 212 (1983); Evans, Testamentary Revocation by Act to the Document and Dependent Relative Revocation, 23 Ky. L.J. 559, 568-70 (1935). See also Atkinson on Wills § 86, at 443. Retention by the lawyer or another of a conformed[5] or photostatic copy of the executed will is of course quite another matter and highly recommended. See J. Price, supra; Johnston, An Ethical Analysis of Common

---

5. A copy of a will is conformed "if it has been clearly marked as a 'copy,' with the date and the names of the testator and witnesses inserted, preferably typed rather than printed or handwritten (e.g., /s/ *Thomas T. Testator*, /s/ *Wilma W. Witness*)." Johnston, An Ethical Analysis of Common Estate Planning Practices—Is Good Business Bad Ethics?, 45 Ohio St. L.J. 57, 131 n.473 (1984).

Estate Planning Practices—Is Good Business Bad Ethics?, 45 Ohio St. L.J. 57 (1984). For more on proper practice in this area, see infra p. 272.

   Proof of Lost or Destroyed Wills. Rebutting the presumption of revocation is not the only barrier to probating a lost or destroyed will. About half of the states, including those that have enacted either the pre-1990 or 1990 UPC,[6] require the will's contents and due execution to be proved by clear and convincing evidence.[7]

   By statute, a few states require proof by *two* witnesses of the will's contents and, in some instances, its proper execution. See, e.g., Mich. Comp. Laws § 700.149. It was this two-witnesses requirement in the Nevada statute, Nev. Rev. Stat. § 136.240(3), that prevented probate of an alleged lost will of Howard Hughes, who died in 1976. See Howard Hughes Medical Inst. v. Gavin, 96 Nev. 905, 621 P.2d 489 (1980). The Howard Hughes Medical Institute (HHMI) produced an unexecuted, unconformed draft of a 1925 will, in which HHMI was the principal devisee. HHMI also submitted the deposition of one witness, who "allegedly read a will signed by Hughes, which left all his estate to HHMI." Other, hearsay evidence was also propounded, including testimony recounting alleged declarations of Hughes himself, but the court held that the latter evidence could not be used to satisfy the two-witnesses requirement. The statute, the court said, requires two witnesses who can testify from personal knowledge, not from the declarations of others. Invoking the statutory two-witnesses require-

---

6. Neither the pre-1990 UPC nor the 1990 UPC contains an explicit provision imposing special requirements of proof in formal testacy proceedings seeking probate of lost or destroyed wills. Hence, the general rules of evidence control proof.

   The Code does make it clear, however, that lost or destroyed wills must be established in formal rather than informal probate proceedings. See UPC § 3-303 (1990) and Comment. Furthermore, the Code specifies that in formal proceedings the petition to establish a lost or destroyed will must "state the contents of the will, and indicate that it is lost, destroyed, or otherwise unavailable." UPC § 3-402 (1990). The Code also makes it clear that the petition must request an order finding the will valid. UPC § 3-405 (1990) governs the court's response to the petition, indicating that the judge may, but need not, "require proof of the matters necessary to support the order sought."

   7. See, e.g., White v. Brennan's Administrator, 307 Ky. 776, 212 S.W.2d 299, 3 A.L.R.2d 943 (1948) (The lawyer who drew the will mailed it, after execution, to the executor. Later, the executor died. Still later, some twelve years after the will's execution, the testator died. The will could not be found. The lawyer produced a carbon copy and testified that the will had been properly executed, though he could not remember the identity of the attesting witnesses. The evidence was held sufficient to prove the will.); Estate of Shaughnessy, 97 Wash. 2d 652, 648 P.2d 427 (1982) (The lawyer who drew the will was a devisee thereunder, and the court held that the "Dead Man's Act" prevented him from testifying as to its contents. Without the lawyer's testimony, the will could not be probated.). See also Estate of Kleefeld, 55 N.Y.2d 253, 433 N.E.2d 521, 448 N.Y.S.2d 456 (1982) (The will that was left with the testator's attorney could not be found after the testator's death. A copy of the will plus testimony of the attorney's secretary that she remembered typing the will but could not remember its contents was held insufficient under N.Y. Surr. Ct. Proc. Act § 1407, requiring clear and distinct proof by "2 credible witnesses or by 1 witness and a copy or draft of the will" of "all the provisions of the will." By later amendment, N.Y. Surr. Ct. Proc. Act § 1407 now allows proof by "a copy or draft of the will proved to be true.")

ment, the trial court granted summary judgment denying probate, which the Nevada Supreme Court affirmed on appeal.

Some of the states with a two-witnesses requirement explicitly provide that a "correct copy"[8] or a "correct copy or draft"[9] takes the place of one witness.

Obviously, claims of lost wills favoring the proponent can be fabricated. But, in the face of situations such as the one in the *Hughes* case,[10] is the two-witnesses requirement, especially without the added provision that a "correct copy," or "correct copy or draft," takes the place of one witness, the wisest way to promote just results? Is the clear-and-convincing-evidence standard sufficient by itself?

Restrictive Lost-Will Statutes. The lost-will statutes of a sizeable number of states not only impose a two-witnesses requirement, but additional requirements as well. A typical statute of this type provides:

> No will of any testator shall be allowed to be proved as a lost or destroyed will, unless the same shall be proved to have been in existence at the time of the death of the testator, or be shown to have been fraudulently destroyed in the lifetime of the testator; nor unless its provisions be clearly and distinctly proved by at least two [2] witnesses, a correct copy or draft being deemed equivalent to one [1] witness.

Ark. Stat. Ann. § 60-304.[11]

This statute, like many others we study in this course, poses a dilemma for the courts. Taken literally, and applied strictly, the statute seems to impede rather than promote donative freedom. By requiring that a lost or destroyed will "be proved to have been in existence at the time of the death of the testator, or be shown to have been fraudulently destroyed in the lifetime of the testator," an unrevoked will whose contents and due execution are adequately established would be denied effect. In such situations, many courts have interpreted the statute in such a way as to render it meaningless. The most popular approach has been to interpret

---

8. See, e.g., Fla. Stat. § 733.207. In Estate of Parker, 382 S.2d 652 (Fla. 1980), the court held the term "correct copy" means "a copy conforming to an approved or conventional standard and that this requires an identical copy, such as a carbon or photostatic copy."

9. See, e.g., Ark. Stat. Ann. § 60-304.

10. See also Creek v. Laski, 248 Mich. 425, 227 N.W. 817 (1929), a case in which a widow, shortly after her husband's death, destroyed his will because she was not satisfied with its terms. Later, she petitioned for probate of the will. In her petition, she set forth the will's alleged provisions, omitting any devise to the plaintiff. The plaintiff intervened, seeking to establish that the will devised $2,000 to her. The lawyer who drafted the will testified in support of the plaintiff's claim, but no other corroborating witness was produced. Hence, the two-witnesses requirement of the Michigan statute was not satisfied, and the will was admitted to probate without any devise to the plaintiff.

The plaintiff then sued the widow in tort to recover damages in the amount of the devise, on the ground of "malicious and fraudulent destruction of the will, which prevented her proving the gift to her and defeated her [devise]." Recovery was allowed. See also Estate of Legeas, 210 Cal. App. 3d 385, 258 Cal. Rptr. 858 (1989), vacating 208 Cal. App. 3d 1516, 256 Cal. Rptr. 117 (1989) (set forth infra p. 266).

11. This statute was applicable but ignored by the court in Tucker v. Stacy, 272 Ark. 475, 616 S.W.2d 473 (1981).

that part of the statute requiring that the will "be proved to have been in existence at the time of the death of the testator" to mean "legal existence." A will is in "legal existence" if it has not been revoked. See, e.g., Eder's Estate, 94 Colo. 173, 29 P.2d 631 (1934); Havel's Estate, 156 Minn. 253, 194 N.W. 633 (1923);[12] Estate of Wheadon, 579 P.2d 930 (Utah 1978).

Another approach has been to interpret the "fraudulently destroyed" part of the statutory language to include constructive as well as actual fraud. The court in Matter of Fox, 9 N.Y.2d 400, 174 N.E.2d 499, 214 N.Y.S.2d 405 (1961), held that destruction by constructive fraud occurs if the destruction was not done by the testator or by her or his authority.[13] Thus the will at issue in *Fox* was held to have been fraudulently destroyed, and therefore entitled to probate, because it was destroyed by fire in Germany in 1944 as the result of a bombing raid on Berlin. (The testator died about nine months after learning of the will's destruction, without having executed another will.)

Are these interpretations of the statute supportable? They were disapproved in Kerckhof's Estate, 13 Wash. 2d 469, 125 P.2d 284 (1942).[14]

In cases where a lost-will statute prevents probate of the will for the purpose of giving effect to its dispositive provisions, does that mean that the will likewise cannot be established for the purpose of revoking an earlier will? Would it make any difference if the lost or destroyed will contained an express revocation clause? In Neubert's Estate, 59 Wash. 2d 678, 369 P.2d 838 (1962), the court held the proof to be insufficient under

---

12. After *Havel*, the Minnesota statute was amended to provide:

Minn. Stat. § 525.261. No such will shall be established unless it is proved to have remained unrevoked nor unless its provisions are clearly and distinctly proved.

13. After *Fox*, the New York statute was amended to provide:

N.Y. Surr. Ct. Proc. Act § 1407. A lost or destroyed will may be admitted to probate only if 1. It is established that the will has not been revoked. 2. Execution of the will is proved in the manner required for the probate of an existing will, and 3. All of the provisions of the will are clearly and distinctly proved by each of at least 2 credible witnesses or by 1 witness and a copy or draft of the will proved to be true and complete.

See Estate of Kleefeld, 55 N.Y.2d 253, 433 N.E.2d 521, 448 N.Y.S.2d 456 (1982). In 1983, the statute was amended again and the legislature substituted the following provision for section 1407(3):

3. All of the provisions of the will are clearly and distinctly proved by each of at least two credible witnesses or by a copy or draft of the will proved to be true and complete.

14. After *Kerckhof*, the Washington statute was amended to provide:

Wash. Rev. Code Ann. § 11.20.070. No will shall be allowed to be proved as a lost or destroyed will unless it is proved to have been in existence at the time of the death of the testator, or is shown to have been destroyed, cancelled or mutilated in whole or in part as a result of actual or constructive fraud or in the course of an attempt to change the will in whole or in part, which attempt has failed, or as the result of a mistake of fact, nor unless its provisions are clearly and distinctly proved by at least two witnesses . . . .

the present Washington statute[15] to establish a lost second will for the purpose of giving it dispositive effect, but that the second will, which contained an express revocation clause, nonetheless revoked an earlier will. Accord Bailey v. Kennedy, 162 Colo. 135, 425 P.2d 304 (1967). See also In re Cunningham, 38 Minn. 169, 36 N.W. 269 (1888).

Fraud. If a person obtains access to a testator's will and wrongfully destroys it, the will is not revoked. The act to the document is ineffective because it is unaccompanied by the testator's intent to revoke. Sadly, perpetrators of this type of fraud are difficult to catch. One was caught in Estate of Legeas, below, and the question arose whether a fraudulent destruction of a will is a tortious act.

Estate of Legeas
210 Cal. App. 3d 385, 258 Cal. Rptr. 858,
vacating 208 Cal. App. 3d 1516, 256 Cal. Rptr. 117 (1989)

POCHE, A.P.J. Foremost among the questions presented by these appeals is whether California will recognize a tort cause of action for the fraudulent destruction of testamentary instruments. We align California with other states which allow recovery in tort for the intentional deprivation of an expected inheritance. . . .

The decedent, Margaret T. Legeas, executed numerous wills and codicils in her old age. The heart of this dispute centered around which of two of those wills would be admitted to probate.

The first will was executed by Mrs. Legeas in September of 1970. Enumerated therein were 27 specific bequests, including $10,000 to sister Jane Connolly; $2,000 to cousin Father Jarlath Heneghan; $20,000 to niece Margaret McInerney; and $20,000 to "my beloved friend, attorney and advisor, Timothy J. McInerney." Mr. McInerney was nominated as executor and given the power to distribute the residue of the estate "to each of my legatees named or otherwise referred to hereinbefore, and in such amounts as my Executor . . . shall in his sole discretion determine, and to such charities as he shall, in his sole discretion, select."

The second will was executed in May of 1979. Among the 17 specific bequests were $3,000 to Father Heneghan and $11,000 to Ms. Connolly. The residue of the estate was bequeathed to Ms. Connolly. Father Heneghan was nominated by Mrs. Legeas as the executor of her estate. There is no mention of either Mr. or Mrs. McInerney.

Between 1970 and 1983, the close friendship between Mrs. Legeas and the McInerneys cooled. Mrs. Legeas felt that Mr. McInerney had unduly profited from a joint business venture and from his handling of the estate of Mrs. Legeas' husband. Mrs. Legeas was annoyed by "lovey-dovey" telephone calls from Mr. McInerney, whom she found intimidating and with whom she wished to avoid personal contact. Her feelings were the same

---

15. The Washington statute is set forth supra note 14.

with respect to Mrs. McInerney, although less intensity of emotion was involved.[16] Mrs. Legeas' antagonism towards Mr. McInerney progressed from distrust to fear and outright hatred. Up to 1983 Mrs. Legeas concealed from the McInerneys knowledge that she had executed the 1979 will.

By May of 1983 Mrs. Legeas' physical condition had deteriorated to the point that Father Heneghan had her placed in a nursing home. In August of that year Mrs. McInerney initiated conservatorship proceedings and was appointed temporary conservator of the person and estate of Mrs. Legeas. Later that month, Mrs. McInerney collected certain assets of the estate such as passbooks, certificates of deposit, and stock certificates, most of which she left with her attorneys. In one of Mrs. Legeas' safety deposit boxes Mrs. McInerney discovered the original of the 1979 will. Surprised at its provisions, Mrs. McInerney put it into her purse and did not turn it over to attorneys representing her in her capacity as Mrs. Legeas' conservator. According to the McInerneys, they gave the will to Mrs. Legeas, who subsequently told them she had torn it up.

Mrs. McInerney's petition to be appointed permanent conservator was successfully opposed by Father Heneghan as well as three of Mrs. McInerney's brothers and sisters on the grounds of (1) Mrs. Legeas' expressed desire that the McInerneys not "have anything to do with my person or my estate" and (2) fears that Mr. McInerney would dominate his wife and thus gain control of Mrs. Legeas' estate. The probate court appointed a bank as permanent conservator of Mrs. Legeas' estate and a charitable organization as permanent conservator of her person.

Mrs. Legeas died in July of 1984 at age 83, leaving an estate valued at approximately $500,000. The following month Mr. McInerney filed a petition asking for admission of the 1970 will to probate, and for his appointment as executor of the estate. Several weeks later Father Heneghan filed a petition for admission to probate of the 1979 will[17] (the original of which was alleged to have been "lost or fraudulently destroyed or [is] being concealed"), as well as his appointment as executor of the estate. The two petitions were consolidated.

In November of that year the McInerneys filed a complaint by which they elected to contest the 1979 will on the grounds that (1) it had been executed at a time when Mrs. Legeas was "mentally incompetent" and acting under the undue influence of the attorney who drafted it,[18] and (2) "in 1983, decedent tore up and destroyed the purported 1979 will . . ., with intent to revoke the same, and with the express intent to revive and make effective, as her last will and testament, the . . . 1970 will."

---

16. During this period Mrs. Legeas was constantly reducing the size of her bequests to the McInerneys.

17. Father Heneghan actually sought admission of the will executed in May of 1979 and a codicil executed by Mrs. Legeas the following month. For purposes of simplicity, subsequent references to "the 1979 will" will be understood as encompassing both the will and the codicil.

18. The parties stipulated at the outset of the trial that Mrs. Legeas' competence would not be put at issue. Nine weeks into the trial the McInerneys asked to be relieved from this stipulation. The trial court refused.

Ms. Connolly responded with a cross-complaint to the McInerneys' probate petition, and with a separate complaint which was given a separate civil action number.[19] In each of these pleadings (as subsequently amended) Ms. Connolly alleged causes of action against the McInerneys for (1) their fraudulent destruction of the 1979 will (2) their "use of fraud[,] undue influence[,] and duress" in procuring the destruction of the 1979 will by Mrs. Legeas (3) their interference with the prospective economic advantage Ms. Connolly would have received under the 1979 will (4) a constructive trust covering the estate assets to which Ms. Connolly would be entitled under the 1979 will should the McInerneys prevail in having the 1970 will admitted to probate (5) the McInerneys' failure to produce the 1979 will as required by Probate Code section 320, and (6) the intentional spoliation of evidence. The new action was ordered "consolidated for purposes of discovery, motions, and trial" with the probate proceedings.

The causes were tried in probate court by a jury which returned two verdicts. The first was a special verdict finding that the 1970 will had been revoked by Mrs. Legeas and that the 1979 will had been fraudulently destroyed. A judgment ordering admission of the 1979 will to probate was entered in due course. The jury also returned a general verdict in the fraud action finding Mr. and Mrs. McInerney liable for compensatory damages of $182,616.60 (which represented the attorneys' fees incurred by Ms. Connolly in connection with all three actions), and further finding Mr. McInerney liable for punitive damages of $150,000. A separate judgment reflecting this verdict was also entered.

Following denial of their motions for new trial and judgment notwithstanding the verdicts, the McInerneys filed a timely notice of appeal from the judgments. Mr. McInerney also appeals from a pretrial order of instruction to the special administrator of Mrs. Legeas estate, and from an order denying his motion for reconsideration. . . .

I. We were more than a little surprised upon reading the parties' briefs by their agreement that California has never taken a position regarding the question whether the fraudulent destruction of a will is an actionable wrong for which tort recovery may be had. Our independent research confirmed that the parties were indeed correct.

The area of transfers from a decedent's estate has proven to be a fertile breeding ground for fraud. Courts have condemned fraud in a constellation of contexts. Its reported manifestations have been organized by commentators into these categories: (1) in inducing or preventing an inter vivos conveyance; (2) in the procuring of the execution of a will; (3) in the prevention of the execution of a will; (4) in causing the revocation or alteration of a will; (5) in the prevention of the revocation or alteration of a will; and (6) in the destruction, concealment, or spoliation of a will. (See Evans, Torts to Expectancies in Decedents' Estates (1944) 93 U. Pa. L. Rev. 187; Annot., Liability in Damages For Interference with Expected

---

19. Ms. Connolly and Father Heneghan were represented throughout these proceedings by the same counsel. Due to their similarity of position, and in the interests of simplicity, Ms. Connolly and Father Heneghan will be collectively designated as "plaintiffs" in this opinion.

Inheritance or Gift (1983) 22 A.L.R.4th 1229; 2 Page on Wills (Bowe-Parker rev. 1960) §§ 24.1, 24.3-24.5; Rest., Restitution, § 184, com. a.) Our concern is with the last grouping.

Judicial aversion to testamentary-related fraud is not a recent phenomenon. The common law of Britain permitted equitable relief to recover a bequest which had been frustrated by the destruction or concealment of a will. . . . Traditional equitable remedies such as the imposition of a constructive trust were, however, deemed inadequate for complete redress. Beginning in 1834, the courts of eight states have explicitly recognized an independent tort action for damages caused in the intentional destruction, concealment, or spoliation of a will. Courts in at least eleven other states have given indications that such a cause of action would probably find a favorable reception. Torts of this nature have also been praised by Prosser (Prosser, Law of Torts (4th ed. 1971) § 130, pp. 950-951) and endorsed by the American Law Institute (Rest. 2d Torts, § 774B; Rest., Torts, § 870, com. b, illus. 2, § 912, com. f, illus. 13).

The reason behind these developments is not hard to fathom. Fraud evokes almost universal repugnance expressed with near-Biblical fervor. . . . The Legislature's attitude toward fraud committed within the testamentary context is particularly intolerant. The forgery of a will has been declared a crime (Pen. Code, § 470), as has the destruction or concealment of an instrument, such as a will, for the purpose of preventing its production in a legal proceeding (Pen. Code, § 135). Additional remedies not of a criminal nature have also been deemed appropriate. This court recently held that "persons who successfully contest a forged will submitted to probate may maintain an action for malicious institution of civil proceedings against those who offered the forged document with knowledge of its falsity." (Steiner v. Eikerling (1986) 181 Cal. App. 3d 639, 645, 226 Cal. Rptr. 694.) California has long made provision for proving fraudulently destroyed wills in probate proceedings.[20] It is thus clear that this state has a general policy against fraud, particularly as it applies to tampering with testamentary transfers.

We believe it is fitting to augment these expressions of disapproving policy with a tort action for damages resulting from the fraudulent destruction, concealment, or spoliation of a will. As we demonstrate, this conclusion is fully compatible with existing law and entails only a small extension of the frontier of common law tort remedies.

---

20. Former Probate Code section 350 provided in pertinent part:

> No will shall be proven as a lost or destroyed will unless proved to have been in existence at the time of the death of the testator, or shown to have been destroyed fraudulently or by public calamity in the lifetime of the testator, without his knowledge; nor unless its provisions are clearly and distinctly proved by at least two credible witnesses. . . .

It was repealed by the Legislature in 1983 (Stats.1983, ch. 842, s 28, p. 3038) upon the recommendation of the California Law Revision Commission that the "extraordinary proof and two-witness requirements for proof of the terms of a missing will . . . is a substantial defect in California law." (Tent. Recommendation Relating to Wills and Intestate Succession (Nov. 1982) 16 Cal. Law. Rev. Com. (1982) pp. 2327-2328; see id. at pp. 2315, 2488-2489.)

This position enjoys a measure of statutory support. Probate Code section 320 provides:

> The custodian of a will, within thirty days after being informed that the maker thereof is dead, must deliver the same to the clerk of the superior court having jurisdiction of the estate, or to the executor named therein. *Failure to do so makes such person responsible for all damages sustained by any one injured thereby.* (Emphasis added.)

The relevant inference which can be drawn from this provision is that the possibility of monetary damages being awarded in response to a judicially-declared cause of action is already within the contemplation of the statutory scheme governing the probate of estates. . . .

II. The damages caused by fraudulent interference with a testamentary disposition which remains undiscovered until after there has been a final distribution of the testator's estate are easily computed; the "direct loss" is amount of the lost legacy. But what damages can be recovered if the intended fraud is discovered and prevented during the course of probating the estate? Citing Code of Civil Procedure section 1021,[21] the McInerneys contend that Ms. Connolly cannot recover compensatory damages measured by the attorneys' fees incurred by her in connection with the will contests.

There is an undeniable plausibility to this claim. By enacting section 1021 "[t]he Legislature has established that in the absence of an express agreement or statute, each party to a lawsuit is responsible for its own attorney's fees." (Davis v. Air Technical Industries, Inc. (1978) 22 Cal. 3d 1, 5, 148 Cal. Rptr. 419, 582 P.2d 1010.) The seeming absoluteness of this general principle is deceptive, for there are a handful of recognized "exceptions . . . created by the courts pursuant to their inherent equitable powers." (Gray v. Don Miller & Associates, Inc. (1984) 35 Cal. 3d 498, 505, 198 Cal. Rptr. 551, 674 P.2d 253.) Prominent among them is the so-called "Prentice exception," which was originally promulgated in these terms:

> A person who through the tort of another has been required to act in the protection of his interests by bringing or defending an action against a third person is entitled to recover compensation for the reasonably necessary loss of time, attorney's fees, and other expenditures thereby suffered or incurred.

(Prentice v. North Amer. Title Guar. Corp. (1963) 59 Cal. 2d 618, 620, 30 Cal. Rptr. 821, 381 P.2d 645.) Strictly speaking, the attorneys' fees damages awarded to Ms. Connolly do not come within this exception because no third party is involved.

Nevertheless, the recovery of attorneys' fees as damages can be upheld by analogy to several situations which are not commonly recognized as additional exceptions to the general rule. Attorneys' fees can be recovered as damages in malicious prosecution actions even if no third party is

---

21. Which provides in pertinent part: "Except as attorney's fees are specifically provided for by statute, the measure and mode of compensation of attorneys and counselors at law is left to the agreement, express or implied, of the parties. . . ."

involved. The same is true with regard to an action for false arrest or imprisonment. Attorneys' fees were also awarded in a fraud action which required resisting a bankruptcy petition which formed an aspect of the fraudulent scheme. As former Presiding Justice Devine of this court put it, attorneys' fees may be recovered as damages where such "fees are of the essence of the loss sustained." (Isthmian Lines, Inc. v. Schirmer Stevedoring Co. (1967) 255 Cal. App. 2d 607, 612, 63 Cal. Rptr. 458.)

Ms. Connolly's situation is essentially no different from these diverse instances of unwarranted prior litigation. Once Mr. McInerney filed the original petition, it was absolutely unavoidable that the probate court would be involved. (See Prob. Code, § 300.) Similarly, it was then utterly foreseeable that Ms. Connolly (who lives in Manchester, England, and has never been to this country) and Father Heneghan (who is attached to the diocese of Seattle) would be obliged to retain local counsel to represent their interests. Ms. Connolly and Father Heneghan were compelled to contest Mr. McInerney's petition for admission of the 1970 will, and to see Father Heneghan's competing petition for admission of the 1979 will become the subject of four months of acrimonious litigation. The lengthy trial would have been unnecessary had not the McInerneys destroyed the original of the 1979 will. Ms. Connolly was in effect subjected to a species of malicious prosecution, which, as we have seen, permits a plaintiff to recover damages for attorneys' fees incurred in antecedent litigation. No logical reason suggests why Ms. Connolly should be denied the recovery afforded to the similarly situated victim of malicious prosecution. (See Civ. Code, § 3511.) The counsel fees for which she became indebted are thus "of the essence of the loss [she] sustained." (Isthmian Lines, Inc. v. Schirmer Stevedoring Co., supra, 255 Cal. App. 2d 607, 612, 63 Cal. Rptr. 458.)

We have it from our Supreme Court that "[a] plaintiff's remedy in tort is compensatory in nature and damages are generally intended . . . to restore an injured person as nearly as possible to the position he or she would have been in had the wrong not been done." (Turpin v. Sortini, 31 Cal. 3d 220, 232, 182 Cal. Rptr. 337, 643 P.2d 954 (1982).) The preceding discussion demonstrates that Ms. Connolly has established her common law entitlement to damages intended to recompense her for the attorneys' fees she incurred solely by reason of the McInerneys' unjustified invocation of the probate court's jurisdiction. As a separate and independent ground for our holding, we also note that Ms. Connolly's recovery of attorneys' fees as damages does enjoy a measure of statutory support.

In Estate of Filtzer (1949) 33 Cal. 2d 776, 205 P.2d 377, the Supreme Court considered whether a family allowance awarded to a minor child pursuant to former Probate Code section 680 properly included attorneys' fees. At the time that statute entitled the minor child " 'to such reasonable allowance out of the estate as shall be necessary for [its] maintenance according to [its] circumstances, during the progress of the settlement of the estate. . . .' " Sustaining the award, the court held that "it would seem proper to conclude that in giving a child the right to an allowance for 'maintenance' against his father's estate, the Legislature intended to comprehend in such term all such elements as would reasonably enter as factors essential to the satisfaction of that obligation, including an allowance for attorney fees necessarily incurred in the prosecution of the statutorily authorized proceedings." (Id. at p. 783, 205 P.2d 377 [emphasis omitted].)

As previously noted, Probate Code section 320 specifies that a custodian's failure to deliver a will to the probate court "makes such person responsible for all damages sustained by any one injured thereby." This statute speaks with particular force to Ms. Connolly's situation. If a custodian does not produce a will, the obvious person who will be "injured thereby" is a beneficiary who would otherwise receive a legacy under the will. It is equally apparent that such a person would attempt to forestall such an injury by resorting to the legal process of the probate court. Such a course of action would ordinarily require the assistance of counsel. The legatee would thus be damaged by the custodian's breach of his or her statutory duty to the extent that such expenses would not have otherwise been incurred. The amount of the attorneys' fees thus incurred would not only be foreseeable; it would, we believe, fit comfortably within the broad guarantee of section 320 that the custodian is "responsible for *all* damages sustained by any one injured thereby." (Emphasis added.) To paraphrase our Supreme Court: "it would seem proper to conclude that in [making a custodian liable for all 'damages'], the Legislature intended to comprehend in such term all such elements as would reasonably enter as factors essential to the satisfaction of that obligation, *including . . . attorney fees necessarily incurred. . . .*" (Estate of Filtzer, supra, 33 Cal. 2d 776, 783, 205 P.2d 377 [emphasis added].) . . .

CHANNELL and PERLEY, JJ., concur.

———

Ethics and the Safeguarding of Clients' Wills. The question of how wills should be safeguarded is discussed in Johnston, supra p. 262, at 124-33:

> Upon execution of a will, an important question is often raised—where should the testator's will be kept? . . . [The] Model Rules of Professional Conduct [do not] contain any provision on safekeeping of wills. Although specific treatment would benefit the profession by providing notice to those attorneys who might otherwise act improperly or by furnishing explicit guidelines to those who seek to stay within ethical bounds, this does not mean that the conduct in question is not circumscribed by broad provisions relating to conflicts of interest and improper solicitation. Even under the general terms of the original Canons of Professional Ethics, which were in effect from 1908 through 1969, an attorney's conduct in keeping a client's will in his or her office was considered subject to certain ethical restraints.
>
> State v. Gulbankian[, 54 Wis. 2d 605, 196 N.W.2d 733 (1972),] appears to be the only reported decision that has denounced the widespread practice of attorney-safekeeping of client's wills. In addition to condemning attorneys' conduct in consistently preparing wills in which the draftsmen name themselves as executors or attorneys for the estate, the Wisconsin Supreme Court was critical of the practice of retaining original wills:

Nor do we approve of attorneys' "safekeeping" wills. In the old days this may have been explained on the ground many people did not have a safe place to keep their valuable papers, but there is little justification today because most people do have safekeeping boxes, and if not, sec. 853.09, Stats., provides for the deposit of a will with the register in probate for safekeeping during the lifetime of the testator. The correct practice is that the original will should be delivered to the testator and should only be kept by the attorney upon specific unsolicited request of the client.

By contrast, a number of ethics opinions deal specifically with safekeeping of testator's wills. The general theme that the various opinions adopt is that the practice of providing this type of custodial service is permissible if the testator has expressly requested that the attorney keep the original will. But if the drafting attorney initially offers to furnish this service, the conduct is considered unethical. Although the difference may seem reasonable on the surface it . . . creates the quandary of attempting to determine whether the testator or the attorney initiated the discussion about maintaining custody of the will, after the testator has died and is no longer able to shed any light on this question. Because of the difficulty of resolving this issue, any effective ethical rule governing the safekeeping of wills should not be based on such a nebulous distinction. Nevertheless, it is important to restrain attorney practices in this area because of the serious ethical problems inherent in such activity.

Before attempting to proscribe rules regulating attorney conduct in this area, the benefits to the client of having the draftsman retain the original will should be balanced against the ethical concerns. There are, of course, certain advantages in having the attorney serve as custodian, principally because this practice precludes the testator's retention of the will in an unsafe place where it might be subject to the whims and caprices of disgruntled heirs and beneficiaries. Thus, leaving the original with the attorney-draftsman serves little purpose that cannot be achieved equally well through some alternative form of safekeeping that does not raise the same ethical questions of solicitation and self-dealing. The attorney should, of course, be certain to retain a copy of the client's will in the office files, so that it can be reviewed periodically to determine if a new will or codicil is necessary or desirable and in order to assist in the probate of a client's will in the event that the original cannot be located after the testator's death. But in either event, retention of a conformed copy will serve the client's purposes.

As an alternative to leaving the original with the attorney who drafted it, the testator might keep the will in his or her own safe-deposit box. Testators are often concerned about such a location for their wills because of the procedure in many jurisdictions of sealing safe-deposit boxes until a state inheritance tax official has inventoried the contents. Lawyers have presumably added their warnings along these lines as an inducement to clients to leave their original wills with them for safekeeping. This drawback, however, has been greatly over-emphasized. In reality, there is usually little delay in making arrangements to obtain the original will from the decedent's box. Furthermore, if a conformed copy is readily available, there is generally no need to have access to the original will immediately upon the testator's death.

If the sealing of safe-deposit boxes presents a substantial problem in a particular jurisdiction, the testator can make arrangements to have the original placed in a relative's box. For example, a husband might keep his wife's will in a box registered in his name, and she should keep her husband's will in her box. Also, a testator who has designated a corporate fiduciary to serve as trustee or executor may prefer to leave the original with the bank, which will often provide a safekeeping service when it has been named to serve in a fiduciary capacity. Although some disadvantages may exist in leaving an original will with a corporate fiduciary under these circumstances, it is a better practice than having the draftsman retain the original for safekeeping.

Another appropriate course of conduct is to file the original will with a county clerk in those jurisdictions that have statutes authorizing such safekeeping. Even though a number of states have enacted these statutes, such custodial services are not well known and therefore are not utilized to the extent they should be. When this alternative is available every estate planner should make it a practice to advise his or her clients of this service and recommend that they consider leaving the original of their wills at the county clerk's office.

Wherever the original is placed, the testator should also keep at least one conformed copy in his or her home. A notation should be placed on the front of the copy specifying the exact location of the original, so that the executor-designate or some appropriate family member will know where to find the will in order to file it for probate. Moreover, the practice of leaving the original will at the lawyer's office for safekeeping has at least several drawbacks in addition to the ethical concerns it raises. It is possible that the drafting lawyer may predecease the testator, retire, change law firms, or otherwise turn his or her practice over to some other attorney or attorneys. If advised of this event the testator might want to reclaim the original and place it somewhere else for safekeeping. Otherwise, on the testator's death the lawyer who happens to have custody of the will at that time is likely to be retained to assist the executor in administration of the estate, even though that attorney did not prepare the will or provide other legal services to the testator. These problems can be avoided if the original will is kept in a safe deposit box in the testator's name, left in a box in the name of one of the testator's relatives, or filed with the local county court.

Professor Johnston's position was examined by an A.B.A. Committee in a preliminary report, Developments Regarding the Professional Responsibility of the Estate Planning Lawyer: The Effect of the Model Rules of Professional Conduct, 22 Real Prop. Prob. & Tr. J. 1, 28 (1987):

> The opinion of the committee is that the practice [of attorney safekeeping] ought to be regarded as ethical, assuming the attorney provides safekeeping merely as an accommodation and makes it clear that his safekeeping is only an alternative to safekeeping by the client, by the fiduciary-designate, or by the county clerk (where authorized by statute). The general theme of the ethics opinions is that attorney safekeeping is permissible if the testator expressly requests it but, if the attorney initiates the safekeeping, the prominent case of State v. Gulbankian indicates that he may be subject to disciplinary sanction for solicitation. Further, retention of the will by the attorney may also be deemed to increase his risk of malpractice exposure for failure to inform the client of changes in the law.

See also J. Price, supra p. 262, at 212 (suggesting attorney safekeeping permissible "if requested by the client to do so").

UPC section 2-515 (1990) authorizes the testator or her or his agent to deposit a will with a court for safekeeping. After death, section 2-516 imposes a duty on any person who has custody of a will to deliver it upon the request of an "interested person" (which is defined in UPC section 1-

201(24) (1990)), to a person able to secure its probate or, if none is known, to an appropriate court.[22] Section 2-516 also provides that a person is liable for damages for a failure to deliver a will.

Is There a Duty to Probate a Will? Must an unrevoked will be probated? Although any "interested person" can petition for probate of a will, the personal representative normally files the petition. If not, the self-interest of one or more of the devisees named in the will can usually be counted on to prompt the filing of a petition.

If, however, the affected parties wish to suppress the will and divide up the decedent's assets in a different way, they normally can do so. See Annot., 29 A.L.R.3d 8 (1970). UPC section 3-912 (1990) authorizes private agreements among successors. See UPC § 1-201(48) (1990) (defining term "successors"). This agreement does not need the consent of the executor. The successors have the power to direct the executor not to probate the will and, if they do so, the executor loses her or his standing to proceed. See UPC § 3-720 (1990), Comment. See supra p. 95 for discussion of problems of obtaining agreement of unascertained successors or successors who lack capacity, discussion of potential adverse tax consequences, and discussion of utilizing disclaimers instead of successors' agreement.

Partial Revocation by Act to the Document. The English Statute of Frauds of 1677 provided that no devise "nor any clause thereof" should be revoked except in the manner specified, including various acts to the document. Under the Wills Act of 1837 the comparable language was "no will . . . or any part thereof." The English courts construed "clause" in the Statute of Frauds to mean "part," see Swinton v. Bailey, L.R. 4 App. Cas. 70, 85 (1878), and the same construction seems to have been taken for granted under American statutes patterned on the Statute of Frauds. See Brown v. Brown, 91 S.C. 101, 74 S.E. 135 (1912).

Section 2-507 of the 1990 UPC allows a will "or any part thereof" to be revoked by revocatory act. Similar provisions appear in most non-UPC statutes. In all, or almost all, of these states, partial revocation by revocatory act seems to be recognized. See Will of Palmer, 359 S.2d 752 (Miss. 1978); Atkinson on Wills § 86, at 444; Rees, American Wills Statutes II, 46 Va. L. Rev. 856, 879-80 (1960). In Dodson v. Walton, 268 Ark. 431, 597 S.W.2d 814 (1980), the Arkansas court qualified this rule by limiting the effect of an interlineation or obliteration of part of a will to cases in which it "does not change the testamentary disposition provided for in the will." If it does operate to make such a change, the attempted partial revocation is ineffective and the will as originally drawn is to be given effect. In Wyoming, a similar rule was announced, but the court permitted the partial revocation to be effective because "the testamentary scheme [after the partial revocation] is basically the same as before." Seeley v. Estate of Seeley, 627 P.2d 1357, 1361 (Wyo. 1981). In *Seeley*, the testator

---

22. Sections 2-515 and 2-516 appeared as §§ 2-901 and 2-902 in the pre-1990 UPC, and (other than renumbering) were carried forward without substantive amendment in the 1990 version.

cut a provision out of her will that granted her son an option to purchase certain property.

In most of the remaining non-UPC states, the revocation statute provides that "no will shall be revoked unless by . . . ." In this group, it is usually held that partial revocation by revocatory act is not permitted. See, e.g., Law v. Law, 83 Ala. 432, 3 S. 752 (1888); Miles' Appeal, 68 Conn. 237, 36 A. 39 (1896); Lovell v. Quitman, 88 N.Y. 377 (1882); Coghlin v. Coghlin, 79 Ohio St. 71, 85 N.E. 1058 (1908). Contra, e.g., Bigelow v. Gillott, 123 Mass. 102 (1877). This is true only of revocation by act to the document. It seems to be everywhere taken for granted that there can be partial revocation by subsequent instrument. See Law v. Law, supra.

In a state that does not allow partial revocation by act to the document, the result is that the will is probated as originally written. Complications arise, however, if the portion of the will that the testator attempted to eliminate cannot be read, and its contents cannot be established by other evidence. This has occurred when the portion was either physically cut out of the paper or so completely obliterated as to be undecipherable. The court's principal choice is between (1) probating the legible portions of the will; or (2) denying probate entirely. Under the first choice, if the legible portions of the will are then given effect, the consequence is that the testator has achieved the results of a partial revocation by a method not recognized in the jurisdiction. Under the second choice, the consequence is the same as though the testator had wholly revoked the will, when in fact she or he intended only a partial revocation. One might expect courts to make the first choice because this will usually give effect to the testator's actual intention, whereas the second choice defeats that intention. Although this has been the tendency of the decisions, there are a few cases that deny probate entirely. See, e.g., Estate of Johannes, 170 Kan. 407, 227 P.2d 148 (1951).

Notes and Problems

1. As originally executed, G's will left the residue of her estate "to my brother, A, *and to my sisters-in-law, X, Y, and Z,* and to my sister B." Thereafter, G crossed out the words in italics, intending thereby to cut out her sisters-in-law. Assuming that the jurisdiction permits partial revocation by revocatory act, who is entitled to the residue of G's estate? See Casey v. Hogan, 344 Ill. 208, 176 N.E. 257 (1931) (refusing to recognize partial revocation by revocatory act).

2. G's will devised "my car *to my friend A* and my house to my daughter B." The will did not contain a residuary clause. G's sole heir was B. After the will was executed, G crossed out the words in italics. Who is entitled to G's car—A or B? See Walpole v. Lewis, 254 Ark. 89, 492 S.W.2d 410 (1973).

3. *Holographic Wills.* The wills in the above cases were attested wills. If they had been holographic wills, the outcome in the cases might have been different. It has been held that the decedent can validly alter a holographic

will by making handwritten changes thereon without signing the will again. See, e.g., Estate of Archer, 193 Cal. App. 3d 238, 239 Cal. Rptr. 137 (1987); Randall v. Salvation Army, 100 Nev. 466, 686 P.2d 241 (1984); Stanley v. Henderson, 139 Tex. 160, 162 S.W.2d 95 (1942); Moyers v. Gregory, 175 Va. 230, 7 S.E.2d 881 (1940).

4. How would Problems 1 and 2 have been affected if the 1990 UPC's dispensing power provision, section 2-503, had been applicable? Or, if 1990 UPC section 2-604 or pre-1990 UPC section 2-606 had been in effect? Should Problems 1 and 2 have been analyzed as dependent relative revocation cases? See infra pp. 300-01.

———

Effect on a Codicil of a Revocation of the Will. The English Wills Act of 1837 provided:

> *7 Wm. 4 & 1 Vict., c. 26, § 20:* That no will or codicil, or any part thereof, shall be revoked otherwise than . . . by another will or codicil executed in manner herein-before required, or by some writing declaring an intention to revoke the same, and executed in the manner in which a will is herein-before required to be executed, or by the burning, tearing, or otherwise destroying the same by the testator, or by some person in his presence and by his direction, with the intention of revoking the same.

In Goods of Turner, L.R. 2 P. & D. 403 (1872), the phrase "no will *or codicil* . . . shall be revoked otherwise than by . . . ." was interpreted to mean that a codicil can be revoked by act only if the act is performed on the codicil. An act performed on the will can revoke the will but not the codicil. This position became generally accepted in English law.

In this country, courts have taken a different tack. The question has usually been made to turn on the relation between the dispositive provisions of the will and codicil, summed up in the following statement of a New York court:

> If they are necessarily interdependent or so interinvolved as to be incapable of separate existence, the revocation of the will ipso facto revokes the codicil, otherwise not.

Francis' Will, 73 Misc. 148, 132 N.Y.S. 695 (Sur. Ct. 1911). The application of this test has been somewhat unpredictable. In the *Francis* case, the codicil revoked a devise to A of one-third of the residuary estate and gave that share equally to B and C. The court held that the codicil was not entitled to probate because of its dependence on the will.

Occasionally a court talks as though the codicil *necessarily* falls with the will. See, e.g., Nokes' Estate, 71 Misc. 382, 130 N.Y.S. 187 (Sur. Ct. 1911). In most decisions, however, this view is either expressly or tacitly rejected. At the other extreme, no American case has been found in which the court held that the codicil necessarily *must* be probated because of the fact that no revocatory act was physically manifested on the codicil as a separate instrument.

Suppose the testator performs a revocatory act on a codicil to her or his will, but performs no revocatory act on the will. What issue does this raise? Does the revocation of the codicil revoke the will? See Estate of Hering, 108 Cal. App. 3d 88, 166 Cal. Rptr. 298 (1980) (discussed infra p. 290).

EXTERNAL REFERENCE. Annot., 84 A.L.R.4th 531 (1991).

PART C. REVOCATION BY CHANGES IN CIRCUMSTANCES—MARRIAGE, DIVORCE, REMARRIAGE

Statutory References: *1990 UPC §§ 2-508, -804*
                              Pre-1990 UPC § 2-508

Martin & Bumpass, Recent Trends in Marital Disruption
26 Demography 37 (1989)

Family life is changing dramatically across virtually all Western industrial societies. Among the most profound of these changes has been the sharp reduction in marital stability, affecting markedly the life course of individuals, the nature of family life, and the household composition of populations. Hence it is not surprising that the recent decline in the U.S. crude divorce rate generated a collective sigh of relief. It is too soon, however, to conclude that the long-term trend has been reversed. We must carefully evaluate this decline in light of the historical context and in light of what we know about composition effects on measures like the crude divorce rate. . . .

Whereas annual rates of divorce have fluctuated with wars and the economy, the likelihood of divorce has increased in a steadily accelerating curve, from 7 percent for first marriages in 1880 to recent levels of more than 50 percent. The duration of this trend strongly suggests that the roots of current patterns of marital instability are deep, and not just a response to recent changes in other domains such as fertility, sex-role attitudes, female employment, or divorce laws.

Increases in divorce since 1965, as well as the declines in marriage and fertility rates, are best seen as a continuation of the long-term reduction of family functions that has occurred in conjunction with the transformation of our economy and an increasing cultural emphasis on individualism. When viewed from this perspective, we must ask whether the underlying changes have run their course. . . .

The U.S. crude divorce rate declined 10 percent between 1980 and 1987. This decline *may* indicate a return to more stable family life; however, it would be foolish to jump to that conclusion from this brief deviation from the trend. The current rate represents a very high level of marital disruption. Moreover, there are a number of reasons why a leveling of divorce rates, or even a slight decline, might occur without any change in values:

1. The acceleration after the mid-1960s cannot continue indefinitely, since an absolute upper limit must soon be reached.

2. Further, it is axiomatic in demography that trends in crude rates may be heavily influenced by shifting composition. Two components are particularly relevant—the increasing age at marriage and the age composition consequences of the baby boom. The marked reduction in marriage rates implies that the composition of recent marriages would tend to make them more stable, all else equal. For example, teenage marriages are much more likely to end in divorce than marriages at older ages, and recent marriages include a lower proportion who married as teenagers. In addition, the lower marriage rate would suggest that at all ages, many of the more tenuous relationships, which previously would have married and divorced, do not now make it to the alter. Independent of the changes in marriage rates, the movement through the population of the large baby boom cohorts first increased, then decreased the proportion of marriages beginning at high-risk young ages. . . .

3. Finally, it is common demographic wisdom that period measures will be inflated to the extent that divorce is occurring progressively earlier in marriage. A downturn in period measures can be expected when timing ceases to change. . . .

Using the marriage histories from the [Census Bureau's June 1985 Current Population Survey], life table procedures yielded estimates that 56 percent of recent first marriages would be likely to disrupt within 40 years of marriage. After adjusting, however, for the well-known underreporting of marital disruption in surveys relative to the vital statistics (and for the underrepresentation of divorces in the [Divorce Registration Area]) we conclude that the best estimate based on these data is that about two-thirds of all first marriages are likely to disrupt.[23] . . .

Surely there will be period variations associated with economic or even attitudinal fluctuations, but we should be slow to interpret plateaus or reversals as turning points in processes with such deep historical roots. The diversity in family life created by patterns of divorce and remarriage are likely an intrinsic feature of modern family life rather than a temporary aberration.

Note

Marriage and Remarriage. Whether the projected divorce rate among first marriages is two-thirds or "only" sixty percent, it is astonishingly high.

---

23. Further work on the data led one of the authors "to suspect that 60% may be closer to the mark." See Bumpass, What's Happening to the Family? Interactions Between Demographic and Institutional Change, 27 Demography 483, 485 (1990). Eds.

Those who divorce are free to remarry and many do. Those whose spouses die are also free to remarry and some of them also do. Data published by the federal government reveal that, within the divorced and widowed population at large, not disaggregated by age, about 83 percent of divorced men and 78 percent of divorced women remarry.[24] U.S. Dep't of Health & Human Services, Pub. No. 89-1923, Remarriages and Subsequent Divorces—United States 12 (1989). The remarriage rate among widowed men and women is much lower and shows a larger discrepancy between men and women. Id. About 21 percent of widowed men and about 8 percent of widowed women remarry. Why is there this discrepancy between widowed men and women?

It is also interesting to note that the average (mean) ages at the time of remarriage of widowed men and women have been steadily increasing, to 60.2 for men and 52.6 for women in 1983, the latest year for which statistics have been published, up from 57.7 for men and 50.3 for women in 1970. The average (mean) ages at remarriages of divorced men and women have also been steadily increasing, but the ages are, of course, much lower. The average (mean) ages for 1983 are 37.3 for men and 33.7 for women, up from 36.7 for men and 32.8 for women in 1970. Id., Table 4, at 24. In 1983, the average intervals between becoming widowed and remarriage for the 65-and-older age group were 3.6 years for men and 7.9 years for women. The average intervals between divorce and remarriage for the same age group were 6.3 years for men and 10.4 years for women. Id. at 13.

The Spencer case, below, is a case of remarriage by a widower. The case involves the not uncommon dispute pitting a decedent's children by a prior marriage against the decedent's second spouse.

Estate of Spencer
60 Haw. 497, 591 P.2d 611 (1979)

OGATA, J. Contestants-appellants (hereinafter appellants), who are children of the deceased testator, appeal from an Order Denying Motion for Declaratory Judgment and from an Order of Probate entered by the court below. The question presented to us on this appeal is whether a will in which the testator gives and bequeaths his entire estate to a woman by her maiden name, is revoked by the subsequent marriage of the testator to that

---

24. The divorce rate among remarried divorced persons is higher than that among the first-married. See, e.g., U.S. Dep't of Health & Human Services, Pub. No. 89-1923, Remarriages and Subsequent Divorces—United States 16 (1989) ("Generally, the more times a divorcing person has been married, the briefer the duration of the marriage. . . . It may be that some selection factor is at work and that people who divorce repeatedly are likely to regard divorce as an acceptable solution to an unpleasant marriage and resort to it with increasing promptness."). See also McCarthy, A Comparison of the Probability of the Dissolution of First and Second Marriages, 15 Demography 345 (1978).

woman by operation of HRS § 536-11 (1975 Supp.).[25] This section provided the following:

> By marriage. If, after the making of a will, the testator or testatrix marries and no provision is made in the will for such contingency, such marriage shall operate as a revocation of the will, and the will shall not be revived by the death of the (testator's) or testatrix's spouse.

We hold that the statute operated to revoke the will and reverse the orders entered by the court below.

The facts in this case are not in dispute. On October 17, 1974, the testator, Robert Stafford Spencer (hereinafter "testator"), then a widower, executed a will in which he left his entire estate to "Sandra Jean Cantwell, of 361 Laleihoku Street, Wailuku, County of Maui, State of Hawaii." On December 28, 1974, testator married Sandra Jean Cantwell (hereinafter "appellee"). On January 10, 1975, the testator died, leaving as survivors, the appellee, his wife, and two children by a prior marriage, who are the parties involved in this dispute.

Appellee filed in the court below a petition for probate of the will executed on October 17, 1974. Appellants thereafter filed an appearance and contest of will, and about two weeks later, filed a motion for declaratory judgment requesting the court to declare that the will submitted for probate had been revoked by the subsequent marriage of their father to Sandra Jean Cantwell, the sole beneficiary. At the hearing on the motion, appellee, over objection by appellants, was permitted to introduce evidence that tended to indicate that, at the time testator executed his will, he intended to marry Sandra Jean Cantwell. This evidence showed that prior to the marriage, on August 21, 1974, testator had designated the testamentary beneficiary as the beneficiary of his interest in the State Employees' Retirement System, under the designation of "Sandra Tarlton Spencer", and had referred to her on such form as his wife; and, that on September 3, 1974, the parties had met with the Reverend Winkler to set a date for their marriage. Upon these facts, the court below found that the testator's will was not revoked by operation of HRS § 536-11 (1975 Supp.). The order denying the motion for declaratory judgment further stated:

> The Court further finds that HRS 536-11 does not automatically revoke a will made prior to marriage where such will names as beneficiary a person who later becomes the spouse of the testator, where there is clear evidence that the testator and such person intended to marry, even though there is no express provision in the will stating that it was providing for the contingency of such marriage;

---

25. HRS § 536-11 (1975 Supp.) was the applicable statute when the will was made and at the time of the testator's subsequent marriage. It was repealed by the [pre-1990] Uniform Probate Code, effective as of July 1, 1977. The [pre-1990] Uniform Probate Code provides for revocation of a will by divorce or annulment only and does not provide for revocation of a will by subsequent marriage.

HRS § 536-11 (1975 Supp.) must be given effect according to its plain and obvious meaning. We have said that this court is bound by the plain, clear and unambiguous language of a statute unless the literal construction would produce an absurd and unjust result and would be clearly inconsistent with the purposes and policies of the statute. . . . We think the language used in HRS § 536-11 (1975 Supp.) is explicitly clear and unambiguous, and the literal construction does not produce a result that is absurd and unjust and clearly inconsistent with the purposes and policies of the statute. The statute provides in clear terms that "[if,] after the making of a will, the testator . . . marries . . . such marriage shall operate as a revocation of the will," unless "provision is made in the will for such contingency". It is clear to us that "contingency" refers to a testator's marriage after having made a will. The will of the testator in the instant case does not contain any provision with respect to the marriage of the testator as the trial court so found in its order denying the motion.

Appellee argues that to revoke the will would produce a result that is absurd and unjust and clearly inconsistent with the purpose of the statute by reducing her share of testator's estate by two-thirds. Notwithstanding revocation of the will, however, the appellee, although no longer entitled to testator's entire estate, is protected by her dower rights under HRS Chapter 533. . . .

Moreover, merely designating "Sandra Jean Cantwell" as the beneficiary of his entire estate did not provide in the will for the contingency of subsequent marriage, for in doing so, the testator did no more than he would have done in leaving any testamentary gift and the statute requires more than this. . . .

The testator's will was revoked by operation of HRS § 536-11 (1975 Supp.) for failure to comply with the statutory requirement. The orders entered by the court below are reversed.

RICHARDSON, C.J., OGATA and MENOR, JJ. concur.

Notes and Questions

1. *Spencer's Interpretation of the Statute.* Was the Hawaii Supreme Court forced by the literal language of the Hawaii statute to frustrate Robert Spencer's intention? Inasmuch as Hawaii had enacted the pre-1990 UPC, under which marriage does not revoke premarital wills, the justices must have known that *Spencer* was likely their last case under the old statute. Should this have freed them from any concern about hard cases making bad law?

2. *Automatic Revocation of Premarital Wills.* At common law, premarital wills of women were revoked upon marriage and premarital wills of men were revoked upon marriage and birth of issue. The wills were revoked as soon as the operative event or events occurred. The fact that the spouse or the spouse and the couple's issue predeceased the testator was accorded no legal significance. See 1 T. Jarman, A Treatise on Wills 152 (2d Am. ed. 1849).

At one time in this country, more than half the states had statutes similar to the now repealed Hawaii statute, which was applicable in the *Spencer* case. Some of these statutes provided for revocation upon marriage alone, others for revocation upon marriage and birth of issue. Relatively few states presently have marriage-revocation statutes.[26] As we shall see in Chapter 8, modern probate codes invoke other means to protect the testator's new spouse and children against unintended disinheritance.

———

Revocation Upon Divorce. Statutes in a large number of states once provided for revocation by operation of law in cases of "subsequent changes in the conditions or circumstances of the testator." Led by Lansing v. Haynes, 95 Mich. 16, 54 N.W. 699 (1893), it was widely held that divorce coupled with a property settlement constituted a subsequent change in the circumstance of the testator sufficient to revoke provisions in a pre-divorce will in favor of the decedent's former spouse. A few states still follow this principle despite the absence of a statute on the subject. See, e.g., Rasco v. Estate of Rasco, 501 S.2d 421 (Miss. 1987) (revocation held not to have occurred under this principle where the divorced couple continued to live together after the divorce and where the property settlement agreement was apparently never carried out).

In the vast majority of states, the generally worded statutes have disappeared,[27] having been replaced by more specific statutory provisions similar or identical to pre-1990 UPC section 2-508,[28] under which the statute specifically provides that revocation occurs by divorce (or annulment) alone.

———

26. By one recent survey, this type of statute remains in only about eleven (possibly twelve) states. The states listed are Connecticut, Georgia, Kentucky, Massachusetts, Nevada, Oregon, Rhode Island, South Dakota, Washington, West Virginia, Wisconsin, and possibly Delaware. See J. Ritchie, N. Alford & R. Effland, Decedents' Estates and Trusts 303 n. 63 (7th ed. 1988).

An Alabama statute that preserved the common-law distinction between a man's and a woman's premarital will, providing for the revocation of a woman's, but not a man's, will upon subsequent marriage alone, was held unconstitutional in Parker v. Hall, 362 S.2d 875, 99 A.L.R.3d 1014 (Ala. 1978).

27. The District of Columbia and New Hampshire seem to be the last remaining jurisdictions. D.C. Code Ann. § 18-109 (see Luff. v. Luff, 359 F.2d 235 (D.C. Cir. 1966) (divorce coupled with a property settlement revokes provisions in a pre-divorce will in favor of former spouse)); N.H. Rev. Stat. Ann. § 551:14.

A couple of other states, notably Massachusetts and Nevada, have statutory provisions stating that a will is revoked "by subsequent changes in the conditions or circumstances of the testator from which a revocation is implied by law," but also have the more specific provision similar to pre-1990 UPC § 2-508 specifying "divorce" as a cause of revocation. (Both of these states also specify "marriage" as a cause of revocation of a premarital will.) See Mass. Gen. Laws ch. 191, §§ 8, 9; Nev. Rev. Stat. §§ 133.120, 133.110, 113.115.

28. In Michigan, for example, the old statute construed in Lansing v. Haynes was repealed in 1979 and replaced by a statute nearly identical to pre-1990 UPC § 2-508. See Mich. Comp. Laws § 700.124(2).

Problem

A and B had no children by their marriage to each other, but each had adult children by a former marriage. During their marriage to each other, A executed a will devising all of his property to B if B survived A. If B failed to survive him, A devised one-half of his property to his children and one-half to B's children. (B also executed a will, which contained reciprocal provisions.)

A and B were subsequently divorced. A died soon after the divorce, survived by B, his children, and B's children. A never revoked his will. How is A's estate to be distributed? Assume that the case arose in a jurisdiction that has a provision similar or identical to pre-1990 UPC section 2-508? See, e.g., Clymer v. Mayo, 393 Mass. 754, 473 N.E.2d 1084 (1985) (set forth infra p. 410); Estate of Coffed, 46 N.Y.2d 514, 387 N.E.2d 1209, 414 N.Y.S.2d 893 (1979).

How would the outcome be changed if the case were governed by UPC section 2-804 (1990)? See also UPC §§ 2-604, -801 (1990).

PART D. REVIVAL OF A REVOKED WILL

Statutory References: *1990 UPC § 2-509*
                            Pre-1990 UPC § 2-509

Consider G, a testator who had previously executed two wills. Will No. 2 expressly revoked Will No. 1. Shortly before her death, G revoked Will No. 2 by drawing a large "X" across each of its pages. Has G died intestate, or is Will No. 1 her valid will? In jurisdictions that follow the view that the execution of Will No. 2 revoked Will No. 1—this is not the view universally followed, as we shall see—the question, framed in legal terminology, is whether Will No. 1 has been "revived." A somewhat different way of thinking about the same question is: Did the revocation of the revoking document (Will No. 2) revoke the revocation (of Will No. 1)?

In England, prior to the Wills Act of 1837, there was no statutory provision on revival. Although the Statute of Frauds of 1677 provided for revocation by later instrument or by act to the document, that statute was silent on the matter of revival. Two approaches emerged in the English decisions: One came from the ecclesiastical courts, which had jurisdiction over succession to personal property; the other came from the common-law courts, which passed on questions of revocation (as well as of due execution) when an issue of title to land was raised.

The Ecclesiastical Rule. Under the ecclesiastical rule, whether G's Will No. 1 would be revived would depend on G's intent. In a lengthy opinion in Williams v. Miles, 68 Neb. 463, 94 N.W. 705 (1903), then Commissioner Roscoe Pound (who later became Dean of the Harvard Law School) canvassed the state of English and American law on revival and described the ecclesiastical rule as follows:

> [T]he ecclesiastical courts . . . , endeavor[ed] in each case to ascertain the testator's intention, . . . making that intention the criterion. In a leading case the doctrine of those courts was stated thus:
>
> > The legal presumption is neither adverse to, nor in favor of, the revival of a former uncanceled [will], upon the cancellation of a later revocatory will. Having furnished this principle, the law withdraws altogether, and leaves the question as one of intention purely, and open to a decision either way, solely according to facts and circumstances.
>
> Usticke v. Bawden, 2 Addams (Eng. Eccle.) 116, [162 Eng. Rep. 238] (1824).

In practice, of course, the proponent of the revoked will presumably has the burden of establishing an intent to reinstate that will. Probate would be denied unless the proponent could produce some evidence of such intent.

The Common-Law Rule. Under the common-law rule, Will No. 1 would be G's valid will, regardless of her intention. The common-law rule is sometimes referred to as a rule of "automatic revival." This is how Commissioner Pound, in Williams v. Miles, described it:

> Lord Mansfield announced a rule, which was followed by the common-law courts when questions as to wills disposing of real property came before them, to the effect that if the first will is preserved, and a subsequent will, revoking it expressly or by implication, is destroyed or canceled, the revocation is repealed, and the original will revived and continued in force, by virtue of these circumstances.

Strictly speaking, Commissioner Pound did not get the common-law rule quite right. Lord Mansfield's actual view, enunciated in the leading case of Goodright v. Glazier, 4 Burr. 2512, 98 Eng. Rep. 317 (1770), was that the first will had never been revoked:

> A will is ambulatory till the death of the testator. If the testator lets it stand till he dies, it is his will: if he does not suffer it to do so, it is not his will. Here, he had two. He has cancelled the second: it had no effect, no operation; it is as no will at all, being cancelled before his death. But the former, which was never cancelled, stands as his will.

The second will in Goodright v. Glazier apparently contained no express revocation clause, but Lord Mansfield later made it clear that the position he had taken would apply even though it had. See Harwood v. Goodright, 1 Cowp. 87, 98 Eng. Rep. 981 (1774).

American Rules on Revival in the Absence of a Statute. In the eleven or so states in which revival is not controlled by statute,[29] there appears to be a

---

29. The Restatement 2d of Property, Statutory Note to § 33.2, lists those states as Connecticut, Delaware, Louisiana, Massachusetts, Mississippi, New Hampshire, Rhode Island, Tennessee, Texas, Vermont, and Wyoming.

preference for the English ecclesiastical rule, though by a fairly narrow
margin. See Pickens v. Davis, 134 Mass. 252 (1883) (burden of proving
intent to revive on proponent of a revoked will); McClure v. McClure, 86
Tenn. 173, 6 S.W. 44 (1887) (burden of proving intent to revive on
proponent of a revoked will, but careful preservation of the revoked will by
the testator raises a presumption of an intent to revive); Hawes v. Nicholas,
72 Tex. 481, 10 S.W. 558 (1889) (intent to revive not shown merely from
destruction of a subsequent will); Gould's Will, 72 Vt. 316, 47 A. 1082
(1900) (burden of proof on proponent of a revoked will; careful preservation of the revoked will by testator can be counted as an indication of an
intent to revive); May v. Estate of McCormick, 769 P.2d 395 (Wyo. 1989)
(in the absence of evidence of an intention to revive, a revoked will was
held not revived by the destruction of a later will that expressly revoked all
prior wills). The English common-law rule also has its adherents, however,
as in Whitehill v. Halbing, 98 Conn. 21, 118 A. 454, 28 A.L.R. 895 (1922);
Succession of Dambly, 191 La. 500, 186 S. 7 (1938). No decisions in the
remaining states appear to exist on the question.

   Statutory Rules on Revival. In England, the common-law rule of "automatic revival" and the ecclesiastical rule giving effect to intention however
proved were abrogated in 1837. The Wills Act of 1837 replaced those rules
by a so called "anti-revival" rule. Under the statutory "anti-revival" rule, G's
Will No. 1 would be revived only if G either reexecuted that will or
executed a codicil showing an intention to revive that will.

   In this country, statutory rules on revival exist in about forty states. See
Restatement 2d of Property, Statutory Note to § 33.2, for a state-by-state
compilation. The statutes in about sixteen or so states maintain the anti-
revival stance of the English Wills Act and require either a reexecution of
the revoked will or the execution of a codicil showing an intention to
revive. The statutes in the remaining twenty-four or so states have
liberalized the strict requirements of the English Wills Act and moved in
the direction of the English ecclesiastical rule. Under the earlier version of
these statutes, revival of Will No. 1 would occur if it "appears by the terms
of" the revocation of Will No. 2 that it was G's intention to revive and give
effect to Will No. 1 or if Will No. 1 was "republished." Today, this version
exists in only about seven states. Many of those in the earlier group have
replaced their more liberal rule with the still more liberal version adopted
by the pre-1990 UPC, which is now in effect in about sixteen or so states,
including Minnesota at the time of Estate of Boysen, below.

Estate of Boysen
309 N.W.2d 45 (Minn. 1981)

   PETERSON, J. Genevieve Thompson appeals from the order of a three-
judge panel of the Dodge County District Court affirming the order of the
county court, probate division, admitting to probate a will of decedent
Chris Boysen. The issue raised by this appeal is whether decedent revived

the will. Because we believe the relevant statute, Minn. Stat. § 524.2-509(a) (1980), was misapplied below, we reverse and remand for a new trial.

Decedent was the father of appellant Genevieve Thompson and respondent Raymond Boysen, proponent of the will in question. Decedent's wife predeceased him by 30 years. Appellant married and moved to Austin, Minnesota. After respondent married, decedent made his home with respondent and his wife in Hayfield, Minnesota. In 1964 respondent was appointed guardian of decedent's person and estate. In 1973 decedent moved from respondent's home to a residence for the elderly located in Hayfield. He lived there until his death in 1977.

Decedent executed the will on March 12, 1964, when he was 75 years old. In the will he devised all his real property—in large part a 200-acre farm near Hayfield—to respondent on the condition that respondent pay appellant $7,000. Decedent bequeathed his personal property to respondent and appellant in equal shares.

After its execution the will was filed with the Dodge County clerk of court. In 1972 the court removed the will from the courthouse vault in order to review it in connection with a proceeding for the dissolution of respondent's marriage. A few years later respondent learned the will had never been returned to the clerk of court's custody. When attempts by decedent's attorney to locate the will proved unsuccessful, decedent discussed the preparation of a new will with a paralegal employed by the attorney. At the probate court hearing the paralegal described their conversation:

> When he came in, he said that his will had been lost so it was necessary for him to make another will, . . . I had been present and witnessed the first will. He thought perhaps I remembered what was in it. I said too long a time had gone by. I didn't . . . could not remember the details of the first will and we had no copy. He said at that time that it was necessary to make one because he wanted the farm to go to Raymond. He said at the first will he had given money to Genevieve, the farm to Raymond and a sum of money to Genevieve. He was indecisive as to this amount of money that he should put in to her because he didn't know what money he'd have, you know, what money there would be left to divide for her. He didn't know what . . . valuations would be to . . . things have changed. So he . . . he did ask if this . . . We discussed and we said, well, how did you determine the first amount of money? And he said, well, he had thought that 3/4 to 1/4 would be a . . . set that sum of money. So we said, 'Well, you can use fractions; you don't have to use sums of money if you don't want to.' And that is why he made a fraction in place of a total sum of money.

Decedent executed the new will on May 13, 1975. It differs from its predecessor in one significant respect: it provides that in order to take decedent's real property respondent must pay appellant a sum equal to one-fourth the property's appraised value. The farm is worth approximately $600,000.

Decedent filed the new will with the clerk of court. He gave respondent an unsigned copy of the will. Respondent put the copy in a safe deposit box.

Efforts to determine the whereabouts of the old will continued. In June 1975 the clerk of court notified decedent's attorney that the old will had been found. In February 1976 the attorney, acting at decedent's direction, withdrew the new will from the court files.

Shortly thereafter, Raymond drove decedent to the attorney's office. The secretary gave decedent the new will and he signed a receipt for it. During the drive back to Hayfield decedent tore the new will in half. At the probate court hearing Raymond testified that decedent handed him the torn will and said:

> They maybe have lost it yet. This will give us . . . some sort of an idea on my likes . . . you take care of it.

Raymond placed the torn will in a locked box at his home. He removed the copy from the safe deposit box and returned it to decedent. Decedent tore the copy in half.

Decedent died in April of the following year. Raymond, as the executor of decedent's estate, filed a petition for probate of the 1964 will. Genevieve objected to the petition and sought an adjudication of intestacy. The probate court found that decedent revived the 1964 will and accordingly admitted the will to probate. A three-judge panel of the district court affirmed the probate court's order. We granted Genevieve leave to appeal to this court from the district court's determination.

Minn. Stat. § 524.2-509(a) (1980) [pre-1990 UPC § 2-509(a)] governs the question whether decedent revived the 1964 will. That statute provides:

> If a second will which, had it remained effective at death, would have revoked the first will in whole or in part, is thereafter revoked by acts under section 524.2-507 [pre-1990 UPC § 2-507], the first will is revoked in whole or in part unless it is evident from the circumstances of the revocation of the second will or from testator's contemporary or subsequent declarations that he intended the first will to take effect as executed.

The 1975 will expressly revoked all prior wills and codicils of decedent. The 1975 will was revoked when decedent tore it in half. Under section 524.2-509(a) the 1964 will is not revived unless from "the circumstances of the revocation" of the 1975 will or from decedent's "contemporary or subsequent declarations" it is evident that he intended the 1964 will "to take effect as executed."

The probate court found that decedent did so intend. The district court panel held the probate court's finding not clearly erroneous. Our review of a factual finding of a court sitting without a jury is likewise limited to the question whether the finding is clearly erroneous. . . . Here, however, we are presented with a case involving the application of a statute we have not previously had occasion to interpret. On this appeal we must initially determine the correct interpretation of section 524.2-509(a) and then decide whether the district court's application of the statute to the facts of this case was consistent with that interpretation.

Where a later will which would have revoked an earlier will is itself revoked, section 524.2-509(a) establishes a presumption against revival of the earlier will. That presumption is rebutted if "the circumstances of the revocation" of the later will or the "testator's contemporary or subsequent declarations" make evident his intent that the earlier will "take effect as executed." In the present case decedent made no declarations indicating such an intent. Our concern, then, is with the meaning of the phrase "the circumstances of the revocation." No court in another jurisdiction that has enacted the [pre-1990] Uniform Probate Code appears to have interpreted this phrase.

The question under section 524.2-509(a) is whether a testator, at the time he revoked a will, intended to die intestate or to revive an earlier will. We believe that in allowing the trier of fact to consider "the circumstances of the revocation" when deciding this question the legislature meant to permit an examination of all matters relevant to the testator's intent. Accordingly, the trier of fact should consider the following:

> 1. Did the testator, at the time he revoked the later will, know whether the earlier will was in existence?
> 2. If the testator did know that the earlier will was in existence, did he know the nature and extent of his property and the disposition made of his property by the earlier will, particularly with respect to persons with a natural claim on his bounty?
> 3. Did the testator, by action or nonaction, disclose an intent to make the disposition which the earlier will directs?

Only if these questions are affirmatively answered should the earlier will be admitted to probate. Because these questions were not addressed below, the district court's order must be reversed and this case remanded for a new trial. By remanding the case we do not intimate an opinion regarding the ultimate result.

Reversed and remanded.

[The dissenting opinion of SCOTT, J. is omitted.]

Notes and Questions

1. *Boysen's Discrete Sub-Requirements Approach.* Is *Boysen* an example of a hard case making bad law? The court was surely correct in saying that "the legislature meant to permit an examination of all matters relevant to the testator's intent" in determining whether one of the statutory require-ments for revival were met. Do you agree, however, that it is appropriate to translate that general statutory prescription into discrete sub-require-ments, all of which must be met? In terms of the rule/standard distinction (supra pp. 153 & 177), the court judicially changed a statutory "standard" into a set of "rules." Such an approach surely makes the proponent's case harder than the legislature intended it to be.

Can there not be cases in which the proponent would be able to establish that it was "evident from the circumstances of the revocation of the second will or from testator's contemporary or subsequent declarations that he intended the first will to take effect as executed," but would not be able to establish that the answer to all three of the court's questions was "Yes"? Is *Boysen* such a case? Would *Boysen* be such a case if the proponent could have established that the testator remembered the contents of his 1964 will, had been told that the 1964 will was in existence, but did not have first-hand knowledge that it existed?

On the actual facts of the *Boysen* case, could the court, without establishing sub-requirements, have concluded that it was *not* "evident from the circumstances . . . or from [the testator's] contemporary or subsequent declarations that [the testator] intended the first will to take effect *as executed*"? On remand in *Boysen*, the trial court applied the supreme court's directives and determined that the 1964 will was not revived. The trial court also, however, applied the doctrine of dependent relative revocation, which we study in Part E, as a way of giving effect to the 1975 will. On appeal, the Minnesota Court of Appeals held that the procedural rules of the prior appeal rendered this determination improper. In the end, Chris Boysen died intestate. See Estate of Boysen, 351 N.W.2d 398 (Minn. Ct. App. 1984).

UPC section 2-509 (1990) continues to employ the same statutory language interpreted in *Boysen*. The Comment to the section, however, explicitly rejects the *Boysen* discrete sub-requirements approach.

2. *Revocation of a Codicil.* In Estate of Hering, 108 Cal. App. 3d 88, 166 Cal. Rptr. 298 (1980), the decedent, Henry Hering, executed an eight-page typewritten will on October 21, 1976. Elaine Bockin was to receive a specific devise of the decedent's personal effects and rent-free use of certain premises. She was to be the income beneficiary of a testamentary trust, with the trustee also having power to invade the corpus of the trust for her benefit. At Elaine's death, any remaining corpus of the trust was to be distributed to the Braille Institute of America, Inc.

On January 13, 1977, Henry executed a typewritten three-page "First Codicil to Will of Henry Richard Hering." The codicil referred to the specific articles of the will containing Elaine's name and amended those articles by deleting her name and inserting the words "Evelyn Salib." The codicil also expressly confirmed and republished the will in all other respects.

On December 2, 1977, in the presence of his attorney and with intent to revoke the codicil, Henry made a large "X" through all of the writing on each page of the codicil and on each page wrote the words, "Revoked December 2, 1977 Henry R. Hering." Henry's attorney testified that, shortly before Henry made these marks on the codicil, Henry stated that he thought that the X's would reinstate the provisions in the original will, devising the income interest to Elaine rather than Evelyn.

When the case was decided, the California statute on revival provided:[30]

---

30. The California provision has now been repealed and replaced by the pre-1990 UPC version of § 2-509. See Cal. Prob. Code § 6123.

If, after making a will, the testator makes a second will, the destruction or other revocation of the second will does not revive the first will, unless it appears by the terms of such revocation that it was the intention to revive and give effect to the first will, or unless, after such destruction or revocation, the first will is duly republished.

The court gave effect to Henry's 1976 will as originally written, but not on the theory that the revoked provisions of the 1976 will had been revived under the above revival statute. The above revival statute was, in fact, held inapplicable to cases of partial revocation by codicil. (Although section 1-201 of the pre-1990 and 1990 UPC defines the term "will" as including a "codicil," California then had no similar statutory provision.[31]) With the legislation held to be inapplicable, the court applied the common-law rule on revival, under which a subsequent revocation of the codicil "leaves the will in force and effect as written."

How would the *Hering* case be decided under UPC section 2-509 (1990)? How would the *Hering* case have been decided under the court's approach and under the approach of the 1990 Code if, just before he made the "X" marks on his 1977 codicil, Henry had said "Now neither Evelyn nor Elaine will get any of my property"?

PART E. DEPENDENT RELATIVE REVOCATION

As we shall see, dependent relative revocation is a remarkable doctrine, ingeniously devised to give a testator a result that comes close to her or his actual intention when that actual intention, though established to the court's satisfaction, cannot be given effect under a state's will execution and revocation statutes.

While the development of the doctrine is laudable, it is still the law of second best. Of prime concern as you study the following materials is whether we cannot do better.

EXTERNAL REFERENCES. Palmer, Dependent Relative Revocation and Its Relation to Relief for Mistake, 69 Mich. L. Rev. 989 (1971); Warren, Dependent Relative Revocation, 33 Harv. L. Rev. 337 (1920).

Estate of Callahan
251 Wis. 247, 29 N.W.2d 352 (1947)

Eva Callahan died in June 1945 at the age of eighty-seven years as a result of an illness with which she was stricken on the preceding January

---

31. One was added in 1983. See Cal. Prob. Code § 88.

21st. Her husband, Dr. John L. Callahan, Sr., died on January 5, 1945 at the age of eighty-four. The Callahans were the parents of two children then living, John Jr. and Albert.

In July 1932 Eva Callahan and her husband executed wills almost identical in their provisions. In December 1936, September 1938, February 1940 and August 1944, further wills were drawn by each clearly evidencing common design and collaboration in their preparation. On the night of January 1, 1945 Quincy H. Hale, an attorney in the city of La Crosse who had drawn the various wills for the Callahans, visited them in the company of his wife. At the conclusion of the visit Dr. Callahan accompanied the Hales to the door and informed them that he and his wife had destroyed their 1944 wills for the purpose of reinstating their 1940 wills, and had done so because Albert had begun drinking heavily again and they desired to put him back in the position he occupied under their 1940 wills. Albert had been addicted to the excessive use of intoxicating liquor and had received less than equal treatment with John in the 1940 wills. In the 1944 wills his position was improved because he had at that time given up drinking. At the time of Dr. Callahan's statement Mrs. Callahan was in the room but said nothing.

The next day, January 2, Mr. Hale determined that the destruction of the 1944 wills did not reinstate the 1940 wills. He drew a new will for Dr. Callahan almost identical with his 1940 will and took it to him for execution. He then informed the doctor and Mrs. Callahan that their 1940 wills had not been revived by destruction of the later wills. He had not been requested to draw the new will by Dr. Callahan either on the preceding night or on the day following, but did so purely of his own volition. He stated that he acted in haste because he was convinced that the doctor would not live long. He did not prepare a similar will for Mrs. Callahan because she was in good health and he was not concerned about her. Dr. Callahan executed the will on January 2 and died three days later.

Mrs. Callahan was stricken on January 21. She was taken to the hospital immediately and died the following June. While she was at the hospital two additional wills were drawn . . . Mr. Hale testified that Mrs. Callahan was incompetent [to execute a will] after she entered the hospital on January 21. . . .

[Mrs. Callahan's] will of 1940 [and] will of 1944 . . . were offered for probate in the alternative. The petition for probate was made by Mr. Hale who had retained a copy of the destroyed 1944 will. John and Albert objected to the probate. [A] decree was entered admitting the 1944 will to probate, from which John and Albert appeal. . . .

RECTOR, J. . . . The appeal of Albert and John from the judgment admitting the 1944 will to probate raises the question whether the trial court properly applied the doctrine of "dependent relative revocation".

That rule is ordinarily applied in cases where a testator having executed one will thereafter revokes it by the execution of a later will which, for some reason fails to become effectual. In such cases revocation of the earlier instrument "is treated as relative and dependent upon the efficiency of the later disposition, which was intended to be substituted." Will of

Lundquist, 1933, 211 Wis. 541, 543, 248 N.W. 410, 411. The revocation of the earlier document is held to be dependent upon the validity of the later one and the later one being invalid, the earlier one stands. . . . The rule has been criticized by some courts and some textwriters, but it is the law in this jurisdiction.

The situation presented here differs somewhat from the usual case in which the doctrine is applied. Here we have a revocation of a later will with an announced intention of reinstating a former one. But the rule was applied to such a situation in Powell v. Powell, 1866, L.R. 1 Prob. 209. The reasoning upon which it is based applies to the same extent that it does in the typical case. Adherence to the rule requires that we apply it here.

It is argued that there is a distinction between this case and other cases in which the rule has been applied. It is said that here the testatrix was advised the destruction of the 1944 will did not reinstate the 1940 will, that she had an adequate opportunity thereafter to prepare a new will if she had desired to do so, and that her failure to prepare a will indicated that her destruction of the 1944 will was not conditioned but was accompanied by an intention to revoke the document absolutely. There is considerable force in the argument. The doctrine of dependent relative revocation is based upon the testator's inferred intention. It is held that as a matter of law the destruction of the later document is intended to be conditional where it is accompanied by the expressed intent of reinstating a former will and where there is no explanatory evidence. Of course if there is evidence that the testator intended the destruction to be absolute, there is no room for the application of the doctrine of dependent revocation. Failure to prepare a new will may or may not be significant. The inferences to be derived from such a failure will vary according to the circumstances. If it were due to lack of opportunity, it would be difficult to attribute any great significance to it. The inferences, as in other factual questions, are to be drawn by the trier of fact.

Here the trial court evidently did not consider the delay in preparing a new will sufficient to establish that the 1944 will was destroyed with the intent to revoke it absolutely. It was justified in arriving at that conclusion.

Three days after Mr. Hale's advice to Mrs. Callahan, her husband died and she was stricken sixteen days after his death with an illness which rendered her incompetent thereafter. Both she and her husband were advanced in years. She was eighty-seven and he was eighty-four. They had lived together for many years. Her grief at his death, the necessity for arrangements that were then required and the loss that she must have felt, constitute adequate explanation of her failure to discuss the matter of a new will in the short time before she became ill.

There is a further argument to the effect that Mr. Hale's testimony as to the testatrix's intention in destroying her 1944 will is incompetent and of no probative force. [The court then held that Dr. Callahan's statement to Mr. Hale was in the course of a social visit and that Mr. Hale's testimony was not incompetent because of a statute prohibiting disclosure by an attorney of communications of a client made to him "in the course of his professional employment."]

So far as the matter of probative force is concerned, it strikes us that the circumstances are persuasive as to the testatrix' intention. We must bear in mind that prior to the doctor's statement to Mr. Hale he and his wife had each executed five wills and these wills carried the clearest indication that they were the result of collaboration and execution of a common design. The fact that they acted in concert in preparing these wills carries an inference that they collaborated in destroying their 1944 wills. Dr. Callahan's statement to Mr. Hale in the presence of Mrs. Callahan that they had acted together must be considered as the statement of one who without doubt had consulted with her in the matter. . . .

Affirmed.

no constr. trust relief b/c no fraud

Notes and Questions

1. *Theory of Dependent Relative Revocation—Mistake or Conditional Revocation?* In the earliest English decision on the general problem, the court based relief partly upon the ground that the revocation "ought to be relieved against and the will set up again in equity, under the head of accident." Onions v. Tyrer, 2 Vern. 742, 23 Eng. Rep. 1085, 1 P. Wms. 343, 24 Eng. Rep. 418 (Ch. 1716). Recognition that the problem is essentially one of giving relief for mistake still appears in some of the cases, but the conventional analysis is the conditional-revocation theory adopted in the *Callahan* case. Commenting on this aspect of the case, Professors Langbein and Waggoner noted:

> Granting that [Callahan's] destruction of her 1944 will was done under a mistake on her part as to the legal consequences of her act, the court was hardly being candid in saying that her revocation was conditional on the correctness of her assumption about the legal consequences of her act. No one who actually intended to effect a conditional revocation of a document would completely destroy it. The truth is that the testatrix meant to revoke her 1944 will, but formed her intention to revoke under the inducement of a mistake.

Langbein & Waggoner, Reformation of Wills on the Ground of Mistake: Change of Direction in American Law?, 130 U. Pa. L. Rev. 521, 544 (1982).

2. *Giving Effect to the Testator's Intention.* As noted in the introductory text to this Part, dependent relative revocation is the law of second best. Callahan's true intention was to revive her 1940 will. She did not intend her destroyed 1944 will to stand unrevoked under the doctrine of dependent relative revocation. The 1940 will could not be given effect because the applicable Wisconsin legislation contained an anti-revival provision similar to the one in the English Wills Act of 1837, requiring reexecution of the revoked will. See Eberhardt's Estate, 1 Wis. 2d 439, 85 N.W.2d 483 (1957).

Presumably, under current Wisconsin law, Callahan's 1940 will would have been revived. Wisconsin has now replaced its earlier provision on revival with one that allows revival "if there is clear and convincing evidence" of an intent to revive (Wis. Stat. § 853.11), which surely existed in the *Callahan* case, especially since the statute specifically allows "proof of testator's statements at or after the act of revocation" to be admissible to establish intent. Although the statute also provides that "a will . . . cannot be revived . . . unless the original . . . is produced in court," this requirement could also have been met in *Callahan*. The 1940 will was not destroyed. The will that was destroyed was the 1944 will, the one to which the court gave effect under dependent relative revocation.

The court in *Callahan* said that application of dependent relative revocation in this type of case depends upon a showing that "the destruction of the later document is . . . accompanied by the expressed intent of reinstating [the] former will . . . ." Extraordinarily, the showing necessary to apply the doctrine of dependent relative revocation and give effect to the 1944 revoked will is the same evidentiary showing that the Wisconsin anti-revival statute was designed to preclude.

Dependent relative revocation cases like *Callahan* should all but disappear in states adopting the more liberal revival rule of section 2-509 of the pre-1990 or 1990 UPC.

3. *Giving Effect to the Testator's Intention in Other Dependent Relative Revocation Cases.* The factual pattern faced by the court in the *Callahan* case—revocation of a later will for the purpose of reviving a former one—is only one of several factual patterns that lend themselves to a dependent-relative-revocation analysis. As the court itself noted:

> The [dependent-relative-revocation] rule is ordinarily applied in cases where a testator having executed one will thereafter revokes it by the execution of a later will which, for some reason, fails to become effectual. In such cases . . . revocation of the earlier document is held to be dependent upon the validity of the later one and the later one being invalid, the earlier one stands.

We will study the cases falling into this category below. As you study them, consider the extent to which enactment of a dispensing power statute like UPC section 2-503 (1990) would give family property law a mechanism by which to give effect to the testator's intention, the later will.

In fact, would it not be the case that a combination of the liberal revival rule of the pre-1990 or 1990 UPC versions of section 2-509 and enactment of UPC section 2-503 (1990) would pretty much make the law of *second* best, as administered under the dependent-relative-revocation doctrine, obsolete?

4. *Giving Effect to Second Best Under Dependent Relative Revocation.* The widespread enactment of UPC section 2-503 (1990) is probably years away. Therefore, it is important to consider how the courts should administer the law of second best. Professor Palmer charts a style of analysis for the courts in the following excerpt from Palmer, Dependent Relative Revocation and Its Relation to Relief for Mistake, 69 Mich. L. Rev. 989, 997-99 (1971):

> [T]he sole justification for the use of dependent relative revocation is to effectuate the decedent's intent as nearly as possible. . . . In most cases the reason for the application of the doctrine is that the known dispositive intent cannot be given effect. Where the act of revocation went to the whole

instrument, the court is left with a choice between giving effect to the dispositions contained in that instrument or letting the property go by intestacy. Usually, neither course will effectuate the decedent's intent exactly, but it will often be possible for the court to conclude that one will come closer than the other. If the testamentary disposition is closer dependent relative revocation should be applied and the will held unrevoked, but if intestacy is closer the doctrine should be held inapplicable. Suppose, for example, that a testator with two heirs, a son John and a daughter Mary, makes a will leaving his entire estate to John, but thereafter cancels the will in connection with an attempt to execute a new will bequeathing his entire estate to Mary. The latter will is invalidly executed so that his intended disposition to Mary cannot be given effect. In such circumstances it should be regarded as clear beyond the possibility of serious argument that dependent relative revocation will not be applied. The result of its application is that the entire estate goes to John, whereas the decedent intended that it should go to Mary; if, in contrast, the court refuses to apply the doctrine so that the property goes by intestacy, Mary takes a one-half interest, which is obviously closer to the intended disposition than the only other choice available to the court.

Although dependent relative revocation is a beneficial doctrine when properly applied, a disturbing fact about the cases is that the kind of analysis just suggested is seldom made. While it appears more frequently in modern decisions than in the older cases, it remains true that in case after case courts apply the analysis mechanically without any attempt to ascertain what might be called the probable intent of the decedent—that is, given the choices available, which would the decedent probably have made had he known that his intended disposition would be ineffective? From the fact that the act of revocation was connected with an attempt to make a different disposition, many courts have thought it followed that the revocation was intended to be conditional on the effectiveness of the disposition. This does not follow, of course, but an important consequence of this view is that the apparent revocation is made presumptively conditional. This will sometimes lead a court to apply the doctrine without even mentioning the terms of the intended disposition. When the relevant facts are fully disclosed, they may be comparable to those in the John-Mary example, in which case the presumption should give way and the doctrine should not be applied. In contrast, in many of the cases in which it has been applied, this was fully warranted by the facts, because of the similarity between the intended dispositions and those contained in the cancelled wills.

Although full recognition of the fact that the case should turn on probable intent has been slow in coming, it is in the process of being achieved.

Ineffective Attempt or Uncompleted Plan to Execute a Subsequent Will. In Carter v. First United Methodist Church, 246 Ga. 352, 271 S.E.2d 493 (1980), Tipton's validly executed 1963 will was found among her personal papers in her dining room chest after her death in 1979. The will was folded together with a handwritten instrument dated May 22, 1978, captioned as her will but unsigned and unwitnessed, purporting to establish what the court described as a "somewhat different" scheme of distribution of her property. Pencil marks had been made diagonally through the dispositive provisions of the 1963 will and through the name of one of the co-executors. The court did not describe the dispositive provisions contained in the 1963 will, nor the changes in them that the 1978 instrument would have achieved, had it been validly executed.

The proponent of the 1963 will was the First United Methodist Church of Albany, Georgia. The contestant (called the caveator) was one Luther Carter, who obviously was Tipton's heir in intestacy, though his relationship to her was not disclosed by the court. The trial court found that from time to time prior to her death, Tipton had made it known to her attorney that she needed his services in order to change or revise her will, or to make a new will. It also found that at one time she had written out some proposed changes on tablet paper to be suggested to her attorney when he prepared a new will for her.

The trial court admitted the 1963 will to probate, and on appeal the supreme court affirmed, saying in part:

> In the present case, the testatrix wrote the 1978 instrument which the parties have conceded (by the absence of their contentions) cannot be admitted to probate because it lacks some of the requisites of a will. The propounder [of the 1963 will] says, in effect, if not in express words, that the testatrix would have preferred the property disposition clauses of the 1963 will over the only other alternative—intestacy. The caveator contends, in essence, that the testatrix would have preferred intestacy. How stands the record?
>
> The fact that the old will, with pencil lines drawn by Mrs. Tipton through the property disposition provisions, was found among her personal papers folded together with the 1978 writing, that makes a somewhat different disposition of her property, is some evidence tending to establish that "the cancellation and the making of a new will were parts of one scheme, and the revocation of the old will was so related to the making of the new as to be dependent upon it." [McIntyre v. McIntyre, 120 Ga. 67, 71, 47 S.E. 501, 503 (1904).] This evidence was sufficient to rebut the statutory presumption of revocation [that arose from the pencil marks made on the 1963 will] and to give rise to a presumption in favor of the propounder under the doctrine of dependent relative revocation or conditional revocation. *McIntyre, supra.* The stipulation that these two instruments were found together thus shifted the burden of proof to the caveator to prove, in essence, that Mrs. Tipton would have preferred intestacy.
>
> [Unlike *McIntyre*,] there is no testimony that the testatrix even told anyone that she had revoked her 1963 will. . . . The presumption against intestacy (or in favor of the continued validity of the 1963 will) stands unrebutted in the present case. . . .
>
> Accordingly, the trial court, as finder of the facts, did not err in admitting the will to probate.

Compare the *Carter* case with Estate of Patten, 179 Mont. 299, 587 P.2d 1307 (1978). Ella D. Patten died in 1973, survived by her two sons, Donald and Robert. In 1970, about three years before her death, she had attempted to execute a will that devised the bulk of her $200,000 estate to Donald. This 1970 will was found in her safe-deposit box after her death, and Donald presented it for probate. Robert, however, successfully contested its validity on the ground of improper execution. See Patten v. Patten, 171 Mont. 399, 558 P.2d 659 (1976).

The 1970 will consisted of two pages. Ella Patten's signature appeared at the bottom of the first page. The second page contained only an attestation clause, with the signatures of three members of her doctor's office staff. The ineffective attempt at proper execution occurred on July 6, 1970. Ella Patten took the will with her to a doctor's appointment. After being attended by her doctor, "a request was transmitted to the office staff to witness her will." Ella, who one witness described as habitually secretive about her personal affairs, folded the document over so that only the second page was visible to the witnesses. Contrary to the will-formality requirements of the then-existing Montana statute,[32] Ella neither signed in the presence of the witnesses nor acknowledged her signature to them.

After failing to get the 1970 will probated, Donald presented for probate a copy of a 1968 will. The original of the 1968 will had been given to Ella by her attorney after its proper execution, but could not be found after her death. The copy presented for probate was a copy retained by her attorney. Like the ineffective 1970 will, the 1968 will devised the bulk of her estate to Donald, although, as the court noted in the excerpt below, there were some differences between the two wills.

Ella was presumed to have destroyed the 1968 will with revocatory intent. Donald's attempt to set its presumed revocation aside under the dependent-relative-revocation doctrine was rebuffed by the court. The court reasoned:

> The doctrine [of dependent relative revocation] is applied with caution. . . . In deciding whether to apply the doctrine in a given case, the testator's "intent" is the controlling factor. The testator must intend that the destruction of the old will is dependent upon the validity of the new will. Evidence of this intent cannot be left to speculation, supposition, conjecture or possibility. The condition that revocation of a will is based upon the validity of the new will must be proved by substantial evidence of probative value. A showing of immediate intent to make a new will and of conditional destruction are required to reestablish a destroyed will under the theory of dependent relative revocation. . . . [T]o prove this intent the proponents of the revoked will must show that the new will was executed concurrently with or shortly after the destruction of the old will and both wills must be similar in content. In the present case, Donald Patten . . . has not proven that decedent intended the destruction of the 1968 will to depend upon the validity of the 1970 will. . . . No one knows when the decedent destroyed her [1968] will or how she did it. The record does not show that the 1970 will was executed concurrently or shortly after the destruction of the 1968 will.
>
> While the content of both wills is similar in some respects, the dissimilarities are such that they reveal decedent's revocation of the 1968 will was not conditioned on the validity of the 1970 will. In the 1968 will, decedent bequeathed $5,000 and $2,500 to her grandchildren, the son and daughter of Robert Patten. In the 1970 will, Donald Patten's name was written in by pen and ink as executor. In the 1968 will, Robert Patten was

---

32. Montana has since enacted the pre-1990 UPC, including § 2-502 thereof. See Mont. Code Ann. § 72-2-302.

the named executor. These differences in the wills show that decedent may not have intended the same dispositive plan.

To what extent did the Georgia and Montana Supreme Courts follow the course of analysis charted for them by the Palmer article, excerpted in Note 4, supra p. 295?

The conditional-revocation theory was previously exposed for what it is—a fiction. In the cases like *Callahan*, where there was a revocation of a later will for the purpose of reviving a former one, it is a fiction to think that when the decedent destroyed the later will, she or he actually formed an intention to make a *conditional* revocation. The decedent merely mistakenly assumed that the former will was revived.

So also, when a decedent destroys a former will, laboring under the mistaken assumption that she or he has validly executed a new will, it is unrealistic to look for proof of an actual intention to make a conditional revocation of the old one. An actual intention to make a conditional revocation of the old will would presuppose that the decedent entertained the possibility of the new one being invalid, even though the decedent had no basis for questioning the new will's validity. The real question in these cases is not one of actual or even implied intent, but one of *imputed* intent: What would the decedent have preferred *if* she or he had known of the mistake and also had known that the mistake could not be corrected? In insisting on affirmative evidence of a conditional revocation, did not the court in the *Patten* case take the conditional-revocation fiction too seriously?

By the same token, did the court in the *Carter* case properly *apply* dependent relative revocation? Was Tipton operating under a mistaken assumption that her new "will" was valid? Obviously, a court cannot make an intelligent decision as to which of two outcomes is second best without knowing the content of first best. A will that the decedent appears to have supposed to be valid, albeit mistakenly, can certainly be counted first best. The question posed by *Carter* is whether *only* such a will can be counted as first best. Put oppositely, can an unexecuted draft such as the one in *Carter* be treated as a sufficiently reliable indication of true (but ineffective) intention from which to judge which of the attainable alternatives comes closer?

Professor Palmer points out that the courts prior to the *Carter* case appear to have insisted upon a will the decedent supposed to be valid:

> [M]ost courts . . . draw the line between an ineffective attempt to make another disposition and an uncompleted plan to do so. This is . . . [for] reasons of policy . . . . [U]nless a new dispositive plan has become definitive—and this does not normally occur until the decedent has executed a testamentary writing which he believes to be effective—the evidence is too uncertain that the decedent's intent to revoke is dependent upon putting the plan into effect. In addition, the existence of a writing containing the terms of the substituted disposition provides some assurance that the testator's true intentions in that regard are known. . . . [T]he doctrine of dependent relative revocation cannot be intelligently applied in the absence of such knowledge. . . .

In [the] group of cases . . . in which the revocation was connected with a new dispositive plan which had not reached the stage of attempted execution of a will, . . . the policy factors [argue for denying the application of dependent relative revocation].

Palmer, supra p. 295, at 994.

Notice how the behavior of Tipton, compared to that of Patten, bears on this point. Tipton preserved her former will with her important papers, along with the unsigned new "will." Patten apparently discarded her former will and preserved only the later one. Which course of action implies that the decedent thought she had not finalized the new "will" and which course of action implies that the decedent was convinced that the new will was valid?

Would Patten's new will stand a strong chance of being upheld under UPC section 2-503 (1990)? Would Tipton's unsigned will? For purposes of dependent relative revocation, must there have been an effort to execute the new "will" sufficient to give effect to that new will under section 2-503?

Despite the fact that the application of dependent relative revocation is troublesome in the *Carter* case, do you not agree with the outcome of the case—giving effect to Tipton's 1963 will? If so, can that outcome be supported by a different theory? Is it fair to analyze the *Carter* facts as *implying* a *true* conditional (or tentative) intent to revoke, as distinguished from the normal dependent relative revocation case where the conditional intent to revoke is imputed (or fictional)?

Some situations concerning an uncompleted plan arguably present an even easier set of facts than *Carter* for applying dependent relative revocation. In Dougan's Estate, 152 Or. 235, 53 P.2d 511 (1936), Dougan made numerous pen and pencil marks on her will and then took the mutilated will to her lawyer, together with an outline of the provisions of a new will, which she requested him to prepare. The will was prepared, but she suffered a stroke and died before she could get to the attorney's office to execute it. The court held that her mutilated will could not be given effect under dependent relative revocation. Why not? Under UPC section 2-503 (1990), could the typewritten will prepared by Dougan's lawyer be given effect?

Partial Revocation by Act to the Document. In Schneider v. Harrington, 320 Mass. 723, 71 N.E.2d 242 (1947), the testator's will provided that her entire estate was to be disposed of in the following manner:

1. To my niece Phyllis H. Schneider, of 2368 Washington Avenue Bronx, New York, one third (1/3).
2. One third (1/3) to my sister, Margaret J. Sugarman, of 177 West 95th Street New York City, New York.
3. One third (1/3) to my sister, Amy E. Harrington, of New York City, New York.

The will contained no residuary clause. At some time after the execution of the will, the testator used a pencil to cross out all of clause 3 and the figures "1/3" in clauses 1 and 2. She then inserted by pencil the figures 1/2 in clauses 1 and 2 leaving uncancelled in these clauses the words "one third."

The testator left no husband or children. Her heirs were four sisters and twenty-two nieces and nephews. The court applied the doctrine of dependent relative revocation by stating:

> We think that the . . . cancellations and the substitutions were inextricably linked together as parts of one transaction; and it is evident that the testatrix intended the cancellations to be effective only if the substitutions were valid. But the substitutions, inasmuch as they were not authenticated by a new attestation as required by statute, were invalid. Consequently the cancellations never became operative. Additional support for this conclusion, if any is needed, may be found in the fact that the will contained no residuary clause, and if the decree entered in the court below should stand there would be a partial intestacy—a result which we think the testatrix did not intend.

Under UPC section 2-503 (1990), could the words written on the will be given effect?[33]

The Massachusetts Supreme Judicial Court said that a partial intestacy as to one-third of the testator's estate was "a result which we think the testatrix did not intend." Accord, e.g., Estate of Uhl, 1 Cal. App. 3d 138, 81 Cal. Rptr. 436 (1969); Wolf v. Bollinger, 62 Ill. 368 (1872); Knapen's Will, 75 Vt. 146 (1903); Appleton's Estate, 163 Wash. 632, 2 P.2d 71 (1931). It is often said in the cases that the revocation is presumed to have been conditioned on the effectiveness of the substituted devise.

At some level of generality, it is probably true that the testator did not intend to die partially intestate. Do you think, however, that if the testator had known that her alterations could not be given effect, she would have preferred that one-third pass by intestacy rather than to her sister, Amy? (Assume that Phyllis' parent, who was the testator's sibling, predeceased the testator.)

Is it proper to characterize the testator as having intended to "revoke" the devises to Phyllis and Margaret, as opposed to the devise to Amy? How might the case have been handled if the testator had done the following: crossed out only the devise to Amy and wrote in the margin "Phyllis and Margaret to divide equally the 1/3 share previously given to Amy"?

Compare *Schneider* with Ruel v. Hardy, 90 N.H. 240, 6 A.2d 753 (1939). A clause of Ethel Smith's will provided:

> To Frank . . . , and to Walter . . . and . . . Lilla . . . , I give five hundred dollars to each one.

---

33. Under conventional law, of course, the testator's actual intention could not be carried out because the alterations were unattested. Even under conventional law, however, the case would be open to proof that the will was in the altered form at the time of execution. See In re Cravens, 206 Okla. 174, 242 P.2d 135 (1952); and cases collected in Annot., 34 A.L.R.2d 619, 630 (1954). Recall also that there is authority holding that the decedent can validly alter a *holographic* will by writing changes thereon without re-signing it. See supra p. 276.

After execution, in an unattested act, Ethel struck out "five" and inserted "one." The residuary devisee was her husband, Benjamin.

The court found dependent relative revocation inapplicable and held that legacies to Frank, Walter, and Lilla were revoked.

> A reduction of eighty per cent of the legacy tends more to show a preference on her part that her legatees should have nothing rather than that they should have the full sum . . . .

Cf. Watson v. Landvatter, 517 S.W.2d 117 (Mo. 1975); Locke v. James, 11 M. & W. 901, 152 Eng. Rep. 1071 (1843).

Express Revocation by Subsequent Instrument. In the preceding cases, the revocation was by act to the document. Can dependent relative revocation be applied to express revocations by subsequent instrument? Most courts have held that it can be. See, e.g., Linkins v. Protestant Episcopal Cathedral Foundation, 187 F.2d 357 (D.C. Cir. 1950); Kaufman's Estate, 25 Cal. 2d 854, 155 P.2d 831 (1945); La Croix v. Senecal, 140 Conn. 311, 99 A.2d 115 (1953); Charleston Library Society v. Citizens & Southern Nat'l Bank, 200 S.C. 96, 20 S.E.2d 623 (1942).

Crosby v. Alton Ochsner Medical Foundation, 276 S.2d 661 (Miss. 1973) (5-to-4 decision), is one of the few cases in which the court refused to apply the doctrine. Hollis Crosby died leaving a will that devised one-half of the residue of his estate to his widow and the other half to the Alton Ochsner Medical Foundation. The devise to the Medical Foundation, having been made in a will executed within ninety days of Hollis's death, was void under the Mississippi mortmain statue. The will contained a clause expressly revoking all former wills.

Hollis's former will, executed more than ninety days prior to death, contained a similar devise to the Medical Foundation. The Medical Foundation argued that the doctrine of dependent relative revocation should be applied so as to render ineffectual the revocation of the devise in its favor in the prior will.

The court rejected the Medical Foundation's argument, saying in part:

> [In Hairston v. Hairston, 30 Miss. 276 (1855)], this Court . . . said: "[When] the will contains an express clause of revocation, . . . there is nothing from which it could be inferred that the testator intended only to revoke conditionally . . . . [I]t would be incompetent to introduce evidence to prove that the declaration was not designed to operate as an absolute, but only as a conditional revocation . . . ." (30 Miss. at 301-303). . . .
>
> We do not think that it can be maintained that *Hairston* was wrongly decided or that its results are detrimental to the public. In fact, we are of the opinion that the law announced therein is sound. A person has a right to make a will and so long as it is in conformity with the law, he or she may leave his or her property as desired. By the same token such person has the right to revoke a will for any reason he or she may have. Due to the construction we have placed on our revocation statute, the only way that a person may be sure that the revocation of a will is unequivocal and certain is by a declaration in writing either in another will or in a separate writing duly attested revoking the former will. When so revoked such a person is

assured that after death no one will be heard to say that he or she did not intend to revoke the former will. We think this is a valuable right and should not be disturbed.

Are you persuaded by the Mississippi court's conclusion and reasoning? If not, how would you answer the court's point that a revocation that is unambiguously and unconditionally declared in a validly executed will cannot be rendered conditional by extrinsic evidence? On the latter question, compare Fleming v. Morrison, 187 Mass. 120, 72 N.E. 499 (1904) (set forth supra p. 209), in which extrinsic evidence was allowed to show that a will was not executed with testamentary intent, even though the will contained unambiguous and unconditional expressions of testamentary intent.

Partial Application of Dependent Relative Revocation. The court in Arrowsmith v. Mercantile-Safe Deposit & Trust Co., 313 Md. 334, 545 A.2d 674 (1988), was asked to apply dependent relative revocation to only one will provision and to treat the rest of the will as revoked. George H. C. Arrowsmith died in 1983, leaving a will dated July 29, 1982. George's 1982 will expressly revoked all prior wills and exercised a testamentary power of appointment over some $7 million in assets of an irrevocable inter-vivos trust created by his mother in 1953.

George's 1982 will did not contain a perpetuity saving clause, a device routinely used by lawyers to avoid violating the Rule Against Perpetuities. See infra p. 1029. In the absence of the perpetuity saving clause, George's exercise of the power of appointment violated the Rule.

George had executed two prior wills, one in 1976 and the other in 1966. His 1976 will expressly revoked all prior wills and exercised his testamentary power of appointment in terms similar to those contained in the 1982 will. The 1976 will also failed to contain a perpetuity saving clause.

George's 1966 will exercised his testamentary power of appointment, but in terms quite dissimilar to the 1982 or 1976 wills. The 1966 will, however, contained a perpetuity saving clause.

The court was asked to apply dependent relative revocation to conclude that the revocation of the perpetuity saving clause in the 1966 will was conditioned upon the validity of the exercise of the power of appointment in the 1976 will and, in turn, in the 1982 will. The court declined to apply dependent relative revocation in this manner, saying:

> Plucking the perpetuities saving clause from the 1966 will and inserting it in the 1982 will is inconsistent with the theoretical justification for the doctrine. . . . [T]he doctrine's underlying theory of conditional revocation limits the relief which a court can grant. If a later will which expressly revokes earlier wills itself fails in whole or in part, the doctrine requires a court to decide whether the decedent would have preferred the prior will to the result under the later will, which may be partial invalidity or intestacy. . . . The doctrine . . . does not present a court with a menu. It is not the judicial function to select some provisions from column A and some provisions from column B in order to put together a valid will.

INTERNAL REFERENCE. See the discussion in Chapter 17 of UPC sections 2-901 to -906 (1990), which incorporates the Uniform Statutory Rule Against Perpetuities (USRAP) into the 1990 UPC. Generally speaking, the effect of USRAP is to insert a perpetuity saving clause into all trusts that contain a perpetuity violation. Had the *Arrowsmith* case been governed by USRAP, George's 1982 will would have been valid and there would have been no reason to go into court to correct the mistaken omission of the perpetuity saving clause.

PROBLEMS CREATED BY THE TIME GAP IN WILLS

There will always be some interval between the time when a will is executed and the time when it takes effect to transfer property. Sometimes the interval will be measured in decades. Older wills, sometimes called "stale" wills, are just as valid as "fresher" ones, but have the potentiality to do mischief because they are so out of date. A challenge for the estate planner is to draft a plan that can accommodate expected and unexpected changes in property and family circumstances. A challenge for the courts and legislatures is to develop rules and doctrines to respond to changes in a manner that is consistent with the testator's manifested estate plan. In this Chapter, we will study the law's response to changes in a testator's property and changes in the circumstances of a testator's devisees.

It is difficult to overemphasize the seemingly obvious point that many of these issues could—and should—be avoided by foresight and careful drafting. The doctrines studied in this Chapter operate as "default rules." They apply because, and only to the extent, the testator and the testator's attorney failed to address the issue in a will provision. As you study the cases, think about what type of will provision you would have advised the testator to have inserted when initially drafting the will or when reviewing the will in light of changed circumstances.

Formal Opinion 210 (March 15, 1941)[1]
Opinions on Professional Ethics 498 (ABA 1967)

An attorney may properly advise a client for whom he has drawn a will of the advisability of reexamining the will periodically and may from time to time send notices to the clients advising him of changes in law or fact which may defeat the client's testamentary purpose, unless the attorney has reason to believe that he has been supplanted by another attorney.

Canon Interpreted: Professional Ethics 27. A member calls attention to the effect on testamentary dispositions of subsequent changes in general economic conditions, of changes in the attitude or death of named fiduciaries in a will, of the removal of the testator to a different jurisdiction where different laws of descent may prevail, of changes in financial conditions, family relationship and kindred matters, and then inquires whether it is proper for the lawyer who drew the will to call attention of the testator from time to time to the importance of going over his will. . . .

The inquiry presents the question as to whether such action on the part of the lawyer is solicitation of legal employment and so to be condemned. Many events transpire between the date of making the will and the death of the testator. The legal significance of such occurrences are [sic] often of serious consequence, of which the testator may not be aware, and so the importance of calling the attention of the testator thereto is manifest.

It is our opinion that where the lawyer has no reason to believe that he has been supplanted by another lawyer, it is not only his right, but it might even be his duty to advise his client of any changes of fact or law which might defeat the client's testamentary purpose as expressed in the will.

Periodic notices might be sent to the client for whom a lawyer has drawn a will, suggesting that it might be wise for the client to reexamine his will to determine whether or not there has been any change in his situation requiring a modification of his will.

External Reference. For a discussion of a lawyer's duty, if any, to notify will clients of changes in the law that may require modifications of their wills, see Johnston, Legal Malpractice in Estate Planning—Perilous Times Ahead for the Practitioner, 67 Iowa L. Rev. 629, 655-58 (1982).

Classification of Devises. Many of the doctrines studied in this Chapter traditionally involve a two-stage analysis. The first stage is classifying the devise as one of four types of devises—specific, general, demonstrative, or residuary. Atkinson on Wills section 132, at 731-32 defines these classes as follows:

> A "specific legacy" is [one] of some specific article or particular fund which the will distinguishes from all the rest of the testator's estate.

---

1. The Canon referred to in this opinion is from the Canons of Professional Ethics, an antecedent of the Model Rules of Professional Conduct. See supra p. 21. Eds.

A "general legacy" is one which is payable out of general assets of the estate and which does not require the delivery of any specific thing or satisfaction from any designated portion of testator's property. A simple pecuniary legacy is a typical case of general legacy.

A "demonstrative legacy" is one of a certain amount or quantity to be satisfied primarily out of a certain fund or particular property, but on failure of the latter, payable generally from the estate.

A "residuary legacy" is one which covers the remainder of testator's property after debts and specific and general legacies have been satisfied.

While it was once held that all devises of land were specific, it is now well recognized that devises may be general or residuary.

The second stage is to apply the doctrine based on the classification of the devise. In other words, the classification of the devise governs the legal outcome.

This two-stage analysis suggests that courts are involved in highly formalistic rule-making. Traditionally, this has been true, and to a great extent still is. The materials that follow, however, also show that courts and legislatures have now begun to erode that formalism by moving to a more generalized inquiry into intention.

PART A. POST-EXECUTION CHANGES IN THE ESTATE

1. Ademption Of Specific Devises By Extinction

Statutory References: *1990 UPC §§ 2-606, 5-426*
Pre-1990 UPC § 2-608

Specific devises are normally used to pass on to particular relatives or friends property the testator holds specially dear. Often, these are items of tangible personal property—a particular piece of jewelry, the piano, a coin or stamp collection, a particular work of art. Also, a piece of real estate is sometimes specifically devised—the family farm, the family home, the vacation house, and so on. In addition, on occasion, testators devise specific financial assets, such as particular stocks or bonds or a savings account.

Although devises of specific financial assets sometimes prove trouble-some, specific devises of tangible personal property or land do not, for the most part, raise many issues. Occasionally, though, the testator might give the piano or the diamond ring to the devisee in advance of death, might sell a particular painting and purchase another one in its place, or might sell the family home and move to another one. Also, as the population ages, more and more elderly testators eventually become incapacitated to some degree. As a testator's financial affairs are taken over by a guardian or conservator, or by an agent acting under a durable power of attorney, specifically devised property becomes more likely to be sold so that the proceeds can be used to pay for nursing care and associated expenses. Occasionally, also, specifically devised property is stolen in a burglary or destroyed in a fire. Finally, it is quite possible that a testator becomes annoyed with the devisee and disposes of the specifically devised property as a method of revoking the devise—revocation by act to the property, so to speak, as opposed to revocation by subsequent instrument or by revocatory act to the will.

Under the doctrine of ademption by extinction, a specific devise is adeemed—ineffective—if the testator no longer owns the specifically devised property at death. As McGee v. McGee, below, shows, the generally accepted interpretation of the doctrine follows the so-called identity theory, which means that the court does not inquire into the reason why the specifically devised property is not found in the estate.

Dispositions by Guardians or Conservators. One type of situation in which the courts have been reluctant wholly to disregard the testator's intention arises where a guardian or conservator, acting on behalf of an incapacitated testator, sold or otherwise disposed of an item of specifically devised property.

In the leading case of Morse v. Converse, 80 N.H. 24, 113 A. 214 (1921), the testator's guardian withdrew a savings bank deposit that had been specifically devised, and used part of the proceeds to buy a Liberty bond, which remained in the estate at the testator's death. The court awarded the Liberty bond to the devisee. As for the part of the withdrawal that had been spent by the guardian, the court held that the devisee had no claim, since "nothing has come to the executor's hands upon which the will can operate." The tendency of the guardianship cases has been in favor of the New Hampshire view,[2] and a few states have adopted that view by statute, so as to provide that the specific devisee "becomes entitled to receive any remaining money or other property."[3]

In Estate of Mason, 62 Cal. 2d 213, 397 P.2d 1005, 42 Cal. Rptr. 13 (1965), the California Supreme Court refused to limit the devisee to the traceable proceeds of the sale. Several years after the testator had executed a will specifically devising her home to Fairbank, she became mentally incompetent and a guardian of her estate was appointed. The guardian sold the home for $21,000, deposited the proceeds into a special account, and spent all but $556 for the support of the testator. The court held that the amount spent should be paid to Fairbank out of the residuary estate.[4] Any

---

2. See, e.g., Stake v. Cole, 257 Iowa 594, 133 N.W.2d 714 (1965); Estate of Graham, 216 Kan. 770, 533 P.2d 1318 (1975); Walsh v. Gillespie, 338 Mass. 278, 154 N.E.2d 906 (1959); Estate of Warren, 81 N.C. App. 634, 344 S.E.2d 795 (1986); Estate of Swoyer, 439 N.W.2d 823 (S.D. 1989). Cases are collected in Annots., 84 A.L.R.4th 462 (1991); 51 A.L.R.2d 770 (1957).

3. See, e.g., N.Y. Est. Powers & Trust Law § 3-4.4 (this is an amended version of an earlier statute that reversed the position adopted by the Court of Appeals in Ireland's Estate, 257 N.Y. 155, 177 N.E. 405 (1931), a case cited in McGee v. McGee, below, as being in opposition to Morse v. Converse).

4. Accord, e.g., 20 Pa. Cons. Stat. Ann. § 2541(16.1), construed in Estate of Fox, 494 Pa. 584, 431 A.2d 1008 (1981).

other result, Justice Traynor said, "would allow the guardian to destroy his ward's testamentary plan even though the guardian was acting to protect the ward's economic interests."

Both the pre-1990 and 1990 UPC explicitly adopt a guardianship exception, adopting the Estate of Mason, rather then Morse v. Converse, view about the amount to which the devisee is entitled. Pre-1990 UPC § 2-608(b); 1990 UPC § 2-606(b). See also UPC § 5-426 (1990) (directing the conservator to take into account the protected person's estate plan when making investment and expenditure decisions and authorizing the conservator to examine the will).

Dispositions by Attorneys-in-fact Acting Under Durable Powers of Attorney. In recent practice, durable powers of attorney—powers of attorney that are not automatically revoked when the principal becomes mentally incompetent—have become popular substitutes for guardianships or conservatorships. See infra p. 437. At least one court has expressly extended the guardianship exception to dispositions made under authority of durable powers. See Estate of Graham, 216 Kan. 770, 533 P.2d 1318 (1975). See also Hobin v. O'Donnell, 115 Ill. App. 3d 940, 451 N.E.2d 30 (1983) ("[A]demption requires some act of the testator indicative of an intention to revoke. . . . If someone other than the decedent sold the stock without permission or if the decedent was incapable of forming the requisite intent, then there was no ademption."); Estate of Warren, 344 S.E.2d 795 (N.C. Ct. App. 1986); Annot., 84 A.L.R.4th 462 (1991).

UPC section 2-606(b) (1990) addresses this problem by explicitly extending the guardianship exception to sales by an agent on behalf of an incapacitated testator under a durable power. To ease the administrative burden of a post-death inquiry into the mental state of the testator, section 2-606(e) establishes a rebuttable presumption that a sale or other disposition by an agent is on behalf of a testator who is incapacitated.

In McGee v. McGee, below, the testator's agent partially disposed of property that the testator had specifically devised. In this case, however, the testator was not incapacitated and in fact approved of her agent's action. As we shall see, the court held that this distinguished the case from others like Morse v. Converse, and held the devise to have been partially adeemed.

McGee v. McGee
122 R.I. 837, 413 A.2d 72 (1980)

WEISBERGER, J. This is a complaint for declaratory judgment, in which the plaintiff administrator, Richard J. McGee (Richard), sought directions from the Superior Court in respect to the construction of certain provisions of the will of his mother, Claire E. McGee, and instructions relating to payment of debts and distribution of assets from the testatrix' estate. The sole issue presented by this appeal concerns the question of the ademption of an allegedly specific legacy to the grandchildren of the decedent and the consequent effect of such ademption upon payment of a bequest in the amount of $20,000 to Fedelma Hurd (Hurd), a friend of the testatrix. The provisions of the will pertinent to this appeal read as follows:

> CLAUSE ELEVENTH: I give and bequeath to my good and faithful friend FEDELMA HURD, the sum of Twenty Thousand ($20,000.00) Dollars, as an expression to her of my appreciation for her many kindnesses.
>
> CLAUSE TWELFTH: I give and bequeath all of my shares of stock in the Texaco Company, and any and all monies standing in my name on deposit in any banking institution as follows:
>
> (a) My Executor shall divide the shares of stock, or the proceeds thereof from a sale of same, *with all of my monies, standing on deposit in my name, in any bank*, into three (3) equal parts and shall pay 1/3 over to the living children of my beloved son, PHILIP; 1/3 to the living children of my beloved son, RICHARD and 1/3 over to the living children of my beloved son, JOSEPH. Each of my grandchildren shall share equally the 1/3 portion given to them. (Emphasis added.)

At the time of the execution of the will and up until a short time before the death of the testatrix, a substantial sum of money was on deposit in her name at the People's Savings Bank in Providence. About five weeks prior to his mother's death, Richard, proceeding pursuant to a written power of attorney as modified by an addendum executed the following month, withdrew approximately $50,000 from these savings accounts. Of this amount, he applied nearly $30,000 towards the purchase of four United States Treasury bonds, commonly denominated as "flower bonds," from the Federal Trust Company in Waterville, Maine (Richard then resided in that state). His objective in executing this transaction was to effect an advantageous method of satisfying potential federal estate tax liability.[5] The bonds, however, did not serve the intended purpose since at the time of Mrs. McGee's death her gross estate was such that apparently no federal estate tax liability was incurred. The remainder of the monies withdrawn from the savings accounts were deposited in Claire McGee's checking account to pay current bills and in a savings account in Richard's name to be transferred to his mother's account as the need might arise for the payment of her debts and future obligations. The sole sum that is now the subject of this appeal is the approximately $30,000 held in the form of United States Treasury bonds.

The complaint for declaratory judgment sought instructions concerning whether the administrator should first satisfy the specific legacy to the grandchildren from the proceeds of the sale of the flower bonds or whether he should first pay the $20,000 bequest to Fedelma Hurd, since the estate lacked assets sufficient to satisfy both bequests.

After hearing evidence and considering legal memoranda filed by the parties, the trial justice found that the bequest to the grandchildren

---

5. Although not otherwise redeemable before maturity, flower bonds may be redeemed at par value, plus accrued interest, upon the owner's death for the purpose of paying the federal taxes on his estate. See Girard Trust Bank v. United States, 602 F.2d 938, 940 n.1 (Ct. Cl. 1979).

contained in the twelfth clause of the will constituted a specific legacy. He held further, however, that Rhode Island regarded the concept of ademption with disfavor and he sought, therefore, to effectuate the intent of the testatrix. He proceeded to determine that since there is an assumption that one intends to leave his property to those who are the natural objects of his bounty, rather than to strangers, the administrator "should trace the funds used to purchase the Flower Bonds and should satisfy the specific legacy to the grandchildren" under the twelfth clause of the will. Consequently, the trial justice held that the legacy to Fedelma Hurd under the eleventh clause of the will must fail. This appeal ensued.

The McGee grandchildren suggest that the principal design of the testatrix' estate plan, ascertainable from a contemplation of the testamentary disposition of her property, was to benefit her family rather than "outsiders." They urge us to consider her intentions—which they assure us were concerned, in part, with protecting the family interests from an anticipated reduction of the estate's value by taxes—in determining whether the transfer of the funds in her accounts did in fact work an ademption. In addition, Richard points out that the decedent did not herself purchase these bonds. On the contrary, Richard acquired them in order to help discharge anticipated tax obligations of the estate and informed his mother of them only subsequently to the purchase. He argues, furthermore, not only that the funds with which he purchased the flower bonds originated in his mother's accounts, but also that since these bonds "are as liquid as cash" they are indeed monies standing in the decedent's name on deposit in a banking institution. He suggests that this description conforms in every respect to the formula drafted into the twelfth clause of her will. Merely the form of the legacy has changed, according to Richard, not its essential character, quality, or substance.

In response, appellant asserts that an ademption occurred by the voluntary act of the testatrix during her lifetime, since her son withdrew the funds as an authorized agent operating under a lawful power of attorney. There is evidence, moreover, that the testatrix subsequently ratified the purchase of the bonds when Richard afterwards told her of his actions and their intended effect upon estate taxes.[6] As a consequence, Hurd asserts that there was no longer any money standing on deposit in the name of the testatrix in any bank with which to discharge the specific legacy to the grandchildren. These transactions resulted in an extinction of the subject matter of the legacy. Hurd argues, in addition, that the intention of the testatrix, even if discernible, is irrelevant to the question of the ademption of the bequest. She therefore contends that her general legacy should be payable from the proceeds of the sale of the flower bonds.

At the outset, we recognize that the instant case concerns specifically the concept of ademption by extinction, a legal consequence that may attend a variety of circumstances occasioned either by operation of law or by the actions of a testator himself or through his guardian, conservator,

---

6. Richard testified his mother "was pleased that (he had) done this because there would be more money available for the children and grandchildren."

or agent. . . . In particular, a testamentary gift of specific real or personal property may be adeemed—fail completely to pass as prescribed in the testator's will—when the particular article devised or bequeathed no longer exists as part of the testator's estate at the moment of his death because of its prior consumption, loss, destruction, substantial change, sale, or other alienation subsequent to the execution of the will. In consequence, neither the gift, its proceeds, nor similar substitute passes to the beneficiary, and this claim to the legacy is thereby barred. Atkinson, Handbook of the Law of Wills § 134 at 741, 743-44 (2d ed. 1953); 6 Bowe & Parker, Page on the Law of Wills § 54.1 at 242, § 54.9 at 256-57 (1962); Note, Wills: Ademption of Specific Legacies and Devises, 43 Cal. L. Rev. 151 (1955).

The principle of ademption by extinction has reference only to specific devises and bequests and is thus inapplicable to demonstrative or general testamentary gifts. . . . In Haslam v. de Alvarez, 70 R.I. 212, 38 A.2d 158 (1944), we prescribed the criteria for determining the character of a legacy, relying on the earlier case of Dean v. Rounds, 18 R.I. 436, 27 A. 515 (1893), wherein we held that "(a) specific legacy, as the term imports, is a gift or bequest of some definite specific thing, something which is capable of being designated and identified." Id. When the testator intends that the legatee shall receive the exact property bequeathed rather than its corresponding quantitative or *ad valorem* equivalent, the gift is a specific one, and when "the main intention is that the legacy be paid by the delivery of the identical thing, and that thing only, and in the event that at the time of the testator's death such thing is no longer in existence, the legacy will not be paid out of his general assets." Hanley v. Fernell, 54 R.I. 84, 86, 170 A. 88, 89 (1934). In particular, the designation and identification of the specific legacy in a testator's will describe the gift in a manner that serves to distinguish it from all other articles of the same general nature and prevents its distribution from the general assets of the testator's estate. . . .

In the case at bar, the trial justice construed the twelfth clause of Mrs. McGee's will as bequeathing a specific legacy to her grandchildren. While it is true that the party who contends the legacy is a specific one must bear the burden of proof on this issue, . . . the trial justice apparently found that petitioner's contentions met the burden and that the testatrix clearly considered the bequest a specific one.

Without a doubt, the trial justice properly interpreted the McGee grandchildren's bequest, primarily because of the tone of the other provisions, the tenor of the entire instrument, and the specificity with which the testatrix described that portion of the twelfth clause relative to the Texaco stock. Additionally, money payable out of a fund—rather than out of the estate generally—described with sufficient accuracy and satisfiable only out of the payment of such fund or a bequest of money deposited in a specific bank is, as a rule, a specific legacy. When a will bequeaths "the money owned by one which is on deposit" in a designated bank, although the amount remains unspecified, the gift is nevertheless identifiable and definite, apart from all other funds or property in the testator's estate; and the legacy is specific. . . . Despite the fact that Mrs.

McGee did not name any particular bank in the twelfth clause of her will, she bequeathed all the money in her name "in any bank." In view of the fact that she expected all of her money remaining at her death to go to her grandchildren and, further, the money to be payable from a particular source—that is, accounts in her name in banking institutions—we conclude that the legacy was sufficiently susceptible of identification to render it a specific one.

Accordingly, since the bequest to the grandchildren is specific, we must now determine whether or not it was adeemed by the purchase of the bonds. . . . In connection with the early theory of ademption, the courts looked to the intention of the testator as the basis of their decisions. . . . But ever since the landmark case of Ashburner v. MacGuire, 2 Bro. C.C. 108, 29 Eng. Rep. 62 (Ch. 1786), wherein Lord Thurlow enunciated the "modern theory," courts have utilized the identity doctrine or "in specie" test. This test focuses on two questions only: (1) whether the gift is a specific legacy and, if it is, (2) whether it is found in the estate at the time of the testator's death. . . . The extinction of the property bequeathed works an ademption regardless of the testator's intent. . . .

The legatees of the twelfth clause argue that the subject matter of the specific bequest, although apparently now unidentifiable in its previous form, actually does exist in the estate of their grandmother but in another form as the result of an exchange or transfer of the original property. But there is a recognized distinction between a bequest of a particular item and a gift of its proceeds, see generally Annot., 45 A.L.R.3d 10 (1972); and the testatrix, in the instant case, did recognize the distinction in the twelfth clause of her will by bequeathing the Texaco stock "or the proceeds thereof from a sale of same" but omitting to include similar provisions regarding proceeds in connection with the language immediately following which described the bank-money legacy. It appears that the testatrix' intention, manifest on the face of her will, was that her grandchildren receive only the money in her bank accounts and not the money's proceeds or the investments that represent the conversion of that money into other holdings. . . .

In accordance with the generally accepted "form and substance rule," a substantial change in the nature or character of the subject matter of a bequest will operate as an ademption; but a merely nominal or formal change will not. In re Peirce, 25 R.I. 34, 54 A. 588 (1903) (no ademption since transfer of stock after consolidation of banks without formal liquidation was exchange and not sale); Willis v. Barrow, 218 Ala. 549, 119 S. 678 (1929) (no ademption by transfer of money from named bank to another since place of deposit was merely descriptive); In re Hall, 60 N.J. Super. 597, 160 A.2d 49 (1960) (no ademption by transfer of the money from banks designated in will to another one since location was formal description only and did not affect substance of testamentary gift).

Since the money previously on deposit in Mrs. McGee's bank accounts no longer exists at the time of her death, the question arises whether the change was one of form only, rather than substance. We have determined that the change effected by Richard was not merely formal but was substantial. There is no language in the will that can be construed as reflecting an intention of the testatrix to bequeath a gift of bond investments to her grandchildren. The plain and explicit direction of the twelfth clause of the will is that they should receive whatever remained in her bank accounts at the time of her death. Since no sums of money were then on deposit, the specific legacy was adeemed. Clearly, this case is dissimilar to those in which the fund, at all times kept intact, is transferred to a different location, as in *Willis* . . ., where the money merely "changed hands," not character. See also In re Tillinghast, 23 R.I. 121, 49 A. 634 (1901) (no ademption by mere act of transferring mortgages to own name since they were in specie at the time of testatrix' death). The fact that Mrs. McGee did not herself purchase the bonds is not significant. Disposal or distribution of the subject matter of a bequest by an agent of the testator or with the testator's authorization or ratification similarly operates to adeem the legacy.

The petitioner improperly relies upon the case of Morse v. Converse, 80 N.H. 24, 113 A. 214 (1921). In that case the testatrix voluntarily placed her property into the hands of a conservator to care for and use for her support. The conservator purchased a Liberty bond out of bank deposits bequeathed in the testatrix' will, and the legacies were not adeemed thereby. But, contrary to the case at bar, the testatrix in Morse neither knew about nor consented to the conservator's acts; therefore, the court explained, the change "furnishes no evidence of an intentional revocation by her." Id. at 26, 113 A. at 215. But see . . . Matter of Ireland's Estate, 257 N.Y. 155, 177 N.E. 405 (1931) (specifically bequeathed stock adeemed even though sold by conservator after testator had become incompetent).

Moreover, under the principles enunciated by Lord Thurlow in Ashburner v. MacGuire, and more fully expressed in the case of Humphreys v. Humphreys, only the fact of change or extinction, not the reason for the change or extinction, is truly relevant. The vast majority of jurisdictions adhere to this rule. See Atkinson, supra § 134 at 741-42; 6 Page, supra § 54.15 at 266-68. This "in specie" theory of ademption, although it may occasionally result in a failure to effectuate the actual intent of a testator, has many advantages. Significant among these advantages is simplicity of application, as opposed to ad hoc determination of intent from extrinsic evidence in each particular case. This theory further has the advantages of stability, uniformity, and predictability. The argument in support of Lord Thurlow's rule is well expressed in 6 Page, supra § 54.15 at 266:

> If the sale or collection of the bequest works an ademption or not depending upon testator's intention as inferred from the surrounding circumstances, many cases will arise in which it is difficult or impossible to ascertain what testator's intention was; and probably, in many cases, testator did not think of the consequences which would follow from his conduct. If the sale or collection of the bequest operates as an ademption or not, depending upon his intentions, and such intention may be shown by his oral declarations, then the controlling evidence in the case will consist of the written will, executed in accordance with statute, together with testator's oral declarations.

This violates both the letter and the spirit of state wills statutes, which insist on the formalities of writing and execution in order to avoid opportunities for perjury. For these reasons, it is now held that the sale, destruction, or collection, of the bequest or devise, adeems it without regard to the actual intention of the testator.

Accordingly, we hold that the trial justice erred in allowing the admission of extrinsic evidence regarding Mrs. McGee's intent. We further hold that the specific legacy in the twelfth clause of the testatrix' will is adeemed and the legatees' claim to this bequest is thereby barred. We direct the trial justice to order the petitioner to satisfy the general pecuniary legacy bequeathed in the eleventh clause of the will from the sale of the flower bonds, with the excess to pass under the residuary (fourteenth) clause of the will.

The respondent's appeal is sustained, the judgment below is reversed, and the cause is remanded to the Superior Court for proceedings consistent with this opinion.

Notes and Questions

1. *Ratification of Agent's Action.* In the *McGee* case, the testator, when told of her agent's action, expressed approval. The court took this to be a ratification of her agent's action. Was the court justified in doing so? In Schreiner v. Scoville, 410 N.W.2d 679 (Iowa 1987) (described infra p. 592), an attorney prepared a will making a specific devise that was later adeemed by an inter-vivos transfer that the same attorney aided the testator in making. The disappointed devisee brought a malpractice action against the attorney, claiming that the attorney failed to advise the testator of the transfer's effect on the devise. The court held that the plaintiff's complaint stated a cause of action.

2. *The Identity Theory vs. The Intent Theory.* *McGee* is a rather stark example of the application of the rule of Ashburner v. Macguire. That rule is sometimes referred to as the "identity" theory of ademption, in contrast to the "intent" theory. According to the identity theory, ademption depends solely upon whether the subject matter of a specific devise exists as part of the testator's estate at death, and the testator's intent concerning the continued validity of the devise is irrelevant. According to the intent theory, ademption depends upon the testator's subjective intent, determined on a case-by-case basis. The difference between these two approaches to questions of ademption amounts to a choice between an inflexible rule and an open-ended standard. Does this choice involve the same contrast between formality and discretion examined supra p. 101? What reasons do you suppose have led courts, in an area of law seemingly dedicated to carrying out the testator's intent, to adopt a rule that disregards intent? In further discussion of ademption, see Paulus, Ademption by Extinction: Smiting Lord Thurlow's Ghost, 2 Tex. Tech. L. Rev. 195 (1971); Paulus, Special and General Legacies of Securities—Whither Testator's Intent, 43 Iowa L. Rev. 467 (1958).

Estate of Austin
113 Cal. App. 3d 167, 169 Cal. Rptr. 648 (1980)

[Lucille Austin's will, executed on March 9, 1977, made two specific bequests to a friend, Betty Guldberg, the appellant. The first specific bequest was of an oil portrait of the testatrix' mother, and the other was of "the promissory note which I own and hold, made by Gary Grenz, together with the deed of trust or mortgage securing said promissory note . . . ." The will also contained nine general bequests, ranging from $2,000 to $15,000, to individuals and organizations. The residue of the estate was given to the respondent, the Shrine Hospital for Crippled Children.

The Grenz note was paid in full on July 1, 1977, about four months after the will was executed. The amount paid was $17,065.88. The payoff was made at the same time that the property, which was the underlying security for the note, was sold. The note did not contain a due-on-sale clause.

Shortly after the note was paid off, the note proceeds were placed in a savings account, which immediately before the deposit had a balance of around $7,700. About a month later, the testatrix withdrew $20,000 from the savings account and loaned it to the Inmans. In return, she received a promissory note secured by a deed of trust. The note was due in six months.

On January 14, 1978, the testatrix died, without having changed her will. The Inman note was paid off to the estate shortly after her death. The trial court held that the specific bequest of the Grenz note was adeemed, so that the proceeds of the Inman note accrued to the residue, for distribution to the Shrine Hospital. An appeal followed.]

ANDREEN, A.J. . . . In discerning the intent of the testatrix, we look first at the will. It is remarkable for the number and diversity of the legacies and bequests. It demonstrates a mind that enjoyed giving to many beneficiaries. Although there is a residuary clause in the will, there is a manifest intention to particularize the disposition of assets.

There is nothing in the record to suggest that the testatrix did anything to initiate the payoff of the Grenz note. It was paid incident to the sale of the property which was the security of the note.

There is nothing to show that the testatrix had a change of mind as to the appellant being a proper beneficiary of her estate. The oil portrait of the testatrix' mother remained a bequest to appellant.

She did nothing with reference to the proceeds except deposit them in a manner which was easily traceable and invested them in an almost identical type of asset—a promissory note secured by a deed of trust.

In determining whether the change is in form only, California courts have lately tended to avoid strict rules of ademption; rather they look to the inferred or probable intent of the testator under the particular circumstances. The reasoning of these more modern cases was crystallized and confirmed by the following statement in Estate of Mason,[7] supra, 62 Cal. 2d [213] at page 215, 42 Cal. Rptr. 13, 397 P.2d 1005:

> Ademption of a specific legacy is the extinction or withdrawal of a legacy in consequence of some act of the testator equivalent to its revocation, or clearly indicative of an intention to revoke. The ademption is effected by the extinction of the thing or fund bequeathed, or by a disposition of it subsequent to the will which prevents its passing by the will, from which an intention that the legacy should fail is presumed. A change in the form of property subject to a specific testamentary gift will not effect an ademption in the absence of proof that the testator intended that the gift fail.

In absence of proof of an intent that the gift fail, there should be no ademption. (Estate of Mason, supra, 62 Cal. 2d 213, 215, 42 Cal. Rptr. 13, 397 P.2d 1005; Estate of Stevens (1945) 27 Cal. 2d 108, 116, 162 P.2d 918; Estate of Holmes (1965) 233 Cal. App. 2d 464, 469, 43 Cal. Rptr. 693.)

We find that there is no indication of an intent by the testatrix to adeem, and that the judgment must be reversed.

We turn to appellant's contention that she is entitled to the amount of the Inman note, which was approximately $3,000 more than the payoff of the Grenz note.

In Estate of Shubin (1967) 252 Cal. App. 2d 588, 60 Cal. Rptr. 678, the court held that there was no ademption and that the beneficiary of the specific devise should receive a more valuable piece of property. The will disposed of a piece of property which was subsequently condemned and the decedent took the proceeds, added approximately $2,000 to it and bought a new piece of property within nine days. The court was aided in determining the testator's intention because he had written the address of the new property in the will next to the dispositive provision.

And in Estate of Cooper (1951) 107 Cal. App. 2d 592, 237 P.2d 699, the testator told his attorney simply "My car to Miss Hage." The attorney wrote "That certain Hudson Automobile, now owned by me." After the will was executed, the testator sold his car and a month later bought a new Hudson, which he owned at his death. The court had no difficulty in finding no ademption, citing a New York case which held that a bequest of a diamond brooch would not be adeemed where subsequent to the execution of the will the testatrix traded it in on a more expensive diamond brooch.

---

7. In an earlier part of the opinion, the court found the *Mason* case to be distinguishable (because it dealt with a sale of specifically devised property by a guardian) but significant, saying:

> The case is significant . . . in that it sets a course away from the strict rules of ademption, and draws a clear distinction between an extinction of a legacy by some act of the testator and the act of a third person. If the testator has disposed of a specific legacy, it may be presumed that he intended that the gift fail. Where it is done by act of a third person, in *Mason* a guardian, no such intent can be presumed.

Eds.

Shubin and *Cooper* are of no assistance to appellant. In each, once the court had found no ademption, it could do nothing other than order the beneficiary to take the property in its present form. The property was unique and there was no practical way to reduce its value to that of the property described in the will.

On the other hand, in this case the note has been converted to cash because it was paid off when due. Money is divisible, and the precise amount of the unpaid balance at the date of death is available.

The judgment is reversed and remanded. The trial court is directed to order that there is no ademption and that appellant take the amount of $17,065.88. . . .

BROWN, P.J., and HOPPER, J., concur.

Notes and Questions

1. *Non-Uniform Probate Code Departures from the Identity Theory.* The identity theory of Ashburner v. Macguire has been generally accepted in this country. *Austin* is not unique, however, in adopting the intent theory. There have been recent departures in circumstances similar to those found in *McGee.* See, e.g., Wachovia Bank & Trust Co. v. Ketchum, 76 N.C. App. 539, 333 S.E.2d 542 (1985) (purchase of a treasury note with cash withdrawn from a specifically devised savings account and certificates by an attorney-in-fact on behalf of a presumably competent testator caused no ademption). In addition, several cases have implicitly extended the guardianship exception to cover actions by persons acting on behalf of the testator over which the testator, even though competent and not under a guardianship, effectively had no control. See, e.g., Estate of Biss, 232 Or. 26, 374 P.2d 382 (1962) (a devise by member of Klamath Tribe of Indians of all money in a specified account was not adeemed where funds were withdrawn under order of Secretary of Interior and placed in trust account).

Finally, at least one non-UPC statute expressly adopts an intent approach to ademption:

> *Ky. Rev. Stat. § 394.360. Conversion or removal of devised property not an ademption unless intended.* (1) The conversion of money or property or the proceeds of property, devised to one (1) of the testator's heirs, into other property or thing, with or without the assent of the testator, shall not be an ademption of the legacy or devise unless the testator so intended; but the devisee shall have and receive the value of such devise, unless a contrary intention on the part of the testator appears from the will, or by parol or other evidence.
>
> (2) The removal of property devised shall not operate as an ademption, unless a contrary intention on the part of the testator is manifested in like manner.

2. *1990 Uniform Probate Code.* UPC section 2-606(a)(6) (1990) changes the pre-1990 UPC (section 2-608) and adopts the intent theory. How would a court have decided *McGee* if subsection (a)(6) had applied?

Avoidance of the Identity Theory. Even in jurisdictions that nominally follow the identity theory, there is no shortage of cases that find one way or another of effectuating intent. Three of the most common avoidance techniques are described below.

Reclassification of the devise. The doctrine of ademption by extinction applies only to specific devises. Especially in the case of devises of financial assets, the courts have exercised discretion in classifying the devises as specific or general. For example, in Will of Blomdahl, 216 Wis. 590, 257 N.W. 152 (1934), the testatrix' will devised "one hundred (100) shares of the common stock of the Ohio Oil Company to Mr. Fred T. Woodford" and "one hundred (100) shares of the common stock of the Ohio Oil Company to the First Church of Christ Scientist, of Milwaukee, Wisconsin." The evidence indicated that the testatrix owned 200 shares of the common stock of the Ohio Oil Company at the time the will was executed, but not at the time of her death.

The court held the devises to be general and, therefore, not adeemed, saying in part:

> The language used by the testatrix in framing her bequest, when read by itself, clearly carries a presumption that she intended, upon her death, to provide the named legatees each with 100 shares of the Ohio Oil Company common stock. If that language in the will is read in connection with the fact that she owned, at the time of the execution of the will, 200 shares of that stock, it might reasonably give rise to the presumption that she was giving away the stock then in her possession. But will such a presumption, if acted upon, carry out the intention of the testatrix? In order to avoid the problematical as far as possible, and as an aid to the rules of law which now apply to the interpretation and construction of wills, we hold that words specifically identifying the property and indicative of possession are necessary in the making of a specific bequest. . . .
>
> It is a generally accepted rule that where the language of the will is clear and unambiguous, it must control and that rule must prevail in this instance. The gift of a certain number of shares of stock without words of identification and possession is a general legacy. The absence of such words in these particular bequests brings this will within the rule accepted by this court and they must be held to be general bequests.

But see, e.g., First Nat'l Bank v. Perkins Inst. for the Blind, 275 Mass. 498, 176 N.E. 532 (1931) (a devise of "all of my stock in . . . Standard Oil Company of New Jersey" was held specific and adeemed, where the stock had been called during the testator's lifetime).

When courts find a devise similar to the one in *Blomdahl* to be general, a question arises whether the personal representative is required to purchase for the devisee an asset of the sort described in the will. Some courts have given the devisee an option to take the value of the asset in cash or to have the asset purchased on her or his behalf. See Annot., 22 A.L.R.2d 457, 464-67 (1952).

Courts have also avoided ademption by classifying the devise as demonstrative rather than specific. Consider the case of Lavender v. Cooper, 248 Ga. 685, 285 S.E.2d 528 (1982). Item Four of the testator's will devised

> unto my daughter-in-law Ollie McDaniel Coody . . . the sum of $8,000.00. Said $8,000.00 bequest to be paid from savings certificate I now hold in Planters Bank, which certificate has the name Ollie McDaniel Coody as co-owner thereon and being the sum of money received by me from the proceeds of an insurance policy on the life of my late son, Dudley. Said . . . sum of money to be the property of Ollie McDaniel Coody to do with as she sees fit.

An $8,000 Planters Bank savings certificate in the names of the testator and Ollie McDaniel Coody was not found among the testator's assets after her death, but an $8,000 Planters Bank savings certificate in her name alone was found among her assets after her death.

Reversing the judgment of the trial court, which had held that the devise was specific and adeemed, the Supreme Court of Georgia said, in part:

> The intention of the testatrix expressed in Item Four of the will . . . was to give the [legatee] "the sum of $8,000.00." That an unconditional gift to the legatee of that sum of money was intended by the testatrix is indicated not only by the foregoing language but as well by her expressed intention that "Said . . . sum of money [is] to be the property of Ollie McDaniel Coody to do with as she sees fit." The gift was of the sum of money, not of the certificate. The certificate merely was designated as the fund or property from which the unconditional gift of the sum of money was to be paid. . . .
>
> The characteristics of the legacy created by the testatrix in Item Four are those of a demonstrative legacy rather than of a specific legacy. A demonstrative legacy designates the fund or property from which it is to be satisfied but nevertheless is an unconditional gift to the legatee of the amount specified. . . . Had the testatrix intended the legatee to have a particular certificate of deposit and none other, instead of a specific sum of money, she doubtless would have used such language in the item of her will establishing the bequest for the legatee, thereby creating a specific legacy of the certificate.

Accord Smith v. Estate of Peters, 741 P.2d 1172 (Alaska 1987).

Change in form. Courts sometimes avoid ademption of a specific devise by holding that, although the subject matter of the devise is not in the estate in its original form, it is in the estate in a changed form. In Goode v. Reynolds, 208 Ky. 441, 271 S.W. 600 (1925), the testator's will made a specific devise to Reynolds of five shares of stock in the Third National Bank of Lexington. During the testator's lifetime, this bank consolidated with another bank in Lexington and, in place of his original five shares, the testator received five shares of stock in the consolidated bank, and also five shares of stock in a realty company organized to take over certain real estate holdings of the old Third National Bank that did not go into the consolidation.

In holding that these new shares were in the estate at death and that they went to Reynolds, the court said, in part:

> In 40 Cyc. 1921, we find:
>
> > A change in the form of a security bequeathed does not necessarily work an ademption. So there is no ademption where notes bequeathed are renewed, where stock bequeathed is exchanged for notes of the company, where stock in a consolidated corporation is accepted by testator in lieu of stock in a component corporation which he had bequeathed or where a state bank, stock in which has been bequeathed, is changed to a national bank.
>
> We believe the rule laid down by these authorities to be the correct one. The likeness of the new shares to the old is more important than their differences. Applying this rule, we think it plain that Miss Reynolds is entitled to the securities given in the consolidation for the securities surrendered.

Accord Stenkamp v. Stenkamp, 80 Or. App. 550, 723 P.2d 336 (1986); UPC § 2-606(a)(5) (1990).

Ademption and the "time-of-death" construction technique. As an initial matter, under both the identity and intent theories of ademption, property that matches the testator's description normally will pass to the devisee whether or not it was the identical property that the testator owned at the time of execution. As stated in Paulus, 2 Tex. Tech. L. Rev., supra p. 315, at 206:

> Although it is commonly stated that "a will speaks at the death of the testator," normal rules of construction demand that the meaning of the words used will be determined in reference to the situation in which the testator finds himself when he executes the will. "The language of a will is to be construed in light of circumstances existing when the will is written; the will operates, however, upon the property existing when death occurs." From an ademption-prevention standpoint, however, it is often helpful to assume that the "words were spoken at death." The will is ambulatory and the testator's lack of revocation or modification suggests that he approves the language of the will in reference to the circumstances that exist at his death.

As indicated, courts sometimes use this time-of-death construction technique to avoid ademption. For example, in Milton v. Milton, 193 Miss. 563, 10 S.2d 175 (1942), a devise of "my home place" was held applicable to the house and lot the testator owned at death, even though they were not the same assets owned when the will was executed.

The time-of-death construction technique applies to specific devises of securities as well as to devises of other kinds of property. Even if, after executing a will making a specific devise of securities, the testator sold the securities and later purchased new securities that fit the description of the will, normally there will be no ademption. In Estate of Russell, 521 A.2d 677 (Me. 1987), a devise of "my shares in the Putnam High Yield Trust" was held to pass to the named devisee all 1,527 shares in the fund held by the estate at death, notwithstanding that the testator purchased 610 of those shares after executing the will.[8]

2. Accessions and Accretions

Statutory References:　　*1990 UPC § 2-605*
　　　　　　　　　　　　　　　Pre-1990 UPC § 2-607

What rights does a devisee have to assets that, after execution of the will, were produced by a devised asset? This is a matter of "accessions" or "accretions." In most situations, the choice is between giving the product to the devisee of the underlying asset or giving it to the residuary devisees. Accession questions can involve many forms of wealth, including corporate stock, mortgages, promissory notes, oil and gas leases, and cultivated farm land.

In general, courts have held that specific devises transfer that specific asset together with accessions and accretions occurring after the testator's death. Thus, for example, rent becoming due after the testator's death goes to the devisee of the land. See Atkinson on Wills § 135, at 750-51. Specific devises do not bear interest, strictly speaking. If the specifically devised asset has not actually produced any income or interest, the devisee is not

---

8. The time-of-death construction technique originated in § 24 of the Wills Act of 1837. From an early time, a will could effectively dispose of all personal property owned by the decedent at her or his death, but it was not until the Wills Act of 1837 that English law permitted a will to operate on land acquired after the will was executed. The church courts had jurisdiction over wills of personal property and borrowed from Roman law the concept that a will could dispose of after-acquired chattels. See 2 F. Pollock & F. Maitland, A History of English Law 315 (2d ed. 1911). The general power of testation over land, however, was first given by the Wills Act of 1540, which the common-law judges soon construed as allowing disposition only of land owned by the testator when the will was made. See Brett v. Rigden, 1 Plow. 340, 344, 75 Eng. Rep. 516, 523 (1568); 7 W. Holdsworth, History of English Law 365 (1926).

By § 3 of the Wills Act of 1837, the old rule as to land was changed in England so as to permit a person to dispose by will of "all real estate and all personal estate which he shall be entitled to, either at law or in equity, at the time of his death." Section 24 of the same Act contained a provision designed to make sure that the courts would not defeat the rule of § 3 by construction. Section 24 provided that a will shall be construed, with reference to the estate, to speak "as if it had been executed immediately before the death of the testator, unless a contrary intention shall appear by the will."

The old rule as to after-acquired land has been eliminated everywhere in this country, in most states by statute. See, e.g., UPC § 2-602 (1990). A few states have also enacted a provision similar to § 24 of the English Act, one of them being Pennsylvania. In Lusk's Estate, 336 Pa. 465, 9 A.2d 363, 125 A.L.R. 787 (1939), the testator devised to his wife "my house and lot in which I now reside, situate in the Second Ward, City of New Castle, Lawrence County, Pennsylvania." Thereafter he sold the house in which he was living when the will was made, and bought another house in the same ward in which he was residing at the time of his death. The court held that the statute was controlling and that the will devised the house owned at death. The word "now" in the will was not a sufficient expression of a contrary intent, since it could "relate to the time when the will became operative." Contra, e.g., Nashville Trust Co. v. Grimes, 179 Tenn. 567, 167 S.W.2d 994 (1943).

entitled to any interest. By contrast, general devises do bear interest, beginning ordinarily one year after the testator's death.

Specific devises of debts or obligations usually carry with them interest accrued but unpaid by the date of the testator's death. Thus specific devises of mortgages or debts pass any accrued but uncollected interest to the devisees. See id. Similarly, courts have held that a specific devise of a bond passes to the devisee an overdue interest coupon that was attached to the bond at the testator's death. See id. Collected interest, however, does not pass to the specific devisee even if it remains part of the testator's estate.

No cases or statutes were found addressing the question of accessions and accretions regarding will substitutes. As you study the materials that follow, consider whether the law's treatment of accessions and accretions for specific devises should be extended to the treatment of gifts found in will substitutes. See infra Chapter 7, Part B. Should a payable-on-death savings account be treated the same as a revocable lifetime trust for purposes of accessions and accretions?

Corporate Stock. The law has had some difficulty in analyzing the effect of post-execution accessions upon devises of corporate securities. This is especially so where the accession results from a corporate restructuring. Corporate restructuring of stock by means of stock splits or stock dividends may affect devises of the stock in fundamental ways, because they potentially alter the economic interests that will be received by the devisee.

Stock split. A *stock split* occurs when a corporation amends its charter to increase the number of shares outstanding and issues these shares on a pro-rata basis to existing shareholders. For example, if a corporation has 1,000,000 shares of stock outstanding selling at $50 per share, a two-for-one stock split will increase the number of shares outstanding to 2,000,000. Existing shareholders will receive two shares for every share they own, but each share will now be worth only $25.

The traditional approach to resolving questions of stock accessions resulting from stock splits has been to depend on the classification of the individual devise as specific or general. If the devise is classified as specific, then the virtually uniform result has been to give to the devisee the increase in the number of shares resulting from a stock split. The devisee does not receive the benefit of the stock split if the courts classify the devise as general.

Pre-1990 UPC section 2-607 adhered to the traditional view concerning stock splits—that whether the devisee is entitled to the additional number of shares resulting from stock splits depends upon the specific-general distinction. This approach has led to some interesting decisions on the classification of the devise at issue.

In Mandelle's Estate, 252 Mich. 375, 233 N.W. 230 (1930), the testatrix's will, executed on September 10, 1923, declared:

> In recognition of his faithful and kindly medical services to me and his contribution to science and humanity, which I wish to facilitate, I give to Charles Jack Hunt, of Mt. Vernon, New York, his heirs and assigns forever, twelve hundred (1200) shares, par value, of the capital stock of Parke, Davis & Company, a corporation, etc., of Detroit, Michigan.

At the time of the execution of her will, the testatrix owned 3,744 shares of the Parke, Davis stock of the par value of $25 each. In February, 1927, the stockholders of Parke, Davis reframed its capital structure in form only, and authorized the exchange of the $25 par value shares for no par value shares in the ratio of one par value share for five no par value shares. In March, 1927, the testatrix exchanged her par value shares for the no par value shares, in accord with the designated ratio. At her death on August 17, 1928, she held the no par shares only. The executors of her estate, being in doubt whether Dr. Hunt was entitled to 6,000 shares of the no par stock (the number of shares equivalent to the 1,200 shares of par value stock), or to only 1,200 shares of the no par stock, petitioned the probate court for instruction.

The probate court held that the devise to Dr. Hunt called for 6,000 shares of the no par stock, together with dividends received upon the 6,000 shares by the executors after the testatrix' death. On appeal by the residuary devisees, the Supreme Court of Michigan affirmed the decision of the probate court, saying in part:

> If the legacy is general, then the legatee takes 1,200 shares of the no par stock and may not participate in any accruals thereon during the course of administration. If the legacy is specific, then the legatee takes 6,000 shares of the no par stock, with all accruals since the death of testatrix. . . .
>
> Upon the question of whether the legacy is specific or general there exist certain general rules all, however, recognizing that the intention of the maker, found in any part of the will or reasonably deducible from the instrument, considered as a whole, must govern construction. . . .
>
> In the forty-second paragraph of the will testatrix declared:
>
>> It is my express wish and desire that all of the above legacies and trust funds shall, as far as possible, be paid in stocks and bonds or other property which I may own at the time of my death.
>
> This expression of purpose is referable to every provision in the will and to the bequest to Dr. Hunt, and discloses that in making the bequest to Dr. Hunt, she intended to give shares of stock then owned by her. In many other paragraphs of the will testatrix gave to the executors, in the capacity of trustees, stocks and bonds to carry out many special trust benefactions therein mentioned. . . .
>
> We think the will, considered as a whole, shows it was the intention of testatrix to constitute her bequest in favor of Dr. Hunt a specific legacy. We think the provisions of the will individualized the shares of stock bequeathed to Dr. Hunt as stock then owned by the testatrix. This brings us to the question of whether there was an ademption by reason of exchange of par value shares of stock for no par value shares. The stock was changed in name and form only and at all times remained substantially the same thing. . . .
>
> There was no ademption accomplished by taking 5 shares of no par stock for each share of par value stock. Testatrix did not initiate the change in form of the shares of stock; the change occurred in consequence of corporate action which she could not control. . . . Dividends, subsequent to death of a testator, on specific legacies of shares of stock, follow the stock.

Fitch's Will, 281 App. Div. 65, 118 N.Y.S.2d 234 (1952), is an example of a case of how far courts will go to allow the devisee of corporate shares to enjoy the advantage of any stock splits. A will contained a devise of 115 "shares of U.S. Steel Co. common stock." The testator owned 115 shares of U.S. Steel when the will was made, but later sold the stock and owned none at his death. After this sale, but before his death, United States Steel Corporation issued three shares of common stock in exchange for each share of the old stock.

The court held that the devise was general, so that there was no ademption. The administrator was ordered to deliver to the devisee "three shares of common stock for each one stated in the will," on the theory that it was "the intent of the testator to bequeath Steel common stock equivalent to the stock that existed when he made his will." The court was not moved by the argument that this "in effect seems to regard the legacies as general legacies for the purpose of avoiding their loss by ademption, but . . . as specific legacies for the purpose of replacing the stock. . . ." Accord, e.g., McFerren's Estate, 365 Pa. 490, 76 A.2d 759, 22 A.L.R.2d 451 (1950).

Bostwick v. Hurstel, below, establishes new precedent by abandoning the specific-general distinction to determine who receives the benefits of stock splits.

Bostwick v. Hurstel
364 Mass. 282, 304 N.E.2d 186 (1973)

QUIRICO, J. This is an appeal by James Bostwick (Bostwick), executor and legatee under the will of Cecile Bostwick (the testatrix), from a decree of the Probate Court to the effect that a bequest in the testatrix's will of twenty-five shares of American Telephone and Telegraph Company (A.T. & T.) common stock to Bostwick was general and not specific, and disallowing a distribution to him of 125 additional shares of A.T. & T. stock resulting from two stock splits. The respondents are two nephews and a niece of the testatrix to whom she bequeathed all her remaining shares of the A.T. & T. stock not included in the bequest to Bostwick.

The will was executed on April 13, 1957. Clause First bequeathed to Bostwick "twenty-five (25) shares of stock in . . . (A.T. & T.) and also all household furniture and furnishings owned by me at the time of my death." Clause Second bequeathed to the respondent nephews and niece "all remaining shares of stock in . . . (A.T. & T.), which I may own at the time of my decease and which is not hereinbefore bequeathed under the First Paragraph of this Will." Clause Nineteenth of the will provides that if assets of the estate which have not been specifically bequeathed or devised under the will are insufficient to pay the debts, expenses of administration and taxes, a bank account specifically bequeathed may first be used, and if that is insufficient then the executors may sell as many shares of A.T. & T. stock as may be necessary, "but such sale of stock shall not affect the specific legacy contained in the First Clause of this Will."

The testatrix died on November 25, 1965, and Bostwick was appointed executor of her will on January 18, 1966. In February, 1966, Bostwick transferred 150 shares of A.T. & T. stock to himself individually, and 1,135 shares to himself as executor. . . .

The primary question raised in this case is whether Bostwick is entitled to the 125 shares of A.T. & T. stock he transferred to himself over and above the twenty-five shares bequeathed to him in the will. . . .

[T]his court has traditionally approached the question whether legatees should benefit from stock splits [as follows]: we have first determined whether the testamentary gift . . . in the will was general or specific, and then applied the result thought to follow automatically from the chosen label. If the bequest was found to be general, indicating that the testator did not have in mind particular property of his own at the time he executed his will, the legatee has only received the exact number of shares specified in the will; if, on the other hand, it was found that the testator intended to separate out and bequeath particular shares then in his possession, the bequest was termed specific and the legatee received the specified shares as well as the accretions created by the stock split. . . .

The approach . . . of first labeling the gift as general or specific and then applying the seemingly automatic consequences is the one we have used in all our . . . cases concerned with shares created by stock splits. . . . It is an approach used frequently in other situations involving the disposition of stock, such as where the ademption of a legacy is involved . . . , or where the court has considered the problem of contribution among legatees to satisfy bequests . . . , or the question of the proper distribution of income earned on bequeathed property during administration . . . .

. . . However, we feel that the problems created by the use of the distinction between general and specific legacies in the stock split situation far outweigh any advantages it might have.

The two principal difficulties with the general versus specific classification approach are that it fails to consider the testator's intent with specific reference to the additional shares created by a stock split and that it also fails to recognize the basic nature of a stock split. As was stated by the Supreme Court of Rhode Island in a case involving the same issue we consider here, "It is readily apparent from an understanding of the basic elementary principles of corporate security law that a change in the number of shares of stock attributable to a split in the stock of the corporation occurring, as it does here, between the execution of the will and the death of the testator should be considered one of form and not substance. . . . A stock split in no way alters the substance of the testator's total interest or rights in the corporation. . . . [It] is merely a dividing up of the outstanding shares of a corporation into a greater number of units without disturbing the stockholder's original proportional participating interest in the corporation." Egavian v. Egavian, 102 R.I. 740, 746, 232 A.2d 789, 793 (1967). . . . It seems to us that the adoption of a different rule comporting more with corporate realities and a testator's intent would be timely and beneficial.

[I]n Egavian v. Egavian, supra, the Rhode Island court stated it believed the distinctions between general and specific gifts were "unnecessary and inappropriate in cases involving stock splits." 102 R.I. at 745, 232 A.2d at 792. . . . [The court in that case concluded:]

> Whereas it has in the past been generally held that a legatee receives the surplus shares of stock split only if the testator is deemed to have specifically bequeathed the stock in question, today we . . . hold that it is presumed that the prime intent of the testator is that the legatee is to benefit from any increased shares coming by way of a stock split provided no contrary intent is evident in the will. 102 R.I. at 747-748, 232 A.2d at 794. . . .

We think that the rule set forth in the Rhode Island . . . and similar decisions . . . reflects a far more realistic approach to the problem of distributing additional shares created by stock splits than the general versus specific bequest distinction which we have heretofore followed. The rule is based on the sound premise that . . . the additional shares created by a stock split merely indicate a change in form, with the stockholder's proportionate interest or ownership in the corporation, his rights to dividends and rights upon dissolution remaining the same. Furthermore, we believe the rule comports more often with a testator's intent regarding such additional shares than is true of our gift classification approach. As observed by several courts, in most cases the probable intent of the testator is to give a legatee the proportion of ownership in a corporation represented by the shares bequeathed on the date of the will's execution, since any other interpretation would mean the testator intended to subject his bequest to change or even negation by subsequent corporate actions over which he probably had little or no control. . . . Finally, it seems that the rule would obviate the necessity for continuously litigating the question whether a particular bequest of stock is general or specific when stock splits are involved, since the rule does not call initially for a determination of fact.

On the strength of the foregoing reasons, we today adopt the rule established in Egavian v. Egavian, 102 R.I. 740, 747-48, 232 A.2d 789 (1967) . . . , and hold that, in the absence of anything manifesting a contrary intent, a legatee of a bequest of stock is entitled to the additional shares received by a testator as a result of a stock split occurring in the interval between the execution of his will and his death.[9]

Our holding does not indicate that we have abandoned the classification of bequests as general or specific for all purposes. We have no occasion at this time to express any opinion on the continuing validity of

---

9. Stock dividends which a testator receives on shares he has previously bequeathed in his will raise questions about distribution similar to those we have discussed in relation to shares created by stock splits. While it is indicated that many courts considering stock dividends in this situation have ruled that they will not pass to the named legatee, see annotation, 46 A.L.R.3d 7, 64-86; Note, 36 Albany L. Rev. 182, 188-92 (1971), the issue of the proper distribution of stock dividends is not before us in this case and we therefore express no opinion on the question.

such distinctions in those cases where abatement or ademption of the legacy is at issue, or where the court is asked to determine the proper order of distribution when the estate is inadequate to satisfy all bequests. . . .

Applying the rule adopted to the facts of the case before us we hold that Bostwick is entitled to the 125 shares in addition to the twenty-five bequeathed. . . .

This case is remanded to the Probate Court for the entry of a decree declaring that under Clause First of the [testator's] will, James Bostwick, legatee, is entitled to 150 shares of stock in the American Telephone and Telegraph Company, and to all dividends received on such 150 shares since the death of the testatrix.

So ordered.

TAURO, C.J., BRAUCHER, KAPLAN, and WILKINS, JJ., concur.

Notes

1. *1990 Uniform Probate Code.* UPC section 2-605 (1990) basically adopts the Massachusetts rule as held in *Bostwick,* which is also now codified in Massachusetts. See Mass. Gen. Law c. 191, § 1A(4).

2. *Stock Dividends.* A stock dividend is a distribution to existing shareholders of stock in lieu of a cash dividend. Usually, stock dividends are distributed from a corporation's own authorized but unissued shares. Sometimes, however, stock dividends are distributed from shares in the stock of other firms that the corporation owns. Courts have had difficulty determining who should receive shares obtained as a result of a stock dividend.

As a first step in examining this question, we need first to note the distinction that courts draw between increases in the market value of stocks and cash dividends. Suppose that a testator devises 100 shares of General Electric stock to A and the residue of her estate to B. At the time of execution, the shares were worth $5,000. Suppose further that General Electric had issued cash dividends to the testator totalling $1,000 between the time the testator executed the will and died and, at the time of testator's death, the market value of the shares increased to $7,500. Under well established principles, if the devise to A is treated as specific, A is entitled to the benefit of the increase in the capital value of the stock but not to the cash dividends, even if they can be traced. The law of devises regards increases in the capital value of stock as part of the asset, but views a cash dividend as a property interest distinct from the underlying asset. Any remaining cash from the dividend will pass to B, the residuary devisee.

The more troublesome question concerns stock dividends. Again, the choice will usually be between the devisee of the stock or the residuary devisee. Both the pre-1990 and 1990 versions of the UPC treat stock dividends the same as stock splits, giving the benefit to the stock devisee. Pre-1990 UPC § 2-607(a)(2); 1990 UPC § 2-605(a)(1). This approach maintains the devisee's percentage of ownership in the issuing firm. The majority of the decisions, however, appear to treat stock dividends the same as cash dividends, denying the benefit of the stock dividend accession to the stock devisee. See Note, 36 Albany L. Rev. 182, 188-92 (1971); Annot., 46 A.L.R.3d 7 (1972). The usual rationale for the majority view is that since stock and cash dividends, but not stock splits, are paid out of the firm's earned surplus (sometimes called "retained earnings"), they should be treated as income on the underlying capital asset rather than as part of the asset itself.

How accessions of stock occurring through splits or dividends should be sorted out depends on what we assume to be the thinking of testators who devise stock. It would seem to be most likely that a testator considers all stock received (other than shares obtained by a post-execution purchase) to be part of the devise. By providing that all stock received by way of stock split or dividend pass to the devisee of the stock, section 2-605 of the 1990 UPC establishes a rule that reflects probable intent.

3. Abatement

Statutory References: *1990 UPC §§ 3-902, -916*

Suppose a will leaves "my antique desk to A, $10,000 to B, $5,000 to C, and the residue of my estate to D." The testator dies owning the antique desk and net assets of $20,000, consisting of stocks and bonds. Because all the provisions of the will can be satisfied leaving a residue of $5,000 for D, there is no problem of funding the specific and general devises.

But if the net assets apart from the antique desk are worth only $10,000, a question arises about how to distribute the decedent's estate. The different systems of reducing the devises, referred to as "abatement" systems, are the subject of this Section. In the absence of a will provision providing for an order of abatement, the default rule of abatement statutes and judge-made law control. As with the doctrine of ademption, the common-law doctrine of abatement turns on classification of the gifts. Under the usual common-law rules, the residuary devisee will take nothing and there will be a pro rata reduction of the general devises to B and C. The devise of the antique desk is specific and abates last, so that A will get the desk unless its sale is necessary to pay debts or expenses of administration. If the will also contained a demonstrative devise, this would be treated as specific for purposes of abatement. See Atkinson on Wills § 136.

Land. The estate included no land in the above example. Abatement may become more complicated when land is involved. At common law, title to personal property passed on the testator's death to the personal representative, but title to land went directly to the devisee. Unless the will provided otherwise, land could not be reached to satisfy the decedent's debts, unless the creditor had a claim secured by a lien on the land. The common-law rules concerning passage of title have persisted to this day, but land is now subject to the decedent's debts. In some states, however, all the personal property abates before any land. In some others, personal property devised in the residuary abates before land devised in the residuary and specifically devised personal property abates before specifically devised land. The UPC eliminates any distinction between real and personal property. See UPC §§ 1-201(10), (39), 3-902 (1990).

Devisees. Many states have statutes covering some or all of the problems of abatement, but they vary considerably in their treatment of the problem. See L. Simes & P. Basye, Model Probate Code 353 (1946) (providing statutory analysis). Some, for example, give priority to specific devises to certain relatives over specific devises to others.[10]

Estate Taxes. Under the federal estate tax, the taxable estate may include nonprobate property. Examples include life insurance and property the decedent gratuitously transferred reserving a life estate. See infra Chapter 6. The position usually taken in the earlier cases followed the "burden on the residue" rule, under which the burden of the estate taxes on nonprobate property was borne by the probate assets.[11] In recent years, a significant number of courts have held that there should be an "equitable apportionment," so as to place a proportionate part of the estate tax burden on nonprobate assets. That is to say, assets not forming a part of the decedent's probate estate but nevertheless includable in her or his taxable estate abate proportionally to pay the federal estate tax liability owed by

---

10. See, e.g., 20 Pa. Cons. Stat. Ann. § 3541. The statute was applied in Estate of Bestwick, 493 Pa. 341, 426 A.2d 580 (1981). The testator's will made devises of 100 shares of "my" Sears and Roebuck stock to his sister, of 100 shares of "my" stock in the same company to his niece, and of 200 shares of "my" stock in the same company to his daughter. At the time of his death, the testator owned only 200 shares of Sears and Roebuck stock. The court construed the devises to be specific and so subject to ademption, but held that the daughter was entitled to all 200 shares of the stock, invoking the Pennsylvania statute, which declares:

> (a) General Rules. Except as otherwise provided by the will, if the assets are insufficient to pay all claimants and distributes in full, the shares of distributees, without distinction between real and personal estate, shall have priority of distribution in the following order:
> (1) Property specifically devised or bequeathed to or for the benefit of the surviving spouse.
> (2) Property specifically devised or bequeathed to or for the benefit of the decedent's issue.
> (3) Property specifically devised or bequeathed to or for the benefit of other distributees.
> (4) Property disposed of by will in the form of a general bequest of cash, stocks or bonds.
> (5) Property disposed of by general devise or bequest and not included in a residuary clause.
> (6) Property devised or bequeathed in a residuary clause.
> (7) Property not disposed of by the will.

11. See, e.g., Ericson v. Childs, 124 Conn. 66, 198 A. 176, 115 A.L.R. 907 (1938); Bemis v. Converse, 246 Mass. 131, 140 N.E. 686 (1923); Fleming, Apportionment of Federal Estate Taxes, 43 Ill. L. Rev. 153, 159 (1948); Sutter, Apportionment of Federal Estate Tax in the Absence of Statute or an Expression of Intention, 51 Mich. L. Rev. 53 (1952).

the estate.[12] Legislation providing for a similar apportionment was enacted in 1930 in New York, and is now in force in about one-half of the states.[13]

The typical provision in the apportionment statutes is similar to that contained in the Uniform Estate Tax Apportionment Act, which is incorporated in UPC section 3-916 (1990). It apportions the burden among all recipients of property, whether probate or nonprobate, included in the taxable estate. The Act provides for an apportionment among those who take probate assets, instead of placing the whole burden on the residuary estate where the decedent dies testate. This goes beyond the decisions favoring an equitable apportionment among nonprobate assets. Do you think treating probate and nonprobate assets alike for purposes of discharging the estate tax liability is likely to coincide with most testators' intent? See Powell, Ultimate Liability for Federal Estate Taxes, 1958 Wash. U. L.Q. 327, criticizing the scope of some of the equitable-apportionment statutes.

Should nonprobate assets also be available to pay debts of the estate other than estate tax liability? Generally, the law requires the probate assets first to bear the burden of the estate's debts. Unsecured estate creditors are allowed to reach some types of nonprobate assets, but typically they can do so only if the probate assets are insufficient. Creditors' rights to nonprobate assets are considered in Chapter 7.

4. Ademption By Satisfaction

Statutory References: *1990 UPC § 2-609*
Pre-1990 UPC § 2-612

If a testator makes a lifetime gift to a devisee, that gift might be treated as satisfying the devise, in whole or in part. The doctrine of satisfaction essentially provides for the situation in which the testator decides to change the timing of a gift to permit the beneficiary to enjoy the gift before the testator's death. It is analogous to the doctrine of advancements that applies to lifetime gifts made by decedents who die intestate. See supra p. 155.

---

12. See, e.g., Estate of Gowling, 82 Ill. 2d 15, 411 N.E.2d 266 (1980) (testate estate); Roe v. Farrell, 69 Ill. 2d 525, 372 N.E.2d 662 (1978) (intestate estate); Kintzinger v. Millin, 254 Iowa 173, 117 N.W.2d 68 (1962); Sebree v. Rosen, 349 S.W.2d 865, 884 (Mo. 1961); Beatty v. Cake, 236 Or. 498, 387 P.2d 355 (1963), rehearing denied 236 Or. 498, 390 P.2d 176 (1964); Industrial Trust Co. v. Budlong, 77 R.I. 428, 76 A.2d 600 (1950). Other cases are cited in Kahn, The Federal Estate Tax Burden Borne by a Dissenting Widow, 64 Mich. L. Rev. 1499, 1506 (1966). See also Minan, The Allocation of Estate Taxes by Judicial Rule: A Case for Reform, 38 Ohio St. L.J. 539 (1977); Note, 1979 U. Ill. L. F. 703.

13. See Kahn, supra note 12, at 1505; Mitnick, State Legislative Apportionment of Federal Estate Taxes, 10 Md. L. Rev. 289 (1949); Scoles & Stephens, The Proposed Uniform Estate Tax Apportionment Act, 43 Minn. L. Rev. 907 (1959).

When the doctrine of satisfaction is applied, the distribution of the property owned at death is not made in accordance with the literal terms of the will. However, if we consider the subject of the gift *as if* it were a part of the distributable estate, then the will can be said to be enforced as written. It is *as if* part of the decedent's estate had been distributed pursuant to the terms of the will in advance of the testator's death. The words "as if" need to be emphasized, because the property given is not treated as part of the estate for other purposes. For example, it is not subject to the claims of creditors of the estate.

Writing. In contrast to advancements, the satisfaction doctrine was not the subject of widespread statutory enactment. In the nineteenth century, a handful of states adopted a writing requirement to prove a satisfaction. Pre-1990 UPC section 2-612 is modeled upon these provisions. Over twenty states presently impose a writing requirement. A writing requirement avoids difficult factual inquiries about whether the testator intended a lifetime gift to be taken into account in distributing the estate. The writing requirement may be satisfied by a provision in the will expressly providing for lifetime advances. An attorney should raise this issue with the client and provide expressly whether lifetime gifts should or should not be taken into account for purposes of distributing the estate. Any other document written by the testator contemporaneously with the gift also qualifies. A satisfaction can also be proven by a writing in which the devisee acknowledges that the gift is in whole or in part satisfaction of a devise.

The 1990 UPC statutory provision concerning satisfaction closely resembles the pre-1990 version, with one exception. It allows the testator to make a gift in satisfaction of a devise to a person other than the devisee. The statutory change is a recognition that testators may want to reduce or eliminate a devise when they make gifts to family members of a devisee. See UPC § 2-609 (1990), comment.

Specific Devise. A lifetime gift can satisfy a specific devise. If the testator makes a lifetime gift of the devised property, the doctrine of ademption applies and no writing is necessary. If the testator makes a lifetime gift of different property, the application of the satisfaction doctrine under both the pre-1990 and 1990 UPC versions depends upon whether the gift was accompanied by a writing. Other than the writing requirement, this is not a change from the common law. The common law recognized that the doctrine could apply even if the nature of the lifetime gift differed significantly from the nature of the devise. In some jurisdictions, however, a substantial difference between the subject matter of the lifetime gift and the devise raises a presumption that the testator did not intend to make a satisfaction. See, e.g., Dugan v. Hollins, 4 Md. Ch. 139 (1853); Scholze v. Scholze, 2 Tenn. App. 80 (1925).

Land. Although the pre-1990 and 1990 UPC and non-UPC statutes eliminate any distinction under the satisfaction doctrine between devises of real and personal property, that was not the early rule. Historically, satisfaction has not been applied to devises of land. If the testator's will devised Blackacre to A and thereafter the testator conveyed the land to B, the courts treated the transfer as a revocation of the devise. They did this even though it could have been regarded as an ademption by extinction. If the testator retained Blackacre, but gave other property to A, intending this as a satisfaction of the devise, this transfer also was regarded as an attempted revocation. When the second situation came before the English courts after the passage of the Statute of Frauds of 1677, which prescribed the methods of revocation, the English courts held that this was not a permitted method and hence was ineffective.[14] See Davys v. Boucher, 2 Y. & C. Ex. 397, 160 Eng. Rep. 757 (1839). Older American cases took the same view: The question was decided, that is, by putting the transaction into the category of an attempted revocation of the devise, instead of an attempted satisfaction of the devise. See, e.g., Burnham v. Comfort, 108 N.Y. 535, 15 N.E. 710, 2 Am. St. Rep. 462 (1888). Whether these older cases would still be followed today is problematical.

Partial Satisfaction. At an early time, a gift of an amount less than the amount of a devise was presumed to have been intended to satisfy the whole devise. The theory was that the testator viewed the gift as a substitute for the devise. This rule is no longer followed. In the absence of evidence that the testator intended a satisfaction in whole, courts now hold that a gift of a part of a devise is a pro tanto satisfaction only.

Pre-1990 UPC section 2-612 and 1990 UPC section 2-609 explicitly address the question of partial satisfaction. Both expressly refer to partial satisfactions when establishing the writing requirement and both provide that for purposes of a partial satisfaction, the lifetime gift of property should be valued when the devisee obtains possession or when the testator dies, whichever occurs first.

EXTERNAL REFERENCE. Barstow, Ademption by Satisfaction, 6 Wis. L. Rev. 217 (1931); Annot., 26 A.L.R.2d 9 (1952).

---

14. One curious aspect of the matter is that after the Statute of Frauds, the court continued to treat an inter-vivos conveyance of devised land as a revocation. Brydges v. Chandos, 2 Ves. Jr. 417, 30 Eng. Rep. 702 (1794). In most instances, theory made no difference, because, regardless of theory, the will could not operate to dispose of land not owned by the testator at her or his death. In some situations, however, theory became important. For example, where the testator conveyed the devised land and later reacquired it so that it was a part of the estate at death, a revocation theory means the will fails to dispose of the land. The holdings that the devise was ineffective in such circumstances could have been put on the ground that a will could not dispose of after-acquired land, so long as that doctrine prevailed. In fact, they were put on the ground of revocation. See, e.g., Grant v. Bridges, L.R. 3 Eq. 347 (1866). With the disappearance of the after-acquired property doctrine, it is vital today in the case of reacquisition to know whether the early rule of revocation by alienation remains good law. Most decisions have rejected it and have held that the reacquired land passes under the devise, but occasional cases still on the books adhere to the older law. See, e.g., Phillippe v. Clevenger, 239 Ill. 117, 87 N.E. 858 (1909); Note, 34 Mich. L. Rev. 1272 (1936).

PART B. POST-EXECUTION CHANGES RELATING TO PERSONS—LAPSE AND ANTILAPSE

Statutory References: *1990 UPC §§ 2-601, -603 to -604, -702*
Pre-1990 UPC §§ 2-601, -603, -605, -606

What happens to a devise if the devisee predeceases the testator? The short answer is that the devise "lapses" (fails). This is because a will transfers property when the testator dies, not when the will was executed, and because property can only be transferred to a living person. All devises, then, are automatically and by law conditioned on survivorship of the testator. A devise fails (lapses) if the devisee predeceases the testator.

120-Hour Requirement of Survivorship. Although at common law, survivorship by only an instant prevents lapse, pre-1990 UPC section 2-601 introduced a 120-hour requirement of survivorship for wills. UPC section 2-702 (1990) extends the 120-hour requirement to all "governing instruments" (as defined in section 1-201).

In Estate of Kerlee, 98 Idaho 5, 557 P.2d 599, 88 A.L.R.3d 1331 (1976), the court held that pre-1990 UPC section 2-601 did not apply to a will that devised property to the testator's sister and provided that "if [she] does not survive me" the property was to go to the North Idaho Children's Home. The testator's sister survived him by 74 hours. The court held that the devise in favor of the testator's sister did not lapse because pre-1990 section 2-601 states that its 120-hour requirement of survivorship is nullified by language in the will "requiring that the devisee survive the testator." See also Estate of Acord, 91-2 USTC ¶ 60,090 (9th Cir. 1991) (the 120-hour rule was nullified by a provision dealing with simultaneous deaths, resulting in the devisee's estate incurring an additional $150,000 in estate taxes). Though unnecessary because of the law-imposed requirement of survivorship, will forms commonly attach boilerplate language of survivorship to devises. How would *Kerlee* be decided under UPC section 2-702 (1990)?

Devolution of a Lapsed Devise. If a devise lapses, what happens to it? In the absence of an applicable antilapse statute and in the absence of an expressly designated alternative taker, lapsed devises devolve in accordance with the following rules.

Lapse of a nonresiduary devise. Where lapse occurs in some part of the will other than the residuary clause, the judicial rule is uniform that lapsed devises of personal property pass to the decedent's residuary devisees. Under early common law, this rule was not followed for land. The view that a will could not dispose of after-acquired land was thought to prevent the residuary clause from passing lapsed nonresiduary devises of land. Thus, they bypassed the residuary clause and passed to the decedent's heirs. Many states have enacted legislation that usually causes real as well as personal property to pass under the residuary clause. A few statutes, however, preserve the common-law rule for land and in at least one state,

Kentucky, the statute provides that personal property also passes by intestacy "unless a contrary intent appears from the will." Ky. Rev. Stat. § 394.500.

Lapse in the residuary. When the residuary devisee predeceases the testator, the residue becomes intestate property. If the residuary clause is in favor of more than one person, and if that clause does not create a class gift,[15] the conventional view is that the death of one or more, but not all, of the residuary devisees before the death of the testator causes an intestacy as to the share intended for the deceased devisee. As the judges follow the rule, they sometimes express dissatisfaction with it. For example, in In re Dunster, [1909] 1 Ch. 103, the court said: "I think the effect of [the rule] is to defeat the testator's intention in almost every case in which it is applied."

A number of decisions have departed from the conventional view and have held that the lapsed share goes to the other residuary devisees, if there are others who survive. See, e.g., Estate of Jackson, 106 Ariz. 82, 471 P.2d 278 (1970); Corbett v. Skaggs, 111 Kan. 380, 207 P. 819 (1922); Niemann v. Zacharias, 185 Neb. 450, 176 N.W.2d 671 (1970); Frolich Estate, 112 N.H. 320, 295 A.2d 448 (1972); Commerce Nat'l Bank v. Browning, 158 Ohio St. 54, 107 N.E.2d 120 (1952); Slack Trust, 126 Vt. 37, 220 A.2d 472 (1966). Other courts, however, have held to the conventional view. See, e.g., Estate of Levy, 415 P.2d 1006 (Okla. 1966); Swearingen v. Giles, 565 S.W.2d 574 (Tex. Civ. App. 1978); Estate of Mory, 29 Wis. 2d 557, 139 N.W.2d 623 (1966).

The pre-1990 and 1990 versions of the UPC are aligned with the trend away from the conventional view. Pre-1990 UPC § 2-606(b); 1990 UPC § 2-604(b).

Estate of Griffen
86 Wash. 2d 223, 543 P.2d 245 (1975)

RoSELLINI, A.J. The will of Kizzie Belle Griffen declared that she was a widow having no child or issue, included one specific bequest to her friend, Mary Hoppe, "provided she survives me," named her stepdaughter, Willa Baughman, as executrix of her estate, and named her attorney alternate executor in the event Willa Baughman should predecease her or be unable or unwilling to serve.

The residue of her estate was disposed of in the following paragraph:

> I do give, devise and bequeath all of the rest, residue and remainder of my estate, wheresoever situated, possessed or owned by me at the time of my death, with all the remainder and remainders, reversion and reversions, together with the appurtenances thereunto belonging, unto my step-daughter, WILLA BAUGHMAN, of Bridgeport, Washington, to have to hold the same unto herself and her heirs forever.

---

15. The different treatment of class gifts is discussed infra p. 343.

The will made no mention of any of the testatrix' heirs at law, all of whom were collateral.

The stepdaughter predeceased the testatrix, leaving as her sole heir an adopted daughter. . . .

It is undoubtedly the general rule that the words "and his heirs" attached to a testamentary gift are words of limitation and not of purchase, and that such a devise or bequest lapses upon the death of the devisee or legatee in the lifetime of the testator, unless an intention on the part of the testator that such words shall effect a substitutionary gift appears from the will itself. See the cases cited in Annots., Devise or bequest to one "or his heirs" or one "and his heirs" as affected by death of person named before death of testator, 128 A.L.R. 94 (1940) and 78 A.L.R. 992 (1932). As the annotations explain, this doctrine had its origin in the technical rule requiring a mention of heirs to pass a fee simple to real property. That rule has long been abolished by statute in most jurisdictions.

Since words of inheritance are no longer needed to convey a fee simple title, it has been argued that where such words are used, they are used for a different purpose, namely, to express an intent that the heirs of the named beneficiary shall take in the event he predeceases the testator. However, the courts have generally rejected this theory, reasoning that lawyers continue to use these words for the purpose of describing the estate, even though it is no longer necessary to do so.

The presumption that the testator intended only to describe the estate and not to express an intent that the heirs of the named beneficiary should take the devise or bequest in the event of the beneficiary's predeceasing him, is not conclusive, however. Where it can be ascertained from the four corners of the will that it was intended that the gift go to the heirs of the named beneficiary under such circumstances, that intent will be given effect. Estate of Hoermann, 234 Wis. 130, 290 N.W. 608 (1940); Estate of Britt, 249 Wis. 30, 23 N.W.2d 498 (1946);[16] Estate of Newby, 146 Colo. 296, 361 P.2d 622 (1961) (recognizing the rule); 6 Bowe-Parker, Page on Wills § 50.8 at 75 (1962); G. Thompson, Law of Wills § 493 (1947, Supp.1962); Annots., 128 A.L.R. Supra at 95, 99; 78 A.L.R. supra at 994, 1004. . . .

Our research has uncovered only one case decided in Washington which construes words of inheritance used in a will or trust. In that case, Shufeldt v. Shufeldt, 130 Wash. 253, 227 P. 6 (1924), the testator had set up a trust and provided that upon a named event the trustee should convey a portion of the trust property to his son-in-law, "his heirs and assigns forever." The son-in-law died before the happening of the event upon which distribution was ordered, and the residuary legatee contended that the gift had lapsed and fallen into the residue. The question was whether, under the will, the son-in-law took a vested or a contingent remainder.

---

16. Another Wisconsin decision reaching the same result is Estate of Mangel, 51 Wis. 2d 55, 186 N.W.2d 276 (1971). Eds.

Observing the rule that the court must give effect to the intent of the testator if it can be gathered from the will, the court quoted from Leeming v. Sherratt, 2 Hare 14, 3 Bro.C.C. 473:

> The question in all the cases has been, whether the testator intended it as a condition precedent that the legatees should survive the time appointed by him for the payment of their legacies, and the answer to this question has been sought for out of the whole will, and not in particular expressions.

Shufeldt v. Shufeldt, 130 Wash. at 259, 227 P. at 8.

This court held that the words "to him, his heirs and assigns forever," as used in the will, indicated an intention to devise a definite and certain estate to the son-in-law, which passed to his heirs upon his death before the date of distribution. It recognized the efficacy of the principle that words of art will not be given their ordinary legal import if the will read as a whole indicates that this was not the meaning intended.

That case differed from this in this respect: There the son-in-law survived the testator but did not live to receive distribution of the trust estate. However, essentially the same question appears in both cases—that is, Did the testator . . . manifest an intent that the heirs of the legatee should receive the bequest as substitute beneficiaries? . . .

We think the [correct construction is] that the testatrix was aware not only of the possibility that a legatee might predecease her, but specifically of the possibility that Willa Baughman might predecease her, for she provided that in that event an alternate executor should administer her estate; furthermore, . . . the specific bequest to Mary Hoppe was expressly contingent upon her surviving the testatrix, while the devise to Willa Baughman was not; finally, . . . the heirs of Willa Baughman were mentioned in the will, while the heirs of the testatrix were ignored.

No reasonable construction of this simple will could lead to the conclusion that the testatrix was unaware of the possibility that she might outlive the named residuary legatee or that she intended in any event to benefit her heirs at law. It is obvious that her affections were centered upon her stepdaughter, and that she desired her estate to go to the stepdaughter's heirs in the event she predeceased the testatrix, just as it would have gone to her natural grandchildren had Willa Baughman been her natural daughter. . . .

As the attorney who drafted the will is undoubtedly now aware, the better practice is to avoid such possible ambiguities as that which appears in the residuary clause by expressly providing that the heirs shall take the legacy in the event the named legatee should predecease the testator. We have no doubt that this is the general practice, since, insofar as we have been able to ascertain, the question has come to this court only twice in its history.

The judgment of the Court of Appeals is affirmed.

STAFFORD, C.J., and FINLEY, HUNTER, HAMILTON, WRIGHT, UTTER, BRACHTEN-BACH and HOROWITZ, JJ., concur.

Notes and Questions

1. *State of the Authorities.* The predominant view is contrary to *Griffen*. In Forester v. Marler, 31 N.C. App. 84, 228 S.E.2d 646 (1976), the testator's will devised all of his property "unto my brother, Jack Freeman, absolutely and in fee simple forever." Jack predeceased the testator by four months. The court held that the testator's estate passed by intestacy, saying that the words "absolutely and in fee simple forever" are

> technical words which define the quantum and quality of the estate granted. They do not indicate an intention that the property affected should remain in the family of Jack Freeman in event he should predecease the testator.

Accord, e.g., Niemann v. Zacharias, 185 Neb. 450, 176 N.W.2d 671 (1970).

2. *Uniform Probate Code.* How would the *Griffen* case have been resolved if it had been governed by UPC section 2-603 (1990)?

3. *Remainder Interest to a Named Person "and Her/His Heirs" vs. Outright Devise.* In *Griffen*, Associate Justice Rosellini said that the *Shufeldt* case raised "essentially the same question" as the one raised by *Griffen*. Do you agree? Suppose Willa (in *Griffen*) had left a valid will devising her estate to persons who were not her heirs. Would they be the appropriate takers according to *Griffen*? Suppose the son-in-law in *Shufeldt* had left a valid will devising his entire estate to persons who were not his heirs. Would they be the appropriate takers?

4. *"Per Stirpes" as Creating an Alternative Devise.* In Richland Trust Co. v. Becvar, 44 Ohio St. 2d 219, 339 N.E.2d 830 (1975), the testatrix devised one-seventh of her residuary estate "to Louise Hummel, per stirpes." Louise predeceased the testatrix by some nine months, leaving no surviving husband, no parents, and no issue. Her heirs were four sisters and the son of a deceased brother. The court held:

> In its technical meaning, "per stirpes" generally relates to the mode of distribution. That is, it refers not to who shall take, but to the manner in which those who shall take come within the class entitled to take. Kraemer v. Hook (1958), 168 Ohio St. 221, 152 N.E.2d 430. However, in the present case, the manner of distribution is expressed, but the class to which that distribution is to be made is not expressed. Nonetheless, it is clear to this court that the testatrix intended a gift to secondary takers in the event that the primary taker, Louise Hummel, did not survive the testatrix. . . . In the absence of an express designation of the class of secondary takers, the class will be assumed to be the heirs at law of the named person, as determined by the statutes of descent and distribution.

See also Restatement 2d of Property § 25.1 comment i, illustration 14. In Estate of Walters, 519 N.E.2d 1270 (Ind. Ct. App. 1988), however, the court held that a residuary devise "to my beloved wife, Jessie E. Walters, per stirpes" lapsed when she predeceased the testator, causing the residue to pass by intestate succession to his children by a former marriage. The claim of her children by a former marriage that the phrase "per stirpes" created a substitutional devise to them was rejected, the court saying:

"There is nothing in the will to indicate that the testator intended to disinherit his own children in favor of stepchildren."[17]

***

Antilapse Statutes. Almost all jurisdictions have antilapse statutes.[18] The "antilapse" label, however, is somewhat misleading. Strictly speaking, antilapse statutes (other than in Maryland and perhaps Iowa) do not reverse the common-law rule of lapse. They do not abrogate the law-imposed condition of survivorship so that devised property passes to the estates of predeceasing devisees. Antilapse statutes leave the law-imposed condition of survivorship intact, but modify the devolution of lapsed devises by providing a statutory substitute gift. The statutory substitute gift is usually to the devisee's descendants who survive the testator.[19]

Antilapse statutes are remedial in nature, tending to preserve equality of treatment among different lines of succession. The statutes commonly provide that the substitute gift takes effect unless a contrary intention is demonstrated. See pre-1990 UPC § 2-603; UPC § 2-601 (1990). What language suffices to make a jurisdiction's antilapse statute inapplicable has been the source of some controversy, as we will see in Detzel v. Nieberding, below.

The statutes were enacted in the belief that the statutory substitute gift for which they make provision is one the testator probably would have made had she or he thought about the matter. At the least, the substitute gifts are thought to produce a result closer to the testator's probable intention than the disposition that results under the common-law doctrine of lapse.

As the chart infra p. 348 makes clear, the antilapse statutes of most jurisdictions apply only to certain classes of devisees—relatives[20] or specified relatives of the testator. Very few statutes apply to any devisee who predeceases the testator leaving descendants who survive the testator. The pre-1990 and 1990 UPC antilapse provisions apply to devisees who are grandparents or descendants of grandparents of the testator. See pre-1990 UPC § 2-605; UPC § 2-603(b) (1990). The 1990 UPC extends its antilapse protection to the testator's stepchildren.

How should the devisee's descendants, as takers of a lapsed devise, be determined? As an example of the kinds of questions that can arise, should a child of unmarried parents participate as a substituted taker under an antilapse statute? Does the answer depend upon whether the nonmarital child would take under the jurisdiction's statute of intestacy, or whether

---

17. See supra p. 81 for discussion of the per-stirpes representation system.

18. For a state-by-state compilation, see Restatement 2d of Property, Statutory Note to § 34.6. See also the chart, infra p. 348.

19. Under the pre-1990 and 1990 versions of the UPC, the substituted descendants must survive the testator by 120 hours. See supra p. 334. Therefore, the UPC antilapse statutes apply even though the devisee survives the testator if the devisee fails to survive the testator by 120 hours.

20. The term "relative" is usually interpreted to mean blood relative. See, e.g., Estate of Bloomer, 620 S.W.2d 365 (Mo. 1981); Estate of Haese, 80 Wis. 2d 285, 259 N.W.2d 54 (1977).

the child would be presumptively included in class gifts under the rules of construction followed in the jurisdiction? See Murray v. Murray, 564 S.W.2d 5 (Ky. 1978); UPC § 1-201(9) (1990).

Detzel v. Nieberding
7 Ohio Misc. 262, 219 N.E.2d 327 (P. Ct. 1966)

DAVIES, J. The evidence in this case discloses that Wilhelmina C. Guenther died testate on July 5, 1965. After making several specific bequests, she provided that the residue of her estate be converted into cash, that certain *contingent* monetary bequests be made to three brothers, a sister, Mary Detzel, a sister-in-law, a niece and a nephew, with a stipulation that the legatee "be living at the time of" the testatrix' death, and that the remainder of the residue be distributed in designated fractions to three named charitable institutions. The monetary bequest to Mary Detzel reads as follows:

> To my beloved sister, Mary Detzel, provided she be living at the time of my death, the sum of Five Thousand Dollars ($5,000.00).

Mary's daughter and sole issue, Helen Detzel, survived her aunt, the testatrix. Mary Detzel predeceased her sister, Wilhelmina.

Helen Detzel has instituted the present action for a declaratory judgment to declare her right as the sole issue of Mary Detzel to take the $5,000.00 bequest made by the testatrix to Mary Detzel under the provisions of Section 2107.52, Revised Code, commonly known as the antilapse statute. The court has been asked to determine, under the provisions of this action, if Helen Detzel will take the $5,000.00 bequest devised to her deceased mother, Mary Detzel; if the bequest will lapse because "a different disposition" of the devise has been made by the testatrix in stipulating in her will that $5,000.00 be given to Mary Detzel "provided she be living at the time of my death"; or if this section has no application to this case.

We have not found any Ohio cases involving the applicability of the Ohio antilapse statute to the exact facts of this case. We have found a number of cases in other jurisdictions in which courts have held that devises or bequests containing provisions similar to the "Detzel" bequest do lapse despite the existence of antilapse statutes in those jurisdictions. . . .

As a summation of the cases which hold that antilapse statutes do not apply to devises or legacies when words of survivorship are used in a will, we quote the following statement found in 92 A.L.R. 857, Section IXa:

> Where the testator uses words of survivorship, indicating an intention that the legatee shall take the gift only if he outlives the testator, it is clear that the statute against lapses has no application. In such a case the condition attached to the gift fails immediately upon the death of the legatee, and there is nothing upon which the statute can operate. This result is so obvious as not to require citation of authority.

Analyses of the . . . cases show that the courts categorically concluded that antilapse statutes do not apply to devises made to relatives when the indicated words of survivorship were used in connection with the devises, because in such events the testators have expressed intentions to nullify the provisions of the statutes. We, frankly, do not agree with the conclusions of the courts that the words of survivorship used by testators . . . leave "no possible room for legal construction to the contrary" or are "so obvious as not to require citation of authority." . . .

Section 2107.52, Revised Code, provides as follows:

> When a devise of real or personal estate is made to a relative of a testator and such relative was dead at the time the will was made, or dies thereafter, leaving issue surviving the testator, such issue shall take the estate devised as the devisee would have done if he had survived the testator. . . .

Antilapse statutes are remedial and should receive a liberal construction. . . . [T]o render statute inoperative contrary intent of testator must be plainly indicated. . . .

To prevent operation of the Ohio antilapse statute when a devise is made to a relative conditioned upon the survival of the testator by the relative, and the relative predeceases the testator leaving issue who survive the testator, it is necessary that the testator, in apt language, make an alternative provision in his will providing that in the event such relative predeceases or fails to survive the testator such devise shall be given to another specifically named or identifiable devisee or devisees.

Since the testatrix, Wilhelmina, made a devise to her sister, Mary, who predeceased the testatrix leaving issue, Helen, surviving the testatrix, and the testatrix did not make by apt language a different disposition of her property under such contingency to prevent the operation of Section 2107.52, Revised Code, Helen will take the $5,000 devised to her deceased mother by substitution under the provisions of said statute.

Judgment accordingly.

Notes and Problems

1. *Survivorship Language.* For a recent case holding (contrary to *Detzel*) that a bare expressly stated requirement of survivorship defeats the antilapse statute, see Estate of Stroble, 6 Kan. App. 2d 955, 636 P.2d 236 (1981).

The question whether survivorship language alone should defeat the antilapse statute is discussed in French, Antilapse Statutes Are Blunt Instruments: A Blueprint for Reform, 37 Hastings L.J. 335, 348-50, 369-70 (1985). Professor French generally approves of the result in *Detzel*, observing that "[c]ourts have tended to accord too much significance to survival requirements when deciding whether to apply antilapse statutes." In contrast, the *Detzel* case is discussed disapprovingly in Roberts, Lapse Statutes: Recurring Construction Problems, 37 Emory L.J. 323, 349-54 (1988). Professor Roberts argues that "express survivorship language should be given effect [to defeat antilapse statutes] unless there is clear and convincing evidence that to do so would be contrary to intent."

2. *1990 Uniform Probate Code.* The 1990 UPC addresses the survivorship-language question explicitly. See UPC § 2-603(b)(3) (1990). UPC section 2-603 also establishes more elaborate rules for determining when the statute's substitute gift takes effect. How would the following problems be resolved under the 1990 UPC? (The cases cited after a problem were decided under the pre-1990 UPC or non-UPC antilapse statutes. They are cited merely to demonstrate the split of authority that exists under conventional antilapse statutes with respect to most of the problems presented. The existence of the wide splits of authority was what led the framers of the 1990 UPC to develop the elaborate statutory provision.)

(a) G's will devised "$10,000 to my sister, S" and "the residue of my estate to X-Charity." S predeceased G, leaving a child, N, who survived G by 120 hours.

(b) G's will devised "$10,000 to my sister, S" and "the residue of my estate, including all failed and lapsed devises, to X-Charity." S predeceased G, leaving a child, N, who survived G by 120 hours. For a case holding that a conventional antilapse statute is counteracted (*i.e.*, X-Charity takes the $10,000 devise; N takes nothing) by this type of provision, see Estate of Salisbury, 76 Cal. App. 3d 635, 143 Cal. Rptr. 81 (1978). Cf. Larson v. Anderson, 167 N.W.2d 640 (Iowa 1969) (antilapse statute counteracted by clause stating that "if any [devisee] die[s] prior to [my death], such gifts shall lapse and become a part of the residue of my estate."); Starkey v. District of Columbia, 377 A.2d 382 (D.C. 1977) (antilapse statute counteracted by clause stating that if "any of the [devisees] do not survive me, then, in that event, his or her devise and bequest shall lapse.").

(c) G's will devised "$10,000 to my surviving children." G had two children, A and B. A predeceased G, leaving a child, X, who survived G by 120 hours. B also survived G by 120 hours. For cases holding that a conventional antilapse statute is counteracted (*i.e.*, B takes $10,000; X takes nothing), see Estate of Price, 75 Wash. 2d 884, 454 P.2d 411 (1969) (6-to-3 decision). Cf. Estate of Fitzpatrick, 159 Mich. App. 120, 406 N.W.2d 483 (1987). For cases holding that a conventional antilapse statute is not counteracted (*i.e.*, X takes $5,000; B takes $5,000) if A was living when G's will was executed, see Henderson v. Parker, 728 S.W.2d 768 (Tex. 1987) (court said: "[W]e read the phrase 'surviving children of this marriage' to mean children 'surviving' at the time the will was executed."). Accord Restatement 2d of Property § 27.2 comment f, illustration 5. Cf. Id. § 27.1 comment e, illustration 6.

(d) G's will devised "$10,000 to my two children, A and B, or to the survivor of them." A predeceased G, leaving a child, X, who survived G by 120 hours. B also survived G by 120 hours. For cases holding that a conventional antilapse statute is counteracted (*i.e.*, B takes $10,000; X takes nothing), see Estate of Burruss, 152 Mich. App. 660, 394 N.W.2d 466 (1986); Estate of Evans, 193 Neb. 437, 227 N.W.2d 603 (1975); Hummell v. Hummell, 241 N.C. 254, 85 S.E.2d 144 (1954); Miner's Estate, 129 Vt. 484, 282 A.2d 827 (1971). For cases holding a conventional antilapse statute is not counteracted (*i.e.*, X takes $5,000; B takes $5,000), see Schneller v. Schneller, 356 Ill. 89, 190 N.E. 121 (1934); Estate of Kehler, 488 Pa. 165, 411 A.2d 748 (1980). Cf. White v. Moore, 760 S.W.2d 242 (Tex. 1988) (court remanded case for a trial on the question of whether testator meant language in will "or to the survivor or survivors of [named devisees]" to mean that the heirs of predeceasing devisees should take).

(e) G's will devised "$10,000 to my two children, A and B, or to the survivor of them." A and B predeceased G. A left a child, X, who survived G by 120 hours; B died childless. For cases holding a conventional antilapse statute is counteracted (*i.e.*, devise lapses and passes under residuary clause; X takes nothing), see Estate of Kerr, 139 U.S. App. D.C. 321, 433 F.2d 479 (1970); Estate of Parker, 15 Misc. 2d 162, 181 N.Y.S.2d 711 (Sur. Ct. 1958). For cases holding a conventional antilapse statute is not counteracted, see Estate of Ulrikson, 290 N.W.2d 757 (Minn. 1980) ("[W]e hold the words of survivorship to be effective [to counteract the antilapse statute] only if there are survivors."). If the statute is not counteracted, does X take $5,000 or $10,000? Cf. Bear v. Bear, 3 N.C. App. 498, 165 S.E.2d 518 (1969) ($5,000).

In considering whether and how the antilapse statute applies, what relevance, if any, would be attributed to the order of deaths between A and B? Cf. Estate of Dittrich, 163 N.J. Super. 449, 395 A.2d 216 (1978) (where A and B predeceased G, B (but not A) leaving descendants who survived G, the court held that B's descendants take the devise; the fact that B predeceased A is irrelevant, for it is "the timing of [the devisees' deaths] *vis-a-vis* the death of [G] alone that ought to invoke the [antilapse] statute.")

(f) G's will devised "$5,000 to my son, A, if he is living at my death; if not, to my daughter, B" and devised "$7,500 to my daughter, B, if she is living at my death; if not, to my son A." A and B predeceased G, both leaving descendants who survived G by 120 hours.

(g) G's will devised "$5,000 to my child, A, if he is living at my death; if not, to A's children, X and Y." A and X predeceased G. A's child, Y, and X's children, M and N, survived G by 120 hours.

Ex.7

———

Class Gifts.[21] Terms of relationship that potentially include more than one person are often used to designate the devisees of property. "Children," "grandchildren," "issue," "descendants," "brothers," "sisters," "nieces," "nephews," and "first cousins" are commonly used terms.

A term of relationship does not necessarily create a class gift. The test for a class gift is often said to be whether the transferor was "group-minded." A more helpful way of framing the "group-minded" test is to pose the following question: Did the transferor intend for the takers to fluctuate in number? If so, a class gift has been created; if not, the language creates

———

21. A more detailed exposition of class gifts and their operation can be found in L. Waggoner, Future Interests in a Nutshell § 13.1 (1981), from which the above textual discussion and examples are drawn. See also infra Chapter 16, Part B.

separate gifts of a fixed fraction of the property in favor of each individually designated taker.

Generally speaking, the question can be answered rather easily using the following rules of thumb. If the takers are referred to by the group label only (such as "to my children"), the gift is presumptively a class gift. If the takers are referred to by a group label and by name (such as "to my children, A, B, and C") or by number ("to my three children"), or by both name and number ("to my three children, A, B, and C"), gifts of a fixed fraction in favor of the designated individuals have presumptively been created—in this case, gifts of one-third to A, one-third to B, and one-third to C. See Restatement of Property § 280.

The major consequence of a class gift, therefore, is the class' ability to fluctuate in size. Fluctuations in size can come about through an increase in the number of takers (caused by births or adoptions) and/or through a decrease in the number of takers (caused by deaths).

Increase in class membership. The ability of the takers to increase in number is unique to class gifts.

> *Example 5.1:* G devised real property "to my children." When the will was executed, G had two children (A and B). Subsequently, but before G's death, a third child (C) was born to G. G was survived by A, B, and C. No children were in gestation at G's death.
>
> G's will presumptively created a class gift. Assuming that this presumption has not been rebutted, the result is that upon G's death, A, B, and C each take an undivided one-third interest in the property.
>
> If, on the other hand, G's will had created individual gifts (suppose, for example, that G's will had said "to my two children, A and B"), the result would have been different. The shares of A and B would not have been decreased to one-third each by C's having been born and having survived G. Instead, the shares of A and B would have remained at one-half each. Not being a class gift, the devise would not have been subject to increase, and C would not have been entitled to share in the property.

Decrease in class membership. The rule of lapse—that devisees must survive the testator to take—applies to class gifts as well as individual gifts. In the absence of an applicable antilapse statute, however, a class gift imports a built-in gift over to the other takers. There is no such gift over in the case of individual gifts.

> *Example 5.2:* G devised property "to my children in equal shares." When the will was executed, G had three children (A, B, and C). One of the children, A, predeceased G, but G's other two children survived him.
>
> G's will presumptively created a class gift. Assuming that this presumption has not been rebutted, and assuming that there is no applicable antilapse statute, the result is that upon G's death B and C each take an undivided one-half interest in the property, probably as tenants in common.
>
> If, on the other hand, G's will had created individual gifts of a one-third share of the property to each of G's three children (suppose, for example, that the language of G's will had been "to my three children, A, B and C"), the result would have been different. The shares of B and C would not have been increased to one-half each by A's having lost his one-third share; the shares

of B and C would have remained unchanged at one-third each. The one-third share to which A would have succeeded if A had survived G would have gone instead, in the absence of an applicable antilapse statute, to G's residuary legatees, or in the unlikely event that there was no residuary clause, to G's heirs by intestate succession.

A class gift such as the one in the above example, where it is an immediate testamentary gift of absolute ownership, is subject to decrease during the interval between the execution of the will and the testator's death. Once the testator has died, the ability to decrease ceases. Thus, if after G's death B dies survived by C, B's one-half interest would not be divested in favor of C.

Do antilapse statutes apply to class gifts? Some courts say no. Their reasoning is that the will makes a devise only to the members of the class who are living at the testator's death. The statute, therefore, has no application to a potential class member who predeceased the testator. In many decisions, however, the statutes have been construed to apply to class gifts and, as the chart infra p. 348 indicates, the UPC and a growing number of non-UPC statutes explicitly apply to class gifts.

The basis for difference of opinion about the applicability of antilapse statutes that do not expressly apply to class gifts is discussed in Hoverstad v. First National Bank & Trust Co., below.

Hoverstad v. First National Bank & Trust Co.
76 S.D. 119, 74 N.W.2d 48, 56 A.L.R.2d 938 (1955)

[The will of Ole Rogn left the residue of his estate "to all my first cousins." Some of the testator's first cousins were dead when the will was executed.]

SMITH, J. . . . Whether our anti-lapse statute, SDC 56.0232, is invoked by the undisputed facts, is the issue. The statute reads:

> If a devisee or legatee dies during the lifetime of the testator, the testamentary disposition to him fails unless an intention appears to substitute another in his place; except that when any property is devised or bequeathed to any child or other relation of the testator, and the devisee or legatee dies before the testator, leaving lineal descendants, or is dead at the time the will is executed but leaves lineal descendants surviving the testator, such descendants take the estate so given by the will in the same manner the devisee or legatee would have done had he survived the testator.

In 57 Am. Jur. 834, Wills, § 1262, it is written:

> Where property is given to legatees who are not named but are referred to in general terms, and it was plain at the time the will was made that the persons who would fall within the group designation used, at the time the gift is to take effect, might in the meantime fluctuate in number, the gift must be regarded as one to a class, unless it otherwise appears that the testator had in mind particular individuals as the object of his bounty.

Cf. Annotation 75 A.L.R. 773. It will be recalled that the words of this testator who wrote his own will are "all the remainder of my estate to all my first cousins." The parties concede that the testator intended to make a gift to a class. The question we must decide therefore is whether the quoted anti-lapse statute is operative upon a gift to a class such as we have under consideration. If the statute is operative its express terms substitute these appealing plaintiffs for the first cousins of Ole Rogn who were dead when the will was executed.

In Page on Wills, Lifetime Ed., § 1062, appears an explanation of the conflict of authority on this question reading as follows:

> Do statutes of this sort apply to gifts to a class? Upon this question there has been a conflict of authority, which is caused, to a large extent, by conflicting views as to the purpose of the legislature in enacting such statutes; and as to the general theory which underlies them. Are such statutes intended to protect the issue of members who die before the testator, if within the designated relationship, or are they only intended to prevent lapse where the gift would have failed at common law? If the former theory is adopted, such statutes should apply to gifts to a class; since the issue of the beneficiary who died before testator need protection as much in this case as in the case of a gift to an individual. If the latter theory is correct, the statute does not apply to a gift to a class; since such gift would not have lapsed by reason of the death of one of the members of the class before testator died, as well as any members of the class surviving testator.

And the author further states:

> By the weight of authority, however, it is held that such statutes are intended to protect the issue of a beneficiary, who is within the designated relationship to testator, and who would have taken under the will if he had survived testator whether the case was a technical case of lapse at common law or not; . . . . Such statutes are, therefore, held to apply to a gift to a class; . . . .

In adopting the position that these statutes apply to a limitation in favor of a class, the authors of Restatement, Property, reason as follows:

> A statutory movement to minimize the hardships of lapse began early in the nineteenth century. These statutes were not, in terms, applicable to a limitation in favor of a class. They provided merely that, under stated circumstances, when a "devisee" died before the testator the descendants of such devisee should be substituted as the takers of what the testator had attempted to give their ancestor. Technically a limitation in favor of a class did not attempt to make a gift to any of the described group who predeceased the testator. Actually, the remedial purpose of these statutes made it reasonable to apply them equally to attempted gifts in favor of specified persons and to an attempted gift couched in the form of a class gift. Thus the rule stated in this Section embodies a liberal construction of these statutes, applying them to certain situations which can arise under limitations in favor of a class as well as to those limitations in favor of individuals which are

clearly within their terms. Thus their remedial purposes are more completely effectuated.

Restatement, Property, Parts 3 & 4, p. 1623, comment a, § 298.

A leading case is that of Woolley v. Paxson, 46 Ohio St. 307, 24 N.E. 599, 600. The reasoning of its author is illuminating. He writes,

> It was upon this ground that a devise of one by name, who predeceased the testator, was held to lapse. The fact that in the latter case the extinguished or lapsed legacy went to the residuary legatees, or to the heir where there were no such legatees, while in the case of death of a member of a class it went to the survivors, supplies no reason for excluding the application of the statute where the devise is to a class. It was not because the extinguished legacy or devise was disposed of by the law in one way rather than another that the statute was adopted, but because it did not go to the issue of the deceased devisee, as the testator, in all probability, supposed it would. In other words, it was not designed to prevent the failure of a legacy by the death of the legatee before the testator,—that were [sic] impossible,—but to make a new disposition by law of such legacy, where the testator had himself failed to do so, in anticipation of the possible death of any one of the chosen objects of his bounty before himself, where such object was a child or other relative of his.

It seems obvious that the statutory exception under consideration was motivated by a purpose to protect the kindred of the testator and by a belief that a more fair and equitable result would be assured if a defeated legacy were disposed of by law to the lineal descendants of the legatees or devisees selected by the testator. Therefore under familiar principles, which require us to so construe an ambiguous statute as to advance the legislative purpose, we feel bound to hold that the measure under consideration applies to a limitation to a class.

Needless to say, this statute will not control if the will of the testator expresses a different intention. Parker State Bank v. Fields, 69 S.D. 605, 13 N.W.2d 302. A different intention is not indicated by the complaint. . . .

All the Judges concur.

CHART—AMERICAN AND ENGLISH ANTILAPSE STATUTES[22]

Takers Substituted by Antilapse Statute

		Issue of Devisee	Heirs	Heirs or Devisees
T a k e r s	Lineal Descendants	Ark.[1], Ill.[1], Ind., Miss., Tex., Gr. Brit.[1]		
P r o t e c t e d	Issue and Siblings	Conn. (child, grandchild, sibling), N.Y.[1,3] (issue and sibling), Pa.[1,4](issue, sibling, and sibling's child)		
	Lineal Descendant of Grandparent	Mich.[2]		
b y A n t i l a p s e	Grandparent or Lineal Descendant Thereof	Ala.[2], Alaska[2], Ariz.[2], Colo.[2], Del.[2] Fla.[2], Hawaii[2], Idaho[2], Me.[2], Minn.[2], Mont.[2], N.J.[2], N.D.[2], S.C.[2], Va.[2], Wyo.[2], UPC[2]		
	Relative/ Kindred/Kinship	Mass.[2], Mo., Neb.[2], Nev., N.M.[2], Ohio, Okla., Or.[1,3], S.D., Vt., Wash., Wis.[1,3]		
S t a t u t e	Spouse and Kindred	Kan. (spouse, lineal descendant, or relative within six degrees)		
	Kindred of Testator and Spouse	Cal.[1,3], (kindred or kindred of a surviving, deceased, or former spouse)		

---

22. Adapted from French, supra p. 341, at 375, and brought up to date by the editors.

Takers Substituted by Antilapse Statute

Protected Taker		Issue of Devisee	Heirs	Heirs or Devisees
P r o t e c t e d	Any Devisee	D.C., Ga., Ky.[1], N.H., R.I., Tenn.[2], W.Va.	Iowa (except spouse)	Md. [1,5]
T a k e r	Other	N.C.[2] (any devisee whose issue would have been an heir of the testator under Intestate Succession Act), Utah[2] (heir of testator)		
	No Statute	La.		

1. Statute expressly applies to class gifts, but does not mention void class gifts.

2. Statute expressly applies to void class gifts as well as to lapsed class gifts.

3. Statute does not apply to class members dead at the execution of will (void class gifts).

4. Devise to sibling or issue of sibling will lapse if taker of lapsed devise would be testator's spouse or issue.

5. Statute does not apply to devisees dead at execution of will.

DIVISION TWO
PROBATE AND NONPROBATE TRANSFERS

TAXATION

Until this point we have concentrated on probate transfers—property owned at death and passing by will or intestacy. Division Two brings nonprobate transfers into the discussion. Nonprobate transfers are of two general types: outright gifts and will substitutes.

The first topic in Division Two is the federal tax system,[1] primarily the federal transfer-tax component of that system. Federal law subjects the gratuitous transfer of property—probate and nonprobate transfers—to an excise tax, which is usually imposed on the donor or the donor's estate. This excise tax can be derived from any of three taxes that make up the transfer-tax component of the federal tax system: the federal gift tax, the federal estate tax, and the federal generation-skipping transfer tax.

The primary purposes of starting Division Two with the tax system are to show how that system integrates taxation of probate and nonprobate transfers and to set the stage for the subsequent chapters of this Division, which take up various aspects of family property law that are belatedly moving in the direction of a similarly integrated treatment. We shall see that the transfer-tax system has from its inception treated will substitutes such as revocable trusts, life insurance, pension death benefits, survivorship annuities, and so on as the equivalent of probate transfers. Of course, treating will substitutes as if they were deathtime rather than lifetime transfers is only one part of the transfer-tax system and so, in this Chapter, we also seek to give an overview of that system as a whole in order to

---

1. Along side the federal tax system are various state tax systems. Many states have inheritance taxes, which tax the recipient of a gratuitous transfer, and estate and gift taxes, which tax the donor. For people of middle-class means, the relative importance of the state tax systems has increased in recent years as the importance of the federal transfer taxes has decreased. Tax saving opportunities are available and state taxes need to be considered in the design of a client's estate plan. Unfortunately, these state taxes vary so greatly in detail that they cannot be summarized in the brief presentation here.

establish a background against which to understand family property law and estate planning techniques. We emphasize that the presentation is merely an overview; it plainly cannot go into the many details that would be covered in a separate course in Federal Transfer Taxation.

PART A. THE FEDERAL TRANSFER TAX SYSTEM

1. The Cumulative Estate and Gift Tax System

The federal estate and gift taxes use progressive rather than flat tax rates. Under a progressive system, the total tax on gratuitous transfers of $2 million are supposed to be more than double the tax on gratuitous transfers of $1 million. To have integrity, a progressive transfer-tax system must therefore be cumulative. That is to say, the tax on the latest round of taxable transfers, whether occurring at death or during life, must take account of all previous taxable transfers.

Until 1976, however, the progressivity of the system was compromised by the fact that the federal estate and gift taxes operated independently rather than cumulatively. The federal estate tax was enacted in 1916 to impose an excise tax on deathtime transfers of property, which as indicated above includes will substitutes as well as probate transfers under the heading of deathtime transfers. The federal gift tax was enacted in 1932 to impose an excise tax on lifetime gifts of property, which for the most part are outright gifts of property. Each tax had its own exemption and progressive rate schedule, but progressivity was compartmentalized. Although the gift tax was cumulative within itself, the estate tax rate applicable to a decedent's taxable estate was not based on the cumulative total of lifetime taxable gifts plus the taxable estate, but only on the taxable estate. A $1 million taxable estate incurred the same estate tax whether the decedent had made no lifetime taxable gifts or lifetime taxable gifts of, say, $5 million.

All this changed with the enactment of the Tax Reform Act of 1976. This act joined the estate and gift taxes into a unified transfer-tax structure with a single exemption and rate schedule and under which the rate applicable to a decedent's taxable estate is based on the cumulative total of the decedent's lifetime taxable gifts and taxable estate. Under the unified system, deathtime transfers are treated as continuations of lifetime gift-giving. The effect of unification is to diminish the opportunity of gaining an overall lower tax rate by splitting estates—particularly large estates—between lifetime and deathtime gifts.

Unified Rate Schedule from IRC § 2001(c)

If the amount with respect to which the tentative tax to be computed is:	The tentative tax is:
Not over $10,000	18 % of such amount.
Over $10,000 but not over $20,000	$1,800, plus 20% of the excess of such amount over $10,000.
Over $20,000 but not over $40,000	$3,800, plus 22% of the excess of such amount over $20,000.
Over $40,000 but not over $60,000	$8,200, plus 24% of the excess of such amount over $40,000.
Over $60,000 but not over $80,000	$13,000, plus 26% of the excess of such amount over $60,000.
Over $80,000 but not over $100,000	$18,200, plus 28% of the excess of such amount over $80,000.
Over $100,000 but not over $150,000	$23,800, plus 30% of the excess of such amount over $100,000
Over $150,000 but not over $250,000	$38,800, plus 32% of the excess of such amount over $150,000.
Over $250,000 but not over $500,000	$70,800, plus 34% of the excess of such amount over $250,000.
Over $500,000 but not over $750,000	$155,800, plus 37% of the excess of such amount over $500,000.
Over $750,000 but not over $1,000,000	$248,300, plus 39% of the excess of such amount over $750,000.
Over $1,000,000 but not over $1,250,000	$345,800, plus 41% of the excess of such amount over $1,000,000.
Over $1,250,000 but not over $1,500,000	$448,300, plus 43% of the excess of such amount over $1,250,000.
Over $1,500,000 but not over $2,000,000	$555,800, plus 45% of the excess of such amount over $1,500,000.
Over $2,000,000 but not over $2,500,000	$780,800, plus 49% of the excess of such amount over $2,000,000.

Through 1992

Over $2,500,000 but not over $3,000,000	$1,025,800, plus 53% of the excess of such amount over $2,500,000.
Over $3,000,000 but not over $10,000,000 ...	$1,290,800, plus 55% of the excess of such amount over $3,000,000.
Over $10,000,000 but not over $21,040,000 ..	$5,140,800, plus 60% of the excess of such amount over $10,000,000.
Over $21,040,000	$11,764,800, plus 55% of the excess of such amount over $21,040,000.

After 1992

Over $2,500,000 but not over $10,000,000 ...	$1,025,800, plus 50 % of the excess of such amount over $2,500,000.
Over $10,000,000 but not over $18,340,000 ..	$4,775,800, plus 55 % of the excess of such amount over $10,000,000.
Over $18,340,000	$9,362,800, plus 50% of the excess of such amount over $18,340,000.

———

The mechanics of the cumulative system are a bit complicated. They incorporate a number of steps in order to arrive at the final tax-due figure. The first of these steps is to compute the *tentative estate tax* by applying the unified rate schedule to the sum of the decedent's "taxable estate" (the decedent's gross estate less deductions) and her or his "adjusted taxable gifts" (the aggregate amount of post-1976 lifetime taxable gifts that she or he made and that are not included in her or his gross estate).[2] The second step is to apply the gift-tax offset, which is done by reducing the tentative estate tax by the aggregate amount of the gift tax that would have been payable with respect to the decedent's post-1976 gifts if the unified rate schedule (as in effect at the decedent's death) had been applicable at the time of the gifts (whether or not the gifts are includable in the gross estate). The result is the *gross estate tax*, a term used in the regulations but not in the Code itself. The third step is to compute the *net estate tax* by subtracting the available credits from the gross estate tax. The principal credit is the "unified credit," which is a quite large amount of $192,800. See IRC §§ 2010, 2505. The other credits include a credit for state death taxes, a credit for federal gift taxes on pre-1977 gifts that are included in the decedent's gross estate, a credit for foreign death taxes, and a credit for federal estate taxes paid on certain prior transfers. The unified credit is the main means by which the federal transfer-tax system restricts its effect to the affluent and wealthy, leaving the middle or working class or the poor unaffected by the system. The unified credit in effect exempts the first $600,000 in transfers from taxation.

> *Example 6.1:* G died with a taxable estate of $1.5 million. If G made no post-1976 lifetime taxable gifts, the decedent's gross estate tax would be $555,800. Assuming that the only credit available is the unified credit, G's net estate tax would be $363,000 ($555,800-192,800).
>
> If, however, G had made post-1976 lifetime adjusted taxable gifts of $1 million, the decedent's gross estate tax would be $872,800, a figure computed by determining the tentative tax on $2.5 million ($1,025,800) and subtracting $153,000, which is the gift tax payable on G's $1 million in lifetime taxable gifts. The gift tax payable of $153,000 is computed by subtracting the unified credit amount of $192,800 from the tentative tax of $345,800 on $1 million.

———

2. As we shall see, few taxable gifts are included in the decedent's gross estate. One of the complications of the transfer-tax system, however, is that the estate and gift taxes are not always mutually exclusive. An example of a gift that is both a taxable gift under the gift tax and is included in the gross estate under the estate tax is an irrevocable gift of a remainder interest in property in which the donor reserves a life estate. The gift of the remainder interest is a taxable gift, but the property is also included in the decedent's gross estate under IRC § 2036 because of the retained life estate. The taxable gift of the remainder interest would therefore not be included in the decedent's "adjusted taxable gifts" because it is already included in the decedent's "taxable estate."

See IRC § 2001(b). Again, assuming that the only credit available is the unified credit, G's net estate tax would be $680,000 ($872,800-192,800).[3]

Before making the computations in this example, the values of G's "taxable gifts" and "taxable estate" must be determined. We turn now to these steps and a more detailed look at each of the transfer taxes, starting with the federal gift tax.

2. The Federal Gift Tax

The federal gift tax now in effect dates back to 1932, when it was enacted as an excise tax on lifetime gifts of property. The 1932 gift tax was not only intended to supplement the estate tax by exacting a cost for making inter-vivos gifts that reduce the donor's taxable estate, but also to supplement the income tax by exacting a cost for making inter-vivos gifts that reduce the donor's taxable income. The 1932 gift tax was preceded by a gift tax that was enacted in 1924 but repealed in 1926. Progressivity under the 1924 gift tax was largely undermined by the fact that the tax was computed on an annual basis, without regard to gifts made in prior years. Unlike its predecessor, the 1932 gift tax is computed on a cumulative basis: Although taxable gifts must be reported and the tax must be paid on an annual basis, the tax rates applicable to a gift are determined by reference to the total amount of taxable gifts made by the donor during her or his lifetime, rather than by reference only to taxable gifts made in a given year. The cumulative aspect of the gift tax system works in a manner similar to the cumulative aspect of the transfer-tax system as a whole, as described and illustrated above in Example 6.1.

> *Example 6.2:* In Year One, G made taxable gifts of $1 million. Using the unified rate schedule, the tentative gift tax on those gifts is $345,800, which is then reduced by the unified credit of $192,800; the gift tax due is $153,000.
>
> In Year Two, G made taxable gifts of $500,000. The tentative gift tax on these gifts is determined by computing the tentative gift tax on $1.5 million ($555,800) and subtracting the tentative gift tax on $1 million ($345,800). G does not have any unified credit available because the Year-One gift exceeded the unified credit equivalent amount of $600,000. Therefore, the gift tax actually due is $210,000 ($555,800-345,800). See IRC § 2502(a).

Until 1976, the gift tax rates were lower than the estate tax rates. This, combined with the fact that before 1976 the estate and gift taxes were not

---

3. While it might appear that there is a double allowance of the unified credit (once against the gift tax and then against the estate tax), in fact this is not the case. The reason is that the $1 million in taxable gifts increased G's tentative estate tax at his death, and the credit reduced the offset allowed for the gift tax payable on those gifts. The reduction of the gift tax offset against the tentative estate tax eliminates any benefit from the apparent duplication of the use of the unified credit.

cumulative, encouraged lifetime gift-giving by the wealthy, for the wealthy can more easily afford to give away part of their property before death. As indicated above, the Tax Reform Act of 1976 adopted a unified rate schedule, which reduced the estate tax savings of making inter-vivos gifts.

While the gift tax supplements both the income and the estate taxes, the sad fact is that the three taxes overlap to some extent, and the treatment accorded a given transaction in the application of the three taxes is not necessarily consistent. Thus, when a gift is made, the donor must resolve three separate questions: (1) whether the transfer is one on which a gift tax is imposed; (2) whether the transferred property will be included in the donor's gross estate on her or his death, notwithstanding the inter-vivos transfer;[4] and (3) whether the donor will continue to be taxed on the post-transfer income generated by the transferred property.

Overview of the Gift Tax. The first step in the determination of a donor's gift tax consequences for a taxable period is to identify the donor's transactions during that period that constitute "gifts" for gift tax purposes and to value the donated property. While a donor's transfer of cash without consideration to her son, B, on B's birthday will almost certainly constitute a gift, there are many less obvious circumstances in which gifts for gift-tax purposes can arise, such as forgiving a loan to a family member, deliberately allowing the statute of limitations to run on the loan, or making the loan at a below-market rate of interest. See IRC § 7872.

The second step is to ascertain what amounts of the "gifts" made by the donor during the taxable period are "taxable gifts." IRC section 2503(b) provides that up to $10,000 of a gift made by a donor during a calendar year to each separate donee is excluded from the donor's taxable gifts, but only gifts that do not constitute "future interests" can qualify for this exclusion. Thus, G can make cash gifts of $10,000 each to all fifteen of his grandchildren this year, next year, and each year thereafter without incurring any gift taxation. Indeed, G will not even be required to file a gift tax return. This exclusion is sometimes called "the annual exclusion."

The third step is to subtract from the amount of gifts made during a taxable period (as reduced by the annual exclusion) any allowable deductions, such as the marital deduction or the charitable deduction, which are discussed infra pp. 371 & 374. The difference between the total value of a donor's gifts and the allowed exclusions and deductions is the amount of taxable gifts of the donor. The unified rate schedule is then applied to the taxable gifts as described above.

Taxable Lifetime Transfers. Retained Powers. If a donor reserves a power to revoke a transfer and revest the property in herself or himself, the transfer is not subject to gift taxation. In gift-tax terminology, the gift is called "incomplete" and the donor continues to be treated as owner of the transferred property for gift and income tax purposes. See Treas. Reg. § 25.2511-2(c); IRC § 676. If a donor transfers property, but retains certain nonbeneficial powers, the gift tax law (and perhaps the income tax laws under IRC section 674) continues to treat the gift as incomplete and the

---

4. See supra note 2.

donor as owner. Although the donor relinquishes the right to enjoy personally the property or the income it produces, the donor retains the power to decide who can enjoy the property or its income. Retaining the right to choose who will enjoy the property is sufficient under the gift tax law (and perhaps under the income tax law) to ignore the transfer. See Treas. Reg. § 25.2511-2(b), (c).

Powers of Appointment. IRC section 2514(b) provides that if a donee of a general power of appointment exercises or releases that power, a gift occurs. As defined in section 2514(c), a general power of appointment is any power that the donee can exercise in favor of herself or himself, her or his estate, her or his creditors, or the creditors of her or his estate. The definition excludes, however, a power to consume the property or invade the trust property if that power is limited by an ascertainable standard relating to the "health, education, support, or maintenance of the donee." See IRC § 2514(c)(1). The definition also excludes a power that can be exercised only in conjunction with the donor or an adverse party. See IRC § 2514(c)(3). See infra Chapter 14 for further discussion of powers of appointment.

One exception to the rule that the release of a general power is a gift concerns a lapse of a general power of appointment with respect to an amount that does not exceed the greater of $5,000 or five percent of the aggregate value of the property subject to the power at the time of the lapse. See IRC § 2514(e). Trusts are often structured to take advantage of this "5 and 5" exception.

> *Example 6.3:* G establishes a trust and gives A an income interest for life and a power to invade corpus up to $5,000 or five percent of the aggregate value of the trust each year during A's life, and also gives B the right to the remaining trust corpus at A's death. Of course, if A invades corpus up to the maximum amount allowed each year, no gift tax consequences occur except to the extent A subsequently makes a gift of the amount A received from the invasions. If A, however, does not invade corpus but allows the power to lapse in any year, that lapse, but for section 2514(e), would have resulted in a gift of the remainder interest to B.

The "5 and 5" power allows a donor to give a donee access to the trust corpus without putting the donee in a position of having to suffer gift taxation upon foregoing withdrawals.

Minimizing Income Tax Liability Through Lifetime Gifts. A donor can reduce her or his federal income taxes by making lifetime gifts. As for the donee, the receipt of lifetime or deathtime gifts of money or other property is not taxable to the recipient as income. See IRC §102. The lifetime gift also has the income tax advantage of causing the post-transfer income from the property generally to be taxed at the donee's rate, which means that the donor can reduce the federal income tax liability of the family by transferring property to family members with lower marginal income tax rates.[5]

The one income tax disadvantage of making lifetime gifts is that, if the gift is of appreciated property or property that later appreciates, the donee will compute the gain from a sale or other disposition of the property received by using the donor's basis (which typically means the donor's cost of having acquired the property) with some adjustment for any gift taxes paid. See IRC § 1015. In contrast, IRC section 1014 provides that a recipient of property included in a decedent's gross estate takes a stepped-up basis equal to the estate tax value of the property, which typically is the value of the property at the decedent's death. In other words, the benefits of having the post-transfer income from property taxed at a donee's lower tax rates must be weighed against the benefit of avoiding tax on any appreciation in the property that occurs between the time the donor acquires the property and the donor's death.

Minimizing Transfer Tax Liability. Five features of the gift tax rules encourage lifetime giving.

Tax-exclusive tax base. As indicated supra p. 358, the gift tax utilizes the same unified rate schedule as the estate tax and the decedent's estate tax rate is determined by taking into account both lifetime and deathtime transfers. In addition, to the extent the unified credit is used to reduce a decedent's gift tax liability, it is in effect unavailable to reduce the decedent's estate tax liability.[6] Although by making a lifetime gift of investment property, the donor can avoid a transfer tax on the investment return from that property, the donor also forgoes the investment return on the amount of any gift taxes paid. The loss of use of the money used to pay gift taxes offsets the benefits of avoiding gift tax on the return from the investment property.[7] Therefore, it would seem that the gift tax does not create incentives for making lifetime gifts on which gift taxes must actually be paid. But, because the gift tax itself is not included in the amount of the gift for gift tax purposes, whereas the estate tax is included in the amount of the estate for estate tax purposes, incentives for making lifetime gifts exist. In other words, the incentives arise from the fact that the gift tax is tax exclusive, but the estate tax is tax inclusive. A com-

---

5. The one major limitation on the opportunity to shift income tax liability is that income that exceeds $1,000 in a year from property owned by a child under 14 is taxed at the parent's marginal tax rate if it is greater than the child's rate. See IRC § 1(i).

6. See supra note 3 and accompanying text.

7. The observation that the benefit of avoiding a transfer tax on the investment return is offset by the cost of losing the investment return on the amount of gift taxes paid can be shown algebraically. If a grantor makes a lifetime gift of investment property I, pays a gift tax at rate **T** out of the investment property, and the donee invests the amount remaining after the grantor pays the gift taxes at interest rate **R**, then the donee will have the amount $I(1 - T)(1 + R)$ one year later. If instead, the grantor does not make a lifetime gift of the investment property I, but instead invests it at interest rate **R** for one year and then dies paying an estate tax at rate T, then the donee will receive the amount $I(1 + R)(1 - T)$ from the estate. The two amounts are equivalent because the commutative principle of multiplication makes the order of multiplication irrelevant.

parison of Examples 6.4 and 6.5, below, demonstrates the tax savings available from making a lifetime gift.

Example 6.4 (lifetime transfer): G makes a gift to A of $100. The gift tax rate is 30%. G pays the government a gift tax of $30 and A receives the gift of $100.

Example 6.5 (deathtime transfer): G dies owning $130 that she devises to B. The estate tax rate is 30%. G's estate pays the government an estate tax of $39 and B receives the remaining $91 ($130 - 39).

These examples show that, to the extent a donor makes gifts exceeding the unified-credit-equivalent amount of $600,000, every dollar of gift tax paid is removed from the donor's taxable estate, tax free.

Annual exclusion. The first $10,000 of gifts made to each donee during the year are not included in the donor's taxable gifts. IRC § 2503(b). Although the original purpose of the annual exclusion was to relieve taxpayers of the need to report and the government of the need to monitor holiday and birthday gifts, the introduction of an amount as high as $10,000 has made it a major tax-minimization tool. An annual gift plan to children, grandchildren, and possibly their spouses or domestic partners can result in the tax-free removal of a significant amount of wealth from the donor's taxable estate.

The annual exclusion is only available with regard to gifts of present interests. If a donor transfers money or other property absolutely, the annual exclusion is, of course, available. It is also available if a donor gives a donee the right to the possession or enjoyment of or the income from the property for life or for a term of years, so long as the right to possession or income begins immediately.

IRC section 2503(c) makes an exception to the present-interest rule for a gift to a minor. The donor can make a gift in trust giving a trustee the discretion to distribute or accumulate the income from the property, so long as the property and any accumulated income is distributed when the minor attains 21. If the minor dies before attaining 21, IRC section 2503(c) requires the trust to provide that the property and any accumulated income be paid to the minor's estate or as the minor directs under a general power of appointment.

Gift splitting. The benefits of the annual $10,000 exclusion are further enhanced by the fact that the Code gives the donor and her or his spouse the right to elect to treat gifts as having been made one-half by the donor and one-half by the donor's spouse. See IRC § 2513. This gift-splitting rule allows a married couple to transfer $20,000 per year to a donee tax free. (A married couple could also accomplish this result by one spouse transferring property to the other tax free in accordance with IRC section 2523, which treats qualified gifts between spouses as tax free. See infra p. 371. That would allow the donee-spouse independently to take advantage of the annual exclusion.)

Tuition-and-medical-expense exclusion. The final advantage of lifetime giving is found in IRC section 2503(e), which excludes from gift taxation any property or money that a donor pays directly to an educational organization for tuition on behalf of a donee or directly to any organization or individual who provides medical care to a donee. Before IRC section 2503(e) was enacted, payments for tuition and medical expenses might not have been taxable if the state law viewed them as discharging the donor's support obligation. See, e.g., Horan, Postmajority Support for College Education—A Legally Enforceable Obligation in Divorce Proceedings?, 20 Fam. L.Q. 589 (1987). IRC section 2503(e) goes far beyond support obligation payments, however, because it applies to tuition and medical payments made on behalf of any donee.

Transfer tax disadvantages of lifetime gifts. Property included in the donor's gross estate at death may enjoy some tax advantages that are not available to property that is transferred during life. IRC section 2032A allows, under certain circumstances, for real property, typically farmland, to be valued at an amount less than its fair market value. IRC section 303 permits the redemption of stock of a closely held corporation for little or no gain (and if there is any gain, it will be a long-term capital gain) to the extent the stock represents a major asset of the estate and the amount received in the redemption does not exceed estate and inheritance taxes and funeral and administration expenses. In the absence of IRC section 303, all of the proceeds of such a redemption (not merely the amount in excess of the shareholder's basis) could be taxed to the shareholder as ordinary income. IRC section 6166 provides for deferral of the payment of estate taxes attributable to closely held businesses at an interest rate of only four percent. That portion of the estate tax may remain entirely unpaid for five years, after which the tax and interest may be paid over ten years. These three tax advantages are only available for property subject to an estate tax and not to a gift tax.

Maximizing the Donor's Distribution Goals. To enjoy these gift tax advantages, the donor must relinquish substantial interests and powers in the property. See IRC §§ 2035-38; infra p. 365. Trusts, however, can be used to allow the donor to retain some degree of control over property and withhold from the donees complete and absolute control. The income and transfer tax laws allow the donor to retain significant investment and management powers over property placed in trust. They also allow the donor to give the trustee, other than designated family members or employees of the donor, broad discretion to distribute income or corpus from the trust, so long as the donor cannot remove the trustee without cause.[8]

---

8. The most significant limitations on who can be trustee are found in the income tax law. See IRC §§ 672(c), 674. Under the income tax law, a donor's power to substitute one trustee for another will not result in income taxation to the donor on the trust's income. See Treas. Reg. § 1.674(d)-2(a). Under the transfer tax laws, however, Rev. Rul. 79-353, 1979-2 C.B. 325, provides that any power given to a trustee will be attributable to the donor if the donor retains the power to remove the trustee without cause. Rev. Rul. 81-51, 1981-1 C.B. 458, provides that Rev. Rul. 79-353 does not apply to transfers made to trusts before October 29, 1979, if the trust was irrevocable on October 28, 1979.

Notwithstanding that the tax laws view independent trustees as beyond the donor's control, the donor's wishes are likely to influence such trustees because they have an economic incentive to please the donor in hopes of receiving other fiduciary appointments. In other words, practical considerations make it possible for donors to retain significant control over investment, management, and distribution of the transferred property. Furthermore, discretionary trusts allow donors to enjoy federal tax savings without having to be concerned that their children or grandchildren will receive the property at too young an age or that their parents or grandparents will feel burdened by investment and management decisions.

Trusts not only facilitate tax planning by allowing donors indirectly to retain control; they also permit donors to transfer property while leaving the ultimate beneficiaries of the income and corpus undetermined. The advantage in this is that it allows the estate plan to take into account later changes in family and economic circumstances. Flexibility can be added by giving the trustee discretionary powers to distribute income and corpus among various beneficiaries at various times. It also can be accomplished by giving beneficiaries the power to appoint income or corpus among designated persons. It is unusual to give a general power to appoint in these circumstances unless the donor wants to qualify the gift for an annual exclusion or a marital deduction. See supra p. 361 and infra p. 371. By giving a nongeneral power, the donor avoids having the property taxed to the donee if she or he exercises the power during life or dies owning the power.

3. The Federal Estate Tax

The federal estate tax was enacted in 1916 as an excise tax on the transfer of property at death. The tax is measured by the deathtime value of the property transferred. The core provision of the estate tax is IRC section 2033, which makes the decedent's probate estate subject to tax. From the beginning, however, Congress recognized that measures had to be taken to subject will substitutes to estate taxation; otherwise, will substitutes could be used as tax avoidance devices to achieve, in effect, tax-free probate transfers. Most of the statutory provisions of the estate tax are devoted to the purpose of taxing will substitutes such as life insurance, joint tenancies and joint accounts, pension death benefits, revocable trusts, and even irrevocable trusts with a retained life estate.

The architecture of the federal estate tax calls for a number of steps to be taken to calculate the amount of estate tax due the federal government. The first step is to determine the property that is included in the decedent's *gross estate* and the valuation thereof. The second step is to determine the *net estate* by subtracting from the gross estate the amount of deductions permitted the decedent's estate. We have already worked through the final three steps—the determinations of the tentative estate tax, the gross estate tax, and the net estate tax. See supra p. 356.

a. The Gross Estate

The decedent's gross estate includes the value of the decedent's probate estate, specified will substitutes, property over which the decedent held a general power of appointment, and certain transfers (QTIPs; see infra p. 372) for which a marital deduction was previously allowed.

Probate Property. Under IRC section 2033, the decedent's gross estate includes "the value of all property to the extent of the interest therein of the decedent at the time of his death." This statutory language describes the decedent's probate estate, the property that passes at her or his death by will or intestacy. Examples would include the value of any real estate owned by the decedent in fee simple absolute and the value of any undivided portion of real estate owned as a tenant in common. The value of any transmissible remainder interest owned by the decedent at death would also be included.

> *Example 6.6:* G's parent created a $1 million trust, directing the trustee to pay the income earned on the principal to G's other parent for life, and at the income beneficiary's death distribute the trust's principal to G. G owns a devisable remainder interest.[9] If G predeceases the income beneficiary, G's remainder interest is part of G's probate estate and is part of her gross estate for federal estate tax purposes under IRC section 2033. If the trust imposed a condition that G survive the income beneficiary and G predeceased the income beneficiary, then the remainder interest would have terminated[10] and its value would not be included either in G's probate estate or her gross estate.

Similarly, an income interest that expires on the death of the income beneficiary is not included in the income beneficiary's probate or gross estates.

> *Example 6.7:* G's parent created a $1 million trust, directing the trustee to pay the income earned on the principal to G for life, and at G's death distribute the trust principal to G's descendants who survive G, by representation; if none, to X-charity.
>
> Because G's income interest expired on her death, nothing is included in her gross estate under IRC section 2033 (other than whatever she still has left of the income payments she received throughout her lifetime or than income payments paid to her estate after her death representing income accrued at her death).

---

9. UPC § 2-707 (1990) adopts a rule of construction that imposes a condition of survivorship on the beneficiary of a future interest under the terms of a trust. Therefore, under the trust described in the text, G's remainder interest would be contingent on G surviving the income beneficiary, unless the trust demonstrated a contrary intention. See UPC § 2-701 (1990).

10. Even if the trust does not explicitly impose a condition that G survive the income beneficiary, UPC § 2-707 (1990) might apply to impose a survivorship condition. See supra note 9.

Lifetime Gifts Within Three Years of Death. The value of certain types of gifts are included in the decedent's gross estate simply because the decedent dies within the three-year period following the gift. The principal focus of this section is on gifts of a life-insurance policy within three years of death. Such a gift causes the full value of the proceeds to be included in the decedent's gross estate. See IRC § 2035(d)(2). This section also applies to a transfer or relinquishment of a retained interest or power within three years of death.

Another feature of the three-year rule is IRC section 2035(c), which provides that the decedent's gross estate includes the amount of any gift tax paid by the decedent on gifts made by the decedent (or her or his spouse) during the three-year period ending on the date of the decedent's death. This provision eliminates the tax-exclusive advantage of making lifetime taxable gifts in those circumstances in which she or he has enjoyed the property until shortly before death.

Retained Property Interests. If a donor makes a lifetime gift of property, but retains certain described interests in that property, the estate tax provides that the gross estate includes the value of that property. By not parting with ownership of the property completely, the donor is treated as if she or he were owner for estate tax purposes.

Retention of an income interest. IRC section 2036(a)(1) provides that if a donor gratuitously transfers a remainder interest in property, in trust or otherwise, while retaining possession or enjoyment or the right to the income for life, then the value of the transferred property at the donor's death is included in the gross estate.[11] The donor is also treated as owner for income tax purposes, except that gains and losses incurred on the sale or exchange of the property usually will not be taxed to the donor. See IRC § 677. The transfer of the remainder interest is subject to the gift tax, but the estate tax computation is designed to treat the gift tax payment as the equivalent of a downpayment on the estate tax owed by the donor's estate. See IRC § 2001(b).

If the donor transfers the retained life estate in the property before death, IRC section 2036(a)(1) is no longer applicable. If, however, the donor transfers the retained life estate within three years of death, IRC sections 2035(a) and 2035(d)(2) operate to include the property valued at the time of the donor's death, and IRC section 2035(c) operates to include the amount of any gift taxes paid with regard to the transfer of the life estate.

Retention of a reversionary interest. If a donor makes a gift of possession in or the income from property for the donee's life or a term of years, IRC section 2033 will include the value of the reversionary interest that the donor retained in the gross estate. Gifts of income interests with retained reversions are unusual since 1986 when Congress amended the income tax law to provide that the donor will be taxed on all income from trusts in

---

11. The period that possession or income must be retained for IRC § 2036(a)(1) to apply is "for . . . [the decedent's] life or for any period not ascertainable without reference to his death or for any period that does not in fact end before his death."

which the donor retains a significant reversionary interest. See IRC §
673(a).

IRC section 2037 addresses transfers in which the donor retains a
reversionary interest that terminates at the donor's death. An example of
this type of transfer is when G transfers property in trust with income to
be paid to A for life, and then to G if G is living, or to B if G is dead. For
IRC section 2037 to apply, three requirements must be met: (1) the donor
must have made a transfer of an interest in which possession or enjoyment
of the property can, through ownership of the interest, be obtained only by
surviving the donor; (2) the donor retained a reversionary interest in the
property; and (3) the value of the reversionary interest immediately before
the donor's death exceeds five percent of the value of the property.[12]
Neither the income tax nor the transfer tax laws create incentives for a
donor to establish trusts of this kind. Donors create irrevocable trusts
reserving reversionary interests typically to meet family or business needs
and not for the purpose of achieving tax savings. If the donor transfers
the retained reversionary interest before death, IRC section 2037 does not
apply. If the transfer occurs within three years of death, however, IRC
sections 2035(a) and (d)(2) include the transferred property in the donor's
gross estate.

Retained Powers; Revocable Trusts. If a donor reserves a power to revoke
a transfer and revest the property in herself or himself, the donor is treated
as owner of the transferred property for estate tax purposes. See IRC §
2038(a)(1). (The donor is also treated as owner for income tax, see IRC §
676(a), and gift tax purposes, see supra p. 358.) Typically donors establish
revocable trusts retaining a right to possession or income from property
along with a power to revoke. These trusts assist donors in asset management and they avoid probate and its potential costs, but they produce no
tax savings. See infra Chapter 7.

If a donor transfers property, but retains certain nonbeneficial powers,
the estate tax law continues to treat the donor as owner.[13] Although the
donor relinquishes the right to enjoy personally the property or the income
it produces, the donor retains the power to decide who can enjoy the
property or its income. Retaining the right to choose who will enjoy the
property or its income is sufficient for the estate tax law to ignore the

---

12. The first federal estate tax statute contained a version of IRC § 2037. For transfers
made before October 8, 1949, only reversionary interests that arise "out of the express terms
of the instrument of transfer" are taken into account. For transfers made on or after October
8, 1949, IRC § 2037 applies even though the reversionary interest is not expressly retained
and arises only by operation of law.

13. IRC § 2036(a)(2) applies to all transfers made on or after March 4, 1931. See IRC §
2036(d). IRC § 2038(a)(1) applies to all transfers made since the inception of the estate tax.
Slightly different rules, however, apply to transfers made on or before June 22, 1936. See IRC
§ 2038(a)(2).

transfer.[14] See IRC §§ 2036(a)(2), 2038(a)(1). See also IRC § 674 (treating donor who retains nonbeneficial powers as owner for income tax purposes).

If the donor relinquishes the retained powers before death, IRC sections 2036 and 2038 generally do not apply. If the transfer occurs within three years of death, however, IRC sections 2035(a) and (d)(2) include the transferred property in the donor's gross estate.

Powers of Appointment. The gross estate also may include property over which the decedent has a power of appointment created by another person in her or him. These are called "donee" powers, as distinguished from "reserved" powers that the donor retains in herself or himself. IRC section 2041(a)(2) provides that if, at the decedent's death, she or he owned a general power of appointment, the value of the property over which she or he owned the general power is included in the gross estate.[15] A general power of appointment is defined in the same manner as it is defined in IRC section 2514(c) for gift tax purposes. See IRC § 2041(b)(1); supra p. 359. Donors typically give general powers of appointment to their donees for the purpose of qualifying the gifts for the annual exclusion, see supra p. 361, or the marital deduction. See infra p. 371.

Donees who receive nongeneral powers of appointment over property will not have that property included in their gross estates. For example, donees who die owning powers to consume property for health or education purposes will not have that property included in their gross estates. Similarly, donees who die owning powers to appoint property to their lineal descendants or even to anyone except themselves, their creditors, their estates, or the creditors of their estates will not have that property included in their gross estates. Although the benefits of these liberal rules regarding powers of appointment have been diminished by the introduction of the generation-skipping transfer tax, see infra p. 374, they continue to play important roles in estate planning as attorneys try to minimize taxes and achieve their clients' distribution schemes.

If the exercise or release of the power is of "such a nature that if it were a transfer of property owned by the [donee of the power] . . . , such property would be includable in the [donee's] . . . gross estate under IRC sections 2035 to 2038, inclusive," then the property over which the power

---

14. Sometimes a transfer is subject to the operation of both IRC §§ 2036 and 2038. In those cases, the Commissioner will rely on IRC § 2036 because it results in the inclusion of the entire value of the property in the decedent's gross estate. In that way, the Commissioner avoids the limitation of IRC § 2038, which requires that the gross estate include only that portion of the property over which the decedent had retained a power to alter, amend, revoke, or terminate.

15. The Revenue Act of 1916, in which the modern estate tax originated, contained no provision specifically dealing with powers of appointment. United States v. Field, 255 U.S. 257 (1921), held that, under this original enactment, the gross estate did not include the value of property subject to an exercised general power of appointment. Congress had since enacted a specific provision in the Revenue Act of 1918 to tax property subject to an exercised general power of appointment.

Amendments in 1942 and 1951 provide that the value of property subject to general powers created after October 21, 1942, is includable in the decedent's gross estate regardless of whether the power is exercised.

is exercised or released should be included in the donee's gross estate. For example, if G establishes a trust and gives B an income interest for life as well as a general power to appoint the remainder interest and B appoints the remainder interest during life to C while retaining the income interest for life, IRC sections 2041(a)(2) and 2036(a)(1) require that the entire value of the trust corpus be included in B's gross estate at B's death. If B wants to remove this property from his gross estate, he must make a lifetime gift of his income interest as well as make a lifetime appointment of the remainder interest.

One exception to the estate taxation rules concerns a lapse of a general power to appoint that does not exceed the greater of $5,000 or five percent of the aggregate value of the trust at the time of the lapse. See IRC § 2041(b)(2); supra p. 359 (discussing analogous gift tax rule). But for IRC section 2041(b)(2), section 2041(a)(2) and sections 2035 through 2038 would operate to include in the donee's gross estate that portion of the trust corpus over which the donee had invasion rights. The 5 and 5 power is useful because it allows a donor to give a donee access to the trust corpus, but that access does not result in estate taxation to the donee.

Jointly Held Property. Jointly held property refers to property held in joint tenancy with right of survivorship, property held in tenancy by the entirety, joint bank accounts, and jointly held U.S. Savings Bonds. A tenancy by the entirety can only be owned by persons who are legally married to each other. Joint ownership with the right of survivorship is popular, especially for people who have small estates, because it effectively avoids probate. The Economic Recovery Tax Act of 1981 greatly simplified the tax treatment of jointly held property and made this pattern of ownership even more desirable.

Unlike property owned in tenancy in common or community property, jointly owned property has a right of survivorship. The right of survivorship means that, when a decedent dies owning jointly held property, the decedent's interest in the property terminates and is, therefore, beyond the reach of IRC section 2033. IRC section 2040 establishes two rules for determining the amount includable in the decedent's gross estate: (1) a fractional-interest rule and (2) a percentage-of-consideration rule.

The fractional-interest rule applies in two situations. First, if the decedent received a jointly held interest as a gift or devise from a person who did not also become a joint tenant, then IRC section 2040(a) includes a fractional share of the property equal to the decedent's fractional cotenancy interest in the decedent's gross estate. Essentially, the survivorship rights are ignored and the decedent's interest is treated as if it were a tenancy in common interest.

The second situation in which the fractional-interest rule applies is when a legally married couple owns jointly held property. IRC section 2040(b) includes one half of the value of the property in the estate of the first spouse to die regardless of how much the decedent spouse contributed to its purchase. The spouses' relative amounts of contribution to the purchase of the jointly held property are also irrelevant for gift tax purposes because IRC section 2523 provides that a gift of property between legal spouses made in a qualified manner is nontaxable. See infra p. 371. Similarly, IRC section 2056(a), which provides that a decedent can deduct the value of property included in the gross estate that passes to the surviving spouse in a qualified manner, in combination with IRC section 2040(b), has the effect of excluding from taxation any portion of the jointly held property until the surviving spouse makes a lifetime gift or dies.

The percentage-of-consideration rule found in IRC section 2040(a) applies for all jointly held property owned by unmarried tenants who acquire the property by purchase. This rule plays an important role for domestic partners who own property jointly with right of survivorship and for others who, to avoid probate and to facilitate financial and personal living arrangements, take property in joint tenancy with right of survivorship. The percentage-of-consideration rule operates to withhold tax advantages from the donor who provided the consideration for the joint property. IRC section 2040(a) creates a presumption that the decedent provided all the consideration for the jointly held property. The decedent's estate has the burden of proving the amount of consideration, if any, that the surviving cotenant or cotenants provided. The amount of jointly held property included in the decedent's gross estate is determined by multiplying the property's value by the percentage of consideration the decedent is deemed to have provided.

Life Insurance. A life-insurance contract on the life of the decedent and paid for by the decedent is a nontestamentary and, therefore, a nonprobate transfer, so long as the beneficiary of the insurance proceeds is someone other than the decedent's estate and the proceeds are not available to the creditors of the decedent's estate. IRC section 2042(2) provides that the insurance proceeds are included in the gross estate if at the decedent's death the decedent retained an "incident of ownership." Incidents of ownership are defined in Treas. Reg. section 20.2042-1(c)(2) to mean "the right of the insured or his estate to the economic benefits of the policy." It includes, among others, the power to change the beneficiary, to surrender or cancel the policy, to assign the policy, to revoke an assignment, to pledge the policy for a loan, or to obtain from the insurer a loan against the surrender value of the policy. Therefore, the only way that a decedent can keep insurance proceeds out of the gross estate is to make a lifetime gift of the policy, to relinquish all rights over the policy during life, and to assure that the proceeds are not paid to the estate or available to pay creditors of the estate.

Annuities. If a decedent purchased an annuity contract that provided for periodic payments for life, the annuity contract would not be part of the decedent's probate or gross estate. This type of annuity, called a nonrefund-single-life annuity, does not lead to any gratuitous transfer, but instead is fully exhausted at the decedent's death. (Of course, if the decedent owns any part of the payments at death, they will be included in the decedent's probate and gross estate.)

A second type of annuity contract is one where the decedent purchases a single-life annuity that pays a refund of a portion of the cost upon the decedent's premature death. If the refund is paid to the decedent's estate, it is included in the gross estate under IRC section 2033. If the refund is paid to a designated beneficiary, it is included in the gross estate under IRC section 2039.

A third type of annuity contract is one where the decedent purchases a joint-and-survivor annuity by which the insurance company obligates itself to make payments to the decedent and to the decedent's designated beneficiary during their joint lives and, upon the death of either, to make payments to the survivor for life. If the decedent dies first, IRC section 2039 includes the value of the survivor's right to future payments in the decedent's gross estate.

A fourth type of annuity contract is one where the decedent purchases a self-and-survivor annuity by which the insurance company obligates itself to make payments only to the decedent and to make payments to the designated beneficiary only after the decedent's death. If the decedent dies first, IRC section 2039 includes the value of the survivor's right to future payments in the decedent's gross estate. The purchase of either a joint-and-survivor annuity or a self-and-survivor annuity is a gift for gift tax purposes.

IRC section 2039(b) provides that "any contribution by the decedent's employer or former employer to the purchase price of such contract . . . shall be considered to be contributed by the decedent if made by reason of his employment." IRC sections 2039(e) and (g), however, exclude from the gross estate up to $100,000 of the value of any annuities receivable by any beneficiary under specified qualified pension plans.

The last three types of annuity contracts do not become a part of the probate estate. The annuity payments, at least in part, are subject to the income tax. See IRC § 72.

b. The Deductions for Expenses, Debts, and Losses

The various deductions the IRC allows serve to reduce the gross estate to the net estate. The deductions are the marital deduction, the charitable deduction, the deduction for funeral and administration expenses, bona fide claims against the decedent's estate, and the deduction for certain losses during administration. There is no deduction for the estate tax payable to the federal government; hence the estate tax is tax-inclusive.

Deductions for Debts, Expenses, and Losses. IRC section 2053 grants a deduction for the decedent's allowable funeral expenses and, subject to certain limitations, the expenses of administering property that was included in the decedent's gross estate. Some administration expenses also constitute allowable income tax deductions, and the executor must elect whether to deduct the expenses as either estate tax or income tax deductions. IRC section 2053 also allows a deduction for outstanding bona fide debts of the decedent, but if a debt is founded on a promise or agreement, the deduction is limited to the extent that the liability was undertaken for an adequate and full consideration in money or money's worth. Mortgage obligations of the decedent, which were contracted in a bona fide manner for adequate and full consideration in money or money's worth, are either deductible or constitute a reduction in the value of the property subject to the mortgage, depending upon whether the decedent was personally liable for the payment of the underlying debt.

IRC section 2054 permits the deduction of casualty and theft losses incurred during the administration of the estate, provided that the loss is not reflected in the valuation of the property where the alternate valuation date, which is allowed by IRC section 2032, was elected.

Marital and Charitable Deductions. Because the estate tax and gift tax allow similar deductions for marital and charitable devises or gifts, these deductions are considered together, below.

4. The Estate and Gift Tax Marital Deduction

The federal estate and gift taxes allow a married donor to transfer property to the donor's spouse without suffering taxation if the property is transferred in a qualified manner. When Congress originally enacted the marital deduction in 1948, the purported rationale of the marital deduction was to grant married citizens of common-law states tax treatment similar to that enjoyed by married couples residing in community-property states. But cf. Jones, Split Income and Separate Spheres: Tax Law and Gender Roles in the 1940s, 6 Law & Hist. Rev. 259 (1988) (arguing that "congressional, judicial, administrative, and taxpayer responses to the question of income splitting . . . were strongly influenced by beliefs about marriage and the family and, necessarily, about the proper roles of women and men in society."). The estate tax deduction was limited to fifty percent of the decedent's adjusted gross estate and the gift tax deduction was limited to fifty percent of the value of the property transferred from one spouse to the other. In 1981, Congress removed all quantitative limitations on transfers between spouses and thereby abandoned the community-property model. Current law treats a married couple as the taxable unit for transfers between spouses. This means that transfers between spouses generally are ignored and that an estate or gift tax is assessed only when one or the other of the spouses transfers property to someone outside the marital unit.

The community-property model continues to play a role in the operation of the transfer tax marital deduction. The rules defining a qualified devise or gift, which were designed to mimic the kind of property a community-property spouse would own, remain applicable. The removal of the quantitative limitations in 1981, however, was also accompanied by the introduction of another type of devise or gift that would qualify for the marital deduction. See IRC §§ 2056(b)(7), 2523(f). Estate planning tools, such as trusts and powers of appointment, are used frequently to meet the qualification requirements.

If donors transfer property to their spouses in absolute-ownership form, the marital deduction is available. For example, if the married couple hold property in joint tenancy and one of the spouses dies, the one-half of the property's value included in the gross estate under IRC section 2040(b), see supra p. 368, qualifies for the marital deduction under IRC section 2056.

If a donor transfers, at death or during life, only an income interest to her or his spouse that expires say in twenty years, however, IRC sections 2056(b)(1) and 2523(b)(1) deny a marital deduction for the value of the term of years. To be deductible, the interest passing to the spouse must not terminate or fail if: (1) an interest in that same property was retained by the donor or donatively transferred to a third person and (2) the donor or the third person would take possession of the property after the interest transferred to the spouse terminated or failed. A donor may enjoy a marital deduction if she or he transfers a copyright or a patent even though these property rights expire, because the donor did not retain or donatively transfer to a third person any interests in the copyright or patent that would take effect upon their termination.

Congress provides for several exceptions to the nondeductible-terminable-interest rule. The exceptions have one thing in common: The interests passing to the spouse will be subject to gift or estate taxation. The two most popular of the exceptions are the "life estate/general power of appointment" and the "QTIP." See IRC §§ 2056(b)(5), (7), 2523(e), (f). Both exceptions have particular and unique requirements. Planners typically find that the requirements can be met efficiently through the trust mechanism. Planners also find that they can infuse the disposition with the flexibility their clients want by using a trust, various types of powers of appointment, and fiduciary powers.

Life Estate/General Power of Appointment. IRC sections 2056(b)(5) and 2523(e) provide that a donor can enjoy a marital deduction if her or his spouse is given an income interest for life along with a power to appoint the property alone to any person and in all events. IRC section 2033 assures that any unconsumed income will be subject to the estate tax. IRC section 2041 assures that the trust corpus will be subject to the estate tax. Similarly, if the spouse makes a gift of the life estate and makes a lifetime appointment of the remainder interest, then IRC sections 2511 and 2514 will operate together to tax the fee.

For the income interest to qualify, the spouse must have an absolute right to be paid the current income at least annually. Regulations make clear that property placed in the trust must be property that produces a current income stream or, at least, that the spouse has the right to compel the trustee to convert any nonincome-producing property into property that will produce a fair current return. See Treas. Reg. §§ 20.2056(b)-5(f)(5), 25.2523(e)-1(f)(4).

For the power to qualify it must be unrestricted, except that IRC sections 2056(b)(5) and 2523(e) provide that a general power only exercisable by will is sufficient. Although the trustee cannot have a power to appoint any part of the property to any person other than the surviving spouse, the trustee can be given additional fiduciary powers to distribute the trust principal to the spouse. Nothing in the statutory requirements precludes a donor from supplementing the spouse's right to a lifetime income interest and general testamentary power with a lifetime power to appoint to a class of beneficiaries, such as the donor's lineal descendants. The exercise of this nongeneral power during life will result in a gift tax, because its exercise operates as a release of the general testamentary power. See IRC § 2514(b).

QTIP. IRC sections 2056(b)(7) and 2523(f) provide that a donor can obtain a marital deduction by transferring a life estate in property to the spouse. For the life estate to qualify under the marital deduction, the donor (for gift tax purposes) or the donor's executor (for estate tax purposes) must elect to have the life estate treated as a qualified terminable interest, and no person, not even the spouse, can have a power to appoint any part of the property to any person other than the surviving spouse during the spouse's life.

To assure that this property does not escape taxation in the donor's and the spouse's respective estates, Congress enacted IRC sections 2044 and 2519. IRC section 2519 treats any disposition of any portion of the life estate as a transfer of the entire remainder interest and thereby assures that the remainder interest is subject to gift taxation. IRC section 2044 includes the value of the property at the spouse's death in the spouse's gross estate, unless IRC section 2519 applied previously. The effect of these two constructive-transfer sections is to assure that property that enjoys a marital deduction in one spouse's estate is taxed in the other spouse's estate.

The life-estate requirements parallel those found under IRC section 2056(b)(5), having to do with the life estate/general power of appointment exception. Just as under IRC section 2056(b)(5), the trustee can have a power to distribute principal to the spouse during the spouse's life. Unlike under IRC section 2056(b)(5), however, the spouse cannot have a lifetime power to appoint to anyone other than herself or himself. In other words, a donor can enjoy a marital deduction if she or he makes a transfer of property in trust giving her or his spouse a current income interest for life to be paid out annually and a power to appoint to the couple's lineal descendants by will and makes the election as directed. A donor cannot enjoy the marital deduction, however, if the power to appoint to the couple's lineal descendants is exercisable during the spouse's life.

Estate Trust. A donor also may enjoy a marital deduction by placing property in trust and giving the trustee discretion to distribute income or principal to her or his spouse so long as the donor also provided that, at the spouse's death, any accumulated income and principal remaining must be distributed to the spouse's estate. The property placed in the trust is deductible under IRC sections 2056 and 2523 because no person other than the spouse received an interest in the property from the donor. Before 1987, this so called estate trust was attractive because it permitted the trustee to accumulate income at the then lower trust income tax rates. After the Tax Reform Act of 1986, that advantage generally has been eliminated. Now an estate trust is only popular for donors who own assets that do not produce current income and who do not want to give the power to the trustee or to the spouse to convert the assets to income-producing property.

5. The Estate and Gift Tax Charitable Deduction

The federal tax system encourages charitable giving. For income tax purposes, a donor can deduct the value of property transferred to a qualifying charitable organization. See IRC § 170. Similarly, a donor can avoid estate and gift taxes for property transferred to a qualifying charitable organization. See IRC §§ 2055, 2522. The three statutes contain slight variations in their definitions of a qualifying charitable organization. Although the income tax deduction is limited to a percentage of adjusted gross income, the transfer tax law places no limitation on the amount deductible from the tax base.

Charitable deductions are available if the donor establishes a trust giving a charity either an income interest (a charitable-lead trust) or a remainder interest (a charitable-remainder trust). The deductibility of transfers to charities of income or remainder interests were significantly restricted by the Tax Reform Act of 1969. Before 1970, if donors transferred income interests to charities and remainder interests to noncharitable beneficiaries, they gave the trustees the power to follow investment policies that resulted in low current yields and high capital appreciation. If donors transferred remainder interests to charities and income interests to noncharitable beneficiaries, they gave the trustees the power to follow investment policies that resulted in high current yields and low capital appreciation. The effect of these strategies was to allow donors to enjoy charitable deductions in amounts that exceeded the economic value of the interests received by the charities because the deductions were computed on the assumption that the trust property would produce a reasonable investment yield. (Before 1970, the applicable rate was 3.5% per year.) The 1969 Act adopted rules to assure that the charities would receive interests that were reasonably related to the amount claimed as a deduction.

The additional requirements imposed by the 1969 Act apply to the estates of decedents dying after 1969. IRC section 2055(e)(3) provides that non-complying trusts qualify for the deduction if the governing instrument is reformed by a state court to comply with the additional requirements imposed by the 1969 Act. See infra pp. 585 & 752.

IRC section 2056(b)(8), which was added by the Economic Recovery Tax Act of 1981, provides that a marital deduction is allowable for certain charitable remainder trusts so long as the trust has no noncharitable beneficiaries other than the surviving spouse. The full value of this type of trust is deductible by virtue of IRC sections 2055 and 2056 by the decedent spouse's estate. The surviving spouse receives only an income interest and, therefore, no portion of the trust property is included in her or his estate at death.

6. The Federal Generation-Skipping Transfer Tax

The federal generation-skipping transfer tax was enacted in 1986 as an excise tax on gratuitous transfers that "skip" a generation. The tax was first introduced in 1976, but the 1976 version was retroactively repealed and replaced in 1986 by the current version. Congress believed that for a transfer tax to approach equity among families, it must apply to each family with approximately the same frequency. To this end, Congress designed the generation-skipping transfer tax to assure generally that a tax is paid whenever property skips a generation or passes through a genera- tion in a form that would allow it to escape gift or estate taxation in the "skipped" generation; in the terminology of the generation-skipping transfer tax, a generation-skipping transfer occurs when property passes to a "skip person."

Skip Person; Transferor; Interest. The generation-skipping transfer tax uses a special terminology. Key interlocking definitions are:

> "Skip person"—either (1) a natural person assigned to a generation that is two or more generations below the generation assignment of the "transferor" or (2) a trust in which all "interests" are held by skip persons or in which no person holds an "interest" and at no time may a distribution, upon termination or otherwise, be made from the trust to a nonskip person. See IRC § 2613.

> "Transferor"—the person who made the transfer insofar as the federal estate or gift tax is concerned, i.e., the decedent if the transfer was subject to the estate tax; the donor if the transfer was subject to the gift tax. See IRC § 2652(a).

> "Interest"—A person has an "interest in property held in trust" if she or he (1) has the right (other than a future right) to receive income or corpus from the trust, (2) is a permissible current recipient of income or corpus from the trust and is not a qualified charity, or (3) is a qualified charity and the trust is a qualified charitable remainder annuity or unitrust or a pooled income fund.[16] See IRC § 2652(c).

$1 million GST Exemption and Computation of the Tax. Like the federal estate and gift taxes, the generation-skipping transfer tax is targeted at the wealthy. IRC section 2631 provides each transferor a $1 million exemption called the "GST exemption." The mechanism by which the GST exemption operates is through the use of an "inclusion ratio," which gives the fraction of a transfer or a trust that is subject to the generation-skipping transfer tax. In the case of "direct skips" (defined below), the inclusion ratio is:

$$1 - \frac{\text{amount of GST exemption allocated to the skip}}{\text{value of the property transferred in the skip}}$$

In cases of "taxable terminations" and "taxable distributions" (defined below), the inclusion ratio is:

---

16. Charitable remainder annuity and unitrusts and pooled income funds are described infra p. 749.

$$1 - \frac{\text{amount of GST exemption allocated to the trust}}{\text{value of the property transferred to the trust}}$$

The transferor can decide how much of her or his $1 million GST exemption to allocate to a direct skip or to a trust; if the transferor makes no election, the exemption is basically allocated to direct skips first and then to trusts with respect to which a taxable distribution or taxable termination might occur. See IRC § 2632. If the transferor allocates her or his full $1 million GST exemption to a $1 million direct skip or $1 million trust, the inclusion ratio will be 0 for that direct skip or for any taxable termination or taxable distribution from the trust. If the transferor allocates $500,000 of GST exemption to a $1 million direct skip or $1 million trust, the inclusion ratio will be .5. And, if the transferor allocates no GST exemption or has none to allocate, the inclusion ratio will be 1.

The generation-skipping transfer tax is a flat-rate tax imposed at the maximum estate tax rate (55 percent through 1992; 50 percent thereafter),[17] not a progressive-rate tax. An inclusion ratio of 1 means that the entire amount of a taxable-event transfer (see below) is subject to the generation-skipping transfer tax, an inclusion ratio of 0 means that none of a taxable-event transfer is subject to the tax, and an inclusion ratio of .5 means that half of a taxable-event transfer is subject to the tax. The tax benefits of the GST exemption encourage wealthy donors to establish long-term trusts that last as long as perpetuity law permits. See infra Chapter 17.

Taxable Events. The generation-skipping transfer tax applies to three types of generation-skipping transfers: direct skips, taxable terminations, and taxable distributions. See IRC § 2611.

Direct skips. A direct skip is a transfer that is subject to either the gift or estate tax and is made to a skip person. See IRC § 2612(c). To the extent that a gift qualifies for the annual exclusion or the tuition-or-medical-expense exclusion, the gift is not subject to the generation-skipping transfer tax. See IRC §§ 2611(b)(1), 2642(c). The generation-skipping transfer tax on a direct skip is computed on a tax exclusive basis, but the transferor's payment of the tax is treated as a taxable gift. IRC § 2515. Liability for payment of the tax is on the transferor or, if the direct skip came from a trust, on the trustee. See IRC § 2603(a)(2), (a)(3).

> *Example 6.8:* G makes an outright taxable gift to her grandchild, X, bypassing her child, A (X's parent). The gift is a direct skip for which the inclusion ratio is 1. The gift is therefore subject to both the gift tax and the generation-skipping transfer tax, the latter based upon a rate of 55% (50% after 1992) of the value of the taxable gift. See IRC §§ 2601, 2612(c), 2641. In addition, G will pay a gift tax on the amount of generation-skipping transfer tax paid. See IRC § 2515. This provision has the effect of treating a

---

17. The higher marginal rates immediately below the top end of the Unified Rate Schedule, supra p. 355, are the result of a mechanism designed to phase out the unified credit and are not to be considered as establishing the "maximum" estate tax rate.

transfer from G to X the same as a transfer from G to A, who in turn uses the transferred property to make a gift to X.[18]

In determining whether a transfer is a direct skip, IRC section 2612(c)(2) allows a "predeceased parent" exception. Under this exception, the transferor's grandchild is treated as the transferor's child if at the time of the gift or devise the grandchild's parent who is the transferor's child is dead. In Example 6.8, G's gift to X would not be a direct skip if A were dead when G made the gift.

Taxable terminations. A taxable termination is the termination (by death, lapse of time, release of power, or otherwise) of an interest in property held in a trust, unless immediately after such termination, a non-skip person has an interest in the property or unless at no time after the termination may a distribution (including a distribution upon termination) be made from the trust to a skip person. See IRC § 2612(a). The generation-skipping transfer tax on a taxable termination is computed on a tax-inclusive basis. Liability for payment of the tax is on the trustee, and hence payable from the corpus of the trust. See IRC § 2603(a)(2).

> *Example 6.9:* G transfers property to a trust directing the trustee to pay income annually to her child, A, for life and at A's death to distribute the corpus to A's descendants. The trust has an inclusion ratio of 1. G will incur a gift tax when she establishes the trust. A dies, survived by his child, X. Because immediately after the termination of A's income interest, the trust corpus passes to a skip person, the termination of A's interest is a taxable termination and the trust will be liable to pay a generation-skipping transfer tax based on the 55% rate (50% after 1992) on the value of the property held in trust when A dies.

Taxable distributions. A taxable distribution is any distribution from a trust to a skip person other than a taxable termination or a direct skip. IRC § 2612(b). The generation-skipping transfer tax on a taxable distribution is computed on a tax-inclusive basis, as liability for payment of the tax is on the transferee. See IRC § 2603(a)(1).

> *Example 6.10:* G transfers property to a trust, authorizing the trustee to distribute income and/or corpus to G's descendants. The trust has an inclusion ratio of 1. The trustee distributes $100,000 of corpus to G's child, A, and

---

18. The numerical example below explains the equivalency.

G makes a gift of $100,000 to A who then uses the $100,000 to make a gift to X (grandchild) as well as pay the gift tax owed on that gift. Assume both G and A are subject to a 55% gift tax rate and that the annual exclusion is unavailable. G would pay a gift tax of $55,000 on her gift of $100,000 to A, thereby reducing her estate by a total of $155,000. A would make a gift of $64,516 to X and pay a gift tax of $35,484. Between G and A, they would pay a total gift tax of $90,484.

The generation-skipping transfer tax obtains the same result if G makes the gift of $64,516 directly to X. G would owe a gift tax of $35,484. In addition, G would owe a generation-skipping transfer tax of $35,484 as well as a gift tax on the amount of generation-skipping transfer tax paid of $19,516. G, X, and the government are left in the same position as they were when G made a gift to A and A made a gift to X: G's wealth is reduced by $155,000 ($64,516 + 35,484 + 35,484 + 19,516); X receives $64,516; and the government receives $90,484.

$100,000 to G's grandchild, X. The distribution to A is not a taxable distribution because A is not a skip person. The distribution to X is a taxable distribution, taxed at the flat rate of 55% (50% after 1992). The transferee, X, is liable for the tax (IRC § 2603(a)(1)); if the trustee pays the tax out of the trust, the amount of the tax paid is itself a taxable distribution (IRC § 2621(b)).

The generation-skipping transfer tax is thought to be essential for the transfer-tax system as a whole to apply in a progressive manner. As the examples show, it prevents the wealthier from avoiding taxation by giving a significant percentage of their wealth to very young or unborn beneficiaries rather than to older beneficiaries. The benefit that the tax disallows is not that the older beneficiaries, were it not for the tax, would have been taxed sooner and the younger beneficiaries would have been taxed later. The benefit is that the older beneficiaries would not have been taxed at all.

Planning for the generation-skipping transfer tax requires consideration of trusts and powers of appointment to maximize flexibility of the plan while minimizing taxes. Trusts and powers of appointment are likely to be used because the tax provides some planning opportunities for transferors who establish QTIP trusts for their spouses. See IRC §§ 2652(a)(3); 2654(b); Priv. Ltr. Rul. 90-02-014.

PART B. FEDERAL TAXATION AND STATE LAW

The assessment of federal income and transfer taxes depends upon the property owner's economic rights and obligations. Economic rights and obligations, with minor exceptions, such as U.S. Savings Bonds, patents, and copyrights, are created and protected by state law. Although state law's characterization or labelling of property interests is not controlling on the federal government's power to tax, state law's determination of a person's economic rights and obligations is controlling. Part B describes the role that state law plays in the federal tax law and how the federal authorities determine that state law.

If the tax dispute turns on state law and the taxpayer has not adjudicated the particular issue in state court, the Internal Revenue Service and the federal courts determine state law in accordance with the *Erie* doctrine. The *Erie* doctrine provides that federal courts must apply state law as announced by state legislation or the state's highest court. See Erie Railroad Co. v. Tompkins, 304 U.S. 64 (1938). If the legislature or the highest court has failed to address the particular issue, then the federal authorities must apply what they find to be state law after giving proper regard to relevant rulings by a state's lower-court decisions.

If the taxpayer has adjudicated the state law question in a state court before having had a final federal determination of her or his tax liability, is the state court's ruling regarding the taxpayer's economic interests and obligations a binding determination of the state law for purposes of determining federal tax liability? The Supreme Court's latest pronounce-ment on this question came in Commissioner v. Estate of Bosch, below.

Commissioner v. Estate of Bosch
387 U.S. 456 (1967)

CLARK, J. These two federal estate tax cases present a common issue for our determination: Whether a federal court or agency in a federal estate tax controversy is conclusively bound by a state trial court adjudication of property rights or characterization of property interests when the United States is not made a party to such proceeding.

In No. 673, Commissioner of Internal Revenue v. Estate of Bosch, 363 F. 2d 1009, the Court of Appeals for the Second Circuit held that since the state trial court had "authoritatively determined" the rights of the parties, it was not required to delve into the correctness of that state court decree. In No. 240, Second National Bank of New Haven, Executor v. United States, 351 F.2d 489, another panel of the same Circuit held that the "decrees of the Connecticut Probate Court . . . under no circumstances can be construed as binding" on a federal court in subsequent litigation involving federal revenue laws. Whether these cases conflict in principle or not, which is disputed here, there does exist a widespread conflict among the circuits over the question and we granted certiorari to resolve it. . . . We hold that where the federal estate tax liability turns upon the character of a property interest held and transferred by the decedent under state law, federal authorities are not bound by the determination made of such property interest by a state trial court. . . .

(a) No. 673, Commissioner v. Estate of Bosch.

In 1930, decedent, a resident of New York, created a revocable trust which, as amended in 1931, provided that the income from the corpus was to be paid to his wife during her lifetime. The instrument also gave her a general power of appointment, in default of which it provided that half of the corpus was to go to his heirs and the remaining half was to go to those of his wife. In 1951 the wife executed an instrument purporting to release the general power of appointment and convert it into a special power. Upon decedent's death in 1957, respondent, in paying federal estate taxes, claimed a marital deduction for the value of the widow's trust. The Commissioner determined, however, that the trust corpus did not qualify for the deduction under [IRC] § 2056(b)(5) . . . and levied a deficiency. Respondent then filed a petition for redetermination in the Tax Court. The ultimate outcome of the controversy hinged on whether the release executed by Mrs. Bosch in 1951 was invalid—as she claimed it to be—in which case she would have enjoyed a general power of appointment at her husband's death and the trust would therefore qualify for the marital deduction. While the Tax Court proceeding was pending, the respondent filed a petition in the Supreme Court of New York for settlement of the trustee's account; it also sought a determination as to the validity of the release under state law. The Tax Court, with the Commissioner's consent, abstained from making its decision pending the outcome of the state court action. The state court found the release to be a nullity; the Tax Court then accepted the state court judgment as being an "authoritative exposition of New York law and adjudication of the property rights involved," . . . and permitted the deduction. On appeal, a divided Court of Appeals affirmed. It held that "[t]he issue is . . . not whether the federal court is 'bound by' the decision of the state tribunal, but whether or not a state tribunal has authoritatively determined the rights under state law of a party to the federal action." . . . The court concluded that the "New York judgment, rendered by a court which had jurisdiction over parties and subject matter, authoritatively settled the rights of the parties, not only for New York, but also for purposes of the application to those rights of the relevant provisions of federal tax law." . . . It declared that since the state court had held the wife to have a general power of appointment under its law, the corpus of the trust qualified for the marital deduction. We do not agree and reverse. . . .

The problem of what effect must be given a state trial court decree where the matter decided there is determinative of federal estate tax consequences has long burdened the Bar and the courts. This Court has not addressed itself to the problem for nearly a third of a century.[19] In *Freuler v. Helvering*, 291 U.S. 35 (1934), this Court, declining to find collusion between the parties on the record as presented there, held that a prior *in personam* judgment in the state court to which the United States was not made a party, "[o]bviously . . . had not the effect of *res judicata*, and could not furnish the basis for invocation of the full faith and credit clause . . . ." At 43. In *Freuler's* wake, at least three positions have emerged among the circuits. The first of these holds that

> . . . if the question at issue is fairly presented to the state court for its independent decision and is so decided by the court the resulting judgment if binding upon the parties under the state law is conclusive as to their property rights in the federal tax case . . . . *Gallagher v. Smith*, 223 F. 2d 218, 225.

The opposite view is expressed in *Faulkerson's Estate v. United States*, 301 F.2d 231. This view seems to approach that of *Erie R. Co. v. Tompkins*, 304 U.S. 64 (1938), in that the federal court will consider itself bound by the state court decree only after independent examination of the state law as determined by the highest court of the State. The Government urges that an intermediate position be adopted; it suggests that a state trial court adjudication is binding in such cases only when the judgment is the result of an adversary proceeding in the state court. . . .

We look at the problem differently. First, the Commissioner was not made a party to either of the state proceedings here and neither had the

---

19. It may be claimed that *Blair v. Commissioner*, 300 U.S. 5 (1937), dealt with the problem presently before us but that case involved the question of the effect of a property right determination by a state appellate court.

effect of *res judicata* . . . ; nor did the principle of collateral estoppel apply. It can hardly be denied that both state proceedings were brought for the purpose of directly affecting federal estate tax liability. Next, it must be remembered that it was a federal taxing statute that the Congress enacted and upon which we are here passing. Therefore, in construing it, we must look to the legislative history surrounding it. We find that the report of the Senate Finance Committee recommending enactment of the marital deduction used very guarded language in referring to the very question involved here. It said that "proper regard," not finality, "should be given to interpretations of the will" by state courts and then only when entered by a court "in a bona fide adversary proceeding." . . . We cannot say that the authors of this directive intended that the decrees of state trial courts were to be conclusive and binding on the computation of the federal estate tax as levied by the Congress. If the Congress had intended state trial court determinations to have that effect on the federal actions, it certainly would have said so—which it did not do. On the contrary, we believe it intended the marital deduction to be strictly construed and applied. Not only did it indicate that only "proper regard" was to be accorded state decrees but it placed specific limitations on the allowance of the deduction as set out in [IRC] §§ 2056 (b), (c), and (d). These restrictive limitations clearly indicate the great care that Congress exercised in the drawing of the Act and indicate also a definite concern with the elimination of loopholes and escape hatches that might jeopardize the federal revenue. This also is in keeping with the long-established policy of the Congress, as expressed in the Rules of Decision Act, 28 U.S.C. § 1652. There it is provided that in the absence of federal requirements such as the Constitution or Acts of Congress, the "laws of the several states . . . shall be regarded as rules of decision in civil actions in the courts of the United States, in cases where they apply." This Court has held that judicial decisions are "laws of the . . . state" within the section. Moreover, even in diversity cases this Court has further held that while the decrees of "lower state courts" should be "attributed some weight . . . the decision [is] not controlling . . ." where the highest court of the State has not spoken on the point. And in West v. A.T.&T. Co., 311 U.S. 223 (1940), this Court further held that "an intermediate appellate state court . . . is a datum for ascertaining state law which is not to be disregarded by a federal court *unless it is convinced by other persuasive data that the highest court of the state would decide otherwise.*" . . . (Emphasis supplied.) Thus, under some conditions, federal authority may not be bound even by an intermediate state appellate court ruling. It follows here then, that when the application of a federal statute is involved, the decision of a state trial court as to an underlying issue of state law should *a fortiori* not be controlling. This is but an application of the rule of Erie R. Co. v. Tompkins, supra, where state law as announced by the highest court of the State is to be followed. This is not a diversity case but the same principle may be applied for the same reasons, *viz.,* the underlying substantive rule involved is based on state law and the State's highest court is the best authority on its own law. If there be no decision by that court then federal authorities must apply what they find to be the state law after giving "proper regard" to relevant rulings of other courts of the State. In this respect, it may be said to be, in effect, sitting as a state court.

We believe that this would avoid much of the uncertainty that would result from the "non-adversary" approach and at the same time would be fair to the taxpayer and protect the federal revenue as well.

The judgment in No. 240 is therefore affirmed while that in No. 673 is reversed and remanded for further proceedings not inconsistent with this opinion.

It is so ordered.

[The dissenting opinions of DOUGLAS, FORTAS, and HARLAN, JJ., are omitted.]

Notes and Questions

1. *"Collusive" Decisions or Reformation of a Mistake.* Why is it wrong to accept the results of a collusive decision? Are there situations in which the federal government should be indifferent about whether a state decision determining property rights is collusive?

Nicholson Estate v. Commissioner, 94 T.C. No. 39 (1990), exemplifies a not uncommon situation. The decedent's attorney made a planning error that came to light after the decedent's death and a state court reformed a trust to correct the error. The trust instrument directed that the decedent's spouse should receive income from the trust "as . . . [she] may from time to time require to maintain . . . [her] usual and customary standard of living . . . ." As written, the trust failed to qualify for the marital deduction under the QTIP provision because it failed to give the surviving spouse the right to all the income from the property. See IRC § 2056(b)(7). The state court determined that the decedent had intended to qualify for the marital deduction and reformed the trust to provide that the trustees were to pay the net income to the surviving spouse in quarterly or more frequent installments. The Tax Court disregarded the state court decision and, based on the following reasoning, held that the trust failed to qualify for the marital deduction:

> While we look to local law in order to determine the nature of the interests provided under a trust document, we are not bound to give effect to a local court order which modifies that document after [the Commissioner] has acquired rights to tax revenues under its terms. . . .
>
> We are not unsympathetic to the contention that the decedent herein would have wished to establish a QTIP trust, but the fact is that he did not do so. . . . Moreover, the decedent wished to spare his widow concerns about providing for her own support. We cannot dismiss the possibility that he might have preferred to have the trustees determine the amount of trust proceeds she required, rather than to force all income to be paid to her, as his adopting of a QTIP trust would mandate.

If the issue is accomplishing the decedent's intent and if a state court determines what the decedent's intent was, why should the Tax Court disregard that holding?[20] Professors Langbein and Waggoner have argued:

> The Treasury occupies the position of an unintended beneficiary in these cases. . . . When the mistake arises in a lawyer-drafted instrument, as is usually the case, the Treasury's posture is particularly unattractive. The Treasury benefits through third-party negligence—a species of wrong-doing—at the expense of the innocent intended beneficiaries.

Langbein & Waggoner, Reformation of Wills on the Ground of Mistake: Change of Direction in American Law?, 130 U. Pa. L. Rev. 521, 550 (1982).

Picking up on this point, Professor Verbit, in Verbit, State Court Decisions in Federal Transfer Tax Litigation: *Bosch* Revisited, 23 Real Prop. Prob. & Tr. J. 407, 457-62 (1988), advocates an abandonment of the *Bosch* rule and the adoption of a rule in which all final decisions of state courts would be binding in federal tax cases. At the core of his argument is an acknowledgment that the courts are deciding cases for the purpose of carrying out the donor's intent:

> Adoption of such an approach would mean that federal courts must accept decisions from state court proceedings that might be characterized as pro forma, a "sham," a "stamp of approval," and similar characterizations. . . . [T]hese decisions allegedly result from the willingness of state court judges to distort the facts or misinterpret or misapply state law as a result of a de facto conspiracy among the court and the parties to do in the federal tax collector. . . .
>
> At the root of this concern about what state judges are doing is the question of why they are doing it. Are they "distorting" the facts or the law solely because they see the issue as one of the hometown crowd against Washington? Is it the case that they are amenable to the pleas and arguments of counsel and parties who are their friends, neighbors or even former colleagues? Are they, as Justice Harlan . . . suggested, simply too busy to devote much time and effort to the issues raised in the state proceeding and thus tend to approve whatever unopposed material is put before them? No reading of the cases yields a complete response to those questions. But it does reveal that many of the *Bosch*-type cases arise in the context of a mistake of law or a mistake in drafting by counsel for a decedent. . . .
>
> *Bosch* itself is one of those cases. . . . The way the Bosch trust was set up, its assets would be taxable in Mr. Bosch's estate by virtue of his retention of a power to revoke the trust and the assets would not be taxable in Mrs. Bosch's estate because her interest in the trust was limited to a life estate and

---

20. Compare Estate of Kraus, T.C.M. (CCH) 1990-399 (trust contained an interpretative-aid savings clause indicating decedent's intent to have the trust qualify for the marital deduction and the state court reformed the trust to qualify it for the marital deduction; the court held that the state court reformation was not binding and did not find the interpretative-aid savings clause controlling, but ultimately found that the trust was a product of mistake); Redd, What Types of Savings Clauses Will Preserve the Marital Deduction?, 14 Est. Plan. 72 (Mar.-Apr. 1987) (analyzing the effectiveness and advocating the use of an interpretative-aid savings clause to clarify a decedent's intent to take advantage of the marital deduction or other similar tax provisions).

a nongeneral power of appointment. It was undisputed that inclusion in Mr. Bosch's estate would not be offset by the estate tax marital deduction because of Mrs. Bosch's limited interest in the trust. This arrangement only made sense if the estate planner thought Mrs. Bosch would die first, which is contrary to experience (most estate planners work on the assumption that the husband will die first). Absent some evidence that Mrs. Bosch was ill or otherwise had a shorter than average life expectancy (and there was none), the principal beneficiary of the Bosch estate plan was the government, which would collect its estate tax sooner rather than later. Was this a tax planner's error? Or was it a scheme for the Bosches to have it both ways—if Mrs. Bosch dies first the trust assets were not then taxable and if Mr. Bosch dies first his tax planner would rush into state court to obtain a ruling to qualify the bequest to Mrs. Bosch for the estate tax marital deduction, thereby postponing taxation until Mrs. Bosch's death? Although this latter scenario was what occurred in *Bosch*, it seems highly unlikely that it was planned in advance, given the fact that it depended on obtaining a state court judgment that, as Judge Friendly pointed out, seemed to be contrary to New York law. Moreover, the consequences of failing to obtain such a ruling were too great—the loss of the estate tax marital deduction meaning that the tax would be payable at Mr. Bosch's earlier death. No competent estate planner would counsel such a course. Instead, *Bosch* appears to be an after-the-fact scramble by attorneys who realized a serious error was made in the Bosch family estate plan.

A second ambiguous case is Newman v. Commissioner, [222 F.2d 131 (8th Cir. 1955),] in which the taxpayer transferred shares of stock worth $30,000 to a trust for the benefit of her daughter. Within three years, the value of the stock had risen to $151,000. In a tax audit of the taxpayer, the agent raised the issue of the trust's revocability because, unlike most states, California law states that a trust is revocable unless the instrument expressly provides otherwise. An action was brought in state court to reform the trust, holding it was irrevocable from the date the instrument was executed. Evidence that the grantor intended the trust to be irrevocable included the filing of California and federal gift tax returns when the trust was established. Nevertheless, it is conceivable (though unlikely) that the omission of language concerning irrevocability was a deliberate attempt by the taxpayer to reserve the power to regain control of the transferred property if that was advantageous to her and claiming it was irrevocable if that was the better position. It is not likely that a taxpayer will play such a sophisticated game. It is far more probable in most of these cases that the drafter simply made a mistake. If a state court finds that a mistake has been made in drafting a trust, it has traditionally had the power to reform the trust retroactively to carry out what it finds to have been the grantor's intent. Nevertheless in *Newman*, the state court judgment was discounted because "no one opposed the entry of the state court order." [222 F.2d at 136.] In similar cases federal courts have reasoned that the state court finding of mistake was an issue of fact rather than law and that federal courts are not bound by state court findings of fact. . . .

At least some of the state decisions that are criticized in federal tax proceedings are attempts to relieve the decedent's estate of the consequences of poor legal advice. Judges would, and frequently do, deny that it is the court's job to compensate for incompetent legal advice and, in particular, to remake the decedent's will. At the same time, however, state courts indicate that, in interpreting instruments, their primary task is to determine the grantor or testator's intent. As the courts are fond of noting, it is difficult to conceive of a testator whose goal is to benefit the Internal Revenue Service at the expense of the natural objects of his or her bounty.

Instead of viewing the actions of state judges as participation in a "Great Treasury Raid," it is equally possible to view the situation as one in which state courts construe and reform instruments to effect the testator's intent while the IRS is attempting to capitalize on every drafting error, however slight. The case in which a taxpayer deliberately chooses to surrender a tax benefit for some non-tax reason, such as to disinherit a spouse, is rare indeed. Contemporary estate planning is often tax-driven. To the extent that is the case, a legitimate question should be considered: Why deny a tax benefit to a taxpayer who has omitted a phrase or used one word too many if the evidence is that the taxpayer intended to qualify for the tax benefit? This is particularly compelling if an error is of essentially a technical nature and the taxpayer is really the innocent victim of a drafter's error. This is not to say that the IRS should accept instruments that do not conform to the requirements of the Internal Revenue Code. But if a state court interprets an instrument to carry out the testator's intent, the IRS *ought* not to be in a position to brush aside such efforts.

2. *The Aftermath of Bosch.* Did the *Bosch* court avoid the uncertainty that concerned it? An excerpt from Verbit, supra, at 438-51, addresses this question, as well as others, as it considers *Bosch*'s aftermath.

Lower Federal Courts Attempt to Apply *Bosch*

[F]ederal courts have taken the following attitude towards state lower court decisions under the guise of following the rule of *Bosch*: (1) that lower state court rulings are entitled to no weight and are therefore not admissible in federal tax proceedings, (2) that lower state court decisions are relevant evidence even though the product of non-adversary proceedings, (3) that lower state court decisions are to be "followed" if they correctly applied state law, and (4) that the existence of the state court decision should be noted but the federal court will thereafter decide the case as if the state court decision did not exist.

Misunderstanding of *Bosch* by the IRS

The scope of *Bosch* has been misunderstood by both the federal courts and the Internal Revenue Service. It is perhaps cited more often in situations in which it is inapposite than when its teaching, such as it is, applies. Thus, while *Bosch* is concerned with the effect to be given a state proceeding that decided an issue now before a federal court, the case is frequently cited as giving general guidance on the sources of state law in federal tax cases.

Perhaps the classic example of the misunderstanding of *Bosch* is illustrated by the course embarked upon by the Internal Revenue Service when, in Revenue Ruling 69-285, it interpreted the holding in *Bosch* as follows:

> A state court decree is considered to be conclusive in the determination of the Federal tax liability of an estate only to the extent that it determines property rights, and if the issuing court is the highest court in the state.

Applying this test to the issue whether a bequest qualified for the section 2055 estate tax charitable deduction, the Service ruled that *Bosch* meant that the allowance of the deduction by the state probate court was "not determinative of whether a charitable deduction is allowable."

There are at least three difficulties with the holding of Revenue Ruling 69-285. First, the state court ruling could not be determinative of deductibility under [IRC] section 2055 in any event because deductibility is a question of federal law and there are substantive federal criteria laid out in that section that must be met. The limited role of state law on the issue of deductibility is to provide some clarity to an otherwise ambiguous will or trust instrument so that a determination whether the requirements of [IRC] section 2055 have been met can be made. In the case discussed in Revenue Ruling 69-285, the will provided that the residuary estate was left to the executor "to be distributed to whatever charities she may deem worthy." The deduction would have been disallowed if the clause permitted the executor to distribute funds to organizations not qualified under [IRC] section 2055. The IRS determined that "[d]ecisions by the Massachusetts Supreme Court indicate that the Massachusetts definition of 'charitable' is at least as restrictive as the Federal definition." At this point the need to refer to state law was at an end. Federal law determines whether the organizations actually selected by the executor met the requirements of [IRC] section 2055 and thus whether distributions to them were deductible under the federal estate tax.

The second difficulty with Revenue Ruling 69-285 is that *Bosch* is not concerned with the general issue of the state law applicable to the interpretation of instruments but, rather, with the more narrow question of the weight to be given a state court *decision* purporting to interpret the instrument in question. In Revenue Ruling 69-285 there was no state court proceeding—highest or lower—interpreting the instrument in question. Instead, the probate court "issued a decree which recited that [the executor] had selected several organizations to receive the residue." Thus, the state court implicitly decided only that the particular organizations selected were charitable according to state law. The criteria that determine whether a gift is deductible under [IRC] section 2055 were apparently not considered by the state court. Thus, *Bosch* was not implicated in the case before the Service.

Finally, in Revenue Ruling 69-285 the Service interpreted *Bosch* as creating a two-part test in order for a state court decision to be binding in a federal tax proceeding: (1) that the state court decree determine property rights, and (2) that it issue from the highest court of the state. Although the Supreme Court in *Bosch* did use the "property rights" language in its opinion, most readers of *Bosch* have considered it as laying down only a one-part test—that the decree be that of the highest court of the state.

The Service's use of the "property rights" language is significant. The Supreme Court seemed to have used the phrase in passing to describe the division of responsibilities of federal and state law as indicated in *Morgan*, that state law determines underlying property rights and federal law identifies those rights that are subject to federal taxation. In using the phrase, the Court in *Bosch* seemed to be saying no more than that there must be a state decree purporting to decide the nature of the property interest the federal government is attempting to tax. But what other sort of state decree might be relevant to a federal proceeding? Nothing in the *Bosch* opinion indicates that the Court was attempting to distinguish between state court decisions by whether they determined property rights. It was assumed that the state decree in question determined property rights. Why then would the Service put such emphasis on "property rights?" The reason has become clear with later administrative rulings; the Service has used the property rights test to bring back into the jurisprudence the discarded collusive proceeding test of *Freuler* and *Blair*.

In Technical Advice Memorandum (TAM) 8346008 the Service was asked to rule on whether a decedent's power under Georgia law was the equivalent of a general power of appointment, requiring inclusion of trust assets in the decedent's estate. The matter first arose when the decedent's estate tax return was being examined. A TAM was issued at that time indicating that the decedent possessed a general power of appointment because his power to encroach upon the trust corpus in the event of an "emergency" was not limited by an ascertainable standard relating to health, education, maintenance or support, within the meaning of [IRC] section 2041(b)(1). This TAM was issued on October 25, 1982. On that very day the Supreme Court of Georgia handed down its decision in Warner v. Trust Company Bank, [296 S.E.2d 553, 555 (Ga. 1982),] which held that the term "emergency" did establish an objective limitation or ascertainable standard against which to measure the extent of a right to invade the corpus. According to the IRS, "the issue presented in this [8346008] request for technical advice is the effect to be given . . . to the recent Georgia Supreme Court decision in Warner v. Trust Company Bank." In resolving the issue, the Service relied upon Revenue Ruling 69-285. In *Warner*, the Service observed, the Supreme Court of Georgia was determining after the decedent's death the extent of his power to invade the trust during his life and, thus, "there was no bona fide determination of *property rights*, that is, the court's determination would not affect or change testator's possible ownership of or rights to property." (emphasis added) Moreover, as the Supreme Court of Georgia had reached its decision in *Warner* by use of the doctrine of *ejusdem generis*, the decision was uniquely tied to the particular will being construed and, therefore, had little value as a precedent. Finally, the Service believed that no "*substantial weight*" should be given to the *Warner* decision because it was the result of a "nonadversary proceeding." (emphasis added) Therefore, the Service concluded, the Service "need not give *any weight* to the *Warner* decision." (emphasis added)

Along with the TAM, the Service published General Counsel Memorandum (GCM) 39183, which amplified the reasons for the Service's views announced in TAM 8346008. The GCM argued that, because there was no actual or justiciable controversy between adverse parties in the *Warner* case, the Georgia trial court did not have jurisdiction to enter a declaratory judgment. Thus "we believe that the Georgia Supreme Court would have held that there was no justiciable controversy in the *Warner* case and would have vacated the *Warner* trial court decision had the court been aware of the true nature of the suit." And "it would be unreasonable to believe that the *Bosch* court intended for the federal courts, as well as the Service, to give binding effect to nonadversary state supreme court proceedings brought solely to determine federal estate tax . . . ." This final statement turns *Bosch* on its head. Nothing could be clearer than that the Supreme Court in *Bosch* discarded the nonadversary proceeding rule in favor of the state supreme court decision rule in the interests of more effective administration. While it seems that the *Bosch* Court never seriously envisioned the possibility of the nonadversary state supreme court decision, even if it had, the opinion seems to indicate that it was willing to trade off that cost for the gain in eliminating the unpredictability of the collusion test. Moreover, the Service gratuitously insulted the Georgia Supreme Court with the allegation that the Georgia Supreme Court failed to perceive the circumstances in which the case had come before it. But most importantly, it is clear that *Bosch* is not implicated here at all. The parties before the Georgia Supreme Court in *Warner* were not the same parties before the

Service in TAM 8346008. Whatever relevance *Warner* had to the issues being considered in TAM 8346008 emanated from the Rules of Decision Act, and not from *Bosch*.

STATE COURT ACTION TO CIRCUMVENT *BOSCH*

Massachusetts has long had a procedure whereby a judge of the probate court "may reserve and report the evidence and all questions of law therein for consideration of the [appeals] court." [Mass. Gen. Laws Ann. ch. 215, § 213 (West 1985).] The appeals court may, in turn, be bypassed when two justices of the Supreme Judicial Court find that the public interest requires a final determination by that body. [Mass. Gen. Laws Ann. ch. 211A, § 10(A) (West 1985 & Supp. 1988).] The Supreme Judicial Court of Massachusetts has utilized these procedures to decide a series of cases in which a probate court judge "reported for [the Supreme Court's] consideration the correctness of his interpretation of the will" even though no party to the probate proceeding challenged that interpretation.

Prior to *Bosch* the Supreme Judicial Court acknowledged that, under *Freuler*, the "conclusiveness" of its construction might depend on "its being made in due course of an adversary proceeding." [Old Colony Trust Co. v. Sillman, 223 N.E.2d 504, 507 (Mass. 1967).] Nevertheless, the court continued to hear nonadversary cases because it believed that the federal courts might find some utility in its pronouncements and because its decisions served as "a precedent for purposes of our own subsequent decisions." [Id.] Subsequent to *Bosch*, the court has made it clear that the main reason it has considered the nonadversary cases is "because the Federal Courts and taxing authorities need not follow an interpretation of state law made by a lower state court." [Perksy v. Hunter, 336 N.E.2d 865, 866 (Mass. 1975).] In fact, the court has interpreted *Bosch* as eliminating the nonadversarial nature of the probate proceedings as a relevant consideration. [See Babson v. Babson, 371 N.E.2d 430, 435 n.5 (Mass. 1977)] Thus, the Massachusetts Supreme Judicial Court has read *Bosch* as a justification for hearing cases that are essentially uncontested.

Will other states emulate Massachusetts in undermining the state supreme court requirement of *Bosch*? Connecticut . . . seems to have developed a technique very similar to that of Massachusetts, allowing a trial court to certify questions to the state supreme court. [See Connor v. Hart, 253 A.2d 9 (Conn. 1968); Gimbel v. Gimbel Foundation, 347 A.2d 81 (Conn. 1974).] New Hampshire has a similar procedure, [See In re Tibbett's Estate, 276 A.2d 919 (N.H. 1971)] but in no state other than Massachusetts has there been a substantial number of cases in which the state supreme court has heard probate matters primarily to create a precedent binding in a federal tax proceeding under the *Bosch* rule.

Aside from the improbability that many states will follow the path blazed by the Massachusetts Supreme Judicial Court is the question whether such a course is desirable. It is difficult to read the series of post-*Bosch* decisions emanating from the Supreme Judicial Court as providing the IRS with a more "even-handed" forum for resolving property law issues having a substantial effect on federal transfer tax consequences. The result of *Bosch*, at least in Massachusetts, was to increase the cost of obtaining a decision that previously would have been available from a lower court. The Massachusetts experience does, however, suggest one possible solution to the problem created for lower courts by *Bosch*.

———

EXTERNAL REFERENCES. Palmer on Restitution § 18.7(b); R. Stephens, G. Maxfield, S. Lind, Federal Estate and Gift Taxation (5th ed. 1983); Boyle, Letting the State Law Dog Wag the Tax Tail, 2 Prob. Prac. Rep. 1 (Feb. 1990); Langbein & Waggoner, Reformation of Wills on the Ground of Mistake: Change of Direction in American Law?, 130 U. Pa. L. Rev. 521, 550-54 (1982); Wolfman, *Bosch*, Its Implications and Aftermath: The Effect of State Court Adjudications on Federal Tax Litigation, 3 Inst. on Est. Plan. ¶ 69,200 (1969).

Chapter 7

REVOCABLE TRUSTS AND OTHER WILL SUBSTITUTES

As noted in Chapter 1, will substitutes have come to equal and perhaps dominate deathtime transmission of wealth. The ideal will substitute allows the donor to retain lifetime enjoyment and control over the asset, while purporting presently to transfer to another person a property interest in (or a contract right to) future possession of that asset. Life insurance, pension accounts, joint accounts, and revocable trusts fit this mold and are widely used.

Joint tenancies, especially if severable, are also counted as will substitutes, because they provide for a right of survivorship. The right to sever, however, does not operate like a power to revoke; it does not allow each joint tenant to regain the fractional portion represented by her or his monetary contribution toward the property's acquisition.[1] Instead, the right to sever means that each joint tenant has the lifetime power to gain a fee simple absolute ownership in her or his fractional interest in the property—a one-half interest if there are two joint tenants, a one-third interest if there are three joint tenants, and so on.

Although the above devices are not wills, they are substitutes for wills. They function to pass property at death without being subject to the

---

1. But see, e.g., Blanchette v. Blanchette, 362 Mass. 518, 287 N.E.2d 459 (1972) (joint tenancy unscrambled because husband, who bought AT&T stock in joint tenancy with his then wife under an employee stock-purchase plan, established that he had not created the joint tenancy with donative intent).

statutory formalities required for executing wills. Also, although the affected property passes at death, it passes outside of probate. Will substitutes are sometimes aptly referred to as probate-avoidance devices, or as nonprobate wills. They do not, of course, eliminate the desirability of having a will. Will substitutes tend to be asset-specific, so a will remains necessary for the decedent's other property. Also, wills are helpful as a back-stop even for property affected by a will substitute, especially joint tenancy property, in case the decedent outlives the other joint tenants.

Because of their will-like characteristics, will substitutes have been exerting increasing pressure on the law of succession, which traditionally invokes somewhat different rules for testamentary and nontestamentary transfers. If will substitutes are not wills for purposes of the statutory formalities, are they wills for other purposes, such as the law of lapse or the revocation of wills by changed circumstances such as divorce? There is no necessary reason why they cannot be treated as wills for some purposes but not for others. As we will see, the law of succession is tending in the direction of a unification of its testamentary and nontestamentary branches. In particular, Article II of the 1990 UPC, in an important departure from the pre-1990 UPC, includes rules that extend the subsidiary law of wills to various will substitute arrangements.

EXTERNAL REFERENCES. Restatement 2d of Property § 32.4; Browder, Giving or Leaving—What Is a Will?, 75 Mich. L. Rev. 845 (1977); Langbein, The Nonprobate Revolution and the Future of the Law of Succession, 97 Harv. L. Rev. 1108 (1984); Ritchie, What Is a Will?, 49 Va. L. Rev. 759 (1963).

PART A. VALIDITY OF WILL SUBSTITUTES—FORM OVER SUBSTANCE

1. Revocable Trusts—The Present-Transfer Test

Property law recognizes the validity of a revocable inter-vivos transfer. Does (and should) property law recognize a difference between manifesting a revocable intent to make a future transfer and an intent to make a present, but revocable, transfer? Consider the next case.

Farkas v. Williams
5 Ill. 2d 417, 125 N.E.2d 600 (1955)

HERSHEY, J . . . . Albert B. Farkas died intestate at the age of sixty-seven years, a resident of Chicago, leaving as his only heirs-at-law brothers, sisters, a nephew and a niece. Although retired at the time of his death, he had for many years practiced veterinary medicine and operated a veterinarian establishment in Chicago. During a considerable portion of that time, he employed the defendant Williams, who was not related to him.

On four occasions (December 8, 1948; February 7, 1949; February 14, 1950; and March 1, 1950) Farkas purchased stock of Investors Mutual, Inc. At the time of each purchase he executed a written application to Investors Mutual, Inc., instructing them to issue the stock in his name "as trustee for Richard J. Williams." Investors Mutual, Inc., by its agent, accepted each of these applications in writing by signature on the face of the application. Coincident with the execution of these applications, Farkas signed separate declarations of trust, all of which were identical except as to dates. The terms of said trust instruments are as follows:

> Declaration of Trust—Revocable. I, the undersigned, having purchased or declared my intention to purchase certain shares of capital stock of Investors Mutual, Inc. (the Company), and having directed that the certificate for said stock be issued in my name as trustee for Richard J. Williams as beneficiary, whose address is 1704 W. North Ave. Chicago, Ill., under this Declaration of Trust Do Hereby Declare that the terms and conditions upon which I shall hold said stock in trust and any additional stock resulting from reinvestments of cash dividends upon such original or additional shares are as follows:
>
> (1) During my lifetime all cash dividends are to be paid to me individually for my own personal account and use;
>
> (2) Upon my death the title to any stock subject hereto and the right to any subsequent payments or distributions shall be vested absolutely in the beneficiary. . . .
>
> (3) During my lifetime I reserve the right, as trustee, to vote, sell, redeem, exchange or otherwise deal in or with the stock subject hereto, but upon any sale or redemption of said stock or any part thereof, the trust hereby declared shall terminate as to the stock sold or redeemed, and I shall be entitled to retain the proceeds of sale or redemption for my own personal account and use.
>
> (4) I reserve the right at any time to change the beneficiary or revoke this trust, but it is understood that no change of beneficiary and no revocation of this trust except by death of the beneficiary, shall be effective as to the Company for any purpose unless and until written notice thereof in such form as the Company shall prescribe is delivered to the Company at Minneapolis, Minnesota. The decease of the beneficiary before my death shall operate as a revocation of this trust.
>
> (5) In the event this trust shall be revoked or otherwise terminated, said stock and all rights and privileges thereunder shall belong to and be exercised by me in my individual capacity. . . .

The applications and declarations of trust were delivered to Investors Mutual, Inc., and held by the company until Farkas's death. The stock certificates were issued in the name of Farkas as "trustee for Richard J. Williams" and were discovered in a safety-deposit box of Farkas after his death, along with other securities, some of which were in the name of Williams alone. . . .

It is conceded that the instruments were not executed in such a way as to satisfy the requirements of the statute on wills; hence, our inquiry is limited to whether said trust instruments created valid inter vivos trusts effective to give the purported beneficiary, Williams, title to the stock in question after the death of the settlor-trustee, Farkas. To make this determination we must consider: (1) whether upon execution of the so-called trust instruments defendant Williams acquired an interest in the subject matter of the trusts, the stock of defendant Investors Mutual, Inc., (2) whether Farkas, as settlor-trustee, retained such control over the subject matter of the trusts as to render said trust instruments attempted testamentary dispositions.

First, upon execution of these trust instruments did defendant Williams presently acquire an interest in the subject matter of the intended trusts?

If no interest passed to Williams before the death of Farkas, the intended trusts are testamentary and hence invalid for failure to comply with the statute on wills. Restatement of the Law of Trusts, section 56.

But considering the terms of these instruments we believe Farkas did intend to presently give Williams an interest in the property referred to. For it may be said, at the very least, that upon his executing one of these instruments, he showed an intention to presently part with some of the incidents of ownership in the stock. Immediately after the execution of each of these instruments, he could not deal with the stock therein referred to the same as if he owned the property absolutely, but only in accordance with the terms of the instrument. He purported to set himself up as trustee of the stock for the benefit of Williams, and the stock was registered in his name as trustee for Williams. Thus assuming to act as trustee, he is held to have intended to take on those obligations which are expressly set out in the instrument, as well as those fiduciary obligations implied by law. In addition, he manifested an intention to bind himself to having this property pass upon his death to Williams, unless he changed the beneficiary or revoked the trust, and then such change of beneficiary or revocation was not to be effective as to Investors Mutual, Inc., unless and until written notice thereof in such form as the company prescribed was delivered to them at Minneapolis, Minnesota. An absolute owner can dispose of his property, either in his lifetime or by will, in any way he sees fit without notifying or securing approval from anyone and without being held to the duties of a fiduciary in so doing.

It seems to follow that what incidents of ownership Farkas intended to relinquish, in a sense he intended Williams to acquire. That is, Williams was to be the beneficiary to whom Farkas was to be obligated, and unless Farkas revoked the instrument in the manner therein set out or the instrument was otherwise terminated in a manner therein provided for, upon Farkas's death Williams was to become absolute owner of the trust property. It is difficult to name this interest of Williams,[2] nor is there any reason for so doing so long as it passed to him immediately upon the creation of the trust. As stated in 4 Powell, The Law of Real Property, at page 87: "Interests of beneficiaries of private express trusts run the gamut from valuable substantialities to evanescent hopes. Such a beneficiary may

---

2. It was a vested remainder subject to divestment. See infra p. 860. Eds.

have any one of an almost infinite variety of the possible aggregates of rights, privileges, powers and immunities."

An additional problem is presented here, however, for it is to be noted that the trust instruments provide: "The decease of the beneficiary before my death shall operate as a revocation of this trust." The plaintiffs argue that the presence of this provision removes the only possible distinction which might have been drawn between these instruments and a will. Being thus conditioned on his surviving, it is argued that the "interest" of Williams until the death of Farkas was a mere expectancy. Conversely, they assert, the interest of Farkas in the securities until his death was precisely the same as that of a testator who bequeaths securities by his will, since he had all the rights accruing to an absolute owner.

Admittedly, had this provision been absent the interest of Williams would have been greater, since he would then have had an inheritable interest in the lifetime of Farkas. But to say his interest would have been greater is not to say that he here did not have a beneficial interest, properly so-called, during the lifetime of Farkas. The provision purports to set up but another "contingency" which would serve to terminate the trust. The disposition is not testamentary and the intended trust is valid, even though the interest of the beneficiary is contingent upon the existence of a certain state of facts at the time of the settlor's death. Restatement of the Law of Trusts, section 56, comment f. In an example contained in the previous reference, the authors of the Restatement have referred to the interest of a beneficiary under a trust who must survive the settlor (and where the settlor receives the income for life) as a contingent equitable interest in remainder.

This question of whether any interest passed immediately is also involved in the next problem considered, namely, the quantum of power retained by a settlor which will cause an intended *inter vivos* trust to fail as an attempted testamentary disposition. Therefore, much of what is said in the next part of the opinion, as well as the authorities cited, will pertain to this interest question.

Second, did Farkas retain such control over the subject matter of the trust as to render said trust instruments attempted testamentary dispositions?

In each of these trust instruments, Farkas reserved to himself as settlor the following powers: (1) the right to receive during his lifetime all cash dividends; (2) the right at any time to change the beneficiary or revoke the trust; and (3) upon sale or redemption of any portion of the trust property, the right to retain the proceeds therefrom for his own use.

Additionally, Farkas reserved the right to act as sole trustee, and in such capacity, he was accorded the right to vote, sell, redeem, exchange or otherwise deal in the stock which formed the subject matter of the trust.

We shall consider first those enumerated powers which Farkas reserved to himself as settlor.

It is well established that the retention by the settlor of the power to revoke, even when coupled with the reservation of a life interest in the trust property, does not render the trust inoperative for want of execution as a will.

Only when it is thought that there are additional reservations present of such a substantial nature as to amount to the retention of full ownership is a court likely to invalidate an inter vivos trust by reason of its not being executed as a will. (See Restatement of the Law of Trusts, section 57.) . . .

However, it is not every so-called additional reservation of power that will be deemed sufficient to invalidate a trust of this nature. In 32 A.L.R.2d 1270, it is stated at pages 1276-1277:

> The later cases, as do the earlier ones, justify the general conclusion that many and extensive rights and power may be reserved by a settlor, in addition to a life interest and power of revocation, without defeating the trust. The instrument is likely to be upheld notwithstanding it includes additionally the reservation of power to amend the trust in whole or in part, or extensive powers over investments, management, or administration, or power to appoint or remove trustees or to appoint interests in remainder, or the right to act as trustee or as one of the trustees, or to enjoy limited rights in the principal, or to withdraw part or all of the principal, or to possess, use, or enjoy the trust property, or to sell or mortgage the property or any of it and appropriate the proceeds.

We conclude therefore, in accordance with the great weight of authority, said powers which Farkas reserved to himself as settlor were not such as to render the intended trusts invalid as attempted testamentary dispositions.

A more difficult problem is posed, however, by the fact that Farkas is also trustee, and as such, is empowered to vote, sell, redeem, exchange and otherwise deal in and with the subject matter of the trusts.

That a settlor may create a trust of personal property whereby he names himself as trustee and acts as such for the beneficiary is clear. Restatement of the Law of Trusts, section 17.

Moreover, the later cases indicate that the mere fact that the settlor in addition to making himself sole trustee also reserves a life interest and a power of revocation does not render the trust invalid as testamentary in character. 32 A.L.R.2d 1286. In 1 Scott, The Law of Trusts, it is stated at pages 353-354:

> The owner of property may create a trust not only by transferring the property to another person as trustee, but also by declaring himself trustee. Such a declaration of trust, although gratuitous, is valid. . . . Suppose, however, that the settlor reserves not only a beneficial life interest but also a power of revocation. It would seem that such a trust is not necessarily testamentary. The declaration of trust immediately creates an equitable interest in the beneficiaries, although the enjoyment of the interest is postponed until the death of the settlor, and although the interest may be divested by the exercise of the power of revocation. The disposition is not essentially different from that which is made where the settlor transfers the property to another person as trustee. It is true that where the settlor declares himself trustee he controls the administration of the trust. As has been stated, if the settlor transfers property upon trust and reserves not only a power of revocation but also power to control the administration of the trust, the trust is testamentary.

> There is this difference, however: the power of control which the settlor has as trustee is not an irresponsible power and can be exercised only in accordance with the terms of the trust.

See also Restatement of the Law of Trusts, section 57, comment b.

In the instant case the plaintiffs contend that Farkas, as settlor-trustee, retained complete control and dominion over the securities for his own benefit during his lifetime. It is argued that he had the power to deal with the property as he liked so long as he lived and owed no enforceable duties of any kind to Williams as beneficiary. . . .

That the retention of the power by Farkas as trustee to sell or redeem the stock and keep the proceeds for his own use should not render these trust instruments testamentary in character becomes more evident upon analyzing the real import and significance of the powers to revoke and to amend the trust, the reservation of which the courts uniformly hold does not invalidate an *inter vivos* trust.

It is obvious that a settlor with the power to revoke and to amend the trust at any time is, for all practical purpose, in a position to exert considerable control over the trustee regarding the administration of the trust. For anything believed to be inimicable to his best interests can be thwarted or prevented by simply revoking the trust or amending it in such a way as to conform to his wishes. Indeed, it seems that many of those powers which from time to time have been viewed as "additional powers" are already, in a sense, virtually contained within the overriding power of revocation or the power to amend the trust. Consider, for example, the following: (1) the power to consume the principal; (2) the power to sell or mortgage the trust property and appropriate the proceeds; (3) the power to appoint or remove trustees; (4) the power to supervise and direct investments; and (5) the power to otherwise direct and supervise the trustee in the administration of the trust. Actually, any of the above powers could readily be assumed by a settlor with the reserved power of revocation through the simple expedient of revoking the trust, and then, as absolute owner of the subject matter, doing with the property as he chooses. Even though no actual termination of the trust is effectuated, however, it could hardly be questioned but that the mere existence of this power in the settlor is sufficient to enable his influence to be felt in a practical way in the administration of the trust. . . .

In the case at bar, the power of Farkas to vote, sell, redeem, exchange or otherwise deal in the stock was reserved to him as trustee, and it was only upon sale or redemption that he was entitled to keep the proceeds for his own use. Thus, the control reserved is not as great as in those cases where said power is reserved to the owner as settlor. For as trustee he must so conduct himself in accordance with standards applicable to trustees generally. It is not a valid objection to this to say that Williams would never question Farkas' conduct, inasmuch as Farkas could then revoke the trust and destroy what interest Williams has. Such a possibility exists in any case where the settlor has the power of revocation. Still, Williams has rights the same as any beneficiary, although it may not be feasible for him to exercise them. Moreover, it is entirely possible that he might in certain situations have a right to hold Farkas' estate liable for breaches of trust committed by Farkas during his lifetime. In this regard, consider what would happen if, without having revoked the trust, Farkas as trustee had given the stock away without receiving any consideration therefor, had pledged the stock improperly for his own personal debt and allowed it to be lost by foreclosure or had exchanged the stock for another security or other worthless property in such manner as to constitute gross impropriety and gross negligence. In such instances, it would seem in accordance with the terms of these instruments that Williams would have had an enforceable claim against Farkas' estate for whatever damage had been suffered. Contrast this with the rights of a legatee or devisee under a will. The testator could waste the property or do anything with it he wished during his lifetime without incurring any liability to those designated by the will to inherit the property. In any event, if Farkas as settlor could reserve the power to sell or otherwise deal with the property and retain the proceeds, which the cases indicate he could, then it necessarily follows that he should have the right to sell or otherwise deal with the property as trustee and retain the proceeds from a sale or redemption without having the instruments rendered invalid as testamentary dispositions.

Another factor often considered in determining whether an *inter vivos* trust is an attempted testamentary disposition is the formality of the transaction. Restatement of the Law of Trusts, section 57, comment g. Historically, the purpose behind the enactment of the statute on wills was the prevention of fraud. The requirement as to witnesses was deemed necessary because a will is ordinarily an expression of the secret wish of the testator, signed out of the presence of all concerned. The possibility of forgery and fraud are ever present in such situations. Here, Farkas executed four separate applications for stock of Investors Mutual, Inc., in which he directed that the stock be issued in his name as trustee for Williams, and he executed four separate declarations of trust in which he declared he was holding said stock in trust for Williams. The stock certificates in question were issued in his name as trustee for Williams. He thus manifested his intention in a solemn and formal manner.

For the reasons stated, we conclude that these trust declarations executed by Farkas constituted valid *inter vivos* trusts and were not attempted testamentary dispositions. It must be conceded that they have, in the words of Mr. Justice Holmes in Bromley v. Mitchell, 155 Mass. 509, 30 N.E. 83, a "*testamentary* look." Moreover, it must be admitted that the line should be drawn somewhere, but after a study of this case we do not believe that point has here been reached. . . .

Reversed and remanded, with directions.

———

Revocability of Inter-Vivos Trusts. Like other inter-vivos transfers of property, an inter-vivos transfer in trust is *irrevocable* unless the grantor expressly retains a power to revoke.[3] This contrasts, of course, with wills, which are revocable without the necessity of an explicit reservation of a power to revoke or amend.

A power to revoke is usually held to include within it the lesser power to alter or amend the terms of the trust. Restatement 2d of Trusts § 331.

Validity of Revocable, Self-Declared Trusts. The Restatement 2d of Trusts supports the position taken by the court in the *Farkas* case. Section 57, comment h, states that a self-declared trust is:

> not testamentary and invalid for failure to comply with the requirements of the Statute of Wills merely because the settlor-trustee reserves a beneficial life estate and power to revoke and modify the trust. The fact that as trustee he controls the administration of the trust does not invalidate it.

Cases in accord with the validity of self-declared trusts similar to the one in *Farkas* include Investors Stock Fund, Inc. v. Roberts, 179 F. Supp. 185 (D. Mont. 1959), aff'd, 286 F.2d 647 (9th Cir. 1961); United Bldg. & Loan Ass'n v. Garrett, 64 F. Supp. 460 (D. Ark. 1946); Estate of Kovalyshyn, 136 N.J. Super. 40, 343 A.2d 852 (1975); Ridge v. Bright, 244 N.C. 345, 93 S.E.2d 607 (1956); Smith v. Deshaw, 116 Vt. 441, 78 A.2d 479 (1951). See also Tex. Prop. Code § 112.033. Contra, Ambrosius v. Ambrosius, 239 F. 473 (2d Cir. 1917) (claimed declaration of trust was quite informal); Mathias v. Fantine, 1990 WL 21466 (Ohio Ct. App. 1990) (surprisingly, court held that grantor's interest as trustee and sole current beneficiary merged, so that no trust was created).

Power in Grantor to Control Administration of Trust. The court in *Farkas* distinguished between the grantor's power to control the administration of the trust as trustee versus retaining that power as grantor:

> [I]f the settlor transfers property upon trust and reserves not only a power of revocation but also power to control the administration of the trust, the trust is testamentary. There is this difference, however: the power of control which the settlor has as trustee is not an irresponsible power and can be exercised only in accordance with the terms of the trust.

Although Restatement of Trusts section 57(3) took the same view, Restatement 2d of Trusts section 57 provides that a trust is not testamentary and invalid "merely because the settlor reserves . . . a power to control the trustee as to the administration of the trust." Cf. National Shawmut Bank v. Joy, 315 Mass. 457, 53 N.E.2d 113 (1944) (power in grantor to control investments did not render trust invalid).

Liability for Breach of Fiduciary Duties? In the *Farkas* opinion, the court suggested that the grantor of a self-declared, revocable trust might be liable, or the grantor's estate might be liable, if the grantor as trustee breached fiduciary duties in the administration of the trust. Is the court

---

3. Statutes in a few states establish the opposite rule. They provide that transfers in trust are revocable unless expressly made irrevocable. See, e.g., Cal. Prob. Code § 15400; Okla. Stat. Ann. tit. 60 § 175.41; Tex. Prop. Code § 112.051.

right about this, or would the breach of fiduciary duties be regarded as an implied exercise of the grantor's power of revocation? According to Restatement 2d of Trusts section 330 comments i & j:

> If the settlor reserves a power to revoke the trust but does not specify any mode of revocation, the power can be exercised in any manner which sufficiently manifests the intention of the settlor to revoke the trust. Any definitive manifestation by the settlor of his intention that the trust should be forthwith revoked is sufficient . . . . If the settlor reserves a power to revoke the trust only in a particular manner or under particular circumstances, he can revoke the trust only in that manner or under those circumstances.

Compare Langbein, The Nonprobate Revolution and the Future of the Law of Succession, 97 Harv. L. Rev. 1108, 1127-28 (1984):

> I suggest that if [the grantor breached a fiduciary duty], the court would treat the case as the analytical equivalent of . . . a two-step transaction—revocation followed by dealings free of trust. In other words, if a plaintiff brought [a lawsuit alleging breach of fiduciary duties]—and of course, no one ever has— the estate of the [grantor] would contend that the interest that the [grantor] retained under the trust was so great that he owed no duty of care to those to whom he might have left something.

But see Breeze v. Breeze, 428 N.E.2d 286 (Ind. Ct. App. 1982). After the grantor's death, the grantor's widow petitioned to have the court declare that the assets of a self-declared, revocable trust were part of the grantor's probate estate, to which she had a claim as heir, rather than pass to the grantor's nieces and nephews, who the trust document designated as the trust beneficiaries after the grantor's death. The court rejected her claim, saying:

> [The widow] submitted evidence that [the grantor] failed to act in a fiduciary capacity. . . . [Her] evidence attempted to prove that [the grantor] treated the property as his own. . . . The essence of [her] argument is that the trust was revoked by [these actions] . . . . We cannot accept [her] argument. . . . [The grantor's failure] to fulfill his duties as trustee may have been grounds for his removal as trustee, but it was not grounds to find the trust was revoked.

Revoking a Self-Declared Revocable Trust. In Barnette v. McNulty, 21 Ariz. App. 127, 516 P.2d 583 (1974), the grantor created a self-declared revocable trust. After his death, the question arose as to whether he had revoked the trust. On this point, the court said:

> As set forth in Restatement (Second) of Trusts § 330, comment i, the [grantor] can revoke a trust by communicating his decision to do so to the trustee. In the case sub judice, the [grantor] is also the trustee. It would be absurd to require the [grantor] to call himself up on the telephone as trustee and tell himself that he is revoking the trust. It would be equally absurd to have the [grantor] send himself a letter as trustee to inform himself as trustee that the trust is to be terminated. The [trust is revoked if it can be shown]

that [the grantor] intended to terminate the trust and some communication on his part to the beneficiary or to a third party manifesting his decision to revoke.

If a revocable trust document is traced to the grantor's possession and cannot be found after her or his death, should a presumption arise that the grantor destroyed the document with intent to revoke the trust?

Rights of the Grantor's Creditors and Creditors of the Grantor's Estate. If a grantor transfers assets to a trust "in fraud of his or her creditors," the grantor's creditors can set the transfer aside to the extent necessary to satisfy the indebtedness, whether the indebtedness arose before or after the transfer. Restatement 2d of Property § 34.3; Unif. Fraudulent Transfers Act (1984) (in effect in about 26 states); Unif. Fraudulent Conveyances Act (1918) (in effect in about 10 states). A transfer "in fraud of creditors" is one made with actual intent to hinder, delay, or defraud a creditor or one that leaves the grantor's remaining assets insufficient to satisfy current debts or debts the grantor intended to incur. A transfer to a trust that is in fraud of creditors can be set aside under the "fraudulent-transfer" principle, whether the trust is revocable or irrevocable.

If the transfer to a *revocable* trust was *not* in fraud of creditors, can the grantor's creditors nevertheless satisfy an indebtedness out of the trust assets on the ground of the revocability of the trust? In National Shawmut Bank v. Joy, 315 Mass. 457, 53 N.E.2d 113 (1944), the court said that an unexercised power to alter, amend, or revoke a trust "is not property, and apart from the Bankruptcy Act cannot be reached by [the grantor's] creditors." This is the traditional position. See Restatement 2d of Trusts § 330 comment o; Scott on Trusts § 330.12.

The Restatement 2d of Property section 34.3(3) and several recent decisions have broken away from the traditional position and allow the grantor's creditors to reach assets in a revocable trust, even though the transfer to the trust was not in fraud of creditors. State Street Bank & Trust Co. v. Reiser, 7 Mass. App. 633, 389 N.E.2d 768 (1979); Estate of Kovalyshyn, 136 N.J. Super. 40, 343 A.2d 852 (1975); Johnson v. Commercial Bank, 284 Or. 675, 588 P.2d 1096 (1978). These cases all involved creditors' claims to the grantor's estate, but the holdings would seem to apply also to creditors' suits brought during the grantor's lifetime. In the *Johnson* case, the Oregon Supreme Court held:

> The proposition that a settlor who retains a life estate in a trust and a *general power of appointment* over the principal of the trust will be treated as the owner with respect to creditors is recognized by A. Scott, The Law of Trusts § 156 (3d ed. 1967); G. Bogert, The Law of Trusts and Trustees § 223 (2d ed. 1965); E. Griswold, Spendthrift Trusts §§ 477-478 (2d ed. 1947). In this case, [the grantor] did not have a general power of appointment, but he *did* retain the right to revoke. . . .
>
> The right to revoke is essentially the same as a general power of appointment since the person having the right to revoke may acquire the property and then appoint or give it to whomever he pleases. There being no practical difference between the right to revoke and a power to appoint, we conclude that the rule stated by the above authorities should apply to this

case. We conclude that [the grantor's estate creditor] was entitled to reach the trust assets to pay her claim.

Several states have enacted statutes that allow the grantor's estate and lifetime creditors to reach assets of a revocable trust. See, e.g., Cal. Prob. Code §§ 18200-18201; Mich. Comp. Laws Ann. § 556.128. See generally Committee Report, Rights of Creditors to Reach Assets of a Revocable Trust After the Death of the Grantor—The Missouri Approach, 20 Real Prop. Prob. & Tr. J. 1189 (1985); Schuyler, Revocable Trusts—Spouses, Creditors and Other Predators, 1974 Inst. on Est. Plan. ¶ 74.1300.

The Bankruptcy Code, adopted in 1978, is less clear than its predecessor on whether the grantor's bankruptcy trustee can reach a revocable trust.[4] If the Bankruptcy Code addresses the question at all, it is by negative implication in the following provision:

> *Bankruptcy Code, 11 U.S.C. § 541. Property of the Estate:* . . . (b) Property of the estate does not include . . . any power that the debtor may exercise solely for the benefit of an entity other than the debtor. . . .

No provision explicitly declares that "property of the estate" *includes* property over which the debtor retains a power exercisable for the debtor's own benefit, such as a power of revocation.

Rights of the Grantor's Surviving Spouse. In some jurisdictions, the grantor's surviving spouse may claim an elective share in the assets of a revocable trust. This subject is considered in Chapter 8.

Federal Taxation of Revocable Trusts: Substance Over Form. The federal system of income, estate, and gift taxation taxes revocable trusts according to their substance, not their form, as illustrated by the following example:

> *Example 7.1:* G transferred property to T, in trust, directing the trustee to pay the net income from the property to G for his lifetime and at his death to deliver the trust corpus to X. G retained a power to revoke the trust at any time and have the trust property returned to him.

The tax consequences of G's transfer are as follows:

> (1) Gift tax consequences: Because of his power to revoke, G's transfer of a remainder interest to X was not a taxable gift. See Treas. Reg. § 25.2511-1(c).
> (2) Income tax consequences: G will continue until his death to be taxed on both the ordinary income generated by the property and also on capital gains (or losses) realized by the trust. See IRC §§ 676, 677(a)(1); Treas. Reg. § 1.671-3(b).
> (3) Estate tax consequences: When G dies, the full value of the corpus of the trust will be included in G's gross estate under IRC § 2036(a)(1) or § 2038.

---

4. Under the predecessor of the Bankruptcy Code, the Bankruptcy Act, 11 U.S.C. § 110(a), the trustee of the estate of a bankrupt was "vested by operation of law with the title of the bankrupt as of the date of the filing of the petition . . . to powers which he [the bankrupt] might have exercised for his own benefit, but not those which he might have exercised solely for some other person."

See supra Chapter 6.

2. Some Other Will Substitutes—
The Present-Transfer Test

Statutory References: *1989 UPC §§ 6-101, -203, -211 to -214*
Pre-1989 UPC §§ 6-101 to -113, 6-201

The present-transfer test of the *Farkas* case is widely used to validate many will substitutes, not only revocable trusts. Though wills in substance, transfers that can be characterized as having presently passed to a donee any *interest in property*, whether present or future, vested or contingent, are not treated as testamentary and their validity does not depend upon compliance with the execution formalities required of wills. Likewise, transfers that can be characterized as presently conferring a *contract right* on another are exempted from the statutory formalities for wills, even though the time of performance of the contract is geared to the time of the transferor's death.

Life Insurance and Life-Insurance Trusts. Compliance with the statutory formalities for wills is not required of beneficiary designations of life-insurance policies. Although life-insurance contracts pay out at death, the beneficiary designation—when made—is treated as conferring a present contract right on the beneficiary. The will-like characteristics of life insurance can, therefore, be ignored, among which are the retained lifetime right of the owner of the policy (who typically is the person whose life is insured by the policy) to terminate the policy or to revoke the beneficiary designation and name a different beneficiary.

An additional will-like characteristic of life insurance is the requirement that the beneficiary survive the insured to be entitled to the policy's proceeds. Conventional antilapse statutes do not cover life-insurance beneficiary designations.

In many states, the proceeds of life-insurance policies are wholly or partly exempt from the claims of the insured's creditors. The statutes vary, and may only apply if the proceeds are payable to specified members of the insured's family.

A popular estate-planning technique is to establish a life-insurance trust. Life-insurance trusts take different forms. One type of life-insurance trust is created by transferring the full ownership of the policy to the trustee. An arrangement in which the grantor irrevocably transfers the policy to the trustee and makes the trust itself irrevocable typically is tax motivated—that is, the arrangement is designed to avoid the inclusion of the value of the proceeds of the policy in the insured's gross estate under IRC section 2042. Trusts of this sort are sometimes "funded"—that is, other assets are irrevocably transferred to the trustee, in addition to the life-insurance policy, with directions to the trustee to pay the life-insurance premiums out of the income generated by the other assets. If the trust is not "funded," the grantor of the trust (the previous owner of the policy and the insured) usually continues to pay the premiums on the policy out of her or his own pocket.

A second type of life-insurance trust is created by naming the trustee as the beneficiary of the life-insurance policy, with directions to the trustee to collect the proceeds on the insured's death and carry out the terms of the trust. Trusts of this sort typically are revocable and hence are not tax motivated. Rather, the motive usually is the administrative convenience of having insurance proceeds added at death to an existing inter-vivos trust. The trust itself is not only revocable, but so is the designation of the trustee as the beneficiary of the policy. The insured, as owner of the policy, retains the right to renounce the beneficiary designation, to terminate the policy, to surrender the policy for its cash value, if any, and so on. Although the validity of this type of trust was at one time in doubt, it now seems settled that this type of arrangement creates a valid trust. As explained by the court in Gordon v. Portland Trust Bank, 201 Or. 648, 271 P.2d 653 (1954):

> Our own view is that the ownership of the . . . policy is actually divided between the [trustee, as the] beneficiary [of the policy] and the insured. . . . [T]he loan and cash surrender values . . . are clearly the property of the insured. On the other hand, the [trustee as the] beneficiary [of the policy] is the owner of a promise to pay the proceeds at the death of insured, subject to insured's right of revocation.

Another decision, Gurnett v. Mutual Life Insurance Co., 356 Ill. 612, 191 N.E. 250 (1934), said:

> The continuing [contract] right to receive the proceeds of an insurance policy is not impaired by the unexercised right or privilege of the insured to designate another beneficiary.

See also A. Smith, Personal Life Insurance Trusts ch. 2 (1960).

Multiple-Party Accounts. Bank and other financial intermediary accounts frequently are registered in the names of more than one person. These multiple-party accounts generally take one of several forms: trust (so-called "Totten" trusts), joint, or payable on death (POD). These forms themselves are ambiguous concerning the depositor's substantive purpose. The depositor may or may not intend to confer on the other party beneficial lifetime rights or survivorship rights or both. For example, if A deposits funds in a savings account registered jointly in the names of "A or B," A may have used the joint form for any one of three different purposes: (1) to give A and B lifetime rights to withdraw funds for their personal benefit, with the survivor receiving funds remaining in the account upon the death of the first to die (a true joint tenancy); (2) to give B the legal power to draw from the account for A's benefit but not B's and no survivorship right (an agency account, in which B acts as A's agent); or (3) to give B the right to any funds remaining in the account at A's death, but no lifetime rights or powers (the equivalent of a payable-on-death account).

Totten trusts. The Totten trust is created when a person deposits her or his funds in a savings or bank account in her or his name "in trust for" another person. The depositor typically retains exclusive control of the account until death, when any remaining funds pass to the beneficiary. Totten trusts have been called the "poor person's will," but as Professor Friedman has observed, "It would be more accurate to call it a middle-class will." Friedman, The Law of the Living, The Law of the Dead: Property, Succession, and Society, 1966 Wis. L. Rev. 340, 369 (1966). Totten trusts are usually created without legal advice, specifically for the purpose of by-passing probate. They are functionally equivalent to a will in every respect; only form distinguishes them from wills.

The Totten trust takes its name from the leading New York case, Matter of Totten, 179 N.Y. 112, 71 N.E. 748 (1904). The court held that such a "trust" was a "tentative trust merely, revocable at will, until the depositor dies or completes the gift in his lifetime by some unequivocal act or declaration, such as delivery of the passbook or notice to the beneficiary."

The Totten trust has been accepted in a substantial number of states besides New York. See, e.g., Brucks v. Home Federal Saving & Loan Association, 36 Cal. 2d 845, 228 P.2d 545 (1951); Seymour v. Seymour, 85 So. 2d 726 (Fla. 1956); Estate of Petralia, 32 Ill. 2d 134, 204 N.E.2d 1 (1965); Estate of Morton, 241 Kan. 698, 740 P.2d 571 (1987); Estate of McFetridge, 472 Pa. 546, 372 A.2d 823 (1977); Reynolds v. Shambeau, 140 Vt. 317, 437 A.2d 1101 (1981). Totten trusts are validated by statute in several states.

Some courts, however, have refused to give effect to the arrangement, either on the ground that it is an attempted testamentary disposition, see, e.g., Fleck v. Baldwin, 141 Tex. 340, 172 S.W.2d 975 (1943), or on the ground that the mere form of the deposit is insufficient evidence of an intent to create a trust, see, e.g., Hoffman's Estate, 175 Ohio St. 363, 195 N.E.2d 106 (1963). A few cases uphold the trust but treat it as irrevocable. See Cazallis v. Ingraham, 119 Me. 240, 110 A. 359 (1920). The question is still open in quite a few jurisdictions.

Courts have held that creditors of the depositor can reach the deposit to satisfy their claims, both while the depositor is living, see Workmen's Compensation Board v. Furman, 106 N.Y.S.2d 404 (Sup. Ct. 1951), and after her or his death, see, e.g., Reich's Estate, 146 Misc. 616, 262 N.Y.S. 623 (1933). Where the beneficiary dies before the depositor, it has been held that the trust "terminated ipso facto, and that the funds on deposit thereafter remained the sole property of the depositor, unimpressed by any trust." See In re United States Trust Co., 117 App. Div. 178, 102 N.Y.S. 271 (1907). A Totten trust may be revoked by appropriate provisions in the depositor's will. See Scanlon's Estate, 313 Pa. 424, 169 A. 106 (1933); infra pp. 407 & 447.

There seems no reason to doubt that a Totten trust can be made irrevocable, but there has been very little discussion of what evidence of intent is needed for this purpose. The question was presented in Estate of Sulovich v. Commissioner, 587 F.2d 845 (6th Cir. 1978); Ingels' Estate, 372

Pa. 171, 92 A.2d 881 (1952); and In re Farrell, 298 N.Y. 129, 81 N.E.2d 51 (1948).

Joint accounts; POD accounts. Like Totten trust accounts, joint bank and other financial organization accounts contain a survivorship feature. The balance on hand in the account at the death of a depositor shifts to the surviving co-account holder without going through probate.

Except in a very few states, however, the funds in a joint account are not owned in joint tenancy (or tenancy by the entirety, if between spouses). That is to say, a deposit into such an account does not transfer an undivided interest therein to the other co-account holder. The fact that each account holder has a right to withdraw the whole of the account masks the true ownership of the funds in the account. The true ownership is that each account holder continues to own her or his own contribution to the balance on hand.[5] If one co-account holder withdraws an amount in excess of her or his own contributions, the other co-account holder normally has a right to force that excess to be returned. This right is routinely waived by inaction, possibly triggering federal gift tax consequences when the statute of limitations expires. See Treas. Reg. § 25.2511-1(h)(4); Estate of Lang v. Commissioner, 613 F.2d 770 (9th Cir. 1980). Consequently, as between the co-account holders, a deposit into a joint bank account is revocable; no federal gift tax consequences are triggered because the tax law treats the deposit as an "incomplete" gift. See supra p. 358.

As with a revocable inter-vivos trust, the validity of the survivorship feature depends upon satisfaction of the present-transfer test. Most courts have found the test to be satisfied on the same theory used to uphold life-insurance beneficiary designations, that is, upon deposit the non-depositing co-account holder acquires a present (though defeasible) contract right to the deposit, payable on the death of the depositor. Legislation in many states also validates or is treated as validating the survivorship feature of joint bank accounts. Finally, in seeming contradiction of the predominant view concerning the rights of each party during life, a group of cases validates the survivorship feature by utilizing a joint-tenancy analysis, especially when the deposit agreement, in tracking the language of a widely enacted bank-protection statute, describes the co-depositors as "joint tenants."

Payable on death (POD) accounts are created when a depositor registers the account in her or his name "payable on death" to another person. Unlike joint accounts, the form of POD accounts discloses the intention to transfer benefits only at the depositor's death. This difference in form has led most courts to treat joint and POD accounts differently. In the absence of validating legislation, POD accounts are generally held to be testamentary, invalidating the attempted transfer of ownership on the depositor's

---

5. In cases involving the rights of a creditor to reach its debtor's interest in a joint account, the applicable case law may ignore underlying beneficial interests and permit the creditor to reach more than its debtor might have withdrawn and retained against the wishes of the other depositor.

death. See, e.g., Truax v. Southwestern College, 214 Kan. 873, 522 P.2d 412 (1974); Compton v. Compton, 435 S.W.2d 76 (Ky. 1968); Matter of Collier, 381 S.2d 1338 (Miss. 1980); Blais v. Colebrook Guaranty Saving Bank, 107 N.H. 300, 220 A.2d 763 (1966); Brown's Estate, 343 Pa. 230, 22 A.2d 821 (1941); Methodist Church v. First Nat'l Bank, 125 Vt. 124, 211 A.2d 168 (1965); Tucker v. Simrow, 248 Wis. 143, 21 N.W.2d 252 (1946). Contra, e.g., Estate of Wright, 17 Ill. App. 3d 894, 308 N.E.2d 319 (1974). See generally McGovern, The Payable on Death Account and Other Will Substitutes, 67 Nw. U. L. Rev. 7 (1972).

POD accounts have fared much better in the legislatures. Legislation in about half the states validates the survivorship feature of such accounts, without requiring compliance with the execution formalities required of wills. Restatement 2d of Property section 32.4 comment e recognizes the validity of POD accounts.

Multiple-party accounts under pre-1989 and 1989 UPC. UPC Article VI deals with non-probate transfers. The pre-1989 version separately identified and defined lifetime and survivorship rights in three types of multiple-party accounts: joint accounts, POD accounts, and trust accounts. Another group of provisions defined various protections for financial intermediaries in making payments according to the terms of account contracts.

Under the pre-1989 version, lifetime ownership of co-account holders in joint accounts was presumptively proportionate to each party's contribution to the balance on deposit. A POD account was owned solely by the depositor and a trust account was owned solely by the trustee.

Concerning survivorship rights, section 6-104 of the pre-1989 version presumptively created a survivorship feature in all accounts that were presently payable to two or more parties, regardless of whether the account form described them as joint tenants or referred in any way to a right of survivorship. The pre-1989 version did recognize, however, that a multiple-party account need not contain a survivorship feature. Although a joint account was presumed to provide survivorship rights, this presumption was rebuttable by clear and convincing evidence of a contrary intent. Section 6-104 also established a presumptive death benefit for the named beneficiary of a trust account, but this presumption similarly was rebuttable by clear and convincing evidence. Finally, the section expressly provided a death benefit for the beneficiary of a POD account. Unlike the death benefits under joint or trust accounts, the death benefit for a POD account beneficiary was unqualified, rather than merely presumptive. Of course, evidence of incapacity, fraud, or undue influence affecting the creation of a POD account was admissable to defeat a beneficiary's claim.

For trust and POD accounts, the pre-1989 version negated survivorship rights among multiple surviving beneficiaries. In contrast, survivorship continued for multiple joint account beneficiaries who survived the death of a third or other co-depositor. Moreover, section 6-104(e) of the pre-1989 version explicitly negated any effort by an owner-party to use a will to alter the death benefit arising from the form of a deposit or the statute, thereby reversing a considerable body of case law involving Totten trusts. Finally, section 6-107 provided that, to the extent the decedent's probate estate proved insufficient, any right of a surviving party or account beneficiary was subject to claims of the decedent's creditors, the payment of estate administration expenses, and statutory allowances to the decedent's surviving family members. This section also included procedures, subject to a two-year limitations period, for recovering sums necessary to satisfy the described charges from surviving account parties and beneficiaries.

The 1989 revision of Article VI's coverage of multiple-party accounts is basically consistent with the pre-1989 version. The major changes include: (1) folding Totten trust account into the definition and coverage of POD accounts; (2) providing statutory forms for joint accounts with or without survivorship, transfer-on-death (TOD) accounts, and joint and single-name accounts designating an agent to act for the owner[6] (3) subjecting survivors' benefits in accounts covered by the legislation to an order (check) of any party who dies before the check is paid; and (4) providing that, when two persons named as parties to a survivorship joint account are married to each other and the account includes one or more additional parties, only the surviving spouse may receive additional ownership of account balances following the other spouse's death. In addition to these changes, the two-year statute of limitations is reduced to one year.

A major goal of the 1989 revision is to encourage financial institutions to use the statutory forms and abandon their practice of routinely offering joint accounts to customers who merely wish to add another person's name to an account for agency, death beneficiary, or multiple-owners-with-no-survivorship purposes. The new statutory forms and depository protection provisions extend greater and more explicit protection to financial institutions in connection with payments they make, pursuant to an agent's instructions, after a principal's death and payments they make to a surviving co-depositor after a party to a "non-survivorship" account has died.

Joint Tenancies; Tenancies by the Entirety. The validity of joint tenancy or tenancy by the entirety forms of ownership does not depend on compliance with the formalities of execution required of wills. This point is beyond argument, for the present-transfer test in these cases is well satisfied: Titling property in joint tenancy or in tenancy by the entirety—like titling property in tenancy in common—irrevocably creates a present undivided interest in the entire property in each co-tenant. Each co-tenant's undivided interest is an equal interest; if there are three joint tenants, for example, each tenant takes an undivided one-third interest in the property. Unless exempted by the marital deduction, unequal contributions to the acquisition of property in joint tenancy triggers federal gift tax consequences for any joint tenant whose contribution exceeds her or his ownership interest. See Treas. Reg. § 25.2511-1(h)(5).

---

6. Accounts in statutory form have statutorily prescribed consequences; accounts in other forms are to be classified according to the parties' intentions, meaning that an account form may be negated by a mere preponderance of the evidence tending to show that there was no intention to create a right of survivorship.

Unlike the interest of a tenant in common, the undivided interest of each joint tenant or tenant by the entirety includes the right of survivorship. Upon death, the interest of a joint tenant or a tenant by the entirety terminates—like a life estate. The property ownership shifts outside of probate to the surviving co-tenant. Since the tenancy-by-the-entirety form of ownership is restricted to spouses, the surviving spouse's interest becomes a fee simple absolute. In the case of a joint tenancy, the interest of a surviving joint tenant also becomes a fee simple absolute, unless there is more than one surviving joint tenant, in which case the surviving joint tenants continue to hold the property in joint tenancy as among themselves.

Since the interest of a joint tenant or a tenant by the entirety terminates upon a co-tenant's death, the creditors of the deceased co-tenant's estate have no claim against the property.

TOD Registration of Securities. The 1990 amendments of Article VI of the Uniform Probate Code also added provisions authorizing a new form of ownership of investment securities, called Transfer on Death (TOD) registration. The new "TOD" provisions, sections 6-301 to -310, are discussed in Wellman, Transfer-On-Death Securities Registration: A New Title Form, 21 Ga. L. Rev. 789 (1987). See also Note, Uniform Probate Code Section 6-201: A Proposal to Include Stocks and Mutual Funds, 72 Cornell L. Rev. 397 (1987).

PART B. WILL SUBSTITUTES AND THE SUBSIDIARY LAW OF WILLS

The question whether will substitutes should be treated as testamentary for purposes of the statutory formalities of execution implicates rules that are mandatory. Apart from a dispensing power provision, such as UPC section 2-503 (1990), wills statute requirements apply regardless of the testator's intent. Indeed, as we have seen, section 2-503 was promulgated to prevent those requirements from defeating the testator's intent.

Other rules of the law of wills, including antilapse statutes and statutes providing for revocation upon changed circumstances, are different in character. These rules yield to contrary intentions of testators. The question that we study in this Part is whether these intent-effectuating rules should apply to wills and will substitutes alike. Put differently, should will substitutes be treated as testamentary for purposes of the subsidiary law of wills even if they are not so treated for purposes of the mandatory requirements of will execution?

1. *Revocation Upon Divorce*

Statutory Reference: *1990 UPC §§ 2-804*
                            Pre-1990 UPC § 2-508

Clymer v. Mayo
393 Mass. 754, 473 N.E.2d 1084 (1985)

HENNESSEY, C.J. . . . At the time of her death in November, 1981, the decedent, [Clara A. Mayo,] then fifty years of age, was employed by Boston University as a professor of psychology. She was married to James P. Mayo, Jr. (Mayo), from 1953 to 1978. The couple had no children. The decedent was an only child and her sole heirs at law are her parents, Joseph A. and Maria Weiss.

In 1963, the decedent executed a will designating Mayo as principal beneficiary. In 1964, she named Mayo as the beneficiary of her group annuity contract with John Hancock Mutual Life Insurance Company; and in 1965, made him the beneficiary of her Boston University retirement annuity contracts with Teachers Insurance and Annuity Association (TIAA) and College Retirement Equities Fund (CREF). As a consequence of a $300,000 gift to the couple from the Weisses in 1971, the decedent and Mayo executed new wills and indentures of trust on February 2, 1973, wherein each spouse was made the other's principal beneficiary. Under the terms of the decedent's will, Mayo was to receive her personal property. The residue of her estate was to "pour over" into the inter vivos trust she created that same day.

The decedent's trust instrument named herself and John P. Hill as trustees. As the donor, the decedent retained the right to amend or revoke the trust at any time by written instrument delivered to the trustees. In the event that Mayo survived the decedent, the trust estate was to be divided into two parts. Trust A, the marital deduction trust, was to be funded with an amount "equal to fifty (50%) per cent of the value of the Donor's 'adjusted gross estate,' . . . for the purpose of the United States Tax Law, less an amount equal to the value of all interest in property, if any, allowable as 'marital deductions' for the purposes of such law . . . ." Mayo was the income beneficiary of Trust A and was entitled to reach the principal at his request or in the trustee's discretion. The trust instrument also gave Mayo a general power of appointment over the assets in Trust A.

The balance of the decedent's estate, excluding personal property passing to Mayo by will, or the entire estate if Mayo did not survive her, composed Trust B. Trust B provided for the payment of five initial specific bequests totalling $45,000. After those gifts were satisfied, the remaining trust assets were to be held for the benefit of Mayo for life. Upon Mayo's death, the assets in Trust B were to be held for "the benefit of the nephews and nieces of the Donor" living at the time of her death. The trustee was given discretion to spend so much of the income and principal as necessary for their comfort, support, and education. When all of these nephews and nieces reached the age of thirty, the trust was to terminate and its remaining assets were to be divided equally between Clark University and Boston University to assist in graduate education of women.

On the same day she established her trust, the decedent changed the beneficiary of her Boston University group life insurance policy from Mayo to the trustees. One month later, in March, 1973, she also executed a change in her retirement annuity contracts to designate the trustees as beneficiaries. At the time of its creation in 1973, the trust was not funded. Its future assets were to consist solely of the proceeds of these policies and the property which would pour over under the will's residuary clause. The judge found that the remaining trustee has never received any property or held any funds subsequent to the execution of the trust nor has he paid any trust taxes or filed any trust tax returns.

Mayo moved out of the marital home in 1975. In June, 1977, the decedent changed the designation of beneficiary on her Boston University life insurance policy for a second time, substituting Marianne LaFrance for the trustees.[7] LaFrance had lived with the Mayos since 1972, and shared a close friendship with the decedent up until her death. Mayo filed for divorce on September 9, 1977, in New Hampshire. The divorce was decreed on January 3, 1978, and the court incorporated into the decree a permanent stipulation of the parties' property settlement. Under the terms of that settlement, Mayo waived any "right, title or interest" in the decedent's "securities, savings accounts, savings certificates, and retirement fund," as well as her "furniture, furnishings and art." Mayo remarried on August 28, 1978, and later executed a new will in favor of his new wife. The decedent died on November 21, 1981. Her will was allowed on November 18, 1982, and the court appointed John H. Clymer as administrator with the will annexed.

What is primarily at issue in these actions is the effect of the Mayos' divorce upon dispositions provided in the decedent's will and indenture of trust. . . .

2. *Validity of "Pour-over" Trust.* The Weisses claim that the judge erred in ruling that the decedent's trust was validly created despite the fact that it was not funded until her death. They rely on the common law rule that a trust can be created only when a trust res exists. Arguing that the trust never came into existence, the Weisses claim they are entitled to the decedent's entire estate as her sole heirs at law.

In upholding the validity of the decedent's pour-over trust, the judge cited the relevant provisions of the Commonwealth's version of the Uniform Testamentary Additions to Trusts Act [pre-1990 UPC § 2-511].

> A devise or bequest, the validity of which is determinable by the laws of the commonwealth, may be made to the trustee or trustees of a trust established or to be established by the testator . . . including a funded or unfunded life insurance trust, although the trustor has reserved any or all rights of ownership of the insurance contracts, if the trust is identified in the

---

7. Upon the decedent's death the benefits under said policy were paid to LaFrance.

will and the terms of the trust are set forth in a written instrument executed before or concurrently with the execution of the testator's will . . . *regardless of the existence, size or character of the corpus of the trust* (emphasis added).

The decedent's trust instrument, which was executed in Massachusetts and states that it is to be governed by the laws of the Commonwealth, satisfies these statutory conditions. The trust is identified in the residuary clause of her will and the terms of the trust are set out in a written instrument executed contemporaneously with the will. However, the Weisses claim that G.L. c. 203, § 3B, was not intended to change the common law with respect to the necessity for a trust corpus despite the clear language validating pour-over trusts, "regardless of the existence, size or character of the corpus." The Weisses make no showing of legislative intent that would contradict the plain meaning of these words. . . .

This court was one of the first courts to validate pour-over devises to a living trust. In Second Bank-State St. Trust Co. v. Pinion, 341 Mass. 366, 371, 170 N.E.2d 350 (1960), decided prior to the adoption of G.L. c. 203, § 3B, we upheld a testamentary gift to a revocable and amendable inter vivos trust established by the testator before the execution of his will and which he amended after the will's execution. Recognizing the importance of the pour-over devise in modern estate planning, we explained that such transfers do not violate the statute of wills despite the testator's ability to amend the trust and thereby change the disposition of property at his death without complying with the statute's formalities.

> We agree with modern legal thought that a subsequent amendment is effective because of the applicability of the established equitable doctrine that subsequent acts of independent significance do not require attestation under the statute of wills.

At that time we noted that "[t]he long established recognition in Massachusetts of the doctrine of independent significance makes unnecessary statutory affirmance of its application to pour-over trusts." It is evident from *Pinion* that there was no need for the Legislature to enact [the Testamentary Additions to Trusts Act] simply to validate pour-over devises from wills to funded revocable trusts.

However, in *Pinion*, we were not presented with an unfunded pour-over trust. Nor, prior to [the Testamentary Additions to Trusts Act], did other authority exist in this Commonwealth for recognizing testamentary transfers to unfunded trusts. The doctrine of independent significance, upon which we relied in *Pinion*, assumes that "property was included in the purported inter vivos trust, prior to the testator's death." Restatement (Second) of Trusts § 54, comment f (1959). That is why commentators have recognized that [the Testamentary Additions to Trusts Act] "[m]akes some . . . modification of the *Pinion* doctrine. The act does not require that the trust res be more than nominal or even existent." E. Slizewski, Legislation: Uniform Testamentary Additions to Trusts Act, 10 Ann. Surv. of Mass. Law § 2.7, 39 (1963). See Osgood, Pour Over Will: Appraisal of Uniform

Testamentary Additions to Trusts Act, 104 Trusts 768, 769 (1965) ("The Act . . . eliminates the necessity that there be a trust corpus").

By denying that the statute effected such a change in the existing law, the Weisses render its enactment meaningless. "An intention to enact a barren and ineffective provision is not lightly to be imputed to the Legislature." Insurance Rating Bd. v. Commissioner of Ins., 356 Mass. 184, 189, 248 N.E.2d 500 (1969). By analogy, in Trosch v. Maryland Nat'l Bank, 32 Md. App. 249, 252, 359 [A.2d] 564 (1976), the court construed Maryland's Testamentary Additions to Trusts Act as "conditionally abrogating the common law rule . . . that a trust must have a corpus to be in existence." Despite minor differences in the relevant language of Maryland's Estates and Trusts Act, § 4-411,[8] and our [Testamentary Additions to Trusts Act], we agree with the court's conclusion that "the statute is not conditioned upon the existence of a trust but upon the existence of a trust *instrument*" (emphasis in original). Id. at 253, 359 N.E.2d 564. The Weisses urge us to follow Hageman v. Cleveland Trust Co., 41 Ohio App. 2d 160, 324 N.E.2d 594 (1974), rev'd on other grounds, 45 Ohio St. 2d 178, 182, 343 N.E.2d 121 (1976), where the court held that an inter vivos trust had to be funded during the settlor's life to receive pour-over assets from a will. However, in reaching this conclusion the court relied on a statute differing from [our Testamentary Additions to Trusts Act], in its omission of the critical phrase: "regardless of the existence, size or character of the corpus of the trust." See Ohio Rev. Code Ann. § 2107.63 (Baldwin 1978).

For the foregoing reasons we conclude, in accordance with [our Testamentary Additions to Trusts Act], that the decedent established a valid inter vivos trust in 1973 and that its trustee may properly receive the residue of her estate. . . .

4. Termination of Trust A. The judge terminated Trust A upon finding that its purpose—to qualify the trust for an estate tax marital deduction—became impossible to achieve after the Mayos' divorce. Mayo appeals this ruling. It is well established that the Probate Courts are empowered to terminate or reform a trust in whole or in part where its purposes have become impossible to achieve and the settlor did not contemplate continuation of the trust under the new circumstances.

The language the decedent employed in her indenture of trust makes it clear that by setting off Trusts A and B she intended to reduce estate tax liability in compliance with then existing provisions of the Internal Revenue Code. Therefore we have no disagreement with the judge's reasoning. See

---

8. Maryland Estates and Trusts Code Ann. § 4-411 (1974), reads:

A legacy may be made in form or in substance to the trustee in accordance with the terms of a written inter vivos trust, including an unfunded life insurance trust although the settlor has reserved all rights of ownership in the insurance contracts, if the trust instrument has been executed and is in existence prior to or contemporaneously with the execution of the will and is identified in the will, without regard to the size or character of the corpus of the trust or whether the settlor is the testator or a third person."

Putnam v. Putnam, 366 Mass. 261, 267, 316 N.E.2d 729 (1974). However, we add that our reasoning below—that by operation of G.L. c. 191, § 9, Mayo has no beneficial interest in the trust—clearly disposes of Mayo's claim to Trust A.

5. *Mayo's Interest in Trust B.* The judge's decision to uphold Mayo's beneficial interest in Trust B was appealed by the Weisses, as well as by Boston University and Clark University. The judge reasoned that the decedent intended to create a life interest in Mayo when she established Trust B and failed either to revoke or to amend the trust after the couple's divorce. The appellants argue that we should extend the reach of G.L. c. 191, § 9 [pre-1990 UPC § 2-508], to revoke all Mayo's interests under the trust.[9] General Laws c. 191, § 9, as amended through St.1977, c. 76, § 2, provides in relevant part:

> If, after executing a will, the testator shall be divorced or his marriage shall be annulled, the divorce or annulment shall revoke any disposition or appointment of property made by the will to the former spouse, any provision conferring a general or special power of appointment on the former spouse, and any nomination of the former spouse, as executor, trustee, conservator or guardian, unless the will shall expressly provide otherwise. Property prevented from passing to a former spouse because of revocation by divorce shall pass as if a former spouse had failed to survive the decedent, and other provisions conferring a power or office on the former spouse shall be interpreted as if the spouse had failed to survive the decedent.

The judge ruled that Mayo's interest in Trust B is unaffected by G.L. c. 191, § 9, because his interest in that trust is not derived from a "disposition . . . made by the will" but rather from the execution of an inter vivos trust with independent legal significance. We disagree, but in fairness we add that the judge here confronted a question of first impression in this Commonwealth.

General Laws c. 191, § 9, was amended by the Legislature in 1976 to provide in the event of divorce for the revocation of testamentary dispositions which benefit the testator's former spouse. St.1976, c. 515, § 6. The statute automatically causes such revocations unless the testator expresses a contrary intent. In this case we must determine what effect, if any, G.L. c. 191, § 9, has on the former spouse's interest in the testator's pour-over trust.

While, by virtue of G.L. c. 203, § 3B, the decedent's trust bore independent significance at the time of its creation in 1973, the trust had no practical significance until her death in 1981. The decedent executed both her will and indenture of trust on February 2, 1973. She transferred no property or funds to the trust at that time. The trust was to receive its funding at the decedent's death, in part through her life insurance policy and retirement benefits, and in part through a pour-over from the will's residuary clause. Mayo, the proposed executor and sole legatee under the

---

9. None of the parties contests the judge's ruling that G.L. c. 191, § 9, revokes those provisions in the decedent's will which benefited Mayo.

will, was also made the primary beneficiary of the trust with power, as to Trust A only, to reach both income and principal.

During her lifetime, the decedent retained power to amend or revoke the trust. Since the trust was unfunded, her co-trustee was subject to no duties or obligations until her death. Similarly, it was only as a result of the decedent's death that Mayo could claim any right to the trust assets. It is evident from the time and manner in which the trust was created and funded, that the decedent's will and trust were integrally related components of a single testamentary scheme. For all practical purposes the trust, like the will, "spoke" only at the decedent's death. For this reason Mayo's interest in the trust was revoked by operation of G.L. c. 191, § 9, at the same time his interest under the decedent's will was revoked.

It has reasonably been contended that in enacting G.L. c. 191, § 9, the Legislature "intended to bring the law into line with the expectations of most people . . . . Divorce usually represents a stormy parting, where the last thing one of the parties wishes is to have an earlier will carried out giving everything to the former spouse." Young, Probate Reform, 18 Boston B.J. 7, 11 (1974). To carry out the testator's implied intent, the law revokes "any disposition or appointment of property made by the will to the former spouse." It is indisputable that if the decedent's trust was either testamentary or incorporated by reference into her will, Mayo's beneficial interest in the trust would be revoked by operation of the statute. However, the judge stopped short of mandating the same result in this case because here the trust had "independent significance" by virtue of c. 203, § 3B. While correct, this characterization of the trust does not end our analysis. For example, in Sullivan v. Burkin, 390 Mass. 864, 867, 460 N.E.2d 572 (1984), we ruled prospectively that the assets of a revocable trust will be considered part of the "estate of the decedent" in determining the surviving spouse's statutory share.

Treating the components of the decedent's estate plan separately, and not as parts of an interrelated whole, brings about inconsistent results. Applying c. 191, § 9, the judge correctly revoked the will provisions benefiting Mayo. As a result, the decedent's personal property—originally left to Mayo—fell into the will's residuary clause and passed to the trust. The judge then appropriately terminated Trust A for impossibility of purpose thereby denying Mayo his beneficial interest under Trust A. Yet, by upholding Mayo's interest under Trust B, the judge returned to Mayo a life interest in the same assets that composed the corpus of Trust A—both property passing by way of the decedent's will and the proceeds of her TIAA/CREF annuity contracts.

We are aware of only one case concerning the impact of a statute similar to G.L. c. 191, § 9, on trust provisions benefiting a former spouse. In Miller v. First Nat'l Bank & Trust Co., 637 P.2d 75 (Okla.1981), the testator also simultaneously executed an indenture of trust and will naming his spouse as primary beneficiary. As in this case, the trust was to be funded at the testator's death by insurance proceeds and a will pour-over. Subsequently, the testator divorced his wife but failed to change the terms of his will and trust. The District court revoked the will provisions favoring the testator's former wife by applying a statute similar to G.L. c. 191, § 9.[10] Recognizing that "[t]he will without the trust has no meaning or value to the decedent's estate plan," the Oklahoma Supreme Court revoked the trust benefits as well. Id. at 77. However, we do not agree with the court's reasoning. Because the Oklahoma statute, like G.L. c. 191, § 9, revokes dispositions of property made by will, the court stretched the doctrine of incorporation by reference to render the decedent's trust testamentary. We do not agree that reference to an existing trust in a will's pour-over clause is sufficient to incorporate that trust by reference without evidence that the testator intended such a result. See Second Bank-State St. Trust Co. v. Pinion, 341 Mass. 366, 367, 170 N.E.2d 350 (1960). However, it is not necessary for us to indulge in such reasoning, because we have concluded that the legislative intent under G.L. c. 191, § 9, is that a divorced spouse should not take under a trust executed in these circumstances. In the absence of an expressed contrary intent, that statute implies an intent on the part of a testator to revoke will provisions favoring a former spouse. It is incongruous then to ignore that same intent with regard to a trust funded in part through her will's pour-over at the decedent's death.[11] See State St. Bank & Trust v. United States, 634 F.2d 5, 10 (1st Cir.1980) (trust should be interpreted in light of settlor's contemporaneous execution of interrelated will). As one law review commentator has noted, "[t]ransferors use will substitutes to avoid probate, not to avoid the subsidiary law of wills. The subsidiary rules are the product of centuries of legal experience in attempting to discern transferors' wishes and suppress litigation. These rules should be treated as presumptively correct for will substitutes as well as for wills." Langbein, The Nonprobate Revolution and the Future of the Law of Succession, 97 Harv. L. Rev. 1108, 1136-1137 (1984).

Restricting our holding to the particular facts of this case—specifically the existence of a revocable pour-over trust funded entirely at the time of the decedent's death—we conclude that G.L. c. 191, § 9, revokes Mayo's interest under Trust B.[12]

6. *Nephews and Nieces of Donor.* According to the terms of G.L. c. 191, § 9, "[p]roperty prevented from passing to a former spouse because of

---

10. Okla. Stat. tit. 84, § 114 (1982), states in part: "If, after making a will, the testator is divorced, all provisions in such will in favor of the testator's spouse so divorced are thereby revoked."

11. Although we need not and do not rely on it, we note that extraneous evidence received by the judge regarding the deteriorating relationship between the decedent and Mayo during the years following the execution of her trust and before her death is consistent with the result we have reached. This evidence included the terms of the Mayos' divorce settlement, the decedent's stated desire to draw up a new will after her divorce, her comments to friends expressing relief that her marriage had ended, and frictions developing between the Mayos as a result of his remarriage.

12. As an alternative ground the appellants argue that the terms of the Mayos' divorce settlement, in which Mayo waived "any right, title or interest" in the assets that later funded the decedent's trust, amount to a disclaimer of his trust interest. We decline to base our holding on such reasoning because a disclaimer of rights "must be clear and unequivocal." Second Bank-State St. Trust Co. v. Yale Univ. Alumni Fund, 338 Mass. 520, 524, 156 N.E.2d 57 (1959), and we find no such disclaimer in the Mayos' divorce agreement.

revocation by divorce shall pass as if a former spouse had failed to survive the decedent . . . ." In this case, the decedent's indenture of trust provides that if Mayo failed to survive her, "the balance of 'Trust B' shall be held . . . for the benefit of the nephews and nieces of the Donor living at the time of the death of the Donor." The trustee is directed to expend as much of the net income and principal as he deems "advisable for [their] reasonable comfort, support and education" until all living nephews and nieces have attained the age of thirty. At that time, the trust is to terminate and Boston University and Clark University are each to receive fifty per cent of the trust property to assist women students in their graduate programs.

The decedent had no siblings and therefore no nephews and nieces who were blood relations.[13] However, when she executed her trust in 1973, her husband, James P. Mayo, Jr., had two nephews and one niece—John and Allan Chamberlain and Mira Hinman. Before her divorce, the decedent maintained friendly relations with these young people and, along with her former husband, contributed toward their educational expenses. The three have survived the decedent.

The Weisses, Boston University, and Clark University appeal the decision of the judge upholding the decedent's gift to these three individuals. They argue that at the time the decedent created her trust she had no "nephews and nieces" by blood and that, at her death, her marital ties to Mayo's nephews and niece had been severed by divorce. Therefore, they contend that the class gift to the donor's "nephews and nieces" lapses for lack of identifiable beneficiaries.

The judge concluded that the trust language created an ambiguity, and thus he considered extrinsic evidence of the decedent's meaning and intent. Based upon that evidence, he decided that the decedent intended to provide for her nieces and nephews by marriage when she created the trust. Because the decedent never revoked this gift, he found that the Chamberlains and Hinman are entitled to their beneficial interests under the trust. We agree. . . .

The appellants . . . argue that even if the decedent had intended to provide for the Chamberlains and Hinman when she executed her indenture of trust, we should rule that the Mayos' divorce somehow "revoked" this gift. According to Boston University, since the beneficiaries are identified by their relationship to the decedent through her marriage and not by name, we should presume that the decedent no longer intended to benefit her former relatives once her marriage ended. General Laws c. 191, § 9, does not provide the authority for revoking gifts to the blood relatives of a former spouse. The law implies an intent to revoke testamentary gifts between the divorcing parties because of the profound emotional and financial changes divorce normally engenders. There is no indication in the statutory language that the Legislature presumed to know how these changes affect a testator's relations with more distant family members. We

---

13. Considering the ages of all concerned, it could not reasonably be argued that the decedent might have contemplated the possibility of siblings to be born after the trust was executed.

therefore conclude that the Chamberlains and Hinman are entitled to take as the decedent's "nephews and nieces" under Trust B. . . .

In sum, we conclude that the decedent established a valid trust under [our Testamentary Additions to Trusts Act], Mayo's beneficial interest in Trust A and Trust B is revoked by operation of G.L. c. 191, § 9; the Chamberlains and Hinman are entitled to take the interest given to the decedent's "nephews and nieces" under Trust B, leaving the remainder to Clark University and Boston University . . . .

So ordered.

WILKINS, ABRAMS, and NOLAN, JJ., concur.

Notes and Questions

1. *Class Gifts; Relatives by Affinity.* At common law, relatives by affinity —such as John and Allan Chamberlain and Mira Hinman in *Clymer*—are presumptively excluded under class-gift terminology. The Restatement 2d of Property provides:

> § 25.6 *Gifts to "Children"—Relatives by Affinity.* When the donor of property describes the beneficiaries thereof as "children" of a designated person, the primary meaning of such class gift term excludes stepchildren, sons-in-law, and daughters-in-law of such person, and excludes other persons related to such person only by affinity. It is assumed, in the absence of language or circumstances indicating a contrary intent, that the donor adopts such primary meanings.

> § 25.8 *Comment e. Application—gift to "nephews and nieces."* The "nephews and nieces" of a designated person are the "children" of the brothers and sisters of the designated person . . . . In common parlance, the children of the brothers and sisters of the designated person's spouse are referred to as such person's nephews and nieces. Since they are related to the designated person by affinity only, they are excluded initially from the primary meaning of "nephews and nieces" of the designated person. The language or the circumstances of the gift to the "nephews and nieces" may fairly easily justify the conclusion that nephews and nieces by affinity are to be included.

By illustration, one of the circumstances cited by the Restatement as rebutting the presumption of exclusion is the fact relied on by the court in *Clymer*—that when the donor executed the governing instrument the donor had no living blood relative to whom the class-gift terminology could apply. Restatement 2d of Property § 25.6 comment b, illustration 2; see also § 25.8 comment d, illustration 5.

The rules of construction in the 1990 UPC also contain provisions expressly on point. Section 2-701 provides that section 2-705 applies not only to "wills" but to any governing instrument containing a donative disposition. Section 2-705, in relevant part, states:

Terms of relationship that do not differentiate relationships by blood from those by affinity, such as "uncles," "aunts," "nieces," or "nephews", are construed to exclude relatives by affinity.

Section 2-701 provides, however, that the rules of construction in Part 7, Article II, of the Code—which include section 2-705—apply only "in the absence of a finding of a contrary intention." Circumstances like those in *Clymer* would undoubtedly support a finding of a "contrary intention."

2. *Will Substitutes and Conventional Revocation-upon-Divorce Statutes.* The Massachusetts revocation-upon-divorce statute is of a type widely enacted throughout the country and is nearly identical to pre-1990 UPC section 2-508. These statutes expressly apply only to "wills."

Should the courts extend the application of these statutes beyond their express scope and apply them to "will substitutes," on the theory that will substitutes are substantively indistinguishable in function from wills? Although the court in *Clymer* moved in this direction, other courts—faced with will substitutes such as life-insurance and pension death-benefit beneficiary designations, have not been willing to do so. Pepper v. Peacher, 742 P.2d 21 (Okla. 1987) (retirement plan); Estate of Adams, 447 Pa. 177, 288 A.2d 514 (1972) (retirement plan); Equitable Life Assurance Society v. Stitzel, 1 Pa.Fiduc.2d 316, 19 D. & C. 3d 55 (Ct. C.P. 1981) (life insurance).[14] Notice, too, that even the court in *Clymer* was reluctant to extend the Massachusetts statute to *all* revocable inter-vivos trusts. The court took care to say that it was "restricting our holding to the particular facts of this case—specifically the existence of a revocable pour-over trust funded entirely at the time of the decedent's death." Would the decedent's divorce attorney have any exposure to a claim for malpractice liability for failing to inquire about and take care of the decedent's life insurance,

---

14. See also Rountree v. Frazee, 282 Ala. 142, 209 S.2d 424 (1968) ("One may take out a life insurance policy on his own life and . . . name anyone as a beneficiary regardless of whether [the beneficiary] has an insurable interest. . . . [D]ivorce per se [does] not affect or defeat any of [the former spouse's] rights as the designated beneficiary."); American Health & Life Ins. v. Binford, 511 S.2d 1250 (La. Ct. App. 1987) ("[T]he description in the policy of Ms. Watson as wife is merely the showing of a relationship in existence at the time of the execution of the contract. The termination of the relationship has no automatic effect on the provisions of the insurance policy."); Gerhard v. Travelers Ins. Co., 107 N.J. Super. 414, 258 A.2d 724 (1969) ("[A] separation agreement . . . which contain[s] a general release of all claims to each other's estate [does] not divest the [former] wife of her interest, as named beneficiary, since her claim under the policy was neither against him nor his estate, but was against the insurance company."); Romero v. Melendez, 83 N.M. 776, 498 P.2d 305 (1972) ("The weight of competent authority seems to support the proposition that where the divorce decree makes a definite disposition of the insurance policies, the [former] wife's interest as a beneficiary can be defeated by such disposition. . . . [C]ases holding conversely do so on the basis of the absence of a clear divorce decree."); Cannon v. Hamilton, 174 Ohio St. 268, 189 N.E.2d 152 (1963) ("[W]here the terms of a separation agreement carried into a divorce decree plainly disclose an intent to remove the [former spouse] from all rights to the proceeds thereof, such agreement may . . . prevent the [former spouse] from claiming the proceeds . . . , but the separation agreement herein did not contain language sufficiently strong or definite to accomplish that result, especially when considered in relation to [the insured's failure] to change the beneficiary in accordance with the terms of the policy [during the 11-year period between the divorce and his death].")

pension benefits, revocable trusts, and so on? See Smith v. Lewis, 13 Cal. 2d 349, 118 Cal. Rptr. 621, 530 P.2d 589 (1975).

3. *Piecemeal Legislation.* A few states have enacted piecemeal legislation providing for revocation of certain will substitutes upon divorce. Michigan and Ohio have statutes transforming spousal joint tenancies in land into tenancies in common upon the spouses' divorce. See Mich. Comp. Laws Ann. § 552.102; Ohio Rev. Code Ann. § 5302.20(c)(5). Ohio, Oklahoma, and Tennessee have recently enacted legislation effecting a revocation of provisions for the settlor's former spouse in revocable inter-vivos trusts. See Ohio Rev. Code Ann. § 1339.62; Okla. Stat. Ann. tit. 60, § 175; Tenn. Code Ann. § 35-50-115 (applies to revocable and irrevocable inter-vivos trusts unless, among other things, "the trust agreement . . . expressly provides otherwise."[15]). Statutes in Michigan, Ohio, Oklahoma, and Texas relate to the consequence of divorce on life-insurance and retirement-plan beneficiary designations. See Ohio Rev. Code § 1339.63; Okla. Stat. Ann. tit. 15, § 178; Mich. Comp. Laws Ann. § 552.101; Tex. Fam. Code §§ 3.632 - .633. See generally Note, Applying the Doctrine of Revocation by Divorce to Life Insurance Policies, 73 Cornell L. Rev. 653 (1988).

4. *Comprehensive Legislation—1990 UPC.* As noted in Part C of Chapter 4, the 1990 UPC significantly revised the former version of section 2-508. As revised and renumbered, section 2-804 expressly calls for the revocation, upon divorce or annulment, of any revocable disposition or appointment of property made by either divorced individual to her or his former spouse, in a deed, will, trust, beneficiary designation, power of attorney, transfer-on-death account, or donative instrument of any other type executed by the divorced individual before the divorce or annulment of her or his marriage to the former spouse. In the revised version, take special note of subsection (b)(2). On what ground is this justified?

5. *Revocation of Benefits to Former Spouse's Relatives.* UPC section 2-804 (1990) not only revokes benefits to the former spouse, but also to the former spouse's relatives. Is this justified? To what result would this statute have led in the *Clymer* case?

———

ERISA Preemption of State Probate Law. Can a state statute provide that divorce alone or a marital property settlement incident to a divorce revokes the designation of an ex-spouse or a member of the ex-spouse's family as beneficiary of a decedent's pension account?

The Employee Retirement Income Security Act of 1974 (ERISA) sought to federalize pension and employee benefit law. Toward that end, section 514(a) of ERISA, 29 U.S.C. § 1144(a), provides that the provisions of Titles I and IV of ERISA "shall supersede any and all State laws insofar as they

———

15. Under this statute, an *irrevocable* inter-vivos trust designed to qualify for the federal gift-tax marital deduction must contain a clause expressly stating that the spouse's powers and beneficial interests are *not* to be revoked in case of a subsequent divorce. Priv. Ltr. Rul. 91-27-005.

may now or hereafter relate to any employee benefit plan" governed by ERISA.

Note the breadth of this preemption provision. Section 514(a) does not merely preempt state law insofar as it conflicts with specific provisions in ERISA. It preempts "any and all State laws" insofar as they "relate to" any ERISA-governed employee benefit plan.

If ERISA contains no provision on a question, but the relevant state law does, does that state law govern? Although with virtual unanimity the federal courts have held that state law does govern in some areas, such as enforcement of state domestic relations decrees against pension accounts, they have been less clear about the effect of state probate law. Compare, e.g., Teamsters Pension Trust Fund v. H.F. Johnson, Inc., 830 F.2d 1009 (9th Cir. 1987) (holding that ERISA preempted the Montana non-claim statute, which is in pre-1990 UPC section 3-803) with Mendez-Bellido v. Board of Trustees, 709 F. Supp. 329 (E.D.N.Y. 1989) (New York "slayer-rule" applied, the court noting that "state laws prohibiting murderers from receiving death benefits are relatively uniform [and therefore] there is little threat of creating a 'patchwork scheme of regulations'" that ERISA sought to avoid.)

One path that is available to reconcile ERISA preemption with state probate law is to develop a federal common law on the basis of state law concepts. The court adopted this approach in Lyman Lumber Company v. Hill, 877 F.2d 692 (8th Cir. 1989). In that case, Jeffrey Hill designated his wife, Colleen, as his primary beneficiary under the Lyman Lumber and Affiliated Companies Profit Sharing Plan (Plan). He named as contingent beneficiaries his parents, E. John and Cassie Hill, and his brother, Seth Hill. Five years later, Jeffrey and Colleen were divorced. The divorce decree stated that Jeffrey "shall have as his own, free of any interest of [Colleen], his interest in the profit-sharing plan of his employer. . . ." Jeffrey died about a year after the divorce, without having changed his Plan beneficiary designation.

The district court held that the divorce decree did not revoke the beneficiary designation to Colleen. On appeal, the district court's judgment was affirmed:

> The Plan is an employee benefit plan governed by the Employee Retirement Income Security Act, 29 U.S.C. §§ 1001-1461 (ERISA). See 29 U.S.C. § 1002(2)(A), (3). None of ERISA's express provisions addresses the issue presented in this case. We therefore must ascertain the proper federal common law principles that should govern. Anderson v. John Morrell & Co., 830 F.2d 872, 877 (8th Cir.1987). In fashioning a body of federal common law, we may look to state law for guidance. See Textile Workers Union of America v. Lincoln Mills of Alabama, 353 U.S. 448, 457 (1957); Scott v. Gulf Oil Corp., 754 F.2d 1499, 1502 (9th Cir.1985).
>
> Under the Plan, each participant may name the beneficiaries who will receive the remainder of his vested account balances upon his death. Plan § 12.01. In the closely analogous area of law involving a former spouse's right to recover life insurance benefits, the general rule is that a divorce does not affect beneficiary designation in a life insurance policy. See Fox Valley and Vicinity Constr. Wkrs. Pension Fund v. Brown, 684 F. Supp. 185, 188

(N.D.Ill.1988) (Fox Valley). The spouse's beneficiary interest can be divested, however, pursuant to a property settlement in a divorce judgment. Id. A number of courts have held that the spouse's rights as a beneficiary are extinguished only by terms specifically divesting the spouse's rights as a beneficiary under the policy or plan. See, e.g., id. (applying federal common law); Prudential Ins. Co. of America v. Cooper, 666 F.Supp. 190, 192 (D. Idaho, 1937) (applying Idaho law), aff'd, 859 F.2d 154 (9th Cir.1988); Lincoln Nat'l Life Ins. Co. v. Blight, 399 F.Supp. 513, 515 (E.D.Pa.1975) (applying Pennsylvania law), aff'd, 538 F.2d 319, 322 (3d Cir.1976); Keeton v. Cherry, 728 S.W.2d 694, 697 (Mo. Ct. App.1987); Haley v. Schleis, 642 P.2d 164, 165 (N.M.1982).

Applying those principles to this case, we conclude that the divorce decree did not divest Colleen of her beneficiary interest in the Plan proceeds. The decree gave Jeffrey his entire interest in the Plan free of any interest of Colleen. It did not, however, specifically refer to and modify the beneficiary interest. See, e.g., Lincoln National Life Ins. Co., 399 F.Supp. at 515-16; National W. Life Ins. Co. v. Schmeh, 749 P.2d 974, 976 (Colo. Ct. App.1987); cf. Fox Valley, 684 F.Supp. at 138 (interpreting settlement agreement as specifically modifying beneficiary interest); Keeton, 728 S.W.2d at 697 (same). The divorce decree thus did not revoke the beneficiary designation, and Colleen is entitled to the Plan benefits.

A more aggressive approach is taken in UPC section 2-804 (1990). The Official Comment to that section urges the federal courts to incorporate section 2-804 into federal common law. Failing that, section 2-804 goes a step further. In the event that federal courts decide that ERISA does preempt section 2-804, subsection (h)(2) imposes an offsetting personal liability on the recipient of the proceeds in the amount of any payment received as a result of preemption.

2. Antilapse Statutes

Statutory References: *1990 UPC §§ 2-702, -706*
                              Pre-1990 UPC §§ 2-601, -605

Antilapse statutes apply by their terms only to "wills." This is true of the antilapse statute contained in the pre-1990 UPC and of almost all the antilapse statutes in the non-UPC states.

Suppose the beneficiary of a revocable inter-vivos trust predeceases the grantor. Or, the beneficiary of a life-insurance policy predeceases the insured, or the beneficiary of a death benefit under a retirement plan predeceases the participant. Should the antilapse statutes be extended to these situations?

As we shall see, the cases so far have concerned only revocable inter-vivos trusts, and the results are conflicting.

Detroit Bank & Trust Co. v. Grout
95 Mich. App. 253, 289 N.W.2d 898 (1980)

[A one-twelfth share (worth about $411,500) of the corpus of a revocable inter-vivos trust was payable on the death of the grantor to "Selden B. Daume of Grosse Pointe Farms, Michigan, his heirs and assigns . . . in absolute legal and equitable ownership." Selden Daume predeceased the grantor, Louise Hill, by about three years. Selden Daume died intestate. He was a friend of Louise Hill's, but bore no relationship by blood or affinity to her.

Mrs. Hill's devisees contended that the gift to Mr. Daume lapsed. The trial court rejected this contention.]

WEBSTER, J . . . . Did the trial court err in determining that the alleged gift and trust did not lapse where the beneficiary predeceased the grantor?

This issue presents an apparent question of first impression in this state. . . . Throughout the term of this trust prior to the death of Mrs. Hill it was revocable either by her act alone or by Mrs. Hill and the trustee. The defendants Grout argue that the law applicable to estates of decedents should be held applicable to the resolution of this issue. It is true that in this state, when a legatee predeceases a testator the bequest or devise is held to lapse and reverts back to the testator's estate, unless the provisions of the anti-lapse statute, M.C.L. § 702.11; M.S.A. § 27.3178(81), apply. That statute provides in pertinent part:

> When a devise or legacy shall be made to any child or other relation of the testator, and the devisee or legatee shall die before the testator, leaving issue who shall survive the testator, such issue shall take the estate so given by the will, in the same manner as the devisee or legatee would have done, if he had survived the testator; unless a different disposition shall be made or directed by the will; Provided, however, That except in the case of a residuary devise or legacy, such issue shall not take the devise or bequest where the relationship of the devisee or legatee to the testator is beyond the fourth degree, but in such case the devise or legacy shall become a part of the residue of the estate.

Obviously, the statute is not applicable in the instant cause since Mr. Daume was not related to Mrs. Hill.

The defendants Daume contend that the general rule found in other jurisdictions pertinent to inter vivos trusts is different from that applicable to estates of decedents. They contend that the words of the trust instrument in this cause created a present interest in Selden B. Daume and his heirs and assigns subject only to revocation by the grantor or settlor during her lifetime. Accordingly, they argue that this Court should follow the weight of authority and hold that Mr. Daume was given a vested remainder subject only to divestment and that accordingly his interest descended to his heirs. In holding that Selden B. Daume's interest did not lapse by reason of his predeceasing Mrs. Hill, the trial court followed the opinion of the Supreme Court of Ohio in The First National Bank of Cincinnati v. Tenney, 165 Ohio St. 513, 60 Ohio Op. 481, 138 N.E.2d 15 (1956). In that case an inter vivos trust was established wherein the settlor reserved a power of revocation. The beneficiary of the trust was to receive the corpus upon the death of the trustor. No alternate beneficiary was named. The beneficiary predeceased the settlor. The Supreme Court of Ohio held that the trust created a vested remainder subject to be divested before revocation. The Court then reasoned that since Ohio statutory and case law states that remainders are alienable, descendible and devisable, a beneficiary's interest passed to the beneficiary's heirs, subject to the same power of revocation. Since the trust was not revoked, the interest of the beneficiary's heirs became indefeasible upon the settlor's death. This principle was re-affirmed in Ohio in Smyth v. The Cleveland Trust Co., 172 Ohio St. 489, 179 N.E.2d 60 (1961). The same issue was decided in Randall v. Bank of America National Trust & Savings Ass'n, 48 Cal. App. 2d 249, 119 P.2d 754 (1941). In that case, the California Court held that since the trust under consideration created a valid vested remainder subject to divestment, the fact that a vested interest was created at the time the trust was created dictated that upon the death of the beneficiary the vested remainder passed to his heirs. In this regard it should be noted that M.C.L. § 554.35; M.S.A. § 26.35 provides:

> Expectant estates are descendible, devisable and alienable, in the same manner as estates in possession.

It is clear in this case that Louise Grout Hill created a vested remainder subject to revocation in Selden B. Daume. An inter vivos trust creates a present interest in property, albeit, as in this case, an expectant interest. Where words of absolute grant are used to create that interest, it must be determined to be a vested interest. The only condition that could defeat Mr. Daume's interest in the Hill trust was revocation by the settlor. Such an interest is, by the weight of authority, and by statutory authority in this state, M.C.L. § 554.35, descendible, devisable and alienable. On the contrary, no present interest in property is created by the execution of a last will and testament. A legatee achieves an interest only upon the death of the testator. Therefore, if the legatee predeceases the testator it is generally held that his interest lapses and reverts to the remainder of the testator's estate, unless he is one of the persons protected by the so-called anti-lapse statute, M.C.L. § 702.11. The only authority that could be said to be *contra* to the above conclusion is In re Estate of Button, 79 Wash.2d 849, 490 P.2d 731 (1971). In that case a Washington Court held that the antilapse statute in that state preserved for the benefit of the heirs of the trustor's mother their interest in the trustor's estate even though the mother predeceased the trustor. That court stated in dicta:

> Whether or not the interest of [the beneficiary] had vested prior to the death of the trustor, it was subject to be divested if she died before the trustor died, under the rule as it existed prior to the enactment of [the anti-lapse statute]. That statute alone, interpreted to apply to trusts as well as to wills, saves her interest for her heirs. 79 Wash.2d 855, 490 P.2d 735.

Thus, the Washington Court would have found in this case, that the interest of Mr. Daume lapsed because it was not protected by the anti-lapse statute. This Court is satisfied that it should follow the weight of authority as established in First National Bank of Cincinnati v. Tenney, supra, Smyth v. Cleveland Trust Co., supra, and Randall v. Bank of America National Trust & Savings Ass'n, supra. The vested remainder of Selden B. Daume did not lapse by reason of his predeceasing Louise Grout Hill and was descendible to his heirs. . . .

Accordingly, the judgment of the trial court is affirmed.

GILLIS, P.J. and BEASLEY, J. concur.

Dollar Savings & Tr. Co. v. Turner
39 Ohio St. 3d 182, 529 N.E.2d 1261 (1988)

[About ten years before his death in 1985, Gus H. Dettman created a revocable inter-vivos trust. The terms of the trust were that the trustee, Dollar Savings & Trust Company, was to pay all of the income to Gus during his life and so much of the principal as Gus should request; on Gus's death, the remaining principal was to be divided into four equal shares, one of which was payable "to my sister, Minnie Applegate, or if she predeceases me, then . . . to her son, Harry Applegate." Both Minnie and Harry predeceased Gus; Harry left issue who survived Gus.]

SWEENEY, J. Both the trial court and the court of appeals concluded that the intent of the settlor was not discernible from the contents of the trust agreement.

We agree that the trust agreement as amended fails to express any specific intent with respect to the disposition of the residuum in the event both Minnie and Harry Applegate predeceased the settlor. It therefore remains to be determined whether R.C. 2107.52 (Ohio's anti-lapse statute) applies to trust agreements. It provides:

> *When a devise of real or personal estate is made to a relative of a testator and such relative was dead at the time the will was made, or dies thereafter, leaving issue surviving the testator, such issue shall take the estate devised as the devisee would have done if he had survived the testator.* If the testator devised a residuary estate or the entire estate after debts, other legacies and devises, general or specific, or an interest less than a fee or absolute ownership to such devisee and relatives of the testator and such devisee and relatives of the testator and such devisee leaves no issue, the estate devised shall vest in such other devisees surviving the testator in such proportions as the testamentary share of each devisee in the devised property bears to the total of the shares of all of the surviving devisees, unless a different disposition is made or required by the *will.* (Emphasis added.)

Appellees maintain and the court of appeals held that R.C. 2107.52 applies only to devises by will. The rationale relied upon is that, inasmuch as the statute is in derogation of the common-law rule that the gift lapses, it must be strictly construed.

Appellants respond that application of the statute to trust agreements furthers the public policy that lapsing of testamentary gifts is not favored. Moreover, appellants maintain that, upon the death of the settlor, the intervivos trust was transformed into a testamentary instrument. Consequently, appellants contend that the intent of the legislature is furthered by application of R.C. 2107.52 to trust agreements.

It is our conclusion that the view urged by appellants represents the better-reasoned approach.

While the contention of appellees that statutes in derogation of the common law should be strictly construed is, in a general sense, a valid statement of the law, it has also been held that remedial statutes are to be afforded a liberal construction. R.C. 1.11. Moreover, this latter rule of statutory interpretation has been deemed to prevail notwithstanding that the remedial legislation represented a departure from a preexisting common-law rule.

Accordingly, this court in Woolley v. Paxson (1889), 46 Ohio St. 307, 314, 24 N.E. 599, 600, observed that the predecessor to R.C. 2107.52 was remedial in nature and was to be liberally construed irrespective of the fact that it was in derogation of the common law:

> The rule as to the lapsing of devises and legacies that prevailed before the statute, defeated, in most cases, the intention of the testator. He generally made his will with reference to the objects of his bounty as they existed at the time and as though his will took effect at the date of its execution—not apprehending that a lapse would occur in case any of them should die before himself, unless some express disposition should be made in anticipation of such event. The statute was passed to remedy such disappointments, and should receive a liberal construction, so as to advance the remedy and suppress the mischief. . . .

Similar application of R.C. 2107.52 is warranted in the case *sub judice*. Considering its status as a remedial statute, R.C. 2107.52 must "be liberally construed in favor of the persons to be benefited." State, ex rel. Maher, v. Baker, 88 Ohio St. [165] at 172, 102 N.E. [732] at 734. With respect to R.C. 2107.52, such persons include both the settlor and the issue of the beneficiary who predeceased him. Equally important is the admonition that a remedial statute should be extended" . . . beyond its actual language to cases within its reason and general intent." Rice v. Wheeling Dollar Savings & Trust Co., 155 Ohio St. [391] at 396, 44 O.O. [374] at 376, 99 N.E.2d [301] at 304.

Thus, while R.C. 2107.52, by its terms, applies only to wills, the intent of the legislature is furthered by its application to trust agreements. Inasmuch as the agreement at issue became testamentary in nature upon the death of Gus Dettman, application of R.C. 2107.52 thereto is wholly consistent with the intent of the General Assembly at the time the statute was enacted.

This view is in accord with the decisions of sister states which have considered analogous statutes. See In re Estate of Button (1971), 79 Wash.

2d 849, 490 P.2d 731; Hester v. Sammons (1938), 171 Va. 142, 198 S.E. 466, 118 A.L.R. 554.

Accordingly, we hold that R.C. 2107.52 is applicable to trust agreements and will operate upon the death of the settlor to prevent the lapse of a gift contained therein so as to vest that portion of the trust res intended for a beneficiary who predeceases the settlor in the issue of the beneficiary.

The judgment of the court of appeals is therefore reversed and the cause is remanded to the trial court for further proceedings. . . .

MOYER, C.J. and LOCHER, HOLMES, DOUGLAS, WRIGHT and HERBERT R. BROWN, JJ., concur.

Notes and Questions

1. *State of the Authorities.* The *Grout* and *Dollar Savings* cases present conflicting views. The weight of authority favors the viewpoint of the *Grout* case. Other cases in accord with *Grout* include Estate of Capocy, 102 Ill. App. 3d 609, 430 N.E.2d 1131 (1981); Hinds v. McNair, 413 N.E.2d 586 (Ind. Ct. App. 1980); May v. Safer, 46 Mich. App. 668, 208 N.W.2d 619 (1973). Although the weight of authority favors the viewpoint of the *Grout* case, the Restatement 2d of Property sides with the *Dollar Savings* case. Comment e to section 27.1 (Class Member Dies Before the Date the Dispositive Instrument is Executed) and comment f to section 27.2 (Class Member Dies After the Date the Dispositive Instrument Is Executed but Before It Takes Effect) state:

> For many purposes the revocable trust operates as a substitute for a will. The reasons that justify the applicability of an antilapse statute to wills are equally present when a revocable trust is involved. Consequently, the statutory language relating to the antilapse statute should be construed to apply to revocable trusts as well as to wills whenever that is possible.

See also Restatement 2d of Property § 34.6(3)(b) and comment b.

The Comment to section 2-603, the antilapse provision contained in the 1990 UPC, states that section 2-603 applies only to wills. See, however, section 2-707, which establishes a similar rule with respect to trusts.

2. *Analysis of the Conflicting Positions.* Although revocable trusts are will substitutes, this does not automatically mean that all the statutory rules pertaining to wills should be judicially extended to them. Several considerations caution against judicial extension of antilapse statutes to revocable trusts.

To start with a very basic point, it must be recognized that a precondition to the need for an antilapse statute is the existence of a requirement of survivorship. Without such a requirement, there is nothing for an antilapse statute to counteract. In the case of a will, the devisee must survive the testator, because the testator's death is when the transfer is made. But there is no comparable common-law rule requiring the holder of a future interest to survive the time of possession or enjoyment. The donee of a future interest need only survive the completion of the gift. A well-established common-law rule of construction—totally overlooked by the Ohio Supreme Court in the *Dollar Savings* case—is that future interests are not subject to a requirement of survivorship to the time of possession.[16]

To illustrate the difference between a devise created by a will and a future interest created by an inter-vivos trust, suppose that G executes a will and creates an inter-vivos trust—on the same day. G's will devises her entire estate to her son, X. G's inter-vivos trust provides for the income to go to G for life, with the remainder in the trust corpus to pass at G's death to X. At common law, if X predeceases G, the devise to X in G's will lapses, giving rise to the need for an antilapse statute. But the remainder interest conferred on X by G's trust—whether G's trust was revocable or irrevocable—does not "lapse"; it continues to be owned by X and thus passes through X's estate to his successor in interest.[17] X's successor in interest becomes entitled to the trust property when G dies.[18]

Were antilapse statutes to be judicially extended to revocable trusts, it would mean that one rule of construction (implying a requirement of survivorship) would apply to future interests created in revocable trusts and the opposite rule of construction (against implying a condition of survivor-

---

16. Like other rules of construction, this rule of construction yields to a contrary intent, such as an expressly stated condition of survivorship in the governing instrument. See infra Chapter 16, Part A.

17. If G's trust was revocable, X's remainder interest would be vested subject to divestment; if G's trust was irrevocable, X's remainder interest would be indefeasibly vested. In either case, it passes through X's estate to his successor in interest.

18. In the *Dollar Savings* case, Harry's remainder interest in his uncle's trust was not expressly conditioned on survivorship. The Supreme Court of Ohio apparently misunderstood the fundamental rule that a future interest not expressly conditioned on survivorship is not subject to a condition of survivorship. Under this fundamental and well-accepted common-law rule, the one-fourth share of the principal payable to Harry should have passed through Harry's estate to his successors in interest. The Ohio court's error is compounded by the fact that it had recognized this fundamental rule in prior decisions concerning revocable inter-vivos trusts. See First Nat'l Bank v. Tenney, 165 Ohio St. 513, 138 N.E.2d 15 (1956), described in the *Grout* case. The court in *Dollar Savings* failed to mention its *First Nat'l Bank* decision.

In *Dollar Savings*, Harry's remainder interest *was* expressly subject to another condition—the condition that his mother, Minnie, not survive the grantor of the trust. Another well-accepted common-law rule, however, is that expressly conditioning a future interest on an event other than survivorship does not implicitly condition that future interest on survivorship. See Bomberger's Estate, 347 Pa. 465, 32 A.2d 729 (1943) (set forth infra p. 895). Harry's remainder interest, therefore, should not have been treated as having been defeated by his failure to survive the grantor.

Having overlooked this point, the Ohio Supreme Court proceeded to operate under the mistaken assumption that Harry's share "lapsed," i.e., that it *was* defeated by his failure to survive the grantor. Thus, in the court's view, the antilapse statute was a "remedial" statute. By extending the statute beyond its terms, the court "saved" Harry's share from "lapsing" without understanding that without the court's bungling the share should not have "lapsed" in the first place.

At this writing, the Ohio State Bar Association is sponsoring an amendment to the Ohio Revised Code that would make it clear that the Ohio antilapse statute only applies to wills, "not [to] inter vivos trust instruments or other instruments not admitted to probate." 1 Prob. L. J. of Ohio 55 (1991).

ship) would apply to future interests created in other governing instruments such as wills, irrevocable trusts, and deeds.

A host of subsidiary questions would also arise. Would the rule implying a condition of survivorship always apply to all future interests in revocable trusts, or only when the beneficiary of the future interest is in the categories protected by the antilapse statute? In the *Grout* case, for example, Selden Daume was a friend but not a relative of the settlor's, and was not in the protected categories. The position of the Restatement 2d of Property section 34.6 comment b, illustration 3, is that the future interest fails when the beneficiary is outside the protected categories.

If the beneficiary of the future interest is in one of the protected categories, what happens if that beneficiary predeceases but leaves no descendants to be substituted? Does the common-law rule then reenter the picture, so that the interest passes through the predeceased beneficiary's estate to her or his successors in interest? Or, as suggested by the theory of the Restatement 2d of Property, does the interest pass to the settlor's successors in interest, as an interest undisposed of by the settlor? While these questions are resolvable, they do suggest that the idea of judicially extending antilapse statutes to revocable trusts requires more thought than merely arguing that antilapse statutes should apply to revocable trusts because such trusts are will substitutes.

A final consideration cautioning against judicially extending antilapse statutes to revocable trusts is the awkwardness of doing so when the distribution of the trust's corpus takes place at the death of someone other than the grantor. This problem does not often arise because the grantor is nearly always the income beneficiary and distribution frequently takes place at the grantor's death (as in the *Grout* and *Dollar Savings* cases). But, suppose that G creates a revocable trust, income to G for life, then income to A for life, remainder in corpus to X. What sense does it make to require X to survive G rather than the time when the corpus is to be distributed—at the death of the survivor of G and A? Consider the following order of deaths: G, then X, then A. Assume that X leaves descendants who outlive A. In such a case, why should the antilapse statute not substitute X's descendants for X as takers of the corpus?

As we will see in Chapter 16, a case can be made for legislatively reversing the common-law rule of construction and imposing an implied condition of survivorship (with an appropriate substitute gift) on future interests in trusts. If this argument is persuasive, would it not be better to have a separate statute substituting X's descendants (who survive the survivor of G and A) for X? Would it also not be better for such a statute to apply to all future interests in trust, not just future interests created in revocable trusts? The UPC (1990) contains such a statutory provision—section 2-707.

3. *Predeceasing Beneficiaries of Life Insurance, Retirement Plan Death Benefits, and POD Accounts.* Although no cases have yet arisen seeking to extend antilapse statutes to other types of will substitutes such as life-insurance beneficiary designations, retirement-plan death benefits, and POD accounts, the case for doing so is much stronger than it is in the case of

revocable inter-vivos trusts. The reason is that beneficiaries of these types of contractual arrangements *do* lose their interests by virtue of predeceasing the decedent because, like wills, the arrangements impose a survivorship requirement on the beneficiaries.

In direct response to this problem, the 1990 UPC contains a new provision, section 2-706, which applies language similar to that of section 2-603 to "beneficiary designations" in favor of the decedent's grandparents, descendants of the decedent's grandparents, and the decedent's step-children. As defined in section 1-201, the term "beneficiary designation" refers to "a governing instrument naming a beneficiary of an insurance or annuity policy, of an account with POD designation, of a security registered in beneficiary form (TOD), or of a pension, profit-sharing, retirement, or similar benefit plan."

Would this section be controlling in the case of an employee benefit plan covered by ERISA? See supra p. 420.

———

Simultaneous or Near Simultaneous Deaths; Uniform Simultaneous Death Act. Under section 5 of the Uniform Simultaneous Death Act (1953), when the person whose life is insured under a life-insurance policy and the person who is the beneficiary of the policy die under circumstances in which there is "no sufficient evidence" that they died otherwise than simultaneously, the proceeds of the policy are to be distributed as if the beneficiary predeceased the insured.

Janus v. Tarasewicz
135 Ill. App. 3d 936, 482 N.E.2d 418 (1985)

[Stanley and Theresa Janus, having just returned from their honeymoon, gathered on September 29, 1982, with other family members to mourn the death of Stanley's brother, who had died earlier that day from ingesting what turned out to be cyanide-laced Tylenol capsules. In the stress of the moment, Stanley and Theresa took some of the Tylenol capsules, not knowing these were poisoned. Within a short while, Stanley fell to the floor. While a neighbor, who was a registered nurse, applied emergency CPR on Stanley, Theresa began having seizures and within a few minutes she fell unconscious. Paramedics testified that Stanley's vital signs disappeared while he and Theresa were in the ambulance en route to the hospital. He was pronounced dead an hour and a half after arriving at the emergency room. Theresa required an artificial respirator in order to breathe by the time she was in the ambulance, but when she arrived at the hospital she did have a palpable pulse and blood pressure. She maintained a "measurable, though unsatisfactory" blood pressure later while she was in the emergency room. The next day, after receiving several tests to assess her brain function, Theresa was diagnosed as having sustained total brain death. Her life support systems were terminated, and she was pronounced dead on October 1, 1982. The death certificates listed Stanley's date of death as September 29, and Theresa's as October 1.

Theresa was the primary beneficiary of Stanley's life-insurance policy. The Metropolitan Life Insurance Company paid the proceeds to the administrator of Theresa's estate. Stanley's mother, Alojza Janus, as the contingent beneficiary of Stanley's policy, brought an action to recover the proceeds, claiming that there was insufficient evidence that Theresa survived Stanley. The trial court found that sufficient evidence that Theresa survived Stanley did exist. On appeal, Alojza's main argument was that there was insufficient evidence to prove that both victims did not suffer brain death before arriving at the hospital on September 29.]

O'CONNOR, J. . . . Dual standards for determining when legal death occurs in Illinois were set forth in the case of In Re Haymer (1983), 115 Ill.App.3d 349, 71 Ill.Dec. 252, 450 N.E.2d 940. There, the court determined that a comatose child attached to a mechanical life support system was legally dead on the date he was medically determined to have sustained total brain death, rather than on the date that his heart stopped functioning. The court stated that in most instances death could be determined in accordance with the common law standard which is based upon the irreversible cessation of circulatory and respiratory functions. If these functions are artificially maintained, a brain death standard of death could be used if a person has sustained irreversible cessation of total brain function. . . .

Even though *Haymer* was decided after the deaths of Stanley and Theresa, we find that the trial court properly applied the *Haymer* standards under the general rule that a civil case is governed by the law as it exists when judgment is rendered, not when the facts underlying the case occur. . . .

Regardless of which standard of death is applied, survivorship is a fact which must be proven by a preponderance of the evidence by the party whose claim depends on survivorship. The operative provisions of the Illinois version of the Uniform Simultaneous Death Act provides in pertinent part:

> If the title to property or its devolution depends upon the priority of death and there is no sufficient evidence that the persons have died otherwise than simultaneously and there is no other provision in the will, trust agreement, deed, contract of insurance or other governing instrument for distribution of the property different from the provisions of this Section:
> (a) The property of each person shall be disposed of as if he had survived. . . .
> (d) If the insured and the beneficiary of a policy of life or accident insurance have so died, the proceeds of the policy shall be distributed as if the insured had survived the beneficiary.

Ill.Rev.Stat.1981, ch. 110 1/2, par. 3-1.

In cases where the question of survivorship is determined by the testimony of lay witnesses, the burden of sufficient evidence may be met by evidence of a positive sign of life in one body and the absence of any such sign in the other. In cases such as the instant case where the death process is monitored by medical professionals, their testimony as to "the usual and customary standards of medical practice" will be highly relevant when considering what constitutes a positive sign of life and what constitutes a criteria for determining death. Although the use of sophisticated medical technology can also make it difficult to determine when death occurs, the context of this case does not require a determination as to the exact moment at which the decedents died. Rather, the trial court's task was to determine whether or not there was sufficient evidence that Theresa Janus survived her husband. Our task on review of this factually disputed case is to determine whether the trial court's finding was against the manifest weight of the evidence. . . . We hold that it was not.

In the case at bar, both victims arrived at the hospital with artificial respirators and no obvious vital signs. There is no dispute among the treating physicians and expert witnesses that Stanley Janus died in both a cardiopulmonary sense and a brain death sense when his vital signs disappeared en route to the hospital and were never reestablished. He was pronounced dead at 8:15 p.m. on September 29, 1982, only after intensive procedures such as electro-shock, medication, and the insertion of a pacemaker failed to resuscitate him.

In contrast, these intensive procedures were not necessary with Theresa Janus because hospital personnel were able to reestablish a spontaneous blood pressure and pulse which did not have to be artificially maintained by a pacemaker or medication. Once spontaneous circulation was restored in the emergency room, Theresa was put on a mechanical respirator and transferred to the intensive care unit. Clearly, efforts to preserve Theresa Janus' life continued after more intensive efforts on Stanley's behalf had failed.

It is argued that the significance of Theresa Janus' cardiopulmonary functions, as a sign of life, was rendered ambiguous by the use of artificial respiration. In particular, reliance is placed upon expert testimony that a person can be brain dead and still have a spontaneous pulse and blood pressure which is indirectly maintained by artificial respiration. The fact remains, however, that Dr. Kim, an intensive care specialist who treated Theresa, testified that her condition in the emergency room did not warrant a diagnosis of brain death. In his opinion, Theresa Janus did not suffer irreversible brain death until much later, when extensive treatment failed to preserve her brain function and vital signs. This diagnosis was confirmed by a consulting neurologist after a battery of tests were performed to assess her brain function. Dr. Kim denied that these examinations were made merely to see if brain death had already occurred. At trial, only Dr. Vatz disagreed with their finding, but even he admitted that the diagnosis and tests performed on Theresa Janus were in keeping with the usual and customary standards of medical practice.

There was also other evidence presented at trial which indicated that Theresa Janus was not brain dead on September 29, 1982. Theresa's EEG, taken on September 30, 1982, was not flat but rather it showed some delta waves of extremely low amplitude. Dr. Hanley concluded that Theresa's

EEG taken on September 30 exhibited brain activity. Dr. Vatz disagreed. Since the trier of fact determines the credibility of expert witnesses and the weight to be given to their testimony . . . , the trial court in this case could have reasonably given greater weight to Dr. Hanley's opinion than to Dr. Vatz'. In addition, there is evidence that Theresa's pupil reacted to light on one occasion. It is argued that this evidence merely represents the subjective impression of a hospital staff member which is not corroborated by any other instance where Theresa's pupils reacted to light. However, this argument goes to the weight of this evidence and not to its admissibility. While these additional pieces of neurological data were by no means conclusive, they were competent evidence which tended to support the trial court's finding, and which also tended to disprove the contention that these tests merely verified that brain death had already taken place.

In support of the contention that Theresa Janus did not survive Stanley Janus, evidence was presented which showed that only Theresa Janus suffered seizures and exhibited a decerebrate posture shortly after ingesting the poisoned Tylenol. However, evidence that persons with these symptoms tend to die very quickly does not prove that Theresa Janus did not in fact survive Stanley Janus. Moreover, the evidence introduced is similar in nature to medical presumptions of survivorship based on decedents' health or physical condition which are considered too speculative to prove or disprove survivorship. Similarly, we find no support for the allegation that the hospital kept Theresa Janus on a mechanical respirator because her family requested that termination of her life support systems be delayed until the arrival of her brother, particularly since members of Theresa's family denied making such a request.

In conclusion, we believe that the record clearly established that the treating physicians' diagnoses of death with respect to Stanley and Theresa Janus were made in accordance with "the usual and customary standards of medical practice." [The physicians'] conclusion that Theresa Janus did not die until October 1, 1982, was based on various factors including the restoration of certain of her vital signs as well as other neurological evidence. The trial court found that these facts and circumstances constituted sufficient evidence that Theresa Janus survived her husband. It was not necessary to determine the exact moment at which Theresa died or by how long she survived him, and the trial court properly declined to do so. Viewing the record in its entirety, we cannot say that the trial court's finding of sufficient evidence of Theresa's survivorship was against the manifest weight of the evidence.

Because of our disposition of this case, we need not and do not consider whether the date of death listed on the victims' death certificates should be considered "facts" which constitute prima facie evidence of the date of their deaths. See Ill.Rev.Stat.1981, ch. 111 1/2, par. 73-25; People v. Fiddler (1970), 45 Ill.2d 181, 184-86, 258 N.E.2d 359.

Accordingly, there being sufficient evidence that Theresa Janus survived Stanley Janus, the judgment of the circuit court of Cook County is affirmed.

Affirmed.

Notes

1. *Definition of Death; Uniform Determination of Death Act.* The definition of death utilized by the Illinois court in *Janus* is similar to that employed in the Uniform Determination of Death Act (1980), set forth supra p. 72. As noted, the Uniform Determination of Death Act has been enacted in 32 states and was incorporated into section 1-107 of the UPC in 1991.

2. *Pre-1990 and 1990 UPC.* As noted supra Chapter 5, section 2-601 of the pre-1990 UPC imposed a 120-hour requirement of survival upon the devisees of a decedent's will. No cases have sought to extend this will provision to all donative provisions, such as beneficiary designations in life-insurance polices. One reason, of course, is that the widely enacted Uniform Simultaneous Death Act (USDA) is inconsistent with a 120-hour require-ment of survival. Insofar as the *Janus* case is concerned, another reason why Stanley's mother did not have the option of making such an argument is that Illinois law has not adopted the pre-1990 UPC or any similar statutory provision even for devisees under wills.

Had *Janus* been governed by the 1990 UPC, the outcome of the case would not only have been different, but the case itself need not have been litigated. Section 2-702 provides that, for purposes of a donative provision of a "governing instrument," a term defined in section 1-201 as including an insurance policy, an individual who is not established by clear and convincing evidence to have survived the death of another individual by 120 hours is deemed to have predeceased that other individual. Theresa's administrator would have had no hope of establishing by clear and convincing evidence that Theresa survived Stanley by 120 hours. The proceeds of Stanley's policy would have gone to Stanley's mother, Alojza, rather than to Theresa's estate and then to her relatives.

Note not only the extension of the 120-hour requirement of survival to all donative provisions of a governing instrument, but also the imposition of a clear-and-convincing standard of proof. Contrast this with the preponderance-of-the-evidence standard of proof under the USDA, as applied in *Janus*. The purposes of section 2-702 are to give a USDA-type result in cases of near-simultaneous as well as simultaneous deaths, to reduce litigation, and to resolve doubtful cases in favor of non-survival.

3. *Joint Tenancies and Multiple-Party Accounts Under 1990 UPC.* Section 2-702 of the 1990 UPC also extends the 120-hour requirement of survival to joint tenancies, tenancies by the entirety, and multiple-party accounts.

4. *Revised Uniform Simultaneous Death Act.* A proposal to revise the USDA along the lines of 1990 UPC section 2-702 was approved by the Uniform Law Commissioners in 1991.

PART C. COORDINATING THE PARTS INTO A COHERENT WHOLE; CONTINGENCY ESTATE PLANNING TECHNIQUES

Inter-vivos trusts, particularly revocable trusts, are staple products in the estate planner's inventory. Inter-vivos trusts can be used to achieve a variety of financial objectives, including tax savings and coordinating life-insurance proceeds with other assets, and to anticipate a variety of contingencies, such as the possibility the grantor will lapse into mental or physical incapacity in later life.

Other legal devices are also useful in contingency estate planning. In particular, so-called durable powers of attorney have proven to be helpful means for persons acting on behalf of incapacitated property owners to respond flexibly to changing circumstances. Durable powers may be used alone, but are better used in conjunction with inter-vivos trusts. In this part, we examine these and other techniques of coordinating the various parts of the plan into a coherent whole.

1. Pour-Over Devises

Statutory References: *1990 UPC § 2-511*
                                      Pre-1990 UPC § 2-511

Supplemental Funding of Inter-Vivos Trusts. After initially funding an inter-vivos trust, the grantor may later want to supplement the trust with additional assets. Supplemental fundings fulfill various objectives. One is tax planning. Grantors who are wealthy enough to worry about federal transfer taxes (recall that the lifetime unified credit shelters transfers up to $600,000, $1.2 million for married couples) frequently take maximum advantage of the gift tax annual exclusion by annually contributing $10,000 (or $20,000 for gifts from a married person) to an irrevocable inter-vivos trust.

Another motive behind supplemental funding of inter-vivos trusts is to coordinate trust assets with other assets, including the grantor's probate estate at death and insurance proceeds. These assets can all be merged into a single trust entity through an arrangement known as the pour-over. To create this arrangement, the grantor creates an inter-vivos trust and then executes a will devising part or all of the estate to the trustee of the receptacle trust. The grantor may also arrange to have life-insurance proceeds added to the receptacle trust by naming the trustee as the insurance beneficiary. Flexibility is maximized if the receptacle trust is revocable, but this comes at the sacrifice of tax savings.

The Common-Law Background of Pour-Over Devises. Prior to statutory authorization of pour-over devises, there was substantial uncertainty about the validity of an attempted pour-over into a revocable trust. Little difficulty was encountered under common-law doctrines when the devise poured over into an irrevocable inter-vivos trust that was established before execution of the will. Most courts seemed willing to accept either the theory that the will incorporated the terms of the trust by reference or the theory that the terms of the trust were facts of independent significance.

More difficulty existed if the trust was revocable or amendable. The likelihood that the court would invalidate the pour-over was greatest where the grantor amended the trust after executing the will.[19] Two issues existed in this situation: first, whether the amendment was effective as to property passing under the pour-over devise and, if not, whether the pour-over was effective at all. Insofar as the pour-over devise is concerned, the amendment could not be given effect under the doctrine of incorporation by reference because it failed the "in-existence" requirement. Eventually, a few courts held that the amendment was effective under the doctrine of facts of independent significance. See, e.g., Canal Nat'l Bank v. Chapman, 157 Me. 309, 171 A.2d 919 (1961); Second Bank-State Street Trust Co. v. Pinion, 342 Mass. 366, 170 N.E.2d 350 (1960). Concerning the second issue, it should have been possible to sustain the testamentary pour-over on the unamended terms of the trust, but at least one court held that the amendment caused the entire pour-over to fail. See President and Directors of Manhattan Co. v. Janowitz, 260 App. Div. 174, 21 N.Y.S.2d 232 (1940). The court's theory was that the attempted devise to the trustee had to fail because it would frustrate the testator's intent to allow the testamentary assets to be administered under the unamended terms of the trust.

Uniform Testamentary Additions to Trusts Act (1960). Acting to facilitate pour-over devises, legislatures began to enact statutes that authorized testamentary additions to revocable or amendable trusts. The Uniform Testamentary Additions to Trusts Act (UTATA) was approved by the Uniform Law Commissioners in 1960, was incorporated into the pre-1990, UPC as section 2-511, and has been adopted in all but seven states. These states have their own statutes largely reaching the same results as the Uniform Act. See Schaefler, Validity of Testamentary Pourovers: ACTEC Study No. 2, in ACTEC Studies (American College of Trust and Estate Counsel, 1979).

The UTATA permits wills to pour probate assets into revocable or irrevocable inter-vivos trusts. Under UTATA, pour-over devises are valid even if the trust is amended after execution of the will. The act requires the testator to identify the trust in her or his will and to state the terms of the trust in a writing (other than the will) executed before or concurrently with execution of her or his final will or the valid final will of another person who predeceased the testator.

---

19. Some courts had even struck down pour-over devises to revocable trusts when the grantor had not exercised the power to revoke. See, e.g., Atwood v. Rhode Island Trust Co., 275 F. 513 (1st Cir. 1921). The court's objection was that the power to revoke or amend the trust itself was impermissible as an attempted power to dispose of probate assets without complying with the wills statute formalities.

1990 UPC Section 2-511. Section 2-511 of the 1990 UPC makes several substantive changes in pre-1990 UPC section 2-511.

The first concerns pour-overs to unfunded inter-vivos trusts. Suppose that a trust instrument is signed by the settlor, but the "trust" is not funded with any property at all—not even a penny. Assuming that the trust instrument was executed before or concurrently with the execution of the testator's will, can the testator's will validly devise property into the "trust," under the UTATA? The court in Clymer v. Mayo, 339 Mass. 754, 473 N.E.2d 1084 (1985) (set forth supra p. 410) said that it can. Accord, Trosch v. Maryland Nat'l Bank, 32 Md. App. 249, 359 A.2d 564 (1976). But see Estate of Daniels, 665 P.2d 594 (Colo. 1983) (pour-over devise failed; before signing the trust instrument, the testator was advised by counsel that the "mere signing of the trust agreement would not activate it and that, before the trust could come into being, [the testator] would have to fund it;" testator then signed the trust agreement and returned it to counsel "to wait for further directions on it;" no further action was taken by the testator prior to death; the testator's will devised the residue of her estate to the trustee of the trust, but added that the residue should go elsewhere "if the trust created by said agreement is not in effect at my death.")

Section 2-511 (1990) makes it clear that the inter-vivos trust receptacle need not have been funded during the testator's lifetime, but can be funded with a trust res by the pour-over devise itself. The UPC also now allows the terms of the trust to be stated in a writing executed after as well as before or concurrently with execution of the testator's will. It further allows the testator's will to provide that the pour-over devise is not to lapse even if the trust terminates or is revoked before the testator's death.

Upon the recommendation of the UPC Drafting Committee, comparable revisions of the UTATA were adopted by the Uniform Law Commissioners in 1991.

2. Durable Powers of Attorney

Statutory References: *1990 UPC §§ 5-501 to -505*

A power of attorney creates an agency relationship between the maker of the power (the principal) and the attorney-in-fact (the agent). Under the traditional law of agency, the authority of the attorney-in-fact is automatically terminated upon the principal's death or incapacity. See Restatement 2d of Agency §§ 120, 122 (1958).

The pre-1990 UPC brought forth a much-desired change in power-of-attorney law by authorizing durable powers of attorney. As opposed to an ordinary power of attorney, a durable power of attorney continues to be valid after the principal has become mentally incapacitated. In addition, the Code provided that death of the principal does not automatically terminate the agent's authority. Under the Code, written powers of attorney, durable or otherwise, continue to be valid after the principal's death; actions taken by the attorney-in-fact in good faith under the power are authorized until the attorney-in-fact gains actual knowledge of the principal's death.

In 1979, the UPC provisions were adopted, with slight modification, as a free-standing Uniform Durable Powers of Attorney Act, which was in turn incorporated into the UPC, as Part 5 of Article V (sections 5-501 through 5-505). Nearly every state now has legislation authorizing the creation of durable powers of attorney. For a state-by-state compilation, see Stiller & Gohn, Durable Powers of Attorney: ACTEC Study No. 17, in ACTEC Studies (American College of Trust and Estate Counsel, 1986).

The next advance in power-of-attorney law was the promulgation of the freestanding Uniform Statutory Form Power of Attorney Act (USFPAA) (1988). The USFPAA authorizes the execution of a fill-in-the-blanks type durable power of attorney that grants the agent the authority to act for the principal in one or more or all of thirteen broad categories, by a check-off procedure, under which the principal checks off those categories in which she or he wants the agent to have power to act. The statute itself supplies the details concerning the exact actions that are authorized within each category checked off.

Durable powers of attorney, including statutory form durable powers, often authorize supplemental fundings of inter-vivos trusts. Trusts, usually revocable trusts with discretionary provisions, provide a better tool for the management of the property of an incapacitated persons than a formal guardianship or conservatorship. Moreover, trusts are more likely to be honored by transfer agents and other third parties than powers of attorney.[20] A technique now catching hold is for a grantor, while fully competent, to create a so-called standby trust, a trust funded with nominal assets such as $100 or $1000. In conjunction with the trust's creation, the grantor executes a durable power of attorney authorizing the attorney-in-fact (who might be the trustee of the trust) to transfer all or a specified portion of the grantor's assets into the trust, if the grantor later loses physical or mental capacity. This technique allows the grantor to retain control of her or his assets while the grantor is still able to manage them, but also to have an arrangement in place by which the assets can be responsibly managed on the grantor's behalf should that become necessary.

EXTERNAL REFERENCES. F. Collin, Jr., J. Lombard, A. Moses & H. Spitler, Drafting the Durable Power of Attorney: A Systems Approach (1987); Lombard, Planning for Disability: Durable Powers, Standby Trusts and Preserving Eligibility for Governmental Benefits, 20 U. Miami Inst. on Est. Plan. Ch. 17 (1986); Stiller & Gohn, Durable Powers of Attorney: ACTEC

---

20. None of the various uniform acts on powers of attorney provide any mechanism that forces financial institutions or any other entity or individual to honor the power of attorney. In response to this problem, the California Law Revision Commission has recommended that a new section be added to California's enactment of the USFPAA that would authorize the agent to bring an action to compel third persons to honor the agent's authority. 20 Cal. L. Rev. Comm'n Report 2629 (1990).

Study No. 17, in ACTEC Studies (American College of Trust and Estate Counsel, 1986).

3. *Custodial Trusts*

Statutory Reference: *Uniform Custodial Trust Act*

In 1987, the Uniform Law Commissioners took another step to facilitate the management of property on behalf of adult beneficiaries, whether incapacitated or not. The Uniform Custodial Trust Act (UCTA), enacted so far in five states, establishes a statutory trust that can be invoked by transferring property to another person "as custodial trustee for (name of beneficiary, who can be the transferor) under the [enacting state] Uniform Custodial Trust Act." The UCTA is designed to provide a statutory standby trust similar to the custodial arrangement for minors established by the Uniform Transfers to Minors Act. The terms of the custodial trust, set forth in the statute itself, provide among other things that if the beneficiary is incapacitated the custodial trustee shall expend so much or all of the custodial trust property as the custodial trustee considers advisable for the use and benefit of the beneficiary. The statute also facilitates a pour-over into a trust designed to coordinate management and distribution of other assets by providing, in section 17(a)(3)(i), that the assets remaining in a custodial trust at the beneficiary's death are to be transferred "as last directed in a writing signed by the deceased beneficiary while not incapacitated and received by the custodial trustee during the life of the deceased beneficiary. . . ."

4. *"Living Wills" and Other Health-Care Decisional Devices*

Use of the durable power of attorney is not limited to funding inter-vivos trusts. The durable power is also used as a device for authorizing one person to make health-care decisions for an incapacitated person, including decisions to withhold or withdraw life support systems. In this context, the durable power is an alternative to the so-called "living will." The living will states the patient's directions concerning termination of medical treatment. The durable power authorizes another person to make health-care decisions.

The following excerpt gives a thumbnail sketch of the use of "living wills," durable health-care powers of attorney, and other devices affecting health-care decisions.

Pickering, Life at All Costs: Pious "Balderdash"
Legal Times, Nov. 13, 1989, at 26

Recent advances in medical science—the ability to prolong life by means such as respirators, dialysis, cardiopulmonary resuscitation, artificial nutrition and hydration, antibiotics, and chemotherapy—have been both a blessing and a curse. They have saved many lives, but they have unnecessarily prolonged the natural process of dying for others, especially the elderly. These new techniques are expensive and have added billions of dollars to our national health-care costs. Accordingly, when and under what circumstances life should be prolonged by these means has been the subject of intense debate within the medical, legal, governmental, academic, and religious communities and in the courts of our nation . . . .

Thirty-nine states and the District of Columbia have statutes permitting living wills, by which competent individuals can give advance instructions as to what treatments they do or do not want in the event of terminal illness. Because of substantial variations of these statutes, the Conference of Commissioners on Uniform State Laws has proposed the Uniform Rights of the Terminally Ill Act. The American Bar Association, acting on recommendation of the Commission on Legal Problems of the Elderly, has approved this uniform act, and the living-will concept generally.

The durable health-care power of attorney is a relatively new concept. These powers are called "durable" because, unlike the common-law power of attorney, they remain in effect if the principal becomes incompetent. All states and the District of Columbia now have statutes authorizing general durable powers of attorney. In addition, 12 states and the District of Columbia have statutes specifically authorizing durable health-care powers of attorney by which the principal can give specific instructions or authority to the agent to act in all health-care decisions for the principal. Although there is some uncertainty, it is believed that the general durable power-of-attorney statutes in other states are broad enough to permit the creation of health-care powers.

Durable health-care powers of attorney have several advantages over living wills. They are not restricted to cases of terminal illness where death is imminent. They can, accordingly, avoid the agonizing litigation over non-terminal vegetative patients like Karen Ann Quinlan and Nancy Cruzan. Moreover, depending on the governing statute, the powers can be detailed or general. They can direct either that *everything* possible be done to preserve the principal's life or that *nothing* be done. They can be flexible to deal with unforeseen developments by giving the agent authority to act as the agent sees fit, or they can specifically limit the agent's authority to act. They can also provide that the power is not effective until the principal is unable to act, and they can direct how the agent is to act then.

In addition to living wills and durable powers, there is a third statutory development that can also eliminate the need for court proceedings. These are the family-consent laws adopted by more than a dozen states. These laws give designated family members the right to withhold or withdraw life-sustaining treatment from incompetent patients in specific situations.

They regularize what now happens naturally in most cases, where the doctor consults with available family members regarding life-sustaining treatment for an incompetent; and if they agree on a level of treatment, that is usually what is done. Nevertheless, problems still arise when family members disagree or when they have interests that conflict with the patient's. Hence, these consent statutes, like living wills and durable powers, do not always provide a complete or satisfactory answer.

The trend of the case and the statutory law has been toward allowing individuals or their surrogates considerable freedom to choose natural death with dignity rather than forcing patients to continue unwanted life-sustaining treatment that is of limited, if any, benefit. Nevertheless, the controversy continues. This trend has been criticized as putting us on the slippery slope to euthanasia and mercy killings. Questions are also asked whether advance directives such as living wills and durable powers really represent what the individual would have chosen if he or she had known the precise circumstances in which choices would later have to be made: Should not one have "a last clear chance" to change one's mind?

These criticisms are not entirely without substance. Decisions to withhold or withdraw life-sustaining treatment are sometimes called passive euthanasia. That sounds bad, but there is a clear distinction between passive and active euthanasia, between omission and commission, between permitting death to occur naturally without artificial prolongation and outright killing. However, the distinction between the two, between passive and active euthanasia, can be blurred in debate and in practice. For instance, the growing hospice-care movement emphasizes palliative care for the terminally ill, but there can be a fine line between the amount of analgesic, such as morphine, that is needed to control pain and the amount that will shorten, or even end, life: indeed, it may be simply a matter of the intention with which the dosage is given.

The controversy over euthanasia is not likely to go away. It may well intensify as medical science continues to find new ways to prolong life even after it has become essentially meaningless or unendurable, as patients and their families see that "death with dignity" can sometimes be slow and horrible, and as social and economic pressures mount from the aging of America. These pressures—the growth of our elderly population and the need to contain our skyrocketing health-care costs—are driving factors that cannot be ignored. If other means are not found to deal with these inescapable facts, euthanasia may come to be considered more favorably, at least as a last resort.

The demographics of aging are dramatic. The fastest-growing segment of our population is the group over 85; that group alone, which is now one percent of the population, is projected to be five percent in the year 2050. Think what enormous challenges these demographics pose for the way we allocate resources and handle such matters as health care, retirement, productivity of the work force, intergenerational pressures, and so on.

Life that can be restored and made productive again by medical science is one thing. Quite another is the artificial prolongation of old age beyond the natural dying process, where there is no hope of functional recovery or restoration to any sort of meaningful existence.

The law has adapted to the pressures of our time and has given a fair amount of freedom for individual choice in matters of life and death, despite countervailing moral, ethical, and religious considerations. Thus far, the court decisions and statutes have provided a reasonably satisfactory framework for these life-and-death health-care decisions—a framework that minimizes the law's intrusion into what are intensely private and personal matters. Whether that framework can meet the challenges of the future depends upon all of us. There must be better communication and understanding among everyone in the health-care loop—the public, individuals and their families, lawyers and doctors, public officials, social workers, nurses, administrators, and other health-care professionals.

Notes

1. *The Cruzan Decision.* The pressure for legislation enabling the creation of durable health-care powers of attorney, living wills, and other similar devices has been intensified in the wake of the United States Supreme Court's decision in Cruzan v. Missouri Department of Health, 497 U.S. 261 (1990). The issue before the Court was the constitutionality of a Missouri statute that allowed a surrogate for a patient to refuse medical treatment, but only if there was clear-and-convincing proof that the refusal corresponded to the patient's wishes. The court held that nothing in the constitution prohibits a state from requiring the heightened clear-and-convincing-evidence standard of proof of the person's wishes. Absent such evidence, which might be furnished by a living will, comparable document, or other evidence, the Court held a state is not constitutionally required to accept the substituted judgment of close family members.

The *Cruzan* decision may be more important for what it did not hold than for what it held. It did not hold that a state is constitutionally required to apply a clear-and-convincing standard of proof of the patient's wishes or even to require any evidence of the patient's wishes at all; absent any specific evidence of what the patient would have wanted, a state would seem to be free to defer to the wishes of the patient's close family members. The Uniform Law Commissioners will soon appoint a drafting committee to begin work on a Uniform Health Care Decisions Act.

2. *Sequel to the Cruzan Case.* Nancy Cruzan, the auto-crash victim who was the subject of the *Cruzan* case, died at the age of 33 on December 26, 1990, twelve days after her feeding tube was removed by order of a Missouri probate court. She had been in a vegetative state for eight years. Although Nancy Cruzan had not signed a living will or a durable health-care power of attorney, the probate court found that there was clear and convincing evidence she would have wanted to die; the finding was based on testimony of former co-workers as to conversations in which she stated that she would never want to live "like a vegetable."

Sample Living Will[21]

I, _____, declare that if I become unable to make my own health care decisions, as determined by my attending physician, such decisions, including those to accept or refuse any treatment, service or procedure used to diagnose, treat or care for me, and to withhold or withdraw life-sustaining measures, shall be made in accordance with my wishes which follow.

I do not want my life prolonged by life-sustaining measures, but want to be allowed to die naturally and to be given all care necessary to make me comfortable and to relieve pain:

    1. If I am diagnosed as having an incurable and irreversible terminal condition; or

    2. If I am diagnosed as being permanently unconscious or in a persistent vegetative state; or

    3. If I am diagnosed as having an incurable and irreversible condition which is not terminal but which causes me to experience severe and progressive physical or mental deterioration and loss of capacities I value, so that the burdens of continued life (with treatment) are greater than the benefits I experience.

In the circumstances described, (a) artificially provided fluids and nutrition, such as by feeding tube or intravenous infusion, should be withheld or withdrawn, (b) if I should suffer cardiac or respiratory arrest, cardiopulmonary resuscitation should not be provided and (c) any other medicine or medical procedures that may be available to prolong my life should not be used.

Any invalid or unenforceable direction shall not affect my other directions.

This document shall not limit the powers given to any existing or future health care agent designated by me.

I understand the purpose and effect of this document and sign it after careful deliberation, this ____ day of _____, 19__.

_____(L.S.)

Residing at: _____

_____

Each of the undersigned declares that the person who signed this document did so in his or her presence; that said person is personally

---

21. This form is reprinted from U.S. Trust Company, Practical Drafting—Trust and Will Provisions. This form is described by the publisher as a "common law" document and as having been prepared on the assumption that applicable state law recognizes its validity and imposes no requirements on its use; should such restrictions or requirements exist, the form must be modified.

known to him or her and appears to be of sound mind and acting willingly and free from duress or undue influence; and that he or she is 18 years of age or older and is not designated as the persons's health care proxy.

_____ residing at _____,

_____

_____ residing at _____,

_____

Sample Durable Health Care Power of Attorney[22]

If my attending physician determines that I am unable to make my own health care decisions, I, _____, appoint _____, residing at _____, _____, as my agent to make all health care decisions for me *except as otherwise provided in this document,* including decisions to accept or to refuse any treatment, service or procedure used to diagnose, treat or care for me, and to withhold or withdraw life-sustaining measures and to direct that artificially provided fluids and nutrition, such as by feeding tube or intravenous infusion, be withheld or withdrawn. This document shall be construed in the broadest possible manner and my agent may act or fail to act to the same extent as I could if I were able to make my own health care decisions, provided that my agent shall do so in accordance with my wishes and instructions as known to my agent or, in their absence, in accordance with my best interests.

If my attending physician shall determine that my agent is unable, unwilling or unavailable to act, I appoint _____, residing at _____, _____, as my health care agent.

Unless revoked, this proxy shall remain in effect indefinitely, even though a guardian or other representative shall be appointed to act on my behalf.

Any invalid or unenforceable power or provision shall not affect the other powers and provisions or the appointment of my health care agent.

I understand the purpose and effect of this document and sign it after careful deliberation, this ___ day of _____, 19__.

---

22. This form is reprinted from U.S. Trust Company, Practical Drafting—Trust and Will Provisions. This form is described by the publisher as a "common law" document and as having been prepared on the assumption that applicable state law recognizes its validity and imposes no requirements on its use; should such restrictions or requirements exist, the form must be modified.

_____(L.S.)

Residing at: _____

_____

Each of the undersigned declares that the person who signed this document did so in his or her presence; that said person is personally known to him or her and appears to be of sound mind and acting willingly and free from duress or undue influence; and that he or she is 18 years of age or older and is not designated as the persons's health care proxy.

_____ residing at _____

_____

_____ residing at _____

_____

———

EXTERNAL REFERENCES. F. Collin, J. Lombard, A. Moses & H. Spitler, Drafting the Durable Power of Attorney: A Systems Approach (1987); G. Alexander, Writing a Living Will: Using a Durable Power of Attorney (1987); Moore, The Durable Power of Attorney as an Alternative to the Improper Use of Conservatorship for Health Care Decisionmaking, 60 St. John's L. Rev. 681 (1986).

PART D. TESTAMENTARY CONTROL OVER WILL SUBSTITUTES

Statutory References: *1990 UPC § 6-213*
                              Pre-1990 UPC § 6-104

To what extent can a will be used to alter the devolution of property subject to a will substitute? The traditional function of a will is to control the succession to *probate* property—property owned in the full technical sense of the term at the time of death. The property subject to a will substitute passes outside the probate system—hence the term "nonprobate" property. Indeed, will substitutes owe their validity to the idea that the arrangements are *lifetime* transfers of a property interest or a contract right, which merely take effect *in possession* at death. How, then, could it be thought that such property could be controlled by the transferor's will?

Recall that one of the attractive features of will substitutes is their amenability and revocability or, in the case of joint tenancies, their severability—even after they have been put into place. In *substance*, the property is still owned, in whole or in part, until death, allowing the "owner" to change her or his mind as to how it will be disposed of after death. Normally, no change of mind occurs and the power to amend, revoke, or sever is never exercised. Occasionally, however, the power is exercised or attempted to be exercised. The question is whether the transferor's power, exercisable at any time until the moment of death, can also be exercised at death in her or his will.

Estate of Lowry
93 Ill. App. 3d 1077, 418 N.E.2d 10 (1981)

[Katherine Lowry established a self-declared, revocable inter-vivos trust in 1972. The power to revoke was set forth in the trust instrument in the following provision:

> I may at any time or times during my lifetime by instrument in writing delivered to the Trustee or Co-Trustees (hereinafter referred to as Trustees) amend or revoke this declaration in whole or in part. The Trust Property to which any revocation relates shall be conveyed to me or otherwise as I direct. This power is personal to me and may not be exercised by my legal representative or others.

Katherine's will, executed in 1977, stated:

> I wish by this instrument, my last will and testament, to revoke, set aside and nullify specifically a certain trust created by me on January 24, 1972 and known as the Katherine Bulkley Lowry Declaration of Trust No. 44995 as amended by amendments no. one through four inclusive.

The trial court upheld the validity of Katherine's revocation of the 1972 trust.]

ROMITI, P.J. . . . The appellants' contention that a will being ambulatory cannot revoke a trust which by its provisions can only be revoked during the settlor's lifetime is supported by language in several cases. Thus it was stated in Rosenauer v. Title Insurance & Trust Co. (1973), 30 Cal. App. 3d 300, 303, 106 Cal. Rptr. 321, 323:

> Accordingly, it is settled that a power to revoke "during the lifetime" of the settlor, which means by a revocation taking effect before the death of the settlor cannot be exercised by a will that in the nature of things cannot take effect before the death of the testator.

Obviously this is true where there is no clause in the will explicitly revoking the trust and as in In re Estate of Anderson (1966), 69 Ill. App.

2d 352, 217 N.E.2d 444 and Merchants National Bank v. Weinold (1959), 22 Ill. App. 2d 219, 160 N.E.2d 174, in such event the will, if it refers to the trust and its assets at all, does nothing more than attempt to dispose of the trust assets. A clause in a will purporting to bequeath property to someone is testamentary and has no effect until the death of the testator. Clearly therefore such a clause would be ineffective to revoke a trust which by its terms could only be revoked during the settlor's lifetime. Likewise, it is clear that even if the will contained a provision expressly purporting to revoke the trust, if any instrument revoking the trust must be delivered to the trustee during the settlor's lifetime and the will is only delivered to the trustee after the settlor's death, the attempted revocation would be ineffective. Neither situation is, however, present here. The language in the first paragraph of the will did not attempt merely to dispose of trust assets; rather it clearly and specifically purported to revoke the trust. Indeed, there can be no question that had that paragraph not been in the will but had been executed, signed and received by the settlor in a separate document, the intended revocation would have been effective. Likewise, unlike the usual case, the settlor was the trustee. Accordingly since she executed and retained the will, it was delivered to her during her lifetime. . . .

In light of the principle that an instrument can act both as a will and as some other legal document, we hold that the first paragraph of the will purporting to revoke the trust was an instrument in writing delivered to the trustee which effectively revoked the trust on March 2, 1977 the day it was executed, which date was during the settlor's lifetime.

For the foregoing reasons the judgment of the trial court is affirmed.

Notes

1. *Conflicting Authorities.* The issue in *Lowry* remains unresolved in the case law. In Estate of Kovalyshyn, 136 N.J. Super. 40, 343 A.2d 852 (1975), for example, the court held that a decedent could not exercise a power to revoke a lifetime trust in a will.

2. *Savings Account Trusts.* In Estate of Bol, 429 N.W.2d 467 (S.D. 1988), the court held that the testator's will effectively revoked her savings account and money-market certificates, all of which were issued in the name of "Henrietta A. Bol, Trustee for Margaret Tompkins [testator's sister]." The will made no specific reference to any of the bank deposits, stating only:

> I give, devise and bequeath all of my estate and property, real, personal or mixed, and wheresoever situated, and over which I have the power to make testamentary disposition, to my brother, ARNOLD F. deBLONK, and my sister, MARGARET E. TOMPKINS, share and share alike . . . .

The South Dakota Supreme Court affirmed the trial court's judgment that the deposits were effectively revoked by the will. The court explained:

Generally, a tentative trust may be revoked by (1) the depositor withdrawing the deposit, (2) the depositor's unequivocal act or declaration of disaffirmance, (3) the beneficiary predeceasing the depositor, (4) the terms of the will of the depositor, and (5) by facts and circumstances resulting in the inadequacy of the estate assets to satisfy the testamentary gifts, funeral and administrative expenses, taxes, and other charges. . . .

Initially, we agree with the majority of jurisdictions holding that a residuary clause in a will, standing alone, is insufficient to impliedly revoke the tentative trust.

Further, we agree with the majority of courts which hold, in cases where the trust was not specifically revoked, that we must resort to a consideration of surrounding circumstances in order to determine whether the true intention of the depositor was to revoke the Totten trust.

In order to determine whether the depositor intended to revoke the tentative trust, courts have considered the following factors: (1) whether subsequent to the alleged revocation (e.g., through a later will), the depositor continued to treat the deposits consistent with the trust (e.g., by maintaining the account in trust form, by activity or inactivity of the account, etc.); (2) retention of possession of the account passbook or certificates; and (3) whether, absent the Totten trust, sufficient assets exist in the estate to effectuate the specific dispositions provided in the will, including directions for the payment of costs and expenses.

We observe, as did the trial court in its findings, that the money market certificates were never cashed or altered, but rather were automatically renewed for a like period at maturity, and there was no evidence offered as to any withdrawals or deposits from the passbook savings account. We further observe that the evidence does not clearly show whether Margaret was notified of the existence of the accounts or whether she had possession of any of the certificates or the account passbook during Henrietta's lifetime. Moreover, Henrietta's will specifically bequeathed her property equally, "share and share alike" to Arnold and Margaret, while disinheriting three other brothers because of Arnold and Margaret's greater need. Finally, we note that if the trusts were not recognized as revoked by the will, Margaret would receive approximately eight and one-half times more of the estate property than Arnold, who would receive merely a negligible distribution of the estate, and that the estate's available liquid assets would be insufficient to pay the debts and costs of administration and expenses of Henrietta's last illness.

The trial court, considering all of the foregoing, concluded that Henrietta's will, read in its entirety and especially considering the lack of liquidity of her estate absent the trust property, evinced her intent to revoke the Totten trust over the deposits.

Although we are not bound by the trial court's interpretation of the will nor by its conclusions of law, we agree with its analysis and holding. When considering and applying all of the appropriate factors, together with the specific language of the will, it is clear that to hold to the contrary would contravene the true intention of Henrietta.

Do you agree with the court's conclusion? Justice Sabers dissented in the case, stating:

I have no trouble with the rule that trusts can be revoked by the terms of a will, as long as the intention to revoke is clear and satisfactory. In this case, however, any intention to revoke the trusts was neither clear nor satisfactory.

See Note, Will Substitutes, Joint Accounts, and Tentative (Totten) Trusts: Uncertainty After *Estate of Bol*, 34 S.D. L. Rev. 381 (1989).

UPC section 6-213(b) provides that a will may not alter the survivorship right in any multiple-party account or POD designation.

See generally Scott on Trusts § 58.4 (Totten trusts), § 330.8 (revocable trusts); Annot., 81 A.L.R.3d 959 (1977) (revocable trusts); Annot., 46 A.L.R.3d 487 (1972) (Totten trusts); Annot., 5 A.L.R.3d 644 (1966) (public pension rights).

3. *Life Insurance.* In Stone v. Stephens, 155 Ohio St. 595, 99 N.E.2d 766 (1951), prior to their divorce in 1944, W was the beneficiary of a life-insurance policy on H's life. After the divorce, H executed a will that bequeathed all his property, including insurance policies, to his grandmother "should I die unmarried."

The court held the will to be ineffective to change the beneficiary designation of his life-insurance policy, saying:

> To hold that a change in beneficiary may be made by testamentary disposition alone would open up a serious question as to payment of life insurance policies. It is in the public interest that an insurance company may pay a loss to the beneficiary designated in the policy as promptly after the death of insured as may reasonably be done. If there is uncertainty as to the beneficiary upon the death of insured, in all cases where the right to change the beneficiary had been reserved there would always be a question as to whom the proceeds of the insurance should be paid. If paid to the beneficiary, a will might later be probated designating a different disposition of the fund, and it would be a risk that few companies would be willing to take, unless some specified time had elapsed after the death of insured, or that there had been some court adjudication as to whom the proceeds should be paid. [quoting from Wannamaker v. Stroman, 167 S.C. 484, 166 S.E. 621, 623 (1932).]
>
> It may also be observed that further delay in the payment of the proceeds of policies might be caused by a contest of such will or by a proceeding involving the construction of such will. The question of law involved herein is not affected by the interpleader of the insurers and their deposit of the disputed funds in court. There is substantial authority for the proposition that rights which become vested on the death of the insured and thus fixed by law can not thereafter be affected by such action of the insurer. 78 A.L.R. 981, and cases cited.

In Connecticut General Life Ins. Co. v. Peterson, 442 F. Supp. 533 (W.D. Mo. 1978), however, the court came to the opposite conclusion. In that case, Wilbur Peterson designated his wife, Anna, as the primary beneficiary of a group life insurance policy insuring his life. His son, Stephen was named as the secondary beneficiary. Shortly after his wife's death, Wilbur executed a will in which he bequeathed

> all of the monies and security which I may have on hand at the time of my death, including but not limited to cash on hand, bank and savings accounts, retirement funds, and/or insurance policies, stocks and bonds of any and all kinds to Mary Katherine Potter [his step-daughter] and Sandra Jacquiline Barnes [his daughter] equally, share and share alike.

The residue of his estate was bequeathed to his son, Stephen.

Holding the will to be effective to change the beneficiary of the life-insurance policy, the court said:

> [U]nder Missouri law, the insured's will effectively changed the beneficiary from Stephen Jesse Peterson to Mary Katherine Potter and Sandra Jacquiline Barnes and judgment will hereafter be rendered accordingly. Therefore, it is not necessary to consider the theory of defendants Potter and Barnes that under the doctrine of election defendant Peterson could not take under Paragraph Fourth of the will and at the same time renounce the effectiveness of Paragraph Second of the will. In passing however, this Court finds that it clearly was not the intention of the testator that defendant Peterson was to receive the proceeds of the life insurance policy and also take under Paragraph Fourth of the will, the residuary clause . . . .
>
> If Paragraph Second is not effective to change the beneficiary on the certificate of insurance the result would be that defendant Peterson would receive approximately $48,000.00 from his father's estate while the daughter and stepdaughter would share approximately $1,350.00 . . . .
>
> The certificate of insurance issued to the decedent contained provisions governing changes of the beneficiary thereof and it is agreed between the claimants in this case that the insured never made any overt attempt whatever to follow the provisions of the certificate in changing the beneficiary from Stephen Jesse Peterson to Mary Katherine Potter and Sandra Jacquiline Barnes . . . .
>
> It is . . . settled law in Missouri that an insurer does waive such provisions, as the insurer has done in this case, by filing an interpleader action, admitting its liability under the policy, paying the funds into court with the prayer that the court determine whichever one of the rival claimants is entitled to the funds . . . .
>
> The insured-testator was the complete owner of the policy. He had the unlimited and unconditional right to change the beneficiary from time to time and at any time he wished. Therefore, this Court feels that if a clear intent was expressed by the insured-testator that the beneficiary be changed, this Court should give effect to that true intent if such is not in violation of established rules of law in Missouri. There appears to be no direct Missouri law on this precise question; however, this Court determines that there is no plausible reason why the sole owner of a certificate of life insurance may not change the beneficiary thereon by his Last Will and Testament and holds that the Last Will and Testament of the insured Wilbur Payne Peterson was effective in changing the beneficiary under the certificate of insurance from Stephen Jesse Peterson to Mary Katherine Potter and Sandra Jacquiline Barnes and renders judgment accordingly . . . .
>
> The Court's decision in this case is not without the support of other authorities as will be reflected by the following: Franklin Life Insurance Company v. Mast, 435 F.2d 1038 (9th Cir. 1970); U. S. v. Pahmer, 238 F.2d 431 (2nd Cir. 1956); Clements v. Neblett, 237 Ark. 340, 372 S.W.2d 816 (1963); and Pan American Life Insurance Company v. De Cobian Alvarez, 160 F.Supp. 292 (D.C.Puerto Rico 1958).

Most of the cases follow the view expressed in *Stone,* but as *Peterson* indicates a few courts have permitted testators to change a life-insurance beneficiary by will. Cases are collected in Annot., 25 A.L.R.4th 1164 (1983). For a case reaching the same result as in *Stone* in the context of an ERISA-covered employee pension benefit plan on the basis of ERISA's preemption of state law, see MacLean v. Ford Motor Co., 831 F.2d 723 (7th Cir. 1987).

———

Equitable Election. Equitable election, a doctrine alluded to in *Peterson*, is a device of ancient origin by which testamentary power over owned property is extended to property owned by another. Suppose, for example, G's will devises $750,000 to A and "my vacation home in East Hampton" to B. Because, however, G and A owned the vacation home in joint tenancy, G lacked the power to devise it to B. Nevertheless, a court is likely to interpret G's will as putting A to a choice, or election; that is, the court is likely to hold that A is entitled to the $750,000 devise only if A transfers the vacation home to B. See, e.g., Estate of Waters, 24 Cal. App. 3d, 100 Cal. Rptr. 775 (1972). In effect, the court would be treating the devise to A as if it were a conditional devise;[23] that is, as if it said: "750,000 to A *if* A transfers the vacation home to B." Is this characterization of the devise to A justified? See Crago, Mistakes in Wills and Election in Equity, 106 L.Q. Rev. 487 (1990) (arguing that G never actually intended the devise to be conditional; rather G's devise of the vacation home to B was merely the product of a mistake on G's part as to his testamentary power to devise it).

Of course, A might decline the election, choosing to keep the vacation home. If this were to happen, A forfeits the $750,000 devise. What, then, becomes of the $750,000? One possibility would be to treat A's action as a disclaimer, in which case the $750,000 devise would pass as if A predeceased G. See UPC § 2-801(d); supra p. 100. If A bore a relationship to G that would trigger an antilapse statute, this might mean that the $750,000 devise would pass to A's descendants. Or, if the antilapse statute were inapplicable, this approach would mean that the $750,000 devise would pass to G's residuary devisees, or heirs.

Perhaps more faithful to G's intent would be to give the $750,000 devise to B, which could be done by applying an equitable doctrine called "sequestration."[24] Cf. Sellick v. Sellick, 207 Mich. 194, 173 N.W. 609 (1919) (set forth infra p. 884); but see Estate of King, 19 Cal. 2d 354, 121 P.2d 716 (1942).

Suppose A died shortly after G and before learning about the election required of her by the terms of the will? In Estate of Kennedy, 135 Cal. App. 3d 676, 185 Cal. Rptr. 540 (1982), the survivor's executor was allowed to make the election.

———

23. Compare cases like Miller v. Miller, 197 Neb. 171, 247 N.W.2d 445 (1976), where G devised real property, owned by G, "to A *on condition that* A pay over $X.00 to B." The court held that this language did not impose a condition on A's devise, but rather imposed an equitable charge or lien on the property in the amount of $X.00 in favor of B.

24. A Wisconsin statute on equitable election codifies the idea of sequestering the failed devise for the disappointed devisee, B, by providing:

Wis. Stat. Ann. § 853.15(1). If [the person put to an election] elects not to take under the will, the bequest or devise given him under the will is to be assigned by the court to the other beneficiary in lieu of the property interest which does not pass under the will.

Community-Property, "Spouse's Election." A modern use of the doctrine of equitable election is the spouse's-election device in community-property states. Under community-property regimes, property acquired during the marriage, other than by gift, inheritance, or devise, becomes community property. Unlike joint tenancy or tenancy by the entirety, community property is a form of co-ownership that operates like a tenancy in common, in that each spouse owns an undivided one-half interest with no right of survivorship in the other. When one spouse dies, that spouse has testamentary power over her or his half of the couple's community property, but not over the survivor's half.

The spouse's-election device seeks to extend the deceased spouse's testamentary power to the *entire* community. In effect, the decedent's will might say to the survivor: I devise my half of the community into a trust, income to you for life, remainder to our descendants, if you agree to contribute your half of the community into the same trust. The survivor is thus put to an election as to whether to (i) keep her or his half of the community outright and forfeit the income interest in the decedent's half or (ii) transfer his or her half into the same trust, thereby enjoying the right to the income from the whole.

Unilateral Severance of a Joint Tenancy. Unless a statute or case law makes joint tenancies indestructible, they are unilaterally severable by any joint tenant.[25] To accomplish a severance, the severing tenant can convey her or his interest to another. Or, if the severing tenant wants to retain ownership (albeit as a tenant in common), the severing tenant can convey her or his interest to a "straw person" who, in turn, conveys the interest back to the severing tenant. Alternatively, the severing tenant can execute a so-called severance deed. Not all states, however, permit the severance-deed method.

There is no requirement that a severing joint tenant notify the other joint tenant, although recordation of the severing instrument may be required to terminate the other joint tenant's right of survivorship. See Cal. Civ. Code § 683.2. Whatever method is used, it must be effected during the severing tenant's lifetime.

---

25. Michigan law adheres to a peculiar pattern under which property titled in the names of two or more persons as "joint tenants" is held in a destructible joint tenancy but property titled as "joint tenants with the right of survivorship" is held in an indestructible joint tenancy. See Albro v. Allen, 434 Mich. 271, 454 N.W.2d 85 (1990).

PART E. HOMICIDE AS AFFECTING SUCCESSION TO PROPERTY

Statutory References: *1990 UPC § 2-803*
                             Pre-1990 UPC § 2-803

Can a killer succeed to her or his victim's property? In cases of homicide, how does the state protect the right of the victim, now dead, to decide that her or his killer is no longer a preferred beneficiary? As indicated earlier, supra p. 103, some state statutes, but not the UPC, provide that spouses and parents forfeit their intestate succession shares if they commit certain statutorily proscribed acts, such as abandonment, nonsupport, or bigamy. In some respects, homicide is just another in the list of reprehensible acts that result in forfeiture because denying an heir the right to take accords with the community's sense of justice and likely reflects the decedent's dispositive preference.

Homicide is different from other wrongful conduct, however, because of the nexus between the killing and the transfer of the victim's property by operation of an intestacy statute, will, or property or contractual arrangement. After all, succession rights are determined by the order of the victim's and killer's deaths. The nexus between the act and property transfers, along with the moral imperative of preventing a killer from succeeding to the victim's property, has led many courts, in the absence of a statutory directive, to deny killers succession rights to their victims' property, and has led many legislatures to enact statutes denying killers succession rights. Neiman v. Hurff, involving realty held in tenancy by the entirety and corporate stock held in joint tenancy, suggests the difficulties in trying to determine what types of property interests the law should prevent the killer from taking.

Neiman v. Hurff
11 N.J. 55, 93 A.2d 345 (1952)

VANDERBILT, C.J. On July 31, 1950 the defendant killed his wife and thereafter pleaded *non vult* to an indictment for second degree murder for which he is now confined in prison. During her lifetime the decedent and the defendant owned a residence in Collingswood, New Jersey, as tenants by the entirety, and certain shares of corporate stock as joint tenants. In her will the decedent named as her sole beneficiary the Damon Runyon Memorial Fund for Cancer Research, Inc.

The plaintiff Alberta A. Neiman as executrix of the decedent sought, first, the direction of the court in regard to the rights of the Cancer Fund and of the defendant respectively in the corporate stock owned jointly by the decedent and the defendant during her lifetime . . . . The Cancer Fund sought an adjudication that the real property held by the entirety and the jointly owned corporate stock be held in trust for it by the defendant and that he be ordered to convey them to it.

The defendant contended that the title to both the realty and the corporate stock vested in him on his wife's death. . . .

The trial court ruled that the decedent having met her death at the hands of the defendant, the title to the realty was vested in him as trustee for himself individually and for the Cancer Fund; that its value at the time of her death was $14,000; that the value of the Cancer Fund's interest was $11,597.98 (this sum representing the difference between $14,000 and "the commuted value as of the date of decedent's death of the net income of one-half of said property for the number of years of defendant's expectancy of life as determined according to the mortality tables used by this Court"); that $11,597.98 was imposed as a lien on the real property in favor of the Cancer Fund; that the defendant pay the Cancer Fund $11,597.98 within 45 days of service of the judgment or that the Cancer Fund have execution issue. The trial court further ruled that the title to the shares of stock likewise be held by the defendant as trustee for himself and the Cancer Fund; that the value of the stock at the time of the wife's death was $2,495.63; that the value of the interest of the Cancer Fund as the sole beneficiary under the decedent's will was $2,062.61 (representing the difference between $2,495.63 and "the commuted value as of the date of the decedent's death of the net income of one-half of the said shares of stock for the number of years of defendant's expectancy of life as determined according to the mortality tables used by this Court"); that $2,062.61 was imposed as a lien in favor of the Cancer Fund and that the defendant pay said sum within 45 days after service of the judgment or that execution issue. . . .

From this judgment the defendant appealed. . . . The question here presented is whether or not a murderer can acquire by right of survivorship and keep property the title to which he had held jointly with his victim. This question has never been before a court of last resort in this State. . . . Some states have held that the legal title passes to the murderer despite his crime and that he may retain it . . . . Some other states have held that the legal title will not pass to the murderer at all . . . . A third group of states has held that legal title passes to the murderer but that equity will treat him as a constructive trustee because of his unconscionable acquisition of the property and compel him to convey it to those to whom it has been devised or bequeathed by the will of his victim, or in the absence of a will to the heirs or next of kin of the decedent exclusive of the murderer. . . .

To permit the murderer to retain title to the property acquired by his crime as permitted in some states is abhorrent to even the most rudimentary sense of justice. It violates the policy of the common law that no one shall be allowed to profit by his own wrong . . . . On the other hand, to divest the surviving murderer of all legal title violates or does violence to the doctrine of vested rights and would conflict with N.J.S. 2A:152-2, N.J.S.A.:

No conviction or judgment for any offense against this state, shall make or work corruption of blood, disinherison of heirs, loss of dower, or forfeiture of estate.

But to follow the principle enunciated in the [third group of states discussed above] does not interfere with vested legal rights, yet by applying the equitable doctrine of a constructive trust force is given to the sound principle of equity that a murderer or other wrongdoer shall not enrich himself by his inequity at the expense of an innocent person. To quote from "Can a Murderer Acquire Title by His Crime and Keep It?" in Ames, Lectures on Legal History (1913), 310, at 321:

> The results reached in these cases must commend themselves to everyone's sense of justice. But all will admit that these results could not be accomplished by common-law principles alone. The common law would make the criminal remainderman in the one case, and the criminal joint tenant in the other case, the absolute owner of the land. Equity alone, by acting *in personam*, can compel the criminal to surrender what, in spite of his crime, the common law has suffered him to acquire.

This doctrine is so consistent with the equitable principles that have obtained here for centuries that we have no hesitancy in applying it, and we find no merit at all in the defendant's argument that the decision below works a corruption of blood or a forfeiture of estate. It would be a strange system of jurisprudence that would be able to grant relief against many kinds of accidents, mistake and fraud, by compelling a defendant to act as a constructive trustee with respect to property vouchsafed him by the common law, and yet be unable similarly to touch the legal rights of a defendant who sought to profit by a heinous crime.

A more difficult question is involved in determining how much, if any, of the realty and of the shares of stock shall be held in constructive trust by the defendant for the benefit of the Cancer Fund. In the ordinary course of events the estate by the entirety in the real property would vest in the survivor absolutely and so would the ownership of the corporate stock, but it is now impossible here to determine whether husband or wife would have survived in the ordinary course of events and thus which would have become the sole owner of the property in question. Inasmuch as the husband by his wrongful act has prevented the determination in the natural course of events of whether he or his wife would survive, it is not inequitable to presume that the decedent would have survived the wrongdoer. In this situation there is no justification for determining survivorship according to the mathematical life expectancies of the decedent and her murderer. The wrongdoer, having prevented the natural ascertainment of the answer to the question of survivorship, should not be permitted to avail himself of mortality tables which may have no applicability as between him and the decedent in respect to their respective individual possibilities of survivorship. Equity therefore conclusively presumes for the purpose of working out justice that the decedent would have survived the wrongdoer. In no other way can complete justice be done and the criminal prevented from profiting through his crime.

This view inevitably leads us to the conclusion that both as to the realty and the corporate stock the Cancer Fund is entitled in equity to an absolute one-half interest and a remainder interest in the other half, subject only to the value of the life estate of the defendant in such half. Thus the defendant will hold the realty in trust for the Cancer Fund subject to a lien thereon for the commuted value at the time of the decedent's death of the net income of one-half of the real property for the number of years of his expectancy of life as determined according to the mortality tables used in our courts, i.e., $2,402.02. Likewise the defendant will hold the shares of stock in trust for the Cancer Fund subject to the commuted value at the date of the decedent's death of the net income of one-half of the shares of stock for the number of years of defendant's expectancy of life as determined according to the mortality tables, or $433.02. . . .

The judgment below is modified in accordance with this opinion but without costs to either party and the cause is remanded for such further proceedings as may be necessary.

Notes

1. *The Remedy in Neiman v. Hurff.* The judgment entered in *Neiman* uses the conventional language of constructive trust, which tends to conceal the nature of the actual decree and thereby causes unnecessary confusion. Literally, the judgment reads as though the husband, who is in prison at the time of judgment, will continue to hold legal title to the property, but as trustee for the wife's estate to the extent indicated. This would make no sense nor would it conform to the role played by a constructive trust, and one may be sure that this is not what the court had in mind. The actual decree in *Neiman* will (or at least should) order the husband to transfer legal title to the property to the wife's estate, upon payment by the latter of the amounts found to be the commuted value of the husband's beneficial interest in the property. (The only reason for finding commuted value was in order to effect such a transfer.) An example of such a decree appears in McCreary v. Shields, 333 Mich. 290, 296, 52 N.W.2d 853, 856, 857 (1952), where the decree also provided that if the defendant failed to deliver a deed "this decree may be recorded in the office of the register of deeds of the county with like effects as though such deed had been executed and delivered."

2. *Forfeiture for Joint Tenancies and Tenancies by the Entirety.* State laws conflict over the treatment of joint tenancies with the right of survivorship.[26] Some states adopt the rule found in *Neiman* that the killer should

---

26. One state goes so far as to deny the killer all rights to the jointly-held property. See Ohio Rev. Code Ann. § 2105.19(A); Oleff v. Holdapp, 129 Ohio St. 432, 195 N.E. 838 (1935); Estate of Fiore, 160 Ohio App.3d 473, 476 N.E.2d 1093 (1984).

retain only a one-half share in the property for life.[27] The majority of state statutes and both the 1990 and pre-1990 UPC section 2-803(b), as well as more recent cases, adopt the rule that the killer should retain a one-half share in fee.

In allowing the killer to retain the present value of only a one-half share in the property for life, the *Neiman* rule seems more appropriate for tenancies by the entirety than for joint tenancies. In a tenancy by the entirety, neither tenant has a unilateral right to sever. Surprisingly perhaps, the courts and statutes that allow a killer to take one-half the property in fee when the killer and victim owned property in joint tenancy extend that result to property owned by the entirety.[28]

After *Neiman* was decided, the New Jersey legislature substantially enacted the pre-1990 UPC version of section 2-803(b).

Subsequently, a case similar to *Neiman* arose, Estate of Karas, 197 N.J. Super. 642, 485 A.2d 1083 (App. Div. 1984). Walter Karas murdered his wife, Krystina Karas. The couple had two infant children. Krystina died intestate. Walter and Krystina owned two improved parcels of land as tenants by the entirety (one being their residence).

The trial judge held that, under the New Jersey counterpart of pre-1990 section 2-803(b), the murder caused a severance of the tenancy-by-the-entirety property. One half passed to Krystina's estate, where it devolved to her two children (Walter being treated as having predeceased her for the purposes of intestate succession). Ownership of the other half went to Walter.

But the court went on to hold that Walter was not entitled to keep his half. The court explained:

> Does the killer take the remaining one-half not only legally but free and clear of the power of equity to impose a constructive trust. Clearly he may not. There is nothing in the Probate Reform Act of 1978 to indicate an intent to invert the strong public policy expressed in Neiman v. Hurff. There was no statement accompanying the legislation to indicate such intent; no commentators have suggested that conclusion. Under those circumstances it is presumed that the legislature did not intend to change the pre-existing common law. Before such intent may be found it must appear clearly and plainly from the legislation.
>
> An exception to that principle of statutory construction is sometimes found where the new statute is part of a complete system of laws covering all aspects of the subject with which it deals so that it may be said that it supersedes all prior law on that subject—whether statutory law or common law. The adoption of the Probate Reform Act of 1978 falls into that category. However, there is nothing in N.J.S.A.3B:7-2 which grants the killer a clear and unequivocal right to *use* his one-half interest.

---

27. Accord Restatement of Restitution § 188 comment b (1937).

28. See, e.g., National City Bank v. Bledsoe, 237 Ind. 130, 144 N.E.2d 710 (1957); UPC § 2-803(b)(2) (1990). But see, e.g., 20 Pa. Cons. Stat. Ann. §§ 8805, 8806 (providing for different rules for joint tenancies and tenancies by the entirety).

The Appellate Division affirmed, holding further that the constructive trust on Walter's remainder interest was to be imposed in favor of Krystina's heirs—the couple's two children.

What is your reaction to the court's analysis? Is *Karas* a reliable precedent for interpreting pre-1990 UPC section 2-803(b).

———

Felonious and Intentional Killing. States generally provide for forfeiture only if the killing is felonious and intentional. The fact the killing was not motivated by greed is appropriately treated as irrelevant to whether the state requires a forfeiture of succession rights, because, regardless of the reason for the intentional killing, the victim lost enjoyment of the property, the opportunity to change the distribution, and the possibility of surviving the killer.

A person who acts in self-defense is not treated as a felonious and intentional killer. See, e.g., State Farm Life Insurance Co. v. Smith, 66 Ill. 2d 591, 363 N.E.2d 785 (1977). The majority of states do not deny succession rights to a killer who was insane at the time of the killing. See, e.g., Ford v. Ford, 307 Md. 105, 512 A.2d 389 (1986). But see, e.g., Ind. Code § 29-1-2-12.1.

A minority of states require the killing to constitute murder before denying the killer the right to succeed to the victim's property. Other states require a person to be convicted of murder or an intentional homicide. Whether a state requires the killing to constitute murder, or whether it requires the killer to be convicted of an intentional homicide, can vary depending on the type of property transfer involved.[29]

In a jurisdiction that does not require a criminal conviction, a civil proceeding is necessary to determine whether a person claiming the decedent's property intentionally killed the victim. Most jurisdictions require that the issue of whether a person feloniously and intentionally killed the decedent be decided by a preponderance of the evidence standard. Both the pre-1990 and 1990 versions of the UPC take this position. A few states impose a clear and convincing standard of proof. See, e.g., Estate of Safran, 102 Wis. 2d 79, 306 N.W.2d 27 (1981); Me. Rev. Stat. Ann. tit. 18-A, § 2-803(e). Most of the statutes provide that a conviction for a felonious and intentional killing conclusively denies the killer succession rights. No jurisdiction, however, treats an acquittal as conclusive evidence of the

---

29. For example, in Seipel v. State Employees' Retirement System, 8 Ill. App. 3d 182, 289 N.E.2d 288 (1972), a widow convicted of voluntary manslaughter of her husband was held barred from receiving death benefits under her husband's state pension by the common-law principle that one may not profit by his own wrong; the pension benefits were ordered paid to the husband's estate. But, in Estate of Seipel, 29 Ill. App. 3d 71, 329 N.E.2d 419 (1975), the same widow was held not barred from succeeding to her husband's estate as his sole heir because, as to the right of inheritance, the state statute barring inheritance in cases of "murder" superseded the common law. But see Life Insurance Co. of North America v. Wollett, 766 P.2d 893 (Nev. 1988) (statutory provision requiring conviction for murder to deny a killer an inheritance preempted the common law and, therefore, killer who entered a plea of voluntary manslaughter received insurance proceeds as beneficiary of a policy on the victim's life).

innocence of the accused or the lawfulness of the killing. This is because of the higher standard of proof necessary to obtain a conviction in a criminal trial.

Property Owned by the Victim. All but a handful of states have statutes that deny the killer the right to receive property from the victim's estate by will or by intestacy and provide that the estate or the failed interest should be distributed in accordance with the fiction that the killer predeceased the victim. In the states without statutes expressly providing for forfeiture, the courts have reached the same result. See, e.g., Wright v. Wright, 248 Ark. 105, 449 S.W.2d 952 (1970) (intestacy); Welch v. Welch, 252 A.2d 131 (Del. Ch. 1969) (will). Under 1990 UPC section 2-803(b), if the decedent died intestate, the estate passes as if the killer disclaimed her or his intestate interest. Under the UPC's disclaimer provision, section 2-801(d), this means that the killer is treated as having predeceased the decedent for purposes of allowing the killer's interest to pass to her or his surviving descendants, if any, but not for purposes of changing the shares.

Will Substitutes. Section 2-803 of the 1990 UPC, while retaining the major thrust of the pre-1990 version, is more comprehensive. Subsection (c) covers property arrangements that were not expressly treated by the pre-1990 version. For example, subsection (c)(1) provides that the felonious and intentional killing of the decedent revokes any revocable disposition made by the decedent to the killer. This includes life-insurance beneficiary designations and interests in revocable trusts.

General Principle. For situations not expressly covered, section 2-803(f) provides that they are controlled by the principle that a killer cannot profit from her or his wrong. Francis Nevins, Jr.'s mystery novel, The 120-Hour Clock (1985), is built around a plot similar to the following: Bradford Haskell dies leaving a will that devises the residue of his estate (worth $10 million) in equal shares to his children, Ann (a child by a prior marriage), Jeffrey, and Eugene. All three children survived Bradford, their father, but Jeffrey's wife arranged for Ann to be killed within the 120-hour period following Bradford's death. Under the 1990 UPC, what result?

Property Not Within the Victim's Control. Even if the victim does not have the power to control the disposition of the property, the killer still may forfeit property interests that are conditioned on survivorship of the victim.

Problems

1. G makes an irrevocable transfer in trust directing the trustee to pay income to A for life; and at A's death, to distribute the corpus of the trust to B. B kills A. Should A's estate be able to obtain an amount equal to the present value of the income interest based on A's life expectancy? Cf. *Neiman.*

2. Same as Problem 1, except the trust directs that if B fails to survive A, the corpus should be distributed to C. Should A's estate be able to obtain an amount equal to the present value of the income interest based

on A's life expectancy or should C receive the entire corpus? See Restatement of Restitution § 188 comment c (1937).

3. Same as Problem 2, except that A kills B. Should A be able to retain her income interest? Should B or C receive the remainder interest?

4. G purchases an insurance policy on her own life and irrevocably names X as primary beneficiary of the proceeds. X feloniously and intentionally kills G. Should X be able to enjoy the proceeds? Should the result be different if the policy does not require X to survive G? See Restatement of Restitution § 189 comment c (1937).

5. W's pension plan, which meets the requirements of the Employee Retirement Income Security Act (ERISA), provides that a surviving spouse shall be entitled to an annuity. H kills W. Should H receive the annuity payments? Should the answer depend on state or federal law? See Mendez-Bellido v. Board of Trustees, 709 F. Supp. 329 (E.D.N.Y. 1989); see also the discussion of federal preemption, supra p. 420.

Property Owned by the Killer. The general, and seemingly appropriate, rule is that the killer should not forfeit any property she or he owns. See, e.g., Luecke v. Mercantile Bank of Jonesboro, 286 Ark. 304, 691 S.W.2d 843 (1985); Meyer's Estate, 276 App. Div. 972, 94 N.Y.S.2d 620 (1950). But see *Neiman* (allowing the killer to take only one-half of the jointly-owned corporate stock for life rather than in fee). Nevertheless, issues can arise that suggest that some exceptions to that rule are warranted. For example, if H feloniously and intentionally killed W and then committed suicide, should W's estate be able to claim an elective share against H's estate? See, e.g., Luecke v. Mercantile Bank of Jonesboro, 286 Ark. 304, 691 S.W.2d 843 (1985); Debus v. Cook, 198 Ind. 675, 154 N.E. 484 (1926); Parker v. Potter, 200 N.C. 348, 157 S.E. 68 (1931). Could W's executor sue H's estate for wrongful death? See F. Harper, F. James & O. Gray, Law of Torts §§ 8.10, 24.5 (2d ed. 1986).

Another troubling case concerns life-insurance policies on the life of the victim where the killer is the owner and primary beneficiary. Should the killer be able to receive the life-insurance proceeds? See, e.g., New York Mutual Ins. Co. v. Armstrong, 117 U.S. 591 (1886). Should the killer be able to obtain the cash surrender value, if any, on the policy? See, e.g., Manufacturers Life Ins. Co. v. Moore, 116 F. Supp. 171 (S.D. Cal. 1953). If the killer named Y to take in the event the killer failed to survive the insured, should Y be able to take? Compare, e.g., First Kentucky Trust Co. v. United States, 737 F.2d 557 (6th Cir. 1984) with, e.g., Manufacturers Life Ins. Co. v. Moore, 116 F. Supp. 171 (S.D. Cal. 1953). See also Seidlitz v. Eames, 753 P.2d 775 (Colo. Ct. App. 1987) (children of the killer received proceeds as named successor-owners and contingent beneficiaries of a policy owned by the killer). Should the insured's estate be able to take? See, e.g., First Kentucky Trust Co. v. United States, supra. Should the insurance company be relieved of all liability? See, e.g., Travelers Ins. Co. v. Thompson, 281 Minn. 547, 163 N.W.2d 289 (1968), appeal dismissed, 395 U.S. 161 (1969); S.D. Cod. Laws § 29-9-13.

EXTERNAL REFERENCES. Palmer on Restitution §§ 20.8-.17; D'Amato, Elmer's Rule: A Jurisprudential Dialogue, 60 Iowa L. Rev. 1129 (1975); Dworkin, The Model of Rules, 35 U. Chi. L. Rev. 14, 23-24, 29-30 (1967); Ehrlich & Posner, An Economic Analysis of Legal Rulemaking, 3 J. Legal Stud. 257, 259 (1974); Fellows, The Slayer Rule: Not Solely a Matter of Equity, 71 Iowa L. Rev. 489 (1986); Maki & Kaplan, Elmer's Case Revisited: The Problem of the Murdering Heir, 41 Ohio St. L.J. 905 (1980); McGovern, Homicide and Succession to Property, 68 Mich. L. Rev. 65 (1969); Wade, Acquisition of Property by Willfully Killing Another—A Statutory Solution, 49 Harv. L. Rev. 715 (1936).

Chapter 8

PROTECTION OF THE FAMILY: LIMITATIONS ON THE FREEDOM OF DISPOSITION

Freedom of disposition is the hallmark of the American law of succession. In the United States, testamentary freedom is abridged only in limited circumstances and only in a limited way. In contrast, in the western European nations, a decedent cannot totally disinherit her or his children and sometimes cannot totally disinherit other blood relatives. In England and the principal commonwealth jurisdictions (the Australian states, most of the Canadian provinces, New Zealand), the statutory scheme known as Testator's Family Maintenance (TFM) is in place, by which the chancery judge is empowered to revise the dispositive provisions of a testator's will (including intestate shares, in an intestate estate) for the benefit of the decedent's relatives and other dependents.[1]

---

1. See, e.g., Inheritance (Provision for Family and Dependents) Act 1975, c. 63 (U.K.). Most commentators have argued that the TFM approach, because of its highly discretionary character, should not be adopted in the United States. Glendon, Fixed Rules and Discretion in Contemporary Family Law and Succession Law, 60 Tul. L. Rev. 1165, 1186-91 (1986); Langbein & Waggoner, Redesigning the Spouse's Forced Share, 22 Real Prop. Prob. & Tr. J. 303, 314 (1987).

In American law, the decedent's spouse is the only relative favored by a protection against intentional disinheritance. The decedent's children and possibly more remote descendants are granted protection only against unintentional disinheritance.

PART A. THE SPOUSE'S ELECTIVE SHARE

Statutory References: *1990 UPC §§ 2-201 to -207*
Pre-1990 UPC §§ 2-201 to -207
Uniform Marital Property Act

1. The Partnership Theory of Marriage

Disinheritance of a surviving spouse brings into question the fundamental nature of the economic rights of each spouse in a marital relationship, of how the institution of marriage is viewed in society. The contemporary view of marriage is that it is an economic partnership.[2] The partnership

---

2. One of the earliest American expressions of the partnership theory of marriage appears in the 1963 Report of the Committee on Civil and Political Rights to the President's Commission on the Status of Women. As quoted in the Prefatory Note to the Uniform Marital Property Act, the Report states:

> Marriage is a partnership to which each spouse makes a different but equally important contribution. This fact has become increasingly recognized in the realities of American family living. While the laws of other countries have reflected this trend, family laws in the United States have lagged behind.

The strength of the attribution to marriage of an economic partnership is evidenced by the recent New Jersey case of Carr v. Carr, 120 N.J. 336, 576 A.2d 872 (1990). In that case, a husband, after having left his wife of seventeen years, died during the pendency of a divorce proceeding initiated by the wife. The husband's will devised his entire estate to his children by a former marriage. The court held that the husband's death terminated the divorce proceeding under which the wife would have been entitled to a share determined under New Jersey's equitable-distribution statute. The wife also had no recourse under New Jersey's elective-share statute because that statute withheld an elective share from a surviving spouse if the decedent and spouse were not living together at the time of the decedent's death. Despite the wife's inability to recover under either the divorce or elective-share statute, the court held:

> We conclude . . . that the principle that animates both [the equitable-distribution and elective-share] statutes is that a spouse may acquire an interest in marital property by virtue of the mutuality of efforts during marriage that contribute to the creation, acquisition, and preservation of such property. This principle, primarily equitable in nature, is derived from notions of fairness, common decency, and good faith. Further, we are convinced that these laws do not reflect a legislative intent to extinguish the property entitlements of a spouse who finds himself or herself beyond the reach of either statute because the marriage has realistically but not legally ended at the time of the other's death.
> In the exercise of their common-law jurisdiction, courts should seek to effectuate sound public policy and mold the law to embody the societal values that are exemplified by such public policy. . . .

theory of marriage, sometimes also called the marital-sharing theory, is stated and supported in various ways. Sometimes it is portrayed "as an expression of the presumed intent of husbands and wives to pool their fortunes on an equal basis, share and share alike." M. Glendon, The Transformation of Family Law 131 (1989). Under this approach, the economic rights of each spouse are seen as deriving from an unspoken or imputed marital bargain under which the partners agree that each is to enjoy a half interest in the fruits of the marriage, that is, in the property nominally acquired by and titled in the sole name of either partner during the marriage (other than in property acquired by gift or inheritance). A decedent who disinherits her or his surviving spouse is seen as having reneged on the bargain. Sometimes the theory is visualized in restitutionary terms, a return-of-contribution notion. Under this approach, the law grants each spouse an entitlement to compensation for non-monetary contributions to the marital enterprise, as "a recognition of the activity of one spouse in the home and to compensate not only for this activity but for opportunities lost." Id. Sometimes the theory is stated in aspirational and behavior-shaping terms:

> [T]he ideal to which marriage aspires [is] that of equal partnerships between spouses who share resources, responsibilities, and risks. . . .
> From a policy standpoint, this partnership framework is desirable both because it encourages cooperative commitments between spouses and because it serves broader egalitarian and caretaking objectives. In effect, sharing principles hold promise for bridging traditional public/private divisions between family and market. A partnership model can cushion the impact of persistent gender biases in couples' private allocation of homemaking tasks and in the public allocation of salaries and benefits. By sharing their total resources, families can spread the risks and benefits of sex-linked roles, the remnants of a socioeconomic system that makes it difficult for any one individual to accommodate a full work and family life. . . .
> Not only do partnership principles promote gender equality; they also support caretaking commitments toward children and elderly dependents.

Rhode & Minow, Reforming the Questions, Questioning the Reforms, in Divorce Reform at the Crossroads 191, 198-99 (S. Sugarman & H. Kay eds. 1990).

A widely-held view is that of the two marital-property systems prevailing in the United States—community property and common-law, or separate property—the community property system implements the partnership theory while the common-law (title-based) system does not. This view is only partly accurate. To understand the differences and similarities between

---

The constructive trust, we believe, is an appropriate equitable remedy in this type of case . . . [that] should be invoked and imposed on the marital property under the control of the executor of [the husband's] estate . . . to avoid the unjust enrichment that would occur if the marital property devolving to [the husband's] estate included the share beneficially belonging to [the wife].

In a footnote, the court noted that efforts were currently pending in the New Jersey legislature to correct the problem of a surviving spouse who falls outside the protection of both statutes.

the community and separate property regimes, we need first to trace the development of the two systems.

a. Community Property and Marital-Property Systems

Separate Property and Community Property. The separate-property (title-based) system derives from English common law, while community property developed in continental Europe and was transplanted to the new world by French and Spanish settlers. The basic distinction between the two systems is this: Under the common law's system of separate property, the husband and wife are separate owners of the assets that each acquires after marriage (except for items that they have agreed to hold jointly). Under the community-property system, husband and wife own all assets acquired by either of them during marriage in equal undivided shares. The particular community-property model followed in the community-property states is derived from the *community of acquests* concept of the Spanish legal system, under which each spouse owns a half interest in the earnings of the other acquired during the marriage, in effect as a tenant in common; property acquired prior to the marriage and property acquired during the marriage by gift, bequest, or inheritance are not counted in the community, and so remain separate property. The other community-property model, called *universal community*, has not appeared in this country. In universal-community systems, each spouse owns a half interest in all the property of the other, regardless of the property's source or time of acquisition.[3]

Historical Background. The distinction between separate and community marital property ideas dates to the thirteenth century. The reasons for the divergence between the systems in England and continental nations remain somewhat obscure. One plausible explanation is that, while England had all of the other ingredients that led to community property in France, it lacked any strong tradition of community within the family, at least one that extended beyond the nuclear family. Professor Donahue has argued: "Without any strong tradition of community, the English lawyers could not group these same [French] elements together and call it community. They lacked at an early stage the social practice around which the legal concept could crystallize and at a slightly later stage the legal concept around which the social practice could crystallize." Donahue, What Causes

---

3. Because both spouses own community property, problems arise concerning management of community assets. Community-property states have statutes prescribing who has power to manage and deal with the assets. These statutes vary considerably in their details, but some generalizations are possible. In Texas, the wife has sole management power over her earnings that are kept separate, and the husband has sole management power over his. In California and several other community-property states either spouse has power, acting alone, to manage community assets. Both spouses, however, ordinarily are required to join in transfers or mortgages of community real property. If one spouse makes a gift of community property to a third party, the non-donor spouse may set it aside entirely or in excess of a stated amount.

Fundamental Legal Ideas? Marital Property in England and France in the Thirteenth Century, 78 Mich. L. Rev. 59, 86-87 (1979).

Although only nine states (Arizona, California, Idaho, Louisiana, Nevada, New Mexico, Texas, Washington, and Wisconsin[4]) can be called community-property states, interest in the community-property system over the years has not been limited to these states. During the 1930s and 40s, before Congress enacted legislation allowing the joint income-tax return for married persons, several separate-property (title-based) states converted their marital-property regimes to community property in order to grant their residents the tax benefits of community property's income-splitting effect. When the income-splitting joint return was adopted in 1948, these states converted back to the separate-property regime, which had the effect of conserving traditional gender roles and power relationships within the marriage. See Jones, Split-Income and Separate Spheres: Tax Law and Gender Roles in the 1940s, 6 Law & Hist. Rev. 259 (1988).

The Uniform Marital Property Act. More recently, interest in community property has been rekindled by a growing conviction in favor of economic equalization between husbands and wives. The idea that both marital partners should share equally acquests from the economic activity of either led to adoption in 1983 of the Uniform Marital Property Act (UMPA). UMPA adopts a version of the community of acquests, although the terminology used in UMPA is different—community property is called "marital property," separate property is called "individual property."[5] Under UMPA, as under community property, the property interest that each spouse acquires in all the assets acquired by the economic activities of either during the marriage is a present, vested ownership right that does not depend on survival of the other spouse. Wisconsin adopted UMPA in 1986 (Wis. Stat. Ann. §§ 766.001-766.979), and is now properly counted as the ninth community-property state.[6]

Elective Share Thought Unnecessary Under Community Property. A unique feature of community-property regimes is that a decedent's surviving spouse is not seen as needing "protection" against disinheritance by means of a so-called "elective" share in the estate of the deceased spouse. The survivor already owns a half interest in the fruits of the marriage. No elective share is provided with respect to the separate or individual property of the other spouse because that property was not attributable to the fruits of the marriage. Contribution having been rewarded, the decedent can be allowed

---

4. Wisconsin's enactment of the Uniform Marital Property Act made it a community property state.

5. With respect to income earned on individual property UMPA follows the minority view and provides in § 4(d) that "income earned or accrued by a spouse or attributable to property of a spouse during marriage . . . is marital property."

6. See Rev. Rul. 87-13, 1987-1 C.B. 20. For tax purposes, the implication of this ruling is that the basis in *both* halves of marital property is stepped up to its value at the date of the decedent's death under IRC § 1014(b)(6). If marital property had been treated for tax purposes as tenancy-in-common property, only the decedent's half would have received a step-up in basis.

unfettered power of disposition over her or his separate or individual property and over her or his half of the community or marital property.

Classification. Under community-property systems and UMPA, the couple's property must be classified upon the first spouse's death and this in turn sometimes requires tracing to source. To help resolve disputes, these systems recognize a presumption that all property is community or marital property. The spouse alleging that an item is separate or individual property must be able to prove it, and this can be a difficult task as assets over time in a marriage are commingled, invested, reinvested, exchanged, and consumed.

To further resolve classification problems, courts have developed subsidiary rules applicable to certain types of transactions. We can give here only a few examples of this highly complex body of law:

Acquisitions where the consideration is partly community, partly separate. Suppose that H purchases a boat under an installment contract executed prior to his marriage to W, and H pays some of the consideration after his marriage. Is the boat separate or community property? Three inconsistent legal theories for classifying ownership are available in this situation: inception-of-title, time-of-vesting, and pro-rata. W would have rights in the boat under the third theory but probably not under the second (depending on whether title transfers at the inception of the transaction or, more likely, when the last payment is made) and certainly not under the first. Compare, e.g., McCurdy v. McCurdy, 372 S.W.2d 381 (Tex. Civ. App. 1963) (applying the inception-of-title theory to a life-insurance policy purchased before the owner/beneficiary's marriage and holding that the proceeds are entirely his separate property) with Cosey v. Cosey, 364 S.2d 186 (La. Ct. App. 1978), rev'd on other grounds, 376 S.2d 486 (La. 1979) (applying the time-of-vesting (or receipt) theory to a premarital land sales contract as to which H paid all of the consideration prior to his marriage but did not receive title until after the marriage and holding the land was not part of the community). No state uses a single theory consistently for all types of acquisitions over time.

Acquisitions on credit. Suppose that W, while married to H, borrows money from a lender, who takes no security interest, and that W still has the borrowed funds on hand when she dies. Are the funds separate or community property? Courts have taken several different approaches to resolving classification questions concerning credit acquisitions by one spouse during marriage. In Texas, for example, all credit acquisitions are community property unless there is "clear and satisfactory evidence that the creditor agreed to look solely to the separate estate or the contracting spouse for satisfaction." Mortenson v. Trammell, 604 S.W.2d 269 (Tex. Civ. App. 1980). In other states, proceeds from unsecured loans given on personal credit of either spouse are presumed community property. In some of these states, the presumption is rebutted by showing that the lender's state of mind was such that it made the loan primarily because the borrower's separate property made repayment likely. See, e.g., Shovlain v. Shovlain, 78 Idaho 399, 305 P.2d 737 (1956); Finley v. Finley, 47 Wash. 2d 307, 287 P.2d 475 (1955). Louisiana follows yet a different test: Loan proceeds are community property unless there is evidence that the borrower intended to repay with separate funds and had the wealth to do so. See, e.g., Succession of Milton, 278 S.2d 159 (La. Ct. App. 1973).

Improvements of separate property with community funds (and vice versa). Suppose that W uses community funds to improve H's separate asset or uses her separate property to improve community assets. Is she entitled to any reimbursement? Courts in several states presume that the improving spouse intends to make a gift when she uses community funds to improve H's separate estate. See, e.g., Marriage of Lucas, 27 Cal. 3d 841, 614 P.2d 285, 166 Cal. Rptr. 853 (1980). Louisiana does not presume a gift in this situation but treats the community as having made a loan to the separate estate. See La. Civ. Code art. 2366.

As these examples indicate, classification issues are highly complex and subject to a bewildering variety of rules. For a discussion of the details of these matters, see W. Reppy & C. Samuel, Community Property in the United States 51-164 (2d ed. 1982).

Classification rules are default rules: Couples in community-property states generally may contract out from under them. By agreement, they may change community property into separate property, separate property into community property, community property into joint tenancy or tenancy in common property, and so on. Such changes in classification are called "transmutation." For further discussion, see id. at 23-49.

Migratory Couples and Quasi-Community Property. If a couple moves from a separate-property state to a community-property state, the surviving spouse may effectively lose protection against disinheritance. The law of the state where the couple domiciled at the time assets were acquired controls ownership of these assets. Thus, assets that either spouse earned during marriage in a separate-property state remain separate property. If one spouse was the sole wage earner and most or all of the couple's assets were registered in her or his name, the surviving spouse who is a non-wage earner may be left with little protection against disinheritance, at least as to those assets. The law of the state of domicile controls the disposition of property of death. If the couple had remained domiciled in a separate-property state at the time of the decedent's death, the surviving spouse would have been protected by that state's elective share statute.

Three of the community-property states, California, Idaho, and Washington, address the problem of migratory couples through the recognition of "quasi-community property." Quasi-community property is property, other than real property located in other states, that would have been community property, but for the fact that it was acquired by the decedent when the couple was domiciled in another state. In California and Washington, the surviving spouse of the acquiring decedent has an automatic half interest in the decedent's quasi-community property. See Cal. Prob. Code §§ 66, 101; Wash. Rev. Code §§ 26.16.220-.250. During the marriage, quasi-community property is regarded for most purposes as separate property of the acquiring spouse.[7] Since this right arises only upon the death of the acquiring spouse, quasi-community property might appropriately be called deferred community property. It is analogous to an elective share in that portion of the decedent's property that was acquired from earnings while the couple was domiciled in a separate property state.

A similar idea, called deferred marital property, is adopted in sections 17 (divorce) and 18 (death) of the UMPA. Idaho, a UPC state, takes a different approach to the survivor's rights in quasi-community property. Rather than granting the survivor an automatic half interest, Idaho applies the UPC's augmented-estate elective-share system to quasi-community property. See Idaho Code §§ 15-2-101, -102. See also Wis. Stat. Ann. § 861.02.

For migrating couples going the other way—*from* a community-property state *to* a common-law or separate-property state—the change in domicile does not change the couple's pre-existing rights, at least not in theory. Community property theoretically retains its character when it is moved to a separate-property state. In practice, however, lawyers and courts in separate-property states, who frequently are unfamiliar with community property, treat community property as analogous to a tenancy in common or, if title is in one spouse's sole name, as separate property subject to a constructive trust for the other spouse.

If a couple moving from a community-property to a separate-property state wishes to retain the community character of their assets, they should take special care to do so. Mingling community property with separate may make tracing impracticable. Furthermore, proceeds from the sale of community assets should be taken in the names of the husband and wife as community property. Alternatively, title may be taken in one spouse's name, while the couple executes a contemporaneous agreement indicating their intention to retain the new assets as community property.

The Uniform Disposition of Community Property Rights at Death Act (1971), enacted in twelve states (Alaska, Arkansas, Colorado, Connecticut, Hawaii, Kentucky, Michigan, New York, North Carolina, Oregon, Virginia and Wyoming), clarifies the rights of a surviving spouse of a couple who move from a community-property to a separate-property state. It creates a rebuttable presumption that property acquired during marriage by either spouse while the couple was domiciled in a community-property state was acquired as and remains property that is subject to the Act. Upon the death of the first to die one-half the property subject to the Act is the property of the surviving spouse and is not subject to the decedent's testamentary control or distributable as her or his intestate estate. Moreover, the one-half which is the decedent's property is not subject to the surviving spouse's elective share. See Johanson, The Migrating Client: Estate Planning for the Couple from a Community Property State, 9 Inst. on Est. Plan. Ch. 8 (1975); Note, Community Property in a Common Law Jurisdiction: A Seriously Neglected Area of the Law, 16 Washburn L.J. 77 (1976).

---

7. Two other states, Arizona and Texas, apply the quasi-community property concept to division of property upon divorce, but do not apply it to division at death. See Ariz. Rev. Stat. § 25-318; Tex. Fam. Code § 3.63(b).

b. Equitable Distribution Upon Divorce

The community-property system, by granting each spouse a one-half interest in the earnings of the other immediately upon acquisition, directly treats a couple's enterprise as collaborative. Nearly all[8] of the separate property states today, however, also give effect, or purport to give effect, to the partnership theory at the time when it perhaps counts most—at dissolution of a marriage upon divorce.[9] Under so-called equitable distribution upon divorce statutes, courts have broad discretion "to assign to either spouse property acquired during the marriage, irrespective of title, taking into account the circumstances of the particular case and recognizing the value of the contributions of a nonworking spouse or homemaker to the acquisition of that property. Simply stated, the system of equitable distribution views marriage as essentially a shared enterprise or joint undertaking in the nature of a partnership to which both spouses contribute—directly and indirectly, financially and nonfinancially—the fruits of which are distributable at divorce." J. Gregory, The Law of Equitable Distribution § 1.03 at 1-6 (1989).

The equitable distribution scheme was first introduced by the Uniform Marriage and Divorce Act (UMDA). As originally promulgated in 1970, UMDA required that "marital" property be distinguished from "nonmarital," or "separate" property. Only the former was subject to distribution at divorce. This distinction, which was drawn from community-property law and generally corresponds to community and separate property, has created various characterization problems. For example, are increases in value of

---

8. In 1989, Professor Oldham reported that "Mississippi is the only state that has not clearly accepted [the equitable-distribution] system. See Jones v. Jones, 532 So.2d 574 (Miss. 1988)." Oldham, Tracing, Commingling, and Transmutation, 23 Family L.Q. 219, 219 n.1 (1989).

For a fascinating account of how this system swept the country, see Glendon, Property Rights Upon Dissolution of Marriages and Informal Unions, in The Cambridge Lectures 245 (N. Eastham & B. Krivy eds. 1981).

9. In Rothman v. Rothman, 65 N.J. 219, 320 A.2d 496 (1974), a landmark case interpreting New Jersey's equitable-distribution statute, the New Jersey Supreme Court stated:

> The statute we are considering authorizes the courts, upon divorce, to divide marital assets equitably between the spouses. . . . [T]he enactment seeks to right what many have felt to be a grave wrong. It gives recognition to the essential supportive role played by the wife in the home, acknowledging that as homemaker, wife and mother she should clearly be entitled to a share of family assets accumulated during the marriage. Thus the division of property upon divorce is responsive to the concept that marriage is a shared enterprise, a joint undertaking, that in many ways it is akin to a partnership. Only if it is clearly understood that far more than economic factors are involved, will the resulting distribution be equitable within the true intent and meaning of the statute. . . . The widely pervasive effect this remedial legislation will almost certainly have throughout our society betokens its great significance.

Id. at 228-29, 320 A.2d at 501-02. Although in this early equitable-distribution case, the court refused to establish a presumptive division of marital assets on a 50/50 basis, see id. at 232 n.6, 320 A.2d at 503 n.6, many courts today do indulge in such a presumption of equal division, and many of the more recently enacted statutes explicitly do so also. See J. Gregory, supra at ¶ 8.03.

admittedly nonmarital property during marriage marital or nonmarital? The statute's approach to characterization was similar to that in a community of acquests regime: a presumption that all assets acquired by either spouse during marriage are marital. Several exceptions to this presumption existed: (1) assets that either spouse brought to the marriage, including assets that can be traced back to such assets; (2) assets that either spouse acquired during marriage other than from earnings; and (3) assets that both spouses have agreed to exclude from distribution upon dissolution of their marriage.

In response to characterization problems that the marital/nonmarital assets dichotomy created, UMDA was subsequently amended to abolish that distinction. Section 307 now describes as the property subject to distribution "property and assets belonging to either [spouse] or both however and whenever acquired. . . ." This provision creates what is called a "hotchpot" property scheme. This change eliminates the characterization problem, but it makes the question how the property should be distributed more difficult. See Levy, An Introduction to Divorce-Property Issues, 23 Fam. L.Q. 147, 151-56, 159-61 (1989).

Among the states that have not adopted UMDA, there are considerable differences in the statutes concerning what property is subject to division.[10] Once the court has determined what property is divisible, however, it has power to order the title-holding spouse to transfer all or a part of divisible assets to the other spouse. The statutes differ as to the criteria by which courts are to make distributive decisions, but, in general, equitable distribution is characterized by a considerable degree of judicial discretion. This feature is an important difference between the equitable-distribution and community-property regimes. Despite this difference, however, equitable distribution approximates community property at divorce by implementing the partnership theory. See Comment, The Development of Sharing Principles in Common Law Marital Property States, 28 UCLA L. Rev. 1269 (1981). The widespread adoption of equitable-distribution statutes is a source of pressure on separate-property states to implement the partnership theory in the other circumstances in which spousal property rights loom large—dissolution of marriage at death.

EXTERNAL REFERENCES. For a collection of excellent essays on divorce-reform laws, see Divorce Reform at the Crossroads (S. Sugarman & H. Kay eds. 1990).

---

10. The various schemes are canvassed, state-by-state, in J. Gregory, supra; J. Oldham, Divorce, Separation and the Distribution of Property (1989); and L. Golden, Equitable Distribution of Property (1983).

c. Conventional Elective-Share Law

All but one of the separate-property states[11] have decided that disinheritance of the surviving spouse at death is one of the few instances in which the decedent's testamentary freedom with respect to her or his title-based ownership interests must be curtailed. No matter what the decedent's intent, the separate-property states recognize that the surviving spouse does have some claim to a portion of the decedent's estate. These statutes, which in all but a few states have replaced the common-law estates of dower and curtesy,[12] provide the spouse a so-called "forced" share. Because the forced share is expressed as an option that the survivor can elect or let lapse during the administration of the decedent's estate, and not as a retitling of the decedent's property that automatically occurs at death, the UPC uses the more descriptive term "elective" share.

Elective-share law in the separate-property states has not caught up to the partnership theory of marriage. Under typical American elective-share law, including the elective share provided by the pre-1990 UPC, a surviving spouse is granted a personal non-transferable right to claim a one-third share of the decedent's estate, not a transmissible right to claim the fifty percent share of the couple's combined assets that the partnership theory would imply.

To illustrate the discrepancy between the partnership theory and conventional elective-share law, consider first a long-term marriage, in which the couple's combined assets were accumulated mostly during the course of the marriage. The elective-share fraction of one-third of the decedent's estate plainly does not implement a partnership principle. The actual result is governed by which spouse happens to die first and by how the property accumulated during the marriage was nominally titled.

Consider Harry and Wilma. Assume that Harry and Wilma were married in their twenties or early thirties. They never divorced, and Harry died somewhat prematurely at age, say 62, survived by Wilma. For whatever reason, Harry left a will entirely disinheriting Wilma. Throughout their long life together, the couple managed to accumulate assets worth $600,000, marking them as a somewhat affluent but hardly wealthy couple.

Under conventional elective-share law, Wilma's ultimate entitlement is governed by the manner in which these $600,000 in assets were nominally titled as between them. Wilma could end up much poorer or much richer than a 50/50 principle would suggest. The reason is that under conventional elective-share law, Wilma has a claim to one-third of Harry's "*estate.*"

---

11. Georgia is the only separate-property state lacking an elective-share statute. For a discussion of the reasons for Georgia's position, including its unusual "year's support" practice, and an argument that elective-share statutes are generally unnecessary, see Chaffin, A Reappraisal of the Wealth Transmission Process: The Surviving Spouse, Year's Support and Intestate Succession, 10 Ga. L. Rev. 447 (1976). For an opposing view, see Note, Preventing Spousal Disinheritance in Georgia, 19 Ga. L. Rev. 427 (1985).

12. The Restatement 2d of Property, Statutory Note to § 34.1, lists five jurisdictions as providing the surviving spouse a dower or dower-like interest in the decedent's real property—Arkansas, District of Columbia, Kentucky, Ohio, and West Virginia.

When the marital assets have been disproportionately titled in the decedent's name, conventional elective-share law often entitles the survivor to less than an equal share. Thus, if Harry "owned" all $600,000 of the marital assets, Wilma's claim against Harry's estate would only be for $200,000—well below Wilma's $300,000 entitlement produced by the partnership/marital-sharing principle. And, if Harry "owned" $500,000 of the marital assets, Wilma's claim against Harry's estate would only be for $166,500 (1/3 of $500,000), which when combined with Wilma's "own" $100,000 yields a less-than-equal share of $266,500 for Wilma—still below the $300,000 figure produced by the partnership/marital-sharing principle.

When, on the other hand, the marital assets have already been more or less equally divided, conventional elective-share law grants the survivor a right to take a disproportionately large share. If Harry and Wilma each owned $300,000, Wilma is still granted a claim against Harry's estate for an additional $100,000.

Finally, when the marital assets have been disproportionately titled in the survivor's name, conventional elective-share law entitles the survivor to magnify the disproportion. If only $200,000 were titled in Harry's name, Wilma would still have a claim against Harry's estate for $66,667 (1/3 of $200,000), even though Wilma was *already* overcompensated as measured by the partnership/marital-sharing theory.

Let us now turn our attention to a very different sort of marriage—a short term marriage, particularly the short-term marriage later in life, in which each spouse typically comes into the marriage with assets derived from a former marriage. In these marriages, the one-third fraction of the decedent's estate far exceeds a fifty/fifty division of assets acquired during the marriage.

To illustrate this sort of marriage, let us turn to the case of Wilma and Sam. Suppose that a few years after Harry's death, Wilma married Sam. Suppose that both Wilma and Sam were in their mid-to-later sixties when they were married. Then suppose that after a few years of marriage—five, let us say—, Wilma died survived by Sam. Assume further that both Wilma and Sam have adult children and a few grandchildren by their prior marriages, and that each would prefer to leave most or all of her or his property to those children.

The value of the couple's combined assets is $600,000, $300,000 of which is titled in Wilma's name (the decedent) and $300,000 of which is titled in Sam's name (the survivor).

Under conventional elective-share law, Sam would have a claim to one-third of Wilma's estate, or $100,000. Keep in mind that when this short-term, late-in-life marriage terminated by Wilma's death, Wilma's assets were $300,000 and Sam's assets were $300,000. For reasons that are not immediately apparent, conventional elective-share law gives the survivor, Sam, a right to shrink Wilma's estate (and hence the share to Wilma's children by her prior marriage to Harry) by $100,000 (reducing it to $200,000) while supplementing Sam's assets (which will likely go to Sam's children by his prior marriage) by $100,000 (increasing their value to $400,000).

Conventional elective-share law, in other words, basically rewards the children of the remarried spouse who manages to outlive the other, arranging for those children a windfall share of one-third of the "loser's" estate. The "winning" spouse—the one who chanced to survive—gains a windfall, for this "winner" is unlikely to have made a contribution, monetary or otherwise, to the "loser's" wealth remotely worth one-third.

How prevalent are marriages like that between Wilma and Sam—the remarriage later in life ending in the death of one of the partners a few years later? Plainly, such marriages do not affect a high proportion of the widowed and divorced population. Nevertheless, government data suggest that the incidence of such marriages may not be insignificant.[13] Equally to the point, when such marriages occur, conventional elective-share law renders results that are dramatically inconsistent with the partnership theory of marriage. That these results are seen as unjust by the children of the decedent's former marriage is both unsurprising and well documented in the elective-share case law.[14] In a case like that of Wilma and Sam—the

---

13. Data published by the federal government reveal that, within the widowed and divorced population at large, not disaggregated by age, about 21% of widowed men and about 8% of widowed women remarry; and about 83% of divorced men and 78% of divorced women remarry. U.S. Dep't of Health & Human Services, Pub. No. 89-1923, Remarriages and Subsequent Divorces—United States 12 (1989). The average (mean) ages at the time of remarriage of widowed men and women have been steadily increasing, to 60.2 for men and 52.6 for women in 1983, the latest year for which statistics have been published, up from 57.7 for men and 50.3 for women in 1970. The average (mean) ages at remarriage of divorced men and women have also been steadily increasing, but the ages are, of course, much lower. The average (mean) ages for 1983 are 37.3 for men and 33.7 for women, up from 36.7 for men and 32.8 for women in 1970. Id., Table 4, at 24.

In 1983, the average intervals between becoming widowed and remarriage for the 65-and-older age group were 3.6 years for men and 7.9 years for women. The average intervals between divorce and remarriage for the same age group were 6.3 years for men and 10.4 years for women. Id. at 13.

Within the 65-years-and-older population, 2.62% of divorced men and .049% of divorced women remarried during 1983. During that same year, the remarriage rate of widowed men and women age 65 and older was 1.68% for men and .019% for women. Within the divorced population ages 60 to 64 for that same year, 4.93% of divorced men and 1.29% of divorced women remarried; figures were not given for the widowed population ages 60 to 64 for that or any other year. The remarriage rates within the 65-and-older divorced and widowed segments of the population have been treading downward, but not in a straight line. The data show peaks and valleys over the course of the 1970-83 period. The peak occurred during the year 1975, when 3.14% of divorced men, .091% of divorced women, 1.95% of widowed men, and .021% of widowed women remarried. Data for 1975 for the 60 to 64 years age group were not reported. Id., Table 3, at 23.

These marriage rates, of course, do not reveal the remarriage rates of divorced or widowed men and women age 65 and older or 60 to 64; they merely reveal the remarriage rates for a given year. Because such remarriages accumulate within the population, the incidence of remarriage later in life appears to be significant.

14. See W. Macdonald, Fraud on the Widow's Share 156-57 (1960). Of the elective-share cases in the law reports up to the time of writing and in which the author could identify the relationships, more than half pitted children of a former marriage against a later spouse.

Statistically, "on average, women ending first marriages had 1.06 children under 18 years, those ending second marriages had 0.64 children, and those ending third marriages had 0.36 children. These differences are due at least in part to the fact that most children are born into first marriages and may not be mentioned on divorce records of subsequent marriages unless

short-term, late-in-life marriage, which produces no children—, a decedent who disinherits or largely disinherits the surviving spouse may not be acting so much from malice or spite toward the surviving spouse, but from a felt higher obligation to the children of her or his former, long-term marriage.

d. The 1990 Uniform Probate Code's Redesigned Elective Share

The 1990 revisions of the UPC contain sweeping changes in the elective share. The purpose is to grant the surviving spouse a right of election that implements the partnership theory for the division of marital property at death. As we have already seen, elective-share law in separate-property states has not caught up with the partnership theory. Under both the traditional type and the augmented-estate type of elective-share statute, a surviving spouse's share is less than the fifty percent share of the couple's combined assets that the sharing theory would imply. The redesigned elective share is intended to change this by bringing elective-share law into line with the partnership theory.

Accrual-Type Elective Share. The redesigned elective-share system can be called an accrual-type elective share.[15] It has three essential features. The first, implemented by section 2-201(a), establishes a schedule under which the elective share adjusts to the length of the marriage. The longer the marriage, the larger the "elective-share percentage." The elective-share percentage starts by providing the survivor, during the first year of marriage, a right to elect the "supplemental elective-share amount" only.[16] After one year of marriage, the surviving spouse's elective-share percentage is three percent and it increases with each additional year of marriage until, after fifteen years of marriage, it reaches the full share, which has been increased to fifty percent.

The second feature of the redesigned system is that the elective-share percentage is applied to the value of the augmented estate, which, as defined in section 2-202(b), includes the couple's *combined* assets. Specifically, the augmented estate consists of the sum of the values of four components: On the decedent's side are (1) the decedent's net probate estate and (2) the decedent's reclaimable estate.[17] On the surviving spouse's side are (3) property to which the surviving spouse succeeds by reason of

---

custody becomes an issue." U.S. Dep't of Health & Human Services, supra note 13, at 3.

15. For a proposal that divorce law utilize an accrual-type system for division of assets, see Sugarman, Dividing Financial Interests on Divorce, in Divorce Reform at the Crossroads 130, 159-60 (S. Sugarman & H. Kay eds. 1990).

16. The supplemental elective-share amount is discussed infra p. 477.

17. The content of the reclaimable-estate component and its role in preventing "fraud on the spouse's share" are discussed infra p. 487.

the decedent's death other than from the decedent's probate estate[18] and (4) property owned by the surviving spouse and amounts that would have been included in the surviving spouse's reclaimable estate had the spouse predeceased the decedent. The purpose behind combining the couple's assets is to implement the marital-sharing theory by denying significance to the possibly fortuitous factor of how the spouses happen to have taken title to particular assets.

The third feature, implemented by section 2-207, is that the surviving spouse's own assets are counted first (or a portion of them in under-fifteen-year marriages) in making up the spouse's ultimate entitlement, so that the decedent's assets are liable only to make up any deficiency.

To illustrate these three features, let us return to Wilma and Sam. Recall that the value of the couple's combined assets was $600,000, of which $300,000 was titled in Wilma's name (the decedent) and $300,000 in Sam's name (the survivor). This having been a marriage that lasted five years, the elective-share percentage prescribed in the statute is fifteen percent. See UPC § 2-201(a)(1990). Sam's elective-share entitlement is $90,000, but this does not mean that he has a $90,000 claim against Wilma's estate. Thirty percent of Sam's own $300,000 in assets (double the elective-share percentage) count in fulfilling Sam's elective-share amount. Since thirty percent of Sam's assets is $90,000, there is no deficiency and hence no claim to any of Wilma's assets.

The redesigned UPC elective-share system differs from the community-property regime in two ways. The rights accorded a spouse under the UPC are conditioned on surviving the decedent. In contrast, under a community-property regime each spouse has a right to control one-half of the marital estate regardless of the order of death. The second difference is that the UPC adds together and then splits all of the couple's assets, including assets acquired before marriage to each other and assets acquired by gift or inheritance, rather than only acquisitions from earnings during marriage to each other. The reason for this more inclusive approach is to make the system more administratively convenient by avoiding the tracing-to-source and related problems that arise under the community-property system. In practice, the gap between the two systems is unlikely to be great. It is unusual for either spouse to bring substantial separate property to a long-duration first marriage. In cases of short-duration marriages, the accrual mechanism abates some of the consequences of an expanded forced share by reducing the vested portion of the survivor's entitlement. Finally, where there is material disparity in the wealth of the parties, they can contract out of the elective-share law through a premarital agreement.

Implementation of a Support Theory; Supplemental Elective-Share Amount. The partnership/marital-sharing theory is not the only driving force behind

---

18. This component covers items such as property held by the decedent and surviving spouse in joint tenancy and life insurance on the decedent's life payable to the surviving spouse.

elective-share law.[19] Another theoretical basis for elective-share law is that the spouses' mutual duties of support during their joint lifetimes should be continued in some form after death in favor of the survivor, as a claim on the decedent's estate. Conventional elective-share law implements this theory poorly. The fixed fraction, whether it is the typical one-third or some other fraction, disregards the survivor's actual need. A one-third share may be inadequate to the surviving spouse's needs, especially in a modest estate. On the other hand, in a very large estate, it may go far beyond the survivor's needs. In either a modest or a large estate, the survivor may or may not have ample independent means, and this factor, too, is disregarded in conventional elective-share law.

The 1990 UPC's redesigned elective-share system seeks to implement the support theory by granting the survivor a supplemental elective-share amount related to the survivor's actual needs. In implementing a support rationale, the length of the marriage is quite irrelevant. Because the duty of support is founded upon status, it arises at the time of the marriage.

Section 2-201(b) of the revised UPC implements the support theory by providing a supplemental elective-share amount of $50,000. Counted first in making up this $50,000 amount are the surviving spouse's own title-based ownership interests, including amounts shifting to the survivor at the decedent's death and amounts owing to the survivor from the decedent's estate under the accrual-type elective-share apparatus discussed above, but excluding amounts going to the survivor under the Code's probate exemptions and allowances and the survivor's Social Security and other governmental benefits. Under section 2-207(b) and (c), if the survivor's assets are less than the $50,000 minimum, then the survivor is entitled to whatever additional portion of the decedent's estate is necessary, up to 100% of it, to bring the survivor's assets up to that minimum level.

The UPC's redesigned elective-share system has been endorsed by the Executive Board and by the Assembly of the National Association of Women Lawyers.

Problems

To evaluate the redesigned system, compare the results that would be reached under that system in the following cases with the results under (i) the pre-1990 UPC elective share (supra p. 473) and (ii) a community-property or UMPA regime. For shorthand purposes, the term "A's estate" is

---

19. One criticism of the partnership theory as applied to divorce law is that it sometimes leaves certain categories of divorced women without an adequate means of support. See, e.g., L. Weitzman, The Divorce Revolution: The Unexpected Social and Economic Consequences for Women and Children in America Ch. 7 (1985); Rhode & Minow, Reforming the Questions, Questioning the Reforms, in Divorce Reform at the Crossroads 191, 201-04 (S. Sugarman & H. Kay eds. 1990); Smith, The Partnership Theory of Marriage: A Borrowed Solution Fails, 68 Texas L. Rev. 689 (1990). For criticism of the Weitzman study, see Sugarman, Dividing Financial Interests on Divorce, in Divorce Reform at the Crossroads 130 (S. Sugarman & H. Kay eds. 1990).

used to mean the assets on the decedent's side that are included in the augmented estate under section 2-202(b)(1) and (2) and the term "B's assets" is used to mean the assets on the surviving spouse's side that are included in the augmented estate under section 2-202(b)(4). (Assume that no assets are covered by section 2-202(b)(3).)

1. Married in their twenties, A and B lived a long life together. A died at age 75, survived by B.

    (a) The value of A's estate totals $500,000; B's assets total $100,000.

    (b) The value of A's estate totals $100,000; B's assets total $500,000.

2. A and B got married late in life, after having previously been married (A had previously been married to X; B had previously been married to Y); each had children by the prior marriage. Five years after their marriage to each other, A died, survived by B.

    (a) The value of A's estate totals $500,000; B's assets total $100,000.

    (b) The value of A's estate totals $100,000; B's assets total $500,000.

    (c) The value of A's estate totals $90,000; B's assets total $10,000.

EXTERNAL REFERENCES. Fisher & Curnutte, Reforming the Law of Intestate Succession and Elective Shares: New Solutions to Age-Old Problems, 93 W. Va. L. Rev. 61 (1990); Waggoner, Spousal Rights in our Multiple-Marriage Society: The Revised Uniform Probate Code, 26 Real Prop. Prob. & Tr. J. 683 (1992).

2. Protection Against Will Substitutes

One of the most troublesome issues regarding elective-share law is the extent to which the surviving spouse's rights extend to will substitutes. An elective share may be of little value to a surviving spouse if it applies only to a fraction of the decedent's probate estate. The decedent could use one or more will substitutes to implement her or his estate plan while simultaneously disinheriting her or his spouse. Many courts, using different approaches, have worked to preserve the effectiveness of the statutory elective share. While legislation has changed elective-share statutes in many states to respond to deficiencies in traditional-type statutes, these judicial doctrines remain important in those states that have not amended their statutes. In these states, the judicial response is the surviving spouse's only protection against disinheritance by will substitutes. We will first examine these judicial approaches and then address the different legislative approaches to will substitutes.

a. Common-Law Theories

The courts have adopted one or the other of two approaches: the *intent* test (also called the *fraudulent-intent* test) and the *illusory-transfer* test. The illusory-transfer test is the predominant view. The leading case adopting the illusory-transfer test is Newman v. Dore, 275 N.Y. 371, 9 N.E.2d 966 (1937). In that case, Ferdinand Straus, an 80-year-old testator, executed trust agreements by which he transferred all his real and personal property to his trustees. The trust agreements were executed three days before his death and when cross actions for dissolution of his marriage were pending. The terms of the trusts reserved to Straus the right to the income for life, the power to revoke the trusts, and the power to control the trustees in all aspects of the trusts' administration; needless to say, Straus' wife of four years, a woman in her thirties, received no beneficial interest in these trusts. She challenged the validity of the transfers to the trustees. The trial court found that Straus' motive in creating the trusts was to evade New York's elective-share statute, and held that the transfers were not valid. In holding that the trusts were illusory, and therefore part of Straus' estate for purposes of his widow's rights, the New York Court of Appeals discussed both the fraudulent-intent test and the illusory-transfer test:

> The Decedent Estate Law . . . regulates the testamentary disposition and the descent and distribution of the real and personal property of decedents. It does not limit or affect disposition of property *inter vivos*. In terms and in intent it applies only to decedents' *estates*. Property which did not belong to a decedent at his death and which does not become part of his estate does not come within its scope. . . .
>
> If the [trust] agreements effectively divested the settlor of title to his property, then the decedent left no estate and the widow takes nothing. The widow has challenged the validity of the transfer to the trustees. . . .
>
> Motive or intent is an unsatisfactory test of the validity of a transfer of property. In most jurisdiction it has been rejected, sometimes for the reason that it would cast doubt upon the validity of all transfers made by a married man, outside of the regular course of business; sometimes because it is difficult to find a satisfactory logical foundation for it. Intent may, at times, be relevant in determining whether an act is fraudulent, but there can be no fraud where no right of any person is invaded. . . .
>
> [I]t would seem that the only sound test of the validity of a challenged transfer is whether it is real or illusory. That . . . test has been formulated in different ways, but in most jurisdictions the test applied is essentially the test of whether the husband has in good faith divested himself of ownership of his property or has made an illusory transfer. "The 'good faith' required of the donor or settlor in making a valid disposition of his property during life does not refer to the purpose to affect his wife but to the intent to divest himself of the ownership of the property. It is, therefore, apparent that the fraudulent intent which will defeat a gift inter vivos cannot be predicated on the husband's intent to deprive the wife of her distributive . . . share as widow." Benkart v. Commonwealth Trust Co., of Pittsburgh, 269 Pa. 257, 259, 112 A. 62, 63. . . .
>
> In this case the decedent . . . retained not only the income for life and power to revoke the trust, but also the right to control the trustees. We need not now determine whether such a trust is, for any purpose, a valid present trust. . . . We assume, without deciding, that except for the provisions of section 18 of the Decedent Estate Law the trust would be valid. . . .
>
> Judged by the substance, not by the form, the testator's conveyance is illusory, intended only as a mask for the effective retention by the settlor of the property which in form he had conveyed. We do not attempt now to

formulate any general test of how far a settlor must divest himself of his interest in the trust property to render the conveyance more than illusory. Question of whether reservation of the income or of a power of revocation, or both, might even without reservation of the power of control be sufficient to show that the transfer was not intended in good faith to divest the settlor of his property must await decision until such question arises. In this case it is clear that the settlor never intended to divest himself of his property. He was unwilling to do so even when death was near.

Although it was by no means the first case to have formulated the general approach it expressed,[20] the decision in Newman v. Dore has had substantial influence on the law in other states.[21]

Although promising in theory, the illusory-transfer doctrine of Newman v. Dore has, for the most part, given the surviving spouse very limited protection against will substitutes. Among the courts accepting the doctrine, one of the most common will substitutes of all, the revocable trust with a retained life estate, has been held not to be illusory. See, e.g., Johnson v. LaGrange State Bank, 3 Ill. 2d 342, 383 N.E.2d 185 (1978) (see also Ill. Rev. Stat. ch. 110 1/2 § 601); Kerwin v. Donaghy, 317 Mass. 559, 59 N.E.2d 299 (1945) (prospectively overruled in Sullivan v. Burkin, 390 Mass. 864, 460 N.E.2d 572 (1984), set forth infra p. 482); Beirne v. Continental-Equitable Trust Co., 307 Pa. 570, 161 A. 721 (1932); see Johnson v. Farmers & Merchants Bank, 379 S.E.2d 752 (W. Va. 1989); Restatement 2d of Trusts § 57 comment c. In a 1944 Ohio decision, such a trust was held ineffective against the claim of a surviving spouse (Bolles v. Toledo Trust Co., 144 Ohio St. 195, 58 N.E.2d 381 (1944)), but the decision was later overruled (Smyth v. Cleveland Trust Co., 172 Ohio St. 489, 179 N.E.2d 60 (1961)). There is even some doubt that a Totten trust is illusory under the illusory-transfer test. Compare Matter of Halpern, 303 N.Y. 33, 100 N.E.2d 120 (1951) and Jeruzal's Estate v. Jeruzal, 269 Minn. 183, 130 N.W.2d 473 (1964), with Montgomery v. Michaels, 54 Ill. 2d 532, 301 N.E.2d 465 (1973). On the other hand, the Supreme Court of Maine seemed to indicate that a revocable trust with a retained life estate might be "illusory" under the illusory-transfer doctrine. See Staples v. King, 433 A.2d 407 (Me. 1981). (Maine has now enacted the augmented-estate concept of the pre-1990 UPC.)

EXTERNAL REFERENCES. The comprehensive work in the field is W. Macdonald, Fraud on the Widow's Share (1960). See also Kwestel & Seplowitz, Testamentary Substitutes—A Time for Statutory Clarification, 23

---

20. In Gentry v. Bailey, 47 Va. (6 Gratt.) 594 (1850), the court observed that it was "not at all material by what motive the husband was actuated in making the disposition of his property." However, the right given the surviving spouse by the election statute was one that "the husband cannot defeat by any contrivance for that purpose: . . . . Whatever may be the form of the transaction, if the substance of it be a testamentary disposition, it cannot be effectual in relation to the wife. If this were otherwise, the statute might be rendered a dead letter at the volition of the husband."

21. In New York, the ruling of the case has been superseded by comprehensive legislation that protects the surviving spouse against specified will substitutes. See N.Y. Est. Powers & Trusts Law § 5-1.1.

Real Prop. Prob. & Trust J. 467 (1988); Schuyler, Revocable Trusts—Spouses, Creditors and Other Predators, 1974 Inst. on Est. Plan. ¶ 74.1300; Annots., 63 A.L.R.4th 1173 (1988); 49 A.L.R.2d 521 (1956); Reporter's Note, Restatement 2d of Property § 13.7, at 101-11.

Sullivan v. Burkin
390 Mass. 864, 460 N.E.2d 572 (1984)

WILKINS, J. Mary A. Sullivan, the widow of Ernest G. Sullivan, has exercised her right, under G.L. c. 191, § 15, to take a share of her husband's estate. By this action, she seeks a determination that assets held in an inter vivos trust created by her husband during the marriage should be considered as part of the estate in determining that share. A judge of the Probate Court for the county of Suffolk rejected the widow's claim and entered judgment dismissing the complaint. The widow appealed, and, on July 12, 1983, a panel of the Appeals Court reported the case to this court.

In September, 1973, Ernest G. Sullivan executed a deed of trust under which he transferred real estate to himself as sole trustee. The net income of the trust was payable to him during his life and the trustee was instructed to pay to him all or such part of the principal of the trust estate as he might request in writing from time to time. He retained the right to revoke the trust at any time. On his death, the successor trustee is directed to pay the principal and any undistributed income equally to the defendants, George F. Cronin, Sr., and Harold J. Cronin, if they should survive him, which they did. . . .

The husband died on April 27, 1981, while still trustee of the inter vivos trust. He left a will in which he stated that he "intentionally neglected to make any provision for my wife, Mary A. Sullivan and my grandson, Mark Sullivan." He directed that, after the payment of debts, expenses, and all estate taxes levied by reason of his death, the residue of his estate should be paid over to the trustee of the inter vivos trust. The defendants George F. Cronin, Sr., and Harold J. Cronin were named coexecutors of the will. The defendant Burkin is successor trustee of the inter vivos trust. On October 21, 1981, the wife filed a claim, pursuant to G.L. c. 191, § 15, for a portion of the estate.[22]

---

22. As relevant to this case, G.L. c. 191, § 15 . . . provides:

The surviving husband or wife of a deceased person . . . within six months after the probate of the will of such deceased, may file in the registry of probate a writing signed by him or by her . . . claiming such portion of the estate of the deceased as he or she is given the right to claim under this section, and if the deceased left issue, he or she shall thereupon take one third of the personal and one third of the real property; . . . except that . . . if he or she would thus take real and personal property to an amount exceeding twenty-five thousand dollars in value, he or she shall receive, in addition to that amount, only the income during his or her life of the excess of his or her share of such estate above that amount, the personal property to be held in trust and the real property vested in him or her for life, from the death of the deceased. . . . If the real and personal property of the deceased which the surviving husband or wife takes under the foregoing provisions exceeds twenty-five thousand dollars in value, and the surviving husband or wife is to take only twenty-five thousand dollars absolutely, the twenty-five thousand dollars, above given absolutely, shall be paid out of that part of the personal property in which the husband or wife is interested; and if such part is insufficient the deficiency shall, upon the petition of any person interested, be

Although it does not appear in the record, the parties state in their briefs that Ernest G. Sullivan and Mary A. Sullivan had been separated for many years. We do know that in 1962 the wife obtained a court order providing for her temporary support. No final action was taken in that proceeding. The record provides no information about the value of any property owned by the husband at his death or about the value of any assets held in the inter vivos trust. At oral argument, we were advised that the husband owned personal property worth approximately $15,000 at his death and that the only asset in the trust was a house in Boston which was sold after the husband's death for approximately $85,000.

As presented in the complaint, and perhaps as presented to the motion judge, the wife's claim was simply that the inter vivos trust was an invalid testamentary disposition and that the trust assets "constitute assets of the estate" of Ernest G. Sullivan. There is no suggestion that the wife argued initially that, even if the trust were not testamentary, she had a special claim as a widow asserting her rights under G.L. c. 191, § 15. If the wife is correct that the trust was an ineffective testamentary disposition, the trust assets would be part of the husband's probate estate. In that event, we would not have to consider any special consequences of the wife's election under G.L. c. 191, § 15, or, in the words of the Appeals Court, "the present vitality" of Kerwin v. Donaghy, 317 Mass. 559, 572, 59 N.E.2d 299 (1945).

We conclude, however, that the trust was not testamentary in character and that the husband effectively created a valid inter vivos trust. Thus, whether the issue was initially involved in this case, we are now presented with the question (which the executors will have to resolve ultimately, in any event) whether the assets of the inter vivos trust are to be considered in determining the "portion of the estate of the deceased" (G.L. c. 191, § 15) in which Mary A. Sullivan has rights. We conclude that, in this case, we should adhere to the principles expressed in Kerwin v. Donaghy, supra, that deny the surviving spouse any claim against the assets of a valid inter vivos trust created by the deceased spouse, even where the deceased spouse alone retained substantial rights and powers under the trust instrument. For the future, however, as to any inter vivos trust created or amended after the date of this opinion, we announce that the estate of a decedent, for the purposes of G.L. c. 191, § 15, shall include the value of assets held in an inter vivos trust created by the deceased spouse as to which the deceased spouse alone retained the power during his or her life to direct the disposition of those trust assets for his or her benefit, as, for example, by the exercise of a power of appointment or by revocation of the trust. Such a power would be a general power of appointment for Federal estate tax purposes (I.R.C. § 2041(b)(1) [1983]) and a "general power" as defined in the Restatement (Second) of Property § 11.4(1) (Tent. Draft No. 5, 1982).

---

shall be paid out of that part of the personal property in which the husband or wife is interested; and if such part is insufficient the deficiency shall, upon the petition of any person interested, be paid from the sale or mortgage in fee, in the manner provided for the payment of debts or legacies, of that part of the real property in which he or she is interested.

We consider first whether the inter vivos trust was invalid because it was testamentary. [The court concluded that the trust was not rendered testamentary by the settlor's retained power to revoke nor by the settlor's power, as trustee, to control the administration of the trust.]

We come then to the question whether, even if the trust was not testamentary on general principles, the widow has special interests which should be recognized. Courts in this country have differed considerably in their reasoning and in their conclusions in passing on this question. See 1 A. Scott, Trusts § 57.5 at 509-511 (3d ed. 1967 & 1983 Supp.); Restatement (Second) of Property, Supplement to Tent. Draft No. 5, reporter's note to § 13.7 (1982); Annot., 39 A.L.R.3d 14 (1971), Validity of Inter Vivos Trust Established by One Spouse Which Impairs the Other Spouse's Distributive Share or Other Statutory Rights in Property. . . .

The rule of Kerwin v. Donaghy, supra 317 Mass. at 571, 59 N.E.2d 299, is that "[t]he right of a wife to waive her husband's will, and take, with certain limitations, 'the same portion of the property of the deceased, real and personal, that . . . she would have taken if the deceased had died intestate' (G.L. [Ter.Ed.] c. 191, § 15), does not extend to personal property that has been conveyed by the husband in his lifetime and does not form part of his estate at his death. Fiske v. Fiske, 173 Mass. 413, 419, 53 N.E. 916 [1899]. Shelton v. Sears, 187 Mass. 455, 73 N.E. 666 [1905]. In this Commonwealth a husband has an absolute right to dispose of any or all of his personal property in his lifetime, without the knowledge or consent of his wife, with the result that it will not form part of his estate for her to share under the statute of distributions (G.L. [Ter.Ed.] c. 190, §§ 1, 2), under his will, or by virtue of a waiver of his will. That is true even though his sole purpose was to disinherit her." . . . The rule of Kerwin v. Donaghy has been adhered to in this Commonwealth for almost forty years and was adumbrated even earlier. The bar has been entitled reasonably to rely on that rule in advising clients. In the area of property law, the retroactive invalidation of an established principle is to be undertaken with great caution. We conclude that, whether or not Ernest G. Sullivan established the inter vivos trust in order to defeat his wife's right to take her statutory share in the assets placed in the trust and even though he had a general power of appointment over the trust assets, Mary A. Sullivan obtained no right to share in the assets of that trust when she made her election under G.L. c. 191, § 15.

We announce for the future that, as to any inter vivos trust created or amended after the date of this opinion, we shall no longer follow the rule announced in Kerwin v. Donaghy. There have been significant changes since 1945 in public policy considerations bearing on the right of one spouse to treat his or her property as he or she wishes during marriage. The interests of one spouse in the property of the other have been substantially increased upon the dissolution of a marriage by divorce.[23] We believe that, when a marriage is terminated by the death of one spouse, the rights of the surviving spouse should not be so restricted as they are by the rule in Kerwin v. Donaghy. It is neither equitable nor logical to extend to a divorced spouse greater rights in the assets of an inter vivos trust created and controlled by the other spouse than are extended to a spouse who remains married until the death of his or her spouse.

The rule we now favor would treat as part of "the estate of the deceased" for the purposes of G.L. c. 191, § 15, assets of an inter vivos trust created during the marriage by the deceased spouse over which he or she alone had a general power of appointment, exercisable by deed or by will. This objective test would involve no consideration of the motive or intention of the spouse in creating the trust. We would not need to engage in a determination of "whether the [spouse] has in good faith divested himself [or herself] of ownership of his [or her] property or has made an illusory transfer" (Newman v. Dore, 275 N.Y. 371, 379, 9 N.E.2d 966 [1937]) or with the factual question whether the spouse "intended to surrender complete dominion over the property" (Staples v. King, 433 A.2d 407, 411 [Me. 1981]). Nor would we have to participate in the rather unsatisfactory process of determining whether the inter vivos trust was, on some standard, "colorable," "fraudulent," or "illusory."

What we have announced as a rule for the future hardly resolves all the problems that may arise. There may be a different rule if some or all of the trust assets were conveyed to such a trust by a third person. Cf. Theodore v. Theodore, 356 Mass. 297, 249 N.E.2d 3 (1969). We have not, of course, dealt with a case in which the power of appointment is held jointly with another person. If the surviving spouse assented to the creation of the inter vivos trust, perhaps the rule we announce would not apply. We have not discussed which assets should be used to satisfy a surviving spouse's claim. We have not discussed the question whether a surviving spouse's interest in the intestate estate of a deceased spouse should reflect the value of assets held in an inter vivos trust created by the intestate spouse over which he or she had a general power of appointment. That situation and

---

23. At the time of a divorce or at any subsequent time, "the court may assign to either husband or wife all or any part of the estate of the other," on consideration of various factors, such as the length of the marriage, the conduct of the parties during the marriage, their ages, their employability, their liabilities and needs, and opportunity for future acquisition of capital assets and income. G.L. c. 208, § 34, as amended by St. 1982, c. 642, § 1. The power to dispose completely of the property of the divorced litigants comes from a 1974 amendment to G.L. c. 208, § 34. See St. 1974, c. 565. It made a significant change in the respective rights of the husband and wife and in the power of Probate Court judges. See Bianco v. Bianco, 371 Mass. 420, 422-423, 358 N.E.2d 243 (1976). We have held that the "estate" subject to disposition on divorce includes not only property acquired during the marriage from the efforts of the husband and wife, but also all property of a spouse "whenever and however acquired." Rice v. Rice, 372 Mass. 398, 400, 361 N.E.2d 1305 (1977). Without suggesting the outer limits of the meaning of the word "estate" under G.L. c. 208, § 34, as applied to trust assets over which a spouse has a general power of appointment at the time of a divorce, after this decision there should be no doubt that the "estate" of such a spouse would include trust assets held in a trust created by the other spouse and having provisions such as the trust in the case before us. [See also Restatement 2d of Property § 34.1(1). Eds.]

the one before us, however, do not seem readily distinguishable. A general power of appointment over assets in a trust created by a third person is said to present a different situation. Restatement (Second) of Property, Supplement to Tent. Draft No. 5, reporter's note to § 13.7 at 29 (1982). Nor have we dealt with other assets not passing by will, such as a trust created before the marriage or insurance policies over which a deceased spouse had control. Id. at 30, 38.

The question of the rights of a surviving spouse in the estate of a deceased spouse, using the word "estate" in its broad sense, is one that can best be handled by legislation. See [pre-1990] Uniform Probate Code, §§ 2-201, 2-202. See also Uniform Marital Property Act, § 18 (Nat'l Conference of Comm'rs on Uniform State Laws, July, 1983), which adopts the concept of community property as to "marital property." But, until it is, the answers to these problems will "be determined in the usual way through the decisional process." Tucker v. Badoian, 376 Mass. 907, 918-919, 384 N.E.2d 1195 (1978) (Kaplan, J., concurring).

We affirm the judgment of the Probate Court dismissing the plaintiff's complaint.

So ordered.

Notes and Questions

1. *Restatement 2d of Property.* The Restatement 2d of Property provides:

> § 34.1 *Effect of Donative Transfer on Spouse of Donor.* . . . . (3) An inter vivos donative transfer to others than the donor's spouse that is a substitute for a will, or that is revocable by the donor at the time of the donor's death, is subject to spousal rights of the donor's spouse in the transferred property that would accrue to the donor's spouse on the donor's death if the transfer had been made by the donor's will.

See also id. § 13.7, the comment to which states that this provision is not restricted to transfers that took place *during* the marriage.

2. *Computation; Contribution.* For purposes of computing the amount of the elective share, the value of a will substitute that is subject to the elective share is added to the value of the decedent's probate estate. In satisfying the elective-share amount, however, is the probate estate used first, so that the beneficiaries of the will substitutes are liable for contribution only to the extent the probate estate is insufficient to satisfy the elective-share amount? See Montgomery v. Michaels, 54 Ill. 2d 532, 301 N.E.2d 465 (1973); Restatement 2d of Trusts § 57. Or, are the beneficiaries of will substitutes liable to contribution of a proportional part of their gifts in making up the spouse's elective share? 1990 and pre-1990 UPC section 2-207 establishes the latter rule. Comment j to section 34.1(3) of the Restatement 2d of Property suggests that the court should try to retain the decedent's dispositive plan as closely as possible. In satisfying the spouse's elective share, the comment states that "consideration might appropriately be given to resorting to intestate property first, then to gifts to others than

relatives, then to gifts to relatives other than descendants. Consideration should also be given to resorting to residuary gifts under a will and will substitutes before resorting to specific gifts."

3. *Will Substitutes and Intestate Estates.* The elective-share provisions of the UPC apply to intestate as well as to testate estates. In Sullivan v. Burkin, the court observed that there seems to be no ready distinction between the situation of a surviving spouse of an intestate and a testate decedent. Surely the court's observation in *Sullivan* was not intended to mean that revocable trusts and possibly other will substitutes might be subject to the spouse's *intestate* share, in an intestate estate in which the spouse did not choose to make an election.

4. *Spousal Protection in Pension Benefits Under Qualified Retirement Plans.* Congress recently stepped in to afford surviving spouses a measure of protection against being cut out of survivor benefits under qualified pension plans. See the Retirement Equity Act of 1984 (REACT), amending the Employee Retirement Income Security Act of 1974 (ERISA). REACT is discussed in J. Langbein & B. Wolk, Pension and Employee Benefit Law 433-39 (1990).

EXTERNAL REFERENCES. Restatement 2d of Property, Statutory Note to § 34.1; Annot., 63 A.L.R.4th 1173 (1988).

b. *The Reclaimable-Estate Component of the Uniform Probate Code's Augmented-Estate System*

Statutory References: *1990 UPC §§ 2-202(b)(2), (4)*
Pre-1990 UPC §§ 2-202(1)

We saw earlier that, under the UPC, the surviving spouse's elective-share percentage is applied to the augmented estate. See supra p. 476. The augmented estate serves two basic functions. By *combining* the couple's assets, it plays a crucial part under the 1990 Code in implementing the marital-sharing theory. See supra p. 477. The other function is to provide a means of dealing with "fraud on the spouse's share." To these ends, the augmented estate consists of the sum of the values of four components: (1) the decedent's net probate estate; (2) the decedent's reclaimable estate; (3) property to which the surviving spouse succeeds by reason of the decedent's death other than from the decedent's probate estate; and (4) property owned by the surviving spouse and amounts that would have been included in the surviving spouse's reclaimable estate had the spouse predeceased the decedent.

We are concerned here with the second of the two functions—preventing "fraud on the spouse's share." This function is performed by the reclaimable-estate component of the augmented estate. Section 2-202(b)(2) gives a detailed list of will substitutes that are included in the decedent's reclaimable estate. Examine section 2-202(b)(2) itself for a complete rundown of the specific types of will substitutes included in the reclaimable estate. You should notice that the listed items are, in general, quite similar to the will substitutes included in a decedent's gross estate for federal estate tax purposes. See supra Chapter 6.

The concept of providing in the statute itself a list of will substitutes to be subjected to the surviving spouse's elective share was pioneered by legislation in New York and Pennsylvania and adopted by the pre-1990 UPC. This approach resolves the problem, illustrated by Newman v. Dore, that the conventional elective-share statute shifts to the courts the burden of deciding the question of whether and under what circumstances will substitutes are subject to the elective share.

The 1990 revisions sought to strengthen the reclaimable-estate component. The pre-1990 version contained several loopholes. The most important of these was life insurance that the decedent purchased, naming someone other than her or his spouse as the beneficiary. Under the 1990 revision, proceeds of these policies are included in the reclaimable estate.

The other important feature of the 1990 revision is that the reclaimable estate now includes property that is subject to a presently exercisable general power of appointment held solely by the decedent. Such powers are viewed as substantively indistinguishable from outright ownership. The power need not have been created by the decedent and need not have been conferred on the decedent during the marriage. The decedent need only have held the power immediately prior to her or his death or have exercised or released the power in favor of someone other than the decedent, the decedent's estate, or the decedent's spouse while married to the spouse and during the two-year period immediately prior to the decedent's death.

Matter of Scheiner
141 Misc. 2d 1037, 535 N.Y.S.2d 920 (Sur. Ct. 1988)

BLOOM, S. All objections filed by the surviving spouse in this contested accounting proceeding, except those relating to her right to elect against certain United States Treasury bills, were withdrawn after conference with the court.

All issues pertaining to the validity of the spouse's right to elect against the Treasury bills, purchased by the decedent in the joint names of himself and his sister prior to his marriage to the electing spouse, were submitted to the court for determination.

Based upon the facts and the circumstances herein, the court determines that these United States Treasury bills cannot be considered testamentary substitutes against which a surviving spouse can elect for the following reasons:

(1) All inter vivos transactions against which a spouse can elect as testamentary substitutes pursuant to EPTL 5-1.1 (b)[24] are exempt from that right where the transaction occurred prior to the marriage (EPTL 5-1.1 [b] [1]). Even if these Treasury bills were usually considered as testamentary substitutes pursuant to the EPTL, which they are not for the reasons set forth later in the decision, the spouse's right to elect against them would be nullified by the fact that they were purchased prior to the marriage even though they rolled over during the course of the marriage.

(2) Certain money transactions, under EPTL 5-1.1 (b) (2), are never deemed to be testamentary substitutes against which a spouse can elect. Included in this exempt category are "any United States savings bonds payable to a designated person" (EPTL 5-1.1 [b] [2] [C]). The Practice Commentary to EPTL 5-1.1 (Rohan, McKinney's Cons Laws of NY, Book 17B, at 18) gives a reason for their omission as testamentary substitutes the fact that their inclusion would conflict with existing Federal regulations and present serious constitutional questions.

The United States Department of the Treasury adopted regulations on July 1, 1986 that are found in 31 CFR part 357 and are known as Treasury Direct. One of the purposes for the enactment of Treasury Direct was to override any inconsistent State law concerning Treasury bills so that they would be treated in the exact manner as United States savings bonds. Evidence of the Government's intent to treat both United States savings bonds and Treasury bills in the same manner thereby enabling them to pass as registered free of the spouse's right of election is clearly set forth in Appendix A (Discussion of Final Rule) to the Federal regulations (31 CFR part 357). It states:

> *Forms of Registration.* The proposed rule provides the investor with a variety of registration options. They are essentially similar to those provided for registered, definitive marketable treasury securities. Investors should be particularly aware that, where the security is held in the names of two individuals, the registration chosen may establish rights of survivorship.
>
> The reason for establishing the rights of ownership for securities held in Treasury Direct is that it will give investors the assurance that the forms of registration they select will establish conclusively the rights to their book-

---

24. EPTL § 5-1.1(b) provides in relevant part as follows:

   (b) Inter vivos dispositions treated as testamentary substitutes for the purpose of election by surviving spouse.

   (1) Where a person dies after August thirty-first, nineteen hundred sixty-six and is survived by a spouse who exercises a right of election under paragraph (c), the following transactions effected by such decedent at any time after the date of the marriage and after August thirty-first, nineteen hundred sixty-six, whether benefitting the surviving spouse or any other person, shall be treated as testamentary substitutes and the capital value thereof, as of the decedent's death, included in the net estate subject to the surviving spouse's elective right: . . . .

   (D) Any disposition of property made by the decedent after August thirty-first, nineteen hundred sixty-six whereby property is held, at the date of his death, by the decedent and another person as joint tenants with a right of survivorship or as tenants by the entirety. . . .

   (2) Nothing in this paragraph shall affect, impair or defeat the right of any person entitled to receive . . . (C) payment of any United States savings bond payable to a designated person, and such transactions are not testamentary substitutes within the meaning of this paragraph.

entry securities. It will also serve to eliminate some of the uncertainties, as well as possible conflicts, between the varying laws of the several States.

A Federal rule of ownership is being adopted by the Treasury for Treasury Direct securities. This regulatory approach is consistent with the one previously taken in the case of United States Savings Bonds. It will have the effect of overriding inconsistent State laws. See, Free v. Bland, 369 U.S. 663 (1962).

Accordingly, the Treasury bills in dispute are not testamentary substitutes against which a spouse can elect. The Federal regulations known as Treasury Direct preempted any existing inconsistent State law by mandating that these securities should pass as registered. In order to be consistent with the regulations in Treasury Direct, EPTL 5-1.1 (b) (2) (C) must be construed to include United States Treasury bills within the term United States savings bonds.

All remaining objections are dismissed.

Notes and Questions

1. *Federal Preemption of State Elective-Share Law.* The decision in *Scheiner* interpreting the Treasury Direct regulations as preempting state law creates an opportunity for individuals to evade the surviving spouse's elective share through United States Treasury bills. In reaching its decision, the court relied on Free v. Bland, 369 U.S. 663 (1962). In *Free,* the husband, who was the manager of the couple's community property under Texas law, purchased United States savings bonds in the names of "Mr. or Mrs." Free. The Treasury Department's savings bonds regulations provided that "the survivor will be recognized as the sole and absolute owner" and that "no judicial impairment will be recognized which would . . . impair the rights of survivorship conferred." 31 C.F.R. §§ 315.20; 315.61.

The wife died first, and her son, Bland, as the devisee under her will claimed that one-half of the savings bonds was part of her estate as community property. The Texas court held that, although Free had full title by virtue of the federal regulations, Bland was entitled to be reimbursed for his mother's one-half interest. The Supreme Court reversed, holding that under the Supremacy Clause of the constitution the savings bonds registration allowed by federal regulations must prevail over Texas's community property law. The Court, however, found that there was an implicit exception in the savings bond regulations in cases of fraud. The Court stated: "The regulations are not intended to be a shield for fraud, and relief would be available in a case where the circumstances manifest fraud or a breach of trust tantamount thereto on the part of the husband while acting in his capacity as manager of the general community property." 369 U.S. at 670. Although *Free* involved savings bond regulations rather than Treasury Direct regulations governing treasury bills, the latter regulations are a clone of the savings bond regulation insofar as they provide that "[r]egistration of a security conclusively establishes owner-ship. . . ." 31 C.F.R. § 357.21[a][1].

The opinion in *Scheiner* does not mention another federal preemption case decided two years after *Free*. In Yiatchos v. Yiatchos, 376 U.S. 306 (1964), the Supreme Court developed the "fraud or breach of trust" exception that it had recognized in dictum in *Free*. In *Yiatchos*, the decedent husband, manager of the community property under Washington law, used community funds to purchase United States savings bonds in his name, payable on his death to his brother. The Court held that, unless the wife had consented to the POD registration or would receive her full half of the community property without the bonds, she was entitled to her one-half community property interest in the bonds. Applying the "fraud or breach of trust" exception, the Court stated: "[W]e shall be guided by state law insofar as the property interests of the widow created by state law are concerned. It would seem obvious that the bonds may not be used as a device to deprive the widow of property rights she enjoys under [state] law and which would not be transferable by her husband but for the survivorship provisions of the federal bonds." 376 U.S. at 309.

Was *Yiatchos* relevant to the problem in *Scheiner*? Unlike a spouse's community-property interest, the elective share is technically not a property interest. Should this fact preclude application of the "fraud or breach of trust" exception to the preemption doctrine? See Gibbs & Ordover, Right of Election by Surviving Spouse, N.Y. L.J., Sept. 13, 1989, 3, col. 4.

Note that section 2-202(f)(2) of the 1990 UPC attempts to handle the preemption problem by imposing a personal liability on the recipient of any item of property or payment made to the recipient resulting from federal preemption.

2. *U.S. Savings Bonds and the Augmented Estate.* Although New York's elective-share statute is an augmented estate-type of statute it expressly excludes from the list of inter-vivos dispositions treated as testamentary substitutes U.S. savings bonds registered jointly or POD in the names of the decedent and another person other than the surviving spouse. See N.Y. Est. Powers & Trusts Law § 5-1.1(b)(2)(C). The reason for this exclusion was the decision in *Free*. Neither the pre-1990 nor the 1990 UPC includes comparable exclusions.

3. The Incapacitated Surviving Spouse

An important feature of modern life is that longevity is on the increase. Many of the country's elderly suffer from some level of mental deficiency during the later portions of their lives, often due to Alzheimer's disease.[25]

---

25. Alzheimer's disease, a form of dementia that progressively impairs intellectual abilities, has become a major problem among the over-65 portion of the American population. A recent study in one geographical area estimates that in excess of ten percent of persons age 65 and older show signs of the disease. See Evans, Prevalence of Alzheimer's Disease in a Community Population of Older Persons, J.A.M.A. Nov. 10, 1989. As American society ages, it is likely that the percentage of the population afflicted with the disease, the incidence of which increases sharply with age, will grow yet higher. Currently, there is no cure or treatment for the disease.

Incompetency raises the questions whether the elective share is available to a mentally incapacitated surviving spouse and, if so, who should have the power to make the election for the spouse and by what standard should that power be exercised. Clarkson v. First National Bank, below, raises these issues.

Clarkson v. First National Bank
193 Neb. 201, 226 N.W.2d 334 (1975)

SPENCER, J. This is an action under section 30-108(2), R.R.S.1943. It involves an election on behalf of an incompetent surviving spouse to either take under or against her husband's will. The District Court vacated an order of the county court electing on behalf of the widow to take the provision made for her in her husband's will. The executor prosecutes this appeal. We affirm.

Joseph D. Clarkson, deceased, married Evelyn Bell Clarkson April 16, 1953. Mr. Clarkson had two daughters from a prior marriage. Mrs. Clarkson had a son and a daughter by a prior marriage. No children were born of the second marriage. Mrs. Clarkson, who is 80 years of age, has been mentally incompetent since June 1965. The record indicates that her chances of recovery were and are nil. The will in question was executed November 18, 1969. The inventory filed in the estate indicates the value of the estate to be $1,229,263.56. The report of the guardian ad litem indicates the net value of the estate is $1,372,224. Only $62,000 is real estate, a Missouri farm valued at $40,000 and the residence property valued at $22,000.

The will makes the following provision for the incompetent:

If my wife, Evelyn Bell Clarkson, survives me, I give, devise and bequeath to the FIRST NATIONAL BANK OF OMAHA, as TRUSTEE for my said wife, an amount equal to one-fourth (1/4) of the value of my net estate as finally determined for Federal Estate Tax purposes, unreduced by any taxes.

The will directs the trustee to pay all income therefrom to Mrs. Clarkson and in addition provides for such amounts of principal to be paid to her from time to time as the trustee deems necessary or desirable to provide for her proper support and maintenance. The will further provides that upon Mrs. Clarkson's death the trust estate shall terminate and the assets remaining in the trust shall then be distributed and disposed of to such persons in such manner as Mrs. Clarkson by her last will and testament shall direct and appoint. If Mrs. Clarkson fails to exercise the general testamentary power of appointment upon her death, the will provides that the remaining assets shall be distributed as follows:

Twenty-five Thousand Dollars ($25,000) thereof shall be paid to each of my wife's children, JERRY W. MENCK and PEGGY LOU McVEA, with the children of either of them who may be then deceased to take equally the share which the parent would have taken if then living; and the balance of said assets remaining shall be distributed to my daughters, HELEN E. CLARKSON and RUTH C. BOLLINGER, share and share alike.

The will was made at a time when Mrs. Clarkson was incompetent. There is no possibility of her exercising the power of appointment granted in the will because her condition cannot improve.

Pursuant to the provisions of section 30-108(2), R.R.S. 1943, the Douglas county court appointed Jack W. Marer as guardian ad litem to make such investigation as he deemed necessary and to report his recommendation to the court as to whether the court should elect on behalf of Mrs. Clarkson to take the provisions made for her under the last will and testament of Joseph D. Clarkson or to take by descent and distribution as provided by law. The guardian ad litem, after investigation, filed a report recommending that the court renounce the provision made for Evelyn Clarkson under the last will and testament of Joseph D. Clarkson and elect to take by descent and distribution as provided by law. The county judge declined to accept the recommendation. He determined her interests were not better served by renouncing the will but that the equities of the matter dictated that the testamentary plan of Joseph D. Clarkson should be adhered to.

The special guardian of the incompetent prosecuted an appeal to the District Court for Douglas County. The District Judge disagreed with the opinion of the county judge and followed the recommendation made by the guardian ad litem. He found an estate in fee title would be of greater value than a beneficial interest in a trust. He specifically determined that the best interests of the surviving spouse would require renouncing the provisions of the will and taking the estate in fee . . . notwithstanding that title would vest in her guardian who would have fiduciary limitations on its disposal.

The incompetent, as the second wife of deceased, would receive one-fourth of the estate if she takes under the statute rather than the will. The parties are in agreement that there is no dollar difference between what Mr. Clarkson left his wife in trust and what she would take by an election. The difference comes about in that a fee title is of much greater value than a beneficial interest in the trust.

While this is a case of first impression in Nebraska, the question has arisen in many other jurisdictions. . . . [T]here is an irreconcilable conflict in the decisions. This conflict arises because of various theories used by the courts in interpreting and defining the meaning of the words "best interests" or similar words which are found in the several statutes under consideration. . . .

In the so-called minority view, all the decisions in one way or another indicate that the best interests of the incompetent will be served by electing the method which is the most valuable to the surviving spouse. This usually means the one having the greater pecuniary value is the one selected.

The language of the various statutes may differ but essentially most of them will provide that the election should be made which is to the best interests, advantage, welfare, or the like of the incompetent person. Our statute provides that the court should make such election as it deems *the* best interests of the surviving wife or husband shall require. This seems to narrow the range of consideration.[26]

The majority view, as stated in Kinnett v. Hood (1962), 25 Ill.2d 600, 185 N.E.2d 888, 3 A.L.R.3d 1, is that all the surrounding facts and circumstances should be taken into consideration by the court in order to make the election to take under the will or against it. . . .

The majority rule emphasizes other considerations than monetary. It characterizes the minority cases as placing the election purely on monetary standards or what would result in the larger pecuniary value, to the detriment of other considerations. We concede that in some instances there may be other considerations than monetary which may promote the best interests of the incompetent. What, however, are those other considerations? It is impractical to delineate factors which could apply in every case or to specify the relative weight which should be given to such other possible considerations. If we follow our statutes, the best interests of an incompetent in most instances will require the election which will result in the larger pecuniary value. We cannot agree that the preservation of the decedent's estate plan is a major consideration as found by the county judge and as it appears to be in many cases espousing the majority view. Under our law the testator's testamentary desires have little or no importance in relation to the best interests of the surviving spouse. . . .

Many of the majority view cases criticize the minority cases, suggesting that they tend to sanction: (1) The interests of the heirs of the incompetent as a consideration; and (2) give too much weight to what the surviving spouse would have done had she made her own election as a consideration. We are in full accord with the view that the interests of possible heirs of the incompetent should play no part in the decision. We would not, however, entirely ignore what the surviving spouse might have done had she made her own election. . . .

It seems a little inconsistent under our law to say, as do some of the majority cases, that the election by the court to renounce the will should be made only if necessary to provide for the widow's needs. This would write a restriction into our statute. The statute requires the court to make the election which it deems is in the best interests of the incompetent spouse. This must be made without reference to whether she may be provided for otherwise. We observe that neither section 30-107 nor section 30-108, which create the right of election and provide the necessary procedural steps, make any mention of or suggest any restrictions under which an election might be made. While a competent surviving spouse may elect to take against the will, even if it would seem obviously against her best interests to do so, a court in making the choice for an incompetent does not have that privilege. It must consider only the best interests of the incompetent.

---

26. Nebraska repealed this statute, incident to enactment of the pre-1990 UPC in 1974. However, § 30-2315, R.R.S. 1943, the Nebraska counterpart of UPC § 2-203, substitutes "in the best interests of" for UPC's "necessary to provide adequate support for," thereby continuing the authority of *Clarkson.* Eds.

On the record we find no considerations other than the monetary value of the estate. We find that an estate in fee is of much greater value than a beneficial interest in a trust. We agree with the District Judge that the best interests of the surviving spouse require taking the estate in fee with full incidents of ownership notwithstanding the title would vest in her guardian who would have fiduciary limitations on its disposal.

The judgment is affirmed.

[The dissenting opinion of McCown, J., in which Newton and Clinton, JJ., joined, is omitted.]

Notes

1. *Pre-1990 Uniform Probate Code.* Section 2-203 of the pre-1990 UPC provided that the right of election can be exercised on behalf of a protected person[27] only after a finding that "exercise is necessary to provide adequate support for the protected person during his probable life expectancy." How does this statute differ from the Nebraska statute that was in effect at the time of the *Clarkson* decision? What is the rationale of the pre-1990 UPC approach to the incompetent spouse's election? See Langbein & Waggoner, Redesigning the Spouse's Forced Share, 22 Real Prop. Prob. & Tr. J. 303, 307-08 n.17 (1987).

2. *1990 Uniform Probate Code.* Section 2-203 of the 1990 UPC includes several innovations. The most important of these is that, under subsection (b), an election made on behalf of a surviving spouse who is an "incapacitated person" under section 5-103(7) requires that the portion of the elective share and supplemental elective-share amounts that are payable from the decedent's probate estate and reclaimable estate under section 2-207(b) and (c) goes into a custodial trust created under the Uniform Custodial Trust Act. The purpose of this provision is to assure that the portion of the elective-share amount that represents involuntary transfers from the decedent is used to benefit the surviving spouse personally rather than the spouse's heirs or devisees. Upon the surviving spouse's death, the remaining custodial trust property passes to the predeceased spouse's residuary devisees or heirs.

---

27. The term "protected person" is defined in § 5-103(18) as a "minor or other person for whom a conservator has been appointed or other protective order has been made. . . ."

4. Premarital and Postmarital Agreements

Statutory References: *1990 UPC § 2-204*
                                       Pre-1990 UPC § 2-204
                                       Uniform Premarital Agreement Act
                                       Uniform Marital Property Act § 10

The right to an elective share (and other death benefits, such as homestead and family allowances) may be waived by premarital or postmarital agreement.[28] In the absence of statute, the validity of these agreements depends upon general principles of contract law. However, because of the confidential relationship between the parties, the law has moved largely to the view that the agreement will be closely scrutinized for any overreaching by either party.

This was not always the standard. In an early Massachusetts decision, the court in Wellington v. Rugg, 243 Mass. 30, 136 N.E. 831 (1922), held that mere failure to disclose a party's true financial situation was not a sufficient ground for setting aside a premarital agreement; it took a showing of actual fraud to avoid enforcement. The rule of the *Wellington* case was prospectively overruled, however, in Rosenberg v. Lipnick, 377 Mass. 666, 389 N.E.2d 385 (1979). In place of the *Wellington* rule, the *Rosenberg* decision announced the following position, believed to reflect the prevailing position today, in the absence of statute:

> [I]n future cases . . . we shall feel free to hold that the parties by definition occupy a confidential relationship and that the burden of disclosure rests upon both of them.
>
> In judging the validity of such an antenuptial agreement, other relevant factors which we may consider are whether (1) it contains a fair and reasonable provision as measured at the time of its execution for the party contesting the agreement; (2) the contesting party was fully informed of the other party's worth prior to the agreement's execution, or had, or should have had, independent knowledge of the other party's worth; and (3) a waiver by the contesting party is set forth. It is clear that the reasonableness of any monetary provision in an antenuptial contract cannot ultimately be judged in isolation. Rather, reference may appropriately be made to such factors as the parties' respective worth, the parties' respective ages, the parties' respective intelligence, literacy, and business acumen, and prior family ties or commitments. . . .
>
> The right to make antenuptial agreements settling property rights in advance of marriage is a valuable personal right which courts should not regulate destructively. Neither should the exercise of that right be looked

---

28. Until recently, agreements pertaining to property rights on *divorce* were held to encourage divorce, and hence unenforceable as against public policy. Today, the prevailing view seems to be that such agreements are enforceable if fair and reasonable. Posner v. Posner, 233 S.2d 381 (Fla. 1970), is the leading decision breaking new ground on the question. One of the most recent states to come over to the *Posner* view is Kentucky. See Edwardson v. Edwardson, 798 S.W.2d 941 (Ky. 1990).

upon with disfavor. Thus, we recognize that antenuptial agreements must be so construed as to give full effect to the parties' intentions, but we are concerned that such agreements be executed fairly and understandingly and be free from fraud, imposition, deception, or over-reaching.[29]

For other decisions adopting a similar set of standards, see Martin v. Farber, 68 Md. App. 137, 510 A.2d 608 (1986); Estate of Benker, 416 Mich. 681, 331 N.W.2d 193 (1982); Juhasz v. Juhasz, 134 Ohio St. 257, 16 N.E.2d 328 (1938); Estate of Crawford, 107 Wash. 2d 493, 730 P.2d 675 (1986). A decision of the Supreme Court of Pennsylvania, Estate of Geyer, 516 Pa. 492, 533 A.2d 423 (1987), also adopted a similar set of standards, but that decision has been reexamined in the *Simeone* decision, below.

Simeone v. Simeone
581 A.2d 162 (Pa. 1990)

FLAHERTY J. At issue in this appeal is the validity of a prenuptial agreement executed between the appellant, Catherine E. Walsh Simeone, and the appellee, Frederick A. Simeone. At the time of their marriage, in 1975, appellant was a twenty-three year old nurse and appellee was a thirty-nine year old neurosurgeon. Appellee had an income of approximately $90,000 per year, and appellant was unemployed. Appellee also had assets worth approximately $300,000. On the eve of the parties' wedding, appellee's attorney presented appellant with a prenuptial agreement to be signed. Appellant, without the benefit of counsel, signed the agreement. Appellee's attorney had not advised appellant regarding any legal rights that the agreement surrendered. The parties are in disagreement as to whether appellant knew in advance of that date that such an agreement would be presented for signature. Appellant denies having had such knowledge and claims to have signed under adverse circumstances, which, she contends, provide a basis for declaring it void.

The agreement limited appellant to support payments of $200 per week in the event of separation or divorce, subject to a maximum total payment of $25,000. The parties separated in 1982, and, in 1984, divorce proceedings were commenced. Between 1982 and 1984 appellee made payments which satisfied the $25,000 limit. In 1985, appellant filed a claim for alimony pendente lite. A master's report upheld the validity of the prenuptial agreement and denied this claim. Exceptions to the master's report were dismissed by the Court of Common Pleas of Philadelphia County. The Superior Court affirmed. . . .

[T]here is need for a reexamination of the foundations upon which . . . and a need for clarification of the standards by which the validity of

---

29. The Massachusetts court subsequently extended the *Rosenberg* rules to the validity of a premarital contract relating to divorce as well as death. Osborne v. Osborne, 384 Mass. 591, 428 N.E.2d 810 (1981).

prenuptial agreements will be judged. There is no longer validity in the implicit presumption that . . . spouses are of unequal status and that women are not knowledgeable enough to understand the nature of contracts that they enter. Society has advanced . . . to the point where women are no longer regarded as the "weaker" party in marriage, or in society generally. Indeed, the stereotype that women serve as homemakers while men work as breadwinners is no longer viable. Quite often today both spouses are income earners. Nor is there viability in the presumption that women are uninformed, uneducated, and readily subjected to unfair advantage in marital agreements. Indeed, women nowadays quite often have substantial education, financial awareness, income, and assets.

Accordingly, the law has advanced to recognize the equal status of men and women in our society. . . . Paternalistic presumptions and protections that arose to shelter women from the inferiorities and incapacities which they were perceived as having in earlier times have, appropriately, been discarded. . . .

Further, [prior law] embodied substantial departures from traditional rules of contract law, to the extent that they allowed consideration of the knowledge of the contracting parties and reasonableness of their bargain as factors governing whether to uphold an agreement. Traditional principles of contract law provide perfectly adequate remedies where contracts are procured through fraud, misrepresentation, or duress. Consideration of other factors, such as the knowledge of the parties and the reasonableness of their bargain, is inappropriate. Prenuptial agreements are contracts, and, as such, should be evaluated under the same criteria as are applicable to other types of contracts. Absent fraud, misrepresentation, or duress, spouses should be bound by the terms of their agreements.

Contracting parties are normally bound by their agreements, without regard to whether the terms thereof were read and fully understood and irrespective of whether the agreements embodied reasonable or good bargains. . . .

Accordingly, we find no merit in a contention raised by appellant that the agreement should be declared void on the ground that she did not consult with independent legal counsel. To impose a per se requirement that parties entering a prenuptial agreement must obtain independent legal counsel would be contrary to traditional principles of contract law, and would constitute a paternalistic and unwarranted interference with the parties' freedom to enter contracts.

Further, the reasonableness of a prenuptial bargain is not a proper subject for judicial review. . . . [E]arlier decisions required that, at least where there had been an inadequate disclosure made by the parties, the bargain must have been reasonable at its inception. Some have even suggested that prenuptial agreements should be examined with regard to whether their terms remain reasonable at the time of dissolution of the parties' marriage.

By invoking inquiries into reasonableness, however, the functioning and reliability of prenuptial agreements is severely undermined. Parties would not have entered such agreements, and, indeed, might not have entered their marriages, if they did not expect their agreements to be strictly enforced. If parties viewed an agreement as reasonable at the time of its inception, as evidenced by their having signed the agreement, they should be foreclosed from later trying to evade its terms by asserting that it was not in fact reasonable. Pertinently, the present agreement contained a clause reciting that "each of the parties considers this agreement fair, just and reasonable. . . ."

Further, everyone who enters a long-term agreement knows that circumstances can change during its term, so that what initially appeared desirable might prove to be an unfavorable bargain. Such are the risks that contracting parties routinely assume. Certainly, the possibilities of illness, birth of children, reliance upon a spouse, career change, financial gain or loss, and numerous other events that can occur in the course of a marriage cannot be regarded as unforeseeable. If parties choose not to address such matters in their prenuptial agreements, they must be regarded as having contracted to bear the risk of events that alter the value of their bargains.

We are reluctant to interfere with the power of persons contemplating marriage to agree upon, and to act in reliance upon, what they regard as an acceptable distribution scheme for their property. A court should not ignore the parties' expressed intent by proceeding to determine whether a prenuptial agreement was, in the court's view, reasonable at the time of its inception or the time of divorce. These are exactly the sorts of judicial determinations that such agreements are designed to avoid. Rare indeed is the agreement that is beyond possible challenge when reasonableness is placed at issue. Parties can routinely assert some lack of fairness relating to the inception of the agreement, thereby placing the validity of the agreement at risk. And if reasonableness at the time of divorce were to be taken into account an additional problem would arise. Virtually nonexistent is the marriage in which there has been absolutely no change in the circumstances of either spouse during the course of the marriage. Every change in circumstance, foreseeable or not, and substantial or not, might be asserted as a basis for finding that an agreement is no longer reasonable.

In discarding the [prior] approach . . . that permitted examination of the reasonableness of prenuptial agreements and allowed inquiries into whether parties had attained informed understandings of the rights they were surrendering, we do not depart from the longstanding principle that a full and fair disclosure of the financial positions of the parties is required. Absent this disclosure, a material misrepresentation in the inducement for entering a prenuptial agreement may be asserted. Parties to these agreements do not quite deal at arm's length, but rather at the time the contract is entered into stand in a relation of mutual confidence and trust that calls for disclosure of their financial resources. It is well settled that this disclosure need not be exact, so long as it is "full and fair." Kaufmann Estate, 404 Pa. 131, 136 n. 8, 171 A.2d 48, 51 n. 8 (1961). In essence therefore, the duty of disclosure under these circumstances is consistent with traditional principles of contract law.

If an agreement provides that full disclosure has been made, a presumption of full disclosure arises. If a spouse attempts to rebut this presumption through an assertion of fraud or misrepresentation then this presumption can be rebutted if it is proven by clear and convincing evidence.

The present agreement recited that full disclosure had been made, and included a list of appellee's assets totalling approximately $300,000. Appellant contends that this list understated by roughly $183,000 the value of a classic car collection which appellee had included at a value of $200,000. The master, reviewing the parties' conflicting testimony regarding the value of the car collection, found that appellant failed to prove by clear and convincing evidence that the value of the collection had been understated. The courts below affirmed that finding. We have examined the record and find ample basis for concluding that the value of the car collection was fully disclosed. Appellee offered expert witnesses who testified to a value of approximately $200,000. Further, appellee's disclosure included numerous cars that appellee did not even own but which he merely hoped to inherit from his mother at some time in the future. Appellant's contention is plainly without merit.

Appellant's final contention is that the agreement was executed under conditions of duress in that it was presented to her at 5 p.m. on the eve of her wedding, a time when she could not seek counsel without the trauma, expense, and embarrassment of postponing the wedding. The master found this claim not credible. The courts below affirmed that finding, upon an ample evidentiary basis.

Although appellant testified that she did not discover until the eve of her wedding that there was going to be a prenuptial agreement, testimony from a number of other witnesses was to the contrary. Appellee testified that, although the final version of the agreement was indeed presented to appellant on the eve of the wedding, he had engaged in several discussions with appellant regarding the contents of the agreement during the six month period preceding that date. Another witness testified that appellant mentioned, approximately two or three weeks before the wedding, that she was going to enter a prenuptial agreement. Yet another witness confirmed that, during the months preceding the wedding, appellant participated in several discussions of prenuptial agreements. And the legal counsel who prepared the agreement for appellee testified that, prior to the eve of the wedding, changes were made in the agreement to increase the sums payable to appellant in the event of separation or divorce. He also stated that he was present when the agreement was signed and that appellant expressed absolutely no reluctance about signing. It should be noted, too, that during the months when the agreement was being discussed appellant had more than sufficient time to consult with independent legal counsel if she had so desired. Under these circumstances, there was plainly no error in finding that appellant failed to prove duress.

Hence, the courts below properly held that the present agreement is valid and enforceable. Appellant is barred, therefore, from receiving alimony pendente lite.

Order affirmed.

PAPADAKOS, J., Concurring. Although I continue to adhere to the [prior] principles . . . I concur in the result because the facts fully support the existence of a valid and enforceable agreement between the parties and any suggestion of duress is totally negated by the facts. The full and fair disclosure, as well as the lack of unfairness and inequity, . . . are supported by the facts in this case so that I can concur in the result.

However, I cannot join the opinion authored by Mr. Justice Flaherty, because, it must be clear to all readers, it contains a number of unnecessary and unwarranted declarations regarding the "equality" of women. Mr. Justice Flaherty believes that, with the hard-fought victory of the Equal Rights Amendment in Pennsylvania, all vestiges of inequality between the sexes have been erased and women are now treated equally under the law. I fear my colleague does not live in the real world. If I did not know him better I would think that his statements smack of male chauvinism, an attitude that "you women asked for it, now live with it." If you want to know about equality of women, just ask them about comparable wages for comparable work. Just ask them about sexual harassment in the workplace. Just ask them about the sexual discrimination in the Executive Suites of big business. And the list of discrimination based on sex goes on and on.

I view prenuptial agreements as being in the nature of contracts of adhesion with one party generally having greater authority than the other who deals in a subservient role. I believe the law protects the subservient party, regardless of that party's sex, to insure equal protection and treatment under the law.

The present case does not involve the broader issues to which the gratuitous declarations in question are addressed, and it is injudicious to offer declarations in a case which does not involve those issues. Especially when those declarations are inconsistent with reality.

McDERMOTT, J., dissenting. I dissent. I would reverse and remand to the trial court for further consideration of the validity of the prenuptial agreement executed by the appellee, Dr. Frederick Simeone, and Catherine Simeone, on the eve of their wedding. . . .

I believe that the door should remain open for a spouse to avoid the application of a pre-nuptial agreement where clear and convincing proof establishes that the result will be inequity and unfairness under the circumstances of the particular case and the public policy of this state. Some pre-nuptial agreements will be unfair and inequitable from their beginning. . . . [R]easonableness at the inception of the agreement necessarily depends upon the totality of all the facts and circumstances existing at the time of the execution of the agreement, including: (a) the financial situation of each spouse; (b) the age of the parties; (c) the number of children each has; (d) the intelligence of the parties; (e) the standard of living each spouse had before marriage and could reasonably expect to have during marriage. . . .

It is also apparent that, although a pre-nuptial agreement is quite valid when drafted, the passage of time accompanied by the intervening events of a marriage, may render the terms of the agreement completely unfair and inequitable. While parties to a pre-nuptial agreement may indeed foresee, generally, the events which may come to pass during their marriage, one spouse should not be made to suffer for failing to foresee all of the surrounding circumstances which may attend the dissolution of the marriage. Although it should not be the role of the courts to void pre-nuptial agreements merely because one spouse may receive a better result in an action under the Divorce Code to recover alimony or equitable distribution, it should be the role of the courts to guard against the enforcement of pre-nuptial agreements where such enforcement will bring about only inequity and hardship. It borders on cruelty to accept that after years of living together, yielding their separate opportunities in life to each other, that two individuals emerge the same as the day they began their marriage.

At the time of the dissolution of marriage, what are the circumstances which would serve to invalidate a pre-nuptial agreement? This is a question that should only be answered on a case-by-case basis. However, it is not unrealistic to imagine that in a given situation, one spouse, although trained in the workforce at the time of marriage, may, over many years, have become economically dependent upon the other spouse. In reliance upon the permanence of marriage and in order to provide a stable home for a family, a spouse may choose, even at the suggestion of the other spouse, not to work during the marriage. As a result, at the point of dissolution of the marriage, the spouse's employability has diminished to such an extent that to enforce the support provisions of the pre-nuptial agreement will cause the spouse to become a public charge, or will provide a standard of living far below that which was enjoyed before and during marriage. In such a situation, a court may properly decide to render void all or some of the provisions of the pre-nuptial agreement.

I can likewise conceive of a situation where, after a long marriage, the value of property may have increased through the direct efforts of the spouse who agreed not to claim it upon divorce or death. In such a situation, the court should be able to decide whether it is against the public policy of the state, and thus inequitable and unfair, for a spouse to be precluded from receiving that increase in the value of property which he or she had, at least in part, directly induced. I marvel at the majority's apparent willingness to enforce a pre-nuptial agreement in the interest of freedom to contract at any cost, even where unforeseen and untoward illness has rendered one spouse unable, despite his own best efforts, to provide reasonable support for himself. I would further recognize that a spouse should be given the opportunity to prove, through clear and convincing evidence, that the amount of time and energy necessary for that spouse to shelter and care for the children of the marriage has rendered the terms of a pre-nuptial agreement inequitable, and unjust and thus, avoidable.

The majority is concerned that parties will routinely challenge the validity of their pre-nuptial agreements. Given the paramount importance of marriage and family in our society, and the serious consequences that may accompany the dissolution of a marriage, we should not choose to close the doors of our courts merely to gain a measure of judicial economy.

Further, although I would continue to allow parties to challenge the validity of pre-nuptial agreements, I would not alter the burden of proof which has been required to sustain such a challenge.

Turning to the facts of the present case, the Master and the trial court agreed that full and fair disclosure had been made as to the value of Dr. Simeone's antique cars. Thus, I agree with the majority that the appellant, Catherine Simeone, cannot seek to avoid the operation of the pre-nuptial agreement on the grounds that full and fair disclosure of financial status was lacking at the time the agreement was executed. However, at issue in the present appeal is the provision of the pre-nuptial agreement which bars appellant's claim for alimony pendente lite. In 1975, the following statutory provision was applicable:

> In the case of divorce from the bonds of matrimony or bed and board, the court may, upon petition, in proper cases, allow a spouse reasonable alimony pendente lite and reasonable counsel fees and expenses.

The Divorce Law, Act of May 2, 1929, P.L. 1237, § 46, as amended, June 27, 1974, P.L. 403, No. 139, § 1; 23 P.S. § 46. This statute was repealed in 1980 with the enactment of the new Divorce Code:

> The court may, upon petition, in proper cases, allow a spouse reasonable alimony pendente lite, spousal support and reasonable counsel fees and expenses. . . .

23 P.S. § 502.

I would remand this matter to provide the appellant with an opportunity to challenge the validity of the pre-nuptial agreement on two grounds. Although alimony pendente lite was mentioned in the pre-nuptial agreement[30] appellant should have an opportunity to establish that the mere recitation of this legal term did not advise her of the general nature of the statutory right she was relinquishing with the signing of the agreement.[31] Appellant must establish this lack of full and fair disclosure of her statutory rights with clear and convincing evidence. Further, I would allow appellant the opportunity, with the same standard of proof, to challenge the validity of the pre-nuptial agreement's support provisions, relating to alimony pendente lite and alimony, for undue unfairness and inequity. I would express no opinion, however, on the appropriate final resolution of these issues. An appellate court should defer to the trial court in these determinations, and the trial court order should not be reversed absent an error of law or an abuse of discretion.

---

30. The agreement stated in relevant part: "Frederick's obligation to make payments to Catherine for her support and maintenance or as alimony (including, without limitation, alimony pendente lite) shall be limited to and shall not exceed the $200 per week as above provided, and Catherine does hereby acknowledge that the foregoing provision for the payment of $200 per week is fair, just and reasonable."

31. This would not apply to any claim for alimony, as the statutory right to alimony did not arise until the enactment of the Divorce Code of 1980.

LARSEN, J., joins this dissenting opinion.

Notes and Questions

1. *Equal Bargaining Power?* Their genders aside, do you think an unemployed twenty-three year old nurse and a thirty-nine year old practicing neurosurgeon are in equal bargaining power as to a premarital agreement drafted by the neurosurgeon's attorney?

Gender *not* aside, consider how the following conclusions bear on the bargaining power of a woman with respect to a premarital agreement presented to her by the man's attorney on the eve of the wedding:

> Despite more than twenty-five years of experience with federal and state laws prohibiting discrimination in employment based on sex, . . . in most cases, marriage is still the most promising opportunity open to women who want to raise their standard of living. If the marriage terminates in divorce, . . . remarriage is the most efficient path to an immediate return to a higher standard of living. Marriage, it seems, is both a long-term cause and a short-term cure of female poverty.

Kay, Beyond No-Fault, in Divorce Reform at the Crossroads 6, 30 (S. Sugarman & H. Kay eds. 1990).

2. *Fairness When?* As alluded to by the majority in *Simeone*, and as accepted by the dissenting judge in that case, some commentators have criticized the doctrine that the validity of premarital agreements are judged by whether they are "fair" or make "adequate" provision for the surviving spouse at the time of execution, rather than at the time of divorce or death. See, e.g., Haskell, The Premarital Estate Contract and Social Policy, 57 N.C. L. Rev. 415 (1979) (arguing that "premarital estate contracts should not be enforceable if this results in financial hardship for the surviving spouse, i.e., if her property is inadequate for her support and she is not capable of earning an adequate living in accordance with a reasonable approximation of her accustomed standard.") For decisions tending in this direction, see Newman v. Newman, 653 P.2d 728 (Colo. 1982); McHugh v. McHugh, 181 Conn. 482, 436 A.2d 8 (1980). In *Newman,* the court said:

> We hold that, even though an antenuptial agreement is entered into in good faith, with full disclosure and without any element of fraud or overreaching, the maintenance provisions thereof may become voidable for unconscionability occasioned by circumstances existing at the time of the marriage dissolution.

3. *Uniform Acts.* No less than three uniform laws contain provisions governing the validity of premarital agreements. Section 2-204 of the pre-

1990 UPC, which applied to a premarital or postmarital "written contract, agreement or waiver," imposed a standard of "fair disclosure."[32]

The Uniform Premarital Agreement Act (1983), which has been enacted so far in 16 states (Arizona, Arkansas, California, Hawaii, Illinois, Kansas, Maine, Montana, Nevada, North Carolina, North Dakota, Oregon, Rhode Island, South Dakota, Texas, and Virginia), applies to written premarital agreements, signed by both parties. Whether or not supported by consideration, the agreements pertaining to property rights on divorce or death are enforceable unless the party against whom enforcement is sought proves (a) that she or he did not execute the agreement voluntarily; or, (b) that the agreement was unconscionable[33] when made *and* that, before execution of the agreements, she or he (1) was *not* provided a fair and reasonable disclosure of the property or financial obligations of the other party, (2) did *not* voluntarily and expressly waive, in writing, any right to disclosure of the property or financial obligations of the other party beyond the disclosure provided, *and* (3) did *not* have, or reasonably could not have had, an adequate knowledge of the property and financial obligations of the other party. The 1990 UPC adopts this approach. See UPC § 2-204 (1990).

UMPA distinguishes between premarital and postmarital agreements. For premarital agreements, the standard of validity is essentially the same as that contained in the Uniform Premarital Agreement Act. A ground of invalidity of a postmarital agreement, however, is that it was "unconscionable" when made. The higher standard for postmarital agreements reflects the idea that married persons stand in a higher confidential relationship to each other and owe each other greater fiduciary duties than persons not yet married.[34]

EXTERNAL REFERENCES. A. Lindey, Separation Agreements and Ante-Nuptial Contracts (1961 & Supp.); Springs & Bruce, Marital Agreements: Uses, Techniques, and Tax Ramifications in the Estate Planning Context, 21 Inst. on Est. Plan. ch. 7 (1987); Clark, Antenuptial Contracts, 50 U. Colo. L. Rev. 141 (1979); Annot., 27 A.L.R.2d 883 (1953).

---

32. The 1990 UPC amended § 2-204 by replacing the "fair disclosure" standard with the standard employed in the Uniform Premarital Agreement Act, except that only the signature of the waiving party is required.

33. The term "unconscionable," derived from § 306 of the Uniform Marriage and Divorce Act, is explained in a Commissioner's Note to § 306 as encompassing overreaching, concealment of assets, or sharp dealings inconsistent with the obligations of marital partners to deal fairly with each other.

34. The initial Wisconsin enactment of UMPA departed from UMPA itself and applied the higher UMPA standard for validity of postmarital agreements to premarital agreements as well. By a trailer amendment, however, Wisconsin replaced the UMPA tests with a requirement that the spouse either have notice of or have received fair and reasonable disclosure, under the circumstances, of the other spouse's property and financial obligations.

5. *Tax Implications of an Election*

In an age in which married partners frequently have children by prior marriages, an aspect of elective-share law that makes election attractive is that, by electing, the spouse receives absolute ownership of all (or part of[35]) her or his entitlement. Absolute ownership means that the spouse has power to give the property to her or his children during life or at death.

To the extent that an elective share confers an absolute-ownership interest on the surviving spouse, it qualifies for the federal estate tax marital deduction. Under the UPC scheme, that part of the elective share made up of augmented-estate property that passes or has passed to the surviving spouse might also qualify for the federal estate tax marital deduction, depending on the terms of the disposition.

As noted in Chapter 6, the Economic Recovery Tax Act of 1981 amended the federal estate tax by allowing a marital deduction for qualified terminable interest property—"QTIPs" in estate-planning parlance. See IRC § 2056(b)(7). The great attraction of QTIPs is that they allow the decedent spouse to create a deductible trust in which the surviving spouse receives only a lifetime income interest in the property. QTIPs are now in widespread use, and may in fact be the predominant method of gaining the marital deduction in estate-planning practice. In a QTIP, of course, the surviving spouse does not have testamentary control over the devolution of the trust property after her or his death.[36]

Consider a surviving spouse who has not been disinherited in any strict sense, but rather, has, been provided for by means of a QTIP trust. The elective-share provisions, as they are currently constituted in non-UPC states, where the forced share entitles the survivor to an absolute-ownership interest, provide this surviving spouse with an incentive to elect the statutory share if she or he has children by a former marriage. To the extent that the electing spouse can take an absolute-ownership interest, as opposed to an interest that expires on her or his death (such as a life estate), the elective share is attractive because it gives the survivor the power to benefit those children upon her or his death.

In an estate large enough to attract a federal estate tax, a more subtle problem pertains to the calculation of the elective share. (The same problem exists, incidentally, in the calculation of the spouse's intestate share in an intestate estate.) The problem is whether the elective-share fraction (or intestate-share fraction) is applied to the estate before or after the federal estate tax has been subtracted. The elective or intestate share will be greater, perhaps substantially greater, under the before-tax approach

---

35. To repeat a point made earlier, however, pre-1990 UPC § 2-207(a) and UPC § 2-207(a)(1) (1990) provide that the elective share is funded first with property interests passing to the surviving spouse that may or may not be absolute ownership interests.

36. Prior to the 1981 tax-law changes, the only methods available for qualifying for the marital deduction required the surviving spouse to be given testamentary control over the property, either through outright ownership of that property or under a general power of appointment. See IRC § 2056(b)(5), supra p. 372.

than under the after-tax approach; also, under the before-tax approach, the federal estate tax itself will be lower, to the extent that the amount of the elective or intestate share qualifies for the marital deduction and reduces the amount subject to estate taxation.

The UPC incorporates as section 3-916 the Uniform Estate Tax Apportionment Act. UPC section 3-916(e)(2) provides that any "deduction allowed by reason of the relationship of any person to the decedent . . . inures to the benefit of the person bearing such relationship. . . ." Because transfers that qualify for the marital deduction are not taxable transfers under the federal estate tax, the import of this provision is that the estate tax should be apportioned only among the recipients of taxable transfers. See supra p. 330 for further discussion of tax-apportionment statutes. Consequently, almost all courts have held, under the Uniform Act or similar tax-apportionment legislation, that the amount of the spouse's elective share (and the amount of the spouse's intestate share in an intestate estate) is calculated on the basis of the estate *before* estate taxes have been subtracted.[37] Wolf's Estate, 307 N.Y. 280, 121 N.E.2d 224 (1954); Rosenfeld Estate, 376 Pa. 42, 101 A.2d 684 (1954); Third Nat'l Bank v. Cotten, 536 S.W.2d 330 (Tenn. 1976); Alexandria Nat'l Bank v. Thomas, 213 Va. 620, 194 S.E.2d 723, 67 A.L.R.3d 190 (1973). Contra, Weinberg v. Safe Deposit & Trust Co., 198 Md. 539, 85 A.2d 50 (1951).

Unfortunately, some non-UPC states do not have tax-apportionment legislation. In the absence of such legislation, the decisions on the question are divided. Spurrier v. First Nat'l Bank, 207 Kan. 406, 485 P.2d 209 (1971), a leading decision for the view that the spouse's elective or intestate share is calculated on a before-tax basis, reasoned:

> When K.S.A. 59-502 providing that all interests by intestate succession are subject to "homestead rights, the allowances . . . , and the payment of reasonable funeral expenses, expenses of last sickness and costs of administration, taxes and debts" was enacted in 1939, the tax advantage of the marital deduction did not exist. . . . We cannot attribute legislative inactivity in this instance as an indication that taxpayers of this state were intended to be deprived of the benefits of the marital deduction.

A pair of leading decisions for the contrary view, that the spouse's elective share and intestate share are calculated on an after-tax basis,[38] are Del Mar v. United States, 390 F.2d 466 (D.C. Cir. 1968) (elective share);

---

37. With respect to the elective share, pre-1990 and 1990 UPC do not rely solely on § 3-916(e)(2). Section 2-202 provides that the fraction (or percentage) applies to an amount "reduced by funeral and administration expenses, homestead allowance, family allowances and exemptions, and enforceable claims." The definition of the word "claims" in § 1-201 carefully states that the "term does not include estate or inheritance taxes. . . ." See pre-1990 UPC § 1-202(4); UPC § 1-201(6) (1990).

38. This approach makes the amount of the forced or intestate share dependent on the amount of the estate tax, which in turn is dependent on the amount of the forced or intestate share! The calculations must be done algebraically. See, e.g., Mertens, Federal Gift and Estate Taxation § 30.12 et seq.

Herson v. Mills, 221 F. Supp. 714 (D.D.C. 1963) (intestate share). In *Del Mar*, the court said:

> Other jurisdictions have permitted the result for which appellants contend, either by specific statute or judicial adoption of general equitable apportionment of estate taxes. However, we are not inclined to modify our settled course of decisions—either to upset the general law of decedents' estates in the District of Columbia merely to allow a dissenting widow a larger portion of the estate at the expense of the remaining legatees and the Government, or to carve out a narrow exception for the widow's intestate share, a course which other states have taken only through actions of their legislatures.
>
> If the marital deduction provision of the tax law reflects a policy that Congress considers applicable to govern local law in the District of Columbia, Congress can easily provide a remedy. If Congress has been sluggish as a local legislature in making available to the District of Columbia benefits it has enabled the various legislatures to provide to the citizens of the states and commonwealths, petitions for relief from this anomaly are properly addressed to Congress.

EXTERNAL REFERENCE. Kahn, The Federal Estate Tax Burden Born by a Dissenting Widow, 64 Mich. L. Rev. 1499 (1966).

PART B. PROBATE EXEMPTIONS AND ALLOWANCES

Statutory References: *1990 UPC §§ 2-401 to -405*
                                        Pre-1990 UPC §§ 2-401 to -404

The elective share in the common-law states and the community interest in the community-property states are not the only protections against disinheritance afforded the surviving spouse. Additional layers of protection routinely run in favor of the decedent's surviving spouse (and often also in favor of the decedent's children, sometimes limited to minor or dependent children). These are the right of homestead, the exempt property allowance, and the family allowance.

Although the statutes vary in considerable detail, the UPC provisions are fairly representative of the type of legislation likely to be found even in non-UPC states, but with one exception: The UPC's homestead allowance is unique, in that it provides for a lump-sum amount rather than a right to occupy the spouses' dwelling house as long as the surviving spouse or minor children wish to do so.

In the 1990 revisions to the UPC, each dollar figure reflects a tripling of the original figures. This was done to align them with the increases in the cost of living that occurred in the twenty or so years between 1969, when the UPC was first promulgated, and 1990, when the UPC was revised.

Effect of the Probate Exemptions and Allowances In Small Estates. Under the UPC, the probate exemptions and allowances—homestead, exempt property, and family allowance (up to the maximum that can be made without special court order)—can be distributed to the surviving spouse without delay, other than as may be necessary for the personal representative to locate, liquidate, and distribute the necessary estate funds or assets in kind. Estates worth as much as $43,000 (in excess of liens) can be closed by distribution of these probate exemptions and allowances, once a personal representative has been appointed. The decedent's will is rendered irrelevant in such cases. However, with the exception of multiple-party accounts in financial institutions (such as checking or savings accounts or certificates) with a right of survivorship or a POD designation,[39] the restraint on testation represented by the probate exemptions and allowances is inapplicable to will substitutes.

Probate Exemptions and Allowances Are Neither Charged Against the Elective Share Nor Against Devises Unless the Decedent's Will So Directs. The UPC clarifies a matter on which many non-UPC statutes are silent, which is whether the exemptions and allowances are in addition to or are charged against devises to the persons entitled to the exemptions and allowances. The UPC does not charge the exemptions and allowances against devises unless the decedent's will directs otherwise. Nor are they charged against the elective share.

Homestead. The homestead allowance provided for by UPC section 2-402 (1990) is derived, in name at least, from a uniquely American contribution to laws giving a decedent's dependent survivors limited protection in the family home.[40] English law is the source of a different idea. Under Magna Carta, the widow had a right, called the widow's quarantine, to "tarry in the chief house of her husband for forty days,"[41] and there are early American decisions recognizing this as a part of the common law. Some American legislation has extended this right for a year,

---

39. UPC § 6-215(a) (1989) provides:

(a) A transfer resulting from a right of survivorship or POD designation under this part is not effective against an estate of a deceased party to transfer sums needed to pay debts, taxes, and expenses of administration, including statutory allowances to the surviving spouse, minor children, and dependent children, if other assets of the estate are insufficient.

Note that § 6-212(a) gives a further right to a surviving spouse in multiple-party accounts by providing:

(a) Except as otherwise provided in this section, on death of a party sums on deposit in a multiple-party account belong to the surviving party or parties as against the estate of the decedent. If two or more parties survive and one is the surviving spouse of the decedent, the amount to which the decedent, immediately before death, was beneficially entitled under Section 6-211 belongs to the surviving spouse. If two or more parties survive and none is the surviving spouse of the decedent, the amount to which the decedent, immediately before death, was beneficially entitled under Section 6-211 belongs to the surviving parties in equal shares, and augments that proportion to which each survivor, immediately before the decedent's death, was beneficially entitled under Section 6-211, and the right of survivorship continues between the surviving parties.

40. The laws are said to have originated in 1839 in the Republic of Texas.
41. The quotation is from 4 J. Kent, Commentaries 61 (1st ed. 1830).

as in Michigan and Ohio,[42] or until dower is assigned, as in Virginia.[43] By contrast, more prevalent American housestead legislation, though framed primarily in terms of exempting the homestead from the claims of the owner's creditors during her or his lifetime, commonly grants a decedent's spouse or minor children a right of occupancy in certain real estate of the decedent that may continue for much longer periods. (A title in fee simple passes to homestead beneficiaries in Wyoming.) These homestead statutes vary markedly in the amount and scope of protection given to family survivors. For example, though homestead titles are typically subject to ceilings of rather low value, the ceiling may be as high as $30,000, as in Massachusetts and Wyoming, or there may be no ceiling at all, as in Minnesota.

The UPC homestead allowance shifts the exemption from a right of occupancy of realty to a money substitute. In doing so, the UPC protects all surviving spouses and minor children, including those of renters, owners of mobile homes not classified as real estate, and decedents who owned no interest in a residence of any sort. The fact that the UPC's homestead allowance does not grant a right of occupancy does not mean that a surviving spouse has no prospect of remaining in possession of realty in the name of the deceased spouse. With the cooperation of the personal representative, a spouse's right to money from an estate can readily be converted into a title to real estate—as a distribution in kind to the spouse, as a sale of land to the spouse, or as some combination of the two. In this connection, it may be noted that under the UPC, a spouse has priority either to serve as the personal representative or to choose who serves, unless a probated will nominates someone else who qualifies and accepts the appointment.

---

42. Mich. Comp. Laws Ann. § 700.288:

In addition to the right to homestead allowance, exempt property, family allowance, and election, the surviving spouse may remain in the dwelling house of the decedent 1 year after the death of the decedent or until the share of the surviving spouse is assigned to him, whichever comes earlier; and the surviving spouse shall not be chargeable with rent, taxes, water bills, repairs except those repairs resulting from the acts, omissions, or negligence of the surviving spouse, insurance premiums, or mortgage or land contract interest or principal payments, but shall be chargeable with public utility bills and, if possession of the dwelling by the decedent had been as a tenant, shall be chargeable with rent. The right of occupancy in this section is exempt from and has priority over all claims against the estate of the decedent.

Ohio Rev. Code § 2117.24:

A surviving spouse may remain in the mansion house of the deceased consort free of charge for one year. . . .

43. Va. Code § 64.1-33:

Until dower or curtesy is assigned, the surviving spouse may hold, occupy and enjoy the mansion house and curtilage.

See generally, "Widow's Right of Quarantine," 126 A.L.R. 796 (1940).

EXTERNAL REFERENCE. On homestead legislation generally, see Restatement 2d of Property, Statutory Note to § 34.1; Am. L. Prop. § 5.114.

PART C. OTHER RESTRICTIONS ON FREEDOM OF DISPOSITION

In this Part, we consider two additional measures of family protection against disinheritance: pretermitted-heir statutes and mortmain statutes. The former protect specified family members from unintentional disinheritance; the latter invalidate specified dispositions in favor of charitable organizations.

1. Protection Against Unintentional Disinheritance

Statutory References: *1990 UPC §§ 2-301 to -302*
                              Pre-1990 UPC §§ 2-301 to -302

Putting aside the probate exemptions and allowances considered in Part B, children may be *intentionally* disinherited in every American state except Louisiana.[44] The power to disinherit one's children is a major difference between American succession law and the system that exists in all civil-law nations. The civil law recognizes the *legitime*, a device that guarantees that close family members will inherit a fixed share of a decedent owner's estate.[45] Although the legitime is frequently said to have originated in Roman law, Professor Dawson has recently pointed out that it owes to classical Roman law not much more than the name. The origins of forced heirship lie elsewhere, he argues:

> The antecedents of these ideas [guaranteed share for the forced heir] lie far back in the forms of social organization among the races of Germanic origin that came to occupy Europe, including Gaul, as Roman power declined.

---

44. Louisiana recently restricted the scope of its forced heirship statute. Effective July 1, 1990, forced heirship protection extends only to two categories of children: those under the age of 23 and those who "ha[ve] been interdicted or [are] subject to being interdicted because of mental incapacity or physical infirmity." La. Civ. Code art. 1493. For a critical analysis of the new statute, arguing, among other points, that it violates the equal protection clauses of the Louisiana and federal constitutions, see Spaht, Lorio, Picou, Samuel & Swaim, The New Forced Heirship Legislation: A Regrettable "Revolution," 50 La. L. Rev. 409 (1990).

45. Early English law also recognized restrictions on an owner's power to disinherit his heirs. The treatise that we know as Glanvill states that an owner could give away to the exclusion of his heirs only a "reasonable" part of his land. See F. Pollock & F. Maitland, History of the Common Law 308-09 (2d ed. 1952). Reference to these restraints disappeared around 1200, probably because they could not be well-enforced in the king's courts. See S. Milsom, The Legal Framework of Feudalism 122 (1976).

They had notions of family solidarity and of subordination of individuals to decisions of family groups that were no part of the heritage from Rome.

J. Dawson, Gifts and Promises 29 (1980).

What advantages might be attributed to this system in modern society? Professor Buchanan, a Nobel laureate in economics, has suggested that fixed shares would reduce waste of economic resources on the part of hopeful beneficiaries attempting to induce gifts and devises to them.[46] What is your reaction to this suggestion? Other commentators have argued that the increasing incidence of multiple marriages increases the need to protect dependent children from intentional disinheritance by noncustodial parents. See Batts, I Didn't Ask to Be Born: The American Law of Disinheritance and a Proposal for Change to a System of Protected Disinheritance, 41 Hastings L.J. 1197 (1990).

Unintentional disinheritance is another matter: Nearly all states have statutes, called "pretermitted-heir" statutes, that grant children a measure of protection from being unintentionally disinherited.[47] Some statutes bear considerable resemblance to pre-1990 UPC section 2-302. Others make no mention of the testator's intention, and provide simply that a child (occasionally, any "issue") not named or provided for in the testator's will takes her or his intestate share.[48] Most statutes protect only children born (or adopted) *after* the execution of the will; a few protect any omitted child. The UPC appears to have broken new ground by providing that nonprobate transfers to a child can defeat that child's statutory protection.[49]

The 1990 UPC substantially revises section 2-302. Two basic changes were made. First, if the testator had no child alive when she or he executed the will, an omitted after-born or after-adopted child takes no portion of the estate if the testator devised all or substantially all of the estate to the other parent of the omitted child and the other parent survives the testator and is entitled to take the property. This extends the rule of pre-1990 UPC section 2-302 that an omitted child does not receive an intestate share if at the time of execution the testator had one or more children and the testator devised substantially all of her or his estate to the other parent of the omitted child. Whether the testator had children at the time of execution, a devise of the bulk of the testator to the other parent of the

---

46. Buchanan, Rent-Seeking, Noncompensated Transfers, and the Laws of Succession, 26 J. L. & Econ. 71 (1983). Similarly, in criticizing the recent amendment to Louisiana's forced heirship statute, Professor Samuel has stated: "Greed, prejudice, jealousy, meanness and fear will henceforth have a much freer hand in influencing a parent's testamentary plan." Moreover, she contends that the old legitime device serves the modern function of "guaranteeing that kids don't get divorced from their inheritance when their parents get divorced from each other." N.Y. Times, Dec. 1, 1989, § B, at 7.

47. For a state-by-state compilation, see Restatement 2d of Property, Statutory Note to § 34.2.

48. The constitutionality of this type of a statute was upheld in Holland v. Willis, 739 S.W.2d 529 (Ark. 1987).

49. For a collection of cases dealing with what constitutes a sufficient indication of a contrary intent, see Annot., 83 A.L.R.4th 779 (1991).

omitted child usually indicates that the testator trusts that parent to use the property to benefit an after-born or after-adopted child.

The other major change concerns situations in which the testator had one or more children alive when the will was executed and devised property to at least one of the then-living children. An omitted after-born or after-adopted child does not take a full intestate share in this situation but only a pro rata share of the property devised to the then-living children.

Although pretermitted-heir statutes are common, protection for the decedent's surviving spouse in that form is rare—apart from the UPC states. The earlier approach to the problem took the form of the common-law doctrines revoking a person's will if she or he later married. See supra p. 282. As elective-share statutes came to replace dower and curtesy, the elective share was thought to provide sufficient protection in the situation of a premarital will. The pre-1990 UPC embarked on a different course by providing, in section 2-301, an omitted-spouse provision in addition to the apparatus of the elective share. The purpose was not only to reduce the frequency of elections under the elective share, but also to provide a share for the surviving spouse more related to the amount the decedent would probably have wanted to give, had she or he gotten around to revising the premarital will.

Problems

In the following problems, the term "net estate" refers to the estate after the deduction of debts, expenses, and allowances, but not after deduction of estate or inheritance taxes.

1. A, a widower, executed a will devising $50,000 to his friend, B, and the residue of his estate to his children. Subsequently, A and B married each other. A later died, leaving a net estate worth $200,000; he was survived by B and by the children of his former marriage. Under the pre-1990 UPC, would B be entitled to the $50,000 devise plus the share of A's estate she would have taken if A had left no will? Compare Estate of Ganier, 418 S.2d 256 (Fla. 1982), with Estate of Christensen, 655 P.2d 646 (Utah 1982). See Comment, The Problem of the "Un-Omitted" Spouse Under Section 2-301 of the Uniform Probate Code, 52 U. Chi. L. Rev. 481 (1985). How would this problem be handled under 1990 UPC section 2-301?

2. H and W enjoyed a long happy marriage to each other, which produced two children, A and B, and three grandchildren, X, Y, and Z. W died at age 70, survived by H, age 68. W's will devised her entire estate to H if he survived her; if not, to A and B in equal shares. H's will, executed at the same time, devised his entire estate to W if she survived him; if not, to A and B in equal shares.

Some few years after W's death, H remarried. He never thought to change his will after the marriage; he assumed that W having predeceased him, his property would be divided equally between A and B. (His new wife, W-2, was financially well off.)

A few months after his second marriage, his son B, age 48, was killed in an airplane crash. B was survived by his wife and by his 19-year-old child, Z. Upon learning of B's tragic death, H suffered a heart attack and died. H was survived (by 120 hours) by his second wife, W-2, and by A, X, Y, and Z.

H's net estate was valued at $150,000. How would H's estate be distributed under the pre-1990 UPC? Under 1990 UPC section 2-301? (W-2's assets at H's death are valued at $500,000.)

Estate of Bartell
776 P.2d 885 (Utah 1989)

ZIMMERMAN, J. Ernest BARTELL died testate, but his will, executed before his marriage to Lola BARTELL, did not mention her. Lola BARTELL sought a declaration from the district court probating her husband's estate that she is an "omitted spouse" within the meaning of section 2-301(1) of the Utah Uniform Probate Code and is therefore entitled to an intestate share of her husband's estate. Utah Code Ann. § 75-2-301 (1978); see Utah Code Ann. § 75-2-102(1)(a) (1978).

After a bench trial, the court found that Ernest intended to provide for Lola by transfers outside his will. The court therefore concluded that she was not entitled to be treated as an omitted spouse. Lola appeals, contending that the evidence was insufficient to support the trial court's determination.

Section 75-2-301 provides:

> If a testator fails to provide by will for his [or her] surviving spouse who married the testator after the execution of the will, the omitted spouse shall receive the same share of the estate he [or she] would have received if the decedent left no will unless it appears from the will that the omission was intentional or the testator provided for the spouse by transfer outside the will and the intent that the transfer be in lieu of a testamentary provision is shown by [1] statements of the testator or [2] from the amount of the transfer or [3] other evidence. Utah Code Ann. § 75-2-301 (1978) (emphasis added).

Under this Code section, the question for the trial court was whether Ernest had provided for Lola outside the will and had intended that this provision be in lieu of her taking under the will. In making this determination, the court could consider the statements of Ernest, the amount transferred, or other evidence of intent.

The trial court found Ernest's statements to be inconclusive as to his intent. However, it did find that Ernest had transferred some $230,000 to Lola in the years immediately preceding his death. The court found that the amount transferred, when considered in light of the fact that only about $100,000 remained in Ernest's estate, was enough to indicate an intent to provide for Lola after his death and was in lieu of a testamentary provision.

As for "other evidence," the trial judge found that Ernest had built a home in Ogden with the help of some close family members and that if Ernest had wanted the home to go to Lola rather than to the close family members who took it under the will, he was sufficiently astute in business matters to have changed his will or transferred the Ogden home into joint ownership with Lola, as he had done with other property. Based on these findings, the trial court determined that Lola was not an omitted spouse under section 2-301(1) and was not entitled to an intestate share. . . . [W]e have considered the evidence and are not persuaded that the trial court's findings regarding the decedent's intent were clearly erroneous.

The judgment is affirmed.

———

EXTERNAL REFERENCE. Note, Premarital Wills and Pretermitted Children: West Virginia Law v. Revised Uniform Probate Code, 93 W. Va. L. Rev. 197 (1990).

2. Mortmain Legislation

In a few states, statutes impose various forms of restraint on gifts by will to charitable or religious organizations. A 1970 report by a national committee of lawyers, ABA Section Committee on Succession, Restrictions on Charitable Testamentary Gifts, 5 Real Prop. Prob. & Tr. J. 290-92 (1970), included the following summary of this legislation:

> The present day restrictions on charitable gifts in the United States have their origins or examples in English statutory law. The early English statutes were enacted, at least in part, to protect the interest of the overlords, and later the crown itself, in the feudal incidents of landholding. The restrictions were also motivated in part by the government's hostility to ecclesiastical and other corporations. The English restrictions on devises for charitable purposes basically took two forms, both of which traversed the Atlantic to the United States in one guise or another. . . .
>
> The earliest mortmain statutes, representing a first type of restriction and beginning with Magna Carta, did not prevent the owner of real estate from transferring the property to a charity or corporation, but directly deprived the charity or corporation of the right to hold real estate. . . .
>
> The second type of restriction was imposed upon the power of an individual to make a testamentary disposition in favor of a corporation. The Georgian Statute of Mortmain prohibited the devise of land to *any* person or corporation for charitable uses, except: "by deed indented, sealed and delivered in the presence of two or more credible witnesses twelve calendar months at least before the death of such donor or grantor. . . ." In the preamble to this statute, it was stated that the purpose of this requirement was to prevent a dying person (possibly affected by fear of an immediate day of judgment) from giving his property to charities to the exclusion of his lawful heirs.
>
> Both types of statute have been repealed in England today. These former English statutory restrictions did not come to the United States as parts of our common law heritage from England. Rather, the only restrictions on charitable

gifts in the United States are statutory. In the United States, the two policies seen to exist in England were implemented in many states by statutes which again restricted either: (i) the power of a corporation to take and hold real and personal property, or (ii) the power of a testator to devise his property to charity, or (iii) a combination of (i) and (ii). The second type of restriction was usually expressed in the form either of a requirement of elapsed time before death or a limitation on the amount which a testator could give to charity or both. . . .

The committee has researched the laws of all states on the general Mortmain area. . . . [A]s of April 1970, . . . nine states—California, Florida, Georgia, Idaho, Iowa, Montana, New York, Ohio and Pennsylvania—plus the District of Columbia have statutes, and one state—Mississippi—has a constitutional provision, which either (a) restrict or prohibit charitable gifts contained in a will which is executed within a certain period prior to the death of the testator (usually one month, three months or six months), or (b) limit the amount of a probate estate which can be given to a charity, or (c) impose a combination of restrictions of both types (a) and (b). . . .

Of the eleven jurisdictions listed in this 1970 report, only Georgia, Idaho, and Mississippi still retain their mortmain provisions.[50] Recently, Florida's mortmain statute was declared unconstitutional under the equal protection clause of the Florida and United States constitutions. Shriners' Hospital for Crippled Children v. Zrillic, 563 S.2d 64 (Fla. 1990).[51]

Contrary to the national trend, the Mississippi constitutional provision and statute were strengthened in 1987. As revised, a charitable devise of any portion of the testator's estate is invalid if the will was executed within 180 days before the testator's death. (The former Mississippi provision only invalidated a charitable devise if the devise was of more than one-third of the testator's estate and if the will was executed within ninety days before the testator's death.)

EXTERNAL REFERENCES. Note, 52 Notre Dame Lawyer 638 (1977); Annot., 6 A.L.R.4th 603 (1981).

---

50. The California statute was repealed in 1971, the District of Columbia and Iowa statutes were repealed in 1980, the Montana and New York statutes were repealed in 1981, and the Ohio statute was repealed in 1985. The former Ohio statute, as applied to the wills of testators who died on or after the repealing statute's effective date, was declared unconstitutional under the equal protection clauses of the state and federal constitutions. See Shriners' Hosp. for Crippled Children v. Hester, 23 Ohio St. 3d 198, 492 N.E.2d 153 (1986). Pennsylvania's statute was declared unconstitutional on substantive due process grounds in Estate of Cavill, 459 Pa. 411, 329 A.2d 503 (1974) and was repealed in 1976. Although the Georgia mortmain statute has not been repealed, its scope was altered in 1982, so that it is inapplicable to that portion of an estate exceeding $200,000 in value.

51. The majority opinion in Zrillic also reasoned that the Florida constitution provides a constitutional right to devise property and that the mortmain statute was an unreasonable restriction on this right. Three members of the court disagreed with this reasoning. According to the majority's reasoning, would the Rule Against Perpetuities violate the Florida constitution?

Chapter 9

WILL CONTRACTS

Part A. Contracts Not to Revoke
Part B. Contracts to Devise

Transfers by will are normally perceived as *donative*, not obligatory. Obligatory transfers by will are also possible, however. A promise, supported by consideration, to leave property by will to the promisee or to third-party beneficiaries can be enforceable as a contract. Such contracts are called *will contracts*, and they take various forms. They may involve a promise to make a will, not to make a will, to revoke a will already made, or not to revoke a will already made. The two most common types of will contracts, however, are (1) contracts not to revoke mutual or joint and mutual wills in favor of third-party beneficiaries and (2) contracts to make a will in favor of the promisee in return for services rendered to the decedent.

PART A. CONTRACTS NOT TO REVOKE

Statutory References: *1990 UPC § 2-514*
                              Pre-1990 UPC § 2-701

Mutual and Joint Wills. Litigation over the existence of a contract not to revoke typically occurs in the context of mutual or joint wills executed by a married couple. Mutual wills are separate wills, executed by each of two persons; they contain similar or reciprocal provisions. Mutual wills are frequently executed by married couples as part of an overall estate plan for the disposition of their property. A *joint will* is a single instrument, executed by two persons, that they intend to operate as the will of each. Typically, joint wills are executed by a husband and wife. Because it acts twice, as the will for each party, a joint will must be probated twice, upon the death of each testator. Joint wills that contain reciprocal provisions, as they commonly do, are sometimes called *joint and mutual*. Because they tend to invite litigation over the existence of a will contract, joint wills are not favored by estate planners.

Where a couple has executed mutual wills or a joint will and the survivor subsequently changes her or his will, the existence of a common scheme expressed by mutual wills or a joint will may lead disappointed beneficiaries later to claim that the original will was executed pursuant to a will contract. The initial question is what evidence is required to prove that a contract not to revoke was made.

Junot v. Estate of Gilliam
759 S.W.2d 654 (Tenn. 1988)

HARBISON, C.J. Appellants brought this action to set aside the probate of a will executed on January 28, 1985, by decedent, Emma Jean Gilliam. The theory of the suit was that Mrs. Gilliam and her deceased husband, Thaddeaus Evans Gilliam, had executed mutual and reciprocal wills in 1974 and that upon the death of Mr. Gilliam in January, 1985, the 1974 will of Mrs. Gilliam had become irrevocable.

Appellants also filed a claim against the estate of Mrs. Gilliam for the portion of the estate which they claim under her 1974 will. Appellee filed a response, alleging that there was no contract between the parties and that the 1985 will of Mrs. Gilliam, already admitted to probate, should stand and be carried out according to its terms. . . .

After a full trial, the judge held that appellants had not carried their burden of proof to establish a contract between Mr. and Mrs. Gilliam that would make her 1974 will irrevocable. The Court of Appeals affirmed. After careful consideration of all of the issues, we also affirm. . . .

The 1974 Wills. Mr. and Mrs. Gilliam were married in 1967. This was the second marriage for each. Mr. Gilliam had three children by his former marriage, and Mrs. Gilliam had two. No children were born to this second marriage.

Prior to February 22, 1974, Mr. and Mrs. Gilliam had discussed making their wills. Mr. Gilliam is shown to have had a separate estate, the amount of which does not appear in the record. It is shown that he owned several pieces of real estate. Whether Mrs. Gilliam had a separate estate does not appear.

On or about February 1, 1974, Mr. and Mrs. Gilliam made an appointment with Mr. Thomas McKinney, Jr., an attorney who had practiced in Kingsport, Tennessee, for several years. He had never met either of the Gilliams previously. He testified that he discussed with them a number of possible dispositions which they might make of their property, including life estates with remainder. There was a general discussion of the subject of wills, the revocation thereof and contracts to make wills irrevocable. Inter vivos gifts were also discussed, but no conclusions were reached during the first meeting.

About three weeks later, on February 22, 1974, Mr. and Mrs. Gilliam returned to the attorney's office and instructed him to write the wills which are in question. They also instructed him to write a warranty deed from Mr. Gilliam to himself and his wife so as to create a tenancy by the entirety in the property on which their residence was situated. This warranty deed was duly executed and was recorded. It is in the record, and there is no issue between the parties concerning it.

The parties executed separate wills on February 22, 1974, which were mutual and reciprocal. In his will, Mr. Gilliam directed payment of debts and funeral expenses. He then left all of his property outright to his wife, Mrs. Gilliam, "except as otherwise directed in Item III hereof. . . ."

In Item III the will provided that if Mrs. Gilliam did not survive the testator, or if she died within 90 days after his death as a result of a common disaster, then all of Mr. Gilliam's estate was to be divided equally among the five children of the parties; that is, Mr. Gilliam's three children and the two children of Mrs. Gilliam.

The will of Mrs. Gilliam was written in exactly the same language, leaving everything to Mr. Gilliam but to the five children of the parties in the event he did not survive her. The same persons witnessed both wills.

Mr. Gilliam died on January 21, 1985. Mrs. Gilliam did survive, and the parties were not involved in "a common accident." She survived for more than 90 days, although she did die a little less than 7 months later, on August 11, 1985.

In the meanwhile, shortly after the death of her husband, Mrs. Gilliam wrote another will, executed on January 28, 1985, leaving the entire estate to her children by her first marriage. They are the executors of her estate and are the appellees herein. There is no evidence of fraud, undue influence or lack of mental capacity, and no claim of such. Mr. McKinney, who also wrote the second will, did state that Mrs. Gilliam appeared to be very emotional and upset after the death of her husband. Her statements to him seem to indicate a feeling of insecurity as to whether Mr. Gilliam's children by his first marriage might be able to take the estate from her and leave her with very few assets. There is no testimony in the record, however, concerning any actual controversy between Mrs. Gilliam and the children of Mr. Gilliam's first marriage, who are the appellants here.

Under the terms of Mr. Gilliam's 1974 will, the entire estate vested in Mrs. Gilliam upon his death, unconditionally and without any kind of restraint or restriction. Unless a contract between the parties could be proved, so as to make her will of the same date irrevocable, she was free to dispose of the estate as she saw fit.

There was very little evidence concerning any such contract. Mr. Gilliam's brother and other witnesses testified that in the eleven years between the execution of the 1974 wills and the death of Mr. Gilliam in January, 1985, Mr. and Mrs. Gilliam made reference that they had "traded wills." Counsel for appellants insist that this is clear evidence that the wills were intended by Mr. and Mrs. Gilliam to be irrevocable after the death of the first of them and resulted from a contract between the parties to that effect.

We respectfully disagree. It is well settled that in order to establish a contract to make or not to revoke a will, where the contract is not otherwise documented, evidence of such a contract must be clear and convincing. The mere fact that parties have executed mutual and reciprocal wills on the same date is not, in and of itself, sufficient to establish the existence of such a contract. That fact, together with other evidence concerning the circumstances of the parties, may be sufficient to establish such a contract. The issue, however, in every case is one of fact, not law, to be determined in light of all of the surrounding circumstances. . . .

In the present case, there is a concurrent finding of fact by the trial court and the Court of Appeals that no such agreement was established by the evidence. That conclusion . . . is binding here if supported by material evidence.

The evidence to establish a contract not to revoke a will must be clear and convincing. The evidence offered by the appellants to show such a contract in the present case was not sufficiently clear or precise to establish a binding contract between Mr. and Mrs. Gilliam that the survivor would not revoke his or her 1974 will. The wills accomplished what each of the spouses apparently desired—that is, each left everything to the survivor provided they were not involved in a common accident with the survivor expiring within 90 days thereafter. Alternate dispositions in each will were identical, but it is clear that the children of the parties were no more than just that—alternate beneficiaries. Legally the entire estate vested in the survivor, and there is nothing in the text of the wills themselves nor in the brief and informal remarks of Mr. and Mrs. Gilliam shown in evidence to establish a firm and binding agreement that the survivor was restricted in any way in his or her subsequent disposition of the property covered by these wills. The residence of the parties, which was the subject of a simultaneous deed, of course, passed to the survivor under the tenancy by the entirety which was created, without restraint, condition or restriction.

Wholly apart from the testimony of the scrivener of the will, Mr. McKinney, the trier of fact was not compelled in this case to conclude that such a contract as contended for by appellants in fact existed. When the testimony of Mr. McKinney is considered, however, it clearly affords material evidence to support the conclusions of the trial court that no such contract was ever made.

Appellants contend that the testimony of Mr. McKinney as to the intention of Mr. and Mrs. Gilliam is inadmissible. In support of that proposition they cite Fisher v. Malmo, 650 S.W.2d 43, 45-46 (Tenn. App. 1983) and Nichols v. Todd, 20 Tenn. App. 564, 101 S.W.2d 486 (1936). Both of these cases hold that the draftsman of a will cannot express an opinion as to the intention of the testator with respect to the interpretation of legal terms such as "heirs."

Even if Mr. McKinney's testimony in the present case may have partly offended that rule, the bulk of it did not. Most of his testimony consisted of his general discussion of the law of wills and several possible dispositions with the parties on February 1, 1974, and his testimony that they expressly disclaimed to him any contractual restrictions upon the survivor when they executed their wills on February 22 which contain no such restrictions.

The judgments of the courts below that the surviving spouse received the estate free of any contractual restrictions are affirmed.

The 1977-78 Statutes. The Court has been furnished excellent briefs by the parties in this case and has been greatly assisted by the able oral argument presented on both sides. The briefs of the parties refer to the numerous cases in Tennessee on the subject of joint wills and of mutual and reciprocal wills.

Probably because of the large body of case law in this state dealing with the subject, the General Assembly has enacted statutes rather rigidly prescribing the requirements of a contract to make a will, not to revoke a will or to die intestate. The first of the statutes was 1977 Tenn. Public Acts, chapter 88, which provided that contracts of this nature might be established in certain ways. This statute was replaced by 1978 Tenn. Public Acts, chapter 745, now codified as T.C.A. § 32-3-107, providing that such contracts can be established only by:

> (1) Provisions of a will stating material provisions of the contract;
> (2) An express reference in a will to a contract and extrinsic evidence proving the terms of the contract; or
> (3) A writing signed by the decedent evidencing the contract.
> (b) The execution of a joint will or mutual wills does not create a presumption of a contract to make a will, or to refrain from revoking a will.

The latter statute . . . is patterned after a model which has been enacted in a number of states. Unlike the provisions in most states, however, this statute contains no provision limiting its effect to wills executed on or after its effective date.

For this reason, counsel for appellees has insisted that the statute should be deemed retroactive and should apply to contracts to make wills entered into before its effective date. It is clear that the 1978 statute is more restrictive than that which was first enacted in 1977. If the 1978 provisions should be applicable to any alleged contract between Mr. and Mrs. Gilliam made in 1974, it is obvious that no contract meeting its requirements has been established.

While the omission from the Tennessee statutes of a provision contained in a model code could have some significance, in our opinion, the 1978 statute, which is the only one remaining in effect, should not be construed as applying retroactively. It prescribes exclusive methods by which a contract to make a will, to revoke a will or to die intestate may be established. There is some authority in other states that such statutes can be given retroactive effect without offending constitutional prohibitions against the impairment of contracts. Appellees particularly cite and rely upon the case of Floerchinger v. Williams, 260 Iowa 53, 148 N.W.2d 410 (1967).

The provisions of the Iowa statute are not the same as those of the Tennessee statute under consideration. Regardless of whether any constitutional limitations may be involved, it is our opinion that the General Assembly did not intend for the 1978 statute to be retroactive. The Legislature replaced a 1977 statute which was merely directory or permissive, prescribing certain ways in which such contracts "may be established." These provisions were replaced by the more stringent terms of the 1978 statute quoted above, to the effect that such contracts "can be established only" in certain prescribed ways.

The 1977 statute did not purport to be exclusive in its terms. The provisions of the 1978 statute were exclusive and mandatory. In our opinion, the rights of parties, contingent or otherwise, which might have come into existence prior to the adoption of the 1978 statute should not be deemed to be affected thereby, and we decline to give retroactive effect to that statute as requested by counsel for appellees.

The judgments of the courts below are affirmed at the cost of appellants. The cause will be remanded to the trial court for collection of costs accrued there and for any other proceedings which may be necessary.

FONES, COOPER, DROWOTA and O'BRIEN, JJ., concur.

Notes and Questions

1. *Proving a Contract Not to Revoke.* Exactly what did the court in *Junot* require the plaintiff to prove in order to establish that a mutual will is subject to a contract not to revoke? Compare the following statement from Wiemers v. Wiemers, 663 S.W.2d 25, 29-30 (Tex. Ct. App. 1983):

> In order to prevail the party asserting a binding contract must prove more than a mere agreement to make reciprocal wills. . . . The agreement must involve the assumption of an obligation to dispose of the property as therein provided, or not to revoke such will, which is to remain in force at the death of the testators.

The majority of decisions hold that contracts not to revoke must be proven by clear and convincing evidence and that the existence of mutual wills does not create a presumption of a contract.

Why are courts typically reluctant to find that mutual wills are subject to contracts not to revoke? Consider the following statement:

> The clear weight of authority, and certainly the sounder view, is that the mere presence of either joint or mutual wills does not raise any presumption that they were executed in pursuance of a contract. Nor is this rule altered by evidence that the parties had "agreed" to the making of such wills. Of course they had so agreed. The mere presence of such wills reveals that the parties must have talked the matter over and must have arrived at an understanding or agreement concerning their testamentary dispositions. Such discussions and such understandings between persons of close affinities, especially between husbands and wives, are not unusual and the fact that they have taken place is no indication that there has been any thought of a binding contract. . . .
>
> It is quite apparent that [the] cases which are contrary to the general rule stated above result from a confusion of evidence of an understanding or a common plan with evidence of a contract. This confusion has resulted in the finding of some contracts on extremely slender evidence and in the occasional suggestion that the presence of reciprocal provisions is sufficient without more to prove the contractual relationship.

B. Sparks, Contracts to Make Wills 27-28, 30 (1956).

2. *Presumptions.* Courts have disagreed on whether a *joint* will with reciprocal provisions is sufficient evidence of a contract. In a few decisions, joint and mutual wills have been *conclusively* presumed contractual. E.g., Estate of Knight v. Knight, 178 Ill. App. 3d 777, 533 N.E.2d 949 (1989) ("The provisions of a valid joint and mutual will become irrevocable upon the death of one of the testators and the survivor may not dispose of the property other than as contemplated in the will."); Rauch v. Rauch, 112 Ill. App. 3d 198, 445 N.E.2d 77 (1983) ("A joint and mutual will must be executed pursuant to a contract between the testators."); Fiew v. Qualtrough, 624 S.W.2d 335 (Tex. Ct. App. 1981) (court applied the established Texas rule that a joint and mutual will is binding on the testators); Estate of Chayka, 40 Wis. 2d 715, 162 N.W.2d 632 (1968) (joint and mutual wills are conclusively presumed contractual, in order that "the legal consequences of executing [such wills] remain clear, fixed and predictable.").[1]

That a joint will with reciprocal provisions is *rebuttably* presumed contractual is the rule adopted by some courts (see, e.g., Glass v. Battista, 43 N.Y.2d 620, 403 N.Y.S.2d 204, 374 N.E.2d 116 (1978)), while other courts reject that idea.

A few cases have extended the inference of a contract to *mutual* wills that are not joint. See, e.g., Hoff v. Armbruster, 125 Colo. 198, 242 P.2d 604 (1952) (overridden by Colo. Rev. Stat. § 153-5-41).

3. *Revocable Trusts.* Do the will-contract principles followed in a jurisdiction, particularly the presumptions, if any, arising from joint or mutual wills, apply to revocable and amendable trusts containing reciprocal provisions? Compare Reznik v. McKee, 216 Kan. 659, 534 P.2d 243 (1975) (holding that they do), with Northern Trust Co. v. Tarre, 86 Ill. 2d 441, 427 N.E.2d 1217 (1981) (holding that they do not).

4. *Statutory Requirements.* The 1978 Tennessee statute held inapplicable in *Junot* is virtually identical to 1990 UPC section 2-514.[2] Its purpose is to reduce the likelihood of litigation in circumstances like that in *Junot* by requiring that all will contracts be reduced to writing.

In the absence of a statute specifically directed at will contracts, most courts have held that the general provision of the Statute of Frauds requiring a writing for contracts for the sale of land applies to contracts to devise *land*. They have further held that the same statutory provision extends to contracts to devise both land and personal property on the theory that these contracts are indivisible. (The provision of the Statute of Frauds relating to contracts not to be performed within one year is held inapplicable to will contracts.)

---

1. As to non-joint wills, Wisconsin legislation provides:

> *Wis. Stat. Ann. § 238.19.* No will shall be construed as contractual unless such fact affirmatively appears in express language on the face of the instrument. This section shall not apply to joint wills which exist as a single document.

2. Section 2-514 appeared without substantial amendment in the pre-1990 UPC as § 2-701.

When the Statute of Frauds does apply and is raised as a defense to the enforcement of an oral will contract, the defense is often unsuccessful *in cases involving joint or mutual wills*.[3] The familiar judicial techniques for avoiding the Statute of Frauds in other contexts may also be available in will-contract litigation. The most important of these theories for taking the case out of the Statute of Frauds are part performance and estoppel. See, e.g., Redke v. Silvertrust, 6 Cal. 3d 94, 98 Cal. Rptr. 293, 490 P.2d 805 (1971); Notten v. Mensing, 3 Cal. 2d 469, 473-74, 45 P.2d 198, 200-01 (1935).

Could a court justifiably adopt either theory to avoid UPC section 2-514?

Shimp v. Huff
315 Md. 624, 556 A.2d 252 (1989)

MURPHY, C. J. . . . In the present case, the issue is whether Lester Shimp's second wife, upon his death, is entitled to receive an elective share and a family allowance under Maryland Code (1974, 1988 Cum.Supp.) § 3-203 and § 3-201 of the Estates and Trusts Article when Lester had previously contracted, by virtue of a joint will with his first wife, to will his entire estate to others.

Section 3-203 . . . provides that "[i]nstead of property left to him by will, the surviving spouse may elect to take a one-third share of the net estate if there is also a surviving issue, or a one-half share of the net estate if there is no surviving issue." As to the family allowance, § 3-201 provides in part, that a surviving spouse is entitled to "an allowance of $2000 for his personal use."

Lester Shimp married his first wife, Clara, in 1941. At the time of their marriage, neither Lester nor Clara possessed any property of consequence. Subsequently, in 1954, they acquired a farm which they sold in 1973; thereafter they bought a home. Lester and Clara took title to both the farm and the home as tenants by the entireties.

On May 8, 1974, in Washington County, the couple executed an instrument titled "Last Will and Testament of Clara V. Shimp and Lester Shimp." It stated in relevant part:

WE, CLARA V. SHIMP AND LESTER SHIMP, of Washington County, Maryland, being of sound and disposing mind, memory and understanding, and capable of making a valid deed and contract, do make, publish and declare this to be our Last Will and Testament, hereby revoking all other Wills and Codicils by each of us made.

---

3. As we shall see in Green v. Richmond, infra p. 534, the Statute of Frauds is a more formidable obstacle in cases of attempted enforcement of an oral promise by the decedent to devise part or all of her or his property in exchange for services rendered to the decedent during life.

After the payment of all just debts and funeral expenses, we dispose of our estate and property as follows:

ITEM I. A. MUTUAL BEQUEST—We mutually give to whichever of us shall be the survivor the entire estate of which we may respectfully own at our death.

B. SURVIVOR'S BEQUEST—The survivor of us gives the entire estate of his or her property which he or she may own at death as follows:

1) Unto James Shimp, if he is living at the death of the survivor of us, the sum of One Thousand ($1,000.00) Dollars.

2) Unto Emma Plotner, if living at the death of the survivor of us, the sum of One Thousand ($1,000.00) Dollars.

3) Unto Mary Virginia Huff and Betty Jane Moats all household goods and machinery to do with as they desire. This bequest is made unto them due to the care that they have given us.

4) All of the rest and residue of the estate of the survivor is hereby devised unto Mary Virginia Huff, Betty Jane Moats, Paul R. Mijanovich and Ruth C. Thomas to be divided equally among them. In the event of the death of any of said persons, their children shall inherit the share to which the parent would have been entitled, if living. . . .

ITEM III. We, the Testators, do hereby declare that it is our purpose to dispose of our property in accordance with a common plan. The reciprocal and other gifts made herein are in fulfillment of this purpose and in consideration of each of us waiving the right, during our joint lives, to alter, amend or revoke this Will in whole or in part, by Codicil or otherwise, without notice to the other, or under any circumstances after the death of the first of us to die. Unless mutually agreed upon, this Last Will and Testament is an irrevocable act and may not be changed.

Clara died in 1975 in Washington County. At the time of her death she did not own property solely in her name and possessed no probate estate. Lester did not offer the will for probate following his wife's death. He did, however, file a petition in the Circuit Court for Washington County seeking declaratory relief and requesting the right to execute a new last will and testament. The court found that the will was revocable, but that the contract under which the will was executed might be specifically enforced in equity or damages recovered upon it at law. Lester appealed to the Court of Special Appeals, and ultimately, by writ of certiorari, the case came before us.

In [Shimp v. Shimp, 287 Md. 372, 412 A.2d 228 (1980)], we found that the Shimps had executed their joint will pursuant to and in accordance with a valid, binding contract. We held that Lester was "entitled to a declaratory decree stating that he may revoke his will but that an enforceable contract was entered into between him and his wife. . . . [and that] [a]t his death it may be specifically enforced in equity or damages may be recovered upon it at law." Thereafter, Lester did not execute another will or otherwise disturb the testamentary plan set forth in the joint will.

On April 4, 1985, in Washington County, Lester married Lisa Mae; they remained married until his death on January 11, 1986. Lester was not survived by any children.

Following Lester's death, Clara and Lester's joint will was admitted to probate in Washington County. Mary Virginia Huff and Wallace R. Huff were appointed Personal Representatives of the Estate on January 30, 1986. Lisa Mae and Lester had not entered into any marital agreement waiving Lisa Mae's marital rights, and she sought payment of a family allowance and filed an election for her statutory share of Lester's estate. On June 4, 1986, the Personal Representatives declined to pay Lisa Mae either her family allowance or her elective share. On July 10, 1986, Lisa Mae filed suit for a declaratory judgment in the Circuit Court for Washington County, requesting that the court pass an order that she was entitled to both a family allowance and an elective share of Lester's estate.

The court (Corderman, J.) . . . found that because Lester, before his marriage to Lisa Mae, had entered into a binding contract to devise all of his estate, he was not seized of an estate of inheritance at the time of his second marriage, but rather was merely a trustee of that estate. Because a widow is entitled to no part of her husband's estate except that of which he dies seized or possessed, the court concluded that since Lester was merely a trustee for the property, there was no estate from which Lisa Mae could take an elective share. Similarly, the court found that Lisa Mae could not claim a family allowance because there were no estate assets from which the allowance could be paid. Lisa Mae appealed to the Court of Special Appeals; we granted certiorari prior to a decision by that court to resolve the important issues raised in the case. . . .

While we have not previously addressed the issue of a surviving spouse's right to take an elective share in conflict with claims under a contract to convey by will, courts in other jurisdictions have examined the issue under varying factual situations.

In a number of these cases one spouse, after entering into a divorce or separation agreement which requires that spouse to leave part or all of the estate to the first spouse, remarries and then dies. In other cases, the decedent has contracted to make a will leaving property to children or other relatives. Still other cases have arisen where the decedent had remarried after entering into an agreement to will property in exchange for services, or for forbearance from legal action, or to facilitate an adoption. In some cases, the decedent has executed a will conforming to the contract, while in others he has breached the contract by executing a nonconforming will or by dying intestate.

The majority of these cases arise from the decedent having breached a contract to devise property by executing a nonconforming will or by dying intestate. In these cases, the claimants under the contract generally proceed on a theory of specific performance. While the rights of beneficiaries of a contract vest after the contract is made, nevertheless, where suit is brought for specific performance of the contract, "the after-acquired rights of third parties are equitable considerations to be regarded in adjudicating the questions." Owens [v. McNally, 113 Cal. 444, 45 P. 710 (1896)]. In determining whether to award specific performance to contract beneficiaries, courts have considered several different factors, including whether the surviving spouse had notice of the contract prior to the marriage, the length of the marriage and the natural affection shared between the decedent and the surviving spouse, whether the surviving spouse would be deprived of the entire estate by enforcement of the contract, and the public policy concerning the marriage relationship and the rights of surviving spouses. In a great many cases consideration of these factors has led the court to determine that the superior equities were with the surviving spouse, while in other cases it has not.

In those cases where the decedent has executed a will conforming to the contract, the claimants cannot seek specific performance, and courts, therefore, do not use equitable powers in resolving these cases. Instead, courts have analyzed the conflicting claims by characterizing the competing claimants as either creditors or legatees and evaluating their claims under the applicable priority rules. In a number of cases involving divorce settlements, the courts have found that where the decedent executes a will, which conforms to the terms of a contract, the beneficiaries take as legatees under the will and not as contract creditors. Consequently, because the applicable statutes give a higher priority to a surviving spouse's elective share than to testamentary bequests, the courts upheld the surviving spouse's claim over the claims of the contract beneficiaries. As the court explained in In Re Hoyt's Estate[, 174 Misc. 512, 21 N.Y.S.2d 107 (Sur. Ct. 1940)]

> . . . [we] hold that the claimants are not creditors under paragraph seventh of the separation agreement, but that the agreement merely created an enforceable obligation to make a testamentary provision for the benefit of the first wife of the testator and his children after her death. The testator performed that agreement. He undertook to do no more. The status of the claimants is therefore that of legatees or beneficiaries under the will. As such legatees or beneficiaries they take subject to the operation of the statutes relating to testamentary dispositions, including the right of the surviving widow to take her intestate share under Section 18 of the Decedent Estate Law. Their rights are also subordinate to all true creditors of the estate. The widow of the testator is therefore entitled to a one-third share of the net estate. The respective interests of the claimants as legatees or beneficiaries must be satisfied out of the balance. 21 N.Y.S.2d at 111.

At least one court, however, has suggested that analyzing the competing claims under the applicable priority statutes should be limited to cases involving divorce settlement agreements. In Rubenstein [v. Mueller, 19 N.Y.2d 228, 278 N.Y.S.2d 845, 225 N.E.2d 540 (1967)], which involved an ordinary contract to devise property rather than a separation agreement, the court distinguished those cases involving marital separation agreements, under which husbands covenanted to make a will, noting that different equitable considerations control in the two situations. The court explained:

> Separation agreements are usually attended by a present division of any jointly held property, and any provision for a future legacy is usually but an incident to the over-all settlement to be made with respect to the husband's individual property and his obligation of support. In the case of the joint will, however, this instrument typically represents the sole attempt by the signatories to effect

a distribution of their collective property in a fashion agreeable to both. Most importantly, in those separation agreements there was no irrevocable obligation concerning the collective property. The husband did not . . . become sole owner of jointly owned property by virtue of surviving the former wife. As the divorced husband's property after the agreement remains his own individual property, to which he holds beneficial as well as legal title, his widow's right of election may be asserted against such assets. 225 N.E.2d at 544, 278 N.Y.S.2d at 850.

Thus, the court suggests that in these cases whether the surviving spouse's claim is given priority does not depend upon whether the contract beneficiaries are characterized as contract creditors or legatees. Instead the court reasoned that this priority is based upon the decedent having held both the legal and beneficial title to the property completely independent of the first spouse as a result of the property division effectuated by the separation agreement—a division which does not occur when one spouse acquires rights in the property pursuant to a joint will.

Courts have cited other reasons for rejecting the practice of categorizing contract beneficiaries as legatees where the decedent has executed a conforming will. These courts acknowledge that technically the contract beneficiary becomes a creditor of the estate only after the decedent breaches the contract by dying intestate or executing a nonconforming will; and that where the decedent executes a conforming will the contract beneficiaries take as legatees under the will. Nevertheless, they note that this analysis leads to the anomalous result that the contract beneficiaries are in a better position where the decedent breaches the contract than where the decedent fully and properly performs in accordance with it. See In Re Erstein's Estate, supra, 129 N.Y.S.2d at 321 ("[i]t would be anomalous if the rights of the promisees would be substantially greater in the case of intestacy than they would be had the testator left a will which carried out his promise").

Other courts have suggested that the resolution of the conflict between the surviving spouse's rights and the rights of contract beneficiaries may be based upon public policy underlying wills statutes. Some courts have held that the right of election is personal to the surviving spouse and cannot be waived or otherwise defeated by the acts of the deceased spouse. . . .

Other courts have upheld the surviving spouse's right to claim an elective share over the claims of contract beneficiaries by relying upon the general principle that the right to will property is not absolute, but instead is a privilege afforded the decedent by the State. Under these cases, the State may impose limitations on that privilege, including the condition that all bequests are subject to the surviving spouse's right to claim an elective share. . . .

Other courts have relied upon the public policy surrounding the marriage relationship as the basis for upholding the surviving spouse's claim to an elective share over the claims of contract beneficiaries. . . . They characterize contracts which require a decedent to devise his entire estate to a third party as being contracts which might restrain or discourage marriage. Therefore, to prevent having these contracts declared void as against public policy, courts have construed the contract to imply that when entering into the agreement the parties contemplated that the testator might remarry. . . .

This case does not present a claim for specific performance because Lester performed his obligation under the contract and died leaving a will which conformed to the contract. Thus, we need not consider whether the superior equities lie with the Personal Representatives or with Lisa Mae.

Because Lester died leaving a will which conformed to the contract, we might consider drawing an analogy between the present case and the divorce cases, wherein courts found that where the decedent died leaving a conforming will, the contract beneficiaries were more properly characterized as legatees rather than contract creditors. Under this approach, we would find the respondents to be legatees under Lester's will whose interest in the estate, like the interest of any other legatee under any will, is subject to the abatement procedure outlined in § 3-208 of the Estates and Trusts Article.[4] Under this procedure Lisa Mae's elective share would have priority over the respondents' claims and their share of the estate would be abated. Nevertheless, we acknowledge . . . that this method of resolving the issue of priority leads to the anomalous result that the contract beneficiaries' rights would be greater where the contract is breached than where the testator performs in accordance with its terms. Consequently, we decline to adopt this theory as the controlling law in this case.

Instead, we find the question of priorities between a surviving spouse and beneficiaries under a contract to make a will should be resolved based upon the public policy which surrounds the marriage relationship and which underlies the elective share statute. . . . The Legislature on several occasions has limited [the right to make a will] by enacting restrictions such as those contained in § 3-203, which grants a surviving spouse the right to receive an elective share of a decedent's estate, regardless of the provisions contained in the decedent's will. In addition, § 3-204 suggests that the right to receive the elective share is a personal right, which cannot be waived by the unilateral acts of others, including the actions of the deceased spouse. These statutes and principles of law suggest that there is a strong public policy in favor of protecting the surviving spouse's right to receive an elective share. This Court on other occasions has recognized the strong public policy interest in protecting the surviving spouse's elective share from the unilateral acts of a deceased spouse. For example, in a number of cases this Court has declared transfers in fraud of marital rights to be void. We have indicated that this doctrine also applies to transfers made prior to the marriage.

In addition to the public policy underlying these statutes, the public policy surrounding the marriage relationship also suggests that the surviving spouse's claim to an elective share should be afforded priority over the claims of beneficiaries of a contract to make a will. Like the majority of other courts, we have recognized the well settled principle that

---

4. Section 3-208(b) provides in relevant part that "[i]f there is an election to take an intestate share, contribution to the payment of it shall be prorated among all legatees."

contracts which discourage or restrain the right to marry are void as against public policy. In executing a will, a testator is presumed to know that a spouse might renounce the will, thus extinguishing or reducing legacies contained in the will, and if the testator does not provide for this contingency then the beneficiaries under the will might lose the property left them. Thus, we find that the respondents' rights under the contract were limited by the possibility that the survivor might remarry and that the subsequent spouse might elect against the will. Consequently, we conclude that their claims under the contract are subordinate to Lisa Mae's superior right to receive her elective share.

Finally, we address the issue of whether Lisa Mae is entitled to a $2000 family allowance under § 3-201. . . .

The respondents' claim upon the estate of Lester Shimp must be characterized as being either that of a general creditor or of a legatee under the will. Under § 8-105, the family allowance receives priority over the claims of both contract creditors and legatees. Therefore, while the respondents' claim is more properly characterized as being that of a legatee, rather than that of a creditor, regardless of which characterization is used, Lisa Mae's claim for a family allowance takes precedence over the respondents' claim. Therefore, Lisa Mae is entitled to receive the family allowance provided for in § 3-201. . . .

JUDGMENT VACATED; CASE REMANDED TO THE CIRCUIT COURT FOR WASHINGTON COUNTY FOR ENTRY OF A DECLARATORY JUDGMENT CONSISTENT WITH THIS OPINION. COSTS TO BE PAID BY THE APPELLEES.

Notes and Questions

1. *1990 Uniform Probate Code.* How would *Shimp* be resolved if it were governed by the 1990 UPC? Had Lester's will not been contractual, what elective-share rights would Lisa Mae have under section 2-201? Would Lisa Mae have any rights to an intestate share under section 2-301? Would Lester's will be found contractual under section 2-514? If so, how would the contractual nature of the will affect Lisa Mae's rights under sections 2-201 and 2-301?

2. *Theories Supporting the Contract Beneficiaries.* Quite a number of courts have held for the contract beneficiaries rather than for the surviving spouse in cases like *Shimp*. In Rubenstein v. Mueller, for example, cited in *Shimp*, the New York Court of Appeals held that the decedent's second spouse had no right to an elective share in the decedent's assets covered by a will contract entered into with his prior, deceased spouse. The reason given was that the will contract transformed the ownership interest in those assets into a life estate in the decedent and a remainder interest in the contract beneficiaries. Other courts have held for the contract beneficiaries on the similar theory that the surviving spouse's statutory rights attach only to assets equitably as well as legally owned by the decedent and that equitably owned assets do not include assets that the decedent received

under a will executed pursuant to a will contract, since a court will impress those assets with a constructive trust for the contract beneficiaries. See, e.g., Estate of Stewart, 69 Cal. 2d 296, 70 Cal. Rptr. 545, 444 P.2d 337 (1968); Bever v. Bever, 364 S.E.2d 34 (W. Va. 1987). Another theory is that breach of the will contract places the contract beneficiary in the position of a creditor and that creditors' rights are superior to the surviving spouse's elective-share right. See, e.g., Estate of Beeruk, 429 Pa. 415, 241 A.2d 755 (1968).

3. *Enforcement of Contractual Wills and Remedies for Breach.* Apart from competing claims of a surviving spouse, most cases brought to enforce a will contract arise because the survivor has breached the contract by making a new will revoking the contractual will. Courts sometimes say that the contractual will became irrevocable. The logical implication of this is that the contractual will is entitled to probate despite the decedent's later attempt to revoke it. Occasionally this is what courts have done. See, e.g., Walker v. Yarbrough, 200 Ala. 458, 76 So. 390 (1917); Helms v. Darmstatter, 34 Ill. 2d 295, 215 N.E.2d 245 (1966) (joint will). But this result conflicts with the long-accepted view that a will is always revocable. In most cases, then, the contract is enforced not by probating the contractual will, but rather through a subsequent proceeding for breach of contract. See, e.g., Estate of Chapman, 239 N.W.2d 869 (Iowa 1976).

This two-step process for enforcing will contracts, probate of the subsequent will followed by a proceeding on the contract, indicates the separate relationship between the contract and the will. The breach-of-contract proceeding may be one at law for damages or in equity for specific performance or a constructive trust. The usual remedy is a constructive trust upon the property passing in violation of the contract.

4. *Survivor's Rights to Consume or Make Gifts.* To what extent is the survivor free to consume or give away during her or his lifetime property that is subject to a will contract? To prevent the survivor from breaching an obligation under a will contract, courts have held that inter-vivos gifts by the survivor of substantial portions of the property can be set aside. See, e.g., Lawrence v. Ashba, 115 Ind. App. 485, 59 N.E.2d 568 (1945); Schwartz v. Horn, 31 N.Y.2d 275, 388 N.Y.S.2d 613, 290 N.E.2d 816 (1972); Estate of Chayka, 47 Wis. 2d 102, 176 N.W.2d 561 (1970). Some courts have analyzed the question under a reasonableness requirement. Under this approach, the survivor is free to make "reasonable gifts"; the question is said to be "one of degree, and depends upon the proportion that the value of the gift bears to the amount of the donor's estate." Dickinson v. Seaman, 193 N.Y. 18, 85 N.E. 818 (1908). Other courts have held that, since the will contract converts the survivor's estate to a life estate, a deed purporting to convey a fee effectively transfers only a life estate for the survivor's life. See, e.g., First United Presbyterian Church v. Christenson, 64 Ill. 2d 491, 356 N.E.2d 532 (1976). It has also been held that the survivor may set aside gifts made by the first to die that are in breach of the will contract. See, e.g., Conitz v. Walker, 168 Mont. 238, 541 P.2d 1028 (1975). Is the survivor protected against testamentary gifts contrary to the contract?

See Duhme v. Duhme, 260 N.W.2d 415 (Iowa 1977); Note, 48 Calif. L. Rev. 858, 862-63 (1960).

5. *What Property Is Covered by a Will Contract?* Questions frequently arise concerning whether a will contract covers property that the survivor acquired after the death of the first to die. Suppose that H died in 1950, survived by W. The value of H's estate, which passed to W pursuant to a contractual will, was $5,000. After H's death, W inherited real estate from a deceased friend, and acquired other property. W left a will devising $5,000 to the beneficiaries of the will contract, but left the remaining portion of her property to others. The terms of the will contract, however, bound the survivor as to "all the property . . . that the survivor may die seized and possessed of." Under these circumstances, courts have held that this language covered the after-acquired property. See, e.g., Wallace v. Turriff, 531 S.W.2d 692 (Tex. Civ. App. 1975); Estate of Jud, 238 Kan. 268, 710 P.2d 1241 (1985).

A similar problem concerns post-death appreciation. Suppose, for example, that when H died in 1948, the value of the combined estates of H and W was approximately $60,000 and that at the time of W's death in 1969, it had grown to over $200,000. Courts have interpreted the contract as covering the entire estate as it existed at W's death. See, e.g., Matter of Wiggins, 45 A.D.2d 604, 360 N.Y.S.2d 129 (1974), aff'd per curiam, 39 N.Y.2d 79, 385 N.Y.S.2d 287, 350 N.E.2d 618 (1976).

6. *Lapse.* Suppose that a contract beneficiary predeceases the surviving contracting party. How should the survivor's estate be distributed? Most courts have held that the contract beneficiary's rights vest upon the death of first of the contracting parties to die. The property covered by the will contract passes through the beneficiary's estate rather than under the otherwise applicable antilapse statute. See, e.g., Rauch v. Rauch, 112 Ill. App. 3d 198, 445 N.E.2d 77 (1983); Estate of Maloney v. Carsten, 178 Ind. App. 191, 381 N.E.2d 1263 (1978); Estate of Duncan, 7 Kan. App. 2d 196, 638 P.2d 992 (1982); Jones v. Jones, 692 S.W.2d 406 (Mo. Ct. App. 1985); Fiew v. Qualtrough, 624 S.W.2d 335 (Tex. Ct. App. 1981). Contra, e.g., Estate of Arends, 311 N.W.2d 686 (Iowa Ct. App. 1981). What theory or theories support the majority view? In this connection, consider the effect of the various approaches to the question of the surviving spouse's elective share. Professor Roberts argues that the majority view that "a beneficiary need not survive when there is a contract not to revoke [can be] intent-defeating." "[T]he lapse rule," she argues, "should still apply [, invoking the antilapse statute,] if applicable. To the extent that [anti]lapse statutes effectuate intent, they would do so in this context as well." Roberts, Lapse Statutes: Recurring Construction Problems, 37 Emory L.J. 323, 384-93 (1988).

7. *Tax Consequences.* Married couples who have children by prior marriages may want special assurance that their property will be split between the two families when the survivor dies. The desirability of using contractual wills for this purpose may be greatly affected by tax consequences. The

cost of using a contract not to revoke may be the loss of the estate-tax marital deduction.[5]

An alternative device, at least for assuring the decedent's control over the disposition of her or his property on the survivor's death, is to devise a life estate (or, more likely, an income interest for life in a trust) to the surviving spouse, coupled with a remainder interest in favor of beneficiaries selected by the decedent. Until the early 1980s, this device suffered the same tax disadvantage—the loss of the estate tax marital deduction. The Economic Recovery Tax Act of 1981, however, amended the Internal Revenue Code so that the life estate/remainder combination, called a "QTIP," can now qualify for the estate tax marital deduction, provided that certain technical requirements are satisfied. See supra Chapter 6. The allowance of a favorable tax consequence for the life estate/remainder combination has made it a more attractive device for controlling the disposition of the decedent's property on the surviving spouse's death than the contract not to revoke. This device, however, does not control after-acquired property.

8. *Planning and Drafting.* Couples who use joint or mutual wills should insert in their wills language clearly indicating whether or not they have contractually bound themselves not to revoke. If the parties *do* want to be contractually bound not to revoke, the contract should be reduced to writing and should spell out what property is covered and the survivor's powers with respect to making gifts.

In preparing this contract, can one lawyer ethically represent both parties, or must each party engage a lawyer? See ABA Model Rules of Professional Conduct, Rules 1.7, 2.1 (1983); Report, Developments Regarding the Professional Responsibility of the Estate Planning Lawyer: The Effect of the Model Rules of Professional Conduct, 22 Real Prop. Prob. & Tr. J. 1, 10-23 (1987). Cf. Whitney v. Seattle-First Nat'l Bank, 16 Wash. App. 905, 560 P.2d 360 (1977); Bank of New York v. United States, 526 F.2d 1012 (3d Cir. 1975).

EXTERNAL REFERENCE: Annot., 85 A.L.R.4th 418 (1991).

---

5. E.g., Estate of Opal v. Commissioner, 450 F.2d 1085 (2d Cir. 1971); Estate of Krampf v. Commissioner, 56 T.C. 293 (1972); Estate of Siegel v. Commissioner, 67 T.C. 662 (1977). The disallowance of the marital deduction applies only to property passing under the decedent's will. Property passing outside of probate—for example, joint tenancy property and life insurance proceeds—can qualify for the estate tax marital deduction even though the surviving spouse is under a contractual obligation as to how this property is to be disposed of on the surviving spouse's death. Rev. Rul. 71-51, 1971-1 Cum. Bull. 274. See also Tech. Adv. Mem. 91-01-002. The tax consequences are discussed in Dobris, Do Contractual Will Arrangements Qualify for Qualified Terminable Interest Treatment Under ERTA, 19 Real Prop. Prob. & Tr. J. 625 (1984); Hess, The Federal Transfer Tax Consequences of Joint and Mutual Wills, 24 Real Prop. Prob. & Tr. J. 469 (1990).

PART B. CONTRACTS TO DEVISE

Claims that a decedent promise to devise property in return for certain services arise in a variety of contexts. In many states the Statute of Frauds prevents enforcement of oral promises to devise either in an action at law for breach of contract damages or in equity for specific performance. Despite non-enforceability of an oral contract to devise, though, the disappointed promisee may bring an action in quantum meruit to recover from the promisor's estate the value of any benefit for services rendered to the promisor.

Green v. Richmond
369 Mass. 47, 337 N.E.2d 691 (1975)

HENNESSEY, J. This is an appeal by the defendant from a judgment rendered against him as the personal representative of the estate of Maxwell Evans Richmond (the decedent). The action was in the nature of quantum meruit and sought recovery for services rendered by the plaintiff in reliance on the decedent's oral promise to leave a will bequeathing his entire estate to her.

A jury trial in the Superior Court resulted in a verdict for the plaintiff in the amount of $1,350,000. . . .

The facts are as follows: The plaintiff testified that she met the decedent in November, 1962, and shortly thereafter accepted his proposal of marriage. She was thirty-six years of age at the time, divorced, and had a fifteen-year old son; she was then employed as a secretary. The decedent was a wealthy, forty-nine year old bachelor whose holdings included licenses to operate three radio stations. Later the plaintiff became a stockbroker, earning about $20,000 a year.

About a year after they met, in October, 1963, the decedent stated that he had a "mental hangup" about marriage and asked to be released from the engagement; he said, however, that if the plaintiff would agree to "stay" with him, he would bequeath his entire estate to her at his death. The plaintiff agreed. There was other evidence directly corroborating the agreement. During the eight-year period between October, 1963, when bargain was made, and October, 1971, when the decedent died, there was evidence that the decedent, on several occasions, made statements to the plaintiff and other persons which could be found to be an acknowledgment by him of the original agreement. The last such occasion was on July 26, 1971, about three months before his death.

There was also evidence from which it could be found that the plaintiff kept her part of the agreement in reliance on the decedent's promise. There was detailed evidence of many services, of a social and domestic as well as of a business nature, performed by the plaintiff for the decedent over the eight-year period. There was evidence of many instances of sexual intercourse between the plaintiff and the decedent. The decedent died in

October, 1971. The inventory value of his estate, which the judge permitted to be shown in evidence, was approximately $7,232,000.

It is clear that the oral agreement involved a promise to make a will, and as such was not binding. G.L. c. 259, § 5. Nevertheless, if the oral agreement were legal and not contrary to public policy, the plaintiff could recover the fair value of her services.

We consider first the defendant's argument that a verdict should have been directed in his favor on the ground that the contract was illegal. The argument offered is that as matter of law the agreement included sexual intercourse or cohabitation as part of the consideration, and that such a contract will not be enforced as against public policy. Further, the argument is that even if the agreement did not expressly include illicit terms, the unlawful performance of the bargain precludes recovery. We conclude that there was no error in the denial of a directed verdict because these issues were properly submitted to the jury under appropriate instructions, and the jury obviously reached conclusions favorable to the plaintiff.[6]

The defendant . . . argues that sexual intercourse was within the scope of the agreement and that the plaintiff therefore can recover nothing for her services; that additionally, or in the alternative, the plaintiff's performance in an illegal manner, by indulging in sexual intercourse, entitles her to no compensation, since her illegal performance was serious and not merely incidental to the agreement; that the illegality of the agreement and the illegality of the performance thereof were established as matter of law by the plaintiff's admissions on the witness stand at the trial, which the defendant argues were binding on her since there was no other evidence more favorable to her as to these issues; and that a directed verdict for the defendant was therefore required. . . .

The judge, in denying the defendant's motion for a directed verdict, submitted to the jury the issue of illegality, both as to the content of the agreement and the nature of the plaintiff's performance. There was no error. . . . Where the evidence is disputed as to the terms or performance of an oral agreement, or the meaning of words used by the parties, the matter should be left to the jury. In this case there was disputed evidence, some of which was sufficiently favorable to the plaintiff to warrant submission of the issues to the jury.

Thus, the plaintiff's testimony as to the terms of the contract contained no reference to sexual intercourse as follows, viz.;

> He said he couldn't lose me, either, and then he said, "I have been thinking about something, and I want you to listen to me." He said: "I have been looking for you all my life. You're the perfect woman for me." He said: "If you will agree to stay with me without marriage, you will be happy. I will see that your life will be happy. There's only one thing you won't have. You won't

---

6. It could persuasively be argued that only naive persons would conclude that sexual intercourse was not central to the arrangement between the parties. Nevertheless that reasoning is not relevant, since the evidence as summarized, infra, warranted the submission of the issues to the jury.

have the emotional security a woman has when she knows she is married, but I will make it up to you. I am going to make my will out right away. Everything I have when I die will be yours. I owe nothing to anyone else."

The defendant contends, however, that other evidence particularly admissions by the plaintiff, required a conclusion that the contract included an agreement for sexual intercourse. The plaintiff had testified of many instances of sexual relations with the decedent. However, on this issue as well as on the related issue of illegality of performance, there was other evidence, including other testimony from the plaintiff, which was more favorable to the plaintiff. Therefore the issue was for the jury's consideration. From the totality of the evidence the jury were warranted in inferring that the illicit relations were no part of the contract, and were no more than an incidental part of the plaintiff's performance.

Thus, inferences favorable to the plaintiff were supported by the evidence. For example, the plaintiff testified that, throughout their relationship, she maintained her own apartment and paid all her own household bills; that the decedent bought her no expensive gifts, furs, cars, jewelry or diamonds and made no contribution to her son's tuition at college; that she did not even accompany him on his annual vacations, customarily taken at Christmastime, until 1966 or 1967, because she felt that she owed it to her son to be home with him during his Christmas vacations from school; and that the decedent, with the plaintiff's knowledge, took another woman with him when the plaintiff could not accompany him on his annual vacation.

Further, the witness Norman Solomon, who shared the decedent's apartment, testified that he never saw the plaintiff or any trace of her at the former residences of the decedent and that the decedent slept in his own apartment every night. The witness recalled only one time when he saw the plaintiff at the decedent's last residence. Solomon further testified that the decedent "traveled a lot with . . . (a certain woman)," both before and after 1962, and "they made many trips together." Solomon quoted the plaintiff as saying, on one occasion, that both she and the decedent were free to "see" whomever of the opposite sex they might want to see.

A female witness, the "certain woman" referred to, supra, called by the defendant, testified that she took trips with the decedent each year between 1954 and 1958, inclusive. During the summer of 1963, she stayed at the defendant's apartment for about ten days. In 1964, she went on a trip to Jamaica with the decedent. In 1965, she went to St. Thomas and Puerto Rico with him. In 1967, she spent a week in Bermuda with him and then spent the entire summer at his apartment in Boston. Over the 1968 New Year's holiday, she went on a thirteen-day cruise with the decedent and, later in that year, went to St. Thomas with him. In 1969, she spent about a week with him at his summer residence in Marblehead and, in November of that year, the two of them went together to Florida for a week.

From all of this evidence the jury were justified in concluding that the sexual aspect of the relationship between the plaintiff and the decedent was no part of the bargain between the two, and no more than incidental to their relationship.

The defendant also argues that if the inventory of the probate estate had been excluded from evidence, as the defendant contends that it should have been, there would have been no evidence before the jury as to the value of the plaintiff's services. For this additional reason, the defendant says, there should have been a directed verdict for the defendant. There is no merit to this contention. Of the many and varied services as to which the plaintiff presented evidence, at least some of them were of such a routine and ordinary nature as to make their fair value a matter of common knowledge for the jury's consideration.

It follows from all that we have said that there was no error in the judge's denial of the defendant's motion for a directed verdict.

2. We turn now to the second issue argued by the defendant, viz.: that it was error to admit in evidence, over the objection and exception of the defendant, the Probate Court inventory showing the value of the estate. Actually there are two related questions raised here: (1) whether evidence as to the value of the estate is admissible and (2) if such evidence is admissible whether the probate inventory is an appropriate form of proof.

We consider first the question of the admissibility of the value of the estate. There is a divergence of opinion in other jurisdictions on the issue whether evidence of the contract terms, including value bargained for, shall be admitted as evidence of the value of the services sought by an action in quantum meruit. This divergence also exists with respect to the narrower question before us, i.e., whether the value of the decedent's estate was properly admitted as evidence of the value of the services rendered by the plaintiff on the basis that the value of the estate is the "price" put on the services by one of the contracting parties. There is precedent in somewhat similar Massachusetts cases for the admission of such evidence and the judge here undoubtedly relied on those decisions in making his rulings. We conclude that those decisions are controlling in the instant case and that the value of the estate was admissible in evidence.

There is substantial authority both judicial and scholarly which favors admissibility. Professor Corbin is emphatic as to the admissibility of this evidence:

> No one doubts, however, that the contract price or rate agreed upon by the parties is admissible in evidence to show what is the reasonable value of the performance that the defendant has received.

Corbin, Contracts, § 1113 (1964). The annotation in 21 A.L.R.3d 9, 18 (1968) is further supportive of admissibility, noting that there is "considerable authority" for admitting the contract price terms as evidence of the value of the services, under the theory that it is an admission against interest and is evidence of the general making and performance of the contract. The annotation further cites authority for admitting the contract price terms although the contract is not enforceable as violative of the statute of frauds, in cases where the promise, as here, is to transfer an estate in consideration of services, and concludes that many courts have admitted the value of the estate in these cases. . . .

We conclude that in the instant case appropriate proof of the value of the decedent's estate was admissible in evidence, and should be admitted at any subsequent retrial of the case.[7] Much of the reasoning advanced in favor of a directed verdict should receive consideration by the judge as substance for cautionary instructions to the jury against misuse of the evidence.

3. We turn now to a consideration of whether the probate inventory was an appropriate form of proof of the value of the estate, and whether, if it was not, it was error to admit the inventory in evidence in this case. We conclude that it was error.

The asset value was shown on the inventory as approximately $7,232,000. We have no way of knowing whether this amount accurately, or even remotely, represents the net value of the estate. We take notice that taxes, debts and other appropriate charges will substantially reduce this gross value. We assume that the inventory amount shown had some basis in fact, but the value of an estate is not shown by a list of its assets alone. . . . [I]n the special circumstances of this case we conclude that a preliminary showing of reliability was required before the amount of the inventory, which may or may not have been reflective of the value of the estate, was disclosed to the jury. . . .

We conclude, therefore, that the judgment should be reversed and the case remanded to the Superior Court for a new trial limited to the issue of damages.

So ordered.

Notes and Questions

1. *Enforceability of the Contract.* If Maxwell Evans had made his promise to leave his entire estate to Bernyce Green in a signed letter to her, would she have been able to recover damages for breach of contract from his estate? Consider the following observations:

> Where there is a contract to devise or bequeath and the promisee fully performs on his part, if the promisor dies without fulfilling his obligation an ordinary action at law for breach of contract will lie. The action is for breach of contract by the deceased and should be brought against the personal representative in the same way as any other contract claim against the estate. The claim is assignable and may be enforced in the name of the assignee. Ordinarily the measure of damages will be the value of the thing promised by the promisor. Where the thing promised is a specific sum of money or a specific item of property the amount of damages is easily determined. If the promise is to give the entire estate or a fractional part thereof an action at law is hardly the appropriate remedy, but if that remedy is entertained the

---

7. An interesting issue has been suggested: As of what date should the value of the estate be shown? Is it the date of the agreement or the date of the death? In the instant case the issue is not pressed, presumably because there was evidence that the decedent renewed his promise just a few months before his death.

value of the thing promised is still the measure of damages. The difficulty here is with the remedy itself. Before the amount of damages can be fixed the net value of the estate must be ascertained. Since a jury is not a satisfactory body to supervise an estate accounting the law court should decline jurisdiction and transfer the case to equity where the parties will find a forum more adapted to their needs. . . .

Recovery in quantum meruit such as is described above should not be confused with an action for damages for breach of the contract where an entirely different measure of damages is demanded. However, recovery in quantum meruit cannot be had unless the contract, even though oral, is proved.

B. Sparks, Contracts to Make Wills 136-40 (1956).

2. *Quantum Meruit Recovery by Unmarried Cohabitors.* Even without an explicit oral promise to devise all or part of the estate in return for services, a surviving cohabitor may have a claim in quantum meruit against the other's estate for the value of services rendered the decedent in the expectation of compensation. See, e.g., Estate of Zent, 459 N.W.2d 795 (N.D. 1990); Suggs v. Norris, 364 S.E.2d 159 (N.C. Ct. App. 1988). See the discussion of unmarried cohabitors' recovery in quantum meruit, supra p. 115.

MISTAKE

Evidence suggesting that the terms of a will vary from actual intention is inherently suspect. This may be especially true when the heart of such evidence consists, as it often does, of testimony as to statements allegedly made by the testator—so-called direct declarations of intent. After death, the testator cannot corroborate or deny the correctness of such evidence. The main protection against fabricated or mistaken evidence is the will itself. After all, the will is a document that is executed in accordance with statutory formalities that have as their underlying purposes the protection of the testator against fraud and undue influence (the so-called protective function), the providing of reliable written evidence of intent (the evidentiary function), the protection of the testator against effectuation of casual or unconsidered declarations of intent (the cautionary function), and the assurance that documents executed in accordance with the prescribed formalities will control the devolution of the property on death (the channeling function).

And yet, it is far from impossible that evidence offered against a will's literal meaning is correct. Mistake in translating intention into legally effective language is a frequent occurrence. Clerical error and, sad to say, the incompetence of a few lawyers practicing in this area make mistakes a phenomenon that is not limited to self-drawn wills.

The dilemma of how the law should respond to allegations of mistake (and uncertainty about the meaning of language) is the subject of the materials in this chapter. Most of the cases deal with wills. A few, however, deal with nonprobate transfers, such as inter-vivos trusts. The first case we present, in fact, concerns the question whether a particular trust arrangement was to be treated as inter vivos or testamentary. The question was decisive to the outcome of the case because, as the opinion makes clear, the conventional view is that instruments effecting gratuitous inter-vivos transfers are reformable on a proper showing of mistake, but that wills cannot be reformed. In Brinker v. Wobaco Trust Ltd., the basic question arose in the context of a pour-over devise, which is a subject we took up supra Chapter 7.

EXTERNAL REFERENCES. Fellows, In Search of Donative Intent, 73 Iowa L. Rev. 611 (1988); Langbein & Waggoner, Reformation of Wills on the Ground of Mistake: Change of Direction in American Law?, 130 U. Pa. L. Rev. 521 (1982).

Brinker v. Wobaco Trust Ltd.
610 S.W.2d 160 (Tex. Civ. App. 1980)

[Norman and Maureen Brinker, husband and wife, had two children, Cynthia and Brenda. Before Maureen's death in 1969, Maureen and Norman established an inter-vivos trust, called the "Norman E. Brinker Family Trusts." The trust instrument named Norman as the "settlor" and named Maureen and a bank, collectively, as the "trustee." The trust was to be principally funded by the proceeds of life insurance on Norman's life, but since Norman was still living at the time of the lawsuit no such proceeds had yet become payable. Maureen's will, however, appointed Norman as trustee of her residuary estate and directed that after a certain period it should pour over into the inter-vivos trust, where it should "be held or disposed of in accordance with the provisions of Article IV" thereof. Article IV of the trust provided that income and ultimately principal be paid to "the issue of settlor." In 1970, after Maureen's death, Norman created two other, separate trusts for the benefit of Cynthia and Brenda. These trusts named Norman as "settlor," and provided that if the principal beneficiary dies without issue, the trust assets are to be paid to the "settlor's issue then living."

In 1971, Norman married Magrit; this marriage produced two children, Christina and Mark. In 1973, Norman conferred with his attorney and decided on a plan to bestow some of Maureen's residuary estate upon the children of this second marriage; to that end he transferred assets of Maureen's residuary estate to another trust he had set up through a banking corporation in the Bahamas. After his second marriage ended in divorce in 1977, Norman had second thoughts and told Cynthia and Brenda what he had done.

Cynthia and Brenda then brought suit to impose a constructive trust on the assets removed form Maureen's estate and to construe or reform the Norman E. Brinker Family Trusts and the two 1970 trusts. The suit asked that Christina and Mark, the children born of their father's second marriage, be excluded as beneficiaries of these trusts. In a bench trial, the court refused to admit evidence seeking to establish Norman's and Maureen's intention in creating the trusts or to show that in the drafting of the trust instruments a mistake had been made that would warrant reformation of the instruments to reflect the true intention.]

CORNELIUS, C.J. . . . On a bill of exceptions, appellants [Cynthia and Brenda] produced evidence that Maureen and Norman Brinker intended for the trusts to benefit only the issue born of their marriage to each other, and that if the term "issue of settlor" as used in the trust indentures meant the issue of Norman Brinker by any other union, a mistake had been made in the drafting of the trust indentures which warranted reformation of the instruments.

The evidence consisted of the testimony of Norman Brinker and Mr. Robert Taylor, a tax lawyer who prepared both the trust indentures and Maureen's will. The evidence may be generally summarized as follows: Mr. Brinker testified that he and Maureen primarily wanted to be certain that whatever assets went into the trust would go for the benefit of their two children at that time, i. e., Cynthia and Brenda. He said they knew Maureen could not have any other children and that they intended for the trust to be just for Cynthia and Brenda. He further testified that neither he nor Maureen was familiar with trusts or wills or legal terminology, and that they depended entirely on their lawyer to correctly put into the trust instruments what they wanted done; that neither he nor Maureen chose to use the word "settlor" or even knew what it meant; that the word was never mentioned or discussed with their lawyer or the bank; and that although they read the trust instruments before executing them they did not understand them, and in effect told their lawyer, "You are the lawyer; we don't understand this, did you do what we asked you to do?", and upon the lawyer's assurance that he had, they completed the transaction.

Mr. Taylor testified in detail. He testified that the Brinkers instructed him to prepare the family trust; in the discussion it was mentioned that Maureen could not have any more children; he understood that they wanted only Cynthia and Brenda to share in that trust; and that was the way he intended to draw the instruments and thought he had done so. When asked if either Norman or Maureen said anything about wanting to include children who might be born of other marriages, he answered "No, just the opposite", although he admitted that they did not specifically tell him to cut out all afterborn children. He further testified that if the trust indentures were written so as to include other children as beneficiaries, he had made a mistake in drafting the trust instruments.

Upon being questioned about Norman alone being named settlor, Mr. Taylor stated that he considered Maureen to be a co-settlor, and had intended to designate her as such in the same manner as he had designated her and the bank as co-trustee, and that was the reason he had her execute the trust indenture along with Norman. He also recalled that Maureen discussed with him the possible remarriage of her husband and that she shared "the normal concern of a wife that her husband, if something happened to her, might remarry and reiterated that she wanted her property to go to Cindy and Brenda."

On cross-examination appellees brought out concessions from Mr. Taylor that the trusts did benefit Cynthia and Brenda, which literally complied with the directions he received from Norman and Maureen, and that the Brinker Family Trust indenture did not contain typographical errors, but contained the actual words he dictated. On the suggestion that many corrections would be necessary to change the trust indenture to designate

Maureen as co-settlor, Mr. Taylor disagreed and said he intended to so designate her and then use the singular of the word "settlor" to refer to both Maureen and Norman as he had done with the singular word "trustee" to refer to Maureen and the bank. Other features of the drafting and signing of the trust indentures were pointed out which could be construed to impeach Mr. Taylor's testimony that a mistake in the drafting had been made.

The foregoing summary demonstrates that a fact issue was made on the question of mistake in the drafting of the trust indenture to correctly express the parties' intention. The evidence raising such issue should have been admitted on appellants' plea for reformation.

If, by mistake, an instrument as written fails to express the true intention or agreement of the parties, equity will grant reformation of the instrument so as to make it correctly express the agreement actually made. The rule applies to express inter vivos trusts as well as to other written instruments. The mistake may be shown by parol evidence. And although a mutual mistake of the parties is required in most instances, if a settlor of a trust receives no consideration for the creation of the trust, a unilateral mistake on his part is sufficient. It is immaterial whether the mistake be one of fact or law. Any mistake of the scrivener which could defeat the true intention may be corrected in equity by reformation, whether the mistake is one of fact or law. The fact that the written instrument is couched in unambiguous language, or that the parties knew what words were used and were aware of their ordinary meaning, or that they were negligent in failing to discover the mistake before signing the instrument, will not preclude relief by reformation. . . .

Appellees contend, however, that because the residuary trust in Mrs. Brinker's will eventually will pour over into the Brinker Family Trust, and Mrs. Brinker's will has now been probated, the Brinker Family Trust, so far as the pour over assets are concerned, has become testamentary and consequently it cannot be reformed. We disagree.

It is true that a testamentary disposition is not subject to reformation. But we hold that the Brinker Family Trust did not become testamentary by reason of Mrs. Brinker's residuary trust pour over.

Prior to the drafting of the Uniform Testamentary Additions to Trusts Act [supra p. 436], there were two legal doctrines concerning the validity and nature of testamentary additions to inter vivos trusts. One was the doctrine of incorporation by reference, which held that the terms of the inter vivos trust became incorporated into the will by reference and became a part of it, thus rendering the trust testamentary insofar as the gift was concerned. . . . The other was the doctrine of independent significance, which held that the trust did not become a part of the will, but that the testamentary bequest or devise simply was added to and augmented the trust corpus to be administered as a part of the trust according to its provisions. Under that doctrine the trust provisions concerning disposition of the gift did not become testamentary. . . . The Uniform Testamentary Additions to Trusts Act was designed to validate testamentary additions to trusts even though such trusts were amendable, and to prevent the trust provisions affecting such gift from becoming testamentary. The Act provides in part as follows:

> . . . the property so devised or bequeathed (a) *shall not be deemed to be held under a testamentary trust of the testator but shall become a part of the trust to which it is given and (b) shall be administered and disposed of in accordance with the provisions of the instrument* . . . setting forth the terms of the trust, ... (Emphasis supplied.)

Texas adopted the Uniform Act in 1961. . . . Although the Texas version does not specifically provide that such a gift will not be deemed to be held under a testamentary trust, in other respects it is essentially the same as the Uniform Act, and it specifically provides that the gift ". . . shall be added to the corpus of such trust to be administered as a part thereof and shall thereafter be governed by the terms and provisions of the instrument establishing such trust. . . ." We hold that the intention of the Texas Act was that the trust provisions would not become testamentary by reason of such a gift, but that the gift would simply augment the corpus of the trust and become a part of it.

Appellees assert that a reformation of the Family Trust would violate that portion of [the Texas version of the Uniform Act] which provides that a gift to a trust will be governed by the trust instrument *and any written amendments or modifications made before the death of the testator.* It is argued that to reform the Family Trust would be the equivalent of amending or modifying it after the death of Maureen Brinker. We cannot agree.

To amend or modify an agreement means to change it. . . . Reformation does not change the agreement; it enforces the agreement. It orders a change in the drafted instrument so that it will correctly express what has been the real agreement from its inception.

The excluded evidence on the issue of reformation is before us in the bill of exceptions, but as indicated in our summary of that evidence it is not so conclusive that it determines the issue as a matter of law and allows us to render a judgment. There is positive evidence of mistake; yet there are circumstances which bear upon the credibility and accuracy of the testimony which might lead reasonable minds to reject it. A fact issue has been created which requires resolution by a trier of fact. The judgment will therefore be reversed and remanded for a new trial.

Note

As *Wobaco* indicates, with respect to inter-vivos instruments courts have been willing to use their equity powers to correct any mistake of the scrivener that could defeat the true intention of the transferor. A case of well-proven mistake—clear and convincing evidence is the standard used—invokes a fundamental principle of the law of restitution: preventing unjust enrichment. If the mistake is not corrected, the mistaken beneficiary is unjustly enriched at the expense of the intended beneficiary.

The *Wobaco* opinion also notes the conventional doctrine that courts do not reform wills. The following materials deal mainly with cases of mistaken wills. What do you suppose are the reasons for the traditional judicial refusal to entertain suits to reform wills?

PART A. CONVENTIONAL LAW

1. *Mistaken Descriptions of Persons or Property*

The No-Reformation Rule. The rule we call the "no-reformation" rule is sometimes known as the "plain-meaning" rule. When the meaning of words of the will is "plain," no deviation can be permitted. The following passage is a familiar statement of the no-reformation (plain-meaning) rule:

> Where there is nothing in the context of a will from which it is apparent that a testator has used the words in which he has expressed himself in any other than their strict and primary sense, and where his words so interpreted are sensible with reference to extrinsic circumstances, it is an inflexible rule of construction, that the words of the will shall be interpreted in their strict and primary sense, and in no other, although they may be capable of some popular or secondary interpretation, and although the most conclusive evidence of intention to use them in such popular or secondary sense be tendered.

J. Wigram, Admission of Extrinsic Evidence in Aid of Interpretation of Wills 18 (5th ed. 1914).

The No-Extrinsic-Evidence Rule. Closely linked to the no-reformation rule is another rule—the no-extrinsic-evidence rule. If equity will not entertain suits to reform wills, no purpose would be served by allowing the introduction of extrinsic evidence to contradict clear and unambiguous terms in a will.

Mahoney v. Grainger
283 Mass. 189, 186 N.E. 86 (1933)

Rugg, C.J. This is an appeal from a decree of a probate court denying a petition for distribution of a legacy under the will of Helen A. Sullivan among her first cousins who are contended to be her heirs at law. The residuary clause was as follows:

> All the rest and residue of my estate, both real and personal property, I give, demise [sic] and bequeath to my heirs at law living at the time of my decease, absolutely; to be divided among them equally, share and share alike;

provided, however, that the real property which I own at my decease shall not be sold or disposed of until five (5) years after my decease, unless there is not sufficient personal property at the time of my decease to pay my specific legatees; in which case said real property may be sold. The income from said real property during said five (5) years is to be distributed among my heirs at law as I have directed.

The trial judge made a report of the material facts in substance as follows: The sole heir at law of the testatrix at the time of her death was her maternal aunt, Frances Hawkes Greene, who is still living and who was named in the petition for probate of her will. The will was duly proved and allowed on October 8, 1931, and letters testamentary issued accordingly. The testatrix was a single woman about sixty-four years of age, and had been a school teacher. She always maintained her own home but her relations with her aunt who was her sole heir and with several first cousins were cordial and friendly. In her will she gave general legacies in considerable sums to two of her first cousins. About ten days before her death the testatrix sent for an attorney who found her sick but intelligent about the subjects of their conversation. She told the attorney she wanted to make a will. She gave him instructions as to general pecuniary legacies. In response to the questions "Whom do you want to leave the rest of your property to? Who are your nearest relations?" she replied "I've got about twenty-five first cousins . . . let them share it equally." The attorney then drafted the will and read it to the testatrix and it was executed by her.

The trial judge ruled that statements of the testatrix

> were admissible only in so far as they tended to give evidence of the material circumstances surrounding the testatrix at the time of the execution of the will; that the words heirs at law were words in common use, susceptible of application to one or many; that when applied to the special circumstances of this case that the testatrix had but one heir, notwithstanding the added words "to be divided among them equally, share and share alike," there was no latent ambiguity or equivocation in the will itself which would permit the introduction of the statements of the testatrix to prove her testamentary intention.

Certain first cousins have appealed from the decree dismissing the petition for distribution to them.

There is no doubt as to the meaning of the words "heirs at law living at the time of my decease" as used in the will. Confessedly they refer alone to the aunt of the testatrix and do not include her cousins.

A will duly executed and allowed by the court must under the statute of wills be accepted as the final expression of the intent of the person executing it. The fact that it was not in conformity to the instructions given to the draftsman who prepared it or that he made a mistake does not authorize a court to reform or alter it or remold it by amendments. The will must be construed as it came from the hands of the testatrix. Mistakes in the drafting of the will may be of significance in some circumstances in a trial as to the due execution and allowance of the alleged testamentary instrument. Proof that the legatee actually designated was not the particular person intended by the one executing the will cannot be received to aid in the interpretation of a will. When the instrument has been proved and allowed as a will oral testimony as to the meaning and purpose of a testator in using language must be rigidly excluded.

It is only where testamentary language is not clear in its application to facts that evidence may be introduced as to the circumstances under which the testator used that language in order to throw light upon its meaning. Where no doubt exists as to the property bequeathed or the identity of the beneficiary there is no room for extrinsic evidence; the will must stand as written.

In the case at bar there is no doubt as to the heirs at law of the testatrix. The aunt alone falls within that description. The cousins are excluded. The circumstance that the plural word 'heirs' was used does not prevent one individual from taking the entire gift.

Decree affirmed.

Note

Ambiguity as the Basis for Admitting Extrinsic Evidence. If, under conventional law, extrinsic evidence of intention cannot be introduced to contradict the "plain meaning" of the will, when *can* extrinsic evidence be introduced? The answer was given in *Mahoney,* when the court said:

> It is only where testamentary language is not clear in its application to facts that evidence may be introduced in order to throw light upon its meaning.

Extrinsic evidence is admissible, in other words, when there is an "ambiguity."

The next case, Arnheiter v. Arnheiter, illustrates the admissibility of extrinsic evidence in cases of ambiguity. It also introduces us to one of the remedial techniques employed in such cases—the deletion of the erroneous parts of a mistaken description, so that what is left accurately describes the testator's intention.

Arnheiter v. Arnheiter
42 N.J. Super. 71, 125 A.2d 914 (1956)

SULLIVAN, J.S.C. Burnette K. Guterl died on December 31, 1953, leaving a last will and testament which has been admitted to probate by the Surrogate of Essex County. By paragraph 2 of said will her executrix was directed "to sell my undivided one-half interest of premises known as No. 304 Harrison Avenue, Harrison, New Jersey," and use the proceeds of sale to establish trusts for each of decedent's two nieces.

This suit comes about because the decedent did not own or have any interest in 304 Harrison Avenue either at her death or at the time her will was executed. At the hearing it was established that the decedent, at the time her will was executed and also at the time of her death, owned an undivided one-half interest in 317 Harrison Avenue, Harrison, New Jersey, and that this was the only property on Harrison Avenue that she had any interest in.

Plaintiff-executrix has applied to this court to correct an obvious mistake and to change the street number in paragraph "2" of the will to read "No. 317 Harrison Avenue" instead of "No. 304 Harrison Avenue." Relief cannot be granted to the plaintiff in the precise manner sought. It matters not that an obvious mistake in the form of a misdescription is proved. A court has no power to correct or reform a will or change any of the language therein by substituting or adding words. The will of a decedent executed pursuant to statute is what it is and no court can add to it.

Plaintiff, however, is not without recourse. In the construction of wills and other instruments there is a principle *"falsa demonstratio non nocet"* (mere erroneous description does not vitiate), which applies directly to the difficulty at hand.

> Where a description of a thing or person consists of several particulars and all of them do not fit any one person or thing, less essential particulars may be rejected provided the remainder of the description clearly fits. This is known as the doctrine of falsa demonstratio non nocet. [Clapp, 5 N.J. Practice, section 114, page 274.]

A leading case involving the application of the above maxim to facts similar to our own is Patch v. White, 117 U.S. 210, 6 S.Ct. 617, 710, 29 L.Ed. 860 (1886). There, the testator bequeathed to his brother land which he described as belonging to himself and as containing improvements, the lot being "numbered six, in square four hundred and three." He did not own the lot so numbered but did own lot number 3, in square 406, which was improved. The lot numbered 6 in square 403 had no improvements. The court applied the principle of *falsa demonstratio non nocet,* and by disregarding or rejecting the words "six" and "three" in the description, concluded that the lot owned by the decedent passed to his brother under this provision of the will.

Turning to the problem at hand and to the description of the property as set forth in paragraph 2 of the will, we find the street number "304" to be erroneous because decedent did not own that property. If we disregard or reject that item of description, the will then directs the executrix "to sell my undivided one-half interest of premises known as Harrison Avenue, Harrison, New Jersey." Since it has been established that the decedent, at the time of her death and also when she executed her will, had an interest in only one piece of property on Harrison Avenue, Harrison, New Jersey; that her interest was an undivided one-half interest; that the property in question is 317 Harrison Avenue; and that decedent made no other specific provision in her will relating to 317 Harrison Avenue, we are led inevitably to the conclusion that even without a street number, the rest of the description in paragraph 2 of the will is sufficient to identify the property passing thereunder as 317 Harrison Avenue.

Judgment will be entered construing decedent's will as aforesaid.

Notes, Questions, and Problems

1. *Problems on Ambiguity.* Applying the conventional distinction between ambiguous and unambiguous descriptions of persons or property, would extrinsic evidence be admissible in the following cases? Could the misdescriptions be remedied by the technique employed in Arnheiter v. Arnheiter and Patch v. White?

(a) Nathaniel Tucker had knowledge of the work of the American Seaman's Friend Society in New York City, and intended to devise a part of his estate to this society. The scrivener who prepared his will knew of only one association for the benefit of seamen, the Seaman's Aid Society of Boston. Nathaniel knew nothing of this society, but the scrivener persuaded him that the society he had in mind went by the name "Seaman's Aid Society of Boston," and this is the way the will was written. See Tucker v. Seaman's Aid Soc'y, 48 Mass. (7 Metc.) 188 (1843). For other cases raising a similar question, see Badman v. American Cancer Soc'y, 26 Wash. App. 697, 615 P.2d 500 (1980); National Soc'y for the Prevention of Cruelty to Children v. Scottish Nat'l Soc'y for the Prevention of Cruelty to Children, [1915] App. Cas. 207 (H.L.); In re Girard Trust Corn Exchange Bank, 418 Pa. 112, 208 A.2d 857 (1965) (inter-vivos deed of trust).

(b) The testator's will devised certain property "to my well-beloved nephews John and William Willard." The testator had two sets of relatives by the names of John and William Willard—grandnephews and grandsons. Evidence was sought to be introduced that the grandnephews were strangers to the testator, never visited him, and never resided near him. The grandsons, however, lived near the testator; he was very intimate and friendly with them, and repeatedly declared that he had bought the devised property for them. The lawyer who drew the will sought to testify that the testator directed that the property in question should be given to the grandsons, but by mistake the lawyer wrote "nephews" instead. See Willard v. Darrah, 168 Mo. 660, 68 S.W. 1023 (1902). For another case raising a similar question, see Siegley v. Simpson, 73 Wash. 69, 131 P. 479 (1913) (devise to "my friend Richard H. Simpson"; extrinsic evidence sought to show that the testator intended Hamilton Ross Simpson, not Richard H. Simpson, to be the devisee; the evidence showed that Hamilton Ross Simpson, whom the testator called "Bill" or "Rotary Bill," was the testator's "friend" and that Richard H. Simpson was merely a remote acquaintance).

2. *Judicial Authority to Delete Words?* As the court noted, the leading case for the view applied in *Arnheiter* is Patch v. White, but the decision in that case was not reached without a struggle. Four justices dissented. They asserted that the action of the court "is not construing the will of the testator; it is making a will for him." 117 U.S. 210 at 227.

This statement from the dissenting opinion raises a challenging question: If courts have no power to reform wills by substituting or adding words to them, by what authority do they have the power to delete words from them?

3. *Attorney Liability?* To what extent is an attorney liable in a malpractice action for drafting a devise in favor of a charitable organization without determining that the name used is the correct name of the charity? How significant is it that the name used in the devise was suggested to the attorney by the testator? See Ventura County Humane Soc'y for the Prevention of Cruelty to Children and Animals v. Holloway, 40 Cal. App. 3d 897, 115 Cal. Rptr. 464 (1974)6); Johnston, Legal Malpractice in Estate Planning—Perilous Times Ahead for the Practitioner, 67 Iowa L. Rev. 629, 662-64 (1982). See also infra Part C.

4. *Significance of Language of Ownership.* Of what significance was it that the devise in *Arnheiter* contained explicit language of ownership: "*my* undivided one-half interest of premises known as No. 304 Harrison Avenue"? (The devise in Patch v. White also said that the devised property "belongs to me.") In Estate of Lynch, 142 Cal. 373, 75 P. 1086 (1904), Lynch devised to his nephew Dennis "that certain lot . . . in Tulare County, State of California, and described as follows, to wit: the S. 1/2 of the N.W. 1/4 of Sec. 1, T. 21, R. 27 E." Lynch never owned this tract but he did own the west half of the southwest quarter of the same section. The court held that the intended devise was ineffective. The court was willing to disregard the "false description," leaving the will as though it read "the 1/2 of the 1/4 of Sec. 1" etc., but in its opinion this left the description too uncertain to be given effect:

> There are four quarter sections within the section, each of which can be divided into halves in four different ways, so that there are sixteen descriptions of land to which this language could apply with equal certainty.

Compare Whitehouse v. Whitehouse, 136 Iowa 165, 113 N.W. 759 (1907). The will devised "the north half of the northwest quarter of section 29, township 80, range 25, Polk County, Iowa." The testator owned only the north half of the northeast quarter of the same section. The court held that extrinsic evidence was admissible to show to which of the north quarters the description should be applied after omitting the word "west." "[T]he presumption should prevail," the court stated, "that the testator is undertaking in his will, without saying so in express terms, to dispose of property which he believed belonged to him, rather than to belong to another."

Latent and Patent Ambiguities. One of the most common statements in the books is that extrinsic evidence can be used where there is a *latent* ambiguity in the will but not where the ambiguity is *patent,* that is an ambiguity that appears on the face of the will. Arnheiter v. Arnheiter and Patch v. White were examples of latent ambiguities.

Another example appears in an Indiana case involving a devise to the "Home for the Aged located at 2007 N. Capitol Avenue, Indianapolis, Indiana." There is nothing in these words to suggest any ambiguity. If there were a home by this exact name at this exact location with which the testator had had some association, and no other claimant to the devise, the matter would have been disposed of without further question. In fact, there was a home for the aged at that address, but it was known as "The Altenheim Home of Indianapolis." There was also "The Indianapolis Home for the Aged, Inc.," located at 1731 N. Capitol Avenue and the extrinsic evidence showed that this was the home the testator had in mind. The court found a latent ambiguity and held that the evidence was admissible "for the purpose of correctly interpreting the language actually employed by the testator in his will." Indianapolis Home for the Aged, Inc. v. Altenheim Home of Indianapolis, 120 Ind. App. 595, 93 N.E.2d 203 (1950).

The distinction between latent and patent ambiguities was given currency by Sir Francis Bacon in his Maxims of the Law, in which he said that patent ambiguity "is never holpen by averrement . . . because the law will not couple and mingle matter of specialty, which is of the higher account, with matter of averrement, which is of inferiour account." F. Bacon, Elements of Common Law 82 (1639), reprinted in F. Bacon, Law Tracts 99 (1737), and 7 F. Bacon's Works 385 (1870).

American scholars of evidence law long ago repudiated Bacon's distinction. In his great Preliminary Treatise on Evidence 424 (1898), James Bradley Thayer described Bacon's distinction as an "unprofitable subtlety," and Dean Wigmore likewise condemned the distinction as resting on a "play upon words." 9 J. Wigmore, Evidence 226, 239 (3d ed. 1940).[1] That the distinction has any important influence on decisions today is doubtful, but it cannot be wholly ignored if for no other reason than that courts occasionally still talk in such terms.

Admissibility of Evidence of Direct Declarations of Intent. In general, then, extrinsic evidence is available as an aid to interpretation and to resolve ambiguity whether latent or patent. But there is one general prohibition on the type of evidence that may be used. Traditionally, testimony as to the testator's statements as to what she or he meant to do in her or his will is not admissible—testimony as to "declarations of intention," as Wigmore called it. 9 Wigmore, supra, at 229.

According to Wigmore, this limitation rests upon the "rule which prohibits setting up any extrinsic utterance to compete with and overthrow the words of a document." He recognized that such declarations could be used, not for this purpose, but rather for that of interpreting the words of the document, yet concluded: "There being two conceivable purposes for which it could be used, the one proper, the [other] improper, it is excluded

---

1. Wigmore had in mind the argument, repeated by the United States Supreme Court in Patch v. White, 117 U.S. 210, 217 (1886), that "as a latent ambiguity is only disclosed by extrinsic evidence, it may be removed by extrinsic evidence."

because of the risk that the latter would dominate and that the temptation to abuse would be too strong." Id. at 229-230.

Equivocations. Despite the traditional inadmissibility of the testator's direct declarations of intent, there is one instance where it is well established that such evidence will be received, that is, where there is an "equivocation." Equivocation exists when the words of the will apply equally to two persons or things.

The English cases have been somewhat more insistent than the American that the words fit the two persons or things more or less equally. In addition, they have tended to limit the equivocation exception to a situation in which the words are a fairly exact description of the two persons or things. An example of this narrow reading of the exception comes from an Ontario case, In re Gray, [1934] Ont. W.N. 17. The testator had one brother whose full name was "John Gray" and another whose full name was "Norman Farquharson Gray." His will left a part of the residue of his estate in equal shares to his brothers and sisters, with a proviso that the share of his brother "John Norman Gray" was to be placed in trust so that he was to have only a life estate instead of an absolute interest. The court rejected evidence of statements by the testator that this special provision was to apply to Norman. "In this case," it said, "the name 'John Norman' cannot be said to be equally applicable in all its parts to each of the brothers . . . although the name so used in the will is in part correctly applicable to each of these brothers." Lacking competent evidence of which of the two brothers was meant, the court held that this part of the will was void because of uncertainty. An occasional American decision also seems to insist that an equivocation only arises from "an *accurate* description that *equally* applies to two or more persons of the same name of things of the same description." Estate of Bergau, 37 Wash. App. 903, 684 P.2d 734 (1984) (emphasis added).

Restatement of Property section 242 comment j, however, defines an equivocation as a description "indifferently applicable to two or more persons or objects." Is it fair to say that, under this definition of an equivocation, ambiguities—latent and patent—are equivocations? For a time it was suggested that the equivocation exception was limited to latent ambiguities. Older cases should have put this artificial distinction to rest. See, e.g., Doe d. Gord v. Needs, 2 Mees. & W. 129, 150 Eng. Rep. 698 (1836). The distinction keeps reappearing in cases, however. See, e.g., Breckner v. Prestwood, 600 S.W.2d 52, 56 (Mo. Ct. App. 1980) (direct declarations of intent are admissible in cases of latent but not patent ambiguities).

Potential Evidentiary Bars to the Admissibility of the Testator's Statements. In addition to the traditional rule against admitting direct declarations of intent, other evidentiary rules may bar admission of the testator's statements.

Dead Man's Acts. In Estate of Thomas, 457 Pa. 546, 327 A.2d 31 (1974), the court disposed of the so-called Dead Man's Act as an obstacle to the admission of the testator's statements, saying:

> Appellant contends finally that the Orphans' Court committed a clear violation of the Dean Man's Statute . . . in permitting the appellee and his

wife to testify as to appellee's conversations with the decedent with reference to the shares of stock and the savings account mentioned in Paragraph Eighth and to decedent's intent to benefit him.[2] This contention is without merit. Where opposing parties in a controversy involving merely the testamentary distribution of property present their claims under the will, either party is competent under language of the Statute to testify as to prior conversations with the testator regardless of any individual interest possessed by them in the testator's property.

But see Estate of Malnar, 73 Wis. 2d 192, 243 N.W.2d 435 (1976); Estate of Christen, 72 Wis. 2d 8, 239 N.W.2d 528 (1976) (incompetency of legatee under prior will to testify as to conversations with the decedent does not extend to spouse of legatee). See generally, Report, Dead Man Statutes: Their Purposes, Effect and Future, 7 Real Prop. Prob. & Trust J. 343 (1972).

Hearsay rule. The Hearsay Rule is not an obstacle to the admission of a testator's statements made before the will was executed. Such statements come within the exception to the Rule for declarations showing a state of mind. As to post-execution statements, however, there is a split of authority, some courts holding their admission barred by the Hearsay Rule, others holding it not barred by that Rule. 6 Wigmore, supra, §§ 1734-40.

Attorney-client privilege. The following analysis of the attorney-client privilege appears in Stevens v. Thurston, 112 N.H. 118, 289 A.2d 398 (1972):

Defendants as contestants moved to discover the contents of the file of the attorney who drafted the will . . . The Trial Court denied [the] motion and reserved and transferred defendants' exceptions.

It appears from the reserved case that the denial of the motion for discovery was based solely on the attorney-client privilege. We recognize and enforce the common-law rule that confidential communications between a client and attorney are privileged and protected from inquiry in the absence of a waiver by the client. . . . We have also held that the privilege continues after the death of the client in actions against the estate and may be waived by the representatives of the decedent. . . .

This appeal from the probate of the will, however, . . . is not an adverse proceeding against the estate . . . , but a contest between parties claiming through the testator. If the defendants are successful, they, rather than the plaintiff, will be the representatives of the testator. Here the privilege is being

---

2. The Dead Man's Statute provides in pertinent part:

Nor, where any party to a thing or contract in action is dead, or has been adjudged a lunatic and his right thereto or therein has passed, either by his own act or by the act of the law, to a party on the record who represents his interest in the subject in controversy, shall any surviving or remaining party to such thing or contract, or any other person whose interest shall be adverse to the said right to such deceased or lunatic party, be a competent witness to any matter occurring before the death of said party or the adjudication of his lunacy . . . unless the issue or inquiry be devisavit vel non, or be any other issue or inquiry respecting the property of a deceased owner, and the controversy be between parties respectively claiming such property by devolution on the death of such owner, in which case all persons shall be fully competent witnesses.

[Footnote by the court. Eds.]

asserted not for the protection of the testator or his estate but for the protection of a claimant to his estate. The authorities uniformly hold that in this situation all reason for assertion of the privilege disappears and that the protection of the testator lies in the admission of all relevant evidence that will aid in the determination of his true will. . . . Defendants' exception to the denial of their motion for discovery is sustained.

Note

Patent Ambiguities. In thinking about the efficacy of the latent/patent ambiguity distinction, consider the following materials, which deal with the question whether the testator's own declarations of intention should be admitted to resolve ambiguities that the courts treated as patent.

In Virginia Nat'l Bank v. United States, 443 F.2d 1030, 1034 (4th Cir. 1971), the court, referring to a patent ambiguity, said:

> Where the provisions of a will are ambiguous Virginia law sanctions the admission of parol evidence of attendant *facts and circumstances* at the time the will was written to show the meaning of the language used by the testator. . . . However, it is not proper to admit direct parol "evidence of the testator's actual intention, such as his declarations of intention, his informal memoranda for his will, his instructions for its preparation, and his statements to the scrivener or others as to the meaning of its language." Coffman's Administrator v. Coffman, 131 Va. 456, 109 S.E. 454, 457 (1921). Thus, we must sift through the parol evidence proffered at trial to determine what portion, if any, was admissible for purposes of clearing up the facial ambiguity in the will. Since *Coffman* held that direct evidence of a testator's actual intention as stated in his declarations of intention or instructions for his will's preparation is inadmissible, the district court was correct in refusing to accept *evidence of what the decedent actually said to the trust officer or to the attorney* who assisted her in the preparation of her will. However, the court should have received and considered, as evidence of attendant facts and circumstances, the *testimony as to what the trust officer and the attorney advised and told the decedent,* since such testimony does not involve her own direct expressions of intention.

Compare with Virginia Nat'l Bank the analysis in Estate of Smith, 119 Ariz. 293, 580 P.2d 754 (Ct. App. 1978). In that case, Hazel Smith's will devised "my money and coin collection to Todd Fehlhaber and Sue Fehlhaber in equal shares, or to the survivor thereof." Included in Smith's estate were a collection of thirty-six coins and six two-dollar bills found in her safe deposit box and appraised at $49.00, and various bank accounts and certificates of deposit valued at close to $107,000. The residuary devisees sought to introduce an affidavit of the attorney who drew the will, in which he stated that he was called to Smith's hospital room about a month before she died. The affidavit further stated:

> 5. At that time Hazel E. Smith stated to me that she intended to change her prior will to leave a collection of coins and bills, which had belonged to her

brother to Todd and Sue Fehlhaber, whose parents are Clinton and Virginia
Fehlhaber.

6. Hazel E. Smith further stated her intent to leave the balance and residue
of her assets, including but not limited to certificates of deposit, savings,
checking account, stock and real estate to [the residuary devisees] Juliet D.
Rolle and Eleanor J. McQuaid, in equal shares. . . .

8. That to effectuate the desires of Hazel E. Smith, I drafted her will and
used the term "my money and coin collection" to denominate the coin and
bill collection that had belonged to her brother. . . . She further indicated the
coins and bills were in her safety deposit box.

The lower court admitted this affidavit into evidence. The court of
appeals affirmed, saying:

> We agree there was an ambiguity in the instant will and it was a patent
> one. The term "money" when used in wills is essentially ambiguous. . . . The
> word may have any meaning which the testamentary intent, as manifested by
> the will read in the light of proper evidence, imparts to it. . . . Once having
> established an ambiguity, parol evidence is admissible for the purpose of
> explaining it. . . . The language used here admits of two constructions. . . .
> It was therefore proper to resort to extrinsic proof, including the statement of
> the attorney who drew up the will.

The issue of the admissibility of direct declarations of intent in instances
of patent ambiguity also occurs in tax cases. An ancillary question in these
cases is whether the federal court must decide whether to apply state law
precedents on the issue. The decisions on this latter question are in
conflict. In Estate of Trunk v. Commissioner, 550 F.2d 81 (2d Cir. 1977),
for example, the court said:

> It would seem that the most compelling evidence of a testator's intent
> would be his own statements concerning it. . . . Although some state courts
> continue to reject testimony of this nature where the ambiguity is patent, . . .
> we see little justification, in a proceeding before the Tax Court, for applying
> different evidentiary rules to latent and patent ambiguities. Proceedings before
> that Court are equitable in nature; and, because the Court is concerned with
> substance and realities rather than form, its search for the truth is not rigidly
> restricted to the contents of writings.

On remand, the Tax Court received testimony from the attorney who
drew the will concerning the testator's statements to him, and on this basis
allowed the estate a federal estate tax marital deduction. 37 TCM (CCH)
497 (1978). Compare Estate of Craft v. Commissioner, 68 T.C. 249 (1977),
aff'd per curiam, 80-1 USTC ¶ 13,327 (5th Cir. 1979), in which the Tax
Court said:

> [We hold] that in those instances where we are called upon to make a
> state law determination as to the existence and extent of legal rights and
> interests created by a written instrument, we must look to that state's parol
> evidence rule in deciding whether or not to exclude extrinsic evidence that
> bears on the disputed rights and interests under the instrument.

To hold otherwise could conceivably lead to an anomalous situation in which, because we had admitted and found convincing parol evidence that would have been excluded by a state court, we might determine and cause to be taxed certain interests and rights that a state court applying state law would find to be nonexistent. Such a result would do violence to that fundamental principle of tax law that state law creates legal rights and property interests while the Federal law determines what, and to what extent, interests or rights, so created, shall be taxed.

Moseley v. Goodman
138 Tenn. 1, 195 S.W. 590 (1917)

NEIL, C.J. E.J. Halley died on October 19, 1910, leaving the following will:

I, E.J. Halley, of a sound mind, will make this my last will and testament. I bequeath to the following people mound set of the names, E.O. Kolley, $500.00, Mr. R.G. Ramsey, $500.00, Miss Elizabeth Berry $500.00. I give to A. Goodman and Armstrong $10,000 a piece, Ed. Hurlburt $5000. Jack Brennan $5000. George Becktall $20,000, Mrs. Moseley $20,000. Mrs. Moseley's housekeeper $20,000, W.M. Palmer $20,000. Mrs. Mergle, Sr., $20,000, Ed. Mergle, $20,000, Theadore Mergle $10,000, the balance of my real estate I give to the St. Peter's Orphan Asylum.

The controversy arises over the legacy: "Mrs. Moseley $20,000, Mrs. Moseley's housekeeper $20,000." That is to say, while the legacy to Mrs. Moseley is the only one directly involved here, it is necessary to consider the legacy to the housekeeper in connection with it, so far as the word "housekeeper" is descriptive of the Mrs. Moseley, intended, as the one who had a housekeeper. . . .

The facts disclosed by the record, by the overwhelming weight of the evidence, are as follows:

The testator was for many years engaged with his mother in business on Main street, in the city of Memphis, in the sale of liquors, tobacco, and cigars. He and his mother bought, through a series of years, cigars from Mr. F.S. Trimble, the husband of Mrs. Lillian E. Trimble. Mr. Trimble was the city salesman for one R.L. Moseley, and, as such, for several years, sold cigars to testator and his mother. Testator generally addressed him as "Moseley," it seems, because he sold the Moseley cigars, and the Moseley sign was very prominently displayed at the front of the building where Trimble worked. It does not appear that testator dealt personally with R. L. Moseley himself at all. Mrs. Trimble, during the same period, bought goods about once a month from testator and his mother, and the testator called her "Mrs. Moseley," and admired her character very greatly. He spoke of her to others as a fine woman. The mother of testator died about January, 1910, and he then fell into the habit of drinking, and became quite dissipated. He made a foreign tour with one Harper, he himself paying all the expenses. His mother had left him about $230,000. He claimed, when he came back, that he had spent $6,000 on this trip. He drank a great deal while he was traveling, and came back in a bad state of health. After his mother died, and before he started on the foreign tour, he engaged a room at an apartment house known as "The Monarch," which was owned, or leased, by Mr. Trimble. Mrs. Trimble had charge of it as manager. When testator started on his foreign tour he gave up his room, but immediately on his return he secured the same or another room at "The Monarch," Mrs. Trimble being still the manager. He still drank heavily and was ill. He stayed at "The Monarch" two or three weeks, and was then removed to the hospital, and died within a day or two thereafter, having made the will Monday night and died Wednesday morning.

Mrs. Trimble, at the time testator returned to "The Monarch," had, as her housekeeper for that institution, Mrs. Anna Lang. Both Mrs. Trimble and Mrs. Lang gave the testator very devoted attention, such attention as a sick man needs, serving night and day. Mrs. Trimble brought him milk and soup and other delicacies. Mrs. Lang ministered to him very assiduously and with great kindness in the way of sponging him and doing other things for his comfort. He appeared to be very grateful for these attentions. He generally called Mrs. Trimble Mrs. Moseley, though occasionally he called her Mrs. Trimble. There is evidence to the effect that he always called her Mrs. Moseley. The witness Rothschild deposed to this fact. He testified that on one occasion, when he was in the room of testator, the latter was talking about Mrs. Moseley quite a good deal, and he asked him who he was referring to, and he said: "Mrs. Trimble; I always call her Mrs. Moseley." He always spoke of Mrs. Lang as "housekeeper," or "the good woman."

It does not appear that he knew Mrs. Lenoir Moseley. It does appear that he knew her husband, R.L. Moseley. Mrs. Moseley herself testified that she did not know Mr. Halley at all. She endeavors to connect herself with the legacy not only by the fact that her name was Mrs. Moseley, but by the further fact that her sister, Miss Jessie Dunlap, was her housekeeper at her private home. It is in proof that the testator incidentally met Miss Dunlap on one occasion at "The Monarch." . . . [T]here is no real evidence that Halley knew that Miss Dunlap was housekeeper to the complainant. However, in our further treatment of the case we shall assume that he did have such information.

If the testimony was competent to the effect that the testator always or generally spoke of Mrs. Trimble as Mrs. Moseley, or generally called her Mrs. Moseley, there was ample evidence to sustain the verdict [in favor of Mrs. Trimble], and that point is not questioned. However, it is said that the evidence was not competent; that when it was proven that there was in existence a Mrs. Moseley, whose legal name was such, this satisfied the language of the will, and the testimony above referred to concerning Mrs. Trimble's being called Mrs. Moseley by the testator could not be used to raise a latent ambiguity. We are of the opinion that this view is erroneous.

The general principle is well stated in Ayres v. Weed, 16 Conn. 290, as follows:

> If a person is commonly called and known by a name which does not properly belong to him, but which properly belongs to another, it cannot

with propriety be said that that name, although a false one, is not in fact descriptive of the former, unless we go so far as to say that a person is not described by the name by which he is known. That would clearly be a case where two different persons would be described by the same name, and where, therefore, parol evidence might be introduced to remove the doubt as to which of them was intended. That the name given to a person is a nickname does not render it the less a description of him, although, indeed, a less correct one, that if his true name were used; and it is well settled that if a legacy is given, or a devise made, to a person by his nickname, parol evidence is admissible to show that the testator usually called him by that name, in order to show that he was intended; much more would it be admissible to show that he was generally known in the community by that name.

Now, there is no evidence in this record that Mrs. Trimble was generally known by the name of Mrs. Moseley; but it was sufficient to indicate the meaning of the testator if it be shown, as it is shown here, that he was accustomed to call her by that name. . . .

[A] devise to a person by any name, however different the name used in the will from the true name of the person, is good, provided it is shown that the name used was one by which the testator was accustomed to designate the person, and such showing may be made by parol proof. . . .

Counsel for the complainant insist that if the court should hold that Mrs. Trimble was the person intended, and so should affirm the judgment of the chancellor and the Court of Civil Appeals decreeing the legacy to her, that would be nothing short of striking the name of Mrs. Moseley from the will, and inserting in its place that of Mrs. Trimble, and so writing a new will for the testator. This argument is clearly fallacious. We look to the evidence merely to ascertain what individual the testator had in mind when he wrote the term "Mrs. Moseley." The evidence recited, if competent, must convince any one, as it did the jury, that he meant Mrs. Trimble, because "Mrs. Moseley" was the name by which he called her, and because of his long acquaintanceship with her, the esteem in which he had long held her, and the kindnesses on account of which he was indebted to her, and because of his associating with her the person whom he always called "the housekeeper," Mrs. Anna Lang. . . .

Judgment will therefore be entered here affirming the judgment of the Court of Civil Appeals, with costs.

Note and Questions

The Personal-Usage Doctrine. Moseley illustrates an established exception to the no-extrinsic-evidence rule, the "personal usage" doctrine. See Restatement of Property § 242 comment d. The language in the will was not manifestly ambiguous, yet the court admitted extrinsic evidence regarding the testator's intent. What do you suppose is the reason for this exception? Was the extrinsic evidence in *Moseley* demonstrably more reliable than that rejected by the court in Mahoney v. Grainger?

2. Mistakes in the Inducement

Statutory Reference: *1990 UPC § 2-302*

Gifford v. Dyer
2 R.I. 99 (1852)

This was an appeal from a decree of the Court of Probate of Little Compton, proving and approving the last will and testament of Abigail Irish. The will was dated December 4, 1850, and the testatrix died December 6, 1850. After several bequests of small sums to the children of Robin Gifford and to others, she gives and bequeaths the rest and residue of her property, one half to John Dyer, who was her brother-in-law, and the other half to her two nephews, Jesse and Alexander Dyer. Robin Gifford, the only child of the testatrix, was not mentioned in the will. It appeared in evidence, that at the date of the will, Robin Gifford had been absent from home, leaving a family, for a period of ten years, unheard from; that all the neighbors considered him dead, and that his estate had been administered upon as of a person deceased. The scrivener who drew the will, testified as follows:

> After I had read the will to her, she asked if it would make any difference if she did not mention her son. I asked if she considered him living. She said she supposed he had been dead for years; she said, if it would make any difference she would put his name in, for they will break the will if they can. I think that was the expression she used. I think she said what she had given her grandchildren was in lieu of what he would have, but am not positive. I think her son left in 1841, and was not heard of to my knowledge. She was speaking of a home at Mr. Dyer's and said, what she had given him would pay him well. She said her grandchildren had not been to see her while she was sick.

It appeared that the testatrix had resided with John Dyer for some time previous to her death. . . .

GREENE, C.J. delivered the opinion of the court. It is very apparent in the present case, that the testatrix would have made the same will, had she known her son was living. She did not intend to give him anything, if living.

But if this were not apparent and she had made the will under a mistake as to the supposed death of her son, this could not be shown *dehors* the will. The mistake must appear on the face of the will, and it must also appear what would have been the will of the testatrix but for the mistake. Thus, where the testator revokes a legacy, upon the mistaken supposition that the legatee is dead, and this appears on the face of the instrument of revocation, such revocation was held void. Campbell v. French, 3 Vesey, 321.

Note

1. *State of the Authorities.* Most of the decisions follow the view reflected in *Gifford*. See, e.g., Bowerman v. Burris, 138 Tenn. 220, 197 S.W. 490 (1917); Carpenter v. Tinney, 420 S.W.2d 241 (Tex. Civ. App. 1967); Clapp v. Fullerton, 34 N.Y. 190, 90 Am. Dec. 681 (1866); Matter of Arnold, 200 Misc. 909, 107 N.Y.S.2d 356 (Sur. Ct. 1951).

In line with the principle announced in *Gifford*, courts have given effect to a will that omitted or gave a nominal amount to a natural object of the testator's bounty even though the will itself recited a reason for the action that was in fact false. See, e.g., Le Flore v. Handlin, 153 Ark. 421, 240 S.W. 712 (1922); Riley v. Casey, 185 Iowa 461, 170 N.W. 742 (1919); Woelk's Estate, 132 Kan. 621, 296 P. 359 (1931); Bedlow's Will, 67 Hun. 408, 22 N.Y.S. 290 (Sup. Ct. 1893); Shumway's Will, 138 Misc. 429, 246 N.Y.S. 178 (Sur. Ct. 1930).

2. *Children Omitted Because Thought Dead; 1990 Uniform Probate Code.* Section 2-302 of the 1990 UPC creates one exception to the general rule that mistakes in the inducement cannot be corrected. If a testator fails to provide for a child living at the time of execution solely because the testator mistakenly believes the child to be dead, the child receives a share of the testator's estate as if the child were an omitted afterborn child. See supra p. 512.

Children can be omitted from a parent's will because thought dead in a variety of settings. By one count, 28,899 children were reported missing between 1984 and 1989. Of these, 10,326 were runaways, 13,062 were abducted by relatives, and 511 were abducted by strangers. Of the 511 abducted by strangers, 22 percent have been found dead, 31 percent have been found alive, and 47 percent are still missing. Newsweek, Nov. 27, 1989, at 95. In war time, children in the armed forces can be listed as missing or killed in action and later show up alive. Some believe that North Vietnam still holds hundreds of members of the American armed forces as prisoners of war.

3. *Relief for Fraud in the Inducement.* As we noted in Chapter 3, supra, courts ordinarily will not relieve a mistake that induced the testator to make a devise, but they will relieve fraud in the inducement.

An example of fraud in the inducement is Huber v. Boyle, 98 Colo. 360, 56 P.2d 1333 (1936). In that case, Samuel Holmes devised his entire estate to his two nieces, Daisy Holmes and Florence Soule, believing that his sister, Ms. Huber, was dead. Huber was alive and, in contesting probate of the will, she sought to establish that Daisy Holmes had written the testator that his sister was dead, knowing that this was false. After Holmes died in Fairplay, Colorado, Daisy went to Fairplay from her home in Michigan and destroyed the letters she had written him. Vacating a directed verdict for the will, the court said this about the proper disposition of the matter in the probate proceeding:

That at the time he executed [the will] Holmes labored under the mistaken belief that his sister was dead, is shown by undisputed evidence. The fact that he was mistaken in that regard would not, of itself, avoid the will. If, however, the mistaken belief was caused by false representations knowingly made by Miss Holmes and Mrs. Soule with the fraudulent purpose of inducing Holmes to make his will in their favor, to the exclusion of his sister, and he so made the will in reliance upon such representations, the will would be void as to both. If such representations were made by one of them, the other not participating in the fraud, the devise and bequest to the wrongdoer would be void, but the devise and bequest to the innocent beneficiary would be valid in the absence of a showing that such devise and bequest were affected by the representations.

4. *Gift Tax Consequences of Mistakenly Induced Inter-Vivos Trusts.* As *Wobaco* indicated, relief is available for mistakes in connection with inter-vivos trusts. Courts have ordered reformation of irrevocable trusts that were mistakenly induced, converting them from irrevocable to revocable trusts. The creation of an irrevocable trust is a transfer subject to federal gift taxation, but the creation of a revocable trust is exempt from gift taxation. What are the gift tax consequences of reforming an irrevocable trust into one that is revocable? In Berger v. United States, 487 F. Supp. 49 (W.D. Pa. 1980), C. William Berger was in line for a high-level position with the federal government. From the press reports he had read, he believed that he had to place all of his assets into an irrevocable trust in order to comply with the Nixon administration's policies on public service conflicts of interest. Berger liquidated all of his property, including even his private residence, and placed the bulk of these assets into two irrevocable trusts with the Pittsburgh National Bank. During the preparation of the trust instrument, a trust officer with the bank suggested that the trust be made revocable. Berger, however, rejected this advice and insisted that the trust be irrevocable in order to comply with the government's conflict of interest rules as he understood them. Subsequently, plans for Berger's job with the government fell through. The Bergers filed a gift tax return that indicated a total transfer of $180,000.00. They did not include payment for the gift tax due on the transfer, however, and they later filed an amended gift tax return alleging that no taxable transfer had occurred and no tax was due.

Berger sought reformation of the trust in state court. The court ordered reformation of the trust instrument, converting the trusts from irrevocable trusts to trusts that were revocable.

The Internal Revenue Service denied the amended tax return on its merits. The Bergers then paid under protest a total of $29,241.70 in taxes and interest of $2,074.38, and brought an action in federal district court seeking a refund of those tax payments.

The federal court granted Berger's motion for summary judgment, saying:

[W]e need not review the state trial court's record to ascertain the soundness of its rulings since the government concedes that but for Mr. Berger's mistaken conception of the conflicts of interest policy he would not have undertaken the transfer. . . . The question remains as to whether or not the state-recognized right to reform the trust from irrevocable to revocable based on the grantor's unilateral mistake can abrogate the gift tax imposed upon the original transaction. The impact of the state right upon the federal tax scheme is a federal question. . . . The federal gift tax accrues to a grantor's transfer of property when the transfer is beyond his dominion and control as to whom will be the beneficiaries of the transferred property. . . .

In the case *sub judice*, the original deed of trust created an irrevocable transfer. . . . Mr. Berger intentionally, albeit as the result of a mistake, relinquished all his legal rights over the property. He did, however, retain an equitable right under Pennsylvania law to reformation based upon the mistaken conveyance. . . .

[U]ntil the grantor relinquished the state law right of revocation, the gift was incomplete and immature and thus, not subject to federal gift tax. . . .

Here, as we have stated, the government has conceded that Mr. Berger acted upon a mistake in creating an irrevocable, hence, taxable, trust; Pennsylvania law permits reformation or revocation of such a gift transfer; Mr. Berger had the trust reformed in Pennsylvania Courts in accordance with Pennsylvania law, and therefore, summary judgment will be entered for the taxpayer.

On the federal tax consequences of a state-court reformation, see supra Chapter 6 and infra p. 585.

3. Mistaken Omissions

Knupp v. District of Columbia
578 A.2d 702 (D.C. Ct. App. 1990)

NEWMAN, J. This is an appeal from a judgment of the Superior Court construing a will. The problem at issue is that the will's sixth paragraph states that the residual estate is to pass to the person specified in the eighth paragraph of the will, but the eighth paragraph does not name a residual legatee. Appellant explains that the inconsistency is a result of an error on the part of the attorney who drafted the will: that although the testator allegedly instructed the attorney to name appellant as the beneficiary of the residual estate, the attorney forgot to insert such a clause in the will. Appellant argued in the construction proceeding in Superior Court that, based upon extrinsic evidence showing that the testator intended the appellant to be the beneficiary of the residual estate, the court should interpret the will to give Appellant the residual estate. The trial court held that it was without power to reform the will by inserting the name of a legatee alleged to have been omitted by mistake. As a consequence, the residue would go to the District of Columbia by escheat. See D.C. Code § 19-701 (1981). We agree with the Superior Court's ruling and, thus, we affirm.

The facts of this case show that the testator, a District of Columbia resident, executed a will from his hospital bed in March 1986 and died approximately one month thereafter. Paragraph Six of the will states:

I direct my Executor to sell or otherwise convert into cash such of the rest and remainder of my estate as, in his judgment, is or may be necessary to pay my just debts, expenses of administration, funeral expenses, expenses of last illness, estate and inheritance (and other) taxes, and the cash legacies specified in subparagraphs A through G, inclusive, of paragraph SEVENTH hereof. I request that the remaining assets of my estate that are not required to be sold in order to pay debts, expenses, taxes, and cash legacies as provided in the preceding sentence be retained in kind by said Executor and distributed in kind to the residual legatee as stipulated in paragraph EIGHTH hereof.

Paragraph eighth of the will states, in pertinent part:

I hereby nominate and appoint RICHARD L. KNUPP, . . . , as Executor of this my last will and testament, and I direct that no bond or security be required of him. I ask that he retain MILTON W. SCHOBER, . . . , as attorney for my estate.

Nowhere does paragraph eighth name a residual beneficiary.

The will was drafted by Milton W. Schober, the attorney referred to in the eighth paragraph of the will and the drafter of the testator's two prior wills. In his two prior wills, the testator left significant bequests to his personal friend, Richard L. Knupp ("Knupp"). Appellant alleges that in this will testator also intended Knupp to benefit. Allegedly, approximately one month prior to his death, the testator told Schober to draft a new will which would leave specific dollar amounts to several named beneficiaries and which would leave the bulk of the estate to Knupp, as residual beneficiary. Schober drafted the new will and the testator signed it. The will, however, did not name the residual legatee. Schober submitted an affidavit to the trial court admitting that he mistakenly failed to designate a residual beneficiary in the will even though the testator had instructed him to name Knupp. Schober also provided the trial court with notes he took of his conversations with the testator to prove that the testator intended Knupp to be the residual legatee.

In an order dated November 16, Judge Barnes found that the will was ambiguous on its face and that the court should consider extrinsic evidence to determine the testator's intent. In a supplemental order, though, Judge Barnes ruled that as a matter of law, specific extrinsic evidence concerning the names of omitted legatees must be excluded.

The general rule in construing a will in the District of Columbia is that the testator's intent is the guiding principle. If the intent is clear from the language of the will, the inquiry ends there. However, "if the language 'upon its face and without explanation, is doubtful or meaningless' . . . a court may examine extrinsic evidence in order to understand the will." Wyman [v. Roesner, 439 A.2d 516, 520 (D.C. Ct. App. 1981)] (quoting Baker v. National Savings & Trust, 86 U.S.App.D.C. 161, 162, 181 F.2d 273, 274 (1950)); accord Starkey v. District of Columbia, 377 A.2d 382, 383 (D.C.1977).

While the intent of the testator is the "polestar in construction of a will," extrinsic facts are not always permitted into evidence in order to prove the testator's intent. Certain conditions must be present to warrant the introduction of extrinsic evidence. First, there must be some ambiguity in order for a court to consider extrinsic evidence. In addition, in all cases in which such evidence is received, it can be "utilized only for the purpose of interpreting something actually written in the will and never to add provisions to the will." [Association of Survivors of the 7th Ga. Regiment v. Larner, 3 F.2d 201, 203 (D.C. Cir. 1925).] As one treatise states:

> evidence of surrounding circumstances is admissible to enable the court to understand the meaning of the words which the testator has used in his will, it is not admissible to add to the will provisions which cannot fairly be inferred from the language which is used therein, or to take from the will provisions which are clearly expressed therein.

4 Bowe-Parker: Page on Wills, § 32.2 at 237.

When an ambiguity exists regarding the testator's intent, often a court will allow extrinsic facts into evidence to clear up the ambiguity. As the Supreme Court noted over a century ago:

> It is settled doctrine that, as a latent ambiguity is only disclosed by extrinsic evidence, it may be removed by extrinsic evidence. Such an ambiguity may arise upon a will, either when it names a person as the object of a gift, or a thing as the subject of it, and there are two persons or things that answer such name or description; or, secondly, it may arise when the will contains a misdescription of the object or subject: as where there is no such person or thing in existence, or, if in existence, the person is not the one intended, or the thing does not belong to the testator.

Patch v. White, 117 U.S. 210, 217 (1886).

Any ambiguity in the will under consideration in this case is not of the sort that can be corrected by the consideration of extrinsic evidence. There is no language in the will that could lead a court to infer that the testator intended Knupp to be the recipient of the residual estate; thus, it was proper for the court not to admit the extrinsic evidence. . . .

For the aforementioned reasons, the decision is hereby
Affirmed.

Notes

1. *Inserting Omitted Language Into Wills by Construction.* Seemingly in conflict with the no-reformation rule are cases in which courts have inserted language mistakenly omitted from wills. Where courts have added the missing language, they have explained their decisions on the theory that they are engaging in a process called "construction." The term "construction" in these cases is being used in the specialized sense of constructing the omitted language by implication from the language that is contained in the will rather than supplying it from extrinsic evidence. The construction theory has produced some curious results. In a pair of

cases decided by the same court on the same day, for example, missing language was inserted in one but not the other.

In Estate of Dorson, 22 Misc. 2d 945, 196 N.Y.S.2d 344 (Sur. Ct. 1959), the testator's will divided the residue of his estate into two trusts, Funds A and B. The testator's widow was the initial income beneficiary of both funds; when her interest terminated, each fund was to be divided into three parts, one part for each of the testator's three children. His daughter Marjorie was the beneficiary of Part 2 of both Fund A and B. Part 2 of Fund A provided for the income to be paid to Marjorie until she reached 35, at which time she was to receive one-third of the corpus; the income from the remaining two-thirds of corpus was to be paid to her until she reached 40, at which time one-half of the remaining corpus was to be paid to her until she reached 45, whereupon she was to receive the entire remaining corpus. Part 2 of Fund B contained identical language, except that the language directing that one-half of the remaining corpus be paid to Marjorie at age 40 was omitted. The court inserted that language into Fund B, saying that "[t]he testator's general dispositive scheme is clearly discernible from a reading of the will. . . ." See also McCauley v. Alexander, 543 S.W.2d 699 (Tex. Civ. App. 1976) (devise in second paragraph of will named the devisee but failed to state what property was devised; omission was filled by word "estate," which appeared in third paragraph of will).

In Estate of Calabi, 22 Misc. 2d 173, 196 N.Y.S.2d 443 (Sur. Ct. 1959), the testator's will, drafted by counsel, divided the residue of his estate into four trusts. Trusts C and D were to receive one-twelfth each of the residue. For Trusts A and B, the will spelled out the trust terms and identified the beneficiaries but the will omitted the terms and beneficiaries for Trusts C and D. The one-sixth of the residue not expressly disposed of was held to pass by intestacy to the testator's heirs, despite an allegation that Trusts C and D were intended to be for the benefit of the testator's grandchildren until each reached the age of 24. The court noted that no supporting evidence of this allegation was submitted, but said that "if such supporting evidence were available it would not be admissible." See also Farmers & Merchants Bank v. Farmers & Merchants Bank, 216 S.E.2d 769 (W. Va. 1975) (devise named the devisee but failed to state the amount of the devise; court held inadmissible lawyers' testimony that the intended amount was $35,000 and that it was inadvertently omitted by lawyer's typist).

Would extrinsic evidence supporting the allegation, if offered in *Calabi*, have been inherently less reliable a basis for correcting the mistake than the basis for relief that the court used in *Dorson*?

2. *Inserting Omitted Language Into Inter-Vivos Trusts.* In contrast with the attitude toward reformation reflected in *Knupp* and *Calabi*, courts have openly reformed revocable trusts on the basis of extrinsic evidence of mistakenly omitted language, even after the settlor's death. A striking example of this incongruity between the law of wills and the law of trusts is Berman v. Sandler, 379 Mass. 506, 399 N.E.2d 17 (1980). Ellen Sandler created a revocable and amendable inter-vivos trust. Later, her attorney found that the first paragraph of section 1 of Article Third of the trust jeopardized the qualification of the trust for the federal estate tax marital

deduction. The attorney drafted a document amending the trust. The amending document, which Sandler signed, directed that section 1 of Article Third be deleted and that certain new language be substituted for it. After Sandler's death, it was discovered that the amendment deleted section 1 in its entirety rather than the first paragraph thereof, as intended. In a suit for reformation brought by the trustee, the court ordered the insertion into the amending document of the mistakenly omitted phrase "the first paragraph of." The court stated:

> It is settled that a written instrument, including a trust, will be reformed on grounds of mistake upon "full, clear, and decisive proof" of the mistake. . . . Since a settlor usually receives no consideration for the creation of a trust, a unilateral mistake on the part of the settlor is ordinarily sufficient to warrant reformation. . . . The additional fact that the settlor in the case at bar has died should not foreclose relief, . . . so long as the evidence of mistake meets the requisite standard of proof. . . . The overwhelming weight of the evidence . . . clearly and decisively points to a scrivener's error as the source of the mistake. . . . Accordingly, judgment shall enter in the court below reforming the trust amendment so as to delete only the first paragraph of the first section of Article Third and to retain the remainder of section 1 as it appears in the original trust agreement.

4. Mistaken Inclusions—Partial Denial of Probate?

Connecticut Junior Republic v. Sharon Hospital
188 Conn. 1, 448 A.2d 190 (1982)

HEALEY, J. The sole issue presented in this case is whether extrinsic evidence of a mistake by a scrivener of a testamentary instrument is admissible in a proceeding to determine the validity of the testamentary instrument. On October 3, 1979, Richards Haskell Emerson, a resident of Lakeville, died at the age of seventy-nine. He had never married and left several cousins as his closest heirs at law. Emerson left a will dated May 19, 1960, and two codicils dated December 4, 1969 (first codicil) and October 24, 1975 (second codicil), all of which were offered for probate by the named executor, the Third National Bank of Hampden County, Springfield, Massachusetts.

The Probate Court for the district of Salisbury admitted the will and codicils on February 19, 1980, after a hearing on the application for probate. This appeal rises out of the court's decision to admit portions of the second codicil which the plaintiffs contend were inserted by mistake of the scrivener and therefore do not embody the dispositions intended by the testator.

Contained in the decedent's will are three articles which set up trusts for the distribution of part of the decedent's estate and designate, as remaindermen, seven named charitable organizations (1960 charities), the defendants in this case. In the first codicil to his will, the decedent deleted the seven 1960 charities and substituted another group of eleven charitable organizations (1969 charities) as remaindermen, which are the plaintiffs in this case. There was only one charity named in both the will and the first codicil.

Subsequently, in 1975, the decedent instructed the trust officer of the Third National Bank of Hampden County to make changes in his will, as amended by the first codicil, so as to qualify the trusts as charitable annuity trusts under the Tax Reform Act of 1969, so that the charitable remainder interests would be allowable as federal estate tax deductions. The trust officer, thereafter, similarly instructed the decedent's attorney. The attorney, however, in drafting the second codicil, not only made the requested changes but also mistakenly reinstated the 1960 charities, which had originally been named in the will, as beneficiaries under two of the three articles of the will which are relevant to this case.[3] The decedent, who had never requested or authorized this change, signed the second codicil apparently without realizing the change in beneficiaries.

At the hearing on the application for the admission of the will and the two codicils, the Probate Court heard evidence on the matter and ruled that Connecticut law does not permit the introduction of extrinsic evidence on the issue of mistake, and found that in the absence of such evidence the presumption of the validity of a testamentary instrument mandated the admission of the entire second codicil to probate.[4] On appeal to the Superior Court, the defendants moved to strike the plaintiffs' reasons of appeal. Practice Book § 194. The Superior Court granted the defendants' motion and held that extrinsic evidence is not admissible to prove that the second codicil, which uses unambiguous language, contained a mistake due to a scrivener's error and, therefore, should not be admitted to probate. The defendants next joined in the executor's motion for summary judgment which was granted by agreement of the parties. From this judgment, the plaintiffs have appealed to this court.

The plaintiffs claim that the lower court erred (1) in failing to find a distinction between a "will construction" proceeding and a proceeding to "admit a will to probate"; (2) in failing to hold that Connecticut cases support the admissibility of extrinsic evidence to prove that material has been mistakenly inserted into a testamentary instrument. . . .

I. The plaintiffs' first argument states that since the issue in this case is the validity of the second codicil and not its meaning, extrinsic evidence

---

3. The remaining article relevant to this case continued to provide for the eleven 1969 charities.

4. The Probate Court made this holding in spite of finding the following:

> Substantial and convincing evidence was offered to establish that the testator had directed that the second codicil to his will be prepared only for the purpose of qualifying the charitable bequests under Paragraphs Seventh and Eighth of the will and first codicil as charitable remainder annuity trusts eligible for an estate tax charitable deduction in the decedent's estate; and that by scrivener's error the "1960 charities" were substituted for the "1969 charities" in the 1975 codicil; and that the proposed 1975 codicil was presented to the testator in a context of innocent misrepresentation of its contents resulting in mistake in the instrument as executed with respect as to which charitable beneficiaries the testator intended to benefit.

should be admissible to prove the scrivener's error. Specifically, they claim that courts which have considered the question have made a distinction between proceedings to admit a will to probate and will construction proceedings, holding or recognizing that extrinsic evidence showing a scrivener's error is admissible in the former but not in the latter proceeding, absent an ambiguity. See annot., 90 A.L.R.2d 924, 931. Because of the scrivener's error, the plaintiffs claim that the mistake in reinstating the 1960 charities into the second codicil should have been allowed to have been proven by extrinsic evidence and should not have been admitted to probate. The lower court rejected this argument. . . .

In Connecticut, our cases have not, to this point, distinguished between the two types of proceedings. See Stearns v. Stearns, 103 Conn. 213, 130 A. 112 (1925) (will construction proceeding); Comstock v. Hadlyme Ecclesiastical Society, 8 Conn. 254 (1830) (proceeding to establish a will); Avery v. Chappel, 6 Conn. 270 (1826) (proceeding to establish a will). Neither the plaintiffs nor the defendants have presented us with any Connecticut authority which recognizes any distinction between the rules of evidence applicable to either of these two forms of proceedings.[5] While it is obvious that the purpose behind each type of proceeding may be different, we are not inclined to establish a rule which would effectuate such a distinction. It would be unwise to maintain a separate rule regarding the admission of extrinsic evidence for each of these two proceedings. This is because a litigant, knowing that more favorable evidentiary rules await those with claims of mistake due to scrivener's error, will always strive to phrase his argument in a way so to state such a claim. . . .

This result would elevate the form over the substance of the argument and transform probate proceedings into mere semantic exercises. As an example, we point to the situation where a beneficiary under an unambiguous will, which also contains a scrivener's error, or words which effectuate a different result than that allegedly intended, knows that the extrinsic evidence demonstrating the mistake or a different intention than that expressed in the will is inadmissible in a will construction proceeding. To avoid this substantive barrier, he can merely rephrase his argument to allege that the scrivener did not follow instructions and, therefore, the will, even though otherwise validly executed, should not be admitted to probate since it does not represent the testator's true intention. Such a situation would expose many wills to litigation merely because a disappointed beneficiary did not receive exactly what he thought the testator would leave him. If a testator, during his lifetime, represented to a beneficiary that he would receive a certain bequest and, later, the testator changed the bequest in his will but neglected to inform the beneficiary, the beneficiary, knowing that extrinsic evidence is admissible in one but not the other proceeding, could certainly at least allege a scrivener's error and challenge the will's admission to probate on the basis that the testamentary document did not

---

5. We do not deem it necessary to undertake any discussion of the matter that jurisdictions outside Connecticut permit extrinsic evidence to prove a mistake in a testamentary instrument.

represent the true intent of the testator. This would tend to produce needless litigation by transforming a simple will construction proceeding into an admission to probate problem where no problem may have actually existed. In order to avoid this, we believe that the better course is to recognize that the same evidentiary rules apply to both types of proceedings.

II. We now turn to the major issue presented by this case. The trial court held that "parol evidence may not be admitted in the instant case to show that the scrivener erred in drafting the codicil or that the testator mistakenly signed it. Connecticut law does not allow extrinsic evidence of a testator's intent to be admitted in cases dealing with either will construction or cases challenging the probate of an instrument. While there is an exception to this rule when there is ambiguity on the face of the will or codicil itself, this exception is not applicable in the instant case." We agree with the trial court. . . .

[The plaintiffs] seek to introduce evidence that the testator's true intent was not to divide his estate among the combined eighteen charitable institutions as appears on the face of the will and codicils, but that his true intent, which was allegedly communicated to the scrivener, was to replace the eleven charitable institutions named in the first codicil with the seven charitable institutions originally named in his will. It is clear that whether this is a "will construction" proceeding or a proceeding to "admit a will to probate," where the claimants seek to introduce extrinsic evidence of a scrivener's error resulting in a disposition of property allegedly contrary to the testator's intention, as expressed to the scrivener, such evidence, absent an ambiguity, is not admissible because "'if such testimony is to be admitted, we do away [with] part at least of the beneficial effect of the statute of frauds, and leave every will exposed to litigation, on a claim of a different intent.'" Stearns v. Stearns, supra, 103 Conn. 224-25, 130 A. 112. See Comstock v. Hadlyme Ecclesiastical Society, 8 Conn. 254, 265-66 (1830);[6] Rapp v. Reehling, 124 Ind. 36, 23 N.E. 777 (1889). "Claimed

---

6. Our holding today is limited to the case where a mistake due to a scrivener's error with no resulting ambiguity is alleged. It is clear that there are certain types of "mistakes" which would merit the introduction of extrinsic evidence as proof thereof. In In re Gluckman's Will, 87 N.J.Eq. 638, 641, 101 A. 295 (1917), the court stated:

Where a testator, in addition to complete testamentary mental capacity, is in full enjoyment of average physical and educational faculties, it would seem that in the absence of fraud or of undue influence, a mistake, in order to defeat probate of his entire will, must in substance or effect really amount to one of identity of the instrument executed; as, for instance, where two sisters, in one case, or a husband and wife, in another, prepared their respective wills for simultaneous execution, and through pure error one executed the other's, and vice versa. Anon., 14 Jur. 402 [1850]; Re Hunt, L.R. 3 P. & D. 250 [1875]; Nelson v. McDonald, 61 Hun. 406, 16 N.Y.Supp. 273 [1891]. Short of this, however, or of something amounting in effect to the same thing, it is against sound public policy to permit a pure mistake to defeat the duly solemnized and completely competent testamentary act. It is more important that the probate of the wills of dead people be effectively shielded from the attacks of a multitude of fictitious mistakes than that it be purged of wills containing a few real ones. The latter a testator may, by due care, avoid in his lifetime. Against the former he would be helpless. . . .

[For a similar argument, see Power, Wills: A Primer of Interpretation and Construction, 51 Iowa L. Rev. 75, 103-06 (1965). Eds.]

errors in the drafting of a will, either by the testator or his scrivener, do not permit the introduction of extrinsic evidence." McFarland v. Chase Manhattan Bank, N.A., 32 Conn.Sup. 20, 37, 337 A.2d 1 (1973), aff'd, 168 Conn. 411, 362 A.2d 834 (1975). We find that this is the relevant public policy as expressed through our cases; therefore, we will not additionally discuss the plaintiffs' fourth claim of error set out above.

We would, however, properly make these observations. It is beyond cavil that "[p]rinciples of law which serve one generation well may, by reason of changing conditions, disserve a later one. . . ." Herald Publishing Co. v. Bill, 142 Conn. 53, 62, 111 A.2d 4 (1955). "Experience can and often does demonstrate that a rule, once believed sound, needs modification to serve justice better. . . ." Herald Publishing Co. v. Bill, supra. . . . The principle of law, which we reiterate today, has been viable for many years and we have not been given nor do we glean any persuasive reason that justice, experience or logic requires it be changed. . . .

There is no error.

[The dissenting opinion of PETERS, J., in which SHEA J., concurred, is omitted.]

Notes and Questions

1. *Ratification of the Mistake by Signing the Will?* In the *Connecticut Junior Republic* case, part of the argument advanced by the proponents of the second codicil was that "whatever error the scrivener may have made was validated and ratified by the testator's act in signing his will." Does the majority opinion confirm this argument? In her dissenting opinion, Justice Peters[7] reacted to this argument as follows:

> Neither American law in general, nor the case law of this state, has ever assigned so conclusive an effect to the reading and subsequent execution of a will. While signing the will creates a strong presumption that the will accurately represents the intentions of the testator, that presumption is a rebuttable one.

Similarly, an English Law Reform Committee expressed this view:

> We have also considered whether any special significance ought to be given to cases in which the will has been read over to the testator, perhaps with explanations, and expressly approved by him before execution. In our view it should not. Some testators are inattentive, some find it difficult to understand what their solicitors say and do not like to confess it, and some make little or no attempt to understand. As long as they are assured that the words used carry out their instructions, they are content. Others may follow

---

7. Prior to her appointment to the Connecticut Supreme Court in 1978, Justice Ellen Ash Peters was professor of law at Yale Law School. Her specialties included Contracts and Commercial Law. She is the first woman to sit on the Connecticut Supreme Court and was appointed Chief Justice in 1984.

every word with meticulous attention. It is impossible to generalise, and our view is that reading over is one of the many factors to which the court should pay attention, but that it should have no conclusive effect.

Law Reform Committee, Nineteenth Report: Interpretation of Wills, Cmnd. No. 5301, at 12 (1973).

2. *English Practice: Partial Denial of Probate.* Under some circumstances, English practice goes so far as to deny probate of particular words of a will that were included by mistake. E.g., Re Reynette-James, [1975] 3 All E.R. 1037; Re Phelan, [1972] Fam. 33; Re Morris, [1971] P. 62; Goods of Boehm, L.R. 16 Prob. 247 (1891).

PART B. A REFORMATION DOCTRINE FOR WILLS?

In this Part, we examine several recent mistake cases and an extract from an article that urges the acceptance of a reformation doctrine for wills similar to the one long in place for instruments effecting inter-vivos transfers. The recent cases do not purport to adopt a general reformation doctrine, but in effect and attitude they depart substantially from most of the decisions we have been reading up to now.

It should be recalled at the outset that the no-reformation and no-extrinsic-evidence rules have not been universally acclaimed or followed. We noted earlier, for example, that Dean Wigmore objected to the no-extrinsic-evidence rule. He contended that "[t]he ordinary standard, or 'plain meaning,' is simply the meaning of the people who did *not* write the document." He further stated, "The fallacy [of the conventional view] consists in assuming that there is or ever can be *some one real* or absolute meaning. In truth, there can be only *some person's* meaning; and that person, whose meaning the law is seeking, is the writer of the document. . . ." 9 J. Wigmore, Evidence 190-92 (3d ed. 1940).

Courts have occasionally departed from the conventional rules. In Estate of Gibbs, 14 Wis. 2d 490, 111 N.W.2d 413 (1961), for example, the court openly substituted a correct term for a mistaken term despite finding no ambiguity. Gibbs' will devised one percent of his estate "to Robert J. Krause, now of 4708 North 46th Street, Milwaukee, Wisconsin." At Gibbs' death, and presumably when the will was executed, there was a Robert J. Krause who lived at the 46th Street address. For this reason, the court said, "there is no ambiguity." Nevertheless, the court held that extrinsic evidence could be introduced to the effect that Gibbs never knew Robert J. Krause of 46th Street, but that he did know and intended to benefit one Robert W. Krause, an employee and friend of Gibbs' for some thirty years. The court explained:

[D]etails of identification, particularly such matters as middle initials, street addresses, and the like, which are highly susceptible to mistake, particularly in metropolitan areas, should not be accorded such sanctity as to frustrate an otherwise clearly demonstrable intent. Where such details of identification are involved, courts should receive evidence tending to show that a mistake has been made and should disregard the details when the proof establishes to the highest degree of certainty that a mistake was, in fact, made.

See also Estate of Ikuta, 639 P.2d 400, 405-06 (Haw. 1981) (in replacing the word "old[e]st" with the word "youngest," the court said: "The purpose of the policy against reformation of a will is to prevent distortion of the testator's intent. Dr. Ikuta's will was reformed to reflect the testator's true intent."); Wilson v. First Florida Bank, 498 S.2d 1289 (Fla.App. 1986) (after making a series of devises of tangible personal property and specified amounts of money, testator's will stated "To the University of Georgia, Financial Aid Department . . . in trust . . . to establish a Scholarship Fund. . . ."; court held the will to be ambiguous, admitted attorney's testimony, along with other corroborating extrinsic evidence, that testator intended the devise to the university to be of the residue of his estate, and directed the residue to be distributed to the university); Will of Goldstein, 46 A.D.2d 449, 363 N.Y.S.2d 147 (1975), aff'd per curiam, 38 N.Y.2d 876, 382 N.Y.S.2d 743 (1976).

Engle v. Siegel
74 N.J. 287, 377 A.2d 892 (1977)

MOUNTAIN, J. The facts in this will construction case are not in dispute. In September, 1973, Albert and Judith Siegel, together with their two children, lost their lives as the result of a tragic hotel fire in Copenhagen, Denmark. All died within thirty days of one another. Albert's will was dated April 2, 1964 and Judith's was dated September 29, 1964. The instruments were admitted to probate October 3, 1973 and Louis Engle, Judith's father, qualified as executor of both. A common disaster clause appears in each will. The provision in Albert's will reads as follows:

> In the event my wife JUDITH and my children predecease me, or (this is the event which occurred) if we all die as a result of a common accident, or within thirty (30) days from the date of my death, then in that event, I give, devise and bequeath all the rest, residue and remainder of my estate and property of every kind and nature unto my mother, ROSE SIEGEL, and my mother-in-law, IDA ENGLE, to be divided between them share and share alike.

The corresponding clause in Judith's will was identical except for appropriate alterations as to names and relationships. Rose Siegel, Albert's mother, predeceased her son and daughter-in-law, having died in or about 1967. Judith's mother, Ida Engle, survived and is a party to this action.

The contest has arisen due to the fact that Rose Siegel, named in each will as a residuary legatee, predeceased her son and daughter-in-law. Ida Engle, the other residuary legatee, takes the position that under these circumstances our statute, N.J.S.A. 3A:3-14, becomes operative to cause the entire residuary estate of each decedent to pass to her. This statute reads as follows:

> When a residuary devise or bequest shall be made to 2 or more persons by the will of any testator dying after July 3, 1947, unless a contrary intention shall appear by the will, the share of any such residuary devisees or legatees dying before the testator and not saved from lapse by section 3A:3-13 of this title, or not capable of taking effect because of any other circumstance or cause, shall go to and be vested in the remaining residuary devisee or legatee, if any there be, and if more than 1, then to the remaining residuary devisees or legatees in proportion to their respective shares in said residue. [N.J.S.A. 3A:3-14]

Appellants, Leo H. Siegel and Judith Siegel Baron, are brother and sister of the decedent, Albert Siegel. All three, of course, are also children of the decedent, Rose. It is these appellants' position that the foregoing statute has no relevance here because, by a proper application of the rule of probable intent, the share of each residuary estate set apart for their mother, should now pass to them in equal shares. The trial court found in favor of Ida Engle and the Appellate Division affirmed. Both opinions are unpublished. We granted certification, 71 N.J. 527, 366 A.2d 682 (1976), and now reverse.

Traditionally, and perhaps rather monotonously, courts have repeated, as we do here again, that in construing the terms of a will, a court's task is always to determine the intent of the testator. But these words may be given different meanings and the quest for intent can be undertaken and pursued in various ways. The generally accepted method of determining testamentary intent was once described by this Court in these words,

> It is elementary principle in the construction of wills that the controlling consideration is the effect of the words as actually written rather than the actual intention of the testator independently of the written words. The question is not what the testator actually intended, or what he was minded to say, but rather the meaning of the terms chosen to state the testamentary purpose . . . [In re Armour, 11 N.J. 257, 271, 94 A.2d 286, 292 (1953)]

This statement can no longer be said accurately to express the law of our State. In Fidelity Union Trust Co. v. Robert, 36 N.J. 561, 178 A.2d 185 (1962) this Court, speaking through Justice Jacobs, announced what has come to be known as the doctrine of probable intent. The rule has been stated thus,

> While a court may not, of course, conjure up an interpretation or derive a missing testamentary provision out of the whole cloth, it may, on the basis of the entire will, competent extrinsic evidence and common human impulses strive reasonably to ascertain and carry out what the testator probably intended should be the disposition if the present situation developed. [In re Estate of Burke, 48 N.J. 50, 64, 222 A.2d 273, 280 (1966)]

It must be clear that the quest for intent projected by this definition is something quite different from the more traditional approach set forth in *Armour*. In applying the new rule a court not only examines "the entire will" but also studies "competent extrinsic evidence"; it attributes to the testator "common human impulses" and seeks to find what he would subjectively have desired had he in fact actually addressed the contingency which has arisen. We are no longer limited simply to searching out the probable meaning intended by the words and phrases in the will. Relevant circumstances, including the testator's own expressions of intent, Wilson v. Flowers, 58 N.J. 250, 262-63, 277 A.2d 199 (1971), must also be studied, and their significance assayed. Within prescribed limits, guided primarily by the terms of the will, but also giving due weight to the other factors mentioned above, a court should strive to construe a testamentary instrument to achieve the result most consonant with the testator's "probable intent." . . .

A search for probable intent was greatly facilitated by this Court's decision in Wilson v. Flowers, supra, 58 N.J. 250, 277 A.2d 199, (1971). There we held that direct statements made by the testator were admissible to show such intent. As Justice Proctor observed,

> If our task is to ascertain and follow the testator's probable intent, we cannot fairly exclude evidence of that intent. [58 N.J. at 262, 277 A.2d at 206] . . .
> In considering *Flowers* it is also important to perceive the breadth of the ruling as to the admissibility of extrinsic testimony.
>
> We do not, of course, mean to imply that [extrinsic] evidence can be used to vary the terms of the will, but rather that *it should be admitted first to show if there is an ambiguity and second, if one exists, to shed light on the testator's actual intent.* [58 N.J. at 263, 277 A.2d at 207; emphasis added] . . .

Respondents rely heavily upon N.J.S.A. 3A:3-14. It is important to consider the nature and purpose of this enactment. It is designed to avoid partial intestacy in those instances where one of several residuary legatees or devisees predeceases the testator and the will contains no limitation over in the event of such contingency. The statute rests upon the legislative judgment that under such circumstances a testator would normally prefer that the presumptive share of the beneficiary so dying should pass to other residuary legatees rather than devolve by intestate succession. It is important to realize fully that the act is in no way intended to pre-empt a testamentary plan that can be discerned by a search for probable intent. . . . Not until a quest for probable intent has proven fruitless, will there be any occasion to resort to the statute.

With these considerations in mind, we turn to the facts of this case.

We are satisfied that the death of Rose Siegel, prior to the tragic deaths of the testators, was a contingency not treated specifically in the wills and not actually foreseen or anticipated by the testators. That inference can be readily drawn from an examination of the wills in their entirety, noting especially the numerous provisions therein for gifts or bequests over to named legatees upon death or failure to survive, indicating clearly enough that the testators were mindful of contingencies of this sort and did anticipate dispositions to be made where this occurred. The failure to make a similar provision in the event of the premature death of either mother, where to do so would be completely logical and in keeping with the tenor of the wills, must be ascribed to inadvertence. It is not to be inferred that that omission was purposeful or that, by implication, and intestacy was intended, or that a gift over by operation of the statute was desired. We thus have no hesitancy in concluding that one element justifying the quest for probable intent has been established in this case, namely, that there has indeed occurred a contingency not foreseen or anticipated when the wills were drafted.

We next turn to the relevant and competent extrinsic evidence which bears upon the probable intention of the testators with respect to this unforeseen situation. The attorney who drafted the will, Samuel J. Zucker, Esq., testified as to his conference with Albert and Judith Siegel preceding the drafting of the will. He testified from memory, aided by notes he had made at the conference. The question as to what disposition should be made of their assets in the event of a common disaster was squarely raised. After conferring together, Albert, speaking for his wife and himself, declared that in that event they would like all of their property to be divided equally between their two families. As Albert put it, "split it down the middle so they (the respective families) each get half . . . ." Mr. Zucker pointed out that the word "family" was inappropriate as being "a broad term." The problem so posed by the attorney was obviously perceived as one of form or draftsmanship. Certainly, the attorney did not suggest that the Siegels should not provide for the persons constituting their "family." Nor can his advice to his clients be interpreted to mean that the Siegels were being told to designate an individual legatee rather than one standing in a representative capacity or an identifiable group or class of persons. The sense of this exchange between Mr. Zucker and the Siegels is that, if it was their intention to benefit the class of persons constituting their respective families, that designation would have to be accomplished with more definite and precise language.

The Siegels, after again conferring together, suggested that, in the event then being considered, their property be equally divided between their respective mothers, Rose Siegel and Ida Engle. The will was, of course, drawn to reflect this decision.

We have no difficulty in reaching the conclusion that the primary wish of each decedent, given the contingency that occurred, would have been to divide the property included in their residuary estates between the Siegel family and the Engle family. The designation of their respective mothers resulted solely from the scrivener's rejection of the word "family" as a term to describe the recipient of a testamentary benefaction. Each mother was obviously thought of as an appropriate representative of a "family."

To give the assets of both estates entirely to Mrs. Engle would seem to fly directly in the face of all the evidence bearing upon probable intent. It is perhaps pertinent to note at this point that the assets constituting the estates of both Albert and Judith were derived almost entirely from Albert's earnings. Judith had no money that had come from her own family.

On the other hand, to divide one-half of each residuary estate equally between Leo H. Siegel and Judith Siegel Baron, now obviously the persons constituting the Siegel "family," would seem completely to carry out probable intent. It may be added that Rose Siegel's will, although never probated because she had no assets, was received in evidence. It left everything to her three children in equal shares. Hence, had the order of the deaths of Rose and her son Albert been reversed, presumably Leo Siegel and Judith Baron would have inherited directly from their mother, the shares of their brother's and sister-in-law's estates set aside for the Siegel "family."

We do not adopt the suggestion that the "Siegel" share of the two estates should be deemed to pass through Rose's estate. Having predeceased her son and daughter-in-law she could hardly qualify as a recipient under their wills. We think rather, as stated above, that one-half of the residuary estate of Albert and one-half the residuary estate of Judith should be divided equally between Leo H. Siegel and Judith Siegel Baron. The other shares of each estate will of course pass to Ida Engle.

The judgment of the Appellate Division is reversed and Louis Engle, as executor of each of the two wills, is directed, as soon as may be appropriate, to effect distribution of the assets of both estates pursuant to what we have said above.

CLIFFORD, J. (dissenting). Even with the decent burial given by the Court to In re Armour, 11 N.J. 257, 271, 94 A.2d 286 (1953), I think I would not consign to the decisional graveyard the following from that case:

> The question is not what the testator actually intended, or what he was minded to say, but rather the meaning of the terms chosen to state the testamentary purpose. . . . [Id. at 271, 94 A.2d at 292].

While this statement no longer carries the dogmatic weight it once did, it retains value as a rule of construction. In the construing of a will the basic statutory policy (N.J.S.A. 3A:3-1 et seq.) of allowing the instrument to speak for the testator as of the date of death must be accorded great respect. I understand the court's function to be to determine the testator's intent from the language employed in the will; only if an ambiguity is shown does the doctrine of probable intent as developed in Fidelity Union v. Robert, 36 N.J. 561, 178 A.2d 185 (1962), and its progeny allow extrinsic evidence to be utilized to construe the document.

Mindful of the difficulties which are often present in determining what is or what is not an ambiguity in any instrument, I nevertheless approach this case with the conviction that the doctrine of probable intent should not be used to create an ambiguity in a will which the doctrine will then be called upon to resolve. I am afraid that is exactly what is happening here.

As I understand the operation of the doctrine of probable intent, an ambiguity in the instrument is the condition which triggers the doctrine's application to change the result which would attend a literal application of the language of the will. Wilson v. Flowers, 58 N.J. 250, 263, 277 A.2d 199 (1971). An ambiguity is a "condition of admitting of two or more meanings, of being understood in more than one way, or of referring to two or more things at the same time. . . ." Webster's Third International Dictionary (1961); cf. Allen v. Metropolitan Life Ins. Co., 83 N.J.Super. 223, 237-38, 199 A.2d 254, (App.Div.1964).

I am unable to discern, anymore than could the trial judge, (as he put it) "any uncertainties of expression [or] latent ambiguities of expression within the testamentary writing . . . which would authorize departure from the result prescribed by N.J.S.A. 3A:3-14." The problem as I see it is simply that the instrument omits the necessary language which would save from lapse a bequest to a predeceased legatee. . . . [T]he "contrary intention" required by the statute is likewise absent.

It seems to me that this is the classic situation the legislature had in mind when it enacted N.J.S.A. 3A:3-14 and we should heed its direction rather than rewrite the testator's will. Having survived his mother by about 6 years, he had the opportunity to undertake that rewriting himself. The testator not having done so, I see no reason why this Court should gratuitously second guess him and perform that service.

Notes and Questions

1. *Cases Giving New Meaning to the Use of Extrinsic Evidence to Establish "Ambiguity." Engle* is a case in which the court engaged in reformation in all but name. The "probable intent" doctrine hid what was actually going on. While that doctrine is peculiar to New Jersey, courts in other states have reached similar results under different rationales. One rationale, of course, is construction.

In Estate of Taff, 63 Cal. App. 3d 319, 133 Cal. Rptr. 737 (1976), the court used the rubric of construction to reform a mistaken description in a will. Pearl Taff devised the residue of her estate

> to my heirs in accordance with the laws of intestate succession, in effect at my death in the State of California, or in effect in such other state or such other place as I may be a resident at the time of my death.

The residue of Taff's estate consisted of community property which she had owned with her previously-deceased husband. Because of the community character of the property and because Pearl died without any surviving issue or spouse, the California intestacy statute provides that one half of the property should go to Pearl's blood relatives and the other half should go to the blood relatives of her deceased husband.

The trial court, however, permitted the attorney who drew Pearl's will to testify that she had instructed him that she wanted the residue "to go to her family, her own blood relatives. She felt she was making adequate provision for Harry's (her predeceased husband's) family in the two specific gifts to Harry's sister which she was providing in her will and she felt no obligation to the other members of Harry's blood relations and was making no gifts to them." In view of this testimony, the trial court held that Harry's blood relatives had no right to any portion of the residuary estate. Affirming this judgment, the appellate court said:

> [I]n Estate of Russell (1968) 69 Cal.2d 200, 70 Cal.Rptr. 561, 444 P.2d 353, our Supreme Court substantially abrogated the "plain meaning" rule. . . . In *Russell,* supra, the trial court admitted extrinsic evidence that a named beneficiary of the testatrix's estate, Roxy Russell, was the decedent's dog. In approving the consideration of the extrinsic evidence, the Supreme Court stated:
>
> > . . . extrinsic evidence of the circumstances under which a will is made (except evidence expressly excluded by statute) may be considered by the court in ascertaining what the testator meant by the words used in the will. If in light of such extrinsic evidence, the provisions of the will are reasonably susceptible of two or more meanings claimed to have been intended by the testator, "an uncertainty arises upon the face of a will" (§ 105) and extrinsic evidence relevant to prove any of such meanings is admissible . . ."
>
> Under *Russell,* supra, extrinsic evidence is admissible both to show that a latent ambiguity exists and to resolve the latent ambiguity. . . . "Extrinsic evidence is now admissible to show that the apparently clear and unambiguous language of the will is in fact ambiguous. . . . If . . . the extrinsic evidence does reveal a reasonable second interpretation, the will is deemed to be ambiguous, and [Prob.Code] section 105 will permit the admission of extrinsic evidence to discover the testator's intent." (22 Hastings Law Journal (1971) pp. 1353-1354.)
> . . . *Russell* . . . clearly ended the vitality of . . . the plain meaning rule . . . by permitting the trial court to consider extrinsic evidence to prove a reasonable second meaning of the language used in the will. Extrinsic evidence contradicting the express terms of a will will be excluded today only where no reasonable ambiguity is made to appear by the extrinsic evidence.
> In the present case the declarations of the decedent to her attorney and her sister exposed a latent ambiguity, i.e., that when the testatrix used the term "my heirs" in her will, she intended to exclude the relatives of her predeceased husband, Harry. Under *Russell,* supra, the extrinsic evidence was properly received both to create the ambiguity in the word "heirs" and to resolve the ambiguity. . . .
> Because the extrinsic evidence is not in conflict as to the decedent's intention to exclude the relatives of Harry C. Taff from taking any part of the residuary estate, and because the term "my heirs" as used in the will is reasonably susceptible to mean that decedent's heirs other than the relatives of Harry Taff, the trial court properly decided as a matter of law that appellants have no right to any portion of the residuary estate.

Professors Langbein and Waggoner have made the following observations about *Taff*:

> In the key passage, the court in *Taff* says that "the extrinsic evidence was properly received both to create the ambiguity in the word 'heirs' and to resolve the ambiguity." But this way of stating the matter obliterates the fundamental distinction between ambiguity and mistake. The disputed term in *Taff* that had been mistakenly employed was quite unambiguous. The effect of the decision in *Taff* was to substitute a phrase such as "my natural heirs" for the inapt phrase that the will had employed ("my heirs in accordance with

the laws of intestate succession, in effect at my death in the State of California"), in order to carry out what the court conceived to be the actual or subjective intent of the testatrix. . . . *Taff* reformed the will without admitting, hence without justifying, this departure from traditional law.

Langbein & Waggoner, Reformation of Wills on the Ground of Mistake: Change of Direction in American Law?, 130 U. Pa. L. Rev. 521 (1982).

Can *Taff* be distinguished from Mahoney v. Grainger, supra p. 546, where the court refused to admit extrinsic evidence of a mistaken description?

Essentially the same approach as *Taff* was taken by the Michigan court in Estate of Kremlick, 417 Mich. 237, 331 N.W.2d 228 (1983). In that case, John Kremlick's will devised half the residue of his estate "to the Michigan Cancer Society. . . ." Competing claims to the devise were made by the Michigan Cancer Society (an affiliate of the Michigan Cancer Foundation) and by the American Cancer Society, Michigan Division. The probate court held that the term "Michigan Cancer Society" was unambiguous and refused to hear extrinsic evidence that the American Cancer Society, Michigan Division, was actually the intended devisee. The Supreme Court of Michigan reversed, holding:

> [N]ot only may extrinsic evidence be used to clarify the meaning of a latent ambiguity, but it may be used to demonstrate that an ambiguity exists in the first place and to establish intent.
>
> In this case, appellants [the American Cancer Society, Michigan Division] produced an affidavit from the executrix of Mr. Kremlick's estate in which she asserted that the intended beneficiary was the American Cancer Society, Michigan Division, instead of the Michigan Cancer Society, an affiliate of the Michigan Cancer Foundation. The executrix stated that she had discussed the provisions of Mr. Kremlick's will with him on many occasions, and that he frequently had mentioned that the American Cancer Society was to be a beneficiary. Appellants also sought to establish that Mr. Kremlick previously had made substantial direct contributions to the American Cancer Society, that the society had helped his wife when she was dying of cancer, and that at the time of her death he requested memorials to the American Cancer Society.
>
> This is the very kind of information that may be used both to establish an ambiguity and to help resolve it. Appellants should have been given the opportunity to do that.[8]

---

8. The *Kremlick* decision has provoked different reactions in the lower Michigan courts. In Estate of Elwen, 141 Mich. App. 423, 375 N.W.2d 738 (1984), the court held:

> In the instant case, respondents argued . . . that the terminology "share and share alike" was ambiguous. The probate court did not agree. . . . The court heard no extrinsic evidence relating to the testatrix' intention with respect to the use of the terminology "share and share alike". The *Kremlick* decision does support the argument that the trial court judge should have admitted extrinsic evidence offered by respondents to demonstrate that a latent ambiguity existed even though on its face "share and share alike" is clear and unambiguous. Based on *Kremlick*, we reverse the decision of the probate court and remand the case to it.

In Estate of Burruss, 152 Mich. App. 660, 394 N.W.2d 466 (1986), a different panel of the Court of Appeals held:

2. *Explicit Reformation.* While the other cases studied so far have been instances of reformation in disguise, one court has openly reformed a mistaken will, although it expressly limited the extent to which it was departing from the traditional rules. In In re Snide, 52 N.Y.2d 193, 437 N.Y.S.2d 63, 418 N.E.2d 656 (1981), an attorney prepared mutual wills for Harvey and Rose Snide, husband and wife. At the execution ceremony, the wills were presented to Harvey and Rose in envelopes, with the envelope marked for each containing the will intended for the other. The attorney, the attesting witnesses, Harvey, and Rose all proceeded with the ceremony without anyone taking care to read the front pages or even the attestation clauses of the wills, either of which would have indicated the error.

After Harvey died, Rose sought to probate the will signed by Harvey (but intended as her will). The Surrogate decreed that it could be admitted to probate, and that it could be reformed to substitute the name "Harvey" wherever the name "Rose" appeared, and the name "Rose" wherever the name "Harvey" appeared. The Surrogate reached this result on general equitable principles, apparently without having understood that reformation had traditionally been refused even for a mistake so obvious. The Appellate Division reversed in a memorandum opinion limited to pointing out that the judgment below ignored contrary New York authority dating back into the 1800's.

The New York Court of Appeals reversed the Appellate Division and sustained the power of the Surrogate to reform the will. The Court of Appeals said:

> Under such facts it would indeed be ironic if not perverse to state that because what has occurred is so obvious, and what was intended so clear, we must act to nullify rather than sustain this testamentary scheme. . . .
>
> In reaching this conclusion we do not disregard settled principles, nor are we unmindful of the evils which the formalities of will execution are designed to avoid; namely, fraud and mistake. To be sure, full illumination of the nature of Harvey's testamentary scheme is dependent in part on proof outside of the will itself. However, this is a very unusual case, and the nature of the

---

Relying on *Kremlick*, appellants argue that a letter from the attorney for decedent should have been considered by the probate court. . . .

We hold that the circumstances of the instant case are distinguishable from those considered in *Kremlick*. Here, there was no latent ambiguity in decedent's will to necessitate going beyond the four corners of the document to determine intent. Here, the "survivorship" language suggests a single meaning. There is no extrinsic "fact" which creates a possibility of more than one meaning. Rather, it is an unsupported interpretation of the language of the will and the appellant's perception of their grandmother's intent that is argued to create such a possibility. The letter received by appellants from decedent's attorney was prepared at appellants' request. That attorney drafted the will for decedent 29 years previously. Under such circumstances, it is doubtful that the letter could even be considered to be reliable or persuasive "evidence" of the decedent's intent.

Surely, *Kremlick* cannot be read to imply that a probate court must look at extrinsic evidence to interpret clear legal language every time there is a potential beneficiary who is displeased with the disposition of property by a will. If we were to adopt appellants' interpretation of *Kremlick*, no will, no matter how clear the language used, would be safe from the possibility of attack through the introduction of extrinsic "evidence". Consequently, we decline appellants' invitation to impair the certainty of testamentary dispositions.

additional proof should not be ignored. Not only did the two instruments constitute reciprocal elements of a unified testamentary plan, they both were executed with statutory formality, including the same attesting witnesses, at a contemporaneous execution ceremony. There is absolutely no danger of fraud, and the refusal to read these wills together would serve merely to unnecessarily expand formalism, without any corresponding benefit. On these narrow facts we decline this unjust course.

Nor can we share the fears of the dissent that our holding will be the first step in the exercise of judicial imagination relating to the reformation of wills. Again, we are dealing here solely with identical mutual wills both simultaneously executed with statutory formality.

In Matter of Provenzano, N.Y. L.J., Dec. 13, 1982 (Sur. Ct.), Joseph Provenzano's will devised all of his property "to my beloved husband, Joseph Provenzano." His widow, Josephine Provenzano, contended that she was the intended devisee of his estate. Her argument was that "the literal form of [the will] is the result of an obvious typographical error, due in part to the similarity of [her] name, Josephine, and the decedent's name, Joseph."

Surrogate Signorelli interpreted the *Snide* decision as holding that "the Surrogate's Court [now has] full equitable power to correct obvious mistakes or drafting errors," and proceeded to exercise the newly conferred power, saying:

> Upon a reading of the will in its entirety and upon all the evidence submitted, the court is satisfied that the testator intended to name his spouse as the sole beneficiary of his estate and that the present form of paragraph "First" of the will propounded exists solely as a result of a typographical error. The circumstances existing in Matter of Snide, supra, were likewise the result of an obvious error, although the facts in the instant case do otherwise differ. Notwithstanding, I believe that Matter of Snide, supra, is controlling here. . . . Accordingly, the court does hereby reform paragraph "First" of decedent's will by substituting the words "wife, Josephine Provenzano" for "my beloved husband Joseph Provenzano."

For a similar case in which the Surrogate exercised his equitable power to reform pursuant to *Snide*, see Estate of Porat, N.Y. L.J., Feb. 18, 1986, at 18 (Sur. Ct.).

3. *Endorsement of Will Reformation by Restatement 2d of Property.* The Restatement 2d of Property section 34.7 comment d endorses reformation where the mistake is "significant enough to justify the conclusion that the donative transfer should be set aside or reformed." The comment further provides that mistake as to the identity of the intended beneficiary or mistake arising from a drafting error in carrying out the donor or testator's intention is sufficiently significant to permit reformation. Illustration 11 applies this principle in the context of a mistaken omission by the testator's lawyer of an intended devise.

Langbein & Waggoner, Reformation of Wills on the Ground of Mistake: Change of Direction in American Law?
130 U. Pa. L. Rev. 521, 524-28 (1982)

The no-reformation rule is peculiar to the law of wills. It does not apply to other modes of gratuitous transfer—the so-called nonprobate transfers—even though many are virtually indistinguishable from the will in function. Reformation lies routinely to correct mistakes, both of expression and of omission, in deeds of gift, inter vivos trusts, life insurance contracts, and other instruments that serve to transfer wealth to donees upon the transferor's death. Alternatively, courts sometimes find it necessary to remedy mistakes in these nonprobate transfers by imposing a constructive trust on the mistakenly named beneficiary in favor of the intended beneficiary.

Courts have been willing to use their equity powers in these nonprobate situations, because a case of well-proven mistake necessarily invokes the fundamental principle of the law of restitution: preventing unjust enrichment. If the mistake is not corrected, the mistaken beneficiary is unjustly enriched at the expense of the intended beneficiary. Moreover, when the mistake results from the wrong of a third party, the courts sometimes speak of a second policy: protecting an innocent party (here, the intended beneficiary) from suffering the consequences of another's wrongdoing.

Judicial intervention to prevent unjust enrichment or to protect the victim of wrongdoing has such a manifestly compelling doctrinal basis that the puzzle is to explain why the courts have not been willing to act similarly when the document affected by the mistake is a will. Unjust enrichment (or third-party negligence) is equally wrong whether the resulting error occurs in an inter vivos transfer or in a will. Both transfers are gratuitous, both unilateral. Accordingly, we emphasize as a starting point that the no-reformation rule for wills cannot rest on the notion that there is no wrong to remedy. Why, then, does equity refuse to remedy unjust enrichment in the case of a mistaken will?

The customary justification has to do with the nature of the evidence in cases of testation. A will is by definition "ambulatory," meaning ineffective to pass property until the death of the testator. Evidence suggesting that the document is affected by mistake—that the will is at variance with the testator's actual intent—must necessarily be presented when death has placed the testator beyond reply. The testimony will typically involve statements allegedly made by the testator, so-called direct declarations of intent, which he can now neither corroborate nor deny. The testator's main protection against fabricated or mistaken evidence is the will itself. Therefore, it is argued, evidence extrinsic to the will should be excluded. And if extrinsic evidence is excluded, the court can have no grounds to reform.

There are, we think, two persuasive answers. First, although the living donor under an inter vivos instrument can take the stand and testify about his true intent, this testimony does not have automatic reliability. The donor's testimony doubtless reflects his current intent, but the matter in issue is his intent at the time the instrument was executed. The instrument may have stated this intent accurately; he may since have changed his mind and now be lying or deceiving himself, or he may be mistaken about what he originally intended. Consequently, even the donor's own testimony is properly regarded as inherently suspect, which is why even such testimony is put to the clear-and-convincing-evidence test.

Second, and still more telling, reformation of documents effecting gratuitous inter vivos transfers is routinely granted even after the death of the donor. In these cases, the extrinsic evidence is inherently suspect for exactly the reason that evidence of a testator's intent is suspect when offered against a will. Nevertheless, in nonprobate transfers when the clear-and-convincing-evidence standard has been satisfied, clauses omitted by mistake have been inserted; mistaken designations of the beneficiaries, of the property intended to have been the subject matter of the gift, and of the extent of the interest intended to have been granted to the beneficiary have been corrected. Documents drafted by lawyers (or others) have not been distinguished from self-drawn documents; enrichment of an un-intended donee at the expense of the intended donee is unjust whether the mistake has been made by the donor or by his lawyer. The essential safeguard in these cases has been the clear-and-convincing-evidence standard, which appellate courts have policed rigorously.

Accordingly, we think that there is no principled way to reconcile the exclusion of extrinsic evidence in the law of wills with the rule of admissibility in the law of nonprobate transfers. Not surprisingly, the no-extrinsic-evidence rule has long been embattled even in the traditional law of wills; it has been subjected to a variety of exceptions . . . ; and it is now on the decline. Wigmore's immensely influential critique of the no-extrinsic-evidence rule underlies its abrogation in California and New Jersey. Wigmore argued that any effort to limit the proofs to the words of a document runs afoul of the "truth . . . that words *always* need interpretation. . . ." Wigmore coined the famous phrase that "the 'plain meaning' . . . is simply the meaning of the people who did *not* write the document."

The Continental legal tradition has for centuries been opposed to our no-extrinsic-evidence rule. The testator's subjective intent predominates over literal meaning; extrinsic evidence is freely admissible, and techniques of supplementary interpretation (*erganzende Auslegung*) allow courts to fashion remedies on the imputed intent principle (what would the testator have desired had he known?). The treatises give no indication that the reception of extrinsic evidence has been anything of a trouble spot. Quite the contrary suggestion was made in evidence to the English Law Reform Committee by the late Professor E.J. Cohn, an experienced practitioner in both England and Germany: "It is my impression that there are rather more disputes on the meaning of wills in this country than in the civilian countries. This may partly be due to the fact that complex rules like [those attempting to exclude extrinsic evidence] invite lawsuits."

We believe that the evidentiary problem, although important, does not in fact explain or justify the no-reformation rule in matters of testamentary mistake. If the courts had not been deeply worried about another policy, namely, compliance with Wills Act formality, we think that they would long ago have followed the evidentiary practice in nonprobate transfers for dealing with claims of mistake. Instead of excluding the evidence, and thereby foreclosing any chance of proving the mistake, the courts would have dealt with the potential unreliability of the evidence by admitting it and testing it against the higher-than-ordinary standard of proof that has worked so well in the law of nonprobate transfers.

Notes and Questions

1. *Commonwealth Reformation Legislation.* One path for changing the traditional common-law rule against reformation of wills is legislation that authorizes the court to correct mistakes in wills. In the United Kingdom, section 20 of the Administration of Justice Act of 1982 provides that "[i]f a court is satisfied that a will is so expressed that it fails to carry out the testator's intentions, in consequence (a) of a clerical error; or (b) of a failure to understand his instructions, it may order that the will shall be rectified so as to carry out his intentions. . . ." Similarly, in Australia, the New South Wales Wills, Probate and Administration (Amendment) Act of 1989 provides in section 29A1 that "[i]f the court is satisfied that a will is so expressed that it fails to carry out the testator's intentions, it may order that the will be rectified so as to carry out the testator's intentions."

2. *Reformation in Limited Cases.* Although no broad reformation legislation yet exists in this country, reformation may be permitted in limited circumstances. One of those circumstances is when the reformation is necessary to obtain certain tax benefits. Despite the general acceptance of the no-reformation rule, for example, state courts seem to be inclined to reform split-interest charitable trusts, created by will or otherwise, to conform them to the federal tax requirements for an estate or gift tax charitable deduction. See, e.g., Estate of Burdon-Miller, 456 A.2d 1266 (Me. 1983). IRC section 2055(e)(3) provides that a charitable deduction shall be allowed for the charitable interest in a split-interest trust "in respect of any qualified reformation." "Qualified reformation" is defined as "a change of a governing instrument by reformation, amendment, construction, or otherwise which changes a reformable interest into a qualified interest but only if . . . such change is effective as of the date of the decedent's death."

Courts have also reformed a will to give a better federal tax result by splitting of a single QTIP trust into three separate QTIP trusts, one of which would be a $ 1 million trust with an "inclusion ratio" of 0. See supra p. 375. The court emphasized that "all interested persons under the present single QTIP trust would remain entitled to precisely the same interests as he or she would have if the will were not construed as proposed," and noted further that "this court has the power to construe and reform testator's will if the will, as written, does not carry out his intention, provided such reformation does not attempt to alter tax consequences retroactively or to change in any respect the dispositive provisions of his will." Will of Choate, 533 N.Y.S.2d 272 (Sur. Ct. 1988). See also First Agricultural Bank v. Coxe, 406 Mass. 879, 550 N.E.2d 875 (1990).

An Oregon statute provides that provisions in a will or trust instrument making a transfer to the donor's spouse with the intent of qualifying for the federal estate or gift tax marital deduction "shall be interpreted consistently with that intent, and the rights, powers and discretion possessed by any fiduciary appointed to administer the will or trust instrument shall be exercisable only in a manner consistent with that intent. The intent to qualify for the marital deduction must be established by a preponderance of the evidence from the language of the will or trust instrument." Or. Rev. Stat. § 118.025.

It is widely recognized that courts have general equity power to reform charitable trusts, whether created by will or otherwise, if the specific charitable purpose becomes impracticable. See infra Chapter 13.

Finally, legislation and judicial authority exists in a number of states authorizing courts to reform dispositive provisions created by will or otherwise that violate the Rule Against Perpetuities. See infra Chapter 17.

3. *Questions.* In many of the cases studied in previous chapters, the testator's intent was apparently frustrated. Examples include Estate of Spencer, supra p. 280, and Crosby v. Alton Ochsner Medical Foundation, supra p. 302. Would the adoption of a general reformation doctrine for wills, as advocated in the Langbein-Waggoner article, provide an avenue for remedying the mistakes that occurred in these cases? What about under section 20 of the U.K. Administration of Justice Act of 1982, supra?

In Connecticut Junior Republic v. Sharon Hospital, supra p. 567, would the denial of probate of the second codicil, as the plaintiffs requested, have prevented the unjust enrichment of unintended takers, or would it have been necessary to reform the second codicil to achieve this objective?

4. *Reformation of Other Transactions.* In Penn Mutual Life Ins. Co. v. Abramson, 530 A.2d 1202 (D.C. 1987), the decedent, Abdur Rahman Y. Ibn-Tamas, purchased a life-insurance policy in 1974, naming as primary beneficiary his second wife, Beverly Ann Ibn-Tamas; and naming as secondary beneficiaries, his three children (two of whom were children of his first marriage and the third of whom was a child of his second marriage). Beverly murdered Abdur. Five months later, Beverly gave birth to their second child (Abdur's fourth child).

A suit was brought to reform the life-insurance beneficiary designation to include the new-born child. Is this an appropriate case for reformation? (The court held that it was not.)

In Webb v. Webb, 301 S.E.2d 570 (W. Va. 1983), Chester G. Webb died intestate, survived by his widow, Lillian Webb, and an adopted son, Chester David Webb. Under the intestacy statute, title to the decedent's house passed to Chester David Webb, subject to the dower interest of Lillian Webb.

Believing that his father wanted his mother to have fee ownership in the house, Chester David Webb (along with his mother) consulted an attorney to see how best to accomplish that objective. Responding to the attorney's question about his marital status, the son stated that he was not married. The attorney did not pursue the inquiry further, and suggested that the son file a disclaimer of his intestate interest in the property. The attorney prepared the disclaimer, which was then executed and recorded. After the disclaimer was recorded, the attorney discovered that the son was divorced and had a child, an infant daughter, who was living with the son's former wife. This meant that under Virginia law, the effect of the son's disclaimer was to vest title to the disclaimed interest in the son's daughter, not the son's mother. A proceeding was brought to set aside the disclaimer, but relief was denied. The Supreme Court of Appeals of West Virginia based its affirmance of the lower court's denial of relief on the following ground:

> In this case the [son] committed a mistake of law and [the attorney] committed a mistake of fact. In both instances the mistake was the result of an omission on the part of the one who committed it. Either person could have, it is assumed, prevented the execution of the disclaimer by acting diligently: the [son], by revealing to counsel facts of which he was aware and which he should have known to have a bearing on the legal result he sought to effect, and counsel, by making further inquiry into the relevant aspects of the [son's] background. In view of the lack of diligence on the part of both the [son] and counsel, we cannot say that the mistakes in this case, taken separately or together, are such that would justify invalidating the disclaimer. Negligence, if any, is a matter between the [son] and counsel, and does not, in our opinion, affect the validity of the disclaimer.

Professor Palmer has stated that this decision "is remarkable for its lack of understanding of the problem. . . . Surely it is time for our courts to put aside the mistake of law rule and apply elementary principles of justice." Palmer on Restitution § 18.6(a) (Supp. 1988).

PART C. ATTORNEY LIABILITY FOR MISTAKE

Would liability for malpractice or for breach of a third-party beneficiary contract be better solutions to the problem of attorney mistake than the adoption of a reformation doctrine? If a reformation remedy were to become available, would there still be room for liability even in cases where the reformation remedy was successfully invoked? Consider the following discussion of these questions in Langbein & Waggoner, Reformation of Wills on the Ground of Mistake: Change of Direction in American Law?, 130 U. Pa. L. Rev. 521, 588-90 (1982):

> Because the error in many mistake cases is sufficiently egregious that a victim might be able to invoke the malpractice liability of the lawyer-draftsman if relief of mistake were denied, the argument can be made the malpractice remedy makes relief for mistake unnecessary. The intended beneficiary whose devise has been frustrated by the lawyer's mistake can be

remitted to his malpractice remedy against the offending draftsman. We think that there are a variety of responses to this contention.

Initially, we note that there is a range of mistake cases that fall outside the scope of malpractice relief, including homedrawn wills and those lawyer-drafted wills where for whatever reason the mistake does not rise to the level of malpractice. Furthermore, in a considerable fraction of lawyer malpractice cases, the draftsman may be wholly or partially judgment-proof, as when he is long since deceased,[9] or when he is uninsured or underinsured. In one region of the country for which a specialist insurance broker has supplied recent data on malpractice coverage to the American Bar Association's Standing Committee on Lawyers' Professional Liability, 51% of the policies in force have $100,000/$300,000 limits, well below the value of significant numbers of testate estates. For devises of unique property, for example, Blackacre or the family bible, relief in damages would not be an adequate substitute.

The malpractice solution is also objectionable because it would channel mistake cases into the tort system. When translated into a tort claim and discounted for the litigation expenses and counsel fees, and for the unpredictability and delay incident to the jury-dominated tort system, a devise frustrated by mistake would be worth but a fraction of the value in the testator's estate.

More fundamentally, the change in theory from devise to tort raises a serious problem of unjust enrichment. Whereas most forms of malpractice inflict deadweight loss that can only be put right by compensation, in these testamentary mistake cases a benefit is being transferred from the intended beneficiary to a mistaken devisee. That devisee is a volunteer lacking any claim of entitlement or justified reliance. The malpractice solution would leave the benefit where it fortuitously fell, thereby creating a needless loss to be charged against the draftsman (or his insurer). So long as the draftsman's error was innocent (which is what distinguishes mistake from fraud), there is no reason to exaggerate his liability in this way. If, on the other hand, the lawyer were charged with the malpractice but subrogated to the tort plaintiff's mistake claim, the mistake doctrine would simply be recognized in a circular and more litigious fashion.

We do not mean to say that negligent draftsmen will be immune from malpractice liability in testamentary mistake cases. When the malpractice causes true loss, that loss should be compensable. One such item of compensable loss may be the reasonable litigation expenses of the parties to the reformation (or other) proceeding occasioned by the mistake. We can also imagine circumstances in which a mistake might come to light after distribution and dissipation of the mistakenly devised property; here the change of position of the mistaken devisee would constitute justified reliance and require that the intended beneficiary be remitted to his malpractice remedy.

Finally, we point once more to the experience under the many existing doctrines that provide partial relief in the field of testamentary mistake. There has been no suggestion in the "mere construction" and other cases [set forth supra Part A] that malpractice should be regarded as an alternative to direct relief.

---

9. A malpractice claim against an attorney may survive the attorney's death. *McStowe v. Borenstein*, 377 Mass. 804, 388 N.E.2d 674 (1979).

Professors Langbein and Waggoner argue that a reformation remedy is a better means of promoting justice than a malpractice remedy. In the malpractice case that follows, consider whether judicial reformation or malpractice liability is the better means of remedying the lawyer's mistake.

Ogle v. Fuiten
102 Ill. 2d 356, 466 N.E.2d 224 (1984)

GOLDENHERSH, J. Plaintiffs, James Elvin Ogle and Leland W. Ogle, initiated this action in the circuit court of Sangamon County against defendants, Lorraine Fuiten, as executrix of the estate of William F. Fuiten, and Robert G. Heckenkamp, who, under the name of Heckenkamp and Fuiten, had been associated with William F. Fuiten in the practice of law. In a two-count complaint plaintiffs alleged that William F. Fuiten had negligently drafted wills for Oscar H. Smith and Alma I. Smith, respectively an uncle and aunt of plaintiffs, and alternatively, that Fuiten failed to properly perform his contract with the Smiths to fulfill their testamentary intentions, and in so doing, failed to benefit the plaintiffs. Defendants moved to dismiss for failure to state a cause of action. The circuit court allowed the motion, and plaintiffs appealed. The appellate court reversed and remanded, and we allowed defendants' petition for leave to appeal.

The appellate court summarized the allegations contained in the complaint as follows:

> Count I essentially alleges: (1) Testators employed defendant Fuiten and the law firm of Heckenkamp and Fuiten to prepare wills in accordance with the testators' intentions; (2) the wills were prepared; (3) neither testator intended their property to devolve by the law of intestate succession; (4) it was their intention that their property be left to plaintiffs if neither testator survived the other by 30 days; (5) this contingency occurred; (6) Fuiten owed plaintiffs the duty of ascertaining the testators' intentions in all foreseeable events and to draft wills which would effectuate these intentions; (7) Fuiten breached this duty and negligently drafted the subject wills; and (8) plaintiffs suffered damage as a direct result of this breach.
>
> Count II essentially alleges the first five allegations noted above and additionally alleges: (6) the purpose of the employment of Fuiten and the firm was to draft wills not only for the benefit of testators, but for the benefit of these plaintiffs; (7) Fuiten and the firm were paid the agreed consideration under the employment agreement; (8) Fuiten and the firm knew plaintiffs were intended beneficiaries of the wills and the employment agreement; (9) Fuiten and the firm had agreed to draft wills leaving the property to plaintiffs in the event neither testator survived the other by 30 days; (10) Fuiten breached this agreement in that the wills failed to fulfill the testators' intentions; and (11) plaintiffs suffered foreseeable, direct damage as a consequence of this breach.

The wills of Oscar H. Smith and Alma I. Smith contained the following provisions:

SECOND: I give, devise and bequeath all of my estate, real, personal and mixed wheresoever situated to my wife, ALMA I. SMITH, if she [my husband, OSCAR H. SMITH, if he] shall survive me within thirty (30) days from the date of my death.

THIRD: I direct that if my wife, ALMA I. SMITH, [my husband, OSCAR H. SMITH] and I die in or from a common disaster that my estate be equally divided between my nephews, JAMES ELVIN OGLE, and LELAND OGLE, share and share alike.

These wills were construed in In re Estate of Smith (1979), 68 Ill.App.3d 30, 24 Ill.Dec. 451, 385 N.E.2d 363, and it was held that because Oscar Smith died suddenly of a stroke on April 10, 1977, and his wife, Alma, died 15 days later from a lingering cancer illness, and neither will contained any other dispositive provisions, their estates passed by intestacy to persons other than plaintiffs.

Because the judgment appealed from was entered upon allowance of defendants' motion to dismiss, all facts properly pleaded in the complaint must be taken as true. A cause of action should not be dismissed on the pleadings unless it clearly appears that no set of facts can be proved which will entitle plaintiffs to recover.

Conceding that under Pelham v. Griesheimer (1982), 92 Ill.2d 13, 64 Ill.Dec. 544, 440 N.E.2d 96, privity is not a prerequisite to an action by a nonclient against an attorney, defendants argue that the complaint fails to allege a duty owed plaintiffs. They argue that the only duty owed by defendants was to provide each testator "with a valid testamentary instrument that disposes of the testators' property at his death in the manner expressly stated in his will." They argue that to permit persons unnamed in the will, or persons named with a precondition which fails to occur, to bring an action against the attorney "creates an unlimited and unknown class of potential plaintiffs." They contend, too, that in order to recover from an attorney, a nonclient must allege and prove "that the primary purpose and intent of the attorney-client relationship itself was to benefit or influence the third party." Defendants argue that under this "intent to directly benefit" test, plaintiffs' cause fails because the testators' intent, as defined in the will-construction action, shows that plaintiffs were to benefit only under certain circumstances which did not occur. Thus, defendants contend, the intent of the testators to benefit plaintiffs is not, as required by Pelham, "clearly evident."

Also citing Pelham, plaintiffs contend that they have alleged facts which show that the testators, in obtaining the services of the defendants in the preparations of the wills, intended to "directly benefit" plaintiffs and that, as held by the appellate court, they have stated a cause of action in both counts of the complaint. . . .

Defendants argue that to state a cause of action plaintiffs should be required to show, from the express terms of the will, that the plaintiff was an intended beneficiary of the relationship between the defendant attorney and the testator. They argue that this would protect against a flood of litigation. Defendants have cited no authority which has applied the rule which they espouse, and we find no basis in the cases which we have examined for imposing such a requirement.

We agree with the appellate court that "the allegations of count I sufficiently state the traditional elements of negligence in tort and count II sufficiently states the traditional elements of a third-party beneficiary/breach of contract theory." We note parenthetically that, unlike Pelham, the defendants' representation of the testators here was of a nonadversarial nature and consisted only of the drafting of the wills which plaintiffs alleged were for their benefit as intended beneficiaries. See Pelham v. Griesheimer (1982), 92 Ill.2d 13, 22, 64 Ill.Dec. 544, 440 N.E.2d 96.

Defendants contend that this action is an impermissible collateral attack upon the judicial determination of the validity of the testators' wills. Defendants' argument appears to be that because the wills were held valid, the question of the testators' intent has been settled, and plaintiffs may not now state a cause of action based on the allegation that the wills do not reflect the true intent of the testators.

In support of their position defendants cite Robinson v. First State Bank (1983), 97 Ill.2d 174, 73 Ill.Dec. 428, 454 N.E.2d 288, and attempt to analogize the claim in Robinson that the testator's attorney, through tortious interference, had prevented the plaintiffs from receiving their inheritance to the allegations here that the testators' attorney, because of negligence or breach of contract, had prevented plaintiffs from receiving the testators' estates. In *Robinson,* holding that the action, in effect, was a tardy will contest, this court affirmed the circuit court's dismissal of the action for tortious interference. Defendants argue that the present action necessarily assumes that the wills are invalid, without having been contested by plaintiffs on that ground within the statutory time.

We find *Robinson* distinguishable in that the basis for the plaintiffs' complaint was that the testator had been subject to the undue influence of her attorney. Claims of undue influence are properly raised in a will-contest action. In the present case, however, the basis for the plaintiffs' complaint is that, because of the attorney's negligence, the testators' true intent is not reflected in the wills. Thus, while the plaintiffs in *Robinson* had the opportunity to pursue their claims in a will-contest action, plaintiffs here had no similar opportunity to do so.

We note further that if plaintiffs here are successful in their action, the orderly disposition of the testators' property is not disrupted, and the provisions of the wills, and the probate administration, remain unaffected. On these facts, the present action is not a collateral attack on the wills. . . .

For the foregoing reasons, the judgment of the appellate court is affirmed.

Notes and Questions

1. *The Privity Problem. Ogle* illustrates the modern trend to abrogate the privity requirement and allow malpractice actions in tort, contract, or both by the intended beneficiaries for mistakes in wills.

A recent article lists five states—Nebraska, New York, Ohio, Texas, and Virginia—as the only ones whose courts have expressly retained the privity barrier in decisions since 1961. See Begleiter, Attorney Malpractice in Estate Planning—You've Got to Know When to Hold Up, Know When to Fold Up, 38 Kan. L. Rev. 193 (1990). The Ohio case cited by the author is Simon v. Zipperstein, 32 Ohio St. 3d 74, 512 N.E.2d 636 (1987). In *Zipperstein*, the court held that a devisee of the testator's will had no cause of action against the drafting attorney for having drafted the will in such a way that the devisee received substantially less than the testator intended. Privity was lacking, the court said, "since [plaintiff], as a potential beneficiary of [testator's] estate, had no vested interest in the estate." A later Ohio case, however, seems somewhat to have backed away from the *Zipperstein* holding. In Elam v. Hyatt Legal Services, 44 Ohio St. 3d 175, 541 N.E.2d 616 (1989), the court held that the devisees of an estate had a cause of action against the executor's attorney for negligently preparing and recording a certificate of transfer that failed to recognize the plaintiffs' remainder interest devised to them by the testator's will. The court held that "a beneficiary whose interest in an estate is vested is in privity with the fiduciary of the estate, and where such privity exists the attorney for the fiduciary is not immune from liability to the vested beneficiary for damages arising from the attorney's negligent performance." In a footnote, the court seemed to admit that it had wrongly decided the *Zipperstein* case; footnote 2 stated: "We note without comment that, while the holding in *Zipperstein* . . . was based largely on the fact that the person in question was only a potential beneficiary, a review of the facts seems to indicate that the person's interest was vested."

The Iowa court has adopted a curious position on the privity question. In Schreiner v. Scoville, 410 N.W.2d 679 (Iowa 1987), attorney Scoville prepared and witnessed Mary Eickholt's will, which devised to Martin Schreiner one-half her interest in a parcel of real estate. Schreiner also received one-half the residuary estate. Scoville subsequently prepared a codicil for Eickholt, reaffirming her intention to leave Schreiner the real estate interest but removing him as residuary devisee. Less than a month after the codicil was executed, Scoville, acting on behalf of Eickholt, brought an action to partition the real estate parcel, which was thereafter sold. Eickholt died several months after receiving the proceeds from the partition sale. In a will construction proceeding, the court concluded that the devise to Schreiner was adeemed and that the proceeds passed under the residuary clause. Schreiner sued Scoville for malpractice, alleging that Eickholt had intended that he (Scoville) receive the proceeds and that Scoville had negligently drafted her will in a way that failed to fulfill her testamentary intent.

Reversing the trial court's dismissal of the action for failure to state a cause of action, the Iowa Supreme Court initially stated that "a lawyer owes a duty of care to the direct, intended, and specifically identifiable beneficiaries of the testator as expressed in the testator's testamentary instruments." The court went on, however, to state a further limitation:

> [W]e hold a cause of action ordinarily will arise only when as a direct result of the lawyer's professional negligence the testator's intent *as expressed in the testamentary instruments* is frustrated in whole or in part and the beneficiary's interest in the estate is lost, diminished or unrealized. . . .
>
> If the testator's intent, as expressed in the testamentary instruments, is fully implemented, no further challenge will be allowed. Thus, a beneficiary who is simply disappointed with what he or she received from the estate will have no cause of action against the testator's lawyer. This limitation, which protects the integrity and solemnity of an individual's testamentary instruments as well as the testator's express intent, will not apply if the lawyer concedes negligence.

Id. at 683 (emphasis added). On the facts, the court held that the complaint stated a cause of action because the proof might show that the will, the codicil, and the partition "were interrelated, were closely connected in time, dealt directly with a specific piece of property, and that Scoville represented Eickholt's interest in all three transactions."

In what situations will malpractice liability lie against Iowa estate planners?

2. Additional Recovery for Emotional Distress? If the intended beneficiaries suffer compensable economic loss as a result of an attorney's negligence, can they also recover for emotional distress? Cf. Tara Motors v. Superior Court, 276 Cal. Rptr. 603, 606, 609 (Cal. Ct. App. 1990) ("[I]t is in the public interest negligent attorneys be held responsible for injury to their clients and not be afforded favored treatment under the law. . . . We find no reason to require a client suffering substantial economic damages to demonstrate willful misconduct in order to recover damages for emotional distress.").

EXTERNAL REFERENCES. Jenkins, Privity—A Texas-Size Barrier to Third Parties for Negligent Will Drafting—An Assessment and Proposal, 42 Baylor L. Rev. 687 (1990); Johnston, Legal Malpractice in Estate Planning—Perilous Times Ahead for the Practitioner, 67 Iowa L. Rev. 629 (1982); Note, Legal Malpractice for the Negligent Drafting of a Testamentary Instrument: Schreiner v. Scoville, 73 Iowa L. Rev. 1231 (1988); Note, Privity as a Bar to Recovery in Negligent Will-Preparation Cases: A Rule Without a Reason, 57 U. Cin. L. Rev. 1123 (1989); Note, *Hale v. Groce*: Lawyer Liability to Intended Beneficiaries of Negligently Drafted Wills—Last Stand of the Immutable Privity Doctrine, 24 Willamette L. Rev. 843 (1988).

Chapter 11

TRUSTS: FORMATION AND FORMALITY

PART A. INTRODUCTION

Bacon said that the use (or trust) "grew to strength and credit by degrees."[1] In 1911, Sir Frederick Maitland looked back on the development of the trust idea and declared it to be "the greatest and most distinctive achievement performed by Englishmen in the field of jurisprudence."[2] Today, without doubt, private trusts and, to a lesser extent, charitable trusts (see Chapter 13) sit at the core of modern estate-planning practice. In 1987, the Federal Reserve Board reported that federally insured commercial and savings banks held 1.4 million personal trust accounts averaging about

---

1. Quoted in Scott on Trusts § 1.2.

2. Maitland, The Unincorporated Body, in 3 F. Maitland, Collected Papers 271, 272 (1911). This is not to suggest, however, that concepts similar to the trust have not been developed by other legal systems. A statutory adoption of the common-law trust is in place in Louisiana. La. Rev. Stat. Ann. §§ 9:1731-9:2252; Lorio, Louisiana Trusts: The Experience of a Civil Law Jurisdiction With the Trust, 42 La. L. Rev. 1721 (1982). And, several civil-law countries have adopted concepts serving similar purposes, such as the German *Treuhand*. See Martinez, Trust and the Civil Law, 42 La. L. Rev. 1709 (1982). Also, the Islamic legal system judicially developed a concept similar to a charitable trust, called the *waghf*, which has been extended by statute in some Islamic states to permit a use similar to the private express trust. E.g., Iranian Civ. Code ch. 2. See Fratcher, The Islamic Wakf, 36 Mo. L. Rev. 153 (1971); Comment, The Influence of the Islamic Law of Waqf on the Development of the Trust in England: The Case of Merton College, 136 U. Pa. L. Rev. 1231 (1988).

$302,000 each in value, for an aggregate value of $422.5 billion.[3] Uncounted in these figures are the vast numbers of personal trusts held by private trustees.

For a definition of a private trust, we turn first to the Restatement 2d of Trusts:

> § 2. *Definition of Trust.* A trust . . . is a fiduciary relationship with respect to property, subjecting the person by whom the title to the property is held to equitable duties to deal with the property for the benefit of another person, which arises as a result of a manifestation of an intention to create it.[4]

1. Historical Development of Trusts

The modern trust described in the Restatement grew out of the *feoffment to uses*. In the thirteenth century, shortly after the Norman Conquest, people (nearly always men) from time to time enfeoffed land to another "to the use" of a third.[5] The maker of the enfeoffment was called the feoffor. In the modern trust, that person is called the *settlor* (or the grantor, trustor, founder, donor, or creator). The one to whom the land was enfeoffed was called the feoffee to uses. Today, we call that person the *trustee*. The third person, the one for whose benefit the land was held, was called the cestui que uses. We know that person today as the *beneficiary* or, less commonly, the cestui que trust. Back then, the evidence suggests that the nearly invariable subject of a use was land.[6] Today, the subject of a trust can still be land, but more commonly it is personal property in the form of investment securities. Whether real or personal property, the subject of the trust is also variously identified as the trust property, the corpus, the principal, or the res.

Normally, there is more than one beneficiary, such as when G transfers property to T, in trust, with a direction to pay income to A for life, then at A's death to transfer the corpus to B. Such a trust gives A an "equitable life estate" and B an "equitable remainder." T's interest is a "legal" estate, probably a fee simple.[7]

---

3. Board of Governors of the Federal Reserve System, Trust Assets of Financial Institutions — 1987, at 8. The aggregate value of the personal trusts is dwarfed by the $1.05 trillion held by those same banks in employee-benefit trusts.

4. The Restatement expressly exempts charitable, resulting, and constructive trusts from this definition.

5. In these early times, the use arrangement was often made for the benefit of the Franciscan friars, whose poverty vows made it impossible for them to own property but who still had to have shelter and land to cultivate.

6. E.g., Maitland, The Unincorporated Body, in 3 F. Maitland, Collected Papers 271, 273 (1911). But see Barbour, Some Aspects of Fifteenth-Century Chancery, 31 Harv. L. Rev. 834, 850 (1918).

7. Subject to a manifestation of a different intention, the Restatement 2d of Trusts § 88 states that the trustee of an interest in land takes such estate "as is necessary to enable him to perform the trust by the exercise of such powers as are incident to ownership of the estate," and a trustee of personal property takes "an interest of unlimited duration and not an interest

The settlor can create a trust during her or his lifetime (an inter-vivos or living trust) or by will (a testamentary trust). An inter-vivos trust can be either irrevocable or, as we know from Chapter 7, revocable. The settlor of an inter-vivos trust can name herself or himself as trustee (a self-declared trust) or name a third-party as trustee. The settlor can also reserve for herself or himself a beneficial interest in the trust; chapter 7 taught us that this often happens in the case of a revocable inter-vivos trust, where the arrangement is essentially a probate-avoidance device, with the settlor commonly being the beneficiary of the income interest.

Nature of the Beneficiary's Interest. The Restatement's definition of a trust, above, might give the impression that the beneficiary's interest is nothing more than a right in personam, enforceable in equity against the trustee. At one time, students of the law of trusts thought of it that way.[8] But a trust is now seen as a property arrangement under which ownership of the property is divided: The trust property's *legal* title goes to the trustee and its *equitable* (or beneficial) title goes to the beneficiary or, more usually, is divided along temporal lines between income beneficiaries and beneficiaries of future interests in corpus.

To say that the trustee holds "legal" title signifies that the law courts recognized the feoffee to uses (the trustee) as the sole owner of the trust property, with the chancery or equity courts recognizing and enforcing the rights of the cestui que uses (the beneficiary). Despite the general merging of law and equity, we still speak of "legal" and "equitable" obligations, though in most states today they are enforced by the same court. To be sure, also, this division-of-ownership idea embraces within it an allocation of rights and duties. Holding legal but not beneficial title carries with it fiduciary duties with respect to the property; holding equitable title confers rights in personam to enforce those duties. But it is now generally agreed that the beneficiary also has rights in rem, an equitable property interest in the assets held in trust.[9] See Restatement 2d of Trusts § 130. Of decisive influence in this regard is the application of the Rule Against Perpetuities to beneficial interests in trust. The Rule Against Perpetuities is strictly a rule of property law. Most perpetuity cases are concerned with the validity of a beneficial interest in trust.

Enforcement. Despite the earlier question about the nature of the beneficiary's interest, one point has long been clear: The trustee's fiduciary

---

limited to the duration of the trust." Comment d declares that "if the trustee is given power to make a sale or mortgage of the fee simple or to convey a fee simple to the beneficiaries, the trustee takes an estate in fee simple in the absence of evidence of a different intention of the transferor."

8. F. Maitland, Equity 29, 107 (2d ed. 1936); J. Ames, Lectures on Legal History 76, 262 (1913); Stone, The Nature of the Rights of the Cestui Que Trust, 17 Colum. L. Rev. 467 (1917). One of the modern-era writers on trusts who espouses this view is R. Powell, Law of Real Property ¶ 515 (rev. ed. 1990).

9. Bogert on Trusts § 183; C. Houston, The Enforcement of Decrees in Equity 136-48 (1915); Scott on Trusts §§ 1, 130; Durfee, Equity in Rem, 14 Mich. L. Rev. 219 (1916); Scott, The Nature of the Rights of the Cestui Que Trust, 17 Colum. L. Rev. 269 (1917).

duties run in favor of the beneficiary. Unless the settlor is also a beneficiary, the settlor has no standing to enforce the trust.

In the beginning stages, the feoffor could do little more than trust to the honor of the feoffee to uses. When that trust was misplaced, the law courts gave no remedy.[10] In such circumstances, it was to be expected that appeals would be made to the Chancellor for relief, and in the first half of the fifteenth century, at the suit of the cestui que use (beneficiary), the Chancellor began to force the feoffee (trustee) to perform his undertakings.[11]

In the same century, the law courts developed the action of assumpsit and thus began the enforcement of simple contracts. It could have happened that assumpsit would be used to enforce the obligations of the trustee, but it did not happen. The idea of privity would have stood in the way of enforcement at the suit of a third-party beneficiary, and for that matter it would today in English law since, on a contract analysis, this would be a contract for the benefit of a third person. A remedy in favor of the feoffor (settlor) would have been within the modes of thought of the law judges, especially since many of the early uses were for the benefit of the feoffor, but none was given. Maitland's explanation is that by the time assumpsit developed "the Chancellor was already in possession, was already enforcing uses by means of a procedure far more efficient and flexible than any which the old courts could have employed."[12] The law court's judgment presumably would have been for money, a judgment that would then have needed to be executed. The Chancellor, however, gave specific relief by directly ordering the feoffee to perform his obligations and by enforcing obedience to that order, if necessary, through contempt. The remedy was given to the cestui que use; if the feoffee was to hold to the use of the feoffor, the latter's suit apparently was in his right as cestui que use, not as creator of the arrangement.

Today, the action against a trustee for breach of duties is not in contract or at law. Except in very limited circumstances, the jurisdiction of equity has remained exclusive.[13] Moreover, the remedy against the trustee remains in the beneficiary. Although the point is not much discussed, it still seems to be taken for granted that the creator of the trust, the settlor, has neither

---

10. Pollock and Maitland suggested that some of the earlier uses "may have been enforced by the ecclesiastical courts." F. Pollock & F. Maitland, History of English Law 232 (2d ed. 1911). Historical evidence has since been uncovered suggesting that Pollock and Maitland were right about this. Professor Helmholz has established that, from the last quarter of the 14th century through the middle of the 15th century, some ecclesiastical courts regularly enforced feoffments to uses. Helmholz, The Early Enforcement of Uses, 79 Colum. L. Rev. 1503 (1979).

11. J. Ames, Lectures on Legal History 237 (1913).

12. F. Maitland, Equity 28 (2d ed. 1936).

13. A legal remedy is available to the beneficiary where the trustee is under an immediate and unconditioned obligation to pay the beneficiary money. Scott on Trusts § 198.1.

a remedy for the trustee's breach, nor otherwise has standing to enforce the trust.[14]

Uses and Abuses. Professor Scott points out that there was "a darker side to the picture." Scott on Trusts § 1. Uses provided a means of defrauding creditors and purchasers. To the annoyance of the overlords and the Crown, they also provided a means of escaping the consequences of many rules of law that landowners had come to regard as burdensome. Through the device of a use, an individual could in effect dispose of land at death at a time when wills of land were not recognized. This was done by conveying land to another to hold to the use of the feoffor and then to the use of such persons as the feoffor should designate in his will. In this way, land could be passed to younger sons or daughters, or even strangers, to the exclusion and chagrin of the eldest son and heir. Furthermore, the burden of feudal obligations could be escaped or lessened by depriving the lord of feudal rights that arose when his tenant died and the land passed to the tenant's heir. In the eyes of the law, legal title to the land was in the feoffee to uses; thus nothing passed on the death of the cestui que use. Of course, the feudal rights attached on inheritance from the feoffee, but inheritance here could be avoided for a long period by placing the title in a large group as joint tenants.[15]

Statute of Uses (1536). The King finally became fed up. Henry VIII, in need of more revenue, insisted that something be done about the situation. Various measures were proposed to Parliament, but they met with opposition.[16] Finally, compromise was reached. In 1536, Parliament enacted the Statute of Uses to eliminate "subtile practiced feoffementes, . . . abuses and errours . . . to the subversion of the good and anncyent laws of the [realm]." The statute itself provided:

> *Statute of Uses, 27 Henry 8, ch. 10.* That where any person or persons stand or be seized . . . of . . . lands . . . to the use, confidence or trust of any person or persons, or of any body politick, . . . in every such case, all and every such person and persons, shall henceforth stand and be seized . . . of . . . the same . . . lands . . . in such like estates as they had or shall have in use, trust or confidence. . . .

Although the statute sought to abolish existing uses, the mechanism used to achieve that objective was not to deprive the cestui que use of his beneficial interest; rather, the statute converted that beneficial interest into a legal interest. In the words of the statute, the cestui shall "henceforth stand and be seized" of the land "in such like estates as they had . . . in

---

14. Note, 62 Harv. L. Rev. 1370 (1949). But see Gaubatz, Grantor Enforcement of Trusts: Standing in One Private Law Setting, 62 N.C. L. Rev. 905 (1984), concluding that "if the grantor has an economic, expectation, or representational interest in the trust, such that he can be trusted to fully and fairly litigate the validity of the transactions that he challenges, and his interest was foreseeable at the time the trust was created, he can maintain the action."

15. F. Maitland, Equity 26-27 (2d ed. 1936).

16. The story is told in J. H. Baker, An Introduction to English Legal History 210-19 (1979). See also Ives, The Genesis of the Statute of Uses, 82 Eng. Hist. Rev. 673 (1967).

use." Converting the cestui's beneficial interest into a legal one brought it under the jurisdiction of the courts of common law rather than the Court of Chancery. For our purposes, conversion rather than abolition was a crucial development, for it meant that, in one form or another, the use was allowed to persist. In addition, the Statute of Wills of 1540 restored the right to devise land by will. As for the Statute of Uses, the common-law judges were inclined to a narrow interpretation.

The modern trust, in fact, arises out of those situations in which the courts held that the statute did not apply. Principally this was in the case of the *active* use. Within a few years after the statute, it was held that it did not apply to an active use. If land was conveyed by G to T to the use of B with B to "take the profits," the statute applied; but if T was to "take the profits and deliver them" to B, it did not apply. Brooke's New Cases, March's Translation 94 (1651). The common use before the statute was "passive," a form of dummy ownership, with the cestui que use in possession of the land and the feoffee holding the bare legal title; this was held to be the only use to which the statute was meant to apply.[17] Hence the modern trust, placing active duties on the trustee, is unaffected by the Statute of Uses so long as the trust remains active.

Remarkably, the statute was also held inapplicable to a use on a use. If G conveyed to X to the use of T to the use of B, the statute executed the first use, so that T got legal title, but did not execute the second use, even though both uses were passive. Sambach v. Dalston, Tothill 188 (1634).[18] Lord Chancellor Hardwicke, in a later case, remarked that this doctrine reduced the statute's effect to "add[ing] at most three words to a conveyance." Hopkins v. Hopkins, 1 Atk. 581, 26 Eng. Rep. 365, 372 (Ch. 1738).

Finally, it was clear from the language of the statute that it did not apply to personal property, but only to a case in which the feoffee was "seized" of land.[19]

In current American law, the Restatement 2d of Trusts sections 69, 70, and 71 carry forward the above three exemptions from the Statute of Uses—the exemption for active trusts, for a use on a use, and for trusts of personal property.

EXTERNAL REFERENCES. Scott on Trusts § 1; Arnold, The Restatement of the Law of Trusts, 31 Colum. L. Rev. 800, 1266 (1931); Scott, The Trust as an Instrument of Law Reform, 31 Yale L.J. 457 (1922).

2. Estate-Planning Uses of Trusts

We began this part by noting that express trusts are at the core of modern estate-planning practice. This is so, basically, because trusts are

---

17. Note, 17 Mich. L. Rev. 87 (1918).
18. See also J. Ames, Lectures on Legal History 243-47 (1913).
19. Scott on Trusts § 1.6.

responsive to so many financial and estate-planning needs. The variety of reasons why settlors create trusts, or are led by their lawyers to create trusts, include probate avoidance, property management, tax reasons, and control through successive generations. Ultimately, all trusts serve donative purposes, but different types of trusts satisfy one or more additional purposes.

As we saw in Chapters 6 and 7, revocable inter-vivos trusts carry no tax advantages, but do avoid probate. They may also provide independent property management, but not if self-declared. A self-declared, revocable inter-vivos trust allows the settlor to retain lifetime management control of her or his own property. A standby trust with an independent trustee, to be more fully funded through the exercise of a durable power of attorney in case of the settlor's incompetence, is a superior alternative to a guardianship or conservatorship.

Whether self-declared or not, a revocable inter-vivos trust acts as a will substitute. On the settlor's death, it may provide for outright distributions, in the manner of outright specific, general, or residuary devises; or, it may provide for the property or a portion of it to continue in trust, in which case it serves the same purposes as a testamentary trust. It may, in fact, receive additional property from the settlor's estate as the result of a pour-over devise.

Irrevocable inter-vivos trusts satisfy entirely different purposes. Chapter 6 surveyed how they can be structured to offer significant tax advantages, by freezing the value of the assets at the date of conveyance and by providing for the receipt of supplemental fundings that qualify for the annual gift-tax exclusion. Pour-over devises from the settlor's estate can also provide additional funding of irrevocable inter-vivos trusts.

In the case of a married testator, testamentary trusts are typically structured to qualify for the estate-tax marital deduction; the continuation after the settlor's death of a revocable inter-vivos trust can also serve this purpose. See the Sample Trust Instrument, set forth below. After the surviving spouse's death, marital-deduction trusts can continue for a further time, for the benefit of successive generations of descendants or down collateral lines. By-pass trusts also can continue for successive generations. The Rule Against Perpetuities in effect places an outer limit on the duration of such trusts. Successive-generation trusts can provide considerable transfer-tax savings, to the extent they come within the protection of the GST exemption from the federal generation-skipping tax. Where the corpus of a trust consists of intangible personal property, such as corporate securities, a trust preserves the integrity of such a fund in a manner not possible in the case of a succession of legal interests not in trust.

Trusts Compared to Other Types of Management Arrangements. There are other kinds of arrangements under which property is managed for persons other than the owners. There are also property arrangements that in the circumstances may leave the nature of the transaction in some doubt.

Sections 5 through 16A of the Restatement 2d of Trusts distinguish "trusts" from a series of arrangements, some of which also create fiduciary relationships. The distinction between a trustee and the *personal representa-*

tive (executor or administrator) of a decedent's estate is more practical than theoretical. Some but not all of the duties of a trustee are imposed upon a personal representative. The latter must be appointed by a court, and her or his duties are limited to winding up the estate of a decedent and so are implicitly temporary in duration. For different reasons, an *officer* or *director* of a corporation is a fiduciary, but not a trustee. So also with a guardian or with a receiver of the property of an insolvent person or corporation. In several of these instances, the fiduciary does not take title to the property involved, whereas a trustee is regarded as taking the legal title to the trust estate.

A *bailee* of personal property owes certain duties to the bailor, but takes only possession of, not legal title to, the property and is not a trustee. Similarly, an *agent* is not a trustee; but the distinction between an agent who is enabled to transfer title to property and a trustee is sometimes not easy to draw.

A conveyance of property upon a *condition subsequent* or subject to a *lien* or an *equitable charge* does not create a trust. The most difficult problem to resolve in a variety of circumstances involves the distinction between trust law and certain aspects of the law of contract, specifically the distinction between a trust and a *debt* or between a trust and a *third-party-beneficiary* contract.

Sample Revocable Inter-Vivos Trust

The following trust instrument is reproduced here to give you some idea of what a modern trust instrument looks like. The instrument suggests especially (a) how a trust can be used to make provision for successive generations, (b) the possibility of giving some flexibility to the dispositions through the use of powers, and (c) the amount of detail commonly found in the administrative provisions of a trust instrument.

This trust agreement is made this _____ day of _____, 19_, between JOHN DOE, the Grantor, and OLD FAITHFUL TRUST COMPANY OF ____, as Trustee.

The Grantor hereby transfers to the trustee the property described in the attached schedule. Such property, and any other property that may be received by the trustee, shall be held and disposed of upon the following trusts:

ARTICLE I

The Grantor may by signed instruments delivered to the trustee revoke the trusts hereunder in whole or in part or amend this agreement from time to time in any manner. No amendment changing the powers or duties of the trustee shall be effective unless approved in writing by the trustee.

ARTICLE II

The trustee shall pay all the net income of the trust estate, and such portions of the principal as the Grantor from time to time directs in writing, to the Grantor, or otherwise as he directs in writing, during his life. In addition, the trustee may in its discretion pay to the Grantor, or use for his benefit, such portions or all of the principal of the trust estate as the trustee determines to be required for the Grantor's support and comfort, or for any other purpose which the trustee determines to be to his best interests.

ARTICLE III

After the Grantor's death the trustee shall hold and dispose of the trust estate as follows:

1. (a) The trustee shall pay all the net income of the trust estate to MARY DOE, wife of the Grantor, during her life, beginning as of the date of the Grantor's death and payable at least as often as quarter-annually. Unproductive property shall not be held as an asset of the trust estate for more than a reasonable time during the life of the Grantor's said wife without her consent.

(b) Whenever the trustee determines that the income of the Grantor's said wife from all sources known to the trustee is not sufficient for her reasonable support and comfort, the trustee shall pay to her, or use for her benefit, so much of the principal of the trust estate as the trustee determines to be required for those purposes.

2. Upon the death of the Grantor's said wife the trustee shall distribute the trust estate to such person or persons, or the estate of the Grantor's said wife, upon such conditions and estates, in trust or otherwise, in such manner and at such time or times as she appoints and directs by will specifically referring to this power of appointment.

3. In default of appointment by the Grantor's wife as aforesaid the trustee shall upon her death, or if she does not survive the Grantor the trustee shall upon the Grantor's death, divide the trust estate into equal funds, one for each child of the Grantor then living and one for the then-living descendants of each child of the Grantor then deceased. Each such fund shall be held and administered as a separate trust and shall be held and disposed of as follows:

(a) While any child of the Grantor is under the age of twenty-one years, the trustee shall use so much of the income of his or her fund for his or her reasonable support, comfort and education as the trustee determines to be required for those purposes. After he or she attains that age, the trustee shall pay all the current net income of his or her fund to him or her.

(b) Whenever the trustee determines that the income of any child of the Grantor from all sources known to the trustee is not sufficient for his or her reasonable support, comfort and education, the trustee shall pay to him or her, or use for his or her benefit, so much of the principal of his or her fund as the trustee determines to be required for those purposes.

(c) When any child of the Grantor shall have attained the age of twenty-five years, the trustee shall distribute to him or her one-third of the principal of his or her fund as constituted at the time of distribution. When he or she shall have attained the age of thirty years, the trustee shall further distribute to him or her one-half of the remaining principal of his or her fund as constituted at the time of distribution. When he or she shall have attained the age of thirty-five years, the trustee shall further distribute to him or her the balance of his or her fund.

(d) Upon the death of any child of the Grantor before he or she becomes entitled to receive the entire principal of his or her fund, the trustee shall distribute his or her fund, or any remaining portion of it, to, or in trust for the benefit of, such person or persons among the Grantor's descendants and their spouses, including such child's own spouse, upon such conditions and estates, in such manner and at such time or times as he or she appoints and directs by will specifically referring to this power of appointment, and in default of such appointment, to his or her descendants then living, by representation, or if there is no descendant of his or her then living, to the Grantor's descendants then living, by representation; provided that if the trustee is then holding another fund or portion hereunder for the primary benefit of any such descendant, his or her share shall be added to and commingled with such other fund or portion and held, or partly held and partly distributed, as if it had been an original part thereof.

(e) The trustee shall distribute each fund set aside for the descendants of a deceased child of the Grantor to such descendants, by representation.

4. Notwithstanding anything in this instrument to the contrary, if any descendant of a deceased child of the Grantor is under the age of twenty-one years when the trustee is directed in the foregoing provisions of this instrument to distribute to him or her any portion of the principal of the trust property, his or her portion shall immediately vest in interest in him or her indefeasibly, but the trustee may in its discretion withhold possession of it and hold it in trust for his or her benefit until he or she attains that age. In the meantime, the trustee shall use so much of the income and principal for his or her reasonable support, comfort, and education as the trustee determines to be required for those purposes.

Article IV

1. If at any time any person to whom the trustee is directed in this instrument to pay any income is under legal disability or is in the opinion of the trustee incapable of properly managing his or her affairs, the trustee may use so much of such income for his or her support and comfort as the trustee determines to be required for the purposes.

2. The trustee either may expend directly any income or principal that it is authorized in this instrument to use for the benefit of any person, or may pay it over to him or her or for his or her use to his or her parent or guardian, or to any person with whom he or she is residing, without responsibility for its expenditure. The trustee shall withhold any such income not so used, and at its discretion add it to principal; provided that during the life of the Grantor's wife the trustee shall in any event pay all the net income of the trust estate to her or use it for her benefit.

3. No interest of any beneficiary in the income or principal of this trust shall be assignable in anticipation of payment or be liable in any way for the beneficiary's debts or obligations and shall not be subject to attachment.

4. Upon the death of my wife, any income accrued or undistributed shall be paid to her estate; upon the death of any other beneficiary, any income accrued or undistributed shall be held and accounted for, or distributed, in the same manner as if it had been income accrued and received after such beneficiary's death.

5. Notwithstanding anything herein to the contrary, the trusts hereunder shall terminate not later than twenty-one years after the death of the last survivor of the Grantor's wife and his descendants living at the Grantor's death, at the end of which period the trustee shall distribute each remaining portion of the trust property to the beneficiaries, at that time, of the income thereof, and in the proportions in which they are beneficiaries of such income.

Article V

1. The trustee shall have the following powers with respect to each trust hereunder, to be exercised as the trustee in its discretion determines to be to the best interests of the beneficiaries:

(a) Subject to Article III, paragraph 1(a), to retain any property transferred, devised, or bequeathed to the trustee, or any undivided interest therein, regardless of any lack of diversification, risk, or non-productivity;

(b) To invest and reinvest the trust estate in any property or undivided interests therein, wherever located, including bonds, notes (secured or unsecured), stocks of corporations, real estate, or any interest therein, and interests in trusts including common trust funds, without being limited by any statute or rule of law concerning investments by trustees;

(c) To sell any trust property, for cash or on credit, at public or private sale; to exchange any trust property for other property; to grant options to purchase or acquire any trust property; and to determine the prices and terms of sales, exchanges, and options;

(d) To execute leases and sub-leases for terms as long as two hundred years, even though such terms may extend beyond the termination of the trust; to subdivide or improve real estate and tear down or alter improvements; to grant easements, give consents, and make contracts relating to real estate or its use; and to release or dedicate any interest in real estate;

(e) To borrow money and to mortgage or pledge any trust property;

(f) To take any action with respect to conserving or realizing upon the value of any trust property, and with respect to foreclosures, reorganizations, or other changes affecting the trust property; to collect, pay, contest, compromise, or abandon demands of or against the trust estate, wherever situated; and to execute contracts, notes, conveyances, and other instruments containing covenants and warranties binding upon and creating a charge against the trust estate, and containing provisions excluding personal liability;

(g) To keep any property in the name of a nominee with or without disclosure of any fiduciary relationship;

(h) To employ agents, attorneys, auditors, depositaries, and proxies, with or without discretionary powers;

(i) To determine the manner of ascertainment of income and principal, and the apportionment between income and principal of all receipts and disbursements, and to select an annual accounting period;

(j) To receive additional property from any source and add it to and commingle it with the trust estate;

(k) To enter into any transaction authorized by this Article with trustees or legal representatives of any other trust or estate in which any beneficiary hereunder has any beneficial interest, even though any such trustee or legal representative is also trustee hereunder;

(l) To make any distribution or division of the trust property in cash or in kind or both, and to allot different kinds or disproportionate shares of property or undivided interests in property among the beneficiaries or portions, and to determine the value of any such property; and to continue to exercise any powers and discretion herein given for a reasonable period after the termination of the trust, but only for so long as no rule of law relating to perpetuities would be violated.

2. To the extent that any such requirements can legally be waived, no trustee shall ever be required to give any bond as trustee or qualify before, be appointed by, or in the absence of breach of trust account to any court, or obtain the order or approval of any court in the exercise of any power or

discretion herein given. No person paying money or delivering any property to any trustee shall be required to see to its application.

3. Any trustee shall be entitled to reasonable compensation for services in administering and distributing the trust property, and to reimbursement for expenses.

ARTICLE VI

1. Any trustee may resign at any time by giving written notice, specifying the effective date of such resignation, to the beneficiaries, at the time of giving notice, of the current income of the trust property.

2. If any trustee at any time resigns or is unable to act, another corporation authorized under the law of any State or of the United States to administer trusts may be appointed as successor trustee, by an instrument delivered to such successor and signed by the beneficiaries, at the time of such appointment, of at least two-thirds of the current income of the trust property, and such beneficiaries may direct the successor trustee to accept the accounts of any former trustee, in which event the successor trustee shall have no responsibility thereof.

3. Every successor trustee shall have all the title, powers, and discretion herein given the trustee, without any act of conveyance or transfer.

4. The guardian or conservator of the estate of a beneficiary under legal disability, or the parents or surviving parent of a minor beneficiary for whose estate no guardian has been appointed, may act for such beneficiary in making any appointment and giving any direction under this Article.

5. If another corporation succeeds to the trust business of any corporate trustee hereunder, such successor shall become trustee hereunder.

ARTICLE VII

After the Grantor's death, the trustee may in its discretion make loans, with or without security, to the executor or administrator of the Grantor's estate, purchase from such executor or administrator, at such value as may be determined by the trustee, any property constituting part or all of the Grantor's estate, and, subject to Article III, paragraph 1(a), retain all or any part of such property regardless of risk, unproductivity, or lack of diversification.

IN WITNESS WHEREOF, the parties hereto have signed and sealed this instrument on the date first above written.

_____(Seal)
                    Grantor

OLD FAITHFUL TRUST
COMPANY OF _____

By _____
                  President

Attest_____
        Trust Officer

————

Constructive Trusts/Resulting Trusts. When we speak of the estate-planning uses of trusts, we are referring to express trusts. Express trusts are intentionally created for the ongoing management of the trust property, whether for private or charitable beneficiaries or for a combination of the two. Express trusts persist over some period of time; in some cases, they persist over a substantial period of time.

We have already mentioned two other trust categories—the constructive trust and the resulting trust. Neither type is truly a "trust," in the sense of requiring ongoing management of trust property. The conventional classification of trusts that emerged in the late nineteenth century identified these as trusts that arise by operation of law rather than by private intention. Some legal scholars, though, who wanted to avoid associating either trust type with collective interference with private intention, attacked this classification scheme. Costigan argued that resulting trusts were "implied in fact," while constructive trusts were "fraud-rectifying." See Costigan, The Classification of Trusts as Express, Resulting, and Constructive, 27 Harv. L. Rev. 437 (1914).

Constructive trusts. The constructive trust is not a trust at all, but a remedy. It is closely associated with quasi contract, which likewise is not a contract but a remedy. In fact, quasi contract is the law's principal answer to unjust enrichment; constructive trust is equity's principal answer.

George Palmer gives the following sketch of this story, at the beginning of his great treatise on restitution (Palmer on Restitution):

> § 1.1. *The Scope of Restitution.* It has been traditional to regard tort and contract as the two principal sources of civil liability at common law, although liability arising out of a fiduciary relationship has developed largely outside these two great categories. There is another category that must be separated from all of these; this is liability based in unjust enrichment. In particularized form this has been a part of our law from an early time, but it has been slow to emerge as a general theory. In present American law, however, the idea of unjust enrichment has been generally accepted and widely applied.
>
> Restitution based upon unjust enrichment cuts across many branches of the law, including contract, tort, and fiduciary relationship, but it also occupies much territory that is its sole preserve . . . .
>
> For a long time restitution developed more or less independently at law and in equity. If the defendant stole the plaintiff's goods and sold them, the plaintiff was given a money judgment in the amount of the proceeds in an action at law. This has come to be known as "quasi contract," although the broader term "restitution" is gaining general acceptance. The action developed out of the common-law action of assumpsit, which was used initially to recover for breach of an express contract. There was of course no express contract by which the thief agreed to pay the proceeds to the plaintiff, but the court treated the situation as though there were for the purpose of making available the writ of assumpsit. If the thief used the proceeds to buy land, courts exercising equity power in this country will order him or her to transfer title to the land to the plaintiff through a remedy almost universally known as constructive trust, though it also can be called specific restitution. The court treats the defendant as though he were a trustee of the land for the

benefit of the plaintiff when in fact there was no express trust, any more than there was an express contract in the first action.

The link that connects these two judgments is the idea of unjust enrichment, just as it is the connecting link in an unending variety of cases in which relief is given. Today, anything like a whole view of the law of restitution must take into account both law and equity . . . .

The term "restitution" . . . is not wholly apt since it suggests restoration to the successful party of some benefit obtained from him or her. Usually this will be the case where relief is given, but by no means always. There are cases in which the successful party obtains restitution of something he did not have before, for example a benefit received by the defendant from a third person which justly should go to the plaintiff.

Resulting trusts. At several points in the succeeding materials, we will also encounter one kind of resulting trust, that is, the kind of "trust" that arises when an express trust fails or does not completely dispose of the trust property. Like the constructive trust, the resulting trust is no trust at all in the sense of prescribing ongoing management of the property. It is, rather, a property interest analogous to the reversion retained by a grantor who conveys one or more legal interests in property for life or for years without creating a remainder thereafter. In other words, a reversion is a legal interest, but the beneficial interest under a resulting trust is equitable, since a resulting trust arises from a conveyance of the legal title in fee simple, but without disposing of the complete beneficial interest.

Another kind of resulting trust is the so-called "purchase-money" resulting trust. The "purchase-money" resulting trust further demonstrates the versatility of the "trust" idea or label, but it is not part of this course. The basic principle is that where property is transferred to one person and the purchase price is paid by another person, a resulting trust presumptively arises in favor of the person who pays the purchase price. For further elaboration of the purchase-money resulting trust, see Restatement 2d of Trusts §§ 440-60; Scott on Trusts §§ 440-60.

EXTERNAL REFERENCE. Alexander, The Transformation of Trusts as a Legal Category, 1800-1914, 5 Law & Hist. Rev. 303 (1987).

PART B. FORMATION OF A TRUST

Modern legal theory defines the trust form in terms of discrete "elements." It is commonly said that in order for any trust to exist there must be a specific trust res, or property, a trustee, identifiable beneficiaries, and specific trust intent. Together, these elements constitute the formal model of the trust. Although aspects of these elements certainly were evident in pre-nineteenth century Equity practice, it was not until the nineteenth century that English and American legal thought abstracted them into constituents of a formal model. As we will see, challenges to this trust model have been made in recent years. These challenges have sought to make the distinction between the trust and other legal forms for disposing of property, such as gift, promise, and agency, less important.

1. The Trust As A Property Arrangement

Trust law requires that there be an identifiable trust property, or res, as it is sometimes called. Restatement 2d of Trusts § 74. The requirement of trust property is sometimes codified, as in the recent California and Texas codifications of the law of trusts. Cal. Prob. Code § 15202; Tex. Prop. Code § 112.005. Any legally recognized property interest that is transferable can be the subject matter of a trust. In most trusts, this requirement presents no difficulties, but occasionally it does, as the next case illustrates.

Brainard v. Commissioner
91 F.2d 880 (7th Cir. 1937)

SPARKS, J. This petition for review involves income taxes for the year 1928. The question presented is whether under the circumstances set forth in the findings of the Board of Tax Appeals, the taxpayer created a valid trust, the income of which was taxable to the beneficiaries under section 162 of the Revenue Act of 1928.[20]

The facts as found by the Board of Tax Appeals are substantially as follows: In December, 1927, the taxpayer, having decided that conditions were favorable, contemplated trading in the stock market during 1928. He consulted a lawyer and was advised that it was possible for him to trade in trust for his children and other members of his family. Taxpayer thereupon discussed the matter with his wife and mother, and stated to them that he declared a trust of his stock trading during 1928 for the benefit of his family upon certain terms and conditions. Taxpayer agreed to assume personally any losses resulting from the venture, and to distribute the profits, if any, in equal shares to his wife, mother, and two minor children after deducting a reasonable compensation for his services. During 1928 taxpayer carried on the trading operations contemplated and at the end of the year determined his compensation at slightly less than $10,000, which he reported in his income tax return for that year. The profits remaining were then divided in approximately equal shares among

---

20. § 162. The net income of the estate or trust shall be computed in the same manner and on the same basis as in the case of an individual, except that— . . .

(b) There shall be allowed as an additional deduction in computing the net income of the estate or trust the amount of the income of the estate or trust for its taxable year which is to be distributed currently by the fiduciary to the beneficiaries, and the amount of the income collected by a guardian of an infant which is to be held or distributed as the court may direct, but the amount so allowed as a deduction shall be included in computing the net income of the beneficiaries whether distributed to them or not.

[Section 162, as amended in certain particulars, now appears as IRC § 661. Eds.]

the members of his family, and the amounts were reported in their respective tax returns for 1928. The amounts allocated to the beneficiaries were credited to them on taxpayer's books, but they did not receive the cash, except taxpayer's mother, to a small extent.

In addition to these findings the record discloses that taxpayer's two children were one and three years of age. Upon these facts the Board held that the income in controversy was taxable to the petitioner as a part of his gross income for 1928, and decided that there was a deficiency. It is here sought to review that decision.

In the determination of the questions here raised it is necessary to consider the nature of the trust, if any, that is said to have been created by the circumstances hereinbefore recited. It is clear that the taxpayer, at the time of his declaration, had no property interest in "profits in stock trading in 1928, if any," because there were none in existence at that time. Indeed it is not disclosed that the declarer at that time owned any stock.[21] It is obvious, therefore, that the taxpayer based his declaration of trust upon an interest which at that time had not come into existence and in which no one had a present interest. In the Restatement of the Law of Trusts, vol. 1, § 75, it is said that an interest which has not come into existence or which has ceased to exist can not be held in trust. It is there further said:

> A person can, it is true, make a contract binding himself to create a trust of an interest if he should thereafter acquire it; but such an agreement is not binding as a contract unless the requirements of the law of Contracts are complied with . . .
>
> Thus, if a person gratuitously declares himself trustee of such shares as he may thereafter acquire in a corporation not yet organized, no trust is created. The result is the same where instead of declaring himself trustee, he purports to transfer to another as trustee such shares as he may thereafter acquire in a corporation not yet organized. In such a case there is at most a gratuitous undertaking to create a trust in the future, and such an undertaking is not binding as a contract for lack of consideration . . .
>
> If a person purports to declare himself trustee of an interest not in existence, or if he purports to transfer such an interest to another in trust, he is liable as upon a contract to create a trust if, but only if, the requirements of the law of Contracts are complied with.

See, also, Restatement, § 30b; Bogert, Trusts and Trustees, vol. 1, § 112. In 42 Harvard Law Review 561, it is said:

---

21. If the "declarer" had owned stock in December, 1927, and had then declared himself trustee of that stock, a trust of that stock would clearly have arisen and any profits realized in trading that stock during 1928 would clearly have been part of the corpus of that trust. Even so, the Internal Revenue Code now contains provisions not part of the Code in the 1920's that would likely make the trust income (probably including realized capital gains) taxable to the transferor or at the transferor's rate. See IRC §§ 644, 671-77. Eds.

> With logical consistency, the courts have uniformly held that an expectancy cannot be the subject matter of a trust and that an attempted creation, being merely a promise to transfer property in the future, is invalid unless supported by consideration.

Citing Lehigh Valley R. R. Co. v. Woodring, 116 Pa. 513, 9 A. 58. Hence, it is obvious under the facts here presented that taxpayer's declaration amounted to nothing more than a promise to create a trust in the future, and its binding force must be determined by the requirements of the law of contracts.

It is elementary that an executory contract, in order to be enforceable, must be based upon a valuable consideration. Here there was none. The declaration was gratuitous. If we assume that it was based on love and affection that would add nothing to its enforceability, for love and affection, though a sufficient consideration for an executed conveyance, is not a sufficient consideration for a promise.

What has been said, however, does not mean that the taxpayer had no right to carry out his declaration after the subject matter had come into existence, even though there were no consideration. This he did and the trust thereby became effective, after which it was enforceable by the beneficiaries.

The questions with which we are concerned are at what times did the respective earnings which constitute the trust fund come into existence, and at what times did the trust attach to them. It is obvious that the respective profits came into existence when and if such stocks were sold at a profit in 1928. Did they come into existence impressed with the trust, or was there any period of time intervening between the time they came into existence and the time the trust attached? If there were such intervening time, then during that time the taxpayer must be considered as the sole owner of the profits and they were properly taxed to him as a part of his income.

It is said in the Restatement of the Law of Trusts, § 75c:

> If a person purports to declare himself trustee of an interest not in existence or if he purports to transfer such an interest to another in trust, no trust arises even when the interest comes into existence in the absence of a manifestation of intention at that time.

This we think is especially applicable where, as here, there was no consideration for the declaration. It is further stated, however, in the Restatement, § 26k:

> If a person manifests an intention to become trustee at a subsequent time, his conduct at that subsequent time considered in connection with his original manifestation may be a sufficient manifestation of intention at that subsequent time to create a trust . . . the act of acquiring the property coupled with the earlier declaration of trust *may be* a sufficient manifestation of an intention to create a trust at the time of the acquisition of the property. (Our italics, here and hereafter.)

In subsection 1 it is said " . . . Mere silence, however, ordinarily will not be such a manifestation. Whether silence is or is not such a manifestation is a question of interpretation." In such interpretation, subsection m is quite pertinent and controlling:

> A promise to create a trust in the future is *enforceable*, if . . . the requirements for an enforceable contract are complied with. Whether a promise to transfer property in trust or to become trustee creates in the promisee a right to recover damages for breach of the promise, and whether such a promise is specifically enforceable, are determined by the law governing contracts. Thus, if the owner of property transfers the property in trust and agrees to pay a sum of money to the trustee to be held upon the same trust, he is not liable for failing to pay the money if the promise was made gratuitously . . . but if the promise was made for consideration . . . the promisor is liable thereon. So also, a promise to create a trust of property if thereafter acquired by the promisor imposes no liability upon the promisor if the promise was gratuitous . . . .

These matters are discussed by Mr. Bogert in his work on Trusts and Trustees, vol. 1, § 112, and we think there is no contrariety of opinion between his conclusions and those of the Restatement. In speaking of the attitudes of courts of law and equity, he says:

> Courts of *law* treat transactions which purport to be present transfers, . . . or trusts of interests in future things as not amounting to *contracts* and as void, with some rare exceptions (referring to potential possession) . . . *Equity* has taken a different attitude toward present efforts to create property interests in future things. It has reasoned that such a transaction could not have been intended to operate as a present transfer because of the inherent impossibility of such an effect. The parties must therefore have expected the only other possible operative result, namely, that there should arise a *contract* to create property interests in the future, by way of absolute transfer, mortgage, trust, or what not . . . Viewed as a *contract* to create property interests in the future, when the things involved are acquired, equity found that in the older common law there was no remedy at all. The law did not recognize the existence of such a *contract*. There was more than inadequacy of remedy; there was total absence of remedy at law. Equity therefore took the position that it would give specific performance or its equivalent. When the things came into existence and into the hands of the intended transferor, they would at once be deemed transferred by way of absolute deed, mortgage, or trust. In other words . . . equity would treat the trust as immediately taking effect and an equitable interest as then passing to the cestui.

For instance, he says:

> The employee under an existing contract has no present interest in wages to be earned. Such right to receive wages when later earned is a future chose in action. An attempted present conveyance or trust of it can only operate as a *contract* to transfer it when and if acquired, which equity will turn into a perfected transfer when the wages are due.

It is obvious that the author's conclusions presuppose . . . the existence of a valid and enforceable contract between the declarer and the beneficiary. Otherwise the law of contracts would be violated, and equity would be in the attitude of establishing a trust upon an invalid and unenforceable contract, or rather upon no contract at all. The authorities cited by the author in support of his last quoted statement involve valid and enforceable contracts which were based on valuable considerations . . . .

The order of the Board is affirmed.

Notes and Questions

1. *Assignment of Future Earnings.* Under existing law, a person can validly assign future earnings from an existing contract. Suppose the taxpayer in *Brainard* had introduced evidence that at the time of his declaration he owned sufficient capital to engage in stock trading. Would (or should) the result change? If so, then, did Brainard lose because of a failure of proof? Assuming that Brainard owned sufficient capital, how could his lawyer have met the trust res requirement?

2. *Assignments and Releases of Expectancies.* The interests of presumptive heirs or legatees of a living person traditionally have been characterized as "expectancies" and not as property. See Simes & Smith on Future Interests § 391. Nevertheless, historically, Equity courts enforced expectancy assignments but only if "value" was given, by which the courts meant that they retained the power to review the fairness of the exchange. Consideration sufficient to support a contract was not by itself sufficient. Quite commonly, the consideration that expectant heirs received for their birthright was insubstantial, the equivalent of the pottage of lentils for which Esau sold his birthright to his brother Jacob, according to Genesis (Genesis 25: 29-34).

Dawson gives the following explanation of Chancery decisions during the formative period:

> The need for special protection arose from prevailing standards of fashionable conduct, which dictated a high level of conspicuous expenditure. It was honorable to maintain a gentlemanly extravagance, even where current income did not suffice; all blame was reserved for those hangers-on of polite society who pandered to extravagance by supplying it with the necessary means. Their special prey was the expectant heir or reversioner, in urgent need of ready cash but precluded from borrowing at moderate rates of interest by the uncertainty of his prospects. The Chancellors of the late seventeenth and eighteenth centuries imposed a firm control on traffic with such persons. In the Chancery reports they published their determination to prevent dispersal of family estates through improvident sales by their prospective owners. The motive was clear—to preserve for a dominant class the economic resources on which its prestige and power depended.

Dawson, Economic Duress—An Essay in Perspective, 45 Mich. L. Rev. 253, 268 (1947).

Quite apart from the protection given the expectant heir or devisee against selling an expectancy for a "mess of pottage," equity did not then give specific performance of a contract under seal (putting aside the special case of an option to purchase). See Jefferys v. Jefferys, Cr. & Ph. 138, 41 Eng. Rep. 443 (1841).

Courts have held that the expectancy of an heir can be *released* voluntarily for valuable consideration, with the result that the heir is excluded from participation as heir in the ancestor's intestate estate. See Martin v. Smith, 404 S.2d 341 (Ala. 1981).

3. *Debts as Trust Property.* Any legally recognized property interest or contract right that is transferrable can be the subject of a trust. If A has a legally enforceable claim against B, A can create a trust of that debt, either by declaration of a trust or by transfer. However, if B declares that she or he holds the debt she or he owes to A in trust for A, no trust is created. B is a debtor, and a debtor cannot be a trustee of her or his own debt. Why might it matter whether B is treated as a debtor or a trustee? See Scott on Trusts § 12.

4. *Uncashed Checks as Trust Property.* Suppose that prior to her death, Susan delivered to her daughter, Emily, a check for $20,000, designating on the check that it was to be held in trust for Emily's minor child. Before Emily was able to cash the check, Susan died. Was a trust created? Is there a legally recognized property interest that can serve as the subject matter of the trust? Compare Estate of Bolton, 444 N.W.2d 482 (Iowa 1989) (holding that an uncashed check is not a completed gift) with Sinclair v. Fleischman, 25 Wash. App. 204, 773 P.2d 101 (1989) (holding that an uncashed check constituted a completed gift because it was legally delivered by the donor and accepted by the donee prior to the donor's death).

Whether gifts by check are complete when the donor dies before the check is cashed has been a problem for federal estate tax purposes. The federal courts, relying on applicable state law, have held that the gift is not complete and therefore that the cash represented by the check is includable in the decedent-donor's gross estate under IRC section 2033. Estate of Dillingham v. Commissioner, 90-1 USTC ¶ 60,021 (10th Cir. 1990); Estate of Gagliardi v. Commissioner, 89 T.C. 1207 (1987). However, where the check was to a charity, the Tax Court has held that the gift became complete upon the delivery of the check. See Estate of Belcher v. Commissioner, 83 T.C. 227 (1984).

2. Intent to Create a Trust

As we have just seen, a trust is a *property* arrangement, requiring a res as its subject. Normally, the property forming the trust res is owned outright by the settlor. The trust is created when the ownership of that property is divided into its legal and equitable portions, with the legal-title portion being transferred to the trustee (or, in the case of a self-declared trust, being retained by the settlor as trustee) and the equitable-title portion being transferred to (and being further subdivided among) the beneficiaries.

The transfer of the equitable title to the beneficiaries does not require the same formalities as would be required for making an outright gift, such as actual, constructive, or symbolical delivery of the subject matter[22] or delivery of a document of transfer or some manifestation that the document is to be presently effective.[23] As the court said in Matter of Brown, 252 N.Y. 366, 169 N.E. 612 (1930):

> [D]elivery is not necessary to constitute a valid trust. While a transfer of the property to a trustee for the purposes of the settlement may be the surest way to create a trust, yet the same result will be accomplished if the owner declares that he himself holds the property in trust for the person designated, and this trust may be created either in writing or, if relating to personal property, by parol. The declaration need not be made to the beneficiary, nor the writing given to him; in fact, his ignorance of the trust is immaterial. There must be proof of a declaration of trust in writing to pass real property, but the declaration varies with the circumstances of each case; it may be contained in a letter, or as here by formal witnessed statement. A declaration implies an announcement of an act performed, not a mere intention, and in most instances to another party. However, a writing formally creating a trust, kept by the donor without delivery to any one, under such circumstances and conditions as to show that a trust was declared, created and intended, will be given effect as such by the courts.

The near absence of formality required to confer upon (transfer to) others the equitable interest in property, making them trust beneficiaries, has led to pressure to treat transactions that would otherwise fail, such as imperfect gifts, as self-declared trusts. This was the argument made, but not accepted, in the next case, Farmers' Loan & Trust Co. v. Winthrop. As background to understanding the *Winthrop* case, remember that, unless modified by statute,[24] an agent's authority under a power of attorney is terminated by the death of the principal. See supra p. 437. Also note that an equitable interest, including the interest of a beneficiary of a trust, can itself be made the subject of a trust. Kekewich v. Manning, 1 DeG. M. & G. 176, 42 Eng. Rep. 519 (1851); Merchants' Loan & Trust Co. v. Patterson, 308 Ill. 519, 139 N.E. 912 (1923).

---

22. See Restatement 2d of Property § 31.1.

23. See Restatement 2d of Property § 32.1 & comment g, stating that the requirement that the donor "manifest in some manner that the document is to be legally operative while the donor is alive" can be satisfied "without any delivery [of the document] to anyone." The requirement would be satisfied, comment g declares, "if the outward and visible acts of the donor recognize the existence of the transfer described in the document" or "if the document itself states that it is presently operative or is not intended as a will, . . . unless other evidence overcomes such result."

24. Section 5-504(a) of the UPC provides:

> The death of a principal who has executed a written power of attorney, durable or otherwise, does not revoke or terminate the agency as to the attorney in fact or other person, who, without actual knowledge of the death of the principal, acts in good faith under the power. Any action so taken, unless otherwise invalid or unenforceable, binds successors in interest of the principal.

Farmers' Loan & Trust Co. v. Winthrop
238 N.Y. 477, 144 N.E. 686 (1924)

CARDOZO, J. On February 3, 1920, Helen C. Bostwick executed her deed of trust to the Farmers' Loan & Trust Company as trustee. It is described as the 1920 deed, to distinguish it from an earlier one made in 1918, which is the subject of another action. By the later of the two deeds she gave to her trustee $5,000, "the said sum, and all other property hereafter delivered to said trustee as hereinafter provided," to be held upon the trusts and limitations therein set forth. The income was to be paid to her own use during life, and the principal on her death was to be divided into two parts—one for the benefit of the children of a deceased son, Albert; the other for the benefit of a daughter, Fannie, and the children of said daughter. The donor reserved "the right, at any time and from time to time during the continuance of the trusts, . . . to deliver to said trustee additional property to be held by it" thereunder. She reserved also a power of revocation.

At the date of the execution of this deed, a proceeding was pending in the Surrogate's Court for the settlement of the accounts of the United States Trust Company as trustee of a trust under the will of [Helen's late husband,] Jabez A. Bostwick. The effect of the decree, when entered, would be to transfer to Mrs. Bostwick money, shares of stock, and other property of the value of upwards of $2,300,000. The plan was that this property, when ready to be transferred, should be delivered to the trustee, and held subject to the trust. On February 3, 1920, simultaneously with the execution of the trust deed, three other documents, intended to effectuate this plan, were signed by the donor. One is a power of attorney whereby she authorized the Farmers' Loan & Trust Company as her attorney "to collect and receive any and all cash, shares of stock and other property" to which she might "be entitled under any decree or order made or entered" in the proceeding above mentioned. A second is a power of attorney authorizing the Farmers' Loan & Trust Company to sell and transfer any and all shares of stock then or thereafter standing in her name. A third is a letter, addressed to the Farmers' Loan & Trust Company, in which she states that she hands to the company the powers of attorney just described, and in which she gives instructions in respect of the action to be taken thereunder:

> My desire is and I hereby authorize you to receive from the United States Trust Company of New York all securities and property coming to me under the decree or order on the settlement of its account and to transfer such securities and property to yourself as trustee under agreement of trust bearing even date herewith executed by me to you.

The decree in the accounting proceeding was entered March 16, 1920. It established the right of Helen C. Bostwick to the payment or transfer of shares of stock and other property of the market value (then or shortly thereafter) of $2,327,353.70. On April 27, 1920, a representative of the Farmers' Loan & Trust Company presented the power of attorney to the

United States Trust Company and stated that he was authorized to receive such securities as were ready for delivery. Shares of stock having a market value of $856,880 were handed to him then and there. No question is made that these became subject to the provisions of the deed of trust. The controversy arises in respect of the rest of the securities, $1,470,473.70 in value, which were retained in the custody of the United States Trust Company, apparently for the reason that they were not yet ready for delivery. During the night of April 27, 1920, Helen C. Bostwick died. She left a will, appointing the Farmers' Loan & Trust Company executor, and disposing of an estate of the value of over $20,000,000. The securities retained, as we have seen, in the custody of the United States Trust Company, were delivered on or about July 13, 1920, to the executor under the will. Conflicting claims of ownership are made by the legatees under the will and the remaindermen under the deed.

We think, with the majority of the Appellate Division, that the gift remained inchoate at the death of the donor. There is no occasion to deny that in the setting of other circumstances a power of attorney, authorizing a donee to reduce to possession the subject of a gift, may be significant as evidence of a symbolical delivery. We assume, without deciding, that such effect will be allowed if, apart from the power, there is established an intention that the title of the donor shall be presently divested and presently transferred . . . . [T]here is here no expression of a purpose to effectuate a present gift. The power of attorney, standing by itself, results, as all concede, in the creation of a revocable agency.

If something more was intended, if what was meant was a gift that was to be operative at once, the expression of the meaning will have to be found elsewhere, in the deed of trust or in the letter. Neither in the one, however, nor in the other, can such a purpose be discerned. Deed and letter alike are framed on the assumption that the gift is executory and future, and this though the addition of a few words would have established it beyond cavil as executed and present. In the deed there is a present transfer of $5,000 and no more. This wrought, there is merely the reservation of a privilege to augment the subject-matter of the trust by deliveries thereafter. The absence of words of present assignment is emphasized when we consider with what simplicity an assignment could have been stated. All that was needed was to expand the description by a phrase:

> The right, title, and interest of the grantor in the securities and other property due or to become due from the United States Trust Company as trustee under the will.

The deed and the other documents, we must remember, were not separated in time. They were parts of a single plan, and were executed together. In these circumstances, a present transfer, if intended, would naturally have found its place in the description of the deed itself. If omitted for some reason there, the least we should expect would be to find it in the letter. Again words of present transfer are conspicuously absent. What we have instead is a request, or at best a mandate, incompetent without more to divest title, or transfer it, serving no other purpose than a memorandum of instructions from principal to agent as a guide to future action. Deed and documents were prepared by counsel learned in the law. With industrious iteration, they rejected the familiar formulas that would have given unmistakable expression to the transfer of a present title. With like iteration, they chose the words and methods appropriate to a gift that was conceived of as executory and future. We must take the transaction as they made it. The very facility with which they could have made it something else is a warning that we are not at liberty, under the guise of construction, to make it other than it is. They were willing to leave open what they might readily have closed. Death overtook the signer before the gap was filled.

Viewed thus as a gift, the transaction was inchoate. An intention may be assumed, and indeed is not disputed, that what was incomplete at the moment should be completed in the future. The difficulty is that the intention was never carried out. Mrs. Bostwick remained free (apart from any power of revocation reserved in the deed of trust) to revoke the executory mandate, and keep the property as her own. Very likely different forms and instrumentalities would have been utilized, if she or her counsel had supposed that death was to come so swiftly. We might say as much if she had left in her desk a letter or memorandum expressing her resolutions for the morrow. With appropriate forms and instrumentalities available, she chose what the course of events has proved to be the wrong one. The court is without power to substitute another.

The transaction, failing as a gift, because inchoate or incomplete, is not to be sustained as the declaration of a trust. The donor had no intention of becoming a trustee herself. The donee never got title, and so could not hold it for another.

There was no equitable assignment. Equity does not enforce a voluntary promise to make a gift thereafter . . . .

One other question is in the case. It concerns the right of the executor to charge a proportionate part of the estate and inheritance taxes upon the interest of the remaindermen under the 1920 deed of trust. For the reasons stated in another action between the same parties involving the 1918 deed, the federal taxes are to be borne by the residuary estate.

The judgment of the Appellate Division should be modified, so as to affirm the judgment entered on the report of the referee in respect of the payment of the federal estate taxes, and, as so modified, affirmed, with a separate bill of costs to each party or set of parties appearing by separate attorney and to the several guardians ad litem, all payable out of the estate.

Notes

1. *Origins of the Winthrop Principle.* That an imperfect gift will not be salvaged by fictitiously attributing to the would-be donor an intent to create a self-declared trust has pretty well been settled since Richards v.

Delbridge, L.R. 18 Eq. 11 (1874). The point is ensconced in the Restatement 2d of Trusts §§ 23, 31 comment a, and codified in the recent California and Texas codifications of trust law. Cal. Prob. Code §§ 15200, 15201; Tex. Prop. Code §§ 112.001, 112.002.

In *Richards*, John Delbridge, shortly before his death, executed a deed of gift assigning his leasehold in a mill to his grandson, Edward Bennetto Richards. Because Edward was a minor, John delivered the deed to Edwards's mother on Edward's behalf. The gift was ineffective under the law of the time (8 & 9 Vict. c. 106, § 3) because the deed was not under seal.

Sir George Jessell, M.R., held that the gift could not be saved by labeling the deed a declaration of trust:

> The principal is a very simple one. A man may transfer his property, without valuable consideration, in one of two ways: he may either do such acts as amount in law to a conveyance or assignment of the property, and thus completely divest himself of the legal ownership, in which case the person who by those acts acquires the property takes it beneficially, or on trust, as the case may be; or the legal owner of the property may, by one or other of the modes recognised as amounting to a valid declaration of trust, constitute himself a trustee, and, without an actual transfer of the legal title, may so deal with the property as to deprive himself of its beneficial ownership, and declare that he will hold it from that time forward on trust for the other person. It is true he need not use the words, "I declare myself a trustee," but he must do something which is equivalent to it, and use the expressions which have that meaning; for, however anxious the Court may be to carry out the man's intention, it is not at liberty to construe words otherwise than according to their proper meaning . . . .
>
> The true distinction appears to me to be plain, and beyond dispute: for a man to make himself a trustee there must be an expression of intention to become a trustee, whereas words of present gift shew an intention to give over property to another, and not retain it in the donor's own hands for any purpose, fiduciary or otherwise.

Prior to *Richards*, there were cases on both sides of the equation. The earliest and most famous of the cases using the self-declared trust label to salvage an imperfect gift was Ex parte Pye, 18 Ves. 140, 34 Eng. Rep. 271 (Ch. 1811). In *Pye*, one William Mowbray, a married English gentleman, wrote a letter to his agent in Paris, Christopher Dubost, instructing Christopher to purchase an annuity of £100 for the benefit of Marie Genevieve Garos for her life, and, to pay for the purchase, to draw £1500 upon William's account. It appears that Marie, though not William's wife, was the mother of three children by him.

Christopher purchased the annuity as instructed, but violated his instructions to put the annuity in Marie's name; he put it in William's name instead, because Marie was then married to another man and also was deranged. Learning of what Christopher had done, William dispatched to Christopher a power of attorney that authorized Christopher to transfer the annuity to Marie. After William's death (in England), but in ignorance thereof, Christopher, in exercise of the power, executed a deed of gift of the annuity to Marie, Marie's husband having died in the meantime, and she having regained mental competency.[25]

In a dispute between William's estate and Marie concerning the ownership of the annuity, Marie argued that under French law, the exercise of the power of attorney in these circumstances was valid, for under French law, a power continues until the agent has knowledge of the principal's death. (Under English law, the exercise of the power would not have been valid because William's death revoked the power.[26])

The Chancellor, Lord Eldon,[27] sustained Marie's claim on a different ground. Apart from the proper construction of French law as to when a power of attorney is revoked, Lord Eldon treated William's power of attorney as a declaration of trust, i.e., that William held this part of his estate in trust for Marie.

Although Lord Eldon's approach of salvaging an imperfect gift has not endured, another aspect of his decision theretofore in doubt has persisted. Lord Eldon took it for granted that no consideration was necessary to support the self-declared trust for Marie. Although English courts resisted this conclusion for a time after that decision, the point is today well settled. Restatement 2d of Trusts §§ 28, 29, 30 (1959); Bogert on Trusts §§ 201, 202; Scott on Trusts § 28. The point is stated explicitly in the recent California and Texas codifications of the law of trusts. Cal. Prob. Code § 15208; Tex. Prop. Code § 112.003. The California statute states:

> § 15208. Consideration. Consideration is not required to create a trust, but a promise to create a trust in the future is enforceable only if the requirements for an enforceable contract are satisfied.

Concerning this aspect of Pye, Professor Alexander has made the following observation:

> [T]he problem that Eldon's decision created relates to the common law's antipathy toward gratuitous promises. For, from one point of view a person's declaration that he henceforth holds some asset in trust for the benefit of another looks very much like a promise to do an act in the future. Suppose, for example, a person declares, "I have decided to give these bonds to Susan when she graduates from college next month." It is not difficult to imagine

---

25. Was there a connection, do you suppose?

26. For American law on this point, see supra note 24 and Chapter 7, Part C.

27. The Chancellorship of Lord Eldon (nee John Scott, 1751-1838), which lasted from 1801 to 1838, is widely considered to have exemplified the interventionist approach to trusts that prevailed in England before notions of economic liberalism began to influence Equity doctrine. Pye may be said to illustrate this outlook.

Eldon's notorious dilatoriness is thought by some to have contributed to the backlog in Chancery practice that Dickens immortalized in the opening scene of his novel Bleak House: "Never can there come fog too thick, never can there come mind and mire too deep, to assort with the groping and floundering condition which this High Court of Chancery, most pestilent of hoary sinners, holds, this day, in the sight of heaven and earth." C. Dickens, Bleak House 1 (Riverside ed. 1956; 1st pub. 1852-53). For a suggestion that Eldon's "legendary lack of expedition on the bench" owed more to "excessive zeal to get things right than to simple tardiness," see S. Gardiner, An Introduction to the Law of Trusts 194 n.44 (1990).

that someone hearing this utterance might understand it to mean the same as the following statement: "I am holding these bonds for Susan until she graduates next month when I will turn them over to her." As a matter of ordinary speech habits, the difference between the two declarations is subtle at best, but the legal difference is very great. The first is a promise to make a gift, unenforceable if not supported by consideration, while the second is a declaration of trust, enforceable in Equity even if it is entirely gratuitous. It is just because the two forms of utterances can sound so much alike that *Pye's* recognition of the trust declaration threatened to undermine the common-law rule on gratuitous promises.

Alexander, The Transformation of Trusts as a Legal Category, 1800-1914, 5 Law & Hist. Rev. 303, 329-30 (1987).

2. *Question.* Should the rule that an imperfect gift will not be salvaged by labeling the transaction a self-declared trust be reexamined? Professor Love has argued that it should. See Love, Imperfect Gifts as Declarations of Trust: An Unapologetic Anomaly, 67 Ky. L.J. 309 (1979).

———

Precatory Language. The next case, Colton v. Colton, explores another aspect of an intent to create a trust—whether, in a given case, "precatory" language in a will or other governing instrument is properly interpreted as creating a trust. The Restatement 2d of Trusts provides:

> § 25. *Precatory Words.* No trust is created unless the settlor manifests an intention to impose enforceable duties.

The distinction, therefore, is between imposing legally enforceable duties on the devisee and merely seeking to impose a moral obligation on the devisee. If the court finds that the imposition of legally enforceable duties was intended, the trust is sometimes called a "precatory trust." The expression "precatory trust" is more confusing than helpful, however, and the following observation of the Kentucky court in Williams v. Williams' Committee, 253 Ky. 30, 32, 68 S.W.2d 395, 396 (1933), dispels the confusion:

> We will be less apt to go astray if we keep in mind that the expression "precatory trust" is a misnomer; it should be called a trust created by precatory words. It is simply a trust after all . . . .

The Restatement 2d of Property gives a somewhat different slant to the interpretation of precatory language:

> § 12.1 *comment d. Precatory words.* Words which merely express a suggestion or wish or desire that a transferee of property will make a certain disposition thereof do not, in the absence of other circumstances, cause the transfer to be less than it would be without the precatory words. This is made unequivocally clear if such words are accompanied with a statement that the transferor "does not intend to create any trust in law or in equity with respect to this transfer." Though precatory words do not cause the transferee to receive any lesser interest than the transferee would otherwise receive, they

may be a sufficient indication of intent to give the transferee a power of appointment over an interest not given to the transferee.

Illustrations:

8. O by will provides: "All tangible personal property owned by me at the time of my death I give to my wife W, if she survives me by thirty (30) days. I express the hope that my said wife will dispose of said tangible personal property according to my wishes expressed in a letter addressed to my wife which is attached to the will." W survives O by thirty days. W is the owner of the tangible personal property disposed of by O's will and is free to disregard O's expressed hope as to the disposition of the tangible personal property. The letter, though incorporated in the will by reference, contains only precatory language.

9. Same facts as Illustration 8 except that the interest specifically given to W is a life interest in the tangible personal property. The letter that is incorporated in the will by reference justifies the conclusion that W is given a power to appoint the tangible personal property in which she has a life interest by deed or by will to the persons referred to in the letter.

In the *Colton* case below, would the Restatement 2d of Property's approach have yielded a satisfactory outcome?

Colton v. Colton
127 U.S. 300 (1888)

These are two bills in equity, one filed by Martha Colton and the other by Abigail R. Colton, each of whom is a citizen of the state of New York, against Ellen M. Colton, a citizen of California.

Martha Colton alleges in her bill that she was a sister of David D. Colton, who died in San Francisco, Cal., on October 9, 1878, and that the defendant, Ellen M. Colton, is his widow; that on October 8, 1878, the said David D. Colton made and executed in due form his last will and testament, a copy of which is made a part of the bill, and is set out as follows:

I, David D. Colton, of San Francisco, make this my last will and testament. I declare that all of the estate of which I shall die possessed is community property, and was acquired since my marriage with my wife. I give and bequeath to my said wife, Ellen M. Colton, all of the estate, real and personal, of which I shall die seized or possessed or entitled to. I recommend to her the care and protection of my mother and sister, and request her to make such gift and provision for them as in her judgment will be best. . . .

The bill then alleges that the estate of David D. Colton thus distributed to the defendant was of the value of about $1,000,000, and that the defendant, though often demanded, has failed, neglected, and refused to make to the plaintiff any gift or provision whatever from the estate of said David D. Colton . . . .

[The bill filed by Abigail, mother of the testator, was much the same as Martha Colton's bill, except that it also alleged that the petitioner was 75 years old and in poor health, that her only income was the interest on a sum of $15,000, and that she was in "very straitened circumstances." A demurrer was sustained to each bill. The trial judge concluded that the "precatory words" of the will did not create a trust. 21 F. 594 (1884).]

MATTHEWS J. These appeals bring before us the will of David D. Colton for construction. The question is whether his widow, Ellen M. Colton, by its provisions, takes the whole estate of which he died seized and possessed absolutely in her own right, or whether she takes it charged with a trust enforceable in equity in favor of the complainants, and, if so, to what extent . . . . No technical language . . . is necessary to the creation of a trust, either by deed or by will. It is not necessary to use the words "upon trust" or "trustee," if the creation of a trust is otherwise sufficiently evident. If it appear to be the intention of the parties from the whole instrument creating it that the property conveyed is to be held or dealt with for the benefit of another, a court of equity will affix to it the character of a trust, and impose corresponding duties upon the party receiving the title, if it be capable of lawful enforcement . . . .

The situation of the testator at the time he framed these provisions is to be considered. He made his will October 8, 1878; he died the next day. It may be assumed that it was made in view of impending dissolution, in the very shadow of approaching death. There is room enough for the supposition that by this necessity the contents of his will were required to be brief; the conception of the general idea to give everything to his wife was simple and easily expressed, and capable of covering all other intended dispositions. The time and the circumstances perhaps disabled him from specifying satisfactory details concerning a provision for his mother and his sister, but he did not forget that he owed them care and protection. That care and protection, therefore, he recommended to his wife as his legatee; but he was not satisfied with that; he wished that care and protection to be embodied in a gift and provision for them out of the estate which he was to leave to her. He therefore requested her to make it, and that request he addressed to his legatee and principal beneficiary as expressive of his will that a gift and provision for his mother and sister should come out of it. . . .

It is an error to suppose that the word "request" necessarily imports an option to refuse, and excludes the idea of obedience as corresponding duty. If a testator requests his executor to pay a given sum to a particular person, the legacy would be complete and recoverable. According to its context and manifest use, an expression of desire or wish will often be equivalent to a positive direction, where that is the evident purpose and meaning of the testator; as where a testator desired that all of his just debts, and those of a firm for which he was not liable, should be paid as soon as convenient after his decease, it was construed to operate as a legacy in favor of the creditors of the latter. Burt v. Herron, 66 Pa. St. 400. And in such a case as the present, it would be but natural for the testator to suppose that a request, which, in its terms, implied no alternative, addressed to his widow and principal legatee, would be understood and obeyed as strictly as though it were couched in the language of direction and command . . . .

On the whole, therefore, our conclusion is that each of the complainants in these bills is entitled to take a beneficial interest under the will of David D. Colton, to the extent, out of the estate given by him to his wife, of a permanent provision for them during their respective lives, suitable and sufficient for their care and protection, having regard to their condition and necessities, and the amount and value of the fund from which it must come. It will be the duty of the court to ascertain after proper inquiry, and thereupon to determine and declare, what provision will be suitable and best under the circumstances, and all particulars and details for securing and paying it. The decrees of the circuit court are accordingly reversed, and the causes remanded, with directions to overrule the demurrers to the several bills, and to take with this opinion; and it is so ordered.

3. Parties To A Trust

a. The Trustee

As explained earlier, an owner of property can create a trust either by declaring herself or himself trustee for designated beneficiaries or by selecting another person as trustee and transferring title to the property to that other person. Once established, the principal relation with respect to the property is between the trustee and the beneficiary, although the settlor may of course retain interests not only as beneficiary but also through retention of various sorts of powers, the commonest being a power to amend or a power to revoke or both. In the remainder of this part, the subjects of study will be the trustee and the beneficiaries, with emphasis on whether either is necessary to establish a trust.

Adams v. Adams
88 U.S. (21 Wall.) 185 (1874)

Appeal from the Supreme Court of the District of Columbia. The case was thus: Adams, a government clerk, in Washington, owning a house and lot there, on the 13th of August, 1861, executed, with his wife, a deed of the premises to one Appleton, in fee, as trustee for the wife. The deed by appropriate words *in praesenti* conveyed, so far as its terms were concerned, the property for the sole and separate use of the wife for life, with power to lease and to take the rents for her own use, as if she was a *feme sole*; the trustee having power, on request of the wife, to sell and convey the premises in fee and pay the proceeds to her or as she might direct; and after her death (no sale having been made), the trust being that the trustee should hold the property for the children of the marriage as tenants in common, and in default of issue living at the death of the wife, then for Adams, the husband, his heirs and assigns.

The deed was signed by the grantors, and the husband acknowledged it before two justices "to be his act and deed." The wife did the same; being separately examined. The instrument purported to be "signed, sealed, and delivered" in the presence of the same justices, and they signed it as attesting witnesses. The husband put it himself on record in the registry of deeds for the county of Washington, D.C., which was the appropriate place of record for it.

Subsequent to this, that is to say in September, 1870, the husband and wife were divorced by judicial decree.

And subsequently to this again, that is to say, in December, 1871—the husband being in possession of the deed, and denying that any trust was ever created and executed, and Appleton, [declining] the wife's request . . . to assert the trust, or to act as trustee, Mrs. Adams filed a bill in the court below against them both, to establish the deed as a settlement made upon her by her husband, to compel a delivery of it to her; to remove Appleton, the trustee named in it, and to have some suitable person appointed trustee in his place . . . .

The bill further alleged the dissolution of the marriage by law, and that the complainant, relying upon the provisions of the deed referred to, neither sought nor obtained alimony in that suit; and further, that she has accepted, and still accepted the benefits of the trust; that Appleton declined to act as trustee, to allow the use of his name, or in any way to aid her in the matter; that her husband, the defendant, was in possession receiving the rents and profits, and declined to acknowledge her rights in the premises . . . .

Appleton also answered, alleging that if any such deed as described was executed, it was executed without his knowledge or consent; that no such deed was ever delivered to him, and that he never accepted any trust imposed by it; that he was never informed of the existence of the deed till 1870, when he was informed of it by the complainant, and that he then declined to act as trustee . . . .

The court below declared the trust valid and effective in equity as between the parties; appointed a new trustee; required the husband to deliver up the deed to the wife or to the new trustee; and to deliver also to him possession of the premises described in the deed of trust, and to account before the master for the rents and profits of it which had accrued since the filing of the bill, receiving credit for any payment made to the complainant in the meantime, and to pay the complainant's costs of the suit.

From a decree accordingly, the husband appealed.

HUNT J. . . . Upon the evidence before us we have no doubt that the deed was executed, acknowledged, and recorded by the defendant with the intent to make provision for his wife and children; that he took the deed into his own possession with the understanding, and upon the belief on his part, that he had accomplished that purpose by acknowledging and procuring the record of the deed, by showing the same to his wife, informing her of its contents, and placing the same in the house therein conveyed in a place equally accessible to her and to himself.

The defendant now seeks to repudiate what he then intended, and to overthrow what he then asserted and believed he had then accomplished.

It may be conceded, as a general rule, that delivery is essential, both in law and in equity, to the validity of a gift, whether of real or personal estate. What constitutes a delivery is a subject of great difference of opinion, some cases holding that a parting with a deed, even for the purpose of recording, is in itself a delivery.

It may be conceded also to have been held many times that courts of equity will not enforce a merely gratuitous gift of mere moral obligation.

These concessions do not, however, dispose of the present case. . . .

We are of opinion that the refusal of Appleton, in 1870, to accept the deed, or to act as trustee, is not a controlling circumstance.

Although a trustee may never have heard of the deed, the title vests in him, subject to a disclaimer on his part. Such disclaimer will not, however, defeat the conveyance as a transfer of the equitable interest to a third person. A trust cannot fail for want of a trustee, or by the refusal of all the trustees to accept the trust. The court of chancery will appoint new trustees. . . .

The defense rests upon the alleged non-delivery by Mr. Adams of the deed of August 13th, 1861, to Mrs. Adams, or for her benefit. We have referred at length to the authorities which show that as matter of law the deed was sufficiently delivered, and that it is the duty of the court to establish the trust.

We think that the decree of the court below was well made, and that it should be

Affirmed.

Notes

1. *Resignation Distinguished from Disclaimer.* In *Adams,* the trustee, Appleton, disclaimed the trust. A trustee can always disclaim (refuse to accept) a trust, but once accepted, the trustee can resign only with the permission of the appropriate court, or in accordance with the terms of the trust, or with the consent of the beneficiaries if they are competent to give such consent. Restatement 2d of Trusts § 106; Scott on Trusts § 106. See also Tex. Prop. Code § 113.081; Cal. Ρ ob. Code § 15640. Trust instruments often provide that the trustee may resign, as in Article VI of the John Doe trust reproduced supra p. 602.

2. *Devolution of a Trustee's Title Upon Death.* At common law, a sole trustee's title to the trust property passed to her or his heirs on the trustee's death intestate and could also be disposed of by will. Restatement 2d of Trusts §§ 104, 105. In some states, this has been changed by statute; New York, for example, provides that title "vests in the supreme court or the surrogate's court, as the case may be, and the trust shall be executed by a person appointed by the court . . . ." N.Y. Est. Powers & Trust Law § 7-2.3. Trust documents commonly take control of this question by expressly designating a successor trustee.

Co-trustees hold title as joint tenants so that, on the death of one, legal title to the trust property is in the survivor. Reichert v. Missouri & Illinois Coal Co., 231 Ill. 238, 83 N.E. 166 (1907); Restatement 2d of Trusts § 103; Scott on Trusts § 103.

3. *Multiple Trustees; Exercise of Powers.* Co-trustees of a private trust must all join in the exercise of their powers as trustees, unless the terms of the trust or of a statute provide otherwise. This rule does not obtain, however, in the administration of charitable trusts, where action may be by a majority of the trustees if there are three or more. Restatement 2d of Trusts §§ 194, 383; Scott on Trusts §§ 194, 383; Cal. Prob. Code § 15620.

4. *Lack of a Trustee.* Suppose that G dies leaving a will that devises her or his entire estate in trust to named beneficiaries. Or, suppose that the will names a trustee but the designated trustee dies prior to G's death. Is there a valid trust? In these circumstances, courts will appoint a trustee to carry out the term of the will, relying on the old saw that a trust will not fail for lack of a trustee. See, e.g., Estate of McCray, 204 Cal. 399, 268 P. 647 (1928); Woodruff v. Woodruff, 44 N.J. Eq. 349, 16 A. 4 (1888); Perfect Union Lodge No. 10 v. Interfirst Bank, 748 S.W.2d 218 (Tex. 1988).

b. The Beneficiaries

(1) UNBORN AND UNASCERTAINED BENEFICIARIES

There is no doubt that a valid trust can be created that includes unborn and unascertained persons among its beneficiaries. Suppose, for example, a parent transfers property to a trustee, directing that the income from the property be paid to the parent for life, corpus at the parent's death to be equally divided among her or his children. The trust would be valid without question, and later born children would be included in the class, also without question.

Can a trust be validly created if *all* of its beneficiaries are unborn, unascertained, or both?

Morsman v. Commissioner
90 F.2d 18, 113 A.L.R. 441 (8th Cir. 1937)

[On January 28, 1929, Robert P. Morsman, president of the United States Trust Company, signed a document declaring himself trustee of certain publicly traded securities; the United States Trust Company was named successor trustee. The securities had substantially appreciated in value during Morsman's ownership. Morsman, being in a high income-tax bracket, hoped that putting the securities into the self-declared trust would cause the ordinary income and any capital gain realized on sale to be taxed to the lower-bracket trust.

The trust document provided that the trust income was to be accumulated and added to principal until January 1, 1934. Thereafter, income was to be paid to Morsman himself for life. On termination of the trust, the principal was to go to his issue, or to his widow if there were no issue, or to his legal heirs if he had neither issue nor a widow then living.

Throughout the period in question, Mr. Morsman was unmarried and had no issue. Apparently his closest blood relative was a brother, who was Morsman's heir apparent.

Shortly after signing the trust document, Morsman sold the securities at a profit. Then, on May 3, 1929, he turned the trust property over to the United States Trust Company as successor trustee. The gains realized on these sales were reported as income of the trust. The Commissioner of Internal Revenue determined that the gains should have been reported as income on Morsman's personal return.]

THOMAS, J. . . . The question for consideration is whether or not the arrangement so devised resulted in the creation of an express trust covering the period and the transactions between January 28 and May 3, 1929. No claim is made that a charitable trust is involved. [Morsman] contends that a private express trust did exist during the period in question and that the profits realized from the sale of the securities should be taxed as income to the trust and not as income to himself individually . . . .

First. With respect to the position of Morsman, it is settled that a trust cannot exist where the same person possesses both the legal and equitable titles to the trust fund at the same time. In such a case the two titles are said to merge . . . . This principle is not denied. The result, of course, is different where one person conveys property to another who agrees to hold in trust for the grantor, as in the case of Doctor v. Hughes, 225 N.Y. 305, 122 N.E. 221. In such a case there is an immediate severance of the legal and equitable titles, and a trust arises at once. In the instant case that provision of the agreement by which [Morsman] undertook to hold for himself, standing alone, therefore, contributes nothing toward the creation of a trust . . . .

Second. With respect to the possibility of issue, it . . . is true that . . . it has been held in several cases that a present trust may be created where the beneficiary of an express trust is an unborn child. [E.g.,] Folk v. Hughes, 100 S.C. 220, 84 S.E. 713. The rationale of these cases, however, is not believed to rest on the theory that an unborn child can be the express cestui of an immediate trust. To so hold would violate fundamental principles of trusts which require a present conveyance of the beneficial interest and the existence of present enforceable duties and it would permit the suspension of the beneficial ownership, a notion repugnant to the requirements of a trust. The rationale of such a case is that the instrument has the effect of creating an immediate resulting trust for the settlor (which will cease if the expected child is born) "with an express trust for the child springing up when and if such child ever materializes." Bogert, Trusts and Trustees, § 163 . . . . So if A, a bachelor, transfers property to B in trust to accumulate the rents and profits and to convey the same to A's eldest son on reaching its majority (Trusts, Restatement, § 112, Illustration 6), a trust will arise at once—B now holding as a resulting trustee for A with the express trust arising if and when the eldest son comes into existence—the resulting trust then to cease. But in that view if A, a bachelor, or any person without issue, declares himself trustee of property for his own eldest son on identical or similar terms, no trust will presently arise. The express trust for the child cannot arise until the child comes into existence, and A cannot hold as a resulting trustee for himself during his lifetime because of the necessary merger in such a case of the legal and equitable interests in the same person. If A should die without issue under these circumstances, the property constituting the so-called trust fund is as much a part of his estate as if he had never made the purported declaration. The distinction thus noted between the case where A declares himself trustee for his unborn issue and where he conveys to B to hold in trust for such issue is vital; and this is the point at which Morsman failed in his attempt to create a present trust . . . .

To hold that a *present* trust arises where the owner of property declares that he holds it in trust for himself and other persons who are as yet nonexistent not only lacks a logical explanation but is incapable of practical application. To a creditor seeking to subject the property to the satisfaction of a debt [Morsman] would say that it was no longer his, but belonged, in equity, to others who were not yet in existence. But if he sought to dissipate the property, there is no person in being who has such an interest that he may go into a court of equity and prevent the dissipation. To say that [Morsman] in this case has an interest in enforcing such an obligation against himself or that the community at large is interested in preserving the rights of issue as yet not conceived is, to say the least, an unwarranted assumption. For the court to regard possible unborn issue as present beneficiaries is to permit the substance and realities of the transaction to be obscured by words and phrases . . . .

Third. With respect to the "heirs" as present beneficiaries and to the possible suggestion that [Morsman's] brother now living may take a present equitable interest under paragraph (8) of the trust agreement, it is observed that one of the elementary rules of law is that "A living person has no heirs". . . . Only on death do heirs come into existence, "for the ancestor during his life beareth in his body (in judgment of law) all his heirs, and therefore, it is truly said that haeres est pars antecessoris." Co. Litt. 22b. Quoted in Doctor v. Hughes, 225 N.Y. 305, 122 N.E. 221, 222. What has been said with reference to the rights of unborn children applies with equal force to the rights of heirs, two classes equally nonexistent. "Heirs," therefore, have no present beneficial interest, and cannot be considered beneficiaries . . . .

Finally, with respect to the status of a widow as a beneficiary, what has been said in reference to the nonexistence of issue and heirs is applicable here. The record, as pointed out above, does not show the existence of a wife. A widow is, therefore, a mere potentiality without existence and with no one to represent her. As a fiction, she belongs to no class. In case of an hypothetical breach of duty of the trustee, no woman in all the world, upon the record here, has a present right to come forward and enforce any rights under the trust agreement, and no existing person is authorized to enforce her imaginary rights.

The trust agreement, therefore, failed to effect the creation of a trust on January 28, 1929. This results from the fact that no existing beneficiaries were named therein and, consequently, there was no present severance of the legal and equitable titles to the property. The question here determined is whether there was a valid declaration of trust operating in praesenti between January 28 and May 3, 1929. That question must necessarily be answered in the negative since there was at that time no person in being who could claim any beneficial interest in the property other than the holder of the legal title. It is true, of course, that in equity a trust may not fail for want of a trustee, nevertheless the courts cannot supply a private express beneficiary . . . .

Affirmed.

GARDNER, J. dissenting. Authority is not wanting to the effect that a trust may be created even though the cestui que trust at the time of its creation is not in existence. For instance, the case of Folk v. Hughes, 100 S.C. 220, 84 S.E. 713, 714, cited in the majority opinion, specifically so holds . . . . But if it be assumed that there must have been in existence at the time of the creation of the trust a cestui que capable of taking, yet a prospective or potential heir, who under the terms of the trust may, under certain contingencies, be a beneficiary, fulfills this requirement.

Note and Questions

Trusts With Unborn Beneficiaries. Compare with *Morsman*, Folk v. Hughes, 100 S.C. 220, 84 S.E. 713 (1915), cited in both the majority and dissenting opinions in *Morsman*. In *Folk*, a father transferred real property to his son under a deed that provided:

> To have and to hold the said described tract of land with all privileges and appurtenances thereof to [my son] for his uses and benefits, and for the maintenance and support of [my son's] children during the term of [my son's] natural life. And I . . . for and in consideration of the love and affection I have for the lawful children of [my son], do hereby grant, release and convey unto the lawful children of [my son] all the above described tract of land. To have and to hold the same immediately after the death of [my son]. Together with all the rights and appurtenances thereto belonging. To have and to hold all and singular the said premises unto the children of [my son], their heirs and assigns forever.

At the time of the transfer, the son was married but childless. A child was born to the son later, however, and the court held that a valid trust had been created for that child at the time of the original transfer. As a consequence, the son was unable by reconveying the property to his father to destroy the contingent remainder in his unborn children. The court said, in part:

It is not necessary to the creation of a trust estate that the cestui que trust should be in existence at the time of its creation. In [Ashurst v. Given, 5 Watts & S. (Pa.) 329], a devise to a father in trust for his children at the time of his death was held to be good, although the father had no children at the time of the vesting of the estate in him as trustee.

A trustee will not be allowed by his own act to defeat or destroy his trust, and those who deal with him in respect of the trust estate, with knowledge of the trust, are bound by the terms of the trust, and if they purchase the trust estate, they take it incumbered with the trust.

Are *Folk* and *Morsman* distinguishable, as the *Morsman* majority thought, or was the dissenting judge right that they are inconsistent? Should it matter that in *Folk* the trust was created by transfer of legal title, while the *Morsman* trust was self-declared?

(2) MERGER: BENEFICIARY AS TRUSTEE

One Person as Both Trustee and Sole Beneficiary. A transfer of legal title to a person to hold in trust for herself or himself, as sole beneficiary, does not create a trust. This is commonly explained, as it was in the *Morsman* opinion, by saying that there is a merger of the legal and equitable titles. But in truth, no separation of legal and equitable title ever occurred so as to bring about a merger—in short, the transfer did not create a trust.

The problem of merger may arise, however, either *after* the inception of an admittedly valid trust or *at* the inception of an intended trust. If title is transferred to A to hold on active trust for B, there is of course a trust at the inception of the arrangement. Should A thereafter die intestate, leaving B as her or his sole heir, in a state in which title to trust property passes to an intestate trustee's heirs, legal and equitable title will have become vested in one person, and there will often be a merger, which will normally put an end to the trust. It is commonly said that equity will prevent a merger in order to effectuate the settlor's intent, and while the maxim is stated more frequently than it is applied there seems little reason to doubt that it will sometimes be applied. In the case just put, for example, if the subject matter of the trust were land, the trust instrument provided that the land was not to be sold for ten years, and the period had not elapsed when A died, the court would probably hold there was no merger and would appoint another trustee in order to effectuate the settlor's wishes.

Much the same issue could arise at the inception of the intended trust. If the trust were testamentary and the named trustee predeceased the testator, the legal title to the trust property might pass to the sole beneficiary as heir or residuary devisee of the settlor. Again, the issue would be whether equity will prevent a merger. If it does, this will have the effect of saving the trust at its inception.

Some statutes specifically recognize certain limited exceptions to the doctrine of merger. See, e.g., Tex. Prop. Code § 112.034; Cal. Prob. Code § 15209.

Multiple Parties, Overlapping Interests as Trustee and Beneficiary. The problems are more complicated once we get beyond the situation of one person as sole trustee and sole beneficiary. Three situations are most troublesome:

> *Category (1)*: G transfers to A and B in trust for A and B, where the beneficial interests are concurrent.
> *Category (2)*: G transfers to A in trust for A and B, where the beneficial interests are concurrent—for example, the beneficiaries are given equal shares in income and principal.
> *Category (3)*: G transfers to A in trust for A and B, where the beneficial interests are successive—for example, income is to be paid to A for life, with principal then to be transferred to B.

A valid trust would be created in all these situations according to Restatement 2d of Trusts section 99. In Category (1), a technical argument favoring validity is that the trustees hold the legal title as joint tenants, while the beneficiaries hold as tenants in common. A purposeful argument is that application of the merger doctrine would defeat the expressed intention of the settlor, which public policy does not require inasmuch as a beneficiary exists who can enforce the trust against a trustee other than herself or himself. Most of the cases that have dealt with the above categories have avoided the merger of interests, and this is certainly the trend. A case in Alabama dealing with Category (1) sustained the trust and overruled a prior case to the contrary. First Alabama Bank v. Webb, 373 S.2d 631 (Ala. 1979). The court said that merger should operate only where one person is both trustee and beneficiary.

A point applicable only to Category (3) is that, at the very least, it should be clear that A holds the remainder interest in trust for B. The only real question should be whether A's equitable life estate, which A holds as beneficiary, merges with the legal life estate, which A holds as trustee, so that A holds the life estate free of trust. The better authority holds that A does not hold the life estate free of trust. The ground, again, is that merger defeats the intention of the settlor for no good reason. Thus the trustee holds the entire legal title in trust, as intended by the settlor; a court should not reduce that legal title to separate undivided interests.

A number of New York cases, however, have held that A does hold the life estate free of trust. Indeed, they have gone even further and held that no trust is created at all: that B holds the remainder interest free of trust. In these cases, the ground offered is not merger but the extent of the trustee's legal title. In New York, the trustee is said to take the legal title only for life, making the trustee the sole beneficiary of the trust. Reed v. Browne, 295 N.Y. 184, 66 N.E.2d 47 (1946).

(3) INDEFINITE BENEFICIARIES

In connection with Clark v. Campbell and the succeeding materials, consider whether a trust is created where G's will purports to create a trust on the following alternative terms:

1. "Income to A for life, remainder in corpus to my (G's) friends"; or

2. "Income to A for life, remainder in corpus to such of my (G's) friends as the trustee shall select"; or

3. "Income to A for life, remainder in corpus to such of my (G's) friends as A shall select."

Clark v. Campbell
82 N.H. 281, 133 A. 166 (1926)

Petition for instructions, by the trustees under the will of Charles H. Cummings. Questions, which appear in the opinion, were reserved without ruling by Sawyer, J.

SNOW, J. The ninth clause of the will of deceased reads:

> My estate will comprise so many and such a variety of articles of personal property such as books, photographic albums, pictures, statuary, bronzes, bric-a-brac, hunting and fishing equipment, antiques, rugs, scrap books, canes and masonic jewels, that probably I shall not distribute all, and perhaps no great part thereof during my life by gift among my friends. Each of my trustees is competent by reason of familiarity with the property, my wishes and friendships, to wisely distribute some portion at least of said property. I therefore give and bequeath to my trustees all my property embraced within the classification aforesaid in trust to make disposal by the way of a memento from myself, of such articles to such of my friends as they, my trustees, shall select. All of said property, not so disposed of by them, my trustees are directed to sell and the proceeds of such sale or sales to become and be disposed of as a part of the residue of my estate.

. . . . By the common law there cannot be a valid bequest to an indefinite person. There must be a beneficiary or a class of beneficiaries indicated in the will capable of coming into court and claiming the benefit of the bequest. This principle applies to private but not to public trusts and charities. Morice v. Bishop of Durham, 9 Vest. 399, 10 Ves. 521.

The basis assigned for this distinction is the difference in the enforceability of the two classes of trusts. In the former, there being no definite *cestui que trust* to assert his right, there is no one who can compel performance, with the consequent unjust enrichment of the trustee; while, in the case of the latter, performance is considered to be sufficiently secured by the authority of the Attorney General to invoke the power of the courts. The soundness of this distinction and the grounds upon which it rests, as applied to cases where the trustee is willing to act, has been questioned by distinguished authorities (5 Harvard Law Review, 390, 394, 395; 65 University of Pennsylvania Law Review, 538, 540; 37 Harvard Law Review, 687, 688) and has been supported by other authorities of equal note (15

Harvard Law Review, 510, 513-515, 530).[28] It is, however, conceded by the former that, since the doctrine was first stated in Morice v. Bishop of Durham, supra, more than a century ago, it has remained unchallenged, and has been followed by the courts in a practically unbroken line of decisions. Although it be conceded that the doctrine is not a legal necessity, the fact that it has never been impeached affords strong evidence that in its practical application it has been generally found just and reasonable. This is a sufficient ground for continued adherence to the rule . . . .

"A gift to trustees to dispose of the same as they think fit is too uncertain to be carried out by the court." Theobald on Wills, 7th ed., 495 . . . .

That the foregoing is the established doctrine seems to be conceded, but it is contended in argument that it was not the intention of the testator by the ninth clause to create a trust, at least as respects the selected articles, but to make an absolute gift thereof to the trustees individually. It is suggested that the recital of the qualifications of the trustees may be considered as investing them with personal and nonofficial character, and that the word "trustees" is merely descriptive of the persons who had been earlier named as trustees, and was not intended to limit the capacity in which they were to act here . . . . If is a sufficient answer to this contention that the language of the ninth clause does not warrant the assumed construction. The assertion of the competency of the trustees to wisely distribute the articles in question by reason of their familiarity with the testator's property, wishes and friendships seem quite as consistent with a design to clothe them with a trusteeship as with an intention to impose upon them a moral obligation only. Blunt v. Taylor, 230 Mass. 303, 305, 119 N.E. 954. If, however, the recited qualifications had the significance ascribed to them the language of the bequest is too plain to admit of the assumed construction. When the clause is ended of unnecessary verbiage the testator is made to say: "I give to my trustee my property (of the described class) in trust to make disposal of to such of my friends as they shall select." It is difficult to conceive of language more clearly disclosing an intention to create a trust. However, if the trust idea introduced by the words "trustees" and in "trust" were not controlling, all the evidence within the will confirms such idea. In the first clause of the will the testator nominates three trustees, and an alternate in case of vacancy. Throughout the will these nominees are repeatedly and invariably referred as "my trustees," whenever the testator is dealing with their trust duties. Whenever rights are conferred upon them individually, as happens in the fifth, sixth, and eighth clauses, they are as invariably severally referred to solely by their individual names. The clause under consideration (ninth) expressly provides for the disposal of only a portion of the classified articles, and imposes upon the trustees the duty of selling the balance thereof and adding the proceeds to the residue which they are to continue to hold, and

---

28. The distinguished authorities referred to are James Barr Ames, 5 Harv. L. Rev. 389 (1892); John Chipman Gray, 15 Harv. L. Rev. 509 (1902); and Austin W. Scott, 65 U. Pa. L. Rev. 527 (1917), 37 Harv. L. Rev. 653 (1924). Eds.

administer in their capacity as trustees. The proceeds thus accruing under this clause are expressly referred to in the eleventh clause in enumeration of the ultimate funds to be distributed by them as trustees "in and among such charitable . . . institutions" as they shall select and designate. The conclusion is inescapable that there was no intention to bestow any part of the property enumerated is the ninth clause upon the trustees for their own benefit. This necessarily follows, since the direction to make disposal is clearly as broad as the gift.

It is further sought to sustain the bequest as a power. The distinction apparently relied upon is that a power, unlike a trust, is not imperative and leaves the act to be done at the will of the donee of the power. But the ninth clause by its terms imposes upon the trustees the imperative duty to dispose of the selected articles among the testator's friends. If, therefore, the authority bestowed by the testator by the use of a loose terminology may be called a power, it is not an optional power, but a power coupled with a trust, to which the principles incident to a trust so far as here involved, clearly apply.

We must therefore conclude that this clause presents the case of an attempt to create a private trust, and clearly falls within the principle of well-considered authorities. Nichols v. Allen, 130 Mass. 211, 212, 39 Am.Rep. 445; Blunt v. Taylor, 230 Mass. 303, 305, 119 N.E. 954. In so far as the cases cited by the petitioners upon this phase of the case are not readily distinguishable from the case at bar, they are in conflict with the great weight of authority.

The question presented, therefore, is whether or not the ninth clause provides for definite and ascertainable beneficiaries, so that the bequest therein can be sustained as a private trust. In this state the identity of a beneficiary is a question of fact to be found from the language of the will, construed in the light of all the competent evidence rather than by the application of arbitrary rules of law. It is believed that in no other jurisdiction is there greater liberality shown in seeking the intention of the testator in this, as in other particulars. We find, however, no case in which our courts have sustained a gift where the testator has attempted to delegate to a trustee the arbitrary selection of the beneficiaries of his bounty through means of a private trust.

Like the direct legatees in a will, the beneficiaries under a trust may be designated by class. But in such case the class must be capable of delimitation, as "brothers and sisters," "children," issue," "nephews and nieces." A bequest giving the executor authority to distribute his property "among his relatives and for benevolent objects is such sums as in their judgment shall be for the best" was sustained upon evidence within the will that by "relatives" the testator intended such of his relatives within the statute of distributions as were needy, and thus brought the bequest within the line of charitable gifts, and excluded all other as individuals. Goodale v. Mooney, 60 N.H. 528, 526, 49 Am. Rep. 334. Where a testator bequeathed his stocks to be apportioned to his "relations" according to the discretion of the trustee, to be enjoyed by them after his decease, it was held to be a power to appoint amongst his relations who were next of kin under the statute of distribution. Varrell v. Wendell, 20 N.H. 431, 436. Likewise where a devise over after a particular estate was to the testator's "next of kin" simpliciter. Pinkham v. Blair, 57 N.H. 226, 243. Unless the will discloses a plain purpose to the contrary, the words "relatives" or "relations," to prevent gifts from being void for uncertainty, are commonly construed to mean those who would take under statutes of distribution or descent.

In the case now under consideration the cestuis que trust are designated as the "friends" of the testator. The word "friends," unlike "relations," has no accepted statutory or other controlling limitations, and in fact has no precise sense at all. Friendship is a word of broad and varied application. It is commonly used to describe the undefinable relationships which exists, not only between those connected by ties of kinship or marriage, but as well between strangers in blood, and which vary in degree from the greatest intimacy to an acquaintance more or less casual. "Friend" is sometimes used in contradistinction to "enemy." "A friendless man is an outlaw." Cowell, Bouvier. Although the word was formerly sometimes used a synonymous with relatives, there is no evidence that it was so used here. The inference is to the contrary. The testator in the will refers to eight different persons, some of them already deceased, by the title of "friends." He never uses the appellation concurrently with "nephew" or "niece," which words occur several times in describing legatees. Nor is there anything to indicate that the word "friends" in the ninth clause was intended to apply only to those who had been thus referred to in the will. There is no express evidence that the word is used in any restricted sense . . . .

It was the evident purpose of the testator to invest his trustees with the power after his death to make disposition of the enumerated articles among an undefined class with practically the same freedom and irresponsibility that he himself would have exercised if living; that is, to substitute for the will of the testator the will and discretion of the trustees. Such a purpose is in contravention of the policy of the statute which provides that

> No will shall be effectual to pass any real or personal estate . . . unless made by a person . . . in writing, signed by the testator or by some one in his presence and by his direction, and attested and subscribed in his presence by three or more credible witnesses.

Where a gift is impressed with a trust, ineffectively declared, and incapable of taking effect because of the indefiniteness of the cestui que trust, the donee will hold the property in trust for the next taker under the will or for the next of kin by way of a resulting trust. . . . The trustees therefore hold title to the property enumerated in the paragraph under consideration to be disposed of as a part of the residue, and the trustees are so advised. This conclusion makes it unnecessary to answer the question reserved, and it has not been considered. . . . Case discharged.

Notes and Questions

1. *Requirement of a Definite Class.* What reasoning explains the rule, applied in *Clark*, that where a fiduciary is under a duty to select the beneficiaries of a trust from amongst a class, the entire membership of the class must be definite and ascertainable? The court in *Clark* pointed to the policy of the statute of wills as a basis for the rule. But a moment's reflection should tell you that this cannot be so.

The first and leading case on the problem was Morice v. The Bishop of Durham, 10 Ves. 522, 32 Eng. Rep. 947 (Ch. 1805), in which property was given by will to the Bishop of Durham upon trust, after the payment of the testatrix's debts and legacies, "to dispose of the ultimate residue to such objects of benevolence and liberality as the Bishop of Durham in his own discretion shall most approve of." The Chancellor, Lord Eldon (whom we met in connection with Ex parte Pye), held that there was no intent that the Bishop take beneficially, and that the Bishop's discretion was not limited to purposes that were charitable, and that, therefore, the trust must fail because it was "for purposes not sufficiently defined to be controlled and managed by this Court." A decree in favor of the next of kin of the testatrix was affirmed.

Prior to this case, Equity judges had been more willing to exercise control over trustees' powers to select beneficiaries. The *Bishop of Durham's* case sharpened the distinction between trust powers and "bare" powers. As a result, Equity embarked on a course that violated donors' intentions in a much wider range of cases. Surveying the changes made by Morice v. The Bishop of Durham, together with Richards v. Elbridge and other Equity decisions of the early nineteenth century, Professor Alexander has offered the following thesis:

> In general, the process of drawing categorical lines between trust and other legal forms served an ideological function. It reinforced the ascendent contractarian mentality, preventing it from being destabilized by the competing non-contractarian principle that is embedded in the very theory of the trust, that is, the notion that at times one has a duty to treat others' interests as though they were one's own. The nineteenth-century categorical structuring of private law allowed the legal systems in both England and the United States to recognize this principle but restrict its scope to an isolated, marginal corner of private law.

Alexander, The Transformation of Trusts as a Legal Category, 1800-1914, 5 Law & Hist. Rev. 303, 336 (1987).

In Nichols v. Allen, 130 Mass. 211, 221 (1881), the leading American case on the problem, the court said:

> The conclusion of the whole matter is, that, the testatrix having given the residue of her property to her executors in trust and not having defined the trust sufficiently to enable the court to execute it, the plaintiff, being her next of kin, is entitled to the residue by way of resulting trust.

Compare this statement with the explanation for the rule put forward by the court in *Clark*.

EXTERNAL REFERENCES. Palmer, Private Trusts for Indefinite Beneficiaries, 71 Mich. L. Rev. 359, 366-67 (1972); Hopkins, Certain Uncertainties of Trusts and Powers, 29 Camb. L.J. 68 (1971).

2. *"Friends" As an Indefinite Class.* Why does the word "friends" create a class too indefinite to sustain a trust? Recall what the court in Clark v. Campbell said about the point:

> The word "friends," unlike "relations," has no accepted statutory or other controlling liitations,   and in fact has no precise sense at all. Friendship is a word of broad and varied application. It is commonly used to describe the undefinable relationships which exist, not only between those connected by ties of kinship or marriage, but as well between strangers in blood, and which vary in degree from the greatest intimacy to an acquaintance more or less casual.

In a recent book, the author Judith Viorst identifies several categories of friendship:

> 1. *Convenience friends.* These are the neighbor or office mate or members of our car pool whose lives routinely intersect with ours. These are the people with whom we exchange small favors. They lend us their cups and silverware for a party. They drive our children to soccer when we are sick. They keep our cat for a week when we go on vacation. And, when we need a lift, they give us a ride to the garage to pick up the Honda. And we do for them.
>
> But we don't with convenience friends, ever come too close or tell too much: We maintain our public face and emotional distance. . . .
>
> 2. *Special-interest friends.* These friendships depend on the sharing of some activity or concern. These are sports friends, work friends, yoga friends, nuclear-freeze friends. We meet to participate jointly in knocking a ball across a net, or saving the world. . . .
>
> 3. *Historical friends.* With luck we also have a friend who knew us . . . way back when. . . .
>
> The years have gone by, [we] have gone separate ways, [we] have little in common now, but [we] still are an intimate part of each other's past. . . .
>
> 4. *Crossroads friends.* Like historical friends, our crossroads friends are important for what was—for the friendship we shared at a crucial, now past, time of life: a time, perhaps, when we roomed in college together; or served a stint in the U.S. Air Force together; or worked as eager young singles in Manhattan together; or went through pregnancy, birth and those first difficult years of motherhood together.
>
> With historical friends and crossroads friends we forge links strong enough to endure with not much more contact than once-a-year letters at Christmas, maintaining a special intimacy—dormant but always ready to be revived—on those rare but tender occasions when we meet.
>
> 5. *Cross-generational friends.* Another tender intimacy—tender but unequal—exists in the friendships that form across generations, the friendships that one woman calls her daughter-mother and her mother-daughter relationships. Across the generations the younger enlivens the older, the older instructs the younger. Each role, as mentor or quester, as adult or child, offers gratifications of its own. And because we are unconnected by blood, our words of advice are accepted as wise, not intrusive, our childish lapses don't

summon up warnings and groans. Without the risks, and without the ferocious investment, which are always a part of a real parent-child connection, we enjoy the rich disparities to be found among our cross-generational friends.

6. *Close friends.* Emotionally and physically (by seeing each other, by mail, by talks on the phone) we maintain some ongoing friendships of deep intimacy. And although we may not expose as much—or the same kinds of things—to each of our closest friends, close friendships involve revealing aspects of our private self—of our private feelings and thoughts, of our private wishes and fears and fantasies and dreams.

J. Viorst, Necessary Losses 197-99 (1986). To which of the above types of "friends" did Charles Cummings' will refer in Clark v. Campbell?

The Restatement 2d of Trusts gives a somewhat different rationale for the indefiniteness of the word "friends":

> § 122 comment a. The class may be such that it is possible to determine that certain persons fall within it and that other persons do not fall within it, but the extent of the class is so indefinite that it is impossible to determine all the persons who fall within it. Thus, the "friends" of the settlor or of another person constitute an indefinite class.

Note also the Canadian case of Re Connor, 10 D.L.R.3d 5 (App. Div., Alberta, Canada 1970). The testatrix's residuary clause provided: "I direct that the residue be divided among my close friends in such a way and at such time as my trustee in her discretion should determine." The trial judge held the trust valid, but on appeal his decision was reversed. McDermid, J.A., construed the residuary clause as requiring that the residue "must be divided amongst all of the close friends," and so the trust failed. He continued:

> Obviously the trustee was not able to designate all of the close friends of the testatrix for the Court ordered that an advertisement be run in the newspaper in six different localities asking any close friend to file an affidavit with the Clerk of the Court setting out the facts on which such person claimed to be a close friend. If a close friend missed reading or hearing about the advertisement owing to absence from the locality or not being a person who habitually read legal notices, such person could be excluded from the gift to which she is entitled. Where advertisements are considered necessary in order to ascertain the members of the class, it indicates the difficulty of ascertaining the class. This is not a case where the members of a class have been ascertained and the advertisements are for the purpose of discovering their whereabouts. Each case, of course, must be decided on its own facts and it is primarily a question of fact to say whether the object of a gift is capable of ascertainment: see Re H. J. Ogden [1933] 1 Ch. 678. Here, as I have said, the mere fact that advertising has to be resorted to in hopes of ascertaining the persons who make up the class demonstrates to my mind the uncertainty.

One judge dissented; he concluded that, since the testator lived in a small town for over forty-two years, "it should be possible without too great difficulty to ascertain who her close friends were."

3. *Meaning of "Relatives."* In Binns v. Vick, 260 Ark. 111, 538 S.W.2d 283 (1976), a testator's residuary clause provided:

> All the rest and residue of my estate . . . I give, devise and bequeath [to] Kenneth Binns [a nephew of the testator and also the testator's executor] to distribute among my relatives as he sees fit.

The trial court held that a trust was intended, but failed for want of definite beneficiaries. The decision was affirmed. The court said that if "relatives" meant legal heirs, the appellant Binns' claim to the property beneficially must be denied because the testator's sole heir was a sister; and that if "relatives" meant all persons related to the testator, the bequest failed for uncertainty.

Compare Restatement 2d of Trusts, which provides:

> § 121. *Relatives as Beneficiaries.* There can be a trust of which the beneficiaries are the relatives of a designated person among whom the trustee is authorized to select who shall take and in what proportions.

See also UPC § 2-711 (1990) (donative disposition of a future interest to an individual's "relatives" or "family" is presumptively a disposition to the individual's heirs); Cal. Prob. Code § 6151 (devise to an individual's "relatives" or "family" is a devise "to those who would be the . . . person's heirs . . . .").

4. *Discretionary vs. Mandatory Powers of Appointment.* This chapter does not deal comprehensively with discretionary powers of appointment, such as the power held by A in Problem 3, supra p. 633. Discretionary powers of appointment are considered in a later chapter, Chapter 14. We are concerned here with a single issue: the distinction between discretionary powers of appointment and mandatory powers of appointment.

Discretionary powers are almost always valid because the test for their validity is so easily satisfied. Discretionary powers are valid unless the group of objects is so indefinite that "it is impossible to identify any person who the donor intended should be objects of the power." Restatement 2d of Property § 12.1 comment h & illustration 18; Restatement of Property § 323 comment h.

Because the tests for validity are so different, the process of identifying which type of power of appointment is created in a given case can be crucial to the outcome. The distinction between mandatory and discretionary powers, however, is not always easily drawn. In Gibbs v. Rumsey, 2 Ves. & B. 294, 35 Eng. Rep. 331 (1813), for example, a will devised the testator's estate to "my said trustees and executors [naming them] to be disposed of unto such person and persons and in such manner and form and in such sum and sums of money as they in their discretion shall think proper and expedient." In upholding the devise, the Master of the Rolls concluded that the will authorized appointment to anyone, including the fiduciaries, and so created "a purely arbitrary power of disposition." In District of Columbia v. Adams, 57 F. Supp. 946 (D.D.C. 1944), however, the court concluded that the following language created a mandatory power rather than a discretionary power in the executor: "I order that my executor shall collect all monies and property of any description due and belonging to me from any bank or insurance company, or from any other source, and dispose of all of the same according to his best judgment." The court held that the trust failed because no general power was intended and "those to whom the property is to be distributed are uncertain."

5. *Reforming the Test for Validity of Mandatory Powers.* Restatement 2d of Trusts section 122 attempts to change the traditional trust rules concerning indefinite beneficiaries and purposes. It provides that even if a trust is unenforceable because of indefinite beneficiaries, if the transferee is given a discretionary or mandatory power to select among members of a class, the power is valid "unless the selection is authorized or directed to be made at a time beyond the period of the rule against perpetuities, or the class is so indefinite that it cannot be ascertained whether any person falls within it."

Though more than three decades old, this provision has yet to exert any significant effect on American law. In the United Kingdom, however, the House of Lords cited this provision in deciding that mandatory and discretionary powers should be subjected to the same test of validity, not different tests. McPhail v. Doulton, [1971] App. Cas. 424 (H.L. 1970); Palmer, Private Trusts for Indefinite Beneficiaries, 71 Mich. L. Rev. 359 (1972).

More recently, in this country, the 1986 Restatement 2d of Property section 12.1 comment e adopted the position of section 122 of the Trusts Restatement. And, a recent California statute moves beyond section 122 by providing that a trust is valid so long as it can be determined that "some person meets the description [of the beneficiary or class of beneficiaries] or is within the class" or if the trust instrument confers on the trustee or some other person a power to select the beneficiaries "based on a standard or in the discretion of the trustee or other person." Cal. Prob. Code § 15205(b). How would this provision have affected the analysis of the hypotheticals with which we opened this section?

Estate of Searight
87 Ohio App. 417, 95 N.E.2d 779 (1950)

HUNSICKER, J. George P. Searight, a resident of Wayne county, Ohio, died testate on November 27, 1948. Item "third" of his will provided:

> I give and bequeath my dog, Trixie, to Florence Hand of Wooster, Ohio, and I direct my executor to deposit in the Peoples Federal Savings and Loan Association, Wooster, Ohio, the sum of $1000.00 to be used by him to pay Florence Hand at the rate of 75 cents per day for the keep and care of my dog as long as it shall live. If my dog shall die before the said $1000.00 and the interest accruing therefrom shall have been used up, I give and bequeath whatever remains of said $1000.00 to be divided equally among those of the following persons who are living at that time, to wit: Bessie Immler, Florence Hand, Reed Searight, Fern Olson and Willis Horn.

At the time of his death, all of the persons, and his dog, Trixie, named in such item third, were living.

Florence Hand accepted the bequest of Trixie, and the executor paid to her from the $1000 fund, 75 cents a day for the keep and care of the dog. The value of Trixie was agreed to be $5. . . .

We do not have, in the instant case, the question of a trust established for the care of dogs in general or of an indefinite number of dogs, but we are here considering the validity of a testamentary bequest for the benefit of a specific dog. This is not a charitable trust, nor is it a gift of money to the Ohio Humane Society or a county humane society, which societies are vested with broad statutory authority, Section 10062, General Code, for the care of animals.

Text writers on the subject of trusts and many law professors designate a bequest for the care of a specific animal as an "honorary trust"; that is, one binding the conscience of the trustee, since there is no beneficiary capable of enforcing the trust.

The rule in Ohio, that the absence of a beneficiary having a legal standing in court and capable of demanding an accounting of the trustee is fatal and the trust fails, was first announced in Mannix, Assignee, v. Purcell, 46 Ohio St. 102, 19 N.E. 572, 2 L.R.A. 753 . . . .

In 1 Scott on the Law of Trusts, Section 124, the author says:

> There are certain classes of cases similar to those discussed in the preceding section in that there is no one who as beneficiary can enforce the purpose of the testator, but different in one respect, namely, that the purpose is definite. Such, for example, are bequests for the erection or maintenance of tombstones or monuments or for the care of graves, and bequests for the support of specific animals. It has been held in a number of cases that such bequests as these do not necessarily fail. It is true that the legatee cannot be compelled to carry out the intended purpose, since there is no one to whom he owes a duty to carry out the purpose.
>
> Even though the legatee cannot be compelled to apply the property to the designated purpose, the courts have very generally held that he can properly do so, and that no resulting trust arises so long as he is ready and willing to carry it out. The legatee will not, however, be permitted to retain the property for his own benefit; and if he refuses or neglects to carry out the purpose, a resulting trust will arise in favor of the testator's residuary legatee or next of kin.

. . . . To call this bequest for the care of the dog, Trixie, a trust in the accepted sense in which that term is defined is, we know, an unjustified conclusion. The modern authorities, as shown by the cases cited earlier in this discussion, however, uphold the validity of a gift for the purpose designated in the instant case, where the person to whom the power is given is willing to carry out the testator's wishes. Whether called an "honorary trust" or whatever terminology is used, we conclude that the bequest for the care of the dog, Trixie, is not in and of itself unlawful. . . .

[As to the common-law Rule Against Perpetuities,] it is to be noted, in every situation where the so-called "honorary trust" is established for specific animals, that, unless the instrument creating such trust limits the duration of the trust—that is, the time during which the power is to be exercised—to human lives, we will have "honorary trusts" established for animals of great longevity, such as crocodiles, elephants and sea turtles. . . .

If we then examine item third of testator's will, we discover that, although the bequest for his dog is for "as long as it shall live," the money given for this purpose is $1000 payable at the rate of 75c a day. By simple mathematical computation, this sum of money, expended at the rate determined by the testator, will be fully exhausted in three years and 238-1/3 days. If we assume that this $1000 is deposited in a bank so that interest at the high rate of 6% per annum were earned thereon, the time needed to consume both principal and interest thereon (based on semi-annual computation of such interest on the average unused balance during such six month period) would be four years, 57 1/2 days.

It is thus very apparent that the testator provided a time limit for the exercise of the power given his executor, and that such time limit is much less than the maximum period allowed under the rule against perpetuities. . . .

We therefore conclude that the bequest in the instant case for the care of the dog, Trixie, does not, by the terms of the creating instrument, violate the rule against perpetuities. . . .

The judgment of the Probate Court is affirmed.

Notes

1. *The Tax Question in Searight.* Believe it or not, *Searight* was a state inheritance tax case. The Ohio Department of Taxation claimed that an inheritance tax was due on the amount devised to Trixie for Trixie's care and on the value of the devise of Trixie to Florence Hand. The Ohio statute imposed an inheritance tax on property passing "to or for the use of a person, institution or corporation." The court held that Trixie herself, a fox-terrier, was not any of these and no inheritance tax was due on the amount devised to Trixie for Trixie's care. An inheritance tax was, however, imposed on the devise of Trixie to Florence Hand. Trixie's value? $5.00.

2. *Honorary Trusts.* Trusts have been upheld that provided for the saying of masses, for the erection of a tombstone, the upkeep of a burial plot, and, as in *Searight*, for the care of a specific animal. Scott on Trusts § 124. One of the few cases going beyond the limited purposes just described is In re Thompson, [1934] Ch. 342, upholding a testamentary trust for the "promotion and furthering of fox-hunting." The court was of the opinion that "the object of the gift has been defined with sufficient clearness and is of a nature to which effect can be given." The devisee was willing to carry out the stated purposes and the court decided that he should be permitted to do so. If he should thereafter misapply the fund, "the residuary legatees are to be at liberty to apply," presumably for an order that the fund be paid over to them on the theory of resulting trust.

Under the common-law Rule Against Perpetuities, a contingent future interest is invalid unless it is certain to vest, if at all, within a life in being plus 21 years from the creation of the interest. See infra Chapter 17. It is now generally recognized that this period applies to honorary trusts and that the trust is invalid if it may last longer than the perpetuities period. Foshee v. Republic Nat'l Bank, 617 S.W.2d 675 (Tex. 1981) (perpetual trust to maintain family burial space in mausoleum). Neither courts nor writers have been in complete agreement on whether such a trust violates the rule against remoteness of vesting itself or only some associated rule. In Smith, Honorary Trusts and the Rule Against Perpetuities, 30 Colum. L. Rev. 60 (1930), the author suggested that the Rule Against Perpetuities was violated, on the theory that the trustee of the honorary trust has a special (nongeneral) power of appointment, and that under perpetuities doctrine such a power is void if it is exercisable beyond a life in being plus 21 years. This position is embraced by other writers on perpetuities. See, e.g., J. Gray, The Rule Against Perpetuities § 909.1 (4th ed. 1942); Scott on Trusts § 124.1.

The Restatement 2d of Trusts states the rule as follows:

> § 124. *Specific Non-charitable Purposes.* Where the owner of property transfers it in trust for a specific non-charitable purpose, and there is no definite or definitely ascertainable beneficiary designated, no enforceable trust is created; but the transferee has power to apply the property to the designated purpose, unless such application is authorized or directed to be made at a time beyond the period of the rule against perpetuities, or the purpose is capricious.

3. *1990 Uniform Probate Code.* Section 2-907 of the 1990 UPC authorizes honorary trusts and trusts for the care of domestic pet animals, authorizes the court to reduce extravagant amounts devised to such trusts, provides a mechanism for their enforcement, and limits their duration to 21 years.

EXTERNAL REFERENCE. R. Powell, Law of Real Property ¶¶ 588-89 (rev. 1990).

PART C. FORMALITIES IN THE CREATION OF A TRUST: THE UNJUST ENRICHMENT DILEMMA

Aside from the substantive requirements just discussed—specific trust property, trust intent, trustee, and at least one definite beneficiary—trust law imposes no formal requirements for creating a trust. Recall, for example, that a declaration of trust of personal property may be entirely oral. However, as the old maxim states, "Equity follows the law." There are two situations in which certain statutory formalities have created problems in proving either trust intent or the substantive terms of the trust. One situation is where the subject matter of the trust is land. If the trust is intended to become effective during the settlor's lifetime, the Statute of Frauds imposes requirements of a signed writing. The other situation involves trusts created at the settlor's death through a will. Testamentary trusts are subject to the requirements of the Statute of Wills.

Both the Statute of Frauds and Statute of Wills impose formalities for evidentiary purposes. In some situations, however, the question arises whether the restitutionary principle of avoiding unjust enrichment should override these evidentiary concerns. In this Part, we examine the problems created by the tension between the unjust enrichment principle and statutory formalities in the creation and enforcement of trusts.

1. Inter-Vivos Trusts of Land: Statute of Frauds Problems

Most states have statutes that require trusts of real property to be evidenced by a signed writing.[29] The statutes vary in their language. Some explicitly provide that trusts of land must be "created or declared" by a writing,[30] while others require that trusts of real property be proved by a writing of the transferor or transferee.[31] Statutes of the latter type are based on section 7 of the English Statute of Frauds of 1677. The conceptual distinction between a writing requirement necessary to effect a transfer and one required only to prove the transfer, however, appears to have had little, if any, influence on the substantive development of the law. It is generally thought that the writing requirement affects the trust's enforcement and not its existence.

Typically, the writing requirement is met by a formal written instrument that is signed by both the settlor and the trustee or, in the case of a self-declared trust, by the settlor alone. In general, in the case of a trust created by transfer, the instrument must be signed either by the settlor before or contemporaneously with the transfer or by the trustee prior to, contemporaneously with, or even subsequent to the transfer (so long as the trustee has not transferred the interest to a third party). See Restatement 2d of Trusts § 42; Stephenson v. Stephenson, 351 Mo. 8, 171 S.W.2d 565 (1943).

It should be mentioned that in a few states, there is no statutory requirement that a trust of land be evidenced by a writing. E.g., Burns v. Equitable Assoc., 220 Va. 1020, 265 S.E.2d 737 (1980). See Bogert on Trusts § 64; Scott on Trusts § 40.1. In these states, the problem becomes

---

29. Oral inter-vivos trusts of personalty are generally valid. Only a few states have statutes that impose a writing requirement for inter-vivos trusts of personalty. E.g., Ind. Code § 30-4-2-1(a); W. Va. Code § 36-1-6 (applicable only to declarations of trust). California requires clear and convincing evidence. Cal. Prob. Code § 15207.

30. E.g., Ga. Code Ann. § 53-12-23; Mass. Gen. Laws ch. 203, § 1; Me. Rev. Stat. Ann. tit. 33, § 851.

31. E.g., Fla. Stat. Ann. § 689.05; Mo. Stat. Ann. 456.010; N.J. Stat. Ann. 25: 1-3; Pa. Stat. Ann. tit. 33, § 2.

one under the parol-evidence rule: May it be shown under a deed absolute in form that the grantee was to hold the land in trust for the grantor or a third person? As Wigmore saw it, the question is "whether the parties, under all the circumstances, appear to have intended the document to cover merely the kind of estate transferred, or to cover all possible aspects of the transfer. . . ." 9 J. Wigmore, Evidence § 2437 (J. Chadbourn rev. 3d ed. 1981). Usually, the former construction is adopted and the extrinsic evidence is received (e.g., Boggs v. Yates, 101 W.Va. 407, 132 S.E. 876 (1926)); however, a few states do not permit proof of the oral trust where the grantor herself or himself was the intended beneficiary. Scott on Trusts § 38; Bogert on Trusts § 64. Restatement 2d of Trusts section 38 provides that where a writing purporting to transfer the property does exist, extrinsic evidence is admissible to show that the transferor intended that the transferee hold the property in trust, either for the transferor or a third person, if the writing does not affirmatively declare "that the transferee is to take the property for his own benefit or that he is to hold it in trust. . . ."

Finally, as indicated earlier, even if the statute states that an oral trust is void, courts have treated such trusts as voidable only. If the trustee does not raise the bar of the Statute of Frauds, the trust is enforceable. In consequence, creditors of an oral trustee cannot defeat the trust if the trustee chooses to recognize it. Courts have held, for example, that where an oral trustee conveys title of land that is the subject matter of the oral trust to the intended beneficiary, the trustee's creditors may not defeat the conveyance as being fraudulent. Hays v. Reger, 102 Ind. 524, 1 N.E. 386 (1885); Berenato v. Gazzara, 346 Pa. 568, 31 A.2d 81 (1943). This result is codified by statute in some states. See, e.g., Tex. Prop. Code § 101.002.[32]

Person v. Pagnotta
273 Or. 420, 541 P.2d 483 (1975)

O'CONNELL, C.J. This is a suit brought by Nellie Person through her conservator to require defendant Michael Pagnotta to reconvey real property previously conveyed to him by Nellie Person on the ground that he holds the property upon a resulting trust. Plaintiff appeals from a decree in favor of defendants.

Plaintiff, an elderly woman, and defendants had a very close relationship over a long period of time. The trial court assessed the evidence as being "strong that the parties treated each other as blood relations." While plaintiff was seriously ill in a convalescent home she executed and delivered to defendant Michael Pagnotta a deed naming him as grantee but reserving to herself a life estate. Michael Pagnotta testified that plaintiff

---

32. Under the federal Bankruptcy Code of 1978, however, if a bankrupt who is the trustee of an oral trust to which the statute of frauds applies under local law attempts to recognize the trust after bankruptcy, the bankruptcy trustee may reach the trust property. 11 U.S.C. § 541(e).

said that she wanted the property to go to the Pagnottas' daughter after plaintiff's death, which she deemed to be imminent. . . .

The trial court held that plaintiff effectively made a gift to defendants' daughter of the remainder interest in the real property. In effect, this recognized that Michael Pagnotta held the remainder interest as trustee for his daughter. Plaintiff contends that this constituted error for the reason that the trust was oral and thus violated the Statute of Frauds. (ORS 93.020).

It will be noted that subsection (2) of [the Oregon Statute of Frauds] makes it clear that the section does not "prevent a trust from arising. . . . by implication or operation of law." A constructive trust is one kind of trust which arises by "operation of law," and is therefore not prevented from arising simply because the evidence necessary to prove it is an oral agreement to hold the property in trust. The question in the present case is, then, whether a constructive trust arose out of Michael Pagnotta's oral agreement to convey to his daughter the real property conveyed to him by plaintiff. The applicable principle is found in Restatement of Restitution § 183, pp. 737-38 (1937):

> Where the owner of an interest in land transfers it inter vivos to another upon an oral trust in favor of a third person or upon an oral agreement to convey the land to a third person, and the trust or agreement is unenforceable because of the Statute of Frauds, and the transferee refuses to perform the trust or agreement, he holds the interest upon a constructive trust for the third person, if, but only if,
>
> [(a) the transferee by fraud, duress or undue influence induced the transferor not to create an enforceable interest in the third person, or]
>
> (b) the transferee at the time of the transfer was in a confidential relation to the transferor, or,
>
> (c) the transfer was made by the transferor in contemplation of death.[33]

The evidence in the case before us clearly establishes that the transferee, Michael Pagnotta, was in a confidential relation to the transferor.[34] As we have already observed, the trial judge found that "the parties treated each other as blood relations." We reach the same conclusion on the basis of the record.

---

33. See also, Restatement (Second) of Trusts § 44 (1959), and Hanscom v. Irwin, 186 Or. 541, 208 P.2d 330 (1949); Harrington v. Harrington, 252 Or. 39, 448 P.2d 364 (1968).

34. Comment c of Section 182, Restatement of Restitution, pp. 734-35 (1937), defines confidential relation as follows:

> A confidential relation exists not only where there is a fiduciary relation such as that between attorney and client, trustee and beneficiary, guardian and ward, partner and partner, and the like, but also where, because of family relationship or otherwise, the transferor is in fact accustomed to be guided by the judgment or advice of the transferee or is justified in placing confidence in the belief that the transferee will act in the interest of the transferor. It might seem, indeed, that wherever the transferee orally agrees to hold the property transferred to him in trust for the transferor or agrees to retransfer it, there is in this very fact a sufficient relation of confidence thereby created to justify imposing a constructive trust upon him if he breaks his promise; but some courts require additional evidence of confidence in the relation between them before imposing a constructive trust (see the Caveat).

There is also evidence that the transfer was made by the transferor in contemplation of death, thus falling within subsection (c) of Section 183.[35] There was testimony that plaintiff made the conveyance in the manner that she did because she "didn't want any probate" and that she "wanted the property to go to . . . (the) daughter after . . . (plaintiff's) death." There was also evidence that plaintiff had previously executed a will in which she devised the property to the daughter.

Since a constructive trust arose in favor of the daughter, this case does not fall within the principle found in Restatement (Second) of Trusts, § 411, p. 333 (1959), relied upon by plaintiff, which states that

> Where the owner of property gratuitously transfers it and properly manifests an intention that the transferee should hold the property in trust but the trust fails, the transferee holds the trust estate upon a resulting trust for the transferor or his estate, unless the transferor properly manifested an intention that no resulting trust should arise or the intended trust fails for illegality.

As we have demonstrated, this is not a case where the "trust fails"; a valid trust in favor of the daughter arose by operation of law. . . .

We hold that the evidence does not support a resulting trust and therefore the decree of the trial court is affirmed.

Notes and Questions

1. *Constructive Trust.* That wrongdoing on the part of the grantee (promisor) provides a ground for the imposition of a constructive trust is well recognized in the cases. The wrongdoing includes that of committing fraud, duress, or undue influence, or of abusing a confidential relationship or the fact that the transferor made the transfer in contemplation of death.

If the grantee orally promised to hold the land in trust for the settlor, the constructive trust is imposed in favor of the settlor. Restatement of Restitution § 182 (1937); Restatement 2d of Trusts § 44. If the grantee orally promised to hold the land in trust for a third person, as in Person v. Pagnotta, the third person can regularly obtain constructive trust relief in her or his own favor. Restatement of Restitution § 183 (1937); Restatement 2d of Trusts § 45(1); Kester v. Crilly, 405 Ill. 425, 91 N.E.2d 419 (1950). Some text-writers have been inclined to disapprove of the latter result, arguing that restitution should be given to the settlor rather than to

---

35. Comment f of § 183, Restatement of Restitution, p. 742 (1937), explains:

Where the owner of an interest in land transfers it to another, and the transferee orally agrees with the transferor at the time of the transfer that he will hold the land in trust for or convey it to a third person, and the transfer was made by the transferor in contemplation of death and intended by him as a substitute for a testamentary disposition of his property, the transferee holds the property upon a constructive trust for the third person (see Restatement of Trusts, § 45, Comment d). This situation is treated as analogous to the situation where a testator devises or bequeaths property to a person in reliance upon his agreement to hold the property in trust for or to convey it to another (see § 186).

the intended beneficiary (Bogert on Trusts § 496; Scott on Trusts § 45.2), but their views seem to have had no influence on the courts. See Palmer on Restitution § 19.3(f)-(g).

Person v. Pagnotta raises an interesting variation of the typical case. The suit was not brought by the intended beneficiary, Michael Pagnotta's daughter. Neither she nor her natural guardian had reason to do so. Why not? The court purported to apply section 183 of the Restatement of Restitution, but neglected to note the absence of a necessary element. What element was absent? Could the court have reached the same result on a different basis? See Palmer on Restitution § 19.3(g) at 127-28 and n.5 (Supp.).

2. *Confidential Relationship.* Although abuse of a confidential relationship is ground for the imposition of a constructive trust, the term "confidential relationship" has not proved easy to define. Some attempts at definition seem to be wholly circular, such as the Illinois court's statement that "the relation exists in all cases where there has been a special confidence reposed in one who is bound to act in good faith and with due regard to the interests of the one reposing the confidence." Dick v. Albers, 243 Ill. 231, 236, 90 N.E. 683, 685 (1910). From one point of view, the concept is so broad as to subsume *all* of the oral trust cases; as said in the Restatement 2d of Trusts:

> § 44 comment c. *Where transferee is in confidential relation to transferor.* It would seem, indeed, that wherever the transferee orally agrees to hold the property transferred to him in trust for the transferor there is a sufficient relation of confidence thereby created to justify imposing a constructive trust upon him if he breaks his promise. . . .

The Restatement's notion could lead to an abandonment of the requirement of a confidential relationship, and this is what occurred in California. In Orella v. Johnson, 38 Cal.2d 693, 242 P.2d 5 (1952), the California Supreme Court accepted the English rule (see below) and based constructive trust relief on the oral promise alone.

Most courts, however, have not been prepared to go that far, so that the search continues for some means of giving content to the idea of a confidential relationship. Since most cases involve conveyances from one family member to another, a recurring problem is whether the family connection alone is enough. Although results are largely unpredictable, it does appear that the number of cases may be increasing in which relief is given where nothing more appears than a close family relationship. Note the further step taken in Person v. Pagnotta, where the court found a confidential relationship between Nellie Person and Michael Pagnotta because they "treated each other as blood relations."

Yet the attitude expressed by the Massachusetts court must be taken into account on the other side. In refusing to find a confidential relationship in a conveyance by father to son on oral trust for the grantor, the court cited numerous Massachusetts cases in which relief had been denied where the conveyances were between members of a family, and concluded: "To adopt the plaintiff's contention would require us to overrule these cases, a course that we are not disposed to follow." Ranicar v. Goodwin, 326 Mass. 710, 96 N.E.2d 853 (1951).

3. *Fraud.* Fraud is another basis for imposition of a constructive trust. Fraud requires establishing that the grantee never intended to keep the oral promise. The grantee's refusal to perform the promise is not usually sufficient, but it may be where the refusal occurred shortly after the promise was made. Lipp v. Lipp, 158 Md. 207, 148 A. 531 (1930).

4. *Value Restitution for Simple Breach?* In the absence of a wrong on the grantee/promisor's part, the case is generally viewed as one of simple breach of an oral and unenforceable promise; no relief is granted if the grantee/promisor raises the Statute of Frauds as a defense. Examples are Funk v. Engel, 235 Mich. 195, 209 N.W. 160 (1926); Horsley v. Hrenchir, 146 Kan. 767, 73 P.2d 1010 (1937).

Most decisions reaching this result make no attempt to relate it to the general law of restitution for breach of an unenforceable agreement. Yet, under the general law of restitution, one who confers a benefit in the performance of an unenforceable agreement will be given restitution of the value of the benefit if the other party repudiates or refuses to perform the agreement. Thus, in a quasi-contract action, a person who has paid money under an oral agreement to purchase land will be permitted to recover the amount paid if the vendor repudiates or refuses to perform. E.g., Ford v. Stroud, 150 N.C. 362, 64 S.E. 1 (1909).

In view of the large number of oral-trust cases that have refused constructive trust relief (specific restitution), it is therefore surprising that there are so few in which the grantor has sought to recover the value of the land (value restitution). This may reflect the widespread professional ignorance of the law of restitution. In Massachusetts, restitution of the value of the land has been allowed, while at the same time the constructive trust remedy has been denied. Kemp v. Kemp, 248 Mass. 354, 142 N.E. 779 (1924); Cromwell v. Norton, 193 Mass. 291, 79 N.E. 433 (1906).

5. *The English View.* Where the grantee was to hold the land on an oral trust for the grantor, English cases from an early date gave constructive trust relief to the grantor based on simple breach of the promise. Hutchins v. Lee, 1 Atk. 447, 26 Eng. Rep. 284 (1737); Bannister v. Bannister, [1948] 2 All E.R. 133.

Where the grantee was to hold on an oral trust for the benefit of a third person, there is no doubt under the English rule that the land will be impressed with a trust, the only issue being whether it will be for the grantor or for the intended beneficiary. A statement in Rochefoucauld v. Boustead, [1897] 1 Ch. 196, 206, that relief will be given to the intended beneficiary, is accepted as a statement of English law in 16 Halsbury's Laws of England 1309 (4th ed. 1976).

Leading American writers on trusts, led by Ames, argued for adoption of the English view, but the great weight of American authority refuses such relief where the only basis for it is simple breach of the oral and unenforceable promise. Ames, Constructive Trusts Based Upon the Breach of An Express Oral Trust of Land, 20 Harv. L. Rev. 549 (1907), reprinted in J. Ames, Lectures on Legal History 425 (1913). Section 16 of the Uniform

Trusts Act provides for specific restitution to the grantor,[36] but the Act is in force in only five states and two of these have omitted this section. Apart from statute, and in addition to the California case of Orella v. Johnson, supra, there are occasional decisions adopting the English view. Eastmond v. Eastmond, 2 N.J. Super. 529, 64 A.2d 901 (1949).

EXTERNAL REFERENCE. Palmer on Restitution § 19.3.

6. *Necessity of a Promise?* In Person v. Pagnotta, Michael Pagnotta expressly promised Nellie Person that he would convey the property to his daughter upon Nellie's death. Is an express promise on the part of the grantee necessary to the imposition of a constructive trust? The next case, Sharp v. Kosmalski, shows that a promise is sometimes implied in fact. The case following *Sharp*, Watts v. Watts, raises questions about imposing a constructive trust on the basis of a promise implied in law.

Sharp v. Kosmalski
40 N.Y.2d 113, 386 N.Y.S.2d 72, 351 N.E.2d 721 (1976)

GARBRIELLI, J. Plaintiff [J. Rodney Sharp] commenced this action to impose a constructive trust upon property transferred to defendant [Jean C. Kosmalski], on the ground that the retention of the property and the subsequent ejection of the plaintiff therefrom was in violation of a relationship of trust and confidence and constituted unjust enrichment. The Trial Judge dismissed plaintiff's complaint and his decision was affirmed without opinion by the Appellate Division.

Upon the death of his wife of 32 years, plaintiff, a 56-year old dairy farmer whose education did not go beyond the eighth grade, developed a very close relationship with defendant, a school teacher and a woman 16 years his junior. Defendant assisted plaintiff in disposing of his wife's belongings, performed certain domestic tasks for him such as ironing his shirts and was a frequent companion of the plaintiff. Plaintiff came to depend upon defendant's companionship and, eventually, declared his love for her, proposing marriage to her. Notwithstanding her refusal of his proposal of marriage, defendant continued her association with plaintiff and permitted him to shower her with many gifts, fanning his hope that he could induce defendant to alter her decision concerning his marriage

---

36. Uniform Trusts Act § 16:

1. When an interest in real property is conveyed by deed to a person on a trust which is unenforceable on account of the Statute of Frauds and the intended trustee or his successor in interest still holds title but refuses to carry out the trust on account of the Statute of Frauds, the intended trustee or his successor in interest, except to the extent that the successor in interest is a bona fide purchaser of a legal interest in the real property in question, shall be under a duty to convey the interest in real property to the settlor or his successor in interest. A court having jurisdiction may prescribe the conditions upon which the interest shall be conveyed to the settlor or his successor in interest.

2. Where the intended trustee has transferred part or all of his interest and it has come into the hands of a bona fide purchaser, the intended trustee shall be liable to the settlor or his successor in interest for the value of the interest thus transferred at the time of its transfer, less such offsets as the court may deem equitable.

proposal. Defendant was given access to plaintiff's bank account, from which it is not denied that she withdrew substantial amounts of money. Eventually, plaintiff made a will naming defendant as his sole beneficiary and executed a deed naming her a joint owner of his farm. The record reveals that numerous alterations in the way of modernization were made to plaintiff's farmhouse in alleged furtherance of "domestic plans" made by plaintiff and defendant.

In September, 1971, while the renovations were still in progress, plaintiff transferred his remaining joint interest to defendant. At the time of the conveyance, a farm liability policy was issued to plaintiff naming defendant and her daughter as additional insureds. Furthermore, the insurance agent was requested by plaintiff, in the presence of defendant, to change the policy to read "J. Rodney Sharp, life tenant. Jean C. Kosmalski, owner." In February, 1973, the liaison between the parties was abruptly severed as defendant ordered plaintiff to move out of his home and vacate the farm. Defendant took possession of the home, the farm and all the equipment thereon, leaving plaintiff with assets of $300.

Generally, a constructive trust may be imposed "[w]hen property has been acquired in such circumstances that the holder of the legal title may not in good conscience retain the beneficial interest." (Beatty v. Guggenheim Exploration Co., 225 N.Y. 380, 386, 122 N.E. 378, 380; 1 Scott, Trusts [3d ed], § 44.2 . . .). In the development of the doctrine of constructive trust as a remedy available to courts of equity, the following four requirements were posited: (1) a confidential or fiduciary relation, (2) a promise, (3) a transfer in reliance thereon and (4) unjust enrichment.

Most frequently, it is the existence of a confidential relationship which triggers the equitable considerations leading to the imposition of a constructive trust. Although no marital or other family relationship is present in this case, such is not essential for the existence of a confidential relation. The record in this case clearly indicates that a relationship of trust and confidence did exist between the parties and, hence, the defendant must be charged with an obligation not to abuse the trust and confidence placed in her by the plaintiff. The disparity in education between the plaintiff and defendant highlights the degree of dependence of the plaintiff upon the trust and honor of the defendant.

Unquestionably, there is a transfer of property here, but the Trial Judge found that the transfer was made "without a promise or understanding of any kind." Even without an express promise, however, courts of equity have imposed a constructive trust upon property transferred in reliance upon a confidential relationship. In such a situation, a promise may be implied or inferred from the very transaction itself. As Judge Cardozo so eloquently observed: "Though a promise in words was lacking, the whole transaction, it might be found, was 'instinct with an obligation' imperfectly expressed." (Sinclair v. Purdy, 235 N.Y. 245, 254, 139 N.E. 255, 258). In deciding that a formal writing or express promise was not essential to the application of the doctrine of constructive trust, Judge Cardozo further observed in language that is most fitting in the instant case:

Here was a man transferring to his sister the only property he had in the world. . . . He was doing this, as she admits, in reliance upon her honor. Even if we were to accept her statement that there was no distinct promise to hold for his benefit, the exaction of such a promise, in view of the relation, might well have seemed to be superfluous (Sinclair v. Purdy, supra, p 254).

. . . . Indeed, in the case before us, it is inconceivable that plaintiff would convey all of his interest in property which was not only his abode but the very means of his livelihood without at least tacit consent upon the part of the defendant that she would permit him to continue to live on and operate the farm. . . .

The salutary purpose of the constructive trust remedy is to prevent unjust enrichment. . . . A person may be deemed to be unjustly enriched if he (or she) has received a benefit, the retention of which would be unjust (Restatement, Restitution, § 1, Comment a). A conclusion that one has been unjustly enriched is essentially a legal inference drawn from the circumstances surrounding the transfer of property and the relationship of the parties. It is a conclusion reached through the application of principles of equity. Having determined that the relationship between plaintiff and defendant in this case is of such a nature as to invoke consideration of the equitable remedy of constructive trust, it remains to be determined whether defendant's conduct following the transfer of plaintiff's farm was in violation of that relationship and, consequently, resulted in the unjust enrichment of the defendant. This must be determined from the circumstances of the transfer since there is no express promise concerning plaintiff's continued use of the land. Therefore, the case should be remitted to the Appellate Division for a review of the facts. In so doing I would emphasize that the conveyance herein should be interpreted "not literally or irrespective of its setting, but sensibly and broadly with all its human implications" (Sinclair v Purdy, 235 N.Y. 245, 254, 139 N.E. 255, 258, supra). This case seems to present the classic example of a situation where equity should intervene to scrutinize a transaction pregnant with opportunity for abuse and unfairness. It was for just this type of case that there evolved equitable principles and remedies to prevent injustices. Equity still lives. . . .

Accordingly, the order of the Appellate Division should be reversed and the case remitted to that court for a review of the facts, or, if it be so advised, in its discretion, to order a new trial in the interest of justice.[37]

---

37. The decision in this case is cited with apparent approval in Kopelman v. Kopelman, 710 F. Supp. 99 (S.D.N.Y. 1989) (applying New York law); Bankers Security Life Ins. Soc'y v. Shakerdge, 49 N.Y.2d 939, 428 N.Y.S.2d 623, 406 N.E.2d 440 (1980).

Watts v. Watts
137 Wis. 2d 506, 405 N.W.2d 303 (1987)

ABRAHAMSON, J.[38] This is an appeal from a judgment of the circuit court for Dane County, William D. Byrne, Judge, dismissing Sue Ann Watts' amended complaint, pursuant to sec. 802.-06(2)(f), Stats. 1985-86, for failure to state a claim upon which relief may be granted. . . .

We test the sufficiency of the plaintiff's amended complaint by first setting forth the facts asserted in the complaint and then analyzing each of the five legal theories upon which the plaintiff rests her claim for relief.

I. The plaintiff commenced this action in 1982. The plaintiff's amended complaint alleges the following facts, which for purpose of this appeal must be accepted as true. The plaintiff and the defendant [James E. Watts] met in 1967, when she was 19 years old, was living with her parents and was working full time as a nurse's aide in preparation of a nursing career. Shortly after the parties met, the defendant persuaded the plaintiff to move into an apartment paid for by him and to quit her job. According to the amended complaint, the defendant "indicated" to the plaintiff that he would provide for her.

Early in 1969, the parties began living together in a "marriage-like" relationship, holding themselves out to the public as husband and wife. The plaintiff assumed the defendant's surname as her own. Subsequently, she gave birth to two children who were also given the defendant's surname. The parties filed joint income tax returns and maintained joint bank accounts asserting that they were husband and wife. The defendant insured the plaintiff as his wife on his medical insurance policy. He also took out a life insurance policy on her as his wife, naming himself as the beneficiary. The parties purchased real and personal property as husband and wife. The plaintiff executed documents and obligated herself on promissory notes to lending institutions as the defendant's wife.

During their relationship, the plaintiff contributed childcare and homemaking services, including cleaning, cooking, laundering, shopping, running errands, and maintaining the grounds surrounding the parties' home. Additionally, the plaintiff contributed personal property to the relationship which she owned at the beginning of the relationship or acquired through gifts or purchases during the relationship. She served as hostess for the defendant for social and business-related events. The amended complaint further asserts that periodically, between 1969 and 1975, the plaintiff cooked and cleaned for the defendant and his employees while his business, a landscaping service, was building and landscaping a golf course.

From 1973 to 1976, the plaintiff worked 20-25 hours per week at the defendant's office, performing duties as a receptionist, typist, and assistant

---

38. Shirley S. Abrahamson was appointed Justice of the Wisconsin Supreme Court in 1976. Prior to then, she was a member of the law faculty at the University of Wisconsin, where she taught Federal Taxation and (best of all) Trusts & Estates. She is the first woman appointed to the Wisconsin Supreme Court.

bookkeeper. From 1976 to 1981, the plaintiff worked 40-60 hours per week at a business she started with the defendant's sister-in-law, then continued and managed the business herself after the dissolution of that partnership. The plaintiff further alleges that in 1981 defendant made their relationship so intolerable that she was forced to move from their home and their relationship was irretrievably broken. Subsequently, the defendant barred the plaintiff from returning to her business.

The plaintiff alleges that during the parties' relationship, and because of her domestic and business contributions, the business and personal wealth of the couple increased. Furthermore, the plaintiff alleges that she never received any compensation for these contributions to the relationship and that the defendant indicated to the plaintiff both orally and through his conduct that he considered her to be his wife and that she would share equally in the increased wealth.

The plaintiff asserts that since the breakdown of the relationship the defendant has refused to share equally with her the wealth accumulated through their joint efforts or to compensate her in any way for her contributions to the relationship.

[The court held that the Wisconsin Family Code, which provides for an equitable distribution of a married couple's property upon divorce, does not apply to unmarried cohabitants and that the defendant was not estopped by his words and conduct from asserting the lack of a legal marriage as a defense against the plaintiff's claim for an equitable division of property pursuant to the Family Code, and continued:]

IV. The plaintiff's third legal theory on which her claim rests is that she and the defendant had a contract to share equally the property accumulated during their relationship. The essence of the complaint is that the parties had a contract, either an express or implied in fact contract, which the defendant breached.

Wisconsin courts have long recognized the importance of freedom of contract and have endeavored to protect the right to contract. A contract will not be enforced, however, if it violates public policy. . . .

Courts have generally refused to enforce contracts for which the sole consideration is sexual relations, sometimes referred to as "meretricious" relationships. See In Matter of Estate of Steffes, 95 Wis.2d 490, 514, 290 N.W.2d 697 (1980), citing Restatement of Contracts Section 589 (1932). Courts distinguish, however, between contacts that are explicitly and inseparably founded on sexual services and those that are not. . . . In this case, the plaintiff has alleged many facts independent from the parties' physical relationship which, if proven, would establish an express contract or an implied in fact contract that the parties agreed to share the property accumulated during the relationship.

The plaintiff has alleged that she quit her job and abandoned her career training upon the defendant's promise to take care of her. A change in one party's circumstances in performance of the agreement may imply an agreement between the parties.

In addition, the plaintiff alleges that she performed housekeeping, childbearing, childrearing, and other services related to the maintenance of the parties' home, in addition to various services for the defendant's business and her own business, for which she received no compensation. Courts have recognized that money, property, or services (including housekeeping or childrearing) may constitute adequate consideration independent of the parties' sexual relationship to support an agreement to share or transfer property.

According to the plaintiff's complaint, the parties cohabited for more than twelve years, held joint bank accounts, made joint purchases, filed joint income tax returns, and were listed as husband and wife on other legal documents. Courts have held that such a relationship and "joint acts of a financial nature can give rise to an inference that the parties intended to share equally." Beal v. Beal, 282 Or. 115, 122, 577 P.2d 507, 510 (1978). The joint ownership of property and the filing of joint income tax returns strongly implies that the parties intended their relationship to be in the nature of a joint enterprise, financially as well as personally.

Having reviewed the complaint and surveyed the law in this and other jurisdictions, we . . . conclude that public policy does not necessarily preclude an unmarried cohabitant from asserting a contract claim against the other party to the cohabitation so long as the claim exists independently of the sexual relationship and is supported by separate consideration. Accordingly, we conclude that the plaintiff in this case has pleaded the facts necessary to state a claim for damages resulting from the defendant's breach of an express or an implied in fact contract to share with the plaintiff the property accumulated through the efforts of both parties during their relationship. Once again, we do not judge the merits of the plaintiff's claim; we merely hold that she be given her day in court to prove her claim.

V. The plaintiff's fourth theory of recovery involves unjust enrichment. Essentially, she alleges that the defendant accepted and retained the benefit of services she provided knowing that she expected to share equally in the wealth accumulated during their relationship. She argues that it is unfair for the defendant to retain all the assets they accumulated under these circumstances and that a constructive trust should be imposed on the property as a result of the defendant's unjust enrichment. In his brief, the defendant does not attack specifically either the legal theory or the factual allegations made by the plaintiff.

Unlike claims for breach of an express or implied in fact contract, a claim of unjust enrichment does not arise out of an agreement entered into by the parties. Rather, an action for recovery based upon unjust enrichment is grounded on the moral principle that one who has received a benefit has a duty to make restitution where retaining such a benefit would be unjust.

Because no express or implied in fact agreement exists between the parties, recovery based upon unjust enrichment is sometimes referred to as "quasi contract," or contract "implied in law" rather than "implied in fact." Quasi contracts are obligations created by law to prevent injustice.

In Wisconsin, an action for unjust enrichment, or quasi contract, is based upon proof of three elements: (1) a benefit conferred on the defendant by the plaintiff, (2) appreciation or knowledge by the defendant of the benefit, and (3) acceptance or retention of the benefit by the defendant under circumstances making it inequitable for the defendant to retain the benefit. . . .

As part of his general argument, the defendant claims that the court should leave the parties to an illicit relationship such as the one in this case essentially as they are found, providing no relief at all to either party. . . .

[But], allowing no relief at all to one party in a so-called "illicit" relationship effectively provides total relief to the other, by leaving that party owner of all the assets acquired through the efforts of both. Yet it cannot seriously be argued that the party retaining all the assets is less "guilty" than the other. Such a result is contrary to the principles of equity. Many courts have held, and we now so hold, that unmarried cohabitants may raise claims based upon unjust enrichment following the termination of their relationships where one of the parties attempts to retain an unreasonable amount of the property acquired through the efforts of both.[39]

In this case, the plaintiff alleges that she contributed both property and services to the parties' relationship. She claims that because of these contributions the parties' assets increased, but that she was never compensated for her contributions. She further alleges that the defendant, knowing that the plaintiff expected to share in the property accumulated, "accepted the services rendered to him by the plaintiff" and that it would be unfair under the circumstances to allow him to retain everything while she receives nothing. We conclude that the facts alleged are sufficient to state a claim for recovery based upon unjust enrichment.

As part of the plaintiff's unjust enrichment claim, she has asked that a constructive trust be imposed on the assets that the defendant acquired during their relationship. A constructive trust is an equitable device created by law to prevent unjust enrichment. To state a claim on the theory of constructive trust the complaint must state facts sufficient to show (1) unjust enrichment and (2) abuse of a confidential relationship or some other form of unconscionable conduct. The latter element can be inferred from allegations in the complaint which show, for example, a family relationship, a close personal relationship, or the parties' mutual trust. These facts are alleged in this complaint or may be inferred. Therefore, we hold that if the plaintiff can prove the elements of unjust enrichment to the satisfaction of the circuit court, she will be entitled to demonstrate further that a constructive trust should be imposed as a remedy. . . .

The judgment of the circuit court is reversed and the cause remanded.

---

39. See, e.g., Harman v. Rogers, 147 Vt. 11, 510 A.2d 161, 164-65 (1986); Collins v. Davis, 68 N.C. App. 588, 315 S.E.2d 759, 761-62 (1984), aff'd, 312 N.C. 324, S.E.2d 892; Mason v. Rostand, 476 A.2d 662 (D.C. 1984); Coney v. Coney, 207 N.J. Super. 63 503 A.2d 912, 918 (1985); In re Estate of Eriksen, 337 N.W.2d 671 (Minn. 1983).

Note

Compare the *Watts* decision with the analysis of the New York Court of Appeals in Morone v. Morone, 50 N.Y.2d 481, 413 N.E.2d 1154 (1980). Although the plaintiff in *Morone* did not seek the imposition of a constructive trust on the ground of unjust enrichment, she did seek a judgment for damages on the bases of two causes of action: breach of an express contract and breach of a contract implied in law.

The Court of Appeals held that the first count stated a cause of action, but that the second did not. The court gave this analysis of the problem of recognizing a contract implied in law:

> Presented by this appeal are the questions whether a contract as to earnings and assets may be implied in law from the relationship of an unmarried couple living together and whether an express contract of such a couple on those subjects is enforceable. Finding an implied contract such as was recognized in Marvin v. Marvin, 18 Cal.3d 660, 134 Cal. Rptr. 815, 557 P.2d 106 to be conceptually so amorphous as practically to defy equitable enforcement, and inconsistent with the legislative policy enunciated in 1933 when common-law marriages were abolished in New York, we decline to follow the *Marvin* lead. Consistent with our decision in Matter of Gorden, 8 N.Y.2d 71, 202 N.Y.S.2d 1, 168 N.E.2d 239, however, we conclude that the express contract of such a couple is enforceable . . . .
>
> Historically, we have required the explicit and structured understanding of an express contract and have declined to recognize a contract which is implied from the rendition and acceptance of services. The major difficulty with implying a contract from the rendition of services for one another by persons living together is that it is not reasonable to infer an agreement to pay for the services rendered when the relationship of the parties makes it natural that the services were rendered gratuitously. As a matter of human experience personal services will frequently be rendered by two people living together because they value each other's company or because they find it a convenient or rewarding thing to do. For courts to attempt through hindsight to sort out the intentions of the parties and affix jural significance to conduct carried out within an essentially private and generally noncontractual relationship runs too great a risk of error. Absent an express agreement, there is no frame of reference against which to compare the testimony presented and the character of the evidence that can be presented becomes more evanescent. There is, therefore, substantially greater risk of emotion-laden afterthought, not to mention fraud, in attempting to ascertain by implication what services, if any, were rendered gratuitously and what compensation, if any, the parties intended to be paid.
>
> Similar considerations were involved in the Legislature's abolition by chapter 606 of the Laws of 1933 of common-law marriages in our State. Writing in support of that bill, Surrogate Foley informed Governor Lehman that it was the unanimous opinion of the members of the Commission to Investigate Defects in the Law of Estates that the concept of common-law marriage should be abolished because attempts to collect funds from decedents' estates were a fruitful source of litigation. Senate Minority Leader Fearon, who had introduced the bill, also informed the Governor that its purpose was to prevent fraudulent claims against estates and recommended its approval. The consensus was that while the doctrine of common-law marriage could work substantial justice in certain cases, there was no built-

in method for distinguishing between valid and specious claims and, thus, that the doctrine served the State poorly.

The notion of an implied contract between an unmarried couple living together is, thus, contrary to both New York decisional law and the implication arising from our Legislature's abolition of common-law marriage. The same conclusion has been reached by a significant number of States other than our own which have refused to allow recovery in implied contract (see Ann., 94 A.L.R.3d 552, 559). Until the Legislature determines otherwise, therefore, we decline to recognize an action based upon an implied contract for personal services between unmarried persons living together.

Is this analysis consistent with the earlier decision of the New York Court of Appeals in Sharp v. Kosmalski, supra p. 651? (The *Morone* opinion itself does not mention *Sharp*.) The contract-implied-in-law/unjust-enrichment analysis of the *Watts* case is examined in Note, Recognizing Contract and Property Rights of Unmarried Cohabitants in Wisconsin: *Watts v. Watts*, 1988 Wis. L. Rev. 1093, 1113-15, 1117-18.

2. Statute Of Wills

Suppose a testator's will devises property to a devisee outright. After the testator's death, a plaintiff alleges that the devisee had promised the testator that the devisee would hold the property for the benefit of the plaintiff. Or, suppose a testator's will expressly indicates that a devisee is to hold the devised property in trust, but neglects to state the substantive terms of the trust, including the intended beneficiary. The two situations involve so-called "secret" and "partially secret" trusts, respectively. Both situations involve issues concerning compliance with the Statute of Wills, analogous to the Statute of Frauds problem in cases of oral inter-vivos trusts of land.

"Secret" Testamentary Trusts. If the plaintiff, who claims to be the intended beneficiary, proves that the devisee promised to hold the property in trust for the plaintiff, whether the promise was made before or after the will was executed, most jurisdictions impose a constructive trust on the devisee in favor of the plaintiff. In the leading case of Trustees of Amherst College v. Ritch, 151 N.Y. 282, 45 N.E. 876 (1897), the court gave this explanation for the result:

If the testator is induced either to make a will or not to change one after it is made, by a promise, express or implied, on the part of a legatee that he will devote his legacy to a certain lawful purpose, a secret trust is created, and equity will compel him to apply property thus obtained in accordance with his promise. . . . The trust springs from the intention of the testator and the promise of the legatee. The same rule applies to heirs and next of kin who induce their ancestor or relative not to make a will by promising, in case his property falls to them through intestacy, to dispose of it, or a part of it, in the manner indicated by him. . . . The rule is founded on the principle that the legacy would not have been given, or intestacy allowed to ensue, unless the promise had been made; and hence the person promising is bound, in equity, to keep it, as to violate it would be fraud. While a promise is essential, it need not be expressly made, for active co-operation or silent acquiescence may have the same effect as an express promise. If a legatee knows what the testator expects of him, and having an opportunity to speak, says nothing, it may be equivalent to a promise, provided the testator acts upon it. Whenever it appears that the testator was prevented from action by the action or silence of a legatee, who knew the facts in time to act or speak, he will not be permitted to apply the legacy to his own use when that would defeat the expectations of the testator. . . .

The trust does not act directly upon the will by modifying the gift, for the law requires wills to be wholly in writing, but it acts upon the gift itself as it reaches the possession of the legatee, or as soon as he is entitled to receive it. The theory is that the will has full effect, by passing an absolute legacy to the legatee, and that then equity, in order to defeat fraud, raises a trust in favor of those intended to be benefited by the testator, and compels the legatee, as a trustee ex maleficio, to turn over the gift to them. The law, not the will, fastens the trust upon the fund, by requiring the legatee to act in accordance with the instructions of the testator and his own promise. Neither the statute of frauds nor the statute of wills applies, because the will takes effect as written and proved; but, to promote justice and prevent wrong, the courts compel the legatee to dispose of his gift in accordance with equity and good conscience.

Although there is little dissent in the cases from the proposition of the *Ritch* case,[40] the result has been criticized. Professor Scott argued that the decisions giving relief in favor of the intended beneficiary are in conflict with the Statute of Wills.[41] In other words, the unjust enrichment should be remedied by imposing the constructive trust in favor of those who would be entitled to the property had the devise not been made. See, however, the following for discussions approving the results of the cases: Palmer on Restitution § 20.6(e); Langbein & Waggoner, Reformation of Wills on the Ground of Mistake: Change of Direction in American Law?, 130 U. Pa. L. Rev. 521, 574-76 (1982). Compare with the results in these cases the treatment of the partially secret trust involved in Olliffe v. Wells, which follows.

Olliffe v. Wells
130 Mass. 221 (1881)

[Ellen Donovan died in 1877. Her will devised the residue of her estate "to the Rev. Eleazer M.P. Wells . . . to distribute the same in such manner as in his discretion shall appear best calculated to carry out wishes which I have expressed to him or may express to him." Her will also nominated the Reverend Wells to be the executor. Donovan's heirs sued, claiming that the residue should be distributed to them. The Reverend Wells claimed the right to carry out Donovan's wishes, which she had expressed to him and

---

40. Cases are collected in Annots., 66 A.L.R. 156 (1930); 155 A.L.R. 106 (1955).
41. Scott on Trusts § 55.1.

to which he had assented before she executed her will. According to Rev. Wells, her intention was that the residue be used to provide for persons who were under the care of the St. Stephen's Mission of Boston.[42] The heirs treated Rev. Wells' allegation as true.]

GRAY, C.J. Upon the face of this will the residuary bequest to the defendant gives him no beneficial interest. It expressly requires him to distribute all the property bequeathed to him, giving him no discretion upon the question whether he shall or shall not distribute it, or shall or shall not carry out the intentions of the testatrix, but allowing him a discretionary authority as to the manner only in which the property shall be distributed according to her intentions. The will declares a trust too indefinite to be carried out, and the next of kin of the testatrix must take by way of a resulting trust, unless the facts agreed show such a trust for the benefit of others as the court can execute. Nichols v. Allen, [130 Mass.] 211. No other written instrument was signed by the testatrix, and made part of the will by reference. . . .

It has been held in England and in other States, although the question has never arisen in this Commonwealth, that, if a person procures an absolute devise or bequest to himself by orally promising the testator that he will convey the property to or hold it for the benefit of third persons, and afterwards refuses to perform his promise, a trust arises out of the confidence reposed in him by the testator and of his own fraud, which a court of equity, upon clear and satisfactory proof of the facts, will enforce against him at the suit of such third persons. . . .

Upon like grounds, it has been held in England that, if a testator devises or bequeaths property to his executors upon trusts not defined in the will, but which, as he states in the will, he has communicated to them before its execution, such trusts, if for lawful purposes, may be proved by the admission of the executors, or by oral evidence, and enforced against them. . . . And in two or three comparatively recent cases it has been held that such trusts may be enforced against the heirs or next of kin of the testator, as well as against the devisee. . . . But these cases appear to us to have overlooked or disregarded a fundamental distinction.

Where a trust not declared in the will is established by a court of chancery against the devisee, it is by reason of the obligation resting upon the conscience of the devisee, and not as a valid testamentary disposition by the deceased. . . . Where the bequest is outright upon its face, the setting up of a trust, while it diminishes the right of the devisee, does not impair any right of the heirs or next of kin, in any aspect of the case; for if the trust were not set up, the whole property would go to the devisee by force of the devise; if the trust set up is a lawful one, it enures to the

---

42. The St. Stephen's Mission was destroyed in the great Boston fire of 1872. Rev. Wells worked to restore the mission, but to no avail. Rev. Wells died in 1878 at age 95. In reading the court's opinion, consider whether these facts might have influenced the result. (We owe information about the St. Stephen's Mission to J. Dukeminier & S. Johanson, Wills, Trusts, and Estates 485-86 n.32 (4th ed. 1990)). Eds.

benefit of the *cestuis que trust*; and if the trust set up is unlawful, the heirs or next of kin take by way of resulting trust. . . .

[In the present case, w]here the bequest is declared upon its face to be upon such trusts as the testator has otherwise signified to the devisee, it is equally clear that the devisee takes no beneficial interest; and, as between him and the beneficiaries intended, there is as much ground for establishing the trust as if the bequest to him were absolute on its face. But as between the devisee and the heirs or next of kin, the case stands differently. They are not excluded by the will itself. The will upon its face showing that the devisee takes the legal title only and not the beneficial interest, and the trust not being sufficiently defined by the will to take effect, the equitable interest goes, by way of resulting trust, to the heirs or next of kin, as property of the deceased, not disposed of by his will. Sears v. Hardy, 120 Mass. 524, 541, 542. They cannot be deprived of that equitable interest, which accrues to them directly from the deceased, by any conduct of the devisee; nor by any intention of the deceased, unless signified in those forms which the law makes essential to every testamentary disposition. A trust not sufficiently declared on the face of the will cannot therefore be set up by extrinsic evidence to defeat the rights of the heirs at law or next of kin. . . .

Decree for the plaintiffs.

Notes and Questions

1. *Contrary Authority.* As the court's opinion in *Olliffe* indicated, the English courts do not differentiate between partially secret and secret testamentary trusts; they uphold both types. The principal decision is Blackwell v. Blackwell, [1929] App. Cas. 318 (H.L.). In that case, Blackwell's will devised £12,000 to five named persons "upon trust . . . for the purposes indicated by me to them." Blackwell communicated to some of the trustees his intention that the fund be used to care for a "woman who was not his wife" and their sixteen-year-old son,[43] and these trustees accepted the trust. The court held that no distinction should be drawn between a case in which the devise was on its face absolute and a case in which the will disclosed that the devisee was to hold the devise in trust. In each case, Lord Warrington said:

The solution is to be found by bearing in mind that what is enforced is not a trust imposed by the will, but one arising from the acceptance by the

---

43. Historically, secret and partially secret trusts were sometimes created by wealthy men who wished to provide for their mistresses and/or non-marital children. See S. Gardner, An Introduction to the Law of Trusts 85-87 (1990). Disclosing the terms of the trust in the will was undesirable because a probated will is a public document. Nowadays, of course, there are other, more effective ways to keep confidential the terms of one's dispositions (including a pour-over will, as we saw in Chapter 7, or a multiple-party bank account), but these techniques were not available until modern times.

legatee of a trust, communicated to him by the testator, on the faith of which the will was made or left unrevoked.

This result is the same as that reached by English courts in cases of secret inter-vivos trusts of land. In both the testamentary and inter-vivos contexts, that is, the result has been to effectuate the trust.

The Restatement of Trusts adopted the English view in 1935 and adhered to it in the 1959 revision. See Restatement 2d of Trusts § 55 comment h. A number of American decisions have followed the Restatement, rejecting *Olliffe*. See Curdy v. Berton, 79 Cal. 420, 21 P. 858 (1889); Linney v. Cleveland Trust Co., 30 Ohio App. 345, 165 N.E. 101 (1928); Hartman's Estate (No. 2), 320 Pa. 331, 182 A. 232 (1936). In Estate of Brandenburg, 13 Wis.2d 217, 108 N.W.2d 374 (1961), the Wisconsin court held that constructive relief is available to the intended beneficiaries, but the court ignored this decision in a case decided the same year in which it held that the heirs took on resulting trust. Estate of Liginger, 14 Wis.2d 577, 111 N.W.2d 407, 3 A.L.R.3d 1372 (1961).

2. *Statute of Frauds Compared.* Very few cases have arisen concerning partially secret trusts contained in deeds of land. One such case is Muhm v. Davis, 580 S.W.2d 98 (Tex. Civ. App. 1979). Perry McNeill conveyed by deed his undivided one-half interest in 300 acres of land to "Cleveland Davis, Trustee." The conveyance was made pursuant to a prior oral agreement under which Davis, McNeill's attorney, agreed to hold the land in trust until McNeill's youngest grandchild reached the age of eighteen, at which time Davis was to convey the land in equal shares to McNeill's two children and three grandchildren. Subsequently, McNeill's youngest grandchild reached eighteen, and Davis carried out his promise.

After McNeill's death, his principal devisee, one of his children, brought an action to set aside the conveyance from McNeill to Davis and the conveyance from Davis to McNeill's children and grandchildren. The trial court granted a motion for summary judgment in favor of the defendants. Affirming, the Texas Court of Civil Appeals said:

> The rule is thoroughly settled "that a trust in land declared by parol only, although wholly unenforceable against the trustee, has yet enough of vitality, so that, if voluntarily executed by the trustee at any time, it will become validated as of the date of the original oral agreement. . . ." Blaha v. Borgman, 142 Wis. 43, 46, 124 N.W. 1047, 1048 (1910).
>
> The seventh section of the English Statute of Frauds which was enacted in many American states commonly provides that trusts of land shall be "void and of no effect", unless manifested or proved by a writing. In these states the word "void" has been held to mean "unenforceable against the objection of the trustee." In Bogert, Trusts and Trustees 2d ed., § 69, the author says that the trustee in an oral trust is not forbidden to carry out his trust. He has a moral obligation to carry out his trust duties, and the performance of the oral trust is a legal and commendable act.
>
> This approach to the problem has been adopted in the Restatement of the Law of Trusts, where the Rule is stated in these words:

> Where an oral trust of an interest in land is created inter vivos, the trustee can properly perform the trust if he has not transferred the interest, although he cannot be compelled to do so.

Restatement (Second) of Trusts, § 43 at 112.

The summary judgment evidence presents no issues of material fact and establishes as a matter of law an executed parol express trust. The trial court did not err in granting summary judgment.

See also Restatement 2d of Trusts § 44 comment e, § 45 comment e.

3. *Questions.* Are the Statute of Frauds and Statute of Wills problems in cases of partially secret trusts strictly comparable? That is, should courts treat partially secret testamentary trusts the same way as they do partially secret inter-vivos trusts of land? Is the distinction that the *Olliffe* court drew between partially secret and secret testamentary trusts sound, or is it evidence that, as one writer has stated, this is "an area of law rife with anomalous distinctions and irreconcilable precedents"? Blumenstein, Secret Trusts, 36 U. Toronto Fac. of L. Rev. 108 (1978).

EXTERNAL REFERENCE. Palmer on Restitution § 20.7.

Chapter 12

SPENDTHRIFT, DISCRETIONARY, AND SUPPORT TRUSTS: A QUESTION OF CONTROL

Now that you have been introduced to the basic requirements necessary to form a trust, we turn your attention to a fundamental question of policy. Once a trust has been properly formed, should the law ensure that it will endure? Or should the law enable the beneficiaries to undo the trust against the wishes of the settlor? The question is one of distributing power between successive property owners, past and present. Where the preferences of present beneficiaries conflict with those expressed by the donor, the law cannot simultaneously respect the autonomy of both, and must choose between them.

The conflict between the donor's wishes and the preferences of current trust beneficiaries arises primarily in the context of three types of trusts: spendthrift, discretionary, and support. Most trusts created today fall into one or more of these categories. The principal features of each are briefly summarized as follows:

Spendthrift Trusts. In the case of a spendthrift trust, a disabling restraint has been imposed on the alienation of the beneficiaries' equitable interests. A disabling restraint on alienation is one that purports to nullify any attempted assignment by a beneficiary of her or his equitable interest and any attempted attachment of a beneficiary's interest by the beneficiary's creditors.

Discretionary Trusts. In the case of a discretionary trust, the trustee is granted discretion to pay to or apply for the benefit of the beneficiary only so much of the income and principal or either as the trustee sees fit.

Support Trusts. In the case of a support trust, the trustee is directed to pay to or apply for the benefit of the beneficiary so much of the income and principal or either as is necessary for the education and support of the beneficiary.

See Restatement 2d of Trusts §§ 154, 155.

To illustrate these types of trusts and the general problem that they pose, consider Example 12.1.

Example 12.1: G has just died at age 75, survived by her 55-year-old daughter, A, and A's 21-year-old son, X. During the last few years of her life, G had been thinking about how to divide her $1 million estate between A and X. G decided to make a will giving most of the benefit of the million-dollar estate, say 80 percent of it, to A. In exploring how to formulate her will with A and X, a choice discussed was simply to devise $800,000 outright to A and $200,000 outright to X. A and X respectfully expressed preference for that form, although A was not so sure that X should be devised such an amount in a lump sum.

Although G did not mention her feelings to A or X, G secretly had reservations about devising lump-sum amounts to either one. G's concern was not about A's lack of maturity or ability to handle money, but she was worried that A's husband, H, who she often referred to as that "no-account bum," might somehow get his hands on the money and squander it on some risky business venture. So, after consulting her lawyer (one of your former classmates), G decided to follow a different path. To the surprise and chagrin of A, H, and X, G's will devised the full $1 million into a trust, the terms of which are that A is to receive the income for life, with the corpus at A's death going to X.

Suppose that, using the actuarial tables currently in use for tax purposes (see IRC § 7520), the present value of A's right to the income from $1 million for life is $800,000 and the present value of X's right to $1 million at A's death is $200,000.

With all due respect for G and her wishes, A and X still prefer the cash. Accompanied by H, they consult you as their lawyer and ask a straightforward question: Can they somehow exchange their trust interests for cash? Well, you tell them, there are two potential sources—the trust and outsiders. A and X could try to find a buyer or buyers for their interests (or find a lender or lenders who would loan them the cash, accepting the beneficial interests as security). Or, A and X could try to terminate the trust and have the $1 million corpus distributed to them on an 80/20 basis.

Putting aside the impracticability of the first option,[1] your examination of G's will reveals that the trust is a spendthrift trust, *i.e.*, it contains a disabling restraint on alienation. Under prevailing American law, disabling restraints on alienation of equitable interests in trust are valid. Moreover, a spendthrift trust is indestructible, *i.e.*, the beneficiaries cannot compel the trustee prematurely to terminate such a trust. See Restatement 2d of Trusts §§ 152, 153, 330 & comment l.

These rules of American trust law represent a shift away from the English law of trusts. Under English law, disabling restraints on the alienation of equitable interests in trust are invalid. This was established by the Chancellor, Lord Eldon, in Brandon v. Robinson, 18 Ves. 429, 34 Eng. Rep. 379 (Ch. 1811). And, English law allows the beneficiaries of any type of trust, irrespective of the settlor's wishes, to undo the trust by demanding the trust property outright and free of trust. This rule was adopted in Saunders v. Vautier, 4 Beav. 115, 49 Eng. Rep. 282 (Ch. 1841), aff'd, Cr. & Ph. 240, 41 Eng. Rep. 482 (Ch. 1841), and solidified in Wharton v. Masterman, [1895] App. Cas. 186 (H.L.). English law, then, empowers trust beneficiaries to control their interests and thereby limits the donor's control. American trust doctrine reverses this allocation of control.

The American shift away from the English rules occurred in the latter part of the nineteenth century. A pair of 1880s decisions of the Supreme Judicial Court of Massachusetts are mainly credited with having engineered these departures from prior law: Broadway National Bank v. Adams (1882), infra p. 669, and Claflin v. Claflin (1889), infra p. 711 .

EXTERNAL REFERENCES. Alexander, The Dead Hand and the Law of Trusts in the Nineteenth Century, 37 Stan. L. Rev. 1189 (1985); Friedman, The Dynastic Trust, 73 Yale L.J. 547 (1964).

---

1. A and X would have difficulty finding buyers for their interests, let alone buyers who would pay full actuarial value. Compare Estate of Vought, infra p. 678. A different situation exists in England, where it has been reported that an organized auction is held once a month at the London Auction Mart for the sale of future interests in property, either vested or contingent. See "Speculation," Newsweek, Jan. 25, 1971, at 66; "Some Britishers Sell Birthrights for More Than Mess of Pottage," Wall St. J., May 10, 1971. In America, no such auction market exists.

PART A.   RESTRAINING ALIENABILITY OF BENEFICIAL INTERESTS/SHIELDING BENEFICIAL INTERESTS FROM CREDITORS

1. Spendthrift Trusts

We begin the study of spendthrift trusts with Broadway National Bank v. Adams. Although *Broadway Bank* was not the first American decision to depart from the English rule by upholding spendthrift trusts, it—along with Justice Miller's dictum in Nichols v. Eaton, 91 U.S. 716 (1875), expressing approval of such trusts—is usually credited with having turned the tide of American law.

To put *Broadway Bank* into perspective, the subject of restraints on alienation of *legal* interests must be briefly examined. (When you read the *Broadway Bank* opinion, note that this is what the court is referring to when it mentions "the rule of the common law.") For our purposes, two types of restraints on alienation are relevant—disabling restraints and forfeiture restraints. The terms are defined and their validity is addressed in the Restatement 2d of Property as follows:

> § 3.1 *Disabling Restraint.* Terms of a donative transfer of an interest in property which seek to invalidate a later transfer of that interest, in whole or in part, constitute a disabling restraint on alienation (hereinafter referred to as a disabling restraint).
>
> § 4.1 *Validity of Disabling Restraint.* (1) A disabling restraint imposed in a donative transfer on an interest in property is invalid if the restraint, if effective, would make it impossible for any period of time from the date of the donative transfer to transfer such interest. . . .

> § 3.2 *Forfeiture Restraint.* Terms of a donative transfer of an interest in property which seek to terminate, or to subject to termination, that interest, in whole or in part, in the event of a later transfer constitute a forfeiture restraint on alienation (hereinafter referred to as a forfeiture restraint). A forfeiture restraint may apply to any attempted later transfer or only to some types of such transfers and may be limited or unlimited in duration. But the person that is to take in the event of a forfeiture must have a valid interest under the rule against perpetuities.
>
> § 4.2 *Validity of Forfeiture Restraint.* (1) A forfeiture restraint imposed in a donative transfer on a life interest in property, or on an interest for a term of years that will terminate at the end of a life (or reasonable number of lives) in being at the time of the transfer, is valid. . . .

In *Broadway Bank*, the beneficiary, Charles Adams, was given an *equitable* life estate, with the statement that it was not to be subject (a) to voluntary alienation by him or (b) to the claims of his creditors. The second provision is often described as a restraint on involuntary alienation, since if a creditor *is* permitted to reach an asset of the debtor the consequence will sometimes be a forced sale of the debtor's interest.

Though it need not do so, the typical spendthrift trust restrains both voluntary and involuntary alienation.[2]

Had Charles Adams been given a *legal* life estate, the restraint would have been void. As the above provisions of the Restatement demonstrate, the general position of the common law is that such "disabling" restraints on legal interests in property are void.

One of Lord Eldon's goals as Chancellor was to move the English rules of equity into greater alignment with those of the common law. This may account for his holding in Brandon v. Robinson voiding disabling restraints on equitable life estates. It may also explain his statement that the equitable interest of the beneficiary could validly have been subjected to a forfeiture restraint, which he expressed in terms of approval of a grant of an equitable interest to a beneficiary "until he shall become bankrupt."

Broadway National Bank v. Adams
133 Mass. 170 (1882)

MORTON, C.J. The object of this bill in equity is to reach and apply in payment of the plaintiff's debt due from the defendant Adams the income of a trust fund created for his benefit by the will of his brother. The eleventh article of the will is as follows:

> I give the sum of seventy-five thousand dollars to my said executors and the survivors or survivor of them, in trust to invest the same in such manner as to them may seem prudent, and to pay the net income thereof, semiannually, to my said brother Charles W. Adams, during his natural life, such payments to be made to him personally when convenient, otherwise, upon his order or receipt in writing; in either case free from the interference or control of his creditors, my intention being that the use of said income shall not be anticipated by assignment. . . .

There is no room for doubt as to the intention of the testator. It is clear if the trustee was to pay the income to the plaintiff under an order of the court, it would be in direct violation of the intention of the testator and of the provisions of his will. The court will not compel the trustee thus to do what the will forbids him to do, unless the provisions and intention of the testator are unlawful. . . .

It is true that the rule of the common law is, that a man cannot attach to a grant or transfer of property, otherwise absolute, the condition that it shall not be alienated; such condition being repugnant to the nature of the estate granted. Co.Lit. 223 a. Blackstone Bank v. Davis, 21 Pick. 42.

---

2. See, for example, the sample clause set forth infra p. 677. In Bank of New England v. Strandlund, 402 Mass. 707, 529 N.E.2d 394 (1988), the court held the following clause restrained involuntary but not voluntary alienation: "[N]o income or principal . . . payable to any beneficiary shall be attachable, trusteeable or in any manner liable for or to be taken for any debts, contracts or obligations of such beneficiary."

Lord Coke gives as the reason of the rule, that "it is absurd and repugnant to reason that he, that hath no possibility to have the land revert to him, should restrain his feoffee in fee simple of all his power to alien," and that this is "against the height and puritie of a fee simple." By such a condition, the grantor undertakes to deprive the property in the hands of the grantee of one of its legal incidents and attributes, namely its alienability, which is deemed to be against public policy. But the reasons for the rule do not apply in the case of a transfer of property in trust. By the creation of a trust like the one before us, the trust property passes to the trustee with all its incidents and attributes unimpaired. He takes the whole legal title to the property, with the power of alienation; the *cestui que trust* takes the whole legal title to the accrued income at the moment it is paid over to him. Neither the principal nor the income is at any time inalienable.

The question whether the rule of the common law should be applied to equitable life estates created by will or deed, has been the subject of conflicting adjudications by different courts. . . . [F]rom the time of Lord Eldon the rule has prevailed in the English Court of Chancery, to the extent of holding that when the income of a trust estate is given to any person (other than a married woman) for life, the equitable estate for life is alienable by, and liable in equity to the debts of, the *cestui que trust*, and that this quality is so inseparable from the estate that no provision, however express, which does not operate as a cesser or limitation of the estate itself, can protect it from his debts. Brandon v. Robinson, 18 Ves. 429. The English rule has been adopted in several of the courts of this country. Other courts have rejected it. . . .

The founder of this trust was the absolute owner of his property. He had the entire right to dispose of it, either by any absolute gift to his brother, or by a gift with such restrictions or limitations, not repugnant to law, as he saw fit to impose. His clear intention, as shown in his will, was not to give his brother an absolute right to the income which might hereafter accrue upon the trust fund, with the power of alienating it in advance, but only the right to receive semiannually the income of the fund, which upon its payment to him, and not before, was to become his absolute property. His intentions ought to be carried out, unless they are against public policy. There is nothing in the nature or tenure of the estate given to the *cestui que trust* which should prevent this. The power of alienating in advance is not a necessary attribute or incident of such an estate or interest, so that the restraint of such alienation would introduce repugnant or inconsistent elements.

We are not able to see that it would violate any principles of sound public policy to permit a testator to give to the object of his bounty such a qualified interest in the income of a trust fund, and thus provide against the improvidence or misfortune of the beneficiary. The only ground upon which it can be held to be against public policy is, that it defrauds the creditors of the beneficiary.

It is argued that investing a man with apparent value tends to mislead creditors, and to induce them to give him credit. The answer is, that creditors have no right to rely upon property thus held, and to give him credit upon the basis of an estate which, by the instrument creating it, is declared to be inalienable by him, and not liable for his debts. By the exercise of proper diligence they can ascertain the nature and extent of his estate, especially in this Commonwealth, where all wills and most deeds are spread upon the public record. There is the same danger of their being misled by false appearances, and induced to give credit to the equitable life tenant when the will or deed of trust provides for a cesser or limitation over, in case of an attempted alienation, or of bankruptcy or attachment, and the argument would lead to the conclusion that the English rule is equally in violation of public policy. . . .

The rule of public policy which subjects a debtor's property to the payment of his debts, does not subject the property of a donor to the debts of his beneficiary, and does not give the creditor a right to complain that, in the exercise of his absolute right of disposition, the donor has not seen fit to give the property to the creditor, but has left it out of his reach. . . .

It follows that, under the provisions of the will which we are considering, the income of the trust fund created for the benefit of the defendant Adams cannot be reached by attachment, either at law or in equity, before it is paid to him.

Bill dismissed.

———

The Dead Hand Dilemma: Whose Freedom of Disposition Do or Should We Protect? Spendthrift trusts raise what Professor Alexander has called the "dead hand dilemma,"[3] which is that the general idea of freedom of disposition can be invoked on either side—for or against the validity of spendthrift trusts. Several writers have opposed the validity of spendthrift trusts, focusing on the infringement of the donee's freedom of disposition. The most outspoken critic of the time was John Chipman Gray, who was prompted by Nichols v. Eaton to write a short book titled Restraints on the Alienation of Property (1883), arguing:

> The fallacy [of validating spendthrift trusts is in the notion] that the only objection to such inalienable life estates is that they defraud the creditors of the life tenant; and the courts labor, with more or less success, to show that these creditors are not defrauded. . . . But, with submission, this is not the ground why equitable life estates cannot be made inalienable and free from debts. The true ground is the same on which the whole law of property, legal and equitable, is based;—that inalienable rights of property are opposed to the fundamental principles of the common law; that it is against public policy that a man "should have an estate to live on, but not an estate to pay his debts with"; Tillinghast v. Bradford, 5 R.I. 205, 212; that a man should have the benefits of wealth without the responsibilities. The common law has recognized certain classes of persons who may be kept in pupilage, viz.

---

3. Alexander, The Dead Hand and the Law of Trusts in the Nineteenth Century, 37 Stan. L. Rev. 1189, 1193 (1985).

infants, lunatics, married women; but it has held that sane grown men must look out for themselves,—that it is not the function of the law to join in the futile effort to save the foolish and the vicious from the consequences of their own vice and folly. It is wholesome doctrine, fit to produce a manly race, based on sound morality and wise philosophy. . . .

That grown men should be kept all their lives in pupilage, that men not paying their debts should live in luxury on inherited wealth, are doctrines as undemocratic as can well be conceived. . . . The general introduction of spendthrift trusts would be to form a privileged class, who could indulge in every speculation, could practice every fraud, and, provided they kept on the safe side of the criminal law, could yet roll in wealth. They would be an aristocracy, though certainly the most contemptible aristocracy with which a country was ever cursed.

Id. at 169-70, 173-74. Gray's opposition to spendthrift trusts was to little avail. In the preface to the second edition of his book, published in 1895, Gray lamented:

State after State has given in its adhesion to the new doctrine. Were it not for an occasional dissenting opinion I should be *vox clamantis in deserto*.

And yet I cannot recant. Doubtless I may exaggerate the importance of the matter; but, so far as it goes, I still believe, as I said in the first edition, that the old doctrine was a wholesome one, fit to produce a manly race, based on sound morality and wise philosophy; and that the new doctrine is contrary thereto.[4]

To the judges (and legislators) of the time (and since), the donor's freedom of disposition has apparently seemed more worthy of protection. This is vividly expressed in the *Broadway Bank* case, where the court said:

The founder of this trust was the absolute owner of his property. . . . His clear intention . . . was not to give his brother an absolute right to the income . . . with power of alienating it in advance, but only the right to receive semiannually the income. . . . His intentions ought to be carried out, unless they are against public policy. . . . We are not able to see that it would violate any principles of sound public policy to permit a testator to give to the object of his bounty such a qualified interest in the income . . . and thus provide against the improvidence or misfortune of the beneficiary.

See also Steib v. Whitehead, 111 Ill. 247, 250-52 (1884).

Does the spendthrift trust doctrine express freedom of disposition? Gray railed against the doctrine as being "socialistic." In what sense are spendthrift trusts socialistic?[5]

---

4. J. Gray, Restraints on the Alienation of Property iv-v (2d ed. 1895).

5. In his autobiography, My United States (1931), Frederic Stimson argued that the spendthrift trust doctrine was responsible for Boston's commercial decline. "No new enterprise could be undertaken [by spendthrift trust beneficiaries, who typically were children of wealthy men], for under the court decision they had no capital to risk," Stimson argued. "Perforce they became coupon-cutters—parasites, not promoters . . . ." Id. at 77. As Professor Lawrence Friedman has pointed out, however, Stimson's dating of the spendthrift trust doctrine—1830—confused that doctrine with another that the Massachusetts court developed,

The term spendthrift trusts is a somewhat of a misnomer, since judicial recognition has not limited such trusts to spendthrifts or to persons who may be in need of special protection. Apart from statute, any person can be the beneficiary of a spendthrift trust in a state recognizing them, without regard to the beneficiary's ability to look after herself or himself and her or his business affairs. Nor has the case law placed any limitation on the amount of income that can be validly protected from the claims of the beneficiary's creditors. In an Illinois case, Congress Hotel Co. v. Martin, 312 Ill. 318, 143 N.E. 838 (1924), the beneficiary was entitled to income of over $171,000 for the year 1921. In that year, she ran up a hotel bill of some $6,700 and the hotel sought to reach income in the hands of the trustee by garnishment. The court denied relief because the will creating the trust included spendthrift provisions.

The Minority View. Only a small number of jurisdictions refuses recognition of spendthrift trusts. One such jurisdiction is New Hampshire. In Brahmey v. Rollins, 87 N.H. 290, 296, 301, 179 A. 186, 191-94 (1935), the New Hampshire court held that, despite a spendthrift clause, a creditor could reach an income interest of his debtor under a trust, saying:

> The view that the right to seize property is in any way an essential attribute of it which the owner may destroy is considered erroneous. It is an exposure to loss of ownership, and not any part of the makeup of title. It is an instrument of attack upon title, and does not enter into it as a constituent. It is a right, not of the owner, but of the creditor. It is not a quality of property, but is wholly external thereto. It is a burden of incidence, and not of inherence. It is a consequence, and not an element of ownership. It is a public regulation of property beyond private control. . . .
>
> If the restraint against alienation is valid, it is because the right to alienate is an inherent element of ownership which the donor may withhold in a gift of the property. . . . If he may bar seizure, why may he not as well bar taxability? . . .
>
> The policy to attach so great weight to the enjoyment of ownership as to permit the owner to prescribe, in a gift of the property owned, special terms which conflict with the general laws of ownership, has no forceful appeal. By the gift the owner parts with all benefit from the property which he may personally enjoy. Why should he have the right to free the property from a burden resting on it while he owns it, during the term the donee in equity may have it, and thereby give or create rights which he himself does not possess? Besides the conflict with general law, there is also the conflict with the general policy that only those needing protective relief should have it.

---

the so-called "prudent man rule" of trust investment law. The latter rule originated in Harvard College v. Amory, 26 Mass. (9 Pick.) 446 (1830). Friedman suggests that the prudent man rule and the spendthrift trust doctrine both contributed to the development of long-term "dynastic" family trusts. Friedman, The Dynastic Trust, 73 Yale L.J. 547 (1964). We will study the prudent investor rule in Chapter 18.

Other cases and statutes adopting the minority view, mainly from Kentucky, Ohio, and Rhode Island,[6] are collected in Scott on Trusts § 152.1 n.3.

Spendthrift-Trust Legislation. Spendthrift trusts are recognized by statute in many states, but the statutes take a variety of forms. No attempt at exhaustive classification is made here; for a state-by-state compilation, see Scott on Trusts § 152.1.

As is true of the common-law decisions, most statutes place no limit on the amount that can be protected by or on who can be the beneficiary of a spendthrift trust, by reference either to need, competency, or relationship to the settlor. In Nevada[7] and Texas,[8] for example, the statute authorizes the creation of spendthrift trusts in terms about as broad as could be devised. Both income and principal may be placed beyond the reach of creditors without regard to the amount of wealth involved. The Nevada statute states explicitly that the validity of such a trust "does not depend on the character, capacity, incapacity, competency or incompetency of the beneficiary." In Alabama,[9] however, the statute limits spendthrift protection to beneficiaries who are the settlor's "child, grandchild, or other relation by blood or marriage."

The New York statute deserves mention because it has been copied in a number of states, in whole or in part. By legislation that had its beginnings in 1828, well before the *Broadway Bank* case was decided, virtually all trusts are automatically made spendthrift trusts by statute, without the need of any provision to that effect in the trust instrument. The central provision in the present New York statute reads:

> N.Y. Est. Powers & Trusts Law § 7-1.5. When trust interest inalienable; exception. (a) . . . (1) The right of a beneficiary of an express trust to receive the income from property and apply it to the use of or pay it to any person may not be transferred by assignment or otherwise unless a power to transfer such right, or any part thereof, is conferred upon such beneficiary by the instrument creating or declaring the trust. . . .

Unlike the judge-approved spendthrift trust, however, the New York statute allows voluntary transfer of any amount of income in excess of $10,000 per year, provided the transfer is made to specified relatives, is gratuitous, and is not expressly prohibited by the trust instrument. N.Y. Est. Powers & Trusts Law § 7-1.5(b). The New York statute also places a limit

---

6. In 1988, Rhode Island enacted a statute declaring:

> *R.I. Gen. Laws § 18-9.1-1. Establishment of spendthrift trust.*—Any person creating an express trust for the benefit of any other person or persons may by the terms thereof establish valid restraints on the voluntary and/or involuntary transfer of interests therein by the beneficiaries thereof, whether by way of anticipation or acceleration, assignment, hypothecation or by virtue of legal process in judgement, execution, attachment, garnishment, bankruptcy or otherwise.

7. Nev. Rev. Stat. §§ 166.010-166.160. But see Ambrose v. First Nat'l Bank, 87 Nev. 114, 482 P.2d 828 (1971), which construed the statute as limiting spendthrift trusts to trusts for support (see infra p. 689).

8. Tex. Prop. Code § 112.035.

9. Ala. Code § 19-3-1.

on the amount of income that can be shielded from the claims of creditors: Creditors can reach income "in excess of the sum necessary for the education and support of the beneficiary." N.Y. Est. Powers & Trusts Law § 7-3.4. This limitation in New York has been substantially vitiated, however, by construing needs to relate to the beneficiary's "station in life."[10] In Kilroy v. Wood, 42 Hun. 636 (N.Y. 1886), for example, creditors were unsuccessful in trying to reach surplus income of a spendthrift trust because they failed to show that the income was more than sufficient for the beneficiary's support. The court said:

> [The beneficiary is] a gentleman of high social standing, whose associations are chiefly with men of leisure, and is connected with a number of clubs, with the usages and customs of which he seems to be in harmony both in practice and expenditure, and it is insisted on his behalf that his income is not more than sufficient to maintain his position according to his education, habits and associations.

Id. at 638. See also E. Griswold, Spendthrift Trusts § 379 (2d ed. 1947); Powell, The Rule Against Perpetuities and Spendthrift Trusts in New York: Comments and Suggestions, 71 Colum. L. Rev. 688, 699 (1971) [hereinafter Powell, Spendthrift Trusts].

The California statute is a variation of the New York scheme. Unlike the New York statute, the restraint on alienation is imposed only if the settlor so provides. Cal. Prob. Code § 15300. But once this has occurred, judgment creditors (as under the New York scheme) can reach any amount "in excess of the amount that is or will be necessary for education and support of the beneficiary"; unlike New York, however, there is apparently an additional cap preventing judgment creditors from reaching more than 25 percent of the amounts otherwise payable. Cal. Prob. Code §§ 15306.5, 15307.

In interpreting the education-and-support limit, the California courts also apply a station-in-life test. But the extremes of the New York cases have arguably been avoided, as the following passage from Canfield v. Security-First Nat'l Bank, 13 Cal. 2d 1, 21-24, 87 P.2d 830, 840-41 (1939), suggests:

> No set sum can be fixed to apply to all cases. The amount varies according to the station in life of the beneficiary. This does not mean, however, that the needs of the beneficiary are to be measured by his extravagance or his ability to spend. It does not mean that an allowance is to be made for extravagant entertaining, and for unbridled luxuries. The manner of living of the beneficiary in the past, if such living was unreasonably extravagant and profuse, is no criterion of the reasonable amount necessary for support and maintenance. Evidence as to cost of living, wages of servants, medical expense and reasonable entertainment, and other reasonably necessary expenses, fixes the amount. . . .

---

10. More recently, provisions of the N.Y. Civil Practice Law and Rules have removed some of the protection previously afforded by this station-in-life test. See Alexander, Spendthrift Trusts and Their Functional Substitutes, in Debtor-Creditor Law ¶ 22A.03[A] (T. Eisenberg ed. 1986).

The cost of living, cost of housing, medical cost, the manner in which the beneficiary has been reared, the number and health of his dependents, his own health, his entire background—all these and perhaps others should be considered. But cost of lavish entertaining, cost of betting on race horses and cost of obvious luxuries, etc.—these are all false factors.

The station-in-life test, even as administered by the California courts, shields from creditors' claims income sufficient to support a fairly luxurious style of living, if this is the style of living to which the beneficiary is accustomed. Dean Griswold and Professor Powell bridled at the station-in-life test and argued for a different approach. In Powell, Spendthrift Trusts, supra, at 704-05, the author argued:

> It would not be wise to prohibit *all* spendthrift trusts. There are occasions when a possessor of substantial wealth has, close to his heart, a relative who lacks the business experience to protect himself from the ever-present vultures. A modest sum, so set up as to protect such a person from dissipating his substance and unreachable by creditors generally, constitutes no threat to social welfare. The trouble arises when the amount entrusted becomes large and the immunities of the beneficiary cease to be reasonable.

Earlier, Dean Griswold had drafted a model spendthrift-trust statute, which provided that all income "in excess of $5000 per annum shall be subject to attachment by a creditor of the beneficiary [of a spendthrift trust] and shall be freely alienable by the beneficiary." E. Griswold, supra, at 648. Griswold wrote this in 1947; in today's dollars, the $5000 figure would translate roughly to $30-35,000 per year.

Griswold's model statute was enacted in Louisiana and Oklahoma. In Louisiana, the $5,000 figure was raised to $10,000 in 1985; in 1987, the limit was repealed altogether.[11] In Oklahoma, the figure remains at $5000 per year.[12] A similar dollar-limitation idea has been adopted in Virginia and a few other states. In Virginia, the idea is expressed in terms of $500,000 of trust principal that can be made the subject of a spendthrift trust.[13]

In 1979, North Carolina repealed its original statute on spendthrift trusts and replaced it with a statute that provides that the interest of a beneficiary shall be alienable, voluntarily or involuntarily, except where the trust is a discretionary trust, a support trust, or a protective trust.[14] A protective trust is defined as one wherein it is provided that the interest of the beneficiary shall cease if the beneficiary alienates or attempts to alienate the interest, if any creditor attempts to reach the interest, or if the beneficiary becomes insolvent or bankrupt. This is a retreat from the full-

---

11. La. Rev. Stat. § 9:2004.
12. Okla. Stat. Ann. tit. 60 § 175.25.
13. Va. Code § 55-19. The statute provides that an estate, "not exceeding $500,000 in actual value, may be holden or possessed in trust upon condition that the corpus thereof and income therefrom, or either of them, shall be applied by the trustee to the support and maintenance of the beneficiaries without being subject to their liabilities or to alienation by them. . . ."
14. N.C. Gen. Stat. § 36A-115.

scale American spendthrift trust and, although the terminology is not entirely the same, amounts substantially to an acceptance of the English law.

Life-Insurance Proceeds. More than half the states have statutes that either automatically shield from the beneficiary's creditors life-insurance proceeds payable under an installment method, or permit the insured to do so by provision in the policy. E. Griswold, Spendthrift Trusts ch. 3 (2d ed. 1947); A. Smith, Personal Life Insurance Trusts app. VI (1950).

Federal Bankruptcy. To the extent that a spendthrift restraint is valid under or automatically imposed by state law or federal law, it is also effective in bankruptcy. The Bankruptcy Code, 11 U.S.C. § 541(c)(2), specifically provides that "a restriction on the transfer of a beneficial interest of the debtor in a trust that is enforceable under applicable nonbankruptcy law is enforceable in a case under this title." On the question generally, see Scott on Trusts § 152.2.

Pension Benefits. Pension plans affected by the Employee Retirement Income Security Act (ERISA) are required to include spendthrift clauses: "Each pension plan shall provide that benefits provided under the plan may not be assigned or alienated." ERISA § 206(d)(1), 29 U.S.C. § 1056(d)(1); Anderson v. Raine, 907 F.2d 1476 (4th Cir. 1990) (holding that ERISA § 206(d)(1) constitutes "applicable nonbankruptcy law" for purposes of Bankruptcy Code section 541(c)(2), supra, and thus a bankrupt's interest in her or his ERISA-covered pension plan cannot be reached by bankrupt's trustee in bankruptcy). ERISA applies to pension plans of employers who engage in or affect interstate or foreign commerce. See also IRC § 401(a)(13). State law also often provides that pension benefits are unassignable and exempt from execution. E.g., Ore. Rev. Stat. § 23.170. See generally Sherman, Spendthrift Trusts and Employee Pensions: The Problem of Creditors' Rights, 55 Ind. L.J. 247 (1980). Various pension plans for federal employees include restraints on alienation. See Scott on Trusts § 157.1 at 200-01.

Boiler-Plate Use of Spendthrift Clauses. In practice, many private trusts drafted by lawyers contain a spendthrift clause. Such clauses are routinely included in law-office and published form-book trust forms. Here is the clause contained in the sample revocable inter-vivos trust reproduced supra p. 602:

> No interest of any beneficiary in the income or principal of this trust shall be assignable in anticipation of payment or be liable in any way for the beneficiary's debts or obligations and shall not be subject to attachment.

The location of the spendthrift clause may also be significant. It is not unusual for a modern trust instrument to be fairly lengthy, consisting of thirty or more typewritten pages. Unlike the testator's will in the *Broadway Bank* case, where the spendthrift restraint was part of the same sentence granting Charles Adams the right to the income, the modern trust forms bury the spendthrift clause in a separate Article toward the end of the document, near the perpetuity saving clause (see infra Chapter 17, Part C). We doubt that very many clients are told the significance of the clause, except where the client expresses concern about one or more of the beneficiaries (such as G did in Example 12.1, supra p. 666). Nor do we think that very many clients notice the clause on their own and inquire about its significance; and, of those that do, we doubt they get much of an explanation of its significance beyond the standard "Oh, that's a technical-legal clause that we put in all the trusts we draft." What risk does this legal practice, to the extent it is true, create for settlors, beneficiaries, or society in general?

Notice that the sample spendthrift clause, supra, applies not only to the interest of the income beneficiary (A, in Example 12.1, supra p. 666), but also to the interest of the remainderman in principal (X, in that Example). Are spendthrift restraints on future interests in principal valid?

Estate of Vought
25 N.Y.2d 163, 303 N.Y.S.2d 61,
250 N.E.2d 343 (1969)

[Chance M. Vought, Sr.,[15] died in 1930, survived by his wife, Edna, and his two sons, Peter Vought and Chance M. Vought, Jr. The will of Chance, Sr., created a trust, the income to be paid to Edna for life, remainder in corpus in equal shares to the two sons. Edna died at age 67 in 1965, survived by Peter. Although Chance, Jr., predeceased his mother by about a year and a half, his remainder interest in half of the corpus (valued at about $1 million) was not conditioned on survivorship to the time of possession or enjoyment and so passed through his estate to his successors in interest, presumably his widow and surviving children.

The trust expressly prohibited alienation of the sons' remainder interests in principal. Nevertheless, Chance, Jr., during his lifetime, purported to assign his remainder interest in the corpus in a series of transactions as follows: (a) on October 27, 1959, he sold to Inheritance Estates Ltd. a right to $450,000, for which he allegedly received $78,750; (b) on October 27, 1959, he sold to the Allied Investment & Discount Corporation a right to $150,000, subject to the prior assignment, for which he allegedly received $15,000; (c) on January 8, 1960, he sold to Lex Company Inc. a right to $500,000, subject to the two prior assignments; and (d) on August 11, 1960, he sold to Leonard P. Levy, all his interest in the principal, subject to the three prior assignments. Chance, Jr., allegedly received $12,000 for these last two assignments.[16] There was evidence that these amounts allegedly received by Chance, Jr. were substantially below the actuarial

---

15. Chance M. Vought, Sr., was one of the pioneers of the American aviation industry. As chief engineer for the Wright brothers' firm, he designed several of the aircraft used in the First World War. After the War, he began his own aviation company, which later merged with Pratt & Whitney Aircraft Company and the Boeing Airplane Company. This merger produced a substantial fortune for him by the time of his death in 1930.

16. The details of the transactions are reported in Estate of Vought, 70 Misc.2d 781, 783, 334 N.Y.S.2d 720, 723 (Sur. Ct. 1972).

values of the interests purportedly assigned by him.[17] There was also evidence that Chance, Jr., was, at the time of these transactions "an alcoholic suffering from chronic relapsing pancreatitis and diabetes and was addicted to the use of drugs as a result of the suffering caused by this condition [and] in the words of one witness [he was also] in 'desperate financial straights'. . . . "[18] The Surrogate's Court held that the clause restraining alienation of Chance, Jr.'s remainder interest in the trust principal was valid and, therefore, that his assignments were void. The Appellate Division affirmed, and the assignees appealed to the Court of Appeals.]

BREITEL, J. . . . The precise question of whether a settlor has the power to make inalienable a principal remainder limited on an entrusted life estate is one of first impression. In this State, although there are many precedents which offer close analogies, they yield no conclusive or authoritative holding or doctrine. It is evident, however, that the prevailing weight of decisional authority in the Nation, based more or less on common-law principles, would sustain the restraint of alienation of a remainder limited on an equitable life interest, if so provided by the creator of the trust. Moreover, in policy, there are no persuasive modern reasons, and aside from conceptual and historical grounds, for nullifying attempts at restraining alienation on transfers in fee absolute, no compelling legal ground why the creator's wishes must be ignored during the measured period involved. Consequently, it is concluded that the determinations of the Surrogate and the Appellate Division should be affirmed. . . .

In the instant case, the issue is whether generally a creator may postpone for a limited period the beneficiary's control of material wealth until a time when the beneficiary is believed to be more able to manage it more wisely. Such a desire is not unnatural in a creator of trusts, nor does it work an undue hardship on those who extend aid to the beneficiary, provided they extend aid with the knowledge that they will not be reimbursed out of the principal against the creator's wishes.

The weight of authority, where not controlled by statute, supports the power to impose inalienability of principal as well as of life interests (see 2 Scott, Law of Trusts [3d ed.], § 153, p. 1170; see, also, 2 Bogert, Law of Trusts and Trustees [2d. ed.], § 222, p. 639, at n. 2). Scott has noted: "The courts seem to feel that the protection of the beneficiary of a trust should extend not merely to his right to receive income but to his right to receive principal in the future, whether in the meantime he or another person is entitled to receive the income" (op. cit., at pp. 1170-1171). As a reflection of a trend in favor of allowing principal inalienability, the Restatement, 2d Trusts, reversing the position of the first Restatement, now allows for inalienability of the principal (compare Restatement, 2d Trusts, § 153, with Restatement, Trusts, § 153). . . .

Given the history of the rules and the statutes expressing the rules, giving only limited value to the ideal of consistency of patterns in the law,

---

17. Estate of Vought, 76 Misc.2d 755, 758, 351 N.Y.S.2d 816, 821 (Sur. Ct. 1973).
18. Id. at 757, 351 N.Y.S.2d at 820-21.

and according substantial weight to modern policy considerations and the purpose of permitting owners enlarged freedom to dispose of their property as they will unless there is injury to the public, the law of this State should conform to the prevailing weight of authority. In this way, the intended beneficiaries of the remainders of principal will be protected as the settlors intend, and the assignees suffer no loss greater than that for which they bargained on the face of the instruments with which they were dealing. Interests in property are not restrained of alienation or transfer for any greater time than the permissible life interests and the legal title of the particular assets . . . is always capable of being transferred [under the trustee's power of sale.]

In the absence of any strong statutory direction or any developed body of precedent restricting provisions making principal inalienable, the will of the testator should be given effect, and the interest of the assignor be deemed unassignable during the life of the trust.

The assignees argue, however, that even if the interest in principal be deemed unassignable, the assignees should be entitled to that interest now that the trust has ended and the principal is now to be paid out. They argue it would be inequitable to have allowed the assignor to renounce the assignment, and urge that his estate be charged with his obligation to facilitate a transfer.

Such a result, however, would render meaningless any provision providing for inalienability of the principal for, indeed, the beneficial owner has no present interest to be protected but the right to receive the principal at a later date. If by an assignment during the life of the trust he is deemed to have transferred this sole right of later possession he has transferred virtually all his interest. Moreover, the creator's wishes would be completely frustrated, the beneficiary not only getting the funds the creator had intended be delayed, but the beneficiary receiving a fraction, after discount, of what was eventually intended.

Thus the courts below correctly determined that the assignees were not entitled to the principal of the trust.

Accordingly, the order of the Appellate Division should be affirmed, with costs to all parties filing briefs payable out of the estate.

FULD, C.J., dissenting. I would reverse on the ground that the estate created in the will for the testator's son constituted both a legal and equitable vested remainder in fee, the alienability of which, under long-established principles, may not be proscribed. (EPTL, 7-1.5 [replacing former Personal Property Law, § 15].) Moreover, the policy considerations in favor of permitting a restraint upon the alienability of property until such time as the beneficiary is believed to be equipped to manage it wisely do not operate where a remainderman is given an absolute and unqualified right to dispose of the property as he chooses, subject only to the prior life estate of another.

Notes and Questions

1. *State of Authorities.* Prior to *Vought,* most of the cases upholding spendthrift restraints on principal interests were cases of postponement-of-enjoyment trusts. Unlike *Vought,* which is a successive-beneficiary trust (income to A for life, remainder in corpus to B), these cases were of the income-to-A-until-A-reaches-30,-then-principal-to-A type. See, e.g., Erickson v. Erickson, 197 Minn. 71, 266 N.W. 161, reh'g denied, 267 N.W. 426 (1936). The original Restatement of Trusts section 153 (1935) restricted the validity of spendthrift restraints on principal interests to this type of trust, i.e., where the principal beneficiary "is entitled to the income from the trust property."

As the New York court pointed out in *Vought,* the position of the original Restatement of Trusts (1935) was reversed in the Restatement 2d of Trusts section 153. According to Scott on Trusts section 153, the "weight of authority today [is that a spendthrift restraint on principal] is valid whether or not the beneficiary is entitled to the income in the meantime." The recent California and Texas codifications of trust law also adopt this position. See Cal. Prob. Code § 15301(a); Tex. Prop. Code § 112.035.

2. *Policy Questions.* The facts of *Vought* made it very tempting to sustain the spendthrift restraint, but is the decision good policy? In terms of the policies for and against spendthrift trusts, should courts distinguish between postponement-of-enjoyment trusts and successive-beneficiary trusts?

3. *Effect of Restraint After Principal/Income Due.* If a spendthrift provision is valid regarding principal, does it continue to be effective once the time has arrived for but prior to actual distribution? Although the decisions are divided on the question (Scott on Trusts § 153), the Restatement 2d of Trusts section 153 states that the restraint becomes ineffective once the beneficiary becomes "entitled to have the principal conveyed to him immediately." This rule is codified in some states. See, e.g., Cal. Prob. Code § 15301.

If a restraint on alienation of a *principal* interest ceases to be effective once the time for distribution has arrived, is a restraint on an *income* interest effective regarding income in the hands of the trustee but not yet paid to the beneficiary? Should it matter whether the time for distribution of such income has arrived? See Restatement 2d of Trusts § 152 comment h & illustration 9; Scott on Trusts § 152.5.

4. *Enforceability of a Contract to Pay Over the Amount of a Spendthrift Trust Payment.* All authorities agree that both income and principal are transferable and attachable once received by the beneficiary. Does it follow that a spendthrift-trust beneficiary who, for value, agrees or purports to transfer her or his interest to another is liable for breach of contract? Substantial authority states that the beneficiary is liable.

In Moffat v. Lynch, 642 S.W.2d 624 (Mo. 1982), James D. Moffat III and his two sisters were the equal income beneficiaries of a testamentary trust that provided that upon the death of any one of the income beneficiaries, her or his portion of the income was to be distributed equally among the survivors of them. The trust contained a spendthrift clause. Several years after creation of the trust, James and his sisters entered into an agreement that upon the death of any one of them, the survivors would pay over to the children of the deceased beneficiary the proportion of the income to which the deceased beneficiary had been entitled while living. After James died, his sisters refused to honor the agreement. James's son sought to enforce the agreement against them. The court held that the agreement was enforceable, reasoning that recovery on the contract by the promisee or contract beneficiary comes out of the general property of the trust beneficiary rather than the beneficiary's interest in the trust. The contract beneficiary, the court said, is reaching no more than any general creditor of the beneficiary could reach. Accord, Restatement 2d of Trusts § 152 comment k; Kelly v. Kelly, 11 Cal. 2d 356, 79 P.2d 1059 (1938); Minot v. Minot, 319 Mass. 253, 66 N.E.2d 5 (1946).

Compare Estate of Vought, 76 Misc. 2d 755, 351 N.Y.S.2d 816 (Sur. Ct. 1973), holding that Chance Vought, Jr.'s estate was neither liable on the contract nor for restitution. The transactions (see supra p. 678), the court found, were unconscionable, usurious, and void; also, the assignees knew of the spendthrift restraint and assumed the risk as to its validity.

2. Discretionary Trusts

Types of Discretionary Trusts. Trusts requiring the trustee to pay the income to a specified beneficiary or divide it equally among a specified group of beneficiaries are sometimes called "straight-income trusts." Another term sometimes used is "successive-beneficiary trusts." In income-tax parlance, the term "simple trust" is somewhat comparable; a simple trust is defined as one in which income is required to be distributed currently, no amounts can be devoted to charitable purposes, and no distribution of corpus is made in the taxable year. Treas. Reg. § 1.651(a)-1. Simple trusts are subject to Subpart B (§§ 651-52) of Subchapter J of the IRC. Generally speaking, this means that for income-tax purposes the ordinary income is taxed to the beneficiary receiving it (or entitled to receive it) rather than to the trust; realized capital gains or losses, however, are taxed to the trust.

By these definitions, the spendthrift trust created by G in Example 12.1, supra p. 666, is a straight-income, successive-beneficiary, simple trust. Note, too, that to qualify for the federal gift-tax or estate-tax marital deduction under IRC section 2523(e) or (f) or IRC section 2056(b)(5) or (b)(7), the spouse must be entitled for life to all the income from the entire interest, or all the income from a specific portion thereof, payable annually or at more frequent intervals. In practical effect, such trusts are quite rigid. See supra p. 371.

To add flexibility and opportunity for post-creation tax planning, trust documents often confer discretionary powers on the trustee. The extent of the trustee's discretionary power varies with the situation. It may relate to income, principal, or both. For example, in Example 12.1, supra p. 666, G might have created a so-called *spray* (or *sprinkle*) trust: Although the trustee would be required to distribute all the income, the trustee would be given a discretionary power to allocate that income all to G's daughter, A; all to A's son, X; or part to A and the remaining part to X. Thus, as time goes along, the trustee would be enabled to adjust the allocation of income to take account of matters such as the different income-tax brackets of A and X and the different needs of A and X. Such a trust, incidentally, would be a "discretionary trust" in trust-law parlance, but would still be a simple trust in income-tax parlance (Treas. Reg. § 1.651(a)-2(b)); it would become a "complex trust," however, if the trustee were authorized to accumulate some or all of the income rather than pay it out.

Even in the case of a marital-deduction trust, where the spouse must be entitled to all the income for life, the trustee often is given a discretionary power exercisable in favor of the spouse to invade the corpus of the trust. Such a power does not disqualify the trust for the marital deduction. E.g., Treas. Reg. § 20.2056(b)-5(i).

Marital-Deduction/By-Pass Trusts. To select one example of many that could be given of the sophisticated use of discretionary powers, consider the standard marital-deduction/by-pass trust combination, illustrated by the following example. Suppose H died, leaving a net estate of $4 million. H's will split his estate into two equal parts, $2 million going into a standard QTIP marital-deduction trust and the remaining $2 million into a standard by-pass trust. The marital-deduction trust provides that W is to receive the entire income for life, and both trusts provide that the remainder in corpus at her death goes to their then-surviving descendants by representation. In this form, the marital-deduction trust is not taxed in H's estate (section 2056) but will be taxed in W's estate when she dies (IRC § 2044); and the by-pass trust is taxed in H's estate (IRC § 2033) but will not be taxed in W's estate when she dies (IRC §§ 2033; 2041).

It was anticipated that the marital-deduction trust would initially produce about $100,000 income annually and that the by-pass trust would initially produce about the same amount. Considering the style of living to which W was accustomed, pre-tax income of roughly $200,000 a year was just about sufficient for her to squeeze by on.

Suppose, however, that H's lawyer, having taken a course from your trusts and estates teacher in law school, knew of the following trick. Instead of requiring the trustee of the by-pass trust to pay out its income to W for life, she drafted the by-pass trust so that the trustee was given a discretionary power to accumulate the income or pay it out to W (or to any one or more of their descendants). And, she drafted the marital-deduction trust so that the trustee was given a discretionary power to invade the corpus for W.

The plan still called for W to receive about $200,000 a year. But, instead of that sum being made up of all the income from the marital-deduction trust and all the income from the by-pass trust, it would be made up of all the income from the marital-deduction trust and, by virtue of an annual exercise of the trustee's discretionary power, an amount of principal from the marital-deduction trust sufficient, after taxes, to give W a yearly pre-tax income of the required $200,000. The trustee was also expected to utilize the discretionary power to accumulate the income from the by-pass trust and add it to corpus. Over time, as the corpus of the marital-deduction trust (which will be taxed in W's estate) dwindles, the corpus of the by-pass trust (which will not be taxed in W's estate) swells.

Both the marital-deduction and the by-pass trust are "discretionary trusts." In income-tax parlance, the marital-deduction trust is a "complex trust" in its termination year and in any prior year in which corpus is paid out to W; the by-pass trust is a "complex trust" throughout its existence, regardless of whether the trustee accumulates the income or pays it out. See Treas. Reg. § 1.661(a)-1. Complex trusts are subject to Subparts C and D of Subchapter J (IRC §§ 661-67). Generally speaking, this means that for income-tax purposes income but not principal distributions are taxed to the beneficiary receiving them; income accumulated is taxed to the trust, subject to a later application of the so-called throwback rules upon actual distribution.

a. Range of the Trustee's Discretion

By conferring discretion, a settlor manifests an intention to trust the trustee's judgment. Restatement 2d of Trusts section 187 provides that a court will not substitute its judgment for that of the trustee, unless the trustee abuses that trust. This, of course, leaves open the question what constitutes an abuse of discretion. On this question, consider the following discussion.

Halbach, Problems of Discretion in Discretionary Trusts
61 Colum. L. Rev. 1425, 1428-33 (1961)

A. Simple Discretion: Absence of Words Indicating Discretion Is Absolute. It is elementary that a court will not interfere with a trustee's exercise of discretion when that exercise is reasonable. Thus, even in cases in which such words as "absolute" and "uncontrolled" do not appear, it is settled that judicial intervention is not warranted merely because the court would have differently exercised the discretion to pay out principal or income. . . . It is equally clear, of course, that a court will not permit the trustee to abuse his discretion. What constitutes an abuse depends on the scope of the discretion conferred and the standards, if any, to be applied by the trustee in its exercise. When there are no words such as "absolute" or "uncontrolled" enlarging the trustee's discretion, a court will intervene if the facts show the payments are an unreasonable means of carrying out the terms of the trust as construed by the court. Typically this occurs in a context in which a beneficiary is entitled to amounts adequate to provide support, or to fulfill some other standard, and the amount being paid is clearly inadequate for that purpose. It is not necessary, however, that the instrument prescribe a clear standard or guide before a good faith decision of the trustee can be deemed so unreasonable as to constitute an abuse.

Naturally, a court will also act to rectify abuses resulting from bad faith or "improper motive," and to prevent abuse through nonexercise of the discretion.

B. *Extended Discretion: Effect of Words Like "Absolute"*. Since, as previously indicated, considerable latitude flows from a grant of simple discretion, it may be asked what can be gained by making discretion "absolute," "unlimited," or "uncontrolled." Since modern cases on this point have placed great emphasis on the language of the *Restatement of Trusts*, it is worthwhile to begin with the position set forth [in section 187 comment j] therein:

> [The words "absolute," "unlimited," or "uncontrolled"] are not interpreted literally but are ordinarily construed as merely dispensing with the standard of reasonableness. In such a case the mere fact that the trustee has acted beyond the bounds of reasonable judgment is not a sufficient ground for interposition by the court, so long as the trustee acts in a state of mind in which it was contemplated by the settlor that he would act. But the court will interfere if the trustee acts in a state of mind not contemplated by the settlor. Thus, the trustee will not be permitted to act dishonestly, or from some motive other than the accomplishment of the purposes of the trust, or ordinarily to act arbitrarily without an exercise of his judgment.

This rule is stated as being applicable "even where there is a standard" by which the extended discretion is to be judged. The statement is made with reference to discretionary powers in general, but its relevance to powers over income and principal is apparent.

All courts agree that if the power involved is a fiduciary discretion rather than a power of appointment, it can not be placed completely beyond the control of the proper court, regardless of the words of the settlor. Thus, as in the case of a simple discretion, nonexercise will not be permitted merely because the discretion is described as absolute, nor will bad faith be tolerated. The difficult question is what conduct will be acceptable to a court on a contested accounting or on petition of a beneficiary when an extended discretion has been exercised and there is no doubt that the trustee acted in good faith. Is it accurate to state that reasonableness will not be required? Or is it just that under an extended discretionary power a wider variety of decisions will appear to be within the bounds of reason—i.e., that it is more difficult to abuse such a power? It is extremely doubtful that a court would refrain from interfering with an unreasonable exercise of an "absolute" discretion, especially when the settlor has provided a standard, such as support, against which reasonableness may readily be measured. No case has been found that has allowed a challenged decision of a trustee to stand when reasonable minds could not have differed. Of course, courts in many cases have refused to interfere with discretionary powers enlarged by such words as "absolute," but no case in which such a power related to distributions of income or principal has been found that actually supports, on its facts, the *Restatement* view that the requirement of reasonableness is dispensed with by such a provision. Language in accord with this view is invariably superfluous, having been added after the decision had already been reached. . . . [I]n numerous cases the trustee's "absolute" or "uncontrolled" discretion has been overturned on much the same ground as that on which simple discretions have often been upset—typically, unreasonably small payments to the beneficiary. Such cases *can* be interpreted as coming within the *Restatement* formulation requiring the trustee to act in the "state of mind . . . contemplated by the settlor," and the modern opinions, almost without exception, have expressed their results in these terms when interfering with the trustee's judgment. Even though language in the decisions tends to perpetuate the *Restatement's* wording of the rule, any distinction between the test of reasonableness and the state-of-mind test is difficult to discern from the holdings of these cases. In fact, the requirements set out in the dicta of some cases, phrased in terms of requiring "reasonable judgment" and "sound discretion," go far in obliterating any such distinction.

It thus appears that a court is likely to require reasonable exercise of an "absolute" discretion, even though it may be necessary to resort to the now customary state-of-mind terminology to justify its result under a local statute or under the general formulation of the common law rule relating to judicial control of such powers. The difference between simple and extended discretion probably is one of degree, not kind. If any other practical consequence flows from extended discretion, it may be that, while the immediate beneficiary can still compel payments that can reasonably be expected to fulfill any prescribed standard or apparent purpose of the trust, the remaindermen will not be heard to complain even if the payments are "unreasonably" generous, so long as the basic purpose of the discretion has not been violated. This consequence is probably consistent with the usual purpose of the draftsman who inserted the provision in the will or trust agreement. Lawyers commonly include such words as "sole, absolute, and uncontrolled" to encourage liberal use of the power, to give the trustee a feeling of security, or to diminish litigation. There seems to be a general fear, and one that does not appear wholly unjustified, that a trustee might otherwise tend to be more conservative than the settlor or his primary beneficiary would desire, especially with respect to principal payments. The draftsman may therefore hope to "loosen" the trustee in the exercise of his discretion. This the provision will probably do; but if it should not and the discretionary beneficiary is paid too little, under the *Restatement* view relief would be difficult to obtain. Therefore, if donative transactions are to be given effect in accordance with the donor's probable intent, the distinction suggested above between simple and extended discretion is likely to be more appropriate than a rule wholly dispensing with the requirement of reasonableness.

———

EXTERNAL REFERENCES. Scott on Trusts §§ 187, 128.3; Bogert on Trusts § 560.

b. Alienability

If a trust is a true discretionary trust, as where the trust instrument gives the trustee discretion, or "uncontrolled" or "absolute" discretion, to pay or not to pay income or principal to the beneficiary, the beneficiary cannot compel the trustee to pay, nor can an assignee or creditor of the beneficiary compel the trustee to pay, any part of the income or principal to her or him. See Restatement 2d of Trusts § 155. In this sense, then, the beneficiary's "interest" in a discretionary trust is inalienable, whether or not the "interest" is subject to a valid spendthrift restriction.

Comment b to section 155 of the Restatement explains this result as follows:

> [A] "discretionary trust" . . . is to be distinguished from a spendthrift trust, and from a trust for support. In a discretionary trust it is the nature of the beneficiary's interest rather than a provision forbidding alienation which prevents the transfer of the beneficiary's interest.

Comment c goes on to say, however, that "the rule stated in the Section is applicable only where the trustee may in his absolute discretion refuse to make any payment to the beneficiary. . . . It is not applicable where the trustee has discretion merely as to the time of payment. . . ."

Protective Trusts. The above rules bring the legal treatment of discretionary trusts to a position that is similar to that given to spendthrift trusts under the majority American rule. In fact, a variation on discretionary trusts, the "protective trust," was developed by English lawyers to achieve much the same purpose as a spendthrift restriction despite English law's non-recognition of spendthrift trusts.[19] At creation, a protective trust typically gives the beneficiary a *right* to the income, but provides that, upon an attempted alienation, voluntary or involuntary, the beneficiary's right is forfeited and the trust becomes a discretionary trust. The protective-trust device takes advantage of the English rule that forfeiture restraints on equitable life estates are valid.

Protective trusts are commonly used as a substitute for a spendthrift trust in the few remaining American jurisdictions that do not recognize spendthrift trusts. See, e.g., Industrial Nat'l Bank v. Budlong, 106 R.I. 780, 264 A.2d 18 (1970).[20]

---

19. In re Bullock, 60 L.J. Ch. 341 (1891). In 1925, England enacted legislation under which a settlor may create a protective trust of income merely by providing that the income is to be held on a "protective trust" for a person for "his life or for any less period." Trustee Act, 1925, 15 Geo. 5, ch. 19, § 33(1).

20. There are limits, however, to the enforceability of protective trusts. As we will learn later, governmental claims for past due income taxes are treated as special even in jurisdictions that do recognize spendthrift trusts. In United States v. Riggs Nat'l Bank, 636 F. Supp. 172 (D.D.C. 1986), a testamentary trust created by the will of Isabel G. Zantzinger provided for payment of a third of the income to her son, William, subject to a spendthrift restraint and a forfeiture provision providing that if William attempts to assign his interest or if his creditors attempt to subject his interest to a levy of execution, writ of attachment, or garnishment, the trustee should have discretion to apply income for the support of William or accumulate it and

Although similar, protective and discretionary trusts are different from spendthrift trusts. At a policy level, one can argue that protective trusts (and forfeiture restraints generally) are less objectionable than spendthrift trusts (and disabling restraints) because they do not create what economists call the "moral-hazard" problem.[21] This problem arises because a device eliminating certain risks may simultaneously increase the probability or the size of a loss by reducing the protected individual's incentive to take desirable precautions. Forfeiture restraints eliminate the moral-hazard problem inherent in spendthrift trusts by creating incentives for beneficiaries to take steps to reduce the probability of a loss of their interest, through refraining from voluntary assignment or building up debt that could lead to creditor action. Does the moral-hazard problem create a sufficient reason to abolish the spendthrift-trust doctrine?

Trustee Liability After Notice of an Assignment. Creditors cannot judicially compel a trustee of a discretionary trust to pay them rather than the beneficiary. One might suppose, therefore, that the trustee may pay the beneficiary without incurring liability to the creditor. According to Restatement 2d of Trusts section 155, however, if there is no spendthrift restraint and if the trustee has knowledge that the beneficiary has assigned her or his interest or if the beneficiary's creditors have served the trustee with process in a proceeding to reach that interest, the trustee is liable to the assignee or the creditor if the trustee first pays the beneficiary.

This principle was established in New York by Hamilton v. Drogo, 241 N.Y. 401, 150 N.E. 496 (1926). In that case, the dowager Duchess of Manchester devised a large sum in trust, giving the trustees "sole and uncontrolled discretion" to pay the income for the benefit of all or any among her son (the ninth Duke of Manchester, who, incidentally, was a genuine spendthrift extraordinaire[22]), his wife, or his descendants. A judgment creditor of the Duke, after an execution was issued and returned unsatisfied, applied for an order that an execution issue against the trust income in the amount of ten percent thereof pursuant to N.Y. Civil Practice

---

add it to corpus. A federal district court held that the protective-trust device was ineffective as against the federal tax lien. The court stated:

> [W]hile [protective] trust clauses create a legitimate property right under state law which can shield the beneficiary from ordinary creditors, such trusts cannot be effective against a federal tax lien, as a matter of federal law. . . . It would be offensive and disruptive to federal tax law for a beneficiary to receive an income stream for years without paying taxes on it, only to have the income stream disappear once the IRS discovers the misfeasance and moves against it.

21. For a succinct description of the moral-hazard problem, see A. Polinsky, An Introduction to Law and Economics 54-55 (1983).

22. See Time, June 17, 1935, at 19. According to Time, the Duke (ne William Angus Drogo Montagu) once owed $5,000 for tennis balls alone.

Law section 684.[23] The court ordered that the execution be granted, relying on this reasoning:

> In the present case no income may ever become due to the judgment debtor. We may not interfere with the discretion which the testatrix has vested in the trustee. . . . But at least annually this judgment must be exercised. And if it is exercised in favor of the duke, then there is due him the whole or such part of the income as the trustee may allot to him. After such allotment, he may compel its payment. At least for some appreciable time, however brief, the award must precede the delivery of the income he is to receive, and during that time the lien of the execution attaches.[24]

California courts later adopted the rule of Hamilton v. Drogo. See, e.g., Canfield v. Security-First Nat'l Bank, 13 Cal. 2d 1, 87 P.2d 830 (1939). The rule is now codified and its scope expanded in the California Probate Code section 15303, which provides that the trustee is liable to the beneficiary's transferee or creditor "to the extent that the payment to or for the benefit of the beneficiary impairs the right of the transferee or creditor." The statute further provides that it applies even if the trust was not a "pure" discretionary trust, i.e., the trust instrument provides a standard for the exercise of the trustee's discretion.[25]

3. Pure-Support Trusts/Discretionary-Support Trusts

Statutory Reference: *Uniform Custodial Trust Act*

A pure-support trust is mandatory, not discretionary. The trustee is required to pay out, and the beneficiary is entitled to receive (or have applied), so much of the income and principal or either as is necessary for the beneficiary's support. This means that the beneficiary's entitlement is to a certain amount of the income or principal or both, such amount specified not in terms of "all" the income or a specified fraction of the income or principal or in dollar terms, but in terms of an objective, ascertainable standard.

---

23. N.Y. Civ. Prac. Law § 684 then provided that "where any . . . income from trust funds . . . are due and owing to the judgment debtor or shall thereafter become due and owing to him," upon application of the creditor the justice must grant "an order directing that execution issue against the . . . income from trust funds of said judgment debtor, and on presentation of such execution . . . to the person . . . from whom such . . . income from trust funds . . . are due and owing or may thereafter become due and owing to the judgment debtor, said execution shall become a lien and a continuing levy upon the . . . income from trust funds . . . due or to become due to said judgment debtor" for "ten percent thereof."

24. This reasoning had been used in an earlier English case involving an assignment by the beneficiary of his interest under a discretionary trust. In re Neil, 62 L.T.R. 649 (1890).

25. An Oklahoma statute also embraces the substance of the Restatement's position, but the statute itself is based upon section 5 of a proposed statute found in E. Griswold, Spendthrift Trusts, app. A (2d ed. 1947). See Okla. Stat. Ann. tit. 60 § 175.25E; First Nat'l Bank v. Clark, 402 P.2d 248 (Okla. 1965).

Pure-support trusts are seldom used in actual practice. More common are what might be called discretionary-support trusts. A discretionary-support trust is a hybrid, containing elements of pure-discretionary and pure-support trusts. The trustee is authorized or directed to pay to the beneficiary so much of the income and principal or either as the trustee, in her or his sole and absolute discretion, determines is necessary for the beneficiary's support. The statutory trust set forth in the Uniform Custodial Trust Act is a discretionary-support trust when it is for an incapacitated beneficiary. Unif. Custodial Trust Act § 9(b) (1987).

a. Range of the Trustee's Discretion

Abravanel, Discretionary Support Trusts
68 Iowa L. Rev. 273, 278-80, 293-95 (1983)

In the case of [a pure-support] trust, as distinguished from the pure discretionary trust, the trustee, in making distributive decisions, is governed by an ascertainable standard. In determining whether to make a disbursement to the support trust beneficiary, the trustee's decision must comport with the following standard: whether the contemplated disbursement will enable the beneficiary to maintain his or her accustomed standard of living.

Although a support trust is deemed to contain an ascertainable standard by which the trustees' distributive decisions can be measured, the trustee is vested with considerable dispositive discretion. The "discretionary" aspect of even a pure support trust arises by reason of the imprecise nature of the support standard. . . .

Frequently, the discretionary element of a support trust is made explicit, as when discretionary language is combined with language that, if taken alone, would be deemed to create a pure support trust. For example, a property owner transfers certain assets "to T, in trust, to pay to W or apply so much of the income or principal of the trust, from time to time, as T shall, *in his uncontrolled discretion, deem necessary for the support and maintenance* of W," with remainder over to some third person upon the termination of the life tenant's interest. This language creates a species of trust termed a discretionary support trust.

It certainly appears that if express discretionary language is added to a support trust, the settlor must have intended that the trustee exercise greater latitude in distributive decisions than would be the case in the absence of the discretionary language. The converse should also hold true. Namely, the scope of the trustee's discretion in the case of a discretionary support trust should be more restricted than would be the case in the absence of the support language. . . .

Subject to a few notable exceptions, the court opinions in this area reflect a singular lack of judicial sensitivity to the distinction between discretionary support trusts, on the one hand, and pure support and pure discretionary trusts, on the other. When confronted with the task of construing a dispositive instrument, the terms of which establish a discretionary support trust, it is probable that a court will simply and, it is contended, erroneously analyze the trust as though it were either a pure discretionary trust or a pure support trust. The courts have been unable or unwilling to appreciate the concept that the hybrid nature of the discretionary support trust results in a trust relationship that is legally distinguishable from the individual elements of which it is composed. . . .

One of the most frequently litigated issues involving support trusts is whether the private resources of the beneficiary must be considered by the trustee in ascertaining the amount properly payable to the beneficiary for support and maintenance. Cases that have addressed this question in the context of a pure support trust are in irreconcilable conflict; beyond a rather simplistic statement that the results turn on the peculiar language of the instrument in question, little in the way of predictive utility is to be derived from a detailed examination of the individual cases. Notwithstanding this confusion in the decisional literature, the *Restatement (Second)* [section 128 comment e] has adopted the position that "[i]t is a question of interpretation whether the beneficiary is entitled to support out of the trust fund even though he has other resources. The inference is that he is so entitled." The pertinent question . . . is whether this same analytic approach is appropriate within the framework of a discretionary support trust. The question posited should be answered in the negative. When a settlor superimposes discretionary language on a support standard, the trustee is not violating a rule of law if he chooses to consider other sources of the beneficiary's income in determining whether to make a distribution to that beneficiary. If the grant of express trustee discretion in the context of a hybrid trust is to be afforded any scope, the trustee should be at liberty to consider or not to consider outside sources of the beneficiary's income. Unfortunately, cases that have addressed this question do not reflect this learning. Instead, the courts have almost uniformly and, in the view of this writer, erroneously adopted a pure support trust model in construing discretionary support trusts in cases involving the issue of the beneficiary's independent resources. Almost no consideration has been given to language in the trust instrument seeking to vest the trustee with discretion relative to the distribution of the trust fund.

Problem

Wilma Brown is a 50-year-old state supreme court justice. Wilma's spouse, Harry, age 47, is a self-employed cello teacher. Wilma and Harry have two children, Sonny and Cher, both of whom are over 18 and are undergraduates at Snootymore University. All members of the family are in good health.

Major assets, liabilities, and annual income and expenses of the family are roughly as follows:

MAJOR ASSETS

House and Furnishings	$300,000
Automobiles	25,000
Investments	200,000
Total	$525,000

MAJOR LIABILITY

Mortgage	$50,000
Net Worth	$475,000

ANNUAL INCOME

Wilma's Salary	$95,000
Harry's Income	10,000
Interest	15,000
Total Income	$120,000

ANNUAL EXPENSES

Automobile Loan Payments Payments	$5,000
Mortgage Payments	12,000
College Expenses for Cher and Sonny	40,000
Taxes (Income and Real Estate)	45,000
Other expenses (Food, clothing, donations, travel, medical, entertainment, etc.)	50,000
Total Expenses	$152,000

1. Justice Brown's mother, Gertrude, died last year; her will, executed five years earlier, devised $3 million in trust. You, as trustee, are directed to pay so much of the income, principal, or both as you, in your absolute and uncontrolled discretion, determine is necessary for Wilma's support and maintenance; unexpended income is to be accumulated and added to principal; upon Wilma's death, the principal (including accumulated income) is to go to Sonny and Cher.

You have invested the $3 million in such a way that it produces income at the rate of about $165,000 per year. In light of Professor Abravanel's discussion and the Restatement, what amount would you decide to distribute to Wilma this year?

2. Same facts as Problem 1, except that Gertrude is Harry's mother, not Wilma's mother, and the beneficiary of the trust is Harry, not Wilma.

3. Same facts as Problem 1, except that the amount Gertrude devised in trust was $800,000, producing income at the rate of about $44,000 per year. See Tidrow v. Director, Missouri State Division of Family Services, 688 S.W.2d 9, 12 (Mo. Ct. App. 1985) (suggesting that the amount of the principal is a factor in deciding whether the beneficiary's other assets or sources of income can or must be taken into account by the trustee).

4. Same facts as Problem 1, except for the additional information that Wilma had been appointed by the governor to fill a vacancy on the state supreme court only two years ago. Prior to that time, Wilma had been a partner in and head of the trusts, estates, and personal financial counseling department of a large law firm, earning about $325,000 per year. The cut in pay Wilma took to become a judge considerably curtailed the style of living to which the family had previously been accustomed.

5. From your perspective as trustee, how could the drafting of Gertrude's trust have been improved?

b. Alienability

Except in cases where the settlor is the beneficiary, the beneficiary's interest in a support trust is inalienable, whether or not it is subject to a valid spendthrift restraint. As in the case of discretionary trusts, the Restatement explains this result on the basis of the "nature" of the beneficiary's interest. See Restatement 2d of Trusts § 154 comment b.

A more persuasive explanation is that the law implies and enforces a restriction on assignments and creditor access to the extent necessary to fulfill the settlor's objective of assuring that the beneficiary's support, education, or other needs are met. See, e.g., Keeler's Estate, 334 Pa. 225, 3 A.2d 413 (1939).

Section 154 of the Restatement restricts support trusts to those in which the trustee is directed to "pay or apply only so much of the income and principal or either as is necessary for the education or support of the beneficiary." Comment e indicates that the inalienability rule does not apply where "the amount to be paid or applied by the trustee is a specified sum or is not limited to what is necessary for the education and support of the beneficiary, although by the terms of the trust it appears that the settlor's motive in creating the trust is to provide for the education or support of the beneficiary." Restatement 2d of Trusts § 154 comment e. Thus, where the trust instrument provides that income is "to be paid to [the beneficiary] for her support," some courts have permitted creditors to reach the beneficiary's interest on the ground that this language merely expresses the settlor's motive rather than restricting the beneficiary's interest to the beneficiary's needs for support. See, e.g., Young v. Easley, 94 Va. 193, 26 S.E. 401 (1897). Other courts have construed the same language as creating a spendthrift trust. See, e.g., Winthrop Co. v. Clinton, 196 Pa. 472, 46 A. 435 (1900). A California statute provides that, when such language is used, the beneficiary's interest is inalienable "to the extent the income . . . is necessary for the education or support of the beneficiary . . . ." Cal. Prob. Code § 15302.

4. Self-Created Spendthrift, Discretionary, and Support Trusts

The law does not permit a settlor to create a spendthrift, discretionary, or support trust for her or his own benefit. Such a "self-created" trust is not void, but the settlor's interest in a spendthrift trust is alienable and can be reached by creditors and the maximum amount that the trustee can pay the settlor or apply for her or his benefit in a support or discretionary trust is alienable and can be reached by creditors. Restatement 2d of Trusts § 156. Although the reason for these rules may seem obvious, a recent textbook states that the "arguments for (and against) spendthrift trusts are largely the same regardless of who created the trusts, so the special status of self-[created] trusts is puzzling.[26] Conceding the *validity* of spendthrift trusts created by others, do you find the law's refusal to extend the same courtesy to self-created spendthrift trusts to be "puzzling"?

In 1986, Congress added a provision to the Social Security Act to prevent a settlor from qualifying herself or himself or her or his spouse for Medicaid by transferring assets to a "medicaid qualifying trust"—a trust defined in the statute as one under which the settlor or the settlor's spouse "may be the beneficiary of all or part of the payments from the trust" and under which "the distribution of such payments is determined by one or more trustees who are permitted to exercise any discretion with respect to the distribution to the [beneficiary]." The "maximum amounts that may be . . . distributed to the [settlor or the settlor's spouse], assuming the full exercise of discretion by the trustee or trustees," are deemed to be available to the settlor or the settlor's spouse in determining her or his eligibility for Medicaid. Social Security Act § 1902(k), 42 U.S.C. § 1396a(k).

The application of the rules against self-created spendthrift trusts is not dependent upon the fraudulent-transfer principle. The right of the settlor's creditors to satisfy their claims from the settlor's beneficial interest does not depend upon the trust having been created in fraud of creditors. (See supra p. 401 for a refresher on the fraudulent-transfer principle.)

Conceding the rules, certain problems remain. Sometimes a trust is only partially for the benefit of the settlor, as where the settlor retains only an income interest or confers a discretionary power over income only. In such cases, only the income interest is affected by the above rules. In some circumstances, such as reciprocal trusts or trusts created or continued as the result of a failure to exercise a general power of appointment, the true

---

26. W. McGovern, S. Kurtz & J. Rein, Wills, Trusts and Estates 347 (1988).

identity of the settlor may not be obvious. See, e.g., McColgan v. Walter Magee, Inc., 172 Cal. 182, 155 P. 995 (1916); American Security & Trust Co. v. Utley, 382 F.2d 451 (D.C. Cir. 1967).

5. Special Categories of Claimants

Hurley v. Hurley
107 Mich. App. 249, 309 N.W.2d 225 (1981)

ALLEN, J. On March 31, 1980, Ingham County Circuit Court ordered garnishee-defendant, Michigan National Bank, to pay accrued and future income of a spendthrift trust to the court in satisfaction of an outstanding judgment for past due child support taken against defendant, James Hurley, former husband of plaintiff, Phyllis Hurley. Garnishee-defendant's motion for rehearing was denied on April 14, 1980. Garnishee-defendant appeals as of right.

The facts before this Court are undisputed. On September 26, 1966, Maybelle Hurley, defendant's mother and a resident of Missouri, executed a will in Missouri. The will devised [approximately one-half of her estate] in a spendthrift trust for James. He was to receive all income from the trust during his lifetime with the principal passing upon James' death into [trusts] for James' two daughters, Linda Kay and Cherri Ann, the decedent's granddaughters. . . .

Plaintiff and defendant were divorced in Missouri approximately six years before the decedent executed her will in September 1966. The decedent did not provide for plaintiff in her will. In 1970, decedent moved from Missouri to Michigan where she remained until her death in 1978. Defendant, James Hurley, moved from Missouri and presently resides in California. He failed to maintain his child support payments. In 1977, plaintiff filed suit in Missouri for past due child support, and in 1979 obtained a Missouri judgment of $19,630 principal plus $5,728 interest. In 1978, Maybelle Hurley died in Michigan, and her will was admitted into probate in Ingham County, Michigan. Garnishee-defendant, Michigan National Bank, was appointed trustee under the will.

In 1979, plaintiff filed a complaint in the Ingham County Circuit Court against defendant and garnishee-defendant, seeking full faith and credit of the Missouri child support judgment. Plaintiff then moved to require the garnishee-defendant, as trustee, to pay plaintiff the past due and future income from defendant's trust to satisfy the outstanding Missouri child support judgment. Garnishee-defendant answered, claiming that the income from the spendthrift trust was not subject to process by the court. On March 31, 1980, the trial court granted plaintiff's motion and ordered garnishee-defendant to pay due and future income into the court to satisfy plaintiff's outstanding judgment. Only garnishee-defendant appeals as of right.

The sole issue before the Court is whether plaintiff, as defendant's former wife, can reach by judicial process the income from a spendthrift trust created in favor of defendant, her former husband, to obtain satisfaction of plaintiff's judgment against defendant for past due child support. The trust established under the terms of Maybelle Hurley's will meets the definition of a spendthrift trust. . . .

Although the issue is one of first impression in Michigan,[27] it has been ruled upon in several other jurisdictions. The majority rule is that, in the absence of a specific state statute, the income of a spendthrift trust of which a former husband is the current income beneficiary may be reached to satisfy his former wife's claim for alimony, separate maintenance, or child support. Restatement, Trusts 2d, § 157, p. 328 provides:

> Although a trust is a spendthrift trust or a trust for support, the interest of the beneficiary can be reached in satisfaction of an enforceable claim against the beneficiary,
> (a) by the wife or child of the beneficiary for support, or by the wife for alimony;[28]
> [(b) for necessary services rendered to the beneficiary or necessary supplies furnished to him;
> (c) for services rendered and materials furnished which preserve or benefit the interest of the beneficiary;
> (d) by the United States or a State to satisfy a claim against the beneficiary.]

See also II Scott on Trusts, 3d ed., § 157.1, pp. 1206-1216.

Several reasons have been advanced in support of the rule. Some courts adhere to the rationale by finding an intention on behalf of the settlor of the trust to allow a wife to enforce a claim for alimony, maintenance, or child support. In Keller v. Keller, 284 Ill. App. 198, 1 N.E.2d 773 (1936), it was held that such an intention will be found unless the trust instrument discloses an intention that such a claim may not be enforced. Other courts have held that child support is not a "debt" contemplated by the spendthrift provision of a trust. . . . Still other courts have held that it would be against public policy to hold that a wife may not enforce child support claims against a recalcitrant husband. . . . In accord with holding a spendthrift provision contrary to public policy is Shelley v. Shelley, 223 Or. 328, 354 P.2d 282 (1960), which opines that if the beneficiary's interest cannot be reached to satisfy claims for alimony or child support, the state may be called upon to support the wife and children. Further, O'Connor v.

---

27. Gilkey v. Gilkey, 162 Mich. 664, 127 N.W. 715 (1910), cited by garnishee-defendant, is not applicable to the present facts. Gilkey involved a discretionary trust, not a spendthrift trust. . . .

28. The special Comment on § 157(a) of the Restatement, Trusts 2d, is as follows:

> Although a trust is a spendthrift trust or a trust for support, the interest of the beneficiary can be reached in satisfaction of an enforceable claim against him for support by his wife or children. In some cases a spendthrift clause is construed as not intended to exclude the beneficiary's dependents. Even if the clause is construed as applicable to claims of his dependents for support, it is against public policy to give full effect to the provision. The beneficiary should not be permitted to have the enjoyment of his interest under the trust while neglecting to support his dependents.

O'Connor, 3 **Ohio Op.2d** 186, 141 N.E.2d 691, 75 Ohio Law Abst. 420 (Oh.Com.Pl., 1957), holds that the husband has a legal duty to support his wife, that a father has a legal duty to support his minor children, and that these elements of public policy outweigh the public policy that an owner of property, such as the settlor of a trust, may dispose of it as he pleases and may impose spendthrift restraints on the disposition of income.

We find all of the above reasons persuasive and affirm, particularly in light of the existing law in Missouri at the time of the execution of the decedent's will and the creation of the present trusts. Missouri law provides, Mo.Rev.Stat. § 456.080:

> All restraints . . . in the form of a spendthrift trust, or otherwise [are] of no effect, as against the claims of any wife, child or children, of [the beneficiary] for support and maintenance, or, as against the claim of any said wife for alimony.

This law was in effect at the time of the creation of the present trusts. Therefore, the trusts as created, even though of a spendthrift nature, could not bar the recovery of the income from the trust for child support. We do not find that the settlor of these trusts intended to exclude such claims but rather intended the trusts to be administered in accordance with the laws of the state in which the trusts were created thereby allowing such claims.

The lower court order . . . was proper and is sustained.

Affirmed.[29]

Notes and Questions

1. *Alimony and Child Support Claims to Spendthrift Trusts.* The view taken in *Hurley*—that a spendthrift clause does not protect a trust beneficiary's interest from claims for child support—represents the prevailing view. Though alimony awards are less common today than they once were, the same view prevails as to the right of a recipient of an alimony award to reached the obligor's interest in a trust despite a spendthrift restraint on that interest. See, e.g., Shelley v. Shelley, 223 Or. 328, 354 P.2d 282 (1960); Restatement 2d of Trusts § 157(a). Several courts, however, have refused to permit a former spouse or children to reach a spendthrift trust to satisfy alimony or child support judgments. An example is Erickson v. Erickson, 197 Minn. 71, 266 N.W. 161, reh'g denied, 267 N.W. 426 (1936). In that case, the court rejected the theory, mentioned in *Hurley*, that the exceptions in favor of alimony and child support claimants are justified, in part, on the basis of the settlor's imputed intent. The court stated: "If alimony or support money is to be an exception to the protection offered by spendthrift provisions it must be by some justifiable interpretation of the

---

29. In Miller v. Department of Mental Health, 432 Mich. 426, 431, 442 N.W.2d 617, 619 (1989), the Michigan Supreme Court noted in dictum that "the interest of a beneficiary of [a spendthrift or a support trust] can be reached to enforce claims by the beneficiary's wife or child for alimony or support. . . ." Eds.

donor's language by which such implied exception may be fairly construed into the instrument of the trust."

From the perspective of the settlor's probable intent, should courts distinguish between the claims of the beneficiary's former spouse and those of the beneficiary's children?[30] As the opinion in *Hurley* indicates, of course, the settlor's imputed intention is not the only rationale for the exceptions in favor of alimony or support claimants.

2. *Alimony and Child Support Claims to Pension Benefits.* Although ERISA requires pension plans to prohibit assignment and alienation of plan benefits (29 U.S.C. § 1056(d)(1)), it also requires such plans to "provide for the payment of benefits in accordance with the applicable requirements of any qualified domestic relations order" for "child support, alimony payments, or marital property rights." 29 U.S.C. § 1056(d)(3).

3. *Tort Creditors.* The text of Restatement 2d of Trusts section 157, quoted in the *Hurley* opinion, does not list tort creditors as having special rights to overcome a spendthrift restraint or the inalienability granted to support trusts. Professor Scott, the Reporter for the Restatement, stated that this was due to the absence of authority on the question. See Scott on Trusts § 157.5. The comments to section 157 do, however, suggest that tort creditors should be included in the special categories.

An unusual twist on this theme occurred in United Mine Workers of America v. Boyle, 418 F. Supp. 406 (D.D.C. 1976), aff'd, 567 F.2d 112 (D.C. Cir. 1977). The United Mine Workers Union unsuccessfully attempted to levy an attachment against a portion of the monthly pension payments due under its union pension trust. The union sought the writ of attachment to satisfy its judgment against three of its officers, W.A. ("Tony") Boyle, George Titler, and John Owens. The judgment, amounting to $239,993.25, was entered for violation of fiduciary duties under the Labor-Management Reporting and Disclosure Act, 29 U.S.C. § 501. Denying the union's petition for a writ of attachment, the court relied on a spendthrift clause contained in the union's pension trust:

> While it can scarcely be denied that there is something shocking in the notion that a settlor may be permitted to immune a beneficiary's interest from the lawful claims of third-party tort creditors by the device of a spendthrift trust, we believe that the considerations are different in a case, such as this, in which the tort victim and trust settlor are one and the same person.
>
> Unlike the hypothetical third-party tort victim, a settlor can preserve his rights against the beneficiary's interest in the trust by circumspection in drafting the trust instrument. In anticipation of existing and foreseeable future obligations, the settlor is at liberty to include or exclude from the trust agreement such terms and conditions as he may deem appropriate, even to deleting a spendthrift clause in its entirety. So here, unlike the third party tort creditor, the UMWA, as settlor of the Pension Trust, could easily have

---

30. Interestingly, a recent article advocating the routine use of spendthrift trusts recommends a clause that specifically states that the interest of any beneficiary "shall be free from the control or interference . . . of any spouse of a married beneficiary," but does not mention claims of children for child support. Roush & Kirkland, Spendthrift Trusts Are Not Limited to Protection of Immature Dependents, 18 Est. Plan. 16, 18 (Jan.-Feb. 1991).

guaranteed the availability of the defendant's beneficial interests for purposes of satisfying a judgment in its favor based upon a tort committed by the beneficiary against the union and unrelated to duties under the Trust. But the UMWA chose to do otherwise.

4. *Claimants Who Provided Necessities/Government Claimants.* The Restatement specifically includes claimants who provided the beneficiary with necessary services or supplies, such as medical personnel, as having special claims on spendthrift and support trusts. Restatement 2d of Trusts § 157(b). The same section also treats government claimants as exempted from spendthrift restrictions. Id. at § 157(d). The comments to section 157 make clear that the focus of subsection (d) is on government claims for unpaid taxes. None of the comments addresses government claimants who provided necessities under government-assistance programs for the needy. The question has become a source of much litigation in recent years. The excerpt that follows provides some background for this litigation.

Owens & Jordan, Estate Planning for Parents of Mentally Disabled Children
126 Tr. & Est. 41, 42-44 (Sept. 1987)

Estate planning is inextricably tied to the laws of each particular jurisdiction. In this regard, the estate planning for parents of mentally disabled children is fraught with local law requirements pertaining to resource programs for the disabled child. The planner, therefore, must be aware of state and local law requirements and should confer with state and local officials with regard to such programs and their administration.

Governmental Benefit Programs. The governmental resource programs available to a disabled child can be divided into three broad categories. The first are need-based programs which are programs made available to individuals who meet fairly rigid financial eligibility requirements. The second involves non-need-based programs which provide financial and other benefits to specified categories of individuals without regard to the availability of other sources of income or assets. Last, but by no means least, some government programs known as "cost-of-care" programs are available to specified individuals without regard to income and assets. However, the cost of such programs will be charged to the recipient in proportion to his or her ability to pay.

[1.] Need-based resource programs provide benefits only to "financially needy" individuals. Supplemental Security Income ("SSI") is by far the largest federal assistance program and is designed to provide a guaranteed annual income to the aged (over 65), blind and disabled individual. Originally conceived as a supplement to social security benefits for the aged, it has evolved into a resource program primarily serving the disabled.

For purposes of the SSI program, a disabled person is defined as one who is "unable to engage in any substantial gainful activity by reason of any medically determinable physical or mental impairment which can be expected to result in death or which has lasted or can be expected to last for a continuous period of not less than 12 months (or, in the case of a child under the age of 18, if he suffers from any medically determinable physical or mental impairment of comparable severity)." Mentally retarded individuals may be qualified as "disabled" for SSI purposes depending on their I.Q. and other factors. However, disabled individuals are generally ineligible for SSI while institutionalized. . . .

SSI eligibility is achieved through establishing need based on an income and a resource (asset ownership) test. A disabled single child is generally eligible for SSI benefits of up to $4,080 annually if he or she has "income" of less than $4,080 (after taking into account certain exclusions), and whose resources are $1,800 or less in 1987 (SSI making up the difference between the $4,080 maximum and the child's "income"). The definition of "income" for SSI purposes is quite broad and encompasses anything received in cash or in kind which can be used "to meet your needs for food, clothing and shelter." Earned income for these purposes includes wages, net earnings from self employment, earned income tax credits and income from sheltered workshops. Unearned income includes social security benefits, worker's or veteran's compensation, annuities, rents, dividends, alimony payments and interest. Further, "income" for SSI purposes specifically includes inherited or gifted property. Not surprisingly, cash distributions made by a trust to or for the benefit of an SSI recipient are also deemed to be "income" for these eligibility purposes irrespective of whether made from the income or principal of the trust. . . .

Apart from the income qualification requirement is the resource or asset ownership qualification. A mentally disabled child will generally qualify under this test, if he or she has assets of no more than $1,800 after taking into account certain excluded assets. . . . [T]he principal of a trust is generally an excluded resource where the beneficiary has limited access to the principal, such as an irrevocable trust in which only the trustee can invade principal. . . .

Disabled individuals may also qualify for the medicaid assistance program, commonly referred to as Medicaid. Medicaid is a medical assistance program administered by the states with federal underwriting which provides medical assistance for needy persons over the age of 65 years, blind, disabled, or members of families with dependent children. Like SSI programs, Medicaid eligibility is likewise subject to stringent resource limitations. . . . Be aware that legislation passed in late 1985 includes as available Medicaid resources, trust assets from a discretionary trust of which an individual is both grantor and beneficiary even if no payments are ever made to such beneficiary so long as the trustee had discretion to do so. [42 U.S.C. § 1396a(k).] This would only come into play where the disabled child has excess assets and is attempting to qualify for Medicaid. Since this legislation is specifically designed to curb perceived Medicaid abuses, it is possible that these assets may not be counted for SSI purposes.

[2.] The second category of government benefits are those that are available without regard to an individual's income or assets. Social security and Medicare fall under this non-need-based umbrella. A disabled child may receive social security benefits either based upon his or her own earnings record provided he or she has worked a certain length of time in a social security covered job or, if the disabled child has been continuously disabled since a time prior to the age of 22 years and is still unmarried, social security benefits may be paid based upon such disabled child being a dependent of an insured parent when that parent retires, dies, or likewise becomes disabled. Note that social security benefits are not paid automatically but must be applied for by the disabled child's representative.

[3.] The third broad category of government benefits are those that are available to all persons who fall within specified categories, but are free only to those persons who cannot afford to pay. If a recipient has the resources to underwrite such payments, the government will seek reimbursement for its services. The most common cost-of-care program is state residential care which is available to disabled persons. Such residential care is usually available regardless of the recipient's financial status. However, state statutes most often require the institutionalized person, his estate or responsible relatives to reimburse the state to the extent of their "financial ability." Cost-of-care programs/benefits which are in this category must be considered when drafting the estate plan for the parents. It is here that careless planning/draftsmanship can lead to a total erosion of the client's assets if the disabled child falls under one or more of the cost-of-care programs and such assets become reachable by the state to pay for the child's costs incurred.

By being familiar with the benefit programs available for which the mentally disabled child may qualify, the estate planner can more accurately design the estate plan of the parents in such a way as to qualify for maximum governmental resource program benefits. At the same time, however, the individual needs of the disabled child are paramount to that of qualifying for governmental assistance programs if parental sources of funds are sufficient to provide otherwise. In other words, do not let the availability of governmental resource programs overshadow the needs of the child, particularly taking into account the modest levels of need-based resource program benefits.

Lang v. Department of Public Welfare
515 Pa. 428, 528 A.2d 1335 (1987)

[Edward LeViseur's mentally disabled son, William, lived in state institutions for thirty years. LeViseur had paid the full cost of William's support until January, 1967, when LeViseur and the state of Pennsylvania agreed to share the cost of William's care at the Cresson State Hospital. Under the agreement LeViseur paid $200.00 per month.

LeViseur executed his will on May 21, 1968, and died on October 7, 1968. Article FOURTH of the will placed assets totalling $118,360.63, or forty-nine percent of the *gross* value of LeViseur's estate in trust for William. The relevant terms of the trust are as follows:

A. The Trustee shall hold, manage, invest and reinvest said Trust estate and shall distribute the net income (hereinafter called "Income") and principal from time to time as follows:

(1) During the lifetime of my son, WILLIAM GEORGE LeVISEUR, if he survives me, the Trustee shall pay the Income periodically to or for the support, maintenance, welfare and benefit of my said son *or may, in the Trustee's discretion, add part or all of the Income to principal, to be invested as such.*

(2) The Trustee *may distribute such part of the Income not necessary for the support of my son,* in equal shares to my three children, MARGARET MARY SMITH, EDWARD JOHN LeVISEUR, JR. and ELIZABETH ELLEN LANG, or to the survivor or survivors of them, provided however, should any of my said children predecease me, or surviving me die prior to the termination of the Trust Estate leaving issue, such deceased child's then living issue shall take the deceased parent's share, per stirpes.

(3) The Trustee shall use so much of the principal *as may in her opinion be advisable therefor,* for the support, maintenance, welfare, comfort and support of my son, WILLIAM GEORGE LeVISEUR. *The Trustee shall have complete discretion as to how much shall be used for such purposes* and may pay the sums to any person or institution having the care of my said son, without liability on the part of the Trustee to see to the application thereof, or directly to or for the benefit of my said son. In the event of the death of my said son, the Trustee is authorized, in her discretion, to pay any part or all of the funeral and burial expenses of my said son.

(4) At the death of my said son, WILLIAM GEORGE LeVISEUR, the Trust shall terminate and the balance of the Trust Estate shall be distributed in equal shares, free and discharged of the Trust, to MARGARET MARY SMITH, EDWARD JOHN LeVISEUR, JR. and ELIZABETH ELLEN LANG, or to the survivor or survivors of them, provided however, should any of my said children not so surviving, leave issue, such deceased child's then living issue shall take the deceased parent's share, per stirpes.

Until 1970, the trustee, William's sister, distributed income of the trust to William's guardian to meet his expenses in excess of his Social Security and Veteran's benefits. By agreement with the Department of Revenue, the trustee paid all of the net income of the trust directly to Cresson from late 1970 through September 1974.

In October 1974, the Pennsylvania legislature amended the Mental Health Act to provide that the liability of any person who had a legal duty to support a patient or resident receiving services under the act would cease when he attained the age of eighteen, or, if he were already eighteen, upon the effective date of the Act, October 12, 1974. After the Department of Public Welfare (DPW) informed the trustee that the new statute relieved the trust of any statutory duty to support William, the trustee exercised her discretion to use trust income to provide William with clothing, gifts, and pocket money.

In January 1984, DPW reversed its position[31] and declared William

---

31. This was probably in response to a Pennsylvania lower court decision in 1983, holding that the mentally-impaired beneficiary of a discretionary support trust similar to that in *Lang* was ineligible for state medical assistance because the trust was a resource available to the

ineligible for state benefits because the trust income and principal were resources available to him. The trustee appealed to DPW's Office of Hearings and Appeals. It upheld the assessment against the trust. The trial court affirmed DPW's decision, holding the testator intended the trust to pay for such support. The Pennsylvania Supreme Court granted the trustee leave to appeal in order to consider the important issues raised by the state's decision to treat the income and assets in the trust as resources available to one of its beneficiaries.]

HUTCHINSON, J. . . . Because William has no income or assets other than what might be available to him under the trust, the underlying question presented by this appeal is whether testator created a duty in trustee, independent of any statutory duty, to provide for William's basic support. If so, William arguably could compel distributions from the trust for his basic support and it thus would be considered available for his use. See Walter's Case, 278 Pa. 421, 123 A. 408 (1924) (State may obtain reimbursement from a support trust under theory of implied contract.) See also 2 A. Scott, The Law of Trusts, § 128.4 at 1020-22 and § 157.2 at 1216-20 (3d ed. 1967) (when a support standard is expressed in a trust instrument, the extent of the interest of the beneficiary depends upon the settlor's intent, and the court will not interfere with the trustee's discretion as long as his judgment is reasonable). If, however, testator gave trustee discretion to consider funding otherwise available from the Commonwealth in determining whether to distribute trust income and principal (or either) for William's support, the trust (or its income or principal) would not be available for William's use and could not be considered his asset or resource. See 2 A. Scott, supra, § 128.3 at 1016-18 (a beneficiary is entitled only to that which the trustee in the proper exercise of his discretion decides to give him, and he cannot obtain a court's assistance to compel a distribution or control this discretion except to prevent an abuse of discretion). See also Abravanel, Discretionary Support Trusts, 68 Iowa L. Rev. 273, 289 (1983) (there should be an exact parallelism between the rights of the beneficiary in and to the trust estate and the rights of his creditors to reach his equitable interest in the estate). . . .

[W]e reject as a matter of public policy [any] implication that it is in a beneficiary's interest not to be "forced to resort to public welfare." The statutory policy of Pennsylvania, particularly with respect to mental health, does not reflect this vision of public assistance as charity and the consequent assumption that a settlor intended to exhaust his family's patrimony before his beneficiary could take advantage of public funds. Our General Assembly acknowledged this in its 1974 amendment of the Mental Health Act relieving those with a legal duty to support persons receiving benefits under the Act from that obligation once the recipient reaches the age of eighteen.

Recognizing that it is the policy of this Commonwealth to support persons over the age of eighteen who qualify for services under the Mental Health Act does not end our inquiry, however. We must still determine

---

beneficiary. Eds.

whether a settlor, here the testator, intended that trust assets be used to support a beneficiary, regardless of the availability of other resources, including state assistance. A settlor's intent must be determined "from all the language within the four corners of the trust instrument, the scheme of distribution and the circumstances surrounding the execution of the instrument." Farmers Trust Co. v. Bashore, 498 Pa. 146, 150, 445 A.2d 492, 494 (1982).

An examination of the language in Article FOURTH of testator's will . . . shows that this instrument is a discretionary trust limited by a support standard based on William's situation. In Paragraph A(1) testator provided that the trustee pay income from the trust "periodically to or for the support, maintenance, welfare and benefit of [William]" or, in her discretion, "add part or all of the Income to principal, to be invested as such." The inclusion of the clause granting trustee the power to add income to principal demonstrates an intent to give her the discretion to do more than merely determine the amount to pay "periodically" for William's support. The use of the words "welfare and benefit" in addition to the usual "support and maintenance" language in the first clause of Paragraph A(1), which defines the support standard, also indicates an intent to give trustee the discretion to do more than ensure a minimum standard of living for William. Paragraph A(3) of the trust gives trustee the power to invade principal as well, leaving it to her "complete discretion" how much to use for William's support or benefit. The use of the word "complete" to describe trustee's discretion again indicates a broad grant of discretion to trustee.[32]

The trust instrument does not expressly state whether testator intended trustee to consider other sources of support available to William, including funds provided by the Commonwealth, in determining whether to distribute income or principal for William's "support, maintenance, welfare and benefit." Several factors support a finding that he wanted his trustee to consider other resources.

Testator chose to set up a discretionary support trust rather than a mandatory form of trust or a "pure" support trust. The addition of discretionary language indicates an intent that trustee exercise greater latitude in her distributive decisions than would be the case in the absence of such discretionary language. See Abravanel, supra, at 277-80.

Testator also chose to set up one trust to benefit all four of his children, rather than four trusts, one to support William and the others to benefit his remaining children. He funded this trust intending to benefit all four of his children with assets valued at sixty-seven percent of his net estate.[33] He

---

32. See 3 A. Scott, supra, § 187 at 1502 (modifiers such as "absolute" or "unlimited" create an enlarged zone of discretion). The Restatement (Second) of Trusts, § 187 comment j (1959), suggests that the use of modifiers such as "unlimited" or "absolute" dispenses with the standard of reasonableness. As commentators have noted, however, courts have rarely implemented this view and have instead held that trustees may not abuse the discretion granted them, however broadly that grant has been expressed. See Frolik, Estate Planning for Parents of Mentally Disabled Children, 40 U.Pitt.L.Rev. 305, 328 (1979).

33. The value of the trust (approximately $118,000 when funded) is small compared with the magnitude of William's expenses (approximately $4,000 per month in 1984). . . .

granted trustee discretion to determine what portion of trust income was necessary for William's welfare and to distribute income that was not *necessary* for that purpose to the other beneficiaries, in equal shares, or to add it to principal. He gave trustee complete discretion to determine whether to invade principal and how much to use for William's benefit, and directed that, at William's death, the balance of the trust estate be distributed to his surviving children or their issue.

The circumstances surrounding the execution of this instrument point strongly to testator's intent to have his trustee consider other resources. William was institutionalized at the time testator executed his will. The cost per month of William's care at Cresson, based on its per diem billing rate, was $543.00. Pursuant to the Maintenance Agreement he had entered with the Commonwealth, however, testator was billed and paid less than thirty-seven percent of the cost of William's care, the agreed amount of $200.00 per month. William's Social Security payments and veteran's benefits available to him as a dependent were used to defray his expenses, and the balance was subsidized by the Commonwealth.

Thus, during his lifetime, testator had accepted the Commonwealth's help in the form of partial subsidization of William's maintenance at Cresson. The Commonwealth had indicated its ability and willingness to provide this help in executing the Maintenance Agreement. When testator died, in 1968, he could not have known that the Legislature would later amend the Mental Health Act. We cannot know for a certainty what form of trust he would have chosen to set up had the Legislature amended the act prior to his death or had he lived to see the amendment relieving him of his legal duty to support William.[34] Given the choices we do know testator made regarding William's support during his lifetime, and the choices he made in setting up his will and the trust, we conclude that testator intended this trust to supplement other resources available to William and to provide for his basic support only to the extent such other resources should prove inadequate or be discontinued. . . .

Courts in several states have directly addressed the issue of whether the state may obtain reimbursement from a trust for an institutionalized beneficiary's care, and have answered in the negative. . . .

Many of these courts have refused to require reimbursement from a trust of state funds expended for an institutionalized beneficiary's care because they considered the trust purely discretionary, though it contained a general standard for the trustee to use in exercising his discretion to provide support. These courts apparently use the designation "support trust"

---

34. During his lifetime, statutory law on the issue of liability for costs of institutionalization was set forth in the Mental Health Act as follows:

[W]henever any person admitted, committed or otherwise receiving any service or benefit under this act shall be unable to discharge the obligation imposed upon him . . . such liability is hereby imposed upon any person owing a legal duty to support the person admitted, committed or otherwise receiving services or benefits under this act.

Mental Health Act, supra, § 502 (amended 1974).

and "discretionary trust" to label, respectively, those trusts from which distribution can be compelled as opposed to those in which the trustee's broad discretion is controlled only by the duty of loyalty and obligation of good faith.

We believe such a rigid categorization is unwarranted and ignores the intent of a settlor who includes both support and discretionary language in his trust instrument, by substituting mechanical rules for individual facts. Interpretation of such a trust as a pure support trust will deplete trust assets if invasion of principal is allowed, leaving nothing for remaindermen and ensuring only a minimal level of support for the institutionalized beneficiary during his lifetime. Once trust assets are gone, the beneficiary must look to his family or the state for care. In the event of an emergency, such care might not be forthcoming, or be inadequate—conditions known from time to time to affect those wholly dependent on public funds and the vagaries of legislative appropriation processes. If the trust is interpreted as purely discretionary, on the other hand, the beneficiary will be unable to compel distributions despite the trustee's failure to follow the standard for such distributions imposed by the governing instrument.

A settlor should not be required to either bankrupt his family or run the risk of leaving a handicapped member destitute or in want because of vagaries in the requirements for public assistance or in the level of funding for such assistance. Nor should he be required to place blind faith in the uncontrolled discretion of an individual trustee, whom the beneficiary may survive, or in a corporate trustee whose ownership, management and policies may change. We believe a settlor is entitled to maintain some control by means of a support standard, and at the same time reasonable flexibility through a grant of considerable discretion to the trustee(s), to ensure his purpose of providing reasonable care to the beneficiary who is or may be institutionalized without effectively disinheriting the other members of his family.

It is our responsibility to interpret this testamentary trust so that the intention of the testator will prevail. Requiring use of trust assets until income is depleted and principal reduced to $1,500 benefits the Commonwealth, not William and the other trust beneficiaries, and nullifies testator's intent.

In this trust, testator intended to provide support for William to the extent it was necessary. If state assistance is available for basic support, use of trust income or principal is not necessary for those basics. Interpreting the trust in the manner suggested by the Commonwealth is contrary to the public policy of this Commonwealth, as reflected in the General Assembly's 1974 amendment of the Mental Health Act. The state may and does properly require use of the income and assets of a person who receives care in a state institution or who is legally obligated to support the recipient of such services before drawing upon public funds. It should not be allowed to extort the assets of one who is under no such legal obligation before providing public support by imputing ownership or attributing a duty to support. Testator's legal obligation to support William ceased upon his death. Were testator alive today, he would have no legal duty to support

William under the 1974 amendment to the Mental Health Act. On this record, it would be anomalous to impose this duty on his trustee.

Should the Commonwealth plainly change its policy of providing public funds to its citizens who are mentally disabled, it could become necessary for William to look to the trust for basic support, and if so, he could compel distribution upon the trustee's unreasonable failure to help him. The trustee would then be required to exercise her discretion in William's favor by the standard set in the trust: "[T]he Trustee shall pay the Income periodically to or for the support, maintenance, welfare and benefit of [William]" and "shall use so much of the principal as may in her opinion be advisable therefor for the support, maintenance, welfare [and] comfort of [William]."

However, trustee does not abuse the broad discretion granted her under this trust by refusing to use income or principal for William's basic support when public funds are available from the Commonwealth. Thus, under the present circumstances, William cannot compel distribution of trust income or assets for his basic support, and they are, therefore, not resources available to him.

Commonwealth Court erred in concluding that the trust is an asset or an "available resource" for purposes of determining William's liability to reimburse the state for the costs of his care or his eligibility for medical assistance. Accordingly, its order is reversed. . . .

Notes

1. *Drafting Implications.* There has been considerable litigation in recent years concerning the question posed in *Lang*, the right of a state to reimbursement from a trust for care of an institutionalized person. Virtually all of these cases involved trusts that simultaneously confer discretion on the trustee and impose a support standard. Unlike the analysis of the court in *Lang*, the standard analysis is that the right of the state turns on whether the trust language creates a discretionary trust or a support trust. If a discretionary trust, then the state's claim is denied on the ground that the beneficiary lacks an ascertainable interest in income or principal that is subject to creditor claims. See, e.g., Miller v. Department of Mental Health, 432 Mich. 426, 442 N.W.2d 617 (1989); First Nat'l Bank v. Dep't of Health & Mental Hygiene, 284 Md. 720, 399 A.2d 821 (1979).

The approach adopted in *Lang* and the other decisions offers estate planners an easy route for achieving the same result as *Lang*, but at minimal risk. Because both *Lang* and the other cases accept the idea that the settlor's intention is to be given effect, the planning lesson is clear: In drafting discretionary or discretionary-support trusts for disabled beneficiaries, explicitly direct the trustee to take into account the benefits of medical or other forms of assistance the beneficiary may receive or be entitled to from any state or federal government or governmental agency; provide that the trust income or income and principal is to be used as a supplement to rather than a replacement of such funds; and provide that the income or income and principal is to be used in such manner as not to forfeit or reduce benefit eligibility where such benefits are available.

Recommendations similar to these abound in the literature. See, e.g., Ass'n for Retarded Citizens, How to Provide for Their Future (1989); Lombard, Planning for Disability: Durable Powers, Standby Trusts and Preserving Eligibility for Governmental Benefits, 20 Inst. on Est. Plan. ch. 17 (1986); Massey, Protecting the Mentally Incompetent Child's Trust Interest from State Reimbursement Claims, 58 Denver L.J. 557 (1981); Verbofsky, Parents of Disabled Children Benefit from Lang Case, 126 Tr. & Est. 16 (Dec. 1987).

2. *Legislation.* A number of states have specifically addressed the problem statutorily, but the thrust and scope of the legislation varies considerably. Perhaps the most troublesome for estate planners is the New Jersey statute, which provides:

> *N.J. Stat. Ann. § 30:4D-6.* Any provision in a . . . will, trust agreement or other instrument which reduces or excludes coverage or payment for goods and services to an individual because of that individual's eligibility for or receipt of Medicaid benefits shall be null and void, and no payments shall be made under this act as a result of any such provision.

The validity of the New Jersey statute is questionable in view of the federal Social Security Act, which requires that state Medicaid plans "provide for taking into account only such income and resources as are, as determined in accordance with standards prescribed by the Secretary, available to the applicant." 42 U.S.C. § 1396(a)(17). The "standards prescribed by the Secretary" provide that "resources are considered available both when actually available and when the applicant or recipient has a legal interest in a liquidated sum and has the legal ability to make such sum available for support and maintenance." 45 C.F.R. § 233.20(a)(3)(D). In Tidrow v. Director, Missouri State Division of Family Services, 688 S.W.2d 9, 13 (Mo. Ct. App. 1985), the court held that the state's determination that the beneficiary of a discretionary-support trust was ineligible for state assistance under its standard of eligibility was erroneous because the broader federal standard under the Social Security Act preempts the more restrictive state standard.

3. *Statutory Discretionary-Support Trusts Under Uniforms Acts.* Under section 9(b) of the Uniform Custodial Trust Act, the custodial trustee for an incapacitated beneficiary is authorized to make expenditures for support "without regard to other support, income, or property of the beneficiary." Note that, in providing a statutory discretionary-support trust for an incapacitated surviving spouse on whose behalf an elective share is taken, the Uniform Probate Code incorporates the Uniform Custodial Trust Act. In doing so, however, the UPC makes certain adjustments to the Custodial Trust Act, including an adjustment to section 9(b). Under UPC section 2-203(c)(2), the custodial trustee is *required* to take "other support, income, and property of the [incapacitated surviving spouse]" into account in making expenditures for support; enacting states, however, are given a choice as to whether the items to be taken into account include or do not

include "benefits of medical or other forms of assistance from any state or federal government or governmental agency for which the [incapacitated surviving spouse] must qualify on the basis of need."

PART B. TERMINATION (OR MODIFICATION) BY THE BENEFICIARIES

As stated at the beginning of this chapter, a fundamental policy question that courts frequently face when the preferences of the settlor and the trust beneficiaries conflict is which side the law should empower. In this part, we consider another aspect of this question: Once a trust has been properly formed, should the law ensure that it will endure? Or should the law enable the beneficiaries to undo or alter the trust against the previously stated or implied wishes of the settlor?

Consider, again, Example 12.1, supra p. 666, where A and X—both of whom are competent adults—prefer cash to their income and remainder interests in the spendthrift trust created by A's mother, G. Recall that under English law, A and X could fulfill their wish by either finding a buyer or buyers for their interests (disabling restraints on alienation being invalid in England) or terminating the trust.

In the United States, however, spendthrift restraints, as we have seen, are valid in the vast majority of states. A and X can neither sell their interests nor borrow against them. In their quest for cash, of course, the inalienability of their interests would not be of much concern if they could terminate the trust. Practically speaking, third-party purchasers are like the "good man" in the song—they're hard to find. The trust itself is a far more promising source of cash.[35]

Under English law, as noted, A and X could compel the termination of the trust. In Saunders v. Vautier, 4 Beav. 115, 49 Eng. Rep. 282 (Ch. 1841), the testator, Richard Wright, died in 1832, devising all his East India stock (worth £2,000) to trustees, in trust, directing them to accumulate the interest and dividends accruing thereon until his great-nephew, Daniel Wright Vautier, became 25; when Daniel became 25, the trustees were to transfer the East India stock, together with the accumulated interest and dividends, to Daniel, absolutely.

Daniel had grander ideas. Promptly upon becoming 21, in March, 1841, Daniel petitioned the court for the fund's immediate transfer to him. Lord Langdale, the Master of the Rolls, upheld Daniel's claim, saying:

---

35. Actually, on termination, the trust assets would probably be distributed in kind; see, e.g., Restatement 2d of Trusts §§ 344-47; Cal. Prob. Code § 15410. Generally speaking, for federal income-tax purposes, the beneficiaries' basis in trust assets distributed to them in kind is the adjusted basis of the property in the hands of the trustee; the trustee can elect, however, to recognize gain or loss on the distribution, in which case the beneficiaries' basis is the fair market value of the property on the date of distribution. IRC § 643(e).

I think that principle has been repeatedly acted upon; and where a legacy is directed to accumulate for a certain period, or where the payment is postponed, the legatee, if he has an absolute indefeasible interest in the legacy, is not bound to wait until the expiration of that period, but may require payment the moment he is competent to give a valid discharge.

On appeal, Lord Langdale's decision was affirmed by the Chancellor, Lord Cottenham. Saunders v. Vautier, Cr. & Ph. 240, 41 Eng. Rep. 482 (1841).

In his article, The Dead Hand and the Law of Trusts in the Nineteenth Century, 37 Stan. L. Rev. 1189, 1201 (1985), Professor Alexander gives this account of the developments following *Saunders:*

> Although the doctrine of *Saunders* was not accepted by the House of Lords until some fifty years later,[36] it was quickly and widely followed in equity practice. In Curtis v. Luken, decided in 1842,[37] the Master of the Rolls explained the *Saunders* doctrine:
>
>> [The beneficiary] has the legal power of disposing of it, he may sell, charge, or assign it, for he has an absolute, indefeasible interest in a thing defined and certain; the Court, therefore, has thought fit . . . to say, that since the legatee has such the legal right and power over the property, and can deal with it as he pleases, it will not subject him to the disadvantage of raising money by selling or charging his interest, when the thing is his own, at this very moment.[38]
>
> The court here explicitly connected the question of a beneficiary's power to compel termination in anticipation of the time prescribed by the trustor with the question of the beneficiary's power to alienate his equitable interest. Since no valid restraint could be imposed upon an equitable fee, a provision postponing possession of the trust estate could not be given effect, since it would be inconsistent with the property given to him. The *Saunders* doctrine thereafter was understood to require premature termination when all parties having an equitable interest in the trust and having legal capacity to consent petitioned for termination and distribution of the trust estate.
>
> The English doctrine was generally followed by American courts prior to 1889.[39] Since American courts had followed the English position on the validity of restraints on alienation of equitable interests, including equitable fees and more limited interests such as life estates in income, it was to be expected that they would not enforce provisions postponing possession of trust property by legally competent beneficiaries who, individually or collectively, held the entire equitable interest.

---

36. Wharton v. Masterman, 1895 App. Cas. 186 (H.L.).

37. 5 Beav. 147, 49 Eng. Rep. 533 (Ch. 1842).

38. Id. at 156, 49 Eng. Rep. at 536.

39. E.g., Sanford v. Lackland, 21 Fed. Cas. 358 (C.C.D. Mo. 1871) (No. 12,312); Gray v. Obear, 54 Ga. 231 (1875); Thompson v. Ballard, 70 Md. 10, 16 A. 378 (1889); Philadelphia v. Girard, 45 Pa. 9, 27 (1863).

Claflin v. Claflin
149 Mass. 19, 20 N.E. 454 (1889)

FIELD, J. By the eleventh article of his will, as modified by a codicil, Wilbur F. Claflin gave all the residue of his personal estate to trustees,

> to sell and dispose of the same, and to pay to my wife, Mary A. Claflin, one-third part of the proceeds thereof, and to pay to my son Clarence A. Claflin, one-third part of the proceeds thereof, and to pay the remaining one-third thereof to my son Adelbert E. Claflin, in the manner following, viz.: Ten thousand dollars when he is of the age of twenty-one years, ten thousand dollars when he is of the age of twenty-five years, and the balance when he is of the age of thirty years.

Apparently, Adelbert E. Claflin was not quite 21 years old when his father died, but he some time ago reached that age, and received $10,000 from the trust. He has not yet reached the age of 25 years, and he brings this bill to compel the trustees to pay to him the remainder of the trust fund. His contention is, in effect, that the provisions of the will postponing the payment of the money beyond the time when he is 21 years are void. There is no doubt that his interest in the trust fund is vested and absolute, and that no other person has any interest in it; and the authority is undisputed that the provisions postponing payment to him until some time after he reaches the age of 21 years would be treated as void by those courts which hold that restrictions against the alienation of absolute interests in the income of trust property are void. There has indeed, been no decision of this question in England by the House of Lords, and but one by a Lord Chancellor, but there are several decisions to this effect by Masters of the Rolls, and by Vice-Chancellors.

These decisions do not proceed on the ground that it was the intention of the testator that the property should be conveyed to the beneficiary on his reaching the age of 21 years, because in each case it was clear that such was not his intention, but on the ground that the direction to withhold the possession of the property from the beneficiary after he reached his majority was inconsistent with the absolute rights of property given him by the will.

This court has ordered trust property conveyed by the trustee to the beneficiary when there was a dry trust, or when the purposes of the trust had been accomplished, or when no good reason was shown why the trust should continue, and all the persons interested in it were *sui juris*, and desired that it be terminated; but we have found no expression of any opinion in our reports that provisions requiring a trustee to hold and manage the trust property until the beneficiary reached an age beyond that of 21 years are void if the interest of the beneficiary is vested and absolute. This is not a dry trust, nor have the purposes of the trust been accomplished, if the intention of the testator is to be carried out. . . .

In the case at bar nothing has happened which the testator did not anticipate, and for which he has not made provision. It is plainly his will that neither the income nor any part of the principal should now be paid to the plaintiff. It is true that the plaintiff's interest is alienable by him, and can be taken by his creditors to pay his debts, but it does not follow because the testator has not imposed all possible restrictions that the restrictions which he has imposed should not be carried into effect.

The decision in Broadway National Bank v. Adams, 133 Mass. 170, rests upon the doctrine that a testator has a right to dispose of his own property with such restrictions and limitations, not repugnant to law, as he sees fit, and that his intentions ought to be carried out, unless they contravene some positive rule of law, or are against public policy. The rule contended for by the plaintiff in that case was founded upon the same considerations as that contended for by the plaintiff in this, and the grounds on which this court declined to follow the English rule in that case are applicable to this; and for the reasons there given we are unable to see that the directions of the testator to the trustees to pay the money to the plaintiff when he reaches the ages of 25 and 30 years are against public policy, or are so far inconsistent with the rights of property given to the plaintiff these restrictions upon the plaintiff's possession and control of the property are altogether useless, for there is not the same danger that he will spend the property while it is in the hands of the trustees as there would be if it were in his own. . . .

Decree affirmed.

Note

State of the Authorities. The *Claflin* doctrine is widely followed in this country. See Scott on Trusts § 337. The American rule, as expressed in Restatement 2d of Trusts section 337, is that the beneficiaries of a trust cannot compel the trust's premature termination (or modification) unless: (i) all beneficiaries consent (and are competent to do so) and (ii) premature termination (or modification) will not defeat a "material purpose" of the trust.

1. Material Purpose

Trusts that contain a "material purpose," precluding their premature termination or modification, are sometimes called indestructible trusts. Basically, postponement-of-enjoyment, spendthrift, support, and discretionary trusts are deemed to contain a material purpose, making them indestructible.

Postponement-of-Enjoyment Trusts. In the case of a postponement-of-enjoyment trust, such as in *Claflin* (and *Saunders*), the settlor wants the beneficiary to have the trust property and its income, but not until the beneficiary reaches a specified age, a certain period of time has elapsed, or a certain date. Obviously, the settlor's purpose ("material" purpose) would be defeated if the beneficiary were permitted to obtain the trust property earlier.

A postponement-of-enjoyment trust sometimes has only one beneficiary. A key factor in making the trusts in *Claflin* and *Saunders* of this single-beneficiary variety was the fact that the beneficiary's interest was indefeasibly vested, giving the beneficiary an equitable fee. This is not a necessary element of a postponement-of-enjoyment trust, however; the beneficiary's interest can be and often is conditioned on surviving the specified age (or on surviving the specified period of time or date certain), with a gift over to another on the beneficiary's failure to survive. Thus the following trust is considered a postponement-of-enjoyment trust:

> *Example 12.2:* G died, devising property in trust, to pay the income to A until A reaches 35 and to pay the principal to A when A reaches that age; but if A dies before reaching 35, to pay the principal to B upon A's death.
> Even though A (age 28) and B desire to terminate the trust, they cannot do so.

Typically, a spendthrift clause is included in postponement-of-enjoyment trusts. Judged by estate-planning practices of today, the trust in *Claflin* is unusual for its absence of a spendthrift restraint. The absence of such a restraint in a similar case, Moxley v. Title Insurance & Trust Co., 27 Cal. 2d 457, 165 P.2d 15 (1946), led Justice Traynor (in dissent) to launch an assault upon the *Claflin* doctrine. Peggy Ann Moxley was the principal beneficiary of a testamentary trust created by her mother, Mabelle E. Kent. By its terms, the trust was to continue until Peggy Ann was 35 years old. Peggy Ann sought termination at age 26, alleging that she was "happily married and living with her husband, capable of managing the estate left in trust by her mother, and is desirous of purchasing a home."

The court refused to order termination of the trust. Dissenting, Justice Traynor argued that a "court will better serve the intentions of the settlor by weighing the actual interests of the beneficiary of a trust in its termination against the benefits intended by its continuance." In other words, since in the absence of a spendthrift restriction the settlor's dominant intention is to benefit the beneficiary, the court should permit premature termination where there is no spendthrift, support, or other more specific motive for the trust. The effect of the decision in *Moxley* was to prevent a beneficiary from using the trust funds for urgent needs or highly desirable purposes. To Justice Traynor, such an effect was incongruous since it would not prevent the beneficiary from selling her equitable interest in the trust. Since a purchaser of that interest could not obtain the trust property before the end of the period specified in the trust instrument, it is unlikely, Traynor argued, that the purchaser would pay a price commensurate with the present value of the interest.

Identifying this incongruity is not a very telling revelation, however. One answer to it is that although theoretically marketable, beneficial interests in indestructible trusts are practically unmarketable. The beneficiary often is unaware of the power to sell, and few willing buyers for such interests exist. See Cleary, Indestructible Testamentary Trusts, 43 Yale L.J. 393, 400 (1934).

Of course, the practical inalienability of beneficial interests such as those held by Adelbert Claflin in the *Claflin* case and Peggy Ann Moxley in the *Moxley* case might largely disappear if the beneficiary's assignee could compel termination of the trust. A supply of willing buyers likely would emerge. Deals could be structured in a variety of ways to ensure assignees a profit, after expenses (including legal fees) and other risks. Consequently, the *Claflin* rule—to have any force—requires that the beneficiary's assignee also be precluded from compelling the termination of the trust. Thus, Comment k to section 337 of the Restatement 2d of Trusts states that provisions postponing termination of the trust are effective against all assignees as well as the original beneficiary. The cases support the Restatement's position on this point, although such cases are not numerous. See, e.g., Stier v. Nashville Trust Co., 158 F. 601 (6th Cir. 1908); Will of Hamburger, 185 Wis. 270, 201 N.W. 267 (1924). But see, e.g., Sanford v. Lackland, 2 Dill. 6, F. Cas. (C.C.D. Mo. 1871) (No. 12,312).

Apart from the practical inalienability of beneficial interests, most indestructible trusts create beneficial interests that are legally inalienable, also.

Spendthrift Trusts. According to the Restatement and substantial case authority, spendthrift trusts are indestructible. See Restatement 2d of Trusts § 337 comment l; Scott on Trusts § 337.2.

The recent California codification of trust law adheres to the traditional view, stating that "the court does not have discretion to permit termination of a trust" on petition of the beneficiaries if the trust "is subject to a valid restraint on transfer of the beneficiary's interest." Cal. Prob. Code § 15403(b). The Texas codification, however, breaks with tradition by stating that "the court shall consider spendthrift provisions as a factor in making its decision whether to modify or terminate, but the court is not precluded from exercising its discretion to modify or terminate solely because the trust is a spendthrift trust." Tex. Prop. Code § 112.054(b).

Support Trusts/Discretionary Trusts. Support trusts and discretionary trusts are indestructible. See Restatement 2d of Trusts § 337 comments m & n; cases cited in Scott on Trusts § 337.4.

Successive-Beneficiary (Straight-Income) Trusts Without Spendthrift Provisions. Are there any trusts that *can* be terminated (or modified) by the beneficiaries, trusts that are not indestructible? The Restatement 2d of Trusts section 337 comment f presumptively treats successive-beneficiary trusts as destructible, for example, income to A for life, remainder in principal at A's death to B. The reason given is that the creation of a successive-beneficiary trust "does not of itself indicate that it was a material purpose of the trust to deprive the beneficiaries of the management of the trust property for the period of the trust." Instead, "the inference is that the only purpose of the trust is to give the beneficial interest in the trust property to one beneficiary for a designated period and to preserve the principal for the other beneficiary. . . ." This is a purpose not deemed to be "material."

Schmucker v. Walker
226 Va. 582, 311 S.E.2d 108 (1984)

STEPHENSON, J. In this appeal, we consider a court's authority to dissolve a testamentary trust before the time of termination expressed in the will.

Appellant, Grace Walker Schmucker, is the trustee of a testamentary trust created by her mother, Elizabeth Sawyer Walker. The appellees,[40] grandchildren of the testatrix, are the remaindermen-beneficiaries of the trust. They filed a bill for declaratory judgment alleging that the purpose of the trust had been accomplished and praying that the trust be terminated and the trust property delivered to them. In her answer, the trustee denied that the trust's purpose had been accomplished and asserted that the powers granted to her by the will should continue until the trust is terminated according to the testatrix's expressed intention.

Following an *ore tenus* hearing, the trial court decreed that the trust be terminated because the trustee "has no further interest, right or responsibility pertaining to the trust property." The decree enjoined the trustee from selling the property and vested fee simple ownership thereof in the appellees. The trustee appeals from this decree.

The clause of the will pertinent to this appeal provides:

> I give, devise and bequeath my property situate at number 3006 McLemore Street in the City of Norfolk, Virginia, together with all improvements thereon, to Grace Walker Schmucker, as Trustee. Said Trustee shall hold said property for the use and benefit of my son, Pealage P. Walker, for and during his lifetime, and upon his death, for the use and benefit of his widow, Edith Lenore Walker, should she be then surviving, until her death or until she should remarry, whichever shall first occur, and upon the death of Pealage P. Walker and the death or remarriage of Edith Lenore Walker, I give and devise this property to their children or the issue of any deceased children, per stirpes, in fee simple. This property, in the sole judgment of my Trustee during the term of any trust, may be sold and disposed of by her in accordance with the general power of sale contained in this my Will.

The will also gives the trustee "full discretionary powers of management" of the trust. These include collecting rents, paying proper costs and expenses, selling trust property, and holding and reinvesting the proceeds "until [they are] finally delivered and distributed" according to the terms of the will.

The testatrix died January 6, 1967. Pealage P. Walker, one of the life beneficiaries, died October 17, 1977. His wife, Edith, the other life beneficiary, continued to live on the property until she moved in April, 1979. In April, 1980, Edith conveyed her interest in the property to the appellees, the remaindermen-beneficiaries of the trust, but the trustee did not join in this conveyance. Edith is still alive and has not remarried.

---

40. The appellees are Pealage P. Walker, IV, Wesley F. Walker, James M. Walker, Rae W. Cox, and Lenore E. Walker.

After Edith moved, the trustee decided to sell the property and to hold and invest the proceeds for Edith's benefit. The appellees initially agreed to a sale, but, after the trustee executed a contract agreeing to sell the property, they changed their minds. Thereafter, they instituted this suit and filed a memorandum of *lis pendens* (Code § 8.01-268) against the property.

While Pealage and Edith lived on the property, they, rather than the trustee, paid the taxes and insurance. The trustee testified, however, that she did not exercise these powers while her brother and his wife occupied the property because she "did not wish to interfere with them." The trustee further testified that she had "nothing to gain financially" by contesting this suit, "but she only wants her deceased mother's wishes and intentions followed."

The appellees contend that since all the beneficiaries are sui juris, they can demand delivery of the trust property and thereby terminate the trust. They rely in the main on Rowley v. American Trust Co., 144 Va. 375, 132 S.E. 347 (1926), and Thom v. Thom, 95 Va. 413, 28 S.E. 583 (1897). The trustee, on the other hand, largely relying upon Telephones, Inc. v. LaPrade, 206 Va. 388, 143 S.E.2d 853 (1965), contends that a voluntary termination of the trust by the beneficiaries runs counter to the testatrix's intention.

We have recognized "that, generally, if all the beneficiaries of a trust are sui juris and all concur in a demand for delivery in kind of the trust assets, the trustees are obligated to make such delivery and thereby terminate the trust." LaPrade at 397, 143 S.E.2d at 859. However, when "no considerations of public policy are involved, and the trust is active, rather than passive," the foregoing rule must yield to the principle that when a settlor expresses a clear intention that the beneficiaries shall not terminate the trust by compelling delivery, the courts must uphold the settlor's expressed intention. Id. This principle of law is especially true when "the [trustee is] vested with broad discretionary powers. . . ." Id.

Applying these principles, we conclude that the trial court erred in terminating the trust. It is apparent that the testatrix intended that the trustee exercise her powers until Edith, the second life beneficiary, either died or remarried. Indeed, the will expressly provides that "[t]his property, *in the sole judgment of my trustee during the term of any trust*, may be sold and disposed of by her in accordance with the general power of sale contained in this my Will." (Emphasis added.) The will also gives the trustee "full discretionary powers" to sell the property, to reinvest the proceeds of sale, and to manage the trust. This language compares favorably with the "absolute discretion" given to the trustees in LaPrade. Id. at 398, 143 S.E.2d at 859.

Obviously, the testatrix intended the trust to be active rather than passive. In a passive trust, the trustee has no active duty to perform but is merely the receptacle of the legal title. G. Bogert, The Law of Trusts and Trustees, § 207 (2d ed. 1979 and Supp.1982).

There is another compelling reason for rejecting the beneficiaries' attempt to terminate the trust. The will states that upon "the death or remarriage of Edith" the property passes to the children of Pealage and

Edith "or the issue of any deceased children per stirpes, in fee simple." Therefore, until the event occurs which will terminate the trust (Edith's death or remarriage), it is not possible to ascertain precisely who will be in the class of remaindermen contemplated by the testatrix. For example, should one of Edith's children die leaving issue before Edith either died or remarried, the class of beneficiaries would open for such issue. Consequently, a premature termination of the trust by the beneficiaries could abridge the rights of undetermined parties. See Roberts v. Scyphers, 128 Va. 85, 104 S.E. 698 (1920).

Rowley and Thom, relied upon by the appellees, are readily distinguishable. In neither case did the trustee have the broad discretionary powers found in LaPrade and the present case. Moreover, both the Rowley and Thom trusts clearly named all the beneficiaries, and, unlike the present case, there was no possibility of the class of beneficiaries changing after the settlor's death.

For these reasons, we will reverse the judgment of the trial court and enter final judgment for the trustee.

Reversed and final judgment.

Notes

1. *Acquiescence by the Trustee.* In the *Claflin* and *Schmucker* cases, the trustees acted in accordance with the settlor's purposes and resisted the beneficiaries' demands for termination of the trusts. Suppose, however, the trustees had breached their trusts by acquiescing in the beneficiaries' demands. The Restatement 2d of Trusts section 342 states that "the trust terminates although the purposes of the trust have not been fully accomplished." The rationale given by the Restatement is that "the beneficiary cannot hold the trustee liable for an act or omission of the trustee as a breach of trust if the beneficiary consented to it." Restatement 2d of Trusts § 342 comment a.

Although case authority exists that directly supports the Restatement position, at least one court has expressed disapproval of such action by a trustee. See Whitney v. Whitney, 317 Mass. 253, 57 N.E.2d 913 (1944).

Does the trustee of a spendthrift trust run even greater risks in acquiescing in the trust's premature termination? The Restatement 2d of Trusts section 342 comment f says no, but decisions from New York and Pennsylvania demonstrate that the trustee runs very real risks in joining with the beneficiaries in putting an end to the trust. See Stambaugh's Estate, 135 Pa. 585, 19 A. 1058 (1890); Matter of Wentworth, 230 N.Y. 176, 129 N.E. 646 (1920). In each of these cases, the trustee in effect terminated the trust in whole or in part by transferring trust property to a third person with the consent of a beneficiary who was protected by a spendthrift clause. The trustee was held accountable to the consenting beneficiary for the amount of his interest diverted to the third person.

2. *Consent of the Settlor.* Although a trust contains a "material purpose," it is widely (though not universally) held that the beneficiaries can compel

its termination (or modification) if they obtain the settlor's consent. See Restatement 2d of Trusts § 338.

3. *Permissible Duration of Indestructible Trusts.* Apart from statute (and an occasional judicial aberration), there is no direct legal limit on the duration of a trust. There probably is, however, a limit on the time during which a trust may be made indestructible. As yet, the cases are far from conclusive as to just what time limit will be imposed, but the writers have usually assumed that it will be the period of the Rule Against Perpetuities, that is, lives in being plus 21 years or a reasonable approximation thereof as established in the Uniform Statutory Rule Against Perpetuities (USRAP). See Restatement 2d of Trusts § 62 comment o; Restatement 2d of Property § 2.1; USRAP § 1 comment.

A trust meant to be indestructible for a longer period is valid, but subject to termination at suit of the beneficiaries, either from the inception of the trust (as some writers assert) or, more probably, and as set forth in the Restatements and the Comment to USRAP, at the expiration of the permissible period. In 1959, California enacted a statute stating that "a provision, express or implied, in the instrument creating the trust that the trust may not be terminated is ineffective insofar as it purports to be applicable beyond" the permissible perpetuity period. Cal. Civ. Code § 716.5.

4. *Annuities.* In Parker v. Cobe, 208 Mass. 260, 94 N.E. 476 (1911), a will devised $75,000 "to be used to purchase an annuity or annuities for Ruth H. Cobe, my niece, the payments thereof to be paid to her quarterly, if that can be done." Ruth demanded the sum of $75,000 instead of the annuity and the court held that she was entitled to it. The court, relying almost entirely on English cases, gave the following reason for its decision:

> The reasoning on which the rule is established is that the legatee can sell the [annuity] as soon as it is bought and the law will not require the performance of a nugatory act.

Is the decision of the Massachusetts court in Parker v. Cobe consistent with its decision in Claflin v. Claflin?

New York took the same position as Massachusetts and for a time the cases from these states were regarded as indicative of the probable course of American law. Later cases, however, have rejected the beneficiary's claim to the capital sum. See, e.g., Morgenthaler v. First Atlantic Nat'l Bank, 80 So.2d 446, 54 A.L.R.2d 353 (Fla. 1955).

New York has changed its rule by a statute providing that the annuitant "may not elect to take the capital sum directed to be used for the purchase of [the] annuity in lieu thereof, unless the will expressly confers such right or except as the will expressly provides for the purchase of an assignable annuity." N.Y. Est. Powers & Trusts Law § 3-3.9. Legislation similar to the New York statute has been adopted in a few other states. See, e.g., Ind. Code Ann. § 29-1-17-10(b); Va. Code § 64.1-69.

2. Beneficiaries' Consent

Premature termination of a trust requires the consent of all of the beneficiaries, none of whom is under a legal incapacity. This is the sole requirement under English law. Under prevailing American law, it is a requirement additional to the no-material-purpose rule.

Problems

1. G, a widow, died, survived by her 55-year-old daughter, A; her 52-year-old son, B; A's 25-year-old child, X; and B's 22-year-old child, Y. G's will devised the residue of her estate in trust, without a spendthrift restraint. Whose consent is necessary to terminate G's trust, if the dispositive terms of the trust provided:

(a) Income to A for life, remainder in principal to X.

(b) Income to A for life, remainder in principal to X if X survives A.

(c) Income to A for life, remainder in principal to A's children.

Compare Bassett's Estate, 104 N.H. 504, 507, 190 A.2d 415, 417 (1963) ("This state rejects the 'notion' there is a conclusive presumption that a man or woman is always capable of bearing children regardless of age, physical condition and medical opinion to the contrary."); Restatement 2d of Trusts § 340 comment e ("If the unascertained beneficiaries are the children of a designated woman, and the woman is beyond the age of child bearing or otherwise physically incapable of bearing children, the court may terminate the trust."); and Cal. Prob. Code §§ 15406, 6152, with Clark v. Citizens & Southern Nat'l Bank, 243 Ga. 703, 706, 257 S.E.2d 244, 246 (1979) ("There is a conclusive presumption of Georgia law that the possibility of issue is not extinct in a female until death. . . . Even if this were not the law in Georgia, the class would be subject to reopening upon the adoption of a child or children by the daughter Elizabeth."). See Saver, Paulson & Lobo, A Preliminary Report on Oocyte Donation Extending Reproductive Potential to Women Over 40, 323 N. Eng. J. Med. 1157 (1990) (reporting that a post-menopausal woman can still become pregnant by implantation of an embryo produced by an egg donated by a younger woman and fertilized by sperm from a man, typically the older woman's husband); Waggoner, Perpetuity Reform, 81 Mich. L. Rev. 1718, 1728-34 (1983) (reporting on the possibility of an older woman (or man) adopting a child).

(d) Income to B for life, remainder in principal to B's children.

(e) Income to A for life, remainder in principal to A's descendants who survive A, by representation; if none, to A's heirs.

2. Would you reach a different answer in any of the cases in Problem 1 if G's trust were an irrevocable inter-vivos trust and if G were alive and gave her consent to the trust's termination?

3. G created a trust, directing the trustee to divide the income equally between A and B for 10 years and to divide the principal equally between A and B at the expiration of the 10-year period. A wants to try to get the

trust terminated, but B refuses to consent. Can A compel termination of half the trust? The Restatement 2d of Trusts provides that even though some of the beneficiaries do not consent to termination or are incapable of giving consent, "the court may decree a partial termination of the trust if the interests of the beneficiaries who do not consent or are under an incapacity are not prejudiced thereby and if the continuance of the trust is not necessary to carry out a material purpose of the trust." Restatement 2d of Trusts § 340 comment g, illustration 9.

4. G created a trust, directing the trustee to divide the income equally between A and B during their joint lives, and on A's death to pay half the principal to X and on B's death to pay the other half of the principal to Y. A and X want to try to get the trust terminated, but B and Y refuse to consent. Can A and X compel termination of half the trust? See Shaller v. Mississippi Valley Trust Co., 319 Mo. 128, 3 S.W.2d 726 (1928).

———

Settlor's Right as Sole Beneficiary to Terminate. In Phillips v. Lowe, 639 S.W.2d 782 (Ky. 1982), the court held that the settlor, who was the sole beneficiary of a trust, could terminate the trust, even though the trust instrument expressly declared that the trust was irrevocable. Accord, e.g., Woodruff v. Trust Co. of Georgia, 233 Ga. 135, 210 S.E.2d 321 (1974); Johnson v. First Nat'l Bank, 386 S.2d 1112 (Miss. 1980); Restatement 2d of Trusts § 339.

It should go without saying that if the settlor is not the sole beneficiary, she or he cannot unilaterally revoke, terminate, or modify an irrevocable trust. Note, however, that the mistake doctrine allows for such a trust to be rescinded or reformed to incorporate a power to revoke if it can be shown that the trust was created as the result of a "material mistake" or that the power was omitted by mistake. See Palmer on Restitution § 18.7(a); Berger v. United States, 487 F.Supp. 49 (W.D. Pa. 1980), supra p. 562.

Consent on Behalf of Minors, Incapacitated Persons, or Persons Under Disability. Section 340(1) of the Restatement 2d of Trusts states that if one or more of the beneficiaries is under an incapacity, "the *others* cannot compel the termination of the trust." Thus, for example, in Problem 1(a), supra p. 719, where the income from G's non-spendthrift trust was to be paid to A for life, remainder in principal to X, A could not compel the termination of the trust if X was a minor or incapacitated in some other way. Is it possible, however, for the court or X's conservator or guardian to join with A in consenting to the trust's termination? Some courts have held that consent can be given on the beneficiary's behalf by the guardian of the incapacitated beneficiary's property or the incapacitated beneficiary's conservator. See, e.g., Randall v. Randall, 60 F. Supp. 308 (S.D. Fla. 1944); Riedlin's Guardian v. Cobb, 222 Ky. 654, 1 S.W.2d 1071 (1928); Flexner's Trust, 56 Misc. 2d 336, 288 N.Y.S.2d 494, aff'd mem., 30 App. Div. 2d 1049, 294 N.Y.S.2d 669 (1968) (New York court expressed approval of a guardian of the property having authority to consent on behalf of his ward, and deferred to the order of a California court, which had held that the guardian had such authority, because California had more significant contacts with the trust). Contra, e.g., Application of Michael, 70 Misc. 2d 161, 333 N.Y.S.2d 301 (Sup. Ct. 1972). See also UPC §§ 5-407, 5-423.

To be contrasted with the problem of gaining consent on behalf of minors, incapacitated persons, or persons under a disability is the problem of unborn or unascertained beneficiaries. Can anyone consent on their behalf? Consider the following case.

Hatch v. Riggs National Bank
361 F.2d 559 (D.C. Cir. 1966)

[In 1923, the settlor created an irrevocable inter-vivos trust with spendthrift provisions, directing the trustees to pay the income to her for life; upon her death, the trustees were to pay the corpus as the settlor should appoint by will; and in default of appointment, the corpus was to go to "such of her next of kin . . . as by the law in force in the District of Columbia at the death of the . . . [settlor] shall be provided for in distribution of an intestate's personal property therein."

The settlor sought to modify the trust to obtain an additional stipend of $5000 a year, out of corpus, "to accommodate recently incurred expenses, and to live more nearly in accordance with her refined but yet modest tastes." The District Court found that there was "no suggestion of extravagance" in the settlor's way of life or in her request for additional funds. She lived in a one-bedroom apartment in a modest residential section of Long Beach, California, and had no assets except limited jewelry, furniture, personal effects, and a medium-priced automobile.

The settlor did not claim that the declaration of trust itself authorized her to revoke or modify the trust. In effect, she invoked the doctrine of worthier title, under which a purported inter-vivos transfer of a future interest to the heirs of the settlor presumptively creates a reversion in the settlor rather than a remainder in the settlor's heirs. She claimed that since she was the sole beneficiary of the trust under this doctrine, and was also the settlor, she had a right to revoke or modify under accepted principles of trust law.

The District Court denied the settlor's claim, and she appealed.]

LEVENTHAL, C.J. [In a part of the opinion reprinted infra p. 962, the court refused to adopt the much-maligned doctrine of worthier title, and continued:]

It is hornbook law that any trust, no matter how "irrevocable" by its terms, may be revoked with the consent of the settlor and all beneficiaries.

The beneficiaries of the trust created by appellant are herself, as life tenant, and her heirs, as remaindermen. Her heirs, if determined as of the present time, are her two sisters. There is no assurance that they will in fact be the heirs who take the remainder under the trust; appellant might survive one or both. Yet their consent is necessary, we think, to revocation, since they are at least the persons who would be beneficiaries if the settlor died today.[41]

In addition, it is necessary to protect the interests of those additional persons, both living and unborn, who may, depending on circumstances, be members of the class of heirs at the time the corpus is distributed. We think that upon an adequate showing, by the party petitioning to revoke or modify the trust, that those who are, so to speak, the heirs as of the present time consent to the modification, and that there is a reasonable possibility that the modification that has been proposed adequately protects the interests of those other persons who might be heirs at the time the corpus is to be distributed, the District Court may appoint a guardian ad litem to represent the interests of those additional persons.

Although the question has not been previously discussed by this court we think basic principles of trust law are in accord with appointment of a guardian ad litem to represent interests of unborn or unascertained beneficiaries, for purposes of consent to modification or revocation of a trust. This use of a guardian ad litem is not uncommon in other jurisdictions. In a number of states authority for such appointments is provided by statute. These statutes reflect a broad sentiment of the approaches that are consistent with the Anglo-American system of law and adopted to promote the objective of justice. Where it is at least debatable whether rulings must await express legislative authorization, this court must take into account the fact that the legislature for the District of Columbia is primarily concerned with awesome questions of national policy, and we should be more ready to accept our obligation as a court to refine and adapt the corpus of law without waiting for a legislative go-ahead. Here we are certainly in a field where it is not inappropriate for courts to act without statutory foundation. . . . "Courts of justice as an incident of their jurisdiction have inherent power to appoint guardians ad litem." [Mabry v. Scott, 51 Cal. App. 2d 245, 124 P.2d 659 (1942).] The efficacy of a guardian ad litem appointed to protect the interests of unborn persons is no different whether he be appointed pursuant to statute or the court's inherent power. Given such protection, the equitable doctrine of representation embraces the flexibility, born of convenience and necessity, to act upon the interests of unborn contingent remaindermen to the same effect as if they had been *sui juris* and parties.

The use of guardians ad litem to represent interests of unborn and/or otherwise unascertainable beneficiaries of a trust seems to us wholly appropriate. Though the persons whose interests the guardian ad litem represents would be unascertainable as individuals, they are identifiable as a class and their interest, as such, recognizable.

The settlor seeking to revoke or modify the trust may supplement his appeal to equity with a quid pro quo offered to the heirs for their consent. In many cases it may well be consistent with or even in furtherance of the interest of the heirs to grant such consent. The case at bar provides a good

---

41. One of the sisters is not *sui juris*. In referring to her consent, we do not mean to exclude consent by her guardian ad litem.

example. Here the interest of all heirs is contingent, since appellant can defeat their remainder by exercising her testamentary power of appointment. If the modification agreed upon not only increased the annual income of the life tenant but also transferred assets in trust for the benefit of the heirs, without any power of alteration in the settlor, the heirs' remainder interest would be secure, and accordingly more valuable than it is now. The pattern of such a modification is clearly available where the remaindermen of a trust are specific named persons, and, we think, should also be available where the remaindermen are recognizable as a class even though the members of the class are not now individually ascertainable.

Appellant, proceeding on a different theory, has not taken steps to obtain the consent of heirs. We think it important to make clear that, in rejecting the doctrine of worthier title, we do not mean to put settlors and life tenants of trusts in which the remaindermen are the settlor's heirs at an unwarranted disadvantage with respect to legitimate efforts to modify trust arrangements concluded largely for their own benefit. Our affirmance of the judgment for appellees is without prejudice to a future submission by appellant on such a basis.

Affirmed.

Notes

1. *Revoking Irrevocable Trusts.* Not infrequently, settlors of irrevocable inter-vivos trusts share a common plight with that of the settlor in the *Hatch* case. Sometimes, the worthier-title doctrine has been successfully invoked. See, e.g., Stewart v. Merchants Nat'l Bank, 3 Ill. App. 3d 337, 278 N.E.2d 10 (1972). This works, however, only if the worthier-title doctrine is followed in the jurisdiction and is applicable to the particular case, i.e., if the beneficial interest is in the "heirs" of the settlor. Otherwise, despite the fact that the inter-vivos trust has proved to be improvident, an order to meet pressing needs of the settlor is often denied because of the impossibility of gaining the consent of unborn or unascertained beneficiaries. Improvidence of the trust is not usually held to provide a ground for rescission. See Palmer on Restitution § 18.7(a). Only occasionally has a decision ordered cancellation. See, e.g., Reuther v. Fidelity Union Trust Co., 116 N.J. Eq. 81, 172 A. 386 (1934).

Legislation in a few states has alleviated the problem, but in a variety of ways. In North Carolina, for example, the settlor is empowered to revoke provisions in favor of persons "not in esse or not determined until the happening of a future event," if the revocation is effected before "the happening of the contingency vesting the future estates" and if the trust instrument does not expressly provide otherwise. N.C. Gen. Stat. § 39-6.

New York authorizes the settlor to revoke a trust with the consent of "all the persons beneficially interested. . . ." N.Y. Est. Powers & Trusts Law § 7-1.9. The phrase "persons beneficially interested" has been interpreted as excluding possible unborn beneficiaries. See, e.g., Smith v. Title Guarantee & Trust Co., 287 N.Y. 500, 41 N.E.2d 72 (1942). Section 7-1.9 further provides that, for purposes of trust termination, a disposition in favor of a class of persons described only as heirs, next of kin, or distributees of the creator of the trust does not create a beneficial interest in such persons.

2. *Consent on Behalf of Unborn or Unascertained Beneficiaries.* The court in *Hatch* found a still different and quite novel solution to the settlor's plight. Many states, to be sure, have statutes authorizing the *appointment* of guardians ad litem to represent certain classes of persons (unborn, unascertained, incapacitated, or protected persons, minors, or persons whose identities or addresses are unknown). See, e.g., UPC § 1-403. But these statutes only authorize the appointment of a guardian ad litem to represent such persons *in litigation*.[42] These statutes address a compelling need, for some machinery is necessary to bind such parties by judgments; otherwise, many cases involving certain kinds of disputes or to establish title to property would be impossible to resolve conclusively. Many statutes, such as UPC section 1-403, apply to any formal proceeding or judicially supervised settlement, while other statutes specify the kinds of judicial proceedings in which the guardian ad litem is authorized to act, such as probate, quiet title, partition, trust accounting, or title registration. The statutes either expressly provide, or seem clearly to imply, that the result of such representation of unborn parties is to make the result of the litigation binding upon any person so represented who later comes into being.

Another doctrine under which unborn or unascertained persons are bound by litigation is that of *virtual representation*. Under this doctrine, which is generally held to be available to courts without legislation, unborn or unascertained persons are held to have been represented by living parties to a suit if the latter have the same or similar interests as those of the later-born or later-ascertained beneficiaries, and if the respective classes of interests are not otherwise adverse to one another. See generally UPC § 1-403; Petition of Wolcott, infra p. 726.

In suggesting the appointment of a guardian ad litem "for the purposes of consent to modification or revocation of a trust," the court in *Hatch* went beyond these traditional limits. Unfortunately, the court did not seem to notice the novelty of its approach. Instead, the discussion concentrated on the power of a court to *appoint* a guardian ad litem without statutory authority, not on the *functions* a guardian ad litem is authorized to perform. The same narrow focus of discussion occurred in a subsequent decision of the District Court in *Hatch*. Following up on the Court of Appeals's suggestion, a guardian ad litem was appointed and a modification agreement was reached. In reaching this agreement, the guardian ad litem acted for the unborn and unascertained beneficiaries; the court did not note whether the guardian ad litem also acted for the settlor's sister who was not *sui juris*. The trustee objected to the guardian ad litem's authority, claiming that the Circuit Court's discussion of this point was dictum. In Hatch v. Riggs Nat'l Bank, 284 F. Supp 396 (D.D.C. 1968), the District

---

42. Indeed, the term "guardian ad litem" means guardian for the purpose of the lawsuit.

Court approved the appointment and the modification agreement. The court did not disclose the terms of the modification agreement, but noted that it was satisfied that the agreed-upon modification "fully protect[s] the interests of any unborn heirs. . . ."

3. *Enabling Legislation.* Although no additional judicial adoption of the idea that a guardian ad litem can consent to a trust termination or modification has as yet been forthcoming, the California legislature has codified the idea in the following provision:

> *Cal. Prob. Code § 15405. Guardian ad litem.* For [the purposes of trust termination or modification], the consent of a beneficiary who lacks legal capacity, including a minor, or who is an unascertained or unborn person may be given in proceedings before the court by a guardian ad litem, if it would be appropriate to do so. In determining whether to give consent, the guardian ad litem may rely on general family benefit accruing to living members of the beneficiary's family as a basis for approving a modification or termination of the trust.

PART C. MODIFICATION (OR TERMINATION) BECAUSE OF UNANTICIPATED CIRCUMSTANCES

If the beneficiaries of a trust can compel its termination, they can instead compel a modification of its provisions. But suppose modification on petition of the beneficiaries is impossible, for example, because there are unborn or unascertained beneficiaries or because one or more of the living beneficiaries refuses to consent. The court still might modify or terminate the trust on the basis of unforeseen circumstances. Thus, the Restatement 2d of Trusts section 167 provides that the court will direct or permit the trustee to depart from the terms of the trust instrument if "owing to circumstances not known to the settlor and not anticipated by him compliance would defeat or substantially impair the accomplishment of the purposes of the trust. . . ." Furthermore, the trustee may deviate from the trust terms without prior court approval if the trustee reasonably believes that there is an emergency and if the trustee has no opportunity to apply for court approval before deviating.

1. Distributive Deviations

A trust beneficiary in need may seek to accelerate or increase her or his right to income or principal beyond that which is granted by the terms of the trust. Such deviations have been permitted in cases of single-beneficiary, postponement-of-enjoyment trusts—trusts, for example, in which the beneficiary is given income and principal upon attaining a certain age or at the end of some other period. See, e.g., Post v. Grand Rapids Trust Co.,

255 Mich. 436, 238 N.W. 206 (1931); Bennett v. Nashville Trust Co., 127 Tenn. 126, 153 S.W. 840 (1912). The deviation in such cases, of course, amounts to a judicially declared power to invade principal for support.[43]

Where, on the other hand, there are other beneficiaries who will be adversely affected by such a deviation, as where the corpus is given to one or more persons other than the income beneficiary, the deviation will usually be denied. See, e.g., Van Deusen's Estate, 30 Cal. 2d 285, 182 P.2d 565 (1947); Staley v. Ligon, 239 Md. 61, 210 A.2d 384 (1965); Matter of Rotermund, 61 Misc. 2d 324, 305 N.Y.S.2d 413 (Sur. Ct. 1969). Arguing that support of the income beneficiary was the testator's or settlor's primary purpose in establishing the trust has usually been to no avail. Justice Traynor's statement in the *Van Deusen's Estate* case is representative of dominant judicial philosophy on this point:

> If the courts could increase the payments under testamentary trusts without the consent of all the beneficiaries merely because the income therefrom is not what it was at the time the will was executed and because at one time or another the testator expressed the desire to provide adequately for the beneficiaries, there would be no stability to any testamentary trust in this state.

The Restatement 2d of Trusts section 168 comment d & illustration 5, however, declare that such a deviation will be judicially authorized "for the necessary support of the beneficiary where the will indicates that the support of the beneficiary was the primary purpose of the testator, even though the testator did not in express terms permit the invasion of the principal." Is Justice Traynor's statement inconsistent with this principle? Is Petition of Wolcott, below, merely an application of this principle, or does it go beyond it?

Petition of Wolcott
95 N.H. 23, 56 A.2d 641 (1948)

[Francis E. Getty died in 1944, leaving a will executed in 1932 that devised $2,500 to his widow, Ada C. Getty, $5,000 each to his two sons, and the residue of his estate in trust. The income from the trust was to be paid to Ada during her lifetime, and on her death the principal was to be paid to his then-living issue or, if none, to his heirs. The will conferred on the trustees broad discretionary powers concerning investment and management of trust assets, including the power to allocate receipts

---

43. Contrast Pierowich v. Metropolitan Life Ins. Co., 282 Mich. 118, 275 N.W. 789 (1937), where a mother, as guardian of the infant beneficiaries under a life-insurance contract, sought a decree for payment to them of sums from the insurance proceeds prior to the times specified in the insurance contract. In denying the petition, the court found that the arrangement created a contract, not a trust, and held that it was without power to modify the terms of a contract.

between income and principal and the power "generally to do all things in relation to the trust fund which the testator could have done if living."

The trustees sought authority to invade principal for Ms. Getty in an amount not to exceed $4,000 per year, on proof of her needs resulting from her advanced age and illness. The income amounted to about $2,300 per year and her needs were estimated at $5,800 per year; the trust principal was valued at $107,000. All living issue—the couple's two sons and an 18-year-old grandson, who was represented by a guardian ad litem—consented to the deviation.]

DUNCAN, J. . . . Despite broad discretionary powers conferred upon the trustees, the will contains no provision for the use of principal for the benefit of the widow. On the other hand, such use is not specifically forbidden. It may fairly be assumed that the beneficiary's need of the principal was not anticipated because of a failure to foresee changes which have occurred since the testator's death, including shrinkage in investment returns, decline in purchasing power, and the expense occasioned by the widow's extreme infirmity. The powers conferred upon the trustees as to investments and the allocation of receipts to income are indicative of a purpose to provide the widow with a liberal income, unrestricted by technical rules. No purpose to transmit any specific residuary amount to the sons or any other issue is disclosed. Fairly construed, the will evidences as its primary purpose "ample and certain provision" for the testator's wife.

What is sought by the petition is not construction of any particular provision of the will but rather authority to deviate from the provisions by which principal would be retained intact during the widow's lifetime. No reliance is placed by the trustees upon their general power "to do all things in relation to the trust which the testator could have done if living." The power is at best obscure in meaning, and if construed independently of other provisions, would have doubtful validity. Clark v. Campbell, 82 N.H. 281, 133 A. 166, 45 A.L.R. 1433. Because of the emergency confronting the life beneficiary, the trustees seek authority to do what the testator presumably would have authorized had he foreseen the emergency.

Where a remainder succeeding a life estate may ultimately vest in persons as yet undetermined and perhaps unborn, courts of equity have at times hesitated or refused to sanction an invasion of principal for the benefit of the life tenant. . . . In one view, permission is sought to appropriate to the use of one beneficiary the property of others without the consent of all. But this view, in our opinion, may be deemed applicable only to the extent the testator's disclosed intention affords it a foundation. Strictly speaking, it may prevent accomplishment of the testator's primary purpose. As is said in 2 Scott, Trusts, § 168, p. 855: "As a matter of strict logic it may be necessary to permit a child to suffer in order to protect the possible children which he may ultimately have, but it is difficult to believe that the settlor would ever desire such a result." Where the testator's desire may be gathered from the will, "strict logic" need not be controlling.

Traditionally, the courts of this jurisdiction have shown a signal regard for the intent of the testator . . . , at times at the expense of other recognized principles deemed less cogent in their application. Cf. Edgerly

v. Barker, 66 N.H. 434, 31 A. 900, 28 L.R.A. 328. In order to prevent impairment of a testator's primary purpose, authority to deviate from the express terms of a gift has been granted in cases of emergency unforeseen by him, even though contingent remainder interests were incidentally affected. . . .

In the will before us, the testator's purpose to furnish reasonable support for his wife is not expressed in words, but is nevertheless implicit in the disposition made of his estate. His direction that his wife should have the income was a means of executing his purpose, and is "properly to be read as subordinate to (his) paramount intention." In re Walker, [1901] 1 Ch. 879, 885. His intent to provide reasonable support to the widow being evident from the will, those whose interests are secondary to hers take subject to the execution of that intent. The remaindermen are deprived of no rights so long as rights which the life tenant was intended to have are not exceeded.

Because of circumstances not provided for by the will and obviously not anticipated by the testator, an emergency threatens accomplishment of his purpose by the means which he provided. Those whose interests are most immediate consent to the authorization sought by the trustees, and there is no objection by the guardian ad litem. If the consent or acquiescence of the parties is not binding upon unborn contingent remaindermen, still they are sufficiently represented by those having like interests to be bound by a decree. . . . In this situation a court of equity need not hesitate to exercise its undoubted power to permit a deviation from the literal provisions of the will. A means of accomplishing the testator's purpose is thereby furnished, which it may reasonably be inferred that he himself would have provided, had he been able to foresee the exigency. . . .

The trustees are advised that principal not in excess of $4,000 a year may be used to supplement the income of the trust, for the purpose of providing the widow with reasonable support, if the trial court shall find in accordance with the uncontroverted allegations of the petition, and it shall appear that the widow has no other income. In view of the discretion vested in the trustees by the testator, there is no reason why they may not safely be left to determine the amount of principal necessary within the limit specified, due regard being given to considerations of what is prudent and reasonable, and best calculated to accomplish the testator's purposes as a whole.

If the requisite findings are made, a decree in accordance with this opinion may be entered by the Superior Court.

Case discharged.

All concurred.

Notes and Questions

1. *Questions.* In what way was the testator's purpose to furnish reasonable support for his widow "implicit in the disposition made of his estate"?

Suppose the testator had directed his personal representative to determine the actuarial value of an income interest for life in favor of a person of his widow's age in a fund the value of his estate (minus the $12,500 pecuniary devises to his wife and sons), directing his executor to use that amount to purchase a straight-life annuity for her. Suppose further that his will had then devised the remaining part of his estate in a separate trust in which the income was to be accumulated during her lifetime and added to corpus, the corpus and accumulated income to be paid over to his then-living descendants at his wife's death or, if none, to his heirs. If the annuity payments later proved insufficient to meet his widow's needs, would the court have ordered an invasion of the principal of the residuary trust to be invaded for her benefit?

2. *Legislation.* A few statutes authorize expansion of a beneficiary's benefits on a showing of need. In Wisconsin, for example, a statute provides:

> *Wis. Stat. Ann. § 701.13. Modification and termination of trusts by court action.*
>
> *(1) Anticipation of directed accumulation of income.* When an accumulation of income is directed for the benefit of a beneficiary without other sufficient means to support or educate himself, the court on the application of such person or his guardian may direct that a suitable sum from the income accumulated or to be accumulated be applied for the support or education of such person.
>
> *(2) Application of principal to income beneficiary.* Unless the creating instrument provides to the contrary, if a beneficiary is entitled to income or to have it applied for his benefit, the court may make an allowance from principal to or for the benefit of such beneficiary if his support or education is not sufficiently provided for, taking into account all other resources available to the beneficiary.

Note that subsection (1) of the Wisconsin statute is within traditional limits, but that subsection (2) goes beyond those limits in much the same way as the *Wolcott* decision. For similar statutes authorizing limited invasions of principal, see N.Y. Est. Powers & Trusts Law § 7-1.6; Pa. Stat. Ann. tit. 20, § 301.2. See also Cal. Prob. Code § 15409; Tex. Prop. Code § 112.054.

In England, the Variation of Trusts Act, 1958, 6 & 7 Eliz. 2, ch. 53, authorizes a court to approve an arrangement varying or revoking a trust, or enlarging the powers of a trustee in administering any of the trust property, on behalf of any beneficiary who is an infant or otherwise incompetent, an unborn or unascertained person, or a person having a discretionary interest under a protective trust.

EXTERNAL REFERENCES. Frolik, Adjustment for Inflation for Fixed-Income Trust Beneficiaries, 54 Notre Dame Law. 661 (1979); Haskell, Justifying the Principle of Distributive Deviation in the Law of Trusts, 18 Hastings L.J. 267 (1967); Committee Report, Modification of Terms Regarding Amount or Time of Payments to Income Beneficiaries, 4 Real Prop. Prob. & Tr. J. 359 (1969).

2. Administrative Deviations

Statutory References: *Uniform Trustees' Powers Act §§ 2, 3(c)(7)*

Requests for deviations from the administrative provisions of a trust are handled differently from requests for distributive deviations. The most common examples of administrative deviations that courts usually permit involve the power of trustees to sell or invest trust assets. These cases involve changes in circumstances which the settlor did not anticipate, and which would defeat or substantially impair the accomplishment of the purposes of the trust. Courts often say that the changed circumstances must produce an exigency or emergency, and it is not enough that a deviation would be beneficial to the beneficiaries. Obviously, this standard is one of degree, making prediction and generalization difficult, as the following materials indicate.

Matter of Pulitzer

139 Misc. 575, 249 N.Y.S. 87 (Sur. Ct. 1931),
aff'd mem., 237 App. Div. 808, 260 N.Y.S. 975 (1932)

FOLEY, S. This is a proceeding for . . . instruction and determination of the court as to the propriety, price, manner, and time of sale of a substantial portion of the assets of the Press Publishing Company, the stock of which constitutes a material part of the assets of the trust here involved. . . . A serious and imperative emergency is claimed to exist, whereby, if such a sale is not made, a valuable asset of the trust estate may be in great part or wholly lost to the trust, the life tenants, and remaindermen. . . .

Joseph Pulitzer[44] died in the year 1911. He left a will and four codicils which were admitted to probate by this court on November 29, 1911. The provisions directly pertinent to the issues here are contained in the first codicil, which is dated March 23, 1909. By its terms he gave the shares of the capital stock of the Press Publishing Company, which were owned by

---

44. A German immigrant to this country, Joseph Pulitzer became one of its wealthiest and most influential journalists. Almost overnight, he converted the New York World, the first modern daily newspaper, from a moribund sheet into the most widely-read daily newspaper in the world. The World's success owed to several innovations that other sensationalist newspapers would later borrow, including multi-columned headlines, pictures and illustrations, and a daily sports page. Using resources generated by its huge circulation, the World mounted stunts that seemed larger than life, including sending Nellie Bly around the world in 72 days to best the fictional record that Jules Verne conceived for Phineas Fogg. The World's editorial page regularly railed against the moneyed elites, although Pulitzer's other newspaper, the St. Louis Post Dispatch was a very different kind of paper, preaching solid middle-class values rather than Mugwump reformism. The World's fascinating story is told in G. Juergens, Joseph Pulitzer and the New York World (1966).

Pulitzer himself was profoundly influenced by the Horatio Alger story of American life and greatly coveted wealth. His estate was a comparatively modest $18,525,116, much less than the thirty to eighty million dollar figure that many had guessed. See W. Swanberg, Pulitzer 413 (1967). The estate would have been larger but for the family's luxurious lifestyle. Eds.

him, and his shares of the Pulitzer Publishing Company, of St. Louis, in trust for the life of each of the two youngest of his sons, Joseph Pulitzer, Jr., and Herbert Pulitzer. . . . There were directions to pay the income in certain fractional shares to his three sons[45] and to certain other persons. . . .

To distinguish it from the residuary trust, the particular trust here has been called the "Newspaper Trust." Its trustees are the testator's three sons, Ralph Pulitzer, Herbert Pulitzer, and Joseph Pulitzer, Jr. The Pulitzer Publishing Company publishes the St. Louis Post Dispatch. The Press Publishing Company publishes the New York World, the Sunday World, and the Evening World. The trustees of the so-called "Newspaper Trust" hold within the trust a very large majority of shares of the Press Publishing Company. The remaining shares are owned by the trustees individually. The paragraph particularly sought to be construed here, which deals with the powers of the trustees and the limitations thereon, is contained in article seventh of the codicil of March 23, 1909, and reads as follows:

> I further authorize and empower my Executors and Trustees to whom I have hereinbefore bequeathed my stock in the Pulitzer Publishing Company of St. Louis, at any time, and from time to time, to sell and dispose of said stock, or any part thereof, at public or private sale, at such prices and on such terms as they may think best, and to hold the proceeds of any stock sold in trust for the beneficiaries for whom such shares were held in lieu thereof, and upon the same trusts. This power is not to be construed as in any respect mandatory, but purely discretionary. This power of sale, however, is limited to the said stock of the Pulitzer Publishing Company of St. Louis, and shall not be taken to authorize or empower the sale or disposition under any circumstances whatever, by the Trustees of any stock of the Press Publishing Company, publisher of "The World" newspaper (to the maintenance and upbuilding of which I have sacrificed my health and strength) in the same spirit which I have striven to create and conduct it as a public institution, from motives higher than mere gain, it having been my desire that it should be at all times conducted in a spirit of independence and with a view to inculcating high standards and public spirit among the people and their official representatives, and it is my earnest wish that said newspaper shall hereafter be conducted upon the same principles.

---

45. In fact, the distribution plan made a flurry of newspaper headlines. Herbert, the youngest child, was given a six-tenths interest in the trust income, three times the size of his eldest brother Ralph's share, while Joseph, Jr., was given only a one-tenth interest. Pulitzer's partiality for Herbert was revealed also by the terms for appointment of trustees. Initially, four independent trustees were appointed, and two of which were to be replaced by Herbert when he reached 21 and by Joseph, Jr., when he reached 30. Ralph, who was 32 at the time of his father's death and had already made his mark in the newspaper business, was the only one of the brothers not given a trusteeship, a fact that led him to make a public statement indicating that the omission might mistakenly suggest "a lack of confidence in me on my father's part." In fact, in an unexecuted will prepared for him in 1911, Pulitzer did name Ralph as a trustee. It is also notable that neither of Pulitzer's two daughters were made trustees or received any interest in the newspaper trust, although they were given income interests in a $1.5 million trust. See W. Swanberg, *supra* note 44, at 414. Eds.

There are fifteen remaindermen in existence. One of them is an adult; the other fourteen are infants. Because of a possible adversity of interest they are represented here by two separate special guardians. The adult life tenants and remaindermen join in requesting the relief sought by the trustees.

Counsel for the trustees contend that the express denial of a power of sale contained in the paragraph was modified and cut down, as a matter of testamentary intent, by Mr. Pulitzer in subsequent language. . . . There is some support to be found in the provisions of the will for these contentions. Indication of an intent to authorize a sale in certain emergencies is thus found in article 6 of the codicil dated May 11, 1910.

But I prefer to place my determination here upon broader grounds and upon the power of a court of equity, in emergencies, to protect the beneficiaries of a trust from serious loss, or a total destruction of a substantial asset of the corpus. The law, in the case of necessity, reads into the will an implied power of sale. . . .

The same rule applies to emergencies in trusts not only where there is an absence of power of sale in a will, but also where there is a prohibition against sale. It has been satisfactorily established by the evidence before me that the continuance of the publication of the newspapers, which are the principal assets of the Press Publishing Company, will in all probability lead to a serious impairment or the destruction of a large part of the trust estate. The dominant purpose of Mr. Pulitzer must have been the maintenance of a fair income for his children and the ultimate reception of the unimpaired corpus by the remaindermen. Permanence of the trust and ultimate enjoyment by his grandchildren were intended. A man of his sagacity and business ability could not have intended that from mere vanity, the publication of the newspapers, with which his name and efforts had been associated, should be persisted in until the entire trust asset was destroyed or wrecked by bankruptcy or dissolution. His expectation was that his New York newspapers would flourish. Despite his optimism, he must have contemplated that they might become entirely unprofitable and their disposal would be required to avert a complete loss of the trust assets. The power of a court of equity, with its jurisdiction over trusts, to save the beneficiaries in such a situation has been repeatedly sustained in New York and other jurisdictions. . . .

The trustees here find themselves in a crisis where there is no self-help available to them. A judicial declaration is necessary, not only as to their general authority, but as to the effect of the words of Mr. Pulitzer contained in his will. The widest equity powers exist in the Surrogate's Court of this state by the grant of the legislative authority contained in section 40 of the Surrogate's Court Act. Matter of Raymond v. Davis' Estate, 248 N.Y. 67, 71, 161 N.E. 421.

I accordingly hold, in this phase of the decision, that the terms of the will and codicils do not prohibit the trustees from disposing of any assets of the Press Publishing Company, that the trustees have general power and authority to act in the conveyance of the assets proposed to be sold, and that this court, in the exercise of its equitable jurisdiction, should authorize them by an appropriate direction in the decree to exercise such general authority. . . .

Notes

1. *Sequel.* The decline in profitability of the *World* newspapers, which led the court to order their sale despite the express provision to the contrary in the will, postdated Joseph Pulitzer's death. After assuming control of the *World* newspapers, Pulitzer's sons changed the papers's style in an effort to appeal to a more educated readership. Circulation and advertising plummeted and, by 1928, all three newspapers were operating with deep deficits. In 1931, the papers were sold to the Scripps-Howard organization for $5 million. The story is told in W. Swanberg, Pulitzer 411-18 (1967).

2. *Legislation on the Trustee's Power of Sale.* The Uniform Trustees' Powers Act (1964), which is approved for inclusion in the Uniform Probate Code as Article VII, Part 4, provides that, unless limited by the trust instrument, a trustee has the power "to acquire or dispose of an asset, for cash or on credit, at public or private sale." Unif. Trustees' Powers Act §§ 2, 3(c)(7).

3. *Permissible Investments.* In Stanton v. Wells Fargo Bank & Union Trust Co., 150 Cal. App. 2d 763, 310 P.2d 1010 (1957), the income of a testamentary trust was given to named persons for life, with a general power in each to appoint the remainder, and in default of appointment the share of the income beneficiary was given to her or his issue, or for want of issue, to surviving life beneficiaries. The will provided that trust investments were to be made only in bonds of the United States or state governments or such other bonds as were rated "AA" by Moody Investor's Service.

In 1951, twenty years after the testator's death, all living beneficiaries sued for modification of the trust to permit investment in securities permitted by the Civil Code, which would include corporate stocks. In favor of the deviation, evidence was offered showing an inflationary trend that had reduced the purchasing power of the dollar, and evidence showing the relative return on stocks and bonds.

In reversing a judgment allowing the deviation, the court said:

The distributable annual income was $88,890.66 in 1938, and by 1954 this had increased to $109,942.84. There is no evidence that any beneficiary is in want or that the distributable net income is not sufficient to supply the reasonable needs of all beneficiaries. No emergency exists. . . . [W]hile the settlor might not have been omniscient [about future economic conditions such as inflationary trends], neither are the beneficiaries nor the courts, omniscient. No one can forecast, with any certainty, future events. Certainly, it is true that misguided restrictions imposed by a settlor should not be permitted to defeat his fundamental trust purpose, but it is equally true that the court should not try to guess what economic conditions may be in a few years by permitting deviations when no real emergency exists or is threatened.

Compare with *Stanton* the decision in Trusteeship With Mayo, 259 Minn. 91, 105 N.W.2d 900 (1960). In that case, Dr. Charles Mayo created two revocable trusts, one in 1917, the other in 1919. Dr. Mayo died in 1939 without having revoked either trust. One trust, by its terms, was to continue until 21 years after the death of the petitioner, a beneficiary; the other was partially to terminate when each child of the petitioner attained the age of 30.

The trusts directed the trustees to invest in "real estate mortgages, municipal bonds or any other form of income bearing property (but not real estate nor corporate stock)." The petitioner sought a deviation from this restriction so as to permit investment in corporate stock. She alleged that, after the settlor's death, inflation had reduced the real value of the trust assets by more than 50 percent, but that the market value of common stock had almost doubled since 1939.

In opposition, the trustees alleged that the testator had witnessed post-World War I inflation, the stock market crash of 1929, and the subsequent depression, and had not amended the trust to permit investment in corporate stock, which indicated that he was satisfied with the terms as written.

The decree below denying the petition was reversed, the court saying:

> It appears without substantial dispute that if deviation is not permitted the accomplishment of the purposes of the trusts will be substantially impaired because of changed conditions due to inflation since the trusts were created; that unless deviation is allowed the assets of the trusts, within the next 20 years, will, in all likelihood, be worth less than one-fourth of the value they had at the time of the donor's death. To avoid this we conclude that in equity the trustees should have the right and be authorized to deviate from the restrictive provisions of the trusts by permitting them, when and as they deem advisable, to invest a reasonable amount of the trust assets in corporate stocks of good, sound investment issues. Through an investment in bonds and mortgages of the type designated by the donor, plus corporate stocks of good, sound investment issues, in our opinion, the trusts will, so far as possible, be fortified against inflation, recession, depression, or decline in prices.

PART D. COMPROMISE OF CONTROVERSIES

Statutory References: *1990 UPC §§ 1-403, 3-1101, -1102*

Adams v. Link
145 Conn. 634, 145 A.2d 753 (1958)

KING, J. The defendants Link and the United States Trust Company of New York are the executors and trustees under the will and codicil of Mildred A. Kingsmill, late of Darien. Mrs. Kingsmill left, as her sole heirs at law, two brothers, Orson Adams, Jr., and Alvin P. Adams, and a sister,

Ethel A. Martin. This action grows out of, although it is distinct from, an appeal by Orson Adams, Jr., and Alvin P. Adams, two of the three heirs at law, from the admission of the will and codicil to probate.

In the view which we take of the case, only the right to terminate the trust created in paragraph sixth of the will need be considered. This paragraph disposed of the residue by a trust. It provided for the payment of the net income for life, in monthly or quarterly installments at their written election, to Joan K. Pringle and Mayes M. Foeppel, neither of whom was an heir at law. At the death of the survivor, the trust was to terminate and distribution of the corpus was to be made to the New York Association for the Blind. In fact, Joan K. Pringle predeceased the testatrix, leaving Mayes M. Foeppel as the sole income beneficiary and entitled, under the terms of the trust, to the entire net income for life.

During the pendency of the appeal from probate, a so-called compromise agreement was entered into between Mayes M. Foeppel, party of the first part, the New York Association for the Blind, party of the second part, and the three heirs at law of the testatrix, parties of the third part. The agreement in effect provided that (1) the appeal from the admission of the will and codicil to probate would be withdrawn; (2) 15 per cent of the residuary estate, i.e. the trust corpus, would be paid outright to the three heirs at law in equal shares; (3) 37 per cent would be paid outright to the New York Association for the Blind; and (4) 48 per cent would be paid outright to Mayes M. Foeppel less a deduction of $15,000 which would be used to establish a new trust, the precise terms of which are not material. Basically, it was for the education of a son of Alvin P. Adams, and upon completion of his education the trust would terminate and any unused corpus and interest would be returned to Mayes M. Foeppel. The compromise agreement was by its express terms made subject to the approval of the Superior Court. The defendant executors and trustees refused to participate in the agreement or to carry it out. The present action, the plaintiffs in which include all parties to the agreement except the New York Association for the Blind, which was made a party defendant, seeks in effect (a) the approval of the agreement by the Superior Court, and (b) a decree compelling the defendant executors and trustees to carry it out. Since the provision for the New York Association for the Blind was a charitable gift, the attorney general was made a defendant to represent the public interest, under the provisions of § 212 of the General Statutes. The court refused to approve the agreement, and from this action the plaintiffs took this appeal. . . .

The fundamental effect of the compromise agreement, if approved by the court, would be to abolish the trust. . . .

Conditions precedent which should concur in order to warrant termination of a testamentary trust by judicial decree are (1) that all the parties in interest unite in seeking the termination, (2) that every reasonable ultimate purpose of the trust's creation and existence has been accomplished, and (3) that no fair and lawful restriction imposed by the testator will be nullified or disturbed by such a result. . . .

The underlying rationale of our rule is the protection, if reasonably possible, of any reasonable, properly expressed, testamentary desire of a decedent. 3 Scott, Trusts (2d Ed.) § 337.

It appears that all the interested beneficiaries have joined in the agreement under consideration. For the purposes of this case only, we will assume, without in any way deciding, that the plaintiffs are correct in their claim that the defendant executors and trustees have no standing to attack the compromise. This assumption is permissible because the compromise was in terms made contingent upon court approval, and this approval could not be compelled by any agreement of the trust beneficiaries among themselves. Thus we may assume, without deciding, that the first condition precedent under our rule is satisfied. The second and third conditions precedent have not, however, been satisfied. The obvious objectives of the testatrix were to provide (a) an assured income for life for Mayes M. Foeppel, and (b) at her death an intact corpus for the New York Association for the Blind. In carrying out these objectives, the testatrix took two important steps. In the first place, the management of the trust corpus was committed to trustees selected by her and in whose financial judgment she is presumed to have had confidence. Secondly, expenditure of any principal by the life beneficiary was precluded. Taken together, these two steps would tend to achieve, and in all reasonable probability would achieve, the testatrix' two basic objectives. To abolish the trust and turn over a fraction of the corpus outright to the life beneficiary would be to enable her in a moment to lose the protection of the practically assured life income provided by the testatrix. The two basic objectives of the trust's creation and existence were reasonable and commendable and cannot be fully accomplished prior to the death of the life beneficiary. Obviously, had the testatrix intended to entrust the life beneficiary with the handling of any part of the corpus, she would have so provided by a simple, outright gift.

The plaintiffs attempt to avoid the impact of our rule by two main claims. The first is that since the protection accorded the life beneficiary could be lost by her voluntary alienation of the income or by its involuntary alienation through attachment or seizure under an order in equity, the testatrix could not have intended to protect the beneficiary. This amounts in effect to a claim that only a spendthrift trust is protected from termination by agreement of all interested beneficiaries. The case against termination under our rule is of course even stronger where a spendthrift trust is involved. But the operation of our rule is not restricted to such trusts. The mere fact that the testatrix failed to provide the maximum possible protection for the life beneficiary by creating a spendthrift trust . . . does not warrant a conclusion that she intended no protection at all, so that we can consider that the trust no longer has any purpose.

The plaintiffs also claim that whatever the rule may be in cases involving no will contest, a more liberal rule applies where, as here, the termination of the trust is a part of the settlement of such a contest. Some support for this position may be found in cases cited in 3 Scott, Trusts (2d Ed.) § 337.6. The rationale of our rule as to the power to set aside or terminate a trust is not, however, such that its applicability would be affected by the mere fact that the motivation of a trust termination agreement is the compromise of a will contest. It is true that such contests are not infrequently compromised by agreements involving the transfer of legacies or devises, in whole or in part, by beneficiaries under the will. Where such gifts are alienable this is permissible, since no violence is done to the provisions of the will. But that is not this case. Here the provisions of the will itself are being drastically changed so as to abolish a trust contrary to our rule. This cannot be done. It follows that the court below was not in error in denying approval of the agreement. Indeed, it was the only decision which could properly have been made. This conclusion makes unnecessary the consideration of the other grounds of appeal.

There is no error.

In this opinion the other judges concurred.

Notes

1. *State of the Authorities.* The Restatement and most authority tend in the direction of Adams v. Link. See, e.g., Restatement 2d of Trusts § 337 comment o; Heritage Bank-North v. Hunterdon Medical Center, 164 N.J. Super. 33, 395 A.2d 552 (Sup. Ct. 1978). There is some authority to the contrary, however. In Budin v. Levy, 343 Mass. 644, 180 N.E.2d 74 (1962), for example, the court, in approving a compromise agreement that prematurely terminated a trust, stated that the agreement's validity did not depend on finding that it did not defeat a material purpose of the trust.

On the tax implications, see Bruce, *Bosch* and Other Dilemmas: Binding the Parties and the Tax Consequences in Trust Dispute Resolution, 18 Inst. on Est. Plan. Ch. 9 (1984).

2. *Uniform Probate Code.* Section 3-1101 of the UPC provides that a compromise of any controversy as to the admission of an instrument offered to formal probate as the testator's will is binding even though it may affect a trust or inalienable interest. Section 3-1102 details the procedure for securing court approval of a compromise agreement. Section 1-403 states that unborn or unascertained beneficiaries who are not otherwise represented in a proceeding are bound by court orders that bind other parties to the extent that their interests are adequately represented by other parties who have a "substantially identical interest" in the proceeding.

CHARITABLE TRUSTS

Charities, an old maxim goes, are a favorite of the law. If this is the case today, it was not always so. As Professor Friedman has observed, "In the early 19th century, charity was associated with privilege, with the dead hand, with established churches, with massive wealth in perpetuity. None of these were particularly popular." L. Friedman, A History of American Law 254 (2d ed. 1985).

Today, the hostile attitude toward charities has largely dissipated. In fact, charitable trusts enjoy some legal privileges. Some of the rules restricting private trusts are suspended for charitable trusts. Not all the restrictive rules are suspended, of course. Like a private trust, a charitable trust is a fiduciary relationship with respect to property, requiring a trust res, an intent to create a trust, compliance with the Statute of Frauds or the Statute of Wills, as appropriate, and so on. But the requirement of definite beneficiaries does not apply to charitable trusts, nor does the Rule Against Perpetuities or associated rules relating to accumulations of income.[1] In addition, charitable trusts enjoy certain tax benefits not accorded private trusts.

Validity of Charitable Trusts. Although the validity of charitable trusts is now universally recognized in the United States, the question was in doubt in the early part of our history. Since charitable trusts are created to accomplish charitable purposes, not to benefit definite beneficiaries, special machinery had to be developed for their enforcement. Such procedure was provided in England by the Statute of Charitable Uses, 43 Eliz. ch. 4 (1601). Some early American courts assumed that authority to enforce charitable trusts originated with and depended upon the English statute.

---

1. Many charitable trusts are in fact designed to last without time limit, through providing that only the income shall be used for the charitable purpose. A perpetual charitable trust facilitated by a warrant from William Penn in 1706 presumably continues today. See Trustees of New Castle Common v. Gordy, 33 Del. Ch. 334, 93 A.2d 509 (1952).

Trustees of Philadelphia Baptist Ass'n v. Hart's Ex'rs, 17 U.S. (4 Wheat.) 1 (1819), held that if that statute was not imported into the state as part of the common law, state legislation was needed for charitable trusts to be created in the jurisdiction. More rigorous historical work showed, however, that the English Court of Chancery had enforced charitable trusts long before the Statute of Charitable Uses, and continued to do so after the enforcement procedure provided by that statute had been repealed. See Vidal v. Girard's Ex'rs, 43 U.S. (2 How.) 127 (1844). On this basis, charitable trusts came to be fully recognized—with or without supporting legislation—as legitimate vehicles for devoting wealth to charitable purposes.

Enforcement of Charitable Trusts. One of the central features of a charitable trust is that it need not have definite beneficiaries. The beneficiaries of a private trust, as we know, are the ones who have standing for its enforcement. Normally lacking definite beneficiaries, however, a charitable trust is principally enforceable by the state Attorney General. The Restatement 2d of Trusts provides:

> § 391. *Who Can Enforce a Charitable Trust.* A suit can be maintained for the enforcement of a charitable trust by the Attorney General or other public officer, or by a co-trustee, or by a person who has a special interest in the enforcement of the charitable trust, but not by persons who have no special interest or by the settlor or his heirs, personal representatives or next of kin.

See also Uniform Supervision of Trustees for Charitable Purposes Act (1954).

Charitable Organizations. A newly created charitable organization can be formed in a variety of ways, including that of a charitable trust or that of a charitable corporation. Existing charitable organizations, including the well-known public charities such as the American Cancer Society and the major charitable foundations such as the Ford Foundation, are usually (but not always) formed as corporations. The rules and principles applicable to charitable trusts are usually applicable to charitable corporations or other organizations, including the cy pres doctrine and the imposition of fiduciary duties on the corporation's Board of Directors and the method of enforcing these duties. See Restatement 2d of Trusts § 348, comment f; § 386, comment b; § 399, comment o. See, e.g., St. Joseph's Hosp. v. Bennett, 281 N.Y. 115, 22 N.E.2d 305 (1939) (cy-pres doctrine); Stern v. Lucy Webb Hayes Nat'l Training School, 381 F. Supp. 1003 (D. D.C. 1974) (fiduciary duties).

Tax-Exempt Status. The income of charitable trusts and charitable corporations is generally exempt from federal income tax. See IRC § 501.

Contributions to Existing Charitable Organizations. A gift or devise to an existing charitable organization is often treated as having created a separate charitable trust with respect to that contribution, with the organization as the trustee. The idea that a charitable trust has been created is more likely if the donor imposed one or more restrictions on the gift or devise. A restriction can take a variety of forms. The donor may restrict the use of the property to one of the purposes for which the charitable organization has been formed; for example, the donor may restrict a donation to an educational institution to the school's scholarship fund. The donor may specify that only the income is to be used, not the principal. Whether or not the transaction is characterized as having created a trust, the rules and principles applicable to charitable trusts are usually applicable to charitable organizations. See Restatement 2d of Trusts § 348, comment f; Scott on Trusts § 348.1.

PART A. CHARITABLE PURPOSES

In this Part, we present cases in which trusts have been challenged on the ground that they are not charitable trusts because their purposes are not "charitable." In the leading English case of Commissioners of Internal Revenue v. Pemsel, [1891] App. Cas. 531, 583 (H.L.), Lord Macnaghten expressed the following understanding of charitable trusts:

> "Charity" in its legal sense comprises four principal divisions: trusts for the relief of poverty; trusts for the advancement of education; trusts for the advancement of religion; and trusts for other purposes beneficial to the community, not falling under any of the preceding heads. The trusts last referred to are not the less charitable in the eye of the law, because incidentally they benefit the rich as well as the poor, as indeed, every charity that deserves the name must do either directly or indirectly.

In this country, Restatement 2d of Trusts section 368 defines charitable purposes as including "(a) the relief of poverty; (b) the advancement of education; (c) the advancement of religion; (d) the promotion of health; (e) governmental or municipal purposes; (f) other purposes the accomplishment of which is beneficial to the community." As you read the cases in this Part, consider why the trust would be invalid as a private trust if it fails to meet the charitable-trust definition.

Tax Deductibility. For qualified gifts to charity, the Internal Revenue Code allows a limited deduction from income taxation and an unlimited deduction from gift taxation; and for qualified devises to charity, the Code allows an unlimited deduction from estate taxation. See IRC §§ 170, 642(c), 2055, 2522. The estate-tax provision, set forth below, is nearly identical to the income and gift tax provisions:

> § 2055. *Transfers for public, charitable, and religious uses.*
> (a) In general.—For purposes of the tax imposed by section 2001, the value of the taxable estate shall be determined by deducting from the value of the gross estate the amount of all bequests, legacies, devises, or transfers—
> (1) to or for the use of the United States, any State, any political subdivision thereof, or the District of Columbia, for exclusively public purposes;
> (2) to or for the use of any corporation organized and operated exclusively for religious, charitable, scientific, literary, or educational purposes,

including the encouragement of art, or to foster national or international amateur sports competition (but only if no part of its activities involve the provision of athletic facilities or equipment), and the prevention of cruelty to children or animals, no part of the net earnings of which inures to the benefit of any private stockholder or individual, which is not disqualified for tax exemption under section 501(c)(3) by reason of attempting to influence legislation, and which does not participate in, or intervene in (including the publishing or distributing of statements), any political campaign on behalf of (or in opposition to) any candidate for public office;

(3) to a trustee or trustees, or a fraternal society, order, or association operating under the lodge system, but only if such contributions or gifts are to be used by such trustee or trustees, or by such fraternal society, order, or association, exclusively for religious, charitable, scientific, literary, or educational purposes, or for the prevention of cruelty to children or animals, such trust, fraternal society, order, or association would not be disqualified for tax exemption under section 501(c)(3) by reason of attempting to influence legislation, and such trustee or trustees, or such fraternal society, order, or association, does not participate in, or intervene in (including the publishing or distributing of statements), any political campaign on behalf of (or in opposition to) any candidate for public office; or

(4) to or for the use of any veterans' organization incorporated by Act of Congress, or of its departments or local chapters or posts, no part of the net earnings of which inures to the benefit of any private shareholder or individual. . . .

Are the trust-law and tax-law definitions of charitable purposes identical? Rev. Rul. 71-447, 1971-2 C.B. 230, states:

Both the courts and the Internal Revenue Service have long recognized that the statutory requirements [of IRC section 501(c)(3)] of being "organized and operated exclusively for religious, charitable, . . . or educational purposes" was intended to express the basic common law concept.

See also Rev. Rul. 67-325, 1967-2 C.B. 113, declaring that the phrase "charitable purposes" in IRC sections 170, 2055, and 2522 is used "in the generally accepted legal sense."

Foreign Beneficiaries. The fact that a charitable trust is for the benefit of a community outside the United States does not prevent the trust from being upheld as a charitable trust or disqualify it for the federal estate or gift tax charitable deduction. Restatement 2d of Trusts § 374, comment i; Scott on Trusts § 374.8; Rev. Rul. 74-523, 1974-2 C.B. 304. For federal income-tax purposes, a contribution or gift *by a corporation* to a trust, chest, fund, or foundation is deductible "only if it is to be used within the United States or any of its possessions . . . ." IRC § 170(c).

1. General Gifts to Charity

Suppose a testator devises property in trust "for such charitable purposes as my trustee shall select" or "to apply the income therefrom, in perpetuity, for the promotion of religion." According to Restatement 2d of Trusts section 396 and most authority, both dispositions create charitable trusts. In Estate of Small, 244 Iowa 1209, 58 N.W.2d 477 (1953), the court upheld a trust created by the will of Dr. W.B. Small. To Dr. Small, divine guidance, though necessary, was not sufficient. His will retained a post-death veto power:

> I direct that my said trustees or their successors shall distribute . . . income . . . for such purposes as they may feel is directed by God the Father, Jesus Christ the Son, and Holy Spirit, *and* as they believe would be acceptable to *me* and meet *my* approval were *I* able to give it . . . . (Emphasis added.)

A charitable trust is also created if the testator simply devises property "to charity" or "to the poor." See Jordan's Estate, 329 Pa. 427, 197 A. 150 (1938) (devise "to charity" upheld as a charitable trust); Restatement 2d of Trusts § 397, comment e; Scott on Trusts § 397. In these cases, of course, the court must select a trustee or frame a scheme for the application of the devise to the intended purpose.

Does a trust authorizing distribution of income "to such charitable organizations as the trustee shall select" qualify for a federal estate or gift tax deduction? See, e.g., Beggs v. United States, 27 F. Supp. 599 (Ct. Cl. 1939) (deduction allowed because court did "not find in the will involved any grant of discretionary authority to the executor to distribute any part of the net proceeds of the estate to other than charities."); Rev. Rul. 71-200, 1971-1 C.B. 272 (deduction denied because there were "no applicable decisions of the courts of the state in which the will was probated that construe similar clauses as limiting the trustees [*sic*] choice of organizations to those qualifying under IRC section 2055 . . . ."); Rev. Rul. 69-285, 1969-1 C.B. 222 (deduction allowed on theory that Massachusetts decisions define "charitable" in a way that is "at least as restrictive as the Federal definition of that term under section 2055."); 5 B. Bittker, Federal Taxation of Income, Estates and Gifts ¶ 130.2 (1984); R. Stephens, G. Maxfield & S. Lind, Federal Estate and Gift Taxation ¶ 5.05[1] (5th ed. 1983).

Devises for purposes not restricted to charitable purposes have generated considerable litigation. Recall the leading case of Morice v. Bishop of Durham, 10 Ves. 522, 32 Eng. Rep. 947 (Ch. 1805), supra p. 637. In that case, Lord Chancellor Eldon held that a devise in trust "to dispose of the ultimate residue to such objects of benevolence and liberality as the Bishop of Durham in his own discretion shall most approve of" failed to create a charitable trust because the purposes were not limited to charity and failed to create a valid private trust because the beneficiaries were indefinite. Some century and a half later, in Chichester Diocesan Fund v. Simpson, [1944] App. Cas. 341 (H.L.), the House of Lords applied the idea that "benevolence" is not restricted to "charity," in the case of a devise to the testator's executors to apply it "for such charitable institution or institutions or other charitable or benevolent object or objects in England as my acting executors or executor may in their or his absolute discretion select."

In this country, most courts have generally agreed with the English view that "benevolence," standing alone, potentially encompasses purposes broader than those that are "charitable." Thus, most American courts have held that a devise "to be used for such benevolent purposes as the trustees shall select" does not create a charitable trust. See, e.g., Estate of Kradwell, 44 Wis. 2d 40, 170 N.W.2d 773 (1969); Adye v. Smith, 44 Conn. 60 (1876). Contra, e.g., Goodale v. Mooney, 60 N.H. 528 (1881). See Restatement 2d of Trusts § 398 comment b; Scott on Trusts § 398.1 n.11.

Can you think of a "benevolent" use of property or income that would not come within the definition of "charity"? Of a "charitable" use that would not come within the definition of "benevolent"? Which of these questions is more important for our purposes? Do you think the distinction between "benevolent" and "charitable" is widely understood by the lay public? By the average lawyer?

Problems

1. G's will devised property in trust, directing her trustee to apply the income therefrom, in perpetuity:

(a) for such "charitable and benevolent purposes" as my trustee shall select.

(b) for such "charitable or benevolent purposes" as my trustee shall select.

(c) for such "charitable or benevolent purpose" as my trustee shall select.

Which version presents the strongest case for validity as a charitable trust? See Restatement 2d of Trusts § 398 comments c & d; Scott on Trusts § 398.1.

2. Would the case for validity in the above cases be strengthened if G's trust had been an inter-vivos trust and if, during G's lifetime, the trustee had administered the trust for purposes clearly "charitable"? Would it matter whether the inter-vivos trust was revocable or irrevocable? In Hight v. United States, 256 F.2d 795 (2d Cir. 1958), the court held that the word "benevolent" has "no fixed meaning which is self-defining." Relying in part on extrinsic evidence concerning the type of institution the testatrix had selected during life for her benefactions, the court upheld as charitable a devise for "such charitable, benevolent, religious or educational institutions as my executors hereinafter named may determine."

Wilson v. Flowers
58 N.J. 250, 277 A.2d 199 (1971)

PROCTOR, J. This is a will construction case. Plaintiffs, trustees under the will of Joseph L.K. Snyder, filed a complaint in the Chancery Division seeking instructions regarding the validity of Article Sixth (C)(12) of the testator's residuary trust of his will which directs them, *inter alia*, to contribute 20% of the residue "to such *philanthropic* causes as my Trustees may select" (emphasis added).

Defendants are the next-of-kin of the testator,[2] and the Attorney General of New Jersey. The latter did not participate in the litigation.

After a hearing, Judge Mintz held that the plaintiffs had established the testator's probable intent that the gifts to "philanthropic causes" be solely charitable in nature. Thus, the gifts were not void and did not pass by intestate succession. Judgment directed 1) that the plaintiffs "shall contribute solely to charitable purposes the income to be disposed under Article Sixth (C)(12) of" the will, 2) that "the dispositions . . . do not violate the rule against perpetuities," and 3) that plaintiffs-trustees "in making contributions to philanthropic causes pursuant to Article Sixth (C)(12) of said will are restricted solely to charities which qualify as charities under [the federal estate tax and the state inheritance tax]." . . .

The primary issue on this appeal is whether the testator, in using the term "philanthropic causes," intended to limit his bounty to charitable causes or whether he intended the term to have a broader meaning. If the trust is not limited to charitable purposes, it is void either for uncertainty or for a violation of the rule against perpetuities. Defendants contend that the trust is void and that it should pass to them by intestate succession.

On February 28, 1965, Joseph L.K. Snyder died leaving a Will dated September 30, 1960 and a Codicil thereto dated December 18, 1964. . . . The great bulk of his estate was disposed of by Article Sixth, which deals with the residuary. By this provision he bequeathed his residuary estate in trust, with directions to pay the income therefrom to three individuals for life (no beneficiary to receive income exceeding an average of $25,000 per year over a period of five consecutive years). Under Subsections (1) to (12) of Section (C) of Article Sixth the decedent directed that the balance of principal and accumulated income of the residuary estate be continued "in perpetual trust" and that the net income be distributed to the beneficiaries in the following proportions: [Here were listed gifts in specified proportions to eleven charitable organizations.] Defendants do not challenge the qualification of the above beneficiaries as charities. Their attack is limited to the language of Subsection (12) by which the remainder of the residue is disposed. That subsection reads in pertinent part:

> (12) To contribute the remaining twenty per cent (20%) thereof, together with income on hand by reason of the defection of any bequest under Subsections (1) through (11) of Section (C) of this Article Sixth, to such philanthropic causes as my Trustees may select, special consideration, however, to be given to charitable, educational and scientific fields, including universities, research laboratories, foundations or organizations formed for the purpose of the combating of and research on degenerative diseases.

It is estimated that the residuary estate will amount to $2,000,000.

Defendants contend that the word "philanthropic" is broader than the word "charitable" both in terms of the testator's intent so far as that intent

---

2. The next-of-kin are Sara Louise Flowers, a daughter of Nevin Snyder, a brother who predeceased testator, and Anna Douds Snyder, executrix under the Will of Jacob Marchand Snyder, a brother who survived testator by six months.

can be gleaned from the four corners of the will and in terms of its generally accepted meaning.

Turning to the second point first, we have been cited to no New Jersey case construing the word "philanthropic." However, there are many cases construing the word "benevolent" which defendants contend is more restrictive than "philanthropic." The cases follow the English rule that "benevolent" is broader than "charitable" and that a trust for such purposes is therefore void.

Defendants urge that since New Jersey courts follow the English cases that hold "benevolent" is broader than "charitable," they must, a fortiori, follow the English cases that hold that "philanthropic" is broader than "charitable." We cannot accept this argument. It is no longer clear that "philanthropic" by legal connotation is broader than "charitable" in its legal connotation. Bogert has stated:

> At the present time it would seem that the intent of a donor who leaves property to be distributed for "benevolent" or "philanthropic" purposes is in most cases charitable. If the duration of the trust is indefinite or perpetual a trust to show mere liberality will be void and in addition it will be subject to heavy tax burdens. Few trustors will desire these results. Common usage has made these words synonyms for charity. . . .

The word "philanthropic" would seem, in its liberal sense, to include all acts of friendliness to mankind, whether conducive to improvement of society or merely to enrichment and enjoyment. In some English cases the word has been construed in this sense, and the result has been that a trust for "philanthropic purposes" has been held non-charitable because it would permit the trustee to perform acts of mere friendliness and generosity, having no connection with the need of the recipients of the benefits and no regard for the effect of the bounty upon the "beneficiaries." This is, however, perhaps a rather bookish meaning of the word. Probably in common use it is taken to mean charity, and some tendency to give it that effect is observable, especially where it is linked with the word "charitable" or with admittedly charitable objects. Bogert, Trusts & Trustees, § 370, p. 69, 70 (2d ed. 1964).

There are a number of cases which have rejected the English cases and have treated "philanthropic" as synonymous with "charitable." E.g., MacKinnon v. MacKinnon (1909) Sess. Cas. 1041 ("charitable or philanthropic" institutions are charitable institutions); Rotch v. Emerson, 105 Mass. 431 (1870) ("for the promotion of agricultural or horticultural improvements, or other philosophical or philanthropic purposes" are charitable purposes); Thorp v. Lund, 227 Mass. 474, 116 N.E. 946 (1917) ("national and philanthropic purposes" are charitable purposes); Brewer v. McCauley (Matter of Loggie), (1954) S.C.R. 645 ("for such charitable, religious, educational or philanthropic purposes as the trustees shall appoint" are charitable purposes) (noted in 33 Can.B.Rev. 334 (1955); Moore v. Sellers, 201 S.W.2d 248 (Tex.Civ.App. 1947) ("charitable, philanthropic, religious and/or educational institutions, societies, organizations or undertakings" are charitable purposes).

But defendants contend that even if philanthropic and charitable have come to mean the same thing, the manner in which the word "philanthropic" is used in the present case indicates a contrary intent. Testator's will directs that 20% of the residue of the estate be given, in trust, "to such philanthropic causes as my Trustees may select, special consideration, however, to be given to charitable, educational and scientific fields." Defendants argue that the "special consideration" clause evidences an intent that charitable, educational and scientific uses must merely be some of the philanthropic uses to which the funds may be given. Thus, they contend "philanthropic" is broader than "charitable" as the testator used it.

It is our duty to follow what we find to be the testator's probable intention. The commonly accepted meaning of words and their context is a strong indication of intent, but that is not the end of the matter. There are frequently other manifestations of intent. In the present case, if we were to accept defendants' argument, we would be left with the conclusion that the testator intended to die intestate. Yet as we noted in Fidelity Union Trust Co. v. Robert, 36 N.J. 561, 572, 178 A.2d 185, 191 (1962), there is a strong presumption that testators do not intend to die intestate, particularly where, as here, the gift is made out of the residuary estate. . . . This presumption is reinforced by the testator's mandate that his trust be perpetual. A perpetual trust for noncharitable purposes would be void, and it is unlikely that the testator intended that result.

There is another factor which indicates the testator intended "philanthropic" to be synonymous with "charitable." The other parts of his will demonstrate an interest in charitable causes. In sections (C)(1) through (C)(11), the testator disposed of 80% of the residuary to eleven specific admittedly charitable causes. Only (C)(12), the remaining section of his residuary trust, is challenged here. An overall feeling of charity pervades section (C) and that the testator should link 11 specific charitable causes with the term "philanthropic causes" is an indication that he intended his entire residuary estate to be devoted to charitable causes. See Bogert, supra at § 370, p. 69, 70.

Of course, these general indications of intent do not answer defendants' argument that the juxtaposition of the language employed shows the testator intended "philanthropic" to be broader than "charitable." But there is direct evidence which answers the argument. . . .

[The Court considered testimony by the scrivener of the will that he had used the word "philanthropic" synonymously with "charitable," and two memoranda by the testator containing expressions of charitable purposes in the making of his will.] . . .

[I]t is apparent that the trial court properly admitted the testator's memoranda and the scrivener's testimony regarding the testator's statements to him and the origin of the disputed word "philanthropic." While "philanthropic" may be technically broader than "charitable," we think that it has come to mean the same thing in modern usage. However, even if it has not, it is ambiguous enough to be construed as such. Most words are susceptible of more than one meaning. . . . Whether the use of a word which admits of more than one meaning is a patent ambiguity in the technical sense is not important; rather, the significant point is that there is an ambiguity at all. And in deciding whether there is an ambiguity, a court should always admit extrinsic evidence including direct statements of intent since experience teaches that language is so poor an instrument for communication or expression that ordinarily all such evidence must be examined before a court can be satisfied of whether an ambiguity exists. We do not, of course, mean to imply that such evidence can be used to vary the terms of the will, but rather that it should be admitted first to show if there is an ambiguity and second, if one exists, to shed light on the testator's actual intent.

In light of the above, it appears clear to us that the testator intended "philanthropic" to have the legal equivalence of "charitable." And if there were any doubt, well established rules of construction would lead us to lean in favor of a construction which upheld the gift as charitable. . . .

The judgment of the Chancery Division is affirmed.

Notes

1. *Curative Legislation.* In 1891, the New York Court of Appeals struck down for indefiniteness a charitable trust that Governor Tilden[3] had attempted to create by his will. The will provided for the establishment of a public library in the city of New York, but granted the trustees broad authority to apply the trust fund to "such charitable educational purposes" as in their judgment would be "most widely and substantially beneficial to mankind." Tilden v. Green, 130 N.Y. 29, 28 N.E. 880 (1891), reh. den., 130 N.Y. 29, 29 N.E. 1033 (1891). Two years later, the "Tilden Act" was adopted.

The current version of the New York statute provides that "[n]o disposition of property for religious, charitable, educational or benevolent uses . . . is invalid by reason of the indefiniteness or uncertainty of the persons designated as the beneficiaries." N.Y. Est. Powers & Trust Law § 8-1.1(a). Similar statutes appear in about ten other states. See, e.g., Mich. Comp. Laws Ann. § 554.351. Statutory citations are listed in Scott on Trusts § 398.1 n.20. The story is told in Katz, Sullivan and Beach, Legal Change and Legal Autonomy: Charitable Trusts in New York, 1777-1893, 3 Law & Hist. Rev. 51 (1985).

2. *Mixed-Purposes Trusts; Separability.* There is nothing unusual about trusts partly for private and partly for charitable purposes. For tax reasons

---

3. Samuel J. Tilden, elected governor of New York in 1874, was the unsuccessful Democratic candidate for President in the infamous 1876 election, narrowly (and perhaps fraudulently) losing to Rutherford B. Hayes. Tilden actually polled more popular votes than Hayes. There were disputed electoral votes in several states, however, and a congressional committee of eight Republicans and seven Democrats, voting along strict party lines, awarded the disputed states to Hayes, making him the winner by a single electoral vote. A reform candidate, Tilden gained his reputation fighting the famed Boss Tweed ring in New York politics. The story of the 1876 Presidential election is interestingly told in Gore Vidal's historical novel, 1876 (1976).

(see below), charitable-remainder trusts and charitable-lead trusts are staples in the modern estate-planner's inventory. A charitable-remainder trust provides for certain payments to a private beneficiary or beneficiaries for life, remainder in principal to a specified charity or for charitable purposes. A charitable-lead trust provides for income to be paid to a specified charity or for charitable purposes for a period of years, remainder in principal to a private beneficiary or beneficiaries.

The fact that such "split-interest" trusts have both charitable and private beneficiaries does not cause them to fail. The charitable portion is separable and upheld. The private portion is also upheld if the private beneficiaries are definite and ascertainable, as they almost always are in such cases. A split-interest trust, however, might fail in part if the remainder interest violates the Rule Against Perpetuities. A charitable remainder preceded by non-charitable interests is not exempt from the Rule Against Perpetuities. But that matter is deferred until Chapter 17.

3. *Tax Deductibility of Split-Interest Trusts.* For federal income, gift, and estate tax purposes, a devise to a *corporation* is deductible only if the corporation was organized and is operated exclusively for charitable purposes. A devise in *trust*, however, is not disqualified merely because the trust has private as well as charitable purposes. Such trusts, called split-interest trusts, either confer current benefits on a private beneficiary for life, and the remainder interest on a charity (charitable-remainder trusts); or confer current benefits on a charity for a term, and the remainder interest on a private beneficiary (charitable-lead trusts). In either case, of course, the deduction is limited to the value of the actual charitable benefit.

If a transfer is made for both charitable and private purposes, the value of the charitable interest is deductible only to the extent that the interest is ascertainable and thus severable from the noncharitable interest. Treas. Reg. § 20.2055-2(a). Prior to 1969, this was the main requirement. The Tax Reform Act of 1969, however, imposed additional requirements. The concern that promoted their imposition was stated by the Treasury Department in its Studies and Proposals and in similar terms by the committee reports accompanying the 1969 Act. See U.S. Treasury Department, 91st Cong., 1st Sess., Tax Reform Studies and Proposals (pt. 3) at 366-367, 381-382 (Committee Print 1969); S. Rep. No. 552, 91st Cong., 1st Sess. 86-93 (1969), in 1969-3 C.B. 423, 479-83; H.R. Rep. No. 413, 91st Cong., 1st Sess. (pt. 1) (1969), in 1969-3 C.B. 200, 237-240. The following is an excerpt from the Treasury Studies:

> [Pre-1969] rules provide[d] that, in the case of split interest transfers, the income beneficiary's interest [was] to be valued on the assumption that the property [would] be invested to yield 3.5 percent interest per year. Obviously, the actual investment experience . . . rarely correspond[ed] to the 3.5 percent assumption. Abuses [arose] because of this fact. For example, assume a charity [was] the income beneficiary for a specified term, the property then to go to the transferor's grandchildren. The transfer [was] exempt for gift tax purposes to the extent of the value of the charity's interest, which [was] based on an assumed 3.5 percent return. But if the property [was] invested to maximize

growth for the benefit of the transferor's grandchildren, then the charity . . . in fact [got] less than assumed. The result [was] that the transferor . . . paid less gift tax than he should have. If the charity [got] the remainder and an individual [had] the income interest, then the abuse possibility [was] the reverse, i.e., the property [could] be invested to maximize the income yield, even at the risk of the principal. Again, a deduction for the charitable transfer [was] permitted in a greater amount than in fact [went] to charity.

Charitable-Remainder Trusts. Under IRC section 2055(e)(2)(A), as amended, where a transfer of a remainder interest is made to a qualified charity and where a beneficiary of all or part of the income interest in the transferred property is someone other than a qualified charity, an estate-tax charitable deduction is granted for the actuarial value of the charity's remainder interest only if one of the following conditions is satisfied:

(1) The transferred property is either a personal residence or a farm; or

(2) The transferred property is realty in which a remainder interest is granted to certain charities (generally, publicly supported charities) for conservation purposes; or

(3) The transfer is made to a "charitable-remainder annuity trust," a "charitable-remainder unitrust," or a "pooled-income fund."

A *charitable-remainder annuity trust* is a trust from which a sum certain (which must be no less than an amount equal to 5 percent of the initial fair market value of all the property transferred to the trust)[4] is payable at least annually to beneficiaries, at least one of whom is not a charitable organization, for a term of years (not to exceed 20 years) or for the life or lives of such individual beneficiaries; and upon the termination of those payments, the trust assets must be transferred to, or for the use of, a qualified charitable organization. No payments may be made to non-charitable beneficiaries other than the annuity payments described in the preceding sentence. IRC § 664(d)(1).

A *charitable-remainder unitrust* is a trust from which a fixed percentage (which must not be less than 5 percent)[5] of the net fair market value of the trust's assets (valued annually) is payable at least annually to beneficia-

---

4. The requirement of a payout of *at least 5%* was explained by the Senate committee report as follows:

> [R]equiring a charitable remainder trust to distribute currently at least the amount of its income (other than long-term capital gains), if this is less than 5 percent payout and the requirement that the charitable remainder interest be valued by assuming at least a 5 percent payout to the income beneficiary will prevent a charitable remainder trust from being used to circumvent the current income distribution requirement imposed on private foundations. In the absence of these rules, a charitable remainder trust could be established which provided for a minimal payout to the noncharitable income beneficiary (substantially less than the amount of the trust income). Since the trust generally is exempt from income taxes this would allow it to accumulate trust income in excess of the payout requirement of the unitrust or annuity trust without tax for the future benefit of charity.

S. Rep. No. 552, 91st Cong., 1st Sess. 90 (1969), in 1969-3 C.B. 423, 482. Note also that § 201(b) of the 1969 Act also amended IRC § 642(c)(2) to preclude a charitable deduction for income permanently set aside for future distribution to a charity.

5. See supra note 4.

ries, at least one of whom is not a charitable organization, for a term of years (not to exceed 20 years) or for the life or lives of such individual beneficiaries; and upon termination of those payments, the trust assets must be transferred to, or for the use of, a qualified charitable organization. In lieu of a percentage payment, the trust instrument may provide for the distribution of trust income to the income beneficiaries in any year in which the trust income is a smaller amount than the percentage payment. It may also provide for the distribution to the income beneficiaries of a year's trust income that is in excess of the percentage payment, but only to the extent that the aggregate trust distributions to the income beneficiaries in prior years was less than the percentage payments would have been. Treas. Reg. § 1.664-3(b). No other amounts may be distributed to them. IRC §§ 664(d)(2), 664(d)(3).

A *pooled-income fund* is a trust, usually run by universities or large charities, to which any number of donors can contribute property. The income from the proportionate part of the fund represented by each donor's contribution is payable to the donor and/or the donor's designated beneficiary or beneficiaries during their lives. At each beneficiary's death, the charity that manages the fund withdraws assets proportionate to the share from which the beneficiary had been receiving income. IRC § 642(c)(5).

Under the 1969 amendment, a deduction is allowable for a charitable remainder subject to a condition only if the likelihood that the charity will not take the property is so remote as to be negligible (Treas. Reg. § 20.2055-2(e)) and if there is no power (other than a power to pay the required annual amount) to invade principal for a noncharitable purpose or beneficiary.

The Internal Revenue Service has promulgated illustrative sample provisions that are *required* to be included in governing instruments creating charitable-remainder annuity trusts or charitable-remainder unitrusts.[6] The Service has also promulgated sample inter-vivos declarations of trust that meet the requirements of IRC section 664(d)(1) for a charitable remainder annuity trust,[7] of IRC section 664(d)(2) for a charitable remainder unitrust,[8] and of IRC sections 644(d)(2) and (3) for a charitable remainder unitrust.[9] Finally, the Service has promulgated sample provisions for the creation of and transfers to pooled-income funds.[10]

Charitable-Lead Trusts. Under IRC section 2055(e)(2)(B), the charitable interest in a charitable-lead trust is deductible only if it is "in the form of

---

6. See Rev. Rul. 72-395, 1972-2 C.B. 340, modified by Rev. Rul. 80-123, 1980-1 C.B. 205, clarified by Rev. Rul. 82-165, 1982-2 C.B. 117, and modified by Rev. Rul. 88-81, 1988-2 C.B. 127.

7. Rev. Proc. 89-21, 1989-1 C.B. 842, amplified by Rev. Proc. 90-32, 1990-1 C.B. 546.

8. Rev. Proc. 89-20, 1989-1 C.B. 841, amplified by Rev. Proc. 90-30, 1990-1 C.B. 534.

9. Proc. 90-31, 1990-1 C.B. 53.

10. Rev. Rul. 82-38, 1982-1 C.B. 96, amplified in Rev. Rul. 90-103, 1990-51 Int. Rev. Bull. 14.

a guaranteed annuity or is a fixed percentage distributed yearly of the fair market value of the property (to be determined yearly)."

Reformation of Defective Instruments. Under IRC section 2055(e)(3), as amended in 1984, a permanent reformation rule is provided for defective split-interest trusts. Under this rule, if certain split-interest trusts that fail to qualify for the charitable deduction are judicially reformed so as to make them qualify, the reformation, subject to the qualifications and limitations set forth in IRC section 2055(e)(3), is recognized for purposes of the estate-tax charitable deduction under federal law. See 5 B. Bittker, Federal Taxation of Income, Estates and Gifts ¶ 130.5.7 (Cum. Supp. No. 4, 1990). For state legislation authorizing reformation of split-interest trusts in certain circumstances and in certain respects, see, e.g., Tex. Prop. Code §§ 112.055, 112.056. See also Estate of Burdon-Miller, 456 A.2d 1266 (Me. 1983).

Combined Marital and Charitable Deductions. The Economic Recovery Tax Act of 1981 added subsection (b)(8) to IRC section 2056. IRC section 2056(b)(8) provides that a marital deduction is allowable for the actuarial value of a surviving spouse's interest in a qualified charitable remainder unitrust or annuity trust so long as the trust has no noncharitable beneficiaries other than the surviving spouse. In such cases, the full value of the trust is deductible—the remainder interest as a charitable deduction under IRC section 2055, the unitrust or annuity interest as a marital deduction under IRC section 2056.

4. *Accumulation of Income.* In the case of private trusts, accumulations of income beyond the perpetuity period are strictly forbidden. See infra Chapter 17. Charitable trusts fall under a different rule, a rule of reasonableness. See Restatement 2d of Property § 2.2. The standard by which reasonableness is to be determined was explored in James' Estate, 414 Pa. 80, 199 A.2d 275 (1964). Frank James died in 1960, devising the residue of his estate (amounting to around $40,000) in trust, with elaborate provisions directing that a portion of the income be accumulated for 400 years, at which time the principal and accumulated income was to be paid over absolutely for the use of the Masonic Homes at Elizabethtown, Pennsylvania. The court held the direction for accumulation to be invalid, saying:

> The will of Frank James supplies no indication of purpose for the 400 year accumulation provision, nor does it, either by express language or by implication, reveal any particular plan or need for retaining accumulations over such an extended period of time. . . .
>
> No case has been cited to us, nor have we been able to locate any authority, which appears to recognize the validity of a proposed gift whose enjoyment is delayed for a period of four centuries without apparent reason.
>
> We hold, therefore, that the provisions for accumulation of income are unreasonable and void as being unnecessary, charitably purposeless and contrary to public policy. . . .

Under the *James' Estate* analysis, would the following trust be valid?

G devised $ 1 million in trust, to accumulate the income until the principal and accumulated income reach the amount of the national debt, at which time the fund is to be paid to the federal government to pay off the country's creditors.

See Girard Trust Co. v. Russell, 179 F. 446 (3d Cir. 1910). Compare Trusts of Holdeen, 486 Pa. 1, 403 A.2d 978, 6 A.L.R.4th 896 (1979) (invalidating accumulation provisions in five inter-vivos trusts of modest initial sums under which income was to be accumulated for periods ranging from 500 to 1000 years, after which time the funds were to be paid to the Commonwealth of Pennsylvania), with Frazier v. Merchants Nat'l Bank, 296 Mass. 298, 5 N.E.2d 550 (1936) (upholding a testamentary trust of about $117,000, under which the trustee was directed to accumulate the income until the principal and accumulated income reached $1,000,000, whereupon income was to be paid perpetually to the Salem Hospital). See also Estate of Orphanos v. Commissioner, 67 T.C. 780 (1977) (allowing a federal estate-tax charitable deduction for a testamentary trust that directed the trustee to accumulate the income until it and the original property reached a "sufficient amount . . . to erect a hospitol [*sic*] in Kerasitsa, Greece. . . ."); cf. Matter of Booker, 37 Wash.App. 708, 682 P.2d 320 (1984).

When a provision for accumulation is found invalid, as in *James' Estate,* how is the trust fund to be administered? On this point, Restatement 2d of Trusts section 401, comment k, states that if the court decides that under all the circumstances the period of accumulation is unreasonably long, it will direct that the property "be applied to the designated charitable purpose either immediately or at a time to be fixed by the court, and, if necessary, will apply the doctrine of cy pres in order to carry out the settlor's general charitable intention." In *James' Estate,* the court noted that the testator "did not point to capital improvements or to any other needs of the charitable institution which ordinarily could not be met by drawing on current funds," and ordered the income to be distributed to the charitable institution currently. See generally Scott on Trusts § 401.9. On tax penalties imposed on private non-operating charitable foundations for accumulating income, see IRC § 4942; R. Stephens, G. Maxfield & S. Lind, Federal Estate and Gift Taxation ¶ 5.05[5][a] (5th ed. 1983).

5. *Mortmain Legislation.* One aspect of the struggle between church and state in England following the Norman Conquest concerned land holdings by religious organizations. The feudal benefits to the king or other overlord, which were dependent upon the heir's succession to land on death of the tenant, disappeared when the land was held by an ecclesiastical corporation, which did not die. Such lands were "in dead hands," and the results must have been particularly objectionable to the Crown where this was to continue in perpetuity. Beginning in the thirteenth century, "mortmain" (dead hand) statutes were passed with the central purpose of prohibiting the acquisition or holding of land by religious bodies. It became possible, however, to avoid these statutes through the device of a use. One of the purposes of the Statute of Uses was to eliminate such practices.

In this country, there is some legislation limiting the amount of land that may be held by a religious organization, but a more important type of statute is that which either (or both) (a) limits the proportion of a decedent's estate that may be devised to charity or (b) provides that a devise to charity is valid only if the will was executed a certain period of time before death. See supra Chapter 8, Part C.2. Certainly the second type of statute, and probably both types, are not at all the product of the factors that led to the early English mortmain acts. The principal objective of such statutes seems to be to prevent a person when death is approaching from disinheriting his or her family or other natural objects of bounty.

2. Specified Purposes

It is usually said that a trust is not a charitable trust if the designated beneficiaries "are not of a sufficiently large or indefinite class so that the community is interested in the enforcement of the trust." Restatement 2d of Trusts § 375. The community is automatically interested in the enforcement of charitable trusts for the benefit of charity in general, for the benefit of the community at large, or for governmental purposes. When a trust is for the benefit of a specified segment of the community, however, the community-interest requirement is met only if the trust purposes relate to the relief of poverty, the advancement of education or of religion, or the promotion of health. Thus, comment a to section 375 explicitly states that when a trust is for any of the latter purposes, "the class of persons who are to benefit directly by the performance of the trust need not be as large as it must be where the trust is simply for the general benefit of the class. . . ."

Shenandoah Valley National Bank v. Taylor
192 Va. 135, 63 S.E.2d 786 (1951)

MILLER, J. Charles B. Henry, a resident of Winchester, Virginia, died testate on the 23rd day of April, 1949. His will dated April 21, 1949, was duly admitted to probate and the Shenandoah Valley National Bank of Winchester, the designated executor and trustee, qualified thereunder. Subject to two inconsequential provisions not material to this litigation, the testator's entire estate valued at $86,000, was left as follows:

> Second: All the rest, residue and remainder of my estate, real, personal, intangible and mixed, of whatsoever kind and wherever situate, . . . , I give, bequeath and devise to the Shenandoah Valley National Bank of Winchester, Virginia, in trust, to be known as the "Charles B. Henry and Fannie Belle Henry Fund", for the following uses and purposes:
> (a) My Trustee shall invest and reinvest my trust estate, shall collect the income therefrom and shall pay the net income as follows:
> (1) On the last school day of each calendar year before Easter my Trustee shall divide the net income into as many equal parts as there are children in

the first, second and third grades of the John Kerr School of the City of Winchester, and shall pay one of such equal parts to each child in such grades, to be used by such child in the furtherance of his or her obtainment of an education.

(2) On the last school day of each calendar year before Christmas my trustee shall divide the net income into as many equal parts as there are children in the first, second and third grades of the John Kerr School of the City of Winchester, and shall pay one of such equal parts to each child in such grades, to be used by such child in the furtherance of his or her obtainment of an education.

By paragraphs (3) and (4) it is provided that the names of the children in the three grades shall be determined each year from the school records, and payment of the income to them "shall be as nearly equal in amounts as it is practicable" to arrange. Paragraph (5) provides that if the John Kerr School is ever discontinued for any reason the payments shall be made to the children of the same grades of the school or schools that take its place, and the School Board of Winchester is to determine what school or schools are substituted for it. . . .

The John Kerr School is a public school used by the local school board for primary grades and had an enrollment of 458 boys and girls so there will be that number of pupils or thereabouts who would share in the distribution of the income.

The testator left no children or near relatives. Those who would be his heirs and distributees in case of intestacy were first cousins and others more remotely related. One of these next of kin filed a suit against the executor and trustee, and others challenging the validity of the provisions of the will which undertook to create a charitable trust. . . .

The sole question presented is: does the will create a valid charitable trust?

Construction of the challenged provisions is required and in this undertaking the testator's intent as disclosed by the words used in the will must be ascertained. If his dominant intent as expressed was charitable, the trust should be accorded efficacy and sustained. But on the other hand, if the testator's intent as expressed is merely benevolent, though the disposition of his property be meritorious and evince traits of generosity, the trust must nevertheless be declared invalid because it violates the rule against perpetuities. . . .

Authoritative definitions of charitable trusts may be found in 4 Pomeroy's Equity Jurisprudence, 5th Ed., sec. 1020, and Restatement of the Law of Trusts, sec. 368, p. 1140. The latter gives a comprehensive classification definition. It is:

Charitable purposes include:

(a) the relief of poverty;
(b) the advancement of education;
(c) the advancement of religion;
(d) the promotion of health;
(e) governmental or municipal purposes; and

(f) other purposes the accomplishment of which is beneficial to the community. . . .

We now turn to the language of the will for from its context the testator's intent is to be derived. . . . In mandatory language the duty and the duty alone to make cash payments to each individual child just before Easter and Christmas is enjoined upon the trustee by the certain and explicit words that it "shall divide the net income . . . and shall pay one of such equal shares to each child in such grades."

Without more, that language and the occasions specified for payment of the funds to the children being when their minds and interests would be far removed from studies or other school activities definitely indicate that no educational purpose was in the testator's mind. It is manifest that there was no intent or belief that the funds would be put to any use other than such as youthful impulse and desire might dictate. But in each instance immediately following the above-quoted language the sentence concludes with the words or phrase "to be used by such child in the furtherance of his or her obtainment of an education." It is significant that by this latter phrase the trustee is given no power, control or discretion over the funds so received by the child. Full and complete execution of the mandate and trust imposed upon the trustee accomplishes no educational purpose. Nothing toward the advancement of education is attained by the ultimate performance by the trustee of its full duty. It merely places the income irretrievably and forever beyond the range of the trust. . . .

In our opinion, the words of the will import an intent to have the trustee pay to each child his allotted share. If that be true,—and it is directed to be done in no uncertain language—we know that the admonition to the children would be wholly impotent and of no avail. . . .

If it be determined that the will fails to create a charitable trust for *educational purposes* (and our conclusion is that it is inoperative to create such a trust), it is earnestly insisted that the trust provided for is nevertheless charitable and valid. In this respect it is claimed that the two yearly payments to be made to the children just before Christmas and Easter produce "a desirable social effect" and are "promotive of public convenience and needs, and happiness and contentment" and thus the fund set up in the will constitutes a charitable trust. 2 Bogert on Trusts, sec. 361, p. 1090, and 3 Scott on Trusts, sec. 368, p. 1972. . . .

Numerous cases that deal with and construe specific provisions of wills or other instruments are cited by appellant to uphold the contention that the provisions of this will, without reference to and deleting the phrase "to be used by such child in the furtherance of his or her obtainment of an education" meet the requirements of a charitable trust. . . . Upon examination of these decisions, it will be found that where a gift results in mere financial enrichment, a trust was sustained only when the court found and concluded from the entire context of the will that the ultimate intended recipients were poor or in necessitous circumstances.

A trust from which the income is to be paid at stated intervals to each member of a designated segment of the public, without regard to whether or not the recipients are poor or in need, is not for the relief of poverty, nor is it a social benefit to the community. It is a mere benevolence—a private trust—and may not be upheld as a charitable trust. . . . Upon examination of these decisions, it will be found that where a gift results in mere financial enrichment, a trust was sustained only when the court found and concluded from the entire context of the will that the ultimate intended recipients were poor or in necessitous circumstances. . . . Payment to the children of their cash bequests on the two occasions specified would bring to them pleasure and happiness and no doubt cause them to remember or think of their benefactor with gratitude and thanksgiving. That was, we think, Charles B. Henry's intent. Laudable, generous and praiseworthy though it may be, it is not for the relief of the poor or needy, nor does it otherwise so benefit or advance the social interest of the community as to justify its continuance in perpetuity as a charitable trust. . . .

No error is found in the decrees appealed from and they are affirmed.

Notes, Questions, and Problems

1. *Scholarships and Awards.* The fact that only one or a small number of persons are to receive the benefits of a trust does not disqualify it from being a valid charitable trust, as long as the class of persons from whom the recipients are to be selected is sufficiently large. Thus, trusts awarding scholarships or awards are generally held to be charitable, even though there may be only one recipient. See, e.g., Estate of Carlson, 187 Kan. 543, 358 P.2d 669 (1961) (upholding a devise in trust to the city of Sylvia, Kansas, to provide funds for the medical education of a young man from Sylvia Township, "upon his promise that he will return to the City of Sylvia, and remain there for the purpose of practicing his profession."); but see, e.g., Estate of Huebner, 127 Cal. App. 244, 15 P.2d 758 (1932) (testamentary trust providing that the income be used "to help defray the expense of some girl or boy in music or art" held not to be charitable.) See generally Scott on Trusts § 375.1.

Trusts to provide education for one's own relatives are non-charitable, but courts have sustained trusts to provide scholarships for needy students in which the settlor expresses a preference for her or his relatives. See, e.g., Estate of Sells v. Commissioner, 10 T.C. 692 (1948) (trust "to provide scholarship first to relatives or other boys or girls" qualified for the federal estate-tax charitable deduction.); but see, e.g., Griffen v. United States, 400 F.2d 612 (6th Cir. 1968) (Trust stated that income was "to be used for the education of my grandchildren and for the education of deserving boys and girls . . . to obtain [a] college education in a Protestant Christian College. . . . It is my intention and desire to make my grandchildren the primary beneficiaries of this trust, and if at any time any grandchild of mine desires to avail himself or herself of the benefits of this trust, he or she shall be entitled to such benefits [not to exceed $750.00 in any one school year] even to the exclusion of all other persons." A state court held that the trust was charitable, but the federal court held that it did not qualify for the estate-tax charitable deduction.) On qualification as a charitable trust under state law, see Restatement 2d of Trusts § 375, comment d; Scott on Trusts § 375.3; Dawn, Charities for Definite Persons, 82 U. Pa. L. Rev. 12 (1933). On qualification for a charitable deduction under the federal tax laws, see Crellin v. Commissioner, 46 B.T.A. 1152 (1944) (deduction denied where principal as well as income was available to relatives, who were sufficient in number to exhaust fund, leaving nothing for educational expenses of non-relatives); Priv. Ltr. Rul. 79-23-001.

2. *Changing Law/Political Purposes/Illegal Purposes.* The Restatement 2d of Trusts section 374 comment j states that

> [a] trust may be charitable although the accomplishment of the purpose for which the trust is created involves a change in existing law. . . . A trust for the improvement of the structure and methods of government is charitable. . . .

Comment k provides, however, that trusts to promote the success of particular political parties are not charitable. Finally, concerning trusts for unpopular causes, comment l states that "[i]f the general purposes for which a trust is created are such as may be reasonably thought to promote the social interest of the community, the mere fact that a majority of the people and the members of the court believe that the particular purpose of the settlor is unwise or not adapted to the accomplishment of the general purposes, does not prevent the trust from being charitable." Of course, trusts that induce or tend to induce the commission of a crime are invalid. See Restatement 2d of Trusts § 377 comment b.

Jackson v. Phillips, 96 Mass. (14 Allen) 539 (1867), is a well-known Massachusetts case contrary to the Restatement position concerning change in existing law. In that case, a testamentary trust was established to be used "to secure the passage of laws granting women, whether married or unmarried, the right to vote" as well as "all other civil rights enjoyed by men." The Massachusetts court struck the trust down as not having been created for a valid charitable purpose:

> This bequest differs from the others in aiming directly and exclusively to change the laws; and its object cannot be accomplished without changing the Constitution also. Whether such an alteration of the existing laws and frame of government would be wise and desirable is a question upon which we cannot, sitting in a judicial capacity, properly express any opinion. Our duty is limited to expounding the laws as they stand. And those laws do not recognize the purpose of overthrowing or changing them, in whole or in part, as a charitable use.

The court adhered to this view as late as 1922, in a case involving a trust for the promotion of women's rights established by the son of Francis Jackson, the testator in Jackson v. Phillips. Bowditch v. Attorney General, 241 Mass. 168, 134 N.E. 796, 28 A.L.R. 713 (1922). This view has found no favor elsewhere. See, e.g., Collier v. Lindley, 203 Cal. 641, 266 P. 526

(1928); Register of Wills v. Cook, 241 Md. 264, 216 A.2d 542 (1966). In Massachusetts today, legislation defines charitable trusts in terms of trusts having tax-exempt status under the federal tax laws (see supra p. 740). Mass. Gen. Laws Ann. ch. 68A.

The distinctions reflected in the Restatement, while generally followed in the cases, make for many close questions. To start with a straightforward example, however, it should be clear that a trust to support the Socialist Party (or the Democrat Party, the Republican Party, or the Libertarian Party) and its candidates is not charitable. But what about a trust providing for payments "to persons, entities and causes advancing the principles of socialism and those causes related to socialism. This shall include, but not be limited to, subsidizing publications, establishing and conducting reading rooms, supporting radio, television and the newspaper media and candidates for public office." See Estate of Breedon, 208 Cal. App. 3d 981, 256 Cal. Rptr. 813 (1989). Or, a trust "to provide a place where the doctrines of socialism could be taught by example as well as by precept"? See Peth v. Spear, 63 Wash. 291, 115 P. 164 (1911). In George v. Braddock, 45 N.J. Eq. 757, 18 A. 881 (1889), the court held that a valid charitable trust had been created where the testator devised property in trust for the purpose of "'spreading the light' on social and political liberty and justice in these United States" by way of distributing the publications of Henry George, whose teachings included the doctrine "that no private, absolute ownership in land can rightfully exist." Is such a trust deductible for federal estate-tax purposes? Leubuscher v. Commissioner, 54 F.2d 998 (2d Cir. 1932), held that it was.

What about a trust to provide for support and education "of such minor Negro child or children, whose father or mother, or both, have been . . . imprisoned . . . as a result of the conviction of a crime or misdemeanor of a political nature"? The will gave examples of the types of crimes the testator had in mind, such as contempt convictions in connection with appearances before the House Un-American Activities Committee. See Estate of Robbins, 57 Cal.2d 718, 21 Cal. Rptr. 797, 371 P.2d 573 (1962).

What about a trust to oppose candidates for public office who favor decriminalization of the use of marijuana? Cf. People ex rel. Hartigan v. National Anti-Drug Coalition, 124 Ill. App.3d 269, 464 N.E.2d 690 (1984).

3. *Influencing Legislation/Political Campaigns/Tax Aspects.* Having a purpose to influence legislation or to support or oppose candidates for public office may jeopardize the tax-exempt status of a charitable organization and jeopardize the deductibility of contributions thereto. Under IRC section 501(c)(3), tax-exempt status is denied to certain charitable organizations if attempting to influence legislation constitutes a "substantial part of the [organization's] activities"[11] or if the organization participates

---

11. IRC § 501(h) permits certain organizations to elect to replace the "substantial part of the activities" test of IRC § 501(c)(3) with limits defined in terms of expenditures for influencing legislation. Under IRC § 4911, the basic permitted level of such expenditures (the "lobbying nontaxable amount") for a year is 20% of the first $500,000 of the organization's exempt purpose expenditures for the year, plus 15% of the second $500,000, plus 10% of the

in or intervenes in "any political campaign on behalf of (or in opposition to) any candidate for public office."

Gifts and devises to an organization or a trust are deductible for income, estate, and gift tax purposes only if the recipient "is not disqualified for tax exemption under IRC section 501(c)(3) by reason of attempting to influence legislation, and . . . does not participate in, or intervene in (including the publishing or distributing of statements), any political campaign on behalf of (or in opposition to) any candidate for public office." IRC §§ 170(c)(2)(D), 2055(a)(2), (a)(3), 2522(a)(2).

Does a bar association that rates candidates for both appointive and elective judgeships at the municipal, state, and federal level as either "approved," "not approved," or "approved as highly qualified" and that communicates its ratings to the public in the form of press releases and publishes them in a regular publication of the association that is sent out to the association's members and approximately 120 other subscribers, including libraries and law schools, qualify for tax-exempt status under IRC section 501(c)(3)? Does it matter that the association evaluates judicial candidates on a nonpartisan basis? That the rating of judicial candidates is not a substantial part of its activities? See Association of the Bar of the City of New York v. Commissioner, 858 F.2d 876 (2d Cir. 1988).

4. *Unpopular Purposes.* According to Professor Scott, "a trust is not a valid charitable trust if [it is for the dissemination of beliefs or doctrines that] are so irrational that it cannot be said that their dissemination can be of any benefit to the community." Scott on Trusts § 370.4. In addition, a trust for the accomplishment of a purpose that is against public policy is one for an illegal purpose and invalid. Restatement 2d of Trusts § 377 comment c. On the other hand, a trust is not invalid merely because the beliefs or doctrines to be disseminated are unpopular or accepted by a minority of the population.

How does a court go about applying the distinction between views that are merely unpopular and those that are so irrational or absurd that their dissemination is of no benefit to the community whatsoever? Some cases are not so difficult. Trusts for the promotion of agnosticism have been held to create valid charitable trusts. See Estate of Connolly, 48 Cal. App. 3d 129, 121 Cal. Rptr. 325 (1975) (promotion of agnosticism serves an educational purpose; court did "not imply that the viewpoint of agnosticism is correct or incorrect," but noted that "the sense of today is all too frequently the nonsense of tomorrow."). Trusts for the promotion of atheism have also been upheld as serving an educational function. See Scott on

---

third $500,000, plus 5% of any additional expenditures. In no event, however, can this permitted level exceed $1,000,000 for any one year. Within these limits, a separate limitation is placed on "grass roots lobbying" (attempting to influence the general public on legislative matters); the "grass roots nontaxable amount" is one fourth of the "lobbying nontaxable amount." An electing organization that exceeds either the "lobbying nontaxable amount" or the "grass roots nontaxable amount" in a taxable year is subject to an excise tax but does not necessarily lose its tax-exempt status. Loss of tax-exempt status occurs only if the organization "normally" makes expenditures of 150% of either limitation.

Trusts § 377. A trust for the promotion of racism would certainly not be upheld.

In Estate of Kidd, 106 Ariz. 554, 479 P.2d 697 (1971), James Kidd's holographic will devised his entire estate, amounting to $175,000, "to go in a reserach (sic) or some scientific proof of a soul of a human body which leaves at death. I think in time their (sic) can be a Photograph of soul leaving the human at death."

The court held that a charitable trust had been created, and that where as here only a charitable purpose is stated, "the court will either appoint a trustee to carry out the purpose or will approve a scheme to carry it out," citing Restatement 2d of Trusts § 397 comment e. The devise was claimed by 102 claimants and the trial court awarded the funds to the Barrow Neurological Institute. On appeal by six other claimants, the award was rejected on the ground that the Institute was not engaged in any research of the kind sought by the testator. The court directed the trial court to select from among two persons and two organizations which of them "is most suitable to carry out the trust expressed in Kidd's will." Since the court was concerned only about who was qualified to carry on the research specified, the decision seems to require, not that a trustee would be appointed to administer the fund, but that the fund would be given directly to a qualified claimant who would be obligated to use it for the specified purpose. On remand, the trial court awarded the fund to the American Society for Psychical Research, which some several years later reported that it had spent the money without having succeeded in photographing the human soul.

PART B. THE CY-PRES DOCTRINE

1. General Principles

The cy-pres doctrine, unique to charitable trusts, is described in section 399 of the Restatement 2d of Trusts in this way:

> If property is given in trust to be applied to a particular charitable purpose, and it is or becomes impossible or impracticable or illegal to carry out the particular purpose, and if the settlor manifested a more general intention to devote the property to charitable purposes, the trust will not fail but the court will direct the application of the property to some charitable purpose which falls within the general charitable intention of the settlor.

Is judicial modification of the terms of a charitable trust under the cy-pres doctrine incompatible with the principle of donative freedom? Consider Judge Posner's explanation:

A policy of rigid adherence to the letter of the donative instrument is likely to frustrate both the donor's purposes and the efficient use of resources. . . .

Where the continued enforcement of conditions in a charitable gift is no longer economically feasible, because of illegality . . . or opportunity costs . . . the court, rather than declaring the gift void and transferring the property to the residuary legatees (if any can be identified), will authorize the administrators of the charitable trust to apply the assets of the trust to a related (*cy pres*) purpose within the general scope of the donor's intent.

R. Posner, Economic Analysis of Law 482-83 (3d ed. 1986).

Application of the cy-pres doctrine requires not only a finding that the charitable purposes articulated in the trust document are or have become impossible, impracticable, or illegal. Its application also requires a finding that the settlor manifested a more general charitable intention than the articulated purposes. The courts have not been willing to dispense with this latter requirement, and hold that the mere failure of the articulated charitable purposes is by itself sufficient to justify diverting the funds to another charitable purpose. Notwithstanding Judge Posner's reliance in part on the public policy of promoting the efficient use of resources, the state courts view the cy-pres doctrine as one that is driven by the policy of intent-effectuation. Evidently, the courts insist on a finding of a general charitable intent because they think cy pres cannot otherwise be comfortably explained in terms of carrying out the settlor's intent; when the court directs the use of the property to some other charitable purpose, it is merely directing its use to one that "falls within the [settlor's] general charitable intention." If no general charitable intent can be found, the impossibility, impracticability, or illegality of the trust's purposes requires the trust to fail entirely, with a resulting trust back to the settlor or the settlor's successors in interest.

How is a general charitable intent to be found in a given case? What is the court to look for? On these questions, consider the following excerpt from Howard Savings Institution v. Peep, 34 N.J. 494, 170 A.2d 39 (1961):

First, the term "general charitable intent" ordinarily used by courts articulating the [cy-pres] doctrine does not require an intention to benefit charity generally. It requires only a charitable purpose which is broader than the particular purpose the effectuation of which is impossible, impracticable or illegal. . . . Second, the inquiry "did the settlor manifest a general charitable intent" is just another way of asking "would he have wanted the trust funds devoted to a like charitable purpose, or would he have wanted them withdrawn from charitable channels." . . . So stated, it can be seen that *cy pres* is an intent-enforcing doctrine. But it is well to keep in mind that it is a surmise rather than an actual intent which the courts enforce through application of the doctrine. Rarely does a settlor contemplate the possible nonfulfillment of his precise purpose. Therefore, the court must make an educated guess based on the trust instrument and relevant extrinsic evidence as to what he would have intended had he been aware of the contingency which has frustrated the exact effectuation of his expressed intent. . . .

On occasion, the terms of the trust make it appear that the settlor *has* contemplated the failure of the trust's purposes. A specific provision, in the form of a condition subsequent or limitation, or otherwise, that the trust should terminate in the event of a failure of its purpose is given effect; cy pres is usually denied, for the provision for termination tends strongly to negate the idea that the settlor had a more general charitable intent than the articulated charitable purpose. Restatement 2d of Trusts § 399 comment c; § 401.

Preliminary to the general-charitable-intent inquiry, of course, is a finding that the trust's articulated purpose is or has become impossible, impracticable, or illegal. Failing this finding, cy pres will be denied regardless of a broader charitable intent. In thinking about how the court should go about deciding whether the trust has become impracticable, consider the next case, which has attracted a great deal of attention in California and elsewhere in recent years.

Estate of Buck

Superior Court of Marin County, California, 1986
[Opinion reprinted from 21 U.S.F.L. Rev. 691 (1987)]

[In 1975, Beryl Buck, a resident of Marin County, California,[12] died a childless widow. Her will devised the residue of her estate to the San Francisco Foundation, a community trust administering charitable funds throughout the five-county San Francisco Bay Area. This devise became known as the "Buck Trust." The will directed that the residue

> shall always be held and used for exclusively non-profit charitable, religious or educational purposes in providing care for the needy in Marin County, California, and for other non-profit charitable, religious, or educational purposes in that county.

Ms. Buck's residuary estate consisted primarily of a block of shares in Belridge Oil Company stock. Belridge, which Buck's father-in-law had founded, was a privately-held company with substantial oil reserves in Southern California. The value of Ms. Buck's interest in the Belridge stock at the time she executed her will was $7 million, and it had not changed significantly by the time she died in 1975. In 1979, however, the value of the Belridge stock in the Buck Trust had shot up to $260 million as a result of a bidding war when Shell Oil bought Belridge. By 1984, when the trial began, the value of the stock had increased to over $400 million, and the trust was generating an annual income of $30 million.

In 1984, the Foundation, having concluded that it was "impractical and inexpedient to continue to expend all of the income from the Buck Trust solely within Marin County," sought judicial authorization to spend some portion of Buck Trust income in the other four counties of the Bay Area.

---

12. Marin County is located north of San Francisco, immediately across the Golden Gate Bridge. It has one of the highest per-capita incomes in the country. Known for its trend-setting ways, it is sometimes called the "hot-tub capital of the world."

Its petition for cy-pres rested upon the theory that the dramatic increase in the trust fund's value was a posthumous "surprise," a change in circumstances raising doubt whether Ms. Buck, had she anticipated its occurrence, would have limited the scope of her charitable objective to Marin County. The Foundation relied on the proposed testimony of Professor John Simon, of the Yale law faculty. Professor Simon, rather than studying whether and how donors have changed their devises after the value of their assets have increased, examined the geographic and subject-matter scope of the sixty-three largest American foundations over the past thirty years. He asserted that charitable behavior by "major American philanthropists" is characterized by breadth of purpose, a desire to serve "a community that is broadly defined in terms of population size and socioeconomic class." His theory was that Ms. Buck should be viewed as a major American philanthropist and in the absence of any evidence explaining her departure from this "philanthropic standard," it is reasonable to assume that she would have wanted some of her money spent elsewhere in the Bay Area.[13]

The Foundation's cy-pres petition stimulated a flurry of legal activity. Marin County intervened in opposition to the petition. (One Marin County official called the Foundation "grave-robbing bastards," and characterized the cy-pres petition as a "criminal attack upon the sanctity of wills.") Forty-six individuals and charitable organizations in the other four counties (called "Objector-Beneficiaries") were allowed to intervene to object to the Marin-only limitation. The California Attorney General, as supervisor of charitable trusts, also intervened, arguing against the petition and asking whether the Foundation was in violation of its fiduciary duties for bringing such a suit and whether it ought to be removed as trustee.

At trial, the Foundation proposed to offer expert testimony from Professor Simon and Professor Mitchell Polinsky of Stanford Law School, both of whom planned to testify that a primary purpose of the cy-pres doctrine was to promote efficiency in the use of charitable resources under changed circumstances. The trial court ruled that Simon's and Polinsky's proposed testimony was inadmissible as evidence of the testator's intent.

Near the close of the respondent's case, the Foundation, strongly criticized by the Marin County authorities, the press, and the state Attorney General, offered to resign as trustee. All the parties except the Objector-Beneficiaries agreed to a settlement, with the trust to be administered by a new Marin-based community foundation. The Objector-Beneficiaries refused to join in the settlement on the ground that it was a "sell-out" of the needy in the Bay Area. On July 31, 1986, the Foundation was permitted to resign, and the court dismissed its cy-pres petition. On August 15, 1986, the trial court issued a judgment against the Objector-Beneficiaries.][14]

---

13. Professor Simon's theory is set out in Simon, American Philanthropy and the Buck Trust, 21 U.S.F. L. Rev. 641 (1987).

14. This statement of facts is based on Malone, McEachron & Cutler, The Buck Trust Trial—A Litigator's Perspective, 21 U.S.F.L. Rev. 585 (1987).

THOMPSON, J. . . .

A. *CY PRES* APPLIES ONLY WHERE THE PURPOSE OF A TRUST HAS BECOME ILLEGAL, IMPOSSIBLE OR PERMANENTLY IMPRACTICABLE OF PERFORMANCE

The purpose of the cy pres doctrine "is to prevent the failure of valid charitable trust gifts." Estate of Zahn (1971) 16 Cal.App.3d 106, 114, cert. denied sub nom. Zahn v. Security Pacific Nat. Bank, 404 U.S. 938. As explained by Professor Scott:

> Where property is given in trust for a particular charitable purpose, the trust will not ordinarily fail even though it is impossible to carry out the particular purpose. In such a case the court will ordinarily direct that the property be applied to a similar charitable purpose. 4 Scott on Trusts (3d ed. 1967), Charitable Trusts, § 399 at 3084.

The words "cy pres" means "as near." The full phrase in Norman French was "cy pres comme possible," meaning "as near as possible." Bogert, Trusts and Trustees (2d ed. 1964) § 431 at 490. Thus, cy pres is a rule "of construction, the object of which is 'to permit the main purpose of the donor of a charitable trust to be carried out as nearly as may be where it cannot be done to the letter.'" Society of California Pioneers v. McElroy (1944) 63 Cal. App.2d 332, 337.

The Restatement (Second) of Trusts, section 399 at 297, describes the cy pres doctrine as follows:

> If property is given in trust to be applied to a particular charitable purpose and *it is or becomes impossible or impracticable or illegal to carry out the particular purpose,* and if the settlor manifested a more general intention to devote the property to charitable purposes, the trust will not fail but the court will direct the application of the property to some charitable purpose which falls within the general charitable intention of the settlor. (Emphasis added).

These eminent authorities, followed by statutory and/or case law in many states, provide that where a purpose of a charitable trust becomes illegal, impossible or impracticable of fulfillment, and the testator manifested a general charitable intention, the court may direct that the property be applied to a similar charitable purpose.[15]

---

15. Bogert includes "inexpedient" as a possible prerequisite for the application of cy pres. He describes the doctrine as follows:

> Roughly speaking, it is the doctrine that equity will, when a charity is originally or later becomes impossible, inexpedient, or impracticable of fulfillment, substitute another charitable object which is believed to approach the original purpose as closely as possible. Bogert, Trusts and Trustees, supra, § 431 at 490.

Although a few California courts have quoted Bogert in dicta, no California court has ever applied cy pres upon finding "inexpediency," or ever applied an "inexpediency" standard for cy pres.

Courts in California, as in other states, exercise extreme caution before they will vary the terms of a charitable trust:

> Basically, "charitable contributions must be used only for the purposes for which they were received in trust." (Holt v. College of Osteopathic Physicians & Surgeons (1964) 61 Cal.2d 750, 754 [40 Cal. Rptr. 244, 394 P.2d 932]). "The policy of the law in favor of charitable gifts requires a court to carry out the dominant purpose of the donor to make a charitable gift for the purposes expressed in the articles of the original corporate donee." (In re Los Angeles County Pioneer Soc. (1953) 40 Cal.2d 852, 865-66). Only when compliance with these foregoing rules becomes impossible does the application of *cy pres* come into play.

California courts have often quoted the language of the Restatement of Trusts setting forth the cy pres standard of illegality, impossibility, or impracticability. The impossibility or impracticability prerequisite, however, has been interpreted in California to require a "permanency of the impossibility or impracticability of carrying out the specific charitable purpose or purposes of the creator of the trust." Estate of Mabury (1976) 54 Cal.App.3d 969, 985 (emphasis in original).

Other California courts have stated that cy pres applies where "the testator has expressed a general charitable intent, and for some reason his purpose cannot be accomplished in the manner specified. . . ." Estate of Gatlin (1971) 16 Cal.App.3d 644, 648; Estate of Klinkner (1978) 85 Cal. App.3d 942, 951.

In practice, cy pres has most often been applied in California in such cases—where the charitable trust purpose is or has become literally impossible to fulfill (it "cannot be accomplished")—or in cases where it has become "reasonably impossible of performance." E.g., Society of California Pioneers v. McElroy, supra, 63 Cal.App.2d 332, 334-35 ("no longer reasonably possible to carry out the testator's intention"), O'Hara v. Grand Lodge of I.O.G.T. (1931) 213 Cal. 131, 140 (method of carrying out the general charitable purpose "has become reasonably impossible of performance").

B. NEITHER INEFFICIENCY NOR INEFFECTIVE PHILANTHROPY CONSTITUTES IMPRACTICABILITY

"Impracticability" has been defined as "impossible" as early as 1850 in Dr. Johnson's famous dictionary (A Dictionary of the English Language (Henry G. Bohn: London, 1850), p. 616). Other prestigious dictionaries have defined impracticability in the same sense, e.g., "incapable of being done or carried out," "a practical impossibility" (Oxford English Dictionary Vol. V. (Oxford University Press: England, 1933), p. 106); "incapable of accomplishment" (The Century Dictionary (The Century Co.: New York, 1897), p. 3014); "incapable of being performed or carried out" (Webster's Third International Dictionary (G.& C. Merriam Co.: Springfield, Massachusetts, 1967), p. 1136); "practically impossible" (The Dictionary of Hard Words (Dodd Mead: New York, 1910), p. 275).

California courts have never adopted a broad interpretation of the term "impracticable" in charitable trust cases. One California court, in Estate of Butin (1947) 81 Cal.App.2d 76, found the trust purpose to be impractical to fulfill. Estate of Butin involved a situation where there was insufficient funds to fulfill the trust purpose. The testatrix had directed the executors of her will to erect in the courthouse park at Madera, California, "a granite tower . . . to contain a carillon of eighteen bells" to be placed in the park at a reasonable cost and with a certain inscription. The testatrix' will also stated that:

> I realize that future conditions are very uncertain and if, for any good reason, it is impractical to erect this type of memorial, my executors are then authorized to use their own discretion as to the type of memorial to be erected and the cost thereof. Id. at 79.

The court indicated that "it appeared impractical to construct the memorial . . ." for the following reasons:

> that a site for the tower to be located on county property could not be procured, that it would interfere with the public business conducted in the courthouse, and that it would cost more than $100,000, which is in excess of the value of the entire estate. Id. at 81.

The court, then, actually applied the standard—i.e., impractical—set forth by the testatrix in her will. The fact situation itself, given the insufficient funds to construct the tower, essentially involved an impossibility. . . .

Like California courts, courts from other states often describe the standard for cy pres as one of "illegality, impossibility or impracticability." In many of those jurisdictions, however, "impracticability" is equated with "impossibility." Dunbar v. Board of Trustees (1969) 170 Colo. 327, 461 P.2d 28, 32 (dicta).

The Restatement (Second) of Trusts, (1959) section 399, comment q at 306, does not require a literal impossibility. Rather, it defines "impracticability" as follows:

> The doctrine of cy pres is applicable even though it is possible to carry out the particular purpose of the settlor, if to carry it out would *fail to accomplish the general charitable intention* of the settlor. In such case it is "impracticable" to carry out the particular purpose. . . . (Emphasis added).

Ineffective philanthropy, inefficiency and relative inefficiency, that is, inefficiency of trust expenditures in one location given greater relative needs or benefits elsewhere, do not constitute impracticability under either view. Such situation is not the equivalent of impossibility; nor is there any threat that the operation of the trust will fail to fulfill the general charitable intention of the settlor.[16] As stated by one court, "the court's power over the disposition of other people's assets is limited to removing restrictions only if they are incompatible with the testator's dominant purpose." Estate of Wilson (1982) 451 N.Y.S.2d 891, 894 aff'd (1983) 465 N.Y.S.2d 900, 452 N.E.2d 1228. In Wilson, although the alternative scheme proposed a gender neutral educational trust, which would have been preferable on public policy grounds, the court stated that:

> there is another competing public policy consideration, namely, preserving the right of the testator to dispose of his property as he wishes. (Citation omitted). This rule becomes even more compelling when applied to the area of private charitable trusts, for one of the very reasons for the rule is to encourage bequests for charitable purposes. Id.

The foregoing policy considerations fully justify the dominant tendency of courts to require a situation of illegality, impossibility or strict impracticability before they will vary the terms of a charitable trust through an application of cy pres.

The present and well-tested law that cy pres will be invoked to save a charitable bequest that has become impossible or impracticable of fulfillment where the testator has a general charitable intent provides an intermediate concept "between the well established rules of construction that a will is to be construed so as to effectuate the intent of the testator, and that a gift to charity should be effectuated whenever possible." Estate of Klinkner, supra, 85 Cal.App.3d 942, 951. Where both the testator's intent and the charitable gift can, in fact, be effectuated, i.e., the specified trust purpose has not become impossible or impracticable of performance, there is no justification for cy pres.

---

16. To the extent that concepts of effective philanthropy or efficiency relate to achieving the greatest benefit for the cost incurred they should not form the basis for modifying a donor's wishes. No law requires a testator to make a gift which the trustees deem efficient or to constitute effective philanthropy. Moreover, calculating "benefit" involves inherently subjective determinations; thus, what is "effective" or "efficient" will vary, depending on the interests and concerns of the person or persons making the determination. Cy pres does not authorize a court to vary the terms of a bequest merely because the variation will accommodate the desire of the trustee.

To the extent that the term efficiency embraces the concept of relative need, it is not an appropriate basis for modifying the terms of a testamentary trust. (The Foundation itself has acknowledged this, and indicated that such a concept "is neither what Mrs. Buck's will contemplates, nor a term which has an readily ascertainable meaning." (San Francisco Foundation's Statement Regarding Attorney General's Supplemental Response to Second Annual Report, judicially noticed on February 6, 1986.)) If it were otherwise, all charitable gifts, and the fundamental basis of philanthropy would be threatened, as there may always be more compelling "needs" to fill than the gift chosen by the testator. Gifts to Harvard or Stanford University, for example, could fail simply because institutions elsewhere are more needy. Similarly, needs in the Bay Area cannot be equated with the grueling poverty of India or the soul-wrenching famine in Ethiopia. Moreover, a standard of relative need would interpose governmental regulation on philanthropy because courts would be required to consider questions of comparable equity, social utility, or benefit, perhaps even wisdom, and ultimately substitute their judgments or those of the trustees for those of the donors.

The cy pres doctrine should not be so distorted by the adoption of subjective, relative, and nebulous standards such as "inefficiency" or "ineffective philanthropy" to the extent that it becomes a facile vehicle for charitable trustees to vary the terms of a trust simply because they believe that they can spend the trust income better or more wisely elsewhere, or as in this case, prefer to do so. There is no basis in law for the application of standards such as "efficiency" or "effectiveness" to modify a trust, nor is there any authority that would elevate these standards to the level of impracticability.

C. Cy Pres May Not Be Invoked Upon the Belief that the Modified Scheme Would Be More Desirable or Would Constitute a Better Use of the Income

Where the income of a charitable trust can be used for the purpose specified by the testator, cy pres may not be invoked on the grounds that a different use of the income would be more useful or desirable. Several cases from other states elaborate on this principle.

The trustees in In re Oshkosh Foundation (1973) 61 Wis.2d 432, 213 N.W.2d 54, for example, sought to expand the geographical limits of the trust from the City of Oshkosh to that city plus the various townships which comprised the Oshkosh area school district. The trustees claimed that it was "impractical" to confine disbursements of trust funds to the city limits, as the city's influence extends far beyond its boundaries, and "[t]o treat [the inhabitants of the City of Oshkosh and those of the surrounding area] differently would be unfair to each group." 213 N.W.2d at 56. The court held that cy pres did not apply. Indicating that an application of cy pres requires a finding that compliance with the trust's stated purpose has become impossible, unlawful or impracticable, the court stated that:

> No argument is here made that the purpose of the trust has become either impossible or illegal. Rather it is claimed that compliance with the trust has become "impracticable" because it has become "unfair." The underlined words are not synonyms. The trustee, in substance, claims only that the use of school district limits would be more useful and desirable than the use of city limits as prescribed in the trust. But *cy pres does not warrant a court substituting a different plan for that set forth in the trust solely because trustee or court, or both, believe the substituted plan to be a better plan.* Where it was neither claimed nor established that there was a lack of qualified scholarship recipients or charitable requests within the limits set by the trust, there is no basis for holding that it has become, in the words of the statute, "impracticable, impossible or unlawful" to comply with the express terms and limits of the trust. Id. at 57 (footnotes omitted) (emphasis added).

Similarly, in In re Petition of Downer Home (1975) 67 Wis.2d 55, 226 N.W.2d 444, the court admonished that a belief that a substituted use "would be a better use of the income" than the designated use "is not the test" for the application of cy pres. 226 N.W.2d at 450.

Courts have also held that terms of a charitable trust may not be modified on the grounds that a different use would be more beneficial to the community or advantageous to the charity. . . .

Thus, cy pres may not be invoked on the grounds that it would be more "fair," "equitable" or "efficient" to spend the Trust funds in a manner different from that specified by the testator.

D. Cy Pres Does Not Authorize the Court To Vary the Terms of a Trust Merely Because the Variation Will Meet the Desire and Suit the Convenience of the Trustee

Nor is cy pres warranted to alleviate the strain or burden a trust has placed on a trustee organization and as stated by Martin Paley [Director of the San Francisco Foundation], to "modify the nature of the Buck Trust to conform to and become compatible with the values and procedures of the Foundation as a whole."

> [T]he cy pres doctrine does not authorize or permit a court to vary the terms of a bequest and to that extent defeat the intention of the testator merely because the *variation will meet the desire and suit the convenience of the trustee.* Connecticut College v. United States (1960) 276 F.2d 491, 497. (Emphasis added).

Rather, "[e]ither impossibility or impracticability of literal compliance with the donor's plan is indispensably necessary if cy pres is applied." Id. . . .

The Foundation accepted the Buck Trust fully cognizant of the increased value of its assets and of the administrative burden such a large trust would impose on a relatively small community foundation. That, in fact, it has caused an administrative burden on the Foundation and is perceived to be a threat to the integrity of the Foundation as a whole does not warrant varying the terms of Mrs. Buck's bequest. . . .

Cy Pres may not be applied to modify the terms of the Buck Trust.

Conclusions

Based upon clear principles of trust law and the overwhelming factual record before the Court . . . the Court makes the following conclusions. . . .

16. The residents of Marin County have substantial unmet needs which are within the scope of the purposes of the Buck Trust. In addition, there are significant opportunities to spend Buck Trust funds on nonprofit charitable, religious or educational purposes in Marin County which could benefit Marin County, and, if appropriate, all of humankind. The entire income of the Buck Trust is presently insufficient, and will remain insufficient in the future, to address all of these needs and opportunities.

17. A Judgment pursuant to this Statement of Decision should be entered denying the Petition for Modification.

Notes and Questions

1. *Aftermath.* The trial court's decision in *Buck* was not appealed. The trial court ordered the creation of the Marin Community Foundation to administer the Buck Trust. The court also appointed a special master to supervise the foundation. The court order required that the trustee expend twenty percent of the trust income annually on major projects "located in Marin County, the benefits from which will inure not only to Marin County but all of mankind." See Mahoney, The Aftermath, 21 U.S.F.L. Rev. 681 (1987).

2. *Surprise, Charitable Inefficiency, and the Testator's Intent.* The San Francisco Foundation's theory had three steps: first, that Ms. Buck would have been surprised by the increase in the value of the trust assets; second, that surprise opens the door to charitable inefficiency; and third, that charitable inefficiency is a proper basis for cy-pres modification. With which of these steps did the trial court disagree? Concerning the first step, that the donor would have been surprised by the size of the trust fund, Ms. Buck, who was well-aware of the world-wide crisis in the oil industry, believed that the Belridge stock someday would be of great value, and she specifically cautioned that the stock should not be sold because "it was a gold mine and it would be for generations to come."

Concerning the second step, what does "charitable efficiency" mean? Does it mean the same thing as economic efficiency, which is usually defined as a resource allocation that places the resource in the hands of the party or parties who value it most highly (measuring value on the basis of willingness to pay)? How would one determine whether the entitlement to receive income from the Buck trust is worth more to the residents of Marin County only or to the residents of the Bay Area generally?

Concerning the third step, what is the relationship between charitable efficiency and the testator's intent? Professors Simon and Polinsky argued that modifying the trust to avoid charitable inefficiency "'enhances the value of the charitable trust to the testator since, if circumstances change, he or she can rely on the trustee and the court to fill in the "gaps" in the charitable trust in a way that promotes the testator's interests.'" Simon, American Philanthropy and the Buck Trust, 21 U.S.F.L. Rev. 641, 644 (1987) (quoting Expert Witness Statement of A. Mitchell Polinsky). What is your reaction to this argument? For an interesting criticism of Professor Simon's suggestion that Beryl Buck's charitable preferences should be constructed according to the behavior of major American philanthropists, see Note, Phantom Selves: The Search for a General Charitable Intent in the Application of the Cy Pres Doctrine, 40 Stan. L. Rev. 973 (1988).

3. *Cy Pres as to Excess Income.* If the articulated purposes of the trust have not become impossible, impracticable, or illegal, but the income or principal exceeds that which is necessary for their accomplishment, the cy-pres power may be applied as to the excess. In Thatcher v. City of St. Louis, 335 Mo. 1130, 76 S.W.2d 677 (1934), for example, a testamentary trust was established in 1851 by Judge Bryan Mullanphy, when St. Louis was the gateway to the West, for the articulated purpose of furnishing

"relief to all poor immigrants and travelers coming to St. Louis on their way, bona fide, to settle in the West." Over time, other westward routes were opened up, and other historical events intervened to make St. Louis no longer the bottleneck for westward travel. Consequently, the trust's income became more than sufficient for the trust's articulated purposes. The court found that Judge Mullanphy's primary intent "was to alleviate a local condition in his home city of St. Louis, which grew out of the mass movement of a great population into the new western lands," rather than "to build up the West by aiding in its settlement." On the strength of this finding, the court applied its cy-pres power as to the excess income, directing that it be applied to "furnishing relief to poor immigrants and travelers generally in the City of St. Louis in need and distress, and found worthy of assistance." Would this decision have supported the use of cy pres in *Buck*?

4. *Gift Over as Blocking Cy-Pres Modification?* A familiar rule of charitable trust law is that upon failure of the initial charitable gift, the existence of a gift over precludes application of cy pres because the gift over shows a specific alternative intent inconsistent with the finding of general charitable intent. In practice, however, the rule operates only as a rule of construction; other factors may indicate that the donor did have a general charitable intent. See Chester, Cy Pres or Gift Over?: The Search for Coherence in Judicial Reform of Failed Charitable Trusts, 23 Suffolk L. Rev. 41 (1989).

5. *Expanded Use of Cy Pres?* Recent commentators have argued that courts should apply cy pres more readily to modify charitable trust provisions in view of changing community needs. See Johnson & Taylor, Revolutionizing Judicial Interpretation of Charitable Trusts: Applying Relational Contracts and Dynamic Interpretation to Cy Pres and America's Cup Litigation, 74 Iowa L. Rev. 545 (1989); Chester, Cy Pres: A Promise Unfulfilled, 54 Ind. L.J. 407 (1979); DiClerico, Cy Pres: A Proposal for Change, 47 B.U.L. Rev. 153 (1967). For an argument that, because of high error and transaction costs, courts should seldom apply cy pres, see Macey, Private Trusts for the Provision of Private Goods, 37 Emory L.J. 295 (1988).

2. Discriminatory Trusts

Over the years, trusts containing terms that discriminate on the basis of race, gender, religion, or other factors have generated considerable cy-pres litigation.

The Girard College Trust Litigation. One of the earliest series of racial discrimination cases in charitable trusts was generated by the will of Stephen Girard, one of the nation's first millionaires. Girard died a widower, without descendants, in 1831. His will devised $2 million out of the residue of his estate to "The Mayor, Alderman, and Citizens of Philadelphia" in trust to establish and maintain in Philadelphia a college to provide for such a number of poor white male orphans, as can be trained in one institution, a better education as well as a more comfortable maintenance than they usually receive from the application of public funds.

The will also provided that "no ecclesiastic, missionary, or minister of any sect whatever, shall ever hold or exercise any station or duty whatever in the said college" or be admitted for any purpose to the premises. In Vidal v. Girard's Ex'rs, 43 U.S. (2 How.) 127 (1844), the United States Supreme Court held that the trust was a valid and enforceable charitable trust under the law of Pennsylvania. The Court rejected the allegation that the trust was "hostile to the Christian religion" and against public policy.

In 1869, the Pennsylvania legislature provided for the appointment of a board, called "Directors of City Trusts," to administer the trusts under Girard's will as well as other trusts of which the city of Philadelphia had been made trustee. The legislation was upheld in Philadelphia v. Fox, 64 Pa. 169 (1870). In 1954, two persons were denied admission to Girard College because of their race. The Supreme Court of Pennsylvania held that this denial, required by the will of Stephen Girard, was not a violation of the equal protection clause of the Fourteenth Amendment. Girard Will Case, 386 Pa. 548, 127 A.2d 287 (1956). The Supreme Court of the United States reversed. In the Court's opinion, the Board of Directors of City Trusts was an agency of the state; thus, the Board's exclusion of the applicants for admission on the ground of race was state action in violation of the Fourteenth Amendment. Pennsylvania v. Board of Directors of City Trusts of Philadelphia, 353 U.S. 230 (1956).

When the case was remanded to the Pennsylvania trial court, it entered an order removing the Board of Directors of City Trusts as the trustee under Girard's will, replaced the Board with thirteen private trustees who were sworn to uphold the letter of the will, and dismissed the petitions seeking admission to the College. This decree was affirmed in Girard College Trusteeship, 391 Pa. 434, 138 A.2d 844 (1958), cert. denied, 357 U.S. 570 (1958).

Thereafter, the plaintiffs sued in federal district court, seeking an injunction against their exclusion from Girard College on the ground of race. The injunction was granted, and on appeal the judgment was affirmed. Pennsylvania v. Brown, 392 F.2d 120 (3d Cir. 1968). The Court of Appeals held that the change in trustees did not succeed in avoiding a violation of the equal protection clause of the Fourteenth Amendment. Under the authority of Evans v. Newton, 382 U.S. 296 (1966) (see infra p. 774) and Shelley v. Kraemer, 334 U.S. 1 (1948), state action was found in the trial court's substitution of private trustees in place of the Board of Directors of City Trusts. The Supreme Court denied certiorari. 391 U.S. 921 (1968).

As an aside, it may be noted that, starting with the original $2 million in 1831, the value of the Girard Trust had grown to $85 million by 1950 and over $90 million by 1959. By 1957, Girard College had the fifth largest endowment among privately endowed educational institutions in the country, exceeded only by Harvard, Yale, Columbia, and the University of Texas. Of Girard himself, Professor Elias Clark has written: "Stephen Girard deserves better than to be discredited by a provision which was seemingly only incidental to his overall design. His career marks him as a creative, generous and, by the standards of his time, tolerant man." Clark, Charitable Trusts, the Fourteenth Amendment and the Will of Stephen Girard, 66 Yale L.J. 979, 984 (1957). And, the Third Circuit in Pennsylvania v. Brown, supra, noted: "Given everything we know of Mr. Girard, it is inconceivable that in this changed world he would not be quietly happy that his cherished project had raised its sights with the times and joyfully recognized that all human beings are created equal." 392 F.2d at 125.

The Baconsfield Litigation. Another celebrated series of discriminatory-charitable-trust cases arose from the will of Senator Augustus O. Bacon of Georgia, who died in 1914 devising land and an endowment fund to the City of Macon as trustee to hold the land in perpetuity as a park and pleasure ground, to be called Baconsfield, for "white women, white girls, white boys and white children of the City of Macon," with discretion in the trustees to admit "white men of the City of Macon, and white persons of other communities." Senator Bacon's will added:

> I am . . . without hesitation in the opinion that the two races should be forever separate and that they should not have pleasure or recreation grounds to be used or enjoyed, together and in common.

In 1963, several African-Americans sought admission to the park in reliance on Pennsylvania v. Board of Directors of City Trusts of Philadelphia, supra, and for a time African-Americans were admitted. Members of the Board of Managers objected and sought to prevent desegregation of the park by way of appointment by the probate court of new private trustees. The city resigned as trustee and new trustees were appointed. This action was affirmed by the Supreme Court of Georgia. The judgment, however, was reversed by the United States Supreme Court in Evans v. Newton, 382 U.S. 296 (1966). The court found that the park had for many years been an integral part of the city's activities, that it was maintained by the city as a park for white persons only, and enjoyed tax exemption. The mere change in trustees, the court said, could not be assumed to have transferred the park from the public to the private sector.

Thereafter, a Georgia trial court held that the accomplishment of the trust's purpose had become impossible, that the trust had failed and was terminated, and that the trust property reverted to Senator Bacon's heirs. The cy-pres doctrine was held inapplicable because of the finding that the racial restriction was so basic to Senator Bacon's purpose that he would have preferred termination to integration. On appeal, the Supreme Court of Georgia affirmed. In Evans v. Abney, 396 U.S. 435 (1970), the Supreme Court reviewed and affirmed the Georgia decision. The Court held:

> The Fourteenth Amendment is not violated where, as here, a state court operating in its judicial capacity fairly applies its normal principles of construction to determine the testator's true intent in establishing a charitable trust and then reaches a conclusion with regard to that intent which, because

of the operation of neutral and nondiscriminatory state trust laws, effectively denies every one, whites as well as Negroes, the benefits of the trust.

Justices Douglas and Brennan dissented.

The import of Evans v. Newton and Evans v. Abney figures prominently in the *Trammell* and *Tinnin* cases that follow.

Trammell v. Elliott
230 Ga. 841, 199 S.E.2d 194 (1973)

[Clem Boyd died in 1962, devising the residue of her estate in equal portions to the Trustees of Georgia Institute of Technology, Emory University, and Agnes Scott College. The articulated purpose of Clem Boyd's devise was to establish an educational scholarship fund in memory of her parents, to be known as the Boyd-McCord Memorial Scholarship. The scholarships were to be provided out of the income of the fund "for [the] benefit of deserving and qualified poor white boys and girls." The trial court determined that the racial restriction was invalid and applied the cy-pres doctrine to remove that restriction.]

Hawes, J. The appeal here is from an order of the Superior Court of Dekalb County entered on motion for summary judgment in a case brought by the executor of the estate of Miss Clem Boyd seeking construction of her will and direction from the court. . . .

Although two of the named universities to act as trustees of the funds are private institutions, the Attorney General representing the Board of Regents of the University System of Georgia has conceded the requisite state interest with regard to the trust administration on behalf of the Georgia Institute of Technology. We proceed, therefore, on the basis that there is sufficient state action involved to invoke the strictures of the Fourteenth Amendment of the United States Constitution and that the racial restrictions in the devise may not be enforced save in violation of equal protection of law. Evans v. Newton, 382 U.S. 296 (1966); Pennsylvania v. Board of Directors of City Trust, 353 U.S. 230 (1957). The single issue before the court with regard to the devise is whether the trial court erred in applying the doctrine of *cy pres* to exclude the offensive and discriminatory classification. . . .

The existence of a general charitable intent is inferred upon the establishment that the grant conforms in subject matter to any of the legitimate subjects of charity . . . . However, in deference to the intent of the testator, *cy pres* will not be applied where there is demonstrated an intention of the settlor contrary to the inference of general charitable intent that the property should be applied exclusively to the purpose which is or has become impracticable or illegal. Evans v. Abney, 224 Ga. 826, 165 S.E.2d 160 (1968). See, also, Restatement, Second, Trusts Vol. 2, § 399 Comment c, p. 299, and IV Scott, Trusts § 399.2 (3rd ed. 1967). In view of the public policy . . . favoring the effectuation of charitable grants promoting the public good and our own rule disfavoring forfeitures, such demonstration of a specific intent of the settlor as would result in a failure of the devise must be clear, definite, and unambiguous. In such event the trust will fail, and a resulting trust will be implied for the benefit of the testator or his heirs. . . .

The appellant has argued on the basis of Evans v. Abney . . . . This argument is not, we believe, of substance. . . . *Evans* . . . stood for the recognized exception in the use of cy pres whereby from the will the specific intent of the testator conclusively negated any general charitable intention.

The will in the present case did not contain language by which the testatrix intended that the charitable trusts be administered exclusively in the manner prescribed. Other evidence supportive of the establishment of a specific and exclusive intention was also absent from the will, for example, for a reverter clause or an alternative gift over in the event of a failure of the grant. On the other hand, in other parts of the will, the testatrix indicated strongly that she desired that no provision of the will should fail and the funds as set aside revert to her heirs. In Item IX, she noted in this regard that "Adults do not need my life's earnings, and the children who need a college education are the ones who interest me most."

We conclude from the foregoing that the evidence on summary judgment was conclusive of the trial court's finding of a general charitable intent on the part of the testatrix and that the doctrine of cy pres was correctly applied in excluding the illegal racial classification from the charitable grant. . . .

Judgment affirmed.

All the Justices concur except JORDAN, J., who dissents from . . . the judgment of affirmance.

Tinnin v. First United Bank
502 S.2d 659 (Miss. 1987)

[Allan R. Hobgood, a bachelor without descendants, died in 1968. His closest surviving relatives and heirs at law were "the Tinnins," a group comprised of Hobgood's aunt of the half-blood and four first cousins. They were omitted from Hobgood's holographic will and codicil, which were executed in 1962 and 1967, respectively, when his mother was still alive. Although Hobgood's will and codicil devised the bulk of his property in trust for the benefit of his mother for life, this part of the trust never took effect because she predeceased him by a month. The lapse of her income interest caused the acceleration of the remainder interest in the trust, which created an educational trust to be named after his parents, T.H. and Allie R. Hobgood. The trust specifically provided:

[M]y trustees shall, in their discretion, make loans to students of a state college or university of and operated by the State of Mississippi, who are found worthy and who are of the Caucassion [*sic*] race and to none other.

In 1969, the trustee, First United Bank, applied on behalf of the trust to the Internal Revenue Service for tax-exempt status. In that application, the trustee declared its intention to make loans from the trust to eligible beneficiaries without regard to race, color, or creed. The Internal Revenue Service granted the trustee's application.

The trustee did not seek judicial approval of its decision to deviate from the terms of the trust, nor did it notify the probate court or Hobgood's heirs, the Tinnins, of its decision to deviate. The Tinnins did not learn of the trustee's action until the early 1980s, when the value of the trust assets was around $293,000. The Tinnins then brought an action in the Chancery Court, arguing that the trust must be terminated and its assets distributed to them. The Chancery Court dismissed the Tinnins' complaint, determining that "the unlawful racial restriction, being only incidental, not integral, to the primary objective of the testator, must be set aside to enable the testator's principal purpose to be carried out." The Tinnins appealed.]

ROBERTSON, J. This case tests our confidence in ourselves as a free pluralistic people. It also tests our fidelity to the rule of law.

On the one hand we are asked to decree that a charitable educational trust be administered in a racially nondiscriminatory manner, notwithstanding the testator's unmistakable language that the beneficiaries be "worthy" college students "who are of the caucassian [sic] race and . . . none other."

On the other hand, the testator's heirs at law ask that we employ the law generally applicable to void or lapsed bequests and give them the trust assets which amount to almost $300,000.00, as the federal constitution prohibits state judicial enforcement of such a racially restrictive provision.

We find the holographic will before us, properly understood, ambiguous. Because the court below proceeded without regard to extrinsic evidence, we cannot say with confidence that its decision striking the racially restrictive clause and otherwise upholding the trust accords the will its most just and reasonable reading consistent with the general plan divined from the will and our positive law. We reverse and remand. . . .

One of the great chapters in the evolution of the rights of man records the winning of the right of testation, the power by will to control from the grave what becomes of one's property. The power derives from legislative grant. Miss.Code Ann. § 91-5-1 (1972). It is exercised by the competent adult as he sees fit, subject to few limitations, and where the testator has acted in conformity with our empowering statutory rules, his will is valid. It becomes in theory almost sacred and in practice judicially enforceable, notwithstanding the testator's death and public or private inconvenience.

A will is privately made law. Like all law, wills are inevitably open textured to one degree or another, notwithstanding the most skillful draftsmanship. Questions of meaning and effect abound. This is more often so with holographic wills. The ultimate authority for the construction of a will lies in the judicial department of the state. The exercise of that authority from time to time requires enforcement of directives not in so many words a part of an otherwise valid will, a task we perform according to certain familiar canons of construction. . . .

As important and central as we regard our duty to implement the testator's intent, even to the point of supplementation or modification in aid thereof, the coin has another side. The testator's right to make his will as he pleases is not unentailed. Our encounter with one of these entailments adds to the difficulty of today's case.

We have often said the testator's intention is given effect only so long as that intent "does not violate the law or public policy." Dealy v. Keatts, 157 Miss. 412, 418, 128 So. 268, 270 (1930); Matter of Griffin's Will, 411 So.2d 766, 767 (Miss.1982). For reasons of social policy, our law has come to provide that one may not wholly disinherit one's spouse, that one may not attempt purchase of a ticket to heaven by leaving his entire estate to the church, that one may not control ownership of property beyond [a] life in being plus twenty-one years. Whatever may once have been the attitudes of many, it is much too late to doubt that a major social policy of our society is that entitlement one is eligible to enjoy on one's merits shall not be denied by reason of one's race, color or creed. This policy is a part of our organic law by virtue of the Equal Protection Clause. There are limitations upon our authority to enforce racially discriminating testamentary trusts. . . .

Without doubt, the T.H. Hobgood and Allie R. Hobgood Educational Trust is a charitable trust . . . . [A]dvancement of education and relief of poverty have been noted as two favorite subjects of charitable trusts. . . .

None of this carries us far, for our question concerns, not the nature or type of testamentary trust before us, but whether the will of Allan Hobgood . . . should be held to have established a non-discriminatory educational trust or, failing that, to direct distribution of the residuum of Hobgood's estate to the Tinnins as his heirs at law.

The Tinnins argue that the racial exclusion was an integral part of the testator's creative scheme and, as it may not be judicially enforced, the trust must fail. The Bank, on the other hand, as trustee, argues that the Court should employ its equitable powers, cy pres variety or otherwise, and strike the racial exclusion from the trust, also for the reason that it may not be judicially enforced. Indeed, all parties conceded at oral argument that judicial enforcement of the racially discriminatory features of the trust is not an available option. It is helpful to consider briefly why and to what extent this is so.

The seminal case is Shelley v. Kraemer, 334 U.S. 1 (1948). There the Court found an equal protection violation in judicial enforcement of a private covenant that prohibited the sale of affected properties to black persons. More specifically, *Shelley* held the action of state courts ordering enforcement of such racially restrictive covenants was state action within the meaning and contemplation of the Fourteenth Amendment. 334 U.S. at 14-18. See also, Evans v. Newton, 382 U.S. 296 (1966).

By way of contrast, the United States Constitution erects no barrier against purely private conduct, however discriminating or offensive.[17] Evans v. Abney, 396 U.S. 435, 445-47 (1970); Shelley v. Kraemer, 334 U.S. at 13. Had the Bank sought to administer the trust adhering to the racial restrictions thereof, *sans* IRS exemption status, of course, and without reliance upon any arm of the state in aid of enforcement thereof, the Fourteenth Amendment may not have been offended.

Assuming nonenforceability of the racial exclusion, what law governs our choice between excision of the offensive restriction or, at the other extreme, declaring the charitable bequest void so that the property passes to those who would take under the statute of descent and distribution?

We find guidance in Evans v. Abney, supra. Evans refused to disturb Georgia's employment of its long-standing and racially neutral law of trusts to decree termination of a charitable trust in the context of the unenforceability of the testator's clearly expressed racially discriminatory enjoyment clause. Holding that the question is one of state law to which the Fourteenth Amendment does not speak, *Evans* expressly

> reaffirms the traditional role of the States in determining whether or not to apply their cy pres doctrines to particular trusts. Nothing we have said here prevents a state court from applying its cy pres rule in a case where the Georgia court, for example, might not apply its rule.

396 U.S. at 447.

By reason of this state's racially neutral and long standing law of wills and trusts, we would give effect to a clause in a testamentary instrument which provided, for example, for a charitable, educational trust

> for worthy college students who are of the Caucasian race and none others; provided, however, that, if for any reason the aforesaid racial restriction is violated or held unenforceable, I direct that all assets then held by my trustee be delivered to my heirs at law.

This view is the consequence of the existence in our law of the power of testation. Such a testamentary directive would vest rights persons might claim and judicially enforce no matter how inconvenient and offensive to others. See In re Brown, 478 So.2d 1033, 1036-37 (Miss.1985).

We have no such will before us. It is thus incorrect to ask, in the context of today's case, whether Allan Hobgood might have prevented any

---

17. Excellent summaries of the present state of the law regarding federal constitutional regulation of private educational trust burdened with racial and other discriminatory selection provisions may be found in Matter of Estate of Wilson, 59 N.Y.2d 461, 465 N.Y.S.2d 900, 452 N.E.2d 1228, 1235-37 (1983); and Shapiro v. Columbia Union National Bank and Trust Co., 576 S.W.2d 310, 316-21 (Mo.1978). These cases consider the point in detail unnecessary to today's decision in light of the parties' concession that judicial enforcement of the racial exclusion is not available. See also cases collected in Annotation, Validity and Effect Of Gift For Charitable Purposes Which Excludes Otherwise Qualified Beneficiaries Because Of Their Race or Religion, 25 A.L.R.3d 736 (1969 and Supp. 1986); Bogert, The Law of Trusts and Trustees § 378, pp. 191-92 (Rev.2d Ed.1977).

of his money from going to black college students, if only he had expressed clearly his intent in that regard in his will. Of course, he could have done that. Our question is, given the options of administration of the trust on a non-discriminatory basis or dismantling the trust and delivery of its assets to the Tinnins, which would Hobgood have preferred? Our polestar consideration, as always, is the intent of the testator, the right our law has given each competent adult to direct from the grave the disposition of his worldly goods. . . .

Although today's question is one of first impression in this state, it has been decided often and variously elsewhere—in varying factual contexts, of course. Most famous is the Girard College case, the subject of much litigation, finally resolved in Pennsylvania v. Brown, 392 F.2d 120 (3d Cir. 1968). A will which provided for an educational institution for "poor male white orphan children" was modified through *cy pres* power to include all poor male orphans regardless of race. . . .

On the other hand, we are impressed by the force of Evans v. Newton, 221 Ga. 870, 148 S.E.2d 329 (1966), affirmed sub nom. Evans v. Abney, 396 U.S. 435 (1970), wherein the Georgia Supreme Court held that the trust which provided the for-whites-only Baconsfield Park in Macon must fail; the doctrine of cy pres, unquestionably a part of Georgia law, could not be applied so as to continue the trust by simply removing restrictive racial provisions. The Georgia Supreme Court made no attempt at second guessing the expressed racially exclusive intent of the testator, the late U.S. Senator Augustus O. Bacon, who designated that the "private" park established as his devise be restricted to whites only. . . .

In the end these cases boil down to a question of whether the court considered the unenforceable racial exclusion "incidental" or "integral" to the testator's purpose. This is the approach of the court below in today's case, its ultimate conclusion being that the racial restriction in Allan Hobgood's will was "only incidental, not integral" and thus "must be set aside." But labels so subjective are of little use, as the judicial eyesight varies widely. Our gaze is upon the choice between two options, each of which bears features we are confident Hobgood did not intend, in the context of which efforts at fitting the racially restrictive language of his will under labels such as "incidental" or "integral" seem vain.

The answer to today's dilemma must be found within the context of our general rules regarding will construction . . . .

We will never know what Allan Hobgood would have preferred to do with his money if he had known that no court would enforce his wish that his money be loaned exclusively to white students. The language he employed leaves no doubt that he did not want any of his money to be loaned to non-whites. Disingenuity attends the suggestion that the racially exclusive language of the will was [incidental] or an afterthought. Given the historical context of the writing of the will—the racial turbulence of the 1960's—it is difficult to hold the words "Caucassion [sic] race and to none other" idly inserted.

Recognition of the unmistakable meaning of this clause, however, leaves us far short of solution to today's construction riddle. The Tinnins' gaze has been so focused upon the tree they have found to their liking that they have given us little help in understanding the complex forest that is Allan Hobgood's reconstructed will. The Chancery Court recognized that the racially restrictive clause should not be viewed in isolation but its world also was too small. That Court looked at the racially restrictive clause and asked whether it was incidental or integral. The Court should have directed its attention to the alternative dispositions argued for and sought a just and reasonable disposition of Allan Hobgood's will as consistent as may be decreed by reference to the general plan reflected by his reconstructed will. More precisely, the alternatives below and here are (a) striking the racially restrictive clause and continuing the trust and (b) causing the trust to fail and the property to be distributed to the Tinnins, the testator's heirs at law. We know for a fact that Allan Hobgood did not wish either of these alternatives. The question is which is less offensive [to] the general plan of his reconstructed will.

The point takes on color in the context of the fact that Lucille Hamilton Hobgood Tinnin, Allan's aunt of the half blood, was not mentioned in his will. Indeed, when the will was made, Allan's mother appears to have been his sole heir at law, so that there is no reason for him to have thought of the possibility that Aunt Lucille would share in his estate, much less that her four children might take it all. While it is true that we construe wills favorably to those who would take under the laws of descent and distribution, unless the testator has manifest[ed] an intent to the contrary, we do so far more readily in favor of next of kin than remote kin. If we understand the facts correctly, Allan's mother was still alive on April 22, 1967, when he made his codicil, meaning that even then it was a near certainty that Allan was unaware that the Tinnins might wind up with his estate. Allan's mother died December 31, 1967, a bare month before her son's death on January 31, 1968. Nothing in the record tells us whether Allan, during January of 1968, was competent to revise his will in light of his mother's death. . . .

The question resolves itself to whether, given the unenforceability of the racially restrictive clause, Allan Hobgood's reconstructed will should be held to direct that the trust continue on a non-discriminatory basis or that all of its assets go to the Tinnins. The will as reconstructed in accordance with the principles . . . above is unclear in this regard. The record before us, which is wholly documentary, is inadequate to enable us to answer this question with confidence.

We hold Allan Hobgood's will, so reconstructed, ambiguous regarding the question before us. The Chancery Court erred when it construed the will wholly upon the documentary record. Resort to extrinsic evidence is desirable, if not essential, to the correct resolution of the weighty claims presented. For example, in deciding whether the Tinnins, as statutory residuary legatees, should prevail it would be helpful to know how close they were to Allan Hobgood, whether they were in fact objects of his affection. On the other hand, the Court should ascertain, if possible, the power and source of Allan Hobgood's interest in helping young people go to college and how important this was vis-a-vis his clearly expressed racially discriminatory intent.

We vacate the Judgment entered October 15, 1984, and remand this case to the active docket of the Chancery Court of Lauderdale County for further proceedings consistent with this opinion. At trial on the merits, and because the will is ambiguous, parol or extrinsic evidence shall be admissible in accordance with our familiar rules.

In the absence of extrinsic evidence which, when coupled with the wording of Allan Hobgood's will reconstructed according to Section III above, will provide a discernible answer to the choice presented by this case, there are certain further principles recognized in our law to which the Chancery Court may resort. Charitable trusts are favored and should be enforced where possible. Instruments . . . purportedly creating charitable trusts will be liberally construed in favor of the charity. Where there are two possible constructions of the instrument in question, one of which will render the charitable gift valid and the other of which will cause it to fail, we will adopt the construction which will sustain the charitable bequest, absent manifest countervailing considerations. Finally, there is a presumption, albeit a rebuttable one, that the testator preferred the charitable trust to survive so far as may be within the law.

REVERSED AND REMANDED.

WALKER, C.J., ROY NOBLE LEE and HAWKINS, P.JJ., and PRATHER, SULLIVAN, ANDERSON and GRIFFIN, JJ., concur. DAN M. LEE, J., concurs in result only.

Notes

1. *Canadian Authority.* In an apparent case of first impression in Canada, Leonard Foundation v. Ontario Human Rights Comm'n, [1990] Ont. J. No. 615 (C.A.), the court held that a trust that restricted scholarships to "white Protestants of British descent" violated public policy and exercised its cy-pres power to delete the discriminatory restrictions.

2. *Tax Deductibility of Discriminatory Trusts.* In Rev. Rul. 67-235, 1967-2 C.B. 79, the Internal Revenue Service disallowed a deduction for a gift to an organization that provided recreational facilities that were open to only a portion of an entire community, on a racial basis. See also Priv. Ltr. Rul. 79-23-001. A three-judge federal court enjoined the Service from allowing a deduction for gifts to fraternal organizations that exclude non-whites from membership. McGlotten v. Connally, 338 F. Supp. 448 (D.D.C. 1972), discussed in Bittker & Kaufman, Taxes and Civil Rights: "Constitutionalizing" the Internal Revenue Code, 82 Yale L.J. 51 (1972).

The tax laws appear to be quite tolerant of non-racial forms of discrimination. In private letter rulings, the Commissioner has determined that devises in trust to provide scholarships for deserving Jewish children of high academic ability or to provide scholarships for male Protestant graduates of a specified high school qualified for the charitable deduction. Priv. Ltr. Rul. 77-44-005; Priv. Ltr. Rul. 77-44-007. In these rulings, the

Commissioner stated that religious and sexual restrictions are permissible in charitable devises.

3. *Tax-Exempt Status.* In Rev. Rul. 71-447, 1971-2 C.B. 230, the Internal Revenue Service, declaring that "racial discrimination in education is contrary to Federal public policy," concluded that "a school not having a racially nondiscriminatory policy as to students is not 'charitable' within the common law concepts reflected in sections 170 and 501(c)(3) of the Code." The Service's position was upheld in Bob Jones University v. United States, 461 U.S. 574 (1983). See also Rev. Proc. 75-50, 1975-2 C.B. 581, which sets forth the following guidelines for determining whether private schools have racially nondiscriminatory policies so as to qualify for tax-exempt status under IRC section 501(c)(3):

> § 3.02. The Service considers discrimination on the basis of race to include discrimination on the basis of color and national or ethnic origin. A policy of a school that favors racial minority groups with respect to admissions, facilities and programs, and financial assistance will not constitute discrimination on the basis of race when the purpose and effect is to promote the establishment and maintenance of that school's racially nondiscriminatory policy as to students.
>
> § 3.03. A school that selects students on the basis of membership in a religious denomination or unit thereof will not be deemed to have a discriminatory policy if membership in the denomination or unit is open to all on a racially nondiscriminatory basis.

In McCoy v. Shultz, 73-1 USTC ¶ 12,906 (D.D.C. 1973), the court dismissed a suit to force the Internal Revenue Service to withdraw tax-exempt status previously granted under IRC section 501(c)(3) to the Portland City Club Foundation, Inc., a private organization that excluded women from membership.

EXTERNAL REFERENCE. Ginsburg, Sex Discrimination and the IRS: Public Policy and the Charitable Deduction, Tax Notes, Jan. 14, 1980, at 27.

4. *Gender and Religious Restrictions/Trust and Property Law.* The Restatement 2d of Trusts is also quite tolerant of gender and religious restrictions in charitable trusts:

> § 369 comment g. *Limitation of beneficiaries to particular place or class.* . . . A trust for the relief of poverty is charitable although the beneficiaries are limited to persons of a particular sex, age, religion, profession or trade or political affiliation.
>
> § 370 comment j. *Limitation of beneficiaries to particular place or class.* . . . [A] trust to establish or maintain a school is charitable although the scholars are limited to persons of a particular sex or religion or to the children of a particular profession or trade. So also, a trust is charitable where it provides for free scholarships although the scholarships are similarly limited.

More recently, however, the Restatement 2d of Property states:

> § 4.2 comment t. *Transferees excluded on the ground of race, color, religion, sex or national origin.* A forfeiture restraint [on alienation of property] which permits alienation to all persons except those of a certain race, or color, or

religion, or sex, or national origin is not reasonable. Such restraints are barred by numerous federal and state statutes (see Statutory Note to Section 3.1, Restatement, Second, Property (Landlord and Tenant)). A restraint on use or occupancy by those of a certain race, or color, or religion, or sex, or national origin is equally not reasonable.

Estate of Wilson
59 N.Y.2d 461, 452 N.E.2d 1228, 465 N.Y.S.2d 900 (1983)

[This case consolidated appeals from lower court judgments in two cases, Estate of Wilson and Estate of Johnson.

Clark W. Wilson devised the residue of his estate to the Key Bank in Central New York, in trust, to apply the income

> to defraying the education and other expenses of the first year at college of five (5) young men [from] Canastota High School, three (3) of whom who shall have attained the highest grades in science and two (2) of whom shall have attained the highest grades in chemistry, as may be certified by the Superintendent of Schools for the Canastota Central School District.

Edwin Irving Johnson devised the residue of his estate to the Board of Education of the Croton-Harmon Union Free School District, in trust, to apply the income

> for scholarships or grants for bright and deserving young men who have graduated from the High School of [the Croton-Harmon Union Free] School District, and whose parents are financially unable to send them to college, and who shall be selected by the Board of Education of such School District with the assistance of the Principal of such High School.

Complaints were filed in both cases with the Civil Rights Office of the United States Department of Education. The allegation was that participation in the selection process by the school districts would violate Title IX of the Education Amendments of 1972, 20 U.S.C. § 1681 et seq., which prohibits gender discrimination in federally financed education programs. The Department of Education notified each school district of its intent to conduct an investigation into the complaints. During the pendency of these investigations, the Canastota Central School District agreed to refrain from again providing names of students to the trustee of the Wilson Trust, and the executor of the Johnson will, the president of the Croton-Harmon Union Free board of education, and the state Attorney General agreed that the Johnson Trust would be administered on a sex-neutral basis, as if Johnson's Trust had used the word "persons" instead of "men."

In the *Wilson* case, the trustee brought an action in Surrogate's Court for a determination of the effect and validity of the above-quoted provision in the Wilson Trust. In *Johnson*, the state Attorney General brought an action in Surrogate's Court for construction of the above-quoted provision in the Johnson Trust.

The Surrogate in *Wilson* held that the school district's participation in the selection process was not unlawful, and ordered the trustee to continue administering the trust. On appeal, the Appellate Division held that the administration of the trust according to its literal terms was rendered impossible by the fact that the school district was under no legal obligation to supply the names of qualified male candidates. The Appellate Division therefore exercised its cy pres power by striking the clause requiring the district's certification; candidates were permitted to apply directly to the trustee.

The Surrogate in *Johnson* held that the administration of the trust according to its literal terms was rendered impossible by the school district's unwillingness to do so. Declining to reform the trust in accordance with the agreement reached among the parties, the Surrogate ordered the school district replaced as trustee with a private trustee who would give effect to the trust as written. On appeal, the Appellate Division held that the Surrogate's substitution of trustees constituted state action and a denial of equal protection of the laws in violation of the fourteenth amendment; the Appellate Division, in exercise of its cy pres power, ordered the gender restriction eliminated from the trust.

Appeals to the Court of Appeals followed in both cases.]

COOKE, C.J. These appeals present the question whether the equal protection clause of the Fourteenth Amendment is violated when a court permits the administration of private charitable trusts according to the testators' intent to finance the education of male and not female students. When a court applies trust law that neither encourages, nor affirmatively promotes, nor compels private discrimination but allows parties to engage in private selection in the devise or bequest of their property, that choice will not be attributable to the State and subjected to the Fourteenth Amendment's strictures.

I. The factual patterns in each of these matters are different, but the underlying legal issues are the same. In each there is imposed a decedent's intention to create a testamentary trust under which the class of beneficiaries are members of one sex. . . .

II. . . . There can be no question that these trusts, established for the promotion of education, are for a charitable purpose within the meaning of the law. . . . Charitable trusts are encouraged and favored by the law. . . . [U]nlike other trusts, a charitable trust will not necessarily fail when the settlor's specific charitable purpose or direction can no longer be accomplished. . . .

The court, of course, cannot invoke its cy pres power without first determining that the testator's specific charitable purpose is no longer capable of being performed by the trust. In establishing these trusts, the testators expressly and unequivocally intended that they provide for the educational expenses of male students. It cannot be said that the accomplishment of the testators' specific expression of charitable intent is "impossible or impracticable." So long as the subject high schools graduate boys with the requisite qualifications, the testators' specific charitable intent can be fulfilled.

Nor are the trusts' particular limitation of beneficiaries by gender invalid and incapable of being accomplished as violative of public policy. It is true that the eradication in this State of gender-based discrimination is an important public policy. Indeed, the Legislature has barred gender-based discrimination in education (see Education Law, § 3201-a), employment (see Labor Law, §§ 194, 197, 220-e; General Business Law, § 187), housing, credit, and many other areas (see Executive Law, § 296). . . . The restrictions in these trusts run contrary to this policy favoring equal opportunity and treatment of men and women. A provision in a charitable trust, however, that is central to the testator's or settlor's charitable purpose, and is not illegal, should not be invalidated on public policy grounds unless that provision, if given effect, would substantially mitigate the general charitable effect of the gift (see 4 Scott, Trusts [3d ed.], § 399.4).

Proscribing the enforcement of gender restrictions in private charitable trusts would operate with equal force towards trusts whose benefits are bestowed exclusively on women. "Reduction of the disparity in economic condition between men and women caused by the long history of discrimination against women has been recognized as . . . an important governmental objective" (Califano v. Webster, 430 U.S. 313, 317). There can be little doubt that important efforts in effecting this type of social change can be and are performed through private philanthropy (see, generally, Commission on Private Philanthropy and Public Needs, Giving in America: Toward a Stronger Voluntary Section [1975]). And, the private funding of programs for the advancement of women is substantial and growing (see Bernstein, Funding for Women's Higher Education: Looking Backward and Ahead, Grant Magazine, vol. 4, No. 4, pp. 225-229; Ford Foundation, Financial Support of Women's Programs in the 1970's [1979]; Yarrow, Feminist Philanthropy Comes Into Its Own, NY Times, May 21, 1983, p. 7, col. 2). Indeed, one compilation of financial assistance offered primarily or exclusively to women lists 854 sources of funding (see Schlacter, Directory of Financial Aids for Women [2d ed., 1981]; see, also, Note, Sex Restricted Scholarships and the Charitable Trust, 59 Iowa L. Rev. 1000, 1000-1001, & nn. 10, 11). Current thinking in private philanthropic institutions advocates that funding offered by such institutions and the opportunities within the institutions themselves be directly responsive to the needs of particular groups (see Ford Foundation, op. cit., at pp. 41- 44; Fleming, Foundations and Affirmative Action, 4 Foundation News No. 4, at pp. 14-17; Griffen, Funding for Women's Programs, 6 Grantsmanship Center News, No. 2, at pp. 34-45). It is evident, therefore, that the focusing of private philanthropy on certain classes within society may be consistent with public policy. Consequently, that the restrictions in the trusts before this court may run contrary to public efforts promoting equality of opportunity for women does not justify imposing a per se rule that gender restrictions in private charitable trusts violate public policy.

Finally, this is not an instance in which the restriction of the trusts serves to frustrate a paramount charitable purpose. In Howard Sav. Inst. v. Peep, 34 N.J. 494, 170 A.2d 39, for example, the testator made a charitable bequest to Amherst College to be placed in trust and to provide scholarships for "deserving American born, Protestant, Gentile boys of good moral repute, not given to gambling, smoking, drinking or similar acts." Due to the religious restrictions, the college declined to accept the bequest as contrary to its charter. The court found that the college was the principal beneficiary of the trust, so that removing the religious restriction and thereby allowing the college to accept the gift would permit administration of the trust in a manner most closely effectuating the testator's intent.

In contrast, the trusts subject to these appeals were not intended to directly benefit the school districts. Although the testators sought the school districts' participation, this was incidental to their primary intent of financing part of the college education of boys who attended the schools. Consequently, severance of the school districts' role in the trusts' administration will not frustrate any part of the testators' charitable purposes. Inasmuch as the specific charitable intent of the testators is not inherently "impossible or impracticable" of being achieved by the trusts, there is no occasion to exercise cy pres power.

Although not inherently so, these trusts are currently incapable of being administered as originally intended because of the school districts' unwillingness to co-operate. These impediments, however, may be remedied by an exercise of a court's general equitable power over all trusts to permit a deviation from the administrative terms of a trust and to appoint a successor trustee.

A testamentary trust will not fail for want of a trustee. . . . Accordingly, the proper means of continuing the Johnson Trust would be to replace the school district with someone able and willing to administer the trust according to its terms.

When an impasse is reached in the administration of a trust due to an incidental requirement of its terms, a court may effect, or permit the trustee to effect, a deviation from the trust's literal terms. This power differs from a court's cy pres power in that "[t]hrough exercise of its deviation power the court alters or amends administrative provisions in the trust instrument but does not alter the purpose of the charitable trust or change its dispositive provisions". The Wilson Trust provision that the school district certify a list of students is an incidental part of the trust's administrative requirements, which no longer can be satisfied in light of the district's refusal to co-operate. The same result intended by the testator may be accomplished by permitting the students to apply directly to the trustee. Therefore, a deviation from the Wilson Trust's administrative terms by eliminating the certification requirement would be the appropriate method of continuing that trust's administration. . . .

III. It is argued before this court that the judicial facilitation of the continued administration of gender-restrictive charitable trusts violates the equal protection clause of the Fourteenth Amendment (see U.S. Const., 14th Amdt., § 1). The strictures of the equal protection clause are invoked when the State engages in invidious discrimination. Indeed, the State itself cannot, consistent with the Fourteenth Amendment, award scholarships that are gender restrictive.

The Fourteenth Amendment, however, "erects no shield against merely private conduct, however discriminatory or wrongful." (Shelly v. Kraemer, 334 U.S. 1). Private discrimination may violate equal protection of the law when accompanied by State participation in, facilitation of, and, in some cases, acquiescence in the discrimination. Although there is no conclusive test to determine when State involvement in private discrimination will violate the Fourteenth Amendment, the general standard that has evolved is whether "the conduct allegedly causing the deprivation of a federal right [is] fairly attributable to the state" (Lugar v. Edmondson Oil Co., 457 U.S. 922, 937). Therefore, it is a question of "state responsibility" and "[o]nly by sifting facts and weighing circumstances can the . . . involvement of the State in private conduct be attributed its true significance" (Burton v. Wilmington Parking Auth., 365 U.S. 715, 722, supra). . . .

The State generally may not be held responsible for private discrimination solely on the basis that it permits the discrimination to occur. Nor is the State under an affirmative obligation to prevent purely private discrimination. Therefore, when the State regulates private dealings it may be responsible for private discrimination occurring in the regulated field only when enforcement of its regulation has the effect of compelling the private discrimination.

In Shelley v. Kraemer (supra), for example, the Supreme Court held that the equal protection clause was violated by judicial enforcement of a private covenant that prohibited the sale of affected properties to "people of Negro or Mongolian Race." When one of the properties was sold to a black family, the other property owners sought to enforce the covenant in State court and the family was ordered to move from the property. The Supreme Court noted "that the restrictive agreements standing alone cannot be regarded as violative of any rights guaranteed to petitioners by the Fourteenth Amendment. So long as the purposes of those agreements are effectuated by voluntary adherence to their terms, it would appear clear that there has been no action by the State and the provisions of the Amendment have not been violated" (334 U.S., at p. 13). The court held, however, that it did [not] have before it cases "in which the States have merely abstained from action leaving private individuals free to impose such discriminations as they see fit. Rather, these are cases in which the States have made available to such individuals the full coercive power of the government to deny petitioners, on the grounds of race or color, the enjoyment of property rights" (id., at p. 19). It was not the neutral regulation of contracts permitting parties to enter discriminatory agreements that caused the discrimination to be attributable to the State. Instead, it was that the State court's exercise of its judicial power directly effected a discriminatory act.

In Barrows v. Jackson, 346 U.S. 249, the court applied the same reasoning when it held that a court's awarding damages against a party who has breached a racially restrictive covenant also violates the equal protection clause. The court reiterated that "voluntary adherence [to the covenant] would constitute individual action only" (id., at p. 253). But, "[t]o compel respondent to respond in damages would be for the State to punish her for failure to perform her covenant to continue to discriminate against non-Caucasians in the use of her property . . . Thus, it becomes not respondent's voluntary choice but the State's choice that she observe her covenant or suffer damages" (id., at p. 254). . . .

A court's application of its equitable power to permit the continued administration of the trusts involved in these appeals falls outside the ambit of the Fourteenth Amendment. Although the field of trusts is regulated by the State, the Legislature's failure to forbid private discriminatory trusts does not cause such trusts, when they arise, to be attributable to the State. It naturally follows that, when a court applies this trust law and determines that it permits the continued existence of private discriminatory trusts, the Fourteenth Amendment is not implicated.

In the present appeals, the coercive power of the State has never been enlisted to enforce private discrimination. Upon finding that requisite formalities of creating a trust had been met, the courts below determined the testator's intent, and applied the relevant law permitting those intentions to be privately carried out. The court's power compelled no discrimination. That discrimination had been sealed in the private execution of the wills. Recourse to the courts was had here only for the purpose of facilitating the administration of the trusts, not for enforcement of their discriminatory dispositive provisions.

This is not to say that a court's exercise of its power over trusts can never invoke the scrutiny of the Fourteenth Amendment. This court holds only that a trust's discriminatory terms are not fairly attributable to the State when a court applies trust principles that permit private discrimination but do not encourage, affirmatively promote, or compel it.

The testators' intention to involve the State in the administration of these trusts does not alter this result, notwithstanding that the effect of the courts' action respecting the trusts was to eliminate this involvement. The courts' power to replace a trustee who is unwilling to act as in Johnson or to permit a deviation from an incidental administrative term in the trust as in Wilson is a part of the law permitting this private conduct and extends to all trusts regardless of their purposes. It compels no discrimination. Moreover, the minimal State participation in the trusts' administration prior to the time that they reached the courts for the constructions under review did not cause the trusts to take on an indelible public character.

In sum, the Fourteenth Amendment does not require the State to exercise the full extent of its power to eradicate private discrimination. It is only when the State itself discriminates, compels another to discriminate, or allows another to assume one of its functions and discriminate that such discrimination will implicate the amendment.

Accordingly, in Matter of Wilson, the order of the Appellate Division should be affirmed, with costs payable out of the estate to all parties appearing separately and filing separate briefs.

In Matter of Johnson, the order of the Appellate Division should be reversed, with costs payable out of the estate to all parties appearing separately and filing separate briefs and the decree of the Surrogate's Court, Westchester County, reinstated.

MEYER, Judge (concurring in Matter of Wilson and dissenting in Matter of Johnson). I would affirm in both cases. Although the Constitution does not proscribe private bias, it does proscribe affirmative State action in furtherance of bias.

In Matter of Wilson the trust is private and the only involvement of a public official (the superintendent of schools) is his certification of a student's class standing, information which is, in any event, available to any student applying to the trustee for a scholarship. There is, therefore, no State action.

In Matter of Johnson, however, the trustee is the board of education, a public body. The establishment of a public trust for a discriminatory purpose is constitutionally improper, as Presiding Justice Mollen has fully spelled out in his opinion. For the State to legitimize that impropriety by replacement of the trustee is unconstitutional State action. The only permissible corrective court action is, as the Appellate Division held, excision of the discriminatory limitation. . . .

Notes

1. *Compensatory Preferences.* In Trustees of University of Delaware v. Gebelein, 420 A.2d 1191 (Del. Ch. 1980), the court considered the validity of Harriott E. Higgins' devise of the residue of her estate to the Trustees of the University of Delaware, to pay the educational expenses of "a young, white, female student" enrolled in the Women's College of the University of Delaware who graduated from the Commodore MacDonough School, a public high school in St. Georges, Delaware. The scholarship recipient was to be selected by the president of the University of Delaware in collaboration with the teaching staff at Commodore MacDonough School, subject only to the restriction "that the young woman is not to be selected from a family with ample means. . . ."

In a prior proceeding, brought by the university trustees in 1979, the court exercised its cy-pres power to eliminate the racial restriction in the trust. In this proceeding, the Attorney General sought removal of the gender restriction; the university trustees opposed the petition. Denying the petition, the court first held that administration of the trust constituted state action. It then concluded that "the benign discrimination set forth in the Higgins' scholarship fund does not subvert equal opportunity, but rather promotes it by compensating for past acts of discrimination." Cf. Mississippi University for Women v. Hogan, 458 U.S. 718 (1982), holding unconstitutional the denial of admission of a male applicant, on the ground of gender, to the School of Nursing of the Mississippi University for Women, a state university.

In Crichfield Trust, 177 N.J. Super. 258, 426 A.2d 88 (1980), the court removed the gender restriction of Frieda Crichfield's devise to the Summit, New Jersey, Board of Education to provide a yearly college scholarship for "worthy boys of Summit High School." The court noted that "[h]ere, no party has defended the discrimination as compensatory for past discrimination." In deciding to apply the cy-pres power to remove the gender restriction, the court further noted that at the time the trust was created few female high school graduates sought scholarships for higher education.

Recently, the United States Department of Education announced that it is reviewing a controversial advisory that said that colleges and universities receiving federal funds would not be allowed to award out of their general scholarship budgets scholarships on the basis of race or ethnicity. (The advisory did not affect scholarships from private donations designated for that purpose or from federal programs established to aid minority students.) The Department advisory said that the policy was based on its legal opinion that "race-exclusive" scholarships are discriminatory and illegal under the Civil Rights Act of 1964. See N.Y. Times, Dec. 19, 1990, at A1. Subsequently, the new Secretary of Education, Lamar Alexander, announced that the controversial advisory was under further consideration. Secretary Alexander said that colleges and universities should continue their current policy regarding scholarships reserved for members of specific racial and ethnic groups. N.Y. Times, March 21, 1991, at A8.

2. *Other Approaches.* Howard Savings Institution v. Peep, 34 N.J. 494, 170 A.2d 39 (1961), the court exercised its cy-pres power to excise discriminatory restrictions in the will of C. Edward McKinney, Jr., who devised the residue of his estate

> to Amherst College . . . to be held in trust to be used as a scholarship loan fund for deserving American born, Protestant, Gentile boys of good moral repute, not given to gambling, smoking, drinking or similar acts. (It being my thought that if a young man has enough funds to allow the waste of smoking, he certainly does not need help.)

Amherst refused to accept the devise unless the "Protestant, Gentile" restriction was removed, on the ground that the administration of such a gift would be contrary to its charter. The appellate court held that cy pres was appropriate because the terms of McKinney's will, including the absence of any gift over upon failure of the trust, indicated that "Mr. McKinney was more interested in benefiting Amherst and its needy students than he was in Protestantism." But cf. La Fond v. City of Detroit, 357 Mich. 362, 98 N.W.2d 530 (1959) (1955 devise of about $25,000 "to the city of Detroit . . . for a playfield for white children"; city resolved to accept the devise "provided the court will . . . make the playfield available to all children without regard to race, color or creed"; held, cy pres denied because "the will does not indicate a general charitable intention to provide for a general charitable purpose rather than for a particular designated object.")

In Lockwood v. Killian, 172 Conn. 496, 375 A.2d 998 (1977), 179 Conn. 62, 425 A.2d 909 (1979), Frank Fuller devised the residue of his estate to the town of East Hartford, Connecticut, to establish a scholarship fund for boys from Hartford high schools "who are members of the Caucasian race and who have severally, specifically professed themselves to be of the Protestant Congregationalist faith . . . ." There was no gift over in case the trust failed. Given the racial, gender, religious, and geographical restrictions, the selection committee found it impossible to find a sufficient number of recipients to expend the annual income. They petitioned the court for instructions. The Connecticut Supreme Court found that Fuller was most concerned about the geographical and religious qualifications, and ordered the others removed. The court stated the selection committee would be unable to attract sufficient applicants for scholarships until the racial and gender restrictions are eliminated because no institution would publicize the availability of these racially and sexually biased scholarships. The court found that enforcement of the religious restriction did not involve state action.

3. *Construction.* Modern trust forms often contain a definitions article. It is not unusual to find in that definitions article a boilerplate clause such as the following:

> *Gender and Form.* The use of any gender herein shall be deemed to be or include the other gender and the use of the singular herein shall be deemed to be or include the plural, and *vice versa*, wherever appropriate.

Had such a clause been included in Clark Wilson's will, would a court have been justified in construing "men" to mean "men or women"? Could "female" in Harriott Higgins' will have been appropriately construed to mean "female or male"? What about construing "boys" in Frieda Crichfield's trust to mean "boys or girls"?

EXTERNAL REFERENCES. Luria, Prying Loose the Dead Hand of the Past: How Courts Apply Cy Pres to Race, Gender, and Religiously Restricted Trusts, 21 U.S.F.L. Rev. 41 (1987); Swanson, Discriminatory Charitable Trusts: Time for a Legislative Solution, 48 U. Pitt. L. Rev. 153 (1986); Leacock, Racial Preferences in Educational Trusts: An Overview of the United States Experience, 28 How. L.J. 515 (1985); Adams, Racial and Religious Discrimination in Charitable Trusts, 25 Clev. St. L. Rev. 1 (1976);

PART C. SUPERVISION OF CHARITABLE TRUSTS

R. Posner, Economic Analysis of Law
484 (3d ed. 1986)

Even where no unforeseen contingencies occur, perpetual charitable gifts raise an economic issue that echoes the concern with the separation of ownership and control in the modern business corporation. A charitable foundation that enjoys a substantial income, in perpetuity, from its original endowment is an institution that does not compete in any product market or in the capital markets and that has no stockholders. Its board of directors is self-perpetuating and is accountable to no one (except itself) for the performance of the enterprise. (Although state attorneys general have legal authority over the administration of charitable trusts, it is largely formal.) At the same time, neither the trustees nor the staff have the kind of property right in the foundation's assets or income that would generate a strong incentive for them to maximize value. Neither the carrot nor the stick is in play.

The incentives to efficient management of foundation assets could be strengthened by a rule requiring charitable foundations to distribute every gift received, principal and income, including the original endowment, within a specified period of years. The foundation would not be required to wind up its operations within the period; it could continue indefinitely. But it would have to receive new gifts from time to time in order to avoid exhausting all of its funds. Since donors are unlikely to give money to an enterprise known to be slack, the necessity of returning to the market for charitable donations would give trustees and managers of charitable foundations an incentive they now lack to conduct a tight operation. Foundations—mostly religious and educational—that market their services or depend on continuing charitable support, and are therefore already subject to some competitive constraints, could be exempt from the exhaustion rule.

The objections to the suggested rule are that it is unnecessary—donors are already free to limit the duration of their charitable bequests—and that it might therefore (why therefore?) reduce the incentives to make charitable gifts. A counterargument is that many perpetual foundations were established at a time when the foundation was a novel institution; a person creating one at that time simply could not have foreseen the problem of inefficient and unresponsive management that might plague a perpetual foundation as a result of the peculiar set of constraints (or lack of constraints) under which they operate.

Note

There is a substantial body of evidence to support Judge Posner's view that closer supervision of charitable trusts is needed. By general recognition, the state attorney general has common-law power to seek judicial enforcement of such trusts, but until recently the power was rarely exercised. The attorney general was usually unaware of the existence of such trusts, and of the possible need for remedial action. The problem is not limited to the prevention of an unlawful diversion of trust funds. In many instances, charitable trusts, particularly the smaller ones, become dormant or nearly so—the fund is not being put to use, although the trustee presumably is collecting fees. Dormancy may be the consequence of a variety of factors, including the obsolescence of a poorly conceived trust.

In 1954, the Uniform Supervision of Trustees for Charitable Purposes Act was promulgated by the National Conference of Commissioners on Uniform State Laws. The Uniform Act has been adopted in four states, California, Illinois, Michigan, and Oregon. A substantial number of other states, although still only a minority, have also enacted statutes designed to correct the misuse or non-use of charitable trust funds. Statutes are collected in Scott on Trusts § 391. The central features of the Uniform Act are that charitable trusts and charitable corporations are covered, with the exception of governments, governmental agencies or subdivisions, and charitable corporations organized and operated primarily for educational, religious, or hospital purposes; that the attorney general must maintain a register of charitable trusts; that trustees must file a copy of the trust and periodic reports with the attorney general; and that the attorney general is authorized to investigate the trust's activities and institute appropriate proceedings to secure compliance with the Act and proper administration of the trust.

Division Three
Powers of Appointment
and Future Interests

Chapter 14

POWERS OF APPOINTMENT

PART A. INTRODUCTION TO POWERS

Powers of appointment are staples in modern estate-planning practice. They are routinely included in trusts for tax reasons and for reasons of adding flexibility to the arrangement.

Power Of Appointment Defined. A power of appointment is generally defined as the authority to designate recipients of beneficial interests in or powers of appointment over property. An owner has the authority with respect to her or his property to designate recipients of beneficial interests in or powers of appointment over property. By creating a power of appointment, the owner confers this authority on someone who is not the property's owner. See Restatement 2d of Property § 11.1.

The property or property interest subject to a power of appointment is called the *appointive property.* The property interest subject to appointment need not be an absolute-ownership interest. In fact, powers of appointment frequently authorize appointment of only a remainder interest in the appointive property, as in the following example.

> *Example 14.1:* G transferred property in trust, income to A for life, remainder in corpus to those of A's descendants as A shall by will appoint; in default of appointment, to X-Charity.
>
> A subsequently dies, leaving a will that exercises her power of appointment in favor of her adult child, B.

Parties. The parties connected to a power of appointment are identified by a special terminology. The *donor* is the person who created the power of appointment—G in the above example. The *donee* (powerholder) is the person upon whom the power of appointment was conferred—A in the above example.

The *objects* (permissible appointees) are the persons in whose favor the power can be exercised—A's descendants in the above example. The donor determines who the objects are by expressly designating them in the instrument creating the power. If the donor does not expressly designate objects, the donee is free in almost all states to appoint in favor of anyone in the world, including the donee, the donee's estate, the donee's creditors, or the creditors of the donee's estate.

The *appointee* is the person to whom an appointment has been made—B in the above example. The appointment makes the appointee the owner of the appointed property interest.

The *taker in default* is the person who takes the appointive property to the extent the power is not effectively exercised—X-Charity in the above example. The taker in default has a property interest that is subject to the power of appointment. Upon A's death, X-Charity's property interest was divested in favor of the appointee, B.

In all cases, there is a donor, a donee, and someone in whose favor an appointment can be made. The other parties are not indispensable. The donee is under no duty to exercise a power of appointment[1] and, therefore, appointees might not always exist. Also, the donor need not expressly designate takers in default.

Powers of appointment are personal to the donee. If the donee dies without having exercised the power, the power expires. Upon the donee's death, an unexercised power is not and cannot be passed along to the donee's successors in interest.

1. Different Kinds Of Powers Of Appointment

Powers of appointment are differentiated in many ways. Two of the most important distinctions are between presently exercisable and testamentary powers; and between general and nongeneral powers. Both of these

---

1. The *nonmandatory* nature of a power of appointment is in that regard distinguishable from the *mandatory* type of power, studied in Chapter 11. See supra pp. 633-41.

distinctions relate to the scope of the donee's authority. An extremely important, overarching principle, set forth in Restatement 2d of Property section 12.2, and followed in almost all states, is that the scope of the donee's authority is presumptively unlimited—that is, the donee's authority as to appointees and the time and manner of appointment is limited only to the extent the donor effectively manifests an intent to impose limits.

Presently Exercisable Powers/Testamentary Powers. When the donee can exercise a power only in the donee's will, the power is called *testamentary.* When the donee can exercise a power *either* in an inter-vivos instrument or in the donee's will, the power is called *presently exercisable.*

Occasionally, the donee can exercise a power only in an inter-vivos instrument. This type of power is sometimes described as a power exercisable by deed alone, although technically speaking the power can be exercised by any instrument or act that is formally sufficient under applicable law to accomplish an inter-vivos transfer. Testamentary exercises of powers to appoint a remainder interest are rarely prohibited, but some powers, such as powers to revoke or amend a trust, or to invade the corpus of a trust, are generally thought to be inherently restricted to inter-vivos exercises.

General Powers/Nongeneral Powers.[2] A *general* power is one that is exercisable in favor of the donee, the donee's estate, the donee's creditors, or the creditors of the donee's estate. See Restatement 2d of Property § 11.4; IRC §§ 2041(b), 2514(c). In accordance with the overarching presumption of unlimited authority, the *absence* of express language excluding the donee, the donee's creditors, the donee's estate, or the creditors of the donee's estate, indicates a general power.[3]

A *nongeneral* power is one in which the donee, the donee's estate, the donee's creditors, or the creditors of the donee's estate are excluded as objects. See Restatement 2d of Property § 11.4 comment b.

The following examples illustrate the overarching presumption of unlimited authority:

> *Example 14.2:* G transferred real property "to A for life, remainder to such person or persons as A shall appoint; in default of appointment, remainder to B."
>
> A's power is a presently exercisable general power. It is presently exercisable because the donor, G, did not expressly restrict the exercise of the power either to a will or to an inter-vivos instrument. The power is general

---

2. Under an older terminology, adopted by the Restatement of Property § 320, but abandoned by the Restatement 2d of Property, there were three types of powers. *General* powers were defined as powers exercisable wholly in favor of the donee or the donee's estate. *Special* (or limited) powers were defined as powers exercisable only in favor of persons, not including the donee, who constitute a group not unreasonably large. All other powers were called *hybrid* powers.

3. In at least one state, however, Maryland, the donee is authorized to appoint to the donee, the donee's estate, the donee's creditors, or the creditors of the donee's estate only if there is express language affirmatively authorizing such an appointment. See, e.g., Frank v. Frank, 253 Md. 413, 253 A.2d 377 (1969).

because the donor did not forbid A from exercising the power in A's own favor.[4]

Example 14.3: G transferred real property "to A for life, remainder to such of A's descendants as A shall by will appoint; in default of appointment, remainder to B."

A's power is a nongeneral testamentary power. It is testamentary because of the donor's insertion of the phrase "by will." Thus any purported inter-vivos exercise of this power by A would be invalid. A's power is nongeneral because A is authorized to appoint only among her own descendants, a group that does not include A.[5]

Example 14.4: G transferred real property "to A for life, remainder to such person or persons except A, A's estate, A's creditors, or the creditors of A's estate, as A shall by will appoint; in default of appointment, remainder to B."

In accordance with the Restatement 2d's categories, A's power is in the same category as A's power in the preceding example—a nongeneral testamentary power.[6]

2. Invalid Powers

Powers Appendant. Another way that powers of appointment are differentiated is on the basis of the donee's property interest, if any, in the appointive property. There are three categories: collateral powers, powers in gross, and powers appendant. Collateral powers and powers in gross are valid; powers appendant are widely thought to be invalid, *i.e.*, to have no separate existence.

A power is a *collateral* power if the donee owns *no* property interest in the appointive property. A power is a *power in gross* if the donee has a property interest in the appointive property that cannot be affected by the exercise of the power. A power of appointment over the remainder interest held by the life tenant or the life income-beneficiary of a trust is a power in gross.

A *power appendant* arises where the donee has a property interest in the appointive property that can be affected by the exercise of the power. In other words, the power of appointment purports to authorize the donee to divest the donee's own property interest and confer it on someone else through an exercise of the power. If the donee owns an equitable property interest that is subject to a spendthrift limitation, see supra p. 668, should the power be treated as a power appendant?

---

4. In Maryland, however, the absence of such a restriction is not sufficient to authorize the donee to appoint to herself or himself; the language would have to say something like: "remainder to such person or persons, *including A or A's estate*, as A shall appoint." See supra note 3.

5. This power would be classified as a *special* power under the older nomenclature because the objects are reasonable in number.

6. The older nomenclature would classify this as a *hybrid* power, not a special power, because the donor did not identify objects that are reasonable in number.

Powers appendant are commonly assumed to be invalid in the United States. The power merges into the property interest owned by the donee and ceases to have any separate existence with respect to that interest. See Restatement of Property § 325; Restatement 2d of Property § 12.3.

> *Example 14.5:* G transferred real property "to such persons as A shall appoint, and until and in default of appointment, to A and her heirs."
>
> Since the power appendant purportedly conferred on A is invalid, A owns a fee simple absolute interest in the property, not a power of appointment and a fee simple subject to divestment by the exercise of the power. If A executes an instrument purporting to exercise the "power," the instrument is construed as a transfer of A's owned interest. See Restatement 2d of Property § 12.3 comment f. If A executes and delivers a deed conveying the property or an interest therein to another, A thereafter has no power to divest the grantee's property interest by a purported exercise of A's "power."

> *Example 14.6:* G transferred property in trust, income to A for life, remainder in corpus to B. A is empowered by the trust instrument to direct the trustee to transfer all or any part of the trust corpus to any one or more of A's descendants as A by deed or will directs.
>
> A has a life income interest in the trust and a presently exercisable nongeneral power of appointment over the *remainder* interest. Despite the terms of the trust instrument, A has no "power of appointment" over A's own income interest. If A directs the trustee to pay out part or all of the trust corpus to an object of the nongeneral power, the transaction is treated as a transfer of A's remaining income interest in the assets and an exercise of A's nongeneral power over the remainder interest.[7]

A power can become a power appendant—and *then* become invalid—at some time after its creation, by the acquisition of the property interest subject to the power.

> *Example 14.7:* G by will devises real property to A for life, remainder to such of A's descendants as A shall appoint; in default of appointment, to B. Subsequently, B dies devising all his estate to A.
>
> Until B's death, A had a valid presently exercisable nongeneral power of appointment over the remainder interest. When B died, A acquired the remainder interest subject to the power, causing the extinguishment of the power. Since A's life estate and remainder interest merge, A owns a fee simple absolute interest in the property, but no power of appointment over it or any interest in it.

Powers that Violate the Rule Against Perpetuities. Powers of appointment (other than general powers presently exercisable) are subject to the Rule Against Perpetuities. A power that violates the Rule is invalid and cannot

---

7. The consequence of invalidating the power with respect to the income interest has important federal gift tax consequences. The exercise of the nongeneral power over the remainder is nontaxable, see IRC § 2514; but the transfer of the remaining portion of the income interest is a taxable gift.

be validly exercised. The question of whether a power is invalid under the Rule is discussed in Chapter 17, Part E.

Powers Without Any Ascertainable Object. A power of appointment is invalid if it has no identifiable objects. A power of appointment has no identifiable objects, and hence the power is invalid, if the objects are described in a way that makes it impossible to identify any person who fits the donor's description of the objects. See Restatement 2d of Property § 12.1 comment h & illustration 18. So long as the donee can appoint to at least one person who fits the donor's description, the courts uphold the power. The fact that the description makes it impossible to know all the objects of the power is not relevant.[8]

3. Creation of a Power of Appointment

A donor creates a power of appointment "if the transferor manifests an intent that [the transfer] shall do so and if the transfer is otherwise effective." Restatement 2d of Property § 12.1. The intent can be manifested by the donor either expressly or by implication. No particular language is necessary; the words "power of appointment" or "appoint" need not be used.

> *Example 14.8:* G transfers "to A for life, remainder, if A dies intestate, to B in fee." This might be construed as implying a general power in A to appoint by will. See Simes & Smith on Future Interests § 892.

Different courts have construed recurring ambiguous dispositive patterns differently and have reached results that are difficult to reconcile. When, for example, property is devised to a devisee "to be disposed of in [the devisee's] discretion," or words of similar import, a court might adopt one of three interpretations. One is that the devisee takes an absolute-ownership interest on the theory that the added language is without legal effect. The language is treated as either precatory or surplusage—merely describing that which any owner of property has power to do as an incident of that ownership.[9] A second interpretation does not regard the

---

8. This test for evaluating a donor's description of objects of a power of appointment is significantly less demanding than the traditional test for evaluating mandatory powers in the United States. See supra pp. 633-41.

9.

> *Example:* (1) G's will devises the residue of her estate "to A to dispose of as A sees fit."
> (2) G's will states: "In case of my death, notify A to dispose of my belongings as A sees fit to."

Although Cases (1) and (2) differ in that in Case (2) there is no language of gift to A, decisions can be found that treat both cases alike. In Cameron v. Parish, 155 Ind. 329, 57 N.E. 547 (1900) (like Case (1)), and Weiss v. Broadway Nat'l Bank, 204 Tenn. 563, 322 S.W.2d 427 (1959) (like Case (2)), the courts held that A took an absolute-ownership interest. In Kuttler's Estate, 160 Cal. App. 2d 332, 325 P.2d 624 (1958) (like Case (2)), and Dormer's Estate, 348 Pa. 356, 35 A.2d 299 (1944) (like Case (1), except that A was G's executor), the courts held that A took a power of appointment. The differing views have obvious differences in result when A dies after G without attempting to dispose of the property.

language as mere surplusage, but as negating ownership and creating only a power of appointment in the devisee. Under this construction, a further question is whether the power is general or nongeneral. The answer has depended on the devisee's relationship to the testator and on whether the testator has indicated by some additional language that the property should be disposed of within a certain class of objects.[10] A third interpretation treats the language as creating a *mandatory* power that is invalid if the class of objects is not definite and ascertainable. See supra pp. 633-41. This interpretation is likely only if the devisee is an independent fiduciary.[11]

Another recurring and perplexing dispositive pattern is the devise to someone for life, remainder to the life tenant's "executors and administrators" or some similar phrase, such as "executors, administrators, and assigns," "heirs, devisees, and legatees," or "estate." Courts have had great difficulty in deciding the import of this type of devise.[12] Some courts hold that the life tenant takes a general power of appointment. See, e.g., Keeter v. United States, 461 F.2d 714 (5th Cir. 1972); Estate of Rosecrans, 4 Cal. 3d 34, 480 P.2d 296, 92 Cal. Rptr. 680 (1971); Powell's Estate, 417 Pa. 164, 207 A.2d 857 (1965). Other courts hold that a life tenant takes a remainder interest. See, e.g., Newlin v. Girard Trust Co., 116 N.J. Eq. 498, 174 A. 479 (1934). One court, Will of Grady, 33 N.C. App. 477, 235 S.E.2d 425 (1977), held that a remainder in favor of the life tenant's "estate" created either (1) a general testamentary power of appointment in the life tenant, with a gift in default in favor of the life tenant's heirs or (2) a remainder in the life tenant's heirs with no power of appointment in the life tenant. It went on to hold that either way, the Rule in Shelley's Case (see infra p. 869) applied to give the life tenant the remainder interest, which then merged with the life estate to give the life tenant absolute ownership!

10.

> *Example:* (1) G's will devises the residue of his estate "to A, my wife, to dispose of among such of my children as she sees fit."
> (2) G's will devises the residue of his estate "to A, my sister, with the request that she dispose of some of the property to my blood relatives."

In McClure's Will, 136 N.Y. 238, 32 N.E. 758 (1892), a case like Case (1), where A was G's second wife and not the mother of his children, the court held that A took a life estate and a nongeneral power of appointment over the remainder interest. In Flynn v. Flynn, 469 S.W.2d 886 (Ky. 1971), a case like Case (2), the court held that A took an absolute-ownership interest and that the language requesting A (who was a blood relative of G's) to dispose of some of the property among G's blood relatives was merely precatory.

11.

> *Example:* G's will devises the residue of her estate "to my executor, E, to distribute among such of my friends as E shall select."

In the much-criticized case of Clark v. Campbell, supra p. 633, the court held that E's power was a *mandatory* power and invalid because the class of objects (G's "friends") was an indefinite class. The Restatement 2d of Property § 12.1 comment e urges courts to construe this type of disposition as conferring on E a *nonmandatory*—discretionary—power of appointment. E's power would be valid under this construction.

12. A possibility that probably can be eliminated is that the life tenant's executors take a beneficial interest or a general power of appointment.

If the remainder to the life tenant's "executors and administrators" is conditioned on some event, such as "income to A for life, and if A dies with issue, to A's executors and administrators," other possible constructions arise. Bredin v. Wilmington Trust Co., 42 Del. Ch. 563, 216 A.2d 685 (1965), held that an implied remainder interest in favor of A's issue was created. In re Clark, 274 A.D. 49, 80 N.Y.S.2d 1 (1948), held that the life tenant took a general power of appointment over the remainder interest. Another possibility would be to hold that A took a *nongeneral* power. Yet another would be that A received a legal remainder in fee (to go with her life estate) on condition that A leaves issue.

PART B. WHO REALLY OWNS THE APPOINTIVE PROPERTY?—FEDERAL TAXES, SPOUSES, CREDITORS

As a technical matter, there is no doubt that the donee of a power of appointment is not recognized as the owner of the appointive property. The conventional distinction between beneficial ownership and a power is stated in Restatement 2d of Property section 11.1 comment b:

> The beneficial owner of an interest in property ordinarily has the power to transfer to others beneficial rights in the owned interest. This power is an incident of the owned interest and the transfer is directly from the owner to the beneficiary of the transfer. A power, however, is the authority to designate beneficial interests in property other than as an incident of the beneficial ownership of the property. When the power is exercised, it is the completion of the terms of a transfer that started with the creator of the power.

Upon exercise of a power of appointment, the notion is that the appointed interest passes directly from the donor to the appointee. This is called the *doctrine of "relation back"*: The donee's appointment is deemed to relate back to and become part of the *donor's* original instrument. The donee is viewed as the donor's agent, as it were; an appointment retroactively fills in the blanks in the original instrument.

> *Example 14.9:* G transferred property in trust, income to A for life, remainder to such of A's descendants as A shall appoint. A makes an intervivos appointment to his child, C. Under the doctrine of relation back, A's appointment is viewed as changing G's original disposition to read: "income to A for life, remainder to C."

Technical ownership aside, when it comes to federal taxation and the rights of the donee's surviving spouse and creditors, the law does not always follow the relation-back doctrine. The likelihood that the donee will be treated as if she or he owned the appointive property is greater in the case of a reserved power, as distinguished from a power conferred on the donee by another.

1. Reserved Powers

a. Federal Tax Consequences

The application of the federal tax laws to the various kinds of powers of appointment is a complicated subject. See supra pp. 359 & 367. For reserved powers, basically, the federal tax laws treat the transferor as still owning the appointive property, whether the reserved power is general or nongeneral.

Federal Estate Tax. If the decedent holds at the time of her or his death, or releases within three years of her or his death, a reserved power over income or corpus of property transferred inter vivos, the value of the property is taxed in the decedent's estate. See IRC §§ 2035, 2036(a)(2), 2038.

Federal Gift Tax. An inter-vivos transfer is not subject to the federal gift tax, to the extent that the transferor reserves to herself or himself a power of appointment over the transferred property, whether the reserved power is a general power (such as a power to revoke the trust) or a nongeneral power (such as a power to amend the trust in any way except for the transferor's benefit). The theory is that the reserved power renders the gift incomplete because the transferor has not parted with sufficient dominion or control over the property. See Treas. Reg. § 25.2511-2.

Federal Income Tax. The transferor of an inter-vivos transfer in which a general or, subject to certain statutory exceptions, a nongeneral power is reserved continues to be taxed on the income generated by the appointive property. The transferor may also be taxed on the income in cases where a power exercisable in her or his own favor, in favor of her or his spouse, or solely in favor of others, is conferred on a "nonadverse party" such as an independent trustee. See IRC §§ 674; 676; 677.

> *Example 14.10:* G transferred property to T, in trust, directing the trustee to pay the income to G for life, remainder in corpus to X. G retained the power to revoke the trust at any time and have the trust property returned to him.
>
> G's transfer of the remainder interest to X was not a taxable gift because of G's reserved general power over the entire trust corpus.
>
> G will continue until his death to be taxed on both the ordinary income generated by the property and also on capital gains (or losses) realized by the trust.
>
> When G dies, the full value of the trust corpus will be taxed in G's estate.

b. *Rights of the Donor-Donee's Surviving Spouse*

Statutory References: *1990 UPC § 2-202*
                            Pre-1990 UPC § 2-202

We have already considered the rights of the donor-donee's surviving spouse in assets over which the donor-donee retained a power to revoke or another type of power of appointment. See supra Chapter 8, Part A.2. Recall Sullivan v. Burkin, supra p. 482, which prospectively adopted the rule that, if the transfer reserving the power occurred during the marriage, the surviving spouse's elective share extends to assets subject to the reserved general power. It is unclear whether that decision would be extended to a reserved general testamentary power.

Recall also that a similar rule was adopted in the Restatement 2d of Property section 13.7. See supra p. 486. The Restatement 2d explicitly requires the reserved general power to have been exercisable by the donor-donee *alone,* but does not require the transfer to have taken place during the marriage or require the reserved general power to have been presently exercisable.

Non-UPC legislation in a few states makes property subject to a reserved general power available to the elective share of the donor-donee's surviving spouse, but only if the donor-donee's will exercised the power or manifested an intent to do so. See, e.g., Mich. Comp. Laws § 5516.116.

Uniform Probate Code. UPC section 2-202(b)(2)(i) (1990) includes in the reclaimable-estate component of the augmented estate, to which the decedent's surviving spouse has a right to an elective share, property subject to "a presently exercisable general power of appointment held by the decedent alone," regardless of when or by whom that power was created. Section 2-202(b)(2)(iv)(B) includes property subject to "a power, exercisable by the decedent alone or in conjunction with any other person or exercisable by a nonadverse party, for the benefit of the decedent or the decedent's estate," but only if that power was created by the decedent during her or his marriage to the surviving spouse. See supra p. 487.

The above provisions replaced provisions of the pre-1990 UPC under which the "augmented estate" merely included the value of property transferred by the decedent *during the marriage* "to the extent that the decedent retained at the time of his death a power, either alone or in conjunction with any other person, to revoke or to consume, invade or dispose of the principal for his own benefit."

c. *Rights of the Donor-Donee's Creditors*

If a reserved power of appointment, even a nongeneral power, was created in a transfer that was in fraud of creditors, the appointive assets can be subjected to the payment of the donor-donee's debts.

Even if the transfer was not in fraud of creditors, the appointive assets are subject to the claims of the donor-donee's creditors if the reserved power is a general power. It makes no difference whether the debt was incurred by the donor-donee before or after the transfer. See Restatement 2d of Property § 13.3; Restatement of Property § 328; Am. L. Prop. § 23.6.

> *Example 14.11:* G transfers property "to G for life, then to such person or persons, including G or G's estate, as G may appoint by deed or by will, and in default of appointment to A and her heirs." Creditors of G can subject not only G's owned life estate to the payment of their claims, but the remainder interest also. On G's death, the claims against G's estate can be satisfied out of the property to the same extent as if G owned the property at G's death and had devised the property to A by will.

Until recently, an anomaly existed with respect to a reserved power to revoke, such as that contained in a revocable inter-vivos trust. The Restatement of Property section 318(2) and comment i excluded powers to revoke from the definition of the term power of appointment, making the rule that a reserved power of appointment subjects the appointive assets to the claims of the donor-donee's creditors inapplicable. Thus it was generally held that the trust assets of a revocable trust were exempt from the claims of the settlor's creditors. See, e.g., National Shawmut Bank v. Joy, 315 Mass. 457, 53 N.E.2d 113 (1944); Restatement 2d of Trusts § 330 comment o; Scott on Trusts § 330.12. Several states now have statutes to the contrary, see, e.g., Mich. Comp. Laws § 556.128, and recent decisions have also held to the contrary. See, e.g., State Street Bank & Trust Co. v. Reiser, 7 Mass. App. Ct. 633, 389 N.E.2d 768 (1979). See supra p. 401.

Another recent development is that the Restatement 2d of Property section 34.3(3) squarely holds that the settlor's creditors are entitled to have their claims satisfied out of property in a revocable trust. The path to the adoption of this rule was cleared by Restatement 2d of Property section 11.1 comment c, which specifically *includes* powers to revoke in the definition of the term "power of appointment." This change in nomenclature resolves the anomaly: It extends the rule of Restatement 2d of Property section 13.3—that the donor-donee's creditors can reach assets subject to a reserved general power of appointment—to powers to revoke in revocable trusts.[13]

---

13. The court in Sullivan v. Burkin, supra p. 482, an elective-share case, considered a power to revoke to be a power of appointment.

2. Donee Powers

a. Federal Tax Consequences

Donee's Tax Consequences—General Powers. Even if the power is not a reserved power, but a donee power (a power conferred on the donee by another), the federal tax laws still treat the donee of a general power of appointment as the owner of the appointive property. For certain purposes, however, a distinction is drawn by the federal estate and gift tax laws between powers created after October 21, 1942 (called "post-42 powers") and powers created on or before October 21, 1942 (called "pre-42 powers"). See supra p. 367.

For estate tax purposes, the value of property subject to a post-42 general power of appointment held by the donee at the donee's death, and conferred on the donee by another, is taxed in the donee's estate regardless of whether the power is exercised. As for pre-42 powers, the value of the appointive property is taxed in the donee's estate only if the power is exercised. See IRC § 2041.

For gift tax purposes, an inter-vivos exercise of a general power of appointment, conferred on the donee by another, is subject to the federal gift tax regardless of when the power was created. A release of a post-42, but not a pre-42, general power of appointment, conferred on the donee by another, is subject to the federal gift tax. See IRC § 2514(a), (b).

For income tax purposes, the donee of a general power of appointment, conferred on the donee by another and presently exercisable by the donee alone, may be taxed on the income generated by the appointive property. See IRC § 678(a).

Donee's Tax Consequences—Nongeneral Powers. For federal income, estate, and gift tax purposes, the donee of a nongeneral power, conferred on the donee by another, is not treated as the owner of the appointive property.

No federal gift tax consequences occur upon the inter-vivos exercise (or release) of a nongeneral power. No federal estate tax consequences occur from holding a nongeneral power at death or from making a testamentary exercise of a nongeneral power. Being the donee of a nongeneral power does not cause the donee to be taxed on the income generated by the appointive property.

Nongeneral powers are implicated by the federal generation-skipping transfer tax. In general, that tax applies whenever property passes to a younger generation of family members without suffering estate or gift taxation in the next oldest generation.

> *Example 14.12:* G's will devises the residue of her estate into a trust, income to her daughter A for life, remainder in corpus to such of A's children as A by will appoints; in default of appointment, to A's children in equal shares. At A's death, her will appoints 50% of the corpus of the trust to one of her children, and the other 50% to be equally divided between her other two children.

Under the federal estate tax, the property is taxed in G's estate and in the estates of A's appointees (G's grandchildren), if they still own the property when they die. The estate tax does not, however, tax the property in A's estate because A's power was a nongeneral power—the estate tax "skips" A's generation. Under the generation-skipping transfer tax, the trust property might no longer go untaxed when A dies.[14]

Donor's Tax Consequences—Why Create a General Power? Apart from the generation-skipping tax, which contains rather liberal exemptions, the considerations discussed so far seem to point in the direction of conferring only nongeneral powers on donees. And it is not only the tax considerations that seem to point in this direction. Conferring a nongeneral power on the donee virtually guarantees the appointive property's freedom from the claims of the donee's creditors and surviving spouse. See infra pp. 810, 812.

The reason why general powers are created is *not* that a general power confers such a greater benefit on the donee that the donor considers its creation to be worth the extra tax and other costs to the donee. At least, this is true if the choice is between conferring a general *testamentary* power or conferring a nongeneral power.[15] The donee of a nongeneral power can be given substantially the same degree of flexibility as the donee of a general testamentary power. The exclusion of the donee, the donee's estate, the donee's creditors, and the creditors of the donee's estate from the list of permissible appointees is an insignificant reduction in the flexibility granted to the donee because donees seldom desire to appoint to their own estates. The scope of objects of a nongeneral power can be so broad as to include virtually every person to whom the donee would conceivably want to appoint.

In addition, in many circumstances, the donor may consider it highly desirable to limit the permissible appointees. The donor who confers a power of appointment on her or his surviving spouse may anticipate remarriage, or her or his surviving spouse may have children by a prior marriage. The donor may, therefore, limit the appointees to assure that the donor's property is not diverted from her or his children or other family members.

Why, then, are general powers ever created? The main reason is that there are certain tax *benefits* to the *donor* that can be obtained by conferring on the donee a general power. The most important of these are

---

14. The part of the property that is taxed is the fractional part, if any, that exceeded the transferor's GST exemption of up to $ 1 million when the trust was created. See IRC § 2631; supra p. 375.

15. General powers presently exercisable are seldom created anyway, except for powers granted to the income beneficiary of a trust to invade the corpus of the trust. Even powers to invade corpus are not considered general powers for estate or gift tax purposes if their exercise is explicitly governed by an ascertainable standard relating to the health, education, support, or maintenance of the donee or if they can be exercised only in conjunction with the donor of the power or a person having a substantial interest in the appointive property that is adverse to the power's exercise in favor of the donee.

to qualify the transfer for either the federal estate or gift tax marital deduction or the federal gift tax annual exclusion. See supra Chapter 6.

Federal Estate and Gift Tax Marital Deduction. A trust qualifies for the federal estate or gift tax marital deduction if the terms of the trust grant the transferor's spouse the right to all the income from the trust for life, payable annually or at more frequent intervals, and a power of appointment over the remainder interest, exercisable by the spouse alone and in all events and in favor of the spouse or the spouse's estate. IRC §§ 2056(b)(5); 2523(e). Until 1981, such a trust—called a power of appointment trust—was the most popular device for creating a trust that qualified for the marital deduction.

The Economic Recovery Tax Act of 1981 added a new subsection to the marital deduction sections that authorizes the use of a "qualified terminable interest property trust"—called a QTIP trust—under which the spouse is granted the right to the income from the trust for life, payable annually or at more frequent intervals; if properly elected, the trust can qualify even if the donor's spouse is given a nongeneral testamentary power of appointment over the remainder interest or no power of appointment at all.

QTIP trusts have now become a very popular marital deduction device, cutting down even further the incidence of the creation of general powers of appointment.

Federal Gift Tax Annual Exclusion. Under IRC section 2503(c), a trust for a minor qualifies for the federal gift tax annual exclusion if, among other requirements, the minor is given a general power of appointment over the remainder interest should the minor die before attaining the age of 21 years; a nongeneral power disqualifies the trust for the gift tax exclusion under this section. A "Crummey" power, named after the case of Crummey v. Commissioner, 397 F.2d 82 (9th Cir. 1968), is another device for qualifying for the annual gift tax exclusion; a Crummey power is a general power conferred on the donee by the donor of a trust that authorizes the donee to withdraw from the corpus all or a specified portion of subsequent contributions into the trust, usually made by the donor annually.

b. Rights of the Donee's Surviving Spouse

Statutory References: *1990 UPC § 2-202*
                          Pre-1990 UPC § 2-202

Common Law. At common law, the surviving spouse of a donee receives less protection than the donee's creditors. As long as the power is not a reserved power, the donee's surviving spouse cannot ordinarily reach the appointive property (against the wishes of the donee), whether the power is general or nongeneral, presently exercisable or testamentary, exercised or unexercised. The explanation offered by the courts is that the surviving spouse's elective-share claim is against the donee's probate estate and the appointive assets are not a part of the probate estate because they are not owned beneficially by the donee.

A relevant consideration, perhaps, is the context that generates a surviving spouse's claim to an elective share in assets subject to a general power conferred on the donee by another. The major reason by far today for conferring a general power on another is to qualify a trust for the federal estate or gift tax marital deduction. In almost all other cases, the creation of a nongeneral power is preferable. The following example is therefore typical. The donee of a general power, conferred on the donee by another, is likely to be the remarried surviving spouse of the donor of the power (in which case the appointive property was originally owned by the donor) and the takers in default are likely to be either the children of the marriage between the donor and donee or the donor's children by a prior marriage.

> *Example 14.13:* G's will devised the residue of his estate into a marital deduction trust, income "to W, my wife, for life, then to such person or persons, including W's estate, as W shall by will appoint; in default of appointment, remainder to my descendants who survive W, such descendants to take by representation, and if none of my descendants survives W, then in default of appointment, to the X charity." W subsequently remarries. At W's death, her will exercises her general testamentary power in favor of the children of her marriage to G. W is survived by her second husband, H-2. H-2 elects to renounce W's will and claim a statutory elective share in W's estate.
>
> The appointive property is not included in the assets in W's estate to which H-2's elective share attaches. The same result has been reached even in cases where W's appointment was in a blending clause or where W's appointment was in favor of her own estate. See Kate's Estate, 282 Pa. 417, 128 A. 97 (1925) (rule of this case codified in 20 Pa. Cons. Stat. § 2203, but restricted to general powers conferred on the donee by another); Restatement 2d of Property § 13.7 illustration 3; Restatement of Property § 332 comment b.

Uniform Probate Code. UPC section 2-202(b)(2)(i) (1990) broke new ground by including in the decedent's reclaimable-estate component of the augmented estate property subject to "a presently exercisable general power of appointment held by the decedent alone," regardless of when or by whom that power was created. Should the framers of the 1990 UPC have gone even further and included property subject to a testamentary general power of appointment? Is the donee's relationship to such property as close to ownership as it is to property subject to a presently exercisable general power? Would the inclusion of property subject to a general testamentary power further encourage the already wide-spread use of the QTIP trust for marital-deduction purposes? A QTIP trust is completely immune from an elective-share claim by the surviving spouse's surviving spouse because the surviving spouse either has no power of appointment or a nongeneral testamentary power over such a trust. The pre-1990 version of UPC section 2-202 did not include in the augmented estate property over which the decedent owned a general power created by another.

Non-UPC Legislation. Legislation in a few other states makes property subject to a general power of appointment, conferred on the donee by another, available to the elective share of the donee's surviving spouse. Unlike the UPC, however, it is available only if the decedent's will exercised the power or manifested an intent to do so. See, e.g., Mich. Comp. Laws § 556.116.

c. Rights of the Donee's Creditors

The majority view at common law is that the donee of a general power, conferred on the donee by another, is treated as the beneficial owner of the appointive property *only if the donee exercises the power.* No distinction is made between a general testamentary power and one that is presently exercisable. See Restatement 2d of Property § 13.2. An early decision enunciating this view, see Gilman v. Bell, 99 Ill. 144 (1881), explained a general power of appointment as the equivalent of an offer. The donee "only receives the naked power to make the property or fund his own." When, however, the donee exercises the power, the donee thereby accepts the offer "and the title thereby vests in him, although it may pass out of him *eo instanti,* to the appointee."

When the donee of a general power exercises the power *by her or his will*, the view that the appointed property is treated as if it were owned by the donee means that the creditors of the donee's estate can reach the appointed property for the payment of their claims. See, e.g., Clapp v. Ingraham, 126 Mass. 200 (1879); Restatement 2d of Property § 13.4. The rule prevails even if this is contrary to the expressed wishes of the donor of the power. See, e.g., State Street Trust Co. v. Kissel, 302 Mass. 328, 19 N.E.2d 25 (1939).

The exercise of the power by will does not confer actual beneficial ownership of the appointive assets on the donee for all purposes. The assets do not ordinarily become part of the donee's probate estate. Thus, in terms of priority, the donee's own estate assets are ordinarily used first to pay estate debts, so that the appointive assets are used only to the extent the donee's probate estate is insolvent. See supra Chapter 5 for further discussion of abatement rules.

In most jurisdictions, the donee's creditors can reach the appointive assets only to the extent the donee's exercise was an *effective* exercise. See Restatement 2d of Property § 13.2 comment b. A few states, however, follow the view that even an ineffective exercise entitles the donee's creditors to reach the appointive assets. See, e.g., Estate of Breault, 63 Ill. App. 2d 246, 211 N.E.2d 424 (1965). Moreover, even in states adhering to the majority view, an ineffective exercise frequently "captures" the appointive assets for the donee's estate, in which case the appointive assets become part of the donee's probate estate for all purposes, including creditors' rights. For an explanation of the "capture doctrine," see infra p. 833.

When the donee of a general power is authorized to and makes an inter-vivos appointment, treating the appointed assets as if they were owned by the donee does not automatically mean that the donee's creditors can subject the appointed assets to the payment of their claims. If the appointment is in favor of a *creditor,* the donee's other, unsatisfied creditors can reach the appointed assets only by having the appointment avoided as a "preference" in bankruptcy proceedings. Apart from bankruptcy, the donee can choose to pay one creditor rather than another with her or his owned assets, and the same is true with respect to appointive assets. If the appointment is in favor of a *volunteer (i.e.,* the appointment is gratuitous), the donee's creditors can reach the appointed assets only if the transfer is the equivalent of a fraudulent transfer under applicable state law.[16]

In a minority of jurisdictions, the donee of a general power, conferred on her or him by another, is not treated as the owner of the appointive property even if the power is exercised. See, e.g., St. Matthews Bank v. DeCharette, 259 Ky. 802, 83 S.W.2d 471 (1935). Of course, if the donee exercises the power in favor of herself or himself or her or his estate, the appointed property becomes owned in the technical sense, and creditors even in states adhering to the minority view would be able to subject the assets to the payment of their claims to the same extent as other property owned beneficially by the donee.

In at least one state, an exercise of a general power in a so-called blending clause (also called a blanket exercise clause) is treated as the equivalent of an appointment in favor of the donee's estate for this purpose. See Stannert's Estate, 339 Pa. 439, 15 A.2d 360 (1940). A blending clause is one that combines owned and appointive assets together, such as:

All the rest, residue, and remainder of my estate, *including property over which I have a power of appointment,* I give, devise, and bequeath to. . . .

A minority of states has enacted legislation that affects the rights of the donee's creditors. The legislation is not uniform. Some of the legislation expands the rights of the donee's creditors and some contracts them. The following is a nonexhaustive sampling of the legislation.

Michigan legislation expands the rights of the creditors of the donee of an *unexercised* general power. During the donee's lifetime, the donee's creditors can subject the appointive property to the payment of their claims if the power is presently exercisable. (If the donee has actually made an inter-vivos exercise of the power, the rules explained above with respect to inter-vivos

---

16. In most states, the applicable state law on fraudulent transfers derives from the Uniform Fraudulent Conveyances Act (1918) (in force in about 10 states) or the newer Uniform Fraudulent Transfers Act (1984) (in force in about 26 states). Under § 4(a) of the Uniform Fraudulent Transfers Act, a transfer is in fraud of present or future creditors if it was made "with actual intent to hinder, delay, or defraud" or "without receiving a reasonably equivalent value in exchange for the transfer" and the transferor "(i) was engaged or was about to engage in a business or a transaction for which the remaining assets of the [transferor] were unreasonably small in relation to the business or transaction; or (ii) intended to incur . . . debts beyond his ability to pay as they became due."

exercises presumably would be applied.) At the donee's death, the donee's creditors can subject the appointive property to the payment of their claims. In both instances, however, the appointive property is available only to the extent that the donee's owned property is insufficient to meet the debts. See Mich. Comp. Laws § 556.123.

Wisconsin legislation adopts the same rules as the Michigan legislation. In addition to general powers, however, powers that are exercisable in favor of anyone but the donee, her or his estate, her or his creditors, and the creditors of her or his estate are subjected to the same rules. See Wis. Stat. § 702.17.

New York legislation expands the rights of the donee's creditors in some particulars but restricts them in other particulars. The legislation adopts the same rules as the Michigan legislation, but limits their application to general powers that are presently exercisable. As to general testamentary powers, the donee's estate creditors can subject the appointive property to the payment of their claims only if the donee, as donor, reserved the power in herself or himself; as to general testamentary powers conferred on the donee by another, the donee's estate creditors cannot reach the appointive property even when the donee's will *exercises* the power! See N.Y. Est. Powers & Trusts Law §§ 10-7.1 et seq.

The federal bankruptcy code implies that a general power presently exercisable passes to the donee's trustee in bankruptcy. A nongeneral power and a general testamentary power clearly do not. See 11 U.S.C. § 541(b).

EXTERNAL REFERENCE. Berger, The General Power of Appointment as an Interest in Property, 40 Neb. L. Rev. 104 (1960).

PART C. EXERCISING A POWER OF APPOINTMENT

Statutory References: *1990 UPC §§ 2-608, -701, -703 to -704*
                               Pre-1990 UPC § 2-610

Capacity of the Donee. An effective appointment can only be made by a donee who has the requisite capacity. The capacity needed to make an effective appointment is the same capacity needed to make an effective transfer of the property if it were owned by the donee.
Compliance With Formalities. An appointment must satisfy the formal conveyancing requirements that would be applicable to a transfer of the property if it were owned by the donee. A testamentary appointment, for example, must be contained in a validly executed will.
Intent to Exercise. A donee must intend to exercise a power in order for the power to be exercised. The recommended method for exercising a power of appointment is by a direct-exercise clause:

I hereby exercise the power of appointment conferred upon me by my mother's will of [date] as follows: I appoint . . . .

Unfortunately, the recommended method is not always used. Often, a so-called blending (blanket-exercise) clause is used. A blanket-exercise clause typically blends the donee's own residuary estate with any property over which the donee has a power of appointment:

All the rest, residue, and remainder of my estate, including any property over which I have a power of appointment, I give, devise, and bequeath as follows: . . . .

Blending clauses, like direct-exercise clauses, clearly express the donee's intent to exercise a power of appointment. They are not recommended, however, because, among other things, they can raise a question about whether the exercise of the power complies with the formality of a specific reference commonly imposed by donors (see below) and because they may subject the appointive property to the claims of the donee's creditors.

In the absence of an express exercise of a power, an intent by the donee to exercise the power can be implied. In the leading case of Blagge v. Miles, 1 Story 426, 3 F. Cas. 559 (C.C. Mass. 1841) (No. 1479), the court described circumstances giving rise to an implied exercise:

Three classes of cases have been held to be sufficient demonstrations of an intended execution of a power: (1) Where there has been some reference in the will, or other instrument, to the power; (2) or a reference to the property, which is the subject, on which it is to be executed; (3) or, where the provision in the will or other instrument, executed by the donee of the power, would otherwise be ineffectual, or a mere nullity; in other words, it would have no operation, except as an execution of the power.[17]

The majority view at common law is that a residuary clause or other clause referring generally to "my estate" or "my property" does not exercise a general or nongeneral power of appointment, unless other facts establish intent. See Restatement 2d of Property § 17.3.

---

17. The Restatement 2d of Property adopted the *Blagge* principles.

§ 17.4 comment a, illustration 1: O, owner of Blackacre in fee simple, by will transfers Blackacre "to D for life, remainder to such one or more of D's children as D shall appoint by her will, and in default of appointment to D's children who survive her and their heirs as tenants in common." D dies and her will provides: "I devise Blackacre to my daughter Mary." D has manifested an intent to exercise her non-general power to appoint Blackacre by her will.

§ 17.5 comment b, illustration 3: O by will transfers $500,000 to T in trust. T is directed "to pay the income to O's daughter D for life and on D's death to pay the trust property to such persons as D may appoint and in default of appointment to pay the same to O's other children who survive D." D executes a will containing $10,000 in pecuniary bequests to servants, $15,000 in pecuniary bequests to distant relatives and a residuary disposition in favor of her three children. At the time D executed her will her owned assets were worth $35,000 . . . . D has manifested an intent to exercise her power.

A minority of jurisdictions follows the so-called Massachusetts view, that a residuary clause is presumed, unless a contrary intent is shown, to exercise a general power of appointment even though no reference is made in the clause to powers.[18] These states recognize the tendency of donees to view general powers as equivalent to ownership. See, e.g., Amory v. Meredith, 7 Allen (Mass.) 397 (1863). A number of jurisdictions have adopted the minority (Massachusetts) view by legislation, and occasionally that view has been extended to nongeneral powers in cases in which the residuary legatees were objects of the nongeneral power.

The 1990 UPC adopts a variation of the minority (Massachusetts) view. Under section 2-608, a general power is presumed exercised by a residuary clause, but only if the donor failed to create a gift in default of appointment. This condition is a recognition of the fact that most general powers are created in marital deduction trusts that include a well-thought-out gift-in-default clause, the terms of which usually represent the shared intent of both the donor and donee. The strict minority (Massachusetts) view defeats that gift-in-default clause, but the UPC view does not.

If there is no gift-in-default clause, the UPC presumes the residuary clause exercises the power. The rationale for this rule is that the alternative would be that the appointive property would return to the donor's estate and require that it be reopened if, as is likely, the donor predeceased the donee. The UPC view is codified in Mich. Comp. Laws § 556.114.

Conflict of Laws. The traditional view is that the law of the donor's domicile governs issues concerning the donee's intent to exercise a power. See, e.g., Beals v. State Street Bank & Trust Co., 367 Mass. 318, 326 N.E.2d 896 (1975); Bank of New York v. Black, 26 N.J. 276, 139 A.2d 393 (1958)). But see, e.g., White v. United States, 680 F.2d 1156 (7th Cir. 1982) (law of donee's domicile governs). See also Restatement 2d Conflict of Laws § 275 (1971) ("Whether a power to appoint by will interests in movables is exercised by a general bequest not mentioning the power is determined by the law governing the construction of the donee's will (see § 264), unless the donor manifested a different intention."); UPC § 2-703 (1990).

EXTERNAL REFERENCES. See (as to movables) Scott on Trusts §§ 629-42 and (as to real property) Restatement 2d of Conflict of Laws §§ 281-82 (1971); Scott on Trusts §§ 661-63. See also Durand & Herterich, Conflict of Laws and the Exercise of Powers of Appointment, 42 Cornell L. Q. 185 (1957).

Specific-Reference Requirements. In creating powers of appointment, it has become common practice for donors to provide that the power can only be exercised by language that specifically refers to the power. Specific-reference clauses were a pre-1942 invention to prevent inadvertent exercises of general powers and thereby avoid federal transfer taxes that applied only if the general power was exercised. See supra p. 808.

---

18. In 1978, Massachusetts itself abrogated that view by adopting a statute similar to pre-1990 UPC § 2-610, which codified the majority common-law view. See Mass. Gen. Laws ch. 191, § 1(A)(4).

Motes/Henes Trust v. Motes
297 Ark. 380, 761 S.W.2d 938 (1988)

HAYS, J. The single issue presented by this appeal is whether a reference in the testator's will to a power of appointment was sufficient to exercise a power of appointment in a trust instrument.

Helen Fay Henes, deceased, executed a will in 1979 containing the following residuary clause:

I give, devise and bequeath all of the remainder and residue of my estate together with *property to which I may have a power of appointment at the time of my death,* to the trustee hereinafter named, to be held in trust for the uses. . . . [Emphasis added.]

In 1982, the Motes/Henes trust was established for Helen Fay Henes and her sister, Elizabeth Henes Motes, in which was placed approximately $6,000,000 from interests the sisters had redeemed from their ownership in certain businesses. The trust contained the following provision:

This trust shall terminate with respect to the separate trust share of each grantor [the two sisters] upon the death of said grantor. Upon such termination, the remaining assets of said separate trust shall be paid to such person or persons or trusts as grantor may, *by specific reference hereto, appoint in her Last Will and Testament.* [Emphasis added.]

Helen Fay Henes died in April 1983 and in February 1988 the trustee of the Motes/Henes trust petitioned for the consolidation of the probate and chancery proceedings and for construction of the power of appointment in the will. Consolidation was granted and following a hearing the trial court held that the language of the will was sufficient to exercise the power of appointment defined in the trust. The trustee and Elizabeth Henes Motes have appealed. Respondent-Appellees are the children of Elizabeth Henes Motes.

The question is: When a power of appointment requires a specific reference to it, as does the trust in this case, will a general reference in the will be sufficient to exercise the power requiring specific reference?

The general rule is defined in Restatement (Second) of Property, (1986):

§ 17.1 Significance of Donee's Intent to Appoint.
In order for a donee to exercise a power effectively it must be established—
(1) That the donee intended to exercise it; and
(2) That the expression of the intention complies with the requirements of exercise imposed by the donor and by rules of law.

The problem here concerns the second requirement and the question we must decide is whether Ms. Henes' will provision, making reference to "property to which I may have a power of appointment at the time of my death," is sufficient to exercise the power of appointment in the trust, or does the law require that she must have made reference to the trust instrument itself.

Finding no cases of our own on this topic, we have turned to other sources for guidance. The Reporter's Note to section 17.1 of the Restatement is primarily devoted to the problem in our case. While the Restatement discusses cases it classifies as "supporting" the rule and those "contrary" to the rule, a closer examination of those cases reveals that the division would be more aptly placed between those cases that construe the "specific reference" requirement literally, and those that favor a flexible interpretation, focusing more on the intent of the donee. See also Annotation, 15 A.L.R. 4th 810 (1982), which distinguishes the cases between those that require specific reference and those that do not.

Our research does not produce a clear majority or trend on either side of the question. We prefer the approach focusing on the intent of the donor, however, as we regard it as the better reasoned view.[19] It is also in keeping with our general approach to the interpretation of wills, which has as its paramount principle that the intention of the testator will govern, as well as the rule that wills should be liberally construed. [I]n Moore v. Avery, 146 Ark. 193, 225 S.W. 599 (1920), in construing a will, we held that the phrase, "all my property," was sufficient to refer to and exercise a power of appointment. While Moore does not involve a "specific reference" requirement, it nevertheless reflects the more liberal approach. See generally, Annotation, Power of Appointment-Execution, 15 A.L.R.3d 346 (1967).

In Roberts v. Northern Trust Co., 550 F. Supp. 729 (N.D. Ill. 1982), the court was faced with the same issue and reviewed Illinois law to determine the correct approach. The court found that in a significant power of appointment case, the Illinois court had drawn on three basic principles of will construction: 1) that the intent of the testator controls and courts should construe wills to give effect to that intention; 2) a devise or bequest should not be voided because of errors in describing the subject matter as long as enough remains to show the testator's intent; and 3) the court will use its equitable powers to correct technical defects in a will in order to effect the testator's intent. From those general rules the court fashioned the following test for the "specific reference" problem:

> Where the evidence of intent is powerful, the question of compliance should be examined in a light which favors fulfillment of both the donor's desire for assurance and the donee's intent. Where, however, evidence of the donee's intent is weak, a liberal construction of the condition of specific reference may well defeat the limitations of both donor and donee.

Following the approach in *Roberts*, supra, we find the evidence of intent in this case is very strong and therefore have no problem with a more liberal construction of the "specific reference" requirement. The evidence of Fay Henes's intent came from the testimony of John L. Johnson, who was

---

19. Other cases favoring the "intent" approach include: Roberts v. Northern Trust Co., 550 F. Supp. 729 (N.D. Ill. 1982); Cross v. Cross, 559 S.W.2d 196 (Mo. App. 1977); First Union National Bank v. Moss, 32 N.C. App. 499, 233 S.E.2d 88 (1977); McKelvy v. Terry, 370 Mass. 328, 346 N.E.2d 912 (1976).

the attorney for both sisters. He had drafted the wills for both, and had also drafted the trust agreement. He testified that at the time of drafting the will he had discussed with Ms. Henes how she wanted to dispose of her property and she told him she wanted her sister to be benefitted and the property to go to her nieces and nephews, her sister's children. The will was drafted to effectuate that intent, giving her sister a life estate through the trust, for her enjoyment during her lifetime, with the property ultimately going to the nieces and nephews.

When Johnson drafted the trust agreement he reviewed Ms. Henes' will and decided there was no need to make any changes in it. He noted that the provision in the will on the power of appointment would operate to exercise all powers of appointment that Ms. Henes would have, to pass the property under a trust arrangement that was set up under her will. Johnson stated that this was absolutely consistent with his view and understanding of Ms. Henes' intent.

Johnson further commented that in drafting the trust, which was irrevocable, he wanted to avoid placing Ms. Henes in the position of being unable to change the beneficiaries of her estate by naming them in the trust instrument. By not putting final testamentary disposition provisions in the trust, it retained for Ms. Henes the ability at any point to change her mind as to the disposition of her estate.

The trial court noted that another significant factor was the problem of estate taxes. If the power was not exercised by the will, double taxation would result, and the trial judge observed that people do not intend tax consequences of that nature. We agree.

Appellant urges that we must ascertain the intent of the testator at the time of the execution of the will, citing *Moore,* supra. That is true, but it does not mean that we eliminate after-acquired property from being disposed by way of a will executed previously. . . . This is also the rule specifically as it relates to powers of appointment. Restatement (Second) of Property, § 17.6 (1986).

In this case, Ms. Henes' will refers first to, "*all* of the remainder and residue of my estate," and then specifically refers to "property to which *I may have a power of appointment at the time of my death.*" It seems clear that the testator's intent at the time of execution was to include any after-acquired property.

Affirmed.

Note and Questions

1. *Restatement 2d of Property.* In *Motes/Henes Trust,* the court referred the section 17.1 of the Restatement 2d of Property. The court did not refer to comment b, however, which provides:

> b. *Requirements imposed by the donor.* The donor may impose formal requirements on the effective exercise of the power. . . . The donor may want to make certain that the donee does not inadvertently exercise the power; and to avoid this possibility, specific reference to the power may be required in

order for it to be effectively exercised. Failure by the donee to comply with the formal requirements imposed by the donor in regard to the exercise of a power may prevent an effective exercise of it even though the intention of the donee to exercise the power is otherwise clearly manifested. . . .

Illustrations:

1. O by will transfers property to T in trust. T is directed to pay the income to W, O's wife, for life. On W's death "T shall pay the trust property to or hold the same for the benefit of such person or persons or the estate of W in such amounts and proportions and for such estates and interests and outright or upon such terms, trusts, conditions, and limitations as W shall appoint by a will executed after O's death referring specifically to the power herein given to W." O's will makes provision for the disposition of the trust property on W's death in default of her exercise of her general power to appoint by will. The residuary clause in W's will provides as follows: "All the rest and residue of my property, wheresoever the same is situated, including any property over which I may have any power of appointment, I hereby bequeath, devise and appoint as follows." The general language of W's residuary clause does not satisfy the requirement imposed by O that specific reference to the power must be made in any exercise of it. W has not effectively exercised her power to appoint, and the appointive property passes to the takers in default of appointment.

2. *Uniform Probate Code.* How would *Motes/Henes Trust* have been decided under UPC sections 2-701 and 2-704 (1990)? How would First National Bank v. Walker, below, have been decided?

First National Bank v. Walker
607 S.W.2d 469 (Tenn. 1980)

BROCK, C.J. Charles Miller died on March 17, 1975, leaving an estate of approximately $800,000.00 which by his last will and testament, dated October 4, 1972, was divided into two trusts, a "marital deduction" trust and a residuary trust. His wife, Allie Bess Walker Miller, was made the lifetime beneficiary of the marital deduction trust and was given a power of appointment over the corpus thereof. However, this power of appointment was limited by the following language:

Such power of appointment shall be exercisable by my said wife exclusively and in all events but shall be exercisable only by specific reference to said power in her last will and testament.

At issue is the question whether Allie Bess effectively exercised the power of appointment thus granted by the language employed in her last will and testament, dated October 17, 1969. That language is as follows:

I give, bequeath and devise all my property both real, personal and mixed to Charles C. Miller, my husband, but if he predeceases me, then I bequeath and devise my property, including all property over which I shall have any power of appointment at my death, to my nephew, William Bryan Walker, Jr., of

Oneonta, Alabama, and to my husband's nephew, Harold Fred Miller, in equal parts. If either of said persons shall be deceased, then their share is to go to their next of kin.

The crucial question is whether Mrs. Miller's reference to ". . . all property over which I shall have any power of appointment . . ." is a sufficient compliance with the stipulation in her husband's will that her power of appointment ". . . shall be exercisable only by a specific reference to said power in her last will and testament."[20]

The Chancellor held that the power of appointment granted to Mrs. Miller had been effectively exercised; but, the Court of Appeals reached a contrary conclusion and reversed the decree of the Chancellor.

The real parties in interest are Mr. Bryan Walker, Jr., of Oneonta, Alabama, and Mr. Harold Fred Miller of Athens, Tennessee. If the power of appointment granted to Mrs. Miller was effectively exercised, upon her death the corpus of the marital deduction trust vested equally in Mr. Walker and Mr. Harold Fred Miller under the will of Mrs. Miller; but, if the power is held to have been not properly exercised, the whole of the corpus would be distributed to Mr. Harold Fred Miller under the residuary trust created by the last will and testament of Mr. Charles Miller.

The material facts have been stated by the Court of Appeals in an opinion by Judge Goddard as follows:

> Harold Fred Miller is the nephew of Charles Miller, deceased. For many years Harold and Charles were very close, and were jointly engaged in various business enterprises. In October, 1973, Charles and Allie Bess Miller adopted Harold as their son. A few days later they deeded him their very substantial farm. William Bryan Walker is the nephew of Allie Bess, but is in no way related to Charles. He was on good terms with both of them and saw them once or twice a year. . . .
>
> The proof shows that Charles made several wills. The first will was executed in 1964 and was drafted by Attorney Thomas Boyd. It contained a marital deduction trust with the power of appointment which provided:

> > Upon the death of my said wife, the trustee shall pay and distribute the entire principal of trust A and any accrued, accumulated or unpaid net income thereof which would have been payable to my said wife had she lived, as she appoint by a provision of her will, specifically referring to this power of appointment (including the power in her to appoint all thereof to her estate and free of trust).

> After executing three codicils, Charles executed a new will in September, 1969, which revoked the 1964 will. The 1969 will contained, verbatim, the above quoted grant of a power of appointment. Then in October, 1969, Attorney Thomas Boyd drafted Allie Bess' last will and testament in which she devised and bequeathed "all property over which I shall [sic] any power of appointment at my death" equally to the appellant and the appellee. Allie Bess' 1969 will revoked a prior will which contained no reference to a power

---

20. Inherent in this question is another: Will the courts recognize the validity of and require compliance with a donor's requirement that the donee of a power of appointment must, to effect an exercise thereof, make "specific reference" to the power.

of appointment. Finally, sometime around 1970, Charles changed attorneys, employing William Biddle in place of Thomas Boyd. In October, 1972, Charles executed his final will containing the previously quoted grant of a general testamentary power of appointment to Allie Bess.

At trial, attorney Boyd testified that when he drafted Allie Bess' last will and testament he had a copy of Charles' 1969 will in his file which contained the marital deduction trust, and that he was aware that it granted her a power of appointment. He testified that he had no personal knowledge of who instructed him to draw Allie Bess' last will, since the instructions came to him through his secretary. He further testified that any instructions to him were always as a result of either a joint consultation with the Millers or a consultation with Charles alone. He was certain that the Millers were aware of the status of each other's will.

In addition to the above, Boyd testified that it was the intent of Allie Bess to make the appellant and the appellee equal beneficiaries of her estate, and that in writing the will it was his intention to exercise the power of appointment granted to Allie Bess and Charles' 1969 will, because that was what she had wanted.

Attorney William Biddle also testified at trial, which testimony will be summarized. Biddle had a special interest in estate planning to avoid federal and state death taxes. He drafted Charles' last will, at which time he was aware of Allie Bess' last will. Charles' major concerns were (1) to avoid as much tax as possible and (2) to provide for Allie Bess without giving her the estate outright. Biddle advised Charles that to qualify for the marital deduction he must give Allie Bess a general power of appointment over the marital deduction trust; but, that the power could be restricted by requiring a specific reference in her will to exercise it. If Allie Bess improperly exercised the power, Charles could designate the beneficiaries under his will to receive the corpus of the trust. Biddle specifically advised Charles that in his opinion the general reference in Allie Bess' will would not exercise the power granted in Charles' will since it required a specific reference.

Our first task, of course, is to ascertain, as best we can, the intent of the testator-donor of the power of appointment. Just what did Charles Miller mean by use of the words ". . . shall be exercisable only by specific reference to said power in her last will and testimony [sic]"? Did he mean a more specific reference than that employed by Allie Bess in her will by use of the words " . . . all property over which I shall have any power of appointment at my death . . . ."? We must determine that intent by making a fair assessment of the words used by the testator-donor in his will, considering the instrument as a whole, read in light of the circumstances known to the testator at the time the will was executed.

We have no reported decision in this state dealing with the particular problem presented. The reported decisions in other jurisdictions, as might be expected, are not unanimous. Some have held that a donor's requirement that the donee make "a specific reference" to the donated power in order to effect its exercise, was intended merely to prevent an inadvertent exercise of such power; whereas, other courts have held that the donor in making such a requirement truly intends to require that the donee refer specifically to the donated power in order to effect an exercise thereof, hoping that the donee will fail to comply with this requirement with the result that the property subject to the power will pass under the will of the donor to recipients of his own choosing rather than to beneficiaries who might be appointed by the donee. Holding that the donor's intent in requiring a specific reference to the power donated was merely to prevent an inadvertent exercise thereof, are Shine v. Monahan, 354 Mass. 680, 241 N.E.2d 854 (1968); McKelvy v. Terry, 370 Mass. 328, 346 N.E.2d 912 (1976); First Union Nat. Bank v. Moss, 32 N.C. App. 499, 233 S.E.2d 88 (1977); Cross v. Cross, Mo. App., 559 S.W.2d 196 (1977). See, also, Restatement of Property, § 347 (American Law Institute). Cases holding that the donor intended a strict and literal compliance with his requirement that the donee exercise the donated power by specific reference thereto are In Re Estate of Schede, 426 Pa. 93, 231 A.2d 135 (1967); Holzbach v. United Virginia Bank, 216 Va. 482, 219 S.E.2d 868 (1975).

The cited cases as well as the instant case may be better understood if we digress for a brief consideration of certain aspects of the federal estate tax laws. Powers of appointment play an important role under the marital deduction trust provisions of the Internal Revenue Code, § 2056. In order to qualify for the marital deduction, the code makes it clear that any property which passes to a spouse without taxation should end up in that spouse's estate and, therefore, cannot be a "terminable interest." Thus, under Internal Revenue Code, § 2056(b)(5), if marital deduction property is placed in trust with income for life to the spouse, that spouse must have a power of appointment which will include the trust corpus in the subsequent estate under Internal Revenue Code, § 2041, that is, some general power of appointment.

It has become a popular estate planning technique for an owner of property to grant to the spouse a life interest and a general power of appointment in order to qualify for the marital deduction, but, to limit the manner in which it can be exercised. Under existing federal law and regulations, such a restriction does not deprive the power of its general character and, thus, does not defeat the marital deduction. Treasury Regulation, § 20-2056(b)-5(g)(4). Under this arrangement, the residual beneficiary under the will of the original grantor will receive the trust corpus unless the spouse has exercised the power of appointment *exactly as directed.* Obviously, this technique was attempted in the case at bar. . . .

Considering Charles Miller's will as a whole and the facts surrounding its execution, we conclude that Charles intended to require of Allie Bess strict compliance with his requirement that in order to exercise her power of appointment she must make "a specific reference" to the power which he had granted her. We further conclude that the general reference contained in her last will and testament was not a compliance with Charles' requirement, although we are satisfied, as found by the Chancellor, that Allie Bess intended the language that she used to be effective to exercise the power that Charles had granted to her. . . .

We find of compelling force the evidence that Charles continued to require a "specific reference" after learning from an attorney schooled in estate planning and death taxes that the general reference to "any power of appointment" contained in Allie Bess' will dated 1969 probably was not an effective exercise of the power of appointment which he had granted to her.

Each case of this kind, of course, must be determined upon its own facts respecting the sometimes elusive intent of the testator. We believe our conclusion to be the correct one, but, it is limited to the peculiar facts of this case.

The decree of the Court of Appeals is affirmed. Costs are taxed against petitioner, William Bryan Walker, Jr., and surety.

FONES, COOPER and HARBISON, JJ., concur.

Notes and Questions

1. *Testator's Intent.* The court in the *Walker* case was concerned about carrying out the testator's intent. In cases such as this, however, there are two testators and their intents conflict. Why did the court prefer Mr. Miller's intent? Mr. Miller's intent was to deprive by all legal means the power of his wife to exercise her general power, an act on her part that he could not directly prohibit. Ms. Miller's intent was to exercise her general power, and she instructed her attorney to that effect. If a general reformation doctrine for wills were to be adopted, would *Walker* have been an appropriate case for reforming Ms. Miller's will—by inserting an appropriately specific reference to her husband's will? See Restatement 2d of Property § 34.7 & comment d, illustration 11; Langbein & Waggoner, Reformation of Wills on the Ground of Mistake: Change of Direction in American Law?, 130 U. Pa. L. Rev. 521, 583 n. 223 (1982).

2. *Restatement 2d of Property.* The *Walker* decision is supported by the Restatement 2d of Property § 17.1 comment b, illustration 1 (set forth supra p. 820).

3. *Quality of Legal Services.* Consider the quality of legal services provided to both the donor and the donee in the *Walker* case. If you were the attorney for Ms. Miller, the donee, and if you knew—as attorney Boyd did—that Mr. Miller's 1969 will contained a specific-reference requirement, would you have drafted her will differently? If you were the attorney for Mr. Miller, and if you knew—as attorney Biddle did—that Ms. Miller's 1969 will was drafted as it was, would you have drafted Mr. Miller's 1972 will differently? See Restatement 2d of Property § 17.1 comment b, illustration 2; Treas. Reg. § 20.2056(b)-5(g)(4).

PART D. EFFECTIVENESS OF THE DONEE'S APPOINTMENT

Statutory References: *1990 UPC § 2-603*
                             Pre-1990 UPC § 2-605

Deceased Appointee. An exercise of a power of appointment in favor of a deceased person is ineffective, except as saved by an antilapse statute. Restatement 2d of Property § 18.5.

Testamentary Appointments—Applicability of Antilapse Statutes. Antilapse statutes in non-UPC states are commonly silent as to their application to the exercise of a power of appointment. Nevertheless, these statutes usually are held to apply to the testamentary exercise of a *general* power in favor of a deceased appointee, as long as the deceased appointee is in the protected relationship to the donee of the power. As to a *nongeneral* power, the authority that exists suggests that the statute does not apply unless the deceased appointee is in the protected relationship to the donee of the power *and* the substituted takers specified in the antilapse statute were objects of the power.[21]

The antilapse statute contained in the 1990 UPC expressly applies to the exercise of a power of appointment, by defining the term "devisee" as including "an appointee under a power of appointment exercised by the testator's will" if the appointee is a "grandparent, a descendant of a grandparent, or a stepchild[22] of either the testator or the donor of the power." UPC § 2-603(a)(4), (b) (1990).

UPC section 2-603 (1990) and Restatement 2d of Property section 18.6 provide that the substitute gift is not defeated merely because the substitute takers are not objects of the power. The 1990 UPC expressly states that "a surviving descendant of a deceased appointee of a power of appointment can be substituted for the appointee under this section, whether or not the descendant is an object of the power." UPC § 2-603(b)(5)(1990).

1. Permissible and Impermissible Appointments

Permissibility of Appointment Not Creating an Absolute-Ownership Interest—Appointment in Trust. The donee of a general power can validly create limited and future interests in her or his appointees, in trust or

---

21. An appointee need not accept an appointment. A disclaimer relates back and operates as a nonacceptance and, therefore, an appointee who disclaims is treated as if she or he predeceased the appointment and an antilapse statute may apply.

22. "Stepchild" is defined as a "child of the surviving, deceased, or former spouse of the testator or of the donor of a power of appointment, and not of the testator or donor." UPC § 2-603(a)(5) (1990).

otherwise, just as if the donee were the owner of the appointive property. By the apparently prevailing view, even an explicit prohibition of this type of an appointment in the language creating the power is ineffective, because it would be useless to try to enforce it. The donee merely could appoint to herself or himself or to her or his estate outright and then convey or devise the owned property as she or he chose. See Restatement 2d of Property § 19.1.

In Equitable Trust Co. v. James, 29 Del. Ch. 166, 47 A.2d 303 (1946), the court stated, contrary to the prevailing view, that an explicit prohibition of less than an outright appointment would be enforced, but also held as a matter of construction that the language must clearly impose this type of prohibition. It held that no prohibition was manifested in the language conferring a power on the donee to appoint the property "in fee simple" to such person or persons as the donee shall by will appoint.

In the absence of a contrary intent manifested in the language creating the power, the prevailing view is that the donee of a nongeneral power can validly create limited and future interests in the objects of the power, in trust or otherwise. See, e.g., Loring v. Karri-Davies, 371 Mass. 346, 357 N.E.2d 11 (1976) (overruling prospectively Hooper v. Hooper, 203 Mass. 50, 89 N.E. 161 (1909)). A manifested prohibition of this type of an appointment, however, is effective. See Restatement 2d of Property § 19.3.

Permissibility of Appointment Creating a New Power. The donee of a general power can confer a new power of appointment on her or his appointee. See Restatement 2d of Property § 19.2.

With respect to a nongeneral power, the better view is that the donee of a nongeneral power can create a general power in an object. See Restatement 2d of Property § 19.4. The fact that the donee of the appointed general power can exercise it in favor of nonobjects of the original power is irrelevant because, had the donee of the original power appointed outright to the object, the object would be free to transfer the property, by gift or otherwise, to a nonobject of the original power. Conferring a general power on an object is the equivalent of appointing outright to the object.

A few courts have held to the contrary, however. These courts take the view that the ability of the donee of the appointed general power to exercise it in favor of nonobjects of the original power precludes the donee of the nongeneral power from conferring a general power on an object. See, e.g., Thayer v. Rivers, 179 Mass. 280, 60 N.E. 796 (1901).

The donee of a nongeneral power can create a nongeneral power in an object so long as the objects of the appointed nongeneral power do not include anyone who is not an object of the first nongeneral power. See Restatement 2d of Property § 19.4.

Example 14.14: G's will devised real property to A for life, remainder to such of A's descendants as A shall appoint. At his death, A exercised his nongeneral power by appointing to his child B for life, remainder to such of B's descendants as B shall appoint. A and B were living at G's death.

A's appointment is valid because all the objects of the nongeneral power conferred on B by A's appointment were objects of A's nongeneral power. If

A had purported to confer on B a power exercisable in favor of B's spouse and descendants as B shall appoint, that part of A's appointment creating the power in B would have been ineffective.

So long as the donee of the appointed nongeneral power is an object, what is the justification for limiting who can be objects of the appointed nongeneral power? See Restatement 2d of Property § 19.4 comment a. Should a donee of a nongeneral power be able to appoint by giving a nonobject a power to appoint among objects of the first nongeneral power? Restatement 2d of Property section 19.4(2) and comment b say yes.

Estate of Kohler
463 Pa. 150, 344 A.2d 469 (1975)

EAGEN, J. This is an appeal from a final decree entered by the Orphans' Court Division of the Court of Common Pleas of Montgomery County sustaining preliminary objections to a petition to reopen an adjudication.

The facts are not in dispute.

Martin Luther Kohler died August 20, 1916, leaving a will which created a trust. According to the terms of the will, income from the trust was to be paid to his two surviving daughters, Ruth K. Bates and Else K. Campbell, during their respective lifetimes. The will provided further:

Upon the death of either of my said daughters then I direct the share of such daughter to be paid to her issue per stirpes as such issue shall arrive at the age of twenty-five years, or that the same be paid to such issue in such manner and in such sums as my said daughters shall by their respective wills direct.

Else K. Campbell died testate. Her will directed that the balance of the residue of her estate, including the power of appointment granted to her by the will of her father, Martin Luther Kohler, was to be divided into four equal shares. One share was bequeathed "to my son, Robert F. Campbell, if he survives me. Should my said son, Robert F. Campbell, predecease me, then his share shall fall into my residuary estate and shall thus increase the shares of the other residuary legatees."

Robert F. Campbell predeceased his mother, Else K. Campbell.

The Fidelity Bank, trustee of the Kohler trust, filed a final account and a petition for adjudication following the death of Else K. Campbell. No notice was given to the children of Robert F. Campbell, and the distribution suggested by the Fidelity Bank made no award to them. On December 6, 1973, the Orphans' Court Division of the Court of Common Pleas of Montgomery County rendered an adjudication confirming the account of, and approving the distribution proposed by the Fidelity Bank.

The children of Robert F. Campbell filed a petition to reopen the adjudication naming as respondents the Fidelity Bank, and the six beneficiaries among whom distribution was awarded by the adjudication. Preliminary objections were filed by the Fidelity Bank. Dismissal of the petition was sought on the ground that the children of Robert F. Campbell lacked standing to file the petition since they were not parties in interest in the trust. The court sustained Fidelity's preliminary objections. The children of Robert F. Campbell then filed this appeal.

The issue presented on this appeal is whether the will of Martin Luther Kohler created an *exclusive* power of appointment in Else K. Campbell or, more specifically, did the will give Else K. Campbell the power to exclude her son's issue from participation in the trust. The appellants contend it did not and maintain that there is nothing in the will of Martin Luther Kohler giving Else K. Campbell "the right to distribute her share of the estate to 'such of her issue' as she might by will appoint". . . .

[T]he appellants argue that the language of the Kohler will, properly interpreted, provides for a gift to Else K. Campbell's issue per stirpes with power in her merely to vary the time and method of distribution. This argument is premised solely upon an interpretation of the words "such issue". . . .

Specifically, appellants contend that the term "such issue" in the clause "or that the same be paid to such issue" has as its antecedent the phrase "issue per stirpes" as used previously in the clause "I direct the share of such daughter to be paid to her issue per stirpes". From this it follows, they assert, that the testator did not intend that either daughter have the power to exclude any of their respective issue from a distributive share of the trust.

Appellants would have us read the disputed language as presenting the following alternatives:

> Upon the death of either of my said daughters, then I direct the share of such daughter to be paid to her issue per stirpes (1) as such issue shall arrive at the age of twenty-five years, or (2) that the same be paid to such issue in such manner and in such sums as my said daughters shall by their respective wills direct.

Such an interpretation, we believe, would render superfluous the words "that the same be paid to such issue". If the power in the daughters to vary the time *for distribution* of the shares of payment were intended merely as an alternative to distribution at the age of twenty-five, there would be no apparent reason to have repeated the words "or the same be paid to such issue".

Given the structure of the language actually used, we feel a much more natural interpretation is the following:

> Upon the death of either of my said daughters then I direct (1) the share of such daughter to be paid to her issue per stirpes as such issue shall arrive at the age of twenty-five years, or (2) that the same be paid to such issue in such manner and such sums as my said daughters shall by their respective wills direct.

With this interpretation no words are superfluous, and the alternatives expressed as noun clauses with identical subjects are in parallel construction. Since wills are to be construed so as to give effect to every word employed by the testator, we deem the latter interpretation preferable.

In addition, appellants' interpretation would have us interpret the term "such issue" to mean "said issue". However, the fact that the testator in the introductory phrases of the contested sentence used the adjective "said" to refer back to his previously mentioned daughters indicates that if he did, in fact, intend to have the term "such issue" refer to an antecedent, he would more likely have used the term "said issue".

In view of the interpretation we adopt, there can be little doubt that the testator intended the power of appointment to be exclusive. A power to appoint to "such" of the class as the donee may select was long ago held to be an exclusive power, permitting the donee to select one or more of the class, to the exclusion of others. Cf. Pepper's Appeal, 120 Pa. 235, 13 A. 929 (1888);[23] Lewis's Estate, 269 Pa. 379, 112 A. 454 (1921).[24]

The appellants argue, nevertheless, that if a power of appointment is intended to be exclusive, it is necessary that the class of possible appointees be introduced by the words "such of". However, an illustration from the Restatement of Property serves to demonstrate the weakness of this contention. Illustration 1 of Section 360 states:

> A by will transfers a fund in trust to pay the income to B for life and then to pay the principal to the children of B as B shall by will appoint and in default of appointment to the children of B equally. B has an exclusive power.

In addition, we have already observed that no particular words are necessary to create a power of appointment.

Decree affirmed. Each side to pay own costs. . . .

ROBERTS, J. (dissenting). I dissent. In my view the language of the will creating the testamentary trust here was intended only to empower the first life tenants to alter the timing and manner of distribution to their issue and not to confer the power entirely to exclude some of their issue from the class of beneficiaries. I would, therefore, vacate the decree and remand for the entry of a decree permitting distribution to appellants herein.

MANDERINO, J., joins in this dissent.

---

23. Therein the language determined to have created an exclusive power of appointment was:

> And from and after his death, then to the use of such of his children and issue, and in such shares and for such estates, as he shall by last will appoint and in default of such appointment. . . .

24. Therein an exclusive power of appointment was held to have been intended by the following:

> To such person or persons, being my lineal descendants, as my said deceased daughter may have appointed by her will, in such shares and amounts as she may choose and direct by such will.

Notes

1. *Exclusive and Nonexclusive Powers Defined.* An *exclusive power* does not require the donee, if she or he exercises the power, to assure that each object receives a part of the appointive assets. One or more of the objects can be omitted or excluded. A *nonexclusive power* requires that, if the donee exercises the power, each object must receive a part of the appointive assets (either via the appointment or as a taker in default).

An example of clear language creating an *exclusive power* would be a power to appoint "to any one or more of the donee's children." An example of clear language creating a *nonexclusive power* would be a power to appoint "to all and every one of the donee's children."

2. *Construction of Ambiguous Language.* When the language is ambiguous, as it was in the *Kohler* case, some courts have adopted the constructional preference in favor of a nonexclusive power. See, e.g., Hopkins v. Dimock, 138 N.J. Eq. 434, 48 A.2d 204 (1946). The Restatement of Property section 360, followed by the court in *Kohler,* adopts the contrary constructional preference.

3. *Doctrine of Illusory Appointments.* Under the *doctrine of illusory appointments,* each object of a nonexclusive power must receive a "substantial part" of the appointive assets, not merely a nominal part. See Restatement of Property § 361(1). The Restatement 2d of Property section 21.2 obviates the necessity of recognizing the doctrine by redefining nonexclusive powers as powers wherein the donor has specified the share of the appointive assets from which an object cannot be excluded.

Estate of duPont
475 Pa. 49, 379 A.2d 570 (1977)

ROBERTS, J. Philip F. duPont died testate in 1928, leaving one-third of the residue of his estate to the Fidelity-Philadelphia Trust Company in trust for the benefit of his daughter, Mrs. Frances duPont Rust. In his will, Mr. duPont created in Mrs. Rust a special testamentary power of appointment over the one-third share of the residue. The will provides that Fidelity-Philadelphia is

> upon her death to transfer, assign, and pay over the principal of her share of (Mr. duPont's) residuary estate unto *such of her children and issue of deceased children,* and in such proportions as she may by her Last Will and Testament or any writing in the nature thereof direct, limit and appoint (emphasis added).

Mrs. Rust died in 1975. In her will, Mrs. Rust appointed a part of this share to appellants William Shore, Harry Devine, and Girard Trust Bank in trust for the benefit of her surviving daughter Carroll (Mr. duPont's granddaughter) for life and then for the benefit of the issue of Carroll (Mr.

duPont's great grandchildren). Mrs. Rust gave appellants the discretion to make periodic payments from principal to Carroll's issue.

Upon Mrs. Rust's death, Fidelity-Philadelphia filed an account in the Orphans' Court Division of the Court of Common Pleas of Chester County. The auditing judge reviewed the objection to Mrs. Rust's exercise of her special power of appointment and concluded that Mrs. Rust exceeded the bounds of her special power by appointing part of the residue for the benefit of the issue of Mrs. Rust's surviving daughter Carroll. Objections to the adjudication of the auditing judge were dismissed by the orphans' court. In this appeal, appellants contend that Mr. duPont authorized Mrs. Rust to appoint to Carroll's issue while Carroll is still living. We do not agree. We agree with the holding of the orphans' court that Mrs. Rust exceeded her special power and therefore affirm.

The orphans' court interpreted "children and issue of deceased children" to include those persons who are either living "children" of Mrs. Rust or "issue of deceased children" of Mrs. Rust at the time of her death. The court concluded that the potential beneficiaries of the special power are confined to those persons within the precise class defined in Mr. duPont's will, and that Mrs. Rust could not alter or expand that group. Hence, the court held invalid the appointment in trust for the benefit of the issue of Mrs. Rust's surviving daughter Carroll because Carroll's issue were not "issue of deceased children" of Mrs. Rust at Mrs. Rust's death.

"The donee of a power is simply a trustee for the donor to carry into effect the authority conferred by the power. In exercising the power, he must observe strictly its provisions and limitations." Rogers' Estate, 218 Pa. 431, 433, 67 A. 762, 762 (1907); Schede Estate, 426 Pa. 93, 231 A.2d 135 (1967). For her exercise of the special power to be effective, Mrs. Rust had to exercise that power within the limits of her authority. Schede Estate, supra; Restatement of Property § 351 (1940); V American Law of Property § 23.52 (Casner ed. 1952).

To validate Mrs. Rust's appointment to Mr. duPont's great grandchildren while their mother Carroll is still living would be to ignore the express language of Mr. duPont's will. Mr. duPont's testamentary plan is explicit: the language "children and issue of deceased children" gives Mrs. Rust the power to benefit her living "children" (Mr. duPont's grandchildren). This language provides in the alternative that if any of those children predecease Mrs. Rust, and if those deceased children are survived by issue, those "issue of deceased children" (Mr. duPont's great grandchildren) should be eligible beneficiaries. Such a scheme is a reasonable method of avoiding the potentially harsh exclusion of the great grandchildren of Mr. duPont whose parent happened to predecease Mrs. Rust. By including "issue of deceased children" as permissible beneficiaries, Mr. duPont allowed Mrs. Rust to appoint to such issue in place of their parent who predeceased Mrs. Rust.

Mr. duPont, in granting Mrs. Rust the power, "upon her death," to benefit "(her) children and issue of (her) deceased children . . . in such proportions" as she should choose, decided that living children of Mrs. Rust are best qualified to see to the needs of their issue; only the issue of deceased children were to be provided for by Mrs. Rust directly. While Mr.

duPont authorized Mrs. Rust to have the power to appoint "in such proportions" as she saw fit, he did not authorize the expansion or alteration of the class of permissible beneficiaries so as to encompass issue of living children. We find such an attempt to be in excess of the limits of Mrs. Rust's powers and therefore hold it invalid.

Mrs. Rust attempted to circumvent Mr. duPont's limitation to appoint only to "issue of *deceased* children" by delegating to appellants the authority to make appointments from principal to Carroll's issue after Carroll's death. Mrs. Rust authorized appellants to exercise at Carroll's death the discretion of Mr. duPont conferred exclusively upon Mrs. Rust to decide how the principal should be apportioned among members of the class of beneficiaries. However, Mr. duPont authorized Mrs. Rust to appoint "by her Last Will and Testament or any writing in the nature thereof." This language reflects an intent that Mrs. Rust exercise her appointment power at the time of her death. The testamentary nature of her special power is inconsistent with her attempt to postpone the choice of beneficiaries beyond the time of her death.

Appellants, at oral argument, contended that the decision of the orphans' court will burden Carroll's issue with harsh tax consequences. That concern does not relieve a court from the duty of discerning the testator's intent as it is expressed in the will and the overall testamentary plan.

> As to the obviation of taxes, it is incontestable that almost every settlor and testator desires to minimize his tax burden to the greatest extent possible. However, courts cannot be placed in the position of estate planners, charged with the task of reinterpreting deeds of trust and testamentary dispositions so as to generate the most favorable possible tax consequences for the estate. Rather courts are obliged to construe the settlor's or testator's intent as evidenced by the language of the instrument itself, the overall scheme of distributions, and the surrounding circumstances.

Estate of Benson, 447 Pa. 62, 72, 285 A.2d 101, 106 (1971).

Decree affirmed. Each party to pay own costs.

POMEROY and NIX, JJ., concur in the result.

Notes

1. *Impermissibility of Direct or Indirect Appointments to Nonobjects.* A direct appointment in favor of a person who is not an object of a non-general power is obviously ineffective. See Restatement 2d of Property § 20.1. Even an appointment in favor of an object is ineffective—a so-called *fraud on the power*—if the donee's purpose was to benefit a nonobject. See Restatement 2d of Property § 20.2.

> *Example 14.15:* G devised the residue of her estate in trust, income to her husband, H, for life, remainder in corpus "to such of G's children by a former marriage as H should by will appoint." On H's subsequent death, H appointed the trust corpus to A, who was one of G's children by her former marriage. Evidence showed, however, that A had agreed, in consideration of the

appointment, to transfer half of the appointive assets to X, H's child of a former marriage.

H's appointment is invalid because his effort to benefit the nonobject, X, constitutes a fraud on his nongeneral power.

2. *Effectiveness of Appointment to Takers in Default.* There is disagreement among the cases as to the effectiveness of an appointment to a taker in default. The rationale of the cases holding that an appointment to a taker in default is ineffective is that the taker in default holds an interest created by the donor that can be defeated or changed by the exercise of the power. A purported exercise of the power in conformity with the interest of the taker in default is a nullity, not an exercise of the power. See Restatement 2d of Property § 24.4.

The capacity in which the person takes, as appointee or taker in default, is of no great concern to the person taking, as long as she or he takes. The significance of whether the appointment is effective or not lies elsewhere. The question usually arises in cases of general powers and the claims of the donee's creditors, usually the donee's estate creditors. By the majority common-law view, an ineffective appointment of a general power does not allow creditors to reach the appointive assets. It takes an effective appointment to subject the appointive assets to the claims of the donee's creditors. See supra p. 812. The issue of whether an appointment to default takers is an exercise of a power may also have tax implications if the donee had a pre-1942 general power. See supra p. 808.

2. Failures to Appoint; Ineffective Appointments

General Powers—Failure to Exercise. If the donee of a general power of appointment fails to exercise the power, the appointive assets pass under the donor's gift-in-default clause. If there is no gift-in-default clause, the appointive assets revert to the donor (or the donor's successor in interest).

Recall that the most likely donee of a general power is the donor's surviving spouse, in which case the power will be a power to appoint the remainder interest in a marital deduction trust. If the donor's estate was well planned, there will be a gift-in-default clause. If the donee does not wish to disturb the gift-in-default clause, the donee should not only refrain from exercising the general power, but should affirmatively declare this intention in the donee's will by a clause such as:

I hereby refrain from exercising the power of appointment conferred on me by my spouse's will of [date].

Ineffective Exercise of General Power—The "Capture Doctrine." If the donee of a general power of appointment makes an ineffective exercise, the appointive property ordinarily goes to the takers in default or, if none, reverts to the donor (or the donor's successor in interest). If, however, the donee's appointment manifests an intent to assume control of the property for all purposes and not merely for the limited purpose of giving effect to the expressed appointment, courts apply the "capture doctrine," which means that the appointive property goes to the donee's estate rather than to the takers in default or to the donor (or the donor's successor in interest). See Restatement 2d of Property § 23.2. Some courts have used the theory that the donee's ineffective appointment constitutes an implied appointment in favor of the donee's own estate.

The donee's intent to assume control of the property for all purposes is manifested by: (1) a blending clause, see, e.g., Fiduciary Trust Co. v. Mishou, 321 Mass. 615, 75 N.E.2d 3 (1947); (2) a residuary clause that presumptively demonstrates an intent to exercise the power pursuant to a statute or rule of common law; (3) a residuary clause that demonstrates an intent to exercise the power because the donee's estate is insufficient to satisfy the donee's bequests; or (4) in the view of some but not all courts, an appointment in trust. Compare Talbot v. Riggs, 287 Mass. 144, 191 N.E. 360 (1934) (capture doctrine applied because donee's ineffective appointment was in trust), with Northern Trust Co. v. Porter, 368 Ill. 256, 13 N.E.2d 487 (1938) (capture doctrine not applied even though donee's ineffective appointment was in trust).

Donors often attempt to protect their gift-in-default clauses against the capture doctrine. A standard clause in frequent use introduces the gift-in-default clause with the phrase:

> To the extent the donee does not effectively exercise this power of appointment, ...

Since one of the theories used to justify an application of the capture doctrine is that, in the circumstances, the import of the donee's ineffective express appointment is an effective implied appointment in favor of her or his own estate, this type of clause may not give the donor the desired protection. Greater protection would be afforded by a slight rewording of the standard clause:

> To the extent the donee does not expressly exercise this power of appointment effectively, ...

Nongeneral Powers. If the donee fails to exercise a nongeneral power of appointment, or makes an ineffective exercise thereof, the property goes to the takers in default. If there are no takers in default, the appointive property will go to the objects of the power if the objects are a defined limited class and not revert to the donor or the donor's successor in interest.

Two different theories are employed to reach this result. Some courts take the view that the donee of a nongeneral power with a defined limited class of objects has a duty to exercise the power, i.e., that the power is a power in trust (also called an imperative or mandatory power). The court will not permit the objects of the power to suffer by the negligence of the donee in failing to appoint or making an ineffective appointment, "but fastens upon the property a trust for their benefit." See, e.g., Daniel v. Brown, 156 Va. 563, 159 S.E. 209 (1931).

Other courts imply a gift in default in favor of the objects of the nongeneral power. See, e.g., Loring v. Marshall, 396 Mass. 166, 484 N.E.2d 1315 (1985); Polen v. Baird, 125 W. Va. 682, 25 S.E.2d 767 (1943); Restatement 2d of Property § 24.2. See also Restatement 2d of Trusts § 120 comment e, § 121 comment a.

> *Example 14.16:* The objects of A's nongeneral power are A's children; there is no express gift in default.
>
> If A dies without exercising the power, or makes an ineffective appointment, the appointive assets will go to his children who survive A (and substituted takers for a deceased child, if an antilapse statute applies). Both the power-in-trust theory and the implied-gift-in-default theory lead to this result. If, however, there are no objects to which the property can pass, the appointive assets revert back to the donor (or the donor's successor in interest).

> *Example 14.17:* The objects of A's nongeneral power are anyone in the world except A, A's estate, A's creditors, and the creditors of A's estate.
>
> If A dies without exercising the power, or makes an ineffective appointment, the appointive assets revert to the donor (or the donor's successor in interest). The power is not a power in trust and there is no implied gift in default because the objects of A's power are not a defined limited class.

3. Contracts to Appoint

Presently Exercisable Powers. A contract by the donee of a presently exercisable power of appointment to make a specified appointment in the future is enforceable if neither the contract nor the promised appointment confers a benefit on a nonobject. See Restatement 2d of Property § 16.1.

If the presently exercisable power is a general power, it follows that a contract to appoint is enforceable, regardless of on whom the benefits are conferred.

If the presently exercisable power is a nongeneral power, a contract to appoint is likely to confer a benefit on a nonobject. If so, the contract is unenforceable, but the promisee, if her or his conduct was not consciously wrongful, is entitled to restitution of the value of the consideration paid for the promise.

> *Example 14.18:* A was the donee of a nongeneral power to appoint among her nephews and nieces. In exchange for consideration of $10,000, A contracted with one of her nephews, X, to appoint all the property to X, to the exclusion of A's other nieces and nephews.
>
> Even though X is an object of the power, the contract is unenforceable because the contract benefitted A, the promisor-donee. A was not an object of the power.

If the donee does not breach the unenforceable contract, but instead abides by it, the donee's appointment may be ineffective on the ground that it constitutes a fraud on the nongeneral power.

Testamentary Powers. A contract to appoint a testamentary power, whether general or nongeneral, violates the donor's intent in limiting the exercise of the power to a testamentary exercise. Thus a contract to appoint a testamentary power is unenforceable. The promisee may, however, be entitled to restitution of the value of the consideration paid for the promise. See Restatement 2d of Property § 16.2.

If the donee does not breach the unenforceable contract, but instead abides by it, the donee's appointment is valid if the power was a general power. See, e.g., Rogers' Estate, 168 Misc. 633, 6 N.Y.S.2d 255 (Sur. Ct. 1938). If the power was a nongeneral power, if the promisee-appointee was an object of the power, and if the promisor-donee received consideration for the promise, it would seem that the appointment should be ineffective as a fraud on the power and that the promisee should then be able to obtain restitution from the promisor-donee (or her or his estate) of the value of the consideration paid for the promise. See, e.g., Pitman v. Pitman, 314 Mass. 465, 50 N.E.2d 69 (1943). The Restatement 2d of Property section 16.2 comment c, however, suggests that the appointment is effective, but also suggests that, to prevent the nonobject-donee-promisor from receiving a benefit, the promisee-appointee should be entitled to receive restitution of the value of the consideration paid for the promise.

4. Releases of Powers

The Restatement 2d of Property sections 14.1 and 14.2 declare that all powers of appointment, general and nongeneral, testamentary and presently exercisable, are releasable in whole or in part, unless the donor has effectively manifested an intent that the power not be releasable. Several states have enacted legislation that is basically or wholly in accord with this proposition.

If the donor of a *general* power expressly provides that the power cannot be released, the donor's intention may not be effective. Its validity still must be examined under the rules governing unreasonable restraints on alienation. See Restatement 2d of Property § 14.1 comment a.

An express provision prohibiting the release of a *nongeneral* power is probably valid. Apart from an express prohibition, the release of a nongeneral power is impliedly prohibited if the nongeneral power is a power in trust (also called an imperative or mandatory power). A nongeneral power is a power in trust if the objects are a defined limited class and if the donor has not provided for a disposition of the property in case the power is not exercised. See Restatement 2d of Property § 14.2 comment d.

The release of a power of appointment, when permissible, is effectively an exercise in favor of the takers in default, even in cases where an actual exercise in favor of the takers in default would be prohibited or ineffective. (An *actual* exercise in favor of the takers in default can be ineffective because the released power was a testamentary power, because one or more of the takers in default died prior to the release, or because the jurisdiction does not recognize an appointment in favor of the takers in default as an effective appointment.)

> *Example 14.19:* G's will devised property in trust, income "to A for life, remainder in corpus to such of A's children as A by will appoints; in default of appointment, to A's children equally. G was survived by A and A's children, X and Y. X then died, leaving all his estate to his wife, W. Then A released her power of appointment.
>
> At the time of the release, the gift in default in favor of A's children became indefeasibly vested. At A's death, the corpus of the trust will go to Y and X's successor in interest (W).

Chapter 15

CLASSIFICATION OF ESTATES AND FUTURE INTERESTS

Having studied the role of powers of appointment in the fashioning of trusts, we now turn to the subject of future interests. If powers of appointment are staples in modern estate-planning practice, future interests are nothing short of indispensable. Future interests are intrinsic to trusts: It is nearly impossible to create a trust without creating one or a set of future interests.

The study of future interests was at one time dominated by—some would say obsessed with—the study of classification. The goal was to teach students to be able to affix the proper label or labels to a possessory or future estate. The preoccupation with classification was appropriate, though tedious, as long as important legal consequences turned on classification. Today, few legal consequences turn on classification. Why, then, study classification at all? Unfortunately, classification is still important in the solving of some legal problems, such as the Rule Against Perpetuities. Additionally, you need to become familiar with the terms associated with classification to understand the legal literature and communicate to others in practice. Thus we study classification in this Chapter, though the subject is presented in less detail than would have been offered in the past.[1]

PART A. CLASSIFICATION: THE HIERARCHY OF ESTATES

As indicated above, classification means fixing the proper label or labels to a possessory or future estate. The hierarchy of estates is a refined, artificial structure that took centuries fully to develop. If it had been designed in one fell swoop, the flexibility it provides estate planners and clients of today could surely be attained with a system of much greater simplicity. A proposal for a simplified system is noted later.

The complexity and artificiality in the current system was not so much designed as evolved, step by step over a fairly long period of time from the struggles of competing interest groups. The owners of the great landed estates, assisted by ingenious lawyers, sought to avoid the estate taxes of the day and to safeguard their estates through generations and generations. As one loophole was plugged in favor of exacting the tax or promoting freer alienability and control for the recipients of the property, the ingenious lawyers found another. The result was that great distinctions were drawn on the basis of the words used in creating dispositions. Through classification, different ways of saying the same thing were accorded different legal consequences. Form controlled over substance. In classification, form still controls over substance. Form controls legal consequences less than before, however, because the legal consequences flowing from classification gradually have been reduced.

As we study the current system, bear in mind also that the system of classification, which was originally developed in feudal times mainly for legal interests in land, has been transposed today to the classification of the beneficial interests in the modern trust. See Browder, Trusts and the Doctrine of Estates, 72 Mich. L. Rev. 1507 (1974).

---

1. For greater detail, see T. Bergin & P. Haskell, Preface to Estates in Land and Future Interests (2d ed. 1984); L. Simes, Handbook on the Law of Future Interests (2d ed. 1966); L. Waggoner, Future Interests in a Nutshell (1981).

Quantum of Estates. According to the hierarchy of estates, the possessory estates are ordered by "quantum." In descending order of quantum, the groupings are: (1) fee simple estate (all fee simple estates are of the same quantum); (2) fee tail; (3) life estate; (4) term of years; (5) estate from period to period; (6) estate at will; and (7) estate at sufferance.

Particular Estate. The term *particular estate* is a term of art denoting any estate that is less than a fee simple—a fee tail, a life estate, a term of years, and so on.

Chart. The following chart of the hierarchy of estates is presented here partly as a point of departure but mainly as a point of retrospection for use as you work your way through the succeeding text.

THE HIERARCHY OF ESTATES*

Possessory Interests	Possible Combinations of Future Interests	
	Nonreversionary (created in a transferee)	Reversionary (retained by or created in transferor or successor)
Fee Simple Absolute	None permissible	None Permissible
Defeasible Fee Simple:		
Fee Simple Determinable**	When none created	Possibility of Reverter
	Executory Interest	If Any, Possibility of Reverter
Fee Simple Subject to a Condition Subsequent***		Right of Entry (Power of Termination)
Fee Simple Subject to an Executory Limitation***	Executory Interest	
Fee Tail****	. . . Same as with Life Estate . . .	
Life Estate	When no remainder created	Indefeasibly Vested Reversion
	Contingent Remainder (subject to a condition precedent); If any, Alternative Contingent Remainder	Reversion Vested Subject to Defeasance (may be merely technical)
	Remainder Vested Subject to Defeasance (conditional); If any, Executory Interest	If any, Possibility of Reverter

	Remainder Vested Subject to Defeasance (limitational);	If any, Reversion either Vested Subject to Defeasance or Indefeasibly Vested Remainder
	Remainder Vested Subject to Open; Executory Interest in unborn class members	None permissible
	Indefeasibly Vested Remainder	None permissible
Life Estate Subject to a Special Limitation*****	. . . Same as with Life Estate . . .	
Life Estate Subject to a Condition Subsequent		Reversion and Right of Entry (otherwise same as with Life Estate)
Life Estate Subject to an Executory Limitation	Remainder and Executory Interest (otherwise, same as with Life Estate)	
Term of Years	. . . Same as with Life Estate . . .	

---

 * Although the chart is believed to be substantially accurate and complete, it does not purport to depict all the combinations of future interests that possibly could follow each possessory interest. A remainder following a life estate might, for example, be in fee simple determinable, in which case the transferor might retain a possibility of reverter in addition to, or instead of, a reversion.

 ** "Fee simple determinable" is the most common name employed to describe this interest. Other names are "base fee," "qualified fee," and "fee simple on a special limitation."

 *** The "fee simple subject to a condition subsequent" and the "fee simple subject to an executory limitation" are created by the same language. The distinction between the two is based on the nature of the future interest following it. If such an estate is followed by both an executory interest and a right of entry, the possessory interest could properly be called a fee simple subject to an executory limitation and a condition subsequent. It may be noted further that the "fee simple subject to an executory limitation" is sometimes called a "fee simple subject to a conditional limitation."

 **** The fee tail interest, though still permissible in a handful of states, has faded from importance.

 ***** Another name for this interest is "determinable life estate."

1. The Possessory Estates

The Estates in Fee Simple. Although there are four fee simple estates, they can be divided into two general categories: fee simple absolute and fee simple defeasible.

The estate in *fee simple absolute* is an estate in land that is not subject to termination; it is unlimited in duration. (The personal-property counterpart of the fee simple absolute is called absolute or outright ownership.) The fee simple absolute is not subject to a special limitation, a condition subsequent, or an executory limitation. A fee simple absolute is never followed by a future interest.

> *Example 15.1:* G conveyed real property "to A and his heirs." A has a fee simple absolute; no future interest follows it.
> The words "and his heirs" are "words of limitation," meaning words defining the estate granted to A, not "words of purchase," meaning words granting an interest in the property to A's heirs.

The *defeasible fee simple* estates are subject to termination upon the happening of an event specified in the grant. There are three defeasible fee simple estates: (1) the fee simple determinable; (2) the fee simple subject to a condition subsequent; and (3) the fee simple subject to an executory limitation. Distinguishing each of these estates from the others requires an understanding of the concept of defeasance.

Defeasance means the loss of ownership—that the holder of the possessory interest (or her or his successor in interest) will lose that interest in the property (including the right to possession) upon the happening of an event that is stipulated in the grant. Defeasance is a broad term that encompasses two categories: condition and limitation. A possessory interest that is subject to defeasance is either subject to a *condition subsequent* or a *limitation*.

Possessory interests that are subject to a "limitation" are said to terminate *naturally* or *by their own terms*. The language in the grant that signifies a "limitation" are words such as "during," "until," "while," "so long as," "for so long as," or simply "for [a designated period]," followed by words such as "at," "upon," or "then." A "special" limitation describes an event that is not certain to happen.

Possessory interests that are subject to a "condition subsequent" (divestment) are said to terminate by being *cut short* or *divested* upon the happening of the stipulated event. The language in the grant that signifies a "condition subsequent" are words such as "on condition that" or "provided that," followed by words such as "but if" or "and if." (In some grants, only the "but if" or "and if" language will appear.)

The *fee simple determinable* is a fee estate that is subject to a *special limitation,* which means that it automatically terminates or expires if the specified event happens; the specified event is an event that is not certain to happen. The future interest following the estate in fee simple determinable, if reversionary, is a possibility of reverter or, if nonreversionary, an executory interest.

Example 15.2: G conveyed real property "to A and her heirs *so long as* A does not allow liquor to be sold on the premises; upon A's allowing liquor to be sold on the premises, the property to revert to me."

Example 15.3: G conveyed real property "to A and her heirs *so long as* A does not allow liquor to be sold on the premises; and upon A's allowing liquor to be sold on the premises, the property to go to B."[2]

The *fee simple subject to a condition subsequent* is a fee estate that is subject to *divestment* in favor of a reversionary future interest called a right of entry (also called a power of termination). The happening of the specified event does not automatically divest the estate; rather, it empowers the grantor or her or his successor in interest to divest the estate by exercising the right of entry.

Example 15.4: G conveyed real property "to A and his heirs *on condition that* A not allow liquor to be sold on the premises, *and if* A allows liquor to be sold on the premises, then the grantor is to have the right to re-enter and take possession of the premises."

The *fee simple subject to an executory limitation* is a fee estate that is subject to *divestment* in favor of a nonreversionary future interest called an executory interest. The happening of the specified event divests the estate.

Example 15.5: G conveyed real property "to A and her heirs, *but if* A allows liquor to be sold on the premises, then to B."

Fee Tail. The fee tail estate is subject to termination if and when the line of the tenant in tail's issue fails. That is, the estate terminates upon the death of the tenant in tail's last living descendant.

The fee tail estate has an interesting history,[3] but its present is no longer very important and its future even less so. In almost all states, the fee tail estate is abolished. Language purporting to create it—"to A and the heirs of his body"—has different consequences in different states. The most predominant results are that it creates a fee simple absolute in A or that it creates a life estate in A, with a remainder in fee in A's issue.

Life Estates and Terms of Years. Life estates and terms of years are estates that are defeasible: As estates that are subject to a *limitation*,[4] they expire naturally (by their own terms) on the life tenant's death or the expiration of the term.

The phrases "equitable life estate" or "equitable term" are sometimes used to describe the interest of a trust beneficiary who has the right to the

---

2. The limitation regarding selling liquor applies only to A and not to A's successors in interest. Therefore, the executory interest to B is valid under the Rule Against Perpetuities because it must vest or fail within A's lifetime.

3. See Restatement of Property Ch. 5; T. Bergin & P. Haskell, supra note 1, at 28-34.

4. "To A *for* life;" "to A *so long as* A lives;" "to A *until* A's death;" "to A *during* A's lifetime;" "to A *for* 10 years."

income from a trust for her or his lifetime or for a term. Equitable terms are most frequently encountered in charitable lead trusts, but they are also used in trusts that give the right to the income to a family member until she or he reaches a specified age.

Life estates and terms of years are by definition defeasible estates, as noted above. Both, however, can be made prematurely defeasible so that they end before the life tenant's death or the expiration of the term. This occurs when either a special limitation or a condition subsequent is added to the grant.

> *Example 15.6:* G transferred real property "to A for life or until A remarries." A's estate is called a "life estate subject to a special limitation." Another name for it is "determinable life estate."

> *Example 15.7:* (1) G transferred real property "to A for life, remainder to B; but if A remarries, to B immediately." A's estate is called a "life estate subject to an executory limitation."
> (2) G transferred real property "to A for life on condition that A not remarry; and if A remarries, G is to have the right to re-enter and take possession of the premises." A's estate is called a "life estate subject to a condition subsequent."

The duration of a life estate need not be measured by the life of the one in possession, but instead it can be measured by the life of another. This type of estate is called a "life estate *pur autre vie.*"

> *Example 15.8:* G transferred real property "to A for the life of B." A predeceases B. A's will devises her entire estate to X. A has a life estate *pur autre vie.* Unlike a life estate that terminates on the life tenant's death, A can devise the remaining portion of her life estate to X. After A's death, X has a life estate *pur autre vie—for the life of B.*

2. Future Interests: Basic Division
Between Reversionary and Nonreversionary Interests

The first step in the process of classification of future interests is to decide whether the future interest is a reversionary interest or a nonreversionary interest. There are five future interests: (1) reversions; (2) possibilities of reverter; (3) rights of entry (also called powers of termination); (4) remainders; and (5) executory interests. Of these, the first three—reversions, possibilities of reverter, and rights of entry—are reversionary interests. Reversionary interests are interests retained by (or created in) the transferor *when the interest was created.* The other two future interests—remainders and executory interests—are nonreversionary interests. Nonreversionary interests are interests *created in* a transferee (someone other than the transferor).

Once made, a classification based on the reversionary/nonreversionary distinction is not altered by subsequent transfers of the interest from one person to another. So, a reversionary interest does not become a nonreversionary interest by virtue of a subsequent transfer of that interest from the transferor to a transferee. And, conversely, a nonreversionary interest does not become reversionary if it subsequently comes into the hands of the transferor. It makes no difference whether the subsequent transfer is inter vivos, testamentary, or the result of intestate succession.

Problems

Classify the future interests in the following problems:
1. G conveyed real property "to A for life."
   (a) Later, G conveyed all her interest in that property to B.
   (b) Instead of conveying her interest to B, G later died leaving a will that did not mention the real property but contained a residuary clause devising and bequeathing all her property not otherwise disposed of to B. G was survived by A and B.
   (c) In Problem 1(b), G died intestate. G was survived by A and by her sole heir, B.
2. G's will devised real property to A for life; the will contained no residuary clause, and so the residue of her estate passed by intestacy to her sole heir, B.
3. G's will devised real property "to A for life, and upon A's death, the property is to go to B."
4. G's will devised real property "to A for life." G's will contained a residuary clause devising "all my property not otherwise disposed of to B."

3. The Reversionary Future Interests: Reversions, Possibilities of Reverter, and Rights of Entry

If a future interest is reversionary, it is either a reversion, a possibility of reverter, or a right of entry.

a. Reversions

Reversions are future interests retained by the transferor (or her or his successors in interest) when she or he transfers out an estate or estates of *less* quantum than she or he had originally. The most common example is that of an owner of property in fee simple absolute who transfers out a particular estate (a possessory interest other than a fee simple interest).

> *Example 15.9:* G conveyed real property "to A for life." G retained a reversionary interest, and that reversionary interest is a reversion.

b. Possibilities of Reverter

Possibilities of reverter are future interests retained by the transferor (or her or his successors in interest) when she or he transfers out an estate or estates of the *same* quantum as she or he had originally. The most common example is that of an owner of property in fee simple absolute who transfers out a fee simple determinable.

> *Example 15.10:* G conveyed real property "to A and his heirs so long as A does not allow liquor to be sold on the premises[, and upon A's allowing liquor to be sold on the premises, the property is to revert to the grantor]." G retained a reversionary interest, and that reversionary interest is a possibility of reverter.

The words contained in the brackets in the preceding example are not necessary to create a possibility of reverter. Possibilities of reverter need not be expressly stated because, like reversions, they constitute an undisposed-of interest remaining in the transferor. See Simes & Smith on Future Interests § 286. In practice, however, it is common expressly to state the possibility of reverter, and a small minority of decisions has held (erroneously) that, without the bracketed words, A takes a fee simple absolute. See, e.g., In re Copps Chapel Methodist Episcopal Church, 120 Ohio St. 309, 166 N.E. 218 (1929).

c. Rights of Entry (Powers of Termination)

Rights of entry—also called powers of termination[5]—are future interests created in the transferor (or her or his successors in interest) when she or he transfers out an estate subject to a condition subsequent (i.e., subject to divestment). (Whether the quantum of the estate is the same as or lesser than that of the transferor's original estate is unimportant.) The most common example is that of an owner of property in fee simple absolute who transfers out a fee simple subject to a condition subsequent and who expressly creates in herself or himself a right to re-enter and retake the premises if and when the condition is broken.

> *Example 15.11:* G conveyed real property "to A and her heirs on condition that A not allow liquor to be sold on the premises, but if A allows liquor to be sold on the premises, the grantor is to have the right to re-enter and take possession of the premises." G retained (more accurately, created in himself) a reversionary interest, and that reversionary interest is a right of entry.

---

5. "Power of termination" is the terminology used in the first Restatement of Property § 155. The Restatement 2d of Property forgoes that terminology and utilizes the older terminology, "right of entry."

A right of entry is not exactly like any other future interest. It is like an executory interest in one sense only—it takes effect in possession by cutting short or divesting the preceding estate. But, unlike the executory interest, it does not take effect in possession automatically when the condition is broken. If A allows liquor to be sold on the premises, this merely gives G a right to elect to take a possessory interest if G so chooses.

It is also unlike the other two reversionary interests because it is not the undisposed-of interest retained by the transferor when she or he transfers other interests.

4. The Nonreversionary Future Interests: Remainders and Executory Interests

If a future interest is nonreversionary, it is either a remainder or an executory interest.

a. Remainders

Remainders are future interests created in a transferee that become possessory if at all upon the *natural termination* of the preceding vested interest. The preceding vested interest (1) must have been created simultaneously with the creation of the future interest and (2) must be a "particular" estate. (Recall that a "particular" estate is a term of art that denotes any possessory interest other than a fee simple interest.) See supra p. 841.

> *Example 15.12:* G transferred real property "to A for life, and upon A's death, to B." B has a remainder, not an executory interest.

b. Executory Interests

Executory interests are future interests created in a transferee that become possessory if at all by *cutting short* or *divesting* the preceding vested interest. The preceding vested interest (1) need not have been created simultaneously with the creation of the future interest and (2) can be a fee simple interest or a particular estate.

> *Example 15.13:* G transferred real property "to A and his heirs on condition that A not allow liquor to be sold on the premises, but if A allows liquor to be sold on the premises, the property is to go to B." B has an executory interest, not a remainder.

Special Case—Executory Interest Succeeds Fee Simple Determinable. In one special case, an executory interest does not "cut short" or "divest" the preceding vested interest, but takes effect on its "natural termination." Since a remainder cannot follow a fee simple interest, a fee simple must always be followed by an executory interest, even when the fee simple is subject to a special limitation.

> *Example 15.14:* G transferred real property "to A and her heirs as long as A does not allow liquor to be sold on the premises, and upon A's allowing liquor to be sold on the premises, the property is to go to B." B has an executory interest, not a remainder.

Springing and Shifting Executory Interests. Executory interests are sometimes divided into two categories—springing and shifting. *Shifting* executory interests potentially divest an interest conferred by the grantor on a transferee. *Springing* executory interests potentially divest an interest retained by the grantor.

> *Example 15.15:* (1) G transferred real property "to A and his heirs, but if A allows liquor to be sold on the premises, to B." B's executory interest is a shifting executory interest.
>
> (2) G transferred real property "to B, to take effect in possession on B's marriage." B's executory interest is a springing executory interest.

Future Interests in Sets. When a set of nonreversionary future interests succeeds a life estate or a term of years, the first future interest will always be a remainder. The other or subsequent future interest(s), however, may be either remainders or executory interests. In determining which they are, the following rules apply:

> *Rule 1:* If the first future interest is a contingent (nonvested) remainder, the other nonreversionary future interests will also be contingent (nonvested) remainders.
>
> *Rule 2:* If the first future interest is a vested remainder subject to divestment, the other nonreversionary future interests will be executory interests.

Problems

After consulting the next section, classify the interests of B and C in the following examples:

1. G transferred real property "to A for life, remainder to B if B survives A, but if not, to C."

2. G transferred real property "to A for life, remainder to B, but if B fails to survive A, to C."

5. Vested and Contingent Future Interests

Future interests are subject to a further level of classification—classification in terms of vesting. There are four categories here: indefeasibly vested,

vested subject to (complete) defeasance, vested subject to open (partial defeasance), and contingent (nonvested).

a. Indefeasibly Vested

An indefeasibly vested future interest is one that is not subject to any conditions or limitations. In other words, the future interest must be certain to become a possessory fee simple *absolute* at some time in the future. See Restatement of Property § 157 comment f. Only remainders and reversions can be indefeasibly vested.

> *Example 15.16:* G transferred real property "to A for life, remainder to B." B's remainder is indefeasibly vested. It is certain to become possessory because A is bound to die. When A dies, B's remainder will become a possessory fee simple absolute.
> Note in this example that B might not be alive when A dies. Except as otherwise provided by statute,[6] B's interest is not subject to a condition of survivorship of A. Therefore, the possibility of B's death before A's death has no bearing on the classification of B's interest. If B dies before A, B's indefeasibly vested remainder will pass at B's death to B's successors in interest—her devisee or, if she dies intestate, her heirs. See infra p. 892 for discussion of survivorship conditions.

> *Example 15.17:* G conveyed real property "to A for life." G's reversion is indefeasibly vested. The comments made in the above example regarding B's remainder apply to G's reversion in this example.

> *Example 15.18:* G conveyed real property "to A for life, remainder to B for ten years." G's reversion is indefeasibly vested. It is certain to become possessory ten years after A's death, and will at that time become a fee simple absolute.
> B's remainder is not indefeasibly vested. Although it is certain to become possessory upon A's death (a certain event), it will not become a fee simple absolute upon A's death. B's remainder is vested subject to defeasance (in the limitational sense). The comments made in the first example regarding survivorship apply to this example.

b. Vested Subject to Defeasance

A future interest that is vested subject to defeasance is one that is subject to either one or more conditions subsequent or one or more limitations. (The term sometimes employed is vested subject to *complete* defeasance in order to distinguish such an interest from one that is vested subject to open.) Future interests, like possessory interests, can be subject to defeasance in either of two senses. A future interest can be subject either to a condition or to a limitation.

---

6. See, e.g., UPC § 2-707 (1990).

A future interest is vested subject to divestment if it is subject to a *condition subsequent*. Only remainders and reversions can be vested subject to divestment. A remainder is vested subject to divestment if it is subject to a condition that is stated in condition subsequent form. A reversion is vested subject to divestment if it is subject to a condition, regardless of whether the condition is stated in precedent or subsequent form. The reason for the difference is that a remainder that is subject to a condition may be either contingent or vested subject to divestment, while a reversion subject to a condition cannot be contingent. *Reversions are always vested.*

> *Example 15.19:* G transferred real property "to A for life, remainder to B, but if B fails to survive A, to C." B's remainder is vested subject to divestment because the condition of survivorship attached to her remainder is stated in condition subsequent form—"to B, but if."
>
> C's executory interest is subject to the condition that B not survive A. This condition is stated in the form of a condition precedent—"if . . . to C." C's executory interest is contingent.
>
> G retained no reversion.

> *Example 15.20:* G conveyed real property "to A for life, remainder to B if B survives A, but if not, to return to me." B's remainder is subject to a condition of survivorship of A, but this time the condition is stated in the form of a condition precedent—"to B if." B's remainder is therefore contingent, not vested subject to divestment.
>
> G's reversion is subject to the condition that B not survive A, and so G's reversion cannot be indefeasibly vested. This condition is stated in the form of a condition precedent. Nevertheless, the rule that reversions are always vested overrides all other rules and, therefore, G's reversion is vested subject to divestment.
>
> This analysis also applies if the phrase "but if not, to return to me" is omitted.

> *Example 15.21:* G conveyed real property "to A for life, remainder to B if B survives A, but if not, to C." B's remainder is subject to a condition of survivorship of A that is stated in the form of a condition precedent—"to B if." B's remainder is therefore contingent, not vested subject to divestment.
>
> C's remainder is subject to the condition that B not survive A. The condition is stated in the form of a condition precedent ("if [B does not survive A], to C") and, therefore, C's remainder is contingent, not vested subject to divestment.
>
> G retained a technical reversion. (There is always a reversion when a particular estate is followed by contingent remainders. In a case such as this example, the contingencies stated with respect to the interests of B and C exhaust all the possibilities; hence, the reversion is said to be merely "technical.") The reversion is vested subject to divestment because it cannot be indefeasibly vested and because it must be vested.

A future interest that is subject to a *limitation* is vested subject to defeasance. Only remainders and reversions can be vested subject to a limitation.

Example 15.22: G transferred real property "to A for life, then to B for life, then to C." B's remainder is vested subject to (limitational) defeasance. It is sometimes referred to simply as a vested remainder for life. Note that B must survive A for his interest to become possessory. This implicit requirement of survivorship is not regarded as a "condition" of survivorship.

C's interest is a remainder because B's interest is subject to a limitation and because it is an estate less than a fee simple. It is an indefeasibly vested remainder because it is subject to no condition or limitation.

Example 15.23: G conveyed real property "to A for life, then to return to me for life, then to C." This is the same as the example above, except that the future interest subject to (limitational) defeasance is a reversion in G rather than a remainder in B.

Example 15.24: G transferred real property "to A for life, then to B for 10 years, then to C." B's remainder is vested subject to (limitational) defeasance. In this case, the time of B's death is irrelevant. If B dies while A is still alive, B's remainder will pass to her devisees or if she died intestate to her heirs. If B dies after A's death but before the 10th anniversary thereof, the remaining portion of B's 10-year term will pass to her devisees or if she died intestate to her heirs.

c. Vested Subject to Open

At inception, only remainders can be vested subject to open. A remainder is vested subject to open when it is subject to no conditions precedent and when it is in favor of a class that contains at least one living member and that is still "open," *i.e.,* where it is possible for additional persons to become class members (typically through birth or adoption). Other and older labels for this type of interest are (i) *vested subject to partial divestment,* or (ii) *vested in quality but not in quantity,* which are descriptive of the phenomenon that each time a new member is added to the class the shares of the existing class members are reduced. Whichever label is used, it is important to note that the existing class member or members are the ones who are regarded as having a vested remainder. The interests of the unborn (or unadopted) class members are contingent on being born (or adopted). They are executory interests because upon birth (or adoption) they partially divest the interests or shares of the living class members.

Example 15.25: G transferred real property "to A for life, remainder to his children." When the transfer was made, A had two children, X and Y. X has a vested remainder subject to open in an undivided half of the property. Y has a vested remainder subject to open in the other undivided half.

Suppose a third child, Z, is born after the transfer occurred. Upon Z's birth, Z's executory interest becomes a vested remainder subject to open in an undivided third of the property, and X's and Y's interests are reduced (or partially divested) to vested remainders subject to open in an undivided third.

The executory interest, the only other nonreversionary future interest, can be in favor of a class that is subject to open, but because executory interests are regarded as contingent, they cannot be *vested* subject to open.

The reversionary interests would never be subject to open at their inception because they are, by definition, retained by the transferor or her or his successors in interest when created. Even if a reversionary interest was originaliy "retained by" the transferor's successors in interest, which might be a group of people, such as her or his heirs, it is not a class subject to open because the membership of this group of takers is determined at the transferor's death.

After their inception, however, reversionary future interests might be transferred to a class that contains at least one living member and that is subject to open. If the reversionary future interest is a possibility of reverter or a right of entry, a transfer to a class would still not make either one of them *vested* subject to open because these interests are regarded as contingent. See infra p. 854. A reversion, however, is vested, and if it was subsequently transferred, it would become vested subject to open.

> *Example 15.26:* G conveyed real property "to A for life." G later died (while A was alive), devising her indefeasibly vested reversion to A's children. Two children of A were living at G's death. These two children receive vested reversions subject to open and A's unborn children receive springing executory interests.

> *Example 15.27:* Same as above except that A had no children at G's death. The situation at G's death would probably be viewed as follows: G carved springing executory interests (in favor of A's unborn children) out of his indefeasibly vested reversion. His indefeasibly vested reversion would thus become vested subject to divestment, and would pass to G's residuary legatee or his heirs, depending on the situation.

d. Contingent (Nonvested)

A future interest is contingent ("nonvested")[7] if it is subject to a *condition precedent*. A condition precedent may be explicit or implicit. An explicit condition precedent exists where the language of the disposition declares that the interest is to become possessory *if* some event occurs. Implicit conditions precedent exist when the future interest is in favor of unborn or unascertained persons.

---

7. The traditional term is "contingent," but the Restatement 2d of Property adopts the term "nonvested."

Remainders can be contingent, but need not be. Executory interests are nearly always contingent.[8] Reversions cannot be contingent but possibilities of reverter and rights of entry are regarded as contingent.

Example 15.28: G conveyed real property "to A for life, remainder to B if B survives A." B's remainder is contingent because the condition of surviving A is stated in the form of a condition precedent—"to B if."

G's reversion appears to be subject to the condition precedent that B not survive A, but G's reversion is vested subject to divestment because of the rule that reversions are always vested. This means that B's remainder in this situation acts like an executory interest because it potentially divests G's reversion. Nevertheless, it is a remainder because its predominant feature is that it takes effect in possession, if at all, on the natural termination of A's life estate.

Example 15.29: G transferred real property "to A for life, remainder to A's children." When the transfer was made, A had no children. A's unborn children have contingent remainders. Their remainders, unlike B's remainder in the example above, are implicitly contingent on being born (or adopted), not on surviving A.

Example 15.30: G transferred real property "to A for life, remainder to A's heirs." The remainder in favor of A's heirs is contingent because it is in favor of unascertained persons. The persons who are A's heirs cannot be ascertained until A's death.

Nevertheless, any person who would be an heir of A if A were to die immediately is called an heir apparent or an heir expectant. The heirs expectant are regarded as having contingent remainders during A's lifetime rather than mere expectancies. Thus it is sometimes said that they take by purchase rather than by succession. Their remainders are of course implicitly contingent on their actually becoming A's heirs when A dies.

Example 15.31: G transferred real property "to A for life, remainder to B, but if B fails to survive A, to C." The condition that B survive A is a condition subsequent as to B's remainder ("to B, but if"), making it vested subject to divestment. C's executory interest is subject to the condition precedent that B not survive A and, therefore, is contingent.

---

8. The typical executory interest is subject to a condition precedent and is classified as contingent (nonvested). In rare cases, an executory interest is created that is unconditional. An example would be if G conveyed real property "to B, to take effect in possession 25 years from now." Another example would be if G conveyed real property "to B, to take effect in possession at my death." It is assumed in each case that the possessory interest retained by G is a fee simple interest, not a term of 25 years or a life estate. This means that B's future interest cannot be a remainder and, therefore, it must be an executory interest. If it were a remainder, it would be classified as indefeasibly vested. The courts have been reluctant to call this type of an executory interest vested. Its classification has been perplexing because it is an executory interest. Nevertheless, it is generally assumed that, like vested interests in general, this type of an executory interest is not subject to the Rule Against Perpetuities. See infra Chapter 17.

Example 15.32: (1) G transferred real property "to A and her heirs on condition that A never allow liquor to be sold on the premises, but if A allows liquor to be sold on the premises, the property is to go to B."

(2) G transferred real property "to A and her heirs for as long as A never allows liquor to be sold on the premises, and upon A's allowing liquor to be sold on the premises, the property is to go to B."

B's executory interest in both cases is subject to the condition that A allow liquor to be sold on the premises. In both cases, the condition is in condition precedent form and, therefore, B's executory interest is contingent in both cases.

Example 15.33: (1) G conveyed real property "to A and his heirs on condition that A never allow liquor to be sold on the premises, but if A allows liquor to be sold on the premises, the grantor shall have the right to re-enter and take possession of the premises."

(2) G conveyed real property "to A and his heirs for a long as A never allow liquor to be sold on the premises, and upon A's allowing liquor to be sold on the premises, the premises are to revert to the grantor."

G's right of entry in the first case and G's possibility of reverter in the second case would appear to be subject to the condition precedent that A allow liquor to be sold on the premises. Most authorities do in fact classify these interests as contingent. See Am. L. Prop. §§ 4.6, 4.12; Simes & Smith on Future Interests §§ 281, 1238. The Restatement of Property § 154 comment e, at 531, classifies possibilities of reverter as contingent but does not classify rights of entry in terms of vesting. It is believed that the contingent classification is proper for both interests.

6. Future Interests Belonging To More Than One Category

Often a future interest will be subject to open but the phrase "subject to open" will not appear in its classification because it is contingent. Or, the phrase might not appear in its classification because it is vested subject to complete defeasance. This does not mean that the interest is not actually subject to open; it merely means that the fact that it is subject to open is not formally expressed as part of its classification.

Example 15.34: G transferred real property "to A for life, remainder to A's children who survive A; but if none of A's children survives A, to B."

The remainders in A's children are contingent. They are also in fact subject to open, but recognition of this fact by using the phrase "contingent subject to open" is not permissible in the classificatory scheme.

Example 15.35: G transferred real property "to A for life, remainder to her children, but if none of A's children survives A, to B." A was alive and had living children when the transfer occurred.

The remainders in A's living children are vested subject to (complete) divestment. They are also subject to open. The Restatement of Property § 157 comment c would classify the remainders as vested subject to (complete) divestment and leave it at that. Nevertheless, it is permissible to say that the interests are vested subject to (complete) divestment and to open because, unlike those in the example above, the interests are vested.

The condition subsequent of survivorship imposed on the interests of A's children in this example is not substantively the same as the condition precedent of survivorship imposed on A's children in the example above. In that example, if at least one of A's children survives A but some predecease her, only the ones who survive A take. But in this example, as long as at least one child survives A, courts can be expected to hold that the interests of those children who predeceased A are not divested. See Restatement of Property § 254 comment a, illustration 2.

TABLE SUMMARIZING THE CATEGORIES OF VESTING

Future Interest	*Permissible Categories of Vesting at Inception*
Remainder	Indefeasibly Vested Vested Subject to Defeasance (Divestment or Limitation) Vested Subject to Open Contingent
Executory Interest	Contingent
Reversion	Indefeasibly Vested Vested Subject to Defeasance (Divestment or Limitation)
Possibility of Reverter	Contingent
Right of Entry	Contingent

7. The Law Favors the Vesting of Estates

Traditionally, vested interests are preferred to contingent interests. Restatement of Property § 243 & comments. Explicit recognition of this idea is colorfully stated in Roberts v. Roberts, 2 Bulst. 123, 80 Eng. Rep. 1002, (K.B. 1613), where it was declared that "the law always delights in vesting of estates, and contingencies are odious in the law, and are the causes of troubles, and vesting and settling of estates, the cause of repose and certainty." The law delights "in preventing of contingencies, which are dangerous. . . ."

The source of the preference is complex, but it is commonly claimed that the desire to avoid certain common-law rules, such as the destructibility rule and the Rule Against Perpetuities, to promote alienability, to promote completeness of the disposition, and to promote equality of distribution among different lines of descent all played important roles.

In general, it can be said that the courts will construe a provision as not imposing a condition precedent if they can do so without contradicting the express language of the instrument, *i.e.*, where there is sufficient ambiguity in the language to permit what might be called an even choice.

Edwards v. Hammond
3 Lev. 132, 83 Eng. Rep. 614 (C.P. 1683)

Ejectment upon *not guilty*, and special verdict, the case was. A copyholder of land, burrough English, surrendered to the use of himself for life, and *after to the use of his eldest son and his heirs, if he live to the age of 21 years: provided, and upon condition, that if he die before 21, that then it shall remain to the surrenderer and his heirs.* The surrenderer died, the youngest son entered; and the eldest son being 17 brought an *ejectment;* and the sole question was, whether the devise to the eldest son be upon condition *precedent,* or if the condition be *subsequent? scil.* that the estate in fee shall vest immediately upon the death of the father, to be divested if he die before 21. For the defendant it was argued, that the condition was *precedent,* and that the estate should descend to the youngest son in the mean time, or at least shall be in contingency and *in abeyance* 'till the first son shall attain to one and twenty; and so the eldest son has no title now, being no more than 17. On the other side it was argued, and so agreed by the Court; that though by the first words this may seem to be a condition *precedent,* yet, taking all the words together, this was not a condition *precedent,* but a present devise to the eldest son, subject to and defeasible by this condition subsequent, *scil.* his not attaining the age of 21. . . .

Notes and Questions

1. *Background of Edwards v. Hammond.* The transferor in the *Edwards* case, the surrenderer, was described as a "copyholder of land, burrough English." Copyholders were free men holding land by unfree tenure. The freehold and seisin of the copyholder's estate resided in his lord. The copyholder's evidence of title was his copy of the roll of the court of the manor; the court's roll served as a form of land registry. The rules governing the landholding of a copyholder were not uniform, but were to be found in the custom of the manor concerned. Borough english was a custom whereby the youngest son, not the eldest son, inherited lands subject to the custom. See A. W. B. Simpson, An Introduction to the History of Land Law 20, 151-62 (3d impress. 1979).

The surrenderer in *Edwards,* engaging in a will substitute of the day, was trying to reverse this rule of inheritance, by transferring (surrendering) his copyhold to his lord who would, upon the surrenderer's death, admit the grantee. The surrender would have been registered on the court rolls by the steward of the manor. The surrender did not completely cut out the surrenderer's youngest son, for by virtue of the custom of borough english, applicable in this case, the surrenderer's youngest son was his heir and, as such, was scheduled to take the land if the eldest son failed to reach 21. Apparently, however, when the surrenderer died, the youngest son was admitted immediately; at least, he entered. This precipitated the action of ejectment, which was brought by the surrenderer's 17-year-old eldest son.

A contingent remainder in a copyhold was not subject to the common-law rule of destructibility of contingent remainders. Copyholds were not freeholds; the seisin remained throughout in the lord of the manor.

2. *Consequences of Classification.* In *Edwards,* the direct result of holding that the remainder was vested subject to divestment was that the surrenderer's 17-year-old eldest son was immediately entitled to possession of the land. If the court had held that the remainder was contingent, the eldest son's right to possession would have been delayed until his 21st birthday, the youngest son having the right to possession in the meantime.

3. *The Mystique of Classification.* As you read the next case, Quilliams v. Koonsman, notice that the court also discussed at some length the proper classification of the future interests. Consider what consequence, if any, turns on how those future interests are classified. Is the *Quilliams* case an example of what Professor Waggoner called the "classificatory mystique"—the notion indulged by some courts that classifying the interests solves what is in fact a straightforward problem of interpreting the meaning of the dispositive language? See Waggoner, Reformulating the Structure of Estates: A Proposal for Legislative Action, 85 Harv. L. Rev. 729, 732 (1972).

Quilliams v. Koonsman
154 Tex. 401, 279 S.W.2d 579 (1955)

CALVERT, J. Our main problem involves the construction of the fourth paragraph of the will of J. J. Koonsman, deceased, which reads as follows:

> I give and devise to my son, Alvin Koonsman, all of my undivided interest in all of the remainder of my real property situated in Scurry County, Texas, which I may own at the time of my death, and to his child or children if any survive him, and in the event of Alvin's death without issue surviving him, then to my son and daughter, Jesse J. Koonsman and Mrs. Cora Quilliams, share and share alike, and to their heirs and assigns forever. . . .

The only evidence in the record before us, other than the will itself and the probate proceedings in connection therewith, is the testimony of Alvin Koonsman that J. J. Koonsman, the testator, died March 6, 1942, and that he (Alvin) has only one child, John Billy Koonsman, born October 15, 1942. From this testimony it appears that John Billy was in esse for the purpose of taking under the will on the date it became effective, that is, the date of J. J. Koonsman's death.

What is the meaning of the words "and to his child or children if any survive him" following the devise to Alvin? We have been cited to and have found no case squarely in point. If the words "if any survive him" had been omitted and we were to follow the weight of authority, heretofore noted, we would be compelled to hold that Alvin and his son, John Billy, took the first estate created as cotenants. But those words were not omitted, and we ascribe to them a two-fold effect: first, they limited the interest of Alvin Koonsman to a life estate, and secondly, they operated to make the remainder to be taken by the child or children of Alvin contingent rather than vested.

The words "if any survive him", qualifying the devise to the children of Alvin, clearly indicate that his children were not to take as cotenants with Alvin but were to take in succession to him, with the result that the devise to Alvin is limited to a life estate. No particular form of words is necessary to the creation of a life estate.

> It has been said that where the construction of a will devising property to one and his children is doubtful, the courts lean toward giving the parent a life estate, and that even a slight indication of an intention that the children shall not take jointly with the parent will give a life estate to the parent with a remainder to the children. 33 Am. Jur. 474.

The conclusion that the remainder in the child or children is contingent rather than vested is also impelled by the words "if any survive him." Survival is made a condition precedent to the vesting of the remainder rather than a condition of defeasance. While it has been said that "The law favors the vesting of estates at the earliest possible period, and will not construe a remainder as contingent where it can reasonably be taken as vested", Caples v. Ward, 107 Tex. 341, 179 S.W. 856, 858, nevertheless, when the will makes survival a condition precedent to the vesting of the remainder, it must be held to be contingent. . . . The rule for determining whether a remainder is vested or contingent is thus stated by Gray in his work on The Rule Against Perpetuities:

> If the conditional element is incorporated into the description of, or into the gift to the remainder-man, then the remainder is contingent; but if, after words giving a vested interest, a clause is added divesting it, the remainder is vested.

3d Ed., § 108(3), page 85. The rule as thus stated has been approved and adopted by the courts of this state. Here the condition of survival is incorporated into the gift to Alvin Koonsman's child or children.

There remains to be determined the nature of the estate devised to Jesse J. Koonsman and Mrs. Cora Quilliams by the fourth paragraph of the will. They are to take the fee "in the event of Alvin's death without issue surviving him." Their estate must be held to be a contingent remainder also. It is to take effect upon Alvin's death, but only if he dies "without issue surviving him". It is an alternative contingent remainder. . . .

The judgments of the trial court and Court of Civil Appeals are reformed to . . . decree that the true meaning and effect of the fourth paragraph of the will is that the plaintiff, Alvin Koonsman, is therein and thereby given an estate for life in the property therein described, with a remainder in fee to the child or children of Alvin Koonsman, conditioned upon their surviving him, and an alternative remainder in fee to Jesse J. Koonsman and Mrs. Cora Quilliams, or their heirs and assigns, conditioned on the death of Alvin Koonsman without a child or children surviving him, and as so reformed the judgments of those courts are affirmed.

Notes and Questions

1. *Reconcilable?* Can you reconcile *Edwards* and *Quilliams? Quilliams* is supported by the Restatement of Property § 278, but a few courts have held that a disposition such as that in *Quilliams* creates a vested remainder subject to divestment. See, e.g., Safe Deposit & Trust Co. v. Bouse, 181 Md. 351, 29 A.2d 906 (1943). Do you think the testator *intends* different consequences by choosing condition precedent, condition subsequent, or even-choice language in describing contingencies? Do you think the testator's attorney might choose one form of conditional language rather than another for the purpose of accomplishing a particular legal result?

2. *Remainders for Life.* In addition to the rule of *Edwards,* another manifestation of the preference for vested interests is the rule that remainders for life are classified as vested subject to defeasance (subject to a limitation, not a condition precedent or subsequent). The remainder for life can be viewed as presenting an even choice to the courts because they could have classified it as contingent (on surviving the primary life tenant).

Consider, now, Example 15.36:

> *Example 15.36:* G transferred real property "to A for life, remainder to B for life if B survives A."

This example presents a further problem for the courts because this remainder for life is expressly conditioned on survivorship of the primary life tenant. Does the inclusion of the phrase "if B survives A" remove this case from the even-choice category, and force a court to hold that B's remainder is contingent? A small number of courts have held that it does. Most courts, however, have held that B's remainder is vested despite the conditional language, suggesting that the preference for vesting is strong. See Simes & Smith on Future Interests § 142. Does the majority view override an obvious attempt by a drafter to rebut the preference for vested interests? Is the classification of remainders for life as vested rather than contingent likely to make any practical or legal difference?

3. *Remainders Subject to a Power.* Frequently someone will be given a power of some sort to divert the property to someone other than the taker of the remainder. In these cases, the remainder is subject to a condition, but the condition is not clearly stated as a condition precedent. The preference for vested estates can, therefore, be viewed as tipping the scale in favor of treating the condition as a condition subsequent.

> *Example 15.37:* G transferred real property "to A for life, empowering A to sell, consume, or otherwise dispose of the property or any part thereof as may be necessary for A's support and maintenance; at A's death the property or such part thereof as may remain unexpended is to go to B." B's remainder is vested subject to divestment in whole or in part by the exercise of the power by A.
>
> The same result would be reached in the case of a remainder interest in a trust where the settlor retained a power to revoke the trust or where the

settlor conferred upon someone else (typically the trustee or the income beneficiary) a power to invade the corpus on behalf of the income beneficiary.

Example 15.38: G transferred real property "to A for life, remainder to such persons as A shall by will appoint, and in default of appointment, to B." B's remainder is vested subject to divestment by the exercise of the power by A. It could be argued in this case that the language expressly imposes a condition precedent (that A will not exercise the power) on B's remainder. Nevertheless, the idea that remainders subject to a power are vested subject to divestment is so well established that B's remainder is not regarded as contingent, even here.

4. *Remainder Subject to a Charge or a Lien.* Transferors occasionally appear to condition a remainder interest on the payment of a sum of money to a designated person. Most courts have held that the remainder is vested and that the taker is entitled to possession on the termination of the prior interest, but subject to a charge or a lien on the property in the designated amount. See, e.g., Miller v. Miller, 197 Neb. 171, 247 N.W.2d 445 (1976); Estate of Marra, N.Y.L.J., May 6, 1987 (Sur. Ct. 1987). This construction is consistent with the general preference for vested interests.

Example 15.39: G transferred real property "to A for life, remainder to B if B pays C $5,000 within one year of A's death." B had not paid C the $5,000 on the first anniversary of A's death. Under the majority view, if B does not pay the $5,000 to C within a reasonable time, C can enforce his charge or lien in that amount against the property. Had the court held B's remainder to have been contingent on B's having paid the money, B would not be entitled to the property and C would not receive the money.

Problems

Classify the future interests in the following problems:

1. A was childless when G made the following two transfers:

(a) G transferred real property "to A for life, then to such of A's children as survive A, but if none survives A, to C."

(b) G transferred real property "to A for life, then to A's children, but if none of A's children survives A, to C."

2. After G's transfer took place, a child (X) was born to A. Does this event alter the original classifications of the future interests in G's dispositions in Problem 1(a) and Problem 1(b)? If so, how?

3. After X was born, A had another child, Y. Years later, X died, survived by A and Y. Then A died, survived by Y. Who becomes entitled to the property at the time of A's death under Problem 1(a)? Problem 1(b)?

4. In the following two cases, B dies while A is still alive. Classify the future interests at the point of their creation and at the point of B's death.

(a) G transferred real property "to A for life, remainder to B, but if B fails to survive A, to C." (It is sometimes said that an executory interest cannot vest until it vests in possession. What is the meaning of this statement?)

   (b) G transferred real property "to A for life, remainder to B if B survives A, but if not, to C."

5. G transferred real property "to A for life, remainder to B if B lives to attain the age of 21." The destructibility rule has been abolished by statute in the jurisdiction. Classify the future interests at the point of their creation and at the following points:

   (a) B reaches 21 while A is still alive.
   (b) A dies; B is then alive but under the age of 21.

Is All This Complexity Necessary? In a word, No. Without sacrificing the slightest degree of flexibility in the planning of family property transactions, classification and the structure of estates could be vastly simplified and the artificiality in the present system could be eradicated. A proposal for a simplified system of estates, in which classification is based on the substance of the disposition rather than the form of its wording, has been put forward in Waggoner, Reformulating the Structure of Estates: A Proposal for Legislative Action, 85 Harv. L. Rev. 729, 755-56 (1972):

> [T]he reformulated structure is based on the premise that the only appropriate distinctions are between certainty and uncertainty as to the termination of possessory interests and between certainty and uncertainty as to the ultimate possession of future interests. Possessory interests, by the terms of the particular transfer, either will not terminate (fee simple absolute), will terminate (life estate or term of years), or will possibly terminate (defeasible interest). Future interests either will become possessory (indefeasibly vested), will become possessory but with a now uncertain number of takers (vested subject to open), or will possibly become possessory (contingent). The reformulated structure is shown in the accompanying chart. . . .

POSSESSORY INTERESTS	FUTURE INTERESTS
Fee Simple Absolute	None permissible
Defeasible Fee Simple	Contingent
Life Estate (may or may not be defeasible)	Contingent (not certain to become possessory); Alternative Contingent Future Interest
	Vested Subject to Open: Contingent (in unborn class members) Indefeasibly Vested
Term of Years	Same as with Life Estate

PART B. SELECTED CONSEQUENCES OF CLASSIFICATION

Classification in all its fine detail is far less important than it once was. This is partly because some of the rules that turned on classification have been widely abolished and partly because many of those rules applied, in any event, only to *legal* future interests in *real property,* which are less often created today. Ironically, the reduced importance of classification has played a roll in keeping the complex and artificial structure in force, by reducing the pressure to reexamine and reformulate it.

At the same time, the importance of certain aspects of classification has not disappeared altogether. This Part elaborates some of the rules that turn on classification. The first two rules—the rule of destructibility of contingent remainders and the Rule in Shelley's Case—are feudal relics, which have no business being part of our law. They have, in fact, been widely, though not completely, abolished. Their decline, in turn, makes the importance of the distinction between remainders and executory interests largely disappear.

1. The Destructibility of Contingent Remainders

The common-law destructibility rule is this: *A legal contingent remainder in real property is destroyed if it does not vest by the time the preceding freehold estate terminates.* The destructibility rule is a rule of law that defeats the intent of the transferor and not a rule of construction that purports to further testator's intent.

Conventional instrumentalist accounts attribute the destructibility rule to the common-law courts' desire to promote societal needs by assuring real property remained alienable. In this respect, it can be viewed as a forerunner of the Rule Against Perpetuities. It was also the product, however, of elaborate conceptual structures.

In part, the destructibility rule reflected a particular conception of conveyancing, which in turn reflected a particular conception of ownership. Under assumptions derived from feudal tenure on "held" land, one was not spoken of as "owner." Holding land was a matter more of status than of right, and that status was dependent on possession. In other words, the right to possession was not fully separated from possession in fact. "Seisin," the word for it, implied possession under a claim to a freehold estate. Seisin was transferred by a transaction called a "feoffment," which required a ritual called "livery of seisin," whereby the parties would go onto the land and the conveyor would express his intent to convey and hand the conveyee a stick, stone, or clod of dirt as symbolizing the transfer of the land itself.

Within this conception of conveyancing, it was not possible for the common-law courts to imagine that a transferor could convey an interest to take effect at a future date or convey an interest to one man on a condition that would shift seisin automatically to another man.

Common-law courts did, however, permit conveyances to one man for life, with remainder, vested or contingent to another man. The courts manipulated the concept of seisin by creating the fiction that the life tenant took the seisin for himself and for the remainderman or the reversioner. Strangely enough, this kind of automatic shift in seisin apparently did not stimulate the common-law courts to design others—not until the Statute of Uses wrought its far-reaching effects upon the structure and conceptions of estates and the modes of conveyancing. In short, the type of future interest that could not be imagined was the executory interest. One of the consequences of the seisin concept was the destruction of legal contingent remainders in real property.

At early common law, no naked future interest could be created that would take effect in possession in the future, and none could be created that would divest a fee simple interest. These rules provided the technical explanation for the destructibility rule: A remainder needed a freehold estate to "support" it. When the supporting freehold estate terminated, there was no problem if the remainder was then entitled to become possessory; seisin passed to the remainderman from the life tenant. But if the remainder was not yet entitled to become possessory—if, for example, a condition precedent to its right to possession was not yet fulfilled—seisin passed to the reversioner whose interest, always regarded as vested, thereupon became possessory. Note that the reversioner did not and could not (since his interest was a fee simple interest) take seisin from the life tenant on behalf of himself and the remainderman. He took it only on his own behalf. Lacking support, the remainder could no longer exist as a future interest, and so it was destroyed.

Despite the fact that seisin was never given more than token recognition even in early America, the destructibility rule was received at least in some of the states as part of our common law. The destructibility rule should be abolished because it applies too narrowly, it is easily avoided, and it is riddled with such technicality that it invariably requires litigation to get it applied. A preferable solution to the problem of land made inalienable by the existence of contingent future interests lies in the doctrine, sometimes codified, by which a life tenant can obtain a judicial order for the sale of the land in fee simple absolute. The proceeds of the sale are put into a kind of trust whereby the life tenant is entitled to the income for life, with the corpus on her or his death going to the persons entitled thereto. See Restatement of Property § 179, at 485-95; Am. L. Prop. §§ 4.98-.99; Simes & Smith on Future Interests §§ 1941-46; L. Simes & C. Taylor, Improvement of Conveyancing by Legislation 235-38 (1960).

The destructibility rule has been abolished by statute in over half the states. The statutes are commonly retroactive in a limited sense: They apply to contingent remainders created, though not destroyed, before the effective date of the Act. The crucial date for this purpose is the date when the supporting freehold terminated. These statutes have survived constitutional challenges that they take property without due process of law.

In the remaining states, the question is largely open. The Restatement of Property section 240 takes the position that the rule is *not* part of our common law. A few courts have on their own openly rejected the rule. Many, but not all, of the American decisions that accepted the rule are from states that subsequently abolished it by statute.

It is doubtful that the rule would be accepted today in states where the question is open, and the time may be ripe for the overruling of decisions that earlier accepted the rule in the other states, even without abolishing legislation.

After the Statute of Uses. When the destructibility rule was developed, remainders were the only type of *legal* future interest that could be created in transferees. However, prior to the Statute of Uses of 1535, the courts of equity had developed their own practice. The Chancellor regularly enforced so called springing and shifting uses.

One of the consequences of the Statute of Uses was to execute (*i.e.,* change into legal interests) these equitable interests. Although it would have then been possible for the law courts to declare springing and shifting interests void, since the Statute of Uses had said nothing about the point, the common-law courts instead recognized executed uses as valid future interests. In this way, executory interests entered the scheme of common-law estates. Executory interests were held to be indestructible, a rule now taken to have been established in Pells v. Brown, Cro. Jac. 590, 79 Eng. Rep. 504 (1620), because seisin could automatically transfer to the holder of an executory interest upon the happening of a future event.

Interests Subject to Rule. Only one interest—the *contingent* remainder—was subject to destruction. Vested remainders, even vested remainders subject to divestment, could not be destroyed. Executory interests, though contingent, also could not be destroyed. The reversionary interests—reversions, possibilities of reverter, and rights of entry—were never subject to destruction.

Only contingent remainders in *real property* were susceptible to destruction because the rule was based in the concept of seisin, a concept that early on became inapplicable to personal property. Similarly, an *equitable* contingent remainder, whether or not in real or personal property, could not be destroyed because seisin remained in the trustee throughout the continuance of the trust.

The destructibility rule only applied if the prior estate was a freehold in accordance with the concept of seisin. Because we are dealing with contingent remainders, the prior possessory estate will always have been a particular estate. (A particular estate is any estate of less quantum than a fee simple.) The only particular estates that are freeholds are fees tail and life estates. Thus a contingent remainder following a term of years was and is not subject to the destructibility rule. The following discussion deals only with contingent remainders following life estates.

Destruction by Merger, Forfeiture, and Time Gap. A legal contingent remainder in real property was destroyed at common law in three basic situations. Two of these—destruction by merger and by forfeiture—were within the control of one or more of the parties and, therefore, can properly be called methods of "intentional destruction." Some commentators have utilized the name of "artificial destruction" for these methods because under both of them the destruction occurs as the result of an artificial termination of the life estate. An artificial termination is one that occurs (or perhaps more accurately, is engineered) during the life tenant's lifetime.

The third situation in which a contingent remainder was destroyed—the time gap situation—is sometimes called "natural destruction" because here the destruction occurs as a consequence of events existing at the natural termination of the life estate, *i.e.*, at the life tenant's death. The events causing the natural destruction are typically outside the lawful control of the parties, and consequently this situation is not a method of intentional destruction.

In most cases the condition precedent attached to a contingent remainder will be resolved one way or the other by the time of the life tenant's death. The typical example is the remainder subject to a condition precedent of surviving the life tenant. Contingent remainders of this sort are not subject to natural destruction—destruction caused by a time gap.

Sometimes, however, a contingent remainder is subject to a condition precedent that can happen after the life tenant's death. If this type of condition has not been fulfilled when the life tenant dies, a time gap or gap in possession arises. That time gap causes the remainder to be destroyed.

> *Example 15.40:* G transferred real property "to A for life, remainder to B if B lives to the age of twenty-one." At A's death, B is under twenty-one. Whether or not the destructibility rule is in force, G's reversion takes effect in possession at A's death. If the destructibility rule is in force, the contingent remainder in favor of B is destroyed. As a result, G's reversion becomes possessory in fee simple absolute.
>
> If B had already reached twenty-one when A died, B's contingent remainder would have become vested before the termination of the life estate, would have avoided destruction, and would have become possessory in fee simple absolute upon A's death.

The indestructibility of executory interests offered an opportunity for saving contingent remainders from destruction. The law courts merely had to accept the proposition that contingent remainders could change into executory interests upon the termination of the supporting freehold prior to the interest's vesting. Acceptance of this proposition would have amounted to an abolition of the destructibility rule, for it would have meant that upon the failure of the supporting freehold (whether this occurred naturally or artificially), a contingent remainder would not be destroyed but would instead change into an interest that did not need a supporting freehold.

Instead, in Purefoy v. Rogers, 2 Wm. Saund. 380, 85 Eng. Rep. 1181 (K.B. 1670), the court prevented the demise of the destructibility rule by saying:

[F]or where a contingency is limited to depend on an estate of freehold which is capable of supporting a remainder, it shall never be construed to be an executory devise, but a contingent remainder only, and not otherwise. . . .

In effect, an interest that is a contingent remainder at its inception cannot avoid destruction by changing into an executory interest later.

The natural destruction of a contingent remainder is only possible when the condition precedent is of a certain type—one that might not be fulfilled by the time of the life tenant's death. Any contingent remainder, however, is susceptible to artificial destruction, even one in which the condition precedent cannot be fulfilled after the death of the life tenant. The artificial destruction of a contingent remainder is made possible by the recognition of the possibility of a premature termination of a life estate. One way of causing a premature or artificial termination of a life estate is by merger.

The doctrine of merger provides: *If, after the creation of a life estate and a successive vested future interest in fee, the two interests come into the hands of the same person, the life estate terminates by being merged into or swallowed up by the other interest.*

Popp v. Bond
158 Fla. 185, 28 S.2d 259 (1946)

TERRELL, J. John B. Franke died testate, leaving his wife, Amelia A. Franke, and a daughter, Lucile Margarite Louise Franke, surviving. The widow has since deceased and the daughter was married and has two minor children, H. Leslie Popp, Jr., and John F. Popp. The father, H. L. Popp, has been duly appointed guardian of the minor children. Paragraph VIII of the John B. Franke will in so far as pertinent is as follows:

> Item VIII. I will and bequeath all the remainder of my property . . . to . . . my daughter, Lucile Margarite Louise Franke . . . to have and to hold for and during (her) natural life . . . and at death . . . , one-half of the remainder and fee thereof to the child or children of my daughter, Lucile Margarite Louise Franke, if any, and one-half thereof to the Theological Seminary of the Evangelical Lutheran Church at Chicago, Illinois . . . if my said daughter shall die without children surviving, then the entire remainder thereof shall go to the said Seminary.

The estate of John B. Franke has been closed and the interest of the Theological Seminary of the Evangelical Lutheran Church, at Chicago, has been acquired by the life tenant, who with her husband, H. L. Popp, individually and as guardian of the minor children, have agreed to sell the real estate demised under Paragraph VIII to the appellee, but he declined to pay for and accept the deed without a court decree holding the title to be merchantable. This cause was instituted by bill of complaint on the part of appellants to coerce specific performance. Appellee answered the bill and the case was heard on an agreed statement of facts. The Chancellor found the title to be not merchantable, decreed accordingly, and this appeal is from the final decree.

The question for determination is whether or not under the facts detailed the life tenant, Mrs. H. L. Popp, joined by her husband individually and as guardian of the minor children, can convey a fee simple title to the real estate devised under Paragraph VIII of the will to appellee, free and clear of all claims of future born children of the life tenant.

In our judgment this question is answered in the affirmative by Blocker v. Blocker, 103 Fla. 285, 137 So. 249. . . .

This holding was predicated on the rule of the common law which is in effect in this State and provides in substance that contingent remainders may be defeated by destroying or determining the particular estate upon which they depend, before the contingency happens whereby they became vested. The contingency involved here was the adverse claim of prospective children of the life tenant. Under the rule as above stated such a contingent remainder was extinguished when the title of the infant remaindermen in being was merged with that of the life tenant in appellee.

An examination of the final decree discloses that the Chancellor held the title not merchantable on authority of Deem v. Miller et al., 303 Ill. 240, 135 N.E. 396, 25 A.L.R. 766, Annotation 770. It is quite true that the Illinois court there held that when a will, as in this case, creates a life estate with remainder to the children of the life tenant, the life tenant and the living children, by making a conveyance, do not destroy the interest of after born children, because the remainder is vested in quality, although contingent in quantity. This holding is in direct conflict with the holding in Blocker v. Blocker and other Florida cases cited, but we are not convinced that we should reverse these cases. In addition to being supported by the rule of the common law they are supported by good logic. It is of course competent for the Legislature to prescribe a different rule, which is doubtless the case in Illinois.

It follows that the judgment appealed from must be and is hereby reversed. . . .

Notes and Questions

1. Did the court in *Popp* get it right?

2. *Merger Method of Destruction.* The merger method allows the destruction of contingent remainders to be easily engineered by the parties: by the life tenant conveying to the reversioner, the reversioner to the life tenant, or the two to a third party. The last of these methods—conveyances by the life tenant and the reversioner to a third party—occasioned the destruction of a contingent remainder in favor of the life tenant's surviving children in the *Blocker* case, relied on by the court in *Popp*.

3. *Termination of the Supporting Freehold by Forfeiture.* Another way at common law by which a life estate could be terminated before the life tenant's death was by forfeiture. Under the feudal doctrine of seisin and

disseisin, a life estate was terminated by forfeiture if the life tenant conveyed—by feoffment (livery of seisin), fine, or common recovery—a greater estate, a fee, than he owned. The conveyee took a tortious fee as a result of the conveyance, destroying any contingent remainder previously supported by the life estate. The conveyee's fee was held to be subject to a right of entry, which arose in the person holding the next vested estate, typically the reversioner. See Loddington v. Kime, 1 Salk. 224 (1695); Archer's Case, 1 Co. Rep. 66b (1597); Chudleigh's Case, 1 Co. Rep. 120 (1595). While under the law of the time, this right of entry was not alienable inter vivos (it was descendible, however), it could be released to the conveyee. It can be seen that these rules enabled the life tenant and the reversioner to transfer a fee simple absolute in the property, much in the fashion of, though in a different form from, the merger method, as discussed above.

Forfeiture of a life estate is not recognized in the United States. The effect of a life tenant's purporting to convey a fee is to transfer only her or his life estate. In other words, a person can convey no greater estate than she or he has. As a result, this method of destroying a contingent remainder is not available even in the states, if any, that still adhere to the destructibility rule.

A life tenant can, however, renounce or disclaim the life estate. Although disclaimer may appear to be the modern-day equivalent of forfeiture, courts that have faced the question have not treated it that way.

> *Example 15.41:* G devised real property "to A for life, remainder to B if he attains twenty-one." A files a disclaimer with G's executor, as authorized by local law. B is fifteen years old at G's death. B's contingent interest is not destroyed. At its inception, it was an executory interest, not a contingent remainder. It is a well accepted principle that a person disclaiming a devise is treated as having predeceased the testator for purposes of the devolution of the disclaimed interest. Therefore, the effect of A's disclaiming is that A is treated as having predeceased G. In other words, no life estate was ever created. It is as if G's will had devised the property "to B if he attains twenty-one," creating an indestructible executory interest in B from the start. See Simes & Smith on Future Interests § 795.

2. The Rule in Shelley's Case

The Rule in Shelley's Case is this: *A remainder interest in real property which is either in favor of the life tenant's heirs or in favor of the heirs of her or his body, and which is of the same quality as that of the life estate, is held by the life tenant.* The Rule in Shelley's Case is derived from Wolfe v. Shelley, 1 Co. Rep. 93b, 76 Eng. Rep. 206 (K.B. 1581), where it was articulated by Lord Coke. The Rule in Shelley's Case is a rule of law and not a rule of construction. It, therefore, operates to defeat the intent of the transferor, rather than to carry it out.

In England, Shelley's Rule was abolished in 1925 by the Law of Property Act. In this country, the Rule apparently continues in force in a small number of states. In most states and in the District of Columbia, the Rule has been abolished by statute.[9] The Restatement 2d of Property section 30.1(3) states that the Rule "should be abolished by judicial decision to the extent it has not been abolished prospectively by statute."

The rule that we now know as the Rule in Shelley's Case was recognized two hundred years prior to Wolfe v. Shelley. Since remainder interests probably were not recognized as valid future interests until the latter part of the 13th century (after the Statute de Donis, 1285), and contingent remainders were not fully recognized until much later, some have speculated that the Rule may have originally been seen as one that gave effect to the intent of the transferor rather than as one that defeated the transferor's intent. The idea is that a conveyance "to A for life, then to his heirs" could only be given effect as a fee simple in favor of A.

Nevertheless, the Rule evolved into a rule of law, not one of construction. Lord Coke described it as a rule of law, and the point was firmly settled in Perrin v. Blake, 1 W. Bl. 672, 96 Eng. Rep. 392 (1769). The probable reason for its existence as a rule of law was made explicit even as early as the Provost of Beverley's Case, Y.B. 40 Edw. IV, Hill. No. 18 (1366): By forcing the remainder to go to the life tenant, the property would pass by descent to the life tenant's heirs on death, rather than to them by purchase; only real property that passed by descent on its owner's death could give rise to the exaction of feudal dues by the lord.

More recent instrumentalist accounts have explained the rule as a device for promoting alienability. It, however, serves this purpose badly because it applies too narrowly, is easily avoided, and is riddled with technicality.

Only one interest—the remainder in real property[10] in favor of the heirs or the heirs of the body of the life tenant—was subject to the Rule in Shelley's Case. Executory interests were not affected by the Rule. The reversionary interests—reversions, possibilities of reverter, and rights of entry—were also not subject to Shelley's Rule. This limitation to remainders is recognized by the Restatement of Property section 312 comment e.[11]

> *Example 15.42:* G transferred real property "to A for life, and one day after A's death, to A's heirs."
>
> The future interest in favor of the life tenant's heirs is an executory interest, not a remainder. Shelley's Rule, therefore, does not apply. A takes a life estate only, and A's heirs take an executory interest.

---

9. For a state-by-state compilation of abolishing statutes, see Restatement 2d of Property, Statutory Note to § 30.1.

10. See Restatement of Property § 312(3). An apparent exception was North Carolina, where in Riegel v. Lyerly, 265 N.C. 204, 143 S.E.2d 65 (1965), the Supreme Court of North Carolina applied the Rule to personal property. In 1987, North Carolina abolished Shelley's Rule by statute. See N.C. Gen. Stat. § 41-6.3. Another exception is Ohio, where in Society Nat'l Bank v. Jacobson, 54 Ohio St. 3d 15, 560 N.E.2d 21 (1990), the Ohio Supreme Court in a muddled opinion applied the Rule to personal property in trust!

11. In Texas, however, a state that has now abolished Shelley's Rule by statute, Darragh v. Barmore, 242 S.W. 714 (Tex. Com. App. 1922), applied the Rule to an executory interest.

Example 15.43: G transferred real property "to A for life, then upon A's death, to A's heirs."

The future interest in favor of the life tenant's heirs is a remainder. Shelley's Rule, therefore, applies. A takes the remainder, which merges with the life estate to give A a fee simple absolute.

For Shelley's Rule to apply, the transferor must be found to have intended that the remainder interest go either to the "heirs" of the life tenant or to the "heirs of the body" of the life tenant, *in the technical sense of these terms.* What *is* the technical sense of these terms?

Finley v. Finley

318 S.W.2d 478 (Tex. Civ. App. 1958),
aff'd in part on another ground,
159 Tex. 582, 324 S.W.2d 551 (1959)

COLLINGS, J. . . . Norman L. Finley . . . sought a construction of the will of his father and mother, E.L. Finley and Ella S. Finley. . . .

E.L. Finley died February 26, 1943, and . . . Ella S. Finley died on July 12, 1950. . . . Norman L. Finley was [their] only child. . . . Norman L. Finley has been married twice, first on July 28, 1920, to which marriage two children were born, to wit Eugene Lee Finley and Ross Alvord Finley; that Norman L. Finley's first marriage was terminated by a divorce in 1940; that he married again in September, 1942; and of the latter marriage one child, Kathy Elizabeth Finley was born. . . .

The pertinent part of the will of Ella S. Finley is as follows:

As to my real estate, I give, devise and bequeath all of my real estate to my son, Norman L. Finley, during his natural life to be used and enjoyed by him so long as he shall live. But upon the death of my son, Norman L. Finley, I give, devise and bequeath said lands to the legal heirs of the said Norman L. Finley. This will, however, shall not be construed to give to Norman L. Finley a fee simple title, but only a life estate in said lands. . . .

Established law in this state requires us to hold that the will of Ella S.Finley comes within the Rule in Shelley's Case and that Norman L. Finley took fee simple title to the land owned by Ella S. Finley at the time of her death. The fairly recent Supreme Court case of Sybert v. Sybert, 152 Tex. 106, 254 S.W.2d 999, 1000, is, in our opinion, squarely in point. In that case there was a bequest of a tract of land to a son of "a life estate only" with the further provision "and after the death of my said son—to vest in fee simple in the heirs of his body." Chief Justice Hickman, speaking for our Supreme Court in that case, stated:

The rule must inevitably apply in the instant case unless there is language qualifying the words "heirs of his body," showing that they were not used in their technical sense, that is, to signify an indefinite succession of takers from generation to generation. Turning now to an examination of the particular provisions of the will under construction we find that the only qualifying words contained therein modify the estate of Fred Sybert—not the words "heirs of his body." The language "a life estate only, to manage, control and use for and during the term of his natural life" is but a statement of the incidents of a life estate. The further language "and after the death of my said son, Fred Sybert, to vest in fee simple in the heirs of his body" does not indicate that the words "heirs of his body" were not used in their usual and technical sense. The expressions "vest in the heirs" and "vest in fee simple in the heirs" are identical in meaning. . . .

The language in the will in this case brings it squarely within the rule, and whether or not the testator so intended is immaterial. While the court may be liberal in construing explanatory language so that the words "heirs" or "heirs of his body" will not be read in their technical sense, we cannot supply that language when it is omitted from the instrument itself.

In the instant case there was no explanatory language in the will of Ella S. Finley which would authorize us to say that the words "legal heirs" should not be read in their technical sense. There was no language which would reasonably permit the words "legal heirs" to be construed to mean "children." There was no language qualifying the words "legal heirs" implying an intention that the land should not pass from person to person through successive generations in regular succession, such as a provision that the "legal heirs" should "share and share alike" or share "equally" in a partition and division of the land.

The provision that "This will, however, shall not be construed to give Norman S. Finley a fee simple title, but only a life estate in said lands" is likewise not controlling. This language does clearly show an intention to limit the interest of Norman L. Finley in the lands to a life estate only. It does not, however, qualify or limit the meaning of the words "legal heirs," which is required to avoid the application of the rule. . . .

The pertinent part of the will of E.L. Finley is as follows:

And I give to my said wife for her sole use and benefit for so long as she shall live, all of the real estate situated in Callahan County, Texas, that I may own or have an interest in at the time of my death. And I direct that upon the death of my said wife, all of said real estate situated in Callahan County, Texas, shall pass to my son, Norman L. Finley, to be used and enjoyed by him so long as he shall live, and I direct that upon the death of my said son all of said Callahan County real estate shall pass to and vest in fee simple in the legal heirs then living of my said son, according to the statutes of descent and distribution now in force in Texas. . . .

In our opinion the words "legal heirs" as used in the will of E.L. Finley did not refer to or contemplate the legal heirs of Norman L. Finley in the technical sense of continuous succession from generation to generation. The will provided that the estate should vest "in fee simple in the *legal heirs then living,*" at the time of Norman L. Finley's death. (Emphasis ours.) It is obvious that the words "legal heirs" as used in the will did not contemplate legal heirs in the technical sense, but that the words were modified so as to designate certain specific heirs and a particular class of persons. The class of persons designated were the heirs of Norman L. Finley living at the time of his death. . . .

[A]ffirmed.

Note

Indefinite versus Definite Line of Succession. The idea that the Rule in Shelley's Case only applies if the transferor used the term "heirs" or "heirs of the body" in the sense of an *indefinite line of succession* was the rule followed in England. As explained in the *Finley* case, the idea of an indefinite line of succession implies a "continuous succession from generation to generation." In affirming the decision in *Finley,* the Supreme Court of Texas questioned the requirement imposed by the Court of Civil Appeals that "heirs" must be intended to mean an indefinite line of succession. Nevertheless, the court found another ground for not applying the Rule in Shelley's Case to the will of E. L. Finley. Do you understand what that other ground might have been?

The English requirement that "heirs" or "heirs of the body" must be used in the sense of an indefinite line of succession has been adopted by a few American courts. See, e.g., Arnold v. Baker, 26 Ill. 2d 131, 185 N.E.2d 844 (1962). The prevailing American view is to the contrary.

The prevailing American view is that of "heirs" or "heirs of the body" being used in the sense of a *definite line of succession.* See Restatement of Property § 313 comment g. See also Restatement 2d of Property § 30.1 comment g. A definite line of succession refers, in the case of "heirs," to the persons who would inherit the real property of the life tenant on her or his death intestate; and, in the case of "heirs of the body," to the persons who as heirs of the body, general or special, would inherit the real property of the life tenant on her or his death intestate.

3. Alienability of Future Interests

Voluntary Alienability. Reversions, remainders, and executory interests are descendible and devisable. If the future interest is either contingent or vested subject to defeasance, it is, of course, descendible and devisable only if the owner's death does not cause the interest to be extinguished.

> *Example 15.44:* G transferred real property "to A for life, remainder to B, but if B fails to survive A, to C." C dies, then B, then A. C's executory interest is contingent on B's not surviving A, but it is not contingent on C himself surviving A. Consequently, C's executory interest was not extinguished by her death before A, and it is descendible and devisable. B's vested remainder subject to divestment was, however, extinguished by his death before A, and so B's remainder is neither descendible nor devisable.

Reversions and vested remainders (even if defeasible) were alienable inter vivos at the common law, but contingent remainders and executory interests were not. Contingent remainders were at first likened to an expectancy—not an interest, but the possibility of an interest arising in the future. When executory interests were later recognized, they were regarded as sufficiently analogous to contingent remainders to warrant the same treatment.

Despite the inalienability of contingent remainders and executory interests, the common law recognizes two ways by which such "inalienable" interests can *in effect* be transferred, and equity recognizes still another. (It may be noted that these three methods of transferring inalienable future interests are also available for transferring non-existent interests, such as expectancies.)

> *Contract to Convey.* A purported transfer, if for adequate consideration, is treated in equity as a contract to convey. The contract becomes specifically enforceable if and when all conditions precedent are satisfied, so as to give the transferor an alienable interest.

> *Estoppel by Deed.* Even without adequate consideration—indeed, without any consideration at all—when a purported transfer is made by a deed that contains a covenant of warranty, the title inures at law by estoppel to the grantee if and when the conditions precedent are later satisfied.

> *Release.* At law, an inalienable future interest can be released to the holder of the interest that would be defeated by the satisfaction of the conditions precedent attached to the released interest. For example, in the case of a disposition "to A for life, remainder to B, but if B fails to survive A, to C," a release of C's executory interest to B would be enforceable at law. Releases do not have to be contained in a warranty deed, nor is consideration necessary. A writing under seal was, however, required at common law, but today where the significance of seals is abolished, an instrument capable of transferring an interest in land would probably be sufficient.

Contingent remainders and executory interests are clearly no longer thought of as mere possibilities of receiving an interest in the future. Rather, they are thought of as present interests in which the right to possession is postponed and uncertain. See Restatement of Property § 157 comment w. Even so, the states take various approaches to the inalienability rule.

In about seven states, the common-law rule of inalienability is still followed. In those states, the equitable contract to convey, the estoppel by deed, and the release methods of transferring inalienable interests are also recognized. Therefore, the inalienability rule followed in those states boils down to this: Purported transfers for inadequate consideration by quit claim deed to someone other than a person in whose favor the interest could have been released are ineffective.

In the other states, the inalienability rule is probably not followed, at least not strictly. By statute or case law in a few states, remainders and executory interests that are contingent as to person (interests in favor of unborn or unascertained persons) are still inalienable, but those that are contingent as to event are alienable.

Example 15.45: G transferred real property "to A for life, remainder to B if B survives A; if not, to B's heirs." B's remainder is contingent as to event, and under this approach it would be alienable. However, the remainder in favor of B's heirs is inalienable under this rule because it is contingent as to person.

In the vast majority of states, mostly by statute but also in some jurisdictions by common-law decision, all contingent future interests are said to be alienable—even those that are contingent as to person. But how can a future interest contingent as to person be alienable? The answer is that these interests are not truly alienable. While the law typically authorizes a specially appointed fiduciary called a guardian ad litem to represent the interests of unborn or unascertained persons in litigation, it is very uncommon to find that this fiduciary can be appointed to join in a transfer of the property interests on behalf of these persons.

Example 15.46: G transferred real property "to A for life, remainder to A's children." If A is childless, no one is authorized to transfer the remainder interest on behalf of A's unborn children. If A has living children, they can, of course, transfer their interests. A is alive, and, therefore, there is a possibility of additional children being born. No one is authorized to transfer the executory interests on their behalf. Thus, the most that A's living children can transfer is a remainder that is subject to open (partial divestment).

What, then, does it mean to say that in the vast majority of jurisdictions even future interests that are contingent as to persons are alienable? The proposition refers to future interests that are in favor of unascertained persons, rather than to those that are in favor of unborn persons as in the example above.

Example 15.47: G transferred real property "to A for life, remainder to B's heirs." B is alive, but if B died now, B's sole heir would be B's child, C. In states in which future interests that are contingent as to persons are said to be alienable, B's heir apparent (C) would be regarded as having a transferable interest, not merely an expectancy, in the subject matter of G's disposition. See Am. L. Prop. § 4.67. If C should transfer her interest, her transferee would, however, receive an interest that is contingent on C's turning out to be B's real heir. See Restatement of Property § 162 comment c. It is thus clear that no one, not even C, can transfer the remainder interest that follows A's life estate. The remainder interest, in other words, is still not truly alienable, C's ability to effect a transfer of her interest notwithstanding. (The notion that C has a property interest in the subject matter of the above disposition should not be confused with the notion that C—as B's heir apparent—has merely an expectancy in B's own property.)

Auctioning Future Interests in England. It is reported that an organized auction is available in England to persons who want to sell their future interests, either vested or contingent. At one of these auctions, a future interest in a trust was sold for $127,000. The future interest was contingent on a woman of thirty-seven surviving the income beneficiary, a woman of sixty-five. The value of the corpus of the trust at the time of sale was $413,219. See Wall St. J., May 10, 1971, at 1.

Based on actuarial methods used by the Internal Revenue Service for valuing gifts made in 1971, the present worth of a future interest that is contingent on a female of 37 surviving another female age 65 is 42.08 percent of the value of the underlying property at the time of the transfer. See Letter from W. E. Wilcox, Chief, Actuarial Branch, Internal Revenue Service, April 10, 1973. On this basis, the purchaser of the future interest in the $413,219 trust got a bargain. The purchaser bought for $127,000 an interest whose actuarially computed worth was $173,882.56.

Involuntary Alienability—Creditors' Rights. Statutes in the various states provide creditors with the right to impound assets of their debtors prior to judgment and the right after judgment to subject assets to sale for its satisfaction. These statutes purport to specify the type of assets that are subject to these procedures, but the statutory language is usually so general that it is within the power of the courts to determine the extent to which the debtor's future interests can be affected.

The general principle followed by the courts under statutes is that if the future interest is voluntarily alienable, it is also subject to the claims of creditors. Indefeasibly vested remainders and reversions, since they are everywhere voluntarily alienable, are automatically available to creditors in the satisfaction of their claims. The same is true of remainders and reversions that are vested subject to defeasance.

Contingent remainders and executory interests, in states where they are not voluntarily alienable, are not subject to the claims of creditors. The fact that the equitable contract to convey, estoppel by deed, and release methods are available in these states does not change the result. Conversely, in states where contingent remainders and executory interests are voluntarily alienable—the vast majority of states—most courts routinely hold interests to be subject to creditors' claims. See, e.g., Everson v. Everson, 264 Pa. Super. 563, 400 A.2d 887 (1979), aff'd as modified, 494 Pa. 348, 431 A.2d 889 (1981). See also Restatement of Property §§ 166, 167.

When the owner of a future interest dies, her or his interest may be transmitted by will even if it was not alienable inter vivos. It may well be argued that the decedent's creditors should be satisfied at this time from these assets, for otherwise they will be deprived of all chance of payment. There appears to be little law on the subject. Some statutes governing the payment of claims against decedents' estates resolve the problem by equating the creditors' rights to property that the decedent could have alienated inter vivos. Text writers and the Restatement of Property section 169 have indicated the same result would probably be reached in situations in which the controlling statute is not so explicit.

In federal bankruptcy proceedings, the rights of creditors are far reaching. The Bankruptcy Reform Act of 1978, 11 U.S.C. § 541(a)(1), treats as part of the bankrupt's estate "all legal or equitable interests" in property owned by the debtor as of the commencement of the case. This language is broad enough to include all types of future interests, even those that are immune from the claims of creditors under state law.

EXTERNAL REFERENCE. Halbach, Creditors' Rights in Future Interests, 43 Minn. L. Rev. 217 (1958).

4. Acceleration of Future Interests— Disclaimers and Other Causes

Statutory Reference: *1990 UPC § 2-801*
                          Pre-1990 UPC § 2-801

When property is given by way of a succession of present and future interests, a prior interest may fail in its inception for a variety of reasons. The question this Section addresses is what effect a failure of the prior interest has upon succeeding interests.

Aberg v. First National Bank
450 S.W.2d 403 (Tex. Civ. App. 1970)

WILLIAMS, J. This is a case of first impression in Texas involving the question of acceleration of contingent remainders caused by renunciation of a prior estate.

The suit was filed by First National Bank in Dallas, as trustee, seeking a declaratory judgment pursuant to Art. 2524—1, Vernon's Ann. Civ. St. of Texas, commonly referred to as the Uniform Declaratory Judgments Act, and also seeking instructions from the court pursuant to the provisions of Art. 7425b—24, V.A.C.S., commonly known as the Texas Trust Act.

The facts are undisputed. T. W. Vardell and wife, Lela Barry Vardell, executed two trust indentures, one dated February 28, 1931 and the other December 31, 1931, in each of which the First National Bank in Dallas was named as trustee. Each trust named the settlors' daughter, Lela Vardell Johnson, as primary beneficiary to receive the net income of each trust during her lifetime. Another daughter, Elizabeth Vardell Goodman, was named as secondary beneficiary in each of the trust instruments. Although there is some variance in the language of the two trust documents, the essential provisions relating to the primary and secondary beneficiaries may be exemplified by quoting from the instrument dated December 31, 1931, as follows:

> (a) The Trustee shall pay the net income to Lela Vardell Johnson for life. . . .
> At the expiration of twenty-one years from the date of the birth of the last child born to Lela Vardell Johnson, or at the death of Lela Vardell Johnson if that be later, the corpus shall be distributed to the then living lineal descendants of the said Lela Vardell Johnson per stirpes. If, however, there

should be no lineal descendant of the said Lela Vardell Johnson then living, the corpus shall thereafter be held in trust by the Trustee for the said Elizabeth Vardell Goodman, if she then be living, and the net income paid to her for life, and after her death the net income shall be paid to her lineal descendants per stirpes until the time hereinafter provided for the distribution of the corpus, the payment of any minor's part to be made to the guardian of the minor's estate. . . . [A]t the expiration of twenty-one years from the date of the birth of the last child born to Elizabeth Vardell Goodman, or at her death if that be later, the corpus shall be distributed to the then living lineal descendants of the said Elizabeth Vardell Goodman per stirpes. . . .

Another provision of the instrument provided:

No assignment or order by any beneficiary by way of anticipation of any part of the income or corpus of this trust shall be valid, but said income and/or corpus shall be paid by the Trustee direct to such beneficiary; nor shall the interest of any beneficiary in the income and/or corpus hereof be subject to the claims of such beneficiary's creditors, or subject to attachment, garnishment or execution or other legal or equitable process or lien brought by or in favor of any of said creditors.

Lela Vardell Johnson subsequently married Kenneth Ellis. She died July 30, 1968 leaving no children, either natural or adopted. Elizabeth Vardell Goodman, the secondary beneficiary, survived her sister, Lela, but she promptly notified the trustee that she was not sure that she cared to accept under the terms of the trust instrument. She later executed a document on October 23, 1968, reading as follows:

KNOW ALL MEN BY THESE PRESENTS:

That I hereby irrevocably renounce and decline to accept any and all interest in or to the corpus and the income therefrom of the two Trusts created by my father, the late T. W. Vardell, by instruments dated February 28, 1931 and December 31, 1931, respectively, primarily for the benefit of my sister, Lela Vardell Ellis, then Lela Vardell Johnson, who died July 30, 1968, of which Trusts, First National Bank in Dallas is now and at all times since their creation, has been Trustee. The effect hereof shall for all purposes be the same as though I had predeceased my sister, Lela.

This document was delivered to the trustee on October 24, 1968. Prior to that date Mrs. Goodman received no benefit of either income or corpus from either of the trusts, and no one demanded of her that her decision concerning renunciation be made at an earlier date. She was solvent and owed no substantial debts.

Elizabeth Vardell Goodman is a widow, approximately sixty-eight years of age. She has had three and only three children, namely, Elizabeth Goodman Aberg, Robert Vardell Goodman and Anne Goodman Wunderlick. All of these children are over the age of twenty-one years. Robert Vardell Goodman is unmarried and without issue. Elizabeth Goodman Aberg and her husband, Charles P. Aberg, Jr., have five children, four of whom are minors. Anne Goodman Wunderlick and her husband, Joseph Thomas

Wunderlick, have nine children, all of whom are minors, the oldest of whom is sixteen years of age and the youngest is two years of age. David M. Kendall, Jr., attorney at law, was appointed by the court to be guardian ad litem for the minor children named. . . .

The matter was submitted to the court, without a jury, upon an agreed statement of facts. The judgment of the court declared: (a) that Mrs. Goodman's renunciation was a valid renunciation; (b) that the renunciation did not operate to accelerate the vesting of the remainder interest but that the remainder interest would not vest until Mrs. Goodman died; (c) that under the trust documents the corpus of the trust should be held until Mrs. Goodman died when such corpus would vest in the descendants of Elizabeth Vardell Goodman per stirpes. In the meantime the income would be distributed to the lineal descendants of Elizabeth Vardell Goodman, per stirpes.

Elizabeth Goodman Aberg, Robert Vardell Goodman and Anne Goodman Wunderlick appeal. They contend, in one point of error, that since the trial court found that Elizabeth Vardell Goodman had made a valid renunciation of her interest in the two trusts involved, the court erred in failing to declare that under the proper construction of the trust instruments such renunciation had the same effect as the death of Elizabeth Vardell Goodman, and operated to accelerate the vesting of the corpus of the trusts in the appellants.

Charles Preston Aberg, the Third, and David M. Kendall, Jr., as guardian ad litem for the minors and unborn descendants of Elizabeth Vardell Goodman, in an able brief, present four counterpoints in which they support the trial court's judgment in denying the doctrine of acceleration because (1) the remainder interests are contingent; (2) the trustors evidenced a clear intention that the corpus of the trusts be maintained until the death of Mrs. Goodman or until the expiration of twenty-one years from the date of the birth of her last child, whichever occurs later; (3) that the persons entitled to take the corpus cannot presently be determined; and (4) the "spendthrift provisions" contained in the trusts manifest a clear intention of the trustors that vesting of the future estate be delayed as long as possible.

Before proceeding to a resolution of the cardinal question presented it is to be observed that the parties are in agreement upon two basic principles of law which are applicable to the factual situation here presented. First, the parties concur, and we agree, that the trial court was correct in finding that Mrs. Goodman's renunciation was timely and fully effective. It is well settled that a beneficiary of a trust who has not, by words or conduct, manifested his acceptance of the beneficial interest, may disclaim such interest. Mrs. Goodman received no portion of the benefits of the legacy or trust and her renunciation was clear, unequivocal and timely made. Secondly, appellants admit, and we agree, that they must be classified as contingent remaindermen, and not vested remaindermen, following the death of their aunt, Lela Vardell Ellis.

While the Texas courts have recognized the doctrine of acceleration where there was a vested remainder appellants concede that our courts have never been called upon to apply the doctrine of acceleration in the instance of a contingent remainder. Much has been written to evidence the fact that there is a clear division of authority in the application of the doctrine of acceleration in favor of a contingent remainder. There are those cases which deny acceleration of contingent remainders based upon the reasoning that the identity of the persons entitled to take the corpus of the trust cannot be determined until the occurrence of the particular contingency specified in the trust instrument. Other cases make no distinction between vested remainders and contingent remainders and apply the doctrine of acceleration following a renunciation by a life tenant unless the trust document contains language clearly showing a contrary intention of the settlor. The cases upon this subject are collated in 5 A.L.R. 460 and 5 A.L.R. 473, supplemented in 164 A.L.R. 1297 and 164 A.L.R. 1433.

The doctrine of acceleration, as applied to the law of property, refers to a hastening of the owner of the future interest towards a status of present possession or enjoyment by reason of the failure of the preceding estate. The Law of Future Interests, Simes and Smith, 2d Ed., § 791, p. 263. Simes and Smith, in § 796 of that treatise, concede that the cases applying acceleration of contingent remainder benefits constitute a deviation from the accepted norms of property law but argue that it is possible to reconcile the apparent conflict in the authorities and that acceleration is justified. In doing so they concede that what the courts are really doing is to rewrite that part of the trust agreement so as to provide for vesting of future estates not only at the death of the last tenant but "upon termination of the life estate." The authors make this very pertinent statement:

> It is believed, therefore, that although the courts may state that contingent remainders are accelerated they are likely to do so only in circumstances when it is reasonable to conclude that the particular condition precedent was not important to the testator in the light of the unanticipated renunciation.

We think this goes to the very heart of the question presented. As stated in Restatement of the Law of Property, Future Interests, § 233, whenever an attempted prior interest is renounced, the desired plan of disposition is inevitably disturbed to some extent.

> The then applicable rules of law are designed to minimize the extent of this disturbance. Normally, this is accomplished by accelerating the succeeding interests (see § 231). When, however, a succeeding interest is created subject to a condition precedent not yet fulfilled, acceleration of such interest would frustrate still further the manifested plan of disposition. . . . Under the rules stated in this Section, an interest is not accelerated so long as it continues to be subject to an unfulfilled condition precedent. . . .

We think that the applicable rule of law is epitomized in Bogert on Trusts, § 172, wherein it is stated that "where the remainder interest is contingent, . . . or where acceleration would defeat the donor's general plan for the distribution of his property" the doctrine of acceleration is not applicable.

We need not be concerned about the provisions of the trust instruments relating to the initial beneficiary, Lela Vardell Johnson (Ellis) for the reason that it is undisputed that she died, without issue. We go immediately to what the settlors said concerning the second beneficiary, their daughter, Elizabeth Vardell Goodman. She was granted a life estate and "then at the expiration of twenty-one years from the date of the birth of the last child born of Elizabeth Vardell Goodman, or at her death if that be later, the corpus shall be distributed to the then living lineal descendants of the said Elizabeth Vardell Goodman per stirpes.". . .

The trustors manifested a clear intent that the trusts terminate upon the death of Elizabeth Vardell Goodman or upon the expiration of twenty-one years after the birth of her last child. Vesting of the estate must be postponed at least until the death of Elizabeth Vardell Goodman. Only at that time may it be definitely determined which of her lineal descendants are then living or whether the birth of her last child has occurred. It is settled law that a person is conclusively presumed to be able to have issue as long as he or she is alive. This rule is applied, not only to cases of the determination of title as against persons who would take if there should be issue, but also in cases of the determination of trusts and specific performance of land contracts. Simes and Smith, The Law of Future Interests, 2d Ed., § 777. Mrs. Goodman is still living so that until her death a determination of who will take pursuant to the trust instruments must await her death. Acceleration at this time would exclude the grandchildren, born and unborn, from a possible right in the beneficial enjoyment of the corpus of the estate. It is impossible to ascertain which of her lineal descendants may predecease her. If one of her married daughters should precede Elizabeth Vardell Goodman in death her children would stand to gain substantially from the distribution of the corpus at the designated time.

We also agree with appellees that the so-called "spendthrift trust" provisions of the documents signed by the settlors in this case should be considered in arriving at the intent of the settlors concerning possible acceleration of the future interests. The provisions of such clause definitely support the belief that the settlors desired to extend the life of the estate as long as possible. It certainly tends to negate the idea that the settlors contemplated termination of the life estate by renunciation and therefore precipitating distribution of the corpus.

A careful exegesis of the trust instruments before us leads us to the conclusion that the trial court was correct in denying the application of the doctrine of acceleration so that appellants would take the corpus of the estate immediately. Accordingly, we sustain appellees' counterpoints.

The judgment of the trial court, denying the doctrine of acceleration to the particular facts involved here, was correct and is here affirmed.

Affirmed.

Problems, Notes, and Questions

1. G died devising $100,000 in trust, "income to my daughter, A, for life, remainder in corpus to such of A's children as survive A; if none, to my younger brother, B." The residue of G's estate was devised to G's husband, C. What do you think should happen to the $100,000 trust in the following alternative circumstances? See 1 Restatement of Property app. at 48-79.

   (a) A predeceased G. G was survived by A's two children, X and Y.

   (b) A survived G, but disclaimed her income interest. At G's death, A was married and 42 years old. A's two children, X and Y, were 17-year-old twins who have just received letters of acceptance from a prestigious private university where the costs of tuition and other charges amount to about $20,000 per year. Although A has not passed the menopause, she certifies that the last thing on her wish list is another child.

   (c) In Problem 1(b), would it make any difference if G's devise had taken the following form: "income to my daughter, A, for life, remainder in corpus to A's children, but if none of A's children survives A, to my younger brother, B"? The Restatement of Property states:

> § 233. *Renunciation—Acceleration Prevented While Succeeding Interest Continues Subject to Unfulfilled Condition Precedent.* When an attempted prior interest fails because it is renounced by the person to whom it is limited, a succeeding interest is not accelerated so long as a condition precedent to such succeeding interest continues unfulfilled.

   (d) Suppose G's devise had stated: "income to my daughter, A, for life, remainder in corpus to A's then-living children; if none, to my younger brother, B." A comment to section 233 of the Restatement of Property states:

> *Comment c. Construction problem as to existence of condition precedent.* The rule stated in [section 233] applies only when the language of a limitation is construed to create a succeeding interest subject to a condition precedent which remains unfulfilled at the time when the creating conveyance becomes operative. . . . In resolving this preliminary problem of construction, the criterion is whether the terms and circumstances of the limitation manifest an intent to benefit persons living at the termination of the preceding interest or at the death of the person to whom such preceding interest was limited.

In Thomsen v. Thomsen, 196 Okla. 539, 166 P.2d 417, 164 A.L.R. 1426 (1946), the court said:

> The doctrine of acceleration is, according to the great weight of authority, a rule of interpretation and is to be applied so as to effect and not defeat the testator's intent. . . . [T]he doctrine . . . proceeds upon the supposition that although the ultimate devise is in terms not to take effect in possession until the death of the life tenant, yet in point of fact it is to be read as a limitation of the remainder to take effect in every event which removes the prior estate out of the way and is applied in promotion of the presumed intention of the testator, and not to defeat his intention.

(e) Assume that the remainder, if stated as in Problem 1(c), can be accelerated because it is subject to a condition subsequent. Would B's interest and the mythical interests of A's unborn and unadopted children be extinguished? Or, would the interests of X and Y somehow remain subject to open and to the condition subsequent of surviving their mother, A? See Restatement of Property § 231 comments h & i (declaring that the accelerated remainder becomes indefeasible). Compare Danz v. Danz, 373 Ill. 482, 26 N.E.2d 872 (1940) (holding the accelerated remainder to be indefeasible, the predominant view according to Simes & Smith on Future Interests § 798), with Hasemeier v. Welke, 309 Ill. 460, 141 N.E. 176 (1923).

2. *Disclaimer Statutes.* Disclaimers, and their consequences on succeeding interests, are now widely regulated by statute. See supra p. 96. If the *Aberg* case had been governed by UPC section 2-801(d) (1990), would there have been a different outcome? Texas now has a disclaimer statute that contains a similar provision. See Tex. Prob. Code § 37A. How would section 2-801(d) change your answers to Problem 1?

In Pate v. Ford, 376 S.E.2d 775 (S.C. 1989), William W. Pate, Sr., died in 1979, leaving an estate valued at approximately $1.6 million. Aletha F. Pate, William's wife, died in 1983, leaving an estate valued at approximately $6.78 million. William's will devised the residue of his estate in trust, with the income going to Aletha for life. At her death, the corpus was to be divided into three equal shares. Aletha's will provided that, if William did not survive her, her estate shall also be divided into three equal shares, to be disposed of under identical terms as those contained in William's will.

Two of the three one-third shares were to continue in trust, one to pay the income to the couple's son, Billy, for life, and the other to pay the income to the couple's other son, Wallace, for life. The provisions for distribution of the corpus were identical:

> On Billy's death, [his one-third] trust shall terminate and . . . my Trustee shall distribute the assets of the trust in equal shares per stirpes to my natural born grandchildren.
> On Wallace's death, [his one-third] trust shall terminate and . . . my Trustee shall distribute the assets of the trust in equal shares per stirpes to my natural born grandchildren.

Wallace has five children. Billy has been thrice married, but has never had any children; Billy's wife is now 32 years old.

Wallace filed a disclaimer of his income interest in his one-third share. Under section 2-801(d) of the Uniform Probate Code (1990), does the remainder interest following Wallace's income interest accelerate?

———

EXTERNAL REFERENCE. Roberts, The Acceleration of Remainders—Manipulating the Identity of Remaindermen, 42 S.C. L. Rev. 295 (1991).

Sellick v. Sellick
207 Mich. 194, 173 N.W. 609 (1919)

FELLOWS, J. This case involves the construction of the will of William J. Sellick, late of Paw Paw, Van Buren county, and the effect as between certain of the legatees of the election of the widow to take [a forced share] under the statute. Mr. Sellick left real estate inventoried at $8,500 and personal property inventoried at upwards of $176,000. He left a widow, Caroline Sellick, and one son, William R. Sellick, the plaintiff, now grown to manhood, who was the child of a former wife. He also left collateral kindred, including the defendants Arthur F. Sellick, a nephew, and Gertrude Sellick, a niece. To his collateral kindred other than defendants he gave varying sums aggregating $15,000. By the second clause of his will he gave to each of the defendants $5,000. The first clause of his will is as follows:

> I give, devise and bequeath to my wife, Caroline Sellick, twenty-five thousand dollars ($25,000), to be used and enjoyed by her during her life and at her death to be equally divided between my nephew, Arthur F. Sellick, and my niece, Gertrude Sellick.

The residue of his estate he gave to his son, the plaintiff. The widow elected to take [a forced share] under the statute. The trial judge construed the first clause of the will, when taken in connection with the second clause, which gave each defendant $5,000, and the residuary clause, as giving the widow absolutely $25,000, and accordingly held that the defendants took nothing under such clause. This rendered unnecessary the determination of the other questions involved. From a decree in accordance with these views the defendants appeal, and it is here urged by their counsel that the first clause of the will gave the widow a life estate, with remainder over to them; that by the election of the widow to take under the statute her life estate is at an end, and that, applying the doctrine of acceleration of remainders, they are now entitled to said sum of $25,000. On the other hand, it is insisted by counsel for the appellee that . . . we should not apply the doctrine of acceleration of remainders, but that such life estate, given to the widow by the will, should be sequestered to reimburse the plaintiff in part for the depletion of his bequest occasioned by the payment out of it of the sums necessary to make up the widow's statutory share. In short, that he is known in the law as a disappointed legatee, and that the doctrine of acceleration of remainders should not be adopted at the expense of disappointed legatees. . . .

It must be conceded at the outset that the decisions of the court of last resort of the state of Pennsylvania sustain the contention of defendants' counsel unequivocally. Is the rule laid down by the Pennsylvania court supported by the weight of authority and by equitable principles? Should the doctrine of acceleration of remainders be applied where by its application the remainderman gets more than the will gave to him and legatees either specific or residuary get less? To these questions we shall now direct our attention.

This court has recognized the doctrine of acceleration of remainders upon the termination of the life estate of the widow by her election to take under the statute. In re Schulz's Estate, 113 Mich. 592, 71 N. W. 1079. But that was a case where none of the legatees were in any way harmed by the application of the doctrine. By the election of the widow to take under the statute their bequests were proportionately diminished, and by the acceleration of their remainders they were proportionately reimbursed. . . .

In the case of Jones v. Knappen, 63 Vt. 391 (22 Atl. 630, 14 L. R. A. 293), the court had before it a case quite similar to the instant case. We quote from the syllabus:

> The election of the widow, who is made life tenant of her husband's property, to take against his will does not accelerate the time for distribution so that it may be made during her lifetime; where the remainder is to be divided between specific and residuary devisees and the result of her election would work inequity by diminishing the residuary, and leaving the specific devisees to be paid in full.

In this case the court quotes the following from Woerner on Administration, 119:

> The rejection by the widow of the provisions made for her by will, generally results in the diminution or contravention of devises and legacies to other parties. The rule in such case is that the devise or legacy which the widow rejects is to be applied in compensation of those whom her election disappoints

—and then says:

> The controlling, and, we think, the more reasonable principle announced in most of these cases is the one expressed by Woerner, supra, viz. to use the renounced devises and legacies given by the will to the widow to compensate, as far as may be, the devises and legacies diminished by such renunciation. When the remaindermen are affected pro rata by such renunciation, acceleration of the enjoyment of their devises or legacies, diminished proportionally, will equitably compensate them, so far as possible for such diminution. But in this case acceleration of enjoyment would increase the specific pecuniary legacies, to the detriment of the residuary legatees, whose shares only are diminished by the renunciation. Applying the principle stated, the life use of the property given by the will to the widow, and renounced by her, should be used to compensate the residuary legatees, the next of kin of the testator and of his wife. . . .

We are persuaded that under the great weight of authority the contention of plaintiff's counsel in this regard must prevail. While the doctrine of acceleration of the time of taking effect of the remainder upon the termination of the life estate by act other than the death of the life tenant (i. e., by the election of the widow to take under the statute) must be recognized and applied in proper cases, such doctrine should not be applied where by the election a portion only of the legacies are diminished in order to make up the amount required by the statute to satisfy the widow's statutory rights. And that this should be true whether the legacy diminished be a specific or a residuary one. Under such circumstances the disappointed legatee may in a court of equity compel the sequestration of the legacy to the refractory legatee for the purpose of diminishing the amount of his disappointment.

Manifestly this is in consonance with equitable principles. In the instant case the residuary fund given to the plaintiff has been diminished by many thousand dollars in order to discharge the claim of the widow resulting from her election. To adopt defendants' claim would give to them the $25,000 many years before the time fixed by the testator for its payment. They would not only receive the amount given them by the will, but they would also receive the widow's life estate renounced by her to the disadvantage of the plaintiff. Equitable principles do not require that this should be done.

We are asked to fix the present worth of the widow's life use of the $25,000 with a view of finally closing the estate and disposing of all matters at once. The parties interested are all of age, and may make such adjustment as they may desire, but we do not feel empowered to fix the present worth of the widow's use and direct its present payment. We see no occasion, however, to longer hold the estate open. A trustee may be appointed to handle this fund of $25,000. He shall annually pay the income thereon to the plaintiff during the life of the widow, and upon her death pay the corpus to defendants in equal shares.

It follows that the decree must be reversed, and one here entered in conformity with this opinion. The defendants will recover costs of this court. Neither party will recover costs of the circuit court.

Note and Question

No Need for Sequestration under Uniform Probate Code. If a UPC-type elective share (see supra Chapter 8) had been in effect in Michigan when the *Sellick* case was decided, the surviving spouse's election would not have occasioned a plea for sequestration of the spouse's income interest. Why not? On the doctrine of sequestration, see generally Restatement of Property §§ 234-35.

5. Failure of a Future Interest—Effect

A future interest can fail for a variety of reasons. The beneficiary might predecease the testator or predecease a subsequent time to which survivorship is required by the terms of the disposition; the future interest might be disclaimed; it might violate the Rule Against Perpetuities; and so on.

In general, a future interest that fails, regardless of the reason, is treated as if it were not created. A particular problem exists, however, if the failed future interest is an executory interest.

Proprietors of the Church in Brattle Square v. Grant
69 Mass. (3 Gray) 142 (1855)

[Lydia Hancock, John Hancock's aunt, died in 1777, leaving a will that provided:

> I give and bequeath unto . . . the Church of Christ in Brattle Street in Boston . . . all that brick dwelling-house and land situated in Queen Street . . . to hold the same . . . upon [the] express condition and limitation . . . that the minister or eldest minister of said church shall constantly reside and dwell in said house, during such time as he is minister of said church; and in case the same is not improved for this use only, I then declare this bequest to be void and of no force, and order that said house and land then [go] to my nephew, John Hancock, Esquire, and to his heirs forever.

The residue of her estate was also devised to John Hancock, who survived her, but died fifteen years later, in 1793.

Some seventy-five or so years after Lydia Hancock's death, the Proprietors of the Church brought a bill in equity, alleging that the conditions had been continuously satisfied and that a sale of the estate had now become necessary to carry out the intent of the devise.

The court held that Lydia Hancock's will created a fee simple subject to an executory limitation in favor of the deacons of the Church; and an executory interest (executory devise) in favor of John Hancock and his heirs. The court further held that John Hancock's executory interest violated the Rule Against Perpetuities (an English invention) and was invalid. (Obviously, the Declaration of Independence had not freed the new American state of all English influence!)

The final question was how the invalidity of John Hancock's executory interest affected the church's fee simple interest.]

BIGELOW, J. . . . Upon this point we understand the rule to be, that if a limitation over is void by reason of its remoteness, it places all prior gifts in the same situation as if the devise over had been wholly omitted. Therefore a gift of the fee or the entire interest, subject to an executory limitation which is too remote, takes effect as if it had been originally limited free from any divesting gift. The general principle applicable to such cases is, that when a subsequent condition or limitation is void by reason of its being impossible, repugnant or contrary to law, the estate becomes vested in the first taker, discharged of the condition or limitation over, according to the terms in which it was granted or devised; if for life, then it takes effect as a life estate; if in fee, then as a fee simple absolute. The reason on which this rule is said to rest is, that when a party has granted or devised an estate, he shall not be allowed to fetter or defeat it, by annexing thereto impossible, illegal or repugnant conditions or limitations.

Such indeed is the necessary result which follows from the manner in which executory devises came into being and were engrafted on the stock of the common law. Originally, . . . no estate could be limited over after a limitation in fee simple, and in such case the estate became absolute in the first taker. This rule was afterwards relaxed in cases of devises, for the purpose of effectuating the intent of testators, so far as to render such gifts valid by way of executory devise, when confined within the limits prescribed to guard against perpetuities.

The result, therefore, to which we have arrived on the whole case is, that the gift over to John Hancock is an executory devise, void for remoteness; and that the estate, upon breach of the prescribed condition, would not pass to John Hancock and his heirs, by virtue of the residuary clause, nor would it vest in the heirs at law of the testatrix. But being an estate in fee in the deacons and their successors, and the gift over being void, as contrary to the policy of the law, by reason of violating the rule against perpetuities, the title became absolute, as a vested remainder in fee, after the decease of the mother of the testatrix, in the deacons and their successors, and they hold it in fee simple, free from the divesting limitation.

Note

1. *Possibility of Reverter.* In First Universalist Society v. Boland, 155 Mass. 171, 29 N.E. 524 (1892), Clark conveyed real property by deed to the First Universalist Society as follows:

> so long as said real estate shall by said society or its assigns be devoted to the uses, interests, and support of [specified] doctrines of the Christian religion; and when said real estate shall by said society or its assigns be diverted from the uses, interests and support aforesaid to any other interests, uses, or purposes than as aforesaid, then the title of said society or its assigns in the same shall forever cease, and be forever vested in the following named persons. . . .

The court held that Clark's conveyance created a fee simple determinable in the Society; and an executory interest in the persons named to take in the case of a diversion from the specified uses. The court further held that the executory interest violated the Rule Against Perpetuities and was invalid.

The court then turned to the question of the effect of that invalidity on the state of the title:

> Since the estate of the plaintiff may determine, and since there is no valid limitation over, it follows that there is a possibility of reverter in the original grantor, Clark. This is similar to, though not quite identical with, the possibility of reverter which remains in the grantor of land upon a condition subsequent. The exact nature and incidents of this right need not now be discussed, but it represents whatever is not conveyed by the deed, and it is the possibility that the land may revert to the grantor or his heirs when the granted estate determines. Clark's possibility of reverter is not invalid for remoteness. It has been expressly held by this court that such possibility of reverter . . . is not within the rule against perpetuities. Tobey v. Moore, 130 Mass. 448; French v. Old South Soc., 166 Mass. 479. If there is any distinction in this respect between such possibility of reverter and that which arises upon

the determination of a qualified fee, it would seem to be in favor of the latter: but they should be governed by the same rule. If one is not held void for remoteness, the other should not be. The very many cases cited in Gray, Prop. §§ 305-312, show conclusively that the general understanding of courts and of the profession in America has been that the rule as to remoteness does not apply, though the learned author thinks this view erroneous in principle. . . . [T]he plaintiff's title must be deemed imperfect, and the entry must be, bill dismissed.

2. *State of the Authorities.* The distinction drawn by the *Grant* and *Boland* decisions has been generally followed. For more modern cases following *Grant*, see Betts v. Snyder, 341 Pa. 465, 19 A.2d 82 (1941); Standard Knitting Mills, Inc. v. Allen, 221 Tenn. 90, 424 S.W.2d 796 (1967). For a case in accord with *Boland*, see City of Klamath Falls v. Bell, 7 Or. App. 330, 490 P.2d 515 (1971). See Agnor, A Tale of Two Cases, 17 Vand. L. Rev. 1427 (1964).

The Restatement 2d of Property section 1.5 comments b & c assert a different position, by suggesting that it might be appropriate to hold that the invalidity of an executory interest following a fee simple determinable as well as a fee simple subject to an executory limitation renders the fee interest absolute. This position was previously urged in Waggoner, Reformulating the Structure of Estates: A Proposal for Legislative Action, 85 Harv. L. Rev. 729, 737-38, 757 (1972).

6. Rule Against Perpetuities As a Consequence of Classification

Before going on to Chapter 16 on construction, we should like to note one final consequence of classification: the Rule Against Perpetuities. Classification is extremely important in determining whether an interest is subject to the Rule Against Perpetuities. Reversions, possibilities of reverter, rights of entry, and vested remainders (including those that are vested subject to defeasance) are not subject to the Rule. The Rule applies to contingent remainders and executory interests.

Once the Rule is determined to be applicable, the next inquiry is whether the particular contingent remainder or executory interest violates the Rule or not. This question is considered infra Chapter 17.

CONSTRUCTION

No greater challenge exists in estate-planning practice than expressing your client's intent without ambiguity. An ability to write clearly is not the only skill necessary. Another is the ability to anticipate, and hence clearly to provide for, the entire range of possible future events that can affect a disposition. Both of these skills can be acquired.

A first step in learning to draft without ambiguity is to examine mistakes that have been made in the past. Too often, the cases in this chapter bring into question the meaning of documents drafted by your predecessors at the bar. We have already seen evidence of this problem in Chapter 10, on Mistake. Whether the document was drafted by a lawyer or not, however, nearly every construction case that we have studied and that we are about to study represents someone's drafting failure.

Drafting failures tend to recur in patterns. With respect to future interests, the subject of this chapter, the same mistakes are made over and over again. Once you know what they are, you will find that drafting to avoid these mistakes is surprisingly easy.

PART A. EXPRESS AND IMPLIED CONDITIONS OF SURVIVORSHIP

Statutory References: *1990 UPC §§ 2-701, -707*

One of the recurring problems in future interests law concerns survivorship: Is a future interest extinguished (terminated) if its holder dies after the creation of the interest but before the time of possession or enjoyment or before reaching a specified age? This is a question of construction, of determining the transferor's intent—not a question of lapse or of classification.

Lapse Distinguished. As we learned in Part B of Chapter 5, the rule of lapse requires a devisee under a *will* to survive the *testator*. The rule of lapse is based on the proposition that a property interest cannot be *transferred* to a deceased person. Thus a devise to a devisee who predeceases the testator lapses, notwithstanding any contrary intent on the testator's part. The rule of lapse is not a question of construction.

The rule of lapse, however, does not require a beneficiary of a future interest to be alive at the time set for possession or enjoyment. Possession or enjoyment of a future interest arises *after*, sometimes long after, the time when the future interest was *transferred* to its recipient. To illustrate, take the simple case of "to A for life, remainder to B." Suppose that this disposition was created in G's will. The common-law rule of lapse requires both A and B to be alive when G dies, for that is the time when both A and B receive their interests. Once the hurdle of surviving G is satisfied, there is no further requirement implicit in the common law necessitating B's survival of A. Consequently, an interest is not rendered subject to a condition of survivorship merely because it is a *future* interest. If a condition of survivorship exists, it derives from a finding of the transferor's intention on the point. The survivorship question is therefore a question of construction, distinguishable from the rule of lapse.

1. Basic Common-Law Rule: Conditions of Survivorship Not Implied

Before proceeding to a discussion of the basic constructional question of survivorship, we digress briefly to set the matter of survivorship into perspective. Future interests are normally held by persons in one or more generations *younger* than that of the income beneficiary. If the income interest is granted to the grantor's surviving spouse, the remainder interest is likely to be granted to the couple's children or descendants; if the income interest is granted to a child of the grantor, the remainder interest is likely to be granted to the child's children or descendants. It is unusual, in other words, to grant an income interest to the grantor's grandchild and follow it with a remainder interest to the grantor's parents.

Consequently, when the beneficiary of a future interest predeceases the time of possession or enjoyment, it is an unexpected event, an event typically caused by the beneficiary's *premature* death. When the unusual or unexpected happens, however, and a beneficiary dies before the time of possession or enjoyment, the first place to look to see if that event was anticipated and provided for is the governing instrument. If the governing instrument *expressly* imposes a condition of survivorship—as, for example, in the disposition "to A for life, remainder to B *if B survives A*"—, then survivorship is required, of course. Conversely, if the governing instrument expressly states that no condition of survivorship is imposed—as, for example, in the disposition "to A for life, remainder to B *whether or not B survives A*"—, then of course B need not survive A.

What happens if the governing instrument *expresses* neither intention—as, for example, in the disposition "to A for life, remainder to B"? *The basic rule of construction at common law is that a condition of survivorship is not implied.* Several rationales are offered in support of this rule. The rule, it is said, (i) furthers the constructional preference for complete dispositions of property, (ii) furthers the constructional preference for equality of distribution among the different lines of descent, and (iii) is supported by the constructional preferences for vested over contingent interests, for vesting at the earliest possible time, and for indefeasible vesting at the earliest possible time. See Restatement of Property § 243 & comments.

While it may be true that the constructional preferences set forth in (iii) played an important role in fashioning the rule against implied conditions of survivorship, one should not equate the two matters—classification and construction.

> Whether a future interest is subject to a requirement of survivorship is a question of construction. Whether a future interest is vested or contingent is a question of classification.

A vested future interest can be subject to a requirement of survivorship. A contingent future interest may reflect conditions keyed to events unrelated to survivorship.

The basic rule of construction against implying conditions of survivorship applies to individual and class gifts.

> *Example 16.1:* G's will devised real property "to A for life, remainder to B." Both A and B survived G. Subsequently, B predeceased A.
>
> B's property interest is not defeated by his death before A. Upon B's death, his remainder interest passes to his successors in interest. There is no implicit condition that B survive A, even though B's remainder is a future interest.

> *Example 16.2:* G's will devised real property "to A for life, remainder in equal shares to B and C." A, B, and C survived G.
>
> The rule of construction against implying conditions of survivorship applies to gifts to more than one individual. Consequently, if either B or C (or both) predeceases A, the predeceased taker's half passes on that person's death through her or his estate to her or his successors in interest.

Example 16.3: G's will devised real property "to A for life, remainder to A's children." At G's death, A and A's daughter, X, were living. During A's lifetime, a son, Y, was born to A. Both X and Y predeceased A. The rule of construction against implying conditions of survivorship applies to class gifts. Restatement 2d of Property § 27.3. Consequently, X's interest passed on her death to her successors in interest, and Y's interest passed on his death to his successors in interest.

EXTERNAL REFERENCES. Halbach, Issues About Issue: Some Recurrent Class Gift Problems, 48 Mo. L. Rev. 333, 361-70 (1983); Halbach, Future Interests: Express and Implied Conditions of Survival (Parts 1 & 2), 49 Calif. L. Rev. 297 & 431 (1961).

The Discredited (?) Divide-and-Pay-Over Rule. Once upon a time, some courts recognized a rule called the divide-and-pay-over rule. The rule was this: If the only language of a disposition directs that property be divided and paid over at a future time, survivorship to that time is required. A trust disposition triggering this rule would be, income "to A for life, then on A's death the trustee is to divide the corpus and pay it over to A's children."

The Restatement of Property rejects this rule:

> § 260. *Direction to Divide and Pay Over at a Future Date.* In a limitation purporting to create a remainder or an executory interest, the fact that the only words of gift to the intended taker thereof consist of a direction to divide and pay over, or to convert, divide and pay over, at the end of the created prior interests or at some other future date is not a material factor in determining the existence of a requirement of survival to the date of distribution.

Today, in most states, the divide-and-pay-over rule has either been overtly repudiated or appears to have fallen into disuse or never to have been followed. See Am. L. Prop. § 21.21. Yet, the rule has not entirely been eradicated. The Supreme Court of Illinois recently found it applicable as a "rule . . . of construction to aid courts in determining whether a gift to a class is a vested or contingent remainder." Harris Trust & Savings Bank v. Beach, 118 Ill. 2d 1, 513 N.E.2d 833 (1987). The Illinois Supreme Court's opinion did not mention the rejection of the rule by the Restatement, cases in other jurisdictions, or scholarly commentary.

Conditions Unrelated to Survivorship. We have seen that, at common law, a future interest to which no express conditions are attached is not subject to an implied condition of survivorship. But what if the future interest is subject to one or more *express* conditions *unrelated* to survivorship? Does the existence of these express conditions automatically subject the future interest to an *implied* condition of survivorship? That is the question posed in the cases below.

Bomberger's Estate
347 Pa. 465, 32 A.2d 729 (1943)

[The testator's will devised $50,000 in trust, income to his niece, Mrs. Lilly Aughinbaugh, for life, corpus on Lilly's death to Lilly's children. The will continued:

> Should [niece Lilly] . . . die without leaving a child or children, I order and direct that the bequest shall be equally divided among my nephews and nieces . . . , then living, the child or children of nieces who may be deceased to have the share their mother would have been entitled to if living.

Lilly died childless, never having had any children. All of the testator's nieces and nephews predeceased Lilly. Ada, one of the nieces who predeceased Lilly, had eight children: seven of them survived Lilly, but one, John, died during Ada's lifetime. Annie, the other niece, had one child, Rachel, who survived Annie but predeceased Lilly.]

STEARNE, J. . . . The language which testator used did not impose the same contingency of survivorship upon the substitutionary gift to child or children of deceased nieces that it did upon the nephews and nieces. For a nephew or niece to take required that he or she be alive when Mrs. Aughinbaugh died without issue. However, if a niece left child or children, their interest was vested. They took in precisely the same manner as if their mother, a niece, had been living at the date of the death of Mrs. Aughinbaugh. There is nothing in the substitutionary gift which expressly states that children of deceased nieces must survive Mrs. Aughinbaugh. . . . The condition of survival to a fixed time is never implied. Such condition must appear plainly, manifestly and indisputably.

"When a condition of survival to the time of distribution has been annexed to the gifts to the first takers, but not to the gifts to the substituted beneficiaries, the condition is not to be implied with respect to the latter": President Judge Van Dusen in Re Carpenter's Estate, 42 Pa. Dist. & Co. R. 367-369. . . .

Costs to be paid from the fund.

Lawson v. Lawson
267 N.C. 643, 148 S.E.2d 546 (1966)

[The testator's will devised land to his daughter Opal Lawson Long for her life, and at her death "to her children, if any, in fee simple; if none, to [Opal's] whole brothers and sisters . . . in fee simple." Fifteen years after the testator's death, Opal died without children. Four of Opal's six whole brothers and sisters survived her. Two of Opal's whole brothers survived the testator but predeceased her; each left descendants surviving Opal.]

SHARP, J. . . . Respondents contend that at the death of the testator, J. Rad Lawson, the six whole brothers and sisters of the life tenant, all of whom were then living, took a vested remainder in the land, and that they, as children of the two whole brothers who predeceased Opal Lawson Long, inherited their interest. The law, however, is otherwise.

This case presents a typical example of a contingent remainder.

> A devises to B for life, remainder to his children but if he dies without leaving children remainder over, both the remainders are contingent; but if B afterwards marries and has a child, the remainder becomes vested in that child, subject to open and let in unborn children, and the remainders over are gone forever. The remainder becomes a vested remainder in fee in the child as soon as the child is born, and does not wait for the parent's death, and if the child dies in the lifetime of the parent, the vested estate in remainder descends to his heirs. 4 Kent's Commentaries, p. 284 quoted in Blanchard v. Ward, 244 N.C. 142, 146, 92 S.E.2d 776, 779.

In Watson v. Smith, 110 N.C. 6, 14 S.E. 649, testator devised land to J for life, and at J's death to such child or children of his that might then be living, but should he die without issue, then to G, W, H, and O in fee. The Court held that the limitation to G, W, H, and O, was a contingent remainder. "Alternative remainders limited upon a single precedent estate are always contingent. Such remainders are created by a limitation to one for life, with remainder in fee to his children, issue, or heirs, and, in default of such children, issue, or heirs, to another or others. . . ." 33 Am. Jur., Life Estates, Remainders, etc. § 148 (1941). . . .

Clearly the interests of the whole brothers and sisters was [sic] contingent and could not vest before the death of the life tenant, for not until then could it be determined that she would leave no issue surviving. "Where those who are to take in remainder cannot be determined until the happening of a stated event, the remainder is contingent. Only those who can answer the roll immediately upon the happening of the event acquire any estate in the properties granted." Strickland v. Jackson, 259 N.C. 81, 84, 130 S.E.2d 22, 25. Respondents' parents, having predeceased the life tenant, could not answer the roll call at her death.

The judgment of the court below is Affirmed.

Notes and Questions

1. *State of the Authorities.* The decision in *Bomberger* reflects the great majority view on the question and the view enunciated in Restatement of Property section 261. See, e.g., Rosenthal v. First Nat'l Bank, 40 Ill. 2d 266, 239 N.E.2d 826 (1968); Bogart's Will, 62 Misc. 2d 114, 308 N.Y.S.2d 594 (Sur. Ct. 1970); Am. L. Prop. § 21.25; Simes & Smith on Future Interests § 594. Some courts have adopted the *Lawson* analysis and have imposed a condition of survivorship on interests that were subject to conditions unrelated to survivorship. See, e.g., Fletcher v. Hurdle, 259 Ark. 640, 536 S.W.2d 109 (1976) (4-to-3 decision); Schau v. Cecil, 257 Iowa 1296, 136 N.W.2d 515 (1965); Jones v. Holland, 223 S.C. 500, 77 S.E.2d 202 (1953).

Professor Roberts, in Class Gifts in North Carolina—When Do We "Call the Roll"?, 21 Wake Forest L. Rev. 1 (1985), noted that the *Lawson* decision seems to have been implicitly overruled by White v. Alexander, 290 N.C. 75, 224 S.E.2d 617 (1976). In *White*, G devised property to S for life, "and if he shall die without heirs of his body . . . to my heirs." S died without heirs of his body, causing the gift to G's heirs to take effect. The class of G's heirs was determined at G's death. Although some of the members of that class predeceased S, the Supreme Court of North Carolina refused to imply a requirement of survivorship as to their interests. Unfortunately, *White* did not expressly overrule *Lawson*. Indeed, the opinion in *White* did not even mention its prior decision in *Lawson*!

2. *Classification and Construction.* Did the court in *Lawson* confuse classification and construction?

It may be true that an interest subject to a requirement of survivorship is often contingent—"to A for life, remainder to B if B survives A." And it may also be true that an interest not subject to a condition of survivorship is often vested—"to A for life, remainder to B whether or not B survives A." However, the two matters are not always coincidental: An interest subject to a requirement of survivorship can be vested ("to A for life, remainder to B, but if B fails to survive A, to C") and an interest not subject to a requirement of survivorship can be contingent ("to A for life, remainder to B if A dies without issue").

Is *Lawson* an example of the mystique of classification, alluded to supra p. 858? The interest of Opal's whole brothers and sisters was clearly contingent when the testator died: It was contingent on Opal's dying without children surviving her. Did the court in *Lawson* think that contingent future interests are necessarily conditioned on survivorship?

Arguably *Lawson* should be limited to class gifts that are expressly contingent on an event unrelated to survivorship. Suppose the disposition were "to A for life, remainder to B if A dies without issue." If A dies without issue, and if B predeceases A, is B's interest defeated in North Carolina because B cannot personally "answer the roll call" at A's death? Professor Roberts indicated that no roll is called in North Carolina in this type of case. See Carolina Power v. Haywood, 186 N.C. 313, 119 S.E. 500 (1923); Britton v. Miller, 63 N.C. 268 (1869); Rawls v. Early, 94 N.C. App. 677, 381 S.E.2d 166 (1989).

Suppose the disposition were "to A for life, remainder to A's children." If one of A's children predeceased A, is that child's interest defeated in North Carolina because the deceased child cannot personally "answer the roll call" at A's death? See Mason v. White, 53 N.C. (8 Jones Eq.) 421 (1862), wherein the court said:

> The question presented is too plain to admit of discussion. . . . [A]lthough the legacy vested, subject to open and let in any persons who might come into existence afterwards and answer the description, yet, there is no ground on which it can be contended that the death of one of the legatees divested her legacy in favor of the surviving legatees. To have this effect, there must be words of exclusion, *e.g.* to the children of A, living at the time of her death.

———

Restricted and Unrestricted Conditions of Survivorship. Restricted conditions of survivorship are said to flow from language phrased in so-called "supplanting" form.

> *Example 16.4:* "To A for life, then to B, but if B predeceases A leaving children, then to such children." B died childless prior to A's death. B's interest is not extinguished. See, *e.g., Krooss,* below; Restatement of Property § 254.

> *Example 16.5:* "To A for life, then to A's children, the children of any deceased child to take their deceased parents' share." Several of A's children survived A, but one child, B, died childless prior to A's death. B's interest is not extinguished. Estate of Houston, 414 Pa. 579, 201 A.2d 592 (1964); Restatement of Property § 254.

Unrestricted conditions of survivorship are said to flow from language phrased in "alternative" form.

> *Example 16.6:* "To A for life, then to B or B's children." B died childless prior to A's death. See, *e.g., Robertson,* below; Restatement of Property § 252. B's interest is extinguished.

Do you think the distinction between "supplanting" and "alternative" language is sensible? Do the two different expressions indicate that the transferors intended the different results accorded by the law? The legal distinction makes sense only within the formalistic doctrine of estates. Whether the legal distinction serves the goal of facilitating the transferor's intent is quite another logical matter.

Matter of Krooss
302 N.Y. 424, 99 N.E.2d 222, 47 A.L.R.2d 894 (1951)

FULD, J. Herman Krooss died in 1932. He was survived by his wife Eliese and his two children, a son, John Krooss, and a married daughter, Florence Maue. By his will, he gave his residuary estate, real and personal, to his wife, "to have and to hold the same for and during the term of her natural life," with the power to use any part of it for her support and maintenance that she deemed necessary; no trust was created. The will further provided:

> Upon the death of my beloved wife, Eliese Krooss, I then give, devise and bequeath all the rest, residue and remainder of my estate, as well real as personal, and wheresoever situate, to my beloved children, John H. Krooss and Florence Maue, nee Krooss, share and share alike, to and for their own use absolutely and forever.
> In the event that either of my children aforesaid should die prior to the death of my beloved wife, Eliese Krooss, leaving descendants, then it is my wish and I so direct that such descendants shall take the share their parent would have taken if then living, share and share alike, to and for their own use absolutely and forever.

Florence Maue died, without having had descendants, in 1947, three years before the life beneficiary Eliese. Some months after Eliese's death, Florence's husband, as executor of his wife's estate, instituted the present proceeding in the Surrogate's Court of Bronx County to compel John Krooss, as executor under Eliese's will and as administrator c. t. a. of Herman Krooss' estate, to render and settle his respective accounts. In order to determine whether the executors of Florence's estate had status to prosecute the proceeding, the surrogate was required, initially, to construe Herman's will. He decided that the interest given to Florence was vested at the testator's death, subject to be divested only in the event of her predeceasing her mother leaving descendants, that it passed under her will, and that her husband, as executor, was entitled to bring the action.[1] The Appellate Division modified that determination. Disagreeing with the surrogate's interpretation, the Appellate Division construed the will as imposing upon each of the remaindermen a condition that he or she survive the life beneficiary; Florence having died without children before Eliese, that condition was not met, and, concluded the court, as to Florence's share in the remainder, Krooss died intestate.

The law has long favored a construction of language in deed and will that accomplishes the vesting of estates; such a result is preferred because, among other things, it enables property to be freely transferred at the earliest possible date. Accordingly, the courts are intent upon restricting defeating events to the exact circumstances specified.

The will under consideration is simple in language and simple in plan. The testator gave his widow a life estate and a power to use the principal if it proved necessary for her maintenance and support. What remained after her death he gave "absolutely and forever" in equal shares to his two children, Florence and John. Had the will stopped at that point, there would be no question that the remainders were vested. And, since that is so, additional language will not be read as qualifying or cutting down the estate unless that language is as clear and decisive as that which created the vested remainder. The further language used by the testator in this case demonstrates, not that he was rendering the vesting of the estates in his children conditional upon survival of the life beneficiary, but that he was willing to have those estates divested only upon the combined occurrences of two further events. He explicitly provided, if either of his children died before his wife, "leaving descendants," then "such descendants shall take the share the parent would have taken if then living". If the words used mean what they say, then, divestiture of the remainder estates depended upon the happening of two plainly expressed and stipulated conditions: (1) the child, Florence or John, must die before the life beneficiary, and (2) the child so dying must leave descendants. Only if

---

1. In her will, Florence left her residuary estate in trust to her husband and to her brother John, as trustees, to pay the net income therefrom to the husband for life; on his death, the principal was to be distributed between Florence's two nephews, the children of her brother John, if living, and to their issue per stirpes if either should die before the termination of the trust.

both of those conditions came to pass was the remainder—by apt and unequivocal language already vested in Florence and John—to be divested and bestowed instead upon the descendants of him or her who might have died.

When a will contains language that has acquired, through judicial decision, a definite and established significance, the testator is taken to have employed that language in that sense and with that meaning in mind. . . .

Over the years, the courts have uniformly held that language such as that used by the testator here, or language substantially identical, creates a vested remainder in fee subject to be divested by the remainderman's failing to survive the life beneficiary, *if, but only if,* such remainderman leaves issue or descendants surviving. . . .

Leading commentators after reviewing the cases, have expressed themselves in similar fashion. (See 2 Powell on Real Property (1950), §§ 330-331, pp. 728-737; 2 Redfield on Law of Wills (1866), § 65, pp. 648-649; 3 Restatement, Property, § 254, Comment a, Illustration 1, particularly Example II, pp. 1284-1286.) Thus, Professor Richard R. Powell of Columbia University Law School and Reporter on Property for the American Law Institute, in his recent work on the Law of Real Property, considers the subject at some length and sums up the law in this way (op. cit., § 330, pp. 729-730):

> Supplanting limitations differ, in that some provide a taker who is to become the substitute whenever the prior taker fails to survive, while others provide a taker who is to become the substitute only under some circumstances. In cases of the second type, the constructional preference for early indefeasibility causes the requirement of survival to be strictly construed, and to operate only under the exact circumstances stipulated. . . . Similarly, in a gift "to my wife B for life, then to my children and the issue of those of my children who may be dead leaving children," the interest of a child of the testator who dies without surviving issue is indefeasible.

Turning to the will before us, we find that, at the expiration of the wife's life estate, the testator "then" gave the remainder to his children "absolutely and forever." The use of the word "then" as an "adverb of time" must be, as it long has been, construed to relate solely "to the time of enjoyment of the estate, and not to the time of its vesting in interest." Hence, the sole combination of events which could divest the "absolute" gift to the daughter Florence was her death before her mother, "leaving descendants". Only one of the specified conditions was fulfilled; although Florence did predecease her mother, she did not leave descendants. Consequently, her absolute gift remained vested and was not defeated. Not only the language employed, but the omission of any "words of survivorship" to indicate an intent that Florence's brother was to take if Florence died without children, illumines the testator's design to give his daughter a vested remainder. . . .

The order of the Appellate Division should be reversed and the decree of the Surrogate's Court affirmed, with costs in this court and in the Appellate Division to all parties, appearing separately and filing separate briefs, payable out of the estate. . . .

Note and Question

Restricted Condition of Survivorship Stated as a Condition Precedent. Would the meaning of Herman Krooss' will have been litigated if the restricted condition of survivorship had been stated in the form of a condition precedent?

As a general rule of thumb, clarity of expression is promoted by stating conditions in precedent form. Conditions stated in subsequent form tend to be lazily formulated and incomplete. Although it takes greater effort and discipline to state conditions in precedent form, the end product is usually worth the effort.

Robertson v. Robertson
313 Mass. 520, 48 N.E.2d 29 (1943)

FIELD, C.J. This petition for partition of certain real estate, in Hudson, was brought in the Probate Court by Ralph A. Robertson and comes before us upon an appeal by Essie Pope, one of the respondents, from a decree of that court for partition.

The case arises upon the following facts which appear in the report of material facts made by the judge: Lillian G. Pope, late of Hudson, died July 12, 1931, leaving a will that has been duly allowed, which contained the following provisions:

> Fourth;—To my daughter, Grace M. Morse and her husband, Alvah W. Morse, the use, income and enjoyment of my homestead estate situated at No. 11 Felton Street, in said Hudson for the term of their natural lives or of the life of the survivor. [Grace and Alvah, or the survivor, were given a power to sell the premises.] In case that at the death of the survivor of said Grace M. Morse and said Alvah W. Morse said homestead has not then been sold then it is to go to [sic] one half part to my said son, Ernest F. Pope, one quarter part of [sic] my said daughter, Ella B. Robertson and one quarter part to my said grandson, Ralph A. Robertson, or to the issue of any that may then be dead by the right of representation.
>
> Fifth;—All the rest and residue of my estate to my children, Ella B. Robertson, Grace M. Morse and my grandchild, Ralph A. Robertson, in equal shares, or to the issue of any who may be dead by the right of representation.

The testatrix left surviving her a son, Ernest F. Pope, married to Essie Pope, a daughter Grace M. Morse, married to Alvah W. Morse, a daughter Ella B. Robertson, and a grandson, Ralph A. Robertson, who, it may be guessed, was the son of Ella B. Robertson although the fact does not appear. The son, Ernest F. Pope, died January 26, 1940, leaving a widow, Essie Pope, and no issue. The daughter Grace M. Morse died June 26, 1940, leaving no issue. Her husband, Alvah W. Morse, had predeceased her. At the time of the death of Grace M. Morse the premises described in the will of the testatrix as her "homestead estate" had not been sold. The record does not disclose what, if any, property the testatrix owned at the time of her death other than the "homestead estate."

Ralph A. Robertson, the grandson of the testatrix, brought the present petition for partition of the "homestead estate," referred to in the fourth clause of the will, and upon this petition a decree was entered that partition of the "homestead estate" be made between the petitioner, Ralph A. Robertson, and Ella B. Robertson in equal shares, and a commissioner was appointed to make such partition. The basis of this decree was that Ella B. Robertson and Ralph A. Robertson each took one quarter part of the "homestead estate" under the fourth clause of the will, but that the devise by that clause of one half part thereof to Ernest F. Pope failed by reason of his death before the death of his sister Grace M. Morse, and therefore was disposed of by the fifth or residuary clause of the will in equal shares to Ella B. Robertson, Ralph A. Robertson, and Grace M. Morse, each of whom took under said clause one sixth part of the "homestead estate," and that the one sixth part of the "homestead estate" that passed to Grace M. Morse went "by purchase from the heirs and legatees under" her will in equal shares to Ella B. Robertson and Ralph A. Robertson, so that each of them took by such transfer one twelfth part of the "homestead estate," with the result that in the aggregate Ella B. Robertson and Ralph A. Robertson each was entitled to one half part of the "homestead estate." Essie Pope, the widow of Ernest F. Pope, appealed from this decree, and contends, in substance, that the one half part of the "homestead estate" devised to her husband by the fourth clause of the will did not fail so that this part fell into the residue of the estate, but rather that it was the property of his estate in which she, as his widow, is entitled to share. The record does not show, however, to what extent she, as his widow, was entitled to share in his estate. . . .

We think that the decree of the Probate Court was based upon the correct interpretation of the will, that Ernest F. Pope took only a contingent remainder in one half part of the "homestead estate," with the result that, since the contingency upon which it depended did not happen, the appellant, Essie Pope, the widow of Ernest F. Pope, is not entitled to share in the partition of the "homestead estate." . . .

The fact that the gift to Ernest F. Pope by the provision of the fourth clause here quoted was subject to being defeated by an exercise of the power of sale . . . did not render the gift to him contingent. A remainder after a life estate is none the less vested because subject to being defeated by the exercise of a power of sale if, apart from the existence of the power, it would be a vested remainder. In these circumstances such a remainder is a vested remainder subject to being divested by the exercise of the power rather than a contingent remainder. . . . And in our opinion the conditional language with reference to the gift in default of sale under the power, "In case that at the death of the survivor of said Grace M. Morse and said Alvah W. Morse said homestead has not then been sold," does not of itself preclude this result so far as the effect of the existence of the power to sell is concerned. If the remainder in one half part of the "homestead estate" given to Ernest F. Pope was contingent rather than vested, it is for reasons other than the existence of the power of sale. . . .

We think that the language of the fourth clause of the will as a whole read in the light of the other provisions of the will discloses an intention on the part of the testatrix to postpone the acquisition by her son, Ernest F. Pope, of a vested interest in one half part of the "homestead estate" until the happening of a future event, that is, the death of the survivor of the life tenants, so that he must be deemed to have taken only a contingent interest—an interest contingent upon his surviving the life tenants, a contingency that did not happen. . . .

[T]he gift to the "issue" of Ernest F. Pope was not a gift by way of substitution in the sense of a supplanting gift. See for the distinction between an "alternative limitation" and a "supplanting limitation" Am. Law Inst. Restatement: Property, § 253, comment c. The gift to the "issue" of Ernest F. Pope ascertained as of the time of distribution, the time of the death of the surviving life tenant, is as direct a gift as the gift to Ernest F. Pope. The language of the will fixes the same time for these gifts to take effect, the time of the death of the surviving life tenant. One half part of the "homestead estate" is "then . . . to go" to Ernest F. Pope or to his "issue," and the gifts are expressly made in the alternative by reason of the use of the conjunction "or" connecting them. The canon of construction stated in Am. Law Inst. Restatement: Property, § 252, relating to an "alternative limitation employing the word 'or'," is as follows:

> In a limitation purporting to create a remainder or an executory interest, in "B or his children," or in "B or his issue," or in "B or his descendants," or by other language of similar import, the alternative form tends to establish as to the interest of B that (a) a requirement of survival to the end of all preceding interests exists; and (b) such survival is a condition precedent of such interest.

This canon of construction is clearly applicable to the language of the will here involved. And in the light of the other considerations herein stated we think that it must be followed with the result that, by reason of the death of Ernest F. Pope before the death of the surviving life tenant, the gift of an interest in one half part of the "homestead estate" to him never vested in him. . . .

The conclusion here reached may seem to rest upon a somewhat technical analysis of the language used by the testatrix. It is, however, to be assumed that this language was used by her advisedly to express her intention, and we "have to go upon slight differences." Lee v. Welch, 163 Mass. 312, 314, 39 N.E. 1112, 1113. If the testatrix had added the words "if he was then living" to the gift of an interest in one half part of the "homestead estate" to Ernest F. Pope, there could be no doubt of the correctness of the conclusion here reached. But it would be even more technical to rest a different conclusion upon the omission of these words when the same intention of the testatrix is shown by other language used by her. . . . The conclusion here reached that the vesting of this interest was intended to be postponed until the death of the surviving life tenant is not in conflict with any intention of the testatrix disclosed by her will.

Decree affirmed.

Notes and Question

1. *Restricted Condition.* Do you think Herman Krooss' intention in *Krooss* was so much different from Lillian Pope's intention in *Robertson*? Why did the court in *Robertson* refuse to consider whether Lillian would have preferred that the primary beneficiaries' interests fail only if they died leaving issue?

2. *Remainders Subject to a Power.* In holding that a remainder interest is not rendered contingent on survivorship of the life tenant by reason of its being subject to a power, the court in the *Robertson* case was well within existing authority. See, e.g., Walker's Estate, 277 Pa. 444, 121 A. 318 (1923); Restatement of Property section 261 illustration 1. See also Note 3, supra p. 860. A few courts have held to the contrary, however. See, e.g., Jarrett v. McReynolds, 212 Va. 241, 183 S.E.2d 343 (1971).

3. *Remainder "to B or his heirs."* Does a remainder "to B or his heirs" present the same or different problems as a remainder "to B or his issue"? The Restatement of Property section 37 comment l states that a devise of a future interest "to B or his heirs" "normally is construed to create an estate in fee simple absolute in [B], if [B] is alive when the limited estate becomes a present interest and in [B]'s heirs if [B] is then dead." This is the result reached in Rowett v. McFarland, 394 N.W.2d 298 (S.D. 1986), and in Landmark Communications, Inc. v. Sovran Bank, 239 Va. 158, 387 S.E.2d 484 (1990). But the Restatement also holds out the possibility that such a devise could be construed as creating an indefeasibly vested remainder in B, as if the devise had been "to B *and* his heirs."

2. Special Case of Multiple-Generation Class Gifts—Class Gifts in Favor of "Issue" or "Descendants"

Statutory References: *1990 UPC §§ 2-708 to -709*

Remainder interests in trusts are commonly given to a class composed of the transferor's or the income beneficiary's "issue" or "descendants." A distinguishing characteristic of these class gifts is that potentially the takers reside in more than one generation. As with most other types of future interests, the recommended form for these class gifts imposes an express condition of survivorship to the time of possession or enjoyment. As Weller v. Sokol, below, demonstrates, a requirement of survivorship commonly is implied for multiple-generation class gifts, even in the absence of one expressly stated. See Restatement of Property § 249 comment i, § 296 comment g; Restatement 2d of Property § 28.2. This result is, of course, contrary to the rules of construction concerning future interests in favor of individuals and in favor of single-generation classes, such as "children," "grandchildren," "nieces and nephews," and so on. Why are class gifts in favor of "issue" or "descendants" treated differently?

A related question in the case of multiple-generation class gifts is the form of distribution among the takers. In Weller v. Sokol, below, a per-stirpes form of distribution was specified in the governing instrument. In cases in which the governing instrument does not specify a form of distribution, the English rule favored a per capita form of distribution.[2] The English preference has now largely disappeared in the United States. Generally speaking, the preferred form of distribution in this country is representational. See Halbach, Issues About Issue: Some Recurrent Class Gift Problems, 48 Mo. L. Rev. 333, 350-55 (1983).

Contrast UPC sections 2-708 and 2-709 (1990) with the positions taken in the Restatements of Property:

> *Restatement 2d of Property § 28.2. Class Gift to "Issue" or "Descendants".* If a gift is made to a class described as the "issue" or "descendants" of a designated person, or by a similar multigenerational class gift term, in the absence of additional language or circumstances that indicate otherwise,
>
> (1) A class member must survive to the date of distribution in order to share in the gift; and
>
> (2) such class member in order to share in the gift must have no living ancestor who is a class member; and
>
> (3) the initial division into shares will be on the basis of the number of class members, whether alive or deceased, in the first generation below the designated person.

> *Restatement of Property § 303. Distribution—Class Described as "Issue of B," or as "Descendants of B," or as "Family of B."* (1) When a conveyance creates a class gift by a limitation in favor of a group described as the "issue of B," or as the "descendants of B," . . . then, unless a contrary intent of the conveyor is found from additional language or circumstances, distribution is made to such members of the class as would take, and in such shares as they would receive, under the applicable law of intestate succession if B had died intestate on the date of the final ascertainment of the membership in the class, owning the subject matter of the class gift.

Although the specifics of intestate distribution among an intestate's descendants take different forms, all such forms are representational in overall approach. See supra Chapter 2, Part B. That is to say, a descendant takes only if no intervening ancestor of that descendant is alive. Any

---

2. Under a per-capita form of distribution, every member of the class takes an equal share, even those with living intervening ancestors. To illustrate, suppose a trust for A for life, remainder in corpus to A's descendants. If A had two children and three grandchildren, each would take a 1/5 share under a per-capita form of distribution. No condition of survivorship of A would be implied. See Restatement 2d of Property § 28.2 comment d, illustration 5.

representational form of distribution, regardless of which type, would justify the rule adopted in Weller v. Sokol on the question of implying a condition of survivorship.

Weller v. Sokol
271 Md. 420, 318 A.2d 193 (1974)

SINGLEY, J. This case combines a number of appeals from a decree of the Circuit Court of Baltimore City which construed the will of the late Arthur Nattans (Arthur Nattans I). While the appeal was originally taken to the Court of Special Appeals, we granted certiorari in order that it could be docketed in this Court.

Although the factual background and particularly the family pedigree are difficult to keep in mind, the case presents two relatively simple issues:

(i) When a will directs a distribution on the death of the testator's last surviving child among "issue and descendants" per stirpes of children of the testator who have died leaving issue surviving, where are the stocks or stirpes to be found?

(ii) Is distribution to be made only to issue and descendants living at the time of distribution?

The chancellor (Ross, J.) determined that the stocks, or stirpes, were to be found among the children of the testator, and not among the grandchildren who were the first takers of an absolute interest, and that distribution was to be made only to descendants living at the time of distribution. For reasons to be developed, we shall affirm.

Arthur Nattans I died domiciled in Baltimore on 17 April 1905, survived by his widow, Jennie Nattans; by three children of a prior marriage; Emily N. Herbert, Addie N. Bachrach, and Samuel A. Nattans, and by five children of his second marriage: Rita Nattans (later Myers), Ralph Nattans, Edith Nattans (later Hecht), Hortense Nattans (later Solomon), and Arthur Nattans (Arthur Nattans II).

The provisions of the Nattans will, executed on 3 October 1903, with which we shall here be concerned are contained in Items Sixth and Tenth. By Item Sixth, 396 shares of stock of Read Drug and Chemical Company of Baltimore City (Read's) owned by Mr. Nattans were bequeathed to trustees to pay the income from specified numbers of shares to the Nattans children, as follows:

Emily N. Herbert	40 shares
Addie N. Bachrach	29 shares
Samuel A. Nattans	29 shares
Rita Nattans (Myers)	60 shares
Ralph Nattans	40 shares
Edith Nattans (Hecht)	60 shares
Hortense Nattans (Solomon)	60 shares
Arthur Nattans II	40 shares

Item Tenth provided:

"*Tenth.* In the event of the death of any of my children above named, during the continuance of this trust, without leaving issue him or her surviving, the income herein given to the child so dying, without issue living at his or her death, shall be divided equally among his or her surviving brothers and sisters annually during the continuance of this trust. And in case of the death of any one of my said children during the continuance of said trust, leaving issue him or her surviving, the income of the share of the one so dying shall go to and become the property of his or her child, if only one, or children, if more than one, equally, share and share alike. Upon the death of the last survivor of all my said eight children this trust shall cease, and thereupon the entire trust property, shall be divided by my said trustees, or their successors in the trust, among the issue and descendants of such of my children as may have died leaving lawful issue him or her surviving *per stirpes and not per capita*. And the said trustees, and their successors in the trust, are authorized and directed to make, execute and deliver all such deeds and instruments of conveyance or assignment as may be necessary to make said division." (Emphasis in original.)

In Ryan v. Herbert, 186 Md. 453, 47 A.2d 360 (1946), our predecessors had occasion to review a declaratory decree which had construed the provisions of Item Tenth relating to devolution of income prior to the termination of the trust. That decree, which was affirmed on appeal, had directed that on the death of a child of Arthur Nattans I prior to the termination of the trust, leaving any issue whatsoever surviving, such issue took a vested interest in the income to which the dying child had been entitled, subject only to defeasance by the termination of the trust.

As a result, when Harold Herbert and Arthur N. Bachrach, grandsons of Arthur Nattans I, died prior to the termination of the trust without leaving descendants surviving, the income which each had been receiving was paid to his respective estate. No consideration was given to the devolution of the corpus at time of termination beyond a recognition that it would certainly pass in proportions which differed from the shares of income, and that it might well pass to persons other than those who had received income from the trust under the determination reached in Ryan. . . .

To us, however, the most compelling argument springs from the very nature of a stirpital distribution. The "issue and descendants" of the children of Arthur Nattans I could not be determined until the termination of the trust. See Restatement of Property, § 296, comment g, §§ 303(1), 304, 311(1). At that time neither Harold Herbert nor Arthur N. Bachrach was alive. While their right to receive income was found to be vested in Ryan, their right to participate in the corpus, under the terms of the will, was implicitly conditioned on survival until distribution. . . .

Decree affirmed, costs to be paid from the assets of the trust estate.

Questions

Why does a future interest in "issue per stirpes" implicitly contain a requirement of survivorship to the time of distribution? Should there be an implicit requirement of survivorship if the future interest is to "issue per capita"? In the case of issue per stirpes, should the requirement of survivorship be restricted or unrestricted? See Restatement of Property § 249 comment i, § 303 (unrestricted); Am. L. Prop. § 21.13, n. 10. Compare Maiorano v. Virginia Trust Co., 216 Va. 505, 219 S.E.2d 884 (1975) (unrestricted), with Elliott v. Griffin, 218 Va. 250, 237 S.E.2d 396 (1977) (restricted).

French, Imposing a General Survival Requirement on Beneficiaries of Future Interests: Solving the Problems Caused by the Death of a Beneficiary Before the Time Set for Distribution
27 Ariz. L. Rev. 801, 801-05 (1985)

This Article addresses the question whether state legislatures should abrogate the venerable preference for indefeasibly vested future interests by imposing a statutory requirement of survival. The conclusion is yes, *but* only if the statute also provides a satisfactory substitution of beneficiaries.

Over its almost four-hundred-year life, the preference for a vested construction has served a number of useful functions in future interests law. When contingent future interests were inalienable and destructible, construing interests as vested served the public interests in promoting alienability of property and in carrying out the donor's intent. Even after contingent interests became alienable and the destructibility doctrine had been generally abolished, the preference for a vested construction proved useful. It promoted marketability by reducing the uncertainties surrounding ownership. It also reduced the number of interests subject to destruction by the Rule Against Perpetuities.

By the middle of the twentieth century, most commentators agreed that these purposes had either become obsolete, or could be equally well served by other doctrines, like the "wait and see" or reformation doctrines in perpetuities law. Commentators began to call for a reevaluation of the rule favoring a vested construction. Several characterized the rule as archaic and without any rational justification. Although a few courts followed their lead, most did not. Within a few years, commentators began to appreciate the significant function the rule performs in avoiding incomplete dispositions.

By their nature, future interests create potential problems of disposition if the intended beneficiary dies before the time set for distribution. . . .

Distribution to the beneficiary's estate is often an attractive solution. When the beneficiary dies, the donor is usually not available to make another disposition of the property, so that a reversion may be an unsatisfactory alternative. The dispositive instrument may not clearly indicate which of the competing claimants the donor would have preferred if he had anticipated the beneficiary's death. Finding the interest a vested one permits the court to avoid admitting extrinsic evidence of the donor's relationships with the various claimants. It also allows the court to avoid writing a substitute gift into the dispositive instrument. Finally, the solution may be attractive because the court believes the donor intended this distribution, or because it avoids a distribution that the donor surely did not intend.

Although distributing the property to the donee's estate presents many attractive features, it is both cumbersome and costly. It is cumbersome because the probate process itself is cumbersome, and to make matters worse, the beneficiary may die long before the property becomes distributable. Too often, the future interest was not recognized as an asset of the beneficiary's estate, and a probate must be opened or reopened years later to receive and then distribute the property.

The process is costly for several reasons. First, the administrative expenses of the probate must be paid. Second, the value of the future interest is taxable as part of the beneficiary's estate. Third, it exposes the property to the claims of the beneficiary's creditors and the claims of forced or pretermitted heirs. Finally, litigation is often required to determine whether the instrument expressed or implied a survival requirement.

Imposing a general survival requirement on the takers of future interests avoids all of these costs. This Article poses the question whether general survival requirements should be imposed by statute. The answer reached is that general survival requirements should be imposed, but only if the current rule's function of providing a useful disposition is filled in another way.

If a statute simply imposed survival requirements without providing a substitute disposition of the property, a situation very much like that produced by the lapse doctrine would result. The lapse doctrine requires that all will beneficiaries survive to the date of the testator's death. The property intended for predeceased beneficiaries passes either to the surviving class members or to the residuary or intestate takers. This produces the same result as finding a reversion after a failed future interest. Widespread unhappiness with this disposition led to almost universal adoption of anti-lapse statutes in the nineteenth century. A similar reaction would surely follow the judicial or statutory imposition of a survival requirement if it did not provide an acceptable substitute disposition.

Notes and Questions

Professor French stressed the need to include an acceptable substitute disposition in any statute purporting to impose a general survival requirement on beneficiaries of future interests. Who should be the substitute takers? Should they be the predeceased beneficiary's descendants who survive the time of possession or enjoyment? What should the statute provide for in cases in which the predeceased beneficiary leaves no descendants who survive the time of possession or enjoyment?

Should the statute allow the transferor to override its provisions by stating in the governing instrument that no condition of survivorship is intended?

Should the statute apply only to wills? Only to wills and will substitutes, such as revocable inter-vivos trusts and life-insurance beneficiary designations? Or, should the statute apply to all future interests, even those created in irrevocable inter-vivos trusts? Should the statute be limited to trusts, or should it also apply to legal future interests?

California amended its probate code in 1983 to require survivorship to the point of possession or enjoyment, but repealed the amendment in 1984 before it became effective. See Cal. Prob. Code § 6146 amendments.

Statutes imposing a general survival requirement in the case of class gifts exist in Pennsylvania and Tennessee. See Pa. Cons. Stat. Ann. tit. 20, § 2514(5); Tenn. Code Ann. § 32-3-104. The Illinois statute, below, is not limited to class gifts.

Illinois Revised Statutes
Chapter 110 1/2

§ 4-11. Legacy to a deceased legatee. Unless the testator expressly provides otherwise in his will, (a) if a legacy of a present or future interest is to a descendant of the testator who dies before or after the testator, the descendants of the legatee living when the legacy is to take effect in possession or enjoyment, take per stirpes the estate so bequeathed; (b) if a legacy of a present or future interest is to a class and any member of the class dies before or after the testator, the members of the class living when the legacy is to take effect in possession or enjoyment take the share or shares which the deceased member would have taken if he were then living, except that if the deceased member of the class is a descendant of the testator, the descendants of the deceased member then living shall take per stirpes the share or shares which the deceased member would have taken if he were then living; and (c) except as above provided in (a) and (b), if a legacy lapses by reason of the death of the legatee before the testator, the estate so bequeathed shall be included in and pass as part of the residue under the will, and if the legacy is or becomes part of the residue, the estate so bequeathed shall pass to and be taken by the legatees or those remaining, if any, of the residue in proportions and upon estates corresponding to their respective interests in the residue. The provisions of (a) and (b) do not apply to a future interest which is or becomes indefeasibly vested at the testator's death or at any time thereafter before it takes effect in possession or enjoyment.

Notes and Problems

The 1990 UPC includes a new section (section 2-707), which provides a rule of construction on survivorship for future interests. Section 2-707 should be read in light of section 2-701.

If the following problems were controlled by the Illinois statute or by UPC section 2-707, what result?

G's will created the following testamentary trusts.

1. Income to my wife, W, for life, remainder in corpus to our child, A. A died before W, leaving descendants who survived W.

2. Income to my sister, S, for life, remainder in corpus to W if W is then living; if not, to A. W predeceased S. A also predeceased S, leaving descendants who survived S.

3. Income to S for life, remainder in corpus to such of her children as survive her; if none, to A. S left no children surviving her. A predeceased S.

    (a) Descendants of A were living at S's death.

    (b) No descendants of A were living at S's death.

4. Income to W for life, remainder in corpus to A if A is then living. G devised the residuary of his estate to X-Charity. A predeceased W, leaving descendants who survived W.

5. Would it make any difference in Problem 1 if the disposition provided the trustee with a discretionary power to invade the corpus on behalf of W? If so, what rationale? Is this statute applicable to inter-vivos transfers?

3. Avoiding Ambiguity in Express Conditions of Survivorship

The routine procedure in estate-planning practice is to impose express conditions of survivorship on the beneficiaries of future interests. This is done for basically the same reasons that prompt proposals for a statute imposing a survivorship requirement when the governing instrument expressly fails to do so. A future interest that passes through a beneficiary's estate is awkward, expensive, and subject to taxation under IRC section 2033. In addition, the absence of an express requirement of survivorship may lead to litigation concerning whether one is to be implied, litigation that may occur decades after the beneficiary's death.

The major advantage of the rule against implying conditions of survivorship—preserving a share of the estate for descending lines in which an ancestor predeceases the time of distribution—is easily accomplished by accompanying an express condition of survivorship with multiple-generation class gifts—future interests in favor of "issue" or "descendants."

Carelessly drafted, however, express conditions of survivorship can themselves be ambiguous and lead to litigation about their meaning.

Problem

At 9:15 p.m. yesterday evening, a tax partner in your firm came into your office, just as you were about to leave for the day. She asked you to examine a 38-page draft she prepared for an irrevocable inter-vivos life-insurance trust. Her client is scheduled to arrive at her office at 9:00 a.m. tomorrow morning to sign the trust.

The tax partner explained to you that the trust is a great device for this client because the client's life insurance policy that will be assigned to the trust has a face value of $6 million and a present value of $1 million. For purposes of the federal generation-skipping transfer tax, the trust will therefore have an "inclusion ratio" of 0, meaning that even though the corpus of the trust will far exceed the client's $1 million GST exemption under IRC section 2631, no generation-skipping tax will ever be incurred.[3] You acted as if you knew what the tax partner was talking about. (To find out, see supra p. 375.) She left to go home. You stayed.

You began reading through the trust. You noticed that the draft provides that after the settlor's death the trustee is to collect the proceeds of the life insurance policy, invest them, and pay the income therefrom to the settlor's son, Arnold, for life. So far, so good, you thought. Then you came to the provisions for the distribution of the corpus of the trust "upon Arnold's death." These provisions state:

(a)   To the surviving descendants of Arnold, by representation; or
(b)   If Arnold shall leave no surviving descendants, then to the surviving descendants of the Settlor, by representation; or
(c)   If the Settlor shall then have no surviving descendants, but he is survived by any of the descendants of his brother, to the descendants of his brother, by representation; or
(d)   If the Settlor is not survived by any of his descendants or by any of the descendants of his brother, to the surviving descendants of his father, by representation; or
(e)   If the Settlor is not then survived by any of the descendants of his father, to the Settlor's surviving heirs at law.

Finish the story. It is now 1:00 a.m.

Boone County National Bank v. Edson
760 S.W.2d 108 (Mo. 1988)

WELLIVER, J. Boone County National Bank brought this action to construe a will. They sought direction as to the proper distribution of a trust estate created by the will. Boone County National Bank is the trustee of a trust

---

3. See, e.g., Brody & Reilly, GSTT Planning Opportunities Continue After TAMRA, 128 Tr. & Est. 24 (May 1989); Blattmachr & Pennell, Adventures in Generation Skipping, Or How We Learned to Love the "Delaware Tax Trap," 24 Real Prop. Prob. & Tr. J. 75 (1989).

established by the Last Will and Testament of Margaret Poindexter Tello (Testatrix). The Boone County Circuit Court found the will clear and unambiguous. . . .

Appellants [Kathie E. Kalmowitz, Judith D. Edson, and Carol E. Thompson] appealed claiming the will, as written, contains a mistake creating an ambiguity. The Court of Appeals, Western District concluded that the will is ambiguous and reversed the judgment. No party disputes the awarding of costs and attorney fees to be paid out of the trust estate. . . . We affirm the trial court.

I. The Testatrix had her attorney write the will in question in 1960. The Testatrix died in 1971 and the will was probated.

The residuary clause of the will created a trust for the support of Lois Tello, Testatrix' daughter. The terms of the trust directed the trustee to pay the income of the trust to Lois and authorized the trustee to invade the corpus of the trust as necessary to properly maintain, support and educate Lois. The will provided for termination of the trust on the death of Lois.

The conditions and directions for distribution of the remaining trust corpus and any undistributed income are set out in paragraph III-G of the will. It provides as follows:

> This trust shall terminate upon the death of my said daughter. At such time my Trustee is directed to pay over all of the remaining corpus of the trust, together with any undistributed income, to the child or children of my said daughter, if she dies with children her surviving, to be divided among her said children in equal shares per stirpes and not per capita. In the event that my said daughter dies without children her surviving, I give, devise and bequeath all of the remaining corpus and undistributed income to my sisters, Jessie P. Moore, of Harlowton, Montana, and Dorothy Edson, of Harlowton, Montana, in equal shares. In the event that my sister, Jessie P. Moore, predeceases me, I desire that her share go to my other sister, Dorothy Edson. In the event that the said Dorothy Edson predeceases me, I give, devise and bequeath her share to her granddaughters, Carol Jane Edson, Kathie Margaret Edson, and Judith Dorothy Edson, or to their survivor, in equal shares.

For convenience and clarity, a diagram of the family relationships follows:

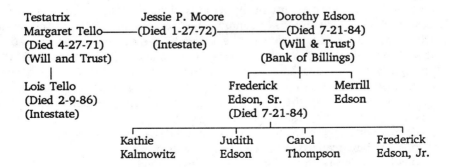

The question presented to us is whether or not the language used in the dispositive provision is ambiguous—that is, did Testatrix intend to use the pronoun "me" in the last two sentences of paragraph III-G or to use the pronoun "her" or the name "Lois."

The Testatrix died in 1971. She was survived by both of her sisters, Jessie P. Moore and Dorothy Edson, and Lois. Jessie P. Moore died intestate in 1972 leaving no spouse or children. Dorothy Edson died testate in 1984 prior to the death of Lois. Dorothy had two sons, Frederick Edson, Sr. (deceased) and Merrill Edson (respondent herein). Frederick was survived by four children, Frederick M. Edson, Jr., and appellants Kathie E. Kalmowitz, Judith D. Edson, and Carol E. Thompson.

Dorothy Edson, by her will, left all of her residuary estate to respondent First Interstate Bank in trust for the benefit of her four grandchildren. She specifically excluded her son, Merrill.

Lois Tello died intestate in 1986 and the trust for her benefit terminated. She was not survived by a spouse or any children.

The deposition of the drafting attorney was taken and offered and was ruled by the trial court to be inadmissable in this proceeding. Relying solely on his memory and not on notes or written memorandums, the attorney testified that it was his memory that the Testatrix intended that either "her" or the name "Lois" should have been used instead of the pronoun "me." He also testified that after the will was typed, it was given to Testatrix to carefully be read before signing.

II. The opposing parties each filed motions for summary judgment after discovery. Each motion incorporated by reference the deposition testimony of the attorney who drafted Testatrix' will. . . .

If the last two sentences of paragraph III-G were construed to read the pronoun "her" or the name "Lois" instead of the pronoun "me," the entire trust corpus would be distributed to appellants Kathie E. Kalmowitz, Judith D. Edson, and Carol E. Thompson, in equal shares.

Our scope of review is established by Murphy v. Carron, 536 S.W.2d 30, 32 (Mo. banc 1976). The judgment must be sustained unless there is no substantial evidence to support it, unless it is against the weight of the evidence, unless it erroneously declares the law or unless it erroneously applies the law.

III. Appellants contend that the trial court erred in overruling their motion for summary judgment. Appellants virtually assume that it was the Testatrix' intent to use the pronoun "her" or the name "Lois", either of which would tie distribution of the assets to the death of Lois instead of the death of the Testatrix. Having so assumed, appellants find the ambiguity which they assert requires construction of the will, and, they then argue that proper construction requires that the court substitute either the pronoun "her" or the name "Lois" in lieu of the pronoun "me" in the last two sentences of paragraph III-G.

One of our rights most sacredly guarded by the law is our right to dispose of our property after death by a will prepared and executed prior to death. To assure the integrity of the instrument, we require formal and verified execution of the instrument. To assure all who would make wills that their intent can and will be carried out following their death, of necessity, we must impose the most strict rules of construction. This we believe the Missouri Courts have done throughout the history of our state. . . .

If a will expresses the intention of the testatrix in clear and unequivocal language, there can be no occasion for construction of the instrument. The courts will not rewrite a will under the guise of construction.

In no case may words be transposed, supplied, substituted or otherwise omitted where the meaning is plain and unambiguous, and any alteration of the language originally employed would create a meaning different from that which it naturally had when the will was written.

The court cannot give the language used a different meaning for the purpose of carrying into effect a conjecture or hypothesis of the testatrix' intention, by supplying or rejecting words.

A. Appellants contend that the trial court misconstrued the will when it failed to substitute the intended pronoun to correct a mistake made by the draftsman. In construing a will, a court cannot correct a mistake made by the draftsman, unless the mistake appears on the face of the instrument, and unless it also appears what would have been the will if the mistake had not occurred. See Annotation, Effect of mistake of draftsman (other than testator) in drawing will, 90 A.L.R.2d 924 (1963). A mistake must be apparent on the face of the will, otherwise there can be no relief. Goode v. Goode, 22 Mo. 518, 524 (1856). Change "this doctrine, and you may as well repeal the statute requiring wills to be in writing, at once. Witnesses will then make wills and not testators." Id. We find the language used is clear and unambiguous on its face, and there is no justification for correcting possible draftsman's mistake. The trial court properly excluded the deposition of the drafting attorney.

B. The Testatrix provided for her daughter by establishing a trust for her care and support. It is clear from reading the will that Testatrix' intent was to provide for Lois. It also is clear the trust was to terminate upon Lois' death. It also is clear the Testatrix wanted the trust corpus to go to Lois' surviving children, if any, but to Testatrix' sisters if no children survived Lois.

Nothing in the will sheds light on whether Testatrix wanted further distribution tied to her death or that of her daughter, except the clear and unambiguous words which she used to tie further distribution to her own death. We can speculate that most people might have done it the other way, or that taxwise it would have been cheaper to do it the other way, but there is nothing on the face of the instrument to show an intent that it go other than by the words used, the words which she read before signing and the words which she signed.

The clear unambiguous words of the instrument mandate that the trial court be affirmed in all respects.

AFFIRMED.

Matter of Gustafson
74 N.Y.2d 448, 548 N.Y.S.2d 625, 547 N.E.2d 1152 (1989)

BELLACOSA, J. In concluding that appellants are not entitled to inherit under the relevant gift provision of this disputed will, we reaffirm two basic principles governing the adjudication of decedents' estates by courts: our primary function is to effectuate the testator's intent and the words used to express that intent are to be given their ordinary and natural meaning.

Testator executed his will in 1955 and it was admitted to probate in 1959. At issue is clause (c) of paragraph FIFTH, which bequeaths part of the residuary of one of two trusts to the "surviving child or children" of testator's brother Leonard, who predeceased the trust's life tenant, testator's widow, Elsie. A "surviving child" of Leonard, Jacqueline, is respondent before us and claims entitlement to the whole of that residuary portion. Appellants are the widow and children of Leonard's other child, Daniel (Jacqueline's brother), who, like his father, predeceased the life tenant. Daniel's children, as appellants, strive to take under paragraph FIFTH'S gift provision and urge the courts to construe the word "children" to include grandchildren so that the collateral descendants of the testator, i.e., the grandnephews and grandnieces, can partake of the testamentary plan. Since they are faced with the fundamental proposition that the word "children" will be given its ordinary and natural meaning unless the will as a whole shows an unmistakable intent that different or remoter persons or classes should be included, they argue that the one-time use of the word "issue" in a different, inoperative clause of the will creates ambiguity and warrants forsaking the general rule of construction. Daniel's widow, as separate appellant, seeks to inherit on an argument that his inchoate share vested in him prior to the death of the life tenant, Elsie, [and passed to her by intestacy from Daniel].

We affirm the order of the Appellate Division, 145 A.D.2d 979, 536 N.Y.S.2d 351, [which awarded all of Leonard's share to Jacqueline, and none of it to Daniel's widow or children,] because a construction which would substitute for the testator's chosen word a broader, judicially applied definition is unwarranted and would be unsettling to the law of descent and distribution. Further, the relevant vesting date can be only the death of the life tenant.

Carl V.E. Gustafson was 59 years old, married and childless when he died in 1959. He disposed of virtually his entire estate through two trusts of equal size with an integrated, complementary residuary plan. The trust established in paragraph SIXTH provided that testator's brothers, Leonard and Roy, were to be equal income beneficiaries, and upon the death of either of them his one-half interest in the trust (that is, a one-fourth interest in the residuary) would pass to "his child or children". When Leonard died in 1978, his children, Jacqueline and Daniel, took equally of Leonard's share in this trust. Roy continues his life tenancy in the other portion of this trust. The half of testator's estate reflected in this trust is not involved in this case.

This case and appeal revolve around the trust created in paragraph FIFTH of the will, in which Elsie, testator's widow, held a life estate. Upon her death, testator's will directed the corpus of this trust be paid as follows:

(a) One-half to my brother, E. Leonard Gustafson.

(b) One-half to my brother, Roy L. Gustafson.

(c) If a brother predeceases Elsie Warren Gustafson, then his share of this Trust shall be paid over to his surviving child or children, share and share alike.

(d) If one of my brothers shall predecease Elsie Warren Gustafson, without issue surviving, then his part of this Trust shall be paid over to his surviving brother.

Roy survived Elsie and took his share pursuant to clause (b). This, too, is not involved in the case.

At issue then is only the portion that would have been Leonard's one-quarter residuary share under clause (a), which, because of Leonard's predeceasing Elsie, must pass through clause (c). Leonard's son, Daniel, having also predeceased Elsie, leaves a widow and children who now seek to take a share of the residuary through this clause, though they are not "surviving child or children".

Courts construing donative instruments are governed by a threshold axiom: a testator's intent, as ascertained "from the words used in the will . . . according to their everyday and ordinary meaning", reigns supreme. . . . In Matter of Villalonga, 6 N.Y.2d 477, 484, 190 N.Y.S.2d 372, 160 N.E.2d 850), the natural and ordinary meaning of the word at issue here was held and applied as follows: "'[c]hildren' means immediate offspring, and we reiterate the rule of the [Matter of] Schaufele [252 N.Y. 65, 67, 168 N.E. 831] case that it will never be held to include grand-children 'unless the will as a whole shows that unmistakable intent.'" (Emphasis added.) The will before us cannot clear that high hurdle.

The order of testator's priorities is straightforwardly expressed in paragraph FIFTH. First, he provided for his widow as long as she lived. Then, upon her death, his brothers would benefit (para FIFTH [a], [b]). If his brother(s) predeceased his widow, then the focus of testator's beneficial intent shifted to the "surviving child or children" of his brother(s) (para FIFTH [c]), a generation proximate to himself. The final subdivision of this paragraph provides that if a brother dies "without issue surviving", the surviving brother takes all. Thus, if neither issue nor children survived one brother, the other brother (or his children or his issue) would take to prevent a lapse. Accordingly, from the four corners of the will's relevant gift provision, assigning to each word its ordinary meaning, the testamentary scheme is reasonably discernible. Carl Gustafson wanted to benefit: (1) his widow while she lived; (2) his brothers who survived his widow; and (3) if a brother did not survive his widow, then the brother's child(ren) who did so survive. Those preferences of the testator as to the order and distribution of his property are not "incoherent", "inequitable", "inconsistent" or "anomalous", but even if they were, testators are privileged to act in any way they see fit to displace the State's otherwise mandated, homogenous distribution by intestacy, so long as they are compos mentis. Courts, on the other hand, are not privileged to put contrary or even additional words into a testator's actual written expression in order retrospectively to effectuate their own notions of "fair" or "equitable" distribution of estates.

Prowitt v. Rodman, 37 N.Y. 41, does not support a different result. There, an exception to the plain meaning of "children" was allowed because "the testator intended that the remote descendants should be takers . . . *if there should be a failure of the immediate offspring of [the trust life tenant]*" (id., at 54 [emphasis added]; see also, Matter of Welles, 9 N.Y.2d 277, 280, 213 N.Y.S.2d 441, 173 N.E.2d 876 ["It seems to us that the only possible occasion justifying a more inclusive meaning (of 'children') would be to avoid failure of the estate."]). There is no failure of an estate here, which is the only justification for the exception to the paramount plain meaning rule of construction.

Nor is this case about the testator's intention to disinherit unknown, collateral descendants two generations removed from him. The law of decedents' affairs recognizes no rule requiring a testator to manifest an intent to disinherit in such circumstances. Rather, our rules relate to the testator's intent to bestow a gift and to whom. In that respect, he was plain, precise and orderly, and appellants' claim to a gift in this trust remainder by implication would wrongly extend the plainly expressed and universally understood words. Our ruling, therefore, is natural, not "narrow", and a faithful application of the holding of the governing precedent, not an "extension" of it. Simply put, children means children in the judicial construction of this will. . . .

We must also address the vesting date with respect to the remainder of the trust at issue. The death of the testator's life tenant, his widow, controls. Rather than "happenstance", this is the common measuring device for the orderly transferences of decedents' assets, a rule providing specificity, not serendipity. The vesting date here is arrived at by an application of well-settled principles of the law of future interests. The language of paragraph FIFTH (c) created a requirement of survival. When the first devisee or legatee takes a life estate, words of survivorship tend to "'establish the time of the termination of all preceding interests as the time to which survival is required'" (Matter of Gautier, 3 N.Y.2d 502, 509, 169 N.Y.S.2d 4, 146 N.E.2d 771, quoting Restatement of Property § 251, at 1266). Here, the preceding interest terminated only upon the death of testator's widow, Elsie, in 1986. Daniel's predecease in 1981 is irrelevant in this respect and precludes his heirs from asserting that any entitlements inchoately vested in him before Elsie's death to accrue later to their benefit.

As we have consistently held, the plain meaning of the testamentary language itself is the surest path to the judicial discernment of a testator's donative intent. Expanding the application of exceptions to that sound general proposition would soon swallow the rule and render less secure the effectuation of testator's relied upon, expressed intentions. Indeed, to create a new exception out of something called "paramount intent", different from the intent clearly expressed on the face of a will and in its only relevant donative provision, would be seriously unsettling because it would sacrifice predictability, an especially crucial element in the field of decedents' estates where "settled rules are necessary and necessarily relied upon". . . .

Accordingly, the order of the Appellate Division should be affirmed, with costs to all parties filing briefs payable out of the residuary trust at issue.

HANCOCK, Judge (dissenting). I would modify the order of the Appellate Division and hold that the term "children" in paragraph FIFTH (c) of the will includes grandchildren and, therefore, that Leonard's share must be divided equally between his son Daniel's surviving children, collectively, and his daughter, Jacqueline.

In my view, construing "children" narrowly here and, thereby, disinheriting the lineal descendants of one of the testator's brothers is unwarranted and represents a distinct—and unfortunate—extension of the "unmistakable intent" rule. In Matter of Villalonga, 6 N.Y.2d 477, 190 N.Y.S.2d 372, 160 N.E.2d 850, where we applied that rule and declined to read "children" broadly, we emphasized that: (1) the will there was "a simple one . . . and not afflicted with the weakness of ambiguity" (id., at 481, 190 N.Y.S.2d 372, 160 N.E.2d 850), (2) "[t]here [was] no interchangeable use made of the terms 'children' and 'issue' " (id., at 481, 190 N.Y.S.2d 372, 160 N.E.2d 850), and (3) "[n]or [did] the general distributive scheme disclose a testamentary purpose to benefit children of predeceased immediate offspring together with surviving immediate offspring" (id.). Those very factors—the absence of which led our court to construe "children" narrowly in *Villalonga*—are present in this case.

The will here is ambiguous. The ambiguity arises, in part, from the interchangeable use of the terms "children" and "issue" in paragraph FIFTH. Also, the use of "issue" in paragraph FIFTH (d) manifests a clear intention to benefit a predeceasing brother's surviving lineal descendants—not just the brother's immediate offspring as a narrow reading of "children" in paragraph FIFTH (c) suggests. Moreover, the intent of the testator as indicated by the language and structure of the entire will seems straightforward: to make gifts to his brothers or their respective family lines, treating them equally. Indeed, there is nothing in the testamentary scheme to suggest that the testator wanted to disinherit the family of his brother's son (Daniel's family), in favor of that brother's other child (Jacqueline), on the seemingly unrelated and meaningless contingency of his brother's son predeceasing his widow.

Significantly, the *Villalonga* court itself reaffirmed the well-established exception to the rule it applied, viz., that where uncertainty exists, "children" should be given a broad construction to avoid an inequitable result (id., at 482-483, 190 N.Y.S.2d 372, 160 N.E.2d 850). Quoting Matter of Paton, 111 N.Y. 480, 486, 18 N.E. 625, our court reiterated that, "[o]f course, if the language employed 'is equally susceptible of one or another interpretation, we should, on every principle of right, and within the spirit of the authorities, give it that which is most equitable and consonant with the dictates of justice' " (6 N.Y.2d, at 484, 190 N.Y.S.2d 372, 160 N.E.2d 850 [emphasis added]. Accordingly, we should construe "children" in paragraph FIFTH (c) as "issue" and, thereby, avoid an incoherent interpretation of paragraph FIFTH (c) and (d) and, at the same time, avoid the patent inequity which otherwise results.

The majority's attempt to reconcile paragraph FIFTH (c) and (d) avoids neither problem. Nor does it withstand scrutiny. Paragraph FIFTH (d) cannot fairly be read—as the majority contends—as providing that, "if neither issue nor children survived one brother, the other brother (or his children or his issue) would take to prevent a lapse." Plainly, the language of paragraph FIFTH (d) does not so provide. It does no more than give the share of the estate in question to the "surviving brother" if the other dies "without issue surviving". There is no language in paragraph FIFTH (d) itself that directs or permits "issue" (or "children") to take. Only paragraph FIFTH (c) can be read as providing for that, and then, only if "children", as used by the testator, is construed to mean "issue".

Indeed, the majority's contention, that paragraph FIFTH (d) permits a devise to a brother's "issue" under certain circumstances, plainly undercuts their position and supports the view taken here. Their contention necessarily recognizes the basic point that "issue" (i.e., children of deceased children) were intended to be beneficiaries in some situations. But because, as noted, such a disposition cannot be effected under paragraph FIFTH (d), it follows that it can only be made under paragraph FIFTH (c)—i.e., by construing "children" in paragraph FIFTH (c) broadly as permitting "issue" to take.

Similarly, other provisions in the will either make little sense or run counter to the testator's over-all design if "children" is narrowly construed. For example, the distribution under paragraph SIXTH, providing for the direct gifts to the testator's two brothers,[4] would have failed if one of them had died with grandchildren or other issue, but with no surviving immediate offspring. And the very same would be true for paragraph EIGHTH—which was explicitly intended to cover any bequest elsewhere in the will that might fail.[5] Under that paragraph, as under paragraphs FIFTH and SIXTH, if "children" is read narrowly, there would be no provision for the very real contingency of a brother dying with no surviving sons or daughters, but with grandchildren or other lineal descendants still alive. Thus, paragraph EIGHTH, intended to avoid intestacy, would actually have permitted intestacy if read strictly.

I would resolve the ambiguities, and avoid the otherwise resulting inconsistencies and anomalies in the will, by broadly construing "children" to mean "issue". Such a construction would, in my view, yield the most reasonable and fair result—i.e., permitting Leonard's son's family (Daniel's family) as well as Leonard's daughter (Jacqueline) to share in the estate—and, thereby, avoid the certainly unintended inequity of depriving Daniel's children on the mere happenstance that their father died before

---

4. Paragraph SIXTH (e) provides: "If a brother predeceases me, then his share of the Trust provided hereby shall be paid over to his child or children, share and share alike."

5. Paragraph EIGHTH provides: "If any Trust or Legacy hereunder shall be voided; or, if any intestacy develops . . . then such legacy or intestacy shall be . . . paid over to my brothers . . . or to the child or children of a deceased brother, share and share alike."

their great uncle's widow. Finally, construing "children" broadly would, thus, give effect to the testator's paramount intent.

WACHTLER, C.J., and ALEXANDER and TITONE, JJ., concur with BELLACOSA, J.

HANCOCK, J., dissents in part and votes to modify in a separate opinion in which SIMONS and KAYE, JJ., concur.

Order affirmed, etc.

Notes and Questions

1. *Restatement of Property.* The court in *Gustafson* relied in part on the Restatement of Property for the proposition that words of survivorship relate to the time of termination of all preceding interests—the death in 1986 of Carl Gustafson's widow, Elsie. The Restatement provides:

> § 251. *Time to Which Survival Is Required by Added Word, Phrase or Clause.* In a limitation purporting to create a remainder or an executory interest, a description of the intended takers as persons "who survive," or who are "living," or by other language of the same import, but which fails to designate the time to which such takers must survive, tends to establish the time of the termination of all preceding interests as the time to which survival is required.

Comment e states that this constructional preference "is a strong one," but also notes that it is opposed "by the preference for early indefeasibility." Consequently, when the preference is "reinforced by a special context indicating survival of a testator as the only survival intended, the tendency stated in this Section is overcome."

2. *Survival of the Time of Substitution?* The dissenting judge in *Gustafson*, Judge Hancock, expressed concern about the outcome of the case, as decided by the majority. Judge Hancock thought that "disinheriting the lineal descendants of one of the testator's brothers is unwarranted and represents a distinct—and unfortunate—*extension* of the 'unmistakable intent' rule." To prevent the disinheritance of Daniel's family, Judge Hancock unsuccessfully argued that "children" should be construed to mean "issue."

Is there another means of preventing the disinheritance of Daniel's family, which Judge Hancock did not notice? Note the order of deaths as between Daniel and his father, Leonard. Daniel died in 1981. Leonard died in 1978. Could the word "surviving" in clause (c) have been held to have related to the time of Leonard's death rather than to the time of Elsie's death? In Will of Colman, 253 Wis. 91, 33 N.W.2d 237 (1949), G's will created a trust, income to her husband, H, for life, remainder in corpus to the couple's children; "but if any of our children predeceases H, that child's share to go to that child's surviving children." G and H had two children, A and B. A survived H. B predeceased H, leaving two children (X and Y) living at B's death. X predeceased H; Y survived H.

The court held that X did not lose his interest by his death before the income beneficiary, H. The word "surviving" required survivorship of B but not of H. The court said:

> The general rule is that when a vested interest is divested by a condition subsequent, such interest immediately vests in the substitutionary legatees unless the will expressly provides otherwise. . . . Once the remainder vested in the children of any of the . . . primary beneficiaries, it was no longer subject to be divested. The law favors a vested rather than a contingent estate; and an absolute rather than a defeasible estate; and a vesting at the earliest possible period.

3. *Survival of the Testator.* Comment e to Restatement section 251, supra Note 1, states that the preference for early indefeasibility, if reinforced by a special context, can overcome the presumption that words of survivorship relate to the termination of all preceding interests. In such a case, words of survivorship can be found to relate to the death of the testator.

A case adopting this construction is Nass's Estate, 320 Pa. 380, 182 A. 401, 114 A.L.R. 1 (1936). George Nass, Sr., died in 1895, leaving a will that disposed of his residuary estate in trust, the income from which was given to his wife for life. On the death of his wife, the trust was to be divided into four equal parts. One part was given to his son, George, absolutely. A half of each of the remaining three parts was given absolutely to each of his daughters, Mary, Amanda, and Julia. The other halves of the remaining three parts were continued in trust, with the income to be paid equally to each of the daughters for life. Upon the death of each daughter, the portion of the principal from which she had been receiving income was to go that daughter's child or children. Nass's will continued:

> In case of the decease of my said Daughters or either of them without leaving lawful issue then and in such case I give devise and bequeath the said part or share hereinbefore given, devised and bequeathed to the said Executors In Trust unto my surviving child or children absolutely and forever.

Nass's wife died in 1915. Mary, one of the daughters, died in 1913 leaving a child who survived Mary (and presumably Nass's wife, also). George died in 1924, leaving issue. Amanda died in 1934, leaving a husband but no children. Julia, the only child still living, claimed the one-eighth share of the principal from which Amanda had been receiving the income. The court rejected Julia's claim, saying:

> Our rule of construction applied to survivorship has been held to refer to the time of death of the testator unless a contrary intent appears in the will. The rule is not without sound reason, for its general effect is to distribute the property among all of testator's descendants rather than to shunt it off into one line where it may pass out of the family. It is apparent that in this case any other construction would work an inequality which would not carry out what was presumably testator's scheme. He intended to treat, not only his own children alike, but his children's children, and no other thought appears in the will. He intended an equal division of his estate among his issue, and

the repeated use of the word "equal" throughout his will is a clear demonstration of this fact. "Where the will shows an intention that the descendants of deceased children shall take, and an evident intention of equality of distribution is manifested, the word "survivors" has been held to apply to the death of the testator." Page on Wills (2d Ed.) p. 1562. If testator's intent be considered otherwise, it results in giving the entire fund to one child, Julia, whose life has been prolonged beyond the lives of the other children, and would tend to prefer her and her heirs over the heirs of other children. . . . Nor is the fact that the person to whom the prior estate is given, though his death is to precede the ultimate limitation, is himself a party entitled to share, sufficient to show an unequivocal intention that he was not to take upon the happening of the contingency.

4. *Question.* Does the Restatement's preference for construing ambiguous words of survivorship as relating to the termination of all preceding interests make more sense when the future interest is to a multiple-generation class such as "issue" or "descendants" than when the future interest is to a single-generation class such as "children" or "nieces and nephews"?

5. *Uniform Probate Code.* If *Gustafson* (supra p. 916), *Colman* (supra Note 2), and *Nass* (supra Note 3) had been governed by UPC section 2-707 (1990), what result?

6. *Problem.* In Smith v. Cockrill, 170 Va. 423, 196 S.E. 681 (1938), Benjamin F. McConchie's will devised certain real property to his daughter, Sarah, for life, remainder in fee simple to the testator's two other children, Mary and James. The will continued:

> But should Mary . . . or James . . . die before Sarah . . . , then his or her one-half . . . is to go to their children to be divided equally amongst their children that may be living at the death of Sarah. . . . And if either Mary . . . or James . . . should die before Sarah . . . without issue, then their one-half interest is to go to my surviving child in fee simple.

First Mary died, then James. James died intestate, apparently without ever having married; he never had any children. Mary was survived by her son, Max. Max also predeceased Sarah, leaving five children, all of whom survived Sarah. It is not clear whether Max survived James. Sarah left the residue of her estate to Rosa E. Smith.

The court held that Max's five children were entitled to the property at Sarah's death:

> We have, therefore, arrived at the conclusion that after the death of Mary . . ., her interest passed to her son, Max . . . , and upon his death and the death of the life tenant, Sarah . . . to his children . . . ; and that upon the death of James . . . his share likewise passed to [Max's five children], they taking the share which Mary . . . would have been entitled to. Rosa E. Smith takes no share of the realty under the will of Sarah. . . . [Benjamin McConchie] wanted to keep it in the family, so to speak.

Does the court's conclusion deserve to be supported with any greater rigor than this? *Can* it be supported with any greater rigor than this? If the case had been governed by UPC section 2-707 (1990), what result?

Assuming the outcome reached by the court carried out Benjamin McConchies's intent, how could the disposition have been drafted so that no litigation would have been required to determine its meaning? How about "to Sarah for life, then to my descendants who survive Sarah, by representation;[6] if none of my descendants survives Sarah, to . . ."?

4. Age Specifications

Dispositions in trust frequently link a beneficiary's right to income or to possession or enjoyment of principal to reaching a specified age. As the following materials demonstrate, age specifications must be drafted with great care. If carelessly drafted, ambiguities in an age specification will probably be resolved by application of various rules of construction that sometimes conflict in a given case. The analysis is likely to begin with the rules of construction laid down in an ancient English case called Clobberie's Case, 2 Vent. 342, 86 Eng. Rep. 476 (Ch. 1677). The full report in this case appears as follows:

> In one *Clobberie's* case it was held, that where one bequeathed a sum of money to a woman, at her age of 21 years, or day of marriage, to be paid unto her with interest, and she died before either, that the money should go to her executor; and was so decreed by my Lord Chancellor Finch.
>
> But he said, if money were bequeathed to one at his age of 21 years; if he dies before that age, the money is lost.
>
> On the other side, if money be given to one, to be paid at the age of 21 years; there, if the party dies before, it shall go to the executors.

The staying power of the constructional rules established in *Clobberie's Case* is remarkable. The Restatement 2d of Property section 27.3 tells us that they are still to be followed:

> *Comment f. Age requirement specified.* . . . The language of the disposition that indicates the age requirement is not a condition but is only a description of the time to which distribution is delayed is when the gift is to the class members "to be paid to each class member at 21" or "when they attain 21 with income in the meantime." If the gift is to the class members "who attain 21," the age requirement is clearly a condition.

See also Restatement of Property §§ 257-59.

---

6. The will should also include a definition of the term "by representation." Cf. UPC § 2-709 (1990).

In re Parker
L.R. 16 Ch. Div. 44 (1880)

[The testator, Mary Elizabeth Parker, died in 1863, leaving a will that devised the residue of her estate in trust, the terms of which were described by the court as follows:

> upon trust to pay the dividends, interest, and income thereof, or such part thereof as my said trustees for the time being shall from time to time deem expedient, in and towards the maintenance and education of my children until my said children shall attain their respective ages of 21 years; and from and immediately after their attaining their respective ages of twenty-one years, then upon trust to pay, assign, and transfer the said stocks, funds, and securities to my said children in equal shares, if more than one, and if but one, then to such one child; and as to each daughter's share, whether original or accruing, upon trust to settle the same," for the benefit of herself and her children. And the testatrix declared "that it shall be lawful for the trustees or trustee for the time being of this my will to assign, transfer, or dispose of any component part, not exceeding one half of the presumptive share of any of my children for the preferment or advancing in life, or preparing for business, or on the marriage of any such child (being daughters) notwithstanding their minorities.

The testator was survived by her two sons and a daughter. One of the sons died in 1873, under the age of 21. The daughter and the other son both reached 21.]

JESSEL, M.R. . . . In my opinion, when a legacy is payable at a certain age, but is, in terms, contingent, the legacy becomes vested when there is a direction to pay the interest in the meantime to the person to whom the legacy is given; and not the less so when there is superadded a direction that the trustees "shall pay the whole or such part of the interest as they shall think fit." But I am not aware of any case where, the gift being of an entire fund payable to a class of persons equally on their attaining a certain age, a direction to apply the income of the whole fund in the meantime for their maintenance has been held to create a vested interest in a member of the class who does not attain that age.

The words here are plain. The trust is of residue: "to pay the dividends, interest, or income thereof, or such part thereof as my said trustees for the time being shall from time to time deem expedient, in or towards the maintenance and education of my children, until my said children shall attain their respective ages of twenty-one years"; so that there is nothing here giving an aliquot share of income to any individual child; the direction being to pay the income of the whole fund in such shares as the trustees shall think fit. I do not think you can infer anything from the direction for the settlement of the daughters' shares.

Then follows a gift of the whole fund to the children equally on attaining twenty-one. I should have felt no difficulty if it had not been for the advancement clause, which speaks of the "presumptive share of any of my children," but I do not think that clause is sufficient to alter the effect of the preceding part of the will.

That being so, I hold that the infant did not take a vested interest in his one-third share of the residue.

Clay v. Security Trust Company
252 S.W.2d 906 (Ky. 1952)

DUNCAN, J. This Declaratory Judgment action seeks a construction of the last will and testament of James T. Clay who died a resident of Fayette County in February, 1932.

The Security Trust Company qualified as trustee and executor under the will, and on January 5, 1952, filed this action in the Fayette Circuit Court. The Bourbon Agricultural Bank and Trust Company, executor under the will of Laura Clay Macey, deceased, Matthew D. Clay, Neal McClure Clay and Charles Wylie, executor under the will of John I. Macey were named defendants. From the construction adopted by the Chancellor, Matthew D. Clay and Neal McClure Clay appeal.

The will under consideration is as follows:

I, James T. Clay, of Lexington, Fayette County, Kentucky, do hereby make this my last will and testament.

First I desire my just debts and funeral expenses be paid.

Second I bequeath to Mrs. Gussie P. Rion, of Latonia, Kentucky, the sum of Ten Thousand ($10,000).

Third All the balance of my estate of whatsoever nature and kind I give to my sister Laura Clay Macey, which is to be held by my Trustee hereinafter named during her life, and the income therefrom is to be paid to her in monthly installments. I desire my Trustee to consult with my said sister in making change of investments of the said fund. At the death of my said sister, Laura Clay Macey, I direct my Trustee to hold the said estate until my nephew John Ireland Macey, the only child of Laura Clay Macey, arrives at the age of thirty-five years, and direct that the income shall be paid to him in monthly installments until the said fund is turned over to him.

I hereby give my Executor and Trustee power to sell and transfer any securities that it may hold for my estate and re-invest the proceeds in such securities or real estate as it may think proper. In the event that my Executor and Trustee should purchase any real estate, it shall have the right to sell the same for re-investment.

Fourth I hereby nominate and appoint the Security Trust Company, Lexington, Kentucky, my Executor and Trustee.

Witness my hand this 21st day of January, 1932.

James T. Clay

At the time of testator's death he was survived by his sister, Laura Clay Macey, two half-brothers, Matthew D. Clay and Neal McClure Clay, and his nephew, John I. Macey (John Ireland Macey), the son of Laura Clay Macey.

John I. Macey predeceased his mother, Laura Clay Macey and died in 1944 before he attained the age of 35. Laura Clay Macey died on February 8, 1951.

The property in question, now being held by the Security Trust Company in trust, consists entirely of personalty and amounts to approximately $42,000.

The sole question in the case is whether the remainder interest given to John I. Macey in the third clause of the will was a vested or contingent remainder. Appellees contend and the lower court found that the interest was a vested one and that the fund in question should be paid to the devisee under the will of John I. Macey. Appellants contend that the interest was contingent upon Macey attaining the age of 35 and that inasmuch as he died prior to his 35th year, the fund descends under the laws of descent and distribution and is payable to the heirs of James T. Clay.

We realize that precedent is not nearly so persuasive in cases involving construction of wills as in other cases. The paramount reason for that fact is that no two wills are exactly alike, whether phrased in the legal terminology of a trained attorney or in the simple and sometimes illiterate language of the testator. We, therefore, hesitate to say that the construction of any given will is absolutely controlled by any previous construction adopted by this court in considering some other will. Our primary concern is to determine, if possible, what the testator meant by the will under consideration.

Rules of construction are not intended as arbitrary means of fixing in every case the rights of parties under the will. However, most of the rules of modern usage are applied where the intention of the testator is otherwise obscure and because it has been determined that by their application the intention of the testator is more nearly reached.

One of the rules of construction of almost universal application is the presumption against partial intestacy. The rule is that where a will is susceptible of two constructions, the law favors that one which disposes of the entire estate. The presumption is even stronger where the will contains a residuary clause.

Another rule of equally general application is that which favors the early vesting of estates. All doubts will be resolved in favor of the construction which accomplishes an early vesting unless a contrary intention clearly appears.

Two other rules of particular applicability to the problem here presented are the following: (1) the absence of a gift or limitation over in the event of failure to attain a specified age is regarded as indicating an intention on the part of the testator that the gift should vest immediately; (2) a gift of the substance to which futurity is apparently annexed is not considered contingent upon the attainment of a specified age where there is a gift of the intermediate use.

In the case of Danforth v. Talbot's Adm'r, 46 Ky. 623, 7 B. Mon. 623, the court had before it for a construction a will the applicable portions of which were as follows:

7th. On the decease of my said wife, the above described farm, &x., &c., shall become the property of my son Cyrus, when arrived at the age of twenty-six years, (excepting the reservation in favor of Ann R.;) but after providing for the support and comfort of his mother, he may be entitled to all the profits arising from the same, except the reserved rights of his sister, Ann R.

In that case the court in a well-reasoned opinion held that the estate devised to Cyrus Talbot was not contingent upon his attaining the age of 26, but that the devise had the effect of merely postponing the time of enjoyment. There it was said:

> And although the event referred to, that is, the arrival of the son at the age of twenty-six, must, when abstractly and precisely considered, be regarded as uncertain and contingent, must it be assumed to have been so regarded by the testator? He evidently did not regard it as contingent. He speaks of it as a thing certainly to happen. He does not even say, "if" he shall arrive, &c., but "when" arrived at the age of twenty-six years; and he makes no devise over upon the event not happening, as he would almost certainly have done if he had regarded the happening of the event as uncertain, or its not happening as a contingency which would give a different direction to the estate. . . .

In the same case the court recognized and applied the rules of construction noted herein which arise from the omission of a devise over upon Cyrus not attaining the age of 26 and the right given him under the will to the intermediate use prior to the time of full enjoyment.

We recognize that the opinion in that case was written more than one hundred years ago. However, that fact does not militate against the weight which should be accorded it if it is sound and the reasons supporting it are valid. . . .

For the reasons indicated, we are of the opinion that the construction adopted by the Chancellor was proper and the judgment is affirmed.

Note and Questions

Drafting Age Specifications. Normally, it will be desirable expressly to require survivorship to the specified age and to provide for alternative takers in the event of a failure to survive. In one situation, however, there may be reason expressly to negate a requirement of survivorship. This arises when the donor wishes to qualify an inter-vivos gift in trust to a minor child for the $10,000 annual gift tax exclusion allowed by IRC section 2503(c).

To qualify for the exclusion under IRC section 2503(c), the property must "pass to the donee on his attaining the age of 21 years, and in the event the donee dies before attaining the age of 21 years, be payable to the estate of the donee or as he may appoint under a general power of appointment. . . ." The custom in estate-planning practice is to use the power of appointment option. But if that option is not chosen, then the governing instrument should clearly state that the death of the donee before reaching 21 does not extinguish the donee's interest. How would you draft the trust to accomplish this result? Should the instrument say "whether or not the donee lives to age 21," or should it track section

2503(c) and say "if the donee dies under 21, then the property is to be paid to the donee's estate"? See Browder, Trusts and the Doctrine of Estates, 72 Mich. L. Rev. 1509, 1522-28 (1974); Fox, Estate: A Word to be Used Cautiously, If at All, 81 Harv. L. Rev. 992 (1968); Annot., 10 A.L.R.3d 483 (1966).

5. Gifts Over on Death or on Death Without Issue

Possessory Interests. G's will devised real property as follows:

    (a) To A and his heirs, but if A should die, to B.
    (b) To A and his heirs, but if A should die without issue, to B.

G died and then A died without issue. B is still alive. Who is entitled to the property, B or A's successors in interest?

In Case (a), the usual construction is that the property goes through A's estate to A's successors in interest.[7] See Restatement of Property § 263.

In Case (b), the usual construction is that A's interest is divested in favor of B.[8] See Restatement of Property § 267. Do you understand the basis for the different constructions?

Woods' Estate
102 N.H. 59, 149 A.2d 865 (1959)

. . . . Elizabeth A. Luce . . . died in 1954. Clara E. Woods died December 30, 1956, and the administratrix was appointed January 5, 1957. Among the assets inventoried in the Woods estate was an undivided one-half interest in certain real estate in Keene.

This property was formerly owned by Mrs. Luce. In her will, after leaving $100.00 to her husband in lieu of all his rights in her estate, she provided that

> all the rest, residue and remainder of my property, whether real or personal, and wherever situated, I give, bequeath and devise in equal shares to my daughter, Jessie Evelyn Starkey, of said Keene, and my sister, Clara E. Woods, of said Keene. In case of the death of either the said Jessie Evelyn Starkey or the said Clara E. Woods, I give, bequeath and devise the share of such decedent to the survivor.

The administratrix of the Woods estate, Evelyn S. Deming, formerly Jessie Evelyn Starkey, claims that as daughter of Mrs. Luce she takes all her

---

7. In Case (a), of course, it makes no difference whether A died with or without issue.
8. The same result would be reached if B survived G but predeceased A; A's interest would be divested in favor of B's successors in interest. See, e.g., Hays v. Cole, 221 Miss. 459, 73 S.2d 258 (1954).

mother's real estate to the exclusion of Clara's heirs. In her petition, she asks us to answer the following questions: "(1) Did the said Clara E. Woods inherit in fee an undivided one-half interest in said real estate under the will of the late Elizabeth A. Starkey Luce? (2) In the event the foregoing question is answered in the negative, should the inventory be amended to exclude said one-half interest in said real estate from the estate of Clara E. Woods?"

BLANDIN, J. The basic question presented is whether Clara E. Woods took a vested interest in fee under the will of her sister, Elizabeth A. Luce, in certain real estate, so that upon her death it descended to Clara's heirs, Florence Cram and Doris Cocco, or whether it passed to Mrs. Luce's only daughter, Evelyn S. Deming. The answer depends on what the testatrix meant when, after bequeathing all the remainder of her estate in equal shares to her daughter and sister, she added the words: "In case of the death of either . . . I give, bequeath and devise the share of such decedent to the survivor." Although as administratrix of Mrs. Woods' estate, Mrs. Deming inventoried a "1/2 interest in Land and buildings" in the disputed real property, she presently claims this was error and that she takes it all as survivor under Mrs. Luce's will.

It is axiomatic that the law favors the early vesting of interests in the interest of certainty, the avoidance of complications, and the expeditious settlement of estates. Furthermore, the common meaning attributed to words of survivorship is that they refer to the death of the devisee in the lifetime of the testatrix. The practical difficulties of applying the construction urged by the administratrix, especially with reference to the disposition of personal estate, are obvious and militate against her claim. Furthermore, the words appear in themselves significant. Since death is certain, there seems no point in using the words "In case" unless they were intended to refer to the death of either of the devisees before that of the testatrix.

We are not unmindful of the administratrix's argument that Mrs. Luce's main concern was her sister, Clara, and her daughter, the administratrix, and that since she did not mention her brother, Samuel Luce, and another sister, Florence Cram, it must have been her intent that neither they nor their children should share in her estate. We agree that her real interest was in her daughter and her sister Clara, but had she been desirous of arranging matters so that no child of her brother or Mrs. Cram should take under her will, she could easily have done so.

In the case of Mulvanity v. Nute, 95 N.H. 526, 68 A.2d 536, cited by the administratrix, the will unequivocally expressed an intention that a joint tenancy be created. The testator gave certain property to his son and sister as "Joint Tenants" and stated that "upon the decease of one the title to vest in the survivor." 95 N.H. at page 527, 68 A.2d at page 536. He expressed the desire that his son and sister have the right to occupy the premises during their lifetime. The Court held that a joint tenancy in fee was created. It added that in order to establish the unusual estate of a life estate with remainder to the survivor, which is what the administratrix claims was created by Mrs. Luce's will, "clear and unambiguous language" would have to be used. Id. at page 528, 68 A.2d at page 537. See also

RSA 477:18. We find no such language in this will indicating an intent to set up such an uncommon estate, but rather it expresses a reasonably plain purpose to make a gift in fee to two persons with the survivor taking all if, but only if, one of them died before the testatrix.

In all the circumstances, we believe the testatrix, when she said "In case of the death of either," referred to death in her lifetime. Since this did not occur, it follows that Clara E. Woods took an undivided one-half interest in fee in the disputed real property which was properly inventoried as part of her estate.

Case remanded.

———

Future Interests. G's will created a trust, the terms of which were:

> (a) Income to L for life, remainder in corpus to A, but if A should die, to B.
> (b) Income to L for life, remainder in corpus to A, but if A should die without issue, to B.

G died, then A died without issue, and then L died. B is still alive. Who is entitled to the property, B or A's successors in interest? The usual construction in both cases is that A's interest is divested in favor of B.[9] See Restatement of Property §§ 264, 269.

G died and then L died. A is still alive. Did A's survival of L render A's interest absolute or does A's interest continue to be defeasible? The majority construction in both cases is that A's survival of L rendered A's interest absolute. See Restatement of Property §§ 264, 269. There is, however, division in the cases on the point, especially regarding Case (b). See Annot., 26 A.L.R.3d 407 (1969).

Definite versus Indefinite Failure of Issue. A further question exists in connection with the dispositions containing a gift over on death without issue. To reintroduce those dispositions, suppose that G disposed of property in her will as follows:

> (a) To A and her heirs, but if A should die without issue, to B.
> (b) To L for life, remainder to A, but if A should die without issue, to B.

After G's death, A died survived by issue. In Case (b), L was still alive when A died.

Does A's death survived by issue render her interest absolute or does her interest continue to be defeasible? The preferred and usual construction is that A's death survived by issue renders her interest absolute. See Restatement of Property § 266. This construction, called a "definite failure of issue" construction, is codified in several states.

An older construction, now nearly universally abandoned, is called an "indefinite failure of issue" construction. Under this construction, which is

---

9. In Case (a), of course, it makes no difference whether A died with or without issue.

the English construction carried over from the fee tail estate, A can still "die without issue" after her death. A's "death without issue" occurs if and when her last living descendant dies. See supra p. 873.

Accrued Shares. G devised a tract of land "to my three sons, A, B, and C; but if any son dies without leaving issue surviving him, the portion devised to such son shall go to my said sons then living."

After G's death, A died without issue; then B died without issue, leaving a will that devised his entire estate to his widow, W. Does C now own the entire tract of land? See Restatement of Property § 271. What happens to the ownership of the land if C dies without issue? What if C dies *with* issue?

PART B. SPECIAL PROBLEMS OF CLASS GIFTS

Class gifts are extremely useful in estate-planning practice, especially multiple-generation class gifts, such as to issue, descendants, or heirs. We are already knowledgeable about many of the features that distinguish class gifts from individual gifts.

In Chapter 5, we studied the definition of a class gift—how to differentiate a class gift ("to my children") from individual gifts ("to my three children, A, B, and C;" "to my three children;" "to my children, A, B, and C"). Chapter 5 also examined the effect of the death of a potential class member before the testator's death and the applicability of anti-lapse statutes in such cases.

Chapter 2 introduced us to the different forms of representation in multiple-generation class gifts—per stirpes, per capita with representation, and per capita at each generation. In addition, the status of adopted children and nonmarital children was also examined.

In Part A of this chapter, we studied the effect of a contingency unrelated to survivorship on a future interest in favor of a single-generation class; and we saw that a condition of survivorship is thought to be implicit in a multiple-generation class gift in which a representational form of distribution is called for.

What is left?

1. Increase in Class Membership: Class Closing and the Rule of Convenience

A unique feature of most class gifts (other than class gifts to heirs) is the ability of new entrants to join the class. Each new entrant increases the number of potential takers and partially divests the shares of the existing class members.

A class is subject to increase—subject to open—as long as it is possible for new entrants to come into the class. The ability of a class to increase ends—the class "closes" to further increase—at the *earlier* of two events: (1) the natural (or physiological) closing of the class; or (2) the artificial (or premature) closing brought about by the application of the so-called *rule of convenience.*

Natural (or Physiological) Class Closing. The natural closing of a class occurs when births (or, if adopted members are within the class description, adoptions) become physiologically impossible. A class gift in favor of a transferor's grandchildren physiologically closes upon the death of the transferor's last living child. A grandchild who is in gestation on the date the class closes is regarded as in being on the closing date.

The physiological closing of a class is traditionally predicated on the assumption that death terminates the possibility of having children. Recent medical developments have shown that the traditional assumption may not always be true. With frozen sperm, ova, and embryos on the contemporary scene, the possibility of having children can exist for years after death. Should a child produced after death be included as a class member? Although the law has not definitively solved this problem, the Introductory Note to Chapter 26 of the Restatement 2d of Property p. 131 states that such after-born children should not be included in the described class "because of the practical considerations of providing assurance for an indefinite period of time that a share in the class gift will be available for such after-born persons." The Introductory Note goes on to say, however, that these after-born persons will be included if the language or circumstances of the gift indicates that the transferor intends to include them. See also UPC §§ 2-108, 2-701, 2-705 (1990).

Of course, in the vast majority of cases, no frozen sperm, ova, or embryos capable of producing a post-death child exists, and the traditional assumption about the parent's death marking the closing of the class prevails and works well. When frozen sperm, ova, or embryos capable of producing a post-death child do exist, the courts or legislatures will probably abide by the Restatement 2d and presumptively close the class under the rule of convenience (see below) no later than at the death of the parent.

Artificial (or Premature) Class Closing: The Rule of Convenience. A class may close earlier than its physiological closing. When this happens, the class has been closed artificially or prematurely. Artificial or premature closing is governed by the rule of convenience.

The rule of convenience is a rule of construction, not a rule of law. It yields to a contrary intent. Although Earle Estate, below, illustrates this point, that case is unusual. In practice, a contrary intent can seldom be shown, and consequently the rule of convenience typically prevails.

Once a class has been closed by the rule of convenience, subsequently conceived or adopted persons are not entitled to participate in the class gift, even though they otherwise fit the class label. New entrants come into a class only if they are conceived[10] or adopted[11] while the class is still open.

Basically, the rule of convenience holds that a class closes when a class member becomes entitled to distribution of her or his share. This rule is founded on two basic premises. First is the premise that the use of only a group or class description indicates that *all* persons who fit the description—whenever born (or adopted)—were intended to share in the gift. In other words, the starting point is that the class was not intended to close until it closes naturally. Second, because of inherent difficulties or "inconveniences" in allowing participation by persons born (or adopted) after distribution, it is believed that the transferor, if she or he had contemplated these difficulties, would have intended to exclude these persons. That is, although the basic intent of the transferor is to keep the class open until it closes naturally, if inconveniences will arise from doing so, the transferor would prefer for the class to be closed prematurely or unnaturally, so that the inconveniences will be avoided.

The inconvenience of a class being kept open after distribution is that the distributees would not take an indefeasible interest. Instead, they would receive a considerably less useful defeasible one. Taking an interest that is subject to being partially divested upon the birth (or adoption) of additional class members would render the property less marketable and, if personal property, would require some device such as the posting of security to protect the interests of unborn (or unadopted) members of the class.

EXTERNAL REFERENCE. Restatement 2d of Property Chapter 26 & Reporter's Notes.

Immediate Class Gifts. As indicated, the rule of convenience comes into operation only if the class has not closed naturally by the time of distribution. In the absence of sperm or ova capable of producing a post-death child, an immediate testamentary devise to the children of the testator will not require premature closing. Similarly, a devise to the children of a person other than the testator will not close prematurely if the person

---

10. As indicated above, a child in gestation when a class closes is regarded as in being at that time. In administering this principle, there is precedent suggesting a rebuttable presumption that the date of conception was nine months before the date of birth. See, e.g., Equitable Trust Co. v. McComb, 19 Del. Ch. 387, 396, 168 A. 203, 207 (1933); In re Wells, 129 Misc. 447, 456, 221 N.Y.S. 714, 724 (1927). To enter the class, the child must be born alive and probably must be born viable. See, e.g., Ebbs v. Smith, 59 Ohio Misc. 133, 394 N.E.2d 1034 (C.P. 1979); Note, 70 Mich. L. Rev. 729, 735 (1972); Restatement 2d of Property §§ 26.1 comment c, 26.2 comment c.

11. With respect to an adopted child, the date of adoption, not the date of conception, is the significant date for inclusion in the class. See, e.g., Estate of Markowitz, 126 N.J. Super. 140, 145, 312 A.2d 901, 903 (1973) ("Born when? . . . Regardless of the time when an adopted child is physically born, he or she does not come into existence as a child of the adoptive parent [in the sense that the law equates the relationship of a biological child with that of an adopted child] until the effective date of the order of adoption."); but see Restatement 2d of Property §§ 26.1 comment d, 26.2 comment d ("By analogy to a child in gestation, a child who is in the process of being adopted is regarded as an adopted child during the period the adoption is in process." To be included in the class, the adoption must be "concluded within a reasonable time" after the closing of the class.)

predeceases the time of distribution. If the person is still living at the time of distribution, however, an application of the rule of convenience is necessary. When at least one member of the class is in existence, an immediate gift closes at the date the gift becomes effective.

> *Example 16.7:* G devised real property "to my grandchildren." When G executed his will, his only son A had a child (X). Subsequently, but before G's death, a second child (Y) was born. G was survived by his son A and by his two grandchildren, X and Y. No grandchildren were in gestation at G's death.
>
> Under the rule of convenience, the class remains open until G's death but closes at that time even though A is still alive and is therefore deemed to be capable of having more children. X and Y each take an undivided interest in one-half of the property in fee simple absolute. In other words, their interests are not subject to partial divestment in favor of any later born (or later adopted) child of A.
>
> Suppose that at G's death, A's wife was pregnant, and that G's third grandchild (Z) was born viable. Z would be considered to have been "in being" at G's death, and consequently he would participate in the class gift. So, X, Y, and Z would each take an undivided one-third possessory interest in the property in fee simple absolute.

In the above example, suppose that A's wife became pregnant with Z shortly after G's death, while G's estate was still in probate. Would Z be included in the class? See Restatement 2d of Property § 26.1 comment g & cases cited in Reporter's Note 6 at pp. 153-54.

There is an exception to the rule that an immediate class gift by will closes at the testator's death. If there is *no* class member then "in being," the class does not close prematurely, but remains open until it closes naturally.

> *Example 16.8:* G devised real property "to my grandchildren." At G's death, her son A was still alive, but A had no living children and none was then in gestation.
>
> The rule of convenience does not close the class at G's death. The class remains open until the death of A. *All* afterborn grandchildren, if any, are entitled to participate.
>
> Note, however, that if a child of A's had been in gestation at G's death, and if that child had been subsequently born viable, then the rule of convenience would have closed the class on G's death, resulting in that child having taken the whole property in fee simple absolute.

Specific-Sum Class Gifts. When a class gift grants a specific sum to each member of the class, as opposed to the more traditional type of class gift in which a proportional share of a fund or item of property is granted to each class member, the class closes when the gift becomes effective, whether or not any class member is then alive. If no class member is then alive, the class gift fails.

Problem

G's will created a trust, income to G's grandchildren until the death of G's last living grandchild, remainder in corpus to M-Charity. When G died, grandchild V and grandchild X were living. Subsequently, grandchild Y was conceived and born, then grandchild Z. To what portion of the income, if any, are the after-born grandchildren entitled?

It may help you in thinking about this problem to note that the Restatement 2d of Property section 26.2 comment g describes each income payment as a "postponed gift."

Earle Estate
369 Pa. 52, 85 A.2d 90 (1951)

LADNER, J. . . . George H. Earle, Jr., died February 19, 1928, leaving a will dated January 24, 1928. In that will he provided by the third paragraph of the Fifth Item of his will as follows:

> In the event that my estate, after the payment of taxes, shall at least amount to the net sum of Five Million ($5,000,000) Dollars or over, I give and bequeath to my Trustees in Trust for the benefit of each and every male child of my sons who shall by birth inherit and bear the name of Earle, the sum of One Hundred Thousand ($100,000) Dollars for each one of such male children. Said sum shall be held in Trust upon the same terms, conditions and uses as provided in Item Third in the trust for the benefit of my granddaughter Louise Dilworth Beggs, and in Item Fourth in trust for the benefit of my granddaughter Edith Earle Lee.

[Items Third and Fourth of the will established trusts for each of the named granddaughters for her life, then for her issue, each trust to continue until the expiration of 21 years after the death of the last surviving grandchild or great-grandchild of the testator who was living at his death. Upon termination, the corpus was to be paid to the issue of each granddaughter then living. If either granddaughter should leave no issue surviving her, the corpus of her trust was to fall into the residuary estate. The residue of the testator's estate was left in trust, the terms of which are not indicated, except that the two named granddaughters were not included, and the trust was to terminate as stated above for the trusts for the granddaughters.]

The reference to the other items of the will makes clear that only the *income* not the principal is given to these grandsons.

The sole question before us on these appeals is whether Anthony Wayne Earle, who was born July 11, 1949, i.e., *after* the testator's death, is entitled to have a $100,000 trust set up for him in accordance with the paragraph quoted.

[When the testator died, his net estate amounted to over $9,000,000. When Anthony Wayne Earle was born, the net value of the residuary trust was $6,842,766. 75 D. & C. 433, 435 (1951).]

. . . . The learned Auditing Judge refused [to set up a trust for Anthony Wayne Earle], holding that the provision of the will in question must be so construed to *exclude* grandsons born *after* testator's death, which ruling was confirmed on exceptions by the court en banc, Judge Bolger dissenting.

With all due deference to the learned judges of the court below, who are distinguished in their respective branch of the law, we must conclude they erred and the decree appealed from must be reversed. . . .

When we peruse the provision in question we see that the testator establishes a class composed of such of his grandsons as are born to his sons and defines the qualifications of members of that class explicitly by the words, "I give and bequeath . . . for the benefit of *each* and *every male* child of my *sons*, who *shall* by birth inherit and bear the name of Earle," etc. Analyzing this language it becomes clear that the phrase "each and every" is an emphatic way of saying "all" and can indicate only an intent that no son of his sons be excluded.

Next we note the testator adds to the phrase "each and every male child" the words "*of my sons*," which indicates *all* male progeny of *both* sons are intended to be included. The use of the plural becomes more important when we view the extraneous circumstances of the family situation from the testator's armchair. . . . The testator at the date of the will had two sons, George H. III, age 37 and married, who had three sons living at the date of the will and at the date of testator's death and one en ventre sa mere born thereafter on September 26, 1928, and Ralph Earle, 35 years of age, who though married had *no* children living at either the date of the will or of testator's death and none so far born since testator's death. Testator was on cordial terms with *both* of his sons for he designated both sons as co-trustees of the trust under his will. These circumstances confirm testator's intent to include any male offsprings of both of his sons whenever born. Certainly it is unthinkable that he intended to cut off sons of Ralph, his younger son, just because he had no sons *then*.

Significant also is the future tense indicated by the word "shall" in the phrase, "who *shall* by birth inherit and bear the name of Earle." To give effect to the future tense, it is reasonable to regard the testator's intent as including in the described class those born *after* his death as well as *before*.

It is equally clear that the motivating purpose that influenced these special bequests of income was pride in the family name and desire to have that name perpetuated by as many lineal male descendants of the *blood and name* as possible. To exclude grandsons that came within the described class merely because they happened to be born after the testator's death would do violence to the very purpose that actuated the gifts. To which may be added that normally if a testator has in mind individual members of a group he would describe them by name; therefore, when he uses a class designation he would seem to mean not only those known to him but all that may come into the class described unless there is some contrary intent manifested. . . .

We have examined the whole will to ascertain if there be any other language that impels such contrary intent and find nothing that compels a narrower construction of the testator's explicit language. . . . Our respect for the learned judges below requires us to examine the reasons advanced in the adjudication and the opinion of the court en banc which led the court below to a different conclusion.

Judge Hunter in his adjudication begins by applying the general rule of construction known as "the rule of convenience" which he states as follows: "that in the case of an *immediate* gift to a class, the class closes as of the death of the testator." However, unless the word "immediate" is understood to mean a gift of principal distributable at the testator's death, the rule is too broadly stated because the rule must be applied with due regard to its origin. As the learned Auditing Judge points out, this rule had its origin in the English case of Ringrose v. Bramham, 2 Cox 384, 30 Eng. Reprint 177 (1794), where the testator provided, "I also give to Joseph Ringrose's children £ 50 to every child he hath by his wife Elizabeth . . . I also give to Christopher Rhodes's children, that he hath by his wife, Peggy, £ 50 to every child. . . ." The court there said, "[I]f I am to let in all the children of these two persons born at any future time, I must *postpone* the *distribution* of the testator's personal estate until the death of Joseph Ringrose and Christopher Rhodes, or their wives . . . until I know how many legacies of £ 50 are payable." (Italics supplied.) It must be remembered this was an executor's account and the rule there adopted solved the very practical difficulty of reserving a sufficient sum to meet the contingency of an unknown number of future births, or in the alternative withhold *all* distribution for an *indefinite* period from other distributees presently entitled. It is to be noted also that the words of this testator "children that he hath by his wife" were of equivocal import so that the rule there adopted was no doubt a proper solution. . . .

In this case [,however,] the basic reason, which gave rise to the "rule of convenience" is *not* present. There is here no gift of principal to any member of the class in question that vested at testator's death. Aside from a few minor legacies given outright to nonmembers of the family by Item Second only *income* is given. No distribution is made of the principal to any family beneficiary and the whole of it is withheld until the date of the termination of the trust as hereinafter noted. Indeed, the learned Auditing Judge admits the reason giving rise to the rule does not here exist and frankly says,

> If this testator intended that the executors pay $100,000 [income] legacies to grandsons living at his death, and that the trustees of residuary estate pay similar legacies to the afterborn, it must be admitted that there is no practical difficulty in so doing. The residuary trust will remain intact until "the expiration of twenty-one (21) years after the death of my (the testator's) last surviving grandchild or great-grandchild living at the time of my decease." Distribution at the termination of the residuary trust will not be delayed, because it does not seem possible that the trust can terminate before the death of testator's two sons, when the class of grandsons will be complete.

It therefore serves no purpose to restrict words of futurity of the gifts here made to the period between the date of the will and testator's death because when such restriction serves no purpose, words of futurity are not to be restricted to date of testator's *death* but are projected at least to the *date of distribution* and it was expressly so held in Heisse v. Markland, 2 Rawle 274 (1830), and Austin's Estate, 315 Pa. 449, 173 A. 278 (1934).

That the rule should not be applied when the reason therefor does not exist has been recognized by . . . the Restatement of Property, Sec. 294, Comment Q, [which] indicates that the rule need not be applied to close a class at testator's death when distribution is not actually delayed. . . . This whether separate sums are given to each member of the class or an aggregate to the whole class: 2 Simes, Future Interests, 1936, Sec. 386, p. 151. . . .

We hold until the time fixed by the testator for the distribution of the corpus of his estate arrives, any son's male child born before that time who qualifies as a member of the class described in par. 3, of Item Fifth, cannot be excluded.

Decree reversed, costs to be paid out of the estate.

[The dissenting opinion of STEARNE, J., is omitted.]

—

Postponed Class Gifts. The basic principle of the rule of convenience is that a class closes when a distribution of the property must be made. Having applied this principle to immediate class gifts, we now turn our attention to class gifts in which distribution is postponed.

Lux v. Lux
109 R.I. 592, 288 A.2d 701 (1972)

KELLEHER, J. [Philomena Lux left the residue of her estate "to my grandchildren, share and share alike." Her will further provided:

3. Any real estate included in said residue shall be maintained for the benefit of said grandchildren . . . until the youngest of said grandchildren has reached twenty-one years of age.

Philomena was survived by one son, Anthony John Lux, Jr., age thirty, and his five children, whose ages ranged from two to eight. The youngest grandchild was born after the will was executed but before Philomena's death.

The court held that clause 3 created a trust for the benefit of the grandchildren, the corpus of which was to be distributed when the youngest grandchild reaches 21; the class of grandchildren should remain open until then. Next, the court turned to the meaning of the term "youngest," saying:]

There are four possible distribution dates depending on the meaning of "youngest." Distribution might be made when the youngest member of the class in being when the will was executed attains twenty-one; or when the youngest in being when the will takes effect becomes twenty-one; or when the youngest of all living class members in being at any one time attains twenty-one even though it is physically possible for others to be born; or when the youngest whenever it is born attains twenty-one. This last alternative poses a question. Should we delay distribution here and keep the class open until the possibility that Philomena's son can become a father becomes extinct? We think not.

We are conscious of the presumption in the law that a man or a woman is capable of having children so long as life lasts. A construction suit, however, has for its ultimate goal the ascertainment of the average testator's probable intent if he was aware of the problems that lead to this type of litigation. It is our belief that the average testator, when faced with the problem presented by the record before us, would endorse the view expressed in 3 Restatement, Property § 295, comment k at 1594 (1940), where in urging the adoption of the rule that calls for the closing of the class when the youngest living member reaches the age when distribution could be made, states:

> When all existent members of the class have attained the stated age, considerations of convenience . . . require that distribution shall then be made and that the property shall not be further kept from full utilization to await the uncertain and often highly improbable conception of further members of the group. The infrequency with which a parent has further children after all of his living children have attained maturity, makes this application of the rule of convenience justifiable and causes it to frustrate the unexpressed desires of a conveyor in few, if any, cases.

We hold, therefore, that distribution of the trust corpus shall be made at any time when the youngest of the then living grandchildren has attained the age of twenty-one. When this milestone is reached, there is no longer any necessity to maintain the trust to await the possible conception of additional members of the class. . . .

Problems

1. When do the classes close in the following cases?

(a) G devised real property "to A for life, remainder to B's children." G was survived by A, B, and B's child (X). A second child (Y) was born to B during A's lifetime. B's third child (Z) was born after A's death. B survived A.

(b) In Problem 1(a), suppose that by the time of A's death, no children had been born to B and that none was then in gestation.

(c) G devised property in trust, income to G's grandchildren, corpus to be equally divided among G's grandchildren when the youngest grandchild attains 21. When G executed her will, her first grandchild (V) had just been born. Subsequently, another grandchild (X) was born. G then died. After G's death, the following events happened, in the order stated: V became 21; another grandchild (Y) was born; X became 21; a fourth grandchild (Z) was born; Y became 21; Z became 21.

No further grandchildren had been born or were in gestation on Z's 21st birthday, but G's children were still living. G's youngest child, E, was a male, age 43; he was contemplating marriage to his 34-year-old female friend, F.

2. G bequeathed $90,000 to those of G's grandchildren who reach the age of 21. (This type of bequest probably would be in trust, and it might provide either for the accumulation of the income until distribution, or for its payment to the grandchildren as it is earned.)

(a) One of G's grandchildren had reached 21 before G's death. Does the class close when that grandchild reached 21 or when G died?

(b) None of G's grandchildren had reached 21 before G's death. Subsequently, the first grandchild (X) reached 21; there were two other grandchildren (Y and Z) then alive. Thereafter, Y died under 21. Then Z reached 21. When did this class close? Who are the ultimate takers and what are their shares?

(c) The income from the trust was to be accumulated and added to the corpus; each grandchild was to receive her or his proportionate part of the corpus upon reaching 21. G was survived by a daughter, age 30, and a son, age 24, both unmarried and childless. Shortly after G's death, the son married a college classmate and the daughter married a widower, age 45, who had two children by his previous marriage. The ages of the widower's two children were 19 and 21. G's son and his bride were childless, but planned on having a family. G's daughter adopted her husband's children. Is the class closed yet? See Silberman's Will, 23 N.Y.2d 98, 242 N.E.2d 736, 295 N.Y.S.2d 478 (1968);[12] Nowels Estate, 128 Mich. App. 174, 339 N.W.2d 861 (1983); Restatement 2d of Property § 25.4; Cal. Prob. Code § 6152; UPC § 2-705 (1990) (see supra pp. 139-49 for further discussion).

3. G bequeathed $90,000 in trust to pay the income to A for life, then to distribute the corpus to those of G's nieces and nephews who reach 21. (Again, the income after A's death, but before distribution of the corpus, might be either accumulated or paid out.)

(a) Prior to A's death, one of G's nieces reached 21. Does the class close when that niece reached 21 or when A died?

(b) None of G's nieces or nephews had attained 21 by the time of A's death. Subsequently, one of the nephews, X, reached 21. Two months after X's 21st birthday, a niece was born. Another niece was born fourteen months after X's 21st birthday. Is either of these nieces included in the class?

4. G devised land "to my grandchildren, but if any grandchild should die before attaining 21, her or his share to go to my then surviving grandchildren." G was survived by children and grandchildren. All of the grandchildren were under 21. Additional grandchildren were born after G's death. How many class gifts are created here? When do they close?

---

12. Discussed in Fetters, The Determination of Maximum Membership in Class Gifts in Relation to Adopted Children, In re Silberman's Will Examined, 21 Syracuse L. Rev. 1 (1969).

2. *Class Gifts to Heirs or Next of Kin*

Statutory References: *1990 UPC §§ 2-701, -711*

The terms "heirs" and "next of kin" have primary meanings that are fixed by statute. Historically, and technically, the two terms have different meanings. *Heirs* are identified by the statute of descent—the term refers to those to whom a decedent's *real property* descends on the decedent's death intestate. *Next of kin* are identified by the statute of distribution—the term refers to those to whom a decedent's *personal property* is distributed upon the decedent's death intestate. A few states still provide for different patterns of takers for real and personal property, but most states, by far, have consolidated the two patterns into a single statute, called a statute of descent and distribution. Consequently, in the vast majority of states, the pattern of intestate succession is the same for real and personal property.

The term "heirs" or "next of kin" is sometimes used in a non-technical sense, to mean children or issue. This usually arises when one or the other term is used interchangeably with children or issue, such as in the disposition "to A for life, remainder to A's heirs, but if A dies without issue, to B." See, e.g., Connor v. Biard, 232 S.W. 885 (Tex. Civ. App. 1921); Restatement 2d of Property § 29.1 comment d. By statute in Georgia, all "limitations over" to "heirs" presumptively mean children and the descendants of deceased children. See Ga. Code Ann. § 44-6-23, interpreted in Dodson v. Trust Co. of Georgia, 216 Ga. 499, 117 S.E.2d 331 (1960). See also N.C. Gen. Stat. § 41-6.

When the term "heirs" or "next of kin" is used in a technical sense, the class gift so created is not subject to open. Once the takers are determined, by application of the relevant intestacy statute, new entrants cannot later join the class.

Matter of Dodge Testamentary Trust
121 Mich. App. 527, 330 N.W.2d 72 (1982)

BEASLEY, P.J. This appeal is taken by various interested parties from an order of the Wayne County Probate Court directing distribution of the trust corpus of a testamentary trust arising under the will of John F. Dodge, deceased. The order was entered pursuant to a thorough and carefully drawn opinion prepared by Judge Willis F. Ward of the Wayne County Probate Court, in which he made findings of fact, conclusions of law and determination of claims.

John F. Dodge, an early and highly successful automobile manufacturer, died testate on January 14, 1920. His will, which was dated April 4, 1918, was admitted to probate in the Wayne County Probate Court. In his will, John F. Dodge created a residuary trust which [set forth comprehensive and lengthy provisions governing the distribution of the income among the testator's widow and four of his six children and their "issue." With respect to the corpus of the trust, Paragraph 20:14(h) of the will provided:]

> [U]pon the death of all of my said children, Winifred Dodge Gray, Isabella Cleves Dodge, Frances Matilda Dodge and Daniel George Dodge, then I direct my said trustees to convey my said estate to the heirs of my said children, Winifred Dodge Gray, Isabella Cleves Dodge, Frances Matilda Dodge and Daniel George Dodge, in such proportion as by law such heirs shall be entitled to receive same.
>
> The provisions I have made in this Will for my son John Duval Dodge, have been made after careful thought and deliberation on my part, un-influenced by any person or persons whomsoever, and I believe these provisions to be the most wise I can make for my said son, John Duval Dodge. I make this explanation in order that it may be known that I have given careful thought to the claims of my said son, John Duval Dodge, and in order that neither my wife, nor any of my children may be accused of having influenced me in reference to the provisions that I have herein made in regard to my said son.

John F. Dodge left surviving him his widow, Matilda R. Dodge (Wilson), and six children, John Duval Dodge, Winifred Dodge Gray (Seyburn), Isabella Cleves Dodge (Sloane), Frances Matilda Dodge (Van Lennep), Daniel George Dodge, and Anna Margaret Dodge. The first three children were born of testator's marriage to Ivy Dodge, who died in 1900, and the second three were born of his marriage to Matilda R. Dodge (Wilson). His widow, Matilda, remarried in 1925 to Alfred Wilson, and they adopted two children, Richard S. Wilson and Barbara Wilson (Eccles). Matilda, who died in 1967, is perhaps best known for her generous bequests which have become the site of Oakland University and the various Meadowbrook cultural events.

Winifred Dodge Gray (Seyburn) was the first-born offspring of John F. Dodge and the last to die in 1980. Her death in 1980 operated to terminate the residuary trust created under the will. Winifred Dodge Gray (Seyburn) had two children as issue of the Gray marriage, Winifred Gray Seyburn Cheston, born in 1917, and Suzanne Gray Seyburn Meyer, born in 1920. Winifred Dodge Gray (Seyburn) also had two children as issue of the Seyburn marriage, Edith Seyburn Quintana, born in 1923, and Isabel Seyburn Harte, born in 1924. These four children of Winifred Dodge Gray (Seyburn) survive.

Isabella Cleves Dodge (Sloane) died March 9, 1962, without issue, while a resident of Florida.

John Duval Dodge, who was substantially disinherited in his father's will, died in 1942, leaving a widow, Dora Dodge, who died in 1950, and a daughter, Mary Ann Dodge (Danaher), who survives.

Anna Margaret Dodge was born June 14, 1919, subsequent to execution of her father's will in 1918. She died intestate on April 13, 1924.

Daniel George Dodge died August 15, 1938, leaving surviving him his widow, Annie Laurine Dodge (Van Etten), and his mother, Matilda R. Dodge (Wilson).

Frances Matilda Dodge (Van Lennep) died in 1971, survived by her husband, Frederick L. Van Lennep, whom she had married in 1949. Also, she left surviving her three children, Judith Frances Johnson (McClung), born in 1941 as issue of Frances' first marriage to James P. Johnson, Jr., whom she divorced in 1948, Fredericka Van Lennep (Caldwell), born in 1951, and John Francis Van Lennep, born in 1952, all of which children survive.

Not mentioned in the will was testator's infant daughter, Anna Margaret Dodge, she having been born June 14, 1919, a year after execution of the will. She took as a pretermitted heir, i.e., the same share she would have received if the testator died intestate. However, she died intestate at age five in 1924, and the devolution of her property was affirmed in In re Dodge's Estate, 242 Mich. 156, 218 N.W. 798 (1928).

John Duval Dodge attacked the validity of his father's will, which case was settled under a then newly-enacted statute authorizing such settlements, which statute was enacted largely as a result of this subject situation. Subsequently, in 1939, John Duval Dodge renewed his will contest and attempted to set aside the settlement agreement. The decision of the circuit court upholding the settlement agreement and rejecting the claim that the will and trust were invalid was affirmed in Dodge v. Detroit Trust Co., 300 Mich. 575, 2 N.W.2d 509 (1942).

In the within proceedings, a guardian ad litem was appointed to represent all unknown claimants to the trust and, after extensive discovery procedures, he reported that there were not any additional interested parties. On this appeal, we consolidate seven separate appeals (files), in some of which there are cross-appeals. We have reviewed at least 30 briefs which have been filed, varying in length from five pages to more than 80 pages.

At the outset, we hold that since the probate court order, which is the subject of all these appeals, affects the rights of the parties with finality, it is a final order, directly appealable to this Court.

In his splendid opinion, the probate judge discussed four issues of law and made detailed rulings cited to authority. First, he dealt with the meaning of the word "heirs" as used in paragraph 20:14(h) of the last will and testament of John F. Dodge, deceased. The issue arises because, in the termination provision of the testamentary trust, the testator said:

> . . . then I direct my said trustees to convey my said estate to the heirs of my said children, Winifred Dodge Gray, Isabella Cleves Dodge, Frances Matilda Dodge and Daniel George Dodge, in such proportion as by law such heirs shall be entitled to receive same.

The question is whether the word "heirs" was used in the will in its technical sense to denote those persons who inherit under the intestacy laws or whether "heirs" as used in the will was intended to designate only the "issue" or "children" of testator's children.

The cardinal rule of law and the predominant rule in the construction and interpretation of testamentary instruments is that the intent of the testator governs if it is lawful and if it can be discovered. This legal proposition finds support in many cases. Unless the will is ambiguous on its face, the testator's intention is derived from the language of the will.

In Brooks v. Parks,[13] which was decided in 1915, about three years prior to the date of execution of the Dodge will, the will in question provided in the residuary clause that one-half would go to a daughter during her lifetime and after her decease to her children and that the other half would go to another daughter during her lifetime and after her decease *to her heirs*. The Court upheld an interpretation that provided that the residue left to the second daughter would pass to her husband, saying that he was an heir of his wife and, as such, would inherit her half. In so holding, the Court declined to interpret the entire will as evidencing a contrary intent. Brooks is authority for defining the word "heir" as designating the persons appointed by law to succeed in case of intestacy and for holding that wherever the word "heir" occurs in a will, unaccompanied by qualifying or explanatory expressions, it must be allowed the meaning the law gives it.

We are satisfied that, in 1918 when the will of John F. Dodge was drawn and signed, the word "heirs" was a technical term with a well and clearly defined meaning, namely, those designated by the statutes of intestate succession to receive one's estate on death and that "heirs" included the spouse of the decedent.[14]

We note that the attorney drawing John F. Dodge's will appears to have been able and experienced in the practice of probate law. He was not a mere tyro, unfamiliar with common and accepted usage in legal circles of words used in the descent and distribution of property upon death.[15]

Thus, we ascribe to the word "heirs", as used in the subject will, its technical meaning as it existed in 1918 when the will was drafted and executed. We decline to conclude that the draftsman of the will made a "mistake" when he used in the will two different words, "issue" and "heirs". On the contrary, we believe that the attorney drawing the will used these two different words in their known, technical legal sense with the intention that the trust corpus descend differently than the trust income.

We acknowledge that a strong, visceral countering argument is made that the testator never intended that any part of his estate, either corpus or income from the testamentary trust, would pass outside of his bloodlines and that the testator intended that the natural objects of his bounty were those in the bloodlines, not spouses of his children, e.g. a son-in-law. At the outset, in weighing the merits of this argument, we note that the law does not permit that we indulge in speculation regarding the testator's intention. We look first to the will and only go beyond the language of the will if convinced that ambiguity is present. The fact that the testator named only his children and their issue to receive trust income, while leaving the residue of the trust corpus upon final termination to the heirs of his children, is not an indication of an ambiguity in the will. . . .

---

13. 189 Mich. 490, 155 N.W. 573 (1915).
14. Brooks v. Parks, supra; In re Shumway's Estate, 194 Mich. 245, 160 N.W. 595 (1916); Menard v. Campbell, 180 Mich. 583, 147 N.W. 556 (1914).
15. 61 Supreme Court Records and Briefs, pp. 346-361 (October Term, 1941).

Thus, we conclude that John F. Dodge did employ a skilled attorney in the preparation of his will, and that the words employed must be given their accustomed technical meaning according to common legal usage. In its legal and technical sense, the word "heir" is understood under established rules of decision as designating persons appointed by law to succeed in the case of intestacy. Wherever the word is employed unaccompanied by qualifying or explanatory expressions, it must be allowed the meaning the law gives it. We hold that the term "heirs", as used in the will, means those persons designated by statute to receive that class of property under the laws of intestate succession.

The second issue decided by the probate court was when should the remainder (corpus) interests of the heirs of the testator's named children vest. Should it be the time of each child's death, or should it be later at the termination of the trust upon the death of the last surviving child?

Unless a testator clearly and unambiguously states to the contrary, vesting of contingent remainders shall be determined as of the date of death of the ancestor. We decline to hold that testator's will in this case clearly and unambiguously established the time of vesting at the date of the termination of the trust. Consequently, we conclude that the date of death of the ancestor is the time of vesting of the contingent remainder interests in this trust.

This conclusion finds support in the case law. In re Jamieson Estate[16] is the leading case and is express authority for Michigan's preference for early vesting, the Court saying:

> [I]t has long been the law in Michigan that vested estates are to be favored, and that conditions of survivorship will not lightly be implied. . . . Indeed, we have characterized as a rule of property not to be disturbed the rule that when ambiguity exists whether a testator intended to condition a remainder-man's taking of an estate merely upon survival of the testator or upon survival of the holder of a precedent estate, the latter condition should not be implied. (Citation omitted.)

In Jamieson, the Court rejected the argument that vesting should be postponed until the time of distribution, saying:

> In the accurate use of language, only those entitled to inherit at the death of another can be called his heirs. Accordingly, unless a contrary intention appears, a gift in a will to the heirs of a person, whether he be the testator or a life tenant or another, will be construed as a gift to such heirs determined as of the time of death of that person.[17]

---

16. 374 Mich. 231, 237-238, 132 N.W.2d 1 (1965). See also, 3 Restatement of Property, § 308, p. 1706, which states that where there is a gift to "heirs", then the statute is applied as of the death of the designated ancestor absent evidence of an intent to the contrary.

17. Jamieson, supra, 374 Mich. at p. 251, 132 N.W.2d 1, citing New England Trust Co. v. Watson, 330 Mass. 265, 267, 112 N.E.2d 799 (1953).

Shortly before decedent's will was drafted in 1918, the Court in In re Shumway's Estate,[18] stated that only the clearest expression of a preference for delayed vesting would justify a departure from the rule favoring early vesting. In Jamieson, supra, the Court quoted Shumway with approval, saying:

> We conclude that unless a contrary intent is manifested, when a testator disposes of property to heirs, the heirs are to be determined upon the death of their ancestor. Such contrary intent will not be deduced from the bare fact that the heirs are secondary remaindermen. Nor will such contrary intent be found to exist simply because some of the testator's language may be strained into ambiguity, but rather "only plain, unambiguous language by the testator will prevent application of that rule [favoring early vesting] in construing a will."[19]

Shumway also indicates that there is nothing particularly unusual about giving trust income to certain life tenants and a non-possessory (remainder) interest to a class of heirs that could include the life tenants themselves.

In the within case, it is contended that the following circumstances suggest that the deceased would have preferred to postpone vesting until termination of the trust: (1) the deceased's express desire to postpone vesting beyond the date of his own death; (2) the indications that the deceased would not have wanted John Duval Dodge to take as an heir of the named life tenants; and (3) the potential for greater federal estate taxation under a theory of successive vesting. These speculations, while interesting, do not justify departure from the established rule favoring early vesting.

As indicated in Shumway, supra, the intention to postpone vesting must be manifested and tangibly expressed in such language as plainly conveys the thought beyond mere surmise, conjecture or supposition. We do not find such clear language in the will, plainly expressing a preference to postpone vesting until the termination of the trust. Postponing vesting beyond the date of his own death is no indication by the testator that he wanted to put it off as long as possible, until the death of his last surviving child which, in fact, turned out to be a period of approximately 60 years.

This is not a circumstance indicating any preference for vesting at the termination of the trust, as opposed to vesting on the dates of the respective deaths of the named children. Neither does the intention of the testator to exclude his son John Duval Dodge from significant[20] trust income during the life of the trust establish any intention to postpone vesting until the termination of the trust.

The argument in this regard is based on the very questionable assumption that the deceased did not even want John Duval Dodge to acquire any vested interest in the corpus of the trust as a possible heir of the four

---

18. 194 Mich. 245, 160 N.W. 595.

19. Jamieson, supra, 374 Mich. at p. 252, 132 N.W.2d 1.

20. The will directed the trustees to pay $150 per month to John Duval Dodge during his lifetime.

named children. The probate court properly rejected this argument that the deceased meant to prohibit John Duval Dodge from inheriting through his brothers and sisters as a contention based entirely upon speculation. The probate court correctly noted that "no language in the will expressly establishes this intention". Even if it were assumed that the testator did intend to preclude John Duval Dodge from taking as an heir of his siblings, the desire was not so plainly expressed as to warrant a departure from the established rule favoring early vesting.

Finally, the idea that the deceased planned to postpone vesting in order to avoid federal estate taxes is without merit. The will does not even refer to federal estate taxes and does not appear to show any concern for them. The federal estate tax was newly enacted in 1918, was quite modest by today's standards, and would hardly have played a major role in the drafting of the will.

In any case, if tax consequences led the testator to prefer to postpone vesting, he should have expressed this preference in clear language in the will. As previously indicated, we do not find error in the conclusion of the probate court favoring vesting as of the time of the death of each ancestor named in the will, i.e., the four named children of the testator.

The third issue discussed and decided by the probate court was whether the word "heirs", as used in the testator's will, should be defined according to the statutes of distribution in effect at the time of the death of each named life income beneficiary, rather than according to the statute of descent in effect at the testator's death. The probate court held that the statutes of distribution in effect at the date of death of the immediate ancestor should be applied in determining the heirs of the children named in the testator's will and in determining the share to which each such heir was entitled. The probate court recited three reasons for this conclusion.

First, the court said that the testator expressed a clear wish in his will that the heirs of his children should take "in such proportion as by law such heirs shall be entitled to receive same". The probate court interpreted this phrase to mean that the testator did not intend that the law at the time of his death would govern determinations to be made many years into the unpredictable future.

Second, the probate court noted that the trust corpus presently in question consists entirely of personal property. No evidence was presented to refute this or to establish that real estate ever was intended to be included in the trust. See Dodge v. Detroit Trust Co., supra, 300 Mich. at p. 598, 2 N.W.2d 509.

Third, the probate court seemed to believe that, since it had already decided that "heirs" is to be defined by reference to the statute in existence at the date of death of the immediate ancestor, it would create a dilemma if it held that the statute was modified by the statute in effect at the date of the execution of the will, citing Brooks v. Parks, supra.

The significance of this issue is that the statute of descent in effect at the time of the testator's death, 1917 P.A. 341; 1915 CL 11795,[21] left nothing to the husband of an intestate woman who died leaving issue to inherit her real estate. However, the statute of descent was amended by 1931 P.A. 79; 1929 CL 13440[22] to allow one-third of any real estate to descend to the surviving husband and the remaining two-thirds to go to the woman's issue. Furthermore, the statute of distribution gave the husband one-third of the woman's personal property.[23]

Thus, if the probate court applied the statute of distribution or the amended statute of descent to determine the "heirs" of the testator's daughter Frances, then it would properly find her surviving husband, Frederick L. Van Lennep, to be entitled to a one-third share of the quarter of trust corpus reserved for her (Frances's) heirs.

On the other hand, if the probate court should have applied the statute of descent in effect at the time of the deceased's death, then Van Lennep was not entitled to take at all, and the entire quarter of the corpus passing to Frances's heirs would go to her children, including appellant, Judith Johnson McClung.

Therefore, in order for appellant McClung to prevail, she must prevail in both of the following propositions: first, that the deceased intended the statutes in effect at the date of his (testator's) death to apply to the determination of his childrens' heirs, and, second, that he intended the statute of descent, rather than the statute of distribution, to apply.

We reject both of these contentions. The language of the will reveals a clear intention to apply future intestacy laws, rather than those in effect at the time the will was drafted. The will provides specifically that the heirs of the testator's four named children should take "in proportion as by law such heirs *shall* be entitled to receive same". Furthermore, since the vesting of the heirs' interests should occur upon the death of each of the four named children, the application of any statutes other than those in effect on the dates of the four named children's respective deaths would be inconsistent and would create a kind of legal dilemma.

---

21. 1915 CL 11795, provides in part:

If such intestate shall die under the age of twenty-one years, and not having been married, all the estate that came to such intestate by inheritance from a parent, which has not been lawfully disposed of, shall descend to the other children and the issue of deceased children of the same parent, if there be such children or issue, and if such persons are in the same degree of kindred to said intestate they shall take equally, otherwise they shall take by right of representation.

22. 1929 CL 13440, provides in part:

If the intestate shall leave a husband or widow and no issue, one-half of the estate of such intestate shall descend to such husband or widow. . . .

If the intestate shall leave a husband or wife and no issue, nor father, mother, brother nor sister, and there be no child of brother or sister, the estate of such intestate shall descend to the husband or wife of such intestate, as the case may be.

23. 1915 P.A. 314; 1915 CL 13913, provides in part:

In any other case the residue, if any, of the personal estate shall be distributed in the same proportion and to the same persons, and for the same purposes, as prescribed for the descent and disposition of the real estate.

As indicated in Brooks v. Parks, supra, there is nothing improper about applying a statute of distribution or descent enacted after the death of the testator. We are satisfied that the inclusion of a single piece of real estate, namely, the boat house, appraised at $40,000 in the inventory of the estate, was an obvious oversight. Thus, we do not believe that those cases which depend for decision on a conclusion that the property involved is "mixed" with both real and personal property are here applicable.

We would not believe that the testator intended to have a trust which had been so painstakingly prepared for the benefit of his named children be invalidated on account of the presence of any real estate. It would appear that the parcel of real estate, which we believe was included only by oversight, amounted to only about one-thousandth of the total value of the trust property. See Dodge v. Detroit Trust Co., supra, 3 Mich. at p. 598, 2 N.W.2d 509. We are not inclined to believe that this "blend" of realty and personalty is the type that was before the courts in the cases cited by appellant[24] and upon which those cases depended for decision.

Furthermore, the real estate parcel included was sold in 1929 and, by the time the first of the four named children who were beneficiaries (Daniel) died in 1938, the trust property consisted entirely of personal property. It was well established at the time the will was drafted and executed that when a devise of personal property is made to the heirs of a given person, the heirs should be identified by application of the statutes in effect at the time of that person's death.[25] Therefore, we conclude that in determining the heirs of each of the four named life income beneficiaries of the trust, it was not error to apply the statute of distribution in effect at the date of each child's death.

The fourth issue considered and determined by the probate court was whether the statutes of the State of Michigan or of the state of domicile of the ancestor determine the "heirs". The issue, which presents a close and difficult question, relates to Isabella Cleves Dodge (Sloane), who died in 1962 while a resident of the State of Florida.

The significance of which state's law controls results from the fact that, in 1962, Florida law[26] provided that collateral kindred of the half blood would inherit only half as much as those of the whole blood while Michigan law[27] provided that heirs of the half blood in these circumstances would take equally with heirs of the whole blood. Thus, under Florida law the heirs of Isabella Cleves Dodge (Sloane) would take as follows: two-fifths to Winifred Dodge Seyburn, two-fifths to Mary Ann Dodge Danaher, and one-fifth to Frances Dodge Van Lennep, the latter being a half-sister because Isabella and Frances had different mothers. Under Michigan law,

---

24. Lyons v. Yerex, 100 Mich. 214, 58 N.W. 1112 (1894); Allison v. Allison's Executors, 101 Va. 537, 44 S.E. 904 (1903).

25. Hascall v. Cox, 49 Mich. 435, 13 N.W. 807 (1882); Turner v. Burr, 141 Mich. 106, 104 N.W. 379 (1905).

26. 1945 Fla.Laws 731.24.

27. 1948 CL 702.84.

Winifred Dodge Seyburn, Mary Ann Dodge Danaher and Frances Dodge Van Lennep would each take one-third.

As previously indicated, the Dodge will provided in paragraph 20:14(h) that, upon termination, the residue of the trust be conveyed to the heirs of the four named children. In Colvin v. Jones,[28] the Court said:

> It is the rule that where the owner of property dies, intestate, . . . his personal property is distributed according to the law of his domicile.

Since Isabella Dodge Sloane died in 1962 domiciled in Florida, it is claimed that technically her heirs should be decided under Florida law. In this connection, 3 Restatement of Property, § 305, pp. 1674-1675 provides as follows:

> When a conveyor describes his conveyees as the "heirs" of a designated person, it is primarily the same as if he had said "those persons who would have succeeded to the property of the named ancestor if he had died intestate." Thus, unless a contrary intent of the conveyor is found from additional language or circumstances, the applicable local law which is used to determine the persons who come within the term "heirs" is the law which would be used to ascertain the heirs of the designated ancestor if he had owned the property in question and had died intestate (see §§ 251 and 308 of the Restatement of Conflict of Laws).

The encyclopedia American Law of Property provides:[29]

> Suppose the subject matter of a devise is located in one state, the testator was domiciled in another state, and the ancestor whose heirs are designated as the beneficiaries is domiciled in still another state. The statute of which state is to be applied? Assuming that the average testator makes a disposition in favor of "heirs", etc., only after he has exhausted his specific desires so that in effect he is saying "Now let the law take its course," the solution in the ordinary case of this conflict of laws problem becomes relatively simple. If the subject matter of the gift is land, the statute is the one in the state in which the land is located, *and if the subject matter is personal property, then the statute should be the one in the state in which the ancestor is domiciled. This seems the desirable resolution of the conflict of laws problem.* (Emphasis added.)

Where personal property is involved, the normal and technical meaning of "heirs" requires the use of the statute of intestacy of the state of the last domicile of the decedent whose heirs are being determined. In holding to the contrary, the probate court placed heavy reliance on In re Sewart Estate,[30] where the Court said:

---

28. 194 Mich. 670, 677, 161 N.W. 847 (1917).
29. 5 American Law of Property, § 22.58(a), which is cited in 53 Harvard L.Rev. 207, 212-213, 228 (1937).
30. 342 Mich. 491, 497, 70 N.W.2d 732; 52 A.L.R.2d 482 (1955).

[T]he basic question in construing the will is the intention of the testatrix. Such intention is to be determined, if possible, from the language of the instrument.

In this case, the testator, John F. Dodge, created a testamentary trust which provided for payment of trust income to four named children, the oldest of whom was under 25 at the time of execution of the will. By its terms, the trust terminated upon the death of the last survivor of the four named children. We assume that the testator contemplated that the trust would continue for many years and that there was nothing in the circumstances to indicate where each named child would die.

The Dodge will does not expressly say that in determining residuary heirs of the four named children, resort should be had to the state of domicile at the time of death of the deceased child. Neither does the Dodge will expressly say that residuary heirs of the four named children should be determined under Michigan law. Under these circumstances, we believe the Sewart decision is controlling.

In 52 A.L.R.2d 482, 495, Sewart is described as illustrative of the general rule that in the absence of anything to indicate a contrary intention on the part of the testator, the "heirs" are ascertained by reference to the law of the testator's domicile.

In Sewart, the Court said, among other things:

> In passing on controversies of this nature courts have repeatedly recognized that the maker of the will was presumably familiar with the laws of his own State and ordinarily without specific information as to statutes in force in other States. Such situation may not be ignored in the construction of the language of a will.[31]

In Sewart, the Court also stated:

> A decision of the supreme court of Kansas in Keith v Eaton, 58 Kan 732; 51 P 271 (1897), is also in point. . . . In holding that the will must be construed in accordance with the law of the domicile of the testator, it was said . . . :
>
>> In the absence of a contrary meaning, to be gathered from the circumstances surrounding a testator or from the instrument as a whole, the sense of the words used by him is to be ascertained in the light of the law of his domicile. Presumptively, he is more familiar with that law than with the law of other jurisdictions. That is the law which is constantly with him, controlling his actions and defining his rights, and more naturally than any other law would be present to his mind in the drafting of an instrument dispository of his property.[32]

We are aware that there are factual differences between Sewart and the within case, but we do not believe they are of a nature to require a different result than that reached by the probate court here. Consequently,

---

31. 342 Mich. 497, 70 N.W.2d 732.
32. 342 Mich. 499-500, 70 N.W.2d 732.

we find that, in accordance with Sewart, the intention of the testator was that the heirs of his four named children be determined under the laws of the State of Michigan. This intention is controlling.

In summary, giving effect to our rulings concerning these four issues discussed by the probate court, we hold that: (1) "heirs" as used in paragraph 20:14(h) of the will means those persons designated by statute to whom the law would give that class of property under the laws of intestate succession; (2) the contingent remainder interest of such "heirs" in the trust corpus vested at the date of death of the respective four named children of the testator; (3) the word "heirs" is defined as of the date of death of each of the four named children of the testator; and (4) in determining the "heirs" of each of the four named children of the testator, we look to the laws of the State of Michigan. However, these rulings do not resolve all of the claims and counter-claims made by the parties on appeal.

[The court then disposed of several claims of individuals who had entered into assignments, agreements, or made elections of various sorts, or had been adopted, and continued:]

Consistent with this opinion, we approve the probate court's conclusion regarding disposition of the trust corpus, the cited fractions representing the fractional interests of the total trust corpus as follows:

1. The "heirs" of Daniel George Dodge (entitled to one-quarter of the trust corpus).

a. Annie Laurine Dodge (Van Etten), the surviving spouse, assigned her one-half share equally to:

Winifred Dodge Gray (Seyburn)	1/24
Isabella Cleves Dodge (Sloane)	1/24
Frances Matilda Dodge (Van Lennep)	1/24

b. The surviving brothers and sisters each shared the remaining half equally as follows:

Winifred Dodge Gray (Seyburn)	1/32
Isabella Cleves Dodge (Sloane)	1/32
Frances Matilda Dodge (Van Lennep)	1/32
(John Duval Dodge)	(1/32)

c. However, the one-thirty-second share which was to go to John Duval Dodge was assigned by him to the following:

Matilda R. Dodge Wilson Fund	1/128
Winifred Dodge Gray (Seyburn)	1/128
Isabella Cleves Dodge (Sloane)	1/128
Frances Matilda Dodge (Van Lennep)	1/128

2. The "heirs" of Isabella Cleves Dodge Sloane (entitled to one-quarter of the trust corpus).

a. The surviving sisters and child of deceased brother, entitled to share equally by right of representation are:

Winifred Dodge Gray (Seyburn)	1/12
Frances Matilda Dodge (Van Lennep)	1/12
Mary Ann Dodge Danaher (daughter of John Duval Dodge)	1/12

3. The "heirs" of Frances Matilda Dodge Van Lennep (entitled to one-quarter of the trust corpus).
a. The surviving spouse entitled to a one-third share is:

Frederick L. Van Lennep	1/12

b. The surviving issue entitled to share equally in the remaining two-thirds are:

Judith Johnson McClung	1/18
Fredericka Van Lennep Caldwell	1/18
John F. Van Lennep	1/18

4. The "heirs" of Winifred Dodge Gray Seyburn (entitled to one-quarter of the trust corpus).
a. The surviving issue entitled to share equally are:

Winifred Seyburn Cheston	1/16
Suzanne Seyburn Meyer	1/16
Edith Seyburn Quintana	1/16
Isabel Seyburn Harte	1/16

Affirmed.

Notes and Questions

1. *Quality of Legal Services.* If nothing else, the will of John F. Dodge disproves the theory that the wealthy need not worry about the quality of legal services provided them. Every litigated question could and should have been anticipated and unambiguously provided for in the will. A lawyer's job is to anticipate such questions, bring them to the client's attention for decision, and effectuate the client's intention without ambiguity.

2. *Uniform Probate Code.* If UPC sections 2-701 and 2-711 (1990) had governed John Dodge's trust, would the case have been litigated? Would the outcome have differed?

3. *Controlling Statute.* In drafting a class gift to a designated person's heirs, the statute to be applied to determine the takers should be expressly identified in the governing instrument. See UPC § 2-703 (1990); Restate-

ment 2d of Property § 29.2 comment c. Failing an express identification, the *Dodge* case held that the controlling statute is: (i) the statute of distribution (ii) of the testator's domicile (iii) in existence when the designated person died.

Using the intestacy statute of the testator's domicile is in line with predominant authority, but the Restatement 2d of Property section 29.2 follows the Restatement of Property section 305 in taking the position that the takers should be governed by the statute that would be used to determine the designated person's actual takers if the designated person had died intestate, owning the subject matter of the gift. In the case of personal property, the position of the Restatements would be that the controlling statute is the statute of distribution of the designated person's domicile. Real property would normally be governed by the statute of descent of the situs.

Using the statute of distribution, when the subject matter is personal property, is also in line with existing authority. When the subject matter is a mixture of real and personal property, the position of the Restatement 2d of Property section 29.3 is that the takers of the personal property are determined under the statute of distribution and the takers of the real property are determined under the statute of descent. There is authority, however, some of which is cited in the *Dodge* case, to the effect that the statute of descent controls the takers of both the real and personal property, in cases of mixtures.

Using the statute in existence at the designated person's death is also the predominant view. See Restatement 2d of Property § 29.4. There is some authority, however, for the view that the statute to be used is the one in existence when the transfer occurred. See Fetters, Future Interests, 23 Syracuse L. Rev. 219, 224-25 (1972), for a discussion of New York cases to this effect.

4. *No Condition of Survivorship.* Once the takers are determined, class gifts to heirs follow the normal rule that no condition of survivorship is imposed unless one is expressly stated. In so holding, the *Dodge* case is consistent with existing authority and the Restatement 2d of Property section 29.5. As is the case with respect to other types of class gifts (see Lawson v. Lawson, supra p. 895), there is a minority view that a class gift to heirs that is contingent on an event unrelated to survivorship is also subject to a condition of survivorship. See, e.g., Continental Illinois Nat'l Bank & Tr. Co. v. Eliel, 17 Ill. 2d 332, 161 N.E.2d 107 (1959). But see Hofing v. Willis, 31 Ill. 2d 365, 201 N.E.2d 852 (1964).

5. *Spouse as an Heir.* Although a person's spouse was not an heir under the common-law canons of descent, modern intestacy statutes include the spouse as an heir. Consequently, as the *Dodge* case illustrates, the designated person's spouse is entitled to participate in a class gift to the designated person's heirs, in the absence of a manifested intent to the contrary on the part of the transferor. See Thomas v. Higginbotham, 318 S.W.2d 234 (Mo. 1958); Restatement 2d of Property § 29.1 comment j.

6. *Division Among Classes and Class Members.* In the *Dodge* case, the class gift was in favor of the heirs of John F. Dodge's four named children. The

court assumed that this meant that the trust corpus was to be divided into four equal shares, the heirs of each named child to get a one-fourth share. This position is supported by the Restatement 2d of Property section 29.8. Also, as held in *Dodge*, the division of each share among the takers within each class is normally determined in accordance with the relevant intestacy statute, rather than on a per capita or some other basis. See Restatement 2d of Property § 29.6.

Although the will of John F. Dodge could certainly have been drafted more clearly on these points, there have been cases exhibiting even poorer drafting. Consider the following:

(a) To A for life, remainder to B and the heirs of A.

(b) To A for life, remainder to A's heirs in equal shares, per stirpes.[33]

(c) To A for life, remainder in equal shares to my heirs and the children of A and the children of B.

7. *Can the State Be an "Heir"?* If, at the time the heirs are to be ascertained, the only claimant is the state by virtue of its right to escheat, section 2-711 of the 1990 UPC takes the position that the state takes. The Restatement of Property section 305 comment n and the Restatement 2d of Property section 29.1 comment k take the position that the class gift fails for want of a taker. Which position do you favor?

8. *Time When Heirs Are Ascertained.* As the *Dodge* case illustrates, the general rule of construction is that heirs or next of kin of a designated person are ascertained at the time of the person's death. See Restatement 2d of Property § 29.4. There are several circumstances, however, in which the general rule of construction does not hold. Ascertainment is often *postponed* if ascertainment at the person's death could result in a complete failure of the gift or in depriving one or more descending lines of a share. To avoid a gap in possession, ascertainment is often *accelerated* or *postponed* if the person is still alive or has predeceased the time when the gift to her or his heirs is to take effect in possession or enjoyment. Consider the following dispositions in the light of the common law and of UPC sections 2-701 and 2-711 (1990):

(a) G devised real property "to A's heirs." A survived G.

(b) G devised real property "to L for life, remainder to A's heirs." A survived both G and L.

(c) G devised real property "to A's heirs." Or, G devised real property "to L for life, remainder to A's heirs." In both cases, A predeceased G. At A's death, A's heirs are her two children, X and Y. X predeceased G. G was survived by Y and X's child, Z.

(d) G devised real property "to A for life, remainder to my (G's) heirs."

---

33. In Pistor's Estate, 53 N.J. Super. 139, 146 A.2d 685 (1958), the court held that the word "equally" indicated that the transferor intended the takers to be the life tenant's descendants (with each descending line receiving an equal share), to the exclusion of the life tenant's surviving spouse, who was among his actual heirs. See also Post's Trust, 61 Misc. 2d 98, 304 N.Y.S.2d 954 (Sur. Ct. 1969). Contra, e.g., Gustafson v. Svenson, 373 Mass. 273, 366 N.E.2d 761 (1977); Eiten v. Eiten, 44 Ill. App. 3d 173, 357 N.E.2d 810 (1976).

(1) G, a widower, was survived by his only descendant, A. Compare Restatement 2d of Property § 29.4 comment f; Restatement of Property § 308 comment k; Hanley v. Craven, 200 Neb. 81, 200 Neb. 701, 263 N.W.2d 79 (1978), with Gross v. Hartford-Connecticut Trust Co., 100 Conn. 332 123 A. 907 (1924).

(2) G, a widower, is survived by his three children, A, B, and C. Cf. Hancock v. Krause, 757 S.W.2d 117 (Tex. Ct. App. 1988).

(e) G devised real property "to A for life, remainder to the persons who would be my (G's) heirs if my (G's) death occurred at the time of A's death."

(f) G devised real property "to A for life, remainder to my (G's) then heirs."

(g) G devised real property "to A for life, then to my (G's) heirs."

(h) G devised real property "to A for life, remainder to my (G's) heirs who survive A." See Love Estate, 362 Pa. 105, 66 A.2d 238 (1949).

EXTERNAL REFERENCES. Restatement 2d of Property § 29.4, comments, & Reporter's Note; Restatement of Property § 308 & comments.

3. Inter-Vivos Transfers to the Grantor's Heirs: The Doctrine of Worthier Title

Statutory Reference: *1990 UPC § 2-710*

Problem

After substantial revision, an irrevocable inter-vivos life-insurance trust provided that after the Settlor's death and the $6 million life insurance proceeds are collected and invested by the trustee, the income is to be paid to the Settlor's son, Arnold, for life. See supra p. 912. Upon Arnold's death, the corpus of the trust is to be distributed as follows:

(a) To the descendants of Arnold who survive Arnold, to be divided among them by representation; or

(b) If Arnold is not survived by any descendants of his own, then to the descendants of the Settlor who survive Arnold, to be divided among them by representation; or

(c) If Arnold is not survived by any descendants of the Settlor, then to the descendants of the Settlor's brother [name of brother] who survive Arnold, to be divided among them by representation; or

(d) If Arnold is not survived by any descendants of the settlor's brother [name of brother], then to the descendants of the Settlor's father [name of father] who survive Arnold, to be divided among them by representation; or

(e) If Arnold is not survived by any descendants of the Settlor's father, then to Arnold's heirs at law.

(f) If the Settlor is not survived by his son, Arnold, then upon the Settlor's death the corpus of the trust is to be distributed to the Settlor's heirs at law.

In the light of the *Dodge* case, it might occur to you that subparagraphs (e) and (f) still need work. Apart from the general need to clarify the term "heirs at law," would it ever have occurred to you that subparagraph (f) was drafted by the settlor's lawyers with the *actual* intention that it constitute a *reversion* in the settlor himself, so that in the unlikely event that subparagraph (f) becomes effective the corpus of the trust would go to the settlor's residuary legatees named in the settlor's will?

One of the tax purposes of this irrevocable inter-vivos life-insurance trust is to avoid the inclusion of the policy proceeds in the settlor's gross estate. Would that purpose be jeopardized in this case if subparagraph (f) is interpreted as a reversion in the settlor rather than a remainder in the settlor's heirs? See IRC § 2042.

Doctor v. Hughes
225 N.Y. 305, 122 N.E. 221 (1919)

CARDOZO, J. The action is brought by judgment creditors to subject what is alleged to be an interest in real property to the lien of a judgment.

In January, 1899, James J. Hanigan conveyed to a trustee a house and lot in the city of New York. The conveyance was in trust to pay from the rents and profits to the use of the grantor the yearly sum of $1,500. The payments might, however, exceed that sum in the discretion of the trustee. Direction was also made for the payment of some debts, and for the payment of two mortgages, then liens upon the property. The trustee was empowered to mortgage, in order to pay existing liens, or to carry into effect the other provisions of the deed. He was also empowered to sell. Upon the death of the grantor, he was to "convey the said premises (if not sold) to the heirs at law of the party of the first part." In case of a sale, he was to pay to the heirs at law "the balance of the avails of sale remaining unexpended." He was authorized at any time, if he so desired, to reconvey the premises to the grantor, and thus terminate the trust.

At the trial of this action, the grantor was still alive. His sole descendants were two daughters. By deed executed in June, 1902, one of the daughters, Mrs. Hughes, conveyed to her husband all her interest in this real estate. Judgment against Mr. and Mrs. Hughes for upwards of $4,000 was afterwards recovered by the plaintiffs. The question to be determined is whether either judgment debtor has any interest in the land. The Special Term held that there passed to Mr. Hughes under the conveyance from his wife an estate in remainder which was subject to the claims of creditors. The Appellate Division held that the creator of the trust did not intend to give a remainder to any one; that his heirs at law, if they receive anything on his death, will take by descent, and not by purchase; and hence that there is nothing that creditors can seize.

We reach the same conclusion. The direction to the trustee is the superfluous expression of a duty imposed by law. "Where an express trust is created, every legal estate and interest not embraced in the trust, and not otherwise disposed of, shall remain in or revert to, the person creating the trust or his heirs." Real Property Law, § 102. (Consol. Laws, c. 50). What is left is not a remainder (Real Property Law, § 38), but a reversion (Real Property Law, § 39). To such a situation neither the rule in Shelley's Case (1 Coke Rep. 104), nor the statute abrogating the rule (Real Property Law, § 54), applies. The heirs mentioned in this deed are not "the heirs . . . of a person to whom a life estate in the same premises is given." Real Property Law, § 54. The life estate belongs to the trustee. The heirs are the heirs of the grantor. . . . The question is whether there is any remainder at all. In the solution of that problem, the distinction is vital between gifts to the heirs of the holder of a particular estate, and gifts or attempted gifts to the heirs of the grantor. "A man cannot, either by conveyance at the common law, by limitation of uses, or devise, make his right heir a purchaser." Pilus v. Milford, 1674, 1 Vent. 372; Read v. Erington, 1594, Cro. Eliz. 322; Bingham's Case, 2 Co. Rep. 91a., 91b; Cholmondaley v. Maxey, 12 East, 589, 603, 604. "It is a positive rule of our law." Hargrave's Law Tracts (1787) p. 571. "If a man make a gift in taile, or a lease for life, the remainder to his own right heirs, this remainder is void, and he hath the reversion in him; for the ancestor during his life beareth in his body (in judgment of law) all his heirs, and therefore, it is truly said that haeres est pars antecessoris." Co. Litt. 22b. To the same effect are all the commentators. 1 Fearne, Contingent Rem. 21; 2 Fearne, 205 (section 389); 2 Washburn on Real Prop. (6th Ed.) § 1525; Vin. Abr. Rem. A, p. 11; Bacon, Abr. Uses, B2; Gilbert, Uses, 20; Preston on Estates, 291; 24 Halsbury's Laws of England, pp. 213, 214. The heirs have a mere expectancy, spes successionis, which may be barred by deed or will. This rule, that a reservation to the heirs of the grantor is equivalent to the reservation of a reversion to the grantor himself, is not to be confused with the rule in Shelley's Case. The two are quite distinct. The one "applies only to the acts of an ancestor as between him and his own heirs." The other is confined to the limitation of estate of inheritance to the heirs of a person who has taken under the same instrument a prior estate of freehold.

At common law, therefore, and under common-law conveyances, this direction to transfer the estate to the heirs of the grantor would indubitably have been equivalent to the reservation of a reversion. In England, the rule has been changed by statute. The Inheritance Act of 1833 provides (3 & 4 Wm. IV, c. 106, § 3) that—

> When any land shall have been limited by any assurance . . . to the person or to the heirs of the person who shall thereby have conveyed the same land, such person shall be considered to have acquired the same as a purchaser by virtue of such assurance, and shall not be considered to be entitled thereto as his former estate or part thereof.

But in the absence of modifying statute, the rule persists to-day, at least as a rule of construction, if not as one of property. There are modern instances of its application to facts hardly to be distinguished from those of the case at bar. Alexander v. De Kermel, 81 Ky. 345; Akers v. Clark, 184 Ill. 136, 56 N. E. 296, 75 Am. St. Rep. 152; Hobbie v. Ogden, 178 Ill. 357,

53 N. E. 104; Robinson v. Blankenship, 116 Tenn. 394, 92 S. W. 854. The reservation of a reversion is not inconsistent with the creation of a trust to continue until the death of the reversioner. We do not say that the ancient rule survives as an absolute prohibition limiting the power of a grantor. At the outset, probably, like the rule in Shelley's Case, it was a rule, not of construction, but of property. But it was never applied in all its rigor to executory trusts, which were "molded by the court as best to answer the intent of the person creating them." We may assume that this is the principle that would control the courts to-day. Executory limitations are no longer distinguished from remainders, but are grouped with them as future estates (Real Prop. Law, §§ 36, 37; Tilden v. Green, 130 N. Y. 29, 47, 28 N. E. 880, 14 L. R. A. 33, 27 Am. St. Rep. 487), and deeds, like wills, must be so construed as to effectuate the purpose of the grantor (Real Property Law, § 240, subd. 3). There may be times, therefore, when a reference to the heirs of the grantor will be regarded as the gift of a remainder, and will vest title in the heirs presumptive as upon a gift to the heirs of others. But at least the ancient rule survives to this extent: That, to transform into a remainder what would ordinarily be a reversion, the intention to work the transformation must be clearly expressed. Here there is no clear expression of such a purpose. No doubt there are circumstances on which it is possible to build an argument. The grantor instructs the trustee, at the end of the life estate, to convey the land (if unsold) to the heirs, and if there has been a sale to pay the proceeds to the heirs. The more appropriate direction, if the grantor retained a reversion, would have been for payment of the proceeds of any sale to the executors or next of kin. "If the ancestor devises his estate to his heir at law by will, with other limitations, or in any other shape than the course of descents would direct, such heir shall take by purchase." 2 Bl. Comm. 241. But the words "heirs" and "next of kin" are often employed as interchangeable. In this instance, the two classes are in fact identical. Nothing in the surrounding circumstances suggests a purpose to vary the course of descent or distribution as it would be regulated by law. If that is so, the courts are not to be controlled by mere inaccuracies of expression. Such slips of speech might be significant if we were construing an admitted remainder. They do not turn into a remainder what would otherwise be a reversion. There is no adequate disclosure of a purpose in the mind of this grantor to vest his presumptive heirs with rights which it would be beyond his power to defeat. No one is heir to the living, and seldom do the living mean to forego the power of disposition during life by the direction that upon death there shall be a transfer to their heirs. This grant by its terms was subject to destruction at the will of the trustee. We think it was also subject to destruction, as against the heirs at law, at the will of the grantor. They had an expectancy, but no estate.

The judgment should be affirmed, with costs. . . .

Note

Post-Doctor v. Hughes Case Authority. In Matter of Burchell, 299 N.Y. 351, 87 N.E.2d 293 (1949), the terms of an irrevocable inter-vivos trust of real property were that the income was to be paid to the grantor for her life. Upon her death, the principal of the trust estate was to go to such persons as the grantor appoints by will; in default of appointment, to the grantor's next of kin as in intestacy.

In an opinion written by Judge Bromley, the court held that the gift in default created a remainder interest in the grantor's heirs, not a reversion in the grantor:

> Confusion as to the nature of an estate when that estate is limited to heirs of the grantor arises because of the existence in our modern jurisprudence of remnants of the ancient doctrine of worthier title (46 Harv. L. Rev. 993). Prior to our decision in Doctor v. Hughes (225 N.Y. 305 . . .), a conveyance by a grantor with a limitation over to his heirs was said to be governed by that doctrine, under which a limitation over to a grantor's heirs resulted in an automatic reversion in the grantor and nullified the limitation over. . . .
>
> It is clear from the cases in this State since Doctor v. Hughes . . . , as admirably analyzed in Richardson v. Richardson ([298 N.Y. 135, 81 N.E.2d 54 (1948)], that, despite the language in that opinion that a reversion exists unless there is clear evidence to the contrary, the rule has been less limited in application. Where a clear intent exists, there is no problem in construing the instrument, since the doctrine no longer exists as a rule of property. But where the grantor's intent is not expressed in unmistakable language, the rule comes into play. Then we look to the instrument for those indicia deemed significant in arriving at the intent of the grantor. In the first of the line of cases following Doctor v. Hughes (supra), (Whittemore v. Equitable Trust Co., 250 N.Y. 298), we applied the rule of construction in the manner indicated in the second interpretation above. We discovered the intent of the grantor from other factors, as shown by the instrument, in order to give full effect to the words of limitation.
>
> While we have not yet adopted a rule, either by statute or judicial construction, under which language limiting an interest to heirs is unequivocally given its full effect, the presumption which exists from the use of the common-law doctrine as a rule of construction has lost much of its force since Doctor v. Hughes (supra). Evidence of intent need not be overwhelming in order to allow the remainder to stand. Whether the rule should be abrogated completely is a matter for the Legislature.
>
> The instant cases furnish sufficient additional indications of the settlor's intent to justify our giving effect to the language of the instrument limiting an estate to the grantor's heirs. Not the least among those indications was the reservation of a testamentary power of appointment as the sole control over the subsequent disposition of the corpus of the trust estate. . . . The fact that the trust agreement reserved a power of appointment is evidence that the settlor believed she had created an interest in the property on the part of others and reserved the power in order to defeat that interest or to postpone until a later date the naming of specific takers. Where we have held that a reversion was intended although a testamentary power of appointment was reserved, the instruments have provided that the trust principal would revert to the grantor upon some contingency or that the grantor retained control over the principal.

In analyzing an instrument and attempting to explore the almost ephemeral qualities which go to prove the necessary intent, many single factors may be considered. Some considered significant in one case may be deemed minimal in another, since their effect may be counteracted by the presence of other factors. It is impossible to set up absolute criteria to serve as a measuring standard for all cases. In the last analysis, the ultimate determination rests on the particular instrument under consideration, aided by the rule which has grown out of the old common-law doctrine and developed over a long line of cases as a rule which allows the language of the instrument creating a remainder to take effect provided some additional evidence pointing the intent of the grantor is present to buttress the language which would create the remainder.

Hatch v. Riggs National Bank
361 F.2d 559 (D.C. Cir. 1966)

LEVENTHAL, C.J. Appellant seeks in this action to obtain modification of a trust she created in 1923. The income terms of the trust instrument are of a spendthrift character, directing the trustees to pay to the settlor for life all the income from the trust estate "for her own use and benefit, without the power to her to anticipate, alienate or charge the same. . . ." Upon the death of the settlor-life tenant, the trustees are to pay over the corpus as the settlor may appoint by will; if she fails to exercise this testamentary power of appointment, the corpus is to go to "such of her next of kin . . . as by the law in force in the District of Columbia at the death of the . . . [settlor] shall be provided for in the distribution of an intestate's personal property therein." No power to appoint the corpus by deed, nor any power to revoke, alter, amend or modify the trust, was expressly retained by appellant, and the instrument states that she conveys the property to the trustees "irrevocably."

Appellant does not claim that the declaration of trust itself authorizes her to revoke or modify the trust. In effect she invokes the doctrine of worthier title, which teaches that a grant of trust corpus to the heirs of the settlor creates a reversion in the settlor rather than a remainder in his heirs. She claims that since she is the sole beneficiary of the trust under this doctrine, and is also the settlor, she may revoke or modify under accepted principles of trust law.

The District Court, while sympathizing with appellant's desire to obtain an additional stipend of $5000 a year, out of corpus, "to accommodate recently incurred expenses, and to live more nearly in accordance with her refined but yet modest tastes,"[34] felt that denial of the requested relief was

---

34. In her complaint, appellant also sought an additional $50,000 from corpus to purchase a residence, but dropped this request at the hearing. The District Court found that there was "no suggestion of extravagance" in appellant's way of life or in her request for additional funds. She now lives in a one-bedroom apartment in a modest residential section of Long Beach, California, and has no assets except limited jewelry, furniture, personal effects, and a medium-priced automobile.

required by this court's decision in Liberty National Bank v. Hicks, 84 U.S.App.D.C. 198, 173 F.2d 631, 9 A.L.R.2d 1355 (1948). Summary judgment was granted for appellees. We affirm.

I. . . . The doctrine of worthier title had its origins in the feudal system which to a large extent molded the English common law which we inherited. In its common law form, the doctrine provided that a conveyance of land by a grantor with a limitation over to his own heirs resulted in a reversion in the grantor rather than creating a remainder interest in the heirs. It was a rule of law distinct from, though motivated largely by the same policies as, the Rule in Shelley's Case. Apparently the feudal overlord was entitled to certain valuable incidents when property held by one of his feoffees passed by "descent" to an heir rather than by "purchase" to a transferee. The doctrine of worthier title—whereby descent is deemed "worthier" than purchase—remained ensconced in English law, notwithstanding the passing of the feudal system, until abrogated by statute in 1833.[35]

The doctrine has survived in many American jurisdictions, with respect to inter vivos conveyances of both land and personalty, as a common law "rule of construction" rather than a "rule of law." In Doctor v. Hughes, 225 N.Y. 305, 122 N.E. 221 (1919), Judge Cardozo's landmark opinion reviewed the common-law history of the doctrine and concluded that its modern relevance was as a rule of construction, a rebuttable presumption that the grantor's likely intent, in referring to his own heirs, was to reserve a reversion in his estate rather than create a remainder interest in the heirs. Evidence might be introduced to show that the grantor really meant what he said when he spoke of creating a remainder in his heirs.

In the decades that followed, the worthier title doctrine as a rule of construction with respect to inter vivos transfers won widespread acceptance.[36] The "modern" rationale for the rule is well stated in an opinion of the Supreme Court of California:

> It is said that where a person creates a life estate in himself with a gift over to his heirs he ordinarily intends the same thing as if he had given the property to his estate; that he does not intend to make a gift to any particular person but indicates only that upon his death the residue of the trust property shall be distributed according to the general laws governing succession; and that he does not intend to create in any persons an interest which would prevent him from exercising control over the beneficial interest. . . . Moreover, this rule of construction is in accord with the general policy in favor of the free alienability of property, since its operation tends to make property more readily transferable.[37]

---

35. 3 & 4 Wm. IV, ch. 106, § 3. For more detailed discussion of the evolution of the doctrine of worthier title at common law, see Annot., 125 A.L.R. 548, 549-550 (1940); Doctor v. Hughes, 225 N.Y. 305, 122 N.E. 221 (1919); In re Burchell's Estate, 299 N.Y. 351, 87 N.E.2d 293, 296 (1949).

36. See Restatement, Property, 314(1) (1940); Restatement (Second), Trusts, 127 comment b (1959); Annot., 16 A.L.R.2d 691 (1951).

37. Bixby v. California Trust Co., 33 Cal.2d 495, 202 P.2d 1018, 1019 (1949). See also McKenna v. Seattle-First Nat'l Bank, 35 Wash.2d 662, 214 P.2d 664, 16 A.L.R.2d 679 (1950).

While the weight of authority, as just indicated, supports the retention of the doctrine of worthier title (unlike its common-law brother, the Rule in Shelley's Case) as a rule of construction, there has been substantial and increasing opposition to the doctrine.[38]

The views of the critics of the doctrine, which we find persuasive against its adoption, and borne out by the experience of the New York courts in the series of cases which have followed Doctor v. Hughes, supra, may be summarized as follows. The common-law reasons for the doctrine are as obsolete as those behind the Rule in Shelley's Case.[39] Retention of the doctrine as a rule of construction is pernicious in several respects.

First, it is questionable whether it accords with the intent of the average settlor. It is perhaps tempting to say that the settlor intended to create no beneficial interest in his heirs when he said "to myself for life, remainder to my heirs" when the question is revocation of the trust, or whether creditors of the settlor's heirs should be able to reach their interest. But the same result is far from appealing if the settlor-life beneficiary dies without revoking the trust and leaves a will which makes no provision for his heirs-at-law (whom he supposed to be taken care of by the trust). In short, while the dominant intent of most such trusts may well be to benefit the life tenant during his life, a subsidiary but nevertheless significant purpose of many such trusts may be to satisfy a natural desire to benefit one's heirs or next of kin. In the normal case an adult has a pretty good idea who his heirs will be at death, and probably means exactly what he says when he states in the trust instrument, "remainder to my heirs."

It is said that the cases in which such is the grantor's intent can be discerned by an examination into his intent; the presumption that a gift over to one's heirs creates a reversion can thereby be rebutted in appropriate cases. But the only repository of the settlor's intent, in most cases, will be the trust instrument itself. Nor would it be fruitful or conducive to orderly and prompt resolution of litigation to engage in searches for other sources of intent. In the typical case of this genre—a stark, unqualified "to myself for life, remainder to my heirs"—the instrument will send forth no signals of contrary intent to overcome the presumption that only a reversion was intended. Yet this is precisely the class of cases in which settlors are likely to have intended to create beneficial interests in their heirs.

A lengthier document may send forth more signals, but they may well be murky. Where other indicia of intent can be discovered in the trust instrument, with the aid of ingenious counsel, the result, as the New York

---

38. See. e.g., Simes, Fifty Years of Future Interests, 50 Harv. L. Rev. 749, 756 (1937); Note, 48 Yale L. J. 874 (1939); Note, 39 Colum. L. Rev. 628, 656 (1939); Comment, 34 Ill. L. Rev. 835, 850-51 (1940). A recent study of the subject by Professor Verrall of the University of California, under the auspices of the California Law Revision Commission, resulted in a strong condemnation of the doctrine. Verrall, The Doctrine of Worthier Title: A Questionable Rule of Construction, 6 U.C.L.A.L. Rev. 371 (1959).

39. The Rule in Shelley's Case (1 Coke Rep. 104) has been abolished by statute in the District of Columbia. D.C. Code 45-203 (1961 ed.).

cases have demonstrated, is a shower of strained decisions difficult to reconcile with one another and generative of considerable confusion in the law.[40] After three decades of observing the New York courts administer the rule of construction announced in Doctor v. Hughes, supra, Professor Powell of Columbia observed that "there were literally scores of cases, many of which reached the Appellate Division, and no case involving a substantial sum could be fairly regarded as closed until its language and circumstances had been passed upon by the Court of Appeals. . . . This state of uncertainty was the product of changing an inflexible rule of law into a rule of construction."[41]

An excellent example of this confusion is the effect to be given the fact that, as in the case at bar, the settlor has reserved the power to defeat the heirs' interest by appointing the taker of the remainder by will. One might well think that the reservation of a power of appointment was an index of intent which buttressed the presumption of a reversion by demonstrating that the settlor did not wish to create firm interests or expectations among his heirs, but intended to retain control over the property. Most courts, including the New York Court of Appeals in its most recent pronouncement on the subject, have disagreed, albeit over the voice of dissent.[42] They have reasoned that the retention of the testamentary power of appointment confirms the intent to create a remainder in the heirs, since the settlor would not have retained the power had he not thought he was creating a remainder interest in the heirs.

We see no reason to plunge the District of Columbia into the ranks of those jurisdictions bogged in the morass of exploring, under the modern doctrine of worthier title, "the almost ephemeral qualities which go to prove the necessary intent."[43] The alleged benefit of effectuating intent must be balanced against the resulting volume of litigation and the diversity and difficulty of decision.[44] We are not persuaded that the policy of upholding the intention of creators of trusts is best effectuated by such a rule of construction, with its accompanying uncertainty.

The rule we adopt, which treats the settlor's heirs like any other remaindermen, although possibly defeating the intention of some settlors, is overall, we think, an intent-effectuating rule. It contributes to certainty of written expression and conceptual integrity in the law of trusts. It allows heirs to take as remaindermen when so named, and promises less litigation, greater predictability, and easier drafting. These considerations are no small element of justice.

We hold, then, that the doctrine of worthier title is no part of the law of trusts in the District of Columbia, either as a rule of law or as a rule of

---

40. The New York cases are admirably summarized and discussed in Verrall, op. cit. supra note 38, at 374-387.

41. Powell, Cases On Future Interests 88 n. 14 (3d ed. 1961).

42. In re Burchell's Estate, 299 N.Y. 351, 361, 87 N.E.2d 293, 297 (1949); see Comment, 34 Ill. L. Rev. 834, 844-45 (1940).

43. In re Burchell's Estate, supra, 299 N.Y. at 361, 87 N.E.2d at 297 (1949).

44. These results led Judge Fuld to call for "clarifying legislation." Dissent in In re Burchell's Estate, supra note 39.

construction. Any act or words of the settlor of a trust which would validly create a remainder interest in a named third party may create a valid remainder interest in the settlor's heirs. It follows that the District Court was correct in granting summary judgment for appellees in this case, since appellant's action is based on the theory that she was the sole beneficiary and hence could revoke the "irrevocable" trust she had created.

II. [The remaining portion of the opinion, discussing the termination or modification of trusts at the suit of the beneficiaries and the use of a guardian ad litem to represent the settlor's heirs in such a proceeding, is reproduced supra p. 721.]

Affirmed.

Notes and Questions

1. *Legislative Abolition of the Worthier-Title Doctrine.* The New York court in *Burchell* seemed to favor complete abrogation of the doctrine of worthier title, but declined to take that step because the court thought abrogation was a matter exclusively for the legislature. Whatever the merits of that idea in New York when *Burchell* was decided, with the experience of Doctor v. Hughes and its progeny, the *Hatch* case shows that abrogation is not necessarily restricted to legislation in jurisdictions that have no such history. In any event, the New York legislature stepped in and abolished the worthier title doctrine in 1966. At least ten other states now have abrogating legislation—Arkansas, California, Illinois,[45] Massachusetts, Minnesota, Nebraska, North Carolina, Tennessee, Texas, and West Virginia. See Restatement 2d of Property, Statutory Note to § 30.2, at 453-55. A statute in Georgia makes application of the doctrine unlikely, by declaring that the word "heirs" is presumed to mean children, unless a contrary intention appears. Ga. Code Ann. § 44-6-23.

Section 2-710 of the 1990 UPC abolishes the worthier-title doctrine.

2. *Post-Hatch Case Authority.* Since 1966, when the *Hatch* case was decided, no state supreme court authority recognizing the validity of the doctrine exists.

3. *Analysis of the Doctrine.* Professor Waggoner has criticized the transformation of the worthier-title doctrine into a rule of construction:

Judge Cardozo, in shifting the inter vivos branch of the worthier title doctrine to a rule of construction, may have been motivated by a desire to soften the old rule of law by allowing it to yield to the grantor's contrary intention. But shifting a rule of law to one of construction is only superficially an enlightened maneuver. Rules of law and rules of construction emanate from

---

45. But see Stewart v. Merchants Nat'l Bank, 3 Ill. App. 3d 337, 278 N.E.2d 10 (1972), where the court seems to have held that the statute only abrogates the worthier title doctrine as a rule of law, not as a rule of construction. See Note, 67 Nw. U. L. Rev. 773 (1973). Harris Trust & Savings Bank v. Beach, 118 Ill. 2d 1, 513 N.E.2d 833 (1987), however, referred to Illinois' "1955 statutory abolition of the doctrine."

entirely different premises. Rules of law defeat intention; rules of construction facilitate the effectuation of intention. Defeating intention is justified only to vindicate goals of sound public policy; the proper function of rules of law is therefore to prohibit individual choices which are deemed to be unduly harmful to society as a whole. Rules of construction, on the other hand, operate in areas where society as a whole is deemed to be indifferent as to whether one or another course of action is taken. The only public policy goal which rules of construction vindicate is the notion that in such areas of societal indifference, private intention ought to be effectuated. Rules of construction seek to facilitate this goal by providing a presumptive meaning—one which is designed to accord with common intention—to words which have failed to express the actual intention of the parties clearly.

When the policy reasons which underlie a rule of law disappear, as is the case with respect to the worthier title doctrine, the normal course is for the legislature to repeal the rule (as the English legislature did in 1833) or for the courts to abrogate it or at least to nibble away at its scope until eventually it ceases to operate. The shifting of the worthier title doctrine from a rule of law to one of construction is therefore not a normal step in the evolutionary process of law.

L. Waggoner, Future Interests in a Nutshell 150-51 (1981). The doctrine was condemned in vehement terms in W. Leach, Property Law Indicted! 56 (1967).

4. *Resurrection of the Doctrine?* The Restatement 2d of Property section 30.2(1) states that the doctrine continues as a rule of construction. Comment a states:

> The continuation of the [inter-vivos branch of the worthier title doctrine] as a rule of construction may be justified on the basis that it represents the probable intention of the average transferor. . . .
>
> The increased alienability of the subject matter of the transfer which results from the application of the [doctrine] is also a justification for it.

This Comment prompted the inclusion of section 2-710 in the 1990 revisions of the UPC.

5. *Drafting Procedures to Avoid the Doctrine.* Consider again subparagraph (f) of the irrevocable life-insurance trust supra at p. 957. Remember, the federal government has considerable revenue to gain if the worthier-title doctrine is applied.[46] If it is applied, and if the life-insurance proceeds are included in the settlor's gross estate, the possibility exists of attorney liability in malpractice. See generally Johnston, Legal Malpractice in Estate Planning—Perilous Times Ahead for the Practitioner, 67 Iowa L. Rev. 629 (1982).

Assuming that the settlor's lawyer notices the worthier-title problem before the irrevocable (and unamendable) trust is signed, the better course is to redraft subparagraph (f) so that it leaves no doubt that it creates a

---

46. On the tax consequences in general of application of the worthier title doctrine, see Johanson, Reversions, Remainders, and the Doctrine of Worthier Title, 45 Tex. L. Rev. 1, 16-27 (1966).

remainder interest in the settlor's heirs. In a world in which the phrase "remainder to my heirs" presumptively means "reversion in myself," how can the settlor's lawyer make it beyond dispute that subparagraph (f) means what it says? Should subparagraph (f) be redrafted to say "to my heirs at law, and I really mean it—no kidding!"? A more lawyer-like way of saying it might be:

> . . . to my heirs at law, such persons to take as purchasers, my intention being to create a remainder interest in favor of my heirs at law; I do not intend to retain a reversion in myself.

Suppose the worthier-title problem in subparagraph (f) was not noticed until *after* the trust was signed and the $6 million life-insurance policy was irrevocably assigned to the trustee. Could the settlor's lawyer successfully petition for reformation of subparagraph (f), to add language making it clear that a remainder was intended? See Palmer on Restitution ch. 18; Langbein & Waggoner, Reformation of Wills on the Ground of Mistake: Change of Direction in American Law?, 130 U. Pa. L. Rev. 521, 524-28 (1982). Would this reformation be controlling for federal tax purposes? See supra pp. 382, 562 & 585. Would it make any difference if the reformation occurred before or after the settlor's death? See Rev. Rul. 73-142, 1973-1 Cum. Bull. 405.

6. *Testamentary Branch of the Doctrine.* At common law, the worthier-title doctrine had two branches—the inter-vivos branch and the testamentary branch. The above materials relate solely to the inter-vivos branch, which as its name implies, applies only to inter-vivos transfers.

The testamentary branch provided that a *devise* of *land* to the testator's heirs was a nullity if the interest devised to them was identical to the interest they would take in intestacy. Like the inter-vivos branch, this was a rule of law, not of construction. See Morris, The Wills Branch of the Worthier Title Doctrine, 54 Mich. L. Rev. 451 (1956). No decision in this country has prolonged the existence of the testamentary branch by holding that it "persists today, at least as a rule of construction, if not as one of property." The Restatement of Property section 314(2) and the Restatement 2d of Property section 30.2(2) declare the testamentary branch not to exist as either a rule of law or of construction. In two states in which no abrogating legislation exists, the rule was recently abolished by court decision (City Nat'l Bank v. Andrews, 355 S.2d 341 (Ala. 1978); Matter of Campbell, 319 N.W.2d 275 (Iowa 1982); Estate of Kern, 274 N.W.2d 325 (Iowa 1979)) and it is doubtful that it remains in effect anywhere today. See Restatement 2d of Property, Reporter's Note 6 to § 30.2, at 471-75.

7. *Continuation of the Inter-Vivos Branch as a Rule of Law?* In a few states that have not enacted abrogating legislation, older cases exist applying the inter-vivos branch of the worthier-title doctrine as a rule of law, not of construction. See Restatement 2d of Property, Reporter's Note 4 to § 30.2, at 470. Whether these decisions would be followed today is problematical.

PART C. INCOMPLETE DISPOSITIONS

Theoretically, the calculus of estates does not admit of a disposition that is incomplete: A transferor is considered to have retained by way of reversionary interest any interest not expressly transferred. For example, in the simple disposition "to A for life," it would be assumed that a reversion in the transferor takes effect upon the death of the life tenant. As we shall see, however, courts sometimes find that a disposition creates a future interest by implication. This process is commonly illustrated by the disposition "to A for life, remainder to B if A dies without issue." If A dies with issue, this disposition has been found to contain an implied remainder interest in their favor. See Restatement of Property § 272.

1. Implication of Interests in Principal

McKinney v. Mosteller, 321 N.C. 730, 365 S.E.2d 612 (1988), provides a striking example of a court adhering to a formal and rigid analysis of dispository language. The court refused to acknowledge a drafting mistake or rectify it. G's will devised the residue of his estate as follows:

> If my wife, W, survives me, then in trust to pay the income to W for life, remainder in corpus to A and B.

W predeceased G. G's sole heir is C.

The court held that C is entitled to the residue of G's estate, not A and B. The court explained:

> [A] gift by implication is not favored in the law and cannot rest upon mere conjecture. . . .
>
> The residuary beneficiaries argue strongly that it is clear that they were to be the secondary object of testator's bounty. Even assuming that extrinsic evidence supports that contention, we are commanded to gather the intent of the testator from the four corners of his will, and such intent should be given effect unless contrary to some rule of law or at variance with public policy. The effect that we give to testator's will is neither offensive to public policy nor contrary to any rule of law. As gleaned from the will itself, the intent of the testator is manifest and unequivocal, that is, the residue is to pass to the named beneficiaries under the residuary clause of the will only if testator's wife survives him. She did not. Therefore, the residue passes to the heirs at law in accordance with the laws of intestacy as enacted by the legislature.
>
> The presumption against partial intestacy is merely a rule of construction and cannot have the effect of transferring property in the face of contrary provisions in the will. The presumption must yield when outweighed by manifest and unequivocal intent.

Hilton v. Kinsey, 185 F.2d 885 (D.C. Cir. 1950), on the other hand, provides an example of a court rectifying a drafting mistake by finding that the omitted language could be implied. James H. Hilton died in 1919, devising his estate in trust, income to his children, J. Franklin Hilton and Catharine Hilton, for life; a cross remainder in the income was provided to the survivor for life. As to the corpus, the will stated:

> In case my son, J. Franklin Hilton, or my daughter, Catharine S. Hilton, should have any [children], such [children], if of J. Franklin Hilton, shall be entitled to his [share] after his death, and if my daughter, Catharine S. Hilton, should have any [children], said [children] shall be entitled to her [share] after her death. . . . Should [they] have no children, then the money of the estate [should be paid to specified charities].

J. Franklin died in 1941, without children; Catharine died in 1947, survived by her daughter, Mary.

The court held that Mary, not the charities or the testator's heirs, was entitled to the half of the corpus from which J. Franklin had been receiving the income prior to his death:

> [W]hen the general plan of the testator for the disposition of his property is considered . . . it is clear that . . . the children of J. Franklin and Catharine, if any, were to be the ultimate beneficiaries of the residuary estate. Under similar circumstances it has been held that although testator's plan is incompletely expressed, it may be implied from the contents of the will as a whole and a cross-remainder of the corpus read into the will. In Boston Safe-Deposit & Trust Co. v. Coffin, [152 Mass. 95, 25 N.E. 30,] the testator, as to one portion of his estate, made the following disposition: The income to grandchildren A, B, and C for life; upon the death of A, or B, or C without issue, the income to be divided among the survivors; upon the death of A, or B, or C with issue, that issue to take the portion of the estate of which the grandchild had enjoyed the interest and income; if A, B, and C all die without issue, the principal to go to the other children of the testator. Both A and B predeceased C, dying without issue. C enjoyed the entire income until his death. He died with issue. It was argued that the issue of C was entitled to the original amount from which C received the income, namely, one-third of the corpus, the remaining two-thirds passing by intestacy. The court rejected this contention, holding that there was an implied cross-remainder of the two-thirds to the issue of C, and, accordingly, that C's children took the entire corpus.
>
> There is a striking similarity between that case and the present one. Franklin predeceased Catharine. Subsequent to his death she was clearly entitled to, and actually received for a period of six years until her death, the income from the entire corpus of the estate. Prior to her death her interest in the estate was not the life income from half the corpus, but the income from the whole. And the gift to the children was to be not a half, but the whole interest of the parent. Therefore, we hold that the provision for a cross-remainder as to the income between the parents had the effect of increasing the share of the children of one should the other die without children.

Warner v. Warner
237 F.2d 561 (D.C. Cir. 1956)

BURGER, C.J. This is an appeal from a decision of the District Court instructing a trustee, on his petition for instructions, as to the distribution of the corpus of a trust created by the will of Brainard Warner, Sr. The pertinent trust provisions are as follows:

All the rest, residue and remainder of my estate, . . . I give, . . . unto The Washington Loan and Trust Company, . . . in trust . . . ; third, to divide the remainder of the net income from this trust estate among my wife, Mary H. Warner and my nine children in equal shares, such payments to commence as soon as practicable after my decease and to continue for and during the term of the life of my said wife.[47] On the death of my said wife, I direct my said trustee to divide the entire residuum of my estate into nine (9) equal parts paying one part thereof unto each of my said children.[48] In the event of the death of any of said children before the decease of my said wife, with issue him or her surviving, then such issue shall take the share of its deceased parent in the income and on the death of my wife the share of the deceased parent in the principal, but if there be no such issue, then the share of the deceased child in the income shall be paid to the survivor or survivors of my said wife and children as the case may be, share and share alike until the death of my said wife, when the final division shall take place.

Five of testator's nine children survived him and the life tenant; one child predeceased testator without issue; three children survived testator but predeceased the life tenant, one leaving issue and two leaving no issue. Plaintiff joined as parties defendant the five surviving children, the three children of the child who died before the life tenant and with issue, and the two sole beneficiaries[49] of the estates of the two children who survived testator but predeceased the life tenant without issue. The plaintiff-trustee asked for instructions on the following questions:

1. Did the testator intend that the interest of those children who survived him and died without issue before the death of the life tenant pass under their respective wills to the distributees thereunder, or

2. Did the testator intend that the interests of those children who survived him and died without issue before the death of the life tenant be divested on death and follow the provision for the payment of income and vest per stirpes in the surviving children or the issue of a deceased child and be distributed accordingly?

---

47. By the time of testator's death in 1916 one child, Southard Parker Warner, had predeceased him, unmarried and without issue.

48. The wife died in 1954 and during the period from the death of the testator until the death of the wife, three more of his children had died as follows: (a) Brainard H. Warner, Jr., who died leaving issue who still survive; (b) Rebecca P. Warner, who died testate and without issue; and (c) Andrew Parker Warner, who died testate and without issue.

49. Jennie M. Warner, widow of Andrew Parker Warner, and Anna Parker Warner, sister of Rebecca P. Warner.

The District Court ruled that an examination of the entire will revealed that testator intended to provide primarily both income and principal for his children and their issue, thereby retaining his estate in the "blood line." The Court stated it was "satisfied that the testator intended to divest the share of the child dying without issue in the principal as well as the income, and the proper construction is that there are cross-remainders both as to the income and principal to surviving children, although the will, being ineptly drawn, fails to include the word 'principal'." In other words the trial court has read the will as though it contained provisions for final division of principal in substantially the same terms as testator used with respect to income.

Jennie M. Warner appealed from this decision, contending that her husband, Andrew Parker Warner, having survived the testator, received a vested remainder which could be divested *only* if he died *with issue* and since Andrew died without issue, Jennie, sole beneficiary under his will, was entitled to his share of the principal. Thus, the issues before us are:

(a) Did Andrew acquire a vested remainder in the principal?

(b) If so, what provision of the will, if any, operates to *divest* Andrew's remainder?

As to the first issue, there is little dispute. The law favors early vesting unless testator manifests a contrary intent. Since Andrew Parker Warner was in being at the death of the testator and had an immediate right to possession upon the expiration of his mother's life tenancy, his remainder interest became vested at the death of the testator.

The second question, then, is what provision of the will, if any, divested Andrew's remainder interest in the principal. Divestiture is not accomplished by the provision that "In the event of the death of any of said children before the decease of my said wife, with issue him or her surviving, then such issue shall take the share of its deceased parent . . . in the principal." A provision, such as this, that the children of deceased remaindermen shall take their parents' share is not sufficient to prevent the remainder from being vested; divestiture occurs only upon death leaving issue—there is no divestiture by death alone without issue.

If divestiture of Andrew's share of the principal is to be accomplished, it must be by implication based on the fact that the will provides for divestment of the interest *in income* of those children dying without issue. Appellees contended, and the District Court held, that since the testator provided for the divestiture of the *income interests* of children dying without issue and set up cross-remainders of such interests in the survivors of his wife and children, similar cross-remainders must be implied as to the interest in principal of children dying without issue, even though the will does not so state.

Appellees rely on two cases[50] in which a cross-remainder of principal was implied when there was a cross-remainder of income. It is clear, however, that these cases do not establish a rule that a cross-remainder of

---

50. Boston Safe-Deposit & Trust Co. v. Coffin, 1890, 152 Mass. 95, 25 N.E. 30, 8 L.R.A. 740; Hilton v. Kinsey, 1950, 88 U.S. App. D.C. 14, 185 F.2d 885, 23 A.L.R.2d 830.

principal *must* be implied in such circumstances. In Boston Safe-Deposit & Trust Co. v. Coffin, the court found that the testator intended each branch of his family to have 1/7th of his estate. Therefore, rather than declare two-thirds of one of the 1/7th interests intestate property, thus taking it away from that branch of the family, the court implied a cross-remainder of principal as to the two-thirds. This was done to prevent partial intestacy and to maintain equality of treatment between different branches of the family. Furthermore, since the will had never made any disposition of the principal interest in suit there was no divestment of a vested interest by implication—i.e., the court supplied a disposition where the will was silent; it did not change a disposition already made.

Hilton v. Kinsey concerned the construction of an extremely "ineptly drawn" will. It was necessary for this court to make certain interpretations; e.g., the word "off-spring" was limited by interpretation to mean "children" in order to prevent the will from violating the rule against perpetuities, and the phrase "his . . . and . . . her interest" was interpreted to mean "share of the corpus." The court then found the general plan of testator was that his grandchildren were to be the ultimate beneficiaries and a cross-remainder of a share of the principal was implied in the surviving grand-child. The alternative interpretation, aside from finding an intestacy, would have resulted in a charity taking, and the court stated that an interpretation was favored which prefers the family and kindred to "utter strangers."[51]

In both of these cases the remainder interest in income, provided by the will, went to a person other than the one in whom the remainder interest in principal was implied. In neither case did the court indicate it was implying the remainder in principal simply because of the existence of the income remainder; both courts relied on other factors which they considered indicative of testators' intent.

Appellant relies on De Korwin v. First Nat. Bank of Chicago, 7th Cir., 1949, 179 F.2d 347, which involved a problem similar to that presented by the Warner will. The court there had to construe the following testamentary provision:

> Sixth:—When the last survivor of my daughters shall have deceased and the youngest surviving child of my daughters shall have attained the age of twenty-one (21) years all of said trust estate then remaining in the hands of said trustee shall be divided in equal shares between my grand-children, the surviving issue of any deceased grand-child to stand in the place of and receive the share which such deceased grand-child would have been entitled to receive if then living.

The court concluded that the words following "grand-children" do not prevent the remainders from vesting on the death of the testator but instead fix the conditions upon which *divestiture* will occur and the gift to the descendants of the deceased remaindermen will take effect. It was

---

51. We do not regard a son's wife as an "utter stranger" to the family and in a position comparable to a charity, even when the son married her after the death of the father.

argued in this case, as here, that testator's central purpose was to keep his estate in the hands of his lineal descendants *because he limited the enjoyment of the trust income to his lineal descendants.* The court held, however:

> But to argue that the testator, because he limited the enjoyment of the trust income to his lineal descendants, intended to follow the same pattern in disposing of the corpus is to indulge, we think, in a non sequitur. Indeed, the clarity of the language with which the testator expressed his intention to restrict to his lineal descendants the enjoyment of the trust income, in contrast with the language employed by him in disposing of the trust corpus, weighs against appellants' contention that he was attempting to follow the same scheme in both instances. And finally, it must be remembered that the best guide to the testator's intent is the particular dispositive language used by him. Here, that language, though perhaps not as plain as some might desire, is substantially equivalent to that which Illinois construes as creating a vested remainder, subject to divestiture only by death with issue in the period prior to distribution.

Since in the case of one of the grand-children (Stanley) the event upon which divestiture was conditioned—death with issue—did not occur, his interest in the corpus passed intestate to his heirs at law.[52]

We cannot agree with the District Court that an examination of the entire will demonstrates testator intended to retain his estate in the blood line and that the will was "ineptly drawn." Standing alone, the fact that testator explicitly provided for the divestiture of the *income* interest of children dying without issue is not the kind of evidence of testator's intent on which courts should rely to divest such childrens' vested remainder in the *principal*. Furthermore, while it is true that the testator provided for the divestment of a deceased parent's share of the *principal* when the parent was survived by issue, this provision alone does not establish that testator wanted all his property to remain in the blood line. If such *were* testator's intent he would more likely have made entirely different provisions—e.g., he might have set up a trust, with his wife and nine children as income beneficiaries, and the trust to terminate when the last one of this group died; at that time the issue of the nine children would take their parents' share of the corpus plus one-ninth of the wife's share; there would be appropriate provisions for the issue of a deceased parent taking the parent's share of the income and cross-remainders of income interests of those parents dying without issue; it would also be provided that the share of principal of a child dying without issue would go to the issue of the other children. Such a provision would have assured that the estate was kept in the blood line for a longer period of time than was

---

52. Plaintiff in this case was the executrix of Joseph De Korwin who had married testator's oldest daughter and was the father of testator's grandchild, Stanley. Stanley's other heirs were a widow and half-sister. Another grandchild, Otto, died without issue and leaving as heirs a widow, father, sister and half-brother. Thus, the court was not impressed by the fact that the estate would pass out of testator's blood line. De Korwin v. First Nat'l Bank of Chicago, D.C.N.D. Ill.1949, 84 F.Supp. 918, 923.

possible under the disposition testator did make. For under the will as *written* any child who survived the wife received the corpus absolutely and could dispose of it in any way he chose—he could leave it in toto to his spouse, charities, etc., by testamentary or inter vivos grants, thus taking it out of the blood line completely. This, it seems to us, tends substantially to neutralize if not entirely negate the "blood line" argument.[53] Contrary to the conclusion of the court below, we feel the will *does not* show an intent to keep the estate in the blood line.

An analysis of the controlling provisions of the will also suggests it was not "ineptly drawn" and that, on the contrary, the will uses the pertinent terms artfully. Testator, with discriminating use of the terms "income" and "principal," specifically provided that issue shall take the share of a deceased parent in the *income* and on death of the life tenant a share in the *principal*. He next provided for a cross-remainder of the *income* interest of a child who predeceased the life tenant without issue and then refers to the "final division." The crucial words he used are all words of art contained in a single sentence and we find it difficult to assume that a testator who was presumably trained and experienced in probate and trust work[54] would make such specific provisions, employing the words "income" and "principal", and intend something *other* than what he said. We are impressed by the fact that if testator *intended* to say what he did in fact say, he chose the simplest way of doing so, even to the point of a terseness which gave rise to the seeming need for judicial instruction. To find for appellees we must rule that, assuming testator meant just what he said, he should have explicitly stated, "Furthermore, there are to be no cross-remainders of principal." We cannot expect testators to rebut, in this fashion, possible interpretations of their words.

To sustain the trial court's holding we must at least do one of two things:

(a) *read out* of the will the words "in the income." or

(b) *read into* the will a whole new clause dealing with "the final division" of *principal* in the event of the death of any of testator's children without issue.

The trial court felt that the testator merely omitted the word "principal." However, the problem is more than a matter of simply supplying the words "and principal" to the phrase dealing with disposition of income. The "income provision" concerns the wife and surviving children and *only* during the life of the wife. The problem of "principal" disposition commences only on the death of the wife and would apply (on the trial court's theory) only to the children then surviving or, if deceased, to their issue. The suggestion that the simple insertion of the words "and principal" after "in the income" solves all over-looks the fact that the first problem involves

---

53. That testator was not concerned that all his property stay in the "blood line" is further evidenced by the fact that he bequeathed $6000 to each of his nine children absolutely, to be paid when they became 21.

54. Testator was president of the Washington Loan and Trust Company, Washington, D.C., for some years prior to making this will.

the wife *and* the children and the second involves only the children and their issue *after* the wife's death.

It seems to us to be beyond the powers of judicial interpretation to say that the last inclusion of the phrase "in the income" was inadvertent or that the testator intended, but omitted to provide, that the principal be disposed of in a pattern similar to the disposition of the income. We must conclude that the will is "ineptly drawn" only if we start with the premise that the testator intended to confine his bounty to "blood relatives" and to eliminate "in-laws."[55] We can find nothing in the will which supports such a premise.

Appellees' final argument in support of an interpretation implying cross-mainders [sic] of principal is that if the court finds the will creates vested remainders subject to divestiture only as to children dying *with* issue, there will be an intestacy as to the share of Southard Parker Warner who predeceased testator without issue. This point was not relied on or discussed by the District Court.

This court has held that the provision in the District of Columbia lapse statute[56] that a devise or bequest which fails shall be deemed included in the residuary clause of the will is inapplicable to devises and bequests *in the residuum* and that as to such devises and bequests there is an intestacy. Appellees argue that since the bequest to Southard was in the residuary clause of the will there will be an intestacy as to a 1/9th share of the principal unless there is implied a cross-remainder of the principal interest of a child dying without issue. Appellees, therefore, contend that we must adopt their interpretation in order to avoid intestacy as to a 1/9th share.

Generally speaking if there are two permissible interpretations of a will courts prefer to adopt the one which will avoid intestacy. However, we do not believe that on the facts of this case, in order to avoid intestacy[57] only as to a 1/9th share of the residuum, we should read precise and controlling words into this will when there is no showing that the testator intended them to be there, especially when the result would be a divestiture of a vested remainder.

It is where the words of an instrument as written produce no rational result whatever that courts, faced with an obligation to resolve the problem by decision, can and do interpret the instrument to produce a result which they regard as consistent with the whole. But where the words as written produce a result which is not irrational or inconsistent with the evident

---

55. As we pointed out above, all parties concede that if testator's son survived the life tenant, the 1/9th share could be given to "in-laws" or any others selected by the son.

56. This statute provides:

> If a devisee or legatee die [sic] before the testator, leaving issue who survive the testator, such issue shall take the estate devised or bequeathed as the devisee or legatee would have done if he had survived the testator, unless a different disposition be made or required by the will. Unless a contrary intention appear [sic] by the will, such property as shall be comprised in any devise or bequest in such will which shall fail or be void or otherwise incapable of taking effect shall be deemed included in the residuary devise or bequest, if any, contained in such will. § 19-110, D.C.Code 1951.

57. We do not decide here whether or not there is an intestacy, but only rule that our decision is not affected by such an assumption.

intent of the instrument then courts should refrain from reading controlling words into or out of the instrument. That this may lead to a partial intestacy is not sufficient to warrant rewriting this will on the basis of the scant evidence we have as to testator's unexpressed intent, since the document can be rationally interpreted and applied without adding or excising words.

Therefore, we hold that this instrument gave testator's children vested remainders in the principal subject to being divested only on death with issue and that the interests of Rebecca P. Warner and Andrew Parker Warner were transmissible by their respective wills to their distributees, Anna Parker Warner and Jennie M. Warner. Since the parties have never explicitly considered the question of the effect of this ruling on Southard's 1/9th share and the trial court did not reach or rule on this point, we shall remand the case for further proceedings not inconsistent with this opinion.

Reversed and remanded.

Estate of Thall
18 N.Y.2d 186, 219 N.E.2d 397, 273 N.Y.S.2d 33 (1966)

FULD, J. Solomon Thall died in September, 1943, survived by his wife, a sister and issue of a deceased brother. By a will executed in 1941, he left his residuary estate in trust for the life of his wife with the income to be shared by her and by the testator's sister Sophie Levitsky and Sophie's two sons, Emanuel Landis and Ben Ami Landis. Upon the death of the widow, the corpus of the trust, after payment of certain legacies, was to go to Sophie, Emanuel and Ben Ami, "share and share alike". There then follow these clauses pertaining to the corpus:

> In the event that my sister Sophie Levitsky shall predecease me or surviving me shall predecease my said wife, I give and bequeath her share to her sons Emanuel Landis and Ben Ami Landis, share and share alike.
>
> Should either Emanuel Landis or Ben Ami Landis predecease me or predecease my said wife, I give and bequeath the share of the one so dying to his surviving child or children, and if more than one, share and share alike.
>
> If either of my said nephews Emanuel Landis or Ben Ami Landis should predecease me or surviving me shall predecease my said wife without leaving any child or children him surviving, I direct that his share shall be paid to his surviving brother.

The testator's widow is still alive. Ben Ami Landis died in 1956 survived by his daughter Barbara Ann. Sophie Levitsky died in 1961, and Emanuel Landis died without issue in 1962.

The will makes no provision for disposition of the income provided for Sophie and her two sons in the event which actually occurred, the death of all of them before that of the testator's widow, and this hiatus renders a construction of the will necessary at this time. The will likewise fails to provide for disposition of the corpus under the circumstance which in fact came to pass, namely, the death of one of Sophie's sons without issue *after* the death of the other son who was survived by a child.

The Surrogate decided that both the net income (after deduction of the widow's interest) and the entire corpus (excluding certain specific bequests) should be equally divided, one half to Ben Ami's daughter, Barbara Ann, and one half to those persons who were the testator's distributees on the date of his death. On appeal, the Appellate Division modified the Surrogate's decree by providing (1) that all of the net *income* was payable to the testator's distributees and (2) that, upon the death of the testator's widow, the entire corpus should be paid to Barbara Ann Landis. In our view, Barbara Ann is entitled to all of that portion of the net income not payable to the widow and, upon the latter's death, is to receive the whole of the corpus, except for the specific bequests.

The first rule of testamentary construction, of course, is that a will be interpreted to reflect the actual intention of the testator and the second that this intention be ascertained from a reading of the document as a whole. If a "general scheme" be found, it is the duty of the courts to carry out the testator's purpose, notwithstanding that "general rules of interpretation" might point to a different result.

Corollary to these broad principles is the doctrine that a court may "give effect to an intention or purpose, indicated *by implication*, where the express language of the entire will manifests such an intention or purpose" and the testator has simply neglected to provide for the exact contingency which occurred. As the Appellate Division wrote [Matter of Selner's Estate,] (261 App.Div. [618,] at pp. 620-621, 26 N.Y.S. [783] at p. 786, supra),

> If . . . the property or estate claimed to be bequeathed or devised by implication, in a contingency which has occurred, has been made the subject of an express bequest or devise in another contingency, which did not occur, then effect may be given to such bequest or devise by implication, in the contingency which did occur, if a reading of the entire will makes manifest that such was the intention of the testator.

In the case before us, the testator's intent, as manifested in his will, is plain. Outside of assuring his wife a minimum income during her lifetime, his paramount concern was for his sister and her two sons. His widow and his collateral relatives were left no part of the bulk of his estate. Indeed, in his bequests to the latter, token $1,000 gifts, he repeated more than once his direction that their legacies were to lapse if they predeceased him—or his widow, in the case of gifts from the trust corpus. Quite different were the provisions of the testator's will for his sister and her sons. In addition to receiving that portion of the trust income not bequeathed to his wife, they were to have the entire trust corpus—except for small gifts to collaterals—upon the wife's death. The testator's interest in his sister and her sons also appears in other parts of his will, for instance, in his bequests of personal property to them.

In disposing of his residuary estate, it is evident that the testator inadvertently neglected to foresee every eventuality. As indicated, he provided that Sophie's share, if she predeceased his widow, was to be divided between Emanuel and Ben Ami; that, if either Emanuel or Ben Ami predeceased the widow, the share of the one so dying was to pass to his surviving children, unless he died without issue, in which event his share was to be paid to his surviving brother. Manifestly, the testator expected that Sophie would die before her sons and that each of the sons thereafter dying would be survived by either a child or a brother. However, he failed to anticipate—what actually came to pass—that the second of the sons would die without issue, survived not by his brother but by the latter's child. Quite obviously, what the testator most desired was that his estate should ultimately go to, and remain within, a particular branch of his family. He could not have intended the descendants of Sophie to be deprived of any portion of his estate by the happenstance that the son (of hers) who was without children died *after*, rather than *before*, the son who left offspring. In short, since the testator desired his sister's descendants to take, there is a necessary "implication" that he did not intend any interest of a grandchild of hers to be defeated by the deaths of Emanuel and Ben Ami, as it were, in the wrong order.

Quite dissimilar are the cases in which the court has decreed an intestacy where the intent of the testator is not sufficiently clear to permit a bequest or devise by implication. [In Matter of Jay's Will, 1 N.Y.2d 897, 154 N.Y.S.2d 649, 136 N.E.2d 720,] for instance, the testator left his residuary estate to his wife for life and upon her death to his issue and, if she died without issue, to his mother or sister or the "survivor". We held that the death of the mother and sister prior to the testator's widow resulted in intestacy. In that case, however, unlike the present, there was no manifest intention by the testator to preserve for a particular branch of his family the interests of the remaindermen who might predecease the life tenant.

It is our conclusion, then, that upon the death of the testator's widow the corpus of the trust, except for specific bequests, is to be turned over to Barbara Ann Landis. It is also our conclusion that she is presently entitled, by reason of section 63 of the Real Property Law, Consol.Laws, c. 50, to the income other than the portion payable to the widow. That section provides that,

> When, in consequence of a valid limitation of a future estate, there is a suspension of the power of alienation, or of the ownership, during the continuance of which the rents and profits are undisposed of, and no valid direction for their accumulation is given, such rents and profits shall belong to the persons presumptively entitled to the next eventual estate.

It is clear that Barbara Ann Landis is the person "presumptively entitled to the next eventual estate", and, consequently, all of the income not otherwise disposed of belongs to her.

We have considered the other arguments advanced by the several parties and agree with the Appellate Division's resolution of them.

The order of the Appellate Division should be modified as herein indicated, with costs to all parties filing briefs payable out of the income of the trust in the same manner as the Surrogate's decree directs the payment of counsel fees and allowances, and, as so modified, affirmed.

Notes and Questions

1. *Death in the "Wrong Order."* In stating that the testator "did not intend any interest of a grandchild of [Sophie's] to be defeated by the deaths of Emanuel and Ben Ami, as it were, in the wrong order," the court seemed to be under the impression that if Emanuel's death without issue had occurred before, rather than after, Ben Ami's death, Emanuel's share of the corpus would have gone to Ben Ami's issue, Barbara Ann. Does the language of the will support the court's assumption?

2. *Comparison With Krooss.* Judge Fuld, who wrote the opinion of the court in *Thall*, also wrote the opinion of the court in Matter of Krooss, supra p. 898. *Krooss* was not cited or discussed in *Thall*. Is *Krooss* relevant to the disposition of Emanuel's share of the corpus? Are *Krooss* and *Thall* reconcilable?

3. *Income to the Persons Entitled to the Next Eventual Estate.* With respect to the trust income, the court invoked section 63 of the New York Real Property Law,[58] which directs that undisposed-of income belongs "to the persons presumptively entitled to the next eventual estate." The application of this section, however, is dependent on the instrument not disposing of the income. Did the instrument dispose of the income? See Browder, Trusts and the Doctrine of Estates, 72 Mich. L. Rev. 1509, 1560-61 (1974).

2. Incomplete or Ambiguous Dispositions of Income

Problems

Consider the proper disposition of the trust income or corpus in the following cases:

1. G devised property in trust, to pay the income from the trust "to A." A died, devising all of her estate to B. See Restatement 2d of Trusts § 128 comment b; Scott on Trusts § 128.2; Browder, Trusts and the Doctrine of Estates, 72 Mich. L. Rev. 1509, 1532-42 (1974). Compare Estate of Bowles, 107 N.M. 739, 764 P.2d 510 (Ct. App. 1988) (will devising income from Blackacre to testator's sister and residue of estate, including Blackacre, to testator's children; held, the will gave the sister only a *life estate* in income from Blackacre).

2. G devised property in trust, to "pay half the income to my child, A, for life and half the income to my child, B, for life; upon the death of the

---

58. This section now appears, in somewhat modified form, as § 9-2.3 of N.Y. Est. Powers & Trusts Law.

survivor of my children, corpus to my then-living descendants, by representation; if none, to X-Charity."

(a) A died without descendants, survived by B. See Restatement of
Property § 115.

(b) A died survived by descendants and by B. See Dewire v. Haveles,
404 Mass. 274, 534 N.E.2d 782 (1989).

3. G devised property in trust, to pay the income "to my children, A and
B, for their respective lives; corpus upon their deaths to their descendants,
by representation; if none, to X-Charity." A died without issue, survived by
B.

4. G devised property in trust, to pay the income "to A and B for 21
years; at the expiration of 21 years, corpus to my then-living descendants,
by representation; if none, to X-Charity." A died five years after G's death,
devising all of her estate to C.

5. G devised property in trust, directing the trustee to pay to A during
A's lifetime so much of the income as the trustee determines is necessary
for A's support and education, corpus on A's death to A's then-living
descendants, by representation; if none, to X-Charity. During A's lifetime,
the income was more than sufficient to pay for A's support and education.
What happens to the surplus income?

6. G devised property in trust, directing the trustee to pay $50,000 per
year to A for A's lifetime, corpus on A's death to A's then-living descendants, by representation; if none, to X-Charity. What happens to the surplus
income if the income exceeds $50,000 in any one year?

7. G devised $600,000 in trust, granting the trustee the discretionary
power to spray the income among G's surviving spouse, H, and G's
descendants; the trust terminates upon H's death, with the corpus then
going to G's then-living descendants, by representation; if none, to
X-Charity.

G's descendants are her two adult children, A and B, and three young
grandchildren, X, Y, and Z. X and Y are A's children; Z is B's child.

Since neither H nor the children, A and B, need any of the income from
the trust, they all agree with the trustee that the trustee's discretionary
power should be exercised in favor of the grandchildren, who are minors
and in low income-tax brackets.

How should the trustee divide the income among X, Y, and Z? Should
half of the income be divided between X and Y, with the other half going
to Z; or should the income be divided among X, Y, and Z equally? A and
B have different views on the matter. Can the trustee allocate any of the
income to the grandchildren, given the fact that they have living ancestors
(A and B)?

EXTERNAL REFERENCES. Browder, Trusts and the Doctrine of Estates, 72
Mich. L. Rev. 1509, 1542-75 (1974); Halbach, Issues About Issue: Some
Recurrent Class Gift Problems, 48 Mo. L. Rev. 333, 355-57 (1983).

Chapter 17

THE RULE AGAINST PERPETUITIES AND RELATED RULES

We now make an abrupt shift, from matters of construction, the purposes of which are to carry out intent, to rules of law that defeat intent for reasons of overriding social policy. Specifically, the main subject of this chapter is the Rule Against Perpetuities. The Rule Against Perpetuities was originally designed to throttle the dead hand from indirectly curtailing the alienability of property for too long a period—in perpetuity. The indirect curtailment of alienability was said to arise from attaching contingencies to future interests in property.

A rule that developed, step by step over time, into the rule known today as the Rule Against Perpetuities was initiated in the much-celebrated Duke of Norfolk's Case, 3 Ch. Cas. 1, 22 Eng. Rep. 931 (1682). The so-called *modern* Rule Against Perpetuities was formulated by Professor John Chipman Gray in the second edition of his book, The Rule Against Perpetuities (2d ed. 1906):

> No [nonvested property] interest is good unless it must vest, if at all, not later than 21 years after some life in being at the creation of the interest.[1]

Nothing resembling this mechanically precise "rule" was stated by the judge in the Duke of Norfolk's Case, the Lord Chancellor, the First Earl of Nottingham. His pronouncements about a prohibition on perpetuities appear to be mere musings:

> But what Time? And where are the Bounds of that Contingency? You may limit, it seems, upon a Contingency to happen in a Life: What if it be limited, if such a one die without Issue within twenty-one Years, or 100 Years, or while *Westminster-Hall* stands? Where will you stop, if you do not stop here? I will tell you where I will stop: I will stop wherever any visible Inconvenience doth appear; . . . .

---

1. This formulation was carried forward, word for word, in subsequent editions of his book. Gray on Perpetuities § 201. A similar formulation was set forth in the first edition of the book published in 1886.

Despite the appearance of imprecision, even casualness, of the Lord Chancellor's statement,[2] the Duke of Norfolk's Case was an exceedingly important case at the time. But not in the way that might at first be imagined: The decision apparently served less as a judicial warning that perpetuities would not be tolerated than as an approval of conveyancers' practices current at the time. The future interest challenged in the Duke of Norfolk's Case was an executory interest. Although the destructibility rule had earlier been held inapplicable to executory interests in Pells v. Brown, Cro. Jac. 590, 79 Eng. Rep. 504 (K.B. 1620), that decision was a sudden and unexpected departure from prior law. Also, a later decision, Purefoy v. Rogers, 2 Wm. Saund. 380, 85 Eng. Rep. 1181 (K.B. 1670), cast some doubt on the continuing validity of *Pells*, by holding that a contingent remainder could not avoid destruction by changing into an executory interest after it was created. The Duke of Norfolk's Case assured the practicing bar that *Pells* remained solid law.

Gradually, over the 150 or so years following the Duke of Norfolk's Case, the pronouncement that a contingency limited to "happen in a Life" was valid, but beyond that, an invalidity would arise "wherever any visible Inconvenience doth appear," grew step by step into the Rule Against Perpetuities stated by Professor Gray, above. The period of a life was enlarged to multiple lives, which in effect is but a single life, the choice being postponed to turn upon which of several is the survivor. Scatterwood v. Edge, 1 Salk. 229, 91 Eng. Rep. 203 (K.B. 1697). To this period was added the period of an actual minority of a beneficiary; and also an actual period of gestation. Some considerable time later, in Cadell v. Palmer, 1 Cl. & F. 372, 6 Eng. Rep. 956 (1833), the minority period was disengaged from an actual minority and allowed as a 21-year period in gross.

Although Professor Gray's book solidified the common-law Rule Against Perpetuities, stunting its further evolution and growth throughout the earlier half of this century, the Rule Against Perpetuities is again undergoing change. The current round of changes has been coming mainly in the form of perpetuity-reform legislation, though there have been some measures of development at common law as well. The most important of the reforms is the promulgation in 1986 of the Uniform Statutory Rule Against Perpetuities (USRAP). USRAP was revised modestly and incorporated into the UPC in 1990. See UPC §§ 2-901 to -906 (1990). The perpetuity-reform movement is discussed infra Part D.

EXTERNAL REFERENCES. On the Duke of Norfolk's Case, see Haskins, Extending the Grasp of the Dead Hand: Reflections on the Origins of the Rule Against Perpetuities, 126 U. Pa. L. Rev. 19 (1977); Haskins, "Inconvenience" and the Rule For Perpetuities, 48 Mo. L. Rev. 451 (1983). On Professor Gray's influence, see Siegel, John Chipman Gray, Legal Formalism, and the Transformation of Perpetuities Law, 36 U. Miami L. Rev. 439 (1982). On the mechanics of the common-law Rule, see Leach, Perpetuities

---

2. Although Nottingham, the Lord Chancellor, did not define a perpetuity, he apparently felt that he would know one if he saw it.

in a Nutshell, 51 Harv. L. Rev. 638 (1938); Leach, The Nutshell Revisited, 78 Harv. L. Rev. 973 (1965). For a comprehensive comparison of the law of a particular jurisdiction with the general common-law Rule, see Chaffin, The Rule Against Perpetuities As Applied to Georgia Wills and Trusts: A Survey and Suggestions for Reform, 16 Ga. L. Rev. 235 (1982).

PART A. MECHANICS OF THE COMMON-LAW RULE AGAINST PERPETUITIES

Interests to Which the Rule Applies. The Rule Against Perpetuities applies to future interests in property, whether legal or equitable, but only if they are nonvested (contingent). Classification of the interests in a disposition is, therefore, a preliminary but crucial step to solving perpetuity questions. Specifically, the Rule applies to contingent remainders and to executory interests, both of which are nonvested future interests. The Rule does not apply to vested remainders, not even to those that are vested subject to defeasance; nor does the Rule apply to reversions, which are always vested.[3] The other two reversionary future interests—possibilities of reverter and rights of entry—are also thought to be exempt from the Rule Against Perpetuities.

Class gifts are also subject to the Rule, and in fact are treated specially. The early English decision of Leake v. Robinson, 2 Mer. 363, 35 Eng. Rep. 979 (Ch. 1817), laid down the proposition that *if the interest of any potential class member might vest too remotely, the entire class gift is invalid.* This is the so-called all-or-nothing rule, by which it is meant that a class gift is either *completely* valid or *completely* invalid. It is not permissible to treat the interest of each class member separately, and say that some class members have valid interests and other class members have invalid interests. More extensive consideration of the special case of class gifts is presented in Part E, infra.

The "Perpetuity Period." The common-law perpetuity period is defined as a life in being plus 21 years. The period can be extended by one or more periods of gestation, *but only when an actual pregnancy makes the extension necessary.*[4] In other words, the period of gestation is not a formal part of the perpetuity period. Cadell v. Palmer, 1 Cl. & F. 372 (H.L. 1883).

The life in being, often called the *measuring life,* must be the life of a person "in being at the creation of the interest." This means that the person whose life is the measuring life must be alive or in gestation when the perpetuity period begins to run. The measuring life must also be a human

---

3. "A vested interest is not subject to the Rule against Perpetuities." Gray on Perpetuities § 205.

4. USRAP § 1(d) (1990 UPC § 2-901(d)) takes a different approach. It provides that, "in determining whether a nonvested property interest [is valid under the common-law Rule], the possibility that a child will be born to an individual after the individual's death is disregarded."

life—the life of a corporation, an animal, or a plant cannot be used. But there are no further restrictions. Theoretically, anyone in the world who was alive or in gestation when the interest was created can be the measuring life. As a practical matter, though, it is not that simple, as we shall see, when one gets down to the problem of identifying the measuring life in actual cases.

Although the 21-year part of the perpetuity period is described by Gray as coming *after* the death of the person who is the measuring life, and we often refer to it as the *tack-on* 21-year period, the 21-year part need not be preceded by a measuring life; it can stand on its own. A testamentary transfer "to such of my grandchildren as are living on the 21st anniversary of my death" would be valid without the necessity of locating a measuring life.

While authority on the question is sparse, it seems to be agreed that the 21-year part cannot come first, followed by a life that is in being 21 years *after* the creation of the interest. This is a consequence of the requirement that the measuring life must be in being *at* the creation of the interest.

> *Example 17.1:* G bequeathed property in trust "to pay the income to G's children for 21 years, then to pay the income of such of G's grandchildren as may then be living for life, and on the death of the survivor to pay the corpus of the trust to G's descendants then living by representation."
>
> If G is survived by one or more children, the remainder interest in the corpus of the trust violates the Rule and is invalid.

As noted above, a child in gestation at the commencement of the perpetuity period can be a measuring life because the child is considered then to be "in being." So also the perpetuity period is expandable at the end to account for an actual period of gestation, if necessary.

1. The Requirement of Initial Certainty

Requirement of Initial Certainty. Implicit in Professor Gray's formulation is the *requirement of initial certainty*, which is that *a nonvested future interest is invalid if, at the creation of the interest, there exists any possible chain of events that might subsequently arise that would allow the interest to remain nonvested beyond a life in being plus 21 years.*

Measuring Life. The "perpetuity period" is a life in being plus 21 years plus, if needed for validity, one or more periods of gestation. The life in being is traditionally called the "measuring life." This suggests that one must identify a particular person as *the* measuring life in *each* case and then test the interest to determine whether or not the interest might remain nonvested beyond 21 years following such person's death. This is *not* the procedure, however. It is wrong to speak as if there is a definite perpetuity period tied into the lifetime of a particular person in the case of both valid and invalid interests. For a life in being to be a "measuring life," the person must satisfy the requirement of initial certainty, which means that *there must be a causal connection between the person's death and the vesting or termination*[5] *of the interest no later than 21 years thereafter.* Only in the case of *valid* dispositions will there be a particular life who has the requisite causal connection and is identified as the so-called *measuring* life. An invalid interest is invalid because there is *no* measuring life that makes it valid—not because it might remain nonvested beyond 21 years after the death of an *identifiable* measuring life. This is what is meant when it is said that invalidity under the common-law Rule depends upon the existence, as of the interest's creation, of an invalidating chain of possible post-creation events. *The search for a "measuring life," therefore, turns out in reality to be a search for a "validating life."*

In Truth, There Is No "Perpetuity Period" at Common Law. The requirement of initial certainty is a mechanism for testing the validity of an interest *in advance* of its actual vesting or termination. With the decision made in advance, the common law has no need to mark off a "perpetuity period" in the case of invalid interests,[6] and no common-law decision has ever declared or even intimated that it does. Here is why: A "perpetuity period" would be necessary only if *actual* post-creation events were to be taken into account to see if an interest for which there is *no* validating life *actually* vests or terminates within that period of time. But the common-law Rule does not permit actual post-creation events to be considered. For interests for which there *is* a validating life, there is no need to trace the actual longevity of that person, for the time of that person's death is immaterial. By definition, the interest *cannot possibly* vest or terminate beyond 21 years after that person's death; the actual time of that person's death does not matter. For valid interests, in other words, the common law uses the life-in-being-plus-21-years "period" in a way that does not require an actual period of time to be marked off by the tracing of the lives of so-called "measuring lives."

2. How to Search for a Validating Life

Goal of the Search: To Find One Person For Whom There Is No Invalidating Chain of Possible Post-Creation Events. The Official Comment to USRAP

---

5. An interest terminates when vesting becomes impossible. In the following example, B's interest terminates if and when she or he predeceases A: "to A for life, remainder to B if B survives A."

6. See J. Ritchie, N. Alford & R. Effland, Decedents' Estates and Trusts 1080 (7th ed. 1988) ("The common law Rule does not allow a time period."); Waggoner, Perpetuities: A Perspective on Wait-and-See, 85 Colum. L. Rev. 1714, 1714-17 (1985); Waggoner, Perpetuity Reform, 81 Mich. L. Rev. 1718, 1720-24 (1983). Professor Dukeminier disputes this. Dukeminier, A Modern Guide to Perpetuities, 74 Calif. L. Rev. 1867, 1868-76 (1986); Dukeminier, Perpetuities: The Measuring Lives, 85 Colum. L. Rev. 1648, 1649-54 (1985). The dispute is in reality a by-product of a different controversy concerning the wait-and-see method of perpetuity reform (see infra Part D); it has no bearing on the solution of perpetuity problems under the common-law Rule, a point that corroborates the position that there is no "perpetuity period" as such at common law.

section 1 sets forth the following guidance for solving a perpetuities problem:

> The process for determining whether a validating life exists is to postulate the death of each individual connected in some way to the transaction, and ask the question: Is there with respect to this individual an invalidating chain of possible [post-creation] events? If one individual can be found for whom the answer is No, that individual can serve as the validating life. As to that individual there will be the requisite causal connection between his or her death and the questioned interest's vesting or terminating no later than 21 years thereafter.

Note that the converse is also true: If no person can be found for whom there is no invalidating chain of possible post-creation events, there is no validating life; an interest for which there is no validating life is invalid.

Only Insiders Need to be Considered. In searching for a validating life, there is no formal rule forbidding the testing of anyone in the world to see if she or he has the causal connection demanded by the requirement of initial certainty. There is, for example, no law against testing your favorite movie star or rock star in each case, if you want to do that. But experience has shown that no outsider will pass the test.

What we mean to say is that you can safely limit the persons you test to insiders—those who are connected in some way to the transaction. Only insiders have a chance of supplying the requisite causal connection demanded by the requirement of initial certainty. The insiders to be tested vary from situation to situation, but would always include the transferor, if living, the beneficiaries of the disposition, including but not restricted to the taker or takers of the challenged interest, the objects and donee of a power of appointment, persons related to the foregoing by blood or adoption, especially in the ascending and descending lines, and anyone else who has any connection to the transaction. If there is any doubt about a particular person, no harm is done by subjecting that person to the test. Usually it takes no more than an instant to resolve whether or not a person arguably on the fringe of the transaction has the requisite causal connection demanded by the requirement of initial certainty.

There is, however, no point in even considering the life of a complete outsider who is clearly unconnected to the transaction—a person selected at random from the world at large—just because the outsider happened to be in being at the creation of the interest. Outsiders in that category have already been tested and found *always* to be wanting. No outsider can possibly fulfill the requirement of initial certainty because there will always be an invalidating chain of possible post-creation events as to every outsider who might be proposed: Any outsider can immediately die after the creation of the interest without having any effect whatsoever on the time when the interest will vest or terminate.

Survivor of Group. In appropriate cases the validating life need not be individuated. Rather, the life can be an as yet (looking at the situation as of the date of the creation of the interests) unidentified member of a group of individuals. It is common in these cases to say that the members of the group are the validating *lives*. This is acceptable, as long as it is recognized that the true meaning of the statement is that the validating *life* is the life of the member of the group who turns out to live the longest. As the court said in Skatterwood v. Edge, 1 Salk. 229, 91 Eng. Rep. 203 (K.B. 1697), "for let the lives be never so many, there must be a survivor, and so it is but the length of that life; for [Justice] Twisden [in Love v. Wyndham, 1 Mod. 50, 54 Eng. Rep. 724, 726 (K.B. 1681)] used to say, the candles were all lighted at once."

Recipient of the Interest as the Validating Life. A well established but sometimes overlooked point is that in appropriate cases the recipient of an interest can be her or his own validating life. See, e.g., Rand v. Bank of California, 236 Or. 619, 388 P.2d 437 (1964). This point is especially useful in cases in which an interest is contingent on the recipient's reaching an age in excess of 21 or is contingent on the recipient's survivorship of a particular point in time that is or may be in excess of 21 years after the interest was created or after the death of a person in being at the date of creation.

Problems

All the nonvested property interests in the following cases satisfy the requirement of initial certainty and are therefore valid. Using the above text as a guide, identify the validating life for each interest.

1. G devised property "to A for life, remainder to such of A's children as attain 21." G was survived by his son (A), his daughter (B), A's wife (W), and A's two children (X and Y).

2. Take the same facts as in Problem 1, but change the disposition to read "to B for life, remainder to such of A's children as attain 21."

3. G devised real property "to such of my grandchildren as attain 21." Some of G's children are living at G's death.

4. (a) G devised real property "to such of A's children as attain 25;" or,

    (b) G devised real property "to such of A's children as are living on the 25th anniversary of my death."

A predeceased G. At G's death, A had three living children, all of whom were under 25.

Multiple Interests. Dispositions of property sometimes create more than one interest that is subject to the Rule. When this happens, the validity of each interest must be tested separately. A validating life that validates one interest might or might not validate the other interests. Consequently, the search for a validating life for each interest must be undertaken.

Problems

1. G devised property "to A for life, then to A's children for their lives, and on the death of each of them to the survivor or survivors of them for life, and on the death of the survivor of them, to B and her heirs."

Do any of the interests created in this disposition violate the common-law Rule Against Perpetuities? See Dodge v. Bennett, 215 Mass. 545, 102 N.E. 916 (1913); Gray on Perpetuities § 207. Suppose the remainder interest to B had been contingent on survivorship of A's last surviving child—that is, suppose it had said "to B if B is then living"?

2. All but one of the future interests in the following cases fail the requirement of initial certainty and are therefore invalid. Explain why there is no validating life in each case. Which future interest is valid and why?

(a) (1) G devised real property "to A and her heirs so long as liquor is not sold on the premises, and upon liquor's being sold on the premises, the property is to go to B;" or

(2) G devised real property "to A and her heirs on condition that no liquor be sold on the premises, but if liquor is sold on the premises, the property is to go to B."

In both cases, G was survived by A and B.

(b) G devised property in trust, directing the trustee to pay the net income therefrom "to A for life, then to A's children for the life of the survivor, and upon the death of A's last surviving child, to pay the corpus of the trust to A's grandchildren." G was survived by A and A's two children, X and Y.

————

Interests That Must Vest or Terminate Within 21 Years. As noted above, there is no need to search for a validating life in the case of interests that are certain to vest or terminate within 21 years after their creation; the 21-year part of the period validates such interests.

In Green v. Green, 9 Ohio Misc. 15, 221 N.E.2d 388 (P. Ct. 1966), an action for a declaratory judgment was brought to construe the will of Roy C. Green, who died on July 24, 1955. Roy was survived by his only child Richard, his sister Helen, Richard's wife Elsie, and their three children, William, Judith, and Betsy. William was born on February 1, 1941, Judith on May 21, 1942, and Betsy on July 28, 1947. Roy's will established a trust that provided:

(6) The trust shall terminate upon the last to happen of the following counts:
(a) The death of my son, Richard C. Green.
(b) The death or remarriage of Elsie L. Green.
(c) The day the youngest living child of my son, Richard C. Green, in being on the date of my death, attains twenty-five (25) years of age.
(d) The death of my sister, Helen Green.
Upon the termination of the trust, the Trustee shall assign, transfer, convey and deliver all of the property then comprising the trust to the lineal descendants of my son, Richard C. Green, per stirpes.

To a contention that the interest in the corpus violated the Rule Against Perpetuities, the court responded:

> Where a trust is to terminate at the time when a designated person attains a specified age, courts have construed this to mean that if the person dies before attaining the required age, the trust terminates immediately upon his death. In re Fishberg's Will, 158 Misc. 3, 285 N.Y.S. 303 (Surr. Ct. 1936); Sammis v. Sammis, 14 R.I. 123 (1883); Butler v. Butler, 40 R.I. 425, 101 A. 115 (1917).
>
> Other courts have held that the trust terminates when the designated person would have attained the specified age had he lived that long. In re Clark's Estate, 13 N.J. Misc. 393, 178 A. 574 (Orphans' Court 1935); Stein v. United States National Bank of Portland, 165 Or. 518, 108 P.2d 1016 (1941).
>
> Basically, the court is trying to find the intention of the testator, and this is reflected in the authorities cited.
>
> Fortunately, we need not analyze the cases to see whether they can be reconciled, nor need we choose between the two views, for under either view the trust in the present case will terminate, the class will close, and the remainders will vest within twenty-one years after lives in being at the date of the testator's death. . . .

What feature of the case allowed the court to declare the interests valid without choosing "between the two views"?

3. Time of Creation

Statutory References: USRAP § 2
                            1990 UPC § 2-902

The time when a property interest is created is important because it fixes the time when the validating life must be "in being." It is also important because it demarks the facts that can be taken into account in determining the validity of an interest. Under the common-law Rule, an interest is valid only if at the time when the interest is created, with the facts *then existing* taken into account, the interest is certain to vest or terminate within a life in being plus 21 years. The facts that *actually* occur from that time forward, with one exception concerning interests created by the exercise of certain powers of appointment (see infra Part E), are irrelevant; all that counts thereafter is what *might* happen.

Property interests created by will are created when the testator dies, not when the testator signs the will. Thus the validating life for testamentary transfers must be a person who was alive (or in gestation) when the testator died, and the facts that can be taken into account in determining the validity of an interest created by will are those existing at the testator's death.

Property interests created by inter-vivos transfers are created when the transfers become effective for purposes of property law generally. This would ordinarily be the date of delivery of the deed or the funding of the trust. Thus the validating life for inter-vivos transfers must be a person who was alive (or in gestation) when the transfer became effective, and the facts that can be taken into account in determining the validity of an interest created by inter-vivos transfer are those existing at that time.

Problem

G conveyed property to a trustee, directing the trustee to pay the net income to herself (G) for life, then to G's son A for his life, then for life to A's children who are living at G's death, and upon the death of the last survivor of such children, the corpus of the trust is to be distributed among A's then-living descendants, by representation. Are any interests in this trust invalid? Suppose:

1. The trust was irrevocable.
2. G retained the power to revoke the trust.

The Postponement Principle. For purposes of the Rule Against Perpetuities, the time of creation of a property interest is postponed in certain cases. One of the leading decisions on the postponement principle is Cook v. Horn, 214 Ga. 289, 104 S.E.2d 461 (1958). In the course of its opinion, the court explained the principle in these terms:

> While there is a scarcity of authority on this question, and none that we have found in Georgia, the prevailing opinion by both the courts of other jurisdictions and recognized text writers is that, when a settlor has the power during his lifetime to revoke or destroy the trust estate for his own exclusive personal benefit, the question whether interests, or any of them, created by an instrument or deed of trust are void because in violation of the rule against perpetuities, is to be determined as of the date of the settlor's death and not as of the date the instrument is executed and delivered. See Ryan v. Ward, 192 Md. 342, 64 A.2d 258, 7 A.L.R.2d 1078; Mifflin's Appeal, 121 Pa. 205, 15 A. 525, 1 L.R.A. 453; Goesele v. Bimeler, 14 How. 589, 14 L.Ed. 554; Manufacturers Life Insurance Company v. von Hamm-Young Co., 34 Haw. 288; Pulitzer v. Livingston, 89 Me. 359, 36 A. 635; City Bank Farmers Trust Company v. Cannon, 291 N.Y. 125, 51 N.E.2d 674, 157 A.L.R. 1424; Equitable Trust Co. v. Pratt, 117 Misc. 708, 190 N.Y.S. 152, affirmed on opinion below 206 App. Div. 689, 199 N.Y.S. 921; Gray, Rule Against Perpetuities, (4th Ed.) 510, par. 524; 45 Harv. L. Rev. 896; 51 Harv. L. Rev. 638; 86 Univ. of Pa.L.Rev. 221; Restatement of Property, § 373 and comments (c) and (d), and Ryan v. Ward, 192 Md. 342, 64 A.2d 258, 7 A.L.R.2d 1078.
>
> While none of these authorities is binding upon this court, the conclusion reached by them is in accord with the aim of and reason for the rule against perpetuities, which is to prevent the tying up of property for an unreasonable length of time and to prohibit unreasonable restraint upon the alienation of property. So long as the settlor of an inter vivos trust has the absolute right to revoke or terminate the trust for his own exclusive personal benefit, there is no tying up of property and no restraint upon the alienability of the property in the trust fund, and thus no reason to include this time during

which the trust is so destructible in determining whether a limitation is violative of the rule against perpetuities. Restatement, Property, sec. 373 states:

> The period of time during which an interest is destructible, pursuant to the uncontrolled volition, and for the exclusive personal benefit of the person having such a power of destruction is not included in determining whether the limitation is invalid under the rule against perpetuities.

We conclude that this rule is a sound one, which does no violence to the rule against perpetuities, but is in complete accord with its aim and purpose.

Does the postponement principle extend to cases other than revocable trusts? Court authority on this question is sparse, if not non-existent, but the commentators believe that it does. See Simes & Smith on Future Interests § 1252. The Restatement of Property section 373, also, declares the principle to be broader: For purposes of the Rule Against Perpetuities, the creation of an interest is postponed so long as the interest "is destructible, pursuant to the uncontrolled volition, and for the exclusive personal benefit of the person having such a power of destruction."

Under this statement of the principle, the power need not be a power to revoke and it need not be held by the settlor or transferor. An *unqualified* and *currently exercisable* power held by *any* person *acting alone* to make herself or himself the beneficial owner of the questioned interest is sufficient. Accord Restatement 2d of Property § 1.2; USRAP § 2(b); UPC § 2-902(b) (1990).

An example of a power that should cause a postponement of the time of creation of the remainder interest under the postponement principle would be a presently exercisable general power of appointment over the remainder interest. Another example would be a power, held by any person who could act alone, to invade the corpus of a trust.

Be sure to notice an important consequence of the idea that a power need not be held by the settlor to postpone the time of creation: It makes postponement available even in cases of testamentary transfers.

> *Example 17.2:* G devised property in trust, directing the trustee to pay the income "to A for life, remainder to such persons as A shall appoint; in default of appointment, the property to remain in trust to pay the income to A's children for the life of the survivor, and upon the death of A's last surviving child, to divide the corpus equally among A's grandchildren." A survived G.
>
> If the perpetuity period commences running on G's death, the remainder interest in favor of A's grandchildren is invalid. But if the Restatement view is followed, thus postponing the running of the period to the expiration (at A's death) of A's presently exercisable general power, the interest is valid. The substance of this transaction is the equivalent of G's having devised the property to A in fee simple absolute and of A's having in turn devised the property at his death in accordance with G's gift in default clause. The Restatement view ought therefore to be followed. Note, however, that if G had conferred on A a *nongeneral* power or a general *testamentary* power, the perpetuity period would clearly commence running on G's death, causing the grandchildren's interest to be invalid.

Problem

In Year One, G created an irrevocable inter-vivos trust, funding it with $20,000 cash. In Year Five, when the value of the investments in which the original $20,000 contribution was placed had risen to a value of $30,000, G added $10,000 cash to the trust. G died in Year Ten. G's will poured the residue of his estate into the trust. G's residuary estate consisted of Blackacre (worth $20,000) and securities (worth $80,000). At G's death, the value of the investments in which the original $20,000 contribution and the subsequent $10,000 contribution were placed had risen to a value of $50,000. G's trust created property interests that are subject to the Rule Against Perpetuities. When are those interests "created" for purposes of determining whether or not they are valid? Cf. USRAP § 2(c); UPC § 2-902(c) (1990).

———

The Rule of Convenience. As noted, in determining whether a nonvested property interest is valid or invalid, the facts existing at the creation of the interest are to be taken into account. This refers not only to the facts as such, but also to the rules of law or construction that those facts trigger. A rule of construction that figures prominently in many perpetuity cases is the rule of convenience.

Problems

Determine the validity of the property interests in the following cases:
1. G devised property in trust, directing the trustee to pay the net income therefrom "to A for life, then to A's children for the life of the survivor, and upon the death of A's last surviving child, to pay the corpus of the trust to A's grandchildren." A predeceased G. G was survived by A's two children, X and Y.
2. G devised real property "to such of A's children as attain 25." At G's death, A (who was then alive) had three living children, all of whom were under 25.
3. In Problem 2, suppose that A's eldest child had reached 25 by the time of G's death.
4. G devised real property "to A for life, then to such of A's children as reach 25." A survived G. By the time of G's death, A's eldest child had reached 25.

4. Constructional Preference for Validity

Gray stated that a will or deed is to be construed without regard to the Rule Against Perpetuities, and then the Rule is to be "remorselessly" applied to the provisions so construed. Gray on Perpetuities § 629. Some courts may still adhere to this proposition. See Colorado Nat'l Bank v. McCabe,

143 Colo. 21, 353 P.2d 385 (1960); Continental Illinois Nat'l Bank & Trust Co. v. Llewellyn, 67 Ill. App. 2d 171, 214 N.E.2d 471 (1966).

Most courts, we believe, would now be inclined to adopt the proposition put forward by the Restatement of Property section 375, which is that where an instrument is ambiguous—that is, where it is fairly susceptible to two or more constructions, one of which causes a Rule violation and the other of which does not—the construction that does not result in a Rule violation should be adopted. Cases supporting this view include First Nat'l Bank v. Jenkins, 256 Ga. 223, 345 S.E.2d 829 (1986); Southern Bank & Trust Co. v. Brown, 271 S.C. 260, 246 S.E.2d 598 (1978); Davis v. Rossi, 326 Mo. 911, 34 S.W.2d 8 (1930).

Does Rust v. Rust, which follows, also represent an application of the constructional preference for validity?

Rust v. Rust
211 S.W.2d 262 (Tex. Civ. App. 1948)

McCLENDON, C.J. Suit to construe the will of John Y. Rust, Jr. The controlling question is whether the provisions of the will disposing of the residuary estate violates Art. I, Sec. 26, Texas Constitution, Vernon's Ann.St., condemning perpetuities. The trial court upheld all provisions of the will, rendered judgment accordingly, and defendant Mrs. Margene Welch Rust, surviving wife of testator, has appealed in her individual capacity, and as guardian of the estate of Margene A. Rust (a minor), the only child of herself and testator.

The pertinent portions of the will (after a $1,000 legacy to Mrs. Rust) read:

> Four. All the remainder of my property of every kind and character, real, personal, mixed or choses in action of which I may die seized or possessed and wheresoever situated, I will, give, devise and bequeath in trust to my executors and trustees hereinafter named and to the survivor thereof and the substitute trustee hereinafter named to hold, manage, use and control for the use and benefit of my daughter, Margene A. Rust.
>
> The property here left for the use and benefit of my daughter, Margene, shall be held in trust by my trustees, the survivor thereof and the substitute trustee until the 17th day of October, 1967, upon which date the trust shall terminate and the property here left in trust shall vest in fee simple in my daughter, Margene A. Rust, free of any restrictions whatsoever.
>
> If my daughter, Margene A. Rust, dies before October 17, 1967, the date upon which the trust herein created terminates, and leaves surviving her issue of her body, then such issue of her body shall become the beneficiary or beneficiaries of this trust and upon the date of its termination the fee simple title to all the property here left in trust shall vest share and share alike in such issue of her body then surviving.
>
> If my daughter, Margene A. Rust, dies before October 17, 1967, the date upon which the trust herein created terminates and does not leave surviving her any issue of her body, then upon her death, all of the property here left in trust shall pass in fee simple share and share alike unto my then living

brothers and sister with the child or children of any brother or sister who then may be deceased, taking the share of the parent per stirpes . . . .

Testator's two brothers George Foster and Armistead Dudley Rust were named independent executors without bond. They, and the survivor of them, were also named as trustees; a bank in San Angelo was named substitute trustee.

The facts are without dispute. They show:

John Y. Rust, Jr., died May 6, 1942. His will was probated May 26, 1942, and his executors promptly qualified and took charge of his estate. His only heirs at law were his surviving wife and daughter. His father, John Y. Rust, Sr., was living. His mother, Agnes B. Rust, died in 1941. The only other children of his father and mother were the two brothers and a sister, Sarah Agnes Rust Gordon. George Foster Rust was married to Minnie Rust. They had no children. Armistead Dudley Rust was married to Sarah J. Rust. They had one child, Nancy Rust, a minor. Mrs. Gordon's husband was Charles R. Gordon. Their only child was a daughter, Jean, married to Charles R. Rainey. Her only child was a three-month old son.

Testator's estate consisted principally of a 1/4 undivided interest in ranch lands—20,394.9 acres in Kimble County, known as Bear Creek Ranch, and 20,895.1 acres in Tom Green County, known as Campbell Ranch. His interest therein was appraised at $116,284.44. The rest of his estate was personalty, appraised at $10,533.05. His total indebtedness was listed at $81,547.75, $73,520.75 of which was in a note to his father for advances to cover excessive living expenses, secured by trust deed upon his interest in the two ranch properties. Net value of his estate was appraised at $45,289.94. The other 3/4 interest in these ranches was owned by his brothers and sister. We give these details regarding his family and estate for whatever light they may shed upon a proper interpretation of the will.

The executors have paid Mrs. Rust's legacy; have renewed the trust deed (now held by a bank); and together with the other joint owners have executed two oil and gas leases upon the ranch properties.

The suit was brought by the two brothers, as executors and trustees, as well as individually, joined in by all the other contingent beneficiaries under the will and the owner of the mineral leases, against Margene W. Rust, individually and as guardian of Margene A. Rust, and against the latter individually. In view of a possible conflict of interest between Margene W. Rust and her ward, the court appointed a guardian ad litem for the latter, who sought to uphold the will, and appears here as an appellee in support of the judgment. . . .

Since, on May 6, 1942 (the date of testator's death) it was within the range of possibilities that Margene A. Rust (born October 17, 1932) might die before October 17, 1946, (21 years prior to the termination of the trust period) and leave a surviving child, the controlling issue is whether, on the one hand, her interest in the property constituted a vested (base) fee subject to defeasance in case of her death prior to October 17, 1967, or, on the other hand, no title would vest in her unless and until she was living on that date. Stated differently, the issue is whether (a) her living until

October 17, 1946, constitutes a condition precedent to the vesting of any title in her (appellants' contention), or (b) her death prior to that date constitutes a condition subsequent divesting the title vested in her as of the date of her father's death. . . .

It is, of course, essential to immediate vesting (possession or enjoyment being postponed) that the person to take be presently in existence and of certain identity. See 2 A.L.I. Rest. Property, § 157, com. q. And it is also well established that the fact that the legal title is vested in trustees, with full discretion as to the application of the income or corpus to the uses of the beneficiary during the trust period, does not militate against the immediate vesting of the beneficial (equitable) title in the beneficiary. . . .

Furthermore, if the beneficial title vested in Margene A. Rust, "it is immaterial that full possession and enjoyment of the property is postponed beyond the period of a life or lives in being and 21 years thereafter with the ordinary period of gestation added." Anderson v. Menefee [Tex. Civ. App., 174 S.W. 907]. . . .

Applying these rules to the bequest to Margene A. Rust, clearly and without substantial doubt, we think, the fee title to the residuary estate vested in her immediately upon the death of her father, defeasible upon the condition subsequent of her death prior to October 17, 1967, and subject to the trust provisions.

The first paragraph of clause Four, standing alone, would vest a fee simple absolute title in her, subject to the trust, since in so many words it unconditionally vests the legal title in the trustees for her "use and benefit."

The second paragraph puts a time limit for the duration of the trust, upon expiration of which her title is to be "free of any restrictions whatsoever." The language, "the trust shall terminate and the property . . . shall vest in fee simple in" her, "free of any restrictions whatsoever," is not reasonably susceptible of the construction that her title had not theretofore vested but was to vest initially as of that date. The words, "free of any restrictions whatsoever," can have no other meaning than that her title should thenceforth be free of the restrictions imposed by the trust, otherwise they would be pure surplusage. The vesting at that time was to be free of these restrictions. Even without this last clause, the language employed is that usually found in instruments creating remainders universally held to be vested, and not contingent. A devise by A to B for life with remainder at his death to C creates a vested remainder in C upon the death of A, subject to B's life estate. The use of "at his death" or words of similar import denote the time when the right of possession and enjoyment of the estate begins, and not the time when the estate in remainder vests.

The third and fourth paragraphs are clearly conditional clauses of defeasance, and as such conditions subsequent. The remaining paragraphs merely detail the powers and duties of the trustees. We find nothing in the language of the will, "read as an entirety and in the light of the circumstances of its formulation," which would call for a construction other than that the contingency of the daughter's dying before October 17, 1967, constituted a condition subsequent divesting her title, and that her living until then was not a condition precedent to its vesting. . . .

The fourth clause vests the fee simple title in the named contingent remaindermen immediately upon the death of the daughter prior to October 17, 1967, without bodily issue. Under no possible contingency could this paragraph create a perpetuity.

The third is the only paragraph which presents any constructional doubt. A doubt which we resolve in favor of a vested remainder upon the death of the daughter prior to October 17, 1967, leaving bodily issue, for reasons we now discuss.

The general plan of the testator seems clear. His primary solicitude was for his daughter, his only child. His principal estate was in extensive ranch property, held in undivided interests, and heavily incumbered. To preserve the estate to his daughter would necessitate wise business management over an extended period of years. He fixed this period as terminating on the daughter's 35th birthday. For obvious reasons he intrusted this management to his two brothers, who owned 2/3 of the remaining interest in the property. The only limitations imposed upon the daughter's otherwise complete fee simple title to the property were (1) the trust provisions which merely postponed her possession and untrammeled enjoyment of the property, and (2) defeasance of her title upon the contingency of her death during the trust period.

His secondary solicitude, should this contingency eventuate, was for his daughter's "bodily heirs", if any, giving them the identical status with reference to the property as that of his daughter. He substitutes them as beneficiaries of the trust and vests complete title at the end of the trust period. The same considerations favoring immediate vesting in the bodily issue and continuing the trust exist in this contingency as originally as to the daughter's title. The considerations as to the trust provisions would not apply in the contingency of the daughter's death without bodily issue.

The only doubt cast upon this immediate vesting is the use of the word "then" before the last word "surviving." In addition to the presumption of early vesting of title, and the general scheme of the testator, there are other considerations which favor construing "then" as referring to the death of the daughter and not the termination of the trust. "Issue of her body," we think, were clearly used in the sense of "children." This appears from use of the words, "share and share alike." As said by the great Oran M. Roberts, in the leading case of Hancock v. Butler, 21 Tex. 804:

> It is presumed it would be difficult to find one case where a man had expressly given his property, to all his descendants, to take per capita—children, grandchildren, great-grandchildren, etc. The general sense of American mind, as exhibited in deeds, wills, and in statutes of descent and distribution, is that it is proper to give property to children, grandchildren, etc., they taking per stirpes.

The possibility of the daughter having any grandchild, the child of a deceased child, prior to 1967, was exceedingly remote.

Another applicable presumption is that against intestacy. "A construction which would render the decedent intestate as to any part of his estate is not favored." 44 Tex. Jur., p. 707, § 148. In case of the death of the daughter before October 17, 1967, leaving a surviving child or children, all of whom including any descendants should die prior to that date, there would be no one to take under the will, if the title had not previously vested in the daughter's "bodily heirs." The only other limitation over (par. 4) was contingent exclusively upon the daughter's dying before October 17, 1967, without leaving any "issue of her body."

Additionally, it is well settled that: ". . . the rule against perpetuities is a rule of property and not one of construction; and where the instrument is capable to two constructions, "one of which would give effect to the whole . . . and the other result in defeating (it) . . . , in whole or in part, preference will be accorded to the construction which will uphold" it. 41 Am.Jur., p. 58, § 12. . . .

If, however, we be mistaken in this construction, and the limitation over to the bodily heirs of the daughter is void as creating a perpetuity, the other provisions of the will would not thereby be affected. In that case the title of the daughter would be defeasible only in case of her death before October 17, 1967, without leaving any heir of her body. A.L.I. Rest. Property, § 229, com. e. Under this construction the surviving bodily heirs of the daughter would take the same title from her by inheritance that they would under the will, construed as valid, subject only to the contingency that the daughter should make no different disposition by will, or otherwise part with her title. . . .

The trial court's judgment is affirmed.

5. Consequences Of Invalidity

When an interest is invalid because it violates the common-law Rule Against Perpetuities, the invalid interest is stricken from the disposition. Unless the doctrine of infectious invalidity applies, see infra p. 1003, the other interests created by the disposition (assuming that none of them violates the Rule) take effect as if the invalid interest had never been created.

> *Example 17.3:* G devised real property "to A for life, then to A's children for the life of the survivor, and upon the death of A's last surviving child, to A's grandchildren." G devised her residuary estate to her husband, H.
>
> Due to the invalidity of the remainder to A's grandchildren, the disposition reads as if *that* remainder interest had never been created: "to A for life, then to A's children for the life of the survivor." Since G's devise did not validly dispose of all interests in the parcel of real property, the undisposed-of interest passes under G's residuary clause to H. This testamentary transfer of the remainder interest to H is deemed to have occurred at G's death. Thus when A's last surviving child dies, the property goes to H (or H's successor in interest).

Note that if G's original devise had been in her residuary clause, the undisposed-of interest would have been intestate property and would have passed at G's death to her heirs at law.

Example 17.4: G devised real property "to A for life, then for life to such of A's children as reach 25, then to B."
The remainder for life to A's children is invalid. The effect of striking it is not to create a gap that must be filled by the residuary clause. Rather it is to accelerate B's remainder: The devise now reads "to A for life, then to B."

In preparation for reading the *Brown* decision, below, consider again the *Grant* and *Boland* cases, supra pp. 887-89.

Brown v. Independent Baptist Church
325 Mass. 645, 91 N.E.2d 922 (1950)

QUA, C.J. The object of this suit in equity, originally brought in this court, is to determine the ownership of a parcel of land in Woburn and the persons entitled to share in the proceeds of its sale by a receiver.

Sarah Converse died seised of the land on July 19, 1849, leaving a will in which she specifically devised it

to the Independent Baptist Church of Woburn, to be holden and enjoyed by them so long as they shall maintain and promulgate their present religious belief and faith and shall continue a Church; and if the said Church shall be dissolved, or if its religious sentiments shall be changed or abandoned, then my will is that this real estate shall go to my legatees hereinafter named, to be divided in equal portions between them. And my will further is, that if my beloved husband, Jesse Converse, shall survive me, that then this devise to the aforesaid Independent Church of Woburn, shall not take effect till from and after his decease; and that so long as he shall live he may enjoy and use the said real estate, and take the rents and profits thereof to his own use.

Then followed ten money legacies in varying amounts to different named persons, after which there was a residuary clause in these words,

The rest and residue of my estate I give and bequeath to my legatees above named, saving and except therefrom the Independent Baptist Church; this devise to take effect from and after the decease of my husband; I do hereby direct and will that he shall have the use and this rest and residue during his life.

The husband of the testatrix died in 1864. The church named by the testatrix ceased to "continue a church" on October 19, 1939.

The parties apparently are in agreement, and the single justice ruled, that the estate of the church in the land was a determinable fee. We concur. The estate was a fee, since it might last forever, but it was not an absolute fee, since it might (and did) "automatically expire upon the occurrence of a stated event." Restatement: Property, § 44. It is also conceded, and was ruled, that the specific executory devise over to the persons "hereinafter named" as legatees was void for remoteness. The reason is . . . that the determinable fee might not come to an end until long after any life or lives in being and twenty-one years, and in theory at least might never come to an end, and for an indefinite period no clear title to the entire estate could be given.

Since the limitation over failed, it next becomes our duty to consider what became of the possibility of reverter which under our decisions remained after the failure of the limitation. First Universalist Society of North Adams v. Boland, 155 Mass. 171, 175, 29 N.E. 524, 15 L.R.A. 231 [supra p. 888]; Restatement: Property, § 228, illustration 2, and Appendix to Volume II, at pages 35-36, including note 2. A possibility of reverter seems, by the better authority, to be assignable inter vivos (Restatement: Property, § 159) and must be at least as readily devisable as the other similar reversionary interest known as a right of entry for condition broken, which is devisable, though not assignable. It follows that the possibility of reverter passed under the residuary clause of the will to the same persons designated in the invalid executory devise. It is of no consequence that the persons designated in the two provisions were the same. The same result must be reached as if they were different.

The single justice ruled that the residuary clause was void for remoteness, apparently for the same reason that rendered the executory devise void. With this we cannot agree, since we consider it settled that the rule against perpetuities does not apply to reversionary interests of this general type, including possibilities of reverter. Proprietors of the Church in Brattle Square v. Grant, 3 Gray, 142, 148, 63 Am. Dec. 725 [supra p. 887]; First Universalist Society of North Adams v. Boland, 155 Mass. 171, 175-176, 29 N.E. 524, 15 L.R.A. 231 [supra p. 888]; Restatement: Property, § 372. See Gray, Rule Against Perpetuities, 4th Ed., §§ 41, 312, 313. For a full understanding of the situation here presented it is necessary to keep in mind the fundamental difference in character between the attempted executory devise to the legatees later named in the will and the residuary gift to the same persons. The executory devise was in form and substance an attempt to limit or create a new future interest which might not arise or vest in anyone until long after the permissible period. It was obviously not intended to pass such a residuum of the testatrix's existing estate as a possibility of reverter, and indeed if the executory devise had been valid according to its terms the whole estate would have passed from the testatrix and no possibility of reverter could have been left to her or her devisees. The residuary devise, on the other hand, was in terms and purpose exactly adapted to carry any interest which might otherwise remain in the testatrix, whether or not she had it in mind or knew it would exist.

We cannot accept the contention made in behalf of Mrs. Converse's heirs that the words of the residuary clause "saving and except therefrom the Independent Baptist Church" were meant to exclude from the operation of that clause any possible rights in the land previously given to the church. We construe these words as intended merely to render the will consistent by excluding the church which also had been "above named" from the list of "legatees" who were to take the residue.

The interlocutory decree entered December 16, 1947, is reversed, and a new decree is to be entered providing that the land in question or the proceeds of any sale thereof by the receiver shall go to the persons named as legatees in the will, other than the Independent Baptist Church of Woburn, or their successors in interest. Further proceedings are to be in accord with the new decree. Costs and expenses are to be at the discretion of the single justice.

So ordered.

Question and Problem

1. *Criticism of Brown.* The *Brown* decision has been criticized on the ground that the testator "did not die twice." Simes, Is the Rule Against Perpetuities Doomed?, 52 Mich. L. Rev. 179 n.4 (1953). What is Simes' point?

2. *Problem.* G devised real property "to A for life, remainder to A's children, but if none of A's children reaches 25, to B." G was survived by A, who had two children, X and Y, neither of whom had reached 25 at G's death. What is the consequence of the invalidity of B's executory interest?

Infectious Invalidity. In appropriate cases, the invalidity of an interest may, under the *doctrine of infectious invalidity*, be held to invalidate one or more otherwise valid interests created by the disposition, or even invalidate the entire will. The question turns on whether the general dispositive scheme of the transferor will be better carried out by elimination of only the invalid interest or by elimination of other interests as well.

This is a question that must be answered on a case by case basis. Several items are relevant to the question, including who takes the stricken interests in place of those designated to take by the transferor. Some jurisdictions have become noted for a greater willingness to apply infectious invalidity than others. See Simes & Smith on Future Interests § 1262; Am. L. Prop. § 24.48 et seq.; Restatement of Property § 402.

6. Separability

When an interest is expressly subject to alternative contingencies, the courts treat the situation as if two interests were created in the same person or class, so that the invalidity of one of the interests does not invalidate the other. This principle was established in Longhead v. Phelps, 2 Wm. Bl. 704, 96 Eng. Rep. 414 (K.B. 1770), and has been followed in this country. See Simes & Smith on Future Interests § 1257; Am. L. Prop. § 24.54; Restatement of Property § 376.

To illustrate, suppose property is devised "to B if X-event or Y-event happens." B in effect has two interests, one contingent on X-event happening and the other contingent on Y-event happening. If X-event might occur too remotely, the consequence of separating B's interest into two is that only one of them, the one contingent on X-event, is invalid. B still has a valid interest—the one contingent on the occurrence of Y-event. Another way of viewing it is to say that the invalid contingency is stricken or excised. Thus the devise is altered to read "to B if Y-event happens." The following examples further illustrate this principle.

> *Example 17.5:* G devised real property "to A for life, then to such of A's children as survive her and reach 25, but if none of A's children survives her or if none of A's children who survives her reaches 25, then to B."
> B takes only if none of A's children survives A; his interest that is contingent on that event is valid. If one or more of A's children survives A, B cannot take even if none of them lives to 25. B's interest that is contingent on none of A's surviving children reaching 25 is invalid. The language "or if none of A's children who survive him reaches 25" is in effect stricken from the devise.
> The interest of A's children is invalid and replaced by a reversion.

The principle of separability is applicable only when the transferor has *expressly* stated the contingencies in the alternative. Where alternative contingencies are merely implicit, no separation will be recognized. See Proctor v. Bishop of Bath and Wells, 2 H. Bl. 358, 126 Eng. Rep. 594 (C.P. 1794).

> *Example 17.6:* G devised real property "to A for life, then to such of A's children as survive him and reach 25, but if none of A's children does so, then to B."
> B has only one interest, and it is invalid. B cannot take even if none of A's children survives A.

PART B. MODERN POLICY OF THE RULE AGAINST PERPETUITIES

Simes, The Policy Against Perpetuities[7]
103 U. Pa. L. Rev. 707, 708, 710, 712-15, 721-24 (1955)

What public policy actuates this rule? If we are to content ourselves with the terse and sometimes superficial pronouncements on the subject scattered through the books, the policy of the Rule has never been in doubt. Ever since it first emerged in the *Duke of Norfolk's Case*, it has been

---

7. Also published in L. Simes, Public Policy and the Dead Hand (1955).

declared to be a rule in furtherance of the alienability of property. . . . [I]f it were not for this Rule, property would be unproductive and society would have less income.

But why should a future interest make property inalienable, and why does inalienability make property unproductive? In answering these questions we must recall that the Rule against Perpetuities developed as a rule restricting future interests in specific land. Viewed thus, the rationale of the Rule is not difficult to perceive. In order to make a profit from land, one must have a type of ownership which insures enjoyment forever or for a fixed and determinable period of time. People who purchase land, whether for profit or for their own use and enjoyment, are not likely to buy unless they can secure either a fee simple absolute or a lease for a fixed term of years. . . .

Now, if the policy of the Rule against Perpetuities is to make property productive, just how far is this policy advanced in the application of the Rule today? Is property still taken out of commerce by remote contingent future interests? *I believe it is no exaggeration to say that, at the present time, due to changes both in the nature of capital investments and in the law, the proposition that contingent future interests make property unproductive is rarely true in the United States and almost never true in England.* I should like to discuss at some length my reasons for this belief.

In the first place, the future interest with which the Rule against Perpetuities is concerned is nearly always an equitable interest in a trust. The modern trust instrument, if well drawn, will contain broad powers of sale and reinvestment. While the beneficiary who has an equitable estate subject to a future interest may have difficulty in selling his property, that does not make it unproductive. As a practical matter, the trustee will have an absolute legal estate which he can sell, and will be empowered to reinvest the proceeds. While at one time in the history of the law, in the absence of express authorization in the trust instrument, the trustee's powers of reinvestments were extremely limited, today the rapidly extending "prudent man rule" gives the trustee a wide field of selection in making trust investments productive.

Moreover, not only is the trustee empowered by the terms of any well-drawn trust instrument to sell and reinvest in productive property; the law requires him to do so. One of the duties imposed by law upon trustees is to use reasonable care in making the trust property productive.

Suppose, however, that the trust instrument is not well drawn, and no express powers of alienation are given to the trustee. Still the trust property is not necessarily taken out of commerce. The law recognizes that, when circumstances change in a matter unforeseen by the settlor, the trustee may secure permission of the court to sell. . . .

Statutes in several states have gone even further in permitting the trustee to sell and reinvest in the absence of a power to do so expressed in the trust instrument. . . .

Of course, it must be recognized that, so far as the common law is concerned, it is perfectly clear that the existence of a power in a trustee to sell and reinvest does not take the case out of the Rule against Perpetuities.

Though courts have rarely discussed the position . . . when they have done so, they have generally dismissed the matter without adequate rationalization.

There is a second reason why future interests do not make property unproductive. Not only is there commonly a power of sale in a trustee where future interests arise in American family settlements; the subject matter of the trust is commonly corporate shares and government or corporate bonds. In the case of corporate shares, the economic value is neither in the interest owned by the beneficiary of the trust, nor is it in the shares in the hand of the trustees. It is the property of the corporation. Certainly that is freely alienable. . . .

There is, moreover, a third situation where, according to American law, the existence of future interests does not render property unproductive. Let us assume that somewhat unusual case where the trust device is not used, and legal future interests in land are created. A devises a particular piece of land to B for life, remainder to B's issue who survive him, in fee simple. Beginning with the case of Bofl v. Fisher,[8] decided in 1850, the American courts have developed a doctrine to this effect: where land is affected with a future interest, a court of equity has power to order a sale and to set up a trust in the proceeds, when this is necessary for the preservation of all interests in the land. . . .

If alienability for purposes of productivity is not the justification of the modern Rule against Perpetuities, then what is the public policy which justifies it?

Before suggesting what I believe to be the true answer, I should like to take a moment to mention two other explanations of the Rule which are sometimes made. First, it is said that the Rule is designed to prevent an undue concentration of wealth in the hands of a few. Professor Leach has indicated that the Rule is intended to remove the "threat to the public welfare from family dynasties built either on great landed estates or on great capital wealth." But, as he points out, that threat is rather effectively removed by our income and estate taxes. I am disposed to agree with him. Indeed, I feel that undue concentration of wealth is an evil which can best be combatted by tax legislation, rather than by perpetuity rules.

A second reason sometimes given for the Rule is as follows: it is socially undesirable for some members of society to have assured incomes and be protected from the economic struggle for existence; the principle of survival of the fittest should apply, so that those who are unable to maintain themselves in the economic struggle for existence should not survive. The American Law Institute, without giving its blessing to this particular rationale, states it as follows: "It is obvious that limitations unalterably effective over a long period of time would hamper the normal operation of the competitive struggle. Persons less fit, less keen in the social struggle, might be thereby enabled to retain property disproportionate to their skills

---

8. 3 Rich. Eq. 1 (S.C. 1850). [See also Am. L. Prop. §§ 4.98-.99; Simes & Smith on Future Interests §§ 1941-46; L. Simes & C. Taylor, Improvement of Conveyancing by Legislation 235-38 (1960); Restatement of Property § 179 at pp. 485-95. Eds.]

in the competitive struggle." Several answers may be made to this argument. The Rule against Perpetuities does permit economic provision for the unfit for one generation, indeed for one generation and during the minority of the next. It would seem almost as bad to permit this sort of thing for the first generation as for succeeding generations. If it be answered that there is a social objection to the continuation of a line of weaklings, the answer is that a restriction on the tying up of property does not eliminate that objection. Modern society, with its elaborate welfare machinery, is not organized on a theory of survival of the fittest, but of survival of the weak. Moreover, if human experience means anything, we may well conclude that the progeny of weaklings are likely to be more numerous in a state of poverty than in a state of wealth.

Thus I believe that neither of these explanations for the Rule is adequate. There are in my opinion, however, two other bases for the social policy of the Rule, the force of which can scarcely be denied.

First, the Rule against Perpetuities strikes a fair balance between the desires of members of the present generation, and similar desires of succeeding generations, to do what they wish with the property which they enjoy. It is almost axiomatic that one of the most common human wants is the desire to distribute one's property at death without restriction in whatever manner he desires. Indeed, we can go farther and say that there is a policy in favor of permitting people to create future interests by will, as well as present interests, because that also accords with human desires. The difficulty here is that, if we give free rein to the desires of one generation to create future interests, the members of succeeding generations will receive the property in a restricted state. They will thus be unable to create all the future interests they wish. Perhaps, they may not even be able to devise it at all. Hence, to come most nearly to satisfying the desires of peoples of all generations, we must strike a fair balance between unrestricted testamentary disposition of property by the present generation and unrestricted disposition by future generations. In a sense this is a policy of alienability, but it is not alienability for productivity. It is alienability to enable people to do what they please at death with the property which they enjoy in life. As Kohler says in his treatise on the philosophy of law: "The far-reaching hand of a testator who would enforce his will in distant future generations destroys the liberty of other individuals, and presumes to make rules for distant times."

But, in my opinion, a second and even more important reason for the Rule is this: it is socially desirable that the wealth of the world be controlled by its living members and not by the dead. I know of no better statement of that doctrine than the language of Thomas Jefferson, contained in a letter to James Madison, when he said: "The earth belongs always to the living generation. They may manage it then, and what proceeds from it, as they please, during their usufruct." Sidgwick, in his *Elements of Politics*, also discusses the problem in the following words: " . . . it rather follows from the fundamental assumption of individualism, that any such posthumous restraint on the use of bequeathed wealth will tend to make it less useful to the living, as it will interfere with their freedom in dealing with it. Individualism, in short, is in a dilemma. . . . Of this difficulty there is, I think, no general theoretical solution: it can only be reduced by some practical compromise."

———

The Know-and-See Theory. Professor Simes said that the Rule "strikes a fair balance between the desires of members of the present generation, and similar desires of succeeding generations, to do what they wish with the property which they enjoy." Where, specifically, is that "fair balance" to be drawn?

Hobhouse suggested a know-and-see theory: "A clear, obvious, natural line is drawn for us between those persons and events which the Settlor knows and sees, and those which he cannot know or see." A. Hobhouse, The Dead Hand 188 (1880).

Leach and Tudor expanded on the know-and-see test:

> The Rule against Perpetuities came into being as a means of preventing inordinate family pride from tying up the soil of England in a manner which would produce undesirable economic and social consequences. In establishing the balance between private right and public interest the courts arrived at a solution which permitted the following: . . . In a will a man of property could provide for all of those in his family whom he personally knew and the first generation after them upon attaining majority.

W. Leach & O. Tudor, The Common Law Rule Against Perpetuities, in Am. L. Prop. § 24.16 at 51. The authors went on to muse that it might have been better if the tack-on 21-year part of the period were not a period in gross, but instead were treated like the period of gestation—allowed only if needed to take account of an actual minority. The fact is, however, that it is now beyond dispute that the 21-year tack-on part of the period is a period in gross; that point was settled long ago in Cadell v. Palmer, 1 Cl. & F. 372, 6 Eng. Rep. 956 (1833).

Professor Waggoner has suggested a further refinement of the theory:

> [T]he [know-and-see] standard [arguably means] that donors should be allowed to exert control through the youngest generation of descendants they knew and saw, or at least one or more but not necessarily all of whom they knew and saw. . . .

Waggoner, The Uniform Statutory Rule Against Perpetuities, 21 Real Prop. Prob. & Tr. J. 569, 587 (1986). Professor Waggoner went on to suggest that the tack-on 21-year part of the period performs a desirable function, especially in a wait-and-see system (see infra Part D), for it allows the inclusion of the after-born members of a generation with respect to which one or more members were "in being"—known and seen by G—at the creation of the interest.

To help us think about and visualize the "know-and-see" theory in action, we think it is useful to present the following charts of four hypothetical four-generation families.[9] Each family is a rather typical two-child family.[10] In each case, G has two children, A and B, four grandchildren (V, X, Y, and Z), eight great-grandchildren (K, L, M, N, P, Q, R, and S), and so on.[11] G's descending line looks the same in each family, as follows:

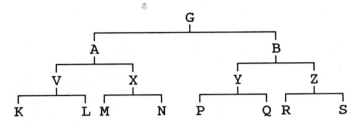

The families differ from one another on when child-bearing takes place. In Family I, the children are born when the parents are 20 and 25, respectively; in Family II, the parents are 25 and 30 when their children are born; in Family III, the parents are 30 and 35; and in Family IV, child-bearing has been deferred until the parents are 35 and 40.

We make no claim that these hypothetical families are frequently duplicated in real life; they are too symmetrical. Nevertheless, in various combinations, and taking due account of the fact that the number of offspring and the timing of child-bearing will vary widely from one family to another and within the same family at each generation and from one descending line to another, we believe that these hypothetical families do, in the aggregate, sufficiently resemble actual families to make the charts illuminating for our purposes.

We present these charts now, and will frequently refer to them as we proceed, for a straightforward reason: As courts and others get absorbed with abnormal post-creation events, we think that normal post-creation events should not be entirely ignored.

---

9. Four-generation families are not unusual. See supra p. 79 n. 21.

10. The latest Census Bureau statistics on fertility rates indicate an average number of children per woman of about 1.85. This is down from the average of 2.5 in 1970 and considerably down from the high of 3.8 in 1957. See U.S. Bureau of the Census, Estimates of the Population of the United States and Components of Change: 1970 to 1985, Table B, at 3 (1986). See also U.S. Bureau of the Census, Statistical Abstract of the United States: 1990, Table 85 at 65 (110th ed. 1990).

11. For the sake of simplicity, the charts do not depict G's spouse or the spouses of G's descendants.

FAMILY I: PARENTS ARE 20 AND 25 WHEN CHILDREN ARE BORN

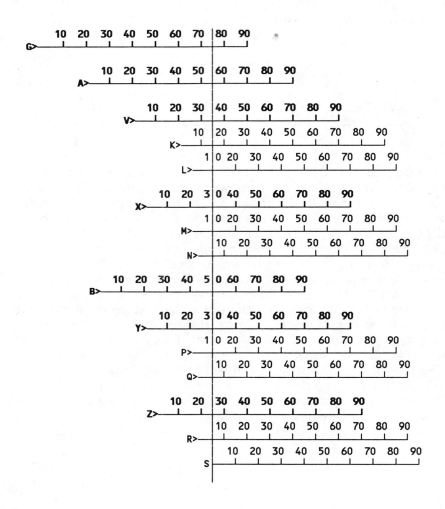

FAMILY II: PARENTS ARE 25 AND 30 WHEN CHILDREN ARE BORN

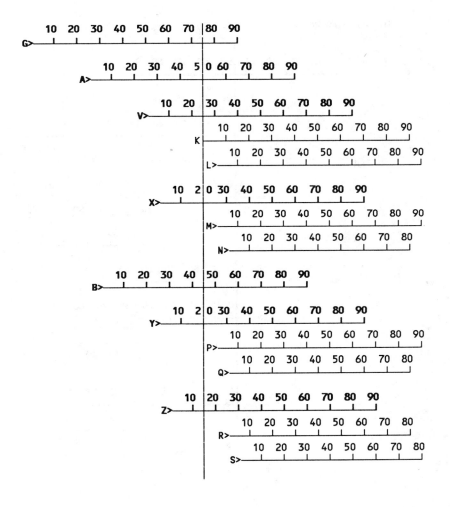

FAMILY III: PARENTS ARE 30 AND 35 WHEN CHILDREN ARE BORN

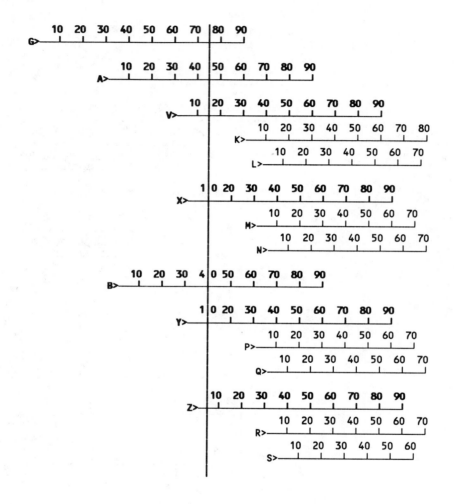

FAMILY IV: PARENTS ARE 35 AND 40 WHEN CHILDREN ARE BORN

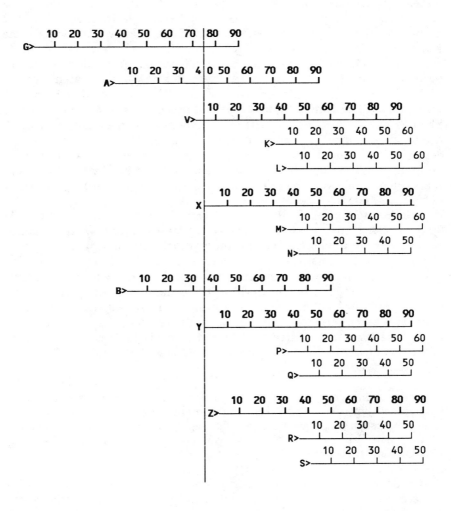

In thinking about the significance of these four charts as they relate to the idea that—in policy—the Rule Against Perpetuities should allow a donor to tie up her or his property through the youngest generation of descendants that the donor knew and saw, keep in mind that statistical life expectancy has now reached 75 years, on average.[12] As shown by the vertical line drawn on each chart, G's hypothesized death at age 75 would mean that the youngest descendant G will have known and seen—the youngest descendant "in being" at G's death, and thus the youngest descendant potentially qualifying as a measuring or validating life for purposes of the Rule Against Perpetuities—is a new-born great-grandchild (S) in Family I, a new-born great-grandchild (K) in Family II, a 5-year-old grandchild (Z) in Family III, and a pair of new-born grandchildren (X and Y) in Family IV. Notice, too, that for G's youngest descendant in being at her or his death to be a child, rather than a grandchild or more remote descendant, G would have to die prematurely—35 or more years prematurely in Family I, 25 or more years prematurely in Family II, 15 or more years prematurely in Family III, and 5 or more years prematurely in Family IV.

Technical Violations of the Rule. How well is the "fair balance"—the "know-and-see" theory—actually served by the common-law Rule Against Perpetuities? In thinking about this question, observe that the requirement of initial certainty makes validity dependent on the full array of *possible* post-creation chains of events, not on the one chain of post-creation events that *actually* happens. In the world of the common-law Rule, every chain of possible post-creation events that can be imagined, no matter how fanciful, is taken seriously—even those that have become impossible by the time of the lawsuit. As stated by Sir Lloyd Kenyon, the Master of the Rolls, in the immensely influential case of Jee v. Audley, 1 Cox 324, 29 Eng. Rep. 1186 (Ch. 1787):

> Another thing pressed upon me, is to decide on the events which have happened; but I cannot do this without overturning very many cases. The single question before me is, not whether the limitation is good in the events which have happened, but whether it was good in its creation; and if it were not, I cannot make it so.

Translation: A *single* chain of imagined events that can postpone vesting (or termination) beyond a life in being plus 21 years spoils the transferor's disposition.

---

12. A dramatic rise in statistical life expectancy has occurred across this century. In 1900, statistical life expectancy at birth was 47 years; in 1910 it was 50 years; in 1930 it was 60 years; and in 1970 it reached 70 years. (The low life expectancies in the earlier half of this century were primarily caused by a high rate of infant mortality, which has now dramatically declined.) Since 1970, life expectancy has been inching up rather more slowly, so that the latest figures show that it reached 75 years in 1982, where it still remains. U.S. Bureau of the Census, Statistical Abstract of the United States: 1990, Tables 103 and 106 at 72, 74 (110th ed. 1990); U.S. Bureau of the Census, Historical Statistics of the United States, Table B107-115 at 55 (Part 1, 1975).

In consequence of the requirement of initial certainty, validity is withheld from interests that are likely to, and in fact would (if given the chance), vest well within the period of a life in being plus 21 years. Reasonable dispositions can be rendered invalid because of exceedingly remote possibilities, such as a woman who has passed the menopause giving birth to (or adopting) additional children, a married individual in her or his middle or late years later becoming remarried to a person born after the transfer, or the probate of an estate taking more than 21 years to complete. Professor Leach called these, respectively, the fertile octogenarian, the unborn widow (we call this case the afterborn spouse), and the administrative contingency. See Leach, Perpetuities in a Nutshell, 51 Harv. L. Rev. 638, 643-44 (1938).[13] None of these dispositions offends the public policy of preventing transferors from tying up property in long-term or even perpetual family trusts. Each disposition seems quite reasonable and violates the common-law Rule on technical grounds only.

1. The Case of the Fertile "Octogenarian"[14]

Fertile-Octogenarian Example. Consider G, a member of Family I, supra p. 1010. G died at age 75, survived by his 55-year-old daughter A, who had passed the menopause, and by A's adult children, V (age 35) and X (age 30). G's will devised property in trust, income "to A for life, then to A's children for the life of the survivor, and upon the death of A's last surviving child, corpus to A's grandchildren."

In thinking about the full array of possible post-creation events, consider the one that seems most likely: A has no more children and V and X live to but not beyond their remaining life expectancies of 42 and 47 more years, respectively.[15] If this happens, the remainder interest in the corpus in favor of A's grandchildren will vest on X's death 47 years after G's death. G knew and saw both V and X. G also knew and saw all four of A's grandchildren (K, L, M, and N), who will succeed to the corpus of the trust when X dies. Even if V or X lives well beyond her or his life expectancy, the remainder in the corpus of the trust still will vest on the death of either V or X, who were "in being" at the creation of G's trust.

---

13. See also Leach, Perpetuities in Perspective: Ending the Rule's Reign of Terror, 65 Harv. L. Rev. 721 (1952); Leach, Perpetuities: Staying the Slaughter of the Innocents, 68 L.Q. Rev. 35 (1952).

14. The term "octogenarian" is not to be taken literally; it refers to persons who are infertile, young or old, male or female.

15. U.S. Bureau of the Census, Statistical Abstract of the United States: 1990, Table 106, at 74 (110th ed. 1990). Notice that we refer to the *remaining* life expectancy of V and X. Although life expectancy at birth is now 75 years, the remaining life expectancy of persons who have lived beyond birth is somewhat greater than 75 years minus their current ages. Why is this is so?

Among the array of "possible" post-creation events exists one that is extremely unlikely: A becomes pregnant and has a third child;[16] or A adopts a child. That third child outlives the following persons by more than 21 years: A, V, X, K, L, M, N, and anybody else one can think of who has any connection to this transaction. Under this chain of events, the interest in the corpus in favor of A's grandchildren vests beyond a life in being plus 21 years.

Jee v. Audley. Jee v. Audley, the early and famous English decision quoted earlier, laid down for perpetuity law the conclusive presumption of lifetime fertility. Again, we quote the words of the judge in that case, Sir Lloyd Kenyon, the Master of the Rolls:

> I am desired to do in this case something which I do not feel myself at liberty to do, namely to suppose it impossible for persons in so advanced an age as John and Elizabeth Jee [both age 70] to have children; but if this can be done in one case it may in another, and it is a very dangerous experiment, and introductive of the greatest inconvenience to give a latitude to such sort of conjecture.

The conclusive presumption of Jee v. Audley has stuck and, due to reported advances in reproductive technology, is perhaps justified:[17] A is conclusively presumed capable of bearing children until she dies. Consequently, the grandchildren's remainder interest in the corpus of G's trust is invalid.

Only one American common-law decision has squarely rejected Jee v. Audley and held in a perpetuity case that the presumption is rebuttable, not conclusive. The Restatement of Property section 377 (1944) squarely supports the conclusive presumption, and there are many perpetuity cases, recent as well as not so recent, that have adhered to it. See, e.g., Abram v. Wilson, 8 Ohio Misc. 420, 423, 220 N.E.2d 739, 742 (P. Ct. 1966) ("Obviously, . . . it is clearly possible for the testator's 75-year-old brother to have children . . . ."); Turner v. Turner, 260 S.C. 439, 445, 196 S.E.2d 498, 501 (1973) ("The possibility of childbirth is never extinct."[18])

The one American common-law decision to hold in a perpetuity case that the presumption of lifetime fertility is rebuttable is Lattouf's Will, next.

Lattouf's Will
887 N.J. Super. 137, 208 A.2d 411 (Super. Ct. App. Div. 1965)

[Sarkis Lattouf, an 80-year old bachelor, died in 1962, leaving a will that devised the residue of his estate in trust, the income from which was

---

16. Reported advances in reproductive technology have apparently made this possible. See supra p. 719.

17. See supra p. 719.

18. In 1987, South Carolina became the first state to enact USRAP, under which a disposition such as the one in *Turner* would almost certainly not be invalid.

to be used in the discretion of the trustee for various specified purposes. The will further provided:

> When the youngest child of my niece, Marie Endres shall have attained, or would have attained the age of twenty-five (25) years, then the trust hereby created shall end, and the principal thereof . . . shall be equally . . . divided among my then living grandnephews and grandnieces.

Surviving the testator were three sisters and forty-one nieces and nephews. The Probate Court held that the trust did not violate the Rule Against Perpetuities, and the contestants appealed.]

GOLDMANN, S.J.A.D. . . . The trial judge held that testator had failed to designate expressly an event or time period at or within which the various interests created by the trust were to vest. Not so; vesting was to occur when the "youngest child of my niece, Marie Endres shall have attained, or would have attained the age of twenty-five (25) years." Not until then would the class of grandnephews and grandnieces close and their identity and number be determined. However, the trial judge considered this language ambiguous and proceeded to construe it as meaning the youngest child living at the time of testator's death, and not the last-born child of Marie Endres. We find no ambiguity in the language employed.

We must look at the *corpus* provision of paragraph Seventh as of the date of testator's death. Would the trust *corpus* vest within a life in being plus 21 years? The answer is clearly no.

Marie Endres had sometime prior to the execution of the will undergone a complete hysterectomy. The parties by stipulation agreed that she was incapable of bearing children when the will was executed and the testator died. The record reveals that testator knew of the hysterectomy when he executed his will.

Defendants-contestants rely upon the ancient legal presumption, often mentioned in our cases, that a woman is presumed legally capable of bearing children at any age. If one were to follow through on contestants' argument that Marie Endres could still have children, there exists the possibility that she might die and leave a child under four years of age. Since the vesting of the trust Corpus among the "then living grandnephews and grandnieces" is to take place when that child "shall have attained, or would have attained" the age of 25, this possibility would violate the requirement of vesting within the period of the rule.

However, we are unwilling to follow the contestants in their reliance upon the ancient presumption. As was said in Trenton Banking Co. v. Hawley, 7 N.J. Super. 301, 307-308, 70 A.2d 896 (Ch. Div. 1950), the presumption should not, merely because of its antiquity, blind us to present realities and conceal demonstrable truth. The hysterectomy, involving complete removal of Marie Endres' procreative organs, rendered her permanently sterile. It logically follows that she could bear no children other than the only child she had when testator died. That child, Linda, it has been stipulated, was just short of three years and ten months old when Lattouf expired.

The rule would be violated were we to take Linda as the measuring life. The trial judge did so, but assumed she was 4 1/2 years old when testator died. This was error. Linda was born December 1, 1958; Lattouf died September 26, 1962, so that the child, as noted, was at least two months short of age 4. Accordingly, had she died immediately after the execution of the will and Lattouf's death, more than 21 years would expire before she "would have attained" age 25.

So, too, were we to take Marie Endres as the measuring life. Had she died immediately after Lattouf, the trust would not have vested within her life and 21 years thereafter.

As our cases have uniformly held, a future interest must vest, if at all, within a period measured by a life in being when the interest was created, plus 21 years. The nine-month period tacked on in case of an existing pregnancy has no application in the circumstances of this case. Marie Endres was not pregnant. She could not be, nor, of course, could the infant Linda. Although plaintiffs' counsel claimed at oral argument that consideration should be given to this extra term of gestation, he has now abandoned the argument, and necessarily so.

Accordingly, we conclude that the trust failed because it was in violation of the rule. . . .

[Case remanded.]

Notes

1. *Avoiding Invalidity in Lattouf.* Is it not ironic that the only American perpetuity decision to have held the presumption of lifetime fertility to be rebuttable[19] and rebutted invalidated part of the disposition anyway? There is an argument supporting the validity of the interest of the grandnephews and grandnieces in the above case, which was apparently not raised. What is it? Can a woman conceive and bear a viable child within a two-month period? Medical evidence today suggests that 23 to 24 weeks after conception is about the shortest period in which a baby can achieve viability, though the Missouri statute whose constitutionality was upheld in Webster v. Reproductive Health Services, 492 U.S. 490 (1989), requires physicians to test for viability at 20 weeks before performing an abortion.

The *Lattouf* case is discussed in Fetters, The Perpetuities Period in Gross and the Child *En Ventre Sa Mere* in Relation to the Determination of Common-law and Wait-and-see Measuring Lives: A Minor Heresy Stated and Defended, 62 Iowa L. Rev. 309 (1976); Waggoner, *In re Lattouf's Will* and the Presumption of Lifetime Fertility in Perpetuity Law, 20 San Diego L. Rev. 763 (1983).

---

19. By statute in Idaho, there is no presumption that a person is capable of having children at any stage of adult life. See Idaho Code § 55-111. By statute in Tennessee, the presumption exists as a prima facie presumption, which is rebuttable by competent evidence. See Tenn. Code Ann. § 24-5-112.

2. *Possibility of Adoption.* Professor Leach was an outspoken critic of the conclusive presumption of lifetime fertility, and wrote extensively in favor of making it rebuttable, as the *Lattouf* court did. See, e.g., Leach, Perpetuities: New Hampshire Defertilizes the Octogenarians, 77 Harv. L. Rev. 279 (1963); Leach & Tudor, The Common Law Rule Against Perpetuities, in Am. L. Prop. § 24.22. Professor Leach argued that perpetuity law should get into step with two other areas of the law in which the presumption was rebuttable—trust termination cases[20] and charitable deduction cases under the federal tax laws.[21] What has happened, however, is that the law in these two areas has more recently moved in the direction of perpetuity law, rather than the other way around. The reason is the same for all three areas: Although it might be possible in a given case, such as *Lattouf*, to establish that the birth of natural children is impossible,[22] it can almost never be established that it is *impossible* for a woman or man to have additional children by adoption. See Clark v. Citizens & S. Nat'l Bank, 243 Ga. 703, 257 S.E.2d 244 (1979) (possibility of adoption would not allow the presumption to be rebutted even it were rebuttable in trust termination cases); Rev. Rul. 74-410, 1974-2 C.B. 187 (possibility of a 60-year-old woman adopting one or more children is not so remote as to be negligible; charitable deduction denied); Rev. Rul. 71-442, 1971-2 C.B. 336 (possibility of a 56-year-old man adopting a child is not so remote as to be negligible; charitable deduction denied); Priv. Ltr. Rul. 80-10-011 (possibility of 60-year-old man adopting a child is not so remote as to be negligible; charitable deduction denied despite medical evidence that man's age and physical condition were such that his ability to father a child was "near zero").

The *Lattouf* court failed to consider the possibility of having children by adoption. Since the trend in the law is strongly toward including adopted children in class gifts, at least in the absence of an expressly stated contrary intent,[23] it is difficult to understand how the *Lattouf* court could hold that the presumption of lifetime fertility had been rebutted: It would hardly be front-page news if an infertile couple in the normal child-bearing years, such as Marie Endres and her husband, decided to adopt a child.[24] As long as the requirement of initial *certainty* remains the test of validity in perpetuity law, we find it hard to understand how—in cases in which adopted children are presumptively included in class gift language and in which the person in question is competent—the presumption of lifetime

---

20. See Scott on Trusts § 340.1.

21. See Waggoner, Perpetuity Reform, supra note 6, at 1730 n.28.

22. Reported advances in reproductive technology cast doubt even on this proposition. See supra p. 719.

23. This is the law in New Jersey. See In re Thompson, 53 N.J. 276, 250 A.2d 393 (1969); N.J. Rev. Stat. §§ 3B:3-48, 3B:5-9 [pre-1990 UPC §§ 2-611, -109].

24. Indeed, even elderly people probably cannot be excluded from adopting children based on their age alone. See Waggoner, Perpetuity Reform, supra note 6 at 1732 n.35.

fertility could ever be properly rebutted—even if the presumption were held to be rebuttable.[25]

3. *Constructional Preference for Validity.* If shifting the presumption of lifetime fertility to a rebuttable presumption holds out little hope for overcoming invalidity in cases in which future children are extremely unlikely (though not strictly impossible), another approach seems more promising. This approach is to apply the constructional preference for validity and hold that the possibility of future children was so remote that the transferor never contemplated it and so did not intend to include such children in the class gift language even if—against the odds—one or more ultimately materializes. So construed, the requirement of initial certainty *is* met, and the interest is valid.[26] See, e.g., Bankers Trust Co. v. Pearson, 140 Conn. 332, 99 A.2d 224 (1953) (testator was held to have meant children in being when he spoke of the children of his brother, age 55, and sisters, ages 52 and 57); Joyner v. Duncan, 299 N.C. 565, 264 S.E.2d 76 (1980) (testator was held to have meant children in being when he spoke of the children of his 47-year-old son). Since the relevant time for determining the intent of a testator is the time of execution of the will—not the time of death—this construction is ordinarily available to a court only if at the time the testator executed the will there was reason to expect that the person in question would not have additional children.

Surprisingly, the Supreme Judicial Court of Massachusetts has seemed unwilling to adopt such a construction even in apparently appropriate cases. See Second Bank-State St. Trust Co. v. Second Bank-State St. Trust Co., 335 Mass. 407, 140 N.E.2d 201 (1957); Sears v. Coolidge, 329 Mass. 340, 108 N.E.2d 563 (1952). The court, in neither case, articulated reasons for denying the construction. It may be significant that other ways of upholding the gifts were found,[27] which allows us to speculate that the construction might have been adopted had another validating method not been available. Is there a different explanation? Although facts known to the testator suggested that she or he never contemplated the possibility of the birth or adoption of additional children, the court might have sensed

---

25. Professor Leach anticipated the problem presented by the possibility of adoption, but nevertheless persisted in pressing his criticism of the conclusive presumption in perpetuity law. His answer to the problem of adopted children was to change the subject: "Ay," he said, noticing the problem of adoption, "there's the rub. . . . This sort of thing is my reason for preferring statutory change on the cy pres principle, *i.e.*, directing the court to reform the disposition to approximate the intention of the testator or settlor within the limits of the Rule." Leach, Perpetuities: New Hampshire Defertilizes the Octogenarians, 77 Harv. L. Rev. 279, 282 (1963).

26. This procedure has been rejected outright in England on the ground that class gifts are unambiguous and therefore extrinsic evidence is inadmissible for the purpose sought. See Ward v. Van Der Loeff, [1924] App. Cas. 653 (Visc. Cave); cf. Estate of Kalouse, 282 N.W.2d 98 (Iowa 1979). The Restatement of Property § 377 comment c, which supports the procedure, answers this point by asserting that it is proper in this situation to utilize the Rule itself as a basis for finding an ambiguity. Cf. Simes & Smith on Future Interests § 1289.

27. In the *Second Bank-State St. Trust Co.* case, the court saved the gift under the subclass doctrine; see infra Part E, p. 1064; in the *Sears* case, the court saved the gift under the second-look doctrine; see infra Part E, p. 1075.

that that does not show that the testator arrived at a specific intent to exclude such children in the unlikely event of their birth or adoption. If this is the explanation for the refusal to apply the construction in the *Second Bank-State St. Trust Co.* or *Sears* cases, it is not entirely persuasive, however: If the testator had been apprised of the fact that their inclusion would cause an invalidity, it is all but certain that she or he *would* have arrived at a specific intent to exclude them. The application of the constructional preference for validity therefore seems justified in those two cases and cases like them.

4. *The Case of the "Precocious Toddler"*[28]—*Young Children and the Presumption of Fertility.* If an elderly person or a person whose physical condition prevents the birth of children is conclusively presumed to be able to have children, are children who have not yet reached puberty subject to the same conclusive presumption? Cases raising this problem are rare. The best known is Re Gaite's Will Trusts, [1949] 1 All Eng. Rep. 459 (Ch.), the facts of which form the basis of Example 17.7.

> *Example 17.7:* G devised property in trust, directing the trustee to pay the net income "to A for life, corpus to such of A's grandchildren living at my death or born within five years thereafter who shall attain the age of 21 years." G was survived by A (a 65-year-old widow) and by A's two children and one grandchild.
>
> If a child under the age of 5 is conclusively presumed to be capable of having a child, the remainder in favor of A's grandchildren who reach 21 is invalid. Although any grandchild of A's born to A's two children who were living at G's death will either reach 21 or die before reaching that age no later than 21 years after the death of the survivor of these two children (who were "in being" at G's death), the conclusive presumption if applicable would say that it is possible that A will conceive and bear a child who will in turn conceive a child, all within 5 years of G's death. Such grandchild therefore might reach 21 more than 21 years after the death of the survivor of A and A's two children and one grandchild who were living when G died.

Notice that in *Lattouf*, which held the presumption to be rebuttable rather than conclusive, the court was willing to indicate that the presumption would be rebutted by age in the case of Marie Endres' 3-year-and-10-month old daughter, Linda. The court's statement was dictum, and rather cryptic: "Marie Endres was not pregnant. She could not be, *nor of course, could the infant Linda.*" (Emphasis added.)

There have been other American cases in which a child shortly after (probable) puberty was conclusively presumed capable of having children. An example is Rust v. Rust, supra p. 996, where the testator's daughter, Margene, who was 9 1/2 years old when the testator died, was apparently conclusively presumed to be able to have a child before her 14th birthday. (Recall that the court found a way to uphold the gift anyway.) This presumption may, of course, be well justified. In early July, 1979, a widely published United Press International newspaper article reported that "a 10-

---

28. Professor Leach's term, again: He cornered the market!

year-old girl gave birth to twin girls at Indiana University Medical Center last week. . . ." According to the report, "Hospital officials . . . said the multiple birth for a mother so young was 'extremely unusual.'"

———

Age Contingencies Exceeding 21. G devised $100,000 in trust, "income to my son B for life, remainder to such of B's children as reach 30; if none reaches 30, to B's descendants who survive B, by representation; if none, to X-Charity." Appropriate provisions for the distribution of the income are made if one or more of B's children is still under 30 when B dies.

Consider how this disposition would play out in all four of the hypothetical families charted supra pp. 1010-13, if G died at his life expectancy of age 75. Consider Family I, first, where B is 50 years old at G's death and his youngest child, Z, is 25 years old; it is, of course, possible—but nevertheless unlikely—that B will have more children. The same prediction is appropriate for Family II, where B is 45 at G's death and Z is 15; concededly, though, the probabilities make it a degree or two less unlikely that additional children will be born to B. Family III is an even closer call, for B is 40 at G's death and Z is 5. Regardless of the possibilities and probabilities, if the charts of Families I, II, and III hold, the *actual* post-creation events are that B will have no more children after G's death. Family IV is different, however, and we will address that family below.

Under the assumption that in Families I, II, and III there will be no more children, B's children would be Y and Z in each family. Z is the younger of the two and therefore will reach 30 later. Z will reach 30 five years after G's death in Family I; fifteen years after G's death in Family II; and twenty-five years after G's death in Family III. In all three families, Z will reach 30 before B's death, if B lives out a normal life expectancy. Both B and Z (and Y, as well) were "in being" at G's death.

Now consider Family IV. There, when G dies, B is 35 and Z's birth is five years away. The post-creation events, if they play out as charted, include an afterborn child. That afterborn child, Z, will reach 30 thirty-five years after G's death, when B is 70 and Y is 35. What would it take for Z's interest to vest more than 21 years after the death of B and Y (B's only descendant who was "in being" at G's death)? *Both* B and Y would have to die *very* prematurely: They would both have to die before Z's ninth birthday, which means that B would have to die under the age of 49 *and* Y would have to die under the age of 14.

We now wish to shift away from the reality of the situation and turn to how the common-law Rule Against Perpetuities looks at it. In the world of the common-law Rule, G's disposition flunks the requirement of initial certainty. At common law, it is assumed that B can have another child after G's death and that that after-born child can outlive B, Y, and (in Families I, II, and III) Z (and anyone else you might think of) by more than 21 years. There is no validating life—no one beyond 21 years of whose death the after-born grandchild's interest *cannot* remain nonvested. Under the all-or-nothing rule for class gifts, that possibility makes the interest of *all* the class members invalid—including the interest of Y, who was "in being" at G's death in all four families, and the interest of Z, who was then "in being" in Families I, II, and III. In addition, the alternative remainders in favor of A's descendants and in favor of X-Charity are invalid because there is no validating life for either of them, either.

Before you ponder this example further on your own, we wish to bring you back specifically to the "know-and-see" *policy* of the Rule Against Perpetuities: Despite the fact that G knew and saw both Y and Z in Families I, II, and III, and despite the fact that G knew and saw Y in Family IV and that Y was in the same generation as that of the afterborn Z, G's gifts to them are invalid! In the case of the common-law Rule Against Perpetuities, there plainly is a gap between policy and operation.

Age Contingencies Not Exceeding 21—The Fertile Decedent and the Child En Ventre Sa Frigidaire![29] G devised $100,000 in trust, "income to my son B for life, remainder to such of B's children as reach 21; if none reaches 21, to B's descendants who survive B, by representation; if none, to X-Charity." Appropriate provisions for the distribution of the income are made if one or more of B's children is still under the age of 21 when B dies.

G's residuary devisees challenge the validity of G's disposition. They argue that the requirement of initial certainty is not met because it is possible that when B dies he will leave sperm on deposit in a sperm bank, and that after B's death B's widow—who could be someone not "in being" at G's death—will become pregnant with that sperm and give birth to a child of B's; B's post-death child cannot reach 21 within 21 years after B's death and will not *necessarily* reach 21 within 21 years after the death of anyone else you might put forward. G's residuary devisees argue that there is no validating life and the remainder interests after B's life estate are invalid.

Do the remainder interests flunk the requirement of initial certainty? How would you answer the argument advanced by G's residuary devisees? See supra p. 932. See also the legislative solution to this problem offered by USRAP section 1(d) and its UPC counterpart, UPC section 2-901(d) (1990).

2. The Case of the Afterborn Spouse

Pound v. Shorter
259 Ga. 148, 377 S.E.2d 854 (1989)

WELTNER, J. When Elizabeth Shorter died in 1929, her will created a trust that provided for her one unmarried son as follows:

---

29. Professor Leach's term: See Leach, Perpetuities in the Atomic Age: The Sperm Bank and the Fertile Decedent, 48 A.B.A.J. 942 (1962).

In trust further, should my son die, either before or after my death, leaving neither child, nor children of a deceased wife surviving him, but leaving a wife surviving him, to pay over the annual net income arising each year from said trust property, in quarterly installments each year, to the wife of my said son, during her life, and upon the death of the wife of my said son, to thereupon pay over, deliver and convey, in fee simple, the corpus of said trust property to the children and descendants of children of my brother . . . and sister. . . .

The son married in 1953 and died in 1987, survived by his widow. He left no descendants. After his death, the trustee bank filed a petition to determine the validity of the trust item. The trial court found that the item created a perpetuity and decreed that the trust be terminated and that the son's widow have fee ownership. Fifty-two lineal descendants of Elizabeth Shorter appeal.

1. The Rule against Perpetuities, adopted first by the legislature in 1863, provides:

Limitations of estates may extend through any number of lives in being at the time when the limitations commence, and 21 years, and the usual period of gestation added thereafter. The law terms a limitation beyond that period a perpetuity and forbids its creation. When an attempt is made to create a perpetuity, the law will give effect to the limitations which are not too remote and will declare the other limitations void, thereby vesting the fee in the last taker under the legal limitations. OCGA § 44-6-1.

2. We have undertaken a study of both the rule against perpetuities and an alternative approach, commonly called "wait and see." Fifteen states have adopted some form of the "wait-and-see" approach and all have done so through legislation. We conclude:

(1) that the traditional rule against perpetuities has been effective so far in Georgia, judging by the few cases brought to invalidate grants, and the even fewer invalidations; and

(2) that the alternative "wait-and-see" approach has many problems, including initial uncertainty (which is avoided by the traditional rule) and the necessity for selecting a method by which to determine the length of the waiting period.[30]

3. We are not convinced that the goals of certainty and early vesting will be served by adopting the alternative, and accordingly decline to do so.

---

30. The problems may be summarized as follows: (1) there is actually no severe problem of grants being invalidated due to a violation of the rule against perpetuities; (2) technical violations of the rule can be avoided by competent drafting, so only unwary counsel is trapped by the rule; (3) there is a big problem of expense and inconvenience during the waiting period; (4) there is an increase in litigation due to the alternative doctrine; (5) much of the testator's estate is diverted to lawyers' fees; (6) most alternative statutes provide for cy pres litigation at the end of the waiting period if the interest has neither vested nor failed, and that litigation is difficult and expensive due to the passage of time; and (7) the alternative does not simplify the perpetuities law. Bloom, Perpetuities Refinement: There is an Alternative, 1987, 62 Wash. L. Rev. 23.

4. As the will encompasses the possibilities that the son might marry a woman who was unborn in 1929 (a life *not* "in being") and then predecease her, it violated the rule against perpetuities.

Judgment affirmed.

All the Justices concur.

Notes

1. *Reality*. Not disclosed but known by the court was the fact that Mildred Shorter, the son's widow, was in being in 1929 when Elizabeth Shorter died.[31] In direct response to the *Pound* decision, the Georgia legislature the following year enacted USRAP, which adopts the wait-and-see method of perpetuity reform.

2. *State of the Authorities*. In accord with Pound v. Shorter are Easton v. Hall, 323 Ill. 397, 154 N.E. 216 (1926); Chenoweth v. Bullit, 224 Ky. 698, 6 S.W.2d 1061 (Ct. App. 1928); Restatement of Property § 370 comment k and illustration 3.

3. *No Violation If Devisees Can Be Their Own Validating Lives*. The possibility of an afterborn spouse does not always create a perpetuity violation. In an appropriate case, the devisees of the remainder interest following the spouse's death are their own validating lives. This would be the case if the contingent remainder were in favor of named individuals (Y and Z perhaps) or a class that was closed at G's death (for example, the children of G's predeceased daughter, A).

Furthermore, if the remainder was not contingent on survivorship, the fact that it was still subject to open at G's death would not invalidate it if the class could not increase beyond lives in being. For example, in the absence of a condition precedent of survivorship, a remainder in favor of G's grandchildren would be valid in the above example. See Lanier v. Lanier, 218 Ga. 137, 126 S.E.2d 776 (1962). But one in favor of G's great-grandchildren would be invalid.

4. *Constructional Preference for Validity*. Even when no other validating lives can be located, the principle of construction favoring validity can often be used to avoid the afterborn-spouse problem. When the language of the instrument fairly allows, some courts have construed G's reference to her or his son's "widow" as referring only to the person to whom the son was married when the will was executed or when G died. See Willis v. Hendry, 127 Conn. 653, 20 A.2d 375 (1941) (G's will referred to "the wife of my said son"); Friend's Will, 283 N.Y. 200, 28 N.E.2d 377 (1940) (G's will

---

31. This is not to suggest that there never are "afterborn spouses." Pablo Casals, the famous cellist, was around 80 when he married his 20-year old student Martita. Of the marriage, Casals wrote: "I was aware at the time that some people noted a certain discrepancy in our ages—a bridegroom of course is not usually thirty years older than his father-in-law." P. Casals, Joys and Sorrows 277 (1970).

In July 1989, newspapers and magazines widely reported that Hugh Hefner, the 63-year old founder of Playboy Magazine and the father of a 36-year old daughter and a 34-year old son, married Kimberley Conrad, the 26-year old 1988 Playmate of the Year.

referred to "the widow of my said son Sol"). However, this procedure is not always used by courts, as the *Pound* case demonstrates.

3. The Case of the Administrative Contingency

This technical violation can occur where a disposition involves the performance by a fiduciary (an executor, a trustee) of some administrative function, the completion of which might but is extremely unlikely to take more than 21 years.

Typical examples are the completion of the probate of a will, the settlement of an estate, the payment of debts or taxes, the sale of estate assets, or the delivery of trust corpus on the termination of a trust.

Administrative-Contingency Example. Consider G, again, in Family I, II, III, or IV. G died at age 75, devising real property "to such of my grandchildren, born before or after my death, as may be living upon final distribution of my estate." G is survived by her children (A and B) and her grandchildren (V, X, Y, and Z in Families I, II, and III; V, X, and Y in Family IV).

The grandchildren's interest is invalid, by the majority view. Though unlikely, there is a possibility that the final distribution of G's estate will not occur within 21 years after G's death.[32] This possibility eliminates validating the interest on the basis of the 21-year part of the period. In addition, there are no lives in being that can validate it. As always, not only are afterborn grandchildren presumed, and but also presumed is the possibility that final distribution of G's estate will occur and that such afterborn grandchildren will outlive by more than 21 years the deaths of A, B, V, X, Y, and (in Families I, II, and III) Z.

As the above example illustrates, the term "administrative contingency" is somewhat misleading. It does not refer to the possibility that the administrative task will never be completed. If it did, all interests that are to take effect in possession upon the completion of an administrative task would be contingent and invalid. But in fact, such gifts are upheld. See cases collected in Am. L. Prop. § 24.23 n.2. Rather, it is accepted as certain that the task will be completed, presumably because of the fiduciary's legal obligation to do so;[33] the uncertainty is that the task might not be

---

32. There have been rare instances of distribution of an estate being delayed for a very long time. See, e.g., Richards v. Tolbert, 232 Ga. 678, 208 S.E.2d 486 (1974) (57 years between death and probate of will); Estate of Hostetter, 75 Ill. App. 3d 1020, 394 N.E.2d 77 (1979) (25 years); Haddock v. Boston & Me. R.R., 146 Mass. 155, 15 N.E. 495 (1888) (63 years between death and probate of will); Garrett Estate, 372 Pa. 438, 94 A.2d 357 (1953) (23 years).

33. But see Miller v. Weston, 67 Colo. 534, 189 P. 610 (1920) (en banc), where the court held that a devise to A "on the admission of this will to probate" is contingent on the probate of the will and invalid because probate "may never happen." The court was unwilling to accept probate as a certainty even if "probate is required by law to be made." In effect, the perpetuity requirement of initial certainty did not allow the possibility of the law's being disobeyed to be ignored!

completed within the perpetuity period. Thus, the administrative contingency problem commonly arises because the interest is contingent on survivorship of the administrative function. These dispositions have the completely rational objective of preventing the actual distribution of property to the estate of a dead person, thereby avoiding unnecessary expenses of administration and possible double estate taxation.[34]

Survivorship of a Period that Might Exceed 21 Years. At bottom, the administrative contingency problem is often one of survivorship of a period of time that might exceed 21 years. Interests that are contingent on survivorship of a period that might exceed 21 years are not always invalid, however. They will be valid if the devisees can themselves be the validating lives, which requires that the questioned interest either be in favor of one or more individual taker or a class that is closed at the testator's death.

> *Example 17.8:* G devised real property "to such of my children as may be living upon final distribution of my estate." G is survived by children.
> The children's interest is valid. Since no children will be born to G after her death, her children are their own validating lives.

Class Subject to Open for More Than 21 Years. When the interest is in favor of a class that is not closed at the testator's death, the administrative contingency problem can also arise even if there is no condition of survivorship.

> *Example 17.9:* G devised real property "to such of my great-grandchildren, born before or after my death, as may be living upon final distribution of my estate." G is survived by children and grandchildren.
> The interest would be invalid even if the phrase "as may be living" were omitted. A great-grandchild could be conceived and born before the completion of the probate of G's estate and more than 21 years after the death of the survivor of G's children and those of G's grandchildren that were living at G's death. Note, however, that the invalidity here is due to the fact that the class of great-grandchildren could not only increase after the testator's death, but also increase after the death of lives in being at his death.

If the class cannot increase after lives in being, the absence of a condition of survivorship will save a gift in favor of a class even though it is not closed at the testator's death. To illustrate this point, suppose the gift in Example 17.9 were in favor of G's grandchildren. Now suppose that the phrase "as may be living" were omitted. This would make the

---

34. Concerns about double estate taxation, under the federal estate tax at least, may be somewhat overdrawn. The reason is that IRC § 2013 provides for a credit against the estate tax of a second decedent in the amount of the estate tax imposed on the estate of the prior decedent. If the two decedents die within two years of one another, the amount of the credit is 100% of the prior decedent's estate tax attributable to the inclusion of the transferred property. The credit is 80% of this amount if the second decedent dies between two and four years after the death of the prior decedent, 60% if the second death occurs between four and six years, 40% for deaths between six and eight years, and 20% for deaths between eight and ten years.

grandchildren's interest valid because no new members could join the class after the death of the survivor of G's children, all of whom were, of course, "in being" at G's death.

The Fiduciary's Obligation. A minority of courts has devised an escape from the administrative-contingency problem. Since the administrative function is to be performed by a fiduciary, the procedure is to hold that the fiduciary's obligation is not only to complete the task, but to do so within a reasonable time, and to hold further that a reasonable time is something less than 21 years. See Belfield v. Booth, 63 Conn. 299, 27 A. 585 (1893); Asche v. Asche, 42 Del. Ch. 545, 216 A.2d 272 (1966); Brandenburg v. Thorndike, 139 Mass. 102, 28 N.E. 575 (1885); cf. In re Taylor, 66 Cal. 2d 855, 59 Cal. Rptr. 437, 428 P.2d 301 (1967) (vesting occurs at time distribution should have been made). The difficulty with this minority view is that, while there may be an obligation to complete fiduciary tasks expeditiously, it is a fiction to say that there is always a violation of a fiduciary duty when the settlement of an estate takes more than 21 years. While rare, there can be cases where protracted and successive litigation over a multitude of issues legitimately ties up an estate for a very long time. Even on a case-by-case basis, it would seem to be impossible to conclude with the certainty required by the Rule and on the basis of the facts existing when the interest was created that no such delay will properly arise.

Constructional Preference for Validity. Depending on the language employed, the principle of construction favoring validity may be available as a method of avoiding invalidity. For example, if a condition of survivorship is ambiguous on the point, it would probably be construed to relate to the death of the testator or of the life tenant rather than to the completion of the administrative task, such as the final distribution of the estate.[35] Indeed, this construction has on occasion been adopted even when the language unambiguously related to the estate's final distribution.[36]

Despite the existence of precedent supporting one or the other of these two salvage devices, the administrative contingency problem has not been solved. Most courts would probably still conclude that devises such as G's in the first example given above violate the Rule and are therefore invalid.[37]

---

35. See First Nat'l Bank v. Jenkins, 256 Ga. 223, 345 S.E.2d 829 (1986) (Will provided that "upon the death of [the life tenant], and after [paying hospital and medical expenses incurred by the life tenant during his life time and at his death paying for his funeral and grave marker], my trustee is directed to divide all the remaining trust property [among various beneficiaries] then living"; held, the remainder interests vested at the life tenant's death, with "only possession or actual payment . . . delayed until his estate is settled, including payments for funeral expenses and the grave marker."); Restatement of Property § 374 comment f.

36. See Malone v. Herndon, 197 Okla. 26, 168 P.2d 272 (1945), where a will providing that on the death of the life tenant leaving issue surviving him, the "trust estate shall be paid over, delivered and conveyed to such issue living at the time of said payment, delivery and conveyance" was construed to require survivorship of the life tenant.

37. See Prime v. Hyne, 260 Cal. App. 2d 397, 67 Cal. Rptr. 170 (1968), for an example of a decision that rejected the notion that the fiduciary's duty guarantees that an estate will be distributed within 21 years of the decedent's death.

PART C. PERPETUITY SAVING CLAUSES—THE PRACTITIONER'S FRIEND

The common-law Rule Against Perpetuities should be and for the most part is less fearsome to practicing estate-planning lawyers than it is to law students and law graduates studying for the bar examination. This is not because estate-planning lawyers have found that the Rule becomes more understandable with experience, but because they have discovered a secret: They need not be greatly concerned about the technicalities of the Rule because they use perpetuity saving clauses.

Formulated and used properly, perpetuity saving clauses mean that no lawyer need ever fear that a trust or other property arrangement she or he drafts will violate the common-law Rule. In addition, unless the trust or other property arrangement is unreasonable—for example, unless it is to continue beyond the death of the last living member of the transferor's youngest descendant living when the trust or other arrangement was created—, the practicing lawyer need not fear that the perpetuity saving clause will have any practical effect other than to save the disposition from a Rule violation. Trusts are routinely created that would violate the Rule, were it not for the perpetuity saving clause; essentially a technicality, a perpetuity saving clause is nevertheless essential in such cases.

In Re Villar
[1929] 1 Ch. 243 (Court of Appeal)

[The testator died on September 6, 1926, survived by his widow, five children (three sons and two daughters), and two infant grandchildren (children of one of his daughters). The testator's will created a residuary trust, the terms of which basically were that an annuity of a specified amount was to be paid to his widow and the remaining part of the income was to be paid to his children and their descendants. All interests in the trust were to vest in the testator's descendants living at the expiration of the "period of restriction." According to the terms of the testator's will, the "period of restriction" was to expire "20 years from the day of the death of the last survivor of all the lineal descendants of Her Late Majesty Queen Victoria who shall be living at the time of my death."]

LORD HANWORTH, M.R. This is an appeal from Astbury J., who had to determine whether or not in the main the will of the testator ought to be declared ineffective. . . . The terms of the residuary gift which are easy to carry out as regards the payment of income at the present time are to be treated as invalid, because of the period of restriction to the end of which distribution of the capital was postponed. The argument is that as the ascertainment of the end of this period will create serious difficulty in time to come, the residuary gift ought to be set aside as invalid. The period of restriction is defined as "the period ending at the expiration of 20 years from the day of the death of the last survivor of all the lineal descendants of Her Late Majesty Queen Victoria who shall be living at the time of my death." We have the evidence of a member of the College of Arms, who says the descendants of Queen Victoria numbered not less than 120 in 1922, and that they might have increased in number by 1926. On the other hand I suppose they might have decreased in number, for I do not know whether the births of new descendants between 1922 and 1926 were sufficient to fill the vacancies among the descendants caused by death. However, it is quite clear that there were a large number of the descendants of Queen Victoria in being on September 6, 1926, and obviously there may be great difficulty in ascertaining whether and when the last of these lineal descendants had passed away. That is what has to be ascertained, and it depends on the existence of one single life out of many others. I recognize that serious difficulty might well arise in the future in ascertaining the date when that life ceased. . . .

But it is said that the Courts ought to take into consideration the difficulty that will arise in the future when, it may be 100 years hence, their successors will be faced with the problem of finding out who is the last survivor of this body of 120 or 130 persons and when he died. That is a difficulty which may arise by reason of the vicissitudes of life, but it may not. It is possible that 120 years hence the Court may find a number of problems relating to the births, marriages and deaths of various persons; but they appear to me to be matters which we ought not to take into account. The difficulties are not insurmountable, and they may in fact never arise. Therefore I return to the view that the only matter I have to consider is whether the residuary gift of the testator can be declared invalid on the ground that it has transgressed some rule of law at the present time. The answer must be that it has not so transgressed, and, if so, we cannot by reference to difficulties that may arise hereafter make a new will for the testator.

I regret the decision, as there is no reason for such a fanciful disposition; but testing it by the rules which have to be applied, I can find no breach of the existing law, and the will must therefore stand. The appellant has suggested that the whole residuary gift should be set aside, but at the present time there is no difficulty in dealing with the estate as directed by the testator. It seems impossible to set aside a gift which works well in the present but which may in the future cause difficulty. I think that the decision of Astbury, J., was right, and that the appeal must be dismissed.

LAWRENCE, L.J., concurring. . . . In my judgment the decision in Thellusson v. Woodford, [11 Ves. Jr. 112, 32 Eng. Rep. 1030 (H.L. 1805)], which is binding on this Court, affords a complete answer to the contention of the appellants that the testator's residuary gift is void, as infringing the rule against perpetuities. In that case Lord Eldon . . . states that "the language of all the cases is, that property may be so limited as to make it unalienable during any number of lives, not exceeding that, to which testimony can be applied, to determine, when the survivor of them drops."

Much stress has been rightly laid by the appellants in the present case on the words "not exceeding that to which testimony can be applied," but in my opinion these words were intended to apply to cases such as In re Moore, [[1901] 1 Ch. 936,] where it is obviously impossible to ascertain the lives specified.[38]

Moreover I think that in cases of that kind the question is not whether the rule against perpetuities has or has not been infringed, but whether the gift is void for uncertainty. If it be impossible to ascertain the lives upon the death of the survivor of which vesting of the capital is to take effect, such vesting is not in fact postponed beyond the permitted limit, but the gift is void for uncertainty. . . .

In the present case there is in my opinion no infringement of the rule against perpetuities. . . . [Nor is the gift void for uncertainty, for] the evidence shows at most that it is difficult at the present time to ascertain who are the lineal descendants in question. . . . In my judgment the evidence falls far short of proving that the number of lives exceeds that to which testimony can be applied to determine when the survivor of them drops. . . .

[The concurring opinion of RUSSELL, L.J. is omitted.]

———

Perpetuity Saving Clauses. The principle of *Villar* provides the platform for the modern perpetuity saving clause. These clauses are a variation of the language in cases like *Villar*, in which the transferor directly governs the term of the trust to a period of time measured by the life of the survivor of a group of designated persons in being at the time of the transfer plus 21 years (20 years, in *Villar* itself). Although perpetuity saving clauses also establish a period of time measured by the life of the survivor of a group of designated persons in being at the time of the transfer plus 21 years, the difference is that saving clauses do not directly govern the term of the trust; they operate as a back-stop just in case the actual term of the trust exceeds the time allotted by the saving clause. That part of a perpetuity saving clause that establishes this period of time is called the *perpetuity-period component*. Saving clauses contain another component, called the *gift-over component*. This component expressly creates a gift over that is guaranteed to vest at the termination of the period established in the perpetuity-period component, but only if the interests in the trust or other arrangement have neither vested nor terminated earlier in accordance with their primary terms.

It is important to note that regardless of what group of persons is designated in the perpetuity-period component of the saving clause, the survivor of the group is not necessarily the person who would be the validating life for the questioned interest in the absence of the saving clause. Without the saving clause, the questioned interest might in fact have been invalid because of the existence of an invalidating chain of

---

38. In In re Moore, the testator created a trust to endure until "twenty-one years from the death of the last survivor of all persons who shall be living at my death." Eds.

possible post-creation events with respect to every person who might be proposed as a validating life. The persons designated in the saving clause, however, become validating lives for all interests in the trust or other property arrangement. The saving clause confers on the last surviving member of the group the requisite causal connection demanded by the requirement of initial certainty. See Norton v. Georgia R.R. Bank & Trust, 253 Ga. 596, 322 S.E.2d 870 (1984) (upholding the validity of a traditional perpetuity saving clause).

In most cases, the saving clause not only avoids a violation of the common-law Rule; it also, in a sense, over-insures the client's disposition against the possibility that the gift over will ever take effect. The period of time established by the perpetuity-period component of the clause provides a margin of safety. Almost always, the length of time is sufficient to exceed—usually by a substantial margin—the time when the interests in the trust or other arrangement actually vest (or terminate) by their own terms. The clause, therefore, is usually a formality that validates the disposition without affecting the substance of the disposition at all.

Royal Lives and Other Ploys. As noted in *Villar*, Thellusson v. Woodford, 11 Ves. Jr. 112, 32 Eng. Rep. 1030 (Ch. 1805), is the source of the so-called uncertainty rule. American authorities take a somewhat stricter view about the matter of uncertainty than was exhibited in *Villar*. The Restatement of Property section 374 comment l declares that a clause like that in *Villar*—called a royal lives clause—would be found invalid by an American court, as would specified similar periods such as one measured by the lives of "those persons whose names appear in the City Directory of the City of X." Accord Restatement 2d of Property § 1.3 comment a; USRAP § 1 Comment, Part B (designation of group is invalid if the group is such "that would cause it to be impracticable to determine the death of the survivor."). Although *Villar* is perhaps the widest group that has ever been upheld, even by an English court,[39] cases of a trust actually being declared invalid are few.[40]

Validity is one thing; discretion and practicability are another. Lord Hanworth said that "there is no reason for such a fanciful disposition" as that in *Villar*, and he was certainly correct. A device sometimes mentioned by commentators is the dozen-healthy-babies ploy, under which the transferor designates a period governed by the life of the survivor of a number of newborn babies in the maternity ward of a specified hospital. A 21-year period is then tacked on after the death of the survivor. Writing in the early 1950's, when life expectancy at birth was about 68 years, Professor Leach said that the period resulting from this device would "add

---

39. Another candidate for the prize comes from In re Warren's Will, 105 Sol. J. 511 (1961), where the period was measured by the life of the survivor of 194 marital issue of Queen Victoria.

40. In In re Moore, [1901] 1 Ch. 936, the testator created a trust to endure until "twenty-one years from the death of the last survivor of all persons who shall be living at my death." In a short opinion, the court held the gift void for uncertainty. "It is impossible to ascertain when the last life will be extinguished," the court said. Cases are collected in Reporter's Note No. 3 to § 1.3, Restatement 2d of Property.

up to about a century."[41] Although it would seem that his mathematics were a little off (68 + 21 = 89, not 100), Professor Leach undoubtedly understood that a group of newborns will almost certainly include several persons who will live beyond her or his life expectancy. Professor Leach apparently estimated that an additional 11 years or so would account for this.

With the current life expectancy at birth standing at 75 years, the total period of time produced by this device today would average out to a period well in excess of the 96 years calculated by adding 21 to 75. In fact, it would yield an average period of about 115 years.[42] Professor Leach rightly condemned such a practice,[43] but he was probably poking at a strawman. To our knowledge, this practice is not used by practicing lawyers. What lawyers actually do is depicted below.

Prototype Trusts Saved by Prototype Perpetuity Saving Clause. We present below two types of trusts as prototypical of trusts that are actually created in practice; we also give you a sample of a type of saving clause frequently used. Were it not for the inclusion of a perpetuity saving clause, the remainder interests in both trusts would flunk the requirement of initial certainty and be invalid. (The first type of trust is more frequently created than the second, but the second type is also used in practice.)

As before, we place G in the families we charted earlier. Assuming that G dies at age 75, G is survived by her or his children (A and B) and grandchildren (V, X, Y, and Z). (In Family IV, however, Z is not "in being" at G's death but is born five years later.)

Example 17.10: Corpus to Grandchildren Contingent on Reaching an Age Exceeding 21. G devised property in trust, income in equal shares to G's children for the life of the survivor, then in equal shares to G's grandchildren, remainder in corpus to G's grandchildren who reach age 30; if none reaches 30, to G's descendants who survive G's last surviving child, by representation; if none, to X-Charity.

Example 17.11: Corpus to Descendants Contingent on Surviving Last Living Grandchild. G devised property in trust, income in equal shares to G's children for the life of the survivor, then in equal shares to G's grandchildren for the

---

41. Leach & Tudor, The Common Law Rule Against Perpetuities, in Am. L. Prop. § 24.16, at 52.

42. The average life expectancy of the longest-living member of a group of twelve newborn babies, selected at random, is 94.2 years. With the 21-year tack-on period, the twelve-healthy-babies ploy would produce, on average, a period of about 115 years (94 + 21).

The 94-year life expectancy was computed by applying a complicated actuarial formula to the data set forth in Table 80CNSMT, in Fed. Est. & Gift Tax Rep. (CCH) ¶ 6415.301 (1989). Starting with an original cohort of 100,000 new-borns, Table 80CNSMT gives the number of people who live to age one (98,740), age two (98,648), and so on to ages 109 (33) and 110 (0).

We would like to express our gratitude to Dr. Cecil Nesbitt, professor emeritus of mathematics at the University of Michigan, for deriving the actuarial formula used in the computation; he derived the formula from the principles set forth in N. Bowers, H. Gerber, J. Hickman, D. Jones & C. Nesbitt, Actuarial Mathematics Ch. 16 (1986).

43. See J. Morris & W. Leach, The Rule Against Perpetuities 13 (2d ed. 1962).

life of the survivor, and on the death of G's last living grandchild, corpus to
G's descendants then living, by representation; if none, to X-Charity.

G's lawyer, to her or his credit, inserted a perpetuity saving clause in
both dispositions. Specifically, the saving clause selected by G's lawyer
says:

> The trust hereby created shall terminate in any event not later than 21 years
> after the death of the last survivor of my descendants who are in being at the
> time this instrument becomes effective, and unless sooner terminated by the
> terms hereof, the trustee shall, at the termination of such period, make
> distribution to the persons then entitled to the income of this trust, and in the
> same shares and proportions as they are so entitled.

Does the use of a saving clause to validate the dispositions in Examples
17.10 and 17.11 extend dead-hand control beyond that which the
common-law Rule allows or should allow, or does it vindicate the
know-and-see policy of the common-law Rule?

Consider each of the four charted families and work out how long
ultimate vesting in Example 17.10 will likely take. As for Example 17.11,
the time of likely final vesting can be projected by determining the number
of years after G's death it will be until G's youngest grandchild, Z, will
reach the end of her or his remaining life expectancy.[44] That will be 51
years after G's death in Family I; 61 years after G's death in Family II; 71
years after G's death in Family III; and 80 years after G's death in Family
IV.

Will the period of time marked off by the perpetuity-period component
of the saving clause exceed the time of projected actual vesting? If so, by
how much? To work this out, you need to add 21 years to the remaining
life expectancy of G's youngest descendant in being at G's death: G's
youngest descendant in Family I is S, a newborn greatgrandchild whose life
expectancy is 75 years; in Family II, the youngest descendant is K, a
newborn greatgrandchild whose life expectancy is 75 years; in Family III,
G's youngest descendant is Z, a 5-year-old grandchild whose remaining life
expectancy is 71 years; and in Family IV, the youngest descendants are X
and Y, newborn grandchildren whose life expectancies are 75 years.

Malpractice Liability. Would G's lawyer be liable in malpractice if she or
he had failed to insert a perpetuity saving clause in the above dispositions?
In the technical violation cases studied earlier, would a lawyer drafting an
irrevocable inter-vivos trust be liable in malpractice if she or he inserts a
perpetuity saving clause that gears the perpetuity-period component to a
group of persons living at the settlor's death?

---

44. Remaining life expectancies are given in U.S. Bureau of the Census, Statistical Abstract
of the United States: 1990, Table 106, at 74 (110th ed. 1990).

Lucas v. Hamm
56 Cal. 2d 583, 15 Cal. Rptr. 821, 364 P.2d 685 (1961)

[After the death of the testator, the attorney who drew the will, in his capacity as counsel of record for the executors, advised the residuary devisees in writing that the residuary trust provision was invalid. The devisees subsequently entered into a settlement agreement with the testator's blood relatives under which the devisees received $75,000 less than they would have received had the trust provision been valid.

In an action for damages brought by the devisees against the drafting attorney, the trial court dismissed the complaint, and the plaintiffs appealed.]

GIBSON, C.J. . . . . [The court held that lack of privity does not insulate an attorney who negligently draws a will from liability in tort to the devisees who lose their testamentary rights because of the attorney's negligence, nor does it insulate the attorney from liability in contract to such devisees as third party beneficiaries if the attorney fails properly to fulfill her or his obligations under the contract with the testator. See supra pp. 589-93. The court then took up the question whether the attorney had been negligent or had breached the contract.]

The complaint, as we have seen, alleges that defendant drafted the will in such a manner that the trust was invalid because it violated the rules relating to perpetuities and restraints on alienation. These closely akin subjects have long perplexed the courts and the bar. Professor Gray, a leading authority in the field, stated: "There is something in the subject which seems to facilitate error. Perhaps it is because the mode of reasoning is unlike that with which lawyers are most familiar. . . . A long list might be formed of the demonstrable blunders with regard to its questions made by eminent men, blunders which they themselves have been sometimes the first to acknowledge; and there are few lawyers of any practice in drawing wills and settlements who have not at some time either fallen into the net which the Rule spreads for the unwary, or at least shuddered to think how narrowly they have escaped it." Gray, The Rule Against Perpetuities (4th ed. 1942) p. xi; see also Leach, Perpetuities Legislation (1954) 67 Harv. L. Rev. 1349 (describing the rule as a "technicality-ridden legal nightmare" and a "dangerous instrumentality in the hands of most members of the bar"). Of the California law on perpetuities and restraints it has been said that few, if any, areas of the law have been fraught with more confusion or concealed more traps for the unwary draftsman; that members of the bar, probate courts, and title insurance companies make errors in these matters; that the code provisions adopted in 1872 created a situation worse than if the matter had been left to the common law, and that the legislation adopted in 1951 (under which the will involved here was drawn), despite the best of intentions, added further complexities. (See 38 Cal. Jur. 2d 443; Coil, Perpetuities and Restraints; A Needed Reform (1955) 30 State Bar J. 87, 88-90.)

In view of the state of the law relating to perpetuities and restraints on alienation and the nature of the error, if any, assertedly made by defendant in preparing the instrument, it would not be proper to hold that defendant failed to use such skill, prudence, and diligence as lawyers of ordinary skill and capacity commonly exercise. The provision of the will quoted in the complaint, namely, that the trust was to terminate five years after the order of the probate court distributing the property to the trustee, could cause the trust to be invalid only because of the remote possibility that the order of distribution would be delayed for a period longer than a life in being at the creation of the interest plus 16 years (the 21-year statutory period less the five years specified in the will). Although it has been held that a possibility of this type could result in invalidity of a bequest (Estate of Johnston, 47 Cal. 2d 265, 269-270, 303 P.2d 1; Estate of Campbell, 28 Cal. App. 2d 102, 103 et seq., 82 P.2d 22), the possible occurrence of such a delay was so remote and unlikely that an attorney of ordinary skill acting under the same circumstances might well have "fallen into the net which the Rule spreads for the unwary" and failed to recognize the danger. We need not decide whether the trust provision of the will was actually invalid or whether, as defendant asserts, the complaint fails to allege facts necessary to enable such a determination, because we have concluded that in any event an error of the type relied on by plaintiffs does not show negligence or breach of contract on the part of defendant. . . .

The judgment is affirmed.

Notes

1. *Criticism.* R. E. Megarry, in 81 L.Q. Rev. 478, 481 (1965), commented on the *Lucas* decision:

> An Englishman's comment on the decision must perforce observe a proper restraint. Doubtless the Supreme Court of California is the best judge of the standard of competence which is to be expected of California lawyers of ordinary skill and capacity. Let it be accepted that [it] is highly unlikely that it would take longer than the perpetuity period for the estate to be distributed. The question then becomes whether an ordinary lawyer who undertakes to draft a will should be expected to know that a gift will be void for perpetuity if there is any possibility, however unlikely, that the perpetuity period will be exceeded. This part of the rule is so fundamental, and so highly stressed by all the books and teachers, that he who does not know it must be expected to know little or nothing of the rest of the rule. The standard of competence in California thus seems to be that it is not negligent for lawyers to draft wills knowing little or nothing of the rule against perpetuities, and without consulting anyone skilled in the rule (a point mentioned by the Court of Appeal but ignored in the judgment of the Supreme Court). If the rule against perpetuities is in this category, what other fundamentals of the law are there of which the California attorney may be ignorant without culpability? How does California translate and apply *spondet peritiam artis?* However bright the future of Lucas v. Hamm may be in England on the score of privity, it is to be hoped that on the standard of professional competence it will prove to be a slur on the profession which, like the mule, will display neither pride of ancestry nor hope of posterity.

See also M. Bloom, The Trouble with Lawyers 72-75 (1968).

2. *Continuing Validity of Lucas?* In Wright v. Williams, 47 Cal. App. 3d 802, 809 n.2, 121 Cal. Rptr. 194, 199 n.2 (1975), the court said: "There is reason to doubt that the ultimate conclusion of Lucas v. Hamm is valid in today's state of the art. Draftsmanship to avoid the rule against perpetuities seems no longer esoteric." See also Millright v. Romer, 322 N.W.2d 30 (Iowa 1982). Cf. Bucquet v. Livingston, 57 Cal. App. 3d 914, 129 Cal. Rptr. 514 (1976); Smith v. Lewis, 13 Cal. 3d 349, 373, 530 P.2d 589, 605 (1975) (Clark J., dissenting).

3. *Model Rules of Professional Conduct,* Rule 1.1 (1983): "A lawyer shall provide competent representation to a client. Competent representation requires the legal knowledge, skill, thoroughness and preparation reasonably necessary for the representation."

EXTERNAL REFERENCE. Johnston, Legal Malpractice in Estate Planning—Perilous Times Ahead for the Practitioner, 67 Iowa L. Rev. 629 (1982).

PART D. WAIT-AND-SEE AND OTHER METHODS OF PERPETUITY REFORM

The need for perpetuity reform is not much in doubt, but controversy persists about the method. Three basic methods have been advanced: (i) discrete statutory repair of the fertile octogenarian, afterborn spouse, and administrative contingency problem areas, along with reduction of age contingencies to 21; (ii) immediately available reformation; and (iii) wait-and-see, with deferred reformation (reformation only if an interest remains contingent at the expiration of the permissible vesting period).

We believe we are accurate in reporting that the only realistic hope for widespread perpetuity reform today is in legislative adoption of the third method—wait-and-see, with deferred reformation. This is the approach of the recently promulgated USRAP. USRAP has been approved by the American Bar Association, on the unanimous recommendation of the Council of the A.B.A. Section of Real Property, Probate and Trust Law; it has also been unanimously endorsed by the Joint Editorial Board for the Uniform Probate Code, the Board of Regents of the American College of Probate Counsel, and the Board of Governors of the American College of Real Estate Lawyers. USRAP has been incorporated into the Uniform Probate Code as Part 9 of Article II, has been enacted in forty percent of the states, making it the single most widely enacted method of perpetuity reform to date, and seems to be on its way to enactment in several others. There is also a chance that a common-law court, without the benefit of legislation, might adopt the similar approach of the Restatement 2d of Property (1983), infra p. 1051.

1. Specific-Statutory-Repair Method

The specific-statutory-repair method is in effect in two jurisdictions—Illinois[45] and New York.[46] Until 1988, this method was also in effect in Florida;[47] it was repealed when Florida enacted USRAP. Until 1991, California had a statute aimed at the afterborn spouse category, but not the other categories of technical violation;[48] this provision was repealed when California enacted USRAP.

Although these statutes differ slightly in detail,[49] we present the Illinois provisions as illustrative of the specific-statutory-repair approach to perpetuity reform.

Illinois Revised Statutes
Chapter 30

§ 194. *Application of the Rule Against Perpetuities.* . . . (c) In determining whether an interest violates the rule against perpetuities:

(1) it shall be presumed (A) that the interest was intended to be valid, (B) in the case of an interest conditioned upon the probate of a will, the appointment of an executor, administrator or trustee, the completion of the administration of an estate, the payment of debts, the sale or distribution of property, the determination of federal or state tax liabilities or the happening of any administrative contingency, that the contingency must occur, if at all, within the period of the rule against perpetuities, and (C) where the instrument creates an interest in the "widow," "widower," or "spouse" of another person, that the maker of the instrument intended to refer to a person who was living at the date that the period of the rule against perpetuities commences to run;

(2) where any interest, but for this subparagraph (c)(2), would be invalid because it is made to depend upon any person attaining or failing to attain an age in excess of 21 years, the age specified shall be reduced to 21 years as to every person to whom the age contingency applies;

(3) if, notwithstanding the provisions of subparagraphs (c)(1) and (2) of this Section, the validity of any interest depends upon the possibility of the birth or adoption of a child, (A) no person shall be deemed capable of having a child until he has attained the age of 13 years, (B) any person who has attained the age of 65 years shall be deemed incapable of having a child, (C) evidence shall be admissible as to the incapacity of having a

---

45. See Ill. Rev. Stat. Ch. 30, § 194(c). The Illinois statute also contains a wait-and-see element applicable only to trusts. See id. at § 195. The statute is explained by its drafter, Professor Schuyler, in Schuyler, The Statute Concerning Perpetuities, 65 Nw. U. L. Rev. 3 (1970).

46. See N.Y. Est. Powers & Trusts Law §§ 9-1.2, -1.3.

47. See Fla. Stat. § 689.22(5)(a)-(d) (repealed).

48. See Cal. Civ. Code § 715.7 (repealed).

49. The differences are recounted and analyzed in Waggoner, Perpetuity Reform, supra note 6, at 1726-50.

child by a living person who has not attained the age of 65 years, and (D) the possibility of having a child or more remote descendants by adoption shall be disregarded.

2. Proper Scope of Perpetuity Reform—The Prevention-of-Unjust-Enrichment Theory

The specific-statutory-repair method of perpetuity reform saves the technical violation cases from invalidity, but leaves other perpetuity violations untouched. The two methods we are about to study—reformation and wait-and-see (with deferred reformation)—affect all perpetuity violations. A theoretical case for this wider scope of perpetuity reform was set forth in Waggoner, Perpetuity Reform, 81 Mich. L. Rev. 1718, 1719-29, 1785 (1983), as follows:

> The original case for perpetuity reform, indeed the only case for reform that has been systematically presented, argues from the technical violation categories and rests on the Rule's "harshness" or "illogicality" in defeating such reasonable dispositions. This case is an argument for reversing the invalidity in the technical violation categories, but not for interfering with the normal operation of the Rule in all cases of perpetuity violation. . . .
>
> The theme of this Article is that there is a respectable case for intercession in all cases of perpetuity violation. The case is grounded upon and is in fact an application of the theme of another article that John Langbein and I recently co-authored, entitled *Reformation of Wills on the Ground of Mistake: Change of Direction in American Law?*, [130 U. Pa. L. Rev. 521 (1982)]. Pointing to the long-recognized reformation doctrine for non-probate transfers, that article advocates the forthright adoption of a similar doctrine for wills. Cases of well-proven mistake of law or fact in the formulation of the terms of gratuitous transfers invoke the fundamental principle of equity jurisprudence: preventing unjust enrichment. If mistakes are not corrected, unintended takers are enriched at the expense of the intended beneficiaries. In one respect, the application of this idea to the perpetuity area is easier than in the generalized cases of mistake that are the main focus of attention in the earlier article. Extrinsic evidence is hardly necessary to show that a perpetuity violation is the product of a mistake, but such evidence is frequently necessary to prove a mistake in other cases.
>
> The application of the prevention-of-unjust-enrichment idea to the perpetuity area is easier, though more subtle, in another respect. Preventing unjust enrichment in generalized cases of mistake requires an open-ended remedy of reformation, to be applied by courts on an ad hoc basis. Because perpetuity violations are relatively homogeneous, the method to be applied in the correction of the mistake can take a common and hence more automatic form. It need not, in fact, be framed overtly as a method of correcting a mistake but can be cast as a legislative reformulation of the Rule Against Perpetuities itself. This approach will be effective as long as it is understood that correction of mistake is the underlying objective of the reformulation, so that the reformulation is shaped by the legislature and administered by the courts in accordance with that objective. . . .

The objective of reform, then, should be to prevent such unjust enrichment, so far as would have been legally possible at the drafting stage of the disposition. . . .

With the theory of reform properly focused on the prevention of unjust enrichment, courts in jurisdictions that have adopted the reformation method should reform offending dispositions by injecting a saving clause into the instrument. And legislatures contemplating perpetuity reform should . . . enact wait-and-see statutes modelled on the [saving-clause principle].

3. Immediately Available Reformation

Statutory References: *USRAP § 5(b)*
1990 UPC § 2-905(b)

Berry v. Union National Bank
262 S.E.2d 766 (W. Va. 1980)

HARSHBARGER, J. This case presents the issue whether a private testamentary trust which violates the rule against perpetuities should be modified to effectuate a testatrix' intent or should fail.

Clara Clayton Post died on June 20, 1975, in Harrison County. Her will and codicil were admitted to probate on June 23, 1975, at which time Josephine H. Berry, appellant, qualified as executrix. After a series of specific bequests to her heirs at law, appellees Ellen Clayton and Arthur Clayton, and to other parties, Ms. Post created a private educational trust for the descendants of her late husband's brothers and sisters, giving her trustee absolute discretion to provide educational expenses for [the descendants of her late husband's brothers and sisters] meeting certain criteria. The trust was to endure for twenty-five years after testatrix' death or until the principal was reduced to less than $5,000.00, whichever should first occur. At the termination of the trust the principal and interest were to be distributed per stirpes to the then living descendants of her husband's brothers and sisters. The Union National Bank of Clarksburg, appellee, was named trustee.

Executrix Berry recognized that the trust potentially violated the rule against perpetuities and entered into a trust termination agreement with the trustee. The agreement amended the twenty-five year provision to twenty-one years and required the executrix to initiate a declaratory judgment action in the Circuit Court of Harrison County to determine *inter alia*, whether the trust violated the rule against perpetuities and whether it was proper for the executrix and trustee to enter into a trust termination agreement. A guardian ad litem was appointed for the unborn beneficiaries on April 26, 1977. The trial court granted summary judgment for the heirs at law, finding that the trust provision violated the rule against perpetuities and was therefore void and without force. The court additionally ruled that the executrix and trustee were not authorized to enter into the trust termination agreement. Executrix Berry appealed. . . .

The analysis of any problem concerning a will must begin with the fundamental principle that a testator's intent shall be ascertained and followed to the extent possible. . . .

The rule against perpetuities is a common law rule which reflects the public policy that a testator or trustor cannot control the devolution of his property for an inordinate period of time. . . .

If a testator creates an estate which vests or has the possibility of vesting after a life in being plus twenty-one years and a period of gestation, the estate violates the rule against perpetuities and the testator's intent will be defeated. . . .

It is here that principles of law collide: a testator may not indefinitely control the devolution of his property; but a testator's intent should be honored and intestacy avoided whenever feasible. To remedy this apparent conflict, we adopt a doctrine of equitable modification which courts should apply to certain devises that on their face appear to violate the rule against perpetuities but meet the conditions enumerated below. Our action accords with a developing trend to ameliorate the harsh consequences of "remorseless application" of the rule. The theory which we endorse today is akin to the doctrine of *cy-pres* which was initially developed in the area of charitable trusts and was legislatively enacted in West Virginia in 1931 for that purpose. W.Va.Code, 35-2-2.

The purpose of equitable modification is to revise an instrument in a fashion that effectuates a testator's general intent within the limitations established by the rule.

We support the underlying policies of the rule against perpetuities and will deny validity to an interest which vests beyond the time limitations provided in the rule. However, before a testamentary scheme is totally obliterated by application of the rule, we will determine whether the testamentary disposition can be equitably modified to comport with the rule's underlying policy.

A non-charitable devise or bequest which violates the rule will be modified if the following conditions are met:

(1) The testator's intent is expressed in the instrument or can be readily determined by a court;
(2) The testator's general intent does not violate the rule against perpetuities;
(3) The testator's particular intent, which does violate the rule, is not a critical aspect of the testamentary scheme; and
(4) The proposed modification will effectuate the testator's general intent, will avoid the consequences of intestacy, and will conform to the policy considerations underlying the rule.

The testamentary trust here meets all these criteria for application of the equitable modification doctrine.

Testatrix clearly expressed her general intent in Section IX of her will when she stated:

> I believe it was the desire of my husband that such funds as I might have at my death should be used to help such persons (who are later defined in this section) obtain educations. This is the only expression I ever heard him make relative to the disposition of such funds.

Her general intention to provide funds for education of her husband's nieces, nephews and their families does not contravene the rule. Her particular intention to have the trust continue for twenty-five years after her death or until the principal was less than $5,000.00 violates the rule. There is no indication that the twenty-five year period is a critical aspect of her testamentary scheme. If the trust is modified to reduce that twenty-five year period to twenty-one years before distribution of the remaining principal to the then living descendants of her husband's siblings, the general intent to provide for their education will be effectuated, intestacy for that portion of her estate will be avoided, and property will not be controlled by her beyond the perpetuities' limitation. . . .

It is not necessary for us to address the other issues raised in the parties' briefs due to our disposition of the main question. We hold, therefore, that the will of Clara Clayton Post should be equitably modified to reduce the duration of the trust from twenty-five years to twenty-one years. The ruling of the circuit court is reversed and the cause remanded for appointment of additional guardians ad litem and further proceedings consistent with this opinion.

Reversed and remanded.

Notes

1. *State of the Authorities.* In 1992, West Virginia enacted USRAP, effectively displacing *Berry* for post-effective date transfers. In decisions antedating *Berry*, the courts in three other jurisdictions had adopted the immediate-reformation approach. See In re Chun Quan Yee Hop, 52 Haw. 40, 469 P.2d 183 (1970) (period in gross lowered from 30 to 21) (in 1992, Hawaii enacted USRAP, effectively displacing the rule of this case for post-effective date transfers); Carter v. Berry, 243 Miss. 321, 140 S.2d 843 (1962) (age contingency lowered from 25 to 21); Edgerly v. Barker, 66 N.H. 434, 31 A. 900 (1891) (age contingency lowered from 40 to 21).

Legislation in Missouri, Oklahoma, and Texas authorizes or directs the courts to reform defective instruments. See Mo. Rev. Stat. § 442.555; Okla. Stat. tit. 60, §§ 75-78; Tex. Prop. Code § 5.043, unnecessarily restricted to charitable gifts in Foshee v. Republic Nat'l Bank, 617 S.W.2d 675 (Tex. 1981); see also Idaho Code § 55-111. Until 1991, California had an immediate-reformation statute, but it was repealed when California enacted USRAP.[50]

Although these judicial decisions and statutes authorize or direct reformation of the defective instrument in a way that comes as close as possible to the transferor's intent without violating the common-law Rule, the cases have all been of a similar type to *Berry* and in each case the courts have reformed the disposition by lowering the period in gross or age contingency to 21. A method of reformation more faithful to the transferor's intention would have been to insert a saving clause into the governing instrument. See Browder, Construction, Reformation, and the Rule Against Perpetuities, 62 Mich. L. Rev. 1 (1963); Waggoner, supra, at 1755-59; Langbein & Waggoner, Reformation of Wills on the Ground of Mistake: Change of Direction in American Law?, 130 U. Pa. L. Rev. 521, 546-49 (1982). Recently, the Supreme Court of Mississippi adopted this method of reformation, but revealed a degree of misunderstanding by also purporting to adopt the wait-and-see method of perpetuity reform without seeming to realize that immediate reformation and wait-and-see are mutually inconsistent methods of perpetuity reform. See Estate of Anderson v. Deposit Guaranty Nat'l Bank, 541 S.2d 423 (Miss. 1989) (court upheld testamentary trust that was to last for 25 years from the date of admission of the will to probate, the income to be used for the education of the descendants of the testator's father, and the corpus at the end of the 25-year period to be paid over to testator's nephew, Howard Davis, or if Howard was not then living, to the heirs of Howard's body; by inserting a saving clause and by adopting the wait-and-see method, court was able to avoid invalidating the trust and to avoid reducing its terms to 21 years.)

In another recent case, Merrill v. Wimmer, 481 N.E.2d 1294 (Ind. 1985), the Supreme Court of Indiana held that judicial reformation to correct a perpetuity violation is forbidden by reason of the fact that in Indiana the common-law Rule was then codified. Do you agree that codification of the common-law Rule precludes the reformation method of perpetuity reform?[51]

2. *Reformation Authorized by USRAP.* Although USRAP adopts the wait-and-see method of perpetuity reform, reformation also plays an important role under USRAP. Section 3 establishes a deferred-reformation rule by directing a court to reform a disposition if, after exhaustion of the permissible vesting period, it violates the Statutory Rule Against Perpetuities. More significant for our purpose here, however, is Section 5 of USRAP. Under that section, the wait-and-see rule adopted by USRAP applies only prospectively; as to pre-existing interests, section 5(b) authorizes immediate reformation. In line with the law review articles listed above, and the recent *Anderson* decision, the Official Comment to section 5(b)

---

50. Cal. Civ. Code § 715.5 (repealed), applied in Estate of Ghiglia, 42 Cal. App. 3d 433, 116 Cal. Rptr. 827 (1974) (age contingency lowered from 35 to 21).

51. "[T]he reformation method . . . does not alter the [common-law] Rule at all. The Rule is left intact, and the disposition is altered to conform to it." Waggoner, Perpetuity Reform, supra note 6, at 1755-56. In any event, Indiana subsequently enacted USRAP, which specifically authorizes reformation of pre-effective-date interests.

urges courts to reform pre-existing perpetuity violations by judicially inserting appropriate saving clauses rather than by lowering age contingencies or periods in gross to 21. The Comment notes that a saving clause would probably have been used at the drafting stage of the disposition had it been drafted competently. In addition, the Comment notes that the period of time marked off by the perpetuity-period component of an appropriate saving clause would ordinarily be more than sufficient to allow the contingencies attached to the nonvested interest to work themselves out to a final resolution under the terms set forth by the transferor.

Clearly, in *Berry* and the other immediate-reformation cases recounted above, the age contingency or period in gross need not have been tampered with.

Section 5(b) only applies to pre-effective date transfers if the judicial proceeding determining the existence of a perpetuity violation was commenced on or after the effective date of enactment. Hopefully, however, courts in enacting states that had previously adopted the immediate-reformation approach, such as Hawaii and West Virginia, and in other enacting states as well, will treat the enactment of USRAP as settling perpetuity policy in the state and, in judicial proceedings commenced before enactment, reform perpetuity violations by inserting an appropriate saving clause geared to lives in being plus 21 years. See, e.g., Fleet Nat'l Bank v. Colt, 529 A.2d 122 (R.I. 1987), infra p. 1049.

4. Wait-and-See/Deferred Reformation

Statutory References: *USRAP §§ 1, 3*
                              1990 UPC §§ 2-901, -903

We know that the basis upon which validity or invalidity depends is the full array of possible post-creation events. In its early stages, the perpetuity-reform movement focused on the technical-violation categories. Since the post-creation chains of possible events that invalidate those interests are so unlikely to happen, it was rather natural to propose that the requirement of initial certainty be abandoned in favor of taking actual post-creation events into account. Instead of invalidating an interest because of what *might* happen, waiting to see what *does* happen seemed then and still seems now to be more sensible. Known as the wait-and-see method of perpetuity reform, this approach is the approach recently promulgated by the two preeminent national organizations concerned with law reform—the American Law Institute and the National Conference of Commissioners on Uniform State Laws.

Neither the ALI's Restatement 2d of Property (1983) nor the NCCUSL's USRAP (1990) alters what may be called the *validating* side of the common-law Rule. Dispositions that would have been valid under the common-law Rule remain valid. Practitioners under either wait-and-see regime can and should continue to use a traditional perpetuity saving clause. The wait-and-see element is applied only to interests that fall prey to the *invalidating* side of the common-law Rule. Interests that would be invalid at common law are saved from being rendered *initially invalid*. To prevent the unjust enrichment of unintended takers caused by a scrivener's mistake in failing to insert a perpetuity saving clause, otherwise invalid interests are, as it were, given a second chance: These interests are valid if they actually vest within the permissible vesting period, and become invalid only if they remain in existence but still nonvested at the expiration of that period.

Shifting the focus from possible to actual post-creation events has great attraction, and wait-and-see has been widely adopted, though still opposed by a small cadre of academics. The greatest controversy over wait-and-see concerns how the permissible vesting period is to be marked off—the permissible period of time for the contingencies attached to an otherwise invalid interest to be worked out to a final resolution.

The conventional assumption has always been that the permissible vesting period should be marked off in time by reference to so-called measuring lives who are in being at the creation of the interest; the permissible vesting period under this assumption expires 21 years after the death of the last surviving measuring life. Controversies raged over who the measuring lives should be and how the law should identify them.

Saving-Clause Principle of Wait-and-See. It now seems to be agreed that wait-and-see is nothing more mysterious than a perpetuity saving clause injected by the law when the governing instrument fails to include one. In effect, the perpetuity-period component of a standard saving clause constitutes a privately established wait-and-see rule. The permissible vesting period under wait-and-see is, or should be, the equivalent of the perpetuity-period component of a well-conceived saving clause.

The saving clause is rounded out by providing the near-equivalent of a gift-over component via a provision for judicial reformation of a disposition in case the interest is still in existence and nonvested when the permissible vesting period expires.

Title in Abeyance. One of the early objections to wait-and-see should be mentioned at this point. It was once widely argued and still occasionally is argued that wait-and-see can cause harm because it puts the validity of property interests in abeyance—no one can determine whether an interest is valid or not. This argument has been shown to be false. Keep in mind that the wait-and-see element is applied only to interests that would be invalid were it not for wait-and-see. These otherwise invalid interests are always nonvested future interests. It is now understood by most, and should be understood by all, that wait-and-see does nothing more than subject that type of future interest to an *additional* contingency. To vest, the other contingencies must not only be satisfied—they must be satisfied within a certain period of time. If that period of time—the permissible vesting period—is easily determined, then the additional contingency causes no more uncertainty in the state of the title than would have been the case had it been explicitly placed in the governing instrument itself. It should also be noted that only the status of the affected future interest in the trust or other property arrangement is deferred. In the interim, the other interests, such as the interests of current income beneficiaries, are carried out in the normal course without obstruction.

The Permissible Vesting Period. As indicated above, the greatest controversy has been over how to mark off the permissible vesting period. This is the subject to which we now turn. The problem arises because the common-law Rule contained no mechanism for marking off an actual period of time to wait to see if an otherwise invalid interest vests or terminates in "due time." The only mechanism the common law provided is the requirement of initial certainty, which as noted supra p. 988, is a mechanism for testing the validity of an interest at the point of its creation. The decision is made at the point of creation, with post-creation events disregarded and, therefore, the common law had no cause to mark off a "perpetuity period" during which post-creation events are allowed to be taken into account. At common law, there either is a validating life or there is no validating life. There is no validating life for invalid interests, hence there is no common-law "perpetuity period" to wait out. A permissible vesting period is necessary only under the wait-and-see method of perpetuity reform.

a. Early Forms of Wait-and-See Legislation

Pennsylvania-Style Statutes. Enacted in 1947, the Pennsylvania statute (20 Pa. Cons. Stat. Ann. § 6104(b)) was the first wait-and-see statute. The statute mistakenly presupposes that there is a common-law perpetuity period, and so it contains no method of marking that period off. The statute provides:

> Upon the expiration of the period allowed by the common law rule against perpetuities as measured by actual rather than possible events, any interest not then vested and any interest in members of a class the membership of which is then subject to increase shall be void.

Pennsylvania-style statutes are also in effect in Ohio,[52] South Dakota,[53] Vermont,[54] and Virginia.[55] The only case ever to apply the Pennsylvania statute or a Pennsylvania-style statute is Pearson Estate, 442 Pa. 172, 275 A.2d 336 (1971), a decision universally condemned for not explaining who the measuring lives were and how they are to be identified under the statute.[56]

Massachusetts-Style Statutes. Enacted in 1954, the Massachusetts-style statute expressly measures the permissible vesting period by the period of

---

52. See Ohio Rev. Code Ann. § 2131.08.
53. See S.D. Codified Laws Ann. § 43-5-6.
54. See Vt. Stat. Ann. tit. 27, § 501.
55. See Va. Code § 55-13.3.
56. See, e.g., Waggoner, Perpetuity Reform, supra note 6, at 1762-76.

one or more life estates in favor of persons in being at the creation of the interest:

> In applying the rule against perpetuities to an interest in real or personal property limited to take effect at or after the termination of one or more life estates in, or lives of, persons in being when the period of said rule commences to run, the validity of the interest shall be determined on the basis of facts existing at the termination of such one or more life estates or lives. In this section an interest which must terminate not later than the death of one or more persons is a "life estate" even though it may terminate at an earlier time.

Massachusetts-style statutes are in effect in Maine[57] and Maryland.[58] Until 1989, this type of statute was also in effect in Connecticut[59] and Massachusetts;[60] it was repealed when Connecticut and Massachusetts enacted USRAP.

Choosing to restrict the permissible vesting period to one or more life estates in favor of persons in being at the creation of the interest does not even reverse the invalidity in a standard administrative-contingency case,[61] nor does it provide appropriate relief in age-contingency-in-excess-of-21 cases. The statutes, in fact, further provide that if at the end of the restricted vesting period, an interest would be invalid because it is "contingent upon any person attaining or failing to attain an age in excess of twenty-one, the age contingency shall be reduced to twenty-one as to all persons subject to the same age contingency." In Second Nat'l Bank v. Harris Trust & Savings Bank, 29 Conn. Supp. 275, 283 A.2d 226 (Super. Ct. 1971), this latter provision was held inapplicable to a trust that was created by the exercise of a general testamentary power of appointment and that provided for the income to go to the testator-donee's daughter, Mary, for 30 years, remainder to Mary, but if she was not then living, to her descendants, per stirpes. The court held that the executory interest in favor of Mary's descendants violated the Rule Against Perpetuities and was invalid; the effect was to render Mary's remainder interest absolute. As for the age-contingency provision of the statute, the court said: "It seems too clear for argument that the remainder to Mary's children is not 'contingent upon any person attaining or failing to attain an age in excess of twenty-one.'"

Clearly, Massachusetts-style statutes fall markedly short of fulfilling the goal of preventing unjust enrichment of unintended takers.

---

57. See Me. Rev. Stat. Ann. tit. 33, § 101.

58. See Md. Est. & Trusts Code Ann. § 11-103(a).

59. See Conn. Gen. Stat. § 45-95 (repealed).

60. See Mass. Gen. Laws Ann. Ch. 184A, § 1 (repealed).

61. Note, however, that in the two states that had such statutes but repealed them, there was a decision upholding a standard administrative-contingency disposition under the common-law Rule, on the theory that the fiduciary has an obligation to complete the administrative task within a period of time less than 21 years. See Belfield v. Booth, 63 Conn. 299, 27 A. 585 (1893); Brandenburg v. Thorndike, 139 Mass. 102, 28 N.E. 575 (1885).

Kentucky-Style Statutes. Enacted in 1960, the Kentucky statute (Ky. Rev. Stat. § 381.216) adopts a permissible vesting period measured by the life of persons who have a "causal relationship" to the vesting or failure of the interest in question:

> In determining whether an interest would violate the rule against perpetuities the period of perpetuities shall be measured by actual rather than possible events; Provided, however, the period shall not be measured by any lives whose continuance does not have a causal relationship to the vesting or failure of the interest.

Kentucky-style statutes are also in effect in Alaska[62] and Rhode Island.[63] Until 1987 and 1992, respectively, this type of statute was also in effect in Nevada[64] and New Mexico;[65] it was repealed when Nevada and New Mexico enacted USRAP.

As we shall see, the meaning of "causal relationship to the vesting or failure of the interest" is much in dispute. One commentator recently concluded: "It is apparent that the 'causal relationship' test does little to clarify the problem of measuring lives under wait-and-see."[66]

Nevertheless, the Supreme Court of Mississippi judicially adopted the wait-and-see method of reform using "causal-relationship" lives. Estate of Anderson, 541 S.2d 423 (Miss. 1989).

Problems and Note

In the following cases, by whose life or lives is the permissible vesting period measured under a Kentucky-style statute?

1. G deeded real property "to A and his heirs, but if the property is used for nonresidential purposes, to X and his heirs."

2. G died, survived by his child, A, and by A's children, X (age 26) and Y (age 21). G's will devised property "to A for life, then to A's children who attain 25."

The architect of the causal-relationship-to-vesting formula and the principal drafter of the Kentucky statute believes that X is the only causal-relationship measuring life in Problem 1 and that X as well as Y are among the causal-relationship measuring lives in Problem 2. See Dukeminier, Perpetuities: The Measuring Lives, 85 Colum. L. Rev. 1648, 1666-67 (Case 6, which is essentially the same as Problem 2), 1705-06 (Case 18, which is essentially the same as Problem 1) (1985).

In a debate centering partially on these examples, Professor Waggoner argued that A, not X, should properly be regarded as the only causal-rela-

---

62. See Alaska Stat. § 34.27.010.
63. See R.I. Gen. Laws § 34-11-38.
64. See Nev. Rev. Stat. § 111.103 (repealed).
65. See N.M. Stat. Ann. § 47-1-17.1 (replealed).
66. Haskell, A Proposal for a Simple and Socially Effective Rule Against Perpetuities, 66 N.C. L. Rev. 545, 554 (1988).

tionship measuring life in Problem 1; that Y but not X should properly be regarded as a causal-relationship measuring life in Problem 2; and that disputes of this sort demonstrate that the causal-relationship-to-vesting formula cannot be counted a responsible means of identifying the measuring lives for wait-and-see. See Waggoner, Perpetuities: A Perspective on Wait-and-See, 85 Colum. L. Rev. 1714, 1719-24 (1985).

Fleet National Bank v. Colt
529 A.2d 122 (R.I. 1987)

[The testator, Samuel P. Colt, died in 1921, survived by his son Roswell and Roswell's daughter, Elizabeth.[67] The testator left a will that created a testamentary trust, under which a one-sixth share of his residuary estate was to pay income to Roswell for life, then to Roswell's children for life, and on the death of each of Roswell's children, to pay to "the child or children of such deceased child . . . , per stirpes and not per capita, his [or] her proportionate share of this trust estate, as an estate vested in fee simple, discharged of all trust."

After the testator's death, several additional descendants were born. Among them were Roswell's son, Caldwell, and Elizabeth's three children and Caldwell's two children. After Roswell's death in 1935, each of his children began receiving a proportionate share of the trust income. Caldwell died in 1985, survived by his two children and by his sister, Elizabeth, and her three children.]

SHEA, J. This case is before the court following a Superior Court granting of a joint motion for certification. . . .

The orthodox rule against perpetuities . . . has been the subject of much criticism and debate by legal scholars and writers. See W. Leach, Perpetuities in Perspective: Ending The Rule's Reign of Terror 65 Harv. L. Rev. 721 (1952). The major criticism of the rule is that it often serves to totally defeat the intent of the testator by invalidating a gift due to remote contingencies based upon improbable happenings. Id. at 723.

In answer to these criticisms Rhode Island, among other states, has enacted a statute to modify the rule. General Laws 1956 (1984 Reenactment) § 34-11-38 modifies the rule against perpetuities by directing that "the period of perpetuities . . . be measured by actual rather than possible events." Our statute requires, however, that the possible measuring lives bear a causal relationship to the vesting or failure of an interest. If, after applying the rule as modified by the statute, a gifted interest is still violative of it, the statute directs that the interest be reformed "to approximate most closely the intention of the creator of the interest."

---

67. The testator was also survived by another son, Russell, and by his brother, LeBaron. Also living at the testator's death were Russell's three children, Lebaron's three children, and LeBaron's five grandchildren. These other relatives were beneficiaries of other shares of the testamentary trust created by the testator's will, but those other shares and these other relatives did not figure in the perpetuity question raised by the case.

Through this statute, our Legislature has adopted both the "wait-and-see" approach and the "cy pres doctrine" as reformation of the rule against perpetuities. Although the statute embodies this state's present method of application of the rule against perpetuities, unfortunately, the statute itself may not be retroactively applied in the case before us because, by its terms, it "shall not be construed to invalidate or modify the terms of any interest which would have been valid prior to May 17, 1983."

We believe § 34-11-38 is a codification of a policy employed by this court prior to the statutory adoption of rule-against-perpetuities reform by the Legislature. . . .

The facts of the case before us present a particularly appropriate situation in which to apply the rule in terms of "wait-and-see actualities" rather than "orthodox possibilities." There is no question that the property at issue in Caldwell's estate is now distributable in fee simple. The only question is who will receive the distribution. Notwithstanding the identity of the persons to inherit, the property will no longer be held unalienable; its transferability is no longer controlled. The purpose of the rule therefore, that of preventing lengthy restraints on the alienation of property, will be fulfilled at this time regardless of who we decide may inherit.

Applying the wait-and-see approach to the rule against perpetuities, we examine the vesting of an interest at the time the contingency upon which it depends occurs. If the facts as they exist at that time allow for vesting within a life or lives in being plus twenty-one years, the gift is valid and the various possibilities that may have prevented vesting when viewed at the death of the testator are irrelevant. Restatement (Second) Property § 1.4 (1983); Note, Understanding the Measuring Life in the Rule Against Perpetuities, 1974 Wash. U.L.Q. 265, 287. Examining the facts, therefore, as they exist at the death of Caldwell rather than at the death of the testator, we must determine whether his shares vest in his children's possession within a life in being plus twenty-one years. This life in being must bear a causal relationship to the vesting of interests under the Will because although the orthodox rule against perpetuities defines a measuring life to be any life whatsoever in being at the death of the testator and requires no causal relationship, the wait-and-see doctrine limits the range of possible measuring lives by requiring that they bear a causal relationship to the vesting of the future interest in question. Note at 290; 61 Am.Jur.2d Perpetuities § 29 at 37 (1981). "The meaning of the causal relationship principle . . . encompasses every relationship that any validating life at common law bears to vesting. It embraces every person who, in the particular situation, can affect vesting." J. Dukeminier, Perpetuities: The Measuring Lives, 85 Col. L. Rev. 1648, 1648 (1985).

At the time of Caldwell's death, his sister Elizabeth . . . [was] the only one of Roswell's . . . children who was alive at the testator's death. . . . She is thus a life in being and an acceptable measuring life. She is causally connected not only to the vesting of the remainder in her own children, but also to the life estate of her siblings and thus to the remainder in her sibling's children. If, for example, Elizabeth had predeceased her father Roswell, the income that Roswell had been receiving as a first life tenant would have been divided [into fewer shares]. Thus, the amount of Caldwell's share, and consequently the amounts of his children's shares, were dependent upon the survival of Elizabeth.

Since Elizabeth is still living today, it is clear that the remainder interests of Caldwell's children have vested within the time period set by the rule against perpetuities. The testator's gift to them, therefore, is valid.

Note and Question

1. *The "Elementary Logic" of the Causal-Relationship Formula.* Commenting on the *Colt* decision, Professor Fletcher said:

> At most, Elizabeth was related to the resolution of only the first uncertainty—the division of shares at Roswell's death. Even here, Roswell's life, not Elizabeth's, is the defensive life. The fact that a class member, such as Elizabeth, happened to be alive at the effective date, is not significant. If, however, we see Elizabeth as significant at Roswell's death, nevertheless she serves no useful function thereafter, and her continued life thereafter should be unusable.
>
> Professor Dukeminier should disapprove of the court's disposition of this case. With respect to the uncertainty in identifying Caldwell's children, Elizabeth is totally useless and should not get on Professor Dukeminier's list; even if he should let her on, he surely would strike her from it the moment Roswell dies.

Fletcher, Perpetuities: Basic Clarity, Muddled Reform, 63 Wash. L. Rev. 791, 832 n.57 (1988).

2. *Retroactivity of the Rhode Island Causal-Relationship Statute.* Are you convinced that application of the Rhode Island causal-relationship wait-and-see statute to the *Colt* case was prevented by the statutory provision that said that the statute "shall not be construed to invalidate or modify the terms of any interest which would have been valid prior to May 17, 1983"?

b. *Restatement 2d of Property (1983)*

In adopting the wait-and-see method of perpetuity reform, the Restatement 2d of Property rejected the causal-relationship formula for determining the measuring lives and chose instead to use a predetermined list of lives. Under section 1.3(2) of the Restatement 2d of Property, the permissible vesting period expires 21 years after the death of the survivor of:

> (a) The transferor if the period of the rule begins to run in the transferor's lifetime; and
>
> (b) Those individuals alive when the period of the rule begins to run, if reasonable in number, who have beneficial interests vested or contingent in the property in which the non-vested interest in question exists and the parents and grandparents alive when the period of the rule begins to run of all beneficiaries of the property in which the non-vested interest exists, and

(c) The donee of a nonfiduciary power of appointment alive when the period of the rule begins to run if the exercise of such power could affect the non-vested interest in question.

If a property interest is still in existence but nonvested at the expiration of the permissible vesting period, section 1.5 provides that "the transferred property shall be disposed of in the manner which most closely effectuates the transferor's manifested plan of distribution and which is within the limits of the rule against perpetuities."

So far, the Restatement 2d's version of wait-and-see has not been directly adopted by any common-law court,[68] nor has it been legislatively enacted by any state. A statute enacted in Iowa was influenced by the Restatement 2d, however; the Iowa statute designates as the measuring lives the beneficiaries and "the grandparents of all such beneficiaries and the issue of such grandparents. . . ." Iowa Code § 558.68(2)(b)(2) (enacted in 1983).

Professor Dukeminier expressed displeasure that the Restatement 2d did not adopt the causal-relationship formula and assailed the Restatement's predetermined list by arguing that it "does not faithfully adhere to any principle at all," is drafted so ambiguously that its words "are like quicksilver" that "slip and slide and elude our grasp," and "may take years of learned analysis and litigation to solve its sphinxine riddles." Dukeminier, Perpetuities: The Measuring Lives, 85 Colum. L. Rev. 1648, 1675, 1681, 1701 (1985).

---

68. It has received favorable comment in a few cases, however. See Hansen v. Stoecker, 699 P.2d 871, 874-75 (Alaska 1985) ("We are persuaded [by the Restatement 2d and other authorities] that the wait-and-see approach should be adopted as the common law rule against perpetuities in Alaska.") The Alaska wait-and-see statute, using causal-relationship-to-vesting measuring lives rather than the Restatement 2d's list, was not applicable in the *Hansen* case because the interest in question was created before the effective date of the statute. The court did not say how it would measure the permissible vesting period under its newly adopted common-law wait-and-see Rule.

See also DeWire v. Haveles, 404 Mass. 274, 534 N.E.2d 782, 785-86 n.7 (1989) (Court suggested that it might follow the Restatement 2d) (note, however, that Massachusetts subsequently enacted USRAP); Nantt v. Pucket Energy Co., 382 N.W.2d 655, 661 (N.D. 1986) (Citing the Restatement 2d of Property, the court said that the wait-and-see rule "is a basic common sense approach to 'perpetuities' today.").

But see Pound v. Shorter, 377 S.E.2d 854 (Ga. 1989), supra p. 1023 (Without mentioning the Restatement 2d, the court rejected wait-and-see as a common-law concept; note, however, that Georgia subsequently enacted USRAP).

c. Uniform Statutory Rule Against Perpetuities
[Uniform Probate Code Article II Part 9 (1990)]

Statutory References: *Uniform Statutory Rule Against Perpetuities (USRAP)*
1990 UPC §§ 2-901 to -906

Introduction. The National Conference of Commissioners on Uniform State Laws promulgated USRAP in 1986, amended it modestly in 1990[69] and brought it into the Uniform Probate Code. The general contour of USRAP is similar to that of the Restatement 2d of Property. The validating side of the common-law Rule is retained but the invalidating side is replaced with wait-and-see and deferred-reformation elements. The major departure from the Restatement approach is that USRAP uses a flat 90-year permissible vesting period under its wait-and-see element rather than a period ending 21 years after the death of the survivor of a predetermined list of measuring lives.

Enactments. So far, USRAP has been enacted in California, Colorado, Connecticut, Florida, Georgia, Hawaii, Indiana, Kansas, Massachusetts, Michigan, Minnesota, Montana, Nebraska, Nevada, New Jersey, New Mexico, North Dakota, Oregon, South Carolina, and West Virginia.

Rationale of the 90-Year Permissible Vesting Period. The most striking feature of USRAP is its use of a flat period of 90 years as the permissible vesting period in its wait-and-see element. The rationale for this step was explained by the Reporter for USRAP as follows:

> [T]he philosophy behind the 90-year period was to fix a period of time that approximates the average period of time that would traditionally be allowed by the wait-and-see doctrine. There was no intention to use the flat-period-of-years method as a means of lengthening the [permissible vesting] period beyond its traditional boundaries. The fact that the traditional period roughly averages out to a longish-sounding 90 years is a reflection of a quite different phenomenon: the dramatic increase in longevity that society as a whole has experienced in the course of the twentieth century. Seen in this light, the 90-year period is an evolutionary step in the development of the wait-and-see doctrine.
>
> [T]he traditional method of delimiting the [permissible vesting] period is to use actual measuring lives plus 21 years. Specifically, under this method, a group of persons—called the measuring lives—is identified. Once the group is identified, the lives of all its members are traced to see which one outlives all the others and when that survivor dies. The [permissible vesting] period extends 21 years beyond the death of that last surviving measuring life.
>
> From its inception, the actual-measuring-lives approach has been plagued by two problems: identification and tracing. The identification problem concerns the method by which the measuring lives are to be chosen. Rival methods have been advanced. Under one method . . . , the measuring lives are identified by testing each disposition to determine the persons whose lives

---

69. The 1990 amendment added subsection (e) to § 1 (UPC § 2-901(e)).

have a "causal relationship" to the vesting or failure of the future interest in question. The actual meaning of causal relationship is in dispute, and the adoption of that method could require front-end litigation to determine the identity of the measuring lives in a given case. Neither the Restatement nor [USRAP] adopted the causal-relationship method. The Restatement specifies the measuring lives in a different way. The Restatement uses a list composed, generally speaking, of the transferor, the beneficiaries of the disposition, the parents and grandparents of the beneficiaries, and, in certain cases, the donee of a nonfiduciary power of appointment; of the foregoing, those who are in being at the creation of the interest are the measuring lives. It soon became apparent that the Restatement's list contained ambiguities, at least at the fringes, which could also require front-end litigation to determine the full complement of measuring lives in a given case. The framers of [USRAP] concluded that an ambiguity-free formulation of the specified-list method would necessitate a complex set of statutory provisions. . . .

The second problem plaguing the actual-measuring-lives approach is that of tracing. No matter how the measuring lives are identified, the lives of those actual individuals must be traced to determine which one is the longest survivor and when he or she died.

The tracing and identification problems are exacerbated by the premise, seemingly accepted under both methods, that the measuring lives cannot always remain a static group, assembled once and for all at the beginning. Instead, individuals who were once measuring lives must be dropped from the group if certain events happen (such as the individual's divorce, adoption out of the family, or assignment of his or her beneficial interest to another); conversely, individuals who were not among the initial group of measuring lives must be included later if certain events happen (such as marriage, adoption into the family, or receipt of another's beneficial interest by assignment or succession) and if they were living when the interest in question was created. This instability within the group of measuring lives heightens the potential for a further round of litigation at one point or another during the running of the [permissible vesting] period.

By opting for a flat period of years, the framers of [USRAP] eliminated the clutter that has heretofore plagued the wait-and-see strategy—the problems of identifying, tracing, and possibly litigating the make-up of a sometimes-fluctuating group of measuring lives. The expiration of a [permissible vesting] period measured by a flat period of years is litigation free, easy to determine, and unmistakable.

The framers of [USRAP] considered objections to replacing the actual-measuring-lives approach with a flat period of years, despite the gain in administrative simplicity that would result. One such objection was the idea that the use of actual measuring lives—especially if determined by the causal-relationship method—generates a [permissible vesting] period that self-adjusts to each situation, somehow extending the dead hand no further than necessary in each case. A flat period of years obviously cannot replicate a self-adjusting function. This objection proved unfounded, however, for the actual-measuring-lives approach also fails to perform a self-adjusting function. Although that approach produces [permissible vesting] periods of different lengths from one case to another, it does *not* generate a [permissible vesting] period that expires at a natural or logical stopping point along the continuum of each disposition, thereby pinpointing the time before which actual vesting ought to be allowed and beyond which it ought not to be permitted. Instead, the actual-measuring-lives approach—under either the specified-list or causal-relationship method—generates a [permissible vesting] period whose length almost always *exceeds* by some arbitrary period of time the point of actual vesting in cases that are traditionally validated by the wait-and-see strategy. The actual-measuring-lives approach, therefore, performs a margin-of-safety function, a function that *can* be replicated by the use of a proxy such as the flat 90-year period under [USRAP].

In standard cases, the rivalry between the causal-relationship and the specified-list methods of identifying actual measuring lives is very little concerned with the length of the [permissible vesting] period. Often, the specified-list method will produce a greater number of measuring lives than the causal-relationship method. In the normal course of events, however, the [permissible vesting] period is not governed by the number of measuring lives, but by the lifetime of the youngest. Unless the additional measuring lives are younger than the others or are clustered in very young age groups, such as under the twelve-healthy-babies ploy, a greater number of measuring lives seldom adds to the length of the [permissible vesting] period. In the normal course of events, the youngest measuring life is the key to the length of the [permissible vesting] period, and no matter which method is used for determining the identity of the measuring lives, the youngest measuring life, in standard trusts, is likely to be the transferor's youngest descendant living when the trust was created. The 90-year period of [USRAP] is premised on this proposition. Using four hypothetical families deemed to be representative of actual families, the framers determined that, on average, the transferor's youngest descendant in being at the transferor's death—assuming the transferor's death to occur between ages 60 and 90, which is when 73 percent of the population die—is about 6 years old. The remaining life expectancy of a 6-year old is about 69 years. The 69 years, plus the 21-year tack-on period, gives [a permissible vesting] period of 90 years. Although this method may not be scientifically accurate to the nth degree, the Drafting Committee considered it reliable enough to support a [permissible vesting] period of 90 years, given the margin-of-safety function that it performs.

Waggoner, The Uniform Statutory Rule Against Perpetuities: The Rationale of the 90-Year Waiting Period, 73 Cornell L. Rev. 157, 162-68 (1988).

Acceptance of the 90-Year Period Under the Federal Generation-Skipping Transfer Tax. In general terms, trusts that were irrevocable on September 25, 1985, are exempt from the federal generation-skipping transfer tax. See Tax Reform Act of 1986 § 1433(b)(2). These trusts are called "grandfathered trusts." Under Treasury Regulations, "grandfathered trusts" can become ungrandfathered if a nongeneral power of appointment is exercised so as to postpone the vesting of an interest beyond the perpetuity period. See Temp. Treas. Reg. § 26.2601-1(b)(1)(v)(B)(2) (1988). Acting in ignorance of the 90-year period of USRAP, the original version of this regulation defined the perpetuity period solely in terms of a life in being plus 21 years. After the 90-year period of USRAP was brought to the attention of Treasury Department officials, the Department issued a letter stating a commitment to amend the regulation to accommodate USRAP's 90-year period. See Letter from Michael J. Graetz, Deputy Assistant Secretary of the Treasury (Tax Policy), to the President of the Nat'l Conf. of Comm'rs on Unif. State Laws (Nov. 16, 1990).

Deferred Reformation—the Approach of USRAP. Section 3 of USRAP directs a court, upon the petition of an interested person, to reform a disposition within the limits of the 90-year permissible vesting period, in the manner deemed by the court most closely to approximate the transferor's manifested plan of distribution, in any one of three circumstances. The "interested person" who would frequently bring the reformation suit would be the trustee.

Seldom will this section become operative. Of the fraction of trusts and other property arrangements that are incompetently drafted, and thus fail to meet the requirement of initial validity under the codified version of the validating side of the common-law Rule, almost all of them will have terminated by their own terms long before any of the circumstances requisite to reformation under section 3 arise.

If, against the odds, the right to reformation does arise, it will be found easier than perhaps anticipated to determine how best to reform the disposition.[70] The court is given two reformation criteria: (i) the transferor's manifested plan of distribution, and (ii) the 90-year permissible vesting period. Because governing instruments are where transferors manifest their plans of distribution, the imaginary horrible of courts being forced to probe the minds of long-dead transferors will not materialize.

The theory of section 3 is to defer the right to reformation until reformation becomes truly necessary. Thus, the basic rule of section 3(1) is that the right to reformation does not arise until a nonvested property interest or a power of appointment becomes invalid; under section 1, this does not occur until the expiration of the 90-year permissible vesting period. By confining perpetuity litigation to those few cases in which the permissible vesting period actually is exceeded, perpetuity litigation is limited to purposive cases. In contrast to the immediately available reformation approach of Berry v. Union Nat'l Bank, 262 S.E.2d 766 (W. Va. 1980), supra p. 1040, which encourages nonpurposive or wasteful perpetuity litigation, USRAP's 90-year wait-and-see and deferred-reformation approach adopts a judicial hands-off policy. See Waggoner, The Uniform Statutory Rule Against Perpetuities: Oregon Joins Up, 26 Willamette L. Rev. 259 (1990).

Not only does the deferred-reformation approach work more efficiently by greatly minimizing the number of reformation suits. It has additional advantages. In the few cases where perpetuity reformation becomes necessary, the deferred-reformation approach minimizes the risk of judicial error by postponing judicial intervention until the time when more information about family circumstances existing at the time of distribution of the trust corpus is known. In addition, any concern that deferring the right to reformation deprives the courts of valuable extrinsic evidence that would be available under the immediate reformation approach is groundless. Under the immediate reformation rule, exemplified by the *Berry* case, the courts have not relied on extrinsic evidence of the transferor's intent. The reason is obvious: The transferor never entertained the possibility that the governing instrument contained a perpetuity violation in the first place.

---

70. Note that reformation under § 3 is mandatory, not subject to the discretion of the court. Consequently, as noted, in the Comment to § 3, the common-law doctrine of infectious invalidity is superseded by USRAP.

Hence, the transferor never formed an intent as to what she or he would have wanted done had she or he been informed of the violation. As expected, therefore, the courts operating under the immediate reformation rule have not determined the transferor's intent by reference to extrinsic evidence, but by reference to the governing instrument. Deferring the right to reformation until after the permissible vesting period has run its course does not deprive the courts of valuable extrinsic evidence. See Fellows, Testing Perpetuity Reforms: A Study of Perpetuity Cases 1984-89, 25 Real Prop. Prob. & Tr. J. 597 (1990).

The deferred-reformation approach is also consistent with the saving-clause principle embraced by USRAP. Deferring the right to reformation until the permissible vesting period expires is the only way to grant every reasonable opportunity for the donor's disposition to work itself out without premature interference. One of the reasons why USRAP specifically rejects the idea of granting a right to reformation at any time on a showing of a violation of the common-law Rule is that the experience under these statutorily or judicially established reformation principles has not been satisfactory. As in *Berry,* the courts have lowered periods in gross or age contingencies to 21. This is a step that amounts to an unwarranted distortion of the donor's intention, a distortion that is avoided by deferring the right to reformation until the contingencies as originally written by the donor have been given a chance to be fulfilled.

To be sure, if the courts utilize the immediate reformation approach to insert a perpetuity saving clause rather than to lower a period in gross or an age contingency to 21, as in Estate of Anderson v. Deposit Guaranty Nat'l Bank, 541 S.2d 423 (Miss. 1989), supra p. 1043, frustration of the donor's intention is avoided, but this comes at the expense of a reformation suit. The insertion-of-a-saving-clause approach is therefore less efficient than wait-and-see with deferred reformation. The period of time produced by a judicially inserted perpetuity saving clause would be about the same in length as that which is automatically granted by USRAP without front-end litigation. The more efficient course is to defer the right to reformation until after the permissible vesting period has run its course. Deferring the right to reformation reduces the necessity and cost of litigation because, as noted, the contingencies attached to most future interests that would otherwise have fallen victim of the common-law Rule will be resolved well within the permissible vesting period. Litigation to reform an offending disposition will seldom become necessary. The Restatement 2d is in accord with this approach. Reformation is provided for in the Restatement only if the nonvested property interest becomes invalid after waiting out the permissible vesting period. See Restatement 2d of Property § 1.5.

At the same time, USRAP is not inflexible, for it grants the right to reformation before the expiration of the 90-year permissible vesting period when it becomes necessary to do so or when there is no point in waiting that period out. Thus subsection (2), which pertains to class gifts that are not yet but still might become invalid under the wait-and-see element, grants a right to reformation whenever the share of any class member is entitled to take effect in possession or enjoyment. Were it not for this subsection, a great inconvenience and possibly injustice could arise, for a class member whose share had vested within the period might otherwise have to wait out the remaining part of the 90 years before obtaining her or his share. Reformation under this subsection will seldom be needed, however, because of the common practice of structuring trusts to split into separate shares or separate trusts at the death of each income beneficiary, one separate share or separate trust for each of the income beneficiary's then-living descendants; when this pattern is followed, the circumstances described in subsection (2) will not arise.

Subsection (3) also grants the right to reformation before the 90-year permissible vesting period expires. The circumstance giving rise to the right to reformation under subsection (3) occurs if a nonvested property interest can vest but not before the 90-year period has expired. Though unlikely, such a case can theoretically arise. If it does, the interest—unless it terminates by its own terms earlier—is bound to become invalid under section 1 eventually. There is no point in deferring the right to reformation until the inevitable happens. USRAP provides for early reformation in such a case, just in case it arises.

Problems

Consider how G's disposition might appropriately be reformed in the following cases.

1. G devised property in trust, directing the trustee to pay the income "to A for life, then to A's children for the life of the survivor, then to A's grandchildren for the life of the survivor, and on the death of A's last surviving grandchild, the corpus of the trust is to be divided among A's then-living descendants by representation; if none, to" a specified charity. G was survived by her child (A) and by A's two minor children (X and Y). After G's death, another child (Z) was born to A. Subsequently, A died, survived by her children (X, Y, and Z) and by three grandchildren (M, N, and O). X, Y, and Z died within the 90-year period following G's death, but some of A's grandchildren were still living at the expiration of the 90-year period.

2. G devised property in trust, directing the trustee to pay the income "to A for life, then to A's children"; the corpus of the trust is to be equally divided among A's children who reach the age of 30. G was survived by A, by A's spouse (H), and by A's two children (X and Y), both of whom were under the age of 30 when G died. After G's death, another child (Z) was born to A. Although unlikely, suppose that at A's death (prior to the expiration of the 90-year period), Z's age was such that he could be alive but under the age of 30 on the 90th anniversary of G's death. Suppose further that at A's death X and Y were over the age of 30.

———

EXTERNAL REFERENCES. USRAP has sparked a lively academic debate. See e.g., Bloom, *Perpetuities Refinement: There Is an Alternative*, 62 Wash. L.

Rev. 23 (1987) (arguing that USRAP is unnecessary because of infrequency of appellate-level perpetuity cases; author proposes own version of perpetuity-reform statute); Dukeminier, The Uniform Statutory Rule Against Perpetuities: Ninety Years in Limbo, 34 UCLA L. Rev. 1023 (1987) (labeling USRAP as "an extraordinarily risky venture" (at 1024), "so bizarre that the mind boggles" (at 1025), "Waggoner's phantom ship" (at 1068), an idea that gives "a bizarre turn to perpetuities reform" (at 1069), and an act that "is deserving of oblivion" (at 1079)); Fellows, Testing Perpetuity Reforms: A Study of Perpetuity Cases 1984-89, 25 Real Prop. Prob & Tr. J. 597 (1990) (testing the various types of perpetuity reform measures and concluding, on the basis of empirical evidence, that USRAP is the best opportunity offered to date for a uniform perpetuity law that efficiently and effectively achieves a fair balance between present and future property owners); Haskell, A Proposal for a Simple and Socially Effective Rule Against Perpetuities, 66 N.C. L. Rev. 545 (1988) (arguing for replacement of both the validating and invalidating sides of the common-law Rule with a statutory rule requiring vesting in possession no later than 125 years after creation).

5. Abolition of the Rule

The ultimate method of perpetuity reform is abolition of the Rule. It may be noted that one of the official advisors to the USRAP Drafting Committee, a respected estate-planning attorney, repeatedly urged the Committee to produce a uniform act that would abolish the Rule entirely.

Recall that a generation-skipping transfer tax has apparently become a permanent fixture—in one form or another—of our federal transfer-tax system. See supra Chapter 6. The generation-skipping transfer tax imposes high costs for creating trusts that persist through more than one generation. This is true, despite the large exemptions: The quite wealthy—whose assets substantially exceed the exemption levels—are more likely to be attracted to the creation of long-term trusts than donors of more modest means.

In this type of tax environment, *is* there a case for abolishing the Rule entirely? In 1969, legislation was enacted in Wisconsin that abolished the common-law Rule Against Perpetuities and rendered a related rule, the rule against the suspension of the power of alienation, inapplicable "if the trustee has power to sell, either expressed or implied, or if there is an unlimited power to terminate in one or more persons in being." Wis. Stat. § 700.16. See also S.D. Codified Laws Ann. § 43-5-8. Compare Idaho Code Ann. § 55.111.

PART E. SPECIAL APPLICATIONS OF AND EXCLUSIONS FROM THE RULE AGAINST PERPETUITIES

1. Class Gifts

a. General Rule: "All or Nothing"

Under the Rule Against Perpetuities, a class gift stands or falls as a whole. This all-or-nothing rule, usually attributed to Leake v. Robinson, 2 Mer. 363, 35 Eng. Rep. 979 (Ch. 1817), is commonly stated as follows:

> If the interest of any potential class member might vest "too remotely," the entire class gift is invalid.

Another way of stating the same rule, which you may find more or less helpful, is set forth in the Restatement of Property sections 371, 383, 384:

> A class gift is entirely invalid if its membership might continue either to increase or decrease (or both) beyond 21 years after the death of a life in being at the creation of the interest.

(The word "decrease" refers to a class gift that is subject to a condition *precedent* of survivorship.)

Although strongly condemned by some (but not all) commentators, the all-or-nothing rule has been squarely rejected by only one American decision, Carter v. Berry, 243 Miss. 321, 140 S.2d 843 (1962).[71] The

---

71. In the *Carter* case, G's will (executed in 1955) created a trust that was to terminate at the earlier of "35 years from the date [of execution] of this will" or "when my youngest grandchild (whether now living or hereafter born) shall become 25 years of age." G was survived by a 22-year-old married daughter who was then childless and by a 24-year-old married daughter who then had three young children. Since the remainder interest in favor of the grandchildren was not subject to an express condition of survivorship of the termination of the trust, the obvious solution to the perpetuity problem was to hold that the gift to the grandchildren was valid in its entirety even under the all-or-nothing rule. In other words, the class was not subject to decrease at all and could not increase after the deaths of G's daughters, who were "in being" at the creation of the interest.

While this possible solution was noted, the court inexplicably thought it "necessary and proper to deal also with the issues in this case on a second basis, namely, that . . . the gift is contingent [on survivorship of the termination of the trust]." This made the class gift one that would be entirely invalid under the all-or-nothing rule.

The court then went on to reject the all-or-nothing rule, the result of which was that the only valid interests were those of the three grandchildren who were living at G's death. This result, the court conceded, would not carry out G's intent because he "wanted all of his grandchildren to take, not just those living at the time of his death." The court nevertheless said that "if this were the only choice, we would not hesitate to take it." But the Mississippi court felt that another choice was available, which was to hold that the cy-pres (reformation)

rationale of the all-or-nothing rule is discussed in L. Waggoner, Future Interests in a Nutshell 237-51 (1981).

The rule has been upheld and applied in numerous cases, including recent ones. See, e.g., Beverlin v. First Nat'l Bank, 151 Kan. 307, 98 P.2d 200 (1940); Thomas v. Citizens & Southern Nat'l Bank, 224 Ga. 572, 163 S.E.2d 823 (1968); In re Lattouf's Will, 87 N.J. Super. 137, 208 A.2d 411 (1965). Also, no American statute reverses the rule.

The following three examples illustrate the all-or-nothing rule: Example 17.12 illustrates a class gift that is invalid because it is subject to decrease "too long," Example 17.13 illustrates a class gift that is invalid because it is subject to increase "too long," and Example 17.14 illustrates a class gift that is invalid because it is subject to both increase and decrease "too long."

> *Example 17.12:* G devised real property "to A for life, then to such of A's children as reach 25." G was survived by A and by A's two children, V and X. V had reached 25 at G's death, but X was under 25.
>
> The class gift in favor of A's children is invalid. There is no validating life because the membership of the class might decrease, though not increase, beyond 21 years after the death of A, V, X, and anyone else who was in being at G's death.

> *Example 17.13:* G devised property in trust, directing the trustee to pay the net income therefrom "to A for life, then to A's children for the life of the survivor, and upon the death of A's last surviving child to pay the corpus of the trust to A's grandchildren." G was survived by A and by A's two children, V and X.
>
> The remainder interest in the corpus in favor of A's grandchildren is invalid. There is no validating life because the membership of the class might increase, though not decrease, beyond 21 years after the death of A, V, X, and any one else who was in being at G's death you might care to propose.

> *Example 17.14:* Same facts and disposition as the above example, except that the remainder upon the death of A's last surviving child was in favor of "A's then-living grandchildren."
>
> The remainder interest in the corpus in favor of A's grandchildren is invalid. The class might increase "too long" and, due to the addition of the condition

---

power could be invoked to reduce the latest time of trust termination to the time when G's youngest grandchild should reach 21, rather than 25 as G had stipulated. This way, the entire class gift was made valid because the court eliminated the possibility of a decrease in class membership beyond 21 years after the deaths of G's two daughters.

In sum, the Mississippi court began with a disposition that was entirely valid, under ordinary precepts of construction. Nevertheless, citing academic criticisms of the all-or-nothing rule, the court proceeded to reject the all-or-nothing rule on the ground that "it is not good logic or sound law," found that the result of rejecting the "ill-considered doctrine of Leake v. Robinson" did not carry out G's intention either because of the real prospect of after-born class members, and so changed G's disposition by lowering the age from 25 to 21.

Two fairly important points the court did not note are: changing the age from 25 to 21 did not carry out G's intention either and it made the rejection of the all-or-nothing rule of no consequence because, as altered by the court, the class gift was *entirely valid* even *under* the all-or-nothing rule.

precedent of survivorship of A's last surviving child, it might also decrease "too long."

Class Gifts Under Wait-and-See. The above discussion relates to the treatment of class gifts under the common-law Rule Against Perpetuities, under which the requirement of initial certainty still reigns. As for the all-or-nothing rule itself, perpetuity reformers have not seen fit to change it. The rule is not reversed in USRAP or under the Restatement 2d of Property. The sting of the all-or-nothing rule, however, is substantially eliminated by the application of the wait-and-see element.[72]

Consider how the above examples would be treated under the wait-and-see element of USRAP (§ 1(a)(2)). If you place G in one of our four charted families, supra pp. 1010-13, and if you posit G's death at around age 75, you will see that it is extremely unlikely that the class gift in Example 17.12 will *actually* decrease beyond the 90-year permissible vesting period after G's death.[73] You will also see that the class gift in Example 17.13 is unlikely to increase beyond the 90-year period and the class gift in Example 17.14 is unlikely to increase or decrease beyond that period.[74] Should the unlikely happen in any of these cases, G's disposition would become subject to reformation under USRAP section 3, the application of which is explained and illustrated in the Official Comment to section 3.

Specific-Sum Class Gifts; Gifts to Sub-Classes. The English courts held the all-or-nothing rule to be inapplicable to specific-sum class gifts and gifts to sub-classes; the American courts have followed suit, sometimes describing the two situations as "exceptions." The two situations are in fact distinguishable from the one to which the all-or-nothing rule applies. See L. Waggoner, Future Interests in a Nutshell 251-58 (1981).

b. *Specific-Sum Class Gifts*

Storrs v. Benbow

3 DeG. M. & G. 390, 43 Eng. Rep. 153 (Ch. 1853)

THE LORD CHANCELLOR. . . . The question arises upon a clause in a codicil which is in these words, —

> Item. I direct my executors to pay by and out of my personal estate exclusively the sum £ 500 a-piece to each child that may be born to either of the children of either of my brothers lawfully begotten to be paid to each of them on her or his attaining the age of twenty-one years without benefit of survivorship.

---

72. See USRAP § 1 Comment Part G.

73. Or beyond the period allowed by the Restatement 2d, measured by 21 years after the deaths of A, V, and X.

74. Or beyond the period allowed by the Restatement 2d, measured by 21 years after the deaths of A, V, and X.

This is a money legacy to each child of any nephew the testator had or might have. The testator had brothers living, but there might be legacies too remote, because the gift included legacies to children of a child not yet born.

The bill was filed twenty or thirty years ago; and the cause was heard before Sir John Leach. The argument then was, that the gift was too remote, but Sir John Leach thought that, according to the true construction of the clause children born in the lifetime of the testator were meant, and therefore he said the gift could not be too remote, for it only let in children that might be born between the date of the will and the death. A decree was accordingly made declaring that the children *in esse* only at the time of the death of the testator were entitled to the legacies, and it was referred to the Master to inquire. &c. The Master found that the Plaintiff was *in esse* in this sense, namely that the testator died in October and the Plaintiff was born six months afterwards; and I think he was so. The question then is whether he is entitled; I am of opinion that he certainly is, for he was a child *in esse* within the meaning put upon the clause by Sir John Leach.

There are three ways in which this gift might be interpreted; it might mean children that were *in esse* at the date of the will; it might mean children that might come into *esse* in the lifetime of the testator; and it might mean children born at any time. I own it seems to me that this gentlemen is entitled *quacunque via*. If it was to the children then in being, he would I think be probably within the meaning of such description; but if it was to children to come *in esse* in his lifetime and afterwards to be born, it seems to me that a child *in ventre sa mere* at the death of the testator was a child "hereafter to be born" within the meaning of the provision.

The rule that makes a limitation of this kind mean children at the death of the testator is one of convenience: a line must be drawn somewhere, otherwise the distribution of the testator's estate would be stopped, and executors would not know how to act; but that rule of convenience cannot be applied to exclude a child certainly within the meaning of the limitation in the absence of any contrary expressed intention of the testator. I think therefore that Sir John Leach was right, supposing the interpretation of the will to be what I have stated, and that this child certainly comes within the description. I must add however that I do not say that the gift was at all remote if it meant a child to be born at any time, because this is not the case of a class: it is gift of a pecuniary legacy of a particular amount to every child of every nephew which the testator then had, or of every nephew that might be born after his death, and is therefore good as to the children of the nephews he then had, and bad as to the children of nephews to be born after his death.

It would be a mistake to compare this with Leake v. Robinson, [2 Mer. 363, 35 Eng. Rep. 979 (Ch. 1817),] and other cases where the parties take as a class, for the difficulty which there arises as to giving it to some and not giving it to others does not apply here. The question of whether or not the children of afterborn nephews shall or shall not take, has no bearing at all upon the question of whether the child of an existing nephew takes: the legacy given to him cannot be bad because there is a legacy given under a similar description to a person who would not be able to take because the gift would be too remote. I give therefore no positive opinion upon the point of remoteness generally in this case, because I think that *quacunque via*, on the construction of the will, there is nothing to justify the exclusion from taking of a child who was conceived at the death of the testator and born six or seven months afterwards. If the words in question meant children who though not then in existence should be in existence at the death, the Plaintiff was in existence at the death; and if they meant children born at any time, he was born and must have been born if at all within such a time as made his legacy not remote. I am therefore of opinion that in any way he is entitled.

c. Gifts to Sub-Classes

American Security & Trust Company v. Cramer
175 F. Supp. 367 (D.D.C. 1959)

YOUNGDAHL, J. Six of the eleven defendants before the Court have moved for summary judgment. A hearing has been held and memoranda of points and authorities have been submitted. Plaintiff, trustee of a testamentary trust, is a stakeholder in this controversy among competing heirs. Since all the material facts have been stipulated, the Court is free to render summary judgment.

Abraham D. Hazen, a resident of the District of Columbia, died in the District on December 4, 1901. His will, executed on October 16, 1900, was admitted to probate on March 11, 1902.

Testator was survived by Hannah E. Duffey, who is referred to in his will as his "adopted daughter". At the time of the testator's death, Hannah had two children: Mary Hazen Duffey (now Cramer), born November 12, 1897, and Hugh Clarence Duffey, born July 11, 1899. After the testator's death, Hannah gave birth to two more children: Depue Hazen Duffey, born October 9, 1903, and Horace Duffey, born July 8, 1908.

The will provided for the payment of debts and certain specific bequests and then provided that the residue of the estate be put in trust for the benefit of testator's wife for life. At her death, one-half of the corpus was to be, and has been, given to testator's sister and brothers; the other half, composed of realty, remained in trust for Hannah for life. At Hannah's death, the income was to go to the children of Hannah "then living or the issue of such of them as may then be dead leaving issue surviving" Hannah, and then "upon the death of each the share of the one so dying shall go absolutely to the persons who shall then be her or his heirs at law according to the laws of descent now in force in the said District of Columbia".

Testator's widow died on October 31, 1916; Hannah died on May 21, 1915.

On October 5, 1917, the heirs of the testator brought an action in equity to have the provisions of the seventh paragraph of the will stricken as being in violation of the rule against perpetuities. The Supreme Court of the District of Columbia held that the interests of Hannah's children under the will were valid and the Court of Appeals affirmed. Hazen v. American Security & Trust Co., 1920, 49 App.D.C. 297, 265 F. 447. The validity of the remainders over, after the death of each child, was expressly not ruled upon as the life estates were not "so intimately connected with the gift over as to require us now to determine the validity of such gifts."

Hugh, one of the four life tenants after the death of the widow and Hannah, died on December 19, 1928 and shortly thereafter the trustee brought a bill for instructions; this time the validity of the remainder over to Hugh's heirs was in issue. On January 2, 1930, Judge Bailey ruled that "the remainder provided by the will after his (Hugh's) death to the persons who shall then be his heirs at law became vested within the period prescribed by law and is valid."

On December 13, 1954, Depue died and for the fourth time a suit concerning this trust was started in this court. The trustees desired instructions as to the disposition of Depue's one-sixth share. While this action was pending, on December 18, 1957, Horace died. A supplemental bill was then filed, asking for instructions as to the disposition of this one-sixth share as well. The remainder over after the death of the sole living life tenant, Mary, cannot yet take effect; however, due to the request of all the parties concerned, and in order to save both the time of this court and the needless expense it would otherwise cost the estate, the Court will also pass on the validity of this remainder.

The law that governs the questions here involved is the law in effect at the time of the testator's death: December 4, 1901.

The . . . effect of the [common-law] rule [against perpetuities] is to invalidate *ab initio* certain future interests that might otherwise remain in existence for a period of time considered inimicable to society's interest in having reasonable limits to dead-hand control and in facilitating the marketability of property. The policy of the law is to permit a person to control the devolution of his property but only for a human lifetime plus twenty-one years and actual periods of gestation. With careful planning, this period could be as long as one hundred years—and this is long enough.

A gift to a class is a gift of an aggregate amount of property to persons who are collectively described and whose individual share will depend upon the number of persons ultimately constituting the class. The members of the class must be finally determined within a life or lives in being plus twenty-one years and actual periods of gestation, or the gift will fail. Put another way, the class must close within the period of the rule against perpetuities, if the class gift is to be valid. Unless a contrary intent is indicated by the testator, the class will close when any member of the class is entitled to immediate possession and enjoyment of his share of the class gift. Applying these basic principles to the trust here involved, it is seen that the life estates to Hannah's children had to vest, if at all, at the termination of the preceding life estates of the widow and Hannah. Since Hannah's children had to be born within Hannah's lifetime, and since Hannah was a life in being, the class (Hannah's children) physiologically had to close within the period of the rule. This has already been so held. Hazen v. American Security & Trust Co., supra, at note 6. Furthermore, the remainder over at Hugh's death has been held valid. The Court now holds that the remainder limited to the heirs of Mary is valid. Both Hugh and Mary were lives in being at the testator's death; the remainders limited to their heirs had to vest, if at all, within the period of the rule. Horace and Depue were born after the testator died; the remainders over at their deaths are invalid.

In applying the rule against perpetuities, it does not help to show that the rule might be complied with or that, the way things turned out, it actually was complied with. After the testator's death, Hannah might have had more children; one of these might have lived more than twenty-one years after the death of all the lives in being at the testator's death. The vesting of the remainder in this after-born's heirs would take place after the expiration of lives in being and twenty-one years, since the heirs could not be ascertained until the after-born's death and an interest cannot be vested until the interest holder is ascertained. Consequently, because of the possibility that this could happen, even though, in fact, it did not, the remainders limited to the heirs of Horace and Depue (both after-borns) are invalid as a violation of the rule against perpetuities.

Counsel have not argued the point of whether the invalidity of the remainders to the heirs of Horace and Depue serves to taint the otherwise valid remainders to the heirs of Mary and Hugh. Of course, the remainder after Hugh's life estate has already been distributed and is not properly in issue. Nevertheless, as shall be demonstrated, it (and the remainder to the heirs of Mary) are not affected by the two invalid remainders, since the four remainders are to subclasses and stand (or fall) separately.

Beginning with Jee v. Audley, 1 Cox Eq.Cas. 324 (1787) and flowering with Leake v. Robinson, 2 Mer. 363, 35 Eng. Rep. 979 (Chancery 1817), there has been the curious anomaly in future interests law that if the interest of any potential member of a class can possibly vest too remotely, the interests of all the members of the class fails [sic]. In other words, the rule is that a class gift is inseparable. For example, T creates a trust to pay the income to A for life and then to pay the corpus over to such of A's children as attain the age of twenty-five. When A dies he might have a child who is not yet four years of age and who was not in being at T's death; this child would not take a vested interest until he satisfied the contingency of reaching the age of twenty-five; since a child under four could not become twenty-five within twenty-one years, the child's interest is void by virtue of the rule against perpetuities. While this much may be sound, the rule in Leake v. Robinson goes on to invalidate the entire class gift. That is, even if the child under four has two brothers who are over twenty-five when A dies, these two brothers take nothing because the invalid interest of their little brother (who, remember, may only be imagined) is contagious—so says Leake. Unless the testator intended to have all of the twenty-five-year-old sons take, or none at all (and this is difficult to imagine in the absence of an express provision in the will), the rule is a dubious one. Fortunately, the Court need not apply it in this case because of the limitation put on it by a long line of cases beginning with Catlin v. Brown, 11 Hare 372, 68 Eng.Rep. 1318 (Chancery, 1853).

In Catlin, the devise was of mortgaged property to A for life, then to the children of A in equal shares during their lives, and after the death of any such child, his share to his children and their heirs. Some of A's children were in being at the time that the testator died; some were born after his death. Counsel conceded that the remainders over to the heirs of those children of A born after the testator's death were invalid. The question was whether those concededly invalid remainders tainted the otherwise valid remainders and rendered them invalid. The Court held that they did not; the remainders to the heirs of the children in being at the testator's death were valid. Leake was distinguished on the ground that it concerned remainders to one class (A's children that reach twenty-five) while the remainders involved in Catlin were to a group of subclasses (the heirs of each of A's children was a subclass). In other words, the limitation placed on Leake by Catlin is that if the ultimate takers are not described as a single class but rather as a group of subclasses, and if the share to which each separate subclass is entitled will finally be determined within the period of the rule, the gifts to the different subclasses are separable for the purpose of the rule.

In the instant case, the language of the will compels the Court to read it as a devise of remainders to subclasses and within the rule of Catlin. The provision in issue reads, in part:

> . . . and *each* of the children of said adopted daughter shall take only for and during the terms of their *respective* lives and upon the death of *each* the share of the *one* so dying shall go absolutely to the persons who shall then be *her or his* heirs at law . . . (Emphasis supplied). . . .

When a remainder in fee after a life estate fails, there is no enlargement or diminution of the life estate; rather there is then a reversion in the heirs of the testator. The two one-sixth shares held invalid shall pass to the successors in interest to the heirs of Abraham D. Hazen. . . .

Notes and Questions

1. *Authority.* The specific-sum and sub-class rules of Storrs v. Benbow and Catlin v. Brown are supported by the Restatement of Property §§ 385, 389.

2. *Infectious Invalidity.* Even though the remainder interests to the heirs of Mary and the heirs of Hugh were valid, would it have been appropriate for the court to have held that the invalidity of the remainder interests to

the heirs of Horace and the heirs of Depue so "infected" the testator's overall scheme that the remainders to the heirs of Mary and the heirs of Hugh should also have been held invalid? The court did not discuss the issue because "counsel have not argued the point." Compare Estate of Morton, 454 Pa. 385, 312 A.2d 26 (1973); Restatement of Property § 389 comment f.

3. *Wait-and-See.* As under the common-law Rule, the remainder interests to the heirs of Mary and the heirs of Hugh would be initially valid under section 1(a)(1) of USRAP. The remainder interests to the heirs of Horace and the heirs of Depue would not be initially invalid, however, but would instead be subject to the wait-and-see element contained in section 1(a)(2). If neither Horace nor Depue outlive the 90-year period, the remainder interests to their heirs will be valid, also. If one or the other outlives the 90-year period, an unlikely event, the court would reform the testator's disposition under USRAP section 3. The provision for mandatory reformation has the effect of abolishing the doctrine of infectious invalidity. See USRAP § 1, Comment Part G.

2. Powers of Appointment

Statutory References: *USRAP §§ 1(b), 1(c)*
1990 UPC §§ 2-901(b), -901(c)

If a power of appointment violates the Rule Against Perpetuities, the power is invalid, and the disposition takes effect as if the power had never been created. If the power itself is valid, some or all of the interests created by its exercise may violate the Rule and be invalid.

a. General Powers Presently Exercisable

Validity of the Power at Common Law. Under the common-law Rule, a general power that is presently exercisable is treated as the equivalent of a *vested* property interest and is therefore not subject to the Rule Against Perpetuities.

If the exercisability of a general power is subject to a condition precedent, the power is treated as the equivalent of a *nonvested* property interest for purposes of the Rule. Although a mouthful, this type of power might be called a *general power not presently exercisable because of a condition precedent.* This is the term used in USRAP section 1(b). The term signifies that once the condition precedent is satisfied, the power becomes presently exercisable. (Note that a power of appointment expires on the donee's death, and so a deferral of a power's exercisability until a future time (even a time certain) imposes a condition precedent on the power's exercisability—the condition precedent being that the donee must be alive at that future time.)

A general power not presently exercisable because of a condition precedent must satisfy the requirement of initial certainty to be valid, which requires a certainty, when the power is created, that the *condition precedent* to its exercise will be resolved one way or the other no later than 21 years after the death of an individual then alive.

Consequently, although (as we shall see) neither a nongeneral power nor a testamentary power can validly be conferred on an unborn person (unless some special restriction is imposed on it forbidding its exercise beyond a life in being plus 21 years), an unborn person can be the recipient of a valid general power that becomes presently exercisable upon the donee's birth. To be valid, of course, the donee's birth must be certain to occur within a life in being plus 21 years.

> *Example 17.15:* G devised real property "to A for life, then to A's first born child for life, then to such persons as A's first born child shall appoint." G is survived by A, who is childless.
>
> The general power conferred on A's first born child is valid. The condition precedent—that A have a child—is certain to be resolved one way or the other within A's lifetime; A is the validating life. If, however, the relevant language had been "then to such persons as A's first born child shall appoint after reaching the age of 25," the additional contingency of reaching 25 would have invalidated the general power, at common law.

Validity of the Power Under Wait-and-See. Under USRAP, the validity of powers of appointment is governed by sections 1(b) and (c).[75] Under section 1(b)(1), a general power of appointment not exercisable because of a condition precedent is initially valid if it satisfies the requirement of initial certainty. If the requirement of initial certainty is not satisfied, the power is not automatically invalid but instead is subject to the wait-and-see element contained in section 1(b)(2). The power is valid if the condition precedent actually occurs within the 90-year period; if it does not, the disposition is subject to reformation under section 3.

Validity of the Exercise at Common Law. In determining the validity of an exercise of a general power presently exercisable, the power is treated as the equivalent of ownership of the property subject to the power. Accordingly, the donee is considered to have created the appointed interests. The exercise is treated as if the donee first exercised the power in her or his own favor and then created the appointed interests out of the now owned property. Consequently the appointed interests are created, for purposes of the Rule, when the exercise becomes effective, with the possibility of postponement in certain cases under the principles outlined supra pp. 993-94.

> *Example 17.16:* G was the life income beneficiary of a trust and the donee of a presently exercisable general power over the succeeding remainder interest. G exercised the power by deed, directing the trustee after her death to pay the income to G's children in equal shares for the life of the survivor,

---

75. A general power presently exercisable is not subject to the Statutory Rule.

and upon the death of her last surviving child to pay the corpus of the trust to her grandchildren.

The validity of the appointed interests depends on whether or not G's appointment was irrevocable. If it was irrevocable, the remainder interest in favor of G's grandchildren is invalid. The appointed interests were created when the deed was delivered or otherwise became effective. If G reserved a power to revoke her appointment, the remainder interest is valid. The appointed interests are created at G's death.

Validity of the Exercise Under Wait-and-See. The only change effected by USRAP is that an exercise that would have been invalid at common law is not initially invalid, but instead is subject to the wait-and-see element of the Statutory Rule. The 90-year period applies, in determining the validity of appointed interests that would have been invalid at common law.

b. Nongeneral Powers and Testamentary Powers

Validity of the Power. A nongeneral power (whether testamentary or presently exercisable) or a general testamentary power is invalid if, when the power is created, it is possible for the power to be *exercised* later than 21 years after the death of an individual then alive.

> *Example 17.17:* (1) G devised real property "to A for life, then to A's first born child for life, then to such persons as A's first born child shall by will appoint;" or
>
> (2) G devised real property "to A for life, then to A's first born child for life, then to such of A's grandchildren as A's first born child shall appoint."
>
> G is survived by A, who is childless.
>
> The power of appointment conferred on A's first born child—general testamentary power in Case (1), a nongeneral power presently exercisable in Case (2)—is invalid. The latest possible time of exercise is at the death of A's first born child, who cannot be the validating life because she or he was not "in being" at the creation of the power.

The lesson is that a nongeneral or testamentary power conferred on an unborn person is invalid.

Problem

G devised property in trust, directing the trustee to pay the income "to A for life, then in equal shares to A's children for their respective lives; on the death of each child, the proportionate share of corpus of the one so dying shall go to such persons as the one so dying shall by will appoint." G was survived by A and A's two children, X and Y. After G's death, another child (Z) was born to A.

1. Are the powers conferred on A's children valid under the common-law Rule? See Restatement of Property § 390 comment f; Am. L. Prop. § 24.32; J. Morris & W. Leach, The Rule Against Perpetuities 141-42 (2d

ed. 19 2). Cf. Slark v. Darkyns, L.R. 10 Ch. App. 36 (C.A. 1874). But see Camden Safe Deposit & Trust Co. v. Scott, 121 N.J.Eq. 3 , 189 A. 63 (1937); Re Phillips, 11 D.L.R. 600 (Ont. 1913).

2. How would the situation be treated under USRAP? Assume that Z was born five years after G's death and that Z died at age 76, leaving a will that purported to exercise her or his power of appointment. See USRAP § 1, Comment Part G, Example 26.

———

Fiduciary Powers. Discretionary powers held by fiduciaries are nongeneral powers of appointment, for purposes of the Rule Against Perpetuities. Discretionary fiduciary powers include a trustee's power to invade the corpus of the trust for the benefit of the income beneficiary or a trustee's power to accumulate the income or pay it out or to spray it among a group of beneficiaries. Purely administrative fiduciary powers, however, are not subject to the Rule Against Perpetuities.

Consider the validity of the fiduciary powers in the following cases, first under the common-law Rule and then under USRAP sections 1(c), 4(2)-(4).

1. G devised property in trust, directing the trustee to pay the income to A for life, then to A's children for the life of the survivor, and on the death of A's last surviving child to pay the corpus to B. The trustee is granted the discretionary power to sell and reinvest the trust assets and to invade the corpus of the trust on behalf of the income beneficiary or beneficiaries. G was survived by A and by A's two children, X and Y.

2. G devised property in trust, directing the trustee to pay the income to A for life, then to A's children; each child's share of principal is to be paid to the child when she or he reaches 40; if any child dies under 40, the child's share is to be paid to the child's estate as a property interest owned by such child. The trustee is given the discretionary power to advance all or a portion of a child's share before the child reaches 40. G was survived by A, who was then childless.

3. G devised property in trust, the terms of which authorized the trustee to accumulate the income or pay it or a portion of it to A during A's lifetime; after A's death, the trustee was authorized to accumulate the income or to distribute it in equal or unequal shares among A's children until the death of the survivor; and on the death of A's last surviving child to pay the corpus and accumulated income (if any) to B. The trustee was also granted the discretionary power to invade the corpus on behalf of the permissible recipient or recipients of the income. G was survived by A, B, and A's two children, X and Y. Compare Gray on Perpetuities §§ 410.1 to 410.6; Lyons v. Bradley, 1 8 Ala. 606, 63 S. 244 (1910); Woodruff Oil & Fertilizer Co. v. Yarborough's Estate, 144 S.C. 18, 142 S.E. 60 (1928), with Andrews v. Lincoln, 96 Me. 641, 60 A. 898 (1901); Bundy v. United States Trust Co., 267 Mass. 72, 163 N.E. 337 (192); Thomas v. Harrison, 24 Ohio Op. 2d 148, 191 N.E.2d 8 2 (P. Ct. 19 2).

Validity of the Exercise—Nongeneral and Testamentary Powers. If a nongeneral or testamentary power passes the appropriate test for validity as set forth above, it can validly be exercised. Whether or not such a power has in fact been validly exercised is the next question.

For the most part, the Rule Against Perpetuities applies to appointed interests (and appointed powers) in the same way it applies to interests (and powers) created by an owner of property. At common law, the requirement of initial certainty applies. Under USRAP, interests (or powers) that do not satisfy the requirement of initial certainty and are therefore not validated by section 1(a)(1) (or, in the case of appointed powers, sections 1(b)(1) or 1(c)(1)), are entitled to a 90-year period to determine their validity. See USRAP §§ 1(a)(2), (b)(2), (c)(2); UPC §§ 2-901(a)(2), (b)(2), (c)(2) (1990). Nevertheless, in the case of nongeneral and testamentary powers, there are some perpetuity questions and doctrines peculiar to appointments.

Industrial National Bank v. Barrett
101 R.I. 89 220 A.2d 517 (1966)

PAOLINO, J. This is a bill in equity brought by the Industrial National Bank of Rhode Island, executor and trustee, and Aline C. Lathan, co-executor, under the will of Mary M. Tilley, deceased, for construction of the latter's will and for instructions to the executors and trustee thereunder. . . .

It appears that Arthur H. Tilley, husband of the deceased, died January 28, 1959. Under the eighth clause of his will, admitted to probate February 5, 1959, he devised the property, which qualified for the full marital deduction, to the Industrial National Bank, in trust, with directions to pay the net income at least quarterly to his wife for life and such amounts of the corpus annually or at more frequent intervals as she should in writing request, for her comfort and support, and without being accountable to any court or remainderman therefor. He also conferred upon her a general testamentary power of appointment over the corpus remaining at her death.

Mary M. Tilley died October 28, 1963. Under the fourth clause of her will, admitted to probate November 7, 1963, she exercised her general testamentary power of appointment to the Industrial National Bank, in trust "to pay over the net income thereof to and for the use and benefit of my granddaughters, Aline C. Lathan and Evelyn M. Barrett . . . equally for and during the term of their natural lives, and upon the death of either of them, to pay over said net income to her issue, per stirpes and not per capita." The trustee was also given uncontrolled discretion to pay over to either of said grandchildren, or the issue of any deceased grandchild, for specific purposes, portions of the principal. Finally, the testatrix provided the trust would terminate "twenty one (21) years after the death of the last survivor of the younger grandchild or issue of either grandchild of mine living at my death. . . ."

On the date of Arthur H. Tilley's death, Aline C. Lathan and Evelyn M. Barrett and one great-grandchild were in being. On the date of Mary M. Tilley's death the aforesaid respondents plus six additional great-grandchildren were in being. One great-grandchild was born subsequent to her death. . . .

The complainants contend that Mrs. Tilley's exercise of the power of appointment created under her husband's will does not violate the rule against perpetuities. . . .

The complainants . . . contend that . . . the better-reasoned authorities hold the perpetuity period should be counted from the date of the power's exercise rather than its creation, which would make the gift here vest within the prescribed time. . . .

It is fundamental law that when the free alienation of a future interest in property is limited, the interest must vest within lives in being plus twenty-one years from the date of the creating instrument. When the persons who will take or the extent of their interests are to be determined by the exercise of a subsequent power of appointment, the rule against perpetuities requires that the vesting time be computed as if the appointment were a part of the instrument creating the limitation, because until it is exercised the limitation is incomplete.

Nevertheless as the primary concern behind the rule is to prevent restraint on alienation, a distinction is made between general and special powers. In the case of a general power of appointment by deed and will, all courts hold that since the donee has absolute disposing power over the property and may bring it into the market place at any time, he has what is tantamount to a fee. Therefore, since whatever estates may be created by one seized in fee may be also created under a general power, the commencement of the limitation is computed from the time of the power's exercise and not its creation.

In the case of a general power of appointment by will, however, the weight of authority counts the perpetuity period from the date of creation on the ground that since the donee cannot freely alienate the property during his life, he is not the practical owner thereof. A minority view disagrees with this position on the theory that the concept of actual ownership clouds the substance of the matter, which is that if the person having the power without the ownership may appoint to whomsoever he pleases at the time he exercises it, he is in the same position in respect to the perpetuity as if he were actually the owner. Thorndike, General Powers And Perpetuities, 27 Harv. L. Rev., pp. 705, 717. Also see Northern Trust Co. v. Porter, 368 Ill. 256, 13 N.E.2d 487, for leading citations on both positions.

Since this is a case of first impression, we have read with interest the authorities supporting the above positions. See Gray, General Testamentary Powers And The Rule Against Perpetuities, 26 Harv. L. Rev., p. 720; Thorndike, General Powers And Perpetuities, supra; Annot., 1 A.L.R. 374; and Northern Trust Co. v. Porter, supra. From this reading it appears that the early English cases in counting the perpetuity period did not distinguish between a general power to appoint by deed and will and a general power to appoint by will only and we think the cases following this position are the more persuasive.

In essence the majority jurisdictions characterize a general power of appointment by will as being in the nature of a special power, and, as such, a part of the creating instrument of the donor. They reach this result solely on the ground that because the donor has tied up ownership of the property until the donee's death, the restraint on alienation is sufficient to count the perpetuity period from the power's creation.

We think that this position misapprehends the fundamental concepts involved here. The law does not prohibit an estate being tied up for the life of any one individual, but prohibits only restraint beyond lives in being plus twenty-one years. See Thorndike, supra. When the donee exercises his power, he is at that time the practical owner thereof, for the purposes of the rule, as he can appoint to anyone of his choice as well as his own estate. Furthermore when he exercises the power he can create, unlike the case of a special power, estates entirely independent from those created or controlled by the donor, and so, as to the donee, the power is a general one. See Perpetuities In Perspective: Ending The Rule's Reign Of Terror, by W. Barton Leach, 65 Harv. L. Rev. 721.

Consequently, we hold the trust created by clause fourth of Mrs. Tilley's will pursuant to her general testamentary power of appointment is valid. We arrive at this conclusion not only because logic favors its adoption but also because we believe it is in line with the trend to obviate the technical harshness of the rule against perpetuities and decide cases on the substance of things. 6 American Law of Property § 24.45 (1952), p. 118; 3 Restatement, Property § 343 (1940), p. 1913; Union & New Haven Trust Co. v. Taylor, 133 Conn. 221, 50 A.2d 168. For a learned discussion of this problem, see Perpetuities In A Nutshell, 51 Harv. L. Rev. 638, and Perpetuities: The Nutshell Revisited, 78 Harv. L. Rev. 973, both being articles by W. Barton Leach. . . .

On July 6, 1966, the parties may present to this court for approval a form of decree, in accordance with this opinion, to be entered in the superior court.

Notes

1. *State of the Authorities.* The position taken by the court in the *Barrett* case is supported by legislation enacted in a few American states.[76] This is

---

76. See Del. Code Ann. tit. 25, § 501; S.D. Codified. Laws § 43-5-5; Wis. Stat. Ann. § 700.16(c). The Delaware and South Dakota statutes apply the same rule to the exercise of nongeneral powers as well as the exercise of general testamentary powers, a position that is responsible for the enactment of IRC § 2041(a)(3). Section 2041(a)(3) was construed in the light of the Wisconsin statute in Estate of Murphy v. Commissioner, 71 T.C. 671 (1979). See Blattmachr & Pennell, Adventures in Generation Skipping, Or How We Learned to Love the "Delaware Tax Trap," 24 Real Prop. Prob. & Tr. J. 75 (1989). Delaware recently added a provision allowing trusts to continue for 110 years after exercise of a nongeneral power (or a general testamentary power). Del. Code Ann. tit. 25, § 503. Any such exercise (and, in certain circumstances, the mere possibility of any such exercise) in a "grandfathered" trust under the federal generation-skipping transfer tax would cause the trust to lose "grandfathered" status. See supra p. 1055.

also the English view, as first enunciated in Rous v. Jackson, L.R. 29 Ch. 521 (1885) and now codified in the Perpetuities and Accumulations Act, section 7. The vast majority view is to the contrary, however. The Restatement 2d of Property section 1.2 comment d, illustration 12, also rejects the reasoning of the *Barrett* case, and supports the majority view, on the ground that the "complete freedom of transfer by will that opens up momentarily on [the donee's] death is not enough to eliminate the interference with unqualified control of beneficial rights . . . that is caused . . . during [the donee's] lifetime." USRAP also supports the majority view. See USRAP § 2(a) and Comment; UPC § 2-902(a) (1990).

2. *Marital Deduction.* Note that general testamentary powers are typically conferred on the donor's surviving spouse in a trust that qualifies for the federal estate tax marital deduction under IRC section 2056(b)(5). If the surviving spouse exercises her or his power by creating a trust, the lawyer drafting the donee-client's will must be especially alert to the fact that the appointed interests and powers are treated as if they were created when the donee-client's power was created; if a perpetuity saving clause is used, the clause must tie the perpetuity-period component into the lives of persons in being at the creation of the donee-client's power, not at the exercise of the donee-client's power.

Estate of Bird
225 Cal. App. 2d 196, 37 Cal. Rptr. 288 (1964)

STONE, J. Jeannette Miller Bird and Geoffrey Andrew Bird, her husband, executed their wills simultaneously February 17, 1961.

Jeannette died June 16, 1961, and her will, which was admitted to probate, provided, insofar as here pertinent: "2. This trust shall exist and continue for and during the life of my said husband, GEOFFREY ANDREW BIRD, and shall cease and terminate upon his death. I give and grant to my husband the exclusive power to dispose of the corpus, and undistributed income, under the terms of his Last Will and Testament. . . ."

Geoffrey Bird died just three months later, September 16, 1961. He exercised the power of appointment created by Jeannette's will, by the following provisions in his will:

FIFTH: I will, devise and bequeath to CITIZENS NATIONAL BANK, in trust, all of the rest, residue and remainder of my property of every nature, kind and description, including the property and assets which are included in the Marital Deduction Trust as set forth in my wife's Will, and I do now specifically exercise my power of testamentary disposition by including such assets in this trust.

(a) Said property is to be held by the Trustee for the following purposes:

Prior to its adoption of USRAP in 1987, Florida had a statute similar to the Delaware and South Dakota provision.

1. The net income shall be distributed in monthly or other convenient installments to or for the benefit of my said children in equal shares for life. . . .

3. This trust shall terminate on the death of the last survivor of my children and my grandchildren living at the time of my death, and the entire corpus and undistributed net income shall go and be distributed to the children of my grandchildren per capita.

Counsel for both appellant and respondent agree that the matter is one of first impression in California, and they pose two questions: First, whether the period prescribed by the rule against perpetuities . . . is determined as of the time the power was created, that is, at Jeannette's death, or at Geoffrey's death when the power was exercised. Second, if the time the power is created governs, is the determination made according to the facts existing at the time of creation of the power, or are the circumstances existing at the time the power is exercised, controlling? We hold that the period is counted from the time the power of appointment is created, but that the facts and circumstances are considered as of the time of its exercise. This holding disposes of both questions raised. . . .

Simes and Smith, in their work, The Law of Future Interests, section 1276, page 214, tell us that the common law rule is:

> . . . in determining the validity of an appointment under a special power or a general testamentary power, though the period is counted from the creation of the power, facts and circumstances are considered as of the time of its exercise. . . .

The Restatement of Property adopted the common law rule applicable to general testamentary powers of appointment. . . . The rule is expressed in section 392 as follows:

> . . . an appointment under either a general testamentary power or a special power is invalid, because of the rule against perpetuities, only to the extent that its limitations, (a) construed in the light of the circumstances existent when the power is exercised, but (b) measured, for the purpose of applying the rule against perpetuities, from the time when the power was created, violate that rule.

In commenting upon the rationale of the rule, the Restatement points out that:

> The element of the stated rule embodied in Clause (a), mitigates the destructive effect of the doctrine of "relation back." In applying the rule against perpetuities to the limitations of an attempted appointment made under either a general testamentary power or a special power, no useful end would be served by finding an invalidity because of some possible uncertainty, present when the power was created, but actually and definitively excluded by the course of events which has already occurred and which is known at the time of the exercise of the power. By the part of the rule embodied in Clause (a) the fiction of "relation back" is prevented from having destructive effects

greater than those required for the reasonable effectuation of the underlying social policy of the rule against perpetuities.

This is in accord with the liberal approach toward the rule against perpetuities taken by the California Supreme Court in the recent case of Wong v. Di Grazia, 60 A.C. 505, [35 Cal.Rptr. 241, 386 P.2d 817]. . . .

The facts of this case demonstrate the reasonableness of the common law rule embodied in section 392 of the Restatement of Property, supra. By reason of the proximate deaths of Jeannette and Geoffrey, only three months elapsed between creation of the power and its exercise. There was no factual change during that short interval. The lives in being at the time the power was exercised were in being when the power was created, so that the power of appointment did not, in fact, violate the rule against perpetuities. To defeat the purposes and the wishes of Jeannette and Geoffrey because a violation of the rule against perpetuities was theoretically possible, but in fact did not occur, seems to us to be unnecessarily restrictive. It is the sort of rigid mechanistic application of the rule which the Supreme Court decried in Wong v. Di Grazia, supra.

In any event, we find Civil Code section 715.2 and the common law rule to which it refers, controlling. Applying his test, there was no violation of the rule against perpetuities at the time the power of appointment was created, when considered in the light of the facts and circumstances as of the time the power of appointment was exercised.

The judgment is reversed.

Notes and Questions

1. *Supporting Authority.* Taking a "second look" at the facts existing at the date of the exercise of a nongeneral or testamentary power is a well established procedure. See Restatement of Property § 392; Am. L. Prop. § 24.35.

2. *Second Look for Gifts in Default.* Can a second look at the facts also be taken in determining the validity of a gift in default in cases in which the power is not exercised? Am. L. Prop. section 24.36, written by Leach and Tudor, supports a second look for gifts in default. Shortly after this treatise was published, this position was adopted in apparently the first American case to consider the question, Sears v. Coolidge, 329 Mass. 340, 108 N.E.2d 563 (1952). Four years later, Simes & Smith on Future Interest section 1276 came out against the decision in *Sears*. Not long after, however, a Canadian court upheld a gift in default by applying the second-look doctrine. See Re Edwards, 20 D.L.R.2d 755 (Ont. 1959). Later, the Pennsylvania court did the same thing, but did so without discussing the issue, except to assert that it was "the better view." See In re Frank, 480 Pa. 116, 389 A.2d 536 (1978). The authority of this decision is undercut by the fact that the Pennsylvania "wait and see" statute was applicable to the case and required the same result, and the court so noted.

Problems

G devised property in trust, income to A for life, remainder in corpus to such persons as A shall by will appoint. A's will appointed the property in a further trust, the terms of which were that the income was to go to A's children in equal shares for their lives; on each child's death, the share of corpus proportionate to the child's share of income was to go to the child's then-living descendants, by representation.

Consider the validity of A's appointment under the common-law Rule and under USRAP in the following circumstances:

1. A died, survived by her two children, X and Y, both of whom were also in being at G's death.

2. A died, survived by her two children, X and Y; X was in being at G's death but Y was born after G's death.

Amerige v. Attorney General
324 Mass. 648, 88 N.E.2d 126 (1949)

[Timothy Leeds left property by will in trust for his brother, James Leeds, for life and then for such persons as James should by will appoint.

James by will expressly blended his own property with that over which he had the power conferred by Timothy, and gave a part of the combined estates in trust for the benefit of his daughter, Mary Elizabeth Williams, for life and then for such persons as she should by will appoint.

Mary Elizabeth by her will also blended her own estate with that over which she had the power conferred by James and left the residue thereof in trust for her two children for life, then to his or her issue, but in default of issue to hold for the life of the survivor, then to his or her issue, but if then there should be no issue of either, to certain charities.

The court held that Mary Elizabeth's appointment violated the common-law Rule Against Perpetuities to the extent it included property from the estate of Timothy.

Among others, James was survived by his daughter Mary Elizabeth, who was also living at Timothy's death, and by Mary Elizabeth's two children, Mary and Edward, neither of whom was living at Timothy's death.]

SPALDING, J. This is a petition for instructions by the trustees under the will of Mary Elizabeth Williams, late of Hopkinton. The case was heard in the Probate Court on a statement of agreed facts and was reserved and reported to this court without decision. . . .

The charities . . . advance the argument that none of the property appointed by Mary Elizabeth Williams is derived from property of Timothy. They invoke the principle that where the donee of a general power of appointment disposes of owned and appointive property as a single fund the appointive property is allocated to the various dispositions of such fund in such manner as to give the maximum effect to such dispositions. That principle is recognized by our decisions, Stone v. Forbes, 189 Mass. 163, 170-171, 75 N.E. 141; Minot v. Paine, 230 Mass. 514, 525, 120 N.E. 167,

1 A.L.R. 365, and by the American Law Institute in § 363 of the Restatement of Property. Thus, it is argued, James Leeds dealt with his own and the appointive property as a single fund and to give the maximum effect to his dispositions the debts, expenses, legacies and residuary gifts must be charged against the appointive property and if this is done that property is exhausted and there is no property of Timothy remaining which Mary Elizabeth Williams could appoint. But that principle is not applicable here. In the case at bar there were successive donees of the power created by Timothy, James Leeds and Mary Elizabeth Williams. The appointments which violate the rule against perpetuities were made by Mary Elizabeth Williams, the second donee. None of the appointments made by James is invalid and no contention is made to the contrary. In all of the cases we have seen where the principle of allocation has been applied the valid and invalid dispositions have been made by the same person in the same will. To give the maximum effect to such dispositions under the principle of allocation the law is attempting to carry out the presumed intent of the testator. The doctrine ought not to be applied in the case of successive donees where the dispositions of the first donee are valid and those of the second invalid. It cannot reasonably be said that James contemplated that Mary Elizabeth Williams would exercise the power improperly with the result that he must be presumed to have intended that this dispositions be charged against the appointive property.

The case is remanded to the Probate Court for further proceedings in conformance with this opinion. . . .

3. Charitable Gifts

With one exception, future interests given to charities are subject to the Rule Against Perpetuities. The Rule applies to charitable interests in the same way it applies to future interests given to private parties. At common law, if there is a condition precedent attached to the interest, and if there is no validating life, the charitable interest fails.

> *Example 17.18:* G devised real property "to A for life, then to such of A's children as reach 25, but if none of A's children reaches 25, to X Charity." Under the wait-and-see modification of the common-law Rule, these interests would not be initially invalid, but would be given a chance to vest or terminate on their own terms within the allowable waiting period.
>
> The remainder in favor of X Charity is invalid. So is the remainder in favor of A's children.

Constructional Preference for Vested Charitable Interests. Charitable interests, like private interests, are not subject to the Rule if they are vested. There is a pronounced tendency in the decisions to construe charitable interests as vested if the language of the instrument permits this classification. Many charitable gifts, which if contingent would have been invalid, have been saved by this device.

Charitable Interests Excluded If Preceded by Another Charitable Interest. As noted above, there is one formal exception to the principle that charitable future interests receive no preferential treatment under the common-law Rule. A future interest held by a charity is excluded from the application of the Rule if the interest was preceded by an interest that is also held by a charity. See Restatement 2d of Property § 1.6; USRAP § 4(5); UPC § 2-904(5) (1990).

The rationale for this exclusion is that, since the law allows a perpetual tying up of property for a single charity, it ought to do so when the transferor provides for a shift from one charity to another, even though the shift might take place beyond the perpetuity period.

> *Example 17.19:* G devised real property "to the X School District so long as the premises are used for school purposes, and upon the cessation of such use, to Y City."
> The executory interest in favor of Y City is valid.

4. Contracts

Owing to its roots as a means by which to curb remotely vesting future interests that made *property* inalienable, especially indestructible executory interests, the Rule Against Perpetuities is inapplicable to legal relationships that do not create property interests. Contracts—even long term contracts —are generally exempt. It has been held that optional modes of settlement for the payment of life insurance proceeds cannot violate the Rule, nor can annuity contracts, even though future payments may be subject to uncertainties that might not be resolved within a life in being plus 21 years. Doyle v. Massachusetts Mutual Life Ins. Co., 377 F.2d 19 (6th Cir. 1967); Holmes v. John Hancock Mutual Life Ins. Co., 288 N.Y. 106, 41 N.E.2d 909 (1942).

5. Commercial Transactions

As noted above, legal relationships that do not create property interests are not subject to the Rule Against Perpetuities. Although this exempts most contracts from the Rule, some contractual arrangements do create property interests, under our classificatory scheme of estates. Many of these legal relationships arise out of commercial transactions.

The Rule Against Perpetuities would seem to be a wholly inappropriate instrument of social policy to use as a control over these arrangements. The period of the Rule—a life in being plus 21 years—may be suitable as a limit on gratuitous transfers of property, but it is not suitable for bargained-for exchanges. Nevertheless, the common-law Rule has been applied to certain types of commercial transactions. The Rule Against Perpetuities argument is usually raised by one of the parties who is seeking to avoid performing on her or his part of the contract.

a. *Commercial Transactions Under the Uniform Statutory Rule Against Perpetuities*

In recognition of the point that the life-in-being-plus-21-year period has no relevance to commercial transactions, USRAP broke new ground by excluding all commercial transactions from the Rule Against Perpetuities. See USRAP § 4(1); UPC § 2-904(1) (1990). Consequently, under USRAP, none of the transactions we are about to consider would be subject to the Rule. The USRAP Drafting Committee took notice of the fact that some of these commercial transactions do restrain the alienability of property, but thought that their control was not, strictly speaking, a Rule Against Perpetuities question and hence was beyond the scope of their project. The Official Comment notes, however, that these transactions are subject to the common-law rules regarding unreasonable restraints on alienation and, in some cases, marketable title acts.

Another approach is to enact a separate set of statutory provisions limiting the duration of certain commercial transactions to a flat period of years, such as 30, as has been done in Illinois (Ill. Rev. Stat. ch. 30, § 194(a)) and Massachusetts (Mass. Gen. Laws Ann. ch. 184A, § 5).

b. *Options In Gross*

A contract right to purchase property is an option in gross if the optionee has no possessory interest in the property, such as a leasehold interest. If the subject of an option is land or a unique chattel, the option is specifically enforceable. Specifically enforceable contracts are treated as creating equitable property interests. Since equitable property interests are subject to the Rule Against Perpetuities, the prevailing view is that options in gross are invalid if they are exercisable beyond a life in being plus 21 years.

> *Example 17.20:* (1) A, the owner of Blackacre, sells an option to B under which A obligates himself, his heirs and assigns at any time in the future to convey Blackacre to B, his heirs and assigns for $X.00.
>
> (2) A, the owner of Blackacre, sells Blackacre to B. As part of the transaction, B obligates himself, his heirs and assigns at any time in the future to reconvey Blackacre to A, his heirs and assigns for $X.00.
>
> Both options are invalid by the great majority view. They are neither specifically enforceable nor are damages for their breach recoverable. Case (2) deserves a special comment. There the option was reserved by the transferor of the property. Although reversionary interests are not subject to the Rule, reserved options are not accorded the same immunity. See Woodall v. Bruen, 76 W. Va. 193, 85 S.E. 170 (1915). Yet the difference between a reserved option and a right of entry may be only a matter of form. For example, suppose the grant of Blackacre in the variation had read: "to B and his heirs, but if the grantor or his heirs should ever tender $X.00 to B, his heirs or assigns, the grantor or his heirs shall have the right to re-enter and retake the

premises." Presumably this change in form would transform A's invalid option into a valid right of entry.

Options that are limited to expire if they are not exercised within a life in being plus 21 years are valid. The options in the above example would have been valid if the obligation had not been to convey Blackacre "at any time in the future," but rather had been to do so "during the lifetime of the survivor of A and B," or "during the next 21 years." Even without so explicit a limitation, a court might construe the language of the option as being so limited. The absence of language such as "his heirs and assigns," for example, might lead a court to hold that the option was to last only during the lifetime of either party or only during their joint lives.

c. Rights of First Refusal (Preemptive Rights)

Unlike options to purchase, rights of first refusal do not obligate the owner of the property to sell it whether she or he wants to or not. Instead, they obligate the owner to offer it first to the preemptioner only if the owner decides to sell. The preemptioner can buy the property, but if she or he declines, the owner is then free to sell to anyone else.

Rights of first refusal have been held to be subject to the Rule Against Perpetuities, and void if they are exercisable beyond a life in being plus 21 years.

It has been suggested that preemptive rights that require merely an offer at the prevailing *market price*, as opposed to a fixed price, ought to be valid even if they are of unlimited duration. See Am. L. Prop. § 26.67. The argument is that this type of a right of first refusal effects no restraint on alienation, direct or indirect. This idea was rejected, however, in Atchison v. City of Englewood, 170 Colo. 295, 463 P.2d 297 (1969), where the court held that the difficulty of ascertaining and locating the owner of the preemptive right at some indefinite time in the future constituted a "sufficiently unreasonable restraint upon the transferability of the property as to justify imposition of the rule against perpetuities." Contra Robroy Land Co., Inc. v. Prather, 622 P.2d 367 (Wash. 1980).

In Continental Cablevision, Inc. v. United Broadcasting Co., 873 F.2d 717 (4th Cir. 1989), the court saved a market-price right of first refusal from invalidity by imposing a 21-year limit on its duration, even though the actual language of the document creating the right of first refusal did not specify an expiration date.

Metropolitan Transportation Authority
v. Bruken Realty Corporation
67 N.Y.2d 156, 492 N.E.2d 379 (1986)

SIMONS, J. In 1966 the State of New York, acting through the Metropolitan Commuter Transportation Authority (now plaintiff Metropolitan

Transportation Authority [MTA]) bought all the capital stock of plaintiff Long Island Railroad from the Pennsylvania Railroad for $65 million. Included among the assets acquired were 65 acres of real property in Queens which had been used by the Long Island Railroad as a freight yard. As part of the consideration, to reduce the purchase price, the State conveyed air rights above this property to Delbay Corporation, a subsidiary of Pennsylvania, together with an easement permitting it to erect columns, piers or foundations and to install utility services necessary to support and service improvements within the air rights. It also executed an "option agreement" granting Delbay the right to purchase 12 lots in the freight yard at market value if MTA subsequently determined that the property was "no longer necessary for [its] transportation operations". The option expired if Delbay, or its successors or assigns, did not exercise it within 99 years. The issue presented on this appeal is whether that option agreement violated the prohibition against remote vesting stated in New York's Rule against Perpetuities (see, EPTL 9-1.1[b]).

On April 16, 1982 MTA notified Delbay that it no longer required six of the lots and that Delbay could acquire them. Delbay thereafter assigned its right to two of the lots to a real estate developer, defendant Bruken Realty Corporation, and Bruken, by letter dated July 13, 1982, notified MTA of its election to purchase them. Although the original agreement provided for arbitration of the market value, the parties agreed to attempt to negotiate the price after obtaining separate appraisals. The air rights conveyed to Delbay had since been acquired by the City of New York in a tax foreclosure proceeding, however, and, with the air rights and the ground rights in separate ownership, the parties were unable to reach agreement. Accordingly, they selected arbitrators and submitted the determination of market value to them. Before hearings could start, plaintiffs instituted this action requesting that the court enjoin the arbitration proceeding and declare that the conveyance to Delbay of the right to acquire the freight yard lots was void. Plaintiffs subsequently moved for summary judgment and Supreme Court denied the motion on alternative legal grounds (125 Misc.2d 497, 479 N.Y.S.2d 646). The Appellate Division affirmed, without opinion, 112 A.D.2d 508, 492 N.Y.S.2d 508, and the matter is before us on a certified question by its leave. We now affirm.

I. The rules limiting the right of owners to indefinitely control title to property developed because of the natural antagonism between society's interest in promoting the free and ready transfer of property and the desire of property owners to control the future disposition of their holdings. Originally intended to restrict family dispositions, usually dispositions by royalty or the landed gentry, the rules have antecedents as old as any known to the common law. Their purpose is to ensure the productive use and development of property by its current beneficial owners by simplifying ownership, facilitating exchange and freeing property from unknown or embarrassing impediments to alienability. The rules are legal prohibitions, based on the public policy of the State. They may not be waived, as could rules enacted for the benefit of the parties alone. When an owner attempts to exert control over the transferability of his property for too long a time, the courts will step in, invalidate the restricting provisions, and permit transfer to take effect uninhibited by the restraint.

In New York an owner's power to dispose of property is limited by three rules. The first two, known as the Rule against Perpetuities, are found in subdivisions (a) and (b) of EPTL 9-1.1. The Rule declares that no estate in property shall be valid (1) if the instrument conveying it suspends the power of alienation for a period longer than lives in being at the creation of the estate plus 21 years[77] and (2) unless it must vest, if at all, before expiration of the same period. Although the statutory period is lives in being plus 21 years, in this case the parties to the agreement were corporations and, inasmuch as no measuring life or lives were stated in the instruments, the permissible period is 21 years. The third rule regulating dispositions is established by common law and invalidates conveyances which impose unreasonable restraints on alienation.

The statutory rule prohibiting remote vesting and the common-law rule against unreasonable restraints serve the same general purpose by limiting the power of an owner to create uncertain future estates. The statutory rule does so indirectly by limiting the time when future interests must vest. The rule against unreasonable restraints on alienation does so directly by forbidding owners to impose conditions on conveyances which block the grantee from freely disposing of the property. While the statutory rule is inflexible, measured solely by the passage of time, the common-law rule is applied by considering the reasonableness of the restraint. Whether a restraint on the disposition of property is unreasonable is a question of fact depending upon its purpose, duration and, where applicable, the designated method for fixing the purchase price. It is generally said that the reason for the common-law rule is that ownership of property cannot exist in one person and the right of alienation in another, but the same general policy concerns underlying the rule against perpetuities also favor a rule against unreasonable restraints.

II. Plaintiff contends that the State's agreement gave Delbay an option to buy the freight yard lots, that options are subject to the rule against remote vesting under the holding of Buffalo Seminary v. McCarthy, 86 A.D.2d 435, 451 N.Y.S.2d 457, aff'd. on opn. below 58 N.Y.2d 867, 460 N.Y.S.2d 528, 447 N.E.2d 76) and that since Delbay's option might not be exercised within the statutory period, it is void. Whether the provision is void or not requires a determination first of the nature of the interest created—whether it is an option or, as Bruken claims, a preemptive right—and, second, if it is a preemptive right, whether the rule applies to it.

[The court held that options in gross are subject to EPTL § 9-1.1, and continued.] Preemptive rights differ significantly from options, however, and we have not yet decided whether they are subject to that rule.

A. The right acquired by Delbay, though called an option by the parties, was a preemptive right to buy the freight yard property. An option grants to the holder the power to compel the owner of property to sell it whether

---

77. The suspension of the power of alienation rule is discussed infra Part F. Eds.

the owner is willing to part with ownership or not. A preemptive right, or right of first refusal, does not give its holder the power to compel an unwilling owner to sell; it merely requires the owner, when and if he decides to sell, to offer the property first to the party holding the preemptive right so that he may meet a third-party offer or buy the property at some other price set by a previously stipulated method. Once the owner decides to sell the property, the holder of the preemptive right may choose to buy it or not, but the choice exists only after he receives an offer from the owner. If the holder decides not to buy, then the owner may sell to anyone. . . .

B. We turn then to whether the rule against remote vesting applies to preemptive rights.

The New York courts which have considered the question have reached different results as have courts from other jurisdictions.

The courts which have declined to apply the rule have tried to distinguish preemptive rights from other interests in property by determining either (1) that the holder of a preemptive right has an interest which vests immediately, not remotely or (2) that the holder acquires only a contract right exercisable at some future date, not an interest in property. Commentators, and this court as well, have criticized both analyses as contrary to established principles of law and have urged that the courts might better concede that although preemptive rights offend the basic policy of the rule against remote vesting, the offense is properly offset by their utility in modern legal transactions and that usefulness justifies excepting them from the operation of the rule (see, 5A Powell, op. cit. ¶ 771[1], at 72-68, 72-70; Simes and Smith, Future Interests § 1154, at 64 [2d ed. 1956]; Leach, Perpetuities: New Absurdity, Judicial and Statutory Correctives, 73 Harv. L. Rev. 1318, 1320).

The courts have reached this conclusion in a number of circumstances involving options and preemptive rights, e.g., for options appurtenant to leases or to mineral rights or to franchise rights or for options to expand an easement or to acquire an interest in a party wall if the optionee decided to build adjacent to the optionor's land (Beloit Bldg. Co. v. Quinn, 145 Kan. 507, 66 P.2d 549). The holder's rights have been recognized because enforcement did not violate the underlying purposes of the rule against remote vesting. Quite the contrary, enforcement of the preemptive right in such cases encouraged the holder to develop the property by insuring his opportunity to benefit from development and to recapture his investment in it. For similar reasons recent decisions have held that, because the management of condominium developments has a valid interest not only in securing the occupancy of the units but also in protecting the ownership of the common areas and the underlying fee, its preemptive rights to repurchase units before sale to third parties should be excepted from the operation of the rule. . . . Finally, Bruken claims that there is a "public interest" exception to the rule prohibiting remote vesting and it urges us to adopt that exception and apply it here (see, Southeastern Pa. Transp. Auth. v. Philadelphia Transp. Co., 426 Pa. 377, 233 A.2d 15). In the Southeastern Pa. Transp. Auth. case, the court enforced an otherwise invalid option to permit a municipal agency to acquire facilities to insure continued mass transportation services in the Philadelphia area. The holding is said to rest upon the rationale that government is similar to a charity and thus not subject to the rule against remote vesting (see, Note, Southeastern Pennsylvania Transportation Authority v. Philadelphia Transportation Co., The Rule Against Perpetuities—Does the Rule Apply to an Option to Purchase Held by a Municipality, 72 Dick. L. Rev. 651, 660, 661).

Implicit in these decisions is a recognition that although preemptive rights unlimited in duration violate the rule against remote vesting they do so only marginally and that application of the rule, because of its inflexibility, may operate to invalidate legitimate transactions. This is so particularly in commercial and governmental activities because neither "lives in being" nor "twenty one years" are periods which are relevant to business or governmental affairs. In such cases the need to insure free alienability is served more effectively if the validity of the preemptive right is assessed by applying the common-law rule prohibiting unreasonable restraints (see, Leach, Perpetuities in a Nutshell, 51 Harv. L. Rev. 638, 660-661; Leach, op. cit., 73 Harv. L. Rev., at 1320; Berg, Long-Term Options and the Rule Against Perpetuities, 37 Cal. L. Rev. 1, 21-22; Simes and Smith, op. cit. § 1154, at 64).

This case illustrates the point. Application of the rule against remote vesting here would defeat the policies underlying the rule because it would invalidate an agreement which promoted the use and development of the property while, at the same time, imposing only a minor impediment to free transferability. Through its agreement with Pennsylvania Railroad, the State advanced its objective, to obtain a substantial reduction in the price it paid to acquire the assets of the Long Island Railroad property, assets the State needed to maintain commuter service to the approximately 260,000 passengers of the New York City and Long Island area who used the transportation facilities of the Long Island Railroad daily. It had no long-term interest in the freight yard property or in the air rights conveyed to Pennsylvania Railroad; it was confronted with the possibility that the Long Island Railroad, previously bankrupt, subsequently reorganized, and in serious financial condition in 1966, might shortly be dissolved. The State's interest was preservation of the passenger transportation facility and it intended to keep the freight yard property only long enough to evaluate the need for the lots in conjunction with operating the commuter service. This agreement gave MTA the opportunity to do so. In the meantime the State conveyed the air rights to Pennsylvania, granting it the necessary easements to develop those rights, and a preemptive right for the future acquisition of the ground rights, so that the interests in air and ground rights could eventually be reunited. The transfer permitted the parties to put both properties, the railroad and the freight yard, to their maximum productive use, a benefit which far outweighed any public interest served by automatic invalidation of the preemptive right to the lots solely because of remote vesting of Delbay's interest. Moreover, because the parties were a State authority and a national transportation corporation engaged in a widely publicized transaction—not private citizens whose interest might never be discovered with the passage of time—it did so without unknown limitations on the title which could inhibit future property transfers. Manifestly whatever obstacles there are to the disposition of property by restrictions such as this are best regulated by the rule against unreasonable restraints on alienation so that the utility of the restriction may be considered, rather than by the inflexible rule against remote vesting.

III. Under the rule prohibiting unreasonable restraints on alienation, the validity of the preemptive right rests on its reasonableness, judged by its duration, price and purpose. The duration of the restraint is not measured by the life of the preemptive right. The rule does not condemn restrictions on transfer, i.e., provisions which postpone sale during the option period; it condemns only the "effective prohibition against transferability itself" (Allen v. Biltmore Tissue Corp., 2 N.Y.2d 534, 542, 161 N.Y.S.2d 418, 141 N.E.2d 812, supra [emphasis in original]). Indeed, dusty New York authority holds that preemptive rights may be perpetual (see, De Peyster v. Michael, 6 N.Y. 467, supra; Jackson ex dem. Lewis v. Schutz, 18 Johns 174 [Spencer, Ch. J., concurring]; Overbagh v. Patrie, 8 Barb. 28, affd. 6 N.Y. 510; see also, Schnebly, Restraints Upon the Alienation of Legal Interests: III, 44 Yale L. J. 1380, 1392-1394). Thus, the reasonableness of Delbay's preemptive right must be determined not by considering the 99-year term, but by considering the 90-day period during which the right could be exercised after the MTA decided to sell.

Reasonableness also depends on price, for the method by which the price is set can be critical in determining whether a preemptive right unlawfully restrains transfers. When the holder has a right to purchase at a fixed price, or at a price less than that offered in the market, it is likely to involve a sacrifice by the owner if he wishes to transfer the property, thus becoming a far more serious interference with alienability (see, Simes and Smith, op. cit. § 1154, at 62-63). A preemptive right, however, usually will not be unlawful when conditioned on payment of market value or a sum equal to a third-party offer (see, Restatement of Property § 413 [1944]; and see generally, Ann., 40 A.L.R.3d 920 § 4). Market value, in some instances, may be less than sale price, but a market value fixed by arbitrators compelled to consider the price a willing seller would accept from a willing buyer at the time of sale can hardly be unreasonable, as a matter of law, notwithstanding the separate ownership of air and ground rights.

Finally, as we have stated, the preemptive right in this case clearly served a beneficial purpose and given its reasonableness in terms of duration and price, it should be enforced.

In sum, we hold that the rule against remote vesting does not apply to preemptive rights in commercial and governmental transactions, that their validity is to be judged by applying the rule against unreasonable restraints and that the preemptive right granted Delbay by the State was under all the circumstances a reasonable restriction on the alienability of the freight yard lots.

Accordingly, the order of the Appellate Division should be affirmed. Question certified answered in the affirmative.

d. Options Appurtenant to Leasehold Interests

Options to renew a lease are not subject to the Rule Against Perpetuities. By the majority American view, options to purchase the property are also immune when held by the lessee of the premises. Thus options appurtenant to leaseholds, even those that are exercisable beyond a life in being plus 21 years, are valid.

e. Leases to Commence in the Future

A lease that is to commence at a fixed time in the future is valid even if the fixed time is or might be beyond a life in being plus 21 years. This is the view of the small handful of cases in which the issue has been decided. These leases are analogous to springing executory interests that are not subject to any contingency.

> *Example 17.21:* (1) A, the owner of Blackacre, leases the premises to B for 30 years. Shortly thereafter A leases the premises to C for 10 years commencing on the expiration of B's term.
> (2) A, the owner of Blackacre, leases the premises to C for 10 years commencing 30 years from date.
> C's lease is valid in both cases.

A lease to commence in the future, if subject to a contingency, is invalid if the contingency might occur beyond a life in being plus 21 years. There has been considerable litigation concerning the validity of so-called "on completion" leases—leases to commence on the completion of a building. These leases would be clearly valid if the lessor was obligated to complete the building within 21 years, but in the absence of an explicit obligation of this sort, some courts have held the lease to be invalid. See, e.g., Southern Airways Co. v. DeKalb County, 115 S.E.2d 207 (Ga. Ct. App. 1960), rev'd on other grounds, 116 S.E.2d 602 (Ga. 1960). Other courts, however, have upheld these leases on the theory that the lessee's interest was vested from the beginning (see Isen v. Giant Foods, Inc., 295 F.2d 136 (D.C. Cir. 1960)), or on the theory that there was an implicit obligation to complete the building within a reasonable time (see Wong v. DiGrazia, 60 Cal.2d 525, 386 P.2d 817 (1963); Singer Co. v. Makad, Inc., 213 Kan. 725, 518 P.2d 493 (1974)).

f. Top Leases and Top Deeds

A common practice in the oil and gas industry is for the owner of land to lease or deed to another, usually an oil company, a working interest or a royalty interest that is to last for a period of a time certain *and* as long thereafter as oil, gas, or other minerals are produced in paying quantities. See 2 H. Williams & C. Meyers, Oil and Gas Law § 322 (1985). The landowner's retained interest in either type of arrangement has been held to be a possibility of reverter, with the lessee or grantee taking a defeasible estate—a fee simple determinable. See Caruthers v. Leonard, 254 S.W. 779 (Tex. Comm'n App. 1923) (lease); York v. Kenilworth Oil Co., 614 S.W.2d 468 (Tex. Civ. App. 1981) (lease); Peveto v. Starkey, 645 S.W.2d 770 (Tex. 1982) (deed). Possibilities of reverter are excluded from the common-law Rule Against Perpetuities. See, e.g., Bagby v. Bredthauer, 627 S.W.2d 190 (Tex. Civ. App. 1981). They are also assignable in many states (see York v. Kenilworth Oil Co., supra; Bagby v. Bredthauer, supra), and since the interest remains a possibility of reverter in the hands of the assignee, the exclusion from the common-law Rule continues even after the assignment (see Bagby v. Bredthauer, supra; Murphy v. Jamison, 117 S.W.2d 127 (Tex. Civ. App. 1938)).

A common commercial practice in the oil and gas industry is to create so-called top leases and top deeds. This type of a lease or deed takes effect on the expiration of a bottom lease or a bottom deed. A bottom lease or a bottom deed is a lease or a deed of the type described in the preceding paragraph. Like the bottom lease or bottom deed, the top lease or top deed is also defeasible—i.e., it is also for the period of a time certain *and* as long thereafter as oil, gas, or other minerals are produced in paying quantities. The validity of this type of an arrangement was the subject of the following case.

Peveto v. Starkey
645 S.W.2d 770 (Tex. 1982)

SONDOCK, J. . . . A.G. Jones and his wife conveyed an undivided three-fourths term royalty interest[78] in several tracts of land to Peveto. The primary term of the royalty deed was "for a period of fifteen years" from April 23, 1960, and "as long thereafter as oil, gas or other minerals, or either of them is produced . . . in paying commercial quantities." . . .

In November of 1973, Jones conveyed to Starkey, by top deed, a three-fourths term royalty interest. This royalty deed was for a primary term of ten years and "as long thereafter as oil, gas or other minerals, or either of them, is produced . . . in paying commercial quantities." The deed contained the following typed provision:

This grant shall become effective only on the expiration of the above described Royalty Deed to R.L. Peveyto [sic] dated April 23, 1960.

---

78. The three-fourths term royalty interest was conveyed by two identical deeds. One was for an undivided one-fourth and the other for an undivided one-half interest. Reference to "the deed" includes both instruments.

Four months before Peveto's deed was to expire, Jones and Peveto executed another instrument. This instrument purported to extend the primary term of Peveto's deed from fifteen years to twenty-five years. . . .

Peveto . . . argues the royalty deed to Starkey violates the Rule against Perpetuities. Article I, section 26 of the Texas Constitution expressly provides: "Perpetuities . . . are contrary to the genius of a free government and shall never be allowed. . . ." Tex.Const. Art. I, § 26. The Rule states that no interest is valid unless it must vest, if at all, within twenty-one years after the death of some life or lives in being at the time of the conveyance. The Rule requires that a challenged conveyance be viewed as of the date the instrument is executed, and it is void if by any possible contingency the grant or devise could violate the Rule.

The deed from Jones conveying the term royalty interest to Starkey was a standard form nonparticipating royalty deed. The printed portion of the granting clause conveyed a presently vested three-fourths royalty interest. However, following the property description, the parties inserted: "this grant shall become effective only upon the expiration of [Peveto's] . . . Deed. . . ." This additional clause causes the Jones-Starkey deed to violate the Rule.

The interest Jones conveyed to Peveto by the first term royalty deed was a determinable fee. This Court defined a determinable fee to be "an interest which may continue forever, but the estate is liable to be determined, without the aid of a conveyance, by some act or event circumscribing its continuance or extent." Stephens County v. Mid-Kansas Oil & Gas Co., 113 Tex. 160, 254 S.W. 290, 295 (1923).

All parties agree the deed from Jones to Starkey is unambiguous. Thus, the intent of the parties must be determined from the four corners of the instrument. The rights of the parties are governed by the language used and the choice of designating words is of controlling importance. The words used here postpone the vesting of Starkey's interest until some uncertain future date. A grant "effective only upon" the termination of a determinable fee cannot vest until the prior interest has terminated. A determinable fee could continue forever, and may not terminate within the time period prescribed by the Rule. The words "effective only upon" created a springing executory interest in Starkey which may not vest within the period of the Rule; therefore, the deed is void.

Because the restrictive language used in the Jones-Starkey deed prevented the grant of the interest from Jones to Starkey from vesting in interest until after Peveto's interest terminated, and since this might not occur within the period prescribed by the Rule, we hold that the instrument violates the Rule against Perpetuities.

Accordingly, we reverse the judgment of the courts below. Judgment is here rendered that the deed from Jones to Starkey is void.

6. Possibilities of Reverter and Rights of Entry

Possibilities of reverter and rights of entry (also known as rights of re-entry, rights of entry for condition broken, and powers of termination) are generally exempt from the common-law Rule Against Perpetuities. See Brown v. Independent Baptist Church, 325 Mass. 645, 91 N.E.2d 922 (1950), supra p. 1001. As rather vividly demonstrated by Peveto v. Starkey,[79] above, their nonreversionary counterpart—the executory interest that follows either a fee simple determinable or a fee simple subject to an executory limitation—is subject to the common-law Rule. When the grantor, Jones, conveyed the royalty deed to Peveto, Jones retained a possibility of reverter; hence, Jones's retained interest was exempt from the Rule. What interest did Jones subsequently convey, by top deed, to Starkey? The classification of Starkey's interest was crucial to its validity. If, as some commentators have urged, Jones's conveyance to Starkey was part of Jones's possibility of reverter—a partial conveyance of a possibility of reverter—Starkey's interest should have been upheld. The Supreme Court of Texas, however, held that the second conveyance created a springing executory interest, which violated the Rule. It would appear that the Supreme Court of Texas made a correct judgment, for when the owner of a possibility of reverter carves out and transfers to another an interest that can divest her or his possibility of reverter, the interest carved out and transferred is a springing executory interest.

By statute in some states, possibilities of reverter and rights of entry expire if they do not vest within a specified period of years (such as 30 years).

Although USRAP does not subject possibilities of reverter and rights of entry to the Statutory Rule or impose a time limit on the duration of these interests, the Official Comment to section 4 urges states enacting USRAP to consider enacting a provision limiting the duration of these interests to a certain period of years, such as 30, if the state has not already done so.

---

79. See also Proprietors of the Church in Brattle Square v. Grant and First Universalist Society v. Boland, supra pp. 887-89.

PART F. A DIVERGENT "RULE AGAINST PERPETUITIES"—PROHIBITION OF THE SUSPENSION OF THE POWER OF ALIENATION

The rule we have been thinking of as the Rule Against Perpetuities is a rule against remotely vesting future interests. Prior to the turn of this century, it was not altogether clear that that rule was *the* rule against perpetuities. A divergent form of the rule existed, called the rule against the suspension of the power of alienation (the anti-suspension rule). In Avern v. Lloyd, L.R. 5 Eq. 383 (1868), the court held that if living persons can together convey a fee, the disposition cannot be invalid, regardless of the time of possible vesting; validity merely required that the power of alienation not be suspended beyond a life in being plus 21 years. To illustrate the difference, consider these dispositions, which would violate the rule against remotely vesting future interests:

> *Example 17.22:* G conveys land "to A and his heirs, but if the land ever ceases to be used for residential purposes, to B and her heirs."
> Because A and B can join together and convey a fee in the land, the power of alienation is not suspended, and the disposition is valid.

> *Example 17.23:* G conveys land "to A and her heirs, but if the land ever ceases to be used for residential purposes, to B and his heirs if B is then living; if not, to B's heirs at law."
> Because B's heirs at law have an interest in the land, an unascertained class, A and B cannot join together and convey a fee in the land. However, B's heirs at law will be ascertained no later than at B's death, a life in being, so this disposition also is valid under the suspension rule.

Professor Gray, in his book on the Rule Against Perpetuities that was first published in 1886, argued strongly that the anti-suspension rule was not *the* rule against perpetuities—the rule against perpetuities was the rule against remotely vesting future interests. Gray won the battle, for the *Avern* decision was disapproved in In re Hargreaves, 43 Ch. Div. 401 (C.A. 1890), and henceforth the rule against remotely vesting future interests became *the* Rule Against Perpetuities in both the United States and England.

Nevertheless, in the United States, statutory support for the anti-suspension rule was already in place, and so that rule was not obliterated altogether; in fact, even today, this is the rule in a few states, as we shall see.

The source of the legislative anti-suspension rule was the New York property reform legislation of 1830. That legislation, including its anti-suspension provision, spread to a number of other states (in some instances with significant modifications). Experience with the anti-suspension provision, however, was not a happy one. The original New York legislation was quite restrictive; it allowed no tack-on 21-year period, and it allowed the power of alienation to be suspended only "during the continuance of not more than two lives in being," not multiple lives.

The quantity of litigation in New York, produced by the necessity for construction of the original statute and efforts to avoid the severity of the perpetuities period it imposed, reflects against the practicability of the legislative doctrine. It has long been the consensus of opinion that the New York effort at perpetuities reform was misguided. As indicated below, a retreat is in full progress, which takes the form either of a reenactment of the common-law Rule in some states that had copied the New York legislation, or in amendments, as in New York itself, which have substantially the same effect.

The current New York legislation is set forth below. You will note that the current statute codifies both the common-law Rule Against Perpetuities and a much-liberalized version of the anti-suspension rule, under which the common-law period of multiple lives plus a 21-year tack-on period is allowed. In effect, the anti-suspension rule has been rendered nearly meaningless, since almost any disposition that violates the anti-suspension rule also violates the common-law Rule.

New York Estates, Powers & Trusts Law

§ 9-1.1. *Rule against perpetuities.*

(a) (1) The absolute power of alienation is suspended when there are no persons in being by whom an absolute fee or estate in possession can be conveyed or transferred.

(2) Every present or future estate shall be void in its creation which shall suspend the absolute power of alienation by any limitation or condition for a longer period than lives in being at the creation of the estate and a term of not more than twenty-one years. Lives in being shall include a child conceived before the creation of the estate but born thereafter. In no case shall the lives measuring the permissible period be so designated or so numerous as to make proof of their end unreasonably difficult.

(b) No estate in property shall be valid unless it must vest, if at all, not later than twenty-one years after one or more lives in being at the creation of the estate and any period of gestation involved. In no case shall lives measuring the permissible period of vesting be so designated or so numerous as to make proof of their end unreasonably difficult.

––––

Suspension Legislation In Other States. As noted above, the original New York legislation spread to other states, in some instances with only minor amendments, in other instances with rather significant changes. The principal difference in this regard was between those states that adopted the "two-lives" period for suspension (Arizona, Michigan, Minnesota, and Wisconsin) and those that substituted a "multiple-lives" period like that under the common-law Rule (California, Idaho, Indiana, Montana, North Dakota, Oklahoma, and South Dakota).

The anti-suspension rule has been repealed or in effect abrogated in all the above states except Idaho (suspension must be restricted to lives in being plus 25 years, modified by a provision allowing reformation of dispositions that violate the suspension rule), South Dakota (suspension must be restricted to lives in being plus 30 years, modified by a wait-and-see element and a provision that declares that there is no suspension of the power of alienation if the trustee has a power of sale), and Wisconsin (suspension must be restricted to lives in being plus 30 years, modified by a provision that declares that there is no suspension of the power of alienation if the trustee has a power of sale). The latter have the anti-suspension rule as their only restriction on perpetuities. The Rule Against Perpetuities does not exist in these states.

EXTERNAL REFERENCES. See Restatement 2d of Property, Statutory Note to § 1.1; Am. L. Prop. chs. 6 and 7; Simes & Smith on Future Interests ch. 41.

PART G. USE OF THE PERPETUITY PERIOD TO CONTROL TRUST INDESTRUCTIBILITY AND INCOME ACCUMULATION

The type of vesting required by the Rule Against Perpetuities is vesting *in interest*, not vesting *in possession*. Consequently, the Rule does not directly limit the *duration* of a trust. A trust can, theoretically, endure beyond the 21-year period following the death of the validating life or, if the wait-and-see modification has been adopted and applies, beyond the permissible vesting period. In effect, however, because of the application of a related rule, the continuance of a trust beyond the perpetuity period can occur only by inaction of the beneficiaries. And, should the beneficiaries allow the trust to continue, another related rule requires the trustee to disgorge the trust's income; no income can therefore be accumulated for future distribution.

1. Permissible Duration of Indestructibility of Trusts

The beneficiaries of a trust can join together to compel the trust's termination and the distribution of its assets, unless the trust is an indestructible trust. An indestructible trust is a trust in which the settlor has expressly or impliedly restrained its premature termination. See supra Chapter 12, Part B.

Restatement 2d of Property

§ 2.1. Duration of Trust. A trust created in a donative transfer, which has not terminated within the period of the rule against perpetuities as applied to such trust, shall continue until the trust terminates in accordance with its terms, except that a trust, other than a charitable trust, may be terminated at any time after the period of the rule against perpetuities expires by a written agreement of all of the beneficiaries of the trust delivered to the trustee, which agreement informs the trustee that the trust is terminated and gives the trustee directions as to the distribution of the trust property.

———

Duration of Indestructibility under USRAP. Under USRAP, the applicable perpetuity period is 90 years with respect to trusts whose validity is governed by the wait-and-see element of section 1(a)(2), (b)(2), or (c)(2). See USRAP § 1, Comment Part G.

———

External References. Restatement 2d of Trusts § 62 comment o; Restatement 2d of Property, Legislative Note & Reporter's Note; Gray on Perpetuities § 121; Scott on Trusts § 62.10(2); Simes & Smith on Future Interests §§ 1391-93.

2. Accumulations of Income

Restatement 2d of Property

§ 2.2 Accumulation of Trust Income.
   (1) An accumulation of trust income under a noncharitable trust created in a donative transfer is valid until the period of the rule against perpetuities expires with respect to such trust and any accumulation thereafter is invalid.
   (2) An accumulation of trust income under a charitable trust created in a donative transfer is valid to the extent the accumulation is reasonable in the light of the purposes, facts and circumstances of the particular trust.
   (3) The trust income released by an invalid accumulation shall be paid to such recipients and in such shares and in such manner as most closely effectuates the transferor's manifested plan of distribution.
   (4) An accumulation of trust income occurs when part or all of the current income of the trust can be and is retained in the trust, or can be and is so applied by the trustee as to increase the fund subject to the trust, and such retention or application is not found to be merely in the course of judicious management of the trust.

Comment:

a. Historical Note: Prior to the death of Peter Thellusson in July, 1797, directions or authorizations to accumulate income were seldom involved in litigation. Probably they were seldom made. Certainly such provisions were not frequently made so as to call for an accumulation of long duration. Thus, the necessity for any rule specifically regulating their creation had not arisen. The will of Peter Thellusson raised the problem in a dramatic manner. He had devised the major part of his very large estate to his eldest male lineal descendant to be ascertained at the end of a period measured by nine lives in being and had directed that the income of his assets should be accumulated from the time of his death to the time of the ascertainment of such ultimate taker. This will was held valid by the House of Lords in Thellusson v. Woodford [11 Ves.Jr. 112, 32 Eng. Reg. 1030 (1805)] and the opinions rendered by the lower and higher courts in this case laid the foundation for what has since been the rule against accumulations. In the House of Lords it was declared that "a testator can direct the rents and profits to be accumulated for that period during which he may direct that the title shall not vest, and the property shall remain unalienable." In England, the presentation of this case in the lower courts had led to the enactment of a statute [39 and 40 Geo. III c. 98 (1800)] considerably more restrictive than the rule affirmed in the Thellusson case. The subsequent English decisions are largely based on the modifications introduced by this statute. In most of the jurisdictions in the United States the law concerning accumulations is still found only in court decisions. The statutory ingredient in the American law of accumulations is set forth in the Statutory Note to Section 2.2. Since the statutes deal only with some aspects of the problem, such as the permissible period, the allowable exceptions to the statute's applicability, and the disposition of released income, a large part of the law of accumulations is non-statutory.

b. Tax considerations. The widespread use of accumulation trusts has been encouraged by the federal income tax advantage of having trust income taxed to the trust as a separate income tax entity in years when the tax rate applicable to the trust was lower than the tax rate applicable to trust beneficiaries to whom the income might be distributed. Also, income accumulated in the trust could be made available to future generations without a federal gift tax or federal estate tax being imposed on the current generation of beneficiaries under the trust. The development of the so-called throwback rule and the extension of its reach by the Tax Reform Act of 1969, with some modifications thereof in the Tax Reform Act of 1976, have undermined the utilization of accumulation trusts to effect significantly, in the long run, federal income tax savings. The introduction in the Tax Reform Act of 1976 of a generation-skipping tax has curtailed to some extent the avoidance of federal gift and estate taxes as the beneficial enjoyment of the trust property moves from one generation of trust beneficiaries to another. Nevertheless, trusts under which the trustee has discretion to pay out or accumulate trust income continue to have substantial attractions for use in estate planning.

c. Tax accounting income contrasted with trust accounting income. Income from a tax accounting standpoint is a broader concept than income from a trust accounting standpoint. Realized capital gain is income from a tax accounting standpoint, but is principal from a trust accounting standpoint. Income in respect of a decedent collected by a trust becomes principal of the trust, but is income for tax purposes. There can be an accumulation of income for the purposes of this section only if income from a trust accounting standpoint is retained in the trust.

d. Discretionary accumulations compared with mandatory accumulations. Most accumulation trusts give the trustee discretion to accumulate the income or pay it out to some trust beneficiary. The discretion will usually relate not only to current income, but also to income accumulated in past years. A mandatory accumulation trust does not provide the desirable flexibility to meet changing conditions that may affect the needs of the beneficiaries. Its use is most appropriate when the trust fund has to be built up to some larger amount to effectuate the purpose the trust is designed to accomplish.

e. Undesirable social consequences provided by accumulations of trust income. Accumulations of trust income do not keep the trust income from use in the economy because such income will be invested in some manner and not taken completely out of circulation. The fiduciary restrictions on trust investments, however, mean that there is not the same freedom of the use of such income in the economy in the hands of the trustee as there would be in the hands of the trust beneficiary.

Accumulations of trust income tend to build up the control of increased amounts of wealth in fewer and fewer people. However, the impact of the higher income tax rates slows down substantially the build-up process referred to.

Accumulations do tend to perpetuate the policies of the transferor who may have established the trust and, as in the case of the rule against perpetuities in relation to vesting, some limit on the period of time such policies should remain in control is desirable.

PART H. RELATED RULES OF SOCIAL POLICY—VALIDITY OF RESTRAINTS ON PERSONAL CONDUCT

In addition to the Rule Against Perpetuities and the rules relating to the duration of the indestructibility of trusts and the duration of accumulations of income, there are a variety of other rules that limit the dead hand. These rules prevent the transferor of property from conditioning her or his benefaction on certain types of personal conduct of the beneficiary. We quote below this series of rules, as set forth in the Restatement 2d of Property.

Restatement 2d of Property

§ 5.1. *Basis for Determining Validity of Restraints on Personal Conduct.* Unless contrary to public policy or violative of some rule of law, a provision in a donative transfer which is designed to prevent the acquisition or retention of an interest in property in the event of any failure on the part of the transferee to comply with a restraint on personal conduct is valid.

§ 5.2 *Effect of Impossibility of Performance.* Impossibility of performance of the terms of a provision in a donative transfer, otherwise valid under the general rule stated in § 5.1, excuses lack of performance if, and only if, this result is the appropriately ascertained intent of the person imposing the restraint.

§ 6.1 *Restraints on Any First Marriage.*

(1) Except as stated in subsection (2), an otherwise effective restriction in a donative transfer which is designed to prevent the acquisition or retention of an interest in property by the transferee in the event of any first marriage of the transferee is invalid. If the restriction is invalid, the donative transfer takes effect as though the restriction had not been imposed.

(2) If the dominant motive of the transferor is to provide support until marriage, the restraint is normally valid.

§ 6.2 *Restraints on Some First Marriages.* An otherwise effective restriction in a donative transfer designed to prevent the acquisition or retention of an interest in the event of some, but not all, first marriages of the transferee is valid if, and only if, under the circumstances, the restraint does not unreasonably limit the transferee's opportunity to marry. If the restriction is invalid, the donative transfer takes effect as though the restriction had not been imposed.

§ 6.3 *Restraints on Remarriage.* An otherwise effective restriction in a donative transfer which is designed to prevent the acquisition or retention of an interest in property by the transferee in the event of the remarriage of the transferee is valid only if:

(1) The transferee was the spouse of the transferor, or

(2) The restraint is reasonable under all the circumstances.

§ 7.1 *Provisions Encouraging Separation or Divorce.* An otherwise effective restriction in a donative transfer which is designed to permit the acquisition or retention of an interest in property by the transferee only in the event of a separation or divorce from the transferee's spouse is invalid, unless the dominant motive of the transferor is to provide support in the event of separation or divorce, in which case the restraint is valid.

§ 7.2 *Provisions Detrimentally Affecting Family Relationship.* An otherwise effective provision in a donative transfer which is designed to permit the acquisition or retention of an interest in property only in the event of either the continuance of an existing separation or the creation of a future separation of a family relationship, other than that of husband and wife, is invalid where the dominant motive of the transferor was to promote such a separation.

§ 8.1 *Provisions Concerning Religion.* An otherwise effective provision in a donative transfer which is designed to prevent the acquisition or retention of property on account of adherence to or rejection of certain religious beliefs or practices on the part of the transferee is valid.

§ 8.2 *Restraints Against Personal Habits.* An otherwise effective provision in a donative transfer which is designed to prevent the acquisition or retention of an interest in property on account of the transferee acquiring or persisting in specified personal habits is valid.

§ 8.3 *Restraints Concerning Education or Occupation.* An otherwise effective provision in a donative transfer which is designed to prevent the acquisition or retention of an interest in property on account of a failure on the part of the beneficiary to acquire or continue an education or occupation is valid.

§ 9.1 *Restraints on Contests.* An otherwise effective provision in a will or other donative transfer, which is designed to prevent the acquisition or retention of an interest in property in the event there is a contest of the validity of the document transferring the interest or an attack on a particular provision of the document, is valid, unless there was probable cause for making the contest or attack.

§ 9.2 *Restraints on Attacks on Fiduciaries.* An otherwise effective provision in a will or other donative transfer, which is designed to prevent the acquisition or retention of an interest in property in the event the propriety of the performance of the fiduciary with respect to the administration of the transferred property is questioned in a legal proceeding, is valid, unless the beneficiary had probable cause for questioning the fiduciary's performance.

§ 10.1 *Restraints on Enforcing Obligations of Transferor or Transferor's Estate.* An otherwise effective provision in a will or other donative transfer, which is designed to prevent the acquisition or retention of an interest in property if there is an attempt to enforce an independent obligation of the transferor or the transferor's estate, is valid.

§ 10.2 *Restraints on Asserting Right to Other Property Owned or Disposed of by Transferor.* An otherwise effective provision in a will or other donative transfer which imposes a condition precedent to the interest of a beneficiary that the transfer, if accepted, is in lieu of an interest in other property owned or disposed of by the transferor, is valid.

DIVISION FOUR
ADMINISTRATION

Chapter 18. Fiduciary Administration

FIDUCIARY ADMINISTRATION

In this Chapter, we discuss selected aspects of fiduciary administration. We concentrate on the fiduciary relationships created when a person becomes a property fiduciary—a personal representative of a decedent's estate, a conservator or guardian of a disabled person's estate, or a trustee. While other relationships, such as attorney and client, principal and agent, corporate officer and stockholder, partner and joint venturer, are also conventionally labelled "fiduciary,"[1] the legal responsibilities imposed on property fiduciaries tend to be more specific and more onerous. Another difference between the fiduciary roles examined here and others is that non-corporate property fiduciaries are more likely to be unaware of the legal implications of the positions they have accepted. Friends and relatives often agree to act as executor or trustee simply to be helpful.

---

1. For general discussions of fiduciary law and obligations, see Frankel, Fiduciary Law, 71 Calif. L. Rev. 795 (1983); Weinrib, The Fiduciary Obligation, 25 U. Tor. L.J. 1 (1975).

PART A. INTRODUCTION: FIDUCIARY ADMINISTRATION OF ESTATES AND TRUSTS

By way of background to the substantive rules regulating property fiduciaries, we first survey the process of administering estates and trusts, focusing particularly on judicial supervision of the three types of property fiduciaries: estate personal representatives, guardians and conservators, and trustees.

1. Personal Representatives

Statutory References: *1990 UPC §§ 1-403, 3-107, -108, -701, -714, -715, -801, -803, -909, -1004, -1006*

Historical Background. After the 1540 Statute of Wills made devises of land possible, testate and intestate devolution of land occurred without special procedures. Title to land passed at death directly to the devisee or heir. The devisee or heir took free of the decedent's debts. Disputes over succession were resolved in actions at law.

As to personal property, there was an office resembling a probate court called the "ordinary" (a judge of the ecclesiastical court), which had authority to accept proof of due execution of wills of personal property and to appoint administrators of intestate personal assets. Executors and administrators were supposed to collect the assets, pay just claims against the decedent, and distribute whatever remained to legatees or distributees. In the absence of controversy, there were no further proceedings once the ordinary had approved a will or appointed an administrator.

American Probate Systems. In the American colonies, the authority of the English ordinary was disbursed among various officials, including courts, legislative creations, and governors' designees. Gradually, these various offices evolved into special courts.

Today, specialized probate courts typically are inferior courts. Appeals usually take the form of de novo proceedings in trial courts of general jurisdiction. In some states, these courts are staffed by elected persons who need not be lawyers. The trend in the states east of the Rockies has been toward more powerful, lawyer-staffed, separate tribunals of restricted subject-matter jurisdiction that includes the probate functions of the English ordinary and chancellor. The California model, widely emulated in the West, makes probate jurisdiction the business of a special docket or division of the trial court of general jurisdiction. In Pennsylvania, a probate official known as the Register of Wills issues papers opening estates, while a court known as the Orphans Court handles other aspects of probate jurisdiction. In New York, the specialized court handling probate matters is called the Surrogate's Court and the judge is called the Surrogate.

Over time, American probate courts have tended to exercise a style of supervision over decedents' estates that is overly formal. A fully adjudicated distribution order is probably unnecessary in most cases. Most estates pass without controversy to a sole surviving heir or a small group of adults who are eager to expedite estate settlement and to release the fiduciary.[2] Nevertheless, personal representatives cannot shortcut mandatory closing procedures. If they do, they are subject to possible sanction by the probate court. The resulting costs and delays may explain the popularity of probate avoidance devices we studied supra Chapter 7.

The Uniform Probate Code was originally drafted in 1969 in response to widely publicized criticisms of typical probate systems. See Wellman, The Uniform Probate Code: A Possible Answer to Probate Avoidance, 44 Ind. L.J. 191 (1969). Article III of the Code, covering probate of wills and administration of decedents' estates, was designed to permit estates of all sizes and asset mixes to be settled with as little procedure as possible. Article IV, devoted to estates located in two or more jurisdictions, permits personal representatives appointed in the decedent's domicile to unify estates[3] for administration purposes merely by filing copies of the domiciliary probate and appointment orders in the local probate office, thereby gaining the powers of a locally appointed personal representative.

UPC Procedures. Under the UPC, probate jurisdiction is assigned to a court that has the stature of a trial court of general jurisdiction, in terms of the qualifications of the judge, the finality of its orders, and the range of matters it may consider. The Code establishes the office of "registrar," to be occupied by an official who is empowered to probate wills and open estates in "informal" (nonadjudicative) proceedings. Informal proceedings do not involve advance notice to interested persons, hearing, or the

---

2. The probate procedures in a few states permit individuals to avoid court supervised estate administration. The first Texas constitution expressly gave testators the ability to direct that their executors be independent of probate court control after opening of the estate. The "independent executor" device appears to be used routinely by knowledgeable estate planners in Texas. The independent executor device also exists in Washington. In Georgia, a statute permitting testators to direct that their executors be excused from "making inventory or returns" allows testate estates to be administered independently of probate court supervision. Independent administration also exists in practice for testate and intestate estates in some areas where officials who control probates and appointments lack the stature, inclination, or tradition of supervising estates.

3. Non-uniform probate laws tend to force separate administrations in each state where land or other assets belonging to the decedent may be located. Succession to land is governed by the law of situs, meaning that local probate procedures are virtually unavoidable in each state where the decedent owned land. Succession to personal and intangible assets is controlled by the law of the decedent's domicile, but procedural rules protect local creditors, and possessors and controllers of out-of-state assets of a decedent may insist on local appointment of an administrator to whom they can make safe payment or delivery. Enactment of Articles III and IV of the UPC by the situs state means that the domiciliary personal representatives from other states can avoid local administrations in the UPC state by filing copies of letters of authority from domicile and copies of duly probated wills with a probate office at the location of the assets. Following these steps, a personal representative can give marketable title by deed in a sale or distribution without court involvement. For a brief discussion of ancillary administrations with and without the UPC, see Wellman, How the Uniform Probate Code Deals with Estates that Cross State Lines, 5 Real Prop. Prob. & Tr. J. 159 (1970).

presentation of testimony. The registrar responds to a detailed application for probate by an interested person.

An estate is opened by the appointment of a personal representative. The statute directs the personal representative to administer and distribute the estate without further contact with the public probate office. Whether the estate is testate or intestate, the personal representative's powers are the same. Persons interested in estates may request "formal" (adjudicated) proceedings as an alternative to informal probate.

In the absence of binding court orders, estates are settled and titles cleared through UPC limitations and purchaser-protection provisions. Under section 3-108, wills may be probated or contested and estates may be opened within three years after death. Section 3-803 provides that claims against an estate, if not otherwise barred by "non-claim" procedures, are barred one year after the decedent's death. Persons to whom estate assets have been wrongfully distributed remain liable to restore the property or its equivalent value. Under section 3-1006, distributee liability to heirs and devisees ends at the later of three years after the decedent's death or one year after distribution.[4] Purchasers and other third persons who assist or deal with a personal representative for value and in good faith are protected by section 3-714. Personal representatives, acting in good faith and in the best interests of those apparently interested in estates, are protected from liability for acts taken in reliance on informal orders of probate and appointment. Section 3-108 gives a remedy "[w]henever fraud has been perpetrated in connection with any proceeding or in any statement filed under this Code or if fraud is used to avoid or circumvent the provisions or purposes of this Code." Action must be commenced against the perpetrator within two years following discovery of the fraud. Innocent beneficiaries of another's fraud are also liable for restitution, but an action against an innocent recipient must be initiated within five years after commission of the fraudulent act.[5]

The view underlying UPC procedures is that state statutes creating and defining rights in decedents' creditors and successors may impose valid qualifications on such rights as necessary to support a system for prompt settlement of estates without binding adjudications by the courts. The recent decision in Tulsa Professional Collection Services, Inc. v. Pope, 485 U.S. 478 (1988), tests the distinction between limitations in probate statutes that may bar claimants without notice and state action in the form of probate court orders. In Mullane v. Central Hanover Bank & Trust Co., 339 U.S. 306 (1949), the Court held that due process in probate court proceedings required notice reasonably calculated to apprise persons whose interests are affected and that, as to known persons, notice by publication

---

4. Distributee liability to decedents' creditors ends no later than one year after death, a period which may be shortened by use of the short non-claim procedure described infra p. 1108.

5. For a more detailed discussion of UPC's informal proceedings and associated safeguards, see Wellman & Gordon, The Uniform Probate Code: Article III Analyzed in Relation to Changes in the First Nine Enactments, 1975 Ariz. St. L.J. 477.

does not meet this requirement. In *Pope*, an Oklahoma law and implementing court order purported to bar unsecured creditors of an estate if they failed to perfect their claims within a statutory period of two months after publication of notice of the opening of the estate to claims. The procedure was held ineffective to bar a decedent's creditor who was known to, or reasonably ascertainable by, the estate fiduciary. The Court conceded that enactment and enforcement of a "self-executing" statute of limitation does not constitute state action implicating the protections of the due process clause. The Court then observed:

> Here, in contrast, there is significant state action. The probate court is intimately involved throughout, and without that involvement the time bar is never activated. The nonclaim statute becomes operative only after probate proceedings have been commenced in state court. The court must appoint the executor or executrix before notice, which triggers the time bar, can be given. Only after this court appointment is made does the statute provide for any notice. . . . Indeed, in this case, the District Court reinforced the statutory command with an order expressly requiring appellee to "immediately give notice to creditors." The form of the order indicates that such orders are routine. . . . Finally, copies of the notice and an affidavit of publication must be filed with the court. . . . It is only after all of these actions take place that the time period begins to run, and in every one of these actions, the court is intimately involved. This involvement is so pervasive and substantial that it must be considered state action subject to the restrictions of the Fourteenth Amendment.

Prior to *Pope*, most probate codes included "short" non-claim time bars allowing creditors from two to six months after the opening of an estate to present in writing claims for allowance or disallowance. In general, pre-*Pope* codes reflected the view that creditors need not be given actual notice of a pending estate administration, but were on their own to ascertain a debtor's death. Most codes also contain "long" non-claim provisions barring claims against unadministered assets after periods ranging from one to several years after the decedent's death. See Falender, Notice to Creditors on Estate Proceedings: What Process is Due?, 63 N.C.L. Rev. 659 (1985).

Are UPC non-claim provisions subject to the *Pope* decision? It is arguable that UPC's "long" non-claim statute, which is unrelated to any notice to creditors and was shortened in 1989 from three years to one year after death, is safe from a *Pope* challenge on the ground that it is a "self-executing" statute of limitations.[6] It is also arguable that UPC's "short" non-claim statute operates independently of state action. The Code's short non-claim provisions are keyed to published notice to creditors, who are given four months after first publication to present claims. See UPC § 3-803.

Publication of notice by the personal representative is mandatory. The duty to do so arises upon acceptance of appointment (§§ 3-701, 3-801), but

---

6. For an opposing view, see Reutlinger, State Action, Due Process, and the New Non-claim Statutes: Can No Notice Be Good Notice If Some Notice is Not?, 24 Real Prop. Prob. & Tr. J. 433 (1990).

an informal proceeding seeking issuance of letters ends with an order making or declining to make an appointment (§ 3-107(4)). The appointing office has no power to sanction a personal representative who neglects to publish. As a result, personal representatives control whether publication and the start of the four month non-claim period will occur. Claims not barred because of a personal representative's failure to publish notice may be barred by limitations running prior to death (§ 3-802) or by the long non-claim period running from death. Until barred, a claim may be pursued against an estate or its distributees (§ 3-1004).

Because of uncertainty regarding the state action question posed by *Pope* as applied to the UPC,[7] the Uniform Law Commissioners approved two modest amendments to the UPC in 1989. One shortened the "long" non-claim period from three years to one year after death. This amendment benefits persons interested in unadministered estates and estates administered without the use of the short non-claim procedure; it hastens the elimination of undischarged claims against a decedent. The other amendment expressly authorizes the use of an optional short non-claim bar operating no earlier than sixty days following actual notice to present claims. The changes do not affect pre-*Pope* Code language purporting to bar known and unknown creditors who are unaware of an administration or fail for other reasons to respond to a published notice to present claims within four months.

If the fact that a state official appoints the personal representative renders the UPC subject to *Pope*, are all acts of a personal representative acts of the state? If so, are UPC's no-notice procedures to secure probate of a will or appointment of a personal representative and related limitations likely to withstand constitutional challenge by an overlooked heir or a devisee claiming under a recently discovered will?

The UPC's basic limitation period expiring three years after death appears to be "self-executing" under *Pope*. Hence, the operation of the Code's informal proceedings may withstand due process challenge.[8]

---

7. A court considering extending the "state action" test to the UPC's short non-claim provision should take account of data indicating that creditors in general are disinterested in the procedural protections traditionally extended to them by probate legislation. See Dunham, The Method, Process and Frequency of Wealth Transmission at Death, 30 U. Chi. L. Rev. 241 (1963); Langbein, The Nonprobate Revolution and the Future of the Law of Succession, 97 Harv. L. Rev. 108 (1984). Hence, costs incurred by imposing new responsibilities upon personal representatives to search for creditors to notify would likely exceed any resulting benefits.

8. For opposing views concerning the constitutional validity of the UPC's informal probate procedures, see Manlin & Martin, Informal Proceedings Under the Uniform Probate Code: Notice and Due Process, 3 U. Mich. J. L. Ref. 38 (1969)(concluding that UPC procedures are constitutional); Note, The Constitutionality of the No-Notice Provisions of the Uniform Probate Code, 60 Minn. L. Rev. 317 (1976).

In Alexander & Pearson, Alternative Models of Ante-Mortem Probate and Procedural Due Process Limitations on Succession, 78 Mich. L. Rev. 89, 107 (1979), the authors argue: "The argument that the entitlement cases apply to probate has a superficial appeal: Succession statutes do explicitly recognize that either the legatees under a will or the heirs at law will assume ownership of the decedent's property. But obviously, despite such statutory provisions, neither category of potential takers can claim present use or enjoyment of the decedent's property. Their interests are wholly prospective and lack recognition as existing property rights.

2. Guardians and Conservators

Statutory References: *1990 UPC §§ 5-207, -209, -309, -409, -423*

Because minor children and incapacitated adults lack competency, they must depend on others for care and property management. All states have judicial procedures for appointing persons to perform these functions. In non-UPC states, the laws providing protective proceedings contemplate two types of guardians: guardian of the person, a fiduciary who is judicially charged with the care and custody of the minor or incapacitated adult, and guardian of the property (or estate), a fiduciary who is responsible for managing assets that a minor or incapacitated adult owns. Under the UPC, a court-appointed "guardian" for a minor or an incapacitated adult is essentially a guardian of the person only, but sections 5-209 and 5-309 confer narrowly limited authority on a guardian to receive and expend funds on behalf of the person under her or his protection. The UPC uses the term "conservator" to refer to a court-appointed fiduciary who is responsible for the estate of a "protected person," who may be a minor or an adult unable to manage business matters. Usually, a UPC conservator has no control of the protected person's custody, but, under section 5-423(a), a conservator whose protected person is an unmarried minor with no parent or court-appointed guardian has the authority of a guardian.

The UPC makes no special provision for a "testamentary conservator." A testator who wants to devise property to a minor or incapacitated devisee can provide management by creating a trust. A UPC conservatorship, which might be necessary if no other protective arrangement has been arranged, offers practically the same advantages as a well-drawn trust except that it involves an initial court appointment, some court supervision, and, in the case of a minor, would end upon the minor's attainment of majority rather than later as might be specified in a trust.

The residency, bond, and court supervision requirement for property fiduciaries under non-UPC statutes resemble those of administrators of intestate estates. The UPC grants considerable managerial powers, protection for purchasers dealing with conservators, and new authority over out-of-state assets to property fiduciaries. Also, an innovative provision, section 5-408, enables a court to approve a proposed plan, such as purchase of an annuity or creation of a trust, as an alternative to protecting an incompetent or disabled person's economic well-being via appointment of a conservator. See Zartman, Planning for Disability, 15 Prob. Notes 11 (Am. Col. of Tr. and Est. Counsel 1989). It remains true, however, that a

---

Indeed, to use the more vivid language of the Supreme Court in [Board of Regents v. Roth, 408 U.S. 564, 577 (1972)], their interests represent nothing more than an abstract desire for the decedent's property or a unilateral expectation of a right to it. For constitutional purposes, a property right arises, if at all, when the inquiry into the existence of a valid will has been completed and the rules of succession have been applied. Only then are the prerequisites of the entitlement cases, particularly justifiable reliance, satisfied. Thus, by the criteria of the entitlement cases themselves, the claim that procedural due process protections extend to probate proceedings—ante-mortem or post mortem—would appear to fail."

well planned, private trust for the protection of property to be managed for a minor or disabled adult generally is preferable to any solution requiring extensive court supervision.

3. Trustees

Statutory References: *1990 UPC §§ 7-101, -102, -103*

Inter-vivos trusts are not subject to judicial involvement until and unless there is litigation between the fiduciary and beneficiaries. However, legislation in a few states permits any person interested in a trust to require that the trust be administered under the continuing supervision of a court. More commonly, legislation requires testamentary trustees to qualify with the court having control of the testator's probate estate before undertaking the office. Qualification may or may not involve submission of the trust administration to continuing court supervision. To qualify, the trustee may be required to post bond unless the trust instrument excuses the requirement. Some statutes provide that non-residents of the state of probate and foreign corporations not qualified to engage in local trust business cannot qualify for appointment as trustee.

Once qualified, a supervised testamentary trustee may be required to submit periodic accountings to the court. Judicial orders settling the accounts of a fiduciary may or may not be binding on all beneficiaries. The scope of the review may indicate a different effect for a regular, periodic accounting to a supervising court as well as for a final accounting seeking discharge of the fiduciary. In both cases, an accounting purporting to bind is ineffective against the interest of a beneficiary to whom inadequate notice has been accorded. In the case of minor or unascertainable beneficiaries, the propriety of any claimed representation other than by a duly appointed guardian ad litem is likely to be governed by legislation, or by equitable principles in the absence of statute. Judicial orders favoring fiduciaries over beneficiaries may be avoided or modified by collateral attack for extrinsic fraud if the fiduciary was guilty of actual or constructive fraud for failure to inform beneficiaries adequately of matters affecting their rights.

UPC Article VII eliminates many of the problems involving court qualification and supervision of testamentary trustees. Article VII identifies a passive, jurisdictional relationship between every trust and a court of the state of principal administration of the trust. It permits mailed notice and provides for representation of unborn or unascertained interests. Furthermore, the UPC neither requires court qualification of trustees nor the posting of bond, filing of inventories, or judicial approval of accounts periodically or at any other time.

UPC section 7-101 requires trustees to register trusts in the court of the principal place of administration. The purpose of trust registration is to assure that a particular court will be available to the parties on a permissive basis, rather than to subject the trust to compulsory continuing court supervision. A trustee registers a trust by filing a short statement acknowledging acceptance of a trust. The statement must identify the trust by the name of the settlor, date of the trust instrument, and the place of probate of the will if the trust is testamentary. Except for trusts created without a writing, the names of the beneficiaries, the nature and value of the assets, and the terms of the trust need not be disclosed. No sanctions for non-registration are provided except that a trustee who refuses to register a trust within thirty days after receipt of a written demand for its registration by a settlor or beneficiary is subject to removal if an interested person petitions for removal. Trust registration has been a controversial innovation. Several states adopting the UPC have omitted the trust registration provisions.

PART B. POWERS, DUTIES, AND LIABILITIES OF PROPERTY FIDUCIARIES

1. The Trust Office

Witmer v. Blair
588 S.W.2d 222 (Mo. Ct. App. 1979)

WELBORN, J. Plaintiffs, beneficiaries of a testamentary trust, filed a two-count action against defendant trustee, seeking an accounting, removal of the trustee, and actual and punitive damages for breach of fiduciary duties. After trial to the court, the court ordered an accounting and removal of the defendant as trustee and entered judgment against defendant for $309 for unaccounted for funds but found against plaintiffs on their claim for damages for breach of fiduciary duties. Plaintiffs appeal from this portion of the decree.

By his Last Will and Testament, Henry F. Nussbaum made a residual bequest and devise of his estate to his niece, Jane Ann Blair, as trustee, "in trust however, for the education of my grandchildren (children of my daughter, Dorothy Janice Witmer) living at the time of my decease, or born within a period of nine months thereafter." In the event that none of his grandchildren survived to inherit the estate, the residue would revert to plaintiff Dorothy Janice Witmer, his daughter and first cousin of defendant trustee.

Nussbaum died in 1960. The trust estate came into the hands of the trustee in 1961. It consisted of $1,905 in checking and savings accounts, $5,700 in certificates of deposit and a house valued at $6,000.00. The house was sold in 1962, netting $4,467 to the trust estate. That amount was deposited in a trust checking account. In 1963, $2,000 in certificates of deposit were acquired by the trust and $500 was so invested in 1964.

As of December 31, 1970, the trust fund assets consisted of $5,847 in checking account, $506 in savings account and $8,200 in certificates of deposit. In 1971 and 1972, the checking account balance was reduced by transfers to the savings account and on December 31, 1975, the trust assets consisted of $2,741 checking account, $5,474 savings account and $8,200 certificates of deposit.

Plaintiff-appellant Marguerite Janice Witmer was the only grandchild of the testator who became a beneficiary of the trust. She was born September 3, 1953. At the time of the trial, she was 23 years of age. She had not attended a college or university. However, various sums of money had been expended from the trust for her benefit, including a typewriter, clothes, glasses, modeling school tuition and expenses and a tonsillectomy. These expenditures totalled some $1,225.00. The trust also provided $350 for dentures for the mother, Dorothy Witmer.

The trust was handled by appellant rather informally. She kept no books for the trust. The expenditures above mentioned were in most cases advanced by her from her personal account and she reimbursed herself from the trust income. In 1965, the bank erroneously credited the trust account with $560 which should have gone to the trustee's personal account. The mistake was not corrected and that amount remained in the trust account. The trustee received no compensation for her services. Asked at the trial whether she had ever been a trustee before, she responded negatively, adding: "And never again." She explained the large checking account balances in the trust account by the fact that college for Janice "was talked about all the way through high school. . . . [I]n my opinion it was the sensible way to keep the money where I could get it to her without any problems at all in case she needed it quickly."

An accountant testified for plaintiffs that if the sum of $800 had been kept in the checking and savings accounts (the $800 was based upon the maximum disbursement in any year) and the balance of the trust placed in one-year certificates of deposit, $9,138 more interest would have been earned as of September 30, 1976, from the trust estate than had been received under respondent's handling of the trust. . . .

In this court, appellants contend that the respondent as trustee was bound to comply with the directions of the trust that she "invest the principal and re-invest the same" and that her failure to invest the trust corpus constituted a breach of her fiduciary duty for which she is liable. The respondent answers that inasmuch as the will failed to specify when and what investments were to be made, such matters were left to the discretion of the trustee and that she exercised such discretion honestly, with ordinary prudence and within the limits of the trust and is not liable for damages.

A concise summary of the law applicable in this situation appears in 76 Am. Jur. 2d Trusts §379 (1975):

> It is a general power and duty of a trustee, implied if not expressed, at least in the case of an ordinary trust, to keep trust funds properly invested. Having uninvested funds in his hands, it is his duty to make investments of them, where at least they are not soon to be applied to the purposes and

objects or turned over to the beneficiaries of the trust. Generally, he cannot permit trust funds to lie dormant or on deposit for a prolonged period, but he may keep on hand a fund sufficient to meet expenses, including contingent expenses, and he need not invest a sum too small to be prudently invested. A trustee ordinarily may not say in excuse of a failure to invest that he kept the funds on hand to pay the beneficiaries on demand.

The trustee is under a duty to the beneficiary to use reasonable care and skill to make the trust property productive.

Restatement (Second) of Trusts §181 (1959). Comment c to this section states:

> *Money.* In the case of money, it is normally the duty of the trustee to invest it so that it will produce an income. The trustee is liable if he fails to invest trust funds which it is his duty to invest for a period which is under all the circumstances unreasonably long. If, however, the delay is not unreasonable, he is not liable.
>
> A breach of trust is a violation by the trustee of any duty which as trustee he owes to the beneficiary.

Restatement (Second) of Trusts §201 (1959). Comment b to this section states:

> *Mistake of law as to existence of duties and powers.* A trustee commits a breach of trust not only where he violates a duty in bad faith, or intentionally although in good faith, or negligently, but also where he violates a duty because of a mistake as to the extent of his duties and powers. This is true not only where his mistake is in regard to a rule of law, whether a statutory or common-law rule, but also where he interprets the trust instrument as authorizing him to do acts which the court determines he is not authorized by the instrument to do. In such a case, he is not protected from liability merely because he acts in good faith, nor is he protected merely because he relies upon the advice of counsel. Compare §297, Comment j. If he is in doubt as to the interpretation of the instrument, he can protect himself by obtaining instructions from the court. The extent of his duties and powers is determined by the trust instrument and the rules of law which are applicable, and not by his own interpretation of the instrument or his own belief as to the rules of law.

Under the above rules, there has been a breach of trust by the trustee in this case and her good faith is not a defense to appellants' claim. When the respondent came into possession of the trust estate in 1962, appellant Marguerite was some nine years of age. Respondent was acquainted with her and was aware of her age. Obviously there was no prospect of the beneficiary's attending college for a number of years. Respondent's failure to invest a large portion of the trust corpus during such time may not be justified on the grounds that during such time she acceded to requests of the beneficiary's mother to provide small sums for the beneficiary or her mother. Respondent's brief acknowledges that such expenditures were not authorized under the trust. A breach of duty by the trustee in that regard cannot justify her further breach of duty to invest the trust corpus.

However, when Marguerite became of college age and was considering a college education, the respondent should not be faulted for keeping readily available a sum of money which would permit the use of the trust fund for such purpose. Marguerite was somewhat less than candid regarding her college plans. She stated that in 1972 when she went to the modeling school, ". . . we had talked about [going to college] but . . . I wasn't sure what I wanted to do. There was a chance I could have gone to college and a chance I couldn't have. There was no definite talk either way." However, her mother, in a letter dated February 6, 1972, had told respondent:

> Jan (Marguerite) has still been inquiring about C.U. Extension and Denver University and Arapahoe Jr. College with the idea of possibly starting this fall semester. She still wants more schooling. For this I am so thankful.

It may be conceded that at sometime thereafter respondent should have become aware that college was not realistically in Marguerite's plans and should have handled the Trust accordingly. However, in 1971 and 1972 she did substantially reduce the trust checking account by transfer to the interest-bearing savings account.

The accountant who testified for appellants calculated that between the opening of the trust and 1971, when college for Marguerite would have been a realistic possibility, had the trust funds, in excess of $100 checking account and approximately $800-1,000 savings account, been invested in one-year certificates of deposit, the trust would have earned additional interest of $2,840.00. In view of the trustee's transfer of a substantial portion of the checking account balance to savings in 1971 and 1972 and in view of the relatively small difference between the return from savings and what might have been earned from certificates of deposit (1/2% to 1-1/2%), no damages should be assessed against the trustee for the handling of the estate during that period. However, the trustee should be held liable for the $2,840 which, according to the measure of damages, invoked by appellants, might have been earned by investment of the trust between 1962 and 1971.

Judgment reversed as to Count II of plaintiffs' petition insofar as it denied plaintiffs' claim for actual damages. Remanded with directions to enter judgment for plaintiffs on Count II for $2,840 actual damages.

Reversed and remanded with directions.

All concur.

Notes and Questions

1. *Exculpatory Clauses.* Jane Blair's announced lack of interest in ever again serving as a trustee is certainly understandable. If widely publicized in the popular press—a big "if"— decisions like *Witmer* would likely deter persons from agreeing to act as trustee as a favor to friends or relations. Often, though, these are just the individuals in whom the settlor had the greatest confidence. Are there steps that a settlor's attorney can take to make the trust office less risky for such persons? One possibility is to insert in the governing instrument an exculpatory clause, which purports to lower

the liability threshold. Should these clauses be enforceable as written? Should parties be able contractually to waive all legally recognized trustee duties, or are these duties (or some of them) mandatory?

The Restatement 2d of Trusts section 222 provides that exculpatory clauses are not effective where the trustee breached the trust in bad faith, intentionally, or with reckless indifference to the interest of the beneficiary. Is this limitation a good idea? Would it be wise to require that exculpatory clauses make specific reference to the trust law rules that they are intended to waive? See generally Note, Directory Trusts and the Exculpatory Clause, 65 Colum. L. Rev. 138 (1965).

2. *Legislation.* Section 11-1.7(a) of the New York Estates, Powers & Trusts Law provides that clauses attempting to exonerate executors or testamentary trustees from liability for failure to exercise reasonable care, diligence, and prudence are contrary to public policy. Why does the statute not include trustees of inter-vivos trusts?

For pensions, which raise concerns that private trusts do not share, ERISA adopts a different approach regarding exculpatory clauses than does the law of private trusts. While trust law treats most rules as default rules, section 410(a) of ERISA prevents the instrument creating the plan from "reliev[ing] a [pension] fiduciary from responsibility or liability." Similarly, section 404(a)(1)(D) prohibits the plan from instituting terms that are not "consistent with the provisions of this title . . . ." These provisions make pension law rules mandatory and bar the use of exculpatory clauses.

3. *Informal Trusts.* Express trusts may be highly informal, created with little or no expression of important trust terms or even whether the arrangement is intended to be a trust. It is common, for example, for grandparents to hand over checks or other assets to children, indicating only that the property is to be used for the grandchildren's benefit (or some narrower purpose, such as education).

The terms of an informal trust are based on the settlor's intention, evidenced by words or conduct. Comment h to section 228 of the Restatement 3d of Trusts provides that in the absence of contrary legislation and intention of the settlor, the trustee's powers and duties regarding investment of trust property are governed by the common-law prudent investor rule, which we take up infra Part C. See also Restatement 3d of Trusts § 228, illustration 14.

2. The Duty of Loyalty

Statutory Reference: *Uniform Trustees' Powers Act § 3(c)(1)*

City Bank Farmers Trust Co. v. Cannon
291 N.Y. 125, 51 N.E.2d 674 (1943)

[By 1928, Mary Cannon had transferred to City Bank Farmers Trust Company, then known as Farmers Loan & Trust Company, as trustee for her revocable trust, 3,000 shares of National City Bank stock. Following the merger of National City Bank and City Bank Farmers Trust Company, the trust company held its own shares of stock. The shares were quoted at an average of $400.00 per share on July 1, 1929, immediately after the merger, indicating a value of $1,200,000 for the 3,000 shares held in trust. When Mary Cannon died in May 1938, the shares had a market value of $18 per share, or a total value of $54,000. A guardian ad litem appointed to represent minor beneficiaries sought to surcharge the trustee for the $1,146,000 difference. The trust instrument expressly authorized the trustee to retain securities "so long as it may seem proper. . . ." Furthermore, after the merger, Cannon expressly consented to retention of the stock.]

THACHER, J. . . . There is no suggestion that these investments were improper when made and both courts below have found that they were made in good faith, upon careful consideration and in the exercise of sound business judgment. It is, however, contended that by the affiliation of the Bank and the Trust Company the latter as trustee became the beneficial owner of its own stock, was thus placed in a position of divided loyalty and should be surcharged for retaining the Bank shares which were inseparable from beneficial ownership of its own shares. . . .

The standard of loyalty in trust relations does not permit a trustee to create or to occupy a position in which he has interests to serve other than the interest of the trust estate. Undivided loyalty is the supreme test, unlimited and unconfined by the bounds of classified transactions. Undivided loyalty did not exist after affiliation of the trustee and the Bank because of the ownership by the trust of the shares of the Bank. The officers of the trustee responsible for the administration of the trust were under a duty with unremitting loyalty to serve both the interest of the Trust Company and the interest of the trust estate. These were conflicting interests insofar as the trust investment in the National City Bank shares required decision whether to hold or to sell the shares in a falling market. The sale of this large number of shares might have seriously affected the interests of the Trust Company by depressing the value of these shares in a rapidly deteriorating market. Consequently, the trustee had conflicting interests to serve in deciding to sell or not to sell. We do not for a moment suggest that the trustee did not act in the utmost good faith. Both courts below so found. But that is not enough for when the trustee has a selfish interest which may be served, the law does not stop to inquire whether the trustee's action or failure to act has been unfairly influenced. It stops the inquiry when the relation is disclosed and sets aside the transaction or refuses to enforce it, and in a proper case, surcharges the trustee as for an unauthorized investment. It is only by rigid adherence to these principles that all temptation can be removed from one acting as a fiduciary to serve his own interest when in conflict with the obligations of his trust. The rule is designed to obliterate all divided loyalties which may creep into a fiduciary relationship and utterly to destroy their effect by making voidable any transactions in which they appear.

In continuing to act as trustee and retaining the shares, the respondent Trust Company violated the rule of undivided loyalty and is accountable for the loss on the shares unless the donor by approving the investment and its retention has estopped the guardian ad litem and the infant remainder-men he represents from objecting to the investment. . . .

A settlor who reserves absolute power of modification and revocation possesses all the powers of ownership and for many purposes is treated as the absolute owner of the property held in trust. . . .

Since the settlor reserved the right to exercise all the powers of ownership insofar as the trust was concerned, we hold that her action in approving the exchange of National City Bank shares for shares carrying a beneficial interest in the shares of the corporate trustee and in opposing sale of the new shares was an effective estoppel not only against her own objections but also against an objection by the recipients of her bounty to the acts of the trustee which she approved. The donor approved the investments and their retention in advance with full knowledge of the resulting divided loyalty and of her own power to remove the trustee or otherwise to revoke or amend the trust and do as she pleased with these shares. She was fully appraised of her legal rights. . . . In this case we are not confronted with any failure to exercise good faith and sound business judgment in retaining the investments and express no opinion upon the question of estoppel in such a case.

The judgment should be affirmed without costs.

Notes and Questions

1. *The "Prophylactic Rule."* The broad proposition stated as dictum in *Cannon* stems from a famous opinion by Judge Cardozo in Meinhard v. Salmon, 249 N.Y. 458, 164 N.E. 545 (1928). In that case, Meinhard was a co-adventurer of Salmon in a profitable hotel enterprise operated on land leased to Salmon for twenty years. Meinhard sued for an accounting when Salmon, four months before expiration of the lease, accepted a long term renewal on adjacent land with an obligation that the old hotel would be razed and a new venture begun. Meinhard was neither informed nor included. Writing for a majority that concluded that Salmon had breached a fiduciary duty to Meinhard, Cardozo wrote the following well-known passage:

> Many forms of conduct permissible in a work a day world for those acting at arms length, are forbidden to those bound by fiduciary ties. A trustee is held to something stricter than the morals of the market place. Not honesty alone, but the punctilio of an honor the most sensitive is then the standard of behavior. As to this there has developed a tradition that is unbending and inveterate. Uncompromising rigidity has been the attitude of courts of equity when petitioned to undermine the rule of undivided loyalty by the "disintegrating erosion" of particular exceptions. . . . Only thus has the level of conduct

for fiduciaries been kept at a level higher than that trodden by the crowd. It will not consciously be lowered by any judgment of this court.[9]

Does the holding in *Meinhard*—as distinguished from Judge Cardozo's dictum—support the court's statement in *Cannon* that a fiduciary duty is breached whenever a trustee fails to act after finding herself or himself in a position involving a possible conflict between personal and fiduciary interests? The prophylactic "no-further-inquiry" rule is that a trustee is liable for losses to the trust regardless of good faith and regardless of causal connection between the trustee's conduct and the loss. Do the reasons for that rule apply where the conflict of interest is neither direct nor substantial? But for the settlor's ratification, would *Cannon* have been an instance of direct, substantial conflict of interest?

2. *Implicit Ratification?* In Bracken v. Block, 561 N.E.2d 1273 (Ill. Ct. App. 1990), the court held that an individual trustee life-beneficiary was not liable for self-dealing where she exercised her discretion to invade the trust principal for her own benefit by selling to herself a trust asset and placing the proceeds in the trust. The trust property was being depleted for the trustee-beneficiary's care. Although the trust instrument did not expressly authorize her to sell the trust assets to herself, the court concluded that the trust indicated that the settlor's primary goal was support of the trustee life-beneficiary, who was his sister, and that the sale to herself was an authorized exercise of her discretion.

3. *Self-Dealing and Corporate Trustee Purchase or Retention of Its Own Shares.* The no-further-inquiry rule is most clearly justifiable in instances of self-dealing by the fiduciary. Self-dealing exists when the trustee sells trust property to itself individually or sells individual property to the trust. In these circumstances, the beneficiaries may set the transaction aside even though it was made in good faith and for a reasonable price. The trustee has committed a breach of trust by placing itself in a position of direct conflict of interest with the beneficiaries. For this breach, the trustee is chargeable with any profit the trustee realized through the breach of trust. If it has made no profit, the trustee is chargeable with any loss to the trust estate resulting from the breach of trust or any profit that would have accrued to the trust estate if there had been no breach of trust.

There is no self-dealing if a corporate trustee, as in *Cannon*, retains for the trust or purchases from others its own shares as trust property.[10] Nevertheless, the practice has been condemned both in the Restatement 2d and 3d of Trusts section 170 comment n on the basis of the possibility of conflict of interest. The Restatement 3d of Trusts adds, however, that it is "ordinarily permissible for a modest amount of the trustee's stock to be held

---

9. Apart from the merits of Judge Cardozo's view, what do you think of his rhetoric? Many lawyers, law teachers, and law students have criticized his opinions over the years for their florid and moralistic style. For an interesting discussion of Cardozo's judicial writing in *Meinhard*, see R. Posner, Cardozo: A Study in Reputation 104-05 (1990).

10. Self-dealing would exist, however, if a corporate trustee purchased for inclusion in the trust other assets, including securities, that the trustee owned.

indirectly through an otherwise appropriate purchase of shares in a pooled investment vehicle."

The inference in *Cannon* is that the trustee would have been liable for the loss in value had the settlor not approved of the retention. What would have been the basis for surcharging the trustee? If a trustee's action resulted in personal gain, liability is justified on the basis of restitution of the gain to the trust, but this theory is not available in *Cannon*. This aspect of the *Cannon* decision is discussed from different points of view in Scott, Retention of its Own Shares by a Corporate Trustee, 57 Harv. L. Rev. 601 (1944) (defending the decision) and Niles & Schwartz, Breach of Trust—Recent Developments, 20 N.Y.U. L. Rev. 165 (1944) (criticizing the decision). It should be noted that the bank affiliation in the *Cannon* case occurred only a few months before the stock market crash of 1929 and that massive losses in common stock values occurred between the crash and 1938 when the settlor died. Niles and Schwartz argue: "[We] have concededly honest trustees who acted in good faith without conscious disloyalty and who followed business practices common to trustees at the time. Nor was the loss . . . due to the supposed default of the trustees. Even had the stock not been that of an affiliate of the trustee, . . . the position of the trustees would in no way be better. The losses sustained would have been the same. Should the beneficiaries now be able to reap a windfall and cast the results of the economic cycle on such trustees. . . .?" Id. at 169. Do you agree?

4. *Legislation.* Some statutes authorize retention but not purchase by a corporate trustee of its own shares in the circumstances described in the statute. See, e.g., Ky. Rev. Stat. § 386.025; 12 Del. Code Ann. § 3305. Section 3(c)(1) of the Uniform Trustees' Powers Act gives a trustee general authority to retain assets "received from a trustor," including those "in which the trustee is personally interested." For a criticism of this aspect of the Uniform Act, see Hallgring, The Uniform Trustees' Powers Act and the Basic Principles of Fiduciary Responsibility, 41 Wash. L. Rev. 801, 813-16 (1966).

5. *Duty to Earmark.* Suppose a trustee causes trust assets to be registered in its name without any indication that it is subject to the trust. If the asset falls in value due to unforeseeable market developments beyond the control of the trustee, should the trustee be able to avoid liability for the loss by explaining away any inference of intentional wrongdoing? Though arguably prohibited by the rule against self-dealing, a distinct duty to earmark a trust investment so as to distinguish it from individual assets of the trustee is recognized by the authorities. See Restatement 2d of Trusts § 179. A breach of the duty to earmark is likely to be treated as a "technical" breach for which the trustee is not chargeable in the absence of bad faith, negligence, or loss causally related to the appearance of an individual holding. See Restatement 2d of Trusts § 205 comment f.

One might question why a purchase transaction between a trust and its trustee acting as an individual should subject the fiduciary to an insurer's liability at the option of beneficiaries, when a loss of a non-earmarked asset may be explained by the fiduciary so as to remain a trust estate loss. A partial answer is that rules formerly governing the liability of securities issuers and transfer agents controlling registrations of securities known to be held in trust produced high transaction costs for transfers involving earmarked securities. As a result, trust instruments commonly relieve trustees from the duty to earmark and non-earmarking is now the order of the day. In the meantime, the old transfer agent problem has been substantially eliminated by enactments in 39 states of the Uniform Act for Simplification of Fiduciary Security Transfers. Section 3 of the act provides: "a corporation or transfer agent making a transfer of a security pursuant to an assignment by a fiduciary . . . may assume without inquiry that the assignment, even though to the fiduciary himself or his nominee, is within his authority and capacity and is not in breach of his fiduciary duties."

The question remains whether a fiduciary who can establish complete good faith, absence of any personal gain, and lack of any realistic causal connection between conduct labeled "breach of trust" and financial harm to the estate should be made an insurer of trust assets. What are the costs and benefits of using this strict liability rule as a deterrent?

6. *Risks of Other Inferences of Disloyalty.* The rules that trustees must account for personal gains and that the court will not inquire into good faith or reasonableness in self-dealing situations led to recoveries by beneficiaries in cases where there is no suggestion of causally related damage to the estate or actual motivation of a fiduciary to take personal advantage of her or his position. Not surprisingly, perhaps, judicial indifference to causal connection between breach and punitive damage awards against trustees also characterizes the more common situation where a fiduciary is unable to disprove an inference of divided loyalty arising from circumstances other than fiduciary gain or self-dealing. The following materials illustrate the point.

Estate of Rothko
43 N.Y.2d 305, 372 N.E.2d 291, 401 N.Y.S.2d 291 (1977)

COOKE, J. Mark Rothko, an abstract expressionist painter whose works through the years gained for him an international reputation of greatness, died testate on February 25, 1970. The principal asset of his estate consisted of 798 paintings of tremendous value, and the dispute underlying this appeal involves the conduct of his three executors in their disposition of these works of art. In sum, that conduct as portrayed in the record and sketched in the opinions was manifestly wrongful and indeed shocking.

Rothko's will was admitted to probate on April 27, 1970 and letters testamentary were issued to Bernard J. Reis, Theodoros Stamos and Morton Levine. Hastily and within a period of only about three weeks and by virtue of two contracts each dated May 21, 1970, the executors dealt with all 798 paintings.

By a contract of sale, the estate executors agreed to sell to Marlborough A.G., a Liechtenstein corporation (hereinafter MAG), 100 Rothko paintings as listed for $1,800,000, $200,000 to be paid on execution of the agreement and the balance of $1,600,000 in 12 equal interest-free installments over a 12 year period. Under the second agreement, the executors consigned to Marlborough Gallery, Inc. a domestic corporation (hereinafter MNY), "approximately 700 paintings listed on a Schedule to be prepared", the consignee to be responsible for costs covering items such as insurance, storage restoration and promotion. By its provisos, MNY could sell up to 35 paintings a year from each of two groups, pre-1947 and post-1947, for 12 years at the best priced obtainable but not less than the appraised estate value, and it would receive a 50% commission on each painting sold, except for a commission of 40% on those sold to or through other dealers.

Petitioner Kate Rothko, decedent's daughter and a person entitled to share in his estate by virtue of an election under EPTL 5-3.3,[11] instituted this proceeding to remove the executors, to enjoin MNY and MAG from disposing of the paintings, to rescind the aforesaid agreements between the executors and said corporations, for a return of the paintings still in possession of those corporations, and for damages. . . . The Attorney-General of the State, as the representative of the ultimate beneficiaries of the Mark Rothko Foundation, Inc., a charitable corporation and the residuary legatee under decedent's will, joined in requesting relief substantially similar to that prayed for by petitioner. On June 26, 1972 the Surrogate issued a temporary restraining order and on September 26, 1972 a preliminary injunction enjoining MAG, MNY, and the three executors from selling or otherwise disposing of the paintings referred to in the agreements dated May 21, 1970, except for sales or dispositions made with court permission. . . . By a 1974 petition, the Attorney-General, on behalf of the ultimate charitable beneficiaries of the Mark Rothko Foundation, sought the punishment of MNY, MAG, Lloyd and Reis for contempt and other relief.

Following a nonjury trial covering 89 days and in a thorough opinion, the Surrogate found: that Reis was a director, secretary and treasury of MNY, the consignee art gallery, in addition to being a coexecutor of the estate; that the testator had a 1969 *inter vivos* contract with MNY to sell Rothko's work at a commission of only 10% and whether that agreement

---

11. The statutory reference is to New York's mortmain legislation, since repealed. Under this law, the excess over 50% of an estate included in a charitable devise could be claimed by a spouse or children if the objectors, under all other terms of the will and applicable intestacy law, would be beneficiaries of the assets denied to the charity. Thus, the legislation invited will draftsmen to avoid the statute by including a devise to one outside the statutory beneficiary class conditioned to take effect to the extent that the charitable devise failed for any reason. Rothko's will, prepared by co-executor Reis who had a law degree but had never practiced law, contained no such saving clause. It included a devise of certain paintings to the Tate Gallery in London, a devise to the artist's wife of the home and contents plus $250,000, and a residuary devise to the Mark Rothko Foundation which had been previously formed and was controlled by Rothko and the three persons named as his executors. Rothko's two children exercised the mortmain election and became entitled to a quarter of the residue. Estate of Rothko, 71 Misc.2d 74, 335 N.Y.2d 666 (1972), affirmed, 43 A.D.2d 819, 351 N.Y.S.2d 940 (1974). This aspect of the *Rothko* case is discussed in Merryman, The Straw Man in the Rothko Case, Art. News, Dec. 1976, p. 32. Also, see L. Seldes, The Legacy of Mark Rothko (1978) for a description of the artist and the post-mortem scramble for his estate that began with his 1970 suicide. Eds.

survived testator's death was a problem that a fiduciary in a dual position could not have impartially faced; that Reis was in a position of serious conflict of interest with respect to the contracts of May 21, 1970 and that his dual role and planned purpose benefited the Marlborough interests to the detriment of the estate; that it was to the advantage of coexecutor Stamos as a "not-too-successful artist, financially", to curry favor with Marlborough and that the contract made by him with MNY within months after signing the estate contracts placed him in a position where his personal interests conflicted with those of the estate, especially leading to lax contract enforcement efforts by Stamos; that Stamos acted negligently and improvidently in view of his own knowledge of the conflict of interest of Reis; that the third coexecutor, Levine, while not acting in self-interest or with bad faith, nonetheless failed to exercise ordinary prudence in the performance of his assumed fiduciary obligations since he was aware of Reis' divided loyalty, believed that Stamos was also seeking personal advantage, possessed personal opinions as to the value of the paintings and yet followed the leadership of his coexecutors without investigation of essential facts or consultation with competent and disinterested appraisers, and that the business transactions of the two Marlborough corporations were admittedly controlled and directed by Francis K. Lloyd. It was concluded that the acts and failures of the three executors were clearly improper to such a substantial extent as to mandate their removal under SCPA 711 as estate fiduciaries. The Surrogate also found that MNY, MAG and Lloyd were guilty of contempt in shipping, disposing of and selling 57 paintings in violation of the temporary restraining order dated June 26, 1972 and of the injunction dated September 26, 1972; that the contracts for sale and consignment of paintings between the executors and MNY and MAG provided inadequate value to the estate, amounting to a lack of mutuality and fairness resulting from conflicts on the part of Reis and Stamos and improvidence on the part of all executors; that said contracts were voidable and were set aside by reason of violation of the duty of loyalty and improvidence of the executors, knowingly participated in and induced by MNY and MAG; that the fact that these agreements were voidable did not revive the 1969 *inter vivos* agreements since the parties by their conduct evinced an intent to abandon and abrogate these compacts. The Surrogate held that the present value at the time of trial of the paintings sold is the proper measure of damages as to MNY, MAG, Lloyd, Reis and Stamos. He imposed a civil fine of $3,332,000 upon MNY, MAG and Lloyd, same being the appreciated value at the time of trial of the 57 paintings sold in violation of the temporary restraining order and injunction. It was held that Levine was liable for $6,464,880 in damages, as he was not in a dual position acting for his own interest and was thus liable only for the actual value of paintings sold MNY and MAG as of the dates of sale, and that Reis, Stamos, MNY and MAG, apart from being jointly and severally liable for the same damages as Levine for negligence, were liable for the greater sum of $9,252,000 "as appreciation damages less amounts previously paid to the estate with regard to sales of paintings." . . . The liabilities were held to be congruent so that payment of the highest sum would satisfy all lesser liabilities including the civil fines and the liabilities for damages were to be reduced by payment of the fine levied or by return of any of the 57 paintings disposed of, the new fiduciary to have the option in the first instance to specify which paintings the fiduciary would accept.

The Appellate Division . . . modified to the extent of deleting the option given the new fiduciary to specify which paintings he would accept. Except for this modification, the majority affirmed the opinion of Surrogate Midonick, with additional comments. Among others, it was stated that the entire court agreed that executors Reis and Stamos had a conflict of interest and divided loyalty in view of their nexus to MNY and that a majority were in agreement with the Surrogate's assessment of liability as to executor Levine and his findings of liability against MNY, MAG and Lloyd. The majority agreed with the Surrogate's analysis awarding "appreciation damages" and found further support for his rationale in Menzel v. List, 24 N.Y.2d 91, 298 N.Y.S.2d 979, 246 N.E.2d 742. . . .

In seeking a reversal, it is urged that an improper legal standard was applied in voiding the estate contracts of May, 1970, that the "no further inquiry" rule applies only to self-dealing and that in case of a conflict of interest, absent self-dealing, a challenged transaction must be shown to be unfair. The subject of fairness of the contracts is intertwined with the issue of whether Reis and Stamos were guilty of conflicts of interest. Scott is quoted to the effect that "[a] trustee does not necessarily incur liability merely because he has an individual interest in the transaction . . . In Bullivant v. First Nat. Bank [246 Mass. 324, 141 N.E. 41] it was held that . . . the fact that the bank was also a creditor of the corporation did not make its assent valid, *if it acted in good faith and the plan was fair*" (2 Scott, Trusts, § 170.24, p. 1384 [emphasis added]). . . .

These contentions should be rejected. First, a review of the opinions of the Surrogate and the Appellate Division manifests that they did not rely solely on a "no further inquiry rule", and secondly, there is more than an adequate basis to conclude that the agreements between the Marlborough corporations and the estate were neither fair nor in the best interests of the estate. . . . The opinions under review demonstrate that neither the Surrogate nor the Appellate Division set aside the contracts by merely applying the no further inquiry rule without regard to fairness. Rather they determined, quite properly indeed, that these agreements were neither fair nor in the best interests of the estate.

To be sure, the assertions that there were no conflicts of interest on the part of Reis or Stamos indulge in sheer fantasy. Besides being a director and officer of MNY, for which there was financial remuneration, however slight, Reis, as noted by the Surrogate, had different inducements to favor the Marlborough interests, including his own aggrandizement of status and financial advantage through sales of almost one million dollars for items from his own and his family's extensive private art collection by the Marlborough interests. . . . Similarly, Stamos benefited as an artist under contract with Marlborough and, interestingly, Marlborough purchased a Stamos painting from a third party for $4,000 during the week in May, 1970 when the estate contract negotiations were pending. . . . The conflicts are manifest. Further, as noted in Bogert, Trusts and Trustees (2d ed.), "The duty of loyalty imposed on the fiduciary prevents him from accepting employment from a third party who is entering into a business transaction with the trust" (§ 543, subd. [S], p. 573). "While he [a trustee] is administering the trust he must refrain from placing himself in a position where his personal interest or that of a third person does or may conflict with the interest of the beneficiaries" (Bogert, Trusts [Hornbook Series—5th ed.], p. 343). Here, Reis was employed and Stamos benefited in a manner contemplated by Bogert. In short, one must strain the law rather than follow it to reach the result suggested on behalf of Reis and Stamos.

Levine contends that, having acted prudently and upon the advice of counsel, a complete defense was established.[12] Suffice it to say, an executor who knows that his coexecutor is committing breaches of trust and not only fails to exert efforts directed towards prevention but accedes to them is legally accountable even though he was acting on the advice of counsel. When confronted with the question of whether to enter into the Marlborough contracts, Levine was acting in a business capacity, not a legal one, in which he was required as an executor primarily to employ such diligence and prudence to the care and management of the estate assets and affairs as would prudent persons of discretion and intelligence accented by "[n]ot honesty alone, but the punctilio of an honor the most sensitive" (Meinhard v. Salmon, 249 N.Y. 458, 464, 164 N.E. 545, 546, supra). Alleged good faith on the part of a fiduciary forgetful of his duty is not enough. He could not close his eyes, remain passive or move with unconcern in the face of the obvious loss to be visited upon the estate by participation in those business arrangements and then shelter himself behind the claimed counsel of an attorney.

Further there is no merit to the argument that MNY and MAG lacked notice of the breach of trust. The record amply supports the determination that they are chargeable with notice of the executors' breach of duty.

The measure of damages was the issue that divided the Appellate Division. The contention of Reis, Stamos, MNY and MAG, that the award of appreciation damages was legally erroneous and impermissible, is based on a principle that an executor authorized to sell is not liable for an increase in value if the breach consists only in selling for a figure less than that for which the executor should have sold. For example, Scott states:

---

12. Counsel advised all three executors that Reis had a conflict of interest. In the same letter, though, the law firm advised them that the Surrogate would not entertain a petition for advance approval of any contracts for liquidating the estate through Marlborough. Surrogate Midonick's opinion stated: "While it is true . . . that Surrogates do not usually give advance approval concerning matters of business judgment which are within the province of executors, no indication was given that the opposite rule governs when a fiduciary faces a conflict of interest." In re Rothko, 84 Misc. 2d 830, 840, 379 N.Y.S.2d 923, 936 (Surr. Ct. 1975). Should the law firm be liable to Levine for negligence? See Cremer, Should the Fiduciary Trust His Lawyer?, 19 Real Prop. Prob. & Tr. J. 786 (1984). For further discussion of the rule that advice of counsel provides no defense for breach of trust, see infra p. 1152. Eds.

The beneficiaries are not entitled to the value of the property at the time of the decree if it was not the duty of the trustee to retain the property in the trust and the breach of trust consisted *merely* in selling the property for too low a price (3 Scott, Trusts [3d ed.], § 208.3, p. 1687 [emphasis added]).

If the trustee is guilty of a breach of trust in selling trust property for an inadequate price, he is liable for the difference between the amount he should have received and the amount which he did receive. He is not liable, however, for any subsequent rise in value of the property sold. (Id., § 208.6, pp. 1689-1690).

A recitation of similar import appears in comment d under Restatement, Trusts, § 205:

d. Sale for less than value. If the trustee is authorized to sell trust property, but in breach of trust he sells it for less than he should receive, he is liable for the value of the property at the time of the sale less the amount which he received. If the breach of trust consists *only* in selling it for too little, he is not chargeable with the amount of any subsequent increase in value of the property under the rule stated in Clause (c), as he would be if he were not authorized to sell the property. See § 208. (Emphasis added).

However, employment of "merely" and "only" as limiting words suggests that where the breach consists of some misfeasance, other than solely for selling "for too low a price" or "for too little", appreciation damages may be appropriate. According to Scott (§ 208.3) and the Restatement (§ 208), the trustee may be held liable for appreciation damages if it was his or her duty to retain the property, the theory being that the beneficiaries are entitled to be placed in the same position they would have been in had the breach not consisted of a sale of property that should have been retained. The same rule should apply where the breach of trust consists of a serious conflict of interest—which is more than merely selling for too little.

The reason for allowing appreciation damages, where there is a duty to retain, and only date of sale damages, where there is authorization to sell, is policy oriented. If a trustee authorized to sell were subjected to a greater measure of damages he might be reluctant to sell (in which event he might run a risk if depreciation ensued). On the other hand, if there is a duty to retain and the trustee sells there is no policy reason to protect the trustee; he has not simply acted imprudently, he has violated an integral condition of the trust.

"If a trustee in breach of trust transfers trust property to a person who takes with notice of the breach of trust, and the transferee has disposed of the property . . . [i]t seems proper to charge him with the value at the time of the decree, since if it had not been for the breach of trust the property would still have been a part of the trust estate." (4 Scott, Trusts [3d ed.], § 291.2; see, also, United States v. Dunn, 268 U.S. 121, 132, 45 S. Ct. 451, 69 L.Ed. 876). This rule of law which applies to the transferees MNY and MAG also supports the imposition of appreciation damages against Reis and Stamos, since if the Marlborough corporations are liable for such damages either as purchaser or consignees with notice, from one in breach of trust, it is only logical to hold that said executors, as sellers and consignors, are liable also *pro tanto.*

Contrary to assertions of appellants and the dissenters at the Appellate Division, Menzel v. List, 24 N.Y.2d 91, 298 N.Y.S.2d 979, 246 N.E.2d 742, supra is authority for the allowance of appreciation damages. There, the damages involved a breach of warranty of title to a painting which at one time had been stolen from plaintiff and her husband and ultimately sold to defendant. Here, the executors, though authorized to sell, did not merely err in the amount they accepted but sold to one with whom Reis and Stamos had a self-interest. To make the injured party whole, in both instances the quantum of damages should be the same. In other words, since the paintings cannot be returned, the estate is therefore entitled to their value at the time of the decree, i.e., appreciation damages. These are not punitive damages in a true sense, rather they are damages intended to make the estate whole. Of course, as to Reis, Stamos, MNY and MAG, these damages might be considered by some to be exemplary in a sense, in that they serve as a warning to others, but their true character is ascertained when viewed in the light of overriding policy considerations and in the realization that the sale and consignment were not merely sales below value but inherently wrongful transfers which should allow the owner to be made whole. . . .

[The balance of the opinion is omitted. It dealt with the trial court's handling of conflicting evidence as to present value of unrecovered paintings, the question of revival of the 1969 contract between MNY and Rothko, and the time of sales held to violate the restraining order and temporary injunction.]

Accordingly, the order of the Appellate Division should be affirmed, with costs to the prevailing parties against appellants, and the question certified answered in the affirmative.

Notes and Questions

1. *Appreciation Damages.* The portion of the majority opinion dealing with the justification for "appreciation damages" merits close scrutiny. Are these damages compensatory, as the court stated, or punitive? Beneficiaries of a trustee's obligation to get a fair price for trust properties that the trustee is required to sell plainly have legitimate expectations to the property's fair market value as of a time when a legitimate sale should have occurred. Is not recovery in excess of such fair market value punitive rather than compensatory?

Professor Wellman has criticized the award of "appreciation damages" as a form of punishment for fiduciary misconduct:

> The costs of penalty awards in cases where a fiduciary's conduct is not obviously wrongful are most severe for estates consisting of unique assets where potential conflicts of interest are common. Testators and settlors whose estates include real property, closely held corporate stock, stamps, books, automobiles, coins, or art understandably select as fiduciaries persons

knowledgeable about those assets. As these persons accept fiduciary positions or deal with associates or potential associates who are fiduciaries, conflicts or potential conflicts of interest must arise. A rule which discourages the selection of persons who are experienced and successful in the handling of the testator's kind of assets is clearly unwise.

Rothko will increase the complexity of these trusteeships. As a precedent, it will encourage fiduciaries to consult their attorneys prior to any transaction possibly tainted with conflict of interest. And, if the attorneys read Surrogate Midonick's opinion carefully, the fiduciaries will be advised to seek a court proceeding with notice for and an opportunity to be heard by all persons interested in the estate, including appropriate state officials if charitable bequests are involved. What could be more wasteful? . . .

Against the argument that *Rothko* may increase a fiduciary's legal costs, it might be argued that a fiduciary faced with possible conflicts of interest will incur these legal costs whether or not *Rothko* penalties are assessed. That is, the standard remedies for disloyalty may induce fiduciaries, before every transaction, to seek legal advice or court instructions concerning possible conflicts of interest. If that is true, the argument runs, the additional risk of liability for appreciation damages will not increase the legal costs of a fiduciary who may have a personal interest in conflict with that of the estate.

This argument is unpersuasive. First, those honest and able fiduciaries in a position of possible conflict may well be willing to administer the estate without extraordinary legal advice or court instructions if they know that the estate's fair market value at the time of its disposition will provide a ceiling on their liability. Honest fiduciaries will be overly cautious only when threatened with surcharges they can neither estimate nor control. Second, if costs will be the same without regard to the fiduciary's honesty, there is absolutely no justification for the award of any penalty surcharge in the name of deterrence. . . .

Finally, as *Rothko* vividly illustrated, disguising appreciation damages as a form of compensation may lead to shattering liabilities that would never be levied in the name of pure punishment. Few if any courts or juries in the land would have assessed a two-million dollar fine against executor Stamos. Stamos was a close friend of Rothko, a fellow artist and the guardian of Rothko's minor children. His disloyalty was simply that he wanted to favor the gallery because the gallery might help him gain recognition for his own works.

Wellman, Punitive Surcharges Against Disloyal Fiduciaries—Is Rothko Right?, 77 Mich. L. Rev. 95 (1978).

2. *Punitive or Compensatory?* Contrast the conduct of Rothko's executors with the trustee's conduct in Jefferson Nat'l Bank v. Central Nat'l Bank, 700 F.2d 1143 (7th Cir. 1983). Central Bank was trustee of a revocable trust until it was revoked just prior to the settlor's death in September, 1976. The trust was funded originally by securities worth $220,000 and a promissory note on which two installments remained unpaid. The settlor, a former officer of Curtis Electro Company (Curtis) and CEO of a Curtis subsidiary, had accepted the note and $150,000 cash from Curtis in exchange for a transfer to Curtis of all of his stock in the company. The unpaid installments on the note, each for about $128,000 and 5 percent interest, were due in early 1971 and early 1972. Though Curtis stock was publicly traded, the company was controlled by the settlor's family, and the settlor's brothers and son (Jerry) held senior management positions.

Sixteen months after the creation of the trust, the settlor suffered a disabling stroke. Thereafter, the trustee agreed with Jerry and the settlor's wife, Betty, to make monthly payments from the trust fund to Betty so that she could meet her husband's medical costs. Betty approved several investment recommendations made by the trustee. The trustee made no effort to communicate with the settlor, who was unable to communicate.

Curtis suffered economic reverses and was unable to pay the note installment due on January, 1971. A couple of months later, the trustee accepted a replacement note with interest at the then prime rate. At a board meeting in September 1971, when the directors, two of whom were Jerry and a commercial loan officer of Central, knew that Curtis had lost $700,000 in 1970, the directors determined that the note installment due in January 1972 could not be paid. Jerry urged Central's trust department to "work out an arrangement" of the Curtis notes, and in March, 1972, the trustee and Curtis entered into a new repayment agreement involving a five year, unsecured note bearing interest at 7-1/2 percent.

Beginning a year or so before the trust was created and continuing thereafter, Central also served as Curtis's principal commercial banker. Prior to mid-1972, the borrower company and the lender bank operated under an unsecured, revolving line-of-credit contract. In August, 1972, the bank and Curtis entered into a new commercial loan agreement involving security for the bank in the form of notes from Curtis subsidiaries, security interests in equipment of subsidiaries, and a security interest in 100 percent of the subsidiaries' stock held by Curtis. In the summer of 1973, the trust department of Central sought payment of overdue installments on the notes held in trust. After delay and being told of a "deep cash crisis," checks making the interest payments current were received. At about the same time, Central's commercial loan department succeeded in getting additional collateral from Curtis in connection with a new loan made to a subsidiary. In late 1973, the trust department contacted the settlor's lawyer and threatened to sue Curtis on the notes, but backed off when informed that a suit would push Curtis into bankruptcy. Curtis filed for Chapter 11 reorganization in April, 1974. The trust department then advised Jerry and Betty that vigorous efforts to collect the Curtis note should be initiated. However, because of conflict between Central's position as a secured creditor of Curtis and its interest as trustee in collecting on the unsecured notes, the trust department advised the family to handle the collection on its own. The family's response was that they would hold Central responsible for any loss on the note. Central denied any improper conduct and claimed that the trust department had simply relied on Jerry's advice. Later, the settlor revoked the trust shortly before death. At trial, the jury awarded $394,475 for loss of value of the note (including $184,000 in pre-judgment interest) to the settlor's estate and rejected Central's cross-complaint that Jerry impliedly warranted that he had authority to act as the settlor's agent.

In affirming, the court of appeals stated:

> It is clear that Central, as Trustee of the Litner Trust, did not discharge its fiduciary duties as prudent individuals would manage their own affairs. On the other hand, Central, where its own dollars were involved as commercial

banker of Curtis, did exactly what an astute investor holding an unsecured note of Curtis would do to protect their individual interest faced with the corporation's dismal financial situation. That prudent and intelligent individual would collateralize the debt just as Central did with their own commercial loan. If subsequently that collateral appeared to be insufficient, the self-interested creditor would demand additional security. This is the course of conduct Central followed in order to safeguard its financial interests vis-a-vis Curtis Electro Corporation. After Central had protected its own interests securing its commercial loans with all of the available assets of Curtis, Central (as Trustee) finally turned its attention to the best interest of the *cestui que* trust.

In its dealings with Curtis it is clear that Central at all times subordinated the interest of Philip Litner, the beneficiary, to that of its own commercial banking division. By the time Central clearly and unequivocally demonstrated. . . . the need to take action to protect the Trust's interests regarding the Curtis notes, the hour was too late for the bank as Trustee to, at last, attempt to properly protect the beneficiary. We agree with the jury and affirm their verdict that Central is liable to the Estate of Philip Litner for the damages proximately caused by its significant breach of his trust.

Regarding the burden of proving damages, the court further stated:

We agree with Central that the burden of proof was on Jefferson National to show that Central wrongfully caused the loss to the Trust but find Central's objection to Judge McGarr's jury instruction [which was that Central had the burden of proving that the loss would have occurred even without the breach] to be without merit. . . . There is more than substantial and overwhelming evidence in the record to support Jefferson National's allegations that Central's conflict of interest, manifesting itself in the Trustee's failure to secure the payment of the Trust's promissory note, while encumbering the assets of Curtis as its commercial lender, was a proximate cause of the financial loss suffered by Philip Litner due to the unenforceability of the promissory note. A "proximate cause" need not be the only cause or the last or nearest cause of a loss. I.P.I.2d § 15.01 (1971).

The record clearly demonstrates that Central imprudently and improperly failed to perform its duties as Trustee of the Litner Trust. The wealth of such evidence easily overcomes any presumption that might have existed that Central had properly performed its duties while acting as the Trustee of the Philip Litner Trust. Central's actions in this case are replete with examples of the causal connection between Central's conflicting roles as Trustee and commercial lender and the unenforceability of the Curtis note. There is no doubt that at the time Curtis filed its bankruptcy petition the promissory note was virtually uncollectible.

Though in different form than the "appreciation damages" awarded in *Rothko,* the *Jefferson* verdict was punitive to the extent that the trustee's liability exceeded its gains and improved the position of the trust beneficiary over that which it probably would have been had there been no conflict. According to *Jefferson,* a disloyal fiduciary has the burden of proving that estate losses equal to those that might have been caused by fiduciary misconduct would have occurred even if there had been no misconduct. The court's formula is facially more favorable to a defaulting fiduciary than the no-further-inquiry rule, which simply requires the fiduciary to restore values that would be in the estate if the questioned conduct had not occurred. The opportunity to prove the consequences of events that did not occur, however, may be of little comfort to a defendant. The *Jefferson* court found a causal connection between divided loyalties of the fiduciary and loss on the estate's note in the circumstance that the commercial side of the bank was able to obtain security for its loan to Curtis while no security was obtained for the trust department's claim against the same debtor. With respect to the ability to get payment or security from a debtor, should the court have distinguished between a creditor furnishing financing for day-to-day expenses of a troubled business and a creditor of the same business whose claim rests on credit extended in a transaction presently contributing little to the debtor's efforts to stay afloat? Is it likely that a trustee without interest in the bank's commercial loan department would have fared any better in efforts to reduce the note held in trust to cash or saleable security? Would the settlor, as an unsecured creditor of Curtis, likely have protested the company's efforts to raise working capital by offering security to its commercial banker?

3. *Commercial Banks as Trustees.* As *Jefferson* illustrates, some conflict of interest questions are virtually unavoidable when the same corporation operates a trust department and engages in commercial lending. Bank regulations create so-called "Chinese walls" to prevent material insider information from flowing between commercial loan and trust departments in violation of SEC Rule 10b-5, as well as to minimize the likelihood of charges of divided loyalties. See Report, Problems of Fiduciaries Under the Securities Laws, 9 Real Prop. Prob. & Tr. J. 292 (1974).

4. *Jury Trials in Trust Litigation.* Note the important role played by the jury in *Jefferson.* The trial court's instructions left the question of causation to the fact-finders. Evidence that the commercial side of Central was able to protect itself against Central's impending insolvency while the trust department was not able to do so sufficed to support a finding of proximate cause between Central's potential conflict and its inability to collect on the note held in trust. Corporate trustees, in particular, probably have added concerns about potential liability for breach of trust when threatened with an action at law and jury trial rather than with the possibly more comforting prospect of a chancery proceeding without a jury.

Prueter v. Bork
105 Ill. App. 3d 1003, 435 N.E.2d 109 (1982)

McNAMARA, J. Plaintiff, Ervin Prueter, brought this action against his sister, Bernice Bork, individually, as executor of the estate of their deceased father Herman Prueter, and as trustee of Prueter Trust No. 3. Other beneficiaries of the trust, Melinda Bork, Maureen Bork, and Marilyn Bork were also named as defendants. Plaintiff alleged that he had a right to certain trust property based on various theories: breach of contract; promissory estoppel; breach of fiduciary duty; and allegations challenging the authenticity of the trust document itself. After a trial without a jury judgment was entered for defendants. Plaintiff appeals.

During his lifetime, Herman Prueter set up a series of trusts for the benefit of his two children, plaintiff and Bernice, designating himself as trustee. The original Prueter Trust dated March 23, 1939, named plaintiff as the sole beneficiary. Plaintiff had the right to all income as well as the proceeds from any disposition of trust assets. In addition, plaintiff had the power to alter, amend or revoke this trust. A similar trust, Prueter Trust No. 2, dated January 20, 1951, designated Bernice as sole beneficiary with the same rights and powers as plaintiff had in the Prueter Trust.

In May 1965 Herman visited plaintiff in his home and, in the presence of plaintiff's wife and children, asked him to "sign off" on the Prueter Trust. Herman explained that he had acquired additional real estate and wanted to set up a new trust which would divide the property equally between plaintiff and Bernice. Plaintiff then signed two documents, one revoking his interest in the Prueter Trust and directing the trustee to convey the assets to Edwin D. Lawler; and the other directing Lawler to convey the assets to Herman as trustee of Prueter Trust No. 3. Plaintiff, his wife and children all testified that plaintiff did not read the documents before signing them. Bernice executed similar directions under Prueter Trust No. 2 and both plaintiff and Bernice signed Prueter Trust No. 3 as beneficiaries.

We first consider plaintiff's contention that the trial court erred in failing to find that Herman, as trustee of Prueter Trust, breached his fiduciary duty to plaintiff, as beneficiary, when he asked plaintiff to revoke that trust in favor of the later trust. Plaintiff also argues that the court erred in not imposing a constructive trust on all the property which was part of the Prueter Trust and in not ordering Bernice to render an accounting as to such property.

The duty of loyalty owed by a trustee to a beneficiary in a trust relationship is more intense than in any other fiduciary relationship. Such duty prohibits the trustee from seeking any benefit for himself during the course of that relationship.

Where the trustee does benefit from a transaction with a beneficiary, such transaction is presumed to be fraudulent. The conclusion is not conclusive but may be rebutted by clear and convincing proof that the transaction was fair and that the trustee did not breach his duty of loyalty to the beneficiary.

While the trial court properly recognized that a fiduciary relationship existed as a matter of Prueter Trust, and plaintiff as its sole beneficiary, it erred in finding that Herman did not benefit from plaintiff's revocation of Prueter Trust. Consequently, the court failed to shift to defendants the burden of proving the fairness of the transaction. Under the original trust plaintiff had the "right to receive the proceeds from income, sales or other disposition of assets. . . ." In addition he held the power to "alter, amend or revoke . . . and [to] withdraw any parcel of real or personal property." Defendant's theory that these powers were illusory has no merit. Although in the original trust Herman did retain the power of trustee "to sell any of the trust property on any terms, [and] to convey with or without consideration . . . ," his power to so deal with the property was strictly limited by his fiduciary duties of care and loyalty to plaintiff as beneficiary. All transactions were required to be solely for plaintiff's benefit.

Conversely, in Prueter Trust No. 3 it was Herman, not plaintiff, who had the power to "alter, amend or terminate . . . [the] trust and . . . [to] withdraw any . . . property therefrom. . . ." Likewise, it was Herman, not plaintiff, who had the present right to all trust income. Although plaintiff was initially named as a beneficiary of Prueter Trust No. 3, he had no right to receive income during Herman's lifetime. Furthermore, plaintiff's future rights to trust property were at all times subject to Herman's right to revoke, a right which Herman did exercise, thus depriving plaintiff of all trust benefits.

When plaintiff revoked the original trust and directed the assets to be transferred to Prueter Trust No. 3, plaintiff suffered a detriment while Herman profited. Since a fiduciary relationship existed between them, this transaction is presumed to be fraudulent. The burden was on defendants to show the fairness of the transaction so as to negate the presumption that Herman breached his fiduciary duty of loyalty to plaintiff. Defendants completely failed to meet this burden.

Important factors in determining whether a particular transaction is fair include a showing by the fiduciary that he made a full disclosure of all relevant information to the subservient party; that the consideration was adequate; and that the principal had competent and independent advice before completing the transaction. Plaintiff was not informed of the difference between his rights under Prueter Trust and Prueter Trust No. 3. Herman's failure to disclose to him this relevant information was fatal to the validity of this transaction. Nor did plaintiff receive any advice prior to executing the documents. Furthermore, a comparison of the interest plaintiff received in Prueter Trust No. 3 with that surrendered by him in Prueter Trust reveals that the consideration was inadequate.

Citing Simpson v. Adkins (1941), 311 Ill. App. 543, 37 N.E.2d 355 and Pernod v. American National Bank & Trust Co. of Chicago (1956), 8 Ill.2d 16, 132 N.E.2d 540, defendants argue that since plaintiff had an opportunity to read the documents and to ascertain the facts for himself he cannot now complain because he failed to do so. Both cases are clearly distinguishable from the present case. In *Simpson* no fiduciary relationship existed. While in *Pernod* there was a fiduciary relationship, the trustee did not profit by the terms of the trust and thus no presumption of invalidity arose. Failure to read a document is normally no excuse for a party who signs it. Where however, as here, a fiduciary relationship exists and where the dominant party benefits from execution of the document by the subservient party, a presumption of invalidity arises. The burden was on defendants to show that plaintiff revoked Prueter Trust with full knowledge of the facts, including knowledge of the legal effect of his signature on the relevant documents. Defendants have failed to meet this burden.

Defendants also maintain that plaintiff's signature on two subsequent documents, an amendment to the trust and a petition for a condemnation proceeding, to both of which a copy of Prueter Trust No. 3 was attached, indicate his consent to or ratification of the terms of the trust. Absent a showing by defendants that plaintiff had full knowledge of the trust terms when he executed these documents these transactions enjoy the same presumption of invalidity accorded his signature on the original documents. . . . Defendants failed to offer any evidence that plaintiff had such knowledge or that the transactions were fair.

Defendants finally contend that plaintiff's action is barred by laches. Although the period of time on which laches is predicated normally begins to run either when the plaintiff learns of the facts on which his rights are based or when a reasonable person would require such knowledge, a different rule applies where a fiduciary relationship is involved. Where a fiduciary has a duty to disclose certain facts to the plaintiff but fraudulently fails to do so, plaintiff's failure to use diligence to ascertain these facts is excused. In such cases, the running of time begins when the fraud is actually discovered by plaintiff.

In the present case it does not appear that plaintiff had actual knowledge of the implications of his revocation of Prueter Trust prior to Herman's death. Since plaintiff filed suit within a reasonable period after Herman's death, laches has no application.

In light of our finding that Herman breached his fiduciary duty to plaintiff, it is unnecessary to consider plaintiff's other contentions of breach of contract, promissory estoppel, and the invalidity of the trust agreement itself.

For the reasons stated, the judgment of the circuit court of Cook County is reversed and the cause is remanded with directions to enter judgment for plaintiff, to order Bernice Bork to render an accounting with regard to that property and income in Prueter Trust No. 3 which was fraudulently derived from Prueter Trust, and for further proceedings consistent with the holdings of this opinion.

Reversed and remanded with directions.

McGillicuddy and Rizzi, JJ., concur.

Notes and Questions

1. *Which Relationship Controls?* In *Prueter*, is it not possible that when Herman succeeded in getting Ervin to "sign off" on Prueter Trust #1 they were acting in the roles of father and son rather than as trustee and beneficiary? Should the court attach any weight to that possibility? Notice the court's approval of the trial court's conclusion that a fiduciary relationship existed as a matter of law.

2. *Fiduciary as Adverse Possessor Against an Estate Beneficiary?* In Venator v. Quier, 285 Or. 19, 589 P.2d 731 (1979), the decedent's widow succeeded as surviving joint tenant to portions of ranch lands that she and her husband had operated as partners. She reasonably believed that she had sole rights to the entire ranch. In fact, the deeds to some acreage in the ranch lacked the magic words of survivorship. Consequently, as to some tracts, the widow succeeded only to a spouse's intestate portion held in

common with her son, whom her husband had adopted. The widow, who was administrator of her husband's estate for two years, later claimed sole ownership of the disputed tract by virtue of oral gifts from her husband followed by adverse possession for the requisite period. The court rejected her claim on the ground that her role as administrator subjected her to the obligation to represent only interests of estate beneficiaries and prevented her possession during the two years as administrator from being adverse to the other heir. According to the court, it did not matter that the widow at all times after the husband's death treated the disputed land as if it belonged to her in her individual capacity.

Along with *Prueter, Venator* illustrates that family members serving as fiduciaries may not be permitted to claim that they acted as individuals rather than in a fiduciary capacity no matter what they and others in the family may have believed. Should courts create an exception for acts that all believed to have been done in a personal rather than in a fiduciary capacity?

Prueter also illustrates the perils confronting a fiduciary who undertakes to bargain with a competent, adult beneficiary for a release of the beneficiary's interest in the subject of a trust or estate. Suppose that someone other than father Herman had been serving as trustee of Prueter Trust No. 1 and that Herman had persuaded his son as sole beneficiary to request the trustee to collapse the trust by a transfer to Herman, or to the son for re-transfer to Herman. What result if the trustee acts as requested and the son later sues the trustee for her or his role in an arrangement that was not well understood by the beneficiary?

PART C. REGULATION OF TRUST INVESTMENTS

1. The Traditional Prudent Investor Rule

Statutory Reference: *1990 UPC § 7-302*

Gordon, The Puzzling Persistence of the Constrained Prudent Man Rule
62 N.Y.U. L. Rev. 52, 57-62 (1987)

A. THE ORIGINAL FORMULATION

The Prudent Man Rule derives from the 1830 case, Harvard College v. Amory,[13] in which the Supreme Judicial Court of Massachusetts, rejecting the English rule requiring investment in government securities, refused to surcharge a trustee for investing in common stocks. The original formulation, which has been adopted by decision or statute in thirty-nine states and the District of Columbia,[14] is a model of flexibility. In investing trust funds, the trustee was enjoined to exercise "sound discretion" and

> to observe how men of prudence, discretion and intelligence manage their own affairs, not in regard to speculation, but in regard to the permanent disposition of their funds, considering the probable income, as well as the probable safety of the capital to be invested.

The rule had two key elements. First, there was a substantive standard of safe investment. The trustee was to acquire investments appropriate for permanent disposition of his own funds, not for speculation. The court realized that absolute safety of investment was impossible. "Do what you will, the capital is at hazard." But it required that within the limits of

---

13. 26 Mass. (9 Pick.) 446 (1830).

14. See G. Bogert & G. Bogert, The Law of Trusts and Trustees § 613, at 57-58 (rev. 2d ed. 1980 & Supp. 1986). Arkansas, California, Colorado, Connecticut, Delaware, Florida, Georgia, Hawaii, Idaho, Illinois, Indiana, Iowa, Kansas, Louisiana, Michigan, Minnesota, Mississippi, Nebraska, Nevada, New Jersey, New York, North Carolina, Oklahoma, Oregon, Pennsylvania, South Carolina, South Dakota, Tennessee, Texas, Utah, Virginia, Washington, and Wyoming have adopted the prudent man standard by statute. See id. at 57 & n.15. Maryland, Massachusetts, Missouri, Rhode Island, and Vermont have adopted the prudent man standard by court decision. See id. at 57-58. The District of Columbia has adopted the prudent man standard by rule of court. See id.

Until the early 1940's, most states had required trustees to select investments from a statutory list (called a legal list) of the (supposedly) safest investment, primarily limited to government bonds, mortgages, and, occasionally, fixed income securities of the most stable companies. The Depression showed that virtually no instrument was immune from default or payment moratorium. . . .

permanent disposition the trustee consider the factors of safety and income. Second, there was a process standard. In making investment judgements, the trustee was subject to the prevailing standard of how prudent men handle their own affairs.

B. The Restatement, the Treatise, and the Constrained Rule

The modern understanding of the Prudent Man Rule was shaped by that great figure in the law of trusts, the late Professor Austin Wakeman Scott. Scott was the reporter of the first and second Restatement of Trusts (the Restatement) completed in 1935 and 1959, respectively, and the author of the leading treatise on trusts, The Law of Trusts (the Treatise), first published in 1939 and successively revised and updated. Scott's work has played a pivotal role in the legal understanding of the trustee's investment management duties. Most cases and commentaries in the area cite as authoritative either the Treatise or the Restatement, or rely on formulations derived from those two sources. Moreover, Scott's teachings on investment management by trustees have remained virtually unmodified over a fifty-year period. The relevant sections and comments of the second Restatement are virtually identical to those of the first Restatement and continue to be regarded as authoritative today.

The investment management sections of the Treatise and the Restatement can be read as an attempt to interpret and apply the Harvard College v. Amory formulation through more specific rules and examples. But Scott's rules and examples are more constraining, and less flexible, than Harvard College required. Perhaps initially useful, these rules and examples no longer conform to our best understanding of prudent investment strategy and thus unwisely restrict trustees. Far more serious, no one has successfully carried forward Scott's project of providing the "better view" in the law of trusts. In a sense Scott has become "Scott," too authoritative to revise. Since the publication of the last editions of the Treatise and the second Restatement, there has been an explosion of theoretical and empirical work by financial economists, leading to new conceptions of investor and market behavior. None of this progress is reflected in "Scott"; indeed, what has been learned contradicts much of what "Scott" states on investment management. . . .

Three key decisions in the Treatise and the Restatement transformed the flexible standard of Harvard College into what has become the constrained Prudent Man Rule. First, Scott altered the Rule to require a more conservative benchmark of prudence than Harvard College. Instead of the prudence of persons seeking "permanent disposition of their funds," Scott prescribed the prudence of one seeking primarily the "preservation of the estate." An investment strategy designed to preserve principal will presumably be more cautious than one aimed at permanent disposition, which could include a buy-and-hold portfolio of common stocks at a higher level of risk and expected return. Moreover, in inflationary times, a mandate to preserve the estate becomes confounding; to preserve the estate in nominal terms may well defeat the testator's objective of transferring wealth to the next generation, but to preserve the estate in real terms requires investment that may risk the loss of principal.

First Alabama Bank of Montgomery, N.A. v. Martin
425 S.2d 415 (Ala. 1982)

TORBERT, C.J. This is a class action. The plaintiffs are beneficiaries of approximately 1,250 individual trusts, of which the bank is trustee. As trustee of these individual trusts, the bank invested certain assets comprising the principal of those trusts in participating units of two common trust funds, a bond fund and an equity fund.

After First Alabama purchased and sold certain units and made certain investments that resulted in substantial losses to those funds, the plaintiffs sought a declaration as to the duty of the bank and its liability to account, a declaration that certain investments were imprudent, and affirmative relief requiring the bank to restore to the common trust funds the losses sustained because of the bank's allegedly improper investments.

Prior to the certification of the class, First Alabama took the position that this action would require a full accounting of each of approximately 1,250 individual trusts. The trial court did not agree. After the original appeal to this Court, First Alabama filed a delayed counterclaim, requesting a full accounting of its own acts as the trustee of the individual trusts. The court subsequently struck this counterclaim, without prejudice to First Alabama's right to maintain individual suits for an accounting. . . .

[T]he court entered an order which found that the defendant as trustee of the common bond fund purchased the following debentures: ATICO Mortgage Investors, Barnett Mortgage Trust, Guardian Mortgage Investors, Justice Mortgage Investors, Midland Mortgage Investors, and Security Mortgage Investors. The trial court concluded that the purchase of these securities by the bank as trustee did not measure up to the "prudent man" standard and were, therefore, imprudent. Because it found the purchase of these securities imprudent, the court found it unnecessary to decide whether the sale of these securities also had been imprudent. These securities were Real Estate Investment Trusts (REITs), as described later in this opinion. . . .

On August 19, 1981, the court ruled against First Alabama on all of its special and affirmative defenses, readopted its class action order of June 24, 1981, and ordered First Alabama to pay $1,226,798.00 into the bond fund and $1,426,354.88 into the equity fund. These sums represented the difference between the purchase and sales prices of the six bond fund securities and twenty-two of the equity fund securities. The bank was further ordered to pay interest on these sums.

At trial, the plaintiffs introduced evidence of a "common trust plan" that had been adopted by First Alabama and approved by the Comptroller of the Currency. Testimony showed that the essential investment purpose of the bond fund was to produce income and that the essential investment purposes of the equity fund were the appreciation of equity and production of income. The plan recognized that the valuation of the investments of the common trust funds would vary periodically and it had specific provisions as to how the funds would be valued quarterly to reflect the market value of investments. The evidence showed that the method of valuation was carefully spelled out in that plan, but that First Alabama did not follow that method.

I. EVIDENCE AS TO IMPRUDENCE OF INVESTMENTS IN THE EQUITY FUND.

In regard to the equity fund, the court found that the purchase of seventeen of the twenty-four designated equity fund securities had been imprudent. As to these seventeen securities, the court found it unnecessary to decide whether their sale was imprudent but did conclude that the sale of five of the remaining seven securities had been imprudent.

Evidence was introduced showing that in 1973 the board of directors of First Alabama reduced to writing what it considered to be minimum standards of safety. Al Byrne, the vice president and senior trust officer of the bank admitted, however, that these standards were followed prior to 1973 as unwritten guidelines and were generally so followed at the time in which the sales and purchases in question were made. These standards were: (1) A rating of B+ or better by the Standard and Poor ratings (S & P) (B+ being an average rating and B being a speculative rating); (2) a minimum of 1,500,000 shares of stock in the hands of the public; and (3) annual sales of at least $100 million. Byrne testified that the bank generally invested in companies with at least ten years' experience in business and a record of increased earnings. He stated that the companies would generally be rated by one of the rating services. First Alabama claimed that the bank's minimum standards were primarily designed for individual trusts, rather than common trust funds, yet Byrne stated that when purchases were made for the two common funds, bank policy required that those minimum standards adopted by the bank be followed. Evidence was also presented showing that deviations were permitted from these standards adopted by the board of directors with the approval of the trust investment committee so as to accomplish its goals.

The plaintiffs offered evidence that these standards had not been followed. For example, Associated Coca-Cola, Cox Broadcasting, Rust Craft Greeting Cards and Sealed Power were rated B+ but failed to meet the Bank's requirement of one hundred million dollars in annual sales. In addition, the following stocks failed to meet the minimum requirement of a B+ rating: American Garden Products; Ames Department Stores; Beverage Canners; CNA Financial; Elixir Industries; First Mortgage Investors; Hav-a-Tampa; Kinney Services; Loomis Corp.; Mortgage Associates; Transamerica Corp.; Universal Oil Products; and Wynn Oil Co.

Dr. Robert Johnston . . . expert witness for the plaintiffs, testified that First Alabama, as trustee, should have invested defensively. According to Johnston, a trustee should first provide for the safety of the principal and then obtain an adequate return. He based his conclusions upon a treatise by Dr. Benjamin Graham, which stated seven criteria for testing the safety of investments. These criteria were (1) a minimum of $100 million in annual sales; (2) a current ratio of at least two to one (current assets should be twice current liabilities); (3) a net working capital to long-term debt ratio of at least one to one (net working capital being current assets less current liabilities and long-term debt meaning obligations that mature in more than one year); (4) earnings stability (positive earnings for the last ten years); (5) a good dividend record; (6) an earnings growth measure of at least one-third per share over a ten-year period, averaging the first three years and the last three years to remove extremes; (7) a moderate price earnings ratio of no more than fifteen to one; and (8) a moderate ratio of price to assets of no more than one and one half to one. Johnston believed that a trustee should not purchase stocks which failed to meet any one of these standards. . . .

The bank, however, contested Johnston's opinion by testimony from Walter McConnell, an investment banker from New York, who stated that Graham's book was intended for amateurs and not trustees. Also, Johnston on cross-examination was forced to admit that only five of the thirty stocks in the Dow Jones industrial average would meet these criteria. Johnston did not believe that a trustee could protect the principal against inflation by investing in common stocks. However, he did believe buying stocks in an old established company which paid high dividends is better than investing in a new venture.

Walter McConnell, as an expert witness for the bank, listed various criteria to be applied in testing the soundness of an investment. Among these were the stability of the company, its financial soundness, its debt/equity ratio, the quality of its management, the company's product, and its standing in the industry. He testified that those criteria would not be affected by market cycles or ups and downs in the market. He stated that in his opinion the investments were prudent, though he could not say that his company had recommended the purchase of these stocks while he was an adviser.

McConnell testified that he believed a trustee must take inflation into account in making trust investments. He stated that the most popular approach was to invest in the very best companies, i.e., the best "growth" companies. The idea was that with companies whose earnings and dividends were growing faster than inflation one would be protected against inflation. Another approach, according to McConnell, was not as popular but was still used by some large banks. This approach was to buy stocks in companies that were not well known, i.e., not well recognized and which were selling at much lower prices than the stocks of better known companies. McConnell analyzed the twenty-four stocks at issue and concluded they had a faster growing rate than the general market, and their earnings were also growing faster than the general market, but they were selling at a lower price-earnings ratio. He concluded that First Alabama used a rational investment approach and that the purchases of these twenty-four stocks were prudent. He further testified that S & P ratings were not intended to be used as investment recommendations and that experienced analysts do not use S & P ratings as a guide to sound investments. He further testified that it would be imprudent to buy or sell solely because of the S & P ratings, because one would not be using judgment in his decisions. Evidence was also introduced showing that the S & P ratings were issued with a warning that they should not be used solely as market recommendations.

Eldon Davis, a former trust investment officer of the bank, who was the trust investment officer at the time the investments were made, testified for First Alabama by deposition. He stated that in 1971 and 1972 the stock market was very high. The "Favorite 50" stocks were selling at extremely high prices so he decided to seek out securities that were undervalued in relation to the higher priced ones. He further stated that he did not rely on prospectuses, because the SEC requires a prospectus to be "plastered with a high degree of risk," and "will not let you say anything good about the securities," i.e., will not allow a prospectus to make favorable forecasts or projections. He likewise stated that he saw little difference in stocks rated B, or speculative, and B+, or median, since the rating services "just don't understand the business they are in." It was Davis's opinion that it is best to buy securities in the growth cycle of a company and not after it has matured. . . .

II. Evidence as to Imprudence of Purchases in the Bond Fund.

Substantial questions arose in regard to the bond fund concerning the purchase of securities of six real estate investment trusts (REIT's). REIT's are entities primarily engaged in mortgage lending on security of real estate, or in a combination of lending with the ownership and commercial development of real estate. One witness called REIT's "the mutual funds of real estate." In September 1971, First Alabama purchased the unsecured debentures of six REITs for $2,608,443.00, which comprised 23.2 percent of the principal of the bond fund. First Alabama suffered a 47.03+% loss on these bonds when they were sold for $1,381,645.00, for a total loss of $1,226,798.00.

Questions were raised as to whether REITs are safe trust investments. Kenneth Campbell, an expert witness for First Alabama, testified that the purchases of the REIT's were prudent investments. Yet he had called REITs "shaky legal undertakings" in his book, New Opportunities in Real Estate Trusts 29 (1978).

Testifying for the plaintiffs, Dr. Johnston stated that REIT's were risky investments. He applied a test set out by Benjamin Graham in his book Security Analysis (4th ed. 1962), which included size of the company, ratio of income to fixed charges, ratio of income to fixed charges in the company's worst year, ratio of income to funded debt, value of property ratio, ratio of net assets to funded debt, and a debt to capital funds ratio. Johnston testified that Graham's standards required one to look at the record of an REIT for a period of seven to ten years before making the investment, in order to determine the ratio of income to fixed charges. This was impossible here, however, because all of the REITs were "too new" to apply this test. Johnston concluded that all six of the REITs failed to meet the test suggested by Graham. Johnston concluded it was a poor decision to purchase REITs because there were other options available which were less risky.

The plaintiffs also offered the prospectuses of the REITs, which contained several pages of risk factors. These risk factors pointed out: (1) That the issuers were mortgage trusts engaged in making high-risk development and construction loans; (2) the competition in that field; (3) the conflict of interest with the sponsor-adviser; and (4) the fact that they operated principally on a leverage basis (that is, borrowing capital to increase earnings). Plaintiffs' evidence showed that the REIT's were making high-risk loans dependent upon the borrower's ability to pay. The plaintiffs contended that if the borrower had good credit, it could borrow directly from the bank and not have to pay the REIT fee.

Campbell, testifying for the bank, stated that the REITs concept has limited if not dangerous application for mortgage lending trusts. John Davis, hired by First Alabama to replace Eldon Davis as trust investment officer, testified that in his opinion the purchase of the six REITs was imprudent because they were all leverage. Davis testified that the REITs would not meet the standards of the Bank today.

Mr. Byrne testified that in 1972 First Alabama's standards for bond purchases were to buy bonds from companies that were well managed, that were generally AA or better, that had the ability to withstand industry trauma, and that were the larger companies available in the bond market. None of the six REITs met those standards. . . .

In its final order the court ordered the defendant to take whatever actions should be necessary to place the common trust funds and beneficiaries in the same position they would have occupied had the bank fully performed its duties. As to the lost principal that was unrecovered, the court determined from the evidence that investment in one-year treasury bills would be fair to the parties. As to the income that the common trust funds would have earned without the transactions complained of, the court ordered First Alabama to calculate the accounts as if it had fully performed the duties as the plaintiffs claimed it should have performed, and to recalculate the accounts as if it had promptly reinvested all the additional income at specified one-year treasury bill rates ranging from 4.61% to 13.23% and averaging 7.5%. . . .

The principal issues to be determined on the merits of this case are whether the trial court erred (1) in finding that the bank acted imprudently in buying or selling the securities, and finding First Alabama to have breached its trust, (2) in assessing interest as a surcharge for imprudent investments, and (3) in ordering a distribution of money damages to the members of the class without identification of the recipients or calculation of their exact damages.

The standard to be followed in determining whether a trustee has breached his duty to the trust was stated in Birmingham Trust National Bank v. Henley, 371 So.2d 883 (Ala.1979):

> The general definition of a trustee's investment duties was first stated by the Supreme Court of Massachusetts in Harvard College v. Amory, 9 Pick. 446, 461, 26 Mass. 446, 461 (1830):
>
>> All that can be required of a trustee to invest, is, that he shall conduct himself faithfully and exercise a sound discretion. He is to observe how men of prudence, discretion and intelligence manage their own affairs, not in regard to speculation, but in regard to the permanent disposition of their funds, considering the probable income, as well as the probable safety of the capital to be invested.
>
> The Restatement of the Law of Trusts 2d, § 227 (1959), states the rule in the following language:
>
>> In making investments of trust funds the trustee is under a duty to the beneficiary
>> (a) in the absence of provisions in the terms of the trust or of a statute otherwise providing, to make such investments and only such investments as a prudent man would make of his own property having in view the preservation of the estate and the amount and regularity of the income to be derived. . . .
>
> Liability cannot be based on the fact it subsequently developed that the investment would have been a good one. This is but the converse of the rule that a trustee is not liable if he makes an investment in a security which subsequently depreciates in value. III Scott on Trusts, § 204, supra, expresses the rule as follows:
>
>> The failure to make a profit which does not result from a breach of trust does not subject the trustee to liability. Thus if by the terms of the trust he is permitted but is not directed to invest in certain securities, he is not liable for failure to make the investment, although the securities subsequently appreciate in value. . . .
>
> The rule has also been summarized by Headley, Trust Investments, (97) Trusts & Estates 739 (1952), as follows:
>
>> The first and all inclusive requirement of the law is that a trustee shall act with complete and undivided loyalty to his trust. Second is that a trustee shall act prudently in the selection and management of investments. The elements of prudence are:
>>　(1) Care—a trustee must gather and weigh the facts and base his decisions on them rather than on rumor or guesswork;
>>　(2) Skill—a trustee must exercise the skill of the average person as a minimum; and if he has more than average skill he must exercise such skill as he has;
>>　(3) Caution—a trustee must not take chances which will imperil the accomplishment of the purposes of the trust. . . .
>>　. . . There must be balance between security of principal and amount and regularity of income; and the governing motive of the trustee must be sound investment for a long period and not speculation for a profit . . .
>
> With specific reference to a trustee's investing in common stocks, this author says:

. . . They represent no promise to return a dollar amount to the investor; their dividends are dependent on earnings and the action of a board of directors; they have always afforded an attractive vehicle for speculation. Nevertheless some of them have demonstrated, over a long period of years, the qualities required for sound permanent investments. Intrinsic values have been maintained and dividends have been adequate and regular. The principal has been reasonably safe for a number of reasons: competent management, sound financing, position in an essential industry, a successful record and an adequate market. . . .

371 S.2d at 894-96. Tested by this standard, we cannot say that the trial court committed reversible error in finding that the defendant did not fulfill its duty of caution, to preserve the trust corpus above all else, while striving for a regularity of income.

As to the imprudence of the equity fund, First Alabama contends that since Alabama is a "legal list" state, and since the beneficiaries had given their permission for the bank to invest in items not on the legal list, then the beneficiaries have no complaint for investments that have gone awry. This argument is without merit. As a trustee, First Alabama has a duty to preserve the trust property and make it productive. III Scott on Trusts § 227 (3rd ed. 1967).

First Alabama also contends that the only reason for holding it liable for the losses on the purchase and/or sale of the securities was that the ratings were below B+ on the S & P chart, and that the only reason for holding it liable for the losses on the REITs was that there was no Moody's or similar rating. First Alabama asserts that to hold it liable here on such evidence would impose a duty upon trustees that would make them absolute insurers against a drop in market price. This, however, is not the case. First Alabama cannot be held liable for its failure to meet its own standards. This is only one factor in the decision. The evidence in this case supports the decision of the trial court that First Alabama failed to fulfill its primary responsibility which was to provide for the safety of the trust's principal. The secondary responsibility was to insure an adequate return.

The difference between speculation and investment is well described by Dr. Headley in Headley, Trust Investments, 97 Trusts & Estates 739 (1952), quoted above in the quotation from Birmingham Trust National Bank v. Henley, 371 S.2d at 895. As Dr. Headley states, one who buys common stocks with the idea of selling them on the market for higher prices is speculating. One who is making a prudent investment examines the stocks' intrinsic values and purchases them for a long-term investment. Walter McConnell, testifying for the defendant, stated that one approach adopted by trust managers is to pick established stocks and not worry about subsequent turns in the market price. It is obvious that neither Headley's standards, nor those mentioned by McConnell, were consistently used by First Alabama.

Dr. Robert Johnston . . . testified that most of the seventeen stocks later found to be imprudent investments would fail to meet his tests. While Walter McConnell, an expert witness for the bank, stated that he believed the purchases to be prudent, he could not say that he, as an investment adviser for a number of trust companies, had ever recommended the purchase of any of the twenty-four stocks at issue.

Finally, the testimony of Eldon Davis, who made the investments at issue, further strengthens the holding of the trial court. As stated above, Mr. Davis testified that he did not look at prospectuses, that he saw little difference between a stock rated B+, or median, and one rated B, or speculative, that he did not think the rating services understood their business, and that he tried to buy undervalued stocks instead of the higher priced, more established ones. All of this evidence, taken together, supports the holding of the trial court that First Alabama was imprudent with regard to purchases made for the equity fund.

We also find no error in the trial court's holding that the sale of the five stocks was imprudent. Even Eldon Davis testified in his deposition that he was against the sale of these stocks and had recommended that they be held. Mr. McConnell, testifying for First Alabama, stated that during the recovery period after the recession the five stocks all had higher recovery rates than the S & P 500. It seems reasonable to state that had these stocks not been sold at the bottom of the market, there would have been no loss. It is true that a trustee will not be held liable under ordinary circumstances for losses due to unforeseen depression or recession of the stock market. Yet, where the course of dealing of the trustee is such that it causes the loss, a trustee will be liable. First Nat. Bank of Birmingham v. Basham, 238 Ala. 500, 191 S. 873 (1939). Here, First Alabama sold these stocks at or near their lowest price levels, against the advice of its own trust officer, and at the time the country was just beginning to recover from the worst recession since the 1930's. We cannot hold as a matter of law that the trial court erred or was plainly and palpably wrong in its conclusion that a reasonable and prudent man would have held these stocks. We therefore affirm the trial court's decision that the sale of the five stocks was imprudent.

It does appear clear from the evidence before the trial court that the investment in six REITs for the common bond fund was imprudent. The six REITs were all three years old or less, they were not listed among the top REITs in the country, and they were among the weakest of the nation's REITs. They did not meet the standards of Al Byrne, Robert Johnston, and Kenneth Campbell, all experts in the case. Thus, we hold that the trial court committed no error in holding against First Alabama as to the purchase of the six REITs. . . .

After careful consideration of the many issues presented on appeal, this Court has determined that the trial court did not err in finding for the plaintiffs. We reaffirm the "prudent man rule," which states that a trustee must only exercise sound discretion, conduct himself faithfully, and manage funds entrusted to him as men of prudence, discretion, and intelligence would manage their own affairs, having due regard for the safety of the corpus and probable income. Harvard College v. Armory, 26 Mass. (9 Pick.) 446 (1830). . . . We conclude that the trial court applied the "prudent man rule." Based upon the foregoing principles and the ore tenus rule, the findings of the trial court are due to be affirmed.

AFFIRMED.

JONES, SHORES, EMBRY, BEATTY and ADAMS, JJ., concur.
FAULKNER, J., recused.

Notes and Questions

1. *Relevance of General Market Conditions.* In 1973 and 1974, when First Alabama Bank made the challenged investments, the prices of stocks generally declined as a result of a bear (*i.e.*, generally declining) market. The *Martin* court did not discuss this background, evidently regarding it as irrelevant. Do you agree?

2. *Prudence Judged Ex Ante.* There is virtual unanimity among the authorities that a trustee, at least in theory, is not chargeable with losses solely because trust investments declined in value. Prudence is judged ex ante rather than ex post, *i.e.*, from the trustee's perspective at the time the investment decision was made and not with the benefit of hindsight. Did the *Martin* court in holding that the sale of five equity stocks when they were "at the bottom of the market" was a breach of trust adhere to the view that hindsight is irrelevant?

3. *Duty to Preserve Purchasing Power.* In *Martin,* part of the bank's explanation for its equity purchases was that it was hedging against inflation. The bank's expert witness testified that investing in growth companies is a sound strategy for coping with inflation. Does the duty to invest prudently mean that trustees are required to maintain purchasing power or merely to prevent nominal loss? The Second Restatement recognizes a duty of trustees to preserve trust property (see Restatement 2d of Trusts § 176), but does not recognize a duty to maintain the purchasing power of a trust's assets. However, the Comment to section 227 lists "likelihood of inflation" as one of ten factors that the trustee should consider when investing trust assets. Restatement 2d of Trusts § 227, at 535. At the same time the Restatement rejects as "speculative" investment strategies designed to increase the trust fund's dollar value. Id. at 531.

Although the Second Restatement's approach represents the traditional view, it has come under attack increasingly in recent years. Commentators have argued that the conventional rules concerning prudence are inappropriate in inflationary times and that trustees should be under a duty to maintain the real economic value of trust assets, not just their nominal value. See Hirsch, Inflation and the Law of Trusts, 18 Real Prop. Prob. & Trust J. 601 (1983). The Restatement 3d of Trusts revised the trustee's duty of impartiality among beneficiaries by providing that this duty "ordinarily includes a goal of protecting the property's purchasing power." Restatement 3d of Trusts § 232 comment c. We will return to the problem of inflation in the next section, discussing the trustee's duty of impartiality.

Notice also that beneficiaries occasionally have been able to compel the trustee to deviate from the terms of the trust to avoid the effects of inflation on trust assets. See, e.g., Trusteeship With Mayo, 259 Minn. 91, 105 N.W.2d 900 (1960), supra p. 734.

4. *The "Anti-Netting" Rule.* The analysis of the *Martin* court illustrates the conventional legal approach to determining the prudence or imprudence of trustee investment decisions, the approach that Professor Gordon calls the "constrained prudent man rule." Under that approach the court evaluates the propriety of each challenged investment in isolation rather than in the context of the entire trust portfolio and its objectives. Clearly consistent with this approach is the "anti-netting" rule, which prohibits a trustee from offsetting gains realized on improper trust investments against liability for loss on improper investments. To illustrate, suppose that a trustee improperly purchases stock in two different firms, A and B, for $10,000 each and later sells stock A for $6,000 and stock B for $12,000. The trustee cannot reduce its liability by offsetting the $2,000 gain against the $4,000 loss from stock A. The beneficiary is entitled to affirm the unauthorized act that resulted in a profit and simultaneously reject the unauthorized act that resulted in a loss.

The usual explanations for this rule are that permitting offsetting would enable the trustee personally to benefit from its dealings with trust property and would create incentives for trustees to engage in speculation to reduce or eliminate liability from improper investments. See, e.g., Cuyler's Estate, 5 D. & C. 317 (Pa. 1924). An important recent decision affirming the anti-netting rule is In re Bank of New York, 35 N.Y.2d 512, 364 N.Y.S.2d 164, 323 N.E.2d 700 (1974).

If the prohibition of offsetting gains against losses is compatible with the traditional asset-by-asset approach to judging prudent investment decisions, is it inconsistent with the modern approach to investment decisions that stresses prudence on a portfolio-wide basis? Comment a to section 213 of the Restatement 3d of Trusts states that the anti-netting rule does not prevent the trustee from relying on an investment strategy that emphasizes the entire trust portfolio. "[T]he rule applies only in ascertaining the amount of the trustee's liability once it has been determined . . . that there has been a breach of trust [in investment matters]."

The anti-netting rule applies only where breaches are separate and distinct. If breaches are not distinct, they are treated as a single breach and offsetting is permitted. Restatement 3d of Trusts § 213. How is one to decide whether breaches are separate or not? Not surprisingly, cases involving similar sets of facts have resulted in inconsistent decisions. Compare, e.g., Creed v. McAleer, 275 Mass. 353, 363, 175 N.E. 761, 765 (1931) with McInnes v. Goldthwaite, 94 N.H. 331, 52 A.2d 795 (1947).

5. *Duty to Diversify: A Contradiction or An Escape?* It is possible to escape the restrictions of the traditional asset-by-asset approach by expanding a corollary rule that has been around for a long time. Decisions in a number of jurisdictions have recognized that an investment may be adequately safe as to type and issuer reputation but nevertheless improper because it is unwise to place so much of a fund available for investment in any single type of investment asset. These precedents recognize that safety in investing involves some diversification to lessen the risk of unforeseeable economic calamity. In jurisdictions rejecting diversification as an element of prudence,

Andrew Carnegie's adage, "Put all your eggs in one basket and watch the basket," has prevailed.

Though an offshoot of the conventional standard in its inception, the duty to diversify shifts some of the inquiry regarding trustee investment judgments away from the merits of each security to concerns for the well-being of the entire trust fund.

Baker Boyer Nat'l Bank v. Garver, 43 Wash. App. 673, 719 P.2d 583 (1986) is an important recent case that illustrates this point. The court, while purporting to apply conventional rules, used the diversification duty to penalize a trustee for keeping all liquid funds of a trust (the trust also included large land holdings) in various tax-exempt municipals. The municipals had suffered a severe decline in market value due to the sharp rise in interest rates during the late 1970s and early 1980s. The court concluded that investing in fixed interest rate bonds was proper only to the extent that vulnerability to rising interest rates was offset by investing part of the fund in common stocks. The court assumed, without discussing the point, that the older view of diversification as a prudent way of reducing unforeseeable risks embraces a duty to consider the gain and risk potentials of different types of investment in, or appropriately considered for, a trustee's portfolio. The downside risks of one type of investment should be offset by another type that is likely to rise in value as a result of factors tending to depress the first.

The Washington trial and appellate courts involved in *Baker Boyer* probably were comfortable with the assumption that trustee investment security holdings should involve a mix of equities (stocks) and obligations (bonds and certificates of deposit). The duty of trustees to avoid favoring either income beneficiaries or remainder beneficiaries and certain trust accounting rules for identifying income and principal (which we will study in Part D, infra) have long served to push trustees to balance portfolio holdings selected for income-generation purposes (usually bonds) with common stocks. The case is noteworthy, however, because both trial and appellate courts used the duty of diversification, rather than the duty of impartiality, to support their rulings.

Section 227(b) of the Restatement 3d of Trusts expressly states that trustees are under a duty to diversify, "unless under the circumstances, it is prudent not to do so." Comment g explains that the diversification requirement is based on more than conservatism. It expresses a warning "against taking bad risks—ones in which there is an unwarranted danger of loss, or volatility that is not compensated by commensurate opportunities for gain." Modern portfolio theory refers to this type of risk as un-compensated risk, distinguished from risks for which the market itself provides compensation. We will consider this distinction and the scope of the diversification duty under the Restatement 3d of Trusts further after first introducing the revolution in financial theory that underlies the new legal thinking on fiduciary prudence.

2. *Rethinking Prudence under Modern Portfolio Theory*

A growing number of practitioners and academics have criticized the conventional interpretation of the prudent investor rule as being at odds with the approach that is reflected in modern portfolio theory and investment practice. While no decisions to date have expressly adopted the new approach, doctrinal change is likely to occur in the future. The recently completed Prudent Investor Rule portion of the Restatement 3d of Trusts revises several provisions of the Second Restatement in light of modern portfolio theory. Also, recently enacted statutory versions of the prudent investor rule depart from the conventional approach to a modern portfolio approach to managing risk in trust investments. See, e.g., Cal. Civ. Code § 2661. Finally, the Uniform Law Commissioners have assigned to the Joint Editorial Board for the Uniform Probate Code a project to develop a Uniform Prudent Investor Act modeled on the approach of the Restatement 3d of Trusts. The excerpts that follow indicate the most important differences between the conventional legal approach to prudence in trust investment and modern portfolio theory and practice.

Note, The Regulation of Risky Investments
83 Harv. L. Rev. 603, 616-21 (1970)

Running throughout the disparate legal approaches to the regulation of risk is a consistent concern with one particular type of risk: the risk of loss. While this regulation may have other objectives, the leitmotiv is an attempt to minimize the probability that the capital value of each investment will be less at some future date than when bought.[15] . . . Statutory legal lists restricting institutional and trust portfolios are explicitly designed to prevent risk of loss by forbidding investment in securities supposedly too susceptible to capital depreciation. The distinction drawn by the modern prudent man rule between "investment" and "speculation" also emphasizes conservation rather than growth. A "speculative" security is one especially likely to be worth less than its cost at some future date.

While this notion of risk savors of common sense, it makes a very peculiar assumption about the proper concerns of investors, policyholders, and trust beneficiaries. The assumption is that these parties are exclusively concerned with the possibility that their investment will sell for less than cost, rather than with all possible future values of their investment. Accordingly, this view ignores the probabilities associated with these other possible future values.

In addition to focusing solely on risk of loss, current regulation is limited to minimizing that risk on each particular security, rather than on the portfolio as a whole. . . . In evaluating the investment of trust funds, the

---

15. It thus includes the risk of decline in capital value of an equity security, the risk of default on a debt obligation, and the risk of interest rate rise with a consequent decline in the capital value of a fixed income security (if the horizon date falls before maturity).

prudent man rule treats each investment separately, instead of considering the portfolio as a whole. . . . Even if risk is viewed narrowly as risk of loss, this focus on individual securities ignores the fact that the risk of a portfolio is not the arithmetic sum of the risks of its component securities. The performance of many different securities may depend on the same future contingent event. A portfolio whose securities strongly covary—are each strongly affected by the same future events—will be riskier than a portfolio composed of securities which covary only slightly. For example, a portfolio consisting of fifty stocks, each of which has an even chance of doing very well or very poorly, carries relatively little risk as long as independent factors determine the success or failure of each security. On the other hand, if the same contingency—for example, the size of next year's defense budget—determines the futures of each security, security performance would covary strongly and portfolio risk would be quite large. Thus, concern should be directed not at the risk profile of each security, but at the marginal effect on total portfolio risk of acquiring each security. . . .

Finally, the law treats risk in isolation from the return an investment may contribute to a portfolio. . . . Each security is evaluated solely by the probability that a capital loss will be incurred. If two securities carry equal risks and only one has a return high enough to justify its risk, current regulatory policy must accept or reject both. . . .

Rigorous economic analysis has devised another concept of risk which may be a better guide to regulatory policy than the current legal concept. This economic concept views the risk of a portfolio as the uncertainty associated with its market value or expected rate or return at some future horizon date. . . . If the portfolio has a wide range of possible future values at the appropriate horizon date, and no one value has a high level of probability, the portfolio is riskier than if all possible prices fell within a narrow range and one possible price was highly probable. One portfolio might thus be riskier than another even though it has a low probability of loss. This is because risk of loss considers only those possible future values which are less than cost. The economic concept considers every possible future value, and thus measures what the investor is actually worried about, the future value of his portfolio.

In addition to being a more appropriate index of risk than risk of loss, the economic concept of risk emphasizes the relationship between the risk of a particular security and the risk of the portfolio. The uncertainty risk of the portfolio is the aggregate of the uncertainty risks of the securities which compose it. This aggregation of risk is not an arithmetic total but recognizes that securities which strongly covary add more to portfolio risk than securities which do not. . . .

B. Longstreth, Modern Investment Management
and the Prudent Man Rule
110-11 (1986)

[T]he law's prudent man bears little resemblance today to prudent men and women in the real world, even those engaged in "safeguarding the property of others." . . .

A modern paradigm for prudence . . . would shift the focus from the disembodied investment to the fiduciary, the portfolio, and its purpose. In light of the over-arching principle . . . that prudence is a test of conduct and not performance, the most promising vehicle for accomplishing that shift is a paradigm of prudence based above all on process. Neither the overall performance of the portfolio nor the performance of individual investments should be viewed as central to the inquiry. Prudence should be measured principally by the process through which investment strategies and tactics are developed, adopted, implemented, and monitored. Prudence is demonstrated by the process through which risk is managed rather than by the labelling of specific investment risks as either prudent or imprudent. Investment products and techniques are essentially neutral; none should be classified prudent or imprudent per se. Investment products and techniques are essentially neutral; none should be classified prudent or imprudent per se. It is the way in which they are used, and how decisions as to their use are made, that should be examined to determine whether the prudence standard has been met.

More specifically, for any investment product or technique employed by a fiduciary or delegate selected by the fiduciary in connection with such employment (including pooled investment vehicles), the test of prudence is care, diligence, and skill demonstrated by the fiduciary in considering all relevant factors bearing on an investment decision. If particular investment products or techniques are not imprudent per se, neither are they per se prudent for all purposes and at all times. Their use, without more, will not suffice. Prudence is not self-evident. Nor will it be enough to point to their use by other fiduciaries. What matters is not that others have used the product or technique (for whatever reasons), but the basis for its use by the fiduciary in question.

Among the relevant factors to be considered are at least the following:

1. The role the investment product or technique is intended to play in the total portfolio.

2. Whether that role is reasonably designed, as part of the total portfolio, to serve the purposes for which the portfolio is being held and invested, taking into account the risk of loss and opportunity for gain associated with the investment product or technique (including such factors as tax effects and informational costs of initiation, monitoring, and termination), the composition of the portfolio in terms of its diversification and systemic risk, and the minimum projected cash flows from income and capital gain over future periods compared with the maximum projected cash demands on the portfolio over those periods.

3. The competence of the fiduciary or the delegates selected by him to employ the product or technique.

4. If delegates are involved, the reasonableness of the terms and conditions of such delegation, taking into account the compensation structure, monitoring mechanisms, and provisions for termination.

Notes

1. *Specific Changes under Restatement 3d of Trusts.* Among the specific legal changes that Mr. Longstreth, a partner in the New York firm of

Debevoise & Plimpton and a former Commissioner of the Securities and Exchange Commission, recommends are recognition of a general duty to diversify, rejection of per se rules prohibiting particular investment products as "speculative," and redefinition of the trustee's duty to avoid risk to conform to the economic concept of risk. The last point specifically means that the trustee must make a deliberate judgment about the suitable level of risk and return in light of the trust portfolio's return requirements, risk tolerance and general purposes, and other circumstances. All of these changes are reflected in the new Restatement.

2. *Diversification and the Market Risk/Specific Risk Distinction.* As mentioned earlier, as part of its portfolio-wide perspective, the Restatement 3d of Trusts expressly provides that trustees are normally under a duty to diversify trust investments. See Restatement 3d of Trusts § 227(b). Understanding the scope of this duty and its rationale requires some background regarding risk management.

Because all investments involve some risk in the sense of possible loss of real, inflation-adjusted value, modern portfolio theory (MPT) defines caution as the prudent management of risk rather than avoidance of risk. In defining prudent risk management the new Restatement draws upon a conceptual distinction made in MPT between uncompensated, or "specific," risk and compensated, or "market" (or "systemic") risk. As the student Note on the regulation of risky investments indicates, investors care about return and risk. Generally, they want the greatest return for the least risk, and they want to be compensated in proportion to the risk they assume. Risk is the probable variability of future returns in relation to the expected rate of return (meaning total return). The greater the risk, the greater the expected return the investor will demand to compensate the risk.

The market does not compensate all types of risk, only that type that affects the market generally. An example is the risk of change in general economic conditions. Almost all investments are affected by this risk the same way, although in different degrees. Another type of risk (loosely called "specific" risk) is that which specifically affects a particular investment or industry but not the market as a whole. The federal defense budget has particular effects on the aerospace industry, while the threat of terrorism affects the travel industry differently than it affects other sectors of the economy. The market does not compensate investors for assuming specific risk, but investors can reduce specific risk through diversification. Investors reduce specific risk by acquiring assets that react in opposite ways to the same events (e.g., the effect of rain on the value of shares in firms manufacturing umbrellas versus those manufacturing suntan lotion). Market risks, by contrast, are not diversifiable because they are systemic. At the same time, there is no reason to diversify them since the market has already rewarded investors for taking them. MPT holds that the investor should hold a broad portfolio in order to reduce specific risk to a low level.

The Restatement 3d's position on diversification of trust investments is compatible with MPT. Comment g to section 227 states that "a trustee's duty of prudent investing normally calls for reasonable efforts to reduce diversifiable risks, while no such generalization can be made with respect to market risk." The appropriate level of market risk for any particular trust depends on that trust's purposes and the relevant trust and beneficiary circumstances. Comment e to the same section also provides that "[f]ailure to diversify on a reasonable basis in order to reduce uncompensated [i.e., specific] risk is ordinarily a violation of both the duty of caution and the duties of care and skill."

The shift to emphasizing total portfolio risk reduction leads the new Restatement to abandon the traditional view that trustees must avoid "speculative" investments. Accordingly, section 227 comment g rejects the rule that treats specific classes of investments or techniques as per se imprudent. An investment that has a high specific risk may be permissible if, as part of a strategy of diversification, it contributes to reducing total portfolio risk. For an argument that trustees of family trusts with small portfolios should not be permitted to invest in volatile stocks regardless of their diversification effects, see Haskell, The Prudent Person Rule for Trustee Investment and Modern Portfolio Theory, 69 N.C.L. Rev. 87 (1990).

3. *Delegation of Fiduciary Duties?* Note that the Longstreth approach takes it for granted that trustees may delegate to investment advisors the responsibility for investment decisions. This practice involves another change in the conventional rules. It is well-settled that trustees may not delegate to others those responsibilities that they can reasonably be required to perform themselves. The line between delegable and non-delegable functions is not always clear. The courts usually articulate the line in terms of an equally uncertain distinction between discretionary and ministerial acts. It is clear, though, that while a trustee may employ investment advisors, delegating the power to select trust investments to an agent is a breach of the duty not to delegate. Restatement 2d of Trusts § 171 comment h. Longstreth and others have criticized this rule on the ground that it inhibits trustees from taking advantage of specialized expertise in an industry that increasingly has become specialized. The question, they argue, should not be whether to delegate but how to delegate in the way most effective for the trust.

The Restatement 3d of Trusts, responding to these criticisms, abandons the traditional non-delegation rule. It subsumes the delegation issue under the trustee's duty to act prudently. Section 227(c)(2) states that the trustee must "act with prudence in deciding whether and how to delegate authority to others . . . ." Expanding on this, comment j states that in investment matters "the trustee has the power, and may sometimes have the duty, to delegate such functions and in such manner as a prudent investor would delegate under the circumstances."

Section 227.1 of the Restatement 2d of Trusts provides that reliance on counsel's advice is no defense to a breach of trust. What implications does the Restatement 3d of Trust's repeal of the non-delegation rule have for section 227.1?

4. *Index Mutual Funds and the Prudent Investor Rule.* Related to the question about the duty not to delegate is the widespread practice of trust investment in mutual funds. It has been noted that this practice to some extent has eroded the traditional no-delegation rule. Langbein & Posner,

Market Funds and Trust Investment Law, 1976 Am. Bar Found. Res. J. 1, 19-24 (1976). Langbein and Posner argue not only that mutual funds are an appropriate trust investment vehicle but that "index" or "market" funds are a particularly effective means of achieving optimal levels of diversification with minimal transaction costs. These are mutual or other investment funds comprised of a securities portfolio that is designed to approximate indexes of market performance, such as the Dow Jones or Standard and Poor's indexes. The theory underlying these funds is that capital markets are highly efficient and attempts to beat the market through a strategy of individually selecting undervalued securities are very likely to fail.[16] Index funds are designed to approximate market performance. Posner and Langbein argue that trust investments in such funds should provide a safe harbor for trustees under the prudent investor rule for three reasons: (1) they are likely to yield higher net returns to the investor, (2) they are better diversified than portfolios constituted by a beat-the-market strategy, and (3) they minimize transaction costs. For a criticism of the index fund proposal, see Fleming, Prudent Investments: The Varying Standards of Prudence, 12 Real Prop. Prob. & Tr. J. 243 (1977) (characterizing the proposal as an "overreaction to a concern for risk-taking involved in individually selected investment portfolios.")

5. *State Legislation.* To date, six states (California, Delaware, Georgia, Minnesota, Tennessee, and Washington) have enacted legislation that adopts a modernized version of the prudent investor rule. These statutes generally authorize but do not require trustees to follow the insights of modern portfolio theory. At the same time, they direct fiduciaries to consider individual investments as part of an overall investment strategy. See, e.g., Cal. Prob. Code § 16040(b).

3. Social Investing and Fiduciary Duties

Fiduciaries have increasingly been under pressure in recent years to take social or political considerations into account in making investment decisions. Social investing covers a wide variety of concerns, ranging from demands that universities and pensions remove from their portfolios investments in firms that conduct business in South Africa to actions such as Harvard University's recent decision to eliminate from its portfolio stock in tobacco companies. The legal issues raised by social investing for trustees primarily concern the prudent investor rule and the duty of loyalty. To date, there is little case law directly dealing with either issue. See Blankenship v. Boyle, 329 F. Supp. 1089 (D.D.C. 1971) (purchase by union pension fund of shares in certain electric utilities to induce them to buy union-mined coal held a breach of duty of loyalty); Associated Students of the Univ. of Or. v. Oregon Inv. Council, No. 78-7502 (Cir. Ct., Lane Co.,

---

16. Empirical work has tended to confirm this theory in revealing that most mutual funds have underperformed market averages over a sustained period of time. See J. Lorie & M. Hamilton, The Stock Market: Theories and Evidence (1973).

Or., Jan. 21, 1985) (proposed university portfolio policy of disinvestment of South Africa-related investments is inconsistent with the prudent investor rule), rev'd on other grounds, 82 Or. App. 145, 728 P.2d 30 (1986), review denied, 303 Or. 74, 734 P.2d 354 (1987); Bd. of Trustees of Employees Retirement System v. Mayor of Baltimore, 317 Md. 72, 562 A.2d 720 (1989); but see Scott on Trusts § 227.17 (stating that trustees may consistently with their duties take social considerations into account in making investment decisions).

In analyzing questions concerning the legal permissibility of social investment, distinctions must be drawn between various types of fiduciaries. The legal standards applicable to charitable institutions such as private foundations, for example, differ in important respects from those governing pension funds. For many pension plans, investment of fund assets is regulated by the Employee Retirement Income Security Act of 1974 (ERISA), which explicitly supersedes state law for non-exempt plans. See Troyer, Slocombe & Boisture, Divestment of South Africa Investments: The Legal Implications for Foundations, Other Charitable Institutions, and Pension Funds, 74 Geo. L. J. 127 (1985). The following excerpts summarize some of the general arguments concerning social investing.

Langbein & Posner, Social Investing and the Law of Trusts
79 Mich. L. Rev. 72, 85-86, 88 (1980)

A portfolio constructed in accordance with social principles will be less diversified than a portfolio constructed in accordance with [modern portfolio theory]. This is because stocks are added to and subtracted from the portfolio by the social investor without regard to the effect on diversification. To be sure, if social responsibility were a random characteristic of firms, so that the set of socially responsible firms differed from the set of socially irresponsible firms only in respect to social responsibility, and not in size, profits, location, or other relevant financial characteristics, the effect on diversification of excluding the socially irresponsible firms from the investment portfolio would be limited to what is called sampling error. . . .

If socially irresponsible firms are not a random draw from the underlying universe of firms, then the use of social-investing criteria to design the portfolio will result not only in sampling error, but also in sampling bias. . . .

The bias imparted by social investing interacts with the problem of sampling error in the following way: a large firm is, by virtue of its size, less likely to survive social-investing screening than a small one [because large firms, by virtue of their size, do more wicked acts], but the exclusion of a large firm from the investment portfolio has a bigger effect in creating sampling error than the exclusion of a small firm. This is because the large firm has a greater weight in the overall performance of the market, and it is that overall performance that one is seeking, through diversification, to track as closely as possible. . . .

In sum, we are skeptical that a portfolio constructed in accordance with consistent, and consistently applied, social principles could avoid serious underdiversification.

Dobris, Arguments in Favor of Fiduciary Divestment of "South African" Securities
65 Neb. L. Rev. 209, 239-40 (1986)

There seems to be something approaching general agreement that portfolios under $50 million can be divested without meaningful effect.[17] It is the larger portfolios that create problems. . . .

It has been suggested "that it is possible to construct passive portfolios that exclude South Africa related securities and that track the S&P 500 reasonably well . . ." but at a higher nonmarket risk.[18] Nonmarket risk is . . . risk that is "uncompensated"; i.e., not likely to lead to reward.[19] So, the passive investor might survive reasonably well.[20] The report further suggests that investments made on the basis of mechanical rules may be accomplished sensibly in a South Africa free investment world.[21] It also suggests that the most vulnerable investor is the active manager who trades a great deal on the basis of company specific research.[22] The point is . . . there may be rational and appropriate investment approaches to South Africa free investing of large portfolios.

Notes and Questions

1. Do Langbein and Posner assume that there is an unavoidable trade-off between the size of a firm in which a trustee or pension fund manager might wish to invest and social investing? Whether or not they do, do you think that social investing requires avoiding investments in large firms?

2. *Standing.* An important question involved in litigation over social investing by state or local government funds (not regulated by ERISA) is who has standing to challenge a public funds investment practices. In Associated Students of the University of Oregon v. Oregon Investment Council, 82 Or. App. 145, 728 P.2d 30 (1986), the court held that student

---

17. See D. Hauck, The Impact of South Africa-Related Divestment on Equity Portfolio Performance 3-4 (1985); Wagner, Emkin & Dixon, [South Africa Divestment: The Investment Issues, Fin. Analysts J., Nov.-Dec. 1984], at 14.

18. See D. Hauck, at 3.

19. See R. Hagin, [The Dow Jones-Irwin Guide to Modern Portfolio Theory (1979)], at 183-84.

20. See D. Hauck, at 3. And, it makes sense to be a passive investor with a large portfolio. The report, moreover, holds out the hope that mathematical modelling of portfolios may allow for sensible investing, even given the possibility of higher nonmarket risk.

21. See id. at 3.

22. See id.

groups lacked standing to challenge the investment policies of the body responsible for investing state university endowment funds.

3. *Social Investment Benefitting a Subgroup of Beneficiaries.* It is useful to distinguish between two types of investment activities that get lumped together under the rubric of "social investing." The first involves use of fiduciary property for social purposes with the effect of suboptimal economic return for the overall portfolio. This type of activity affects all beneficiaries. A second type of social investing economically benefits one group of beneficiaries while harming others. Plans to create jobs for union members are an example of this second type. Where the plan involves state or local pension funds, common-law trust rules apply. In Withers v. Teacher Retirement System, 447 F. Supp. 1248 (S.D.N.Y. 1978), aff'd mem, 595 F.2d 1210 (2d Cir. 1979), the New York City Teachers Retirement System committed over $800 million in pension assets to purchase bonds from New York City, which was nearly bankrupt at the time, on terms that the city could not have obtained from another lender. The court held that the deal did not violate the trustees' duty of loyalty because, the court found, the investment was in the interest of all the beneficiaries. This finding, however, overlooks the fact that had the city defaulted, more senior beneficiaries, such as retirees, who had the largest claims could have been harmed by the trustee's decision. More junior beneficiaries, however, were benefited since their ultimate retirement benefits depended on the city remaining solvent. See Fischel & Langbein, ERISA's Fundamental Contradiction: The Exclusive Benefit Rule, 55 U. Chi. L. Rev. 1105, 1144-47 (1988).

For plans regulated by ERISA, such investment practices raise issues concerning ERISA's exclusive benefit rule. Section 404(a)(1)(A) of ERISA requires plan fiduciaries to discharge their duties for "the exclusive purpose of . . . providing benefits to participants and their beneficiaries." This provision is the ERISA counterpart to the common-law duty of loyalty. One might suppose that the exclusive benefit rule precludes investment of ERISA-regulated pension funds for the purpose of benefitting some but not all plan participants. In Donovan v. Walton, 609 F. Supp. 1221 (S.D. Fla. 1985), aff'd per curia, sub nom. Brock v. Walton, 794 F.2d 586 (11th Cir. 1986), however, the court rejected a Department of Labor challenge to an investment program that did not benefit all participants. In that case, trustees of a multi-employer pension fund offered bargain-rate mortgage loans to plan participants for the purpose of creating more employment for union members. The fund was a construction-industry pension fund in Broward County, Florida, an area where the industry was in a serious slump in the early 1980's. The trustees tried to stimulate construction by developing a tract of real estate with union labor. If then offered mortgage loans on office space in the completed building at 2 1/8 percentage points below the area's market rate. The Secretary of Labor complained that the program violated the trustees' duties of loyalty and prudent investing. The court emphasized that the trustees consulted experts and that the interest rate on loans was higher than on other parts of the fund's portfolio. On the ERISA exclusive benefit rule generally, see Fischel & Langbein, supra.

4. Duty to Follow the Terms of the Trust Instrument and Related Matters

Dickerson v. Camden Trust Co.
1 N.J. 459, 64 A.2d 214 (1949)

VANDERBILT, C.J. The several appeals in this cause stem from a decree of the former Court of Chancery surcharging the defendants Camden Trust Company and Woodward Tingle Dickerson by reason of their administration of the estate of Edwin Stuart Dickerson, deceased.

The decedent died on October 9, 1930, leaving a will executed in August, 1930, in which he designated the Camden Safe Deposit and Trust Company, the predecessor of the Camden Trust Company, and his son, Woodward Tingle Dickerson, executors and trustees of his estate. After making several relatively small bequests and disposing of his residence and household effects, the testator gave the residue of his estate to his executors, in trust, "to invest said estate in legal securities and from the income therefrom arising to pay" certain annuities to his widow and two sons, other relatives and employees, with gifts over of the principal upon stated contingencies.

Almost immediately after qualifying, the defendant executors and trustees took possession of the assets of the estate, which consisted of realty and personalty valued at $526,430.46 as of the date of death. The great bulk of the personalty, amounting to more than $490,000, was composed of bonds, stocks, notes and other investments, purchased by the testator during his lifetime, which were not legal investments for fiduciaries in this State. Although general economic conditions, both preceding and following the commencement of the administration of this estate, were such that the value of securities of the type constituting the assets of the estate was rapidly declining, the executors, notwithstanding the direction contained in the will, retained almost all of the securities without making any attempt to dispose of them. Indeed, upon the conclusion of their administration as executors, the defendants turned over to themselves as trustees the greater part of these securities which, with minor exceptions, they still held at the time the present suit was instituted.

The executors filed their first accounting in December, 1931, and their second and final accounting in June, 1934, in the Camden County Orphans' Court. In the statement of assets annexed to each of the accounts, the executors set forth a complete schedule of the securities held by the estate, listing them, however, at the inventory value at the date of the testator's death. Thus, while the market value of the estate assets had depreciated to approximately $190,000 as of the date of filing the final account, it carried them at $330,000. Although this appears to have been the practice prevailing in those years, it should be noted in passing that, since the 1941 revision of the rules of the Prerogative Court and of the Orphans' Court, it has been incumbent upon an accountant to set forth in the statement of assets the true value of the assets of the estate, as well as the inventory value, Prerogative Court Rule 35; Orphans' Court Rule 27; Rule 3:95-2. All parties in interest, including the complainants, were duly notified of the filing of both accounts, but no exceptions were taken with respect to the propriety of the retention by the executors of the nonlegal investments. The decree allowing the final account charged the executors with the sum of $330,567.20 as being in their hands, which after the payment of commissions and counsel fees totalling $12,000, was "to be disposed of according to law."

Upon the allowance of their final account as executors, the defendants turned over to themselves as trustees all of the assets of the estate, accepting them at inventory value instead of the then depreciated market value. On November 21, 1938 they filed their first account as trustees, scheduling and charging themselves with the assets of the estate at inventory value, again as of the date of the testator's death. Prior to the allowance of this account, the present suit was commenced by several of the cestuis, seeking in essence to surcharge the defendant fiduciaries for the losses accruing to the estate as a result of the decline in value of the non-legal investments. The former Court of Chancery thereupon assumed general jurisdiction of the administration of the estate and trusts under the will of the testator and directed the removal to it of the proceedings under the trustees' first accounting, then pending in the Camden County Orphans' Court.

The final decree advised by the learned Vice Chancellor ordered the immediate sale and conversion of all the non-legal securities remaining in the hands of the trustees and the investment of the proceeds into authorized securities, and surcharged the defendant trustees for the difference between the value at which the non-legal securities had been accepted by them on taking over the assets as trustees and the sum actually received from the sale of said securities, as well as for the consequent loss of income. . . .

It is the position of the defendant fiduciaries that, under the terms of the will and the applicable statutes, they were authorized to retain any non-legal investments which were made by the testator and received by them as part of the assets of the estate. Although it is true that under the provisions of the law in force at the time of the testator's death an executor or a testamentary administrator or trustee was empowered "in the exercise of good faith and reasonable discretion" to continue investments made by his testator, P.L.1899, c. 103, § 1, N.J.S.A. 3:16-12, this authority was expressly qualified by the terms of section 3 of that act which stipulated that the act should not apply in cases where the will "specially directs in what manner the trust fund shall be invested", P.L.1899, c. 103, § 3. In the face of the plain and explicit direction of the testator here to "invest said estate in legal securities", we can perceive no justification for the retention of these securities by the defendant fiduciaries. It was their absolute duty as executors to dispose of the non-legal investments within a reasonable time after receiving them and to invest the proceeds in securities which were proper investments, 2 Scott, The Law of Trusts, § 230.

There is no merit in the suggestion that by reason of the authorization contained in section 1 of the Act of 1899 investments made by a testator became legal securities for a fiduciary to the same extent as those within the statutory list of specific securities. Though the statute made it lawful to retain a testator's investments it did not thereby constitute such investments legal securities within the usual and normal connotations of that phrase. The commonly accepted meaning of the term relates to the statutory list of designated securities in which a fiduciary is permitted to invest the funds of his estate, P.L.1898, c. 234, § 137, N.J.S.A. 3:16-1, P.L. 1899, c. 103, § 2, as amended and supplemented. Thus a testamentary direction to invest in legal securities constituted an effective prohibition against the retention of non-legal investments made by a testator under the provisions of the Act of 1899.

Nor may the continuance of the testator's investments be defended upon the ground that they were retained in the exercise of reasonable care and discretion in good faith. In the absence of any authority to retain the non-legal securities this test has no application. It is only when the fiduciary is acting within the limits of his powers that that standard becomes pertinent.

The liability of these defendants as executors for their breach of duty in failing to dispose of the improper investments within a reasonable time, however, is dependent upon the effect to be accorded the orphans' court decrees approving and allowing their two accounts. Each of the accounts as filed had annexed a statement of assets upon which were listed all of the investments held by the estate and the corresponding values of each, which were in fact in most instances the same values set up in the original inventory. In these circumstances, both the executors and the beneficiaries are concluded by the decree of the Orphans' Court approving and allowing the accounts and the executor's administration of the estate may not be challenged in the present proceedings either with respect to the propriety of the investments or as to the value thereof as stated in the accountings.

But as trustees whose power of investment was restricted to legal securities and who had no authority to continue non-legal investments of the testator, the defendants were under an unqualified duty upon assuming the administration of the trust to accept for the trust estate only cash or legal securities valued at the then market value. . . . Instead the trustees took over all of the assets held by themselves as executors, consisting in large part of non-legal investments, accepting them at the original inventory value of the estate. Having accepted the securities at inventory value in breach of their trust they are charged with and required to account for the assets at the values at which they received them. As stated in 3 Bogert, Trusts and Trustees, § 583, pp. 15, 16: ". . . The trustee owes a duty to the cestui on taking over property from the executor to examine the property tendered and see whether it is that which he ought to receive. If the executor is under a duty to deliver money to the trustee, and tenders corporate stock in which the executor has wrongfully invested the funds of the estate, the trustee may render himself liable to the cestui by accepting such a tender. . . ."

This principle would be applicable whether the trustee accepts securities in which the executor has wrongfully invested or whether he accepts securities which the executor has improperly retained. The fiduciary obligation which is breached is the same in each instance—the acceptance of improper assets. And where, as in the present cause, the trustees take over non-legal securities at values in excess of actual worth, they are liable to surcharge for the difference between the values at which the securities were accepted and the amounts realized upon the disposition of such securities. It follows as a necessary consequence that the trustees are liable also for the loss of income to the estate resulting from their breach of trust.

[The decree of the Vice Chancellor was affirmed.]

Notes and Questions

1. *"Legal Investments"*. The New Jersey statutes mentioned in *Dickerson* have been repealed. The current New Jersey statute, called the "Prudent Investor Law," N.J. Rev. Stat. § 3B:20-12 et seq., contains no "legal list" of kinds of investments approved for fiduciaries. Rather, it authorizes fiduciaries to invest "in any investments whatever," subject, of course, to the general rule of prudence and to any contrary provisions in the controlling trust instrument. Id. § 3B:20-14. The enactment also redefines "legal investments" as used in any trust instrument to mean "any investment of the kind authorized by this article." Id. § 3B:20-16. Would retention of originals by the *Dickerson* trustee have been wrongful under present New Jersey law? Might a court construe a trust instrument like the will of Edwin Dickerson to require sale and reinvestment even though the jurisdiction no longer had a statutory legal list?

Statutory legal lists like New Jersey's "permissive list" referred to in *Dickerson* have become somewhat uncommon, though state laws usually declare various governmental obligations to be "legal investments" for all fiduciaries. Obviously, reference in a trust instrument to "legal" securities still may be construed quite restrictively, meaning that legislation like that in New Jersey establishing a preference for a non-restrictive meaning is needed. Legislative definitions of language like "legal investments" comparable to that now found in New Jersey have been enacted recently in California (Cal. Civ. Code § 2261, applicable only to trusts created on or after Jan. 1, 1985) and Washington (Wash. Rev. Code § 11.100.010-.140, applicable to instruments effective before or after Jan. 1, 1985). Was it necessary or desirable for California to limit its enactment to future instruments?

2. *Duty to Receive Due Performance by a Prior Fiduciary*. In In re First Nat'l Bank 37 Ohio St. 2d 60, 307 N.E.2d 23 (1974), the Ohio Supreme Court, relying on *Dickerson*, surcharged a testamentary trustee who had failed to challenge its own executor's account to the probate court for negligent overpayment of inheritance tax. Several years later, at the urging of the Ohio State Bar Association, the Ohio General Assembly enacted legislation applicable to all fiduciaries providing:

Ohio Rev. Code § 1339.42B. A fiduciary, or a custodian, who is a transferee of real or personal property that is held by a fiduciary other than the person or entity serving as the transferee, is not required to inquire into any act, or audit any account, of the transferor fiduciary, unless the transferee is specifically directed to do so in the instrument governing him unless the transferee has actual knowledge of conduct of the transferor that would constitute a breach of the transferor's fiduciary responsibilities.

Notice that the statute would not have affected the result in *Dickerson* or the Ohio case following *Dickerson*. A Georgia statute, enacted in 1968 as a part of legislation bringing the Uniform Testamentary Additions to Trusts Act into the state, applies only to the relationship between an executor of a will affecting a pour-over and the receiving trustee. Arguably applicable to entities serving in the dual role of executor and inter-vivos trustee provides:

Ga. Code § 53-14-3. The trustee or trustees of a trust established by the testator or others . . . shall not be required to inquire into or audit the actions of the executor or executors of the testator's estate or to make any claim against the executor or executors unless specifically directed to do so by the trustor or trustors in the trust instrument.

The responsibility of successor fiduciaries regarding the activities of prior fiduciaries would seem to be especially worrisome to corporate fiduciaries named to succeed a settlor or a member of the settlor's family as trustee of an inter-vivos trust that may have been mismanaged. The careful drafter will anticipate and avoid this peril by provision in the governing trust instrument.

3. *Beneficiary Consent to Breach of Trust.* If one or more but less than all of the beneficiaries of a trust appear to have consented to or waived a breach of trust by a trustee, are other beneficiaries affected?

The question involves two inquiries. First, it must be determined whether the consenting beneficiary was sufficiently informed by the trustee to be able to signal an effective consent to breach. In Estate of Cook, 20 Del. Ch. 123, 171 A. 730 (1934), the court made this observation:

Evidence was introduced at the hearing that the exceptant, the beneficiary, knew of the investments made by the trustee and made no objection thereto. This circumstance was shown, I take it, in order to raise an estoppel against the beneficiary based on consent. That consent of a beneficiary, under some circumstances, may afford protection to a trustee against the consequences of a breach of duty, may be conceded. But before exonerating consent can be made out, it must appear that the cestui que trust knew all the facts, was apprised of his legal rights, was under no disability and acted freely, deliberately and advisedly with the intention of confirming the transaction which he knew, or might or ought, with reasonable or proper diligence, to have known to be impeachable. A trustee cannot relieve himself of the responsibility of an investment by the simple expedience of informing the beneficiary that the investment had been made. The cestui que trust is under no duty to act as adviser to his trustee. Consent, such as to foreclose the beneficiary from objecting, is not evidenced by failure to complain. Silence is not affirmation and approval.

A beneficiary may be precluded from holding a trustee liable for breach of trust not only by approving the act in advance but also by affirming or ratifying the act after it occurred. She or he is in a position that bears some analogy to that of a party to a bargain transaction who has the right to avoid the transaction, for example for fraud, but may lose the right by conduct constituting an affirmance.

Even a mere failure of the beneficiary to object may bar her or him from holding the trustee liable for breach. Suppose, for example, that a trustee invested $10,000 in shares of stock in a new, untried venture that the law would consider too speculative for a trust investment. The usual remedy to correct this breach of trust is to order the trustee to pay $10,000 into the estate, with interest from the time of the purchase. The trustee thereupon will take title to the stock individually and will be credited with any dividends on it that went into the trust. If the stock has depreciated in value, the beneficiary is apt to seek this relief. On the other hand, if the stock has increased in value, the beneficiary may decide not to challenge the investment while it continues to be profitable, but may seek to surcharge the trustee should the stock thereafter fall below the purchase price. To leave her or him with this choice over any long period of time after she or he is aware of her or his rights means that the beneficiary has an investment on which she or he may gain, without risk of losing the amount of the initial investment. When in such circumstances a beneficiary is barred by failure to assert her or his rights, the decision may be put on the ground of estoppel, affirmance by acquiescence, or laches.

Once it is determined that a beneficiary has effectively consented to or waived a breach of trust, the effect of such conduct on other beneficiaries must be determined. As a general rule, one beneficiary's consent to a breach of trust cannot affect the legal rights of another beneficiary. However, the effective consent or waiver by a beneficiary holding a general power of appointment over the trust estate is effective to bar all persons taking through exercise or in default of exercise of the power. Restatement 2d of Trusts § 216 comments h and i. In other words, the holder of a general power of appointment, including one that is exercisable only by will, is treated for this purpose as if she or he were the sole beneficial owner of the property subject to the power. The rule is especially important to persons named to take as successor trustees to settlors of revocable declarations of trust, for it serves to neutralize the worrisome duty of a successor fiduciary discussed above. Notice the inconsistency between the significance of a general testamentary power of appointment for purposes of consenting to a breach of trust and the significance of such a power in relation to the vesting requirement of the Rule Against Perpetuities. See USRAP § 2; supra Chapter 17, Part E.

PART D. THE DUTY OF IMPARTIALITY: ALLOCATIONS BETWEEN INCOME AND PRINCIPAL BENEFICIARIES

Statutory Reference: *Revised Uniform Principal and Income Act*

Typically, trusts include multiple beneficiaries who have differing interests in income and principal. This situation creates the potential for conflicting preferences among beneficiaries. For example, beneficiaries who have a remainder interest in principal usually prefer that the trustee emphasize capital appreciation in making investment decisions, while life income beneficiaries prefer an investment strategy that emphasizes income-production. Conflicts also frequently exist among concurrent beneficiaries. Concurrent life beneficiaries, for example, may have different tax positions or different preferences between income and growth. Responding to these problems, trust law has long recognized a duty on the trustee to act impartially between income and principal beneficiaries. The duty of impartiality is involved in decisions about how to allocate receipts and expenditures between income and principal. It also applies in the context of decisions concerning trust investments. The case that follows illustrates the relationship between trust duties of investment and the duty of impartiality.

1. Depreciating Property

Dennis v. Rhode Island Hospital Trust National Bank
744 F.2d 893 (1st Cir. 1984)

BREYER, C.J. The plaintiffs are the great-grandchildren of Alice M. Sullivan and beneficiaries of a trust created under her will. They claimed in the district court that the Bank trustee had breached various fiduciary obligations owed them as beneficiaries of that trust. The trust came into existence in 1920. It will cease to exist in 1991 (twenty-one years after the 1970 death of Alice Sullivan's last surviving child). The trust distributes all its income for the benefit of Alice Sullivan's living issue; the principal is to go to her issue surviving in 1991. Evidently, since the death of their mother, the two plaintiffs are the sole surviving issue, entitled to the trust's income until 1991, and then, as remaindermen, entitled to the principal.

The controversy arises out of the trustee's handling of the most important trust assets, undivided interests in three multi-story commercial buildings in downtown Providence. The buildings (the Jones, Wheaton-Anthony, and Alice Buildings) were all constructed before the beginning of the century, in an area where the value of the property has declined markedly over the last thirty years. During the period that the trust held these interests the buildings were leased to a number of different tenants, including corporations which subsequently subleased the premises. Income distribution from the trust to the life tenants has averaged over $34,000 annually.

At the time of the creation of the trust in 1920, its interests in the three buildings were worth more than $300,000. The trustee was authorized by the will to sell real estate. When the trustee finally sold the buildings in 1945, 1970, and 1979, respectively, it did so at or near the lowest point of their value; the trust received a total of only $185,000 for its interests in them. These losses, in plaintiffs' view, reflect a serious mishandling of assets over the years.

The district court . . . while rejecting many of plaintiffs' arguments, nonetheless found that the trustee had failed to act impartially, as between the trust's income beneficiaries and the remaindermen; it had favored the former over the latter, and, in doing so, it had reduced the value of the trust assets. To avoid improper favoritism, the trustee should have sold the real estate interests, at least by 1950, and reinvested the proceeds elsewhere. By 1950 the trustee must have, or should have, known that the buildings' value to the remaindermen would be small; the character of downtown commercial Providence was beginning to change; retention of the buildings would work to the disadvantage of the remaindermen. The court ordered a surcharge of $365,000, apparently designed to restore the real value of the trust's principal to its 1950 level.

On appeal, plaintiffs and defendants attack different aspects of the district court's judgment. [The court then announced that it affirmed the district court's judgment.]

I. a. The trustee first argues that the district court's conclusions rest on "hindsight." It points out that Rhode Island law requires a trustee to be "prudent and vigilant and exercise sound judgment," Rhode Island Trust Co. v. Copeland, 39 R.I. 193, 98 A. 273, 279 (1916), but "[n]either prophecy nor prescience is expected." Stark v. United States Trust Co. of New York, 445 F.Supp. 670, 678 (S.D.N.Y.1978). It adds that a trustee can indulge a preference for keeping the trust's "inception assets," those placed in trust by the settlor and commended to the trustee for retention. How then, the trustee asks, can the court have found that it should have sold these property interests in 1950?

The trustee's claim might be persuasive had the district court found that it had acted *imprudently* in 1950, in retaining the buildings. If that were the case, one might note that every 1950 sale involved both a pessimistic seller and an optimistic buyer; and one might ask how the court could expect the trustee to have known then (in 1950) whose prediction would turn out to be correct. The trustee's argument is less plausible, however, where, as here, the district court basically found that in 1950 the trustee had acted not imprudently, but *unfairly*, between income beneficiaries and remaindermen.

Suppose, for example, that a trustee of farmland over a number of years overplants the land, thereby increasing short run income, but ruining the soil and making the farm worthless in the long run. The trustee's duty to take corrective action would arise from the fact that he knows (or plainly ought to know) that his present course of action will injure the remaindermen; settled law requires him to act impartially, "with due regard" for the "respective interests" of both the life tenant and the remainderman. Restatement (Second) of Trusts § 232 (1959). See also A. Scott, The Law of Trusts § 183 (1967); G.G. Bogert & G.T. Bogert, The Law of Trusts and Trustees § 612 (1980). The district court here found that a sale in 1950 would have represented one way (perhaps the only practical way) to correct this type of favoritism. It held that instead of correcting the problem, the trustee continued to favor the life tenant to the "very real disadvantage" of the remainder interests, in violation of Rhode Island law.

To be more specific, in the court's view the problem arose out of the trustee's failure to keep up the buildings, to renovate them, to modernize them, or to take other reasonably obvious steps that might have given the remaindermen property roughly capable of continuing to produce a reasonable income. This failure allowed the trustee to make larger income payments during the life of the trust; but the size of those payments reflected the trustee's acquiescence in the gradual deterioration of the property. In a sense, the payments ate away the trust's capital.

The trustee correctly points out that it did take certain steps to keep up the buildings; and events beyond its control made it difficult to do more. In the 1920's, the trustee, with court approval, entered into very longterm leases on the Alice and Wheaton-Anthony buildings. The lessees and the subtenants were supposed to keep the buildings in good repair; some improvements were made. Moreover, the depression made it difficult during the 1930's to find tenants who would pay a high rent and keep up the buildings. After World War II the neighborhood enjoyed a brief renaissance; but, then, with the 1950's flight to the suburbs, it simply deteriorated.

Even if we accept these trustee claims, however, the record provides adequate support for the district court's conclusions. There is considerable evidence indicating that, at least by 1950, the trustee should have been aware of the way in which the buildings' high rents, the upkeep problem, the changing neighborhood, the buildings' age, the failure to modernize, all together were consuming the buildings' value. There is evidence that the trustee did not come to grips with the problem. Indeed, the trustee did not appraise the properties periodically, and it did not keep proper records. It made no formal or informal accounting in 55 years. There is no indication in the record that the trust's officers focused upon the problem or consulted real estate experts about it or made any further rehabilitation efforts. Rather, there is evidence that the trustee did little more than routinely agree to the requests of the trust's income beneficiaries that it manage the trust corpus to produce the largest possible income. The New Jersey courts have pointed out that an impartial trustee

must view the overall picture as it is presented from all the facts, and not close its eyes to any relevant facts which might result in excessive burden to the one class in preference to the other.

Pennsylvania Co. v. Gillmore, 137 N.J.Eq. 51, 43 A.2d 667, 672 (1945). The record supports a conclusion of failure to satisfy that duty.

The district court also found that the trustee had at least one practical solution available. It might have sold the property in 1950 and reinvested the proceeds in other assets of roughly equivalent total value that did not create a "partiality" problem. The Restatement of Trusts foresees such a solution, for it says that

> the trustee is under a duty to the beneficiary who is ultimately entitled to the principal not to . . . retain property which is certain or likely to depreciate in value, although the property yields a large income, unless he makes adequate provision for amortizing the depreciation.

Restatement (Second) of Trusts § 232, comment b. Rhode Island case law also allows the court considerable discretion, in cases of fiduciary breach, to fashion a remedy, including a remedy based on a hypothetical, earlier sale. In, for example, Industrial Trust Co. v. Parks, 190 A. at 42, the court apportioned payments between income and principal "in the same way as they would have been apportioned if (certain) rights had been sold by the trustees immediately after the death of the testator" for a specified hypothetical value, to which the court added hypothetical interest. In the absence of a showing that such a sale and reinvestment would have been impractical or that some equivalent or better curative steps might have been taken, the district court's use of a 1950 sale as a remedial measure of what the trustee ought to have done is within the scope of its lawful powers.

In reaching this conclusion, we have taken account of the trustee's argument that the buildings' values were especially high in 1950 (though not as high as in the late 1920's). As the trustee argues, this fact would make 1950 an unreasonable remedial choice, other things being equal. But the record indicates that other things were not equal. For one thing, the district court chose 1950, not because of then-existing property values, but because that date marks a reasonable outer bound of the time the trustee could plead ignorance of the serious fairness problem. And, this conclusion, as we have noted, has adequate record support. For another thing, the district court could properly understand plaintiffs' expert witness as stating that the suburban flight that led to mid-1950's downtown decline began before 1950; its causes (increased household income; more cars; more mobility) were apparent before 1950. Thus, the court might reasonably have felt that a brief (1948-52) downtown "renaissance" should not have appeared (to the expert eye) to have been permanent or longlasting; it did not relieve the trustee of its obligation to do something about the fairness problem, nor did it make simple "building retention" a plausible cure. Finally, another expert testified that the trustee should have asked for power to sell the property "sometime between 1947 and 1952" when institutional investors generally began to diversify portfolios. For these reasons, reading the record, as we must, simply to see if it contains adequate support for the district court's conclusion as to remedy (as to which its powers are broad), we find that its choice of 1950 as a remedial base year is lawful.

Contrary to the trustee's contention, the case law it cites does not give it an absolute right under Rhode Island law to keep the trust's "inception assets" in disregard of the likely effect of retention on classes of trust beneficiaries. The district court's conclusion that the trustee should have sold the assets if necessary to prevent the trust corpus from being consumed by the income beneficiaries is reasonable and therefore lawful.

c. The trustee challenges the district court's calculation of the surcharge. The court assumed, for purposes of making the trust principal whole, that the trustee had hypothetically sold the trust's interests in the Wheaton-Anthony and the Alice buildings in 1950, at their 1950 values (about $70,000 and $220,000, respectively). It subtracted, from that sum of about $290,000, the $130,000 the trust actually received when the buildings were in fact sold (about $40,000 for the Wheaton-Anthony interest in 1970 and about $90,000 for the Alice interest in 1979). The court considered the difference of $160,000 to be a loss in the value of the principal, suffered as a result of the trustee's failure to prevent the principal from eroding. The court then assumed that, had the trustee sold the buildings in 1950 and reinvested the proceeds, the trustee would have been able to preserve the real value of the principal. It therefore multiplied the $160,000 by 3.6 percent, the average annual increase in the consumer price index from 1950 to 1982, and multiplied again by 32, the number of full years since 1950. Finally, the court multiplied again by an annual 0.4 percent, designed to reflect an "allowance for appreciation." It added the result ($160,000 X 4 percent X 32), about $205,000, to the $160,000 loss and surcharged the trustee $365,000. We are aware of a number of mathematical problems with this calculation. (Why, for example, was no account taken of inflation when subtracting sale receipts from 1950 values?) But, in the context of this specific litigation, fairness as between the parties requires us to restrict our examination to the two particular challenges that the trustee raises.

First, the trustee claims that the court improperly ascertained the 1950 values of the trust's interests because it simply took a proportionate share of the buildings' values. That is to say, it divided the total value of the Alice Building by four to reflect the fact that the trust owned a 1/4 undivided interest. The trustee argues that the building's values should have been discounted further to reflect the facts that the trust owned a fractional interest in the buildings and that fractional interests (with their consequent problems of divided control) typically sell at a discount.

This particular matter in this case, however, was the subject of conflicting evidence. On the one hand, the trustee showed that the marketplace ordinarily discounted the value of fractional interests. On the other hand, the plaintiffs introduced an expert study giving the 1950 values of the trust's interests at precisely the figure shown by the district court. When the trustee finally sold the trust's interests (in 1970 and 1979), their value was *not* significantly discounted. And, since the trustee also controlled (as a trustee) other fractional interests in the same building, the trustee arguably could have arranged to sell the entire building in 1950 as it did in 1970 and 1979. Evaluating this evidence and the merits of these arguments is a matter for the district court. We see no abuse of the district court's powers to make reasonable judgments as to hypothetical values in its efforts to devise an appropriate remedy for the trustee's breach of duty.

Second, the trustee argues that the district court should not have applied to the 1950 hypothetical sales value a 4 percent interest factor—a factor designed to compensate for 3.6 percent average annual inflation and for 0.4 percent "appreciation." We do not agree with the trustee in respect to the 3.6 percent.

Rhode Island law simply requires that the court's approach be reasonable and its calculations grounded in the record's facts. See generally Industrial Trust Co. v. Parks, supra. The trustee does not claim that it requires the court to follow any one particular calculation method, such as that, for example, contained in Restatement (Second) of Trusts § 241. And, we believe the inflation adjustment meets Rhode Island's broader requirements.

For one thing, it seems reasonable for the court—in devising a remedy for the trustee's violation of its duty of impartiality—to assume that a fair trustee would have maintained the property's real value from 1950 through 1982. Such an assumption is consistent with basic trust law policies of providing income to income beneficiaries while preserving principal for the remaindermen, and, consequently, of avoiding investment in wasting assets. Moreover, it is consistent with readily ascertainable general economic facts that wages and many asset values as well as prices have on average kept pace with inflation. See generally K. Hirsch, Inflation and the Law of Trusts, 18 Real Prop., Prob. & Tr. J. 601 (Win.1983); Comment, Investment and Management of Trust Funds in an Inflationary Economy, 126 U. of Pa.L.R. 1171, 1197 (1978). While the value of long term bonds has fallen, the value of common stocks and much property has risen. See generally R. Ibbotson & R. Sinquefield, Stocks, Bonds, Bills and Inflation: The Past and the Future (1982); J. Wiedemer, Real Estate Investment (1979). Where a court is trying to create, not a measure of the trustee's duty, but simply a plausible reconstruction of what would have occurred to a hypothetical 1950 reinvestment, we see nothing unreasonable in assuming that the value of the corpus would have kept pace with inflation.

We reach a different conclusion, however, in respect to the additional 0.4 percent, designed to reflect "appreciation." Neither the court nor the parties have provided us with any reason to believe that the trustee would have outperformed inflation. There is no evidence in the record suggesting that a hypothetical reinvestment of hypothetical proceeds from a hypothetical 1950 property sale would have yielded real appreciation over and above inflation's nominal increase. We have found no information about the performance of an average, or typical, trust. And the general publicly available sources offer insufficient support for a claim of likely real increase. See R. Ibbotson & R. Sinquefield, supra. Moreover, one can imagine reasonable disagreement about whether any such hypothetical real appreciation would belong to the life tenant or to the remainderman. These factors lead us to conclude that, in adding 0.4 percent interest for real appreciation, the district court exceeded its broad remedial powers. Our recalculation, omitting the 0.4 percent, reduces the surcharge from $365,781.67 to $345,246.56.

d. The trustee objects to the court's having removed it as trustee. The removal of a trustee, however, is primarily a matter for the district court. A trustee can be removed even if "the charges of his misconduct" are "not made out." Petition of Slatter, 108 R.I. 326, 275 A.2d 272, 276 (1971). The issue here is whether "ill feeling" might interfere with the administration of the trust. The district court concluded that the course of the litigation in this case itself demonstrated such ill feeling. Nothing in the record shows that the court abused its powers in reaching that conclusion. [The balance of the opinion, rejecting the plaintiff's contentions that (1) prejudgment interest should have been awarded, and (2) that defendant should have been charged personally with plaintiff's attorneys fees, is omitted.]

The judgment of the district court is modified and as modified affirmed.

Note

Trust Law Definitions of Income and Principal. The *Dennis* opinion notes the possibilities of sale, or retention plus larger expenditures from rental income for maintenance, as possible approaches for a trustee who wishes to hold deteriorating real estate while acting impartially toward life and remainder beneficiaries. Is there not another possible course of action? Suppose the *Dennis* trustee, recognizing that the properties were becoming dated and unlikely to continue to command preferred location rentals, had regularly treated a portion of current rents as corpus to be retained and invested in prudently selected securities. Could a trustee safely establish a reserve serving to translate high rental income into rental commensurate with the real value of the buildings *and* a growing collection of other investments that would offset real estate losses?

Though seemingly responsive to a fiduciary's obligation to be equally considerate of beneficiaries of present and future interests in a trust estate, the course of action just suggested probably would be prohibited under the default rules in present law. See infra pp. 1169-73. Paradoxically, the problem stems from specific trust accounting rules designed to protect successive beneficiaries that govern the classification of receipts and expenditures by trustees. In many states, the traditional rules have been replaced by either of two versions of the Uniform Principal and Income Act. The original act was adopted by the Uniform Law Commissioners in 1931 and the revised act was adopted in 1962. The 1931 Act has been enacted into law in thirteen states, including Connecticut, Pennsylvania, and Texas. The 1962 Act has been enacted in twenty-six states, including California, Florida, Illinois, Michigan, Minnesota, Montana, New York, North Dakota, and Ohio. The Uniform Law Commissioners have a project underway to update the 1962 Act in light of modern portfolio theory.

The trust law rules for defining income and principal apply in cases where the trust instrument provides that current returns from all or a portion of the trust assets should be paid to present interest beneficiaries, leaving the income-producing fund to future interest beneficiaries. By and large the rules are irrelevant in situations where the instrument directs the trustee to pay a fixed or computed sum periodically to present interest beneficiaries.

2. Trustee Discretion over Allocation Decisions

The trust allocation rules are default rules, at least in theory. They control the classification of receipts and expenditures between income and principal in the absence of any provision in the trust instrument dealing with the question. Drafters frequently include in trust instruments provisions giving the trustee discretion over allocation questions. The following case illustrates how courts often construe such trustee discretion clauses.

Clarenbach's Will
23 Wis. 2d 71, 126 N.W.2d 614 (1964)

[In 1962, a trust created under the will of Hildegard Clarenbach realized net capital gains totalling $19,858.63 on the sale of shares of stock in several corporations that were part of the trust estate. From this amount, the trustees, who were the testator's children, distributed $10,000 to themselves as life income beneficiaries. A guardian ad litem, representing the remainder beneficiaries, who were children of the trustees, objected to their petition for an accounting of this distribution.]

DIETERICH, J. The crux of the instant appeal is the interpretation to be placed upon clause 7(G) of the trust provisions of the will, which reads:

> (G) I hereby grant to my executors the power to determine how all receipts, whether realized or accrued (inclusive of stocks, rights, securities received upon reconversion or upon reorganization, or other securities) and all disbursements, whether paid or accrued, shall be charged or apportioned as between income and principal in making current or final distributions, and the decision of the executors shall be final and not subject to question by any court or by any beneficiary hereof.

While the above quoted clause speaks of executors and not trustees, it is conceded that the trustees succeeded to the same discretionary power conferred upon the executors.

The appellant trustees contend in effect that irrespective of whether or not they consider profits realized from the sale of trust corpus securities to be income or corpus, they have the uncontrolled discretion under this clause to distribute such part of these profits to themselves so long as they do not abuse their discretion. They point to the fact that they have not distributed all of such profits to themselves but only approximately half thereof and that this moderation on their part absolves them from any charge of abuse of discretion. The guardian ad litem, on the other hand, contends that the clause must be construed as conferring upon the trustees the discretion to determine in good faith whether any particular receipt of the trust is income or principal from an accounting standpoint; and, only after having made the decision in good faith that a particular receipt is income, may the trustees lawfully distribute the same to themselves as the life beneficiaries of the trust.

The Uniform Principal and Income Act was adopted in Wisconsin in 1957,[23] and sec. 231.40(3)(b) of that act provides that "any profit . . . resulting upon any change in form of principal shall enure . . . upon principal." The instant profits from sale of trust securities fall in to that category. However, sec. 231.40(2) authorizes the person creating a trust to vary this provision of the act by granting discretion in the trustees to apportion receipts contrary to the other provisions of the act.[24] In these two respects, the act is but a codification of the common law of this state which existed prior to its enactment.

However, in another respect the Uniform Principal and Income Act . . . operated so as to materially change the common law of Wisconsin. This is the provision of sec. 231.40(5)(a) which provides that stock dividends "shall be deemed principal." [P]rior to enactment of the act in 1957, Wisconsin followed the Pennsylvania rule with respect to apportioning stock dividends between trust principal and income, and this often presented an acute accounting problem. The instant will was drafted prior to enactment of the act, and the fact that Wisconsin followed the Pennsylvania rule with respect to stock dividends may well have been one of the reasons which prompted testatrix to include clause 7(G) in her will. This probability is one of the factors that motivates this court toward adopting the interpretation of that clause advanced by the guardian ad litem. Another fact is that nowhere else in the will is there any provision which grants discretion to the trustees to invade the corpus, even to a limited extent, for the benefit of the life beneficiaries. However, the interpretation advanced by the trustees would convert clause 7(G) into exactly that type of device. We cannot bring ourselves to the opinion that this was what the testatrix intended by that clause.

It is our considered judgment that the purpose of clause 7(G) was to protect the trustees from any liability after they exercised their good faith judgment that a particular receipt was to be treated as either income or principal for accounting purposes, or for the purpose of apportionment

---

23. The statute to which the court is referring is the 1931 Uniform Principal and Income Act. Eds.

24. Sec. 231.40(2), Stats., provides in part: ". . . and the person establishing the principal may himself direct the manner of ascertainment of income and principal and the apportionment of receipts and expenses or grant discretion to the trustee or other person to do so, and such provision and direction where not otherwise contrary to law shall control notwithstanding this section."

between the life beneficiaries and remaindermen. We, therefore, so construe it and reject the broader interpretation advanced by the trustees.

It might be argued that the guardian ad litem has not adduced any proof that, interpreting clause 7(G) as we do, there has been any abuse of discretion by the trustees, viz., a failure to make a good faith decision that $10,000 of the $19,858.63 of the profits realized from the sale of trust securities constituted trust income and not principal. We consider that the account filed by the trustees, together with their arguments on the issue of abuse of discretion advanced on this appeal, clearly establish that the trustees did not make a good faith decision that the $10,000 of profits constituted income and not principal. In the recapitulation at the end of the account all the profits from the sale of securities are lumped together under the one item "Capital Gains—1962, $19,858.63," although earlier in the account there is a detailed table showing the cost, the selling price and the profit realized on each sale of stock. The account further shows that $5,000 of these profits was disbursed to each of the two life beneficiaries on December 31, 1962, the disbursement being labeled "Cap. Gains Dist." No profit realized on the sale of these securities was in round figures, but all were amounts ending in odd cents. No attempt was made by the trustees to allocate the $10,000 to any particular stock or stocks sold. There is no logical reason why an even figure of $10,000 should have been segregated out of the $19,858.63 total profits as being income and the remaining $9,858.63 be treated as principal. The only justification advanced by the trustees for this arbitrary distribution was that they were given discretion to do this by clause 7(G).

The trustees place great reliance upon Dumaine v. Dumaine (1938), 301 Mass. 214, 16 N.E.2d 625, 118 A.L.R. 834. There, a trust clause bearing some similarity to clause 7(G) of the trust in the instant action was broadly construed as permitting a partial invasion of principal. This result was not reached by the application of any different principle of law than we have herein acknowledged. If the person creating the trust intended such broad interpretation of the particular trust clause, then there is no breach of trust in the trustees acting pursuant to such clause so broadly interpreted. However, there are three facts that are different in the Dumaine Case which may have influenced the Massachusetts court in interpreting the clause before it as it did. First, there was no change made in the Massachusetts law after the inception of the trust with respect to how stock dividends were to be apportioned between income and principal. At all times Massachusetts followed the simple rule that stock dividends were principal and not income. Also, profits from sale of assets composing the trust principal were to be treated as principal. Therefore, it is arguable that the trustor by the clause must have intended it as a power to invade receipts from such sources else the clause would serve no purpose. Second, the Dumaine Case clause did not have the bracketed words "(inclusive of stocks, rights, securities received upon reconversion or upon reorganization, or other securities)" found in clause 7(G) of the Clarenbach trust which indicates the particular type of situation the testatrix in the instant action had in mind in granting discretion to her trustees. Third, in the Dumaine trust, the trustees had discretion to pay out trust income to the life beneficiaries for their needs, or to accumulate it. The Massachusetts court in its opinion emphasized this particular wide discretion in arriving at the broad interpretation it did with respect to the clause bearing similarity to clause 7(G) of the instant trust. This is not the situation involved in the instant appeal, and consequently the Dumaine Case is not controlling. Thus we affirm the judgment of the trial court.

Judgment affirmed.

GORDON, J. (dissenting). I respectfully dissent. In my opinion, clause 7(G) of the will gave to the trustees the power to determine whether capital gains on the sale of the trust property should be attributed in whole or in part to principal or to income.

This is precisely what the testatrix had in mind when she granted her trustees power to determine "how all receipts . . . shall be . . . apportioned as between income and principal." I know of no reason why this discretionary power should not be fully respected by the court. The fact that the testatrix went on to say that the decision shall not be "subject to question by any court or by any beneficiary hereof" merely serves to stress the breadth of the trustees' discretion. . . .

In my opinion, Mrs. Clarenbach intended to give to her trustees the power to determine what was principal and what was income. While this is not an absolute discretion, there is applicable thereto what the Massachusetts court said in Dumaine v. Dumaine (1938), 301 Mass. 214, 16 N.E.2d 625, 630, 118 A.L.R. 834:

> The discretion conferred is not an empty one. It confers an important responsibility to make a determination which, if honestly exercised, calls for no revision by the court.

There has been no showing of fraud, bad faith or dishonest conduct on the part of the trustees, and, therefore, I believe that the exercise of the broad powers which were awarded to them by the testatrix should not be disturbed. . . .

Notes and Questions

1. *Discretionary Allocation Clauses.* Would discretionary trustee allocation clauses like that in *Clarenbach's Will* provide support for a general trustee discretion approach to allocation problems? Corporate trustees have strongly opposed adoption of a broadly discretionary approach as a general alternative to the existing legal rules for resolving allocation problems. Why do you suppose they do not welcome the kind of discretion that Hildegard Clarenbach's will seemingly conferred? See Panel Discussion on the Uniform Revised Principal and Income Act, 101 Tr. & Est. 894, 896 (1962).

For another example of judicial reluctance to permit trustees, acting under discretionary allocation clauses, to depart from the existing legal rules, see Englund v. First Nat'l Bank, 381 S.2d 8 (Ala. 1980).

2. *Invasion-of-Principal Clauses.* The discretionary power to allocate receipts between income and principal involved in *Clarenbach's Will* presents a different question than does a clause that permits a trustee to invade principal for life beneficiaries. Invasion-of-principal clauses are attempts to provide for the life beneficiaries' needs by anticipating the unforeseen. The life beneficiaries' needs provide a standard by which the trustee may exercise discretion. See supra Chapter 12 Part A.2-.3. In contrast, allocation problems of the sorts studied here are foreseeable, and clauses like that in *Clarenbach's Will* provide no guide to help the trustee balance the interests of income and principal beneficiaries. Not all courts, however, have kept the distinction between the two types of clauses straight, as the Wisconsin court did. See, e.g., Citizens & Southern Nat'l Bank v. Haskins, 254 Ga. 131, 327 S.E.2d 192 (1985) (treating discretionary trustee allocation clause as an invasion-of-principal clause).

3. The Time Factor in Income

Trust estates sometimes include assets that generated income during a period that began before the asset was transferred into the trust. Two questions of time are involved in determining whether the income beneficiary (or the beneficiary's estate) is entitled to such income items. One question concerns the time when the income beneficiary's right to income accrues. A related question is whether the income that the trust receives is apportionable. Concerning the second question, the common-law rule was that rent is non-apportionable. This rule developed in the context of landlord-tenant law, where no trust was involved. See Bank of Pennsylvania v. Wise, 3 Watts 394 (Pa. 1834). Both versions of the Uniform Principal and Income Act reject this rule. On the other hand, both acts have continued the judicial view that no part of an ordinary corporate dividend is earned for an income beneficiary at least until it is declared. The 1962 Act did depart from the common-law rule that receipts of apportionable items always must be divided between income and principal when the receipt is for a period that is not entirely within the span of the life beneficiary's interest. The following case illustrates the problem.

Stern's Trust
87 N.Y.S.2d 128 (Sup. Ct. 1949)

GREENBERG, J. This is an application by the National City Bank of New York, as trustee, to settle and approve its account and for the construction of the inter vivos trust agreement with respect to the trustee's investment powers. . . .

Emil Stern, the settlor of the trust, on December 15, 1924, executed an agreement with the National City Bank of New York, by the terms of which certain bonds with coupons attached were assigned, transferred and set over to the trustee, to be held in trust by it for the purposes named in the indenture. The securities which were delivered pursuant to the terms of the agreement and the additions to the trust fund were inventoried at their respective market values, but these values did not include the interest on the bonds which had accrued from the last interest date to the date of the transfer of the securities to the trustee.

When the first interest coupon became due on each of the bonds, the entire amount thereof, including the amount of the interest accrued to the date of the gift, was allocated and paid to the income beneficiaries. These payments of accrued interest present the first legal challenge to the account filed by the trustee. The guardians of the infants contend that the accrued interest became part of the principal, and therefore should not have been paid over to the income beneficiaries. The trustee, the settlor of the trust, and the income beneficiaries take the contrary position.

There is very respectable authority for the proposition that the interest which had accrued on the bonds at the time the transfer was made to the trustee should be treated and accounted for as principal, and not as income. A different result would follow only if the settlor evidenced that there should be no apportionment of the interest. . . . An intent of this character is not to be found in the indenture. Paragraph IV of clause Third of the trust agreement does not supply this omission. It reads:

> The trustee shall apply the entire income of all the securities at any time held by it hereunder, to the use of the beneficiary for whom they are held, irrespective of the price paid for them or of their market value at any time: it being intended hereby that no part of such income shall be applied as a sinking fund to offset the gradual loss of the premium upon, or market value of such securities. All stock dividends shall be treated as principal and added to the trust fund so far as permitted by law.

In the court's judgment, had the provision quoted ended with a comma after the word "held," it conceivably might be construed as a direction against any apportionment and support the argument of the trustee. However, a literal reading of the language dictates the conclusion that the purpose of the provision was to obviate the legal requirement that the premiums on the purchase of securities be amortized. Its clear purport was to avoid the application of income as against the loss of premium or market value of the securities. If the settlor had intended that all income should be paid to the income beneficiaries, it would have been a simple matter for him to provide that income accrued on the property at the time of the transfer to the trustee, whether or not then due or payable, be considered as income, and this is precisely what he did in the 1932 trust which was created by him and which is the subject of another proceeding.

The trustee, in an endeavor to sustain its position, has offered a letter recently written by the settlor stating that it was his intention when the trust was established that accrued as well as accruing income be paid to the life beneficiaries. This letter may not be considered by the court in derogation of the clear and unambiguous language of the trust indenture. . . .

The second objection to the account arises by virtue of the trustee's charge of principal commissions based on capital increments. The trustee and the settlor entered into a specific agreement which provided for the payment of commissions, as follows:

> A total principal fee of 2% of the first $350,000, of market value, and 1-1/2% on the next $250,000. This fee is payable as follows:
>
> 1% on the creation of the trust as to the securities then placed in trust.
>
> 1% on each subsequent addition, up to a total of $250,000. 3/4 of 1% on any subsequent additions after the $250,000 aggregate has been reached; a similar percentage when the trust finally terminates.

This agreement is silent on the trustee's right to charge principal commissions on capital increments, whether net or gross. It, however, specifically specifies a certain rate of commissions to be charged for receiving and paying principal. While the agreement does refer to "subsequent additions," such phrase obviously applies to the additional deposit of securities contemplated at the time by the settlor.

In light of the fact that the agreement fails to mention any contingency for charging commissions other than those referred to, the court would not be justified in reading into the agreement an intention not disclosed by the language itself. . . .

Accordingly, (1) the trustee and life beneficiaries are directed to restore to principal the amount of accrued interest which was paid over as income, (2) the principal commissions on increment are disallowed. . . .

Notes and Questions

1. *Revised Uniform Principal and Income Act.* In 1965, New York adopted the Revised Uniform Principal and Income Act. How would *Stern's Trust* have been decided under that statute? Suppose that the income beneficiary died sometime during a period in which interest on the bonds was accruing. Who would be entitled to the next interest payment under the revised Act?

2. *Bond Premiums and Discounts.* Trustees often purchase bonds at a premium or discount from the face value. A bond purchaser pays a premium when the interest rate on the bond exceeds the prevailing market rate at the time of purchase. A discount is simply the reverse. The amount of premium or discount depends on two factors: the variance between the bond's interest rate and the market interest rate and the time remaining before the bond matures.

The authorities indicate that a trustee who purchases a bond at a premium may, and perhaps must (the jurisdictions are divided), amortize the premium by allocating an appropriate amount of each interest payment to capital. See Scott on Trusts § 239.2. Amortization means that an amount is set aside which, when added to the value of the bond at maturity, will equal the amount paid for the bond. The same approach is not followed, however, for bonds bought at a discount. The trustee may not give the income beneficiary any part of the bonus over cost received when the bond matures or is later sold for a lower discount from par. See, e.g., Old Colony Trust Co. v. Comstock, 290 Mass. 377, 195 N.E. 389 (1935); Bogert on Trusts § 826. Both the original (section 6) and revised (section 7) Principal and Income Acts include a default rule against amortization of bond premiums.

Not surprisingly, many older trust instruments contain a provision like that in the Stern trust.

4. Corporate Distributions and Related Problems

Statutory References: *Revised Uniform Principal and Income Act §§ 6, 12, 14*

First Wyoming Bank v. First National Bank & Trust of Wyoming
628 P.2d 1355 (Wyoming 1981)

[Charles W. Burdick, a successful lawyer and businessman in Cheyenne, executed his will on May 7, 1919. It appointed his daughter, Margaret Burdick Hewlett, and her husband, George Hewlett, as "joint trustees of my estate," and devised to them "as joint trustees" all of his estate with instruction to pay the income to Margaret for her life and upon her death to certain named remainder beneficiaries. Six months after executing his will, Burdick transferred 12,000 shares of stock in Standard Oil Company of Indiana to Margaret in trust to pay Burdick the income for his life and upon his death to transfer the stock "to the trustee or trustees of the estate of said grantor [Burdick] who have been or may be named and designated by said grantor in his Last Will and Testament." Burdick died in 1927, and Margaret and George Hewlett were appointed executors of his estate.

In 1929, Standard Oil, having declared a 50% stock dividend, issued 6,000 additional shares of its stock to Margaret as trustee of Burdick's inter vivos trust. A year later, Margaret and George, as executors, filed a petition for a final accounting. The petition listed as inventory of the estate 12,000 shares of Standard Oil stock and also noted that 6,000 additional shares issued had been issued to Margaret as trustee following a stock dividend declaration. The executors' petition requested that Margaret and George be appointed trustees of the testamentary trust, that the 6,000 shares of Standard Oil stock issued under the stock dividend be distributed to Margaret as income beneficiary of the testamentary trust, and that the 12,000 shares be transferred to Margaret and George as trustees of the same trust. A guardian ad litem was appointed to represent the remainder interests (which were held by either minors or non-residents), and following notice of the petition no one filed objections. The probate court entered a decree allowing the petition.

Following Margaret's death in 1976, persons holding remainder interests challenged the distribution of the 6,000 shares to Margaret on the ground that the probate court lacked jurisdiction over these as the assets of an inter vivos trust that never passed through probate. The trial court ruled against them on res judicata grounds, and they appealed.]

RAPER, J. This litigation represents an attempt by the remaindermen of a trust to charge the estate of the life beneficiary-trustee for her allegedly wrongful appropriations of trust property. The value of their claims total in excess of five million dollars. . . .

In order to resolve th[e] question [whether the probate court decree is res judicata], the language of the inter vivos trust must be analyzed and compared to that appearing in the will. The trust agreement provided:

> For a valuable consideration the grantor has set over, assigned, transferred and delivered to the trustee, her successors in trust and assigns, twenty four hundred (2,400) shares of capital stock of Midwest Refining Company.
> TO HAVE AND TO HOLD all and singular the said shares of stock, in trust nevertheless . . . and upon the death of the said grantor shall transfer, pay over and deliver the said shares of stock to the trustee or trustees of the estate of said grantor who have been or may be named and designated by said grantor in his Last Will and Testament. (Emphasis added.)

Mr. Burdick's will also used the term "joint trustees of my estate." Even the codicils used this terminology. The probate court appointed the persons who were named joint trustees of the estate as the executors, apparently having concluded that the terms were intended to be synonymous. Since the trust agreement was executed six months after the will, the conclusion follows that the term joint "trustees of the estate" as used in that agreement in all probability would have the same meaning the court determined was ascribed to it in the will. Therefore, under the trust agreement, upon Charles Burdick's death, the trust property passed to the executors and into the estate, and from there, in accord with the provisions of the will, it passed on into the testamentary trust. Since the property would have first become a part of the estate, the conclusion then follows that it was subject to the probate court's jurisdiction [and, therefore, the question concerning whether the distribution of the 6,000 shares to Margaret was appropriate is res judicata.]

CLAIM TO
STANDARD OIL OF NEW JERSEY STOCK

Between the years 1948 and 1963, Standard Oil of Indiana declared certain dividends to its stockholders, payable in shares of stock of Standard Oil of New Jersey. Standard Oil of Indiana had acquired these shares in 1932 when it transferred certain of its foreign properties to Standard Oil of New Jersey.

When paying on the dividends, Standard Oil of Indiana had designated that the value of distribution be of dividends in kind, payable in Standard Oil of New Jersey stock. The distribution was charged against the earned surplus of Standard Oil of Indiana. The dividends were not denominated as a return of capital. In every year in which such a dividend was paid,

Standard Oil of Indiana sent notices to all stockholders receiving the dividends advising them to treat the dividends as income for the taxable year in which they were received.

Standard Oil Company of Indiana had sufficient earnings and earned surplus against which such charge was made. There is no evidence of record demonstrating that the stock dividend, in kind, of Standard of New Jersey, declared to the owners of Standard Oil Company of Indiana impinged upon the capital of Standard of Indiana, or amounted to a partial liquidation of Standard of Indiana. Further, the distribution of the stock dividend in kind of Standard Oil Company of New Jersey does not appear to have been made by Standard Oil Company of Indiana pursuant to a court decree or final administrative order by a government agency ordering distribution of the particular assets.

In Margaret Hewlett's estate, 18,298 shares of Standard Oil of New Jersey were attributable to dividends taken by Margaret Hewlett as income on the trust, the corpus of which was originally the 12,000 shares of Standard Oil of Indiana.

Currently, § 34-18-106, W.S.1977,[25] is the controlling statute for deciding whether the distribution of corporate stock is principal or income. As part of the Uniform Principal and Income Act (1962 version), the statute was passed in 1963. Therefore, it is not controlling unless it can be applied retroactively to the transactions occurring in this case between 1948 and 1963. . . . [I]t would be improper to apply the statute to the situation here since the legislation evinces a legislative intent that it not apply to receipts obtained before the effective date of the act. . . . Therefore, we are constrained to try and reconstruct what the law would have been before the passage of the statute.

The only Wyoming case which bears on the subject is Allith-Prouty Co. v. Wallace, 1925, 32 Wyo. 392, 233 P. 144, reh. den. 234 P. 504. There in dictum Justice Blume hinted that Wyoming would follow the Massachusetts rule. This rule was to the effect that dividends paid in stock of the declaring corporation were principal while dividends paid in either cash or in stock of another corporation were income unless they amounted to a partial liquidation of the corporate assets. The Massachusetts rule has long since the Allith-Prouty Co. decision become the majority rule and been embodied in the Restatement, Trust 2nd § 236. . . . We believe that the Restatement is consistent with Allith-Prouty Co. and also reflects the majority view of the country during the time in question. It is the law to be applied to the dividends paid in this case.

Turning to the facts in this case, since the dividends were distributed in stock of another corporation, the ultimate question for us to resolve is whether the payment of these dividends amounted to a partial liquidation of Standard Oil of Indiana. . . .

Standard Oil of Indiana had received the shares of Standard Oil of New Jersey along with cash in 1932 when it transferred certain foreign property

---

25. Section 34-18-106, W.S.1977, is a verbatim version of the Revised Uniform Principal and Income Act § 6. Eds.

to Standard Oil of New Jersey. Sixteen years later Standard Oil began paying out the shares of stock as dividends. The dividends were charged against the earned surplus of Standard Oil of Indiana. There is no evidence that the capital of the corporation was impinged upon in any way. In light of the facts adduced before the district court, we must conclude that the payment of Standard Oil of New Jersey stock as dividends by Standard Oil of Indiana did not amount to a partial liquidation; therefore, the dividends were properly treated as income.

OIL ROYALTIES

At the time of his death, Charles Burdick was the owner of certain oil royalty interests located in Natrona County. These interests were overriding oil royalty interests arising out of federal leases. Prior to Mr. Burdick's death, oil wells had been drilled and he was receiving royalty payments. In accord with the provisions in the will, the royalty interests were placed in the testamentary trust. From the date of commencement of said trust down to the date of death of Margaret Hewlett, the total amount of royalties paid was in the sum of over six hundred thousand dollars. All of these payments were turned over to Margaret Hewlett and she treated the total amount thereof as income. No part of the payments were treated by her or accounted for by her as corpus of the trust and no reserve was set up for the benefit of the remaindermen of the trust.

The best statement of the law currently with respect to the rights of owners of successive legal interest in the mineral lands can be found in Scott on Trusts, Vol. III, § 239.3. There it is stated:

> . . . Where the owner of such land creates a legal life estate in one person and a remainder in another, and it is not otherwise provided by the terms of the instrument by which the successive estates are created, it is held that if mines were opened prior to the creation of the estates the life tenant is entitled to continue to work the mines and to take the proceeds as his own without deduction for depletion. On the other hand, where no mines were opened prior to the creation of the estates, neither the life tenant nor the remainderman is entitled to open the mines without the consent of the other. If the life tenant does open mines, the proceeds will be treated as principal. . . . (Footnotes omitted.)

Here, the oil wells were producing before Mr. Burdick's death. . . .

The purpose of the so-called "open mine" rule is to try and match testator's intent. Presumably where she/he has been receiving oil royalty payments she/he considers them to be income. Thus, absent some words of limitation in instrument creating a trust, it is assumed that testator intended the life tenant to enjoy the property in the same fashion and to the same extent it had been enjoyed by the testator. . . .

In the present case, no words of restriction appear in the will creating the testamentary trust. Thus, Margaret Hewlett was entitled to enjoy the royalty interests in the same manner that they had been enjoyed by her father. As a result she was able to take the royalty payments and treat them as income.

The Uniform Principal and Income Act does not dictate a different result. As stated in § 34-18-109(b), W.S.1977:

> (b) If a trustee, on the effective date of this act, held an item of depletable property of a type specified in this section he shall allocate receipts from the property in the manner used before the effective date of this act, but as to all depletable property acquired after the effective date of this act by an existing or new trust, the method of allocation provided herein shall be used.

Thus, by its own terms, this trust was exempted from coverage since the corpus was acquired nearly forty years before the act.

Affirmed.

McCLINTOCK, J., dissenting in part. I agree that the "open-mine" principle should be applied if the mineral rights were producing royalties at the time the trust was created. I also agree that the "Massachusetts rule," espoused by this court in Allith-Prouty Co. v. Wallace, 32 Wyo. 392, 233 P. 144, 39 A.L.R. 513 (1925), reh. denied 234 P. 504, and essentially stated in Restatement of Trusts, Second, § 236, that dividends "in property other than in shares of the holding corporation," should govern the treatment to be given the distribution of shares in New Jersey Standard by Indiana Standard.

However, the probate judge's ruling that the stock dividends consisting of 6,000 shares of Standard Oil Company of Indiana stock were income and should be distributed to Margaret Hewlett was contrary to the law of Wyoming. Four years prior to the probate court's ruling this court stated: ". . . Ordinarily a dividend declared in stock is to be deemed capital and not income. The interest of stockholders in a corporation remains unchanged upon the latter declaring a stock dividend. . . ." Allith-Prouty Company v. Wallace, supra, 32 Wyo. at 408 and 234 P. at 506.

As this court explained in Allith-Prouty, when a corporation declares a stock dividend it is merely increasing the number of shares that a stockholder owns without increasing the stockholder's interest in the corporation. By allowing Margaret Hewlett to treat the stock dividend as income, the probate judge reduced the percentage of the trust's ownership of the corporation. In other words, the principal of the trust and the contingent remaindermen's interest were substantially diminished. Therefore, the probate judge erred when he declared that the stock dividends were income of the trust and the remaindermen should be entitled to recover these shares of stock from Margaret Hewlett's estate.

The majority avoids this very logical and proper result by treating the action of the probate court of Laramie County as an error committed in the exercise of proper jurisdiction and, therefore, correctable only by timely appeal. I cannot agree either that the probate court had jurisdiction or that the action before us, instituted by the remaindermen some years after the original estate had been closed, is barred by limitations or laches. . . .

I cannot agree with the majority when they conclude . . . that the inter vivos trust property passed to the estate in accordance with the provisions of the will. While the 12,000 shares of Indiana were included in the inventory the probate judge did not treat them as part of the testamentary estate of Charles W. Burdick. What he did was to give effect to an instrument not before him and direct a person (the trustee of the inter vivos trust) likewise not before him to transfer part of the corpus of the trust to one entity (the testamentary trust) and another part of that corpus to another party (the life beneficiary). . . .

Appellees contend that appellants are barred from asserting the present claims by reason of the statute of limitations and laches. Once again, I cannot agree. Appellants did not have a right of action until the life estate was terminated. As a general rule neither the applicable statute of limitations nor laches will bar an action brought by remaindermen until the remaindermen are entitled to possession of the estate. . . . I find the theory behind this general rule particularly compelling in the case of contingent remaindermen like those in the case at bar because their interest may never become vested. Here the remaindermen's cause of action is not barred by the statute of limitations or laches. . . .

Notes and Questions

1. *Reverse Pour-Over.* The inter-vivos trust in *First Wyoming Bank* was a "reverse" pour-over arrangement. Upon termination at the grantor's death, the contents of the trust pour into the testamentary trust created by the grantor's will. The assets are transferred directly to the trustee of the testamentary trust and are not part of the grantor's probate estate. Under what theory, then, did the probate court have jurisdiction to award to Margaret, as income beneficiary of Burdick's testamentary trust, the 6,000 shares of Standard Oil (Indiana) stock that were issued as a stock dividend while the estate was in probate? Did you find the court's reasoning persuasive? Why might the court have been anxious to avoid hearing the principal beneficiaries' objection?

2. *Corporate Distributions.* The stock dividends under which Margaret Hewlett, the income beneficiary in *First Wyoming Bank*, took additional shares of Standard Oil of Indiana stock and shares of Standard Oil of New Jersey stock raise allocation questions that have been perhaps the most controversial in this area of law. It is well settled that income beneficiaries receive ordinary cash dividends and that principal beneficiaries receive any capital gains if the stock is sold. The states have divided, however, over allocation of extraordinary cash dividends and stock dividends. The so-called "Pennsylvania rule" allocates extraordinary dividends payable in cash or in kind to income to the extent that the dividend came from earnings that accrued to the corporation during the term of the trust and to principal to the extent that the dividend came from earnings that accrued prior thereto. The same rule also apportions stock dividends payable in the distributing entity's own stock, but not stock splits, on the same basis. The complex fact-finding and accounting that the Pennsylvania rule required created what has justly been called "a trustee's nightmare." See Flickinger,

A Trustee's Nightmare: Allocations of Stock Dividends Between Income and Principal, 43 B.U. L. Rev. 199 (1963). Happily, the spectre of this complexity has been greatly reduced by the widespread acceptance of the so-called "Massachusetts rule." That rule, which the court in *First Wyoming Bank* followed, allocates all ordinary and extraordinary dividends payable in cash or property (including the shares of another corporation) to income unless the dividend is a return of capital. All stock dividends in shares of the issuing corporation are allocated to principal. The Revised Uniform Principal and Income Act adopts the Massachusetts rule, despite its emphasis on form over substance, on the view that the high costs of applying a rule of apportionment greatly outweigh the gains that such a rule produces. Section 6 of the Act provides that "[c]orporate distributions of shares of the distributing corporation, including . . . a stock split or stock dividend, are principal."

3. *Retroactive Application of the Revised Act Rules?* It would simplify trust administration if one set of rules could be applied to all trusts, but there was initial doubt as to whether the original statute could be constitutionally applied to previously created trusts. Section 14 of the Revised Uniform Principal and Income Act provides that the Act applies to "any receipt or expense received or incurred after the effective date of this Act by any trust or decedent's estate whether established before or after the effective date. . . ."

A New Jersey case, In re Arens, 41 N.J. 364, 197 A.2d 1 (1964), is of possibly greater importance to simplication efforts in states that accepted the original Uniform Act in its non-retroactive form. In *Arens*, the court created a common-law rule of non-apportionability of stock dividends, resolving the dilemma posed by the state's enactment of the original Uniform Act. The court stated:

> While the theory of the Massachusetts rule is the only basic alternative, we think a new common law rule for old trusts in this State can be most beneficial by conforming exactly with the provisions of the [original Uniform Act] in its present form . . . and as it may be hereafter amended. This will give us a single, clear formula for the administration of all trusts. . . .
>
> [W]e find nothing unfair in any broad sense in changing the common law rule as to prior created trusts. Since some rule was made necessary by the lack of expression of intention or presumably of any thought about the subject on the part of the settlor, it is difficult to conceive of any realistic reliance by him on any particular rule. Probably the most that could be said is, that if there was reliance on anything, it was only on the general proposition that "income" would mean what the courts would say it did as situations arose.

Five months after the *Arens* decision, the New Jersey legislature amended the statute to make it apply to "trusts and estates created or established before or after May 9, 1952, except that it shall not affect or apply to any apportionment or allocation of principal or income which was in fact made by the fiduciary prior to [the enactment date]."

4. *Rethinking Allocation Rules for Corporate Distributions.* Criticizing the Massachusetts rule for giving short shrift to income beneficiaries, commentators have suggested as an alternative a percentage allocation approach.

According to one version of this approach, all receipts would initially be treated as principal. On each date for payment to income beneficiaries, those beneficiaries would receive a fixed percentage of the value of the principal. See Comment, Effectuating the Settlor's Intent: A Formula for Providing More Income for the Life Beneficiary, 33 U. Chi. L. Rev. 783 (1966). A similar approach is suggested in Comment, Range of Return: A New Approach to the Allocation of Trust Gains and Losses, 21 Stan. L. Rev. 420 (1969). Also deviating from the Massachusetts rule are a few statutes providing that any stock dividend of less than six percent counts as income. See, e.g., N.Y. Est. Powers & Trusts Law § 11-2.1(e)(2).

The growing acceptance of modern portfolio theory, which underlies current efforts to revise the Prudent Investor Rule, also has led to rethinking the existing rules regarding allocations of corporate distributions to income and principal. The following excerpt from Professor Jeffrey Gordon's article describes the basis for this rethinking.

Gordon, The Puzzling Persistence of the Constrained Prudent Man Rule
62 N.Y.U. L. Rev. 52, 100-01 (1987)

A division of a firm's return between income and capital gain is highly artificial from the perspective of financial economics. Imagine two firms, *A* and *B*. For every one hundred dollars of shareholders' equity, each earns ten dollars. *A*, thinking its primary business has reached a no-growth steady state, pays out all earnings as dividends. *B*, thinking its business provides additional investment opportunities, reinvests all earnings, which leads to an increase in the price of its shares. Each firm is providing comparable economic return to its shareholders; only the form is different. But a trustee holding *A* must pay out all dividends to income beneficiaries, even if, because of inflation, the purchasing power of the remainder interest, the *A* stock in the portfolio, is meanwhile depreciating. A trustee holding *B* can pay out nothing to income beneficiaries, even if the remainder interest is increasing because of *B*'s decision to reinvest earnings that would otherwise be available to an income beneficiary.

To assure fairness between income beneficiaries and remaindermen, the trustee may have to adopt an investment policy that mixes *A* and *B* stock. Alternatively, present law apparently allows the trustee to refuse to hold *B*. The result in either case will be a portfolio that is not optimally diversified; it has not been assembled with the objective of producing the greatest expected returns for the risk. It is easy to see why systematic exclusion of companies with low dividends but high reinvestment rates will upset a diversification scheme. But there is no assurance that a portfolio that emphasizes balance between high and low dividend-paying securities will be well-diversified in other respects. The allocation of total returns between income and principal compelled by settled trust law is profoundly inconsistent with the portfolio theory paradigm.

Notes and Questions

1. *Implementing Modern Portfolio Theory.* How might a statute or language in a trust instrument defining the benefits of current beneficiaries implement the total return concept of modern portfolio theory? Professor Gordon has identified five possible approaches: (1) "Prudent trustee payout" (comparable to discretionary trustee powers to allocate receipts and expenditures between income and principal accounts); (2) "Fixed nominal payout" (comparable to a fixed annuity that neither increases to reflect inflation nor decreases to reflect portfolio losses); (3) "Fixed real payout" (an annuity fixed in real terms to produce a stream of income for life beneficiaries that is adjusted according to some inflation measure); (4) "Fixed portfolio percentage payout" (life beneficiaries periodically receive a fixed percentage of the portfolio's current value); (5) "Payout of adjusted real yield" (life beneficiaries periodically receive payouts geared to the portfolio's real yield; the payout is based on the total portfolio return, corrected for any loss in real value due either to inflation or capital loss). What advantages and disadvantages do you see for each of these approaches? See Gordon, supra, at 102-08.

2. *Allocation Rules for Not-for-Profit Institutions.* Unlike private trusts, which are subject to the allocation rules just studied, particularly the Revised Uniform Principal and Income Act, most charitable institutions are subject to a statute that permits them to implement a total return approach. The Uniform Management of Institutional Funds Act (UMIFA) allows charitable trustees and directors of non-profit institutions to count appreciation, realized and unrealized, in the value of a fund for purposes of establishing an income stream that balances corpus and operating needs.

Wasting Assets. The question in *First Wyoming Bank* regarding allocation of royalties from oil wells illustrates one aspect of allocation problems involving wasting assets, *i.e.*, assets whose value is expended by current payments. When a trust includes such assets as mineral rights, patents, copyrights, leaseholds, and artists' royalties, the question is what portion, if any, should the trustee allocate to principal. If no portion is allocated to principal, the income beneficiaries may eventually receive its entire value. As to royalties from rights in minerals and similar natural resources, section 9(a)(3) of the Revised Uniform Principal and Income Act adopts an approach different from that taken in *First Wyoming Bank*. It provides that 27 1/2 percent of mineral royalties be allocated to principal and the balance to income. In some states the statute bases the percentage allocated to principal on the portion of the gross receipts allowed as a deduction for depletion in computing taxable income for federal income tax purposes. See. e.g., N.Y. Est. Powers & Trusts Law § 11-2.1(h)(1). For other types of wasting assets, section 11 of the revised act provides the income beneficiary a right to an investment return up to 5% of the asset's inventory value. For a general discussion of apportionment problems with wasting assets, see Abravanel, Apportioning Receipts from Wasting Assets under the Uniform Laws: A Proposal for Legislative Reform, 58 N.C. L. Rev. 255 (1980).

Where a trustee has received as an original asset of the trust a building that produces rental income, courts have generally held that the trustee is not permitted to set aside a depreciation reserve for the principal beneficiaries unless the governing instrument provides otherwise. That is, courts have not applied the rules relating to wasting assets. In part, this is due to the influence of the law governing rights between owners of successive legal interests. A life tenant of land is entitled to rents and profits without any deduction for depreciation of buildings on the land, and the New Jersey court concluded that the same rule applies to land held in trust. In re Roth, 139 N.J. Eq. 588, 52 A.2d 811 (1947). Other courts have concluded that the settlor did not intend that the income beneficiary's receipts be reduced by depreciation. Chapin v. Collard, 29 Wash. 2d 788, 189 P.2d 642 (1948). Restatement 2d of Trusts section 239 comment h takes the position that if "the trust estate includes a building used for business purposes, such as a factory, a hotel or an apartment house, the trustee is ordinarily under a duty to set aside a part of the income as a reserve for depreciation, in accordance with the ordinary business customs with respect to depreciation and obsolescence." There is very little case authority for this view, however. The Revised Uniform Principal and Income Act adopts a different approach. Section 13 imposes a duty on the trustee to charge against income a "reasonable allowance for depreciation on property subject to depreciation under generally accepted accounting principles. . . ." However, recognizing that this provision departs from the common law and the 1931 act, the revised act excepts "any property held by the trustee on the effective date of this Act for which the trustee is not then making an allowance for depreciation."

Unproductive Property. Unproductive (and underproductive) assets present the opposite problem from that created by wasting assets. The income generated by unproductive assets is less rather than more than a return provided by normal trust investments. The trustee's duty of impartiality usually means that such assets must be sold. See Restatement 2d of Trusts § 240. Section 12 of the Revised Uniform Principal and Income Act provides that upon sale of unproductive property the income beneficiary is entitled to a portion of the proceeds upon sale as "delayed income," whether or not the trustee is under a duty to sell. The Restatement provides for allocation only where the trustee was obligated to sell but was delayed in doing so. See Restatement 2d of Trusts § 241. To determine the amount that is allocated to principal from the sale proceeds, both the Restatement and the revised act use the same formula:

$$\text{Principal} = \frac{\text{net proceeds}}{1 + (\text{period of years held} \times \text{interest rate})}$$

If the settlor directs that the trustee retain an unproductive asset, the apportionment rules usually do not apply. There is disagreement about what to do, however, where unproductive property is an original trust asset but the settlor does not expressly direct its retention. Some courts have refused to order apportionment under these circumstances (see, e.g., Creed v. Connolly, 272 Mass. 241, 172 N.E. 106 (1930)), while other courts imply both a duty to dispose of unproductive assets and a duty to apportion upon sale (see, e.g., Rowland's Estate, 273 N.Y. 100, 6 N.E.2d 393 (1937)).

5. Income During Probate Administration

Statutory Reference: *Revised Uniform Principal and Income Act § 5*

Proctor v. American Security & Trust Company
98 F.2d 599 (D.C. Cir. 1938)

VINSON, J. This case is before us upon an agreed statement of facts. Stephen L'Hommedieu Slocum, a resident of the District of Columbia, died testate on December 14, 1933. He was possessed of a large estate, which, after satisfaction of just debts, specific devises and legacies, he devised and bequeathed to the American Security and Trust Company, in trust, with direction to the trustees to convert all the "rest, residue and remainder" of his estate into cash and sound securities and to divide this residue into equal shares, the net income of these shares to be paid to several named life beneficiaries, and with remainders over. . . .

Costs of administration, debts, specific devises and legacies amounted to approximately $800,000. The gross estate amounted to some $3,000,000. . . .

During the course of administration, the securities of the estate, which were sold to raise money for the payment of the costs of administration, debts, and legacies, produced before sale earnings of $28,328.64. The sole question in this case is the proper disposition of this amount. The appellants contend that this amount should be considered income distributable to the life beneficiaries of the residuary trusts. Appellees maintain that it should be added to the residuary trust and become part of its corpus. The lower court found that it should, upon distribution to the trustee, be added to the corpus of the residuary trusts.

In the long ago, the life beneficiary of a residuary trust received no income during the administration of the estate. After payment of costs of administration, debts and legacies, the residue was transferred to the trustee. Income produced thereafter was paid to the life beneficiary. The reason for such rule, as generally expressed, was that during the period of administration the residue had not been ascertained. All monies earned upon the property of the testator during the administration of the estate, not having been disposed of by will, were a proper part of the residue.

Life beneficiaries suffered hardships. Delay in the administration occurred through proper cause, or through inaction or non-action of the executor. It was then argued that the life beneficiary of a residuary trust was closer to the heart of the testator than the remainderman, such life beneficiary having been named first to benefit from the residuary trust. And it was successfully contended that such life beneficiary should have the income from the clear residue from the date of testator's death.

It is the now accepted rule that, in the absence of controlling language in a will, the life beneficiary is entitled to the income of the clear residue as afterwards ascertained, to be computed from the date of the death of testator. . . .

In this jurisdiction it is settled that a life beneficiary of a residuary trust is entitled to income thereon from the date of testator's death.

The item of the will, XVI, with which we are here concerned, covers 9 printed pages of the transcript. In this item the testator provided for a conversion of all the "rest, residue and remainder" of his entire estate into cash and sound securities and a division into "equal parts or shares." These "equal parts or shares" were given in trust to the American Security and Trust Company which was to pay the income earned by this share to the named beneficiary. We take the "part" of which Margaret O. F. Proctor was beneficiary as typical of the careful way in which the testator devised and bequeathed his property. The will provided for the payment of the "net income" arising therefrom to her for life. Upon death, if there should be surviving issue, the trust was to cease, and the trustee was ordered to pay over such part or share, "*together with any undistributed accumulations of net income*" to the surviving issue. If the beneficiary should survive the testator but thereafter die leaving no issue surviving her, the "part" theretofore held in trust for her, "*Together with any undistributed accumulations of net income*" should be divided into two equal portions. One such portion was to be subdivided into halves. Each half was to be added to and become a part of one of the subsequently created "equal parts or shares" of the "rest, residue and remainder" of the estate. Then, there are elaborate interlocking directions to the end that the residuary trusts would not fail so long as the beneficiaries or their issue, all of whom were his kin, survived him.

There is nothing in the will to indicate that testator would prefer the first life beneficiaries to receive a larger sum during the administration of the estate than thereafter, or larger than that which subsequent life beneficiaries would receive; particularly when, by such increase of income during the administration of the estate, the corpus of the residuary trust would be diminished. There is nothing to indicate that such "windfall" to the life beneficiaries, during the course of administration, was intended. . . .

It is fair to say that there are two irreconcilable rules which have grown up in this country in respect to the point involved. There is the general rule, supported by the decided weight of authority in this country, and, likewise, the English cases, that the earnings upon testator's property, derived during the course of administration, used to pay costs of administration, debts and legacies, if not disposed of by the express terms of the will, are added to the residuary trust as part of its corpus. Then there is the so-called Massachusetts rule, which crystallized in 1929, which holds that the earnings upon testator's property used to pay costs of administration, debts and legacies derived during the course of administration if not disposed of by the express terms of the will, are distributable to the life beneficiary as income.

The general rule finds support in the courts of New York, Maryland, Connecticut, Kentucky, New Hampshire, Delaware, New Jersey and the English cases. The Massachusetts rule is followed in the courts of Rhode Island and North Carolina.

It is necessary, therefore, for this court to determine which rule shall prevail in this jurisdiction. The pointed question to be answered is whether the life beneficiaries of the residuary trusts are only entitled to receive the "net income" of such residuary trusts, as stated in the will, or whether, in addition to such "net income," they shall receive, *as income*, the earnings derived from property used to pay costs of administration, debts and legacies during the course of the administration of the estate.

We are of the opinion that the general rule is supported by better reason and we follow it in this jurisdiction.

We are unable to get away from the idea that when this testator set up these residuary trusts and directed that the "rest, residue and remainder" of his estate should be transferred to such trusts and that the life beneficiaries thereof were to receive the "net income" therefrom he meant what he said. From the earliest decisions, as we read them, the "rest, residue and remainder" of an estate meant all property not expressly disposed of by the will. After subtracting the costs of administration, debts, specific devises and legacies from the entire estate then existing, that which remains is the "rest, residue and remainder." Thereupon such property was transferred to the residuary trust, and it was the net income from such trust that such life beneficiaries were entitled to receive. . . .

Under the will involved in the case at bar the life beneficiaries are only entitled to "*net income*" upon the "rest, residue and remainder." The Massachusetts rule must proceed upon the theory that all property of the testator at the date of his death is the "rest, residue and remainder," or that all property at the date of the death of the testator is "rest, residue and remainder" until wanted. We cannot agree with either position. The earnings involved, to-wit, $23,328.64, were not a part of the estate at the time testator died. As a matter of fact, the earnings involved were not in existence at the date of testator's death. Further, the earnings were derived from property that has never been, and never will be, a part of the residuary trusts. It is *net income* from the residuary trusts that the live beneficiaries are entitled to receive.

We find that the sum representing the earnings during the course of administration upon property used to pay costs of administration, debts and legacies is not expressly disposed of by the will and therefore it should be transferred to the residuary trust as a part of its corpus. With this treatment, every life beneficiary, whether original or a successor, would, for their respective lives, receive the income from such funds. Thereafter it would be found intact in the corpus of the residuary trusts available for the remaindermen.

Counsel for the appellants stress the complexity of computation involved under the general rule. It may be that the Massachusetts rule is the more simple in computation, but we do not feel that we should break away from the long applied rule, supported by authority, reason and fairness to parties involved because of the difficulty in computing the amount of the trust funds. Moreover, the question of complexity urged by appellant is not before us for consideration. It was expressly stipulated in the court below by agreement of all counsel that should it be adjudged that the earnings derived from property used to pay costs of administration, debts and legacies should be added to the corpus of the residuary trusts, the full amount involved herein, $23,328.64 was the sum to be so added to corpus. We do not decide the method of computation.

The decree of the lower court is affirmed.

Notes and Questions

1. In Webb v. Lines, 77 Conn. 51, 58 A. 227 (1904), the testator's will created five separate trusts of amounts ranging from $15,000 to $120,000, providing in each instance that income was to be paid to a named beneficiary for life, with remainders to other persons. The will also made various cash devises in amounts ranging from $1,000 to $25,000. As to the cash devises, the court applied the usual rule that "general legacies do not, in the absence of a contrary testamentary direction, bear interest until one year from the death of the testator." As to the cash amounts devised in trust, however, the court held that the income beneficiaries were entitled to income from the testator's death. The funds were not placed in the separate trusts until the end of one year after the testator's death, but during that year the average rate of income on the estate was 4.14 percent. The court held that each trust was entitled to a proportionate part of this average income.

The courts generally have followed the distinction drawn in Webb. They usually state that general pecuniary devises draw interest from the time the devises are "due and payable," and this is generally at the end of one year after the testator's death (the normal period of probate administration). See, e.g., State Bank of Chicago v. Gross, 344 Ill. 512, 176 N.E. 739 (1931). As to money devises in trust, there are many cases that accept the position taken in Webb, but a few defer commencement of income for one year. See, e.g., Rowe v. Rowe, 113 N.J. Eq. 344, 167 A. 16 (1933). Similarly, nearly all courts hold, as in Proctor, that the rights of the income beneficiary of a residuary trust commence at the testator's death. See, e.g., In re King Estate, 367 Mich. 503, 116 N.W.2d 897 (1962).

In states following the rule of Proctor rather than the Massachusetts rule, it is not altogether clear how to ascertain the amount of income that is to be added to corpus. Proctor seems to suggest that the amount consists of actual earnings on the property sold to pay costs of administration, debts, and devises, but the issue was not before the court since the parties had stipulated the amount in controversy. Alternatively, commentators have suggested that income should be attributed to the assets sold on the basis of the average rate of return from the whole estate and the length of time the assets were held. See Scott on Trusts § 234.4. The Restatement 1st of Trusts section 234 comment g, approved the English computation method, which seeks to equalize the income to the life tenant during and after administration. The Restatement described this method as follows:

> A proper method of determining the extent to which legacies, debts and expenses of administration should be paid out of principal is by ascertaining the amount which with interest thereon at the rate of return received by the executor upon the whole estate from the death of the testator to the dates of payment would equal the amounts paid.

The Maryland court followed this method in Tilghman v. Frazer, 199 Md. 620, 87 A.2d 811 (1952). Before that decision, Maryland had adopted the Massachusetts rule by statute, but the statute was held inapplicable to the estates of persons dying before its passage. Restatement 2d of Trusts section 234 comment g rejects the English method and adopts the Massachusetts rule.

2. *Legislation.* There has been a clear tendency in recent years in favor of the Massachusetts rule, reflected partly in case law but more strongly in legislation. However, only about one-third of the states have statutes on the question. Statutes are collected and analyzed in Bogert on Trusts section 817.

Section 5(b) of the Revised Uniform Principal and Income Act appears to accept the distinction, recognized in *Webb*, between non-residuary pecuniary devises that are outright and those that are in trust. It provides that, unless the will states otherwise, income from property used to discharge liabilities is payable as follows: (1) specific devisees receive the net income from the devised property earned during administration; (2) all other devises, except devisees of non-trust pecuniary devisees, receive a proportionate share of the balance of the net income. Devisees of outright cash devises receive none of the income earned during probate administration under this provision.

The Uniform Probate Code section 3-904 provides that "[g]eneral pecuniary devises bear interest at the legal rate beginning one year after the first appointment of a personal representative until payment, unless a contrary intent is indicated by the will." Is this provision consistent with section 5 of the Revised Uniform Principal and Income Act? Suppose that a testator makes a nonresiduary devise of $100,000 in trust for an elderly parent and that a significant period of time passes prior to distribution of the estate and funding of the trust. If there is no probate income (perhaps, for example, administrative expenses and losses during administration are high), is there statutory interest on the pecuniary devise at time of distribution, under UPC section 3-904, or does the trust for the parent receive only the stated pecuniary amount under the Uniform Principal and Income Act since the devise was in trust?

3. *Effect on Shares of Residuary Beneficiaries of Tax or Other Payments Chargeable to Less Than All.* Iandoli's will gave one-half of his entire estate

to his widow, one-half to his daughter by a prior marriage, and nominated the widow as personal representative. The will made no provision regarding the burden of estate taxes. Consequently, all estate taxes were charged to the daughter's share as a result of a Florida statute similar to UPC section 3-916, the Uniform Estate Tax Apportionment Act. In re Estate of Iandoli, 9 Fla. Sup. 2d 162 (Cir. Ct. 1985). Later, more litigation developed between the widow and the daughter regarding the size of the shares of the residuary beneficiaries in the assets remaining after payment of the taxes. The value of the estate's principal asset, a shopping center, had appreciated substantially during the course of probate administration. As a result, the entire estate appraised originally at about $7.6 million and after reduction by estate tax payments of approximately $1.15 million, was worth about $9.5 million at the time of the later proceeding.

In 1986, the probate court ruled that the interests of the residuary beneficiaries in the remaining residuary estate were 59.91 percent for the widow, and 40.09 percent for the daughter. The ruling expressly rejected a contention by the daughter that the payment chargeable to the daughter should be treated as a loan from the residuary estate to the daughter to be repaid by adjustment at final distribution based on the daughter's continuing 50 percent share of all residuary assets. After observing that the daughter's theory would work to the disadvantage of the daughter if estate assets had fallen in value rather than appreciated, the trial court observed:

> The only equitable rule is one in which both beneficiaries share ratably in gain as well as loss. . . . There is no question but that the interests of the two beneficiaries of the Iandoli estate started out as equal fifty percent shares. [Upon payment of estate taxes] chargeable solely to the daughter, . . . the asset pool constituting the estate was reduced by almost $1,150,000 . . . [reducing] the income and appreciation potential of the beneficiaries' interests in remaining assets. . . . The widow's interest prior to tax payments was a vested present interest, and such interests implicitly reflect the right to income and appreciation in assets which are the subject of the interest. If the widow's interest as viewed prior to the tax payment is to remain intact after estate tax payments (as it must remain if it is to be deductible under the estate marital deduction) the participation of the widow's interest in estate income and appreciation must not be diluted by tax payments. . . . The p.r. must be guided by a rule that is equitable in all cases. The p.r. cannot be responsible for making predictions, based on uncertain future events beyond her control that may determine who, among co-beneficiaries with conflicting interests will be hurt or helped.

The court also relied on Florida's enactment of section 5(b)(2) of the Revised Uniform Principal and Income Act, observing: "The Court recognizes that the Principal and Income law . . . deals in express terms only with the allocation of income on estate assets. The rationale of, and method prescribed by the principal and income law is properly applied to the capital appreciation in the instant case. . . ." Estate of Iandoli, 22 Fla. Supp. 2d 8 (Cir. Ct. 1986), aff'd, 547 S.2d 664 (Fla. Ct. App. 1989) ("Our review of the authorities leads us to conclude that there is no clear-cut line of authority which compels a uniform approach to computation of shares of the residue in relation to payment of death taxes . . . [T]he lower court tribunal is in the best position to measure the fairness and logic embodied in a particular scheme of distribution. In the absence of an abuse of discretion, this court will not attempt to second-guess this basic fact-finding exercise.") Was the appellate court suggesting that if the daughter rather the widow had been named executor, the fiduciary might have properly treated the residuary shares as equal following the tax payments? See Cantrill, Fractional or Percentage Residuary Bequests: Allocation of Postmortem Income, Gain and Unrealized Appreciation, 10 Prob. Notes 322 (Am. Col. Tr. & Est. Counsel 1985).

6. Compensation of Fiduciaries

Statutory References: *1990 UPC §§ 3-719, -721*

Estate of Davis
509 A.2d 1175 (Maine 1986)

WATHEN, J. On a petition to review fees filed by personal representative Stuart E. Hayes, the Somerset County Probate Court approved a fee of $44,700 for services as personal representative of the estate of Linea A. Davis. Benjamin D. Harrington, Sr., and James B. Harrington, Jr., residual beneficiaries under the will of Linea Davis, appeal the Probate Court's order, challenging the reasonableness of the fee, which Hayes admitted was based on a fixed percentage of the decedent's estate, under the Maine Probate Code. We conclude that the court erred in its determination of reasonableness, and accordingly, we vacate the Probate Court's order.

Hayes, an attorney, testified that he calculated his fee on a percentage basis. From decedent's gross estate, valued at $1,388,000, he deducted a total of $590,400 attributable to real and personal property situated in Florida, leasehold property located in Maine, and lifetime transfers made by the decedent. He then charged five percent of the remaining $797,600 value of the estate and five percent of $96,000 in income earned by the estate, for a total fee of $44,700.

Hayes testified that the handling of the Davis estate required performance of numerous tasks. The will listed many charities as beneficiaries but did not provide addresses for the various charitable legatees. Name changes increased the difficulty of locating some of the charities. In addition, payment to one individual beneficiary was impossible because she was incompetent and, as best Hayes could ascertain, did not have a representative to handle her affairs. The federal estate tax return had to be prepared under some time pressure due to delay in resolving a dispute between beneficiaries regarding the valuation of certain property. Hayes also testified that he encountered difficulty in obtaining information from various institutional trustees regarding four trusts created by decedent during her lifetime.

With regard to certain leasehold property held by the estate, Hayes testified that he had to negotiate the transfer of the leases to the beneficiaries and also described becoming embroiled in a dispute between beneficiaries as to whether the personal representative should undertake repairs on the leased property. Hayes was also responsible for overseeing the maintenance and subsequent sale of Florida real estate. Finally, Hayes testified that he timed certain distributions to minimize the beneficiaries' ultimate tax liability.

The record reveals that Hayes was familiar with the decedent's estate. He had acted as personal representative of the estate of decedent's husband in 1978. Thereafter, he prepared decedent's will in which he was named personal representative. Later, the decedent granted him a power of attorney to handle her financial affairs. Pursuant to the power of attorney, he had maintained the decedent's Florida real estate and had taken steps toward eventual sale of that property. After decedent's death, the maintenance arrangements previously made with respect to the property were simply continued. In addition, he stated that he did not participate in the actual sale of the property. Hayes stated that he was familiar with the trusts that the decedent created during her lifetime, having drafted one or two of them and having prepared income tax returns for all of the trusts.

Hayes admitted that, in general, the negotiations involved in handling the estate were not particularly difficult. He also stated no tax issues were presented beyond those normally encountered in estate work and that, in fact, the estate presented no novel legal issues of any kind. At the time of hearing on his petition, Hayes had spent 112 hours on the estate. In addition, Hayes' secretary and bookkeeper had 100 hours and 35 hours, respectively, invested in the case.

The Probate Court made the following factual findings: Attorney Hayes is an experienced, able, and reputable practitioner of probate law. Personal representatives in the locality customarily charge five percent of the taxable estate for their services. Hayes and his staff spent approximately 250 hours working on the estate. The estate required considerable skill on the part of the personal representative and was handled in an efficient and competent manner. Finally, the court found that under the circumstances of this case, the fee charged constituted reasonable compensation for Hayes' services as personal representative.

The Harringtons argue that the Probate Court's decision must be vacated because the personal representative based his fee on a percentage of the estate, a practice the Legislature has sought to eliminate. We agree that with the enactment of the Maine Probate Code in 1981, the Legislature intended to abolish the prevailing practice of determining compensation for personal representatives as a percentage of the estate and to substitute a system based on reasonable compensation.

Prior to 1981, personal representatives were authorized by statute to charge up to five percent of the personal assets of an estate for their services. 18 M.R.S.A. § 554, *repealed by* P.L. 1979, ch. 540 (eff. January

1, 1981). A commission created by the Legislature to study and recommend changes in Maine's probate law urged a change in the prevailing system as follows:

> One important, and highly undesirable, aspect of the . . . present Maine system is the tying of compensation to various percentages of the estate's value. It is precisely this kind of approach that has led to criticism of probate expense and has given rise to anti-trust problems when used as a general and pervasive standard for attorneys' fees throughout the bar. . . . Compensation should be based on the amount and value of the work done, under a variety of relevant circumstances.

Maine Probate Law Commission, *Report of the Commission's Study and Recommendations Concerning Maine Probate Law* 305 (October 1978). The Maine Probate Code, enacted in 1981, implemented the commission's recommendation regarding fees for personal representatives. Section 3-719 states that a personal representative "is entitled to reasonable compensation for his services." 18-A M.R.S.A. § 3-719 (1981). Section 3-721 sets forth the following criteria for determining the reasonableness of a fee:

> (1) The time and labor required, the novelty and difficulty of the questions involved, and the skill requisite to perform the service properly;
> (2) The likelihood, if apparent to the personal representative, that the acceptance of the particular employment will preclude the person employed from other employment;
> (3) The fee customarily charged in the locality for similar services;
> (4) The amount involved and the results obtained;
> (5) The time limitations imposed by the personal representative or by the circumstances;
> (6) The experience, reputation and ability of the person performing the services.

18-A M.R.S.A. § 3-721(b) (1981).[26]

The current provisions of the Probate Code, along with the legislative history surrounding their enactment, demonstrate that the Legislature intended to abolish the determination of fees for personal representatives on a percentage basis and to mandate that in all cases, such fees be governed by a standard of reasonable compensation. The clear expression of legislative intent is not dispositive of the present case, however, because the order of the Probate Court recites consideration of most[27] of the factors

---

26. 18-A M.R.S.A. § 3-719 is identical to section 3-719 of the Uniform Probate Code. The formulation of the factors designated in 18-A M.R.S.A. § 3-721(b) for determining the reasonableness of a fee, is not contained in the uniform act. Other states, however, have adopted similar additions to the Uniform Probate Code. See, e.g., Colo.Rev.Stats. § 15-12-721 (1974); Fla.Stat.Ann. § 733.617 (West Supp.1986).

27. The Probate Court made no findings regarding the extent to which work on the estate precluded Hayes from accepting other employment, § 3-721(b)(2), or as to time constraints involved in handling the estate, § 3-721(b)(5). In his petition to review fees, Hayes admitted that work on this estate did not preclude his accepting other employment. The only evidence in the record as to time constraints was noted above with regard to filing of the federal estate

set forth in section 3-721 and ultimately finds the fee assessed to be reasonable. The determination of a reasonable fee is reviewed only for abuse of discretion, and the court's factual findings are final unless demonstrated to be clearly erroneous.

The Probate Court's findings as to the reputation and experience of the personal representative, the time expended and skill required to handle the estate, the efficient manner in which the estate was handled, and the customary fee in the locality are all supported by evidence in the record. Nevertheless, the court abused its discretion in concluding that a fee of $44,700 constitutes reasonable compensation for the services provided in this case.

Section 3-721 places complexity of the services required and the time and skill necessary to perform those services first among the factors to be considered in arriving at a reasonable fee. Courts in other jurisdictions with similar statutory provisions have emphasized that the reasonableness of a fee depends on the services actually performed rather than on the size of the estate. In re Estate of Painter, 39 Colo.App. 506, 508, 567 P.2d 820, 822 (1977); In re Estate of Kottrasch, 63 Ill.App.3d 370, 374-75, 20 Ill.Dec. 349, 352, 380 N.E.2d 26, 29 (1978). Although the estate in this case cannot be described as simple, the personal representative himself testified that it involved no difficult negotiations or litigation and presented no novel legal questions. In cases such as this, when the services required are routine rather than extraordinary, the amount of time expended should be the predominant factor.

The Probate Court found that Hayes and his staff devoted 250 hours to handling the estate. Utilizing this figure, over half of which consists of secretarial and bookkeeping time, the fee amounts to an hourly rate of $180. If only the hours put in by attorney Hayes are considered, the hourly rate exceeds $400. It is evident that in finding such extraordinary hourly compensation to constitute a reasonable fee, the Probate Court relied heavily on the local custom of charging a five percent fee for estate work. Given that sections 3-719 and 3-721 embody a legislative intent to abolish the percentage fee system, any continuing practice of charging percentage fees should carry little or no weight in evaluating the reasonableness of a fee under the new statutory scheme. The Probate Court's reliance on the local custom of percentage charges was improper.

Because we conclude that the Probate Court abused its discretion, we vacate the order and remand for further proceedings. On remand, the personal representative may present evidence as to any additional time expended on the settling of this estate after the date of the original hearing in this case.

The entry is:

Order allowing fee vacated.

Case remanded to the Probate Court for further proceedings consistent with the opinion herein.

All concurring.

tax return . . . .

Note

1. *Sequel.* In response to an inquiry from the editors, Jon R. Doyle, Esq., of Augusta, Maine, counsel for B. Harrington and J. Harrington in the principal case, advised us as follows regarding the case and its ultimate disposition:

> We ultimately settled on an amount for fees without resorting back to the Probate Court of Somerset County in the amount of $14,000. My judgment was that that was an appropriate settlement amount and correctly reflected the value of the services provided.
>
> The case was an interesting one to prepare and present. I was pleased we were able to prevail. I suspect that the atmosphere in the original probate court which is in rural Maine, in Skowhegan, Maine, is not unlike rural areas in your state. Before I started trying the case the probate judge told me quite candidly that I would lose and that it had been the practice before him for some time to use a flat percentage rate which seemed to me to be prohibited by the statute. The net result was that we did try the case and obviously lost in the lower court and ultimately prevailed in our court of final jurisdiction.
>
> The dynamics of the case meant as well that the other members of the probate bar both in Somerset County where the case originated and in Piscataquis County, another rural nearby county in which the practice was the same, lost and will continue to lose some substantial income. I think I would have settled the case for approximately $20,000 or perhaps $22,000 the day of the hearing.

2. *Fiduciary Compensation Practices.* Clients, of course, are keenly interested in the fees charged by fiduciaries, including trustees and estate personal representatives. In the past, many states statutorily set the personal representative's fee. The typical statute provided a schedule of fees based on a percentage of the estate. The UPC abandons the fee schedule approach and provides that the estate personal representative and the attorney representing the estate are entitled to "reasonable compensation." UPC §§ 3-719, 3-721. The UPC permits personal representatives to establish their fees and those of estate attorneys with formal court approval. Because this is a marked departure from the conventional practice, section 3-721 emphasizes that any interested person can require court review of these fees.

For inter-vivos trusts, the trustee's fee is usually established by the terms of the trust agreement. In the absence of any explicit agreement, the reasonable compensation standard is applied. See Bogert on Trusts § 975.

Clients are especially likely to be concerned about fees if the fiduciary is a corporate fiduciary (*i.e.*, a bank or trust company). Corporate fiduciaries typically recommend including in wills or trust instruments compensation provisions that permit them to be paid without prior court approval. In addition, the suggested compensation provisions might state that the testator or grantor "recognizes that such compensation may exceed the compensation for [fiduciary] services in effect from time to time under applicable law."

Corporate fiduciaries' commission policies vary, of course, but to illustrate these policies we have taken the following information from the January 1991 commission policy statement of a major firm, United States Trust Company. Acting as estate personal representative, the company applies the rates currently permitted by New York law:

  5% on the first $100,000
  4% on the next $200,000
  3% on the next $700,000
  2 1/2% on the next $4,000,000
  2% on the balance.

The company charges a minimum fee of $25,000.

For trusts, the company charges an annual fee consisting of two parts, a base fee of $2,000 per trust plus a variable fee. The variable fee is:

  1% on the first $3,000,000 of principal
  3/4 of 1% on the next $2,000,000 of principal
  1/2 of 1% on the next $5,000,000 of principal
  3/8 of 1% on the balance.

Additional compensation is required for acquisition of special investments, for closely-held companies, and for certain other estates and trusts services.

E. THE TRUST AND OUTSIDERS—
CREDITORS AND THE EPA

Statutory Reference: *1990 UPC §§ 3-808, 5-429, 7-306*

Creditors' Claims. The common-law rule is that a trustee is personally liable on any contract that the trustee makes regardless of whether the trustee had the power to enter into the contract. One with whom the trustee contracts cannot obtain a legal judgment against the trustee as trustee so as to collect the judgment against trust assets. The trustee does not avoid personal liability merely by signing in its fiduciary role. See, e.g., Dolben v. Gleason, 292 Mass. 511, 198 N.E. 762 (1935). The trustee is entitled to be indemnified out of trust assets, but if the contract is beyond the trustee's powers there is no right to indemnity. Moreover, the trustee is personally liable to the extent that the trust estate is insufficient to indemnify the trustee.

The contract may expressly relieve the trustee of personal liability if the trustee had authority to enter into the contract. Under these circumstances, the creditor does have recourse against trust assets on the theory that the creditor is enforcing the trustee's right to indemnity (but only to the extent of the trustee's right of indemnification). The other theory upon which creditors may recover against trust assets is unjust enrichment. If the creditor has conferred a benefit upon the trust estate, the trustee is entitled to recover directly from the trust estate to that extent.

The trustee's tort liability follows the same general approach. The trustee is personally liable for torts committed by the trustee or the trustee's employee in the course of trust administration. The trustee, if not personally at fault, is entitled to indemnification from trust assets. See, e.g., Matter of Lathers, 137 Misc. 226, 243 N.Y.S. 366 (1930). It is likely that a court that permits a contract creditor to reach trust assets through substitution of the creditor for the trustee's right to indemnity will reach the same result when a tort claimant tries to reach trust assets, but courts have been somewhat cautious in committing themselves to this position. See, e.g., Johnston v. Long, 30 Cal. 2d 54, 181 P.2d 645 (1947).

Commentators have criticized the traditional rules as unfair to both creditors and the trustee where the trustee is not personally at fault and trust assets are insufficient to indemnify the trustee. See Johnston, Development in Contract Liability of Trusts and Trustees, 42 N.Y.U. L. Rev. 483 (1966). Reacting to these criticisms, recent statutes have reversed the traditional rules. Section 7-306 of the Uniform Probate Code is an example. It permits both tort and contract creditors to proceed against the trustee in her or his representative capacity whether or not the trustee is personally liable. Comparable provisions apply to the liability of estate personal representatives (§ 3-808) and conservators of an incompetent's property (§ 5-429).

Environmental Protection Agency. Suppose it turns out that part of the corpus of a trust is land in which hazardous chemicals are buried. Under the Comprehensive Environmental Response, Compensation and Liability Act of 1980 (CERCLA), 42 U.S.C. §§ 9601-75, the Environmental Protection Agency (EPA) can sue the current owner of the land for the clean-up costs, even if the current owner is not responsible for the contamination and was unaware of it. Recently, several bills have been introduced in Congress to grant some measure of relief for fiduciaries in these circumstances. In the meantime, trustees are seeking ways of ridding their trusts of contaminated land through disclaimers and other means of protection.

EXTERNAL REFERENCES. Adams, Clean Hands in a New Context: Environmental Hazards for Fiduciaries, 25 Univ. Miami Inst. Est. Plan. 12-1 (1991); Anderson & Lowet, The Fouled Fiduciary: Seeking Relief from Toxic Waste Liability, 2 Probate and Property, No. 6, p. 14 (November/December 1988); Medlin, Environmental Liability: A Hazard for Fiduciaries, 3 Prob. Prac. Rep. 1 (March 1991); Pendygraft, Plews, Clark & Wright, Who Pays for Environmental Damage: Recent Developments in CERCLA Liability and Insurance Coverage Litigation, 21 Ind. L. Rev. 117 (1988); Shi & Moxley, New Hazards for Fiduciaries: Environmental Liability, 4 Probate and Property, No. 6, p. 36 (November/December 1990); Slap & Israel, Private CERCLA Litigation: How to Avoid It? How to Handle It?, Hazmat 90: Hazardous Materials Management Conference & Exhibition/International (1990); Warchall & Crough, Environmental Risk-Reduction Considerations for Trustees, 130 Tr. & Est. 24 (April 1991).

Index

References are to Pages

0-88277-904-4